| 103d Congress 2d Session | COMMITTEE PRINT | 103–111 |

NUCLEAR PROLIFERATION FACTBOOK

PREPARED FOR THE

COMMITTEE ON GOVERNMENTAL AFFAIRS UNITED STATES SENATE

BY THE

CONGRESSIONAL RESEARCH SERVICE LIBRARY OF CONGRESS

DECEMBER 1994

Printed for the use of the Committee on Governmental Affairs

U.S. GOVERNMENT PRINTING OFFICE
WASHINGTON : 1995

80–936 CC

For sale by the U.S. Government Printing Office
Superintendent of Documents, Mail Stop: SSOP, Washington, DC 20402-9328
ISBN 0-16-046780-2

COMMITTEE ON GOVERNMENTAL AFFAIRS

JOHN GLENN, Ohio, *Chairman*

SAM NUNN, Georgia
CARL LEVIN, Michigan
JIM SASSER, Tennessee
DAVID PRYOR, Arkansas
JOSEPH I. LIEBERMAN, Connecticut
DANIEL K. AKAKA, Hawaii
BYRON L. DORGAN, North Dakota

WILLIAM V. ROTH, JR., Delaware
TED STEVENS, Alaska
WILLIAM S. COHEN, Maine
THAD COCHRAN, Mississippi
JOHN McCAIN, Arizona
ROBERT F. BENNETT, Utah

Leonard Weiss, *Staff Director*
Randy Rydell, *Professional Staff Member*
Franklin G. Polk, *Minority Staff Director and Chief Counsel*
Michal Sue Prosser, *Chief Clerk*

FOREWORD

Congress of the United States,
Washington, D.C., December 2, 1994.

Halting the global spread of nuclear explosive devices has been a goal of American policy for over a half a century. It predates even the first detonation of such a device in 1945. There is no weapon on earth that matches the instantaneous destructive power of the Bomb, which can devastate whole cities in the blink of an eye. Nonproliferation counted then and counts all the more today as a top national security priority.

Achieving this goal has not been easy and by all indications it will not get any easier to achieve in the years ahead. Nonproliferation efforts will continue to be hampered by the rapid pace of technological change, the greed of unscrupulous exporters of dangerous goods and technologies, the passions of nationalism, the mindless inertia of bureaucracies, and the belief that political power grows out of an implosion package. Yet two of the gravest dangers may well be the easiest to cure: ignorance and complacency.

It is, therefore, vital for members of the Congress and the public to have an easily accessible shelf reference to consult for answers to questions relating to the history of nonproliferation efforts, the basic technology of bombs and how they are made, regional problems, legislation, treaties, regulations, and other such vital data.

This volume represents the fifth edition of the *Nuclear Proliferation Factbook*, which is intended to address just such issues. The Congress and all readers of this volume will be indebted to the labors of the staff of the Congressional Research Service, particularly Zachary Davis, Carl Behrens, and former Senior Specialist Warren H. Donnelly, who has recently retired after a long and distinguished career. In recognition of his long service, I would like to take this opportunity to dedicate this volume to Dr. Donnelly.

JOHN GLENN
Chairman, Committee on Governmental Affairs
United States Senate

LETTER OF SUBMITTAL

CONGRESSIONAL RESEARCH SERVICE
THE LIBRARY OF CONGRESS
Washington, D.C., December 1, 1994

HON. JOHN GLENN,
Chairman, Committee on Governmental Affairs, Washington, D.C.

DEAR MR. CHAIRMAN: I am submitting this edition of the factbook on proliferation, which has been prepared at your request.

This is the fifth in a series begun and directed by Warren H. Donnelly, for many years Senior Specialist at the Congressional Research Service. The current edition was assembled by Zachary Davis, Analyst in International Nuclear Policy, and by Carl E. Behrens and Robert L. Bamberger, Specialists in Energy Policy, in the Environment and Natural Resources Policy Division.

The dramatic end to the Cold War has added a new perspective to most non-proliferation issues, and added new ones. In addition to a wide selection of historical documents, this factbook includes data and discussions of a wide variety of technical and political topics.

We hope this fifth edition of the factbook will continue to serve your needs as well as others who are concerned with non-proliferation in the post-Cold War world.

Sincerely,

DAN MULHOLLAN
Director.

TABLE OF CONTENTS

	Page
Foreword	III
Letter of Submittal	V
Contents	VII
U.S. Nonproliferation Policy Documents	1
U.S. Nonproliferation Legislation	215
International Treaties, Agreements and Laws	371
Technical Aspects	461
Fuel Cycle	473
Plutonium	543
Nuclear Weapons	595
Disposal	709

U.S. NONPROLIFERATION POLICY DOCUMENTS

CONTENTS

Page

The Truman Administration
 The Baruch Plan, presented to the United Nations Atomic Energy Commission by Bernard Baruch, the U. S. Representative, 14 June 1946 2

The Eisenhower Administration
 President Eisenhower's address before the United Nations General Assembly on the peaceful uses of nuclear energy (Atoms for Peace), 8 December 1953 13
 Executive Order 10841, 30 September 1959, as amended by Executive Order 10956, 12 August 1961, providing for the carrying out of certain provisions of the Atomic Energy Act of 1954 as amended, relating to international cooperation 22

The Kennedy Administration
 Executive Order 11057, 18 October 1962, authorization for the communication of restricted data by the Department of State 23
 President Kennedy's address at American University in Washington announcing unilateral suspension of atmospheric nuclear tests, 10 June 1963 24

The Johnson Administration
 The Committee on Nuclear Proliferation (Gilpatric Committee), Report to the President, 21 January 1965 30
 President Johnson's statement accompanying release of the U.S.-Soviet draft treaty on Nonproliferation of Nuclear Weapons, 24 August 1967 38
 William C. Foster, U.S. Representative to the Conference of the Eighteen-Nation Disarmament Committee, statement made in plenary session of the Conference, 24 August 1967 38

The Nixon Administration

President Nixon's Message to the Senate urging action on the Nuclear Nonproliferation Treaty, 5 February 1969 42

William Rogers, Secretary of State, statement before the Senate Committee on Foreign Relations, 18 February 1969 43

The Ford Administration

Henry Kissinger, Secretary of State, "An Age of Interdependence: Common Disaster or Community", address before the United Nations General Assembly, 23 September 1974 (excerpt) 45

Executive Order 11902, procedure for an export licensing policy as to nuclear materials and equipment, 2 February 1976 46

President Ford's statement on nuclear policy, 28 October 1976 48

The Carter Administration

Presidential Directive/NSC-8, Nuclear Non-Proliferation Policy, 24 March 1977 63

Statement by President Carter on decisions reached following a review of U.S. nuclear power policy, 7 April 1977 66

President Carter's remarks following a review of U.S. policy, 7 April 1977 (excerpt) 68

Message of President Carter to Congress and accompanying White House fact sheet transmitting his proposed Nuclear Nonproliferation Policy Act of 1977 (27 April 1977) 70

White House fact sheet on the proposed Nuclear Nonproliferation Policy Act of 1977, issued 27 April 1977 71

President Carter's remarks before the first plenary session of the International Nuclear Fuel Cycle Evaluation Conference, Washington, D.C., 19 October 1977 74

President Carter's statement on signing into law The Nuclear NonProliferation Act of 1978, (P.L. 95-242), 10 March 1978 77

Executive Order 12055, export of special nuclear material to India, 27 April 1978 79

Executive Order 12058, functions relating to nuclear nonproliferation, 11 May 1978 81

Joseph S. Nye, Jr., deputy to the undersecretary of state for security assistance, science, and technology, statement on nuclear fuel exports to India, to the House Committee on International Relations, 23 May 1978 83

	Page
Joseph S. Nye, Jr., deputy to the undersecretary of state for security assistance, science, and technology, statement before the Subcommittee on International Economic Policy and Trade of the House Committee on International Relations, 3 October 1978	86
Edmund S. Muskie, Secretary of State, and Senator Frank Church, exchange of letters, and a White House statement, concerning nuclear fuel shipments to India, 9, 10, and 24 September 1980	89
John H. Glenn, Senator from Ohio, "Disapproval of Enriched Uranium to India", floor statement, 23 September 1980	90

The Reagan Administration

	Page
Presidential Directive/NSC-6, United States Non-Proliferation and Peaceful Nuclear Cooperation Policy, 16 July 1981	98
President Reagan's statement on U.S. nuclear non-proliferation policy, 16 July 1981	102
Presidential Determination No. 82-7, determination to authorize security assistance for Pakistan, 10 February 1982	104
"Reprocessing and Plutonium Use," statement by the Department of State, 9 June 1982	105
Richard T. Kennedy, undersecretary of state for management and U.S. permanent representative to the IAEA, statement before the Subcommittee on Energy, Nuclear Proliferation, and Government Processes of the Senate Committee on Government Affairs, 9 September 1982 (excerpts)	106
Richard T. Kennedy, U.S. permanent representative to the IAEA, statement before a joint hearing of the Senate Foreign Relations Committee and the Subcommittee on Energy, Nuclear Proliferation, and Government Processes of the Senate Committee on Governmental Affairs, 30 September 1983	115
Richard T. Kennedy, U.S. permanent representative to IAEA, "Reprocessing and Plutonium Use in Civil Nuclear Programs," statement before the Subcommittees on Arms Control, International Security, and Science and on International Economic Policy and Trade of the House Foreign Affairs Committee, 24 July 1985	121

	Page
Kenneth L. Adelman, director of the Arms Control and Disarmament Agency, Richard T. Kennedy, U.S. permanent representative to IAEA and special adviser to the secretary of state on nonproliferation policy and nuclear energy affairs, and Paul D. Wolfowitz, assistant secretary of state for East Asian and Pacific Affairs, U.S.-China Nuclear Cooperation Agreement, statement before the House Foreign Affairs Committee, 31 July 1985	125
John H. Glenn, Senator from Ohio, "Nuclear Proliferation: The Current and Future Threat," *Issues in Science and Technology*," Winter 1985	130
Presidential determination no. 86-03, pursuant to Section 620E(e) of the Foreign Assistance Act of 1961, as amended, 25 November 1985	141
President Reagan's statement on U.S.-China nuclear cooperation agreement, 16 December 1985	142
Presidential determination no. 87-3, pursuant to Section 620E(e) of the Foreign Assistance Act of 1961, as amended, certifying that Pakistan does not possess a nuclear explosive device. 27 October 1986	143
Office of the Legal Advisor, Department of State, definition of "possession" of nuclear weapon	144
White House statement concerning nonproliferation agreement with allies, 16 April 1987	145
J. Stapleton Roy, deputy assistant secretary for East Asian and Pacific Affairs, statement before the Subcommittee on Asian and Pacific Affairs of the House Foreign Affairs Committee, concerning South Pacific nuclear free zone, 9 June 1987	146
Richard W. Murphy, assistant secretary for Near Eastern and South Asian affairs, "Pakistan and the Nuclear Issue," statement before the Subcommittees on Asian and Pacific Affairs and on International Economic Policy and Trade of the House Foreign Affairs Committee, 22 July 1987	149
President Reagan's message to Congress concerning U.S.-Japan nuclear cooperation agreement, 9 November 1987	151
Presidential determination no. 88-4, pursuant to Section 620E(e) of the Foreign Assistance Act of 1961, as amended, certifying that Pakistan does not possess a nuclear explosive device. 17 December 1987	152
White House statement concerning continuation of aid to Pakistan, 15 January 1988	153

	Page
Presidential determination no. 88-5, pursuant to Sections 670(a) and 620(E)(d) of the Foreign Assistance Act of 1961, as amended, certifying that Pakistan does not possess a nuclear explosive device. 15 January 1988.	154
Leonard Weiss, Staff Director of the Senate Committee on Governmental Affairs, "The Concept of 'Timely Warning' in the Nuclear Nonproliferation Act of 1978," inserted in the Congressional Record, 21 March 1988	155
Presidential determination no. 89-7, pursuant to Section 620E(e) of the Foreign Assistance Act of 1961, as amended, certifying that Pakistan does not possess a nuclear explosive device. 18 November 1988	179
Statement on talks between the United States and the Soviet Union on nonproliferation, 15 December 1988	180

The Bush Administration

	Page
Presidential determination no. 90-1, pursuant to Section 620E(e) of the Foreign Assistance Act of 1961, as amended, certifying that Pakistan does not possess a nuclear explosive device, 5 October 1989	181
Soviet-United States Joint Statement on Nonproliferation, 4 June 1990	182
White House Fact Sheet, Middle East Arms Control Initiative, 3 June 1991	186
Excerpts from a joint ministerial news conference held by Secretary Baker and other ministers concerning North Korea's nuclear weapons threat, 14 November 1991	189
President Bush's statement, "Non-proliferation Efforts Bolstered," and accompanying fact sheet, 13 July 1992	190
President Bush's statement on the purchase of highly enriched uranium from the Russian Federation	193

The Clinton Administration

	Page
Warren Christopher, Secretary of State, Message of support to the Nuclear Suppliers Group meeting in Lucerne, Switzerland, 1 April 1993	194
White House Fact Sheet: "Non-Proliferation and Export Control Policy", 27 September 1993	195
Les Aspin, Secretary of Defense, Remarks before the National Academy of Sciences Committee on International Security and Arms Control, 7 December 1993	197
Daniel Poneman, Special Assistant to the President, Memorandum "Agreed Definitions", 18 February 1994	205
Office of the Deputy Secretary of Defense, "Report on Nonproliferation and Counterproliferation Activities and Programs", May 1994 (Executive Summary)	206

U.S. NONPROLIFERATION LEGISLATION

CONTENTS

	Page
The Atomic Energy Act of 1954 as amended (excerpts)	216
The Foreign Assistance Act of 1961 as Amended (excerpts)	277
The Atomic Weapons and Special Nuclear Materials Rewards Act of 1955 as amended (excerpts)	284
The International Atomic Energy Agency Participation Act of 1957 as amended	286
The EURATOM Cooperation Act of 1958 as amended, with Congressional Resolution and Executive Orders on cooperation with EURATOM	290
International Bank of Reconstruction and Development as amended, sec. 701, 1977 (excerpts)	295
Export-Import Bank Act of 1945 as amended, 1977 (excerpts)	296
Nuclear Non-Proliferation Act of 1978, as amended (excerpts)	298
Export Administration Act of 1979 (excerpt)	314
U.S. Exports of Low-Enriched Uranium Fuel. Joint resolution (S.J. Res. 89) permitting the supply of additional low enriched uranium, 18 June 1980	315
Convention on the Physical Protection of Nuclear Material Implementation Act of 1982 (excerpts)	316
Nuclear Waste Policy Act of 1982 (excerpt)	320
Agreement for Nuclear Cooperation between the United States and China, 1985	321
Anti-Terrorism Act of 1987 (excerpt)	323
National Defense Authorization Act for Fiscal Year 1994 (excerpts)	325
Arms Control and Nonproliferation Act of 1994 (Title VIIA of Foreign Relations Authorization Act, FY1994 and FY1995)	341
Nuclear Proliferation Prevention Act (Title VIII of Foreign Relations Authorization Act, FY 1994 and FY1995)	353

INTERNATIONAL TREATIES AGREEMENTS AND LAWS

CONTENTS

	Page
Treaty on the Non-Proliferation of Nuclear Weapons (NPT)	372
Bruce Unger, "Participation in the Review Conferences of the Parties to the Treaty on the Non-Proliferation of Nuclear Weapons"	376
Treaty Banning Nuclear Weapon Tests in the Atmosphere, in Outer Space, and Under Water	384
Treaty for the Prohibition of Nuclear Weapons in Latin America (Treaty of Tlatelolco)	386
South Pacific Nuclear Free Zone Treaty	396
Convention on the Physical Protection of Nuclear Material	404
United Nations Resolution 255 on Security Assurance to Non-Nuclear Weapon States	411
The Structure and Content of Agreements between the International Atomic Energy Agency (IAEA) and States Required in Connection with the Treaty on Non-Proliferation of Nuclear Weapons (NPT)	412
Guidelines for Nuclear Transfers, agreed upon by the members of the Nuclear Supplier Group (the London Club)	426
Multilateral Nuclear Export Control Regimes	433
The Missile Technology Control Regime	437
Meeting of Adherents to the Nuclear Suppliers Guidelines, Statement on Full Scope Safeguards, 3 April 1992	441
Guidelines for Transfers of Nuclear-related Dual-use Equipment, Material and Related Technology	443
United Nations Security Council, Resolution 687, 3 April 1991 (excerpts)	449
United Nations Security Council, Declaration on Disarmament, Arms Control and Weapons of Mass Destruction, 31 January 1992	452
Commonwealth of Independent States, "Declaration on Nuclear Arms", 22 December 1991	453
Mutual Defense Treaty between the Republic of Korea and the United States of America, 1 October 1953 (18 November 1954)	455

	Page
Joint Declaration of the Denuclearization of the Korean Peninsula, 19 February 1992	456
Agreed Framework between the United States of America and the Democratic People's Republic of Korea, 23 October 1994	457

TECHNICAL ASPECTS

CONTENTS

	Page
Glossary, Abbreviations, Acronyms, and Conventions	462
Glossary	469

Fuel Cycle

Nuclear Devices and the Nuclear Fuel Cycle	474
Research Reactors: Country-by-Country Listing	501
Fuel Cycle Facilities	509
Flow Schemes for Light Water Nuclear Power Reactors	521
The Liquid Metal Fast Breeder Reactor	522
Heavy Water Reactor	523
High Temperature Gas-Cooled Reactor	523
Fuel Cycles for Commercial Power Reactors	524
Nuclear Fuel Cycles	525
Schematic Diagram of Flows of Fissile Material in the Civil and Military Nuclear Establishment	526
Summary of the Diversion Points in the LWR Fuel Cycle	527
Number of Shipments in the Nuclear Fuel Cycle Projected to the Year 2000	528
Uranium Enrichment	529
Important Enrichment Technique Property Ratings According to their Contribution to Proliferation Sensitivity	540
Technological Thresholds to Proliferation	540
A Schematic Drawing of a Calutron	541

Plutonium

Frank Barnaby, "Plutonium and Its Production"	544
J. Carson Mark, "Reactor-Grade Plutonium's Explosive Properties" (Washington, D.C.: Nuclear Control Institute, August 1990)	550
Plutonium Production in Various Types of Reactors	556
Improving the Proliferation Resistance of the Plutonium Cycle	556
Current Methods for Producing Weapon-Grade Plutonium	557
Weapon-Grade Plutonium from Reactor Production and Blending	557
An Estimate of the Global Amounts of Weapons Grade Plutonium	558

	Page
Nuclear Weapon Destructiveness	650
Weapon Damage Equivalents	650
Kill Probabilities against Hard Targets	650
Fission Weapons: Gun Mechanism, Implosion Technique; Thermonuclear Weapon	651
Schematic Description of a Nuclear Explosive of the Gun Barrel Type	652
Model of Hiroshima Uranium Bomb	652
Schematic Description of a Nuclear Explosive of the Implosion Type	653
Implosion Lens System	653
Model of Nagasaki Plutonium Bomb	654
Model of Israeli Plutonium Bomb	655
Schematic Drawing of a Fusion Nuclear Explosive	656
Nuclear Test Sites and Seismic Stations	657
Estimated Average Annual Expenditures on Strategic Nuclear Forces	658
Military Personnel in Strategic Nuclear Forces	658
U.S. Department of Energy: Atomic Energy Defense Activities and Expenditures, 1990	658
U.S. Nuclear Warhead Production, 1945-85	659
Nuclear Warheads in Full Scale Production and Research and Development, 1985-90	661
Nuclear Weapons Production and Naval Propulsion Fuel Cycle	662
The Effects of Nuclear Explosions	663
The Radioactive Cloud of a Nuclear Explosion	663
Prompt Radiation from Nuclear Explosions	663
Heat Damage from Nuclear Explosions	664
Air Blast and Wind from Nuclear Explosions	665
Idealized Fallout Dose Contours	666
Fallout Pattern Shape	667
Fraction of Maximum Dose	667
Estimated Fallout Contours for the Bravo Test (15 Megatons)	667
Decay of Radioactivity from a One-Megaton Nuclear Explosion	668
Influence of Duration of Exposure	669
Mortality from Whole-Body Radiation Exposure	669
Short-Term Effects of Acute Radiation Exposure	669
Casualties from a One-Megaton Attack on Detroit	670
Prompt Death and Injuries from a Nuclear Attack on U.S. Cities	670
Blast Effects on Detroit	671
Fallout Pattern from a One-Megaton Surface Burst in Detroit	671
Recent Weapons Effects Tests	672
Senate Committee on Governmental Affairs, "Intelligence Views on Proliferation: Comparison between Public Russian and U.S. Assessments", Proliferation Watch, January-February 1993	673
Department of Energy, "Declassification of Pre-1961 Pacific Nuclear Test Yields", 7 December 1993	679

	Page
Department of Energy, "Declassification of Unannounced Nuclear Tests at the Nevada Test Site", 7 December 1993	686
"Known Nuclear Tests Worldwide, 1945-1993", *The Bulletin of the Atomic Scientists*, May/June 1994	706

Disposal

Thomas L. Neff, "Integrating Uranium from Weapons into the Civil Fuel Cycle"	710
Office of Technology Assessment, "Dismantling the Bomb and Managing the Nuclear Materials", September 1993 (Summary)	717
Committee on International Security and Arms Control, National Academy of Sciences, "Management and Disposition of Excess Weapons Plutonium", Executive Summary, 1994	734

U.S. NONPROLIFERATION
POLICY DOCUMENTS

The Baruch Plan, Presented to the United Nations Atomic Energy Commission, June 14, 1946

My Fellow Members of the United Nations Atomic Energy Commission, and My Fellow Citizens of the World:

We are here to make a choice between the quick and the dead. That is our business.

Behind the black portent of the new atomic age lies a hope which, seized upon with faith, can work our salvation. If we fail, then we have damned every man to be the slave of Fear. Let us not deceive ourselves: We must elect World Peace or World Destruction.

Science has torn from nature a secret so vast in its potentialities that our minds cower from the terror it creates. Yet terror is not enough to inhibit the use of the atomic bomb. The terror created by weapons has never stopped man from employing them. For each new weapon a defense has been produced, in time. But now we face a condition in which adequate defense does not exist.

Science, which gave us this dread power, shows that it *can* be made a giant help to humanity, but science does *not* show us how to prevent its baleful use. So we have been appointed to obviate that peril by finding a meeting of the minds and the hearts of our peoples. Only in the will of mankind lies the answer.

It is to express this will and make it effective that we have been assembled. We must provide the mechanism to assure that atomic energy is used for peaceful purposes and preclude its use in war. To that end, we must provide immediate, swift, and sure punishment of those who violate the agreements that are reached by the nations. Penalization is essential if peace is to be more than a feverish interlude between wars. And, too, the United Nations can prescribe individual responsibility and punishment on the principles applied at Nürnberg by the Union of Soviet Socialist Republics, the United Kingdom, France, and the United States—a formula certain to benefit the world's future.

In this crisis, we represent not only our governments but, in a larger way, we represent the peoples of the world. We must remember that the peoples do not belong to the governments but that the governments belong to the peoples. We must answer their demands; we must answer the world's longing for peace and security.

In that desire the United States shares ardently and hopefully. The search of science for the absolute weapon has reached fruition in this country. But she stands ready to proscribe and destroy this instrument—to lift its use from death to life—if the world will join in a pact to that end.

In our success lies the promise of a new life, freed from the heart-stopping fears that now beset the world. The beginning of victory for the great ideals for which millions have bled and died lies in building a workable plan. Now we approach fulfilment of the aspirations of mankind. At the end of the road lies the fairer, better, surer life we crave and mean to have.

Only by a lasting peace are liberties and democracies strengthened and deepened. War is their enemy. And it will not do to believe that any of us can escape war's devastation. Victor, vanquished, and neutrals alike are affected physically, economically, and morally.

Against the degradation of war we can erect a safeguard. That is the guerdon for which we reach. Within the scope of the formula we outline here there will be found, to those who seek it, the essential elements of our purpose. Others will see only emptiness. Each of us carries his own mirror in which is reflected hope—or determined desperation—courage or cowardice.

There is a famine throughout the world today. It starves men's bodies. But there is a greater famine—the hunger of men's spirit. That starvation can be cured by the conquest of fear, and the substitution of hope, from which springs faith—faith in each other, faith that we want to work together toward salvation, and determination that those who threaten the peace and safety shall be punished.

The peoples of these democracies gathered here have a particular concern with our answer, for their peoples hate war. They will have a heavy exaction to make of those who fail to provide an escape. They are not afraid of an internationalism that protects;

they are unwilling to be fobbed off by mouthings about narrow sovereignty, which is today's phrase for yesterday's isolation.

The basis of a sound foreign policy, in this new age, for all the nations here gathered, is that anything that happens, no matter where or how, which menaces the peace of the world, or the economic stability, concerns each and all of us.

That, roughly, may be said to be the central theme of the United Nations. It is with that thought we begin consideration of the most important subject that can engage mankind—life itself.

Let there be no quibbling about the duty and the responsibility of this group and of the governments we represent. I was moved, in the afternoon of my life, to add my effort to gain the world's quest, by the broad mandate under which we were created. The resolution of the General Assembly, passed January 24, 1946 in London, reads:

"*Section V. Terms of Reference of the Commission*

"The Commission shall proceed with the utmost despatch and enquire into all phases of the problem, and make such recommendations from time to time with respect to them as it finds possible. In particular the Commission shall make specific proposals:

"(a) For extending between all nations the exchange of basic scientific information for peaceful ends;

"(b) For control of atomic energy to the extent necessary to ensure its use only for peaceful purposes;

"(c) For the elimination from national armaments of atomic weapons and of all other major weapons adaptable to mass destruction;

"(d) For effective safeguards by way of inspection and other means to protect complying States against the hazards of violations and evasions.

"The work of the Commission should proceed by separate stages, the successful completion of each of which will develop the necessary confidence of the world before the next stage is undertaken. . . ."[1]

Our mandate rests, in text and in spirit, upon the outcome of the Conference in Moscow of Messrs. Molotov of the Union of Soviet Socialist Republics, Bevin of the United Kingdom, and Byrnes of the United States of America. The three Foreign

[1] *Department of State Bulletin*, Feb. 10, 1946, p. 198.

Ministers on December 27, 1945 proposed the establishment of this body.²

Their action was animated by a preceding conference in Washington on November 15, 1945, when the President of the United States, associated with Mr. Attlee, Prime Minister of the United Kingdom, and Mr. Mackenzie King, Prime Minister of Canada, stated that international control of the whole field of atomic energy was immediately essential. They proposed the formation of this body. In examining that source, the Agreed Declaration, it will be found that the fathers of the concept recognized the final means of world salvation—the abolition of war. Solemnly they wrote:

"We are aware that the only complete protection for the civilized world from the destructive use of scientific knowledge lies in the prevention of war. No system of safeguards that can be devised will of itself provide an effective guarantee against production of atomic weapons by a nation bent on aggression. Nor can we ignore the possibility of the development of other weapons, or of new methods of warfare, which may constitute as great a threat to civilization as the military use of atomic energy." ³

Through the historical approach I have outlined, we find ourselves here to test if man can produce, through his will and faith, the miracle of peace, just as he has, through science and skill, the miracle of the atom.

The United States proposes the creation of an International Atomic Development Authority, to which should be entrusted all phases of the development and use of atomic energy, starting with the raw material and including—

1. Managerial control or ownership of all atomic-energy activities potentially dangerous to world security.
2. Power to control, inspect, and license all other atomic activities.
3. The duty of fostering the beneficial uses of atomic energy.
4. Research and development responsibilities of an affirmative character intended to put the Authority in the forefront of atomic knowledge and thus to enable it to comprehend, and therefore to detect, misuse of atomic energy. To be effective, the Authority must itself be the world's leader in the field of atomic knowledge

---
² *Department of State Bulletin*, Dec. 30, 1945, p. 1031.
³ *Ibid.*, Nov. 18, 1945, p. 781.

and development and thus supplement its legal authority with the great power inherent in possession of leadership in knowledge.

I offer this as a basis for beginning our discussion.

But I think the peoples we serve would not believe—and without faith nothing counts—that a treaty, merely outlawing possession or use of the atomic bomb, constitutes effective fulfilment of the instructions to this Commission. Previous failures have been recorded in trying the method of simple renunciation, unsupported by effective guaranties of security and armament limitation. No one would have faith in that approach alone.

Now, if ever, is the time to act for the common good. Public opinion supports a world movement toward security. If I read the signs aright, the peoples want a program not composed merely of pious thoughts but of enforceable sanctions—an international law with teeth in it.

We of this nation, desirous of helping to bring peace to the world and realizing the heavy obligations upon us arising from our possession of the means of producing the bomb and from the fact that it is part of our armament, are prepared to make our full contribution toward effective control of atomic energy.

When an adequate system for control of atomic energy, including the renunciation of the bomb as a weapon, has been agreed upon and put into effective operation and condign punishments set up for violations of the rules of control which are to be stigmatized as international crimes, we propose that—

1. Manufacture of atomic bombs shall stop;
2. Existing bombs shall be disposed of pursuant to the terms of the treaty; and
3. The Authority shall be in possession of full information as to the know-how for the production of atomic energy.

Let me repeat, so as to avoid misunderstanding: My country is ready to make its full contribution toward the end we seek, subject of course to our constitutional processes and to an adequate system of control becoming fully effective, as we finally work it out.

Now as to violations: In the agreement, penalties of as serious a nature as the nations may wish and as immediate and certain in their execution as possible should be fixed for—

1. Illegal possession or use of an atomic bomb;
2. Illegal possession, or separation, of atomic material suitable for use in an atomic bomb;
3. Seizure of any plant or other property belonging to or licensed by the Authority;

4. Wilful interference with the activities of the Authority;

5. Creation or operation of dangerous projects in a manner contrary to, or in the absence of, a license granted by the international control body.

It would be a deception, to which I am unwilling to lend myself, were I not to say to you and to our peoples that the matter of punishment lies at the very heart of our present security system. It might as well be admitted, here and now, that the subject goes straight to the veto power contained in the Charter of the United Nations so far as it relates to the field of atomic energy. The Charter permits penalization only by concurrence of each of the five great powers—the Union of Soviet Socialist Republics, the United Kingdom, China, France, and the United States.

I want to make very plain that I am concerned here with the veto power only as it affects this particular problem. There must be no veto to protect those who violate their solemn agreements not to develop or use atomic energy for destructive purposes.

The bomb does not wait upon debate. To delay may be to die. The time between violation and preventive action or punishment would be all too short for extended discussion as to the course to be followed.

As matters now stand several years may be necessary for another country to produce a bomb, *de novo*. However, once the basic information is generally known, and the Authority has established producing plants for peaceful purposes in the several countries, an illegal seizure of such a plant might permit a malevolent nation to produce a bomb in 12 months, and if preceded by secret preparation and necessary facilities perhaps even in a much shorter time. The time required—the advance warning given of the possible use of a bomb—can only be generally estimated but obviously will depend upon many factors, including the success with which the Authority has been able to introduce elements of safety in the design of its plants and the degree to which illegal and secret preparation for the military use of atomic energy will have been eliminated. Presumably no nation would think of starting a war with only one bomb.

This shows how imperative speed is in detecting and penalizing violations.

The process of prevention and penalization—a problem of profound statecraft—is, as I read it, implicit in the Moscow statement, signed by the Union of Soviet Socialist Republics, the United States, and the United Kingdom a few months ago.

But before a country is ready to relinquish any winning weapons it must have more than words to reassure it. It must have a guarantee of safety, not only against the offenders in the atomic area but against the illegal users of other weapons—bacteriological, biological, gas—perhaps—why not?—against war itself.

In the elimination of war lies our solution, for only then will nations cease to compete with one another in the production and use of dread "secret" weapons which are evaluated solely by their capacity to kill. This devilish program takes us back not merely to the Dark Ages but from cosmos to chaos. If we succeed in finding a suitable way to control atomic weapons, it is reasonable to hope that we may also preclude the use of other weapons adaptable to mass destruction. When a man learns to say "A" he can, if he chooses, learn the rest of the alphabet too.

Let this be anchored in our minds:

Peace is never long preserved by weight of metal or by an armament race. Peace can be made tranquil and secure only by understanding and agreement fortified by sanctions. We must embrace international cooperation or international disintegration.

Science has taught us how to put the atom to work. But to make it work for good instead of for evil lies in the domain dealing with the principles of human duty. We are now facing a problem more of ethics than of physics.

The solution will require apparent sacrifice in pride and in position, but better pain as the price of peace than death as the price of war.

I now submit the following measures as representing the fundamental features of a plan which would give effect to certain of the conclusions which I have epitomized.

1. General. The Authority should set up a thorough plan for control of the field of atomic energy, through various forms of ownership, dominion, licenses, operation, inspection, research, and management by competent personnel. After this is provided for, there should be as little interference as may be with the economic plans and the present private, corporate, and state relationships in the several countries involved.

2. Raw Materials. The Authority should have as one of its earliest purposes to obtain and maintain complete and accurate information on world supplies of uranium and thorium and to bring them under its dominion. The precise pattern of control for various types of deposits of such materials will have to depend upon the geological, mining, refining, and economic facts involved in different situations.

The Authority should conduct continuous surveys so that it will have the most complete knowledge of the world geology of uranium and thorium. Only after all current information on world sources of uranium and thorium is known to us all can equitable plans be made for their production, refining, and distribution.

3. Primary Production Plants. The Authority should exercise complete managerial control of the production of fissionable materials. This means that it should control and operate all plants producing fissionable materials in dangerous quantities and must own and control the product of these plants.

4. Atomic Explosives. The Authority should be given sole and exclusive right to conduct research in the field of atomic explosives. Research activities in the field of atomic explosives are essential in order that the Authority may keep in the forefront of knowledge in the field of atomic energy and fulfil the objective of preventing illicit manufacture of bombs. Only by maintaining its position as the best-informed agency will the Authority be able to determine the line between intrinsically dangerous and non-dangerous activities.

5. Strategic Distribution of Activities and Materials. The activities entrusted exclusively to the Authority because they are intrinsically dangerous to security should be distributed throughout the world. Similarly, stockpiles of raw materials and fissionable materials should not be centralized.

6. Non-Dangerous Activities. A function of the Authority should be promotion of the peacetime benefits of atomic energy.

Atomic research (except in explosives), the use of research reactors, the production of radioactive tracers by means of non-dangerous reactors, the use of such tracers, and to some extent the production of power should be open to nations and their citizens under reasonable licensing arrangements from the Authority. Denatured materials, whose use we know also requires suitable safeguards, should be furnished for such purposes by the Authority under lease or other arrangement. Denaturing seems to have been overestimated by the public as a safety measure.

7. Definition of Dangerous and Non-Dangerous Activities. Although a reasonable dividing line can be drawn between dangerous and non-dangerous activities, it is not hard and fast. Provision should, therefore, be made to assure constant re-examination of the questions and to permit revision of the dividing line as changing conditions and new discoveries may require.

8. Operations of Dangerous Activities. Any plant dealing with uranium or thorium after it once reaches the potential of dangerous use must be not only subject to the most rigorous and competent inspection by the Authority, but its actual operation shall be under the management, supervision, and control of the Authority.

9. Inspection. By assigning intrinsically dangerous activities exclusively to the Authority, the difficulties of inspection are reduced. If the Authority is the only agency which may lawfully conduct dangerous activities, then visible operation by others than the Authority will constitute an unambiguous danger signal. Inspection will also occur in connection with the licensing functions of the Authority.

10. Freedom of Access. Adequate ingress and egress for all qualified representatives of the Authority must be assured. Many of the inspection activities of the Authority should grow out of, and be incidental to, its other functions. Important measures of inspection will be associated with the tight control of raw materials, for this is a keystone of the plan. The continuing activities of prospecting, survey, and research in relation to raw materials will be designed not only to serve the affirmative development functions of the Authority but also to assure that no surreptitious operations are conducted in the raw-materials field by nations or their citizens.

11. Personnel. The personnel of the Authority should be recruited on a basis of proven competence but also so far as possible on an international basis.

12. Progress by Stages. A primary step in the creation of the system of control is the setting forth, in comprehensive terms, of the functions, responsibilities, powers, and limitations of the Authority. Once a charter for the Authority has been adopted, the Authority and the system of control for which it will be responsible will require time to become fully organized and effective. The plan of control will, therefore, have to come into effect in successive stages. These should be specifically fixed in the charter or means should be otherwise set forth in the charter for transitions from one stage to another, as contemplated in the resolution of the United Nations Assembly which created this Commission.

13. Disclosures. In the deliberations of the United Nations Commission on Atomic Energy, the United States is prepared to make available the information essential to a reasonable understanding of the proposals which it advocates. Further disclosures must be dependent, in the interests of all, upon the effective ratification of the treaty. When the Authority is actually created, the United States will join the other nations in making available the further information essential to that organization for the performance of its functions. As the successive stages of international control are reached, the United States will be prepared to yield, to the extent required by each stage, national control of activities in this field to the Authority.

14. International Control. There will be questions about the extent of control to be allowed to national bodies, when the Authority is established. Purely national authorities for control and development of atomic energy should to the extent necessary for the effective operation of the Authority be subordinate to it. This is neither an endorsement nor a disapproval of the creation of national authorities. The Commission should evolve a clear demarcation of the scope of duties and responsibilities of such national authorities.

And now I end. I have submitted an outline for present discussion. Our consideration will be broadened by the criticism of the United States proposals and by the plans of the other nations, which, it is to be hoped, will be submitted at their early convenience. I and my associates of the United States Delegation will make available to each member of this body books and pamphlets, including the Acheson-Lilienthal report, recently made by the United States Department of State, and the McMahon Committee Monograph No. 1 entitled "Essential Information on Atomic Energy" relating to the McMahon bill recently passed by the United States Senate, which may prove of value in assessing the situation.[4]

All of us are consecrated to making an end of gloom and hopelessness. It will not be an easy job. The way is long and thorny, but supremely worth traveling. All of us want to stand erect, with our faces to the sun, instead of being forced to burrow into the earth, like rats.

The pattern of salvation must be worked out by all for all.

The light at the end of the tunnel is dim, but our path seems to grow brighter as we actually begin our journey. We cannot yet light the way to the end. However, we hope the suggestions of my Government will be illuminating.

Let us keep in mind the exhortation of Abraham Lincoln, whose words, uttered at a moment of shattering national peril, form a

---

[4] Department of State publication 2498; for excerpts from the Acheson-Lilienthal report see *Department of State Bulletin*, Apr. 7, 1946, p. 553. The text of the McMahon bill is S. Rept. 1211, 79th Cong.

complete text for our deliberation. I quote, paraphrasing slightly:

"We cannot escape history. We of this meeting will be remembered in spite of ourselves. No personal significance or insignificance can spare one or another of us. The fiery trial through which we are passing will light us down in honor or dishonor to the latest generation.

"We say we are for Peace. The world will not forget that we say this. We know how to save Peace. The world knows that we do. We, even we here, hold the power and have the responsibility.

"We shall nobly save, or meanly lose, the last, best hope of earth. The way is plain, peaceful, generous, just—a way which, if followed, the world will forever applaud."

My thanks for your attention.

President Eisenhower's Address Before the General Assembly of the United Nations on the Peaceful Uses of Nuclear Energy, December 8, 1953

Madame President, Members of the General Assembly:

When Secretary General Hammarskjold's invitation to address this General Assembly reached me in Bermuda, I was just beginning a series of conferences with the Prime Ministers and Foreign Ministers of Great Britain and of France. Our subject was some of the problems that beset our world.

During the remainder of the Bermuda Conference, I had constantly in mind that ahead of me lay a great honor. That honor is mine today as I stand here, privileged to address the General Assembly of the United Nations.

At the same time that I appreciate the distinction of addressing you, I have a sense of exhilaration as I look upon this Assembly.

Never before in history has so much hope for so many people been gathered together in a single organization. Your deliberations and decisions during these somber years have already realized part of those hopes.

But the great tests and the great accomplishments still lie ahead. And in the confident expectation of those accomplishments, I would use the office which, for the time being, I hold, to assure you that the Government of the United States will remain steadfast in its support of this body. This we shall do in the conviction that you will provide a great share of the wisdom, the courage, and the faith which can bring to this world lasting peace for all nations, and happiness and well-being for all men.

Clearly, it would not be fitting for me to take this occasion to present to you a unilateral American report on Bermuda. Nevertheless, I assure you that in our deliberations on that lovely island we sought to invoke those same great concepts of universal peace and human dignity which are so clearly etched in your Charter.

Neither would it be a measure of this great opportunity merely to recite, however hopefully, pious platitudes.

I therefore decided that this occasion warranted my saying to you some of the things that have been on the minds and hearts of my legislative and executive associates and on mine for a great many months—thoughts I had originally planned to say primarily to the American people.

I know that the American people share my deep belief that if a danger exists in the world, it is a danger shared by all—and equally, that if hope exists in the mind of one nation, that hope should be shared by all.

Finally, if there is to be advanced any proposal designed to ease even by the smallest measure the tensions of today's world, what more appropriate audience could there be than the members of the General Assembly of the United Nations?

I feel impelled to speak today in a language that in a sense is new—one which I, who have spent so much of my life in the military profession, would have preferred never to use.

That new language is the language of atomic warfare.

The atomic age has moved forward at such a pace that every citizen of the world should have some comprehension, at least in comparative terms, of the extent of this development of the utmost significance to every one of us. Clearly, if the peoples of the world are to conduct an intelligent search for peace, they must be armed with the significant facts of today's existence.

My recital of atomic danger and power is necessarily stated in United States terms, for these are the only incontrovertible facts that I know. I need hardly point out to this Assembly, however, that this subject is global, not merely national in character.

On July 16, 1945, the United States set off the world's first atomic explosion. Since that date in 1945, the United States of America has conducted 42 test explosions.

Atomic bombs today are more than 25 times as powerful as the weapons with which the atomic age dawned, while hydrogen weapons are in the ranges of millions of tons of TNT equivalent.

Today, the United States' stockpile of atomic weapons, which, of course, increases daily, exceeds by many times the explosive equivalent of the total of all bombs and all shells that came from every plane and every gun in every theatre of war in all of the years of World War II.

A single air group, whether afloat or land-based, can now deliver to any reachable target a destructive cargo exceeding in power all the bombs that fell on Britain in all of World War II.

In size and variety, the development of atomic weapons has been no less remarkable. The development has been such that atomic weapons have virtually achieved conventional status within our armed services. In the United States, the Army, the Navy, the Air Force, and the Marine Corps are all capable of putting this weapon to military use.

But the dread secret, and the fearful engines of atomic might, are not ours alone.

In the first place, the secret is possessed by our friends and allies, Great Britain and Canada, whose scientific genius made a tremendous contribution to our original discoveries, and the designs of atomic bombs.

The secret is also known by the Soviet Union.

The Soviet Union has informed us that, over recent years, it has devoted extensive resources to atomic weapons. During this period, the Soviet Union has exploded a series of atomic devices, including at least one involving thermo-nuclear reactions.

If at one time the United States possessed what might have been called a monopoly of atomic power, that monopoly ceased to exist several years ago. Therefore, although our earlier start has permitted us to accumulate what is today a great quantitative advantage, the atomic realities of today comprehend two facts of even greater significance.

First, the knowledge now possessed by several nations will eventually be shared by others—possibly all others.

Second, even a vast superiority in numbers of weapons, and a consequent capability of devastating retaliation, is no preventive, of itself, against the fearful material damage and toll of human lives that would be inflicted by surprise aggression.

The free world, at least dimly aware of these facts, has naturally embarked on a large program of warning and defense systems. That program will be accelerated and expanded.

But let no one think that the expenditure of vast sums for weapons and systems of defense can guarantee absolute safety for the cities and citizens of any nation. The awful arithmetic of the atomic bomb does not permit of any such easy solution. Even against the most powerful defense, an aggressor in possession of the effective minimum number of atomic bombs for a surprise attack could probably place a sufficient number of his bombs on the chosen targets to cause hideous damage.

Should such an atomic attack be launched against the United

States, our reactions would be swift and resolute. But for me to say that the defense capabilities of the United States are such that they could inflict terrible losses upon an aggressor—for me to say that the retaliation capabilities of the United States are so great that such an aggressor's land would be laid waste—all this, while fact, is not the true expression of the purpose and the hope of the United States.

To pause there would be to confirm the hopeless finality of a belief that two atomic colossi are doomed malevolently to eye each other indefinitely across a trembling world. To stop there would be to accept helplessly the probability of civilization destroyed—the annihilation of the irreplaceable heritage of mankind handed down to us generation from generation—and the condemnation of mankind to begin all over again the age-old struggle upward from savagery toward decency, and right, and justice.

Surely no sane member of the human race could discover victory in such desolation. Could anyone wish his name to be coupled by history with such human degradation and destruction.

Occasional pages of history do record the faces of the "Great Destroyers" but the whole book of history reveals mankind's never-ending quest for peace, and mankind's God-given capacity to build.

It is with the book of history, and not with isolated pages, that the United States will ever wish to be identified. My country wants to be constructive, not destructive. It wants agreements, not wars, among nations. It wants itself to live in freedom, and in the confidence that the people of every other nation enjoy equally the right of choosing their own way of life.

So my country's purpose is to help us move out of the dark chamber of horrors into the light, to find a way by which the minds of men, the hopes of men, the souls of men everywhere, can move forward toward peace and happiness and well being.

In this quest, I know that we must not lack patience.

I know that in a world divided, such as ours today, salvation cannot be attained by one dramatic act.

I know that many steps will have to be taken over many months before the world can look at itself one day and truly realize that a new climate of mutually peaceful confidence is abroad in the world.

But I know, above all else, that we must start to take these steps—*now*.

The United States and its allies, Great Britain and France, have over the past months tried to take some of these steps. Let no one say that we shun the conference table.

On the record has long stood the request of the United States, Great Britain, and France to negotiate with the Soviet Union the problems of a divided Germany.

On that record has long stood the request of the same three nations to negotiate an Austrian Peace Treaty.

On the same record still stands the request of the United Nations to negotiate the problems of Korea.

Most recently, we have received from the Soviet Union what is in effect an expression of willingness to hold a Four Power Meeting. Along with our allies, Great Britain and France, we were pleased to see that this note did not contain the unacceptable preconditions previously put forward.

As you already know from our joint Bermuda communique, the United States, Great Britain, and France have agreed promptly to meet with the Soviet Union.

The Government of the United States approaches this conference with hopeful sincerity. We will bend every effort of our minds to the single purpose of emerging from that conference with tangible results toward peace—the only true way of lessening international tension.

We never have, we never will, propose or suggest that the Soviet Union surrender what is rightfully theirs.

We will never say that the peoples of Russia are an enemy with whom we have no desire ever to deal or mingle in friendly and fruitful relationship.

On the contrary, we hope that this coming Conference may initiate a relationship with the Soviet Union which will eventually bring about a free intermingling of the peoples of the East and of the West—the one sure, human way of developing the understanding required for confident and peaceful relations.

Instead of the discontent which is now settling upon Eastern Germany, occupied Austria, and the countries of Eastern Europe, we seek a harmonious family of free European nations, with none a threat to the other, and least of all a threat to the peoples of Russia.

Beyond the turmoil and strife and misery of Asia, we seek peaceful opportunity for these peoples to develop their natural resources and to elevate their lives.

These are not idle words or shallow visions. Behind them lies a story of nations lately come to independence, not as a result of war, but through free grant or peaceful negotiation. There is a record, already written, of assistance gladly given by nations of the West to needy peoples, and to those suffering the temporary effects of famine, drought, and natural disaster.

These are deeds of peace. They speak more loudly than promises or protestations of peaceful intent.

But I do not wish to rest either upon the reiteration of past proposals or the restatement of past deeds. The gravity of the time is such that every new avenue of peace, no matter how dimly discernible, should be explored.

There is at least one new avenue of peace which has not yet been well explored—an avenue now laid out by the General Assembly of the United Nations.

In its resolution of November 18th, 1953, this General Assembly suggested—and I quote—"that the Disarmament Commission study the desirability of establishing a sub-committee consisting of representatives of the Powers principally involved, which should seek in private an acceptable solution . . . and report on such a solution to the General Assembly and to the Security Council not later than 1 September 1954."

The United States, heeding the suggestion of the General Assembly of the United Nations, is instantly prepared to meet privately with such other countries as may be "principally involved," to seek "an acceptable solution" to the atomic armaments race which overshadows not only the peace, but the very life, of the world.

We shall carry into these private or diplomatic talks a new conception.

The United States would seek more than the mere reduction or elimination of atomic materials for military purposes.

It is not enough to take this weapon out of the hands of the soldiers. It must be put into the hands of those who will know how to strip its military casing and adapt it to the arts of peace.

The United States knows that if the fearful trend of atomic military buildup can be reversed, this greatest of destructive forces can be developed into a great boon, for the benefit of all mankind.

The United States knows that peaceful power from atomic energy is no dream of the future. That capability, already proved, is here—now—today. Who can doubt, if the entire body of the world's scientists and engineers had adequate amounts of fissionable material with which to test and develop their ideas, that this capability would rapidly be transformed into universal, efficient, and economic usage.

To hasten the day when fear of the atom will begin to disappear from the minds of people, and the governments of the East and West, there are certain steps that can be taken now.

I therefore make the following proposals:

The Governments principally involved, to the extent permitted by elementary prudence, to begin now and continue to make joint contributions from their stockpiles of normal uranium and fissionable materials to an International Atomic Energy Agency. We would expect that such an agency would be set up under the aegis of the United Nations.

The ratios of contributions, the procedures and other details would properly be within the scope of the "private conversations" I have referred to earlier.

The United States is prepared to undertake these explorations in good faith. Any partner of the United States acting in the same good faith will find the United States a not unreasonable or ungenerous associate.

Undoubtedly initial and early contributions to this plan would be small in quantity. However, the proposal has the great virtue that it can be undertaken without the irritations and mutual suspicions incident to any attempt to set up a completely acceptable system of world-wide inspection and control.

The Atomic Energy Agency could be made responsible for the impounding, storage, and protection of the contributed fissionable and other materials. The ingenuity of our scientists will provide special safe conditions under which such a bank of fissionable material can be made essentially immune to surprise seizure.

The more important responsibility of this Atomic Energy Agency would be to devise methods whereby this fissionable material would be allocated to serve the peaceful pursuits of mankind. Experts would be mobilized to apply atomic energy to the needs of agriculture, medicine, and other peaceful activities. A special purpose would be to provide abundant electrical energy in the power-starved areas of the world. Thus the contributing powers would be dedicating some of their strength to serve the needs rather than the fears of mankind.

The United States would be more than willing—it would be proud to take up with others "principally involved" the development of plans whereby such peaceful use of atomic energy would be expedited.

Of those "principally involved" the Soviet Union must, of course, be one.

I would be prepared to submit to the Congress of the United States, and with every expectation of approval, any such plan that would:

First—encourage world-wide investigation into the most effective peacetime uses of fissionable material, and with the certainty that they had all the material needed for the conduct of all experiments that were appropriate;

Second—begin to diminish the potential destructive power of the world's atomic stockpiles;

Third—allow all peoples of all nations to see that, in this enlightened age, the great powers of the earth, both of the East and of the West, are interested in human aspirations first, rather than in building up the armaments of war;

Fourth—open up a new channel for peaceful discussion, and initiate at least a new approach to the many difficult problems that must be solved in both private and public conversations, if the world is to shake off the inertia imposed by fear, and is to make positive progress toward peace.

Against the dark background of the atomic bomb, the United States does not wish merely to present strength, but also the desire and the hope for peace.

The coming months will be fraught with fateful decisions. In this Assembly; in the capitals and military headquarters of the world; in the hearts of men everywhere, be they governors or governed, may they be the decisions which will lead this world out of fear and into peace.

To the making of these fateful decisions, the United States pledges before you—and therefore before the world—its determination to help solve the fearful atomic dilemma—to devote its entire heart and mind to find the way by which the miraculous inventiveness of man shall not be dedicated to his death, but consecrated to his life.

I again thank the delegates for the great honor they have done me, in inviting me to appear before them, and in listening to me so courteously. Thank you.

NOTE: The President's opening words referred to Mme. Vijaya Pandit, President of the United Nations General Assembly.

EXECUTIVE ORDERS

(3) **Executive Order 10841, September 30, 1959, 24 F.R. 7941, 3 CFR 1959-63 Comp., p. 375; as amended by Executive Order 10956, August 12, 1961, 26 F.R. 7315, 3 CFR 1959-63 Comp., p. 482**

PROVIDING FOR THE CARRYING OUT OF CERTAIN PROVISIONS OF THE ATOMIC ENERGY ACT OF 1954, AS AMENDED, RELATING TO INTERNATIONAL COOPERATION

By virtue of the authority vested in me by the Atomic Energy Act of 1954, as amended (42 U.S.C. 2011 et seq.), herein referred to as the Act, and section 301 of title 3 of the United States Code, and as President of the United States, it is ordered as follows:

Section 1. Whenever the President, pursuant to section 123 of the Act, has approved and authorized the execution of a proposed agreement providing for cooperation pursuant to section 91c, 144a, 144b, or 144c of the Act (42 U.S.C. 2121(c), 2164(a), 2164(c)), such approval and authorization by the President shall constitute his authorization to cooperate to the extent provided for in the agreement and in the manner provided for in section 91c, 144a, 144b, or 144c, as pertinent. In respect of sections 91c, 144b, and 144c, authorizations by the President to cooperate shall be subject to the requirements of section 123d of the Act and shall also be subjected to appropriate determinations made pursuant to section 2 of this order.

Sec. 2. (a) The Secretary of Defense and the Atomic Energy Commission are hereby designated and empowered to exercise jointly, after consultation with executive agencies as may be appropriate, the following described authority without the approval, ratification, or other action of the President:

(1) The authority vested in the President by section 91c of the Act to determine that the proposed cooperation and each proposed transfer arrangement referred to in that section will promote and will not constitute an unreasonable risk to the common defense and security.

(2) The authority vested in the President by section 144b of the Act to determine that the proposed cooperation and the proposed communication of Restricted Data referred to in that section will promote and will not constitute an unreasonable risk to the common defense and security: *Provided,* That each determination made under this paragraph shall be referred to the President and, unless disapproved by him, shall become effective fifteen days after such referral or at such later time as may be specified in the determination.[1]

(3) The authority vested in the President by section 144c of the Act to determine that the proposed cooperation and the communication of the proposed Restricted Data referred to in that section will promote and will not constitute an unreasonable risk to the common defense and security.

(b) Whenever the Secretary of Defense and the Atomic Energy Commission are unable to agree upon a joint determination under the provisions of subsection (a) of this section, the recommendations of each of them, together with the recommendations of other agencies concerned, shall be referred to the President, and the determination shall be made by the President.

Sec. 3. This order shall not be construed as delegating the function vested in the President by section 91c of the Act of approving programs proposed under that section.

Sec. 4. (a) The functions of negotiating and entering into international agreements under the Act shall be performed by or under the authority of the Secretary of State.

(b) International cooperation under the Act shall be subject to the responsibilities of the Secretary of State with respect to the foreign policy of the United States pertinent thereto.

---

[1] This provision was added by Executive Order 10956, Aug. 12, 1961, 26 F.R. 7315.

Executive Order 11057, October 18, 1962, 27 F.R. 10289

AUTHORIZATION FOR THE COMMUNICATION OF RESTRICTED DATA BY THE DEPARTMENT OF STATE

By virtue of the authority vested in me by the Atomic Energy Act of 1954, as amended (hereinafter referred to as the Act; 42 U.S.C. 2011 et seq.), and as President of the United States, it is ordered as follows:

The Department of State is hereby authorized to communicate, in accordance with the terms and conditions of any agreement for cooperation arranged pursuant to subsection 144b of the Act (42 U.S.C. 2164(b)), such Restricted Data and data removed from the Restricted Data category under subsection 142d of the Act (42 U.S.C. 2162(d)) as is determined

"(i) by the President, pursuant to the provisions of the Act, or (ii) by the Atomic Energy Commission [1] and the Department of Defense, jointly pursuant to the provisions of Executive Order No. 10841, as amended,

to be transmissible under the agreement for cooperation involved. Such communications shall be effected through mechanisms established by the Department of State in accordance with the terms and conditions of the agreement for cooperation involved: *Provided,* That no such communication shall be made by the Department of State until the proposed communication has been authorized either in accordance with procedures, adopted by the Atomic Energy Commission [1] and the Department of Defense and applicable to conduct of programs for cooperation by those agencies, or in accordance with procedures approved by the Atomic Energy Commission [1] and the Department of Defense and applicable to conduct of programs for cooperation by the Department of State.

---

[1] Functions of the Atomic Energy Commission under this Executive order were modified so that such functions would be exercised by the Secretary of Energy and the Nuclear Regulatory Commission, pursuant to sec. 4(a)(1) of Executive Order 12038, Feb. 3, 1978, 43 F.R. 4957.

232 Commencement Address at American University in Washington. *June 10, 1963*

President Anderson, members of the faculty, board of trustees, distinguished guests, my old colleague, Senator Bob Byrd, who has earned his degree through many years of attending night law school, while I am earning mine in the next 30 minutes, ladies and gentlemen:

It is with great pride that I participate in this ceremony of the American University, sponsored by the Methodist Church, founded by Bishop John Fletcher Hurst, and first opened by President Woodrow Wilson in 1914. This is a young and growing university, but it has already fulfilled Bishop Hurst's enlightened hope for the study of history and public affairs in a city devoted to the making of history and to the conduct of the public's business. By sponsoring this institution of higher learning for all who wish to learn, whatever their color or their creed, the Methodists of this area and the Nation deserve the Nation's thanks, and I commend all those who are today graduating.

Professor Woodrow Wilson once said that every man sent out from a university should be a man of his nation as well as a man of his time, and I am confident that the men and women who carry the honor of graduating from this institution will continue to give from their lives, from their talents, a high measure of public service and public support.

"There are few earthly things more beautiful than a university," wrote John Masefield, in his tribute to English universities—and his words are equally true today. He did not refer to spires and towers, to campus greens and ivied walls. He admired the splendid beauty of the university, he said, because it was "a place where those who hate ignorance may strive to know, where those who perceive truth may strive to make others see."

I have, therefore, chosen this time and this place to discuss a topic on which ignorance too often abounds and the truth is too rarely perceived—yet it is the most important topic on earth: world peace.

What kind of peace do I mean? What kind of peace do we seek? Not a Pax Americana enforced on the world by American weapons of war. Not the peace of the grave or the security of the slave. I am talking about genuine peace, the kind of peace that makes life on earth worth living, the kind that enables men and nations to grow and to hope and to build a better life for their children—not merely peace for Americans but peace for all men and women—not merely peace in our time but peace for all time.

I speak of peace because of the new face of war. Total war makes no sense in an age when great powers can maintain large and relatively invulnerable nuclear forces and refuse to surrender without resort to those forces. It makes no sense in an age when a single nuclear weapon contains almost ten times the explosive force delivered by all of the allied air forces in the Second World War. It makes no sense in an age when the deadly poisons produced by a nuclear exchange would be carried by wind and water and soil and seed to the far corners of the globe and to generations yet unborn.

Today the expenditure of billions of dollars every year on weapons acquired for the purpose of making sure we never need to use them is essential to keeping the peace. But surely the acquisition of such idle stockpiles—which can only destroy and never create—is not the only, much less the most efficient, means of assuring peace.

I speak of peace, therefore, as the necessary rational end of rational men. I realize that the pursuit of peace is not as dramatic as the pursuit of war—and frequently the words of the pursuer fall on deaf ears. But we have no more urgent task.

Some say that it is useless to speak of world peace or world law or world disarmament—and that it will be useless until the leaders of the Soviet Union adopt a more enlightened attitude. I hope they do. I believe we can help them do it. But I also believe that we must reexamine our own attitude—as individuals and as a Nation—for our attitude is as essential as theirs. And every graduate of this school, every thoughtful citizen who despairs of war and wishes to bring peace, should begin by looking inward—by examining his own attitude toward the possibilities of peace, toward the Soviet Union, toward the course of the cold war and toward freedom and peace here at home.

First: Let us examine our attitude toward peace itself. Too many of us think it is impossible. Too many think it unreal. But that is a dangerous, defeatist belief. It leads to the conclusion that war is inevitable—that mankind is doomed—that we are gripped by forces we cannot control.

We need not accept that view. Our problems are manmade—therefore, they can be solved by man. And man can be as big as he wants. No problem of human destiny is beyond human beings. Man's reason and spirit have often solved the seemingly unsolvable—and we believe they can do it again.

I am not referring to the absolute, infinite concept of universal peace and good will of which some fantasies and fanatics dream. I do not deny the value of hopes and dreams but we merely invite discouragement and incredulity by making that our only and immediate goal.

Let us focus instead on a more practical, more attainable peace—based not on a sudden revolution in human nature but on a gradual evolution in human institutions—on a series of concrete actions and effective agreements which are in the interest of all concerned. There is no single, simple key to this peace—no grand or magic formula to be adopted by one or two powers. Genuine peace must be the product of many nations, the sum of many acts. It must be dynamic, not static, changing to meet the challenge of each new generation. For peace is a process—a way of solving problems.

With such a peace, there will still be quarrels and conflicting interests, as there are within families and nations. World peace, like community peace, does not require that each man love his neighbor—it requires only that they live together in mutual tolerance, submitting their disputes to a just and peaceful settlement. And history teaches us that enmities between nations, as between individuals, do not last forever. However fixed our likes and dislikes may seem, the tide of time and events will often bring surprising changes in the relations between nations and neighbors.

So let us persevere. Peace need not be impracticable, and war need not be inevitable. By defining our goal more clearly, by making it seem more manageable and less remote, we can help all peoples to see it, to draw hope from it, and to move irresistibly toward it.

Second: Let us reexamine our attitude toward the Soviet Union. It is discouraging to think that their leaders may actually believe what their propagandists write. It is discouraging to read a recent authoritative Soviet text on *Military Strategy* and find, on page after page, wholly baseless and incredible claims—such as the allegation that "American imperialist circles are preparing to unleash different types of wars . . . that there is a very real threat of a preventive war being unleashed by American imperialists against the Soviet Union . . . [and that] the political aims of the American imperialists are to enslave economically and politically the European and other capitalist countries . . . [and] to achieve world domination . . . by means of aggressive wars."

Truly, as it was written long ago: "The wicked flee when no man pursueth." Yet it is sad to read these Soviet statements—to realize the extent of the gulf between us. But it is also a warning—a warning to the American people not to fall into the same trap as the Soviets, not to see only a distorted and desperate view of the other side, not to see conflict as inevitable, accommodation as impossible, and communication as nothing more than an exchange of threats.

No government or social system is so evil that its people must be considered as lacking in virtue. As Americans, we find communism profoundly repugnant as a negation of personal freedom and dignity. But we can still hail the Russian people for their many achievements—in science and space, in economic and industrial growth, in culture and in acts of courage.

Among the many traits the peoples of our two countries have in common, none is stronger than our mutual abhorrence of war. Almost unique, among the major world powers, we have never been at war with each other. And no nation in the history of battle ever suffered more than the Soviet Union suffered in the course of the Second World War. At least 20 million lost their lives. Countless millions of homes and farms were burned or sacked. A third of the nation's territory, including nearly two thirds of its industrial base, was turned into a wasteland—a loss equivalent to the devastation of this country east of Chicago.

Today, should total war ever break out again—no matter how—our two countries would become the primary targets. It is an ironic but accurate fact that the two strongest powers are the two in the most danger of devastation. All we have built, all we have worked for, would be destroyed in the first 24 hours. And even in the cold war, which brings burdens and dangers to so many countries, including this Nation's closest allies—our two countries bear the heaviest burdens. For we are both devoting massive sums of money to weapons that could be better devoted to combating ignorance, poverty, and disease. We are both caught up in a vicious and dangerous cycle in which suspicion on one side breeds suspicion on the other, and new weapons beget counterweapons.

In short, both the United States and its allies, and the Soviet Union and its allies, have a mutually deep interest in a just and genuine peace and in halting the arms race. Agreements to this end are in the interests of the Soviet Union as well as ours—and even the most hostile nations can be relied upon to accept and keep those treaty obligations, and only those treaty obligations, which are in their own interest.

So, let us not be blind to our differences—but let us also direct attention to our common interests and to the means by which those differences can be resolved. And if we cannot end now our differences, at least we can help make the world safe for diversity. For, in the final analysis, our most basic common link is that we all inhabit this small planet. We all breathe the same air. We all cherish our children's future. And we are all mortal.

Third: Let us reexamine our attitude toward the cold war, remembering that we are not engaged in a debate, seeking to pile up debating points. We are not here distributing blame or pointing the finger of judgment. We must deal with the world as it is, and not as it might have been had the history of the last 18 years been different.

We must, therefore, persevere in the search for peace in the hope that constructive changes within the Communist bloc might bring within reach solutions which now seem beyond us. We must conduct our affairs in such a way that it becomes in the Communists' interest to agree on a genuine peace. Above all, while defending our own vital interests, nuclear powers must avert those confrontations which bring an adversary to a choice of either a humiliating retreat or a nuclear war. To adopt that kind of course in the nuclear age would be evidence only of the bankruptcy of our policy—or of a collective death-wish for the world.

To secure these ends, America's weapons are nonprovocative, carefully controlled, designed to deter, and capable of selective use. Our military forces are committed to peace and disciplined in self-restraint. Our diplomats are instructed to avoid unnecessary irritants and purely rhetorical hostility.

For we can seek a relaxation of tensions without relaxing our guard. And, for our part, we do not need to use threats to prove that we are resolute. We do not need to jam foreign broadcasts out of fear our faith will be eroded. We are unwilling to impose our system on any unwilling people—but we are willing and able to engage in peaceful competition with any people on earth.

Meanwhile, we seek to strengthen the United Nations, to help solve its financial problems, to make it a more effective instrument for peace, to develop it into a genuine world security system—a system capable of resolving disputes on the basis of law, of insuring the security of the large and the small, and of creating conditions under which arms can finally be abolished.

At the same time we seek to keep peace inside the non-Communist world, where many nations, all of them our friends, are divided over issues which weaken Western unity, which invite Communist intervention or which threaten to erupt into war. Our efforts in West New Guinea, in the Congo, in the Middle East, and in the Indian subcontinent, have been persistent and patient despite criticism from both sides. We have also tried to set an example for others—by seeking to adjust small but significant differences with our own closest neighbors in Mexico and in Canada.

Speaking of other nations, I wish to make one point clear. We are bound to many nations by alliances. Those alliances exist because our concern and theirs substantially overlap. Our commitment to defend Western Europe and West Berlin, for example, stands undiminished because of the identity of our vital interests. The United States will make no deal with the Soviet Union at the expense of other nations and other peoples, not merely because they are our partners, but also because their interests and ours converge.

Our interests converge, however, not only in defending the frontiers of freedom, but in pursuing the paths of peace. It is our hope—and the purpose of allied policies—to convince the Soviet Union that she, too, should let each nation choose its own future, so long as that choice does not interfere with the choices of others. The Communist drive to impose their political and economic system on others is the primary cause of world tension today. For there can be no doubt that, if all nations could refrain from interfering in the self-determination of others, the peace would be much more assured.

This will require a new effort to achieve world law—a new context for world discussions. It will require increased understanding between the Soviets and ourselves. And increased understanding will require increased contact and communication. One step in this direction is the proposed arrangement for a direct line between Moscow and Washington, to avoid on each side the dangerous delays, misunderstandings, and misreadings of the other's actions which might occur at a time of crisis.

We have also been talking in Geneva about other first-step measures of arms control, designed to limit the intensity of the arms race and to reduce the risks of accidental war. Our primary long-range interest in Geneva, however, is general and complete disarmament—designed to take place by stages, permitting parallel political developments to build the new institutions of peace which would take the place of arms. The pursuit of disarmament has been an effort of this Government since the 1920's. It has been urgently sought by the past three administrations. And however dim the prospects may be today, we intend to continue this effort—to continue it in order that all countries, including our own, can better grasp what the problems and possibilities of disarmament are.

The one major area of these negotiations where the end is in sight, yet where a fresh start is badly needed, is in a treaty to outlaw nuclear tests. The conclusion of such a treaty, so near and yet so far, would check the spiraling arms race in one of its most dangerous areas. It would place the nuclear powers in a position to deal more effectively with one of the greatest hazards which man faces in 1963, the further spread of nuclear arms. It would increase our security—it would decrease the prospects of war. Surely this goal is sufficiently important to require our steady pursuit, yielding neither to the temptation to give up the whole effort nor the temptation to give up our insistence on vital and responsible safeguards.

I am taking this opportunity, therefore, to announce two important decisions in this regard.

First: Chairman Khrushchev, Prime Minister Macmillan, and I have agreed that high-level discussions will shortly begin in Moscow looking toward early agreement on a comprehensive test ban treaty. Our hopes must be tempered with the caution of history—but with our hopes go the hopes of all mankind.

Second: To make clear our good faith and solemn convictions on the matter, I now declare that the United States does not propose to conduct nuclear tests in the atmosphere so long as other states do not do so. We will not be the first to resume. Such a declaration is no substitute for a formal binding treaty, but I hope it will help us achieve one. Nor would such a treaty be a substitute for disarmament, but I hope it will help us achieve it.

Finally, my fellow Americans, let us examine our attitude toward peace and freedom here at home. The quality and spirit of our own society must justify and support our efforts abroad. We must show it in the dedication of our own lives—as many of you who are graduating today will have a unique opportunity to do, by serving without pay in the Peace Corps abroad or in the proposed National Service Corps here at home.

But wherever we are, we must all, in our daily lives, live up to the age-old faith that peace and freedom walk together. In too many of our cities today, the peace is not secure because freedom is incomplete.

It is the responsibility of the executive branch at all levels of government—local, State, and National—to provide and protect that freedom for all of our citizens by all means within their authority. It is the responsibility of the legislative branch at all levels, wherever that authority is not now adequate, to make it adequate. And it is the responsibility of all citizens in all sections of this country to respect the rights of all others and to respect the law of the land.

All this is not unrelated to world peace. "When a man's ways please the Lord," the Scriptures tell us, "he maketh even his enemies to be at peace with him." And is not peace, in the last analysis, basically a matter of human rights—the right to live out our lives without fear of devastation—the right to breathe air as nature provided it—the right of future generations to a healthy existence?

While we proceed to safeguard our national interests, let us also safeguard human interests. And the elimination of war and arms is clearly in the interest of both. No treaty, however much it may be to the advantage of all, however tightly it may be worded, can provide absolute security against the risks of deception and evasion. But it can—if it is sufficiently effective in its enforcement and if it is sufficiently in the interests of its signers—offer far more security and far fewer risks than an unabated, uncontrolled, unpredictable arms race.

The United States, as the world knows, will never start a war. We do not want a war. We do not now expect a war. This generation of Americans has already had enough—more than enough—of war and hate and oppression. We shall be prepared if others wish it. We shall be alert to try to stop it. But we shall also do our part to build a world of peace where the weak are safe and the strong are just. We are not helpless before that task or hopeless of its success. Confident and unafraid, we labor on—not toward a strategy of annihilation but toward a strategy of peace.

NOTE: The President spoke at the John M. Reeves Athletic Field on the campus of American University after being awarded an honorary degree of doctor of laws. In his opening words he referred to Hurst R. Anderson, president of the university, and Robert C. Byrd, U.S. Senator from West Virginia.

THE WHITE HOUSE
WASHINGTON

SECRET [Declassified]   January 21, 1965

A REPORT TO THE PRESIDENT
BY
THE COMMITTEE ON NUCLEAR PROLIFERATION

At your request, we have studied the problem of preventing the spread of nuclear weapons. In our examination, we consulated widely with your principal officers from relevant agencies of the Government. In the process, we considered a range of possible policies for the future and their consequences for the Nation. We have noted a significant diversity of views within the government about the feasibility and the costs of preventing nuclear proliferation, and consequently about a appropriate policies for the United States.

Among ourselves there was also a diversity of opinions at the outset of our study. As a result of our study, however, the Committee is now unanimous in its view that preventing the further spread of nuclear weapons is clearly in the national interest despite the difficult decisions that will be required. We have concluded, therefore, that the United States must, as a matter of great urgency, substantially increase the scope and intensity of our efforts if we are to have any hope of success. Necessarily, these efforts must be of three kinds: (a) negotiation of formal multilateral agreements; (b) the application of influence on individual nations considering nuclear weapons acquisition, by ourselves and in conjunction with others; and (c) example by our own policies and actions.

Specifically, we have concluded that:

1.   <u>The spread of nuclear weapons poses an increasingly grave threats to the security of the United States.</u> New nuclear capabilities, however primitive and regardless of whether they are held by nations currently friendly to the United States, will add complexity and instability to the deterrent balance between the United States and the Soviet Union, aggravate suspicions and hostility among states neighboring new nuclear powers, place a wasteful economic burden on the aspirations of developing nations, impede the vital task of controlling and reducing weapons around the world, and eventually constitute direct military threats to the United States.

As additional nations obtained nuclear weapons, our diplomatic and military influence would wane, and strong pressures would arise to retreat to isolation to avoid the risk of involvement in nuclear war. Nevertheless, even then, we could not escape the problem. There would be additional nuclear powers -- perhaps some in this hemisphere -- individually possessing the capability of destroying millions of American lives. Major defensive efforts might help substantially to diminish such limited threats, but millions of American lives would always be at risk.

2. <u>The world is fast approaching a point of no return in the prospects of controlling the spread of nuclear weapons.</u> Nuclear power programs are placing within the hands of many nations much of the knowledge, equipment and materials for making nuclear weapons. The recent Chinese Communist nuclear explosion has reinforced the belief, increasingly prevalent throughout the world, that nuclear weapons are a distinguishing mark of a world leader, are essential to national security, and are feasible even with modest industrial resources.

[Next two paragraphs blacked out].

We are convinced, therefore, that energetic and comprehensive steps must be taken in the near future to discourage further acquisition of nuclear weapons capabilities or an accelerating increase in the number of nations engaged in nuclear weapons programs will occur -- possibly beginning within a matter of months.

3. <u>Success in preventing the future spread of nuclear weapons requires a concentrated and intensified effort.</u> Although non-proliferation has been declared part of United States foreign policy since 1945, we must now greatly intensify our efforts -- both to obtain appropriate multilateral agreements and to affect directly the motivations of individual nations -- if we are to have any hope of success in halting the spread of nuclear weapons.

We have been impressed in the course of our study by the fact that actions affecting the spread of nuclear weapons also related to a very broad range of United States interests; relations with our allies and with other nations, weapons deployments at home and abroad, programs in peaceful atomic energy, and commerce with foreign nations. In order that our efforts to stop nuclear proliferation may succeed, each of these areas on interest, as well as the agencies of government which deal with them, must be truly responsive to our non-proliferation policies, and must give such non-proliferation policies far greater weight and support than they have received in the past.

We must acknowledge the importance of participation by the Soviet Union in efforts to stop proliferations. Furthermore, it is unlikely that others can be induced to abstain indefinitely from acquiring nuclear weapons if the Soviet Union and the United States continue in a nuclear arms race. Therefore, lessened emphasis by the United States and the Soviet Union on nuclear weapons, and agreements on broader arms control measures must be recognized as important components in the overall program to prevent nuclear proliferations.

4. <u>A major effort on our part has promise of success in halting or retarding the spread of nuclear weapons.</u> The dangers of proliferation affect all countries, creating a widespread common interest in early and effective steps to halt the nuclear spread. To date, initiatives within the United Nations and in disarmament negotiations have been only partially successful, but the Irish Resolution of 1961 and the limited nuclear test ban treaty of 1963 continue to offer a basis on which to take more comprehensive an effective steps. There remains broad support for multilateral measures to control nuclear proliferation.

We believe that the Soviet Union, because of its growing vulnerability to proliferation among its neighbors, probably shares with us a strong interest in preventing the further spread of nuclear weapons. Further, we believe that the change of leadership in the Soviet Union and the possible resulting review of Soviet nuclear policies may not provide an immediate opportunity for joint or parallel action in the near future to stop the nuclear spread.

Of course, even major efforts on our part may not be successful in halting or greatly retarding the spread of nuclear weapons. But we are unanimous in our agreement that such efforts should be made. The rewards of long-term success would be enormous, and even partial success world be worth the costs we can expect to incur.

RECOMMENDATIONS

We therefore recommend that the United States undertake the following measures to implement its policy to prevent the spread of nuclear weapons.

1. <u>Multilateral agreements.</u>

Measures to prevent particular countries from acquiring nuclear weapons are unlikely to succeed unless they are taken in support of a broad international prohibition applicable to many countries. We should seek to obtain on a multilateral basis formal treaty commitments of three kinds:

    a. <u>Non-proliferation agreements</u>. We should intensify our efforts for a non-proliferation agreement and seek the early conclusion of the widest and most effective possibly international treaty on non-dissemination and non-acquisition of nuclear weapons.

[next 3/4 page blacked out].

    b. <u>Comprehensive test ban</u>. We should renew our efforts to negotiate a verified comprehensive test ban with the Soviet Union.

[Next sentence blacked out].

We should be prepared to accept the minimum number of on-site inspections in the Soviet Union that would be consistent with a viable treaty. In this connection, we should consider our anticipated improved capabilities for seismic detection and identification, and our other relevant unilateral intelligence capabilities. Inspection procedures and quotas covering other countries should also be reviewed to facilitate the widest and most effective application of the treaty. We should be prepared to propose an exception to such a treaty for peaceful nuclear explosions if a satisfactory procedure can be promptly devised that would preclude the development of nuclear weapons under the guise of a peaceful explosives program and if such an exception would be acceptable to other nations. An early approach should be made to the Soviet Union, and we should seek the widest adherence to the agreement and be prepared to bring strong influence to bear on significant countries to participate in it.

    c. <u>Nuclear free zones</u>. We should actively support the establishment of Latin American and African (including, if possible, Israel-UAR) nuclear free zones. To facilitate such agreements, we should be prepared to modify our requirement for verification and our position on transit tights and declarations with respect to United States nuclear weapons to the maximum extent consistent with demonstrable United States security needs.

2. <u>Policies towards non-nuclear powers</u>.

In conjunction with the multilateral measures described above, we should intensify our efforts on country-by-country basis to influence the decision of individual non-nuclear powers not to undertake the development or acquisition of nuclear weapons and to secure workable commitments to this effect. We should ourselves refrain from actions that would contribute to or suggest a future contribution to the development of nuclear weapons by these countries.

The State, Treasury and Commerce Departments should develop programs of economic restrictions and other measures which could be quickly imposed by Executive action and which would be strong enough to produce a reversal of any decision to manufacture or otherwise acquire nuclear weapons.

[Next 7 pages blacked out]

c. <u>Soviet Union</u>. In view of the great importance of Soviet support and cooperation in connection with efforts to stop nuclear proliferation, we should undertake new initiatives to obtain such support. We should make early approaches to the Soviets, seeking cooperation on as broad a basis as possible in achieving the objectives described in this report, and to the extent possible, the relevant specific actions set forth in paragraphs 1,2 and 5 of these recommendations.

In addition to the direct non-proliferation measures describe in paragraph 1 above, we should undertake early initiatives toward the following United States-Soviet arms control agreements as a means both of reducing tensions between the United States and the Soviet Union and creating an atmosphere conducive to wide acceptance of restraints on nuclear proliferation:

(1) A verified fissile materials production cutoff for weapons purposes, to be established by treaty (with appropriate provisions permitting the production on tritium).

(2) A verified strategic delivery vehicle freeze coupled with significant agreed reductions (e.g. 30%) in strategic force levels, to be established by treaty.

(3) An 18 to 24-month halt in the construction of new ABM or ICBM launchers, to be accomplished by reciprocal Executive action based on unilateral verification capabilities.

[Next 1/2 page blacked out].

5. <u>Peaceful uses of atomic energy</u>.

While we recognize that in the long run fissionable materials will probably be available in all industrial countries as a result of nuclear power program, we believe that every effort should be made at this time to ensure that peaceful atomic energy programs do not unreasonably contribute to potential proliferation of nuclear weapons capabilities. We should in all cases insist on adequate safeguards for all peaceful programs which will advance the economic development of friendly countries; and we should not press such programs with special subsidies. Careful consideration should be given to the political stability and reliability of countries where such programs are undertaken. We should make an effort to get all potential suppliers to agree to offer materials and facilities only under adequate safeguards.

We should take the following actions with regard to IAEA and Euratom:

    a. IAEA.

        (1) We should increase our efforts to build up the IAEA, including broader responsibilities, increased operational activities, larger budgets and improved technical capabilities.

        (2) We should exert stronger influence on all nations, including supplying nations and the Soviet Bloc to accept IAEA safeguards on reactors and separation plants and should offer, in return, to extend safeguards to additional United States facilities.

        (3) We should explore additional means on establishing control practices with respect to uranium and fuel elements which would reduce the risk of nuclear power facilities being used for military purposes.

    b. Euratom.

        (1) We should press Euratom in order to obtain satisfactory United States verification of Euratom safeguards.

        (2) We should work toward Euratom acceptance of IAEA safeguards and IAEA acceptance of Euratom.

While we recognize that the peaceful uses of nuclear explosives (Project Plowshare) may have long-term economic importance, we do not believe that the program should be allowed to jeopardize a comprehensive test ban treaty or to encourage interest in nuclear weapons. Undue emphasis on such programs tends to make nuclear explosives appear desirable, necessary and acceptable for countries presently considering undertaking nuclear weapons programs. In addition, attempts to incorporate provisions permitting such programs under a comprehensive test ban treaty may be difficult, if not impossible, without providing a loophole under which nuclear weapons could be developed. We should not, therefore, actively seek to interest other countries in such programs until we better understand their relationship to the comprehensive test ban and the general nuclear proliferation problem.

6. <u>United States weapons policies</u>.

If we are to minimize the incentives for others to acquire nuclear weapons, it is important that we avoid giving an exaggerated impression of their importance and utility and that we stress that current and future important role of conventional armaments. It is also important that our physical arrangements minimize the possibility of unauthorized seizure or compromise of design information regarding United States nuclear weapons deployed aborad. Accordingly, we should take the following actions: *[blacked out]*

b. <u>Physical security</u>. *[Next sentence blacked out]*. Intensified research to develop improved safeguards against seizure of unauthorized use should be continued. We should consider appropriate assistance to the United Kingdom, France and the Soviet Union in connection with the development of *[word blacked out]* and safety devices for their respective weapons.

c. <u>Research and development</u>. The Department of Defense should reexamine future requirements in the light of the policies recommended in this memorandum. Consideration should be given, among other matters, to damage limitation systems effective against lesser nuclear threats; to detection and identification systems related to such threats; and to the development of any weapons systems necessary to back our commitments to nations electing not to develop their own nuclear weapons.

The program outlined above should not preclude other measures to prevent nuclear proliferation and the appropriate agencies of the Government should be called upon to undertake to develop additional proposals to that end. All agencies should carefully consider the implications for nuclear proliferation of all their actions and information policies, and their progress on non-proliferation matters would, we think, be followed closely by you and your senior advisers.

Arthur H. Dean	James A. Perkins
Allen W. Dulles	Arthur K. Watson
Alfred M. Gruenther	William Webster
George B. Kistiakowksy	Herbert F. York
John J. McCloy	Roswell L. Gilpatric
	Chairman

Draft Treaty on Nonproliferation of Nuclear Weapons Submitted to Geneva Disarmament Conference

Following are statements made on August 24 by President Johnson and by William C. Foster, U.S. Representative to the Conference of the Eighteen-Nation Disarmament Committee, together with the text of the draft treaty.

STATEMENT BY PRESIDENT JOHNSON

White House press release dated August 24

Today at Geneva the United States and the Soviet Union, as cochairmen of the Eighteen-Nation Disarmament Committee, are submitting to the Committee a draft treaty to stop the spread of nuclear weapons.

For more than 20 years, the world has watched with growing fear as nuclear weapons have spread.

Since 1945, five nations have come into possession of these dreadful weapons. We believe now—as we did then—that even one such nation is too many. But the issue now is not whether some have nuclear weapons while others do not. The issue is whether the nations will agree to prevent a bad situation from becoming worse.

Today, for the first time, we have within our reach an instrument which permits us to make a choice.

The submission of a draft treaty brings us to the final and most critical stage of this effort. The draft will be available for consideration by all governments and for negotiation by the Conference.

The treaty must reconcile the interests of nations with our interest as a community of human beings on a small planet. The treaty must be responsive to the needs and problems of all the nations of the world—great and small, alined and nonalined, nuclear and nonnuclear.

It must add to the security of all.

It must encourage the development and use of nuclear energy for peaceful purposes.

It must provide adequate protection against the corruption of the peaceful atom to its use for weapons of war.

I am convinced that we are today offering an instrument that will meet these requirements.

If we now go forward to completion of a worldwide agreement, we will pass on a great gift to those who follow us.

We shall demonstrate that—despite all his problems, quarrels, and distractions—man still retains a capacity to design his fate rather than be engulfed by it.

Failure to complete our work will be interpreted by our children and grandchildren as a betrayal of conscience in a world that needs all of its resources and talents to serve life, not death.

I have given instructions to the United States Representative, William C. Foster, which reflect our determination to insure that a fair and effective treaty is concluded.

The Eighteen-Nation Committee on Disarmament now has before it the opportunity to make a cardinal contribution to man's safety and peace.

STATEMENT BY AMBASSADOR FOSTER [1]

A major milestone on the path toward achievement of a nonproliferation treaty is marked today.

An important initial milestone was the unanimous adoption of the Irish resolution in 1961.[2] Public debate, here and in New York, private negotiations and additional action by the General Assembly and the U.N. Disarmament Commission followed in the succeeding years.

1965 was marked by the public presentation

---

[1] Made in plenary session of the Conference of the Eighteen-Nation Disarmament Committee at Geneva on Aug. 24.
[2] U.N. doc. A/RES/1665; adopted Dec. 4, 1961.

of concrete treaty texts, by the submission of an eight-nation joint memorandum on nonproliferation, and by the adoption of General Assembly Resolution 2028.[3] As a result, multilateral negotiations in this Committee and in the General Assembly took on new meaning.

Given this new direction and impetus, the 1966 negotiations in this Committee succeeded in identifying with greater clarity the major obstacles to agreement. At the end of the ENDC session that year, the eight-nation joint memorandum made the following comment:

> The eight delegations regret that it has not so far been possible to arrive at an agreement on a treaty acceptable to all concerned. They are deeply conscious of the danger inherent in a situation without an agreement that prevents proliferation of nuclear weapons. They view with apprehension the possibility that such a situation may lead not only to an increase of nuclear arsenals and to a spread of nuclear weapons over the world, but also to an increase in the number of nuclear weapon Powers, thus aggravating the tensions between States and the risk of nuclear war.
>
> The eight delegations are aware that a main obstacle to an agreement has so far been constituted by differences concerning nuclear armaments within alliances, a problem mainly discussed between the major Powers and their allies.

Today, for the first time, conclusion of a nonproliferation treaty is within reach. The members of this Committee, all of whom helped bring the negotiations to this point, share in the achievement we mark today. As will be seen from a careful examination of the draft, it is based upon the principles enunciated in the joint memoranda and Resolution 2028.

The draft nonproliferation treaty we are presenting today is a recommendation for discussion and negotiation in the ENDC and for the consideration of all governments. We have worked long and hard over it. We have sought to take into account the interests of all potential adherents. This draft reflects constructive suggestions made by other delegations here and by other governments. We could not, of course, expect governments to be committed to this draft at this point, since all governments would want to be able to consider improvements which might be suggested here.

We recognize the interest of governments not represented on this Committee to have their views on the nonproliferation treaty draft made known during this next and crucial stage in the elaboration of the treaty. A procedure already exists for the circulation within the Committee of the views of nonmembers.

Let me now present a brief explanation of the provisions of the draft.

Obligations of Nuclear and Nonnuclear States

Article I deals with the obligations of nuclear-weapon states. First, they cannot transfer nuclear weapons, or control over them, to any recipient whatsoever. Second, they cannot assist non-nuclear-weapon states to manufacture or otherwise acquire nuclear weapons. Third, these prohibitions are applicable not only to nuclear weapons but also to other nuclear explosive devices.

Article II deals with the obligations of non-nuclear-weapon states and is the obverse of article I. First, such states cannot receive the transfer of nuclear weapons, or control over them, from any transferor whatsoever. Second, they cannot manufacture or otherwise acquire nuclear weapons or seek or receive assistance for such manufacture. Third, these prohibitions are applicable not only to nuclear weapons but also to other nuclear explosive devices.

We have already made clear the reasons for including such devices in the prohibitions of the treaty. These devices could be used as nuclear weapons and the technology for making them is essentially indistinguishable from that of nuclear weapons.

Provision on Peaceful Nuclear Explosions

The United States recognizes that the benefits which may some day be realized from nuclear explosions for peaceful purposes should be available to the nonnuclear states. In his message of February 21 to the ENDC, President Johnson stated:[4]

> The United States is prepared to make available nuclear explosive services for peaceful purposes on a non-discriminatory basis under appropriate international safeguards. We are prepared to join other nuclear states in a commitment to do this.

My delegation has elaborated on this proposal in interventions at our 295th and 303d meetings.

We are pleased that the preamble of the draft nonproliferation treaty contains a forthright provision on peaceful nuclear explosions. It states:

---

[3] For text, see BULLETIN of Nov. 29, 1965, p. 884.

[4] For text, see *ibid.*, Mar. 20, 1967, p. 447.

... potential benefits from any peaceful applications of nuclear explosions should be available through appropriate international procedures to non-nuclear-weapon States Party to this Treaty on a non-discriminatory basis and that the charge to such Parties for the explosive devices used should be as low as possible and exclude any charge for research and development.

Article III, the safeguards article, has been left blank, although there are several references to safeguards in the preamble. The article is blank because the cochairmen have not yet been able to work out a formula which would be acceptable to all states which wish to support this treaty. The cochairmen are continuing their consultations with a view to drafting an agreed text for this article. In the meantime, I hope that ENDC plenary discussion will focus on the provisions which have been submitted today, with the safeguards discussion being deferred for the time being while the cochairmen work on the problem.

Peaceful Uses of Atomic Energy Encouraged

Article IV results from many suggestions by non-nuclear-weapon countries that the treaty contain an article on peaceful uses of atomic energy. Indeed, the idea for such an article was originally derived from the treaty of Tlatelolco, Mexico.[5]

The article describes two recognized rights of parties with respect to peaceful uses. First, it makes clear that nothing in the treaty draft interferes with the right of the parties to develop their research, production, and use of nuclear energy for peaceful purposes in compliance with articles I and II, which, of course, include provisions on peaceful nuclear explosive devices. Second, it recognizes the right of the parties to participate in the fullest possible exchange of information for, and to contribute alone or in cooperation with other states to, the further development of the applications of nuclear energy for peaceful purposes.

These two rights are specific elaborations of the principle, stated in the preamble that "the benefits of peaceful applications of nuclear technology . . . should be available for peaceful purposes to all Parties to the Treaty, whether nuclear-weapon or non-nuclear-weapon States."

As the preamble also makes clear, this principle includes not only modern reactor technology and the like, but "any technological

---

[5] For background, see *ibid.*, Mar. 13, 1967, p. 436.

by-products which may be derived by nuclear-weapon States from the development of nuclear explosive devices."

These provisions make clear that the treaty would promote, not discourage, national development and international cooperation with respect to peaceful applications of atomic energy. This applies to research, production, and use as well as to information, equipment, and materials.

Amendments and Review

Article V deals with amendments and review. Paragraph 1 states how amendments may be initiated and is derived from the test ban treaty. Paragraph 2 describes how amendments enter into force.

It provides that an amendment must be approved by a majority of the parties who are members of the IAEA [International Atomic Energy Agency] Board of Governors.

The last paragraph of article V provides for a conference after 5 years to review the treaty's operation with a view to assuring that its purposes and provisions are being realized. This will provide an opportunity for nonnuclear and nuclear-weapon states alike to assess whether the treaty is accomplishing its primary purpose of preventing the spread of nuclear weapons and also its purposes of easing international tensions and facilitating agreement on cessation of the nuclear arms race and on disarmament. The review conference is thus relevant to the question of further measures of disarmament, a question which has been of such interest to many members of this Committee.

Arms Control and Disarmament

The draft also contains preambular provisions on arms control and disarmament, including a declaration of intention to achieve a cessation of the nuclear arms race at the earliest possible date. The "declaration of intention" form was, of course, suggested in the eight-nation joint memorandum on nonproliferation of last August. In a similar vein, a later preambular paragraph calls for the cessation of production of nuclear weapons and the elimination of nuclear weapons and delivery vehicles from national arsenals, pursuant to a treaty on general and complete disarmament under strict and effective international control.

These preambular provisions state the purposes of the treaty. Steps toward achievement of these purposes would be reviewed by the review conference to which I have referred. Thus, while no specific obligation for nuclear disarmament would appear, the preambular provisions, combined with the review paragraph in article V, would provide the most realistic approach to this problem.

We share the general desire for early progress to halt the nuclear arms race and to begin the process of reducing and ultimately eliminating nuclear weapons from national arsenals. The United States has proposed, and will continue to pursue, various measures to achieve these objectives. But we all know why it would not be feasible to incorporate specific obligations to this end in the treaty itself. The differences that have prevented agreement on these measures have not as yet been resolved. Any attempt to incorporate specific nuclear arms limitation obligations in the treaty would inevitably also inject these differences into the consideration of the treaty itself and could only jeopardize its prospects.

Let us therefore agree to pursue these nuclear arms limitations measures with a greater sense of urgency and, I would hope, in a spirit of greater cooperation. Let us also all agree that this treaty must be regarded as a step toward the achievement of these other necessary measures. We are convinced that the treaty will create a more favorable environment for agreement on them. That is why we believe we must concentrate now on ways to expedite and facilitate the conclusion of this treaty and avoid actions which would delay or jeopardize it. The situation requires that our efforts be focused on achieving a realistic agreement as soon as possible.

Other Treaty Provisions

Article VI contains signature and entry into force provisions derived from those of the test ban treaty. It would require that a certain number of non-nuclear-weapon states in addition to the nuclear-weapon signatories would have to ratify before the treaty would enter into force. We have not expressed a view on the precise number. The United States believes it should be sufficiently large so that the treaty will begin to achieve its purposes when it enters into force.

Article VII states that the treaty shall be of unlimited duration. It contains a withdrawal clause similar to that of the test ban treaty, with one significant improvement. The notice of withdrawal, together with a statement of reasons therefor, would be submitted to the U.N. Security Council as well as to the parties. The withdrawal provision is central to this treaty. States will adhere to the treaty if they believe it is consistent with their security interests. Under the proposed clause, a party can cease to be bound by the treaty if it decides that its supreme interests have been jeopardized by extraordinary events related to the subject matter of the treaty.

Article VIII provides depositary procedures for the treaty text. It also states that the treaty will be equally authentic in each of the five official languages of the United Nations.

Lessening the Danger of Nuclear War

We recognize that the problem of security assurances, which is of concern to some nonalined countries, remains to be considered. The United States maintains the view that this is a matter which, because of its complexity and the divergent interests involved, cannot be dealt with in the treaty itself. We are, however, exploring various possible solutions, including action which could be taken in the context of the United Nations, whose primary purpose is the maintenance of peace and security. We expect that the cochairmen will be exploring this problem further with a view to presenting recommendations to this Committee in the course of our consideration of the treaty.

Mr. Chairman, if the draft presented today leads to a generally accepted treaty, our generation will pass on a gift to future generations. Such a treaty will lessen the danger of nuclear war. It will stimulate widespread, peaceful development of nuclear energy. It will improve the chance for nuclear disarmament. It will help reduce tensions. Like the test ban and outer space treaties, it will constitute a major step toward a more peaceful world. It will be a treaty for all of us—but most of all for our children and our grandchildren.

Mr. Chairman, the future safety of mankind requires prompt action to halt the spread of nuclear weapons. An unprecedented opportunity to do so now awaits us. Let us seize this opportunity while we can.

President Nixon Urges Senate Action on Nuclear Nonproliferation Treaty

President Nixon's Message to the Senate [1]

To the Senate of the United States:

After receiving the advice of the National Security Council, I have decided that it will serve the national interest to proceed with the ratification of the Treaty on Non-Proliferation of Nuclear Weapons.[2] Accordingly, I request that the Senate act promptly to consider the Treaty and give its advice and consent to ratification.

I have always supported the goal of halting the spread of nuclear weapons. I opposed ratification of the Treaty last fall in the immediate aftermath of the Soviet invasion of Czechoslovakia. My request at this time in no sense alters my condemnation of that Soviet action.

I believe that ratification of the Treaty at this time would advance this Administration's policy of negotiation rather than confrontation with the USSR.

I believe that the Treaty can be an important step in our endeavor to curb the spread of nuclear weapons and that it advances the purposes of our Atoms for Peace program which I have supported since its inception during President Eisenhower's Administration.

In submitting this request I wish to endorse the commitment made by the previous Administration that the United States will, when safeguards are applied under the Treaty, permit the International Atomic Energy Agency to apply its safeguards to all nuclear activities in the United States, exclusive of those activities with direct national security significance.

I also reiterate our willingness to join with all Treaty parties to take appropriate measures to insure that potential benefits from peaceful applications of nuclear explosions will be made available to non-nuclear-weapon parties to the Treaty.

Consonant with my purpose to "strengthen the structure of peace," therefore, I urge the Senate's prompt consideration and positive action on this Treaty.

RICHARD NIXON

THE WHITE HOUSE,
February 5, 1969.

---

[1] Transmitted on Feb. 5 (White House press release).
[2] For background, see BULLETIN of July 29, 1968, p. 126; for text of the treaty, see BULLETIN of July 1, 1968, p. 9.

Department Emphasizes the Importance of the Nuclear Nonproliferation Treaty

Statement by Secretary Rogers [1]

I am happy to appear before your committee to express the administration's support for the Treaty on the Nonproliferation of Nuclear Weapons.[2] The policy of the administration was set forth by President Nixon in his letter of February 5 to the Senate, and I quote:[3]

> I believe that ratification of the Treaty at this time would advance this Administration's policy of negotiation rather than confrontation with the USSR. ...
> Consonant with my purpose to "strengthen the structure of peace," therefore, I urge the Senate's prompt consideration and positive action on this Treaty.

Of course, as the committee knows, the treaty, which has now been signed by 87 countries and ratified by nine, is the culmination of many years of effort in both Republican and Democratic administrations. Beginning with the Baruch plan and the McMahon Act in 1946, the United States has searched for ways to curb the spread of nuclear weapons. President Eisenhower's Atoms for Peace plan and the resulting International Atomic Energy Agency helped to lay the foundations on which a realistic and verifiable nonproliferation treaty could be built. Now, after long, patient negotiations by William C. Foster, Adrian Fisher, and a very able team, during the administrations of both President Kennedy and President Johnson, we have before us a carefully drafted and carefully balanced international agreement which can contribute to this country's nonproliferation goal.

In his press conference of February 6,[4] President Nixon stated that, in asking the Senate to approve the treaty, "I did not gloss over the fact that we still very strongly disapproved of what the Soviet Union had done in Czechoslovakia and what it still is doing. But on balance, I considered that this was the time to move forward on the treaty and have done so."

But the invasion of Czechoslovakia was not the sole cause of concern to President Nixon in his consideration of the Nonproliferation Treaty. He also wanted an opportunity to address the concerns of our allies, with whom we expect to have further discussions next week during the deliberations of the Senate.

In this connection, I want to reiterate that the Nonproliferation Treaty will not adversely affect our existing defense alliances.

As Secretary Rusk noted during the July hearings before this committee,[5] we provided our NATO allies during the negotiation of the treaty with answers to questions they had raised concerning articles I and II. They are set forth in Executive H [90th Cong., 2d sess.]. I want to confirm at this time this administration's complete concurrence in those answers. We stand by them and will continue to do so.

With respect to the broader question of security assurances, I wish to make clear that the Nonproliferation Treaty does not create any new security commitment by the United States abroad and that it does not broaden or modify

---

[1] Made before the Senate Committee on Foreign Relations on Feb. 18 (press release 38).
[2] For text of the treaty, see BULLETIN of July 1, 1968, p. 9.
[3] BULLETIN of Feb. 24, 1969, p. 162.
[4] *Ibid.*, p. 157.
[5] BULLETIN of July 29, 1968, p. 131.

any existing security commitments abroad. My understanding of the effect and significance of U.N. Security Council Resolution 255 (1968) [6] and the related U.S. declaration [7] is in complete accord with that expressed in the committee's report on the treaty last September.

With respect to the safeguards article of the treaty (article III), I would like to stress the fact that this article was included at the insistence of the United States, following intensive consultation with our allies. We believe it should make an important contribution to the U.S. objective of safeguarding against diversion to nuclear weapons of the vast quantities of plutonium becoming available throughout the world as a byproduct of the operation of peaceful nuclear reactors. Moreover, we believe that the three guiding principles enunciated by the United States (set forth at pages IX and X of Executive H) constitute important and useful guidelines for the successful implementation of article III.

The fact that I have explicitly referred to certain prior United States statements this morning but not to others should, of course, not be taken as in any way altering or denying the positions reflected in such other statements. This administration has considered the many technical issues raised by this treaty, and we find ourselves in agreement with the positions previously taken by the United States. In this connection, I request that there be included in the record of these hearings the letter dated January 17, 1969, and accompanying memorandum from my predecessor, Dean Rusk,[8] relating to the issues raised in the minority views of this committee.

In conclusion, Mr. Chairman, I would like to point out that the United States has for many years been in the forefront of the many countries which realize the awesome insecurity that could result from the spread of nuclear weapons. There is no effort of greater importance than the endeavor to prevent such an eventuality. Thus I sincerely hope that this committee will again report favorably on this treaty and that the Senate will give its advice and consent to ratification as soon as it reasonably can, in the light of the treaty's importance.

[6] BULLETIN of July 8, 1968, p. 58.
[7] *Ibid.*, p. 57.
[8] Not printed here.

An Age of Interdependence: Common Disaster or Community

Address by Secretary Kissinger [1]

The Nuclear Dimension

The second new dimension on our agenda concerns the problem of nuclear proliferation.

The world has grown so accustomed to the existence of nuclear weapons that it assumes they will never be used. But today, technology is rapidly expanding the number of nuclear weapons in the hands of major powers and threatens to put nuclear-explosive technology at the disposal of an increasing number of other countries.

In a world where many nations possess nuclear weapons, dangers would be vastly compounded. It would be infinitely more difficult, if not impossible, to maintain stability among a large number of nuclear powers. Local wars would take on a new dimension. Nuclear weapons would be introduced into regions where political conflict remains intense and the parties consider their vital interests overwhelmingly involved. There would, as well, be a vastly heightened risk of direct involvement of the major nuclear powers.

This problem does not concern one country, one region, or one bloc alone. No nation can be indifferent to the spread of nuclear technology; every nation's security is directly affected.

The challenge before the world is to realize the peaceful benefits of nuclear technology without contributing to the growth of nuclear weapons or to the number of states possessing them.

As a major nuclear power, the United States recognizes its special responsibility. We realize that we cannot expect others to show restraint if we do not ourselves practice restraint. Together with the Soviet Union we are seeking to negotiate new quantitative and qualitative limitations on strategic arms. Last week our delegations reconvened in Geneva, and we intend to pursue these negotiations with the seriousness of purpose they deserve. The United States has no higher priority than controlling and reducing the levels of nuclear arms.

Beyond the relations of the nuclear powers to each other lies the need to curb the spread of nuclear explosives. We must take into account that plutonium is an essential ingredient of nuclear explosives and that in the immediate future the amount of plutonium generated by peaceful nuclear reactors will be multiplied many times. Heretofore the United States and a number of other countries have widely supplied nuclear fuels and other nuclear materials in order to promote the use of nuclear energy for peaceful purposes. This policy cannot continue if it leads to the proliferation of nuclear explosives. Sales of these materials can no longer be treated by anyone as a purely commercial competitive enterprise.

The world community therefore must work urgently toward a system of effective international safeguards against the diversion of plutonium or its byproducts. The United States is prepared to join with others in a comprehensive effort.

Let us together agree on the practical steps which must be taken to assure the benefits of nuclear energy free of its terrors:

—The United States will shortly offer specific proposals to strengthen safeguards to the other principal supplier countries.

—We shall intensify our efforts to gain the broadest possible acceptance of International Atomic Energy Agency (IAEA) safeguards, to establish practical controls on the transfer of nuclear materials, and to insure the effectiveness of these procedures.

—The United States will urge the IAEA to draft an international convention for enhancing physical security against theft or diversion of nuclear material. Such a convention should set forth specific standards and techniques for protecting materials while in use, storage, and transfer.

—The Treaty on the Non-Proliferation of Nuclear Weapons, which this Assembly has endorsed, warrants continuing support. The treaty contains not only a broad commitment to limit the spread of nuclear explosives but specific obligations to accept and implement IAEA safeguards and to control the transfer of nuclear materials.

Mr. President, whatever advantages seem to accrue from the acquisition of nuclear-explosive technology will prove to be ephemeral. When Pandora's box has been opened, no country will be the beneficiary and all mankind will have lost. This is not inevitable. If we act decisively now, we can still control the future.

---

[1] Made before the 29th United Nations General Assembly on Sept. 23 (text from Office of Media Services news release).

No. 11902

Feb. 2, 1976, 41 F.R. 4877

PROCEDURES FOR AN EXPORT LICENSING POLICY AS TO NUCLEAR MATERIALS AND EQUIPMENT

The Energy Reorganization Act of 1974 transferred to the United States Nuclear Regulatory Commission the licensing and related regulatory functions previously exercised by the Atomic Energy Commission under the Atomic Energy Act of 1954, as amended.

The exercise of discretion and control over nuclear exports within the limits of law concerns the authority and responsibility of the President with respect to the conduct of foreign policy and the ensuring of the common defense and security.

It is essential that the Executive branch inform the Nuclear Regulatory Commission of its views before the Commission issues or denies a license, or grants an exemption.

NOW, THEREFORE, by virtue of the authority vested in me by the Constitution and statutes of the United States of America, including the Atomic Energy Act of 1954, as amended (42 U.S.C. 2011 et seq.), and as President of the United States of America, it is hereby ordered as follows:

Section 1. (a) The Secretary of State is designated to receive from the Nuclear Regulatory Commission a copy of each export license application, each proposal by the Nuclear Regulatory Commission to issue a general license for export, and each proposal by the Nuclear Regulatory Commission for exemption from the requirement for a license, which may involve a determination, pursuant to the Atomic Energy Act of 1954, as amended, that the issuance of the license or exemption from the requirement for a license will, or will not, be inimical to or constitute an unreasonable risk to the common defense and security.

(b) The Secretary of State shall ensure that a copy of each such application, proposed general license, or proposed exemption is received by the Secretary of Defese, the Secretary of Commerce, the Administrator of the United States Energy Research and Development Administration, hereinafter referred to as the Administrator, the Director of the Arms Control and Disarmament Agency, hereinafter referred to as the Director, and the head of any other department or agency which may have an interest therein, in order to afford them the opportunity to express their views, if any, on whether the license should be issued or the exemption granted.

Sec. 2. Within thirty days of receipt of a copy of a license application, proposed general license, or proposed exemption, the Secretary of Defense, the Secretary of Commerce, the Administrator, the Director, and the head of any other agency or department to which such copy has been transmitted, shall each transmit to the Secretary of State his views, if any, on whether and under what conditions the license should be issued or the exemption granted.

Sec. 3. The Secretary of State shall, after the provisions of section 2 of this order have been complied with, transmit to the Secretary of Defense, the Secretary of Commerce, the Administrator, the Director, and the head of any other department or agency who has expressed his views thereon, a proposed position of the Executive branch as to whether the license should be issued or the exemption granted, including a proposed judgment as to whether issuance of the license or granting of the exemption will, or will not, be inimical to or constitute an unreasonable risk to the common defense and security.

Sec. 4. If the heads of departments and agencies specified in section 2 of this order are unable to agree upon a position for the Executive branch, the Secretary of State shall refer the matter to the Chairman of the Under Secretaries Committee of the National Security Council in order to obtain a decision. In the event the Under Secretaries Committee is unable to reach a decision, the Chairman of that Committee shall refer the matter to the President for his decision.

Sec. 5. The Secretary of State, after taking the actions required by this order, shall notify the Nuclear Regulatory Commission of the position of the Executive branch as to whether the license should be issued or the exemption granted, including the judgment of the Executive branch as to whether issuance of the license or granting of the exemption will, or will not, be inimical to or constitute an unreasonable risk to the common defense and security. The Executive branch position shall be supported by relevant information and documentation as appropriate to the proceedings before the Nuclear Regulatory Commission.

GERALD R. FORD

THE WHITE HOUSE,
February 2, 1976.

PRESIDENT FORD

Statement on Nuclear Policy. *October 28, 1976*

WE HAVE known since the age of nuclear energy began more than 30 years ago that this source of energy had the potential for tremendous benefits for mankind and the potential for unparalleled destruction.

On the one hand, there is no doubt that nuclear energy represents one of the best hopes for satisfying the rising world demand for energy with minimum environmental impact and with the potential for reducing dependence on uncertain and diminishing world supplies of oil.

On the other hand, nuclear fuel, as it produces power also produces plutonium, which can be chemically separated from the spent fuel. The plutonium can be recycled and used to generate additional nuclear power, thereby partially offsetting the need for additional energy resources. Unfortunately—and this is the root of the problem—the same plutonium produced in nuclear powerplants can, when chemically separated, also be used to make nuclear explosives.

The world community cannot afford to let potential nuclear weapons material or the technology to produce it proliferate uncontrolled over the globe. The world community must ensure that production and utilization of such material by any nation is carried out under the most stringent security conditions and arrangements.

Developing the enormous benefits of nuclear energy while simultaneously developing the means to prevent proliferation is one of the major challenges facing all nations of the world today.

The standards we apply in judging most domestic and international activities are not sufficiently rigorous to deal with this extraordinarily complex problem. Our answers cannot be partially successful. They will either work, in which case we shall stop proliferation, or they will fail and nuclear proliferation will accelerate as nations initially having no intention of acquiring nuclear weapons conclude that they are forced to do so by the actions of others. Should this happen, we would face a world in which the security of all is critically imperiled. Maintaining international stability in such an environment would be incalculably difficult and dangerous. In times of regional or global crisis, risks of nuclear devastation would be immeasurably increased—if not through direct attack, then through a process of ever-expanding escalation. The problem can be handled as long as we understand it clearly and act wisely in concert with other nations. But we are faced with a threat of tragedy if we fail to comprehend it or to take effective measures.

Thus the seriousness and complexity of the problem place a special burden on those who propose ways to control proliferation. They must avoid the temptation for rhetorical gestures, empty threats, or righteous posturing. They must offer policies and programs which deal with the world as it is, not as we might wish it to be. The goal is to prevent proliferation, not simply to deplore it.

The first task in dealing with the problem of proliferation is to understand the world nuclear situation.

More than 30 nations have or plan to build nuclear powerplants to reap the benefits of nuclear energy. The 1973 energy crisis dramatically demonstrated to all nations not only the dangers of excessive reliance on oil imports but also the reality that the world's supply of fossil fuels is running out. As a result, nuclear energy is now properly seen by many nations as an indispensable way to satisfy rising energy demand without prematurely depleting finite fossil fuel resources. We must understand the motives which are leading these nations, developed and developing, to place even greater emphasis than we do on nuclear power development. For unless we comprehend their real needs, we cannot expect to find ways of working with them to ensure satisfaction of both our and their legitimate concerns. Moreover, several nations besides the United States have the technology needed to produce both the benefits and the destructive potential of nuclear energy. Nations with such capabilities are able to export their technology and facilities.

Thus, no single nation, not even the United States, can realistically hope—by itself—to control effectively the spread of reprocessing technology and the resulting availability of plutonium.

The United States once was the dominant world supplier of nuclear material equipment and technology. While we remain a leader in this field, other suppliers have come to share the international market—with the U.S. now supplying less than half of nuclear reactor exports. In short, for nearly a decade the U.S. has not had a monopoly on nuclear technology. Although our role is large, we are not able to control worldwide nuclear development.

For these reasons, action to control proliferation must be an international cooperative effort involving many nations, including both nuclear suppliers and customers. Common standards must be developed and accepted by all parties. If this is not done, unrestrained trade in sensitive nuclear technology and materials will develop—with no one in a position to stop it.

We in the United States must recognize that interests in nuclear energy vary widely among nations. We must recognize that some nations look to nuclear energy because they have no acceptable energy alternative. We must be sure that our efforts to control proliferation are not viewed by such nations as an act to prevent them from enjoying the benefits of nuclear energy. We must be sure that all nations recognize that the U.S. believes that nonproliferation objectives must take precedence over economic and energy benefits if a choice must be made.

Previous Action

During the past 30 years, the U.S. has been the unquestioned leader in worldwide efforts to assure that the benefits of nuclear energy are made available widely while its destructive uses are prevented. I have given special attention to these objectives during the past 2 years, and we have made important new progress, particularly in efforts to control the proliferation of nuclear weapons capability among the nations of the world.

In 1974, soon after I assumed office, I became concerned that some nuclear supplier countries, in order to achieve competitive advantage, were prepared to offer nuclear exports under conditions less rigorous than we believe prudent. In the fall of that year, at the United Nations General Assembly, the United States proposed that nonproliferation measures be strengthened materially. I also expressed my concern directly to my counterparts in key supplier and recipient nations. I directed the Secretary of State to emphasize multilateral action to limit this dangerous form of competition.

At U.S. initiative, the first meeting of major nuclear suppliers was convened in London in April 1975. A series of meetings and intensive bilateral consultations followed. As a result of these meetings, we have significantly raised international standards through progressive new guidelines to govern nuclear exports. These involve both improved safeguards and controls to prevent diversion of nuclear materials and to guard against the misuse of nuclear technology and physical protection against theft and sabotage. The United States has adopted these guidelines as policy for nuclear exports.

In addition, we have acted to deal with the special dangers associated with plutonium.

—We have prohibited export of reprocessing and other nuclear technologies that could contribute to proliferation.

—We have firmly opposed reprocessing in Korea and Taiwan. We welcome the decisions of those nations to forego such activities. We will continue to discourage national reprocessing in other locations of particular concern.

—We negotiated agreements for cooperation with Egypt and Israel which contain the strictest reprocessing provisions and other nuclear controls ever included in the 20-year history of our nuclear cooperation program.

—In addition, the United States recently completed negotiations to place its civil nuclear facilities under the safeguards of the International Atomic Energy Agency—and the IAEA has approved a proposed agreement for this purpose.

New Initiatives

Last summer, I directed that a thorough review be undertaken of all our nuclear policies and options to determine what further steps were needed. I have considered carefully the results of that review, held discussions with congressional leaders, and benefited from consultations with leaders of other nations. I have decided that new steps are needed, building upon the progress of the past 2 years. Today, I am announcing a number of actions and proposals aimed at:

—strengthening the commitment of the nations of the world to the goal of nonproliferation and building an effective system of international controls to prevent proliferation;

—changing and strengthening U.S. domestic nuclear policies and programs to support our nonproliferation goals; and

—establishing, by these actions, a sound foundation for the continued and increased use of nuclear energy in the U.S. and in the world in a safe and economic manner.

The task we face calls for an international cooperative venture of unprecedented dimensions. The U.S. is prepared to work with all other nations.

Principal Policy Decisions

I have concluded that the reprocessing and recycling of plutonium should not proceed unless there is sound reason to conclude that the world community can effectively overcome the associated risks of proliferation. I believe that avoidance of proliferation must take precedence over economic interests. I have also concluded that the United States and other nations can and should increase their use of nuclear power for peaceful purposes even if reprocessing and recycling of plutonium are found to be unacceptable.

Vigorous action is required domestically and internationally to make these judgments effective.

—I have decided that the United States should greatly accelerate its diplomatic initiatives in conjunction with nuclear supplier and consumer nations to control the spread of plutonium and technologies for separating plutonium.

Effective nonproliferation measures will require the participation and support of nuclear suppliers and consumers. There must be coordination in restraints so that an effective nonproliferation system is achieved, and there must be cooperation in assuring reliable fuel supplies so that peaceful energy needs are met.

—I have decided that the United States should no longer regard reprocessing of used nuclear fuel to produce plutonium as a necessary and inevitable step in the nuclear fuel cycle, and that we should pursue reprocessing and recycling in the future only if they are found to be consistent with our international objectives.

We must ensure that our domestic policies and programs are compatible with our international position on reprocessing and that we work closely with other nations in evaluating nuclear fuel reprocessing.

—The steps I am announcing today will assure that the necessity increase in our use of nuclear energy will be carried on with safety and without aggravating the danger of proliferation.

Even with strong efforts to conserve, we will have increasing demands for energy for a growing American economy. To satisfy these needs, we must rely on increased use of both nuclear energy and coal until more acceptable alternatives are developed. We will continue pushing ahead with work on all promising alternatives such as solar energy but now we must count on the technology that works. We cannot expect a major contribution to our energy supply from alternative technologies until late in this century.

To implement my overall policy decisions, I have decided on a number of policies that are necessary and appropriate to meet our nonproliferation and energy objectives.

—First, our domestic policies must be changed to conform to my decision on deferral of the commercialization of chemical reprocessing of nuclear fuel which results in the separation of plutonium.

—Second, I call upon all nations to join us in exercising maximum restraint in the transfer of reprocessing and enrichment technology and facilities by avoiding such sensitive exports or commitments for a period of at least 3 years.

—Third, new cooperative steps are needed to help assure that all nations have an adequate and reliable supply of energy for their needs. I believe, most importantly, that nuclear supplier nations have a special obligation to assure that customer nations have an adequate supply of fuel for their nuclear powerplants, if those customer nations forego the acquisition of reprocessing and uranium enrichment capabilities and accept effective proliferation controls.

—Fourth, the U.S. must maintain its role as a major and reliable world supplier of nuclear reactors and fuel for peaceful purposes. Our strong position as a supplier has provided the principal basis for our influence and leadership in worldwide nonproliferation efforts. A strong position will be equally important in the future. While reaffirming this Nation's intent to be a reliable supplier, the U.S. seeks no competitive advantage by virtue of the worldwide system of effective nonproliferation controls that I am calling for today.

—Fifth, new efforts must be made to urge all nations to join in a full-scale international cooperative effort—which I shall outline in detail—to develop a system of effective controls to prevent proliferation.

—Sixth, the U.S. must take new steps with respect to its own exports to control proliferation, while seeking to improve multilateral guidelines.

—Seventh, the U.S. must undertake a program to evaluate reprocessing in support of the international policies I have adopted.

—Finally, I have concluded that new steps are needed to assure that we have in place when needed, both in the U.S. and around the world, the facilities for the long-term storage or disposal of nuclear wastes.

Actions To Implement Our Nuclear Policies

In order to implement the nuclear policies that I have outlined, major efforts will be required within the United States and by the many nations around the world with an interest in nuclear energy. To move forward with these efforts, I am today taking a number of actions and making a number of proposals to other nations.

I. *Change in U.S. Policy on Nuclear Fuel Reprocessing*

With respect to nuclear fuel reprocessing, I am directing agencies of the executive branch to implement my decision to delay commercialization of reprocessing activities in the United States until uncertainties are resolved. Specifically, I am:

—Directing the Administrator of the Energy Research and Development Administration (ERDA) to:

• change ERDA policies and programs which heretofore have been based on the assumption that reprocessing would proceed;

• encourage prompt action to expand spent fuel storage facilities, thus assuring utilities that they need not be concerned about shutdown of nuclear reactors because of delays; and

• identify the research and development efforts needed to investigate the feasibility of recovering the energy value from used nuclear fuel without separating plutonium.

II. *Restraint in the Transfer of Sensitive Nuclear Technology and Facilities*

Despite the gains in controlling proliferation that have been made, the dangers posed by reprocessing and the prospect of uncontrolled availability of plutonium require further, decisive international action. Effective control of the parallel risk of spreading uranium enrichment technology is also necessary. To meet these dangers:

—I call upon all nations to join with us in exercising maximum restraint in the transfer of reprocessing and enrichment technology and facilities by avoiding such sensitive exports or commitments for a period of at least 3 years.

This will allow suppliers and consumers to work together to establish reliable means for meeting nuclear needs with minimum risk, as we assess carefully the wisdom of plutonium use. As we proceed in these efforts, we must not be influenced by pressures to approve the export of these sensitive facilities.

III. *Assuring an Adequate Energy Supply for Customer Nations*

—I urge nuclear suppliers to provide nuclear consumers with fuel services, instead of sensitive technology or facilities.

Nations accepting effective nonproliferation restraints have a right to expect reliable and economic supply of nuclear reactors and associated, nonsensitive fuel. All such nations would share in the benefits of an assured supply of nuclear fuel, even though the number and location of sensitive facilities to generate this fuel is limited to meet nonproliferation goals. The availability of fuel-cycle services in several different nations can provide ample assurance to consumers of a continuing and stable source of supply.

It is also desirable to continue studying the idea of a few suitably-sited multinational fuel-cycle centers to serve regional needs, when effectively safeguarded and economically warranted. Through these and related means, we can minimize incentives for the spread of dangerous fuel-cycle capabilities.

The United States stands ready to take action, in cooperation with other concerned nations, to assure reliable supplies of nuclear fuel at equitable prices to any country accepting responsible restraints on its nuclear power program with regard to reprocessing, plutonium disposition, and enrichment technology.

—I am directing the Secretary of State to initiate consultations to explore with other nations arrangements for coordinating fuel services and for developing other means of ensuring that suppliers will be able to offer, and consumers will be able to receive, an uninterrupted and economical supply of low-enriched uranium fuel and fuel services.

These discussions will address ways to ensure against economic disadvantage to cooperating nations and to remove any sources of competition which could undermine our common nonproliferation efforts.

To contribute to this initiative, the United States will offer binding letters of intent for the supply of nuclear fuel to current and prospective customers willing to accept such responsible restraints.

—In addition, I am directing the Secretary of State to enter into negotiations or arrangements for mutual agreement on disposition of spent fuel with consumer nations that adopt responsible restraints.

Where appropriate, the United States will provide consumer nations with either fresh, low-enriched uranium fuel or make other equitable arrangements in return for mutual agreement on the disposition of spent fuel where such disposition demonstrably fosters our common and cooperative nonproliferation objectives. The United States seeks no commercial advantage in pursuing options for fuel disposition and assured fuel supplies.

Finally, the United States will continue to expand cooperative efforts with other countries in developing their indigenous nonnuclear energy resources.

The United States has proposed and continues to advocate the establishment of an International Energy Institute, specifically designed to help developing countries match the most economic and readily available sources of energy to their power needs. Through this Institute and other appropriate means, we will offer technological assistance in the development of indigenous energy resources.

IV. *Strengthening the U.S. Role as a Reliable Supplier*

If the United States is to continue its leadership role in worldwide nonproliferation efforts, it must be a reliable supplier of nuclear reactors and fuel for peaceful purposes. There are two principal actions we can take to contribute to this objective:

—I will submit to the new Congress proposed legislation that will permit the expansion of capacity in the United States to produce enriched uranium, including the authority needed for expansion of the Government-owned plant at Portsmouth, Ohio. I will also work with Congress to establish a framework for a private, competitive industry to finance, build, own, and operate enrichment plants.

U.S. capacity has been fully committed since mid-1974 with the result that no new orders could be signed. The Congress did not act on my full proposal and provided only limited and temporary authority for proceeding with the Portsmouth plant. We must have additional authority to proceed with the expansion of capacity without further delay.

—I will work closely with the Congress to ensure that legislation for improving our export controls results in a system that provides maximum assurance that the United States will be a reliable supplier to other nations for the full period of agreements.

One of the principal concerns with export legislation proposed in the last Congress was the fear that foreign customers could be subjected to arbitrary new controls imposed well after a long-term agreement and specific contracts for nuclear powerplants and fuel had been signed. In the case of nuclear plants and fuel, reliable long-term agreements are essential, and we must adopt export controls that provide reliability while meeting nonproliferation objectives.

V. *International Controls Against Proliferation*

To reinforce the foregoing policies, we must develop means to establish international restraints over the accumulation of plutonium itself, whether in separated form or in unprocessed spent fuel. The accumulation of plutonium under national control, especially in a separated form, is a primary proliferation risk.

—I am directing the Secretary of State to pursue vigorously discussions aimed at the establishment of a new international regime to provide for storage of civil plutonium and spent reactor fuel.

The United States made this proposal to the International Atomic Energy Agency and other interested nations last spring.

Creation of such a regime will greatly strengthen world confidence that the growing accumulation of excess plutonium and spent fuel can be stored safely, pending reentry into the nuclear fuel cycle or other safe disposition. I urge the IAEA, which is empowered to establish plutonium depositories, to give prompt implementation to this concept.

Once a broadly representative IAEA storage regime is in operation, we are prepared to place our own excess civil plutonium and spent fuel under its control. Moreover, we are prepared to consider providing a site for international storage under IAEA auspices.

The inspection system of the IAEA remains a key element in our entire nonproliferation strategy. The world community must make sure that the Agency has the technical and human resources needed to keep pace with its expanding responsibilities. At my direction, we have recently committed substantial additional resources to help upgrade the IAEA's technical safeguards capabilities, and I believe we must strengthen further the safeguard functions of the IAEA.

—I am directing the Secretary of State and Administrator of ERDA to undertake a major international effort to ensure that adequate resources for this purpose are made available, and that we mobilize our best scientific talent to support that Agency. Our principal national laboratories with expertise in this area have been directed to provide assistance, on a continuing basis, to the IAEA Secretariat.

The terrible increase in violence and terrorism throughout the world has sharpened our awareness of the need to assure rigorous protection for sensitive nuclear materials and equipment. Fortunately, the need to cope with this problem is now broadly recognized. Many nations have responded to the initiatives which I have taken in this area by materially strengthening their physical security and by cooperating in the development of international guidelines by the IAEA. As a result of consultations among the major suppliers, provision for adequate physical security is becoming a normal condition of supply.

We have an effective physical security system in the United States. But steps are needed to upgrade physical security systems and to assure timely international collaboration in the recovery of lost or stolen materials.

—I have directed the Secretary of State to address vigorously the problem of physical security at both bilateral and multilateral levels, including exploration of a possible international convention.

The United States is committed to the development of the system of international controls that I have here outlined. Even when complete, however, no system of controls is likely to be effective if a potential violator judges that his acquisition of a nuclear explosive will be received with indifference by the international community.

Any material violation of a nuclear safeguards agreement—especially the diversion of nuclear material for use in making explosives—must be universally judged to be an extremely serious affront to the world community, calling for the immediate imposition of drastic sanctions.

—I serve notice today that the United States will, at a minimum, respond to violation by any nation of any safeguards agreement to which we are a party with an immediate cutoff of our supply of nuclear fuel and cooperation to that nation.

We would consider further steps, not necessarily confined to the area of nuclear cooperation, against the violator nation. Nor will our actions be limited to violations of agreements in which we are directly involved. In the event of material violation of any safeguards agreement, particularly agreements with the IAEA, we will initiate immediate consultations with all interested nations to determine appropriate action.

Universal recognition of the total unacceptability of the abrogation or violation of any nonproliferation agreements is one of the most important steps which can be taken to prevent further proliferation. We invite all concerned governments to affirm publicly that they will regard nuclear wrongdoing as an intolerable violation of acceptable norms of international behavior, which would set in motion strong and immediate countermeasures.

VI. *U.S. Nuclear Export Policies*

During the past 2 years, the United States has strengthened its own national nuclear export policies. Our interests, however, are not limited to controls alone. The United States has a special responsibility to share the benefits of peaceful nuclear energy with other countries. We have sought to serve other nations as a reliable supplier of nuclear fuel and equipment. Given the choice between economic benefits and progress toward our nonproliferation goals, we have given, and will continue to give priority to nonproliferation. But there should be no incompatibility between nonproliferation and assisting other nations in enjoying the benefits of peaceful nuclear power if all supplier countries pursue common nuclear export policies. There is need, however, for even more rigorous controls than those now commonly employed, and for policies that favor nations accepting responsible nonproliferation limitations.

—I have decided that we will henceforth apply new criteria in judging whether to enter into new or expanded nuclear cooperation:

• Adherence to the nonproliferation treaty will be a strong positive factor favoring cooperation with a nonnuclear weapon state.

• Nonnuclear weapons states that have not yet adhered to the nonproliferation treaty will receive positive recognition if they are prepared to submit to full fuel cycle safeguards, pending adherence.

• We will favor recipient nations that are prepared to forego, or postpone for a substantial period, the establishment of national reprocessing or enrichment activities or, in certain cases, prepared to shape and schedule their reprocessing and enriching facilities to foster nonproliferation needs.

• Positive recognition will also be given to nations prepared to participate in an international storage regime, under which spent fuel and any separated plutonium would be placed pending use.

Exceptional cases may occur in which nonproliferation will be served best by cooperating with nations not yet meeting these tests. However, I pledge that the Congress will not be asked to approve any new or amended agreement not meeting these new criteria unless I personally determine that the agreement is fully supportive of our nonproliferation goals. In case of such a determination, my reasons will be fully presented to the Congress.

—With respect to countries that are current recipients of U.S. nuclear supply, I am directing the Secretary of State to enter into negotiations with the objective of conforming these agreements to established international guidelines, and to seek through diplomatic initiatives and fuel supply incentives to obtain their acceptance of our new criteria.

We must recognize the need for effective multilateral approaches to nonproliferation and prevent nuclear export controls from becoming an element of commercial competition.

—I am directing the Secretary of State to intensify discussions with other nuclear suppliers aimed at expanding common guidelines for peaceful cooperative agreements so that they conform with these criteria.

In this regard, the United States would discuss ways of developing incentives that can lead to acceptance of these criteria, such as assuring reliable fuel supplies for nations accepting new restraints.

The reliability of American assurances to other nations is an asset that few, if any, nations of the world can match. It must not be eroded. Indeed, nothing could more prejudice our efforts to strengthen our existing nonproliferation understandings than arbitrary suspension or unwarranted delays in meeting supply commitments to countries which are dealing with us in good faith regarding effective safeguards and restraints.

Despite my personal efforts, the 94th Congress adjourned without passing nuclear export legislation which would have strengthened our effectiveness in dealing with other nations on nuclear matters.

—In the absence of such legislation, I am directing the Secretary of State to work closely with the Nuclear Regulatory Commission to ensure proper emphasis on nonproliferation concerns in the nuclear export licensing process.

I will continue to work to develop bipartisan support in Congress for improvements in our nuclear export laws.

VII. Reprocessing Evaluation Program

The world community requires an aggressive program to build the international controls and cooperative regimes I have just outlined. I am prepared to mount such a program in the United States.

—I am directing the Administrator of ERDA to:

• Begin immediately to define a reprocessing and recycle evaluation program consistent with meeting our international objectives outlined earlier in this statement. This program should complement the Nuclear Regulatory Commission's (NRC) ongoing considerations of safety safeguards and environ-

mental requirements for reprocessing and recycling activities, particularly its Generic Environmental Statement on Mixed Oxide Fuels.
* Investigate the feasibility of recovering the energy value from used nuclear fuel without separating our plutonium.

—I am directing the Secretary of State to invite other nations to participate in designing and carrying out ERDA's reprocessing and recycle evaluation program, consistent with our international energy cooperation and nonproliferation objectives. I will direct that activities carried out in the U.S. in connection with this program be subjected to full IAEA safeguards and inspections.

VIII. *Nuclear Waste Management*

The area of our domestic nuclear program dealing with long-term management of nuclear wastes from our commercial nuclear powerplants has not in the past received sufficient attention. In my 1977 Budget, I proposed a fourfold increase in funding for this program, which involves the activities of several Federal agencies. We recently completed a review to determine what additional actions are needed to assure availability in the mid-1980's of a federally-owned and managed repository for long-term nuclear wastes, well before significant quantities of wastes begin to accumulate.

I have been assured that the technology for long-term management or disposal of nuclear wastes is available but demonstrations are needed.

—I have directed the Administrator of ERDA to take the necessary action to speed up this program so as to demonstrate all components of waste management technology by 1978 and to demonstrate a complete repository for such wastes by 1985.

—I have further directed that the first demonstration depository for high-level wastes which will be owned by the Government be submitted for licensing by the independent NRC to assure its safety and acceptability to the public.

In view of the decisions announced today, I have also directed the Administrator of ERDA to assure that the waste repository will be able to handle spent fuel elements as well as the separated and solidified waste that would result if we proceed with nuclear fuel reprocessing.

The United States continues to provide world leadership in nuclear waste management. I am inviting other nations to participate in and learn from our programs.

—I am directing the Secretary of State to discuss with other nations and the IAEA the possibility of establishing centrally located, multinationally controlled nuclear waste repositories so that the number of sites that are needed can be limited.

Increased Use of Nuclear Energy in the United States

Even with strong conservation efforts, energy demands in the United States will continue to increase in response to the needs of a growing economy. The only alternative over the next 15 to 20 years to increased use of both nuclear energy and coal is greater reliance on imported oil which will jeopardize our Nation's strength and welfare.

We now have in the United States 62 licensed nuclear plants, providing about 9 percent of our electrical energy. By 1985, we will have from 145 to 160 plants, supplying 20 percent or more of the Nation's electricity.

In many cases, electricity from nuclear plants is markedly cheaper than that produced from either oil or coal-fired plants. Nuclear energy is environmentally preferable in a number of respects to other principal ways of generating electricity.

Commercial nuclear power has an excellent safety record, with nearly 200 plant-years of experience (compiled over 18 chronological years) without a single death from a nuclear accident. I have acted to assure that this record is maintained in the years ahead. For example, I have increased funds for the independent Nuclear Regulatory Commission and for the Energy Research and Development Administration for reactor safety research and development.

The decisions and actions I am announcing today will help overcome the uncertainties that have served to delay the expanded use of nuclear energy in the United States. While the decision to delay reprocessing is significant, it will not prevent us from increasing our use of nuclear energy. We are on the right course with our nuclear power program in America. The changes I am announcing today will ensure that we continue.

My decisions today do not affect the U.S. program of research and development on the breeder reactor. That program assumes that no decision on the commercial operations of breeder reactors, which require plutonium fuel, will be made before 1986.

Conclusion

I do not underestimate the challenge represented in the creation of a worldwide program that will permit capturing the benefits of nuclear energy while maintaining needed protection against nuclear proliferation. The challenge is one that can be managed only partially and temporarily by technical measures.

It can be managed fully if the task is faced realistically by nations prepared to forego perceived short-term advantages in favor of fundamental long-term gains. We call upon all nations to recognize that their individual and collective interests are best served by internationally assured and safeguarded nuclear fuel supply, services, and storage. We ask them to turn aside from pursuing nuclear capabilities which are of doubtful economic value and have ominous implications for nuclear proliferation and instability in the world.

The growing international consensus against the proliferation of nuclear weapons is a source of encouragement. But it is certainly not a basis for complacency.

Success in meeting the challenge now before us depends on an extraordinary coordination of the policies of all nations toward the common good. The United States is prepared to lead, but we cannot succeed alone. If nations can work together constructively and cooperatively to manage our common nuclear problems, we will enhance our collective security. And we will be better able to concentrate our energies and our resources on the great tasks of construction rather than consume them in increasingly dangerous rivalry.

THE WHITE HOUSE
SECRET[Declassified]   WASHINGTON

<u>Presidential Directive/NSC-8</u>   March 24, 1977

TO: The Vice President
               The Secretary of State
               The Secretary of Defense
               The Director, Arms Control and Disarmament Agency
               The Administrator, Energy Research and
                  Development Administration
       ALSO: The Director of Central Intelligence
               The Chairman, Nuclear Regulatory Commission
               The Assistant to the President for
                  Energy Policy

SUBJECT: Nuclear Non-Proliferation Policy (U)

It shall be a principal U.S. security objective to prevent the spread of nuclear explosive -- or near explosive -- capabilities to countries which do not now possess them. To this end U.S. non-proliferation policy shall be directed at preventing the development and use of sensitive nuclear power technologies which involve direct access to plutonium, highly enriched uranium, or other weapons useable material in non-nuclear weapons states, <u>and</u> at minimizing the global accumulation of these materials.

1. Specifically, the U.S. will seek a pause among all nations in sensitive nuclear developments in order to initiate and actively participate in, an intensive international nuclear fuel cycle re-evaluation program (IFCEP) whose technical aspects shall concern the development and promotion of alternative, non-sensitive, nuclear fuel cycles. This program will include both nuclear supplier and recipient nations.

2. For its part, the United States Government will:

   -- Indefinitely defer the commercial reprocessing and recycle of plutonium in the U.S.

   -- Restructure the U.S. breeder reactor program so as to emphasize alternative designs to the plutonium breeder, and to meet a later date for possible commercialization. As a first step the need for the current prototype reactor, the Clinch River project, will be reassessed.

- Redirect the funding of U.S. nuclear research and development programs so as to concentrate on the development of alternative nuclear fuel cycles which do not involved access to weapons useable materials.

- Provide incentives, in the area of nuclear fuel assurances and spent fuel storage, to encourage the participation of other nations in the International Fuel Cycle Evaluation Program. Detailed studies of these programs shall be carried out by the NSC Ad Hoc Group established herein, and submitted to me as directed in the accompanying memorandum.

- Initiate a program of assistance to other nations in the development of non-nuclear means of meeting energy needs.

- Increase production capacity for nuclear fuels.

3. It shall also be U.S. policy to strengthen the existing non-proliferation regime: by encouraging the widest possible adherence to the Non-Proliferation Treaty, and to comprehensive international safeguards; by strengthening and improving the IAEA; and by providing stronger sanctions against the violation of nuclear agreements. Therefore the U.S. will announce its intention to terminate nuclear cooperation with any non-nuclear weapons state that hereafter

   - detonates or demonstrably acquires a nuclear explosive device; or

   - terminates or materially violates international safeguards of any guarantees it has given to the United States.

4. In order to implement these policies to perform the necessary studies, and to coordinate departmental activities in the non-proliferation field, I hereby establish an NSC Ad Hoc Group, to be chaired by the Department of State, and to include the Presidential Assistant for Energy. This group shall establish task forces, chaired by the appropriate agencies, to perform, among others, the tasks detailed in the accompanying memorandum.

The NSC Ad Hoc Group, established in PD-8, is directed to:

-- prepare and submit by March 31 a comprehensive list of all activities, facilities and technologies related to nuclear power, which involve direct access to weapons useable materials;

-- prepare and submit by April 1, a review of the Fiscal 1978 budget with appropriate recommendations to implement the policies set for in the accompanying Presidential Directive;

-- prepare and submit by April 5, proposed nuclear export policies, including: a summary of current applications for export of Highly Enriched Uranium and plutonium; criteria which should be applied to nuclear exports at the licensing stage; a list of criteria and conditions which should be required for new and amended agreements for cooperation, and necessary revisions in existing agreements; explicit options covering U.S. policies on consent to retransfer, reprocess, reexport and reuse U.S.-supplied fuels, Highly Enriched Uranium, plutonium, and materials irradiated in U.S.-supplied facilities; and legislative proposals to implement these recommendations;

-- prepare and submit by May 1, a detailed study of measures the U.S. might take so as to be able to offer nuclear fuel assurances to nations participating in the International Fuel Cycle Evaluation Program, including: rigorous revised estimates of future nuclear energy demand; measures to expand U.S. enrichment capacity; analysis and justification of U.S. stockpile programs; recommendations for appropriate terms and conditions for future toll enrichment contracts; assessments of the benefits of declaring an open season on enrichment contracts; exploration of international undertakings and agreements; and other short and long-term options for providing nuclear fuel assurances and collaborating with other suppliers;

-- prepare and submit by May 1, a thorough study of measures the U.S. might take concerning nuclear fuel storage including: measures to expand U.S. spent fuel storage and transportation capacity; proposals for meeting the storage needs of those participant in the International Fuel Cycle Evaluation Program;

-- prepare and submit by May 1, a program for promoting the development of non-nuclear energy alternatives and for assisting other nations with non-nuclear means to meet their energy needs.

PRESIDENT CARTER

Nuclear Power Policy
Statement on Decisions Reached Following a Review. April 7, 1977

There is no dilemma today more difficult to resolve than that connected with the use of nuclear power. Many countries see nuclear power as the only real opportunity, at least in this century, to reduce the dependence of their economic well-being on foreign oil—an energy source of uncertain availability, growing price, and ultimate exhaustion. The U.S., by contrast, has a major domestic energy source—coal—but its use is not without penalties, and our plans also call for the use of nuclear power as a share in our energy production.

The benefits of nuclear power are thus very real and practical. But a serious risk accompanies worldwide use of nuclear power—the risk that components of the nuclear power process will be turned to providing atomic weapons.

We took an important step in reducing the risk of expanding possession of atomic weapons through the nonproliferation treaty, whereby more than 100 nations have agreed not to develop such explosives. But we must go further. The U.S.

is deeply concerned about the consequences for all nations of a further spread of nuclear weapons or explosive capabilities. We believe that these risks would be vastly increased by the further spread of sensitive technologies which entail direct access to plutonium, highly enriched uranium, or other weapons usable material. The question I have had under review from my first day in office is how can that be accomplished without forgoing the tangible benefits of nuclear power.

We are now completing an extremely thorough review of all the issues that bear on the use of nuclear power. We have concluded that the serious consequences of proliferation and direct implications for peace and security—as well as strong scientific and economic evidence—require:
— a major change in U.S. domestic nuclear energy policies and programs; and
— a concerted effort among all nations to find better answers to the problems and risks accompanying the increased use of nuclear power.

I am announcing today some of my decisions resulting from that review.

First, we will defer indefinitely the commercial reprocessing and recycling of the plutonium produced in the U.S. nuclear power programs. From our own experience, we have concluded that a viable and economic nuclear power program can be sustained without such reprocessing and recycling. The plant at Barnwell, South Carolina, will receive neither Federal encouragement nor funding for its completion as a reprocessing facility.

Second, we will restructure the U.S. breeder reactor program to give greater priority to alternative designs of the breeder and to defer the date when breeder reactors would be put into commercial use.

Third, we will redirect funding of U.S. nuclear research and development programs to accelerate our research into alternative nuclear fuel cycles which do not involve direct access to materials usable in nuclear weapons.

Fourth, we will increase U.S. production capacity for enriched uranium to provide adequate and timely supply of nuclear fuels for domestic and foreign needs.

Fifth, we will propose the necessary legislative steps to permit the U.S. to offer nuclear fuel supply contracts and guarantee delivery of such nuclear fuel to other countries.

Sixth, we will continue to embargo the export of equipment or technology that would permit uranium enrichment and chemical reprocessing.

Seventh, we will continue discussions with supplying and recipient countries alike, of a wide range of international approaches and frameworks that will permit all nations to achieve their energy objectives while reducing the spread of nuclear explosive capability. Among other things, we will explore the establishment of an international nuclear fuel cycle evaluation program aimed at developing alternative fuel cycles and a variety of international and U.S. measures to assure access to nuclear fuel supplies and spent fuel storage for nations sharing common nonproliferation objectives.

We will continue to consult very closely with a number of governments regarding the most desirable multilateral and bilateral arrangements for assuring that nuclear energy is creatively harnessed for peaceful economic purposes. Our intent is to develop wider international cooperation in regard to this vital issue through systematic and thorough international consultations.

Nuclear Power Policy

Remarks and a Question-and-Answer Session With Reporters on Decisions Following a Review of U.S. Policy. April 7, 1977

* * *

The second point I'd like to make before I answer questions is concerning our Nation's efforts to control the spread of nuclear explosive capability. As far back as 30 years ago, our Government made a proposal to the United Nations that there be tight international controls over nuclear fuels and particularly those that might be made into explosives.

Last year during the Presidential campaign, both I and President Ford called for strict controls over fuels to prevent the proliferation—further proliferation of nuclear explosive capability.

There is no dilemma today more difficult to address than that connected with the use of atomic power. Many countries see atomic power as their only real opportunity to deal with the dwindling supplies of oil, the increasing price of oil, and the ultimate exhaustion of both oil and natural gas.

Our country is in a little better position. We have oil supplies of our own, and we have very large reserves of coal. But even coal has its limitations. So, we will ourselves continue to use atomic power as a share of our total energy production.

The benefits of nuclear power, particularly to some foreign countries that don't have oil and coal of their own, are very practical and critical. But a serious risk is involved in the handling of nuclear fuels—the risk that component parts of this power process will be turned to providing explosives or atomic weapons.

We took an important step in reducing this risk a number of years ago by the implementation of the nonproliferation treaty which has now been signed by approximately a hundred nations. But we must go further.

We have seen recently India evolve an explosive device derived from a peaceful nuclear powerplant, and we now feel that several other nations are on the verge of becoming nuclear explosive powers.

The United States is deeply concerned about the consequences of the uncontrolled spread of this nuclear weapon capability. We can't arrest it immediately and unilaterally. We have no authority over other countries. But we believe that these risks would be vastly increased by the further spread of reprocessing capabilities of the spent nuclear fuel from which explosives can be derived.

Plutonium is especially poisonous, and, of course, enriched uranium, thorium, and other chemicals or metals can be used as well.

We are now completing an extremely thorough review of our own nuclear power program. We have concluded that serious consequences can be derived from our own laxity in the handling of these materials and the spread of their use by other countries. And we believe that there is strong scientific and economic evidence that a time for a change has come.

Therefore, we will make a major change in the United States domestic nuclear energy policies and programs which I am announcing today.

We will make a concerted effort among all other countries to find better answers to the problems and risks of nuclear proliferation. And I would like to outline a few things now that we will do specifically.

First of all, we will defer indefinitely the commercial reprocessing and recycling of the plutonium produced in U.S. nuclear power programs.

From my own experience, we have concluded that a viable and adequate economic nuclear program can be maintained without such reprocessing and recycling of plutonium. The plant at Barnwell, South Carolina, for instance, will receive neither Federal encouragement nor funding from us for its completion as a reprocessing facility.

Second, we will restructure our own U.S. breeder program to give greater priority to alternative designs of the breeder other than plutonium, and to defer the date when breeder reactors would be put into commercial use.

We will continue research and development, try to shift away from plutonium, defer dependence on the breeder reactor for commercial use.

Third, we will direct funding of U.S. nuclear research and development programs to accelerate our research into alternative nuclear fuel cycles which do not involve direct access to materials that can be used for nuclear weapons.

Fourth, we will increase the U.S. capacity to produce nuclear fuels, enriched uranium in particular, to provide adequate and timely supplies of nuclear fuels to countries that need them so that they will not be required or encouraged to reprocess their own materials.

Fifth, we will propose to the Congress the necessary legislative steps to permit us to sign these supply contracts and remove the pressure for the reprocessing of nuclear fuels by other countries that do not now have this capability.

Sixth, we will continue to embargo the export of either equipment or technology that could permit uranium enrichment and chemical reprocessing.

And seventh, we will continue discussions with supplying countries and recipient countries, as well, of a wide range of international approaches and frameworks that will permit all countries to achieve their own energy needs while at the same time reducing the spread of the capability for nuclear explosive development.

Among other things—and we have discussed this with 15 or 20 national leaders already—we will explore the establishment of an international nuclear fuel cycle evaluation program so that we can share with countries that have to reprocess nuclear fuel the responsibility for curtailing the ability for the development of explosives.

One other point that ought to be made in the international negotiation field is that we have to help provide some means for the storage of spent nuclear fuel materials which are highly explosive, highly radioactive in nature.

I have been working very closely with and personally with some of the foreign leaders who are quite deeply involved in the decisions that we make. We are not trying to impose our will on those nations like Japan and France and Britain and Germany which already have reprocessing plants in operation. They have a special need that we don't have in that their supplies of petroleum products are not available.

But we hope that they will join with us—and I believe that they will—in trying to have some worldwide understanding of the extreme threat of the further proliferation of nuclear explosive capability.

I'd be glad to answer a few questions.

Nuclear Nonproliferation Policy Act of 1977 Transmitted to the Congress

Following is the text of a message from President Carter to the Congress dated April 27, together with a fact sheet issued by the White House that day.

MESSAGE FROM PRESIDENT CARTER

White House press release dated April 27

To the Congress of the United States:

The need to halt nuclear proliferation is one of mankind's most pressing challenges. Members of my Administration are now engaged in international discussions to find ways of controlling the spread of nuclear explosive capability without depriving any nation of the means to satisfy its energy needs. The domestic nuclear policies which I have already put forward will place our nation in a leadership position, setting a positive example for other nuclear suppliers as well as demonstrating the strength of our concern here at home for the hazards of a plutonium economy. Today I am submitting to the Congress a bill which would establish for the United States a strong and effective non-proliferation policy.

This bill relies heavily upon work which the Congress has already done, and I commend the Congress for these valuable initiatives. I look forward to working with the Congress to establish a strong, responsible legislative framework from which we can continue strengthened efforts to halt the spread of nuclear weapons.

Among our shared goals are: an increase in the effectiveness of international safeguards and controls on peaceful nuclear activities to prevent further proliferation of nuclear explosive devices, the establishment of common international sanctions to prevent such proliferation, an effort to encourage nations which have not ratified the Non-Proliferation Treaty to do so at the earliest possible date, and adoption of programs to enhance the reliability of the United States as a supplier of nuclear fuel.

This bill differs from pending proposals, however, in several respects:

1. It defines the immediate nuclear export conditions which we can reasonably ask other nations to meet while we negotiate stricter arrangements. The proposals currently before Congress would impose criteria that could force an immediate moratorium on our nuclear exports, adversely affecting certain allies whose cooperation is needed if we are to achieve our ultimate objective of non-proliferation.

2. It defines additional nuclear export conditions which will be required in new agreements for civil nuclear cooperation. In particular, we will require as a continuing condition of U.S. supply that recipients have all their nuclear activities under IAEA [International Atomic Energy Agency] safeguards. I view this as an interim measure and shall make it clear to all potential recipients and to other nuclear suppliers that our first preference, and continuing objective, is universal adherence to the Non-Proliferation Treaty.

3. For the near future, it attempts to tighten the conditions for U.S. nuclear cooperation through renegotiation of existing agreements to meet the same standards as those we will require in new agreements. I believe that this approach will better meet our non-proliferation objectives than will the unilateral imposition of new export licensing conditions.

May 16, 1977

4. It increases the flexibility we need to deal with an extremely complex subject. For example, instead of requiring countries that want our nuclear exports to foreswear fuel enrichment and reprocessing for all time, it allows us to draft new agreements using incentives to encourage countries not to acquire such facilities. It also permits me to grant exceptions when doing so would further our basic aim of non-proliferation. All new cooperation agreements would, of course, be subject to Congressional review.

This bill is intended to reassure other nations that the United States will be a reliable supplier of nuclear fuel and equipment for those who genuinely share our desire for non-proliferation. It will insure that when all statutory standards have been met, export licenses will be issued—or, if the judgment of the Executive Branch and the independent Nuclear Regulatory Commission should differ, that a workable mechanism exists for resolving the dispute.

Since I intend personally to oversee Executive Branch actions affecting non-proliferation, I do not think a substantial reorganization of the responsibility for nuclear exports within the Executive Branch is necessary. This conclusion is shared by the Nuclear Regulatory Commission.

The need for prompt action is great. Until domestic legislation is enacted, other countries will be reluctant to renegotiate their agreements with us, because they will fear that new legislation might suddenly change the terms of cooperation. If the incentives we offer them to renegotiate with us are not attractive enough, the United States could lose important existing safeguards and controls. And if our policy is too weak, we could find ourselves powerless to restrain a deadly world-wide expansion of nuclear explosive capability. I believe the legislation now submitted to you strikes the necessary balance.

JIMMY CARTER.

THE WHITE HOUSE, *April 27, 1977.*

WHITE HOUSE FACT SHEET

White House press release dated April 27

The Nuclear Non-Proliferation Policy Act of 1977, the domestic nuclear policies announced by the President on April 7, and the additional policy decisions included in this fact sheet are key components of the Administration's nuclear nonproliferation policy. The President's policy decisions include:

—New conditions we will require for the granting of nuclear export licenses.

—Additional new conditions we will require in new U.S. agreements for cooperation. These agreements are the formal bilateral undertakings which form the basis for civil nuclear interactions with other nations.

—Policies the executive branch will follow in making recommendations to the Nuclear Regulatory Commission on the export of sensitive items such as plutonium and highly enriched uranium (the weapons-usable form of uranium, known as HEU).

—Policies the executive branch will follow in deciding whether to approve a request by another nation to retransfer U.S.-supplied fuel to a third nation for reprocessing.

—Policies to improve U.S. reliability as a nuclear fuel supplier by introducing greater clarity and predictability into the export licensing process.

Together, all these policies will place the United States in a leadership position among nuclear suppliers, and will establish a strong and effective nonproliferation policy. These policies have been developed, and must be evaluated, as a complete package. They are intended as a delicately balanced blend of:

—*Denials:* for those items, such as reprocessing plants, which we believe create such a large risk that their export should be avoided whenever possible;

—*Controls:* over those items and technologies, required by ongoing programs, where improved safeguards and conditions for physical security will substantially reduce the risk. These controls will be backed up by stiff sanctions which would be imposed on violators.

—*Incentives:* The United States fully recognizes that there is no such thing as an effective unilateral nonproliferation policy. We must gain the support of other nations—both suppliers and recipients—if we are to reach our common goal of limiting the spread of nuclear weapons. Hence the Administration's program includes substantial elements of incentives, particularly in the areas of: uranium resource assessment; guaranteed access to nonsensitive, low enriched uranium (LEU) nuclear fuel; and spent fuel storage.

The following are key features of the Nuclear Non-Proliferation Policy Act of 1977 and related Administration policies:

1. The bill establishes for the first time a statutory requirement forbidding the independent Nuclear Regulatory Commission (NRC) from granting a license to export nuclear materials or facilities until it has been notified by the executive branch of its judgment that the issuance of a license "will not be inimicable to the common defense and security." This judgment will be reached by the Departments of State, Defense, Commerce, the Arms Control and Disarmament Agency, and the Energy Research and Development Administration.

In arriving at these judgments, the executive branch will adhere to the following policies not detailed in the act:

—Continue to embargo the export of enrichment and reprocessing plants.

—Avoid new commitments to export significant amounts of separated plutonium except for gram quantities for research and analytical uses.

—Avoid new commitments to export significant quantities of highly enriched uranium except when the project is of exceptional merit and the use of low enriched fuel or some other less weapons-usable material is clearly shown to be technically infeasible.

—Require direct Presidential approval for any supply of HEU greater than 15 kilograms (the approximate amount needed for a bomb).

—Undertake efforts to identify projects and facilities which might be converted to the use of LEU instead of HEU.

—Take steps to minimize inventories of weapons-usable uranium abroad.

2. The bill defines the immediate nuclear export conditions which we can reasonably expect other nations to meet while we negotiate stricter agreements for cooperation. These conditions include:

—A requirement for International Atomic Energy Agency (IAEA) safeguards on all exported items and on any other plutonium or enriched uranium that might be used in the exported facility or produced through its use.

—A requirement that no U.S. export be used for research or production of any nuclear explosive device.

—A requirement that no U.S. export be retransferred by a recipient nation to any other nation without the prior approval of the United States.

—A requirement that no fuel exported from the United States be reprocessed without the prior approval of the United States.

These criteria differ from proposals currently before Congress which include criteria that could force an immediate moratorium on U.S. nuclear exports. Such a moratorium would seriously damage U.S. relations with certain allies whose cooperation is essential if we are to achieve our nonproliferation objectives.

3. The bill defines additional nuclear export conditions which will be required in new agreements for cooperation. These include:

—A requirement, in the case of non-nuclear-weapons states, that IAEA safeguards cover all nuclear materials and equipment regardless of whether these have been supplied by the United States. Fulfillment of this requirement will be a condition of continuing U.S. nuclear supply.

The President has also directed that this requirement be viewed only as an interim measure and that the United States' first preference, and continuing objective, is universal adherence to the Non-Proliferation Treaty.

—The stipulation that U.S. cooperation under the agreement shall cease if the recipient detonates a nuclear device or materially violates IAEA safeguards or any guarantee it has given under the agreement.

—A requirement for IAEA safeguards on all U.S.-supplied material and equipment for indefinite duration, whether or not the agreement for cooperation remains in force.

—The U.S. right of approval on retransfers extended to all special nuclear material produced through the use of U.S. equipment.

—The U.S. right of approval on reprocessing extended to all special nuclear material produced through use of U.S. equipment.

4. For the near future, the bill proposes to tighten the conditions for U.S. nuclear cooperation through the renegotiation of existing agreements to meet the same standards as those we will require for new agreements (as specified in 3 above). This approach will better meet U.S. nonproliferation objectives than would an attempt to impose unilaterally new export-licensing conditions.

5. The bill provides the flexibility needed to deal with the many different situations and nations involved. For example, it makes the necessary exceptions for licenses under existing multilateral agreements. It also establishes an efficient mechanism for the President and Congress to review cases where the executive branch and the independent NRC differ on the granting of a proposed export license. And it permits the President to grant exceptions from the stiff new conditions required for new agreements for cooperation, if he considers that this is in our overall nonproliferation interest.

6. The bill creates sanctions against the violation of nuclear agreements by providing that no nuclear export shall be granted to any non-nuclear-weapons state that, after enactment of this legislation:

—Detonates a nuclear explosive device.

—Terminates or abrogates IAEA safeguards.

—Is found by the President to have materially violated an IAEA agreement or any other guarantee it has given under an agreement for cooperation with the United States;

unless the President determines that such a cutoff would hinder the achievement of U.S. non-proliferation objectives or would jeopardize the common defense and security.

7. The legislation proposes the establishment of an international Nuclear Fuel Cycle Evaluation Program, aimed at furthering the development of alternative nuclear fuel cycles which do not provide access to weapons-usable material, as announced by the President in his April 7 statement.

8. As an essential element of the international evaluation program, the legislation proposes a number of policies to assure that adequate nuclear fuel supply will be available to all nations as a nonproliferation incentive. These include:

—A policy to assure adequate U.S. uranium enrichment capacity.

—A policy assuring that nuclear exports will be licensed on a timely basis once statutory requirements are met.

—U.S. initiatives to promote international consultations to develop multilateral means for meeting worldwide nuclear fuel needs.

The bill further requires the President to report to the Congress on the progress of these discussions and to propose any legislation he may consider necessary to promote these objectives.

9. The bill commits the United States to work with other nations to strengthen the International Atomic Energy Agency through: contribution of technical resources, support, and funding; improving the IAEA safeguards system; and by assuring that that IAEA receives the data needed for it to administer an effective comprehensive international safeguards program.

Organizing Conference of the International Nuclear Fuel Cycle Evaluation Meets in Washington

The Organizing Conference of the International Nuclear Fuel Cycle Evaluation (INFCE) was held in Washington, D.C., October 19-21. Following are a press release announcing the meeting, President Carter's remarks before the first plenary session of the conference on October 19, and the text of the final communique issued on October 21.

Press release 463 dated October 14

The United States will be host on October 19-21 to a major international meeting, the Organizing Conference of the International Nuclear Fuel Cycle Evaluation. The President referred to this conference in his recent address to the U.N. General Assembly.[1] The conference will be the first step in a new joint international effort to find better ways of reducing the danger of the spread of nuclear weapons while permitting all countries to meet their peaceful nuclear energy needs. The conference will set in motion an evaluation of all aspects of the nuclear fuel cycle to explore practical means of attaining these goals, including alternative technical approaches and ways to improve safeguards. We expect over 30 countries and 4 international organizations will attend the conference and take part in the subsequent evaluation.

The President first called for an international nuclear fuel cycle evaluation in his April 7 nuclear policy statement.[2] Since then we have discussed the matter with more than 30 countries which have a major interest in nuclear energy, including the six other London summit countries. We have received broad indications of interest in taking part in such an evaluation, including expressions of interest from all of the London summit countries.

* * *

REMARKS BY PRESIDENT CARTER

Weekly Compilation of Presidential Documents dated October 24

About 25 years ago I was a student doing graduate work in nuclear physics and reactor technnology, not too many years after the first atomic weapons had been used to destroy human beings. My study was the peaceful use of this tremendous force, working under Admiral [Hyman] Rickover in the development of atomic submarine powerplants.

And now we have come to a time when we can look back with a clear historic perspective at what has transpired during this quarter century. It is a great honor for us to have you leaders come from, I believe, 40 nations and 4 international organizations to think back to 1945, to remember our own President Eisenhower's proposal called Atoms for Peace, part of which was adopted; the later establishment of an International Atomic Energy Agency (IAEA) which has provided for us so far a very effective mechanism by which explosions could be reduced and power could be produced. We then went into a time of at least embryonic discussions of nuclear test bans, and now we have one that still permits the testing of weapons which have the equivalent of 150,000 tons of TNT. Even this has been recognized as an achievement.

---
[1] For text of address, see BULLETIN of October 24, 1977, p. 547.
[2] For text of statement, see BULLETIN of May 2, 1977, p. 429.

And, of course, we are discussing with the Soviet Union means by which we can eliminate sometime in the future our dependence upon atomic weapons altogether. We have lived under the threat which so far has not been realized, and I pray that it never shall.

In the last 32 years there have been no people killed by the use of atomic weapons. But with the rapidly increasing price of oil and the scarcity of fuel which we have taken for granted in years gone by, there is an increasing pressure for expanding atomic power use. And commensurate with that use is also the threat of the proliferation of nuclear explosives among nations that have foregone voluntarily that opportunity up until now.

We have seen regional actions taken in the southern part of this hemisphere. The treaty of Tlatelolco [Treaty for the Prohibition of Nuclear Weapons in Latin America] is now being ratified by the last nations, we hope, to prevent the deployment of any atomic explosions or explosives in that part of the world. We hope that this will prevail in many other parts of the world.

We have also seen progress made recently between ourselves and the Soviet Union. We are eager to see drastic reductions in the deployment of nuclear weapons. And we are now negotiating with the Soviet Union and with Great Britain for a complete elimination of the testing of atomic explosions.

At the same time, the challenge presents itself to this group and to me, as one of the world leaders, to find a means by which the consuming nations who need atomic power to produce electricity and to serve peaceful purposes, to draw a distinction between that need which is legitimate and the threat of the development of atomic explosions themselves.

I have a feeling that the need for atomic power itself for peaceful uses has perhaps been greatly exaggerated and I hope that all the nations represented here and others will assess alternatives to turning to this source of power, if for no other reasons than because of economic considerations.

Recent studies that I have read show that we can gain the equivalent of a barrel of oil per day by conservation measures at very little or any cost, often zero cost or up to $3,500. North Sea oil costs capital investment about $10,000 for every barrel of oil per day derived from that source. Our own Alaskan oil will cost $20,000 in capital investment for every barrel of oil per day or its equivalent derived at the ultimate site of use. And for the equivalent of a barrel of oil per day at the end-use site of atomic power, the capital investment is between $200,000 and $300,000. So there is a tremendous cost even for the potential peaceful use of atomic power. Even so, we recognize that there will be a need, and we are eager to cooperate.

It is important that we understand your problems; that those nations that supply enriched uranium—ourselves, the Canadians, others—those who have major deposits of uranium ore that have presently not been exploited, like Australia, understand the need of nations that are not well blessed with uranium fuel supplies. It is important that you understand from those of us who unfortunately are nuclear-weapon nations our special commitment to reducing this threat.

I believe that in this brief session that you will have this week, followed by weeks and months of tedious, I am sure, argumentative but productive discussions and debates, that common knowledge will benefit us all. It is important that we combine our ingenuity, our foresight, our own experience, our research and development efforts, so that we don't duplicate the very expensive efforts to use atomic power in a useful way. And this exchange of ideas among us will be very helpful.

It is important that we know what potential nuclear fuel cycles are available to us, the quantity and the location of uranium and thorium and other nuclear fuels, the methods used for extraction, the methods used and the costs for enrichment, possible distribution systems, the proper design and use, standardization of powerplants, safety of people who live near them, proper siting considerations, the political objections to atomic powerplants themselves, the possible need for breeder reactors, the handling of spent fuel, the need or absence of a need for reprocessing the spent fuel, and international safeguards that will prevent the development of explosives.

We are eager to cooperate as a nation which is a consumer and also a supplier. We want to be sure that where there is a legitimate need and where there is a mutually agreed upon proliferation restraint, that there be an adequate supply of nuclear fuel. I think an international fuel bank should be established so that if there is a temporary breakdown in the bilateral supply of nuclear fuel, that there might be a reservoir of fuel to be supplied under those circumstances. And we will certainly contribute our own technical ability and our own portion of the enriched uranium supplies for that purpose.

We are very eager also to help solve the problem of the disposal of spent nuclear fuel itself. We cannot provide storage for the major portion of the world's spent fuel but we are willing to cooperate. And when a nation demonstrates to us your need for spent nuclear fuel storage, we hope to be prepared to accept that responsibility working closely with you. All the costs of the nuclear fuel cycle should be accurately known, as well as possible. And there should be an open-minded approach to this very controversial and very difficult subject.

I hope, as the President of our country, to learn from you and I will welcome your advice and your counsel. I welcome your caution and, on occasion, your criticism about American policies. And I believe that we will find a common ground on which we can work together in harmony to make sure that our people do have a better quality of life, that alternate fuel supplies are evolved in an effective and adequate way, that energy is conserved to an optimum degree, and that the threat of nuclear destruction is minimized.

I want to congratulate all of you on being willing to come here to meet together, because there has been an inclination to avoid controversy. This question is inherently controversial. The interests on occasion are highly divergent, and many of these matters have not been discussed adequately in the past.

I am very grateful that the International Atomic Energy Agency is here because there is no conflict between this effort and the tremendous contribution that that Agency has been making and will make in the future. We want to do everything we can to strengthen the safeguard system already established. And if there is a recommendation from this group that the functions of the International Atomic Energy Agency should be expanded, we will certainly be willing to contribute our own financial and other support to make that possible.

In closing, let me thank you for being willing to participate in this international discussion. I am very eager to study your own debates and derive information from you. We will cooperate in every possible way that we can to give our people of the world adequate power sources and at the same time to keep their lives from being endangered.

TEXT OF FINAL COMMUNIQUE, OCTOBER 21

The participants in the Organizing Conference of the International Nuclear Fuel Cycle Evaluation are conscious of the urgent need to meet the world's energy requirements and that nuclear energy for peaceful purposes should be made widely available to that end. They are also convinced that effective measures can and should be taken at the national level and through international agreements to minimize the danger of the proliferation of nuclear weapons without jeopardizing energy supplies or the development of nuclear energy for peaceful purposes.

The following countries which participated in the Organizing Conference have therefore agreed that an International Nuclear Fuel Cycle Evaluation (INFCE) will be conducted to explore the best means of advancing these objectives:

Algeria
Argentina
Australia
Austria
Belgium
Brazil
Canada
Czechoslovakia
Denmark
Egypt
Finland
France
German Democratic Republic
Federal Republic of Germany
India
Indonesia
Iran
Ireland
Israel
Italy
Japan
Korea
Mexico
Netherlands
Nigeria
Norway
Pakistan
Philippines
Poland
Portugal

NUCLEAR POLICY:
Non-Proliferation Act of 1978

Statement by President Carter

I am pleased to sign into law today H.R. 8638, the Nuclear Non-Proliferation Act of 1978. Enactment of this legislation takes us a major step toward fulfillment of an objective which the United States shares with other nations—a halt in the spread of nuclear weapons capability while preserving the peaceful use of nuclear energy.

The Congress has responded to this challenge with both care and courage in establishing a framework for insuring that we meet these objectives. Senators Ribicoff, Glenn, and Percy; Representatives Zablocki, Bingham, and Findley; their collegues on the committees which developed this bill; and their staffs have my respect and my thanks for their leadership on this issue. It has been a privilege for me, as it has been for Secretary Vance and other members of my Administration, to work with them on the Nuclear Non-Proliferation Act of 1978.

Our efforts to prevent the spread of nuclear weapons began more than 30 years ago, when we went to the United Nations with an offer to place certain aspects of nuclear energy under international ownership and control. The passage of the Atomic Energy Act of 1954 and the adoption of the Non-Proliferation Treaty by the United Nations in 1968 and now this law, each has moved us further toward attainment of our nonproliferation goals.

On April 7 and 27 of last year, I outlined the policies and programs which we would implement to diminish proliferation risks.[1] Today, I want to reaffirm this Administration's strong commitment to that policy. We also recognize that nuclear power technologies now in operation, which do not involve nuclear fuel reprocessing, can and must provide an important source of energy for our nation and for other countries. Our current once-through fuel cycle is and will continue to be a significant contributor to our energy supply. Properly managed, it can function without increasing the risks of proliferation. Our policy takes a responsible course between forgoing the energy benefits of nuclear power and becoming committed to commercialized use of plutonium before we know that we can deal safely with its risks.

I continue to oppose making premature and unnecessary commitments to commercialization of the fast breeder reactor and reprocessing, as exemplified in the United States by the Clinch River and Barnwell projects.

We and the other nations of the world must use the time we now have and pause to develop safer technologies, better institutional arrangements, and improved safeguards which will permit all nations to achieve their energy objectives while preventing the spread of nuclear weapons.

More than 40 nations have already joined with us in an International Nuclear Fuel Cycle Evaluation [INFCE] to explore and assess our means of meeting these twin goals. During this period of examination, the uranium-fueled reactors now in widespread operation can be used without incurring new proliferation risks. If our common search for improved institutions and technologies is to be successful, however, all nations will be required to avoid those steps which prejudice the outcome of the INFCE.

The Nuclear Non-Proliferation Act sets the conditions and criteria which will govern U.S. cooperation with other nations in our efforts to develop the peaceful use of nuclear energy. The encouragement of universal ratification of the Non-Proliferation Treaty is central to the act, as is the establishment of a comprehensive set of controls, including application of International Atomic Energy Agency safeguards and provision of a stable framework for international nuclear cooperation and commerce. The act will also make our export licensing process more predictable.

We also will be taking steps to strengthen the safety and security of the fuel cycle we now have in operation and to insure that it continues to be an efficient and reliable source of energy, both domestically and abroad.

Over the course of this year, we will develop comprehensive policies for management and disposal of radioactive waste, including implementation of the spent fuel storage program announced last October. To insure our ability to continue as a reliable supplier of uranium fuel to those who share our nonproliferation objectives, we are moving ahead with a new enrichment plant at Portsmouth, Ohio.

Preventing nuclear proliferation will not be easy—some have called this task impossible. I believe, however, that halting the spread of nuclear weapons is imperative. We must press forward in our efforts. Fear of failure cannot be allowed to become a self-fulfilling prophecy.

In our first year, we have made substantial progress. The nuclear-supplying countries have agreed upon and published guidelines for the export of nuclear fuel and technology. The International Nuclear Fuel Cycle Evaluation is underway. As this legislation now becomes law, we are establishing clear criteria and incentives for nuclear cooperation, as well as sanctions against violations of safeguards.

Although I still have reservations about the numerous provisions in this act which state that Congress may invalidate or approve executive branch action by concurrent resolution, I am signing it because of its overwhelming importance to our nonproliferation policy. I do wish to make clear, however, that by signing this act, I am not agreeing that the Congress can overturn authorized executive actions through procedures not provided in the Constitution.

In conclusion, I am persuaded that the new criteria, incentives, and procedures in this act will help solve the problems of proliferation. They will help to insure that access to nuclear energy will not be accompanied by the spread of nuclear explosive capability. While I recognize that some of these provisions may involve adjustments by our friends abroad, this more comprehensive policy will greatly increase international security. I believe that they will ultimately join us in our belief that improved world security justifies the steps which we all must take to bring it about. Control over the spread of nuclear weapons on our planet is one of the paramount questions of our time.

If the world is to benefit from the great potential of nuclear power, we must act now to protect ourselves and future generations from its worst dangers. We in the United States will dedicate our expertise and technical resources to this task, and we urge other countries to do the same. Let us continue to work together to achieve these goals. ☐

Made on signing H.R. 8638 into law on Mar. 10, 1978 (text from Weekly Compilation of Presidential Documents of Mar. 13). As enacted H.R. 8638 is Public Law 95-242, approved Mar. 10.

[1] For text of President Carter's April 7, 1977, statement, see BULLETIN of May 2, p. 429; for text of his message to the Congress of April 27, see BULLETIN of May 16, p. 477.

Export of Special Nuclear Material to India

Executive Order 12055, April 27, 1978, 43 F.R. 18157

By virtue of the authority vested in me as President by the Constitution of the United States of America and by Section 126b(2) of the Atomic Energy Act of 1954 (42 U.S.C. 2155), as amended by Section 304(a) of the Nuclear Non-Proliferation Act of 1978 (Public Law 95-242, 92 Stat. 131), and having determined that withholding the export proposed pursuant to Nuclear Regulatory Commission export license application XSNM-1060 would be seriously prejudicial to the achievement of the United States non-proliferation objectives, that export to India is authorized; however, such export shall not occur for a period of 60 days as defined by Section 130g of the Atomic Energy Act of 1954, as amended.

PRESIDENT'S MESSAGE TO THE CONGRESS, APR. 27*

I am transmitting herewith, pursuant to Section 126b(2) of the Atomic Energy Act of 1954, as amended, an Executive Order authorizing the export of 7,638 Kgs. of low-enriched uranium to India for use in the fueling of its Tarapur Atomic Power Station.

In our Agreement for Cooperation with India, the United States agreed to supply all of the fuel requirements for that Power Station, and India agreed to operate it exclusively on U.S.-supplied fuel. We contracted to supply the specific fuel here involved a number of years ago.

An application for a license to export this fuel was submitted to the Nuclear Regulatory Commission early last year. This application was carefully reviewed within the Executive Branch, which concluded that the proposed export would not be inimical to the common defense and security, that it would meet all the immediate statutory criteria under the then pending Nuclear Non-Proliferation Act, and that the license should be issued. Later that month, the Commission was officially notified of the Executive Branch findings and recommendations.

On April 20, the Nuclear Regulatory Commission found itself unable to agree upon the issuance of this license, being divided by a 2-2 vote. The Nuclear Nonproliferation Act of 1978 wisely provided for just such a contingency. Previously, there was no clear way of dealing with a situation in which the Commission was unable to decide upon the issuance of an export license, and no way of ensuring that in cases where the licensing process would lead to a result that the President believed would be seriously prejudicial to the achievement of United States non-proliferation objectives, such prejudice could be avoided.

I have determined that this is such a case. The Government of India has given us its commitments to use our exports only at the Tarapur Atomic Power Station and not for any explosive or military purpose, and I have the highest confidence that it will honor these commitments. I am convinced that denial of this export would seriously undermine our efforts to persuade India to accept full-scope safeguards, and would seriously prejudice the achievement of other U.S. non-proliferation goals. I intend to pursue these matters further with the Government of India.

A period in which to seek agreement to full-scope safeguards was clearly provided for in the Act. The Act permits a continuation of exports during this period, including exports in cases where there are questions as to whether and when that objective may be achieved. Rather than prejudice the prospects for success in such efforts by refusing to fulfill an existing commitment that is important to India's power supply, we should be using this period to find, in the light of the new legislation's requirements, mutually acceptable ways of meeting both India's need for continued operation of the Tarapur Atomic Power Station and our need for full-scope safeguards and the attainment of other non-proliferation objectives.

In transmitting this Executive Order to you pursuant to Section 126b(2) of the Act, I wish to make clear that I am not departing from the reservations I expressed at the time I signed the Nuclear Non-Proliferation Act of 1978 concerning the constitutionality of provisions of that Act which purport to allow Congress to overturn my decisions by actions not subject to my veto power.

JIMMY CARTER ☐

---

*Text from Weekly Compilation of Presidential Documents of May 1, 1978, which also contains the text of Executive Order 12055.

Executive Order 12058, May 11, 1978, 43 F.R. 20947
FUNCTIONS RELATING TO NUCLEAR NON-PROLIFERATION

By virtue of the authority vested in me by the Nuclear Non-Proliferation Act of 1978 (Public Law 95-242, 92 Stat. 120, 22 U.S.C. 3201) and the Atomic Energy Act of 1954, as amended (42 U.S.C. 2011 et seq.), and Section 301 of Title 3 of the United States Code, and as President of the United States of America, it is hereby ordered as follows:

Section 1. Department of Energy. The following functions vested in the President by the Nuclear Non-Proliferation Act of 1978 (92 Stat. 120, 22 U.S.C. 3201), hereinafter referred to as the Act, and by the Atomic Energy Act of 1954, as amended (42 U.S.C. 2011 et seq.), hereinafter referred to as the 1954 Act, are delegated or assigned to the Secretary of Energy:

(a) That function vested by Section 402(b) of the Act (92 Stat. 145, 42 U.S.C. 2153a).

(b) Those functions vested by Sections 131a(2)(G), 131b(1), and 131f(2) of the 1954 Act (92 Stat. 127, 42 U.S.C. 2160).

(c) That function vested by Section 131f(1)(A)(ii) of the 1954 Act to the extent it relates to the preparation of a detailed generic plan.

Sec. 2. Department of State. The Secretary of State shall be responsible for performing the following functions vested in the President:

(a) Those functions vested by Sections 104(a), 104(d), 105, 403, 404, 407, and 501 of the Act (92 Stat. 122, 123, 146, 147, and 22 U.S.C. 3223(a), 3223(d), 3224, and 42 U.S.C. 2153b, 2153c, 2153e, and 22 U.S.C. 3261).

(b) That function vested by Section 128a(2) of the 1954 Act (92 Stat. 137, 42 U.S.C. 2157(a)(2)).

(c) That function vested by Section 601 of the Act to the extent it relates to the preparation of an annual report.

(d) The preparation of timely information and recommendations related to the President's functions vested by Sections 126, 128b, and 129 of the 1954 Act (92 Stat. 131, 137, and 138, 42 U.S.C. 2155, 2157, and 2158).

(e) That function vested by Section 131c of the 1954 Act (92 Stat. 129, 42 U.S.C. 2160(c)); except that, the Secretary shall not waive the 60-day requirement for the preparation of a Nuclear Non-Proliferation Assessment Statement for more than 60 days without the approval of the President.

Sec. 3. Department of Commerce. The Secretary of Commerce shall be responsible for performing the function vested in the President by Section 309(c) of the Act (92 Stat. 141, 42 U.S.C. 2139a).

Sec. 4. Coordination. In performing the functions assigned to them by this Order, the Secretary of Energy and the Secretary of

State shall consult and coordinate their actions with each other and with the heads of other concerned agencies.

Sec. 5. General Provisions. (a) Executive Order No. 11902 of February 2, 1976, entitled "Procures for an Export Licensing Policy as to Nuclear Materials and Equipment," is revoked.

(b) The performance of functions under either the Act or the 1954 Act shall not be delayed pending the development of procedures, even though as many as 120 days are allowed for establishing them. Except where it would be inconsistent to do so, such functions shall be carried out in accordance with procedures similar to those in effect immediately prior to the effective date of the Act.

NUCLEAR POLICY: *Nuclear Fuel Exports to India*

by Joseph S. Nye, Jr.

Statement before the House Committee on International Relations on May 23, 1978. Mr. Nye is Deputy to the Under Secretary for Security Assistance, Science, and Technology.[1]

I am pleased to have this opportunity to discuss with you the Administration's view on the proposed export of nuclear fuel for India's Tarapur reactors. In my prepared statement today, I would like to focus specifically on the basis for the Administration's judgment, as highlighted in the President's April 27 message to the Congress, that withholding this export would be seriously prejudicial to the achievement of U.S. nonproliferation objectives.

This matter is before you today because of differing views—on which the Nuclear Regulatory Commission (NRC) divided evenly—regarding the application of specific requirements of the recently enacted Nuclear Nonproliferation Act. Among other things, that act wisely foresaw the need to provide for Presidential and congressional review under such circumstances.

Policy Objectives

The particular difference which brings us here, regarding the new law's requirements, is an important one and I look forward to addressing it shortly. While the issue has arisen in the context of an individual export license application, representing only about 4 months' supply for the Tarapur operation, we are actually addressing the broader question of continuing cooperation and supply during the 18–24-month "grace period" provided by law. At the outset, therefore, I believe it most important to consider some of the fundamental policy objectives which, in my view, the law is meant to serve.

• It sets forth the principles which govern our nuclear exports, in the form of immediately applicable export criteria, with a view toward insuring further that these principles are met and toward enhancing the predictability of our nuclear trade activity under these principles.
• It incorporates requirements for new and amended agreements for cooperation and other objectives, to be sought in negotiations with cooperating countries, with a view toward upgrading our supply arrangements and achieving international acceptance of more stringent nuclear safeguards and controls.
• It establishes a future full-scope safeguards criterion with a view toward clarifying our resolve on the importance we attach to such safeguards.

Each of these policy objectives is embodied in the law in a manner which recognizes that the success of our nonproliferation efforts fundamentally depends upon the cooperation of other countries, that the negotiations to achieve this require time, and that a moratorium on our cooperation in the meantime would not serve our objectives.

None of the three basic objectives listed above would, in the Administration's view, be served by withholding this proposed export to India. On the contrary, we believe that failure to continue supply during the period provided by law would, in fact, undermine the dialogue we now have with India. This would greatly diminish the likelihood not only of reaching the goals we are seeking but also of finding the most acceptable arrangements, consistent with broad foreign policy and overall nonproliferation considerations, with respect to a discontinuation of U.S. supply if this were to become necessary. In this light, withholding this export would risk both what we hope to achieve and what we wish to avoid in our nonproliferation dialogue with India.

Nonproliferation Dialogue

It is within this context that I would like to review the U.S.-India nonproliferation dialogue and two significant developments that have occurred in this regard over the past 12 months.

First, the United States has increased its efforts worldwide to gain acceptance of policies more in keeping with our overall nonproliferation objectives. There has been a considerable number of exchanges with the Government of India on:

• Nuclear arms control and related nonproliferation problems;
• Steps that need to be taken by nuclear-weapon states to control vertical proliferation;

- Common approaches to prevent horizontal proliferation (including nuclear export policies designed to control the spread of nuclear-weapon capabilities);
- The ground rules for future cooperation with the United States; and
- Developing mutually satisfactory arrangements for the disposition of spent fuel at Tarapur.

Nonproliferation matters were a key subject of discussion during the President's visit to India in January of this year.[2]

Second, there has been a new government in India which, among other things, has provided certain assurances in this area and has pursued this dialogue in a candid and cooperative manner. Not long after coming into office, Prime Minister Desai publicly expressed strong opposition to atomic explosions, defining his policy from the very beginning in terms of India having "no need whatsoever for an atomic bomb." These statements have been supplemented by assurances from the Prime Minister that he will not authorize further explosions such as the one in 1974. As the Desai government informed the Indian Parliament early this year, India "will unilaterally desist from making nuclear tests."

We should not underestimate the importance of this particularly positive development to the nonproliferation goals shared by most nations. Moreover, Prime Minister Desai has unequivocally assured us that no U.S. material will be used for any nuclear explosive purposes and that, so long as the U.S. honors its obligations under the agreement for cooperation, India will abide by all the terms and conditions of our agreement. We have every confidence that India will abide by these commitments.

India also concluded an agreement with the International Atomic Energy Agency (IAEA) last fall to place the second Canadian-supplied reactor at Rajasthan under international safeguards and to extend the international safeguards, which India had maintained after Canada broke off cooperation in the wake of India's 1974 nuclear test, on the first Canadian-supplied reactor at Rajasthan. Today, all three operational power reactors in India and the near-operational reactor at Rajasthan are subject to IAEA safeguards.

Third, in the context of continued U.S. cooperation, India has taken a cooperative approach in our discussions to date on the disposition of spent fuel at the Tarapur reactors. U.S. and Indian officials have held discussions on various aspects of this matter, and the executive branch has established an interagency group to develop possible approaches concerning the long-term disposition of Tarapur spent fuel.

Pending development with India of arrangements for such long-term disposition, the executive branch has focused efforts on assisting India in developing an acceptable interim storage plan, under effective safeguards, in view of the acute shortage of storage capacity at the Tarapur facility and U.S. policy on reprocessing. With respect to fuel cycle and disposition matters in the broader context, India is actively involved in the International Nuclear Fuel Cycle Evaluation, a comprehensive international review of conventional reprocessing and alternatives with the aim of developing more proliferation-resistant fuel cycles.

Despite these positive developments and cooperative approaches by India, we still have a difference of views over full-scope safeguards. However, during discussions with the President, a U.S. congressional delegation, and British Prime Minister Callaghan in January of this year, Prime Minister Desai indicated that India could accept full-scope safeguards when at least the U.S., the U.S.S.R., and the United Kingdom agreed to a complete nuclear test ban, agreed not to add further to their nuclear arsenals, and came to agreement to have a gradual reduction of nuclear stockpiles with a view to their eventual elimination. I would note that the thrust of these goals is, in its own right, basically consistent with our ultimate objectives on controlling the nuclear arms competition as stated in the President's inaugural address.

At this stage, we have no assurance that India will have safeguards on all its peaceful nuclear activities within the time frame provided in the law. However, India is fully aware of the recently enacted Nonproliferation Act that establishes that a recipient country must, within 2 years, have all its peaceful nuclear activities subject to IAEA safeguards as a condition for U.S. supply after that time. India is, of course, also aware of the time when this requirement comes into effect.

We intend to continue every effort toward this end as well as toward other nonproliferation objectives. We believe that these efforts can move forward only within a cooperative context. As I noted at the outset, the Nonproliferation Act clearly recognizes that negotiations to obtain strengthened controls require time and an atmosphere which does not entail a moratorium on our cooperation or accusations of bad faith during such negotiations.

Statutory Requirements

Moreover, the executive branch believes that the proposed export to India meets all statutory requirements. The basis for our conclusion on the export criteria was detailed in our submissions to the NRC as previously provided to the committee. This conclusion on the applicable criteria was, as you know, also reached by [NRC]Chairman [Joseph M.] Hendrie, [NRC] Commissioner [Richard T.] Kennedy, and the NRC staff as a result of their own reviews.

It is important to note that, after extensive review by the executive branch and then by the NRC staff and the Commission, no question has resulted regarding the fulfillment of the applicable criteria under conditions of continued cooperation or continued U.S. supply of fuel for the Tarapur reactors as provided for under the framework of the agreement for cooperation. Moreover, as the executive branch noted in its submissions to the NRC, India has adhered to all the terms and conditions of its agreement with the United States.

A central question raised in this matter, on which the NRC evenly divided, has been whether we should require as a condition of export that the applicable criteria will continue to be fulfilled under circumstances where the United States ceased cooperation and fuel supply in conformance with the act. This has come to the fore largely in view of the future full-scope safeguards requirement in the law, even though it is not now in effect, and the fact that India has not accepted safeguards on all its peaceful nuclear activities.

The executive branch strongly believes that we should stand by the ground rules which have been set by law for our negotiating partners, including India. Not to do so, or to withhold this export on the basis of speculation with respect to the outcome of our negotiation efforts, would seriously prejudice achievement of the objective we are seeking, as I discussed previously, and would not be consistent with our understanding of the intent of the Nonproliferation Act.

Both the immediately applicable export criteria and future full-scope safeguards requirement were carefully crafted in full consultations between the Congress and the executive branch. These requirements provide a statutory basis for the principles governing our nuclear cooperation and trade with other countries while, at the same time, both avoiding a moratorium on exports and providing time for negotiations with other countries.

The Senate Report [No. 95–46] on the law reflects this by noting that "As currently drafted, these 'Phase I' export criteria will not result in an immediate moratorium on U.S. nuclear exports. Although the actual language in our existing agreements for cooperation varies, and seldom corresponds precisely to the language of these criteria, it is our understanding that each of these basic requirements and rights are contained in those agreements . . ." except those with the IAEA and EURATOM [European Atomic Energy Community].

With respect to the application of the "Phase II" full-scope safeguards criterion, the law grants an 18-month to 2-year "grace period" to provide an opportunity for seeking such safeguards with any cooperating country that has not accepted them. Conversely, this period also provides an opportunity for finding the most acceptable arrangements with respect to a discontinuation of U.S. supply in the event this became necessary.

Further, the law distinguishes between immediately applicable export criteria and the more comprehensive objectives to be sought through negotiations with other countries. For example, all new or amended agreements for cooperation are to contain explicit assurances that "safeguards will be maintained irrespective of the duration of other provisions or whether the agreement is terminated." This is, indeed, one of the concerns addressed in the separate views of [NRC] Commissioners [Victor] Gilinsky and [Peter A.] Bradford. However, the law makes it clear that the explicit assurances are goals to be sought in the renegotiation of agreements for cooperation. In this respect, the law further stipulates that the amendments to section 123 on negotiation of new or amended agreements "shall not affect the authority to continue cooperation pursuant to agreements for cooperation entered into prior to" March 10, 1978.

In summary, regardless of precisely how one reads the export criteria, "the President's obligations are broader" as noted in the separate views of Commissioners Gilinsky and Bradford. The statute specifically provides that the President may authorize an export when he determines that withholding it would be "seriously prejudicial to the achievement of the United States non-proliferation objectives," and the President has made such a determination in this case. As I have indicated, the executive branch considers it essential that the purposes which the law is to serve be kept to the forefront when considering incremental supply during the "grace period" provided by law. These purposes are the very objectives which we share and to which our negotiations are geared. To alter or reinterpret now the ground rules which we have just clearly set for our negotiating partners, including India, would seriously handicap these efforts. ☐

[1] The complete transcript of the hearings will be published by the committee and will be available from the Superintendent of Documents, U.S. Government Printing Office, Washington, D.C. 20402.
[2] For material relating to President Carter's trip, see BULLETIN of Feb. 1978, p. 1.

U.S. Policy on Reprocessing of U.S.-Origin Nuclear Material

by Joseph S. Nye, Jr.

Statement before the Subcommittee on International Economic Policy and Trade of the House Committee on International Relations on October 3, 1978. Mr. Nye is Deputy to the Under Secretary for Security Assistance, Science, and Technology.[1]

I am pleased to be here today to discuss U.S. policy on retransfer of U.S.-origin nuclear material for reprocessing in the United Kingdom and France. Before discussing the cases which are before us, I would like to review briefly how our policy on retransfers relates to our broader nonproliferation objectives.

The basic objective of U.S. nonproliferation policy is to develop an international framework that will minimize both the incentives and opportunities for nuclear proliferation. To this end, we are working toward the development of an international regime of norms and institutions that will provide the widest possible separation between peaceful applications and potential military uses, while enabling countries to meet their energy needs. One key element in bringing about such a development is the International Nuclear Fuel Cycle Evaluation (INFCE) which is examining more proliferation-resistant alternatives to the present nuclear fuel cycle.

The United States sees INFCE as a cooperative effort to evaluate the role of nuclear energy technology in an international context and help develop an objective appreciation of the nonproliferation, economic, and other implications of different fuel cycle approaches. INFCE provides a 2-year period in which nations can re-examine assumptions and find ways to reconcile their somewhat different assessments of the risks involved in and the timescale for commercialization of the various aspects of the nuclear fuel cycle. While INFCE has a technical cast, it is part of the process of laying a basis for a stable international regime to govern nuclear energy through the end of the century.

A stable regime should be designed to minimize the global distribution of weapons-usable materials and vulnerable points in the fuel cycle while adequately meeting the energy needs of all countries. One can visualize five basic norms for a strengthened international regime: full-scope safeguards, avoidance of the unnecessary spread of sensitive facilities, use of diversion-resistant technologies, multinational control of sensitive facilities, and institutions to insure the availability of the benefits of nuclear energy.

The United States does not, of course, have all the answers for how a safer nuclear order may be structured, nor are we in a position to dictate the norms to be followed. Indeed, success in building a safer nuclear order depends critically on the cooperation of other countries. It is in this broader context that we look at the specific matter of U.S. policy on requests for the retransfer of U.S.-origin material for reprocessing in the United Kingdom and France during this 2-year period of INFCE.

The Nuclear Nonproliferation Act of 1978 sets forth criteria in addition to other requirements of the law to be applied to requests for retransfers for reprocessing. The law specifies that:

• With respect to facilities which had not processed power reactor fuel assemblies or been the subject of a subsequent arrangement prior to March 10, 1978, the Secretary of Energy may not enter into a subsequent arrangement for such retransfer for reprocessing of any special nuclear material exported by the United States unless, in his judgment, and that of the Secretary of State, such reprocessing or retransfer will not result in a significant increase of the risk of proliferation beyond that which exists at the time that approval is requested. Among the factors in making this judgment, foremost consideration will be given to whether or not the reprocessing or retransfer will take place under conditions that will insure timely warning to the United States of any diversion well in advance of the time at which the non-nuclear-weapon state could transform the material into a nuclear explosive device.

• For facilities that have processed power reactor fuel or been subject to a subsequent arrangement prior to March 10, 1978, the Secretary of Energy will attempt to insure that such reprocessing or retransfer will take place under conditions comparable to those above.

Retransfer to the United Kingdom

In both cases now before us, we believe that the above criteria for approval are met. In the Tokyo Electric Power Company (TEPCO) case we have addressed this question in the revised analysis under section 131 (b) (2) of the act.

In addition to the requirements of the law, the President has established policy criteria regarding requests for retransfer for reprocessing. Approval of such requests has been on a case-by-case basis when there is clear showing of need (i.e. spent fuel congestion), and then only provided that the United States retains the right of approval over subsequent transfer of the separated plutonium and the requesting country has made appropriate efforts to expand its spent fuel storage capacity. Three approvals have been made under these criteria since April 1977.

The Tokyo Electric Power Company requests to transfer approximately 24 tons of spent nuclear power reactor fuel to Great Britain for reprocessing at Windscale would be the fourth such case. The basis for our determination that there is a need for the transfer has been spelled out in the analysis forwarded to the committee.

Both Japan and the United Kingdom have also been cooperative in nonproliferation areas. Both are parties to the Nonproliferation Treaty (NPT), both are active participants in the International Atomic Energy Agency (IAEA), in the Nuclear Suppliers Group, and more recently in INFCE, and both have a strong political commitment to preventing the further spread of nuclear weapons. They have both worked to further common nonproliferation objectives.

Furthermore, in connection with INFCE and as reflected in the Tokai-Mura communique of last September, Japan stated that it shares the view that plutonium poses a serious proliferation danger, that its recycle in light-water reactors is not ready at present for commercial use, and that its premature commercialization should be avoided. Japan also agreed to undertake experimental coprocessing work at its operational test laboratory and, if such coprocessing is found to be technically feasible and effective in light of this work and INFCE, to convert the Tokai reprocessing facility to coprocessing at the end of the initial period of operation. In addition, Japan has agreed to defer the construction of its planned plutonium conversion facility at Tokai-Mura for 2 years and is now studying possible alterations for a combined uranium/plutonium product. Japan is also working with the IAEA at the Tokai reprocessing facility to test the application of advanced safeguards instrumentation.

This is not to say that our policies and those of the other countries in-

January 1979

volved in these transfers are always identical. There was, for example, a frank difference of opinion between the United States and the United Kingdom over the timing of the Windscale/Thorp project, with the United States preferring deferral of the project at least pending the outcome of INFCE. As the committee knows, the project has not been deferred. However, in parliamentary debate supporting the project, the British Government noted that, since actual construction of the reprocessing plant itself would not begin before 1981 or 1982, the design could still be adjusted to accommodate any results of INFCE.

Finally, we believe that the proposed retransfer for reprocessing will not result in a significant increase in the risk of proliferation, with due consideration of whether we would have timely warning of any diversion well in advance of the time at which the non-nuclear-weapon state could transform the diverted material into a nuclear explosive device. We believe this conclusion is supported, among other considerations, by the nonproliferation credentials of the countries involved, by where the reprocessing will occur, and by the fact that the derived plutonium may not be returned to Japan or transferred to another country without specific U.S. consent.

Retransfer to France

The second case which I would like to discuss with you today, the request by Japan's Kansai Electric Power for the transfer of 29 tons of spent fuel to France for reprocessing in the existing UP-2 Cogema facility differs from the cases previously approved. While it meets all other aspects of our approval criteria, it is not based on a spent fuel storage congestion problem. For this reason, the matter was forwarded to the President with a recommendation of the State Department, Department of Energy, and Arms Control and Disarmament Agency that our nonproliferation objectives would be best served by approval. The President agreed with this recommendation.

Kansai and the Japanese Government have asked for approval of this transfer on the basis that the contract concerning the shipment was concluded in 1975, before the current U.S. policy had been enunciated; that public assurances had been given to the local community, on the basis of the contract, that the spent fuel would be transferred; and that it will have to pay substantial financial penalties if the spent fuel does not move on schedule. Although the utility was aware that U.S. approval for the retransfer would be required to fulfill the contract, it could not have foreseen that U.S. policy would change from a permissive policy on retransfers to a policy where approval would be granted only as a "last resort."

The executive branch has carefully weighed all aspects of this matter and has determined that approval would best serve U.S. nonproliferation and broader foreign policy interests. This decision does not represent any basic change in the U.S. view of reprocessing. Requests for retransfers for reprocessing will continue to be considered on their merits and on a case-by-case basis, giving primacy to the test of "need."

However, the President has decided that the Administration will consider approval of this limited set of requests that involve contracts predating 1977 if the requesting country is actively cooperating in exploring more proliferation-resistant methods of spent fuel disposition and if approval would directly further nonproliferation objectives. In this regard we have Japanese agreement to join the United States in discussions of possible international spent fuel storage centers. These discussions will complement studies in the United States and INFCE on developing spent fuel storage regimes, something that is essential if we are to be successful in deferring reprocessing.

U.S. Considerations

In every case, we would continue, among other things, to retain a veto over transfer of plutonium. This limited change in our policy was explained to the countries concerned when we notified them of the decision on the TEPCO and Kansai requests.

We have added "pre-existing contracts" as a factor to be considered in approving reprocessing for the following reasons.

• As the President made clear in his April 7, 1977, statement, our policy has never assumed that ongoing activities in the United Kingdom, France, West Germany, and Japan would be "turned off" during INFCE. The INFCE communique provides that INFCE will be carried out without jeopardizing other countries' fuel cycle policies or international cooperation, agreements, and contracts.

• Holders of reprocessing contracts entered into prior to current U.S. policy can argue with some justification that they have been caught in the middle when the rules changed. This modification will allow us to take this factor into consideration while we continue to encourage the expansion of spent fuel storage capacity.

• Only four countries have reprocessing contracts which predate our policy (Japan, Switzerland, Sweden, and Spain). Moreover, several of the concerned facilities are expanding their spent fuel storage capacities (in part due to our urging in previous retransfer approvals). This will limit the number of requests we are faced with during the INFCE period.

Most importantly, our approach to such reprocessing requests is inextricably related to achievement of a fundamental objective of our nonproliferation strategy that I described above: the development of an international consensus on norms for a more proliferation-resistant framework for nuclear energy. Achieving this objective depends on the cooperation of other countries. The results of INFCE are beginning to be shaped and total inflexibility now in dealing with key participants is likely to give us less influence over the shape of the outcome.

Thus we believe that this interim approach to handling requests for reprocessing in the United Kingdom and France during the INFCE period is consistent with our longer term nuclear nonproliferation objectives and, at the same time, affords sufficient protection against the erosion of our policy on reprocessing. To take the alternative course, would, in our view, have weakened the prospects for developing the cooperative framework on which the achievement of our larger nonproliferation objectives depends.

Spent Fuel Storage in U.S.

The example the United States sets in its own programs is also key to effective pursuit of our nonproliferation program. In this context I would like to address the questions of spent fuel storage in the United States, in particular the development of an away-from-reactor (AFR) spent fuel storage capacity to implement the President's spent fuel policy announced in October 1977.

On March 13, 1978, the President established an interagency nuclear waste management task force to formulate recommendations for Administration policy with respect to long-term management of nuclear wastes. This interagency task force is chaired by the Department of Energy and includes State and other concerned agencies.

The task force is now in the process of preparing a draft report for the President which we expect to circulate for public comment in early October. Early availability of additional AFR capacity would demonstrate concrete progress in our domestic program and

Reprocessing Cont'd

is highly desirable if we are to focus international attention on alternatives to reprocessing, including the economic and technical feasibility of storing spent fuel in the interest of common nonproliferation goals.

In addition to this task force, we continue to argue in INFCE that spent fuel can be stored safely and securely for long periods and that reprocessing is not a requirement for effective waste management. While we have not made any specific commitments, direct or indirect, regarding acceptance of foreign power reactor spent fuel in the United States, and are mindful that the law would require congressional review of any such commitment, we are continuing to discuss the possibility of multilateral and bilateral waste management questions with other countries.

Long-term solutions to all the complex problems we face in regard to nuclear energy will require international cooperation. The policy that I have described today is designed to strengthen the prospects for such cooperation.

Summary

In closing, I would like to summarize this policy. For the interim INFCE period, we will approve retransfer for reprocessing on a case-by-case basis under the following carefully defined conditions.

● Requests involving a clear showing of need (i.e. spent fuel congestion) will continue to be approved on a case-by-case basis if the requesting country has made appropriate efforts to expand its spent fuel storage capacity;

● Requests not meeting the physical need standard, but involving contracts predating 1977, such as the Kansai request, will be considered for approval on a case-by-case basis if the requesting country is actively cooperating in exploring more proliferation-resistant methods of spent fuel disposition and approval will directly further major nonproliferation objectives;

● We will continue to require prior U.S. approval over the subsequent transfer, including return to the country which has title to the material, of any plutonium resulting from the reprocessing. □

---

[1] The complete transcript of the hearings will be published by the committee and will be available from the Superintendent of Documents, U.S. Government Printing Office, Washington, D.C. 20402.

Nuclear Fuel Shipments to India

Following is an exchange of letters between Secretary Muskie and Senator Frank Church, Chairman of the Senate Foreign Relations Committee, and a White House statement.

SENATOR CHURCH'S LETTER

September 9, 1980

Dear Mr. Secretary:

The Foreign Relations Committee will consider on September 10 what recommendation it wishes to make to the Senate regarding Executive Order 12218 of June 19 authorizing nuclear exports to India. This is an extremely difficult issue that has caused me personal concern. I would like to support the President on this matter of national security significance. I recognize the nuclear non-proliferation and foreign policy benefits of the course of action taken by the President.

I am concerned, however, that a less than adequate case has been made by the Administration that both fuel shipments really are needed by India at this time. In this regard, as you know, during the past weeks our staffs have discussed in depth the non-proliferation and foreign policy issues related to the President's June 19 decision. In those discussions, several matters were identified on which I believe further administration assurances would make it easier for the Committee and the Senate to support the President's decision.

First, I would like to request your assurance that the Administration will not permit the second fuel shipment to be exported before it is needed to ensure the efficient and continuous operation of the Tarapur Power Station. I understand the time period involved is about a year. This will provide additional time for the Administration to continue to seek to narrow U.S. non-proliferation differences with India.

Second, I would appreciate your commitment to consult with Congress well in advance of permitting the second shipment to be made. We would expect to review with you the progress that is being made in discussions with India on safeguards and other non-proliferation objectives at that time. This will help Congress to determine whether India is willing to strengthen its non-proliferation policies and commitments.

Third, I would like your assurance that the second fuel shipment will not be permitted to occur at all if the President finds India has exploded a nuclear device, is preparing to explode a nuclear device, or is engaging in other activities that would require termination of exports under section 129 of the Atomic Energy Act. In other words, I seek a commitment that, if these sanctions become applicable, the President will not propose to the Congress that these particular provisions be waived in order to permit the second fuel shipment.

I think both the Administration and the Congress must agree that approval of these exports will not constitute a precedent for treatment of future export license applications. Therefore, I request that you provide me your assurance that the Administration will regard the full-scope safeguards licensing criterion as set forth in section 128 a (1) of the Atomic Energy Act as applicable to any future license applications for the export of fuel to Tarapur.

It is my belief that the Administration should provide the Committee these commitments in writing. This will demonstrate our seriousness of purpose in working together to find a solution to this difficult issue, a solution that will serve the national interest and be widely supported.

Sincerely,

FRANK CHURCH

The Honorable Edmund S. Muskie
Secretary of State
Washington, D.C. 20520

SECRETARY MUSKIE'S LETTER

September 10, 1980

Dear Frank:

Thank you for your letter of September 9 concerning the Foreign Relations Committee's consideration of the President's Executive Order authorizing the export of two nuclear fuel shipments to India. I understand the concerns you raised in your letter and appreciate your desire to find a mutually acceptable solution. The course you propose is acceptable to the Administration.

During the past weeks we have discussed in depth with the members of Congress the non-proliferation and foreign policy benefits we see in proceeding with these exports. As you point out, questions have been raised as to whether the two fuel shipments are both needed in India at this time. In this regard, the Hyderabad fuel fabrication plant in India, which fabricates fuel for Tarapur, is currently out of fresh fuel and urgently needs the first shipment. Once the first export is received the fuel fabrication plant will be able to operate for approximately one year before it is ready to begin work on the second shipment. Since air transport of the fuel is much more expensive than the normal surface transportation, the second shipment should be released in sufficient time to allow India to arrange for surface shipment of the second export (although it will certainly need to air ship the first).

In this light, I wish to assure the Congress that, while the first shipment of Tarapur fuel should leave the United States as promptly as possible after the Executive Order becomes effective, the Administration will not permit the second shipment to leave the United States until it is needed to assure continuity of operations at the Hyderabad fuel fabrication plant, which has consistently been considered by both India and the United States as necessary for the efficient and continuous operation of the Tarapur Atomic Power Station. We will consult with Congress well in advance of the date of the export of the second shipment on the progress that is being made in discussions with India on safeguards and other non-proliferation objectives.

I want to further assure the Congress that export of the second fuel shipment will not be permitted to occur at all if the President finds that India has exploded a nuclear device, is preparing to explode a nuclear device, or is engaging in other activities that would require termination of exports under Section 129 of the Atomic Energy Act. The President will not propose to Congress that these provisions be waived in order to permit the second fuel shipment.

I agree that approval of these exports will not constitute a precedent for the treatment of future export license applications. The full-scope safeguards export licensing criterion as set forth in Section 128 a (1) of the Atomic Energy Act will apply to any future license applications for the export of nuclear fuel to Tarapur.

The foregoing conditions are intended to demonstrate the continued strong commitment of the United States to the policy of nuclear non-proliferation. I hope you will agree that these conditions will ensure that the exports here at issue will be carried out in a manner that is fully consistent with that commitment.

The proposed exports will assure the continuation in force of important safeguards applicable to Tarapur. We will use the time gained by these exports to seek to reduce our non-proliferation differences with India. I believe it is essential that the Congress not deprive the President of the opportunity to pursue constructive negotiations on this subject.

With best wishes, I am

Sincerely,

EI

Honorable Frank Church, Chairman,
Committee on Foreign Relations,
United States Senate ■

WHITE HOUSE STATEMENT SEPT. 24, 1980[1]

We are pleased that the Senate, in a display of bipartisanship, has supported the President's decision on shipment of fuel to the Tarapur Atomic Power Station. The Senate action will help further the administration's policy of seeking to prevent nuclear proliferation and adds support to our discussions with the Government of India toward bringing all of that nation's nuclear facilities under international safeguards.

---
[1] Text from Weekly Compilation of Presidential Documents of Sept. 29, 1980. ■

DISAPPROVAL OF ENRICHED URANIUM TO INDIA
Floor Statement by Senator John H. Glenn
September 23, 1980

Mr. President, if anyone had told me 2 years ago that I would be standing here arguing against a position taken by the Carter administration on nuclear nonproliferation, I would have, indeed, found that hard to believe. I would have found it even harder to believe that the issue would concern an administration decision to continue sending nuclear fuel to India, the first country in the history of the nuclear age to divert nuclear materials from a civilian program for the purpose of conducting nuclear explosions.

Mr. President, I was with the President for the ceremony on March 10, 1978, when the Nuclear Nonproliferation Act, the NNPA, was signed into law. At the time, the President said:

The Nuclear Nonproliferation Act sets the conditions and criteria which will govern U.S. cooperation with other nations in our efforts to develop the peaceful use of nuclear energy. The encouragement of universal ratification of the Nonproliferation Treaty, (the NPT) is central to the act, as is the establishment of a comprehensive set of controls, including the application of IAEA safeguards and provision of a stable framework for international nuclear cooperation and commerce.

The President has always been a strong advocate of the NPT, as I have been. When I introduced Senate Concurrent Resolution 109 on July 25, of this year, I quoted some statements from one of the President's speeches, when he was a candidate in 1976, concerning the NPT. In May of that same year, before a U.N. sponsored conference on Nuclear Energy and World Order, the President made an even more direct supportive statement concerning the NPT. He said at the time:

There are still a dozen or more important countries with active nuclear power programs which have not joined the Treaty. Hopefully, some of these nations may decide to become members, but in the case of several of them, this is unlikely until the underlying tensions behind their decision to maintain a nuclear weapons option are resolved... The advanced countries have not done nearly enough in providing (nuclear power benefits) to convince the member states that they are better off inside the Treaty than outside. In fact, recent commercial transactions by some of the supplier countries have conferred special benefits on non-Treaty members, thereby largely removing any incentive for such recipients to join the Treaty. They consider themselves better off outside. Furthermore, while individual facilities in these non-treaty countries may be subject to international safeguards, others may not be and India has demonstrated that such facilities may provide the capability to produce nuclear weapons.

Now, if I add to that the statement that the President made later in 1976, that the State Department had become India's "chief advocate and apologist," one can understand my surprise at standing here today and having to oppose a Presidential Executive order that overturned a unanimous NRC decision to the effect that India was not in compliance with a cornerstone provision of the Nuclear nonproliferation Act—an act that was passed with the wholehearted support of the President.

Let me say, I tried very hard to get the President not to send his Executive order up here, at least not now, not yet.

I sent a letter to Secretary Muskie, which I understand he did discuss personally with the President, setting out a number of reasons why it would have been better to have waited until next year and have reviewed the issue at that time.

The situation on the South Asian subcontinent would have been much more clear and we would have had the benefit of a 3-year review by the GAO of our entire nonproliferation policy and the working of the NNPA.

We wrote that into the individual bill, that at the end of the 2 years an examination of the effectiveness of that legislation would start and be presented at the end of the third year so we could see if any changes were necessary in the NNPA, so we could improve it, make it more effective.

That study will not be available until—it was deadlined for next March 15. But we could have had it around the first of the year, probably; we could have speeded it up some. But the President did not wait.

Now we must make our decision. Despite my efforts, the President made his. Now we must make ours. The issues involved in the Tarapur fuel export controversy fall naturally into three categories. They are issues involving nonproliferation, issues involving general foreign policy, and issues involving legal considerations. I would like to say a few words about each one of them.

NONPROLIFERATION ISSUES

It is very difficult Mr. President, to discuss the nonproliferation questions raised by the pending fuel shipments to India without getting into a little bit of history. India exploded a nuclear device in 1974 using U.S. heavy water in a Canadian reactor.

This was a violation of the sales agreement because our agreement said that everything that we sent to India under it would be used only for peaceful purposes.

In 1970, 4 years before that explosion, 4 years before that bomb was built, we had some indication that something was going on in India that we considered a misuse of the material we had sent. So we sent an aide memoire to the Indian Atomic Energy Commission in Bombay on November 16, 1970.

This was classified secret until last Friday when I asked it be declassified, which it was. It spells out in very certain terms what our view of our 1956 contract with Indian concerning the sale of heavy water was. It states as follows:

The United States Government has noted various affirmations of Indian interest in developing the technology of peaceful nuclear explosions, as well as statements that the Government of India is not planning for a nuclear explosion.

Occasionally, in the public debate on the nuclear issue, the question has been raised as to whether, under extant agreements, the Government of India could legitimately use foreign-supplied nuclear technology or materials to manufacture an explosive device to be used in detonating a peaceful nuclear explosion.

We believe the Government of India is aware of the American interpretation of agreements under which the United States has assisted India's development in the field of atomic energy. However, we would like to reiterate the American view in the interest of clarity and to obviate any misunderstanding.

The American position, reflected in the Non-Proliferation Treaty, is that the technology of nuclear explosives for peaceful uses is indistinguishable from that of nuclear weapons, and that any nuclear explosive device, though it be intended for benign economic purposes, could also be used for destructive purposes. The development of such explosives, therefore, is tantamount to the development of nuclear weapons. Any other position would be inconsistent with United States obligations under the Non-Proliferation Treaty and the United States Atomic Energy Act.

Consequently, the United States would consider it incompatible with existing United States-Indian agreements for American nuclear assistance to be employed in the development of peaceful nuclear explosive devices. Specifically, for example, the use, for the development of peaceful nuclear explosive devices of plutonium produced therefrom, would be considered by the United States a contravention of the terms under which the American materials were made available.

The United States interprets the safeguards and guarantees provisions of the Tarapur agreement as prohibiting the use of American materials and equipment, or materials produced from such materials and equipment, for research on or development of any nuclear explosive devices, regardless of stated applications.

The contract of March 16, 1960, under which the United States sold heavy water to India for the CIRUS Reactor states: "The heavy water sold hereunder shall be for use only in India by the Government in connection with research into and the use of atomic energy for peaceful purposes. . . ." The United States would not consider the use of plutonium produced in CIRUS for peaceful nuclear explosives intended for any purpose to be "research into and use of atomic energy for peaceful purposes."

That was delivered to the Indian Atomic Energy Commission in 1970, 4 years before they went ahead and used our material to make the nuclear explosion.

Besides being a violation of the sales agreement with the United States under which the heavy water was supplied, the Indian explosion was a shock to the foundations of the entire international nonproliferation regime—a shock that is still causing reverberations today. The Canadians, much to their credit, tried further negotiations then terminated nuclear cooperation with India following the 1974 explosion—and I should add that the Canadians today and the Australians as well, will not engage in nuclear trade with any country that does not accept safeguards on all its nuclear facilities, so-called full-scope safeguards. In contrast, the United States continued nuclear trade with India, continuing negotiations but we did pass the NNPA 2 years ago which said that after March 10, 1980, no nuclear exports would go from the United States to any country that did not accept full-scope safeguards, which was passed largely because of the situation that had developed in India.

That provided a 2-year negotiating period from March 10, 1978 to March 10, 1980. In these 2 years, there has been not one whit of progress in the negotiations with India. She has adamantly refused to even entertain the notion of full-scope safeguards, and the unsafeguarded facilities that she is presently constructing will provide her with the capability of obtaining thousands of kilograms of plutonium by the end of this decade that can be translated into hundreds of nuclear warheads.

Mr. President, India of course, is not a member of the NPT, a treaty signed by 114 nations. All 111 non-weapons states in the NPT must accept full-scope safeguards and foreswear nuclear weapons if they want nuclear trade and assistance. I think we should ask ourselves why a nation would want to join or remain a member of the NPT, and make the political commitment to subject themselves to full-scope safeguards in return for nuclear assistance, when countries like India can obtain nuclear assistance without making a similar commitment. It is supposed to be U.S. policy to strengthen the NPT. Does the President's decision regarding the Tarapur export support U.S. policy? I do not believe so. I believe the decision undermines the NPT.

Another point to be made is that by continuing trade with India under these conditions, we are also undermining our own effort to try to get other nuclear supplier nations to accept full-scope safeguards as a requirement for their own nuclear trade. As I mentioned earlier, Australia and Canada already require full-scope safeguards as a condition for exports. If we are to get other suppliers such as France and West Germany to do the same, how can we take the position that in the case of the worlds first nuclear violator we will ignore our own advice?

Let us recall that we passed the NNPA only 2 short years ago by a vote of 88 to 3. The pending fuel exports to Tarapur constitute a first landmark test of whether the U.S. Senate was serious about enacting the full-scope safeguards requirement into law. If we back down at the first test, especially in the case of India, the country with the worst history of any of our trading partners, what does that do to the credibility of our nonproliferation policy? What, in particular, will that do to our present goal of curbing the spread of sensitive facilities capable of producing weapons—usable high-enriched uranium and plutonium?

Why should our nuclear trading partners, many of whom have strong nonproliferation credentials, acquiesce in restrictions on their nuclear activities for the sake of nonproliferation when we are unwilling to enforce our most basic standards against India?

FOREIGN POLICY ISSUES

I am aware that nonproliferation is not the be-all and end-all of foreign policy. I am realistic enough to know that there may be times when it is necessary to take a step backward temporarily in our nonproliferation effort in order to advance a broader foreign policy objective. Like the President, I, too, would like India to be more sympathetic to our national security concerns stemming from events in that part of the world. But where is the evidence that nuclear trade has had or will have a positive impact on Indian foreign policy? What kind of foreign policy line did

India take following the President's promise to Mrs. Gandhi to send the fuel? Was she sympathetic to our concerns in the last few months? Here is the record of Indian decisions after the President's promise to send the fuel. India concluded a $1.6 billion arms deal with the Soviet Union, a deal that had been, to be sure, in the mill for some time but which India then went ahead with, anyway.

India then became the only non-Communist country to recognize the pro-Soviet regime in Kampuchea, after we requested them not to do so.

India abstained from the U.N. resolution condemning the Soviet invasion of Afghanistan; and, finally, to add injury to insult, she negotiated a long-term trade agreement with Iran that undercuts our ability to apply pressure for the release of our hostages. The Iran agreement was announced on June 14, 1980, by the well-known New Delhi newspaper, The Statesman, with a headline, "India to Help Iran Beat U.S. Sanctions." (Copy at end of remarks). If that is not enough to make every American unhappy, I do not know what is: "India to Help Iran Beat U.S. Sanctions."

FROM OUR SPECIAL REPRESENTATIVE

NEW DELHI, Friday.—India is to send grain and a number of other industrial products believed to be worth several hundred million dollars to Iran to enable her to meet shortages arising out of the sanctions imposed by the USA and the EEC.

After a couple of other paragraphs, it says:

What remains to be finalized is the financing of the deals since India wants assurances on payments. . . .

In effect, the result of the talks is that India has agreed to help Iran to beat the U.S. and ECC sanctions imposed because of the hostages issue. Iran presented a long shopping lists to India of items that she needs urgently and much of her needs are to be met.

So much for the foreign policy implications of shipping nuclear fuel to India.

The State Department argument that sending nuclear fuel to India improves United States-Indian relations simply has no substance. That is not to say that there is nothing the United States can do to improve Indo-United States relations. We are presently engaged in $2 billion worth of trade with India. We are providing hundreds of millions of dollars in various forms of economic assistance and we recently completed arrangements for sending India 3,700 TOW antitank missiles. Our relations with India could be far more positively affected by changes in our policy on countervailing duties—affecting textile sales—than by the sale of nuclear fuel, but the administration is not proposing anything along that line, quite the contrary.

Much has been made about the fact that if we do not send fuel for Tarapur the Indians may turn to the French or the Soviets. The administration has provided no evidence that India's nonalined status or the orientation of her present foreign policy would be significantly altered by such a move. There is no reason to believe that India's drive toward nuclear independence will falter as a result of receiving Soviet fuel in addition to the Soviet heavy water she has imported in the past. From a nonproliferation point of view, even if the Soviets were to step in as an alternate fuel supplier the Soviets have invariably required strict safeguards and other nonproliferation controls on nuclear projects they have aided.

According to the respected trade journal, Nucleonics Week, there is debate going on in India about whether to place heavy water in one of the Indian reactors—with arguments being made by some Indian scientists urging that India hold off because, if the Russian heavy water is not used in the reactor, the reactor would not have to be safeguarded. In other words, they believe Soviet nuclear fuel restrictions are "tough." Should we, therefore, take a backward step in our nonproliferation policy in order to prevent the Indians from buying 38 tons of nuclear fuel from the Russians? I believe not.

There are other foreign policy issues involved here as well. The Washington Post ran two front-page stories, regarding Swiss nuclear aid to Pakistan that will enable the Pakistanis to obtain high-enriched uranium, a weapons-usable material. The Carter administration has been unsuccessful in trying to get the Swiss to turn off the spigot of supplies to Pakistan. We ourselves have cut off Pakistan from economic and military assistance as a result of Pakistan's efforts to obtain the facilities needed to make a nuclear weapon.

We have tried to get the Pakistanis to accept full-scope safeguards on all her nuclear facilities. How likely is it that we will succeed in our effort with the Pakistanis if we continue to send nuclear materials to India without the same requirement? How likely is it that we can convince the Swiss not to send nuclear materials to Pakistan if we do not set an example of not trading with countries that are deliberately keeping a nuclear weapons option open?

Mr. President, the administration has not made a convincing case that providing nuclear fuel to India is indispensable toward achieving our foreign policy objectives in South Asia. On the contrary, I am convinced that the achievement of our goals in that region and elsewhere will be enhanced by resoluteness on the part of the United States. Not changing direction again. Our action on this issue will be carefully noted in every capitol in the world, not just for what it says about our nonproliferation policy, but for what it says about the ability of the United States to prevent itself from being bullied by other nations. To send this fuel because of veiled Indian threats regarding what they might do with previous shipments makes a mockery of our position as a world power. Those who are concerned about the Indians buying nuclear fuel from the Soviets ought to worry about the signal being sent to the Soviets by a lack of American resolve to follow a justifiably tough policy on nonproliferation.

LEGAL ISSUES

Mr. President, I beileve the administration knows that it has no case in favor of these shipments on foreign policy grounds and it has no case in favor of these shipments on nonproliferation grounds, especially when one looks at the impact on countries outside of India. The administration has therefore chosen to make its case on the basis of a very weak legal argument that the United States might be in violation of the 1963 Agreement for Cooperation with India and the fuel contract written pursuant to it. The administration argues that if the Indians see the cutoff as a breach of the agreement they will feel free to disregard their obligations under the agreement which are to retain safeguards on the Tarapur reactor and the U.S.-origin spent fuel emanating from it.

First of all, the agreement says that the United States will supply uranium fuel "as needed" for Tarapur pursuant to the "terms, conditions, and delivery schedule set forth in a contract to be made between the parties." The contract, when it was signed in 1966, said that the United States will make this material available "subject to such conditions and licenses as the seller (the United States) may require." In 1971 this part of the contract was amended and amplified and India agreed to "procure all necessary licenses or permits and comply with all applicable laws, regulations, and ordinances of the United States and of any State, territory, or political subdivision" in conjunction with the export of nuclear fuel.

All these were commitments to abide by what were to be quite clearly future regulations that the U.S. Government would define.

The American Law Division of the Congressional Research Service was asked to analyze the agreement and the fuel contract and after a detailed analysis they wrote a report which contains the following conclusion:

> India's refusal to submit to the adoption of full-scope safeguards and inspections for all nuclear facilities is not in conformance with its 1971 undertaking to comply with all applicable U.S. laws. As a consequence, congressional rejection of the pending export may be regarded not as a violation of the agreement, but rather as an appropriate action proximately caused by India's refusal to live up to its undertaking to comply with applicable U.S. legal requirements. As such, India may be the party in actual or potential breach of the agreement and in ordinary circumstances cannot walk away from the bargain previously struck. Generally, the election to abandon a contractual obligation upon the occasion of material breach is available only to the injured party. There is no obligation on the injured party to make such an election and it may waive the breach and accept or insist on performance after such breach of the contract. The United States, accordingly, may continue to regard the existing agreement and contract as effective and seek to persuade India that it stands ready and willing to meet its obligation to supply India's fuel requirements when the latter indicates its willingness to stand by its contractual obligation to comply with U.S. legal requirements including the NNPA's provision for the adoption of full-scope safeguards and inspection of its nuclear facilities.

In other words, Mr. President, the United States will not be in violation of the agreement or the fuel contract by refusing the present shipments. Undaunted by this, the administration then argues as follows: Suppose the Indians go ahead and act as if we violated the agreement, seizing the spent fuel and reprocessing it without our permission. Is not that something we should be concerned about? The answer to that, of course, is yes—we should be concerned about it. But we need to look at the larger picture. The U.S. spent fuel at Tarapur is soon going to be a very small part of the materials that India will have available to her for the production of weapons.

By the end of this decade, according to a Congressional Research Service calculation, India's unsafeguarded facilities—these are facilities other than Tarapur (which is under safeguards)—will produce thousands of kilograms of plutonium that will make the amount of plutonium in the U.S.-origin spent fuel look small by comparison.

The administration is trying to convince us that keeping control of the U.S.-origin spent fuel is worth the demise of our nonproliferation policy around the globe. Does that sound like a reasonable tradeoff? It certainly does not to me.

Mr. President, the administration has not looked carefully at the implications of its own argument on this issue. They are saying, in effect, "keep sending the Indians nuclear fuel, because if you do not, you risk the possibility of their making weapons with the plutonium from past fuel shipments." The implication of this argument is that the State Department is as suspicious of the Indian nuclear program as I am. And well they should be, considering India's history in this area. The question is: If they are so suspicious of Indian intentions, why are they advocating continued shipments of nuclear fuel?

Mr. President, not only is the present State Department position on this issue illogical, it is not even consistent with their past stated policy on Tarapur. Two years ago, when the issue of the first Tarapur shipments following the passage of the NNPA came up, the State Department said that it was their intention to ship fuel up until the NNPA deadline unless there were "materially changed circumstances" in India. This was said during the Desai regime. Since then, India has had two governments, and is now headed by the same Mrs. Gandhi who produced the policy that led to the 1974 explosion, and who says that further explosions will be produced whenever India deems them in that country's national interest. That certainly sounds like "materially changed circumstances" to me. Even the Indians say that a change has occurred. Yet, the State Department, despite its own written policy, pretends that everything is the same as before, and we should send the fuel.

I will say only one more word about the logic of the administration's argument in this case. The administration claims that fullscope safeguards should not apply to these shipments, but they will be glad to apply it to future shipments. But their argument about the breach of contract also applies to future shipments. If the administration seeks to convince us that we should send the fuel in order to prevent the Indians from claiming a breach of contract they are in effect arguing that no matter when fullscope safeguards would apply, we should ignore the criterion and send the fuel because otherwise the Indians will do all those terrible things they have threatened. That is a policy of supply without end, a policy of appeasement, a policy of caving in to extortion. If we follow this policy, Mr. President, I submit that the United States will have take another giant step down the road of erosion of its power and influence around the world, a step with the gravest implications for our future national security.

Mr. President, not since the efforts with regard to SALT have we seen such a lobbying effort as the administration has mounted on undecided Senators in the last few days. I have talked to a number of Senators today who have talked about getting calls from *Air Force One* flying around the country, from ACDA, from the State Department, and from the Secretary of Defense.

And that is fair enough to lobby on this, although I must admit with the manpower I have out of my office and the committee we are somewhat outgunned in this area. It is very impressive to receive a call from *Air Force One* to be lobbied on this particular subject.

Mr. President, let me talk a moment about past intent, the past intent of those who have spoken on this subject, and I ask the question in advance, did they really mean what they said?

For example, 4 years ago the President said:

We have done little to encourage the dozen or more non-NPT countries with active nuclear programs to join. In fact, we have given more assistance to those countries who have not signed the treaty than we have to those who have. For example, in recent hearings before the Nuclear Regulatory Commission on continuation of nuclear aid to India, the State Department has become that country's chief advocate and apologist, even though India, not an NPT party, used our past aid to explode a nuclear device—and even though there are no safeguards to prevent this from happening again.

Did the President mean what he said? Did the State Department mean what it said 2 years ago when it indicated that it would reconsider support for continued supply for Tarapur if there were materially changed circumstances in India?

This was said during the regime of Prime Minister Desai, who stated there would be no explosion of any kind of whatever type as long as he was the Prime Minister. But since then Mrs. Ghandi has been reelected and has clearly stated if it is in India's interests, India will produce further nuclear explosions. That certainly seems like a change and even the Indians believe this and say a significant change has occurred. But the question is did the State Department mean what it said? Mr. President, did the Senate mean what it said 2 years ago at the time of the examination of the first Tarapur explosions following the passage of the Nuclear Nonproliferation Act? The vote on this particular resolution of disapproval that I propose to the Senate in the Senate Foreign Relations Committee, though, was 8 to 7.

So we did act in committee to support our previous view on this. At that time, after our expression of opinion had taken place, after we had voted for the Nuclear Nonproliferation Act, we felt concerned enough about what was going to happen that the committee asked our chairman at that time, Senator Sparkman, to send a letter to the President expressing our view of what should happen in the future, and I quote from that letter which Senator Sparkman signed and sent to the President:

The committee requested that I write to

you to communicate the following views of the committee:

Substantial progress at an early date for placing all peaceful nuclear activities in India under international safeguards is of critical importance. The executive branch should make a vigorous effort to secure Indian agreement to full-scope safeguards within 18 months of the enactment of the Nuclear Nonproliferation Act of 1978.

The executive branch and the Indian Government should base their discussions on the anticipation that if full-scope safeguards are not achieved, it is highly unlikely that a waiver allowing continued exports would be acceptable.

I think the members of the committee were correct in voicing that concern about whether we would allow exports to Tarapur after 2 years of fruitless negotiations, and that is our position today on it, that we still do not have one shred of indication of any progress toward the safeguards that we wrote about at that time.

Mr. President, it is important to understand what we are dealing with here. The State Department would have us believe we are dealing with a situation that is not precedent setting. By means of a narrowly drawn legalistic argument they seek to convince us that the full-scope safeguards criteria of the NNPA will be preserved somehow despite sending these shipments to India.

But their argument immediately runs up against two severe problems. The first is that we, they, and virtually every foreign government around the world did, in fact, view the 24-month hiatus from the date of enactment as leading to, in fact, a hard and fast cutoff point. There was a State Department cable sent out to all U.S. diplomatic posts just after the Nonproliferation Act was passed so that our embassy officials could explain the act to foreign governments, and it stated:

IAEA safeguards on all peaceful activities in nonnuclear weapons states will be required, after 24 months following enactment, as a condition of continued U.S. exports.

So the State Department believed in what we had passed, believed what I believed in, what the committee believed in, what the Senate, everyone, believed in, including the President at that time. So if the first major problem is that people inside the Government who have read past State Department explanations of the NNPA are unconvinced of State's latest reinterpretation, the second major problem is that people outside the Government are also unconvinced.

Mr. President, comments from across the country would be of interest. We have identified 90 editorials that have appeared on the subject of Tarapur, all opposing the exports.

I asked the staff, after they came up with that, to go back and find somebody who was in, editorially commenting in, favor of the exports. They said they would try again. So they found four, I believe is the grand total, that had editorialized in favor of this shipment. But every major paper in the country in every major city, almost without exception, has editorialized against this shipment.

Mr. President, just a few days ago the New York Times, as one example, ran an editorial against the shipments which put the problem in a nutshell. The Times stated that Mr. Carter's dilemma was either alienating the Government of India or undermining his own policies against nuclear proliferation. The Times said that, "In June he chose the latter course."

Mr. President, I view this as a step backward in the pursuit of nonproliferation goals in order to achieve a broader foreign policy objective.

The State Department has made only assertions, without evidence, that providing the uranium for India will enhance the achievement of broad foreign policy objectives in that area of the world or elsewhere.

Let us examine the evidence. President Carter has told Mrs. Ghandi apparently last winter that he would send the fuel for Tarapur. Foreign policy decisions since then have been, Indian foreign policy decisions have been, recorded in the chronology which we have distributed on the floor here to all Senators. This shows that Mrs. Ghandi announced her government will not hesitate in carrying out nuclear explosions in the national interest.

As I said before, India, at the same time, has closed a $1.6 billion arms sale with the Soviet Union; is in the process of coming to a major trade agreement with Iran, undercutting our U.S. embargo on exports to Iran; recognized the pro-Soviet government in Kampuchea, and abstained in the U.N. condemnation vote.

In the end, Mr. President, we all know the issue before us is not just United States-India relations. These relations are going to evolve and either prosper or deteriorate because of factors which have little to do with the nuclear trade.

We have $2 billion in trade with India, we have several hundred million dollars in economic aid; we recently completed the deal sending them 3,700 antitank missiles. Surely these elements are much more important to the question of United States-Indian relations than the question of uranium for Tarapur.

But in the end the issue is what signal will the United States be sending to the rest of the world and, particularly, to potential proliferators elsewhere by taking this manifestly backward step in nonproliferation policy?

I believe the answer is self-evident. We will have undermined the policy. We will have removed the standard that we worked so hard to establish 2 years ago that made our policy a model for others to follow. I might add we worked very hard on that in tandem, Senator PERCY and myself, and we find ourselves on opposite ends of the log at this time, and I am sorry that this is the case. But we see this particular situation in a different light.

Mr. President, if we are to ship this fuel, then I would submit that we are in fact changing our nuclear policy.

To say that the NNPA, the Nuclear Nonproliferation Act, will go ahead as always in spite of this fuel shipment to India would be nothing but a charade, and I will not be party to that.

This will not leave us with a policy, if we make this shipment, that says unequivocally, "Here we stand," and for what we stand. As I see it, it will be but a chameleon policy changing color against every new background that happens to come along.

Mr. President, in my remarks here today I have dealt with foreign policy, I have dealt with contract questions, I have dealt with being a reliable supplier, and I would say my major bottom line concern, Mr. President, is this:

The most important reason for barring these exports is that a U.S. capitulation to India could eviscerate our nonproliferation efforts around the world. The 111 nations, nonnuclear weapons nations which have already signed the NPT, and agreed to full scope safeguards would very validly question the value of continued adherence if India receives nuclear assistance without a similar commitment.

Second, current negotiations with non-NPT countries on the full scope safeguards question would be undermined if we continue business as usual with the world's first nuclear violator.

Third, nuclear supplier nations, some of whom now require full scope safeguards as a precondition to sales, such as Australia and Canada and others who may be moving in that direction, perhaps, and West Germany and France, might reassess their conditions as they become convinced that the United States is reversing itself on this vital issue.

Finally, if America is to demonstrate its ability to conduct consistent foreign and national security policies, it is imperative that we shun even the appearance of appeasement. In his testimony, congressional testimony, 2 years ago, Joseph Nye, then a State Department official, stated that in the absence of progress in the full scope safeguard issue it was 'highly unlikely" that the United States would supply India with nuclear materials after the NNPA deadline.

Mr. President, I want to see us retain leadership in trying to get the nations of the world to sign up under NPT. I think we meant what we said 2 years ago. I meant what I said, and I think at that time, at least, the President meant what he said. I know Senator PERCY meant what he said, the Senate Foreign Relations Committee meant what its vote said. In fact, that was our policy, and we thought that it was going to last. Now we find ourselves at this first test saying that the policy may not be valid.

I do not think it is time for us to lay down this policy. I think we must meet the policy's first test.

THE WHITE HOUSE
WASHINGTON

SECRET [Declassified]   July 16, 1981

NATIONAL SECURITY DECISION
DIRECTIVE NUMBER 6

UNITED STATES NON-PROLIFERATION AND PEACEFUL NUCLEAR COOPERATION POLICY

I have reviewed the interagency report on United States non-proliferation and peaceful nuclear cooperation policy and related guidelines, along with the agencies' recommendations, and have approved the policies set forth below.

The United States will:

- Seek to prevent the spread of nuclear explosives to additional countries as a fundamental security and foreign policy objective.

- Strive to reduce the motivation for acquiring nuclear explosives by working to improve regional and global stability and to promote understanding of the legitimate security concerns of other states.

- Continue to support adherence to the Treaty on the Non-Proliferation of Nuclear Weapons and to the Treaty for the Prohibition of Nuclear Weapons in Latin America (Treaty of Tlatelolco) by countries that have not accepted those treaties.

- View a material violation of these treaties or of an international safeguards agreement as having profound consequences for international order and United States bilateral relations, and also view any nuclear explosion by a non-nuclear-weapon state with grave concern.

- Strongly support and continue to work with other nations to strengthen the International Atomic Energy Agency (IAEA) to provide for an improved international safeguards regime for cooperation in the areas of nuclear safety and environmentally sound waste management.

- Work more effectively with other countries to forge agreement on measures for combatting the risks of proliferation.

- Undertake prompt efforts to enhance the credibility and reliability of the United States as a responsible nuclear supplier.

- Maintain a strong intelligence collection and assessment capability as an integral part of United States non-proliferation policy and actions pursuant to that policy.

Achieving United States objectives will require making distinctions among states based on the degree of proliferation risk. The United States will cooperate with other nations in the peaceful uses of nuclear energy, including civil nuclear programs to meet their energy security needs, under a regime of adequate safeguards and controls.

To provide the basis for further action and decision, I hereby direct that:

1. The Secretary of State, in consultation with the Department of Energy and other interested agencies, will make a concerted effort with other supplier nations to seek uniform nuclear supply conditions and, in particular, to

   (a) prevent transfers to non-nuclear-weapon states of any significant nuclear material, equipment, or technology not subject to IAEA safeguards;

   (b) inhibit transfers of sensitive nuclear material, equipment, and technology, particularly where the danger of proliferation demands;

   (c) require IAEA safeguards on all nuclear activities in non-nuclear-weapon states as a condition for any significant new nuclear supply commitment;

   (d) increase the effectiveness of international nuclear export control lists; and

   (e) consider multinational undertakings as an alternative to the development of national facilities for reprocessing or enrichment.

2. The Secretary of State, the Director of the Arms Control and Disarmament Agency, the Secretary of Defense, and the Chairman of the Joint Chiefs of Staff will promptly coordinate action to obtain the Senate's advice and consent to ratification of Protocol I to the Treaty for the Prohibition of Nuclear Weapons in Latin America.

3. *[Paragraph blacked out]*

4. All Executive Branch agencies having responsibilities for determinations or authorizations related to nuclear exports and request under agreements for peaceful nuclear cooperation will

   (a) take steps promptly to ensure that such actions are carried out expeditiously where the necessary statutory requirements are met and that authorization for retransfer of nuclear material or equipment prior to use in reactors is, absent unusual circumstances, decided on by the time an export license is issued;

   (b) give favorable consideration to requests for the retransfer of spent fuel for reprocessing in the United Kingdom and France if the necessary statutory requirements are met; and

   (c) consider requests for the disposition or use of plutonium on the merits of each case pending development of further policy on reprocessing and plutonium use.

I also request that the Nuclear Regulatory Commission act expeditiously in carrying out its nuclear export licensing responsibility and its consultative responsibilities on other nuclear activities with other countries where the necessary statutory requirements are met.

In addition, I have noted that a number of actions will be undertaken by the Secretary of State in a timely manner and working with the interested agencies. These include, in particular:

1. review of what steps might be appropriate, consistent with United States non-proliferation objectives, to facilitate or remove any unnecessary impediments to commercial relations in the field of nuclear energy and review of applicable laws, regulations, and procedures to determine whether changes should be sought;

2. work to ensure effective physical protection for nuclear material, to support the Convention on the Physical Protection of Nuclear Material, and to substitute lower enriched fuels for research reactors at the earliest possible time;

3. negotiation of a convention for nuclear safety cooperation and assistance in civil nuclear emergencies;

4. *[Paragraph blacked out]*

5. support of ongoing international efforts in the areas of international plutonium storage, spent fuel management, assurances of supply and improved safeguards, particularly for large and advanced nuclear facilities.

The Secretary of Energy, in consultation with the interested agencies, shall ensure that adequate capacity is available to provide enrichment services for domestic and foreign customers.

I direct that the Secretary of State, working with other interested agencies, give priority attention to efforts to reduce proliferation risks, to enhance the international non-proliferation regime and, consistent with United States security interests, to re-establish a leadership role for the United States in international nuclear affairs. These decisions do not imply any requirements for additional federal funding.

PRESIDENT REAGAN

Statement on United States Nuclear Nonproliferation Policy
July 16, 1981

Our nation faces major challenges in international affairs. One of the most critical is the need to prevent the spread of nuclear explosives to additional countries. Further proliferation would pose a severe threat to international peace, regional and global stability, and the security interests of the United States and other countries. Our nation has been committed on a bipartisan basis to preventing the spread of nuclear explosives from the birth of the atomic age over 35 years ago. This commitment is shared by the vast majority of other countries. The urgency of this task has been highlighted by the ominous events in the Middle East.

The problem of reducing the risks of nuclear proliferation has many aspects, and we need an integrated approach to deal with it effectively. In the final analysis, the success of our efforts depends on our ability to improve regional and global stability and reduce those motivations that can drive countries toward nuclear explosives. This calls for a strong and dependable United States, vibrant alliances and improved relations with others, and a dedication to those tasks that are vital for a stable world order.

I am announcing today a policy framework that reinforces the longstanding objectives of our nation in nonproliferation and includes a number of basic guidelines.

The United States will:
• seek to prevent the spread of nuclear explosives to additional countries as a fundamental national security and foreign policy objective;
• strive to reduce the motivation for acquiring nuclear explosives by working to improve regional and global stability and to promote understanding of the legitimate security concerns of other states;
• continue to support adherence to the Treaty on the Non-Proliferation of Nuclear Weapons and to the Treaty for the Prohibition of Nuclear Weapons in Latin America (Treaty of Tlatelolco) by countries that have not accepted those treaties;
• view a material violation of these treaties or an international safeguards agreement as having profound consequences for international order and United States bilateral relations, and also view any nuclear explosion by a nonnuclear-weapon state with grave concern;
• strongly support and continue to work with other nations to strengthen the International Atomic Energy Agency to provide for an improved international safeguards regime;
• seek to work more effectively with other countries to forge agreement on measures for combating the risks of proliferation;
• continue to inhibit the transfer of sensitive nuclear material, equipment and technology, particularly where the danger of proliferation demands, and to seek agreement on requiring IAEA safeguards on all nuclear activities in a nonnuclear-weapon state as a condition for any significant new nuclear supply commitment.

I am also announcing that I will promptly seek the Senate's advice and consent to ratification of Protocol I of the Treaty of Tlatelolco.

The United States will cooperate with other nations in the peaceful uses of nuclear energy, including civil nuclear programs to meet their energy security needs, under a regime of adequate safeguards and controls. Many friends and allies of the United States have a strong interest in nuclear power and have, during recent years, lost confidence in the ability of our nation to recognize their needs.

We must reestablish this Nation as a predictable and reliable partner for peaceful nuclear cooperation under adequate safeguards. This is essential to our nonproliferation goals. If we are not such a partner, other countries will tend to go their own ways, and our influence will diminish. This would reduce our effectiveness in gaining the support we need to deal with proliferation problems.

To attain this objective, I am:
- instructing the executive branch agencies to undertake immediate efforts to ensure expeditious action on export requests and approval requests under agreements for peaceful nuclear cooperation where the necessary statutory requirements are met;
- requesting that the Nuclear Regulatory Commission act expeditiously on these matters.

The administration will also not inhibit or set back civil reprocessing and breeder reactor development abroad in nations with advanced nuclear power programs where it does not constitute a proliferation risk.

The United States will support IAEA programs and other international cooperative efforts in the areas of nuclear safety and environmentally sound nuclear waste management.

To carry out these policies, I am instructing the Secretary of State, working with the other responsible agencies, to give priority attention to efforts to reduce proliferation risks, to enhance the international nonproliferation regime and, consistent with United States security interests, to reestablish a leadership role for the United States in international nuclear affairs.

Presidential Determination No. 82-7 of February 10, 1982

Presidential Determination To Authorize Security Assistance for Pakistan

Memorandum for the Honorable Alexander M. Haig, Jr., the Secretary of State

By the authority vested in me as President by the Constitution and statutes of the United States of America, including sections 620E and 670(a)(2) of the Foreign Assistance Act of 1961, as amended ("the Act"), I hereby:

(1) determine, pursuant to section 620E(d) of the Act, that the provision of assistance to Pakistan under the Act through September 30, 1987, is in the national interest of the United States and therefore waive the prohibitions of section 669 of the Act with respect to that period;

(2) determine and certify, pursuant to section 670(a)(2) of the Act, that not providing assistance referred to in section 670(a)(1) of the Act to Pakistan would be seriously prejudicial to the achievement of United States nonproliferation objectives and otherwise jeopardize the common defense and security;

(3) authorize the provision of assistance referred to in sections 669(a)(1) and 670(a)(1) of the Act to Pakistan beginning thirty (30) days following submission of this determination and certification to the Congress.

This determination and certification together with the statement setting forth specific reasons therefore shall be submitted to the Congress immediately.

This determination shall be published in the Federal Register.

Reprocessing and Plutonium Use

DEPARTMENT STATEMENT, JUNE 9, 1982[1]

You will recall that the presidential policy statement on nuclear cooperation and nonproliferation of July 16, 1981, directed the Secretary of State, in cooperation with other responsible agencies, to give priority attention to efforts to reduce proliferation risks, to enhance the international nonproliferation regime, and, consistent with U.S. security interests, to reestablish a leadership role for the United States in international nuclear affairs. Under this mandate, one of the follow-on reviews has focused on approaches for a more predictable policy for exercising U.S. rights to approve reprocessing and use of plutonium subject to U.S. control under our peaceful nuclear cooperation agreements.

That review has now been completed, and the President has decided that in certain cases, the United States will offer to work out predictable, programmatic arrangements for reprocessing and plutonium use for civilian power and research needs, in the context of seeking new or amended agreements as required by law. These agreements would involve only countries with effective commitments to nonproliferation, where there are advanced nuclear power programs, and where such activities do not constitute a proliferation risk and are under effective safeguards and controls.

U.S. approval will be given only if U.S. statutory criteria are met and will be valid only as long as these criteria and other conditions in the agreements continue to apply.

It should be noted that the United States has been approving reprocessing requests on an *ad hoc*, case-by-case basis under existing agreements for many years. What the President has now approved is a new approach to granting long-term approvals in certain cases for the life of specific, carefully defined programs, as long as the conditions I have described are met.

---

[1] Read to news correspondents by acting Department spokesman Alan Romberg. ■

STATEMENT OF UNDER SECRETARY OF STATE RICHARD T. KENNEDY BEFORE THE SUBCOMMITTEE ON ENERGY, NUCLEAR PROLIFERATION AND GOVERNMENT PROCESSES, COMMITTEE ON GOVERNMENT AFFAIRS, UNITED STATES SENATE. September 9, 1982. (Excerpt)

Mr. Chairman:

I appreciate the opportunity to testify before this committee to discuss recent developments in U.S. non-proliferation policy, most particularly the approach of this Administration toward the reprocessing of nuclear material subject to U.S. consent rights and the use of plutonium produced from that material in certain countries. This hearing comes at an especially appropriate time in view of the numerous misunderstandings and mischaracterizations of the reprocessing and plutonium use policy which President Reagan approved in June of this year. It is very important to set the record straight on this matter since in my view our approach represents the most realistic and effective means of advancing our non-proliferation objectives at this time. In the course of explaining what our policy on these issues is and what it is not, I will seek to answer the specific questions which you have asked.

In his July 16, 1981, message on nuclear cooperation and non-proliferation, President Reagan stressed a number of key themes. Two themes are particularly relevant to the Administration's position on foreign reprocessing and plutonium use.

247

First, he stated that as one of the many elements of the Administration's overall non-proliferation policy, the United States would continue to inhibit the transfer of sensitive nuclear material, equipment and technology, particularly where the danger of proliferation demands. Underlying this policy is a long-standing US recognition of the serious risks associated with reprocessing and other sensitive technologies, the need for great caution and restraint in dealing with them, and the importance of limiting sensitive facilities and activities to as few locations as possible under adequate safeguards and only where there is no significant risk of proliferation.

The President also emphasized that an essential step in achieving our non-proliferation goals must be the reestablishment of this nation as a reliable partner for nuclear cooperation under adequate safeguards. In this connection, he announced that the U.S. will not inhibit or setback civil reprocessing and breeder reactor development abroad in nations with advanced nuclear power programs where it does not constitute a proliferation risk.

Consistent with this position, in June the President decided on a modified and limited approach toward the reprocessing of material subject to U.S. consent rights and the use of plutonium derived from that material in certain countries.

248

This approach is primarily designed to give our close allies in EURATOM and Japan a firmer and more predictable basis upon which to plan their vital energy programs while at the same time furthering our non-proliferation objectives, including strengthened controls over civil plutonium.

Specifically, we are offering Japan and the countries of EURATOM new, long-term arrangements for implementation of U.S. consent rights over the reprocessing and use of material subject to our agreements for peaceful nuclear cooperation. This advance, long-term approval would apply only for facilities and activities which we determine meet our strict statutory criteria. We are also prepared to state our intention to consent to such activities in future programs when we have sufficient information about them to make the necessary determinations under our law.

These offers are being made in the context of seeking new or amended peaceful nuclear cooperation agreements with Japan and EURATOM, which would be subject to Congressional review. The approvals would be valid only as long as the conditions provided in the agreement, including non-proliferation and statutory conditions, continue to be met. Our willingness to take these steps presumes the continued strong commitment of these countries to our common non-proliferation efforts and to developing and implementing more effective controls over plutonium.

249

Providing advance consent will not open the floodgates to the widespread use of plutonium. We are proposing this arrangement only to those few nations which have well-defined and coherent, advanced nuclear programs and where reprocessing and plutonium use do not constitute a proliferation danger. The President's decision limits the offer of advance consent for these activities, therefore, to Japan and the countries of EURATOM, nations which regard the uses of plutonium as crucial to meeting their future nuclear energy needs. Moreover, some of these countries already have reprocessing technology as well as active research, development and demonstration programs for advanced nuclear fuel cycles using plutonium. They already possess sizeable quantities of separated plutonium. Our policy does not endorse or encourage the spread of reprocessing and plutonium; it recognizes that major programs already exist and that we must work realistically with our most important allies to ensure vigorous safeguards and controls over sensitive technology and materials, and to otherwise advance our non-proliferation objectives.

This policy acknowledges that our close allies with advanced nuclear programs which pose no proliferation risk must be distinguished from others. Such a distinction is based upon genuine differences between countries, and we need to tailor our policies to deal with those differences. Past efforts to challenge the carefully considered programs of Japan and EURATOM countries led only to rancorous debates which soured our relations with key allies without enhancing our non-proliferation goals. At the same time we must and we will continue to hold the line against the spread of sensitive nuclear activities particularly where the danger of proliferation demands.

Moreover, our approach would not entail a blanket endorsement of the programs of Japan and EURATOM. We will grant advance consent for reprocessing and the use of plutonium only for those facilities and activities which we can determine satisfy the strict criteria contained in the Atomic Energy Act of 1954, as amended. We are offering this approach in the context of seeking new or amended agreements and the law requires that the President must "determine in writing that the proposed agreement will promote, and will not constitute an unreasonable risk to the common defense and security." In addition, since the advance consent arrangement involves reprocessing, we will also determine before entering into the arrangement that our approval will not result in a significant increase of the risk of proliferation, as would be required under Section 131 of the Act.

251

In making that determination foremost consideration will be given to whether or not the reprocessing will take place under conditions that will ensure timely warning to the U.S. of any diversion.

For other countries with which we have cooperation agreements, we will be working to provide advance, long-term consent for retransfers of U.S.-origin spent fuel to the United Kingdom and France for reprocessing in facilities which meet the applicable statutory criteria. Disposition of the recovered plutonium would be subject to further US consent. Such arrangements will also be made in the context of seeking new or amended peaceful nuclear cooperation agreements.

During the past two administrations, requests for reprocessing or retransfer of plutonium were approved on a case-by-case basis. Past approvals have involved primarily reprocessing in Japan at Tokai Mura or the shipment of spent fuel from Japan and a few other countries to France and the UK for reprocessing. Both previous administrations and this administration have always approved such requests. However, the case-by-case approach was resented by these countries because it caused considerable uncertainty in their nuclear power planning.

252

The previous Administration was considering ways to reduce that uncertainty during its last year in office and was consulting with our key allies on possible approaches including the provision of more extended approvals. Our approach is thus not a major break with past practices but a logical progression from them. It is also consistent with the approaches recently adopted toward Japan and EURATOM by Canada and Australia which presently insist as a general policy on consent rights similar to ours.

Our approach includes as well an effort to strengthen our agreements for cooperation, safeguards and other controls on civil plutonium. As you know, the present agreements between the U.S. and EURATOM do not provide for U.S. consent rights over the reprocessing of nuclear material which we export to the Community. We are required by the Nuclear Non-Proliferation Act of 1978 (NNPA) to seek such consent rights in EURATOM and to expand the ones we have presently with Japan. The countries of EURATOM are not likely to give the U.S. such rights nor is Japan likely to agree to expanding existing ones unless they are confident that we will exercise those rights in a responsible and predictable manner. I believe our new approach will go a long way toward convincing these countries that their agreement to new or expanded consent rights will place our nuclear relations on a more sound and orderly basis.

253

In addition, advance, long-term approval of reprocessing with EURATOM and Japan is clearly premised on the expectation of strengthened and broadened cooperation on non-proliferation matters, particularly in dealing with pressing proliferation problems in sensitive regions of the world and in implementing more effective controls on civil plutonium. Such approvals would be premised on continued commitments to improve the application of IAEA safeguards at reprocessing plants and other facilities which process, use or store plutonium as well as commitments to assure adequate physical security measures for plutonium.

Such cooperation from the major advanced nuclear countries is essential if we are to succeed in strengthening these aspects of the non-proliferation regime. The US no longer enjoys a position as the monopoly supplier of nuclear materials equipment and technology. Today we supply only some 35% of the non-communist enrichment market whereas we accounted for virtually all of it just a few years ago. But if we are to have the full cooperation of the other advanced nuclear powers in pursuing our non-proliferation objectives, we cannot continue to press a policy which is hostile to their reprocessing and breeder programs or which needlessly creates uncertainties and difficulties for their nuclear power planning affecting capital investments in the billions of dollars. In that kind of atmosphere, U.S.

254

proposals to modify the design features of those facilities to strengthen the application of safeguards and other steps to ensure more vigorous controls on the use of plutonium would be viewed with skepticism, if not as an effort to  breeder programs. It is, therefore, essential that we take steps to remove tensions that have marred our nuclear relations with our close allies over the past few years so that we can work more effectively together..

* * *

Nonproliferation: Where We Are and Where We're Going

by Richard T. Kennedy

Statement before a joint hearing of the Senate Foreign Relations Committee and the Subcommittee on Energy, Nuclear Proliferation, and Government Processes of the Senate Committee on Governmental Affairs on September 30, 1983. Ambassador Kennedy is U.S. permanent representative to the International Atomic Energy Agency (IAEA) and Ambassador at Large and special adviser to the Secretary on nonproliferation policy and nuclear energy affairs.[1]

I welcome the opportunity to meet with you today to discuss the Administration's program for preventing the spread of nuclear weapons. It has been about a year since we have had an oversight hearing on this important issue before your committees. You have invited me to discuss a number of very significant topics, including the International Atomic Energy Agency (IAEA); the question of spare parts for the Tarapur reactors in India; recent discussions we have had with the Soviet Union, the People's Republic of China, Argentina, and Brazil; our plutonium use policy and the status of negotiations with the European Energy Community (EURATOM) and Japan; the hexapartite safeguards agreement; and the impact of the Supreme Court's *Chadha* decision. These are very significant issues and I will attempt to cover each of them in this statement.

As you may recall, in a previous appearance before you, I outlined the responsibilities and organizational relationships in the nonproliferation area—relationships which were contemplated by the President and Secretary Shultz when nominating me as Ambassador at Large with responsibility for nonproliferation matters. In that role, I coordinate the efforts of the executive branch and act as the special representative of the Secretary and the President in discussions and negotiations with other countries on nonproliferation. I am pleased to note that over the past many months, these organizational relationships have worked well and have provided an increasingly cohesive approach to a complex, difficult, and vital task. In particular, I want to express my admiration and appreciation for the excellent work done by the staff in the Bureau of Oceans and International Environmental and Scientific Affairs of the State Department and, indeed, by all of the various bureaus of the Department which contribute to a fully coordinated effort. I also want to note the effective contributions of the Arms Control and Disarmament Agency, Department of Energy, and Department of Defense, which work together with us in support of the effort. They contributed greatly to the progress which we have made. And, of course, the Nuclear Regulatory Commission (NRC) continues its important export licensing role, as well as assisting other nations with their own nuclear regulation activities. Through this effective coordinated relationship, we have been able to focus attention on the problem of proliferation, as we believe the Congress had intended.

All of our nonproliferation efforts, of course, are conducted under the guidelines provided by the President in his statement of July 16, 1981. In that statement, the President laid out seven basic guidelines.

• The United States will seek to prevent the spread of nuclear explosives to additional countries as a fundamental national security and foreign policy objective.

• The United States will strive to reduce the motivation for acquiring nuclear explosives by working to improve regional and global stability and to promote understanding of the legitimate security concerns of other states.

• The United States will continue to support adherence to the Treaty on the Non-Proliferation of Nuclear Weapons and to the Treaty for the Prohibition of Nuclear Weapons in Latin America (treaty of Tlatelolco) by countries that have not accepted those treaties.

• The United States will view a material violation of these treaties or an international safeguards agreement as having profound consequences for international order and U.S. bilateral relations and also view any nuclear explosion by a non-nuclear-weapons state with grave concern.

• The United States will strongly support and continue to work with other nations to strengthen the IAEA to provide for an improved international safeguards regime.

• The United States will seek to work more effectively with other countries to forge agreement on measures for combatting the risks of proliferation.

• The United States will continue to inhibit the transfer of sensitive nuclear material, equipment, and technology, particularly where the danger of proliferation demands, and to seek agreement on requiring IAEA safeguards on all nuclear activities in a non-nuclear-weapons state as a condition for any significant new nuclear supply commitment.

To these guidelines, I would like to add one additional concept which underlies our policy and which I have asserted in numerous fora—that is that the United States will never allow its nonproliferation objectives to be undercut for commercial gain. Our policy is to put in place the most effective nonproliferation regime which we, in combination with other concerned nations, can achieve.

I would now like first to bring you up to date on several important events which have taken place since we last met and then turn to the specific areas which you asked me to address.

Update on Recent Events

President Reagan's Comprehensive Safeguards Initiative. U.S. law requires IAEA safeguards on all existing nuclear activities in the recipient non-nuclear-weapons state as a condition for major U.S. nuclear exports. President Reagan has called upon all supplier states to require comprehensive safeguards for their own exports. Our objective must be the establishment of agreed norms which all suppliers will honor. We have pursued this objective through bilateral consultations in capitals and in a number of discussions in Washington. These discussions will continue.

Additional Parties to the Nonproliferation Treaty. The United States strongly supports universal adherence to the Nuclear Nonproliferation Treaty (NPT). The Administration continues active diplomatic efforts to encourage countries not yet party to the treaty to ratify this central instrument of the international nonproliferation regime. During 1982 four additional states became parties—Papua New-Guinea, Nauru, the Socialist Republic of Vietnam, and Uganda. There are now more than 115 states which are parties to the NPT, making it the most widely accepted multilateral arms control agreement. We also are taking steps to encourage implementation of the treaty of Tlatelolco.

New Bilateral Agreements for Cooperation in the Peaceful Uses of Atomic Energy. As you know, Section 404 of the Nuclear Nonproliferation Act of 1978 requires that the United States seek to renegotiate agreements of cooperation under Section 123 of the Atomic Energy Act of 1954. We have renegotiated our agreement with the IAEA, entered into force May 6, 1980; Canada entered into force July 9, 1980; Australia entered into force January 16, 1981; and Colombia (not yet in force). We anticipate that revised agreements with Norway and Sweden will be submitted to the Congress in the near future. We have also concluded new agreements of cooperation with several nations—Morocco (entered into force May 16, 1981), Bangladesh (entered into force June 12, 1982), Peru (entered into force April 15, 1982), Indonesia (entered into force December 30, 1981), and Egypt (entered into force December 29, 1981).

Bilateral Consultations. During the past year, U.S. officials have consulted with more than a dozen countries in Europe, Latin America, and Asia on how to pursue more effectively our common goal of preventing proliferation. In these talks, we have paid specific attention to improving nuclear export controls, including the difficult task of controlling "dual-use" commodities—items which have both conventional and potential nuclear uses. These meetings have helped others to understand our policies and have contributed significantly to an improved nonproliferation regime.

Improvement of U.S. Nuclear Export Regulations. On February 4, 1983, the Department of Energy issued revised and strengthened regulations which serve to control the transfer of unclassified and unpublished nuclear technology, the "part 810" regulations.

U.S. Reprocessing of Research Reactor Fuel. The Department of Energy extended through 1987 its policy of receiving and making financial settlement for U.S.-origin spent fuels from research reactors. This policy applies to highly enriched uranium fuels which raise proliferation concerns because of their potential use in nuclear explosives.

Implementation of Voluntary Safeguards Offer. The U.S. voluntary offer, made several years ago, to accept safeguards on civil nuclear facilities entered into force during 1980. Under this offer, four U.S. facilities were selected by the IAEA for the application of safeguards, and in 1982, the detailed arrangements under which they are now being safeguarded were brought into force. The most significant of these four is the Exxon fuel fabrication plant where valuable experience has been gained in the effective implementation of safeguards.

Nuclear Export Alerts. Steps to make it more difficult technically for a sensitive country to acquire particular equipment or materials in pursuit of a nuclear weapons capability can buy time for other initiatives to reduce its motivations to acquire those weapons. The United States has worked in close and frequent consultation with other supplier states to shut off specific export transactions of proliferation concern. During the 1982 calendar year, approximately 100 such export alerts were pursued, and about 50 have been issued so far this year.

Assistance to Non-Nuclear-Weapons States in Spent Fuel Storage and Disposal. Under Section 223 of the Nuclear Waste Policy Act of 1982, a *Federal Register* notice has been published offering to augment U.S. international cooperative arrangements in the area of spent fuel storage and disposal. Non-nuclear-weapons states were contacted through diplomatic channels to solicit expressions of interest. The United States was the host for a major IAEA international conference on radioactive waste management in Seattle, Washington, in May 1983.

Emerging Suppliers. A potential problem which the Administration has begun to address is the expansion in the number of nations capable of exporting nuclear materials, equipment, and technology. Consultations with other nations have been directed toward alerting these new suppliers to the need for effective controls on their nuclear trade to assure that it is not misused for explosives developments, thereby undermining the current system of nuclear supplier guidelines.

Ratification of Physical Security Convention. President Reagan sought and obtained enactment of domestic legislation making certain acts involving nuclear materials serious Federal crimes. This law implements certain provisions in the Convention on the Physical Protection of Nuclear Material. In late 1982, the United States ratified this convention, a major step in dealing with threats of nuclear terrorism and proliferation. The Administration also remains committed in its efforts to work with other countries to assure the adequacy of physical security measures, especially where nuclear materials of U.S.-origin are involved.

***Chadha* Decision and the Legislative Veto.** Various provisions of the Atomic Energy Act as amended by the Nuclear Nonproliferation Act of 1978 have provided for a legislative veto by the Congress of Presidential determinations to permit nuclear exports. Basically these statutory provisions contain three distinct elements.

First, they establish very strict and specific standards which limit the export of nuclear items.

Second, they authorize the President to waive certain restrictions and permit exports if he makes certain findings. There are also requirements that such waivers and findings be reported to the Congress with specified waiting period before those actions may become effective.

The **third** was the legislative veto.

The Department of State made its position clear on this issue last July when Deputy Secretary Kenneth Dam testified before this committee and at a hearing before the House Foreign Affairs Committee. Secretary Dam testified that the Department of State considers that those standards and that waiver authority, as well as the statutory requirement of notification to Congress and the observance of a waiting period, continue to be valid. We will continue to wait through the period during which the Congress, in the past, deliberated over its veto. During that time, the Congress may use its constitutional authority to enact new legislation if it chooses. The only provision that is invalid is the third, which permitted a legislative veto by concurrent resolution.

Secretary Dam emphasized last July, and I reiterate today, that neither the Department nor the Administration intends to take advantage of the situation created by the *Chadha* decision to take any action which would disturb the relationship of cooperation and collaboration we have developed with the Congress over the years in the area of nuclear nonproliferation. We intend to continue consulting regularly with the Congress and its committees and taking your counsel and advice into account in reaching important decisions. Our commitment to that spirit of cooperation is strengthened rather than diminished by the *Chadha* decision. As Secretary Dam said last July: "If anything, I believe *Chadha* will make the departments and agencies of the executive branch more, not less, conscious that they are accountable for their actions."

Spare Parts for the Tarapur Reactors in India

With regard to India's Tarapur atomic power station, the Government of India is seeking to obtain from the United States and other countries spare parts for the Tarapur reactors, which were designed and built by U.S. companies. India considers the continued operation of this facility, which is subject to IAEA safeguards, as vital to meet its electric power needs. The parts it seeks are important to furthering the safe operation of the plant. We are principally concerned with the health and safety of individuals working at the Tarapur facility and those living nearby.

It was in these circumstances that Secretary Shultz informed the Government of India during his recent visit to New Delhi that the President would be prepared to take measures designed to ensure the availability from the United States of required parts that could not be supplied from other sources.

Notwithstanding the significant health and safety aspect involved, the steps which have been taken so far in this matter—and the steps we will take in the future—will be with full and careful attention to the nonproliferation considerations involved, both from the standpoint of our overall policy and that policy vis-a-vis India.

To date, we have not been able to determine whether all of the required parts will be available from non-U.S. sources. Discussions between India and potential non-U.S. suppliers are continuing.

Discussions With the People's Republic of China

Over the course of the last several years, the People's Republic of China (P.R.C.) has developed plans for an ambitious program for the installation of a substantial number of nuclear power stations in those areas of the country where coal and hydroelectric resources are not available. Those plans call for the importing of the initial plants and, at the same time, the acquisition of the technology and the facilities to permit China's industry to manufacture much of the equipment required for the later plants.

The Chinese authorities have expressed an interest in obtaining the services of experienced U.S. firms in implementing that program. Accordingly, since 1981, the possibility of a bilateral agreement for cooperation in the peaceful uses of atomic energy, as required by the Atomic Energy Act for significant exports of the kind that would be sought by the P.R.C., has been discussed with China. This Administration believes that, under appropriate conditions, such cooperation would be in the interest of the United States. Conclusion of an agreement for cooperation within the terms of the Atomic Energy Act would demonstrate the readiness of the United States to expand its relationship with the P.R.C. in areas of mutual interest and could lead to cooperation in other areas as well. It would also provide additional opportunities to encourage China to adopt nonproliferation policies, including those related to its exports of nuclear materials, equipment, and technologies—policies which would be consistent with those which have been developed and adopted by the major suppliers.

The most recent discussions with the Chinese authorities took place in July, when a delegation visited Washington at the invitation of Secretary Shultz. In those discussions, nonproliferation matters were addressed extensively. Overall, good progress was made in clarifying the views of both sides. At that time, we were told that the P.R.C. was considering joining the IAEA. Since then, Director General Blix has visited Beijing to discuss the P.R.C.'s interest in membership, and just recently its formal application has been submitted. We welcome this action by the P.R.C. as an indication of its intention to play a constructive role in nonproliferation and international cooperation in the peaceful uses of atomic energy.

Within the next few days, I will lead a delegation to Beijing to continue the discussions with the P.R.C. We will seek to confirm that we share the same basic principles regarding nonproliferation as a basis for further discussion of possible cooperation.

Bilateral Discussions With the Soviet Union

The United States and U.S.S.R. have held two rounds of bilateral meetings on a broad range of nonproliferation issues. The first session was in Washington December 15-17, 1982, and the second took place in Moscow June 14-16, 1983. I headed the U.S. delegation at both sessions, and the Soviet side was headed in December by Ivan Morozov, until recently Deputy Chairman of the State Committee on the Utilization of Atomic Energy, and in June by A. M. Petrosyants, Chairman of the State Committee. The talks during both rounds were frank and positive, with a very constructive exchange of views.

The discussions were divided into plenary and working group sessions. In the plenary, a wide range of issues was covered. These included prospects for strengthening the international nonproliferation regime, assuring the safe development of nuclear energy, and encouraging additional countries to sign and ratify the NPT and the newly established Convention for the Physical Security of Nuclear Materials. Discussions also took place on ways to strengthen the IAEA and on preparations for the third review conference for the NPT to be held in 1985.

Working groups held detailed discussions on specific issues, such as export controls, and multilateral issues, including the IAEA and its safeguards system.

The two sides agreed that the IAEA safeguards system was crucial to the success of the international nuclear nonproliferation regime. They agreed to take steps to try to strengthen that system and also agreed that other IAEA-sponsored activities, such as the work of the Committee on Assurances of Supply and Technical Assistance and Cooperation activities, should also be strongly supported. The Soviets expressed support for the concept of comprehensive safeguards, as recently proposed by the President, but believe the policy cannot be effective until all major suppliers adopt it.

On export issues, it was clear that the United States and the Soviets share the view that meaningful controls over nuclear exports can make a significant contribution to achieving our nonproliferation goals. The need to ensure that controls evolve in respect to technological change and the spread of nuclear capabilities was dealt with in some detail. The Soviets also agreed with us that it will be important for emerging new suppliers to apply meaningful export controls and adopt standards equivalent to those in the current international nonproliferation regime.

The two rounds of discussions and the accompanying exchange of views with the Soviets on nonproliferation issues have made a useful contribution to our efforts to restrain the spread of nuclear explosives.

EURATOM and Japan Negotiations—Plutonium Use

Regarding the EURATOM and Japan negotiations on plutonium use, you may recall that in September 1982, I testified before the Subcommittee on Energy, Nuclear Proliferation, and Government Process of the Senate Committee on Government Affairs on the policy decisions made by the President in June 1982 on these matters. At that time, the President decided on a new approach to give our close allies in EURATOM and Japan a firmer and more predictable basis upon which to plan their vital energy programs, while at the same time furthering our nonproliferation objectives, including strengthened controls over civil plutonium.

At that time, I reported that the United States was offering Japan and the countries of EURATOM new, long-term arrangements for implementation of U.S. consent rights over the reprocessing and use of materials subject to our agreements for peaceful nuclear cooperation. This advance, long-term approval would apply only to facilities and activities which we determine meet our strict statutory criteria. The United States would be prepared to state its intention to consent to other facilities and activities in these programs when we have sufficient information about them to make the necessary determinations under our law.

Finally, I noted that these offers were being made in the context of seeking new or amended peaceful nuclear cooperation agreements with Japan and EURATOM and that the approvals would be valid only as long as the conditions provided in the agreement, including nonproliferation and statutory conditions, continued to be met. Our willingness to take these steps presumed a continuing strong commitment of these countries to our common nonproliferation efforts and to developing and implementing more effective controls over plutonium.

We have provided detailed proposals on this subject to the Government of Japan and in the last year have had seven negotiating sessions with the Japanese, in Washington and Tokyo, in an effort to reach agreement both on the long-term arrangement for plutonium use and on the peaceful nuclear cooperation agreement. I can report to you that we have made significant progress in a number of areas but that there are important matters that remain to be resolved as well. As the substance of these issues is under negotiation between the two governments, I cannot go into the details in open session. I can say, however, that both sides continue serious and intense efforts to find solutions and approaches that will permit them to reach agreement at an early date. As I have always done, I will keep the Congress briefed on significant developments.

Progress with EURATOM is slower. This is understandable, since negotiations with EURATOM are complex by their nature, given the institutional arrangements that apply within the European Communities, and the need for the EC Commission to consult with member states. I can report that we provided the EC with details of our new proposals last spring. The EC Commission requested time to study those proposals and to consult informally with member states. This month we have just received a number of detailed questions concerning our proposals, and we would anticipate early talks with the commission to clarify our proposals and to agree on how to proceed thereafter.

Trigger List Upgrade

You have requested an update on our efforts to improve international guidelines for controlling exports which could be used for nuclear explosives development. As you know, there are two internationally agreed trigger lists adopted by nuclear suppliers in the mid-1970s to control their export activities. They are called "trigger lists" because the export of any listed item triggers the application of safeguards on that item. The first list is linked to the NPT which requires safeguards on items "especially designed or prepared" for the processing or production of fissionable material. This list is implemented through the 21-member NPT Exporters Committee—also called the Zangger committee, after its Swiss chairman. In addition to the Zangger list, there is a substantially identical trigger list not linked to the NPT but which was implemented through the informal nuclear suppliers' group—often referred to as the London group because it initially met in the United Kingdom.

Both these lists have been extremely important for the effort to control sensitive nuclear exports to countries of proliferation risk. Over the past few years, however, it has become clear to us, and several other suppliers, that it would be useful to further refine and clarify the lists, in response to technological developments and the spread of nuclear capabilities to additional nations.

I am pleased to report that substantial progress has been made on this initiative. We have made a commitment to other participating governments that the detailed status of the negotiations would remain confidential until administrative arrangements can be completed. This will take a few months. I would be pleased to go into specifics with you or members of your staff in closed session; however, I can make a few comments in open session which give a general picture of our approach and the progress achieved so far.

We have decided to approach the trigger list upgrade on a technology-by-technology basis, with a small group of the key technology holders in that field. Once a technical consensus has been achieved on what refinements in the trigger list are necessary, the discussions have been expanded to other nations. The additional nations may not be centrally involved with the industrial applications of a particular technology, however; they may nonetheless be able to export certain items related to that process. Therefore, the participation of such nontechnology holders is important if the control regime is to be effective.

We began our efforts over a year ago with the gas centrifuge uranium enrichment process because of its sensitivity and the interest being shown in the process by nations of proliferation concern. After much effort, we are near final agreement on a revised trigger list for this technology. We are making good progress on other sensitive nuclear processes, but it will take sustained effort to achieve broad agreement on the range of technologies which must be considered.

In concluding my remarks on this subject I would like to emphasize two points.

First, we regard this important initiative as fully consistent with our nonproliferation obligations under Article III of the NPT and other commitments we have undertaken in the nuclear suppliers group. The group's guidelines recognize that periodic review and updating of the trigger lists may be necessary to assure that they remain effective. We are committed to this process of continuing review.

Second, implementing strict nonproliferation controls and revising them periodically is not an exercise in technology denial, as some have charged. If nuclear power is to play a

December 1983

role in meeting the world's energy needs, world public opinion must be assured that this technology will not be diverted from its intended peaceful purposes to explosives development. Our export control system plays a key role in providing that assurance. Therefore, all nations have a stake in a nonproliferation regime which clearly demonstrates that nuclear technology will not be misused, a regime which adjusts to meet changed circumstances—whether technical or political.

Hexapartite Safeguards Project

As you may know, we have recently concluded an important international effort to strengthen IAEA safeguards. In this effort, known as the hexapartite safeguards project, the countries which have developed gas centrifuge uranium enrichment technology assisted the IAEA inspectorate—and the EURATOM inspectorate—in the development of a safeguards approach for enrichment plants using this new technology.

Several years ago several countries had developed gas centrifuge enrichment technology to the point where they began to build demonstration or commercial scale plants and, pursuant to their NPT obligations, make these plants available for IAEA safeguards. The IAEA at that time had no experience safeguarding gas centrifuge enrichment plants—or any other type of enrichment plant, all of which had been located in nuclear weapons states. At the urging of the United States, a special international project was established, comprising technical experts from the six countries that have this technology and from the safeguards inspectorates of the IAEA and EURATOM. During the next 2½ years, these experts developed a safeguards approach that provides effective safeguards while properly protecting the technology.

In April 1983, the project was concluded, and the six technology holders undertook, in an exchange of diplomatic notes in Vienna, to permit the implementation of international safeguards based on the limited frequency unannounced access approach at their existing and planned commercial gas centrifuge uranium enrichment plant. Four of the project participants have gas centrifuge enrichment plants in operation or under construction. The operating plants include the two URENCO facilities at Almelo in the Netherlands and at ... in the United Kingdom and the Japanese pilot plant at Ningyo Toge.

In the United States, the Department of Energy's gas centrifuge enrichment plant is currently under construction and is expected to begin recycle operations in the summer of 1984, with actual production scheduled for late summer of 1985.

We understand that the facility attachment negotiations for the Dutch and Japanese plants will be begun in the near future. The United Kingdom has listed its Capenhurst plant as eligible for IAEA safeguards under the U.K. voluntary offer; the IAEA has selected this plant for safeguards, and facility attachment negotiations are also expected to begin in the near future.

For our part, following the exchange of notes, we immediately took steps to place our gas centrifuge enrichment plant on the list of facilities eligible for safeguards under the U.S. voluntary offer, as required by our commitment in that offer to make available for safeguards all U.S. facilities deemed not to be of direct national security significance. Following notification to Congress, the IAEA was informed that this plant was eligible for selection for safeguards, and the IAEA was invited to participate in a facility orientation visit to the plant. At the end of July, the IAEA formally selected the gas centrifuge enrichment plant for safeguards, and the first IAEA inspection was conducted in early August, as the first small quantity of nuclear material was brought onto the site. The IAEA team responsible for negotiating facility attachments for all gas centrifuge enrichment plants was given a special orientation briefing and tour of the facility at this time. Once plant construction is sufficiently advanced, we will provide the appropriate design information to the IAEA and initiate facility attachment negotiations. We expect to provide the design information sometime around the first of next year.

To summarize then, all the hexapartite safeguards project participants are currently engaged in the implementation of their respective undertakings, as made at the conclusion of the project. We fully expect that by the time that the facility attachment for our gas centrifuge enrichment plant is completed and enters into force, the other parties will have completed similar arrangements with respect to their existing gas centrifuge enrichment plants.

Reestablishing Dialogue—Brazil and Argentina

A key element in our nonproliferation efforts has been to reestablish or strengthen a dialogue on nuclear cooperation and nonproliferation matters with states where such dialogue may have languished. This effort is perhaps best exemplified in the cases of Brazil and Argentina. For several years our relations with these two countries in the nuclear area were severely strained. The export of nuclear fuel and facilities to these countries had been prohibited by the Nuclear Nonproliferation Act unless full-scope safeguards were adopted and each country has indigenously developed nuclear facilities which have not been submitted to safeguards. Both countries have declined to sign the Nonproliferation Treaty, although both have signed, but not brought into force, the treaty of Tlatelolco.

We have stressed to both Brazil and Argentina the importance of the Nonproliferation Treaty, the benefits of full adherence to IAEA safeguards, and we have urged both countries to waive into force the treaty of Tlatelolco. We have urged both to strengthen their support for the IAEA and its safeguards programs. Meanwhile, we believe it important to carry on a dialogue on nuclear matters with those countries so that we can create a stronger sense of mutual confidence and an informed understanding of each other's nonproliferation concerns and objectives. In this respect, the Administration is looking to limited nuclear cooperation in the area of nuclear safety and waste management, consistent with the Atomic Energy Act, while engaging these countries in renewed discussions regarding our nonproliferation goals.

Our discussions with Brazil have taken place under the aegis of the U.S.-Brazil joint working group, which was established jointly by President Reagan and President Figueiredo, following President Reagan's trip to Brazil last winter. The working group was tasked with exploring bilateral problem areas and exploring new opportunities for cooperation. Five subgroups were established, one of which dealt with nuclear matters.

Last May, I led a U.S. delegation for the first meeting of the nuclear subgroup in Brasilia. At that time we outlined potential areas of nuclear cooperation and also had a full discussion of nonproliferation matters, including the importance of controls over nuclear exports and adherence to the treaty of Tlatelolco. Significantly, the Brazilian side stressed that by virtue of signing the treaty of Tlatelolco, Brazil considered itself legally and morally bound by its principles even though the treaty was not yet in force.

The U.S.-Brazil nuclear subgroup met again in Washington in August and agreed to pursue a number of areas of nuclear cooperation, including nuclear safety, spent fuel and waste management, and reduced enrichment for research and test reactors. The meeting also afforded the opportunity to discuss President Reagan's initiatives on comprehensive safeguards and a series of nonproliferation and multilateral issues, including reducing politicization in the IAEA, the IAEA Committee on Assurances of Supply, and the prospects for an international plutonium storage regime.

We also discussed the U.S.-Brazil enrichment services contract. We have been unable to complete our side of the contract in the existing circumstances because we cannot export the enriched product to Brazil given the limits of the Nonproliferation Act. Accordingly, the United States and Brazil agreed that it would be in their mutual interest to suspend indefinitely the contract, as to which we had already suspended the first reload. We will continue discussions with Brazil concerning safeguards matters and would hope that a situation could be developed which would permit reinstating the fuel supply contract.

We believe that the working group meetings were highly successful and have led to a renewed spirit of cooperation between the United States and Brazil. For our part, we will be continuing these contracts, taking the opportunities to discuss with Brazil our nonproliferation concerns.

Argentina has presented a similar situation for many years. Our relations in the nuclear area have been strained, and it has been difficult to find opportunities to pursue our nonproliferation objectives with the Government of Argentina. For this reason, the Administration is also working to regain a dialogue with Argentina—a dialogue which would encompass renewed discussion of our nonproliferation goals, while at the same time we seek areas where the United States and Argentina can cooperate, within the limits of our law.

During my trip to South America last May, I had extensive discussions with Admiral Castro Madero, the President of the Argentine Atomic Energy Commission. I stressed the importance of bringing into force the treaty of Tlatelolco, the necessity of strengthening IAEA safeguards, the desirability of comprehensive safeguards, the need for emerging nuclear suppliers, such as Argentina, to follow agreed rules of nuclear trade, and the need to support and strengthen the IAEA. As in the case of Brazil, we discussed possible areas of nuclear cooperation between the United States and Argentina.

Argentina has since followed up on our discussions and indicated an interest in pursuing cooperation in nuclear safety, waste management and spent fuel technical assistance, systems of accounting and control, reduced enrichment for research and test reactors, and laboratory-to-laboratory exchanges. Over the next few weeks, we will be examining these possibilities with a view to further talks during the IAEA general conference in October.

Again, I believe that our initiative toward a dialogue is proving productive. Our discussions were frank and cordial and, while differences of view are evident, our talks have shown that there is a considerable measure of agreement on the need for common efforts to prevent the spread of nuclear weapons.

South Africa

South Africa is another country with which we are re-establishing a dialogue on nonproliferation matters. In the absence of South Africa's acceptance of full scope safeguards, the United States has not permitted the export of significant nuclear materials or equipment to South Africa since 1978. Unfortunately, over the same period our discussions with South Africa on nonproliferation matters had languished.

During the past year, we have revived our discussions with South Africa across a broad range of safeguards and nonproliferation matters, including adherence to comprehensive safeguards and the Nonproliferation Treaty, strengthening the IAEA safeguards regime, and requiring safeguards on all significant nuclear fuel and facilities placed in international commerce. We have also taken the opportunity to stress to the South Africans the benefits of placing their enrichment facilities under IAEA safeguards. At the same time, we have also discussed the possibility of resolving our differences on the existing uranium enrichment services contract between South Africa and the U.S. Department of Energy.

We believe that South Africa recognizes the importance of safeguards, as they might apply to their semicommercial enrichment facility. We also believe that South Africa understands the importance of safeguards on international nuclear commerce. As these discussions continue, I plan to keep the Congress fully and currently informed on any developments which may occur.

International Atomic Energy Agency

Since I last testified before the committee, a great deal has occurred in the International Atomic Energy Agency. As you are aware, we left last September's general conference in protest against the illegal rejection of the credentials of the Israeli delegation. Since then, we have been pleased that our message to the IAEA membership seems to have been heard and heeded. Our extensive consultations with many members demonstrated that the great majority agreed with us on the need to reduce politicization in the IAEA. Following an extensive reassessment of U.S. participation in the IAEA, the President approved the resumption of U.S. participation and agreed that the IAEA safeguards system performs a critical role for U.S. national security, nonproliferation, and peaceful nuclear cooperation interests. Significantly, both the February and June meetings of the IAEA Board of Governors were businesslike and devoid of excess rhetoric or divisive dispute.

Thus, we are encouraged that the majority of the membership appears to agree that (1) the IAEA is a useful and worthwhile organization, (2) that extraneous political posturing and actions which threaten to destroy the IAEA are counterproductive, and (3) it is time to concentrate on the main objectives of the IAEA—to spread the benefits of peaceful nuclear technology under appropriate safeguards.

Nevertheless, I cannot claim that this year's general conference will be totally free from problems. We will continue, however, to take strong measures to protect Israel's rights of membership in the IAEA, to assert our view that the agency must act in accordance with the precepts of its statute and concentrate on its mandate to assure the benefits of the peaceful uses of nuclear energy with safeguards to guard against its misuse.

---

[1]The complete transcript of the hearings will be published by the committee and will be available from the Superintendent of Documents, U.S. Government Printing Office, Washington, D.C. 20402. ■

Reprocessing and Plutonium Use in Civil Nuclear Programs

by Richard T. Kennedy

Statement before the Subcommittees on Arms Control, International Security, and Science and on International Economic Policy and Trade of the House Foreign Affairs Committee on July 24, 1985. Ambassador Kennedy is U.S. permanent representative to the IAEA and special adviser to the Secretary on nonproliferation policy and nuclear energy affairs.[1]

I would like to thank you for this opportunity to appear before the committee to discuss U.S. policy on cooperation with other nations in the areas of nuclear spent fuel reprocessing and use of the derived plutonium in civil nuclear power programs.

I would like to begin by saying that in this area, as in other areas of the civil nuclear fuel cycle, the overriding objective of this Administration is to insure that the policies we follow are fully consistent with achieving our nonproliferation goals. In a policy statement made soon after he took office, President Reagan declared that preventing the spread of nuclear explosives is one of the most critical challenges facing our nation in international affairs. Further proliferation, he said, would pose a severe threat to international peace, regional and global stability, and the security interests of the United States and other countries. He pledged that the United States would seek to prevent the spread of nuclear explosives as a fundamental national security and foreign policy objective.

In a major address before the UN Association of the USA on November 1, 1984, Secretary of State Shultz strongly reaffirmed this basic commitment to reducing the dangers to world peace and global stability posed by the potential spread of nuclear weapons. "It is no exaggeration," he declared, "to say that controlling the spread of nuclear weapons is critical to world peace and, indeed, to human survival. It is a cause that deserves and receives a top priority in our foreign policy."

To underscore the depth of our conviction on this point, I can only reaffirm in the strongest terms this Administration's commitment never to sacrifice its nonproliferation principles for commercial gain or political adavantage and its belief that this standard should be a universal norm for all countries.

It is not enough, however, simply to proclaim a nonproliferation policy. That policy must bring results. And to bring results, it must first find support with the world's other nuclear suppliers. The day is long past when the United States could unilaterally dictate the terms and conditions of international nuclear commerce. We no longer enjoy a monopoly over nuclear technology and the ability to supply or deny it as suits our interest. We are not even close to enjoying this privileged position anymore.

We must, therefore, face reality. If our nonproliferation policy is to succeed, we must persuade other countries of the benefits and desirability of supporting U.S. views on critical supply, safeguards, and other nonproliferation issues. We are making good progress in this direction, and I am convinced that it offers by far the best road to insuring that the peaceful use of nuclear energy does not lead to further nuclear explosives proliferation.

And so, as a necessary complement to our strong nonproliferation policy, we are also committed to cooperation with other nations in the peaceful uses of nuclear energy under adequate safeguards and controls.

Motivating Factors for Nuclear Development

Many of the world's industrial and industrializing nations have not been blessed with abundant domestic sources of fossil or other organic fuels. They regard the development of nuclear energy as vital to their national well-being and energy security needs. In order to exploit the potential of nuclear energy to the fullest, a very few of them—certain West European countries and Japan—have developed plans to reprocess spent fuel from existing nuclear power reactors and to use the separated plutonium as fuel to generate additional electric power. Their plans include the development of breeder and other types of advanced reactors and the use of mixed plutonium oxide and uranium oxide (MOX) fuel in light water power reactors (so-called thermal recycle).

The economic justification for these programs may be debatable. But economics is not the principal motivating factor. Much more important is a determination on the part of these countries to achieve the highest possible degree of self-sufficiency in energy production capability. The oil shocks of the 1970s, along with other developments such as the sweeping changes that occurred in U.S. laws and policies in the late 1970s concerning U.S. nuclear exports, have caused considerable uncertainties in the energy plans of other nations. These nations believe it essential to develop an energy infrastructure less vulnerable to the changing demands of outside energy suppliers.

There are, of course, other motivating factors as well. Some countries with advanced nuclear programs regard reprocessing as a potentially important tool for managing nuclear waste, not just technologically but politically as well. In some countries, it is only the promise that nuclear waste will be reprocessed rather than stored indefinitely that permits governments to overcome opposition to their nuclear power programs on environmental grounds. In these countries U.S. opposition to or interference with reprocessing would be regarded as jeopardizing not just some marginal adjunct to their nuclear programs but the programs themselves.

These are serious concerns, just as plutonium's potential for use in nuclear explosives is a serious concern. We have been faced with the need to develop a realistic policy that takes both sets of concerns into account. And I think we have managed to do this.

Stated very succinctly, it is the policy of the United States not to seek to inhibit or set back such civil reprocessing and civil plutonium use in countries with advanced nuclear power programs where it does not constitute a proliferation risk, provided that certain strict conditions and controls are maintained.

The Reagan Administration recognizes full well that plutonium is a dangerous material, the use of which must be carefully controlled and safeguarded. The President has categorically reaffirmed our commitment to inhibiting the transfer of sensitive nuclear material where the danger of proliferation requires restraint. We believe that sensitive nuclear facilities and activities should be limited to those countries where their presence results in no significant risk of proliferation. We have urged that this view be accepted as an international norm. We have initiated and participated in a number of multilateral efforts to improve safeguards on plutonium and to reduce the risk of its use for nonpeaceful purposes. These have included efforts to revise and upgrade the Zangger committee trigger list on exports of reprocessing equipment and close cooperation with the International Atomic Energy Agency (IAEA) and other nations on developing more efficient and effective measures for safeguarding reprocessing plants and facilities where plutonium is present.

We are thus alert to the potential risks and are at the forefront of efforts to minimize them. But at the same time we are simply not in a position to dictate or prescribe a policy on reprocessing and plutonium use to developed countries with advanced nuclear programs that value the capability to use plutonium in meeting their future energy needs.

Misconception About U.S. Consent Rights

There is a misconception that the United States controls the world's plutonium and that all we have to do is say no and reprocessing and plutonium use will quickly come to an end. I would like to correct this misconception. In the case of the European Atomic Energy Community (EURATOM), where much of the planning for breeder reactor development and thermal recycle is taking place, the United States does not presently have consent rights over EURATOM's reprocessing of U.S.-origin spent fuel. According to a recent study by Mr. Myron Kratzer of International Energy Associates, Ltd., by the year 2000, the EURATOM countries will have accumulated in spent fuel and in separated form more than 330 metric tons of fissile plutonium, none of it subject to U.S. reprocessing controls. Even assuming a new or revised agreement for cooperation granting the U.S. consent rights over all U.S.-origin material, including material we have previously supplied as well as material we might supply in the future, nearly 290 of the 330 metric tons will still not be subject to U.S. consent rights, because it will be derived from non-U.S. sources. I might note that these estimates are based on conservative assumptions regarding the rate of plutonium production in EURATOM from now until the end of the century.

In the case of other advanced nuclear countries where the United States currently does enjoy consent rights, these rights apply only to a portion of the material now present or expected to be present. According to Mr. Kratzer's study, by the year 2000, Japan will have accumulated 11.3 metric tons of fissile plutonium not subject to U.S. control, Spain 18.9 metric tons, Sweden 2.4 metric tons, and Switzerland 4.2 metric tons.

The implication is clear: The United States has no legal basis, nor can it hope to acquire a legal basis, for preventing the advanced nuclear nations of Western Europe and Japan from using large quantities of plutonium in their thermal recycle or fast breeder-reactor programs.

It has been argued, of course, that even in the absence of enforceable consent rights, the United States should seek to persuade these countries against plutonium use, if necessary, by exercising other forms of leverage. But here too some hard facts must be reckoned with.

Use of Plutonium for Energy

The nations of EURATOM and Japan have repeatedly made clear that they regard plutonium use as essential, even crucial, to their civil energy plans. Indeed, they already have large investments in reprocessing technology of their own; active programs of research, development, and demonstration for advanced nuclear fuel cycles using plutonium; and sizable quantities of separated plutonium already available for use. They are intimately familiar with the arguments against civil plutonium use and they do not find them compelling. If, in the face of this clearly expressed determination on the part of EURATOM and Japan to proceed on their present course, the United States was to attempt to dissuade them by resorting to pressure in this or other areas of our relationship, it would risk a serious unravelling of cooperation not only in nonproliferation matters but also in other areas equally vital to U.S. interest. The price could be heavy, indeed.

It is sometimes argued that reprocessing and use of plutonium in civil nuclear power programs by the industrialized countries will set a "bad example" for countries with developing nuclear programs, which will inevitably seek to imitate the former in this regard. But it is by no means clear that a simple desire to emulate the industrialized world has ever been the primary motivation for any Third World nuclear program. To the extent that emulation is a factor at all, it is much more likely to manifest itself as a desire to match a neighboring country's program step-for-step. And, more importantly, there is no evidence that self-denial on the part of the industrialized world is likely to lead to similar forbearance on the part of Third World nations. It was analogously argued in the late 1970s that U.S. forbearance in reprocessing and civil plutonium use would prompt other countries with advanced nuclear programs to follow a similar path.

Another argument of those who oppose the present U.S. policy on reprocessing and plutonium use is that by encouraging such activities or at least permitting them to go forward it hastens the day when plutonium will be a commodity in routine commercial use and thus more susceptible to diversion or access by nuclear terrorists. It is sometimes added, as a corollary, that the present Administration is not doing enough to defend against nuclear terrorism.

Protections for Plutonium

It is true that increasing use of plutonium in civil nuclear power programs poses new challenges for providing adequate safeguards and physical protection. But we believe these challenges can be met. The United States has taken the lead in developing improved physical protection techniques requisite to insure that plutonium will not fall into terrorist hands. Plutonium is *not* just another commodity, and it is not and will not be treated as such.

As to the Administration's position on nuclear terrorism, we regard it as a potentially very grave threat to the nation's security. We have taken and will continue to take the necessary and appropriate steps to prevent nuclear terrorism. It was at the initiative of the executive branch that Congress enacted tough criminal legislation in 1982 to cover potential terrorist acts involving nuclear material. Internationally, the Administration has worked vigorously to promote agreement among the major nuclear suppliers to require adequate physical security measures as a condition for their nuclear exports. And it is strongly urging all countries that have not yet signed and/or ratified the Convention on the Physical Protection of Nuclear Material to do so at the earliest possible date.

Implementing U.S. Policy

Let me turn now to the ways in which we are implementing our policy on reprocessing and plutonium use. We are proceeding with caution and prudence.

We have continued the practice of previous Administrations of approving, on a case-by-case basis, requests by advanced nuclear countries, such as Japan and Switzerland, to reprocess U.S.-controlled nuclear material for peaceful use in their civil nuclear programs.

In addition, in the context of seeking new or amended agreements for cooperation that incorporate the more stringent nonproliferation conditions called for by the Nuclear Nonproliferation Act, and in order to help restore confidence in the United States as a reliable supplier, we have discussed with Japan and the countries of EURATOM certain long-term arrangements for reprocessing of material subject to U.S. control and use of the derived plutonium.

More specifically, we have discussed with Japan an advance-consent arrangement for reprocessing, retransfers for reprocessing, and use of plutonium from U.S.-controlled material in a Japanaese program for which we have sufficient information to make the necessary statutory determinations. Section 123 of the Atomic Energy Act provides that the President must make a determination that a proposed agreement will promote, and will not constitute an unreasonable risk to, the common defense and security. In addition, we would not approve reprocessing and retransfers of plutonium for further use unless we determined that these activities would meet the requirements of Section 131 of the act, namely that they not be inimical to the common defense and security and not result in a significant increase in the risk of proliferation.

We envisage that this advance-consent arrangement could include:

• The retransfer of U.S.-origin spent fuel from Japan to facilities in France and the U.K. for reprocessing;
• The reprocessing of U.S.-origin spent fuel at Japan's Tokai-Mura reprocessing plant as well as future reprocessing plants;
• The use of U.S.-origin plutonium in Japan's breeder, advanced reactor, and thermal recycle programs; and
• The return of U.S.-origin separated plutonium from France and the U.K. to Japan for use in the Japanese program.

With respect to EURATOM, the United States does not currently have a right of consent over the reprocessing of U.S.-origin material. In accordance with Section 404 of the Nuclear Nonproliferation Act, we are seeking a new or amended agreement for cooperation with EURATOM containing, *inter alia*, such a right of consent. In the context of seeking this new or amended agreement, we have discussed with EURATOM arrangements for advance, long-term approvals for reprocessing and plutonium use that are essentially the same as those we have discussed with Japan.

In the case of other countries with which we have cooperation agreements, we are prepared to offer advance consent for the transfer of U.S.-origin material to France and the United Kingdom for reprocessing in facilities for which we are able to make the necessary statutory determinations. By way of example, our new agreements for cooperation with Norway and Sweden, which entered into force last year, and our new agreement with Finland, which is now before the Congress, provide U.S. consent in advance to these countries to transfer material subject to the agreements to specified reprocessing facilities in the United Kingdom or France without rechecking with the United States prior to each transfer. In turn, Norway, Sweden, and Finland are required to keep records of any such transfers and to notify the United States of each one. They are also required to obtain prior confirmation from EURATOM that the material will be held within EURATOM subject to the U.S.-EURATOM agreement for cooperation, to retain legal control over any plutonium separated as a result of the transfer, and to obtain prior agreement for any subsequent transfers to another country or for any use of the plutonium.

It should be noted that these U.S. offers of advance, long-term consent have only been made subject to the stringent conditions in new or amended agreements for cooperation continuing to be met, including adequate safeguards and physical security. Moreover, before entering into such an arrangement, we carefully review whether authorizing these activities will result in a significant increase in the risk of proliferation beyond that existing at the time the approval is requested, giving foremost consideration to whether the reprocessing or transfer will take place under conditions that would insure timely warning to the United States of any diversion. We also retain the ability to terminate the arrangement if we ever judge these conditions no longer to be met.

It is our policy, finally, to permit the export of sensitive U.S. reprocessing technology and equipment to Japan and EURATOM provided that the necessary statutory requirements and Nuclear Supplier Group guidelines are satisfied and provided that the recipient has a continuing commitment to nonproliferation and to strengthening IAEA safeguards and physical protection measures at facilities using or deemed to be derived from the U.S.-supplied sensitive technology or equipment. This policy, too, does no more than recognize reality. Japan and several EURATOM countries are building and will continue to build these facilities with or without U.S. technology and equipment. Our maximum attainable objective thus becomes to insure the strongest possible safeguards and physical protection. Our direct involvement in helping design and equip the facilities will help us to achieve our objective in two ways: It gives us some standing to express our views, and it makes U.S. expertise available to help accomplish the objective.

Let me make a few general observations regarding our overall policy:

First, it is not one that endorses or encourages the spread of reprocessing and civil plutonium use. Rather, it is one that recognizes that certain major civil nuclear programs involving reprocessing and plutonium use already exist in countries with advanced nuclear programs posing no proliferation risk, that these programs will go forward regardless of any U.S. attempt at dissuasion, and that a more realistic course is, therefore, to work *with* these select countries to help improve safeguards and controls over the sensitive technology and materials that they are using.

Second, it is not a radical departure from past practice. The previous two Administrations, as well as the present one, have acted favorably on requests by certain West European countries and Japan for U.S. consent to reprocessing. These requests have pertained to the reprocessing of U.S.-origin fuels by Japan at Tokai-Mura and the shipment of spent fuel from Japan and a few other advanced countries to France or the United Kingdom for reprocessing. Some of the U.S. approvals, although not contained in agreements for cooperation, have run for a number of years and have not been limited to specific quantities of nuclear material. For example, the U.S. approvals for Japanese reprocessing of U.S.-origin material at Tokai-Mura have permitted reprocessing of U.S.-origin fuel for the Japanese research and development program over a several-year period.

Third, it is a policy that makes rational distinctions between close allies and friends that have advanced nuclear programs, share our nonproliferation objectives, and pose no proliferation risk, on the one hand, and countries that could or do pose such a risk, on the other. We continue to seek to inhibit the spread of sensitive materials and technology to countries and regions where there is a risk of proliferation.

In sum, ours is a carefully circumscribed, measured, and restrained policy that we believe will substantially increase the ability of the United States to influence foreign nuclear programs in ways that will help us to achieve our nonproliferation goals. It is a policy consistent with the approaches adopted by Canada and Australia, counties that have strong nonproliferation policies and, like the United States, insist on consent rights as part of their nuclear export policies.

I would like to close with a few additional thoughts on the theme of constancy in U.S. policy. It is quite apparent that the sharp turns in U.S. nuclear policy in recent years have led to serious friction with our nuclear trading partners and a consequent decline in our ability to win their support for important nonproliferation objectives. Only now, after several years of determined effort and relative stability in our policies, are we beginning to reestablish the United States as a predictable and reliable partner for peaceful nuclear cooperation under a regime of adequate safeguards and controls. It would damage the national interest to jeopardize these hard-won gains by taking actions that would prompt our close nuclear trading partners once again to question the constancy and reliability of the United States as a partner in peaceful nuclear cooperation.

I cannot emphasize too strongly that a successful nuclear policy must proceed from a basis of mutual respect and trust. The confidence of our allies and friends in the nuclear area is vital. We must be able to work with them if we are to strengthen the nonproliferation regime.

Some may argue that our ability to work with others counts for little if it does not induce them to forego plutonium use. But such an "all-or-nothing" attitude is shortsighted and lacks appreciation of the possibilities open to us. Our leverage, though certainly limited, can pay substantial dividends if realistically applied. Only if we indicate a willingness to understand the needs and objectives of our friends and allies, we can expect them to work with us to assure needed stringent safeguards and security for plutonium use. We are convinced that this is the course most likely to result in the ever stronger nonproliferation regime we seek.

---

[1] The complete transcript of the hearings will be published by the committee and will be available from the Superintendent of Documents, U.S. Government Printing Office, Washington, D.C. 20402. ∎

U.S.-China Nuclear Cooperation Agreement

Statements by Kenneth L. Adelman, Director of the Arms Control and Disarmament Agency (ACDA), Ambassador Richard T. Kennedy, U.S. permanent representative to the IAEA and special adviser to the Secretary of State on nonproliferation policy and nuclear energy affairs, and Paul D. Wolfowitz, Assistant Secretary for East Asian and Pacific Affairs, before the House Foreign Affairs Committee on July 31, 1985.[1]

MR. ADELMAN

I am pleased to appear before this distinguished committee today to discuss the peaceful nuclear cooperation agreement between the United States and China—the first agreement with a nuclear-weapon state since the Nuclear Non-Proliferation Act.

Before addressing how this agreement advances important nonproliferation interests, I should place it into the broad picture of enhanced U.S.-Chinese consultations on arms control. This type of consultation followed on the heels of the President's April 1984 visit to China. Soon thereafter, in the summer of 1984, I led a delegation of American officials to Beijing to concentrate on arms control. The Chinese reciprocated by having their arms control experts come here just last month.

Nonproliferation has been a key topic in these discussions with the Chinese. I explained to the Chinese that nonproliferation is one of the highest U.S. priorities as well as the one area of arms control which has been perhaps the most successful. This agreement continues that record.

This committee has, of course, already received ACDA's Nuclear Proliferation Assessment Statement on the agreement, which we provided to the President prior to his approval of the agreement. The prime question before you now—as before the President on July 23—is: "Does this new agreement contribute to U.S. nonproliferation efforts?" I believe the answer is a resounding "yes." Why? Because our agreement with China helps ensure that they are part of the nonproliferation solution rather than part of the problem.

China's Nonproliferation Policy

During the 1960s and 1970s, China rejected nonproliferation norms. They actually portrayed proliferation in a favorable light by openly declaring that the spread of nuclear weapons around the globe would diminish the power of the United States and the Soviet Union and enhance the opportunities for revolution. China denied that a world of more nuclear-weapon states would enhance the risk of nuclear war.

China also undertook no international legal obligations and had no policy to require safeguards and other controls on its nuclear exports. This naturally quickened our concerns about Chinese actions that could help other countries acquire nuclear explosives. Clearly, herein lay the potential for great harm to global nonproliferation efforts in both word and deed. And, needless to tell this committee, words are exceedingly important in this realm. They affect the strength of the international norms and standards upon which nonproliferation ultimately rests.

Against this background, the United States opened talks on peaceful nuclear cooperation with China—first in 1981 and then more intensively in 1983—with ACDA participating in all stages of the negotiations.

After 2 years of negotiations, an agreement was initialed during President Reagan's visit to China. It then became necessary to engage in further discussions with China to clarify matters related to implementation of its nuclear policies. We did not want to proceed until we were completely satisfied. We were willing to wait as long as need be. These discussions concluded successfully at the end of June.

Over these past 2 years, the Chinese Government has taken a number of important nonproliferation steps.

First, it made a pledge that it does "not engage in nuclear proliferation" nor does it "help other countries develop nuclear weapons." The substance of this pledge has been reaffirmed several times by Chinese officials both abroad and within China. In fact, China's sixth National People's Congress made this policy a directive to all agencies of that large and complex government. As such, it constitutes a historic and positive change in China's policies. It helps bolster rather than break down those critical norms and standards that comprise the nonproliferation regime.

Second, in January 1984, China joined the over 100 members of the International Atomic Energy Agency (IAEA), which plays such a critical role in international nonproliferation efforts. This was a necessary step in China's evolution toward acceptance of the basic norms of nuclear supply.

Third, China adopted a policy of requiring IAEA safeguards on its nuclear exports to non-nuclear-weapon states. This, too, was a big plus. Not only could a supplier that did not accept this basic norm directly contribute to spreading uncontrolled nuclear equipment and material to potential nuclear-weapon states, it could also undermine the consensus of supplier countries that has been painstakingly constructed over the past decade.

Fourth, during our hours and hours of discussions, the Chinese have made it clear that they will implement their policies in a manner consistent with the basic nonproliferation practices we and others support so vigorously.

In the short span of 2 years, China has embraced nonproliferation policies and practices, which it had eschewed so vociferously for a quarter of a century. This clearly is a turnabout of historic significance in our efforts to prevent the spread of nuclear weapons. The Chinese are to be applauded for such a change of course.

We can take a measure of pride in this as well. For I believe that the lengthy discussions by the United States and other supplier nations with China, combined with the prospect of agreements for peaceful nuclear cooperation, contributed heavily to these Chinese actions.

Protecting U.S. Interests

We will, of course, watch Chinese practices closely to satisfy ourselves that China's actions are consistent with its words, with our expectations, and with our policies and laws. The Chinese know that. They know that nuclear cooperation with us rests on their strict adherence to basic nonproliferation practices discussed and clarified at such great length. The agreement before you rests on that foundation. It could rest on no other.

As presented in ACDA's Nuclear Proliferation Assessment Statement, all statutory requirements for such agreements have been fully met. Two issues that were subject to protracted negotiations are worth mentioning.

• The agreement before you contains a provision for "mutually acceptable arrangements for exchanges of information and visits" in connection with transfers under its terms. This was done to help ensure that all the agreement's provisions will be scrupulously honored. The specifics of visits and information exchanges will be worked out with the Chinese before any licenses are issued for nuclear exports. They will permit visits by U.S. personnel to sites in China wherever our material or equipment, subject to this agreement, is located.

• The second issue concerns the right of prior approval over reprocessing of spent fuel subject to the agreement. The agreement notes that neither party contemplates reprocessing such material. In fact, activities of this kind are not likely to become an issue in China for at least 15 years. While the language dealing with this issue does differ from that in other agreements, it is clear that China cannot reprocess without U.S. approval.

Other aspects of our assessment statement can be fully explained in response to your questions. Let me just add now that U.S. interests are fully protected. This agreement includes many written guarantees and controls to ensure that material, equipment, or technology supplied by the United States will not be misused.

If they are misused, or if China's nonproliferation policies do not live up to their pledges and to our expectations, we have clear recourse. We hope and expect that this agreement will lead to significant peaceful nuclear commerce with China—otherwise the President would not have sent it to you—but the agreement is only an umbrella agreement. That is, it permits, but does not require, the export of any nuclear items. Thus, if Chinese behavior ever became inconsistent with our understandings, we would suspend the licensing of exports. The Chinese know that.

Conclusion

China's recent nonproliferation steps are and will be critical to our mission of bolstering vital nonproliferation norms and standards. Our long talks with the Chinese, as well as the prospects of civil nuclear cooperation with the United States and other suppliers, contributed to these major improvements in China's nonproliferation policies. Further, as I said, the agreement will enhance our efforts to cooperate to strengthen nonproliferation norms and actions.

Thus, I believe this agreement is fully in U.S. national interests. I trust that, after a thorough consideration of all the issues, you and the whole Congress will agree.

AMBASSADOR KENNEDY

I am pleased to have this opportunity to speak to you today on the proposed agreement between the United States and the People's Republic of China (P.R.C.) concerning the peaceful uses of nuclear energy. This agreement was signed in Washington on July 23. We believe this agreement is important to the interests of both countries and supportive of our shared nonproliferation objectives.

The agreement establishes the basis for cooperation in a variety of the peaceful applications of nuclear energy. It provides the basis for export of nuclear reactors, fuel, components, and the exchange of technology including cooperation in health, safety, and the environmental implications of the peaceful uses of nuclear energy. The agreement is not, however, a commitment to supply. Rather, it provides the legal framework within which nuclear cooperation may take place. Once the agreement enters into force, nuclear reactors, components, and nuclear fuel may be exported under licenses issued by the Nuclear Regulatory Commission, in accordance with existing law and regulations.

The agreement permits nuclear cooperation between the United States and China exclusively in the peaceful uses of nuclear energy. It contains reciprocal commitments by the United States and China that nuclear facilities and materials subject to the agreement will not be used for any nuclear explosive or military purpose. This guarantee, as well as other assurances and controls in the agreement, will help preserve the distinction between the civil and military use of nuclear energy. It is also important to stress that cooperation under the agreement is limited to nonsensitive aspects of the nuclear fuel cycle. It expressly excludes the transfer of any sensitive nuclear technology such as enrichment or reprocessing. Nor does it in any way require that technology of strategic or military significance be transferred.

Provisions of the Agreement

I would now like to turn to a brief examination of the specific provisions of the agreement we have signed with the People's Republic of China. The text of the agreement and supporting documents developed during its review within the executive branch have been transmitted to the Congress by the President. The text, in most respects, does not differ significantly from new and renegotiated agreements for peaceful nuclear cooperation which we have concluded with other countries since enactment of the Nuclear Non-Proliferation Act of 1978 and which have been before Congress for review. The agreement with China fully meets all the requirements specified in Section 123 of the Atomic Energy Act of 1954, as amended, for nuclear cooperation agreements with nuclear-weapon states.

Specifically, section 123 requires that such agreements contain several guarantees by the cooperating partner.

The first guarantee is that no nuclear materials or equipment subject to the agreement will be used for any nuclear explosive device, for research on or development of any nuclear explosive device, or for any other military purpose. This requirement is met by article 5, paragraph 3, of the proposed agreement with the P.R.C.

The second guarantee required is that no nuclear material or equipment subject to the agreement will be transferred beyond the jurisdiction or control of the cooperating party without the agreement of the United States. This requirement is met by article 5, paragraph 1, of the agreement.

The third guarantee required is that adequate physical security will be maintained with respect to any nuclear material subject to the agreement. This requirement is met by article 6 of the agreement.

The fourth guarantee required is that no nuclear material subject to the agreement will be enriched, reprocessed, altered in form or content, or (in the case of weapons-usable materials) stored without the prior agreement of the United States. This requirement is met by article 5, paragraph 2, of the agreement.

The Chinese understood U.S. legal requirements, said they had no plans to undertake the activities in question, and were concerned that, in the event of possible future Chinese changes of plans, the United States would give a timely response. While the language that was negotiated is different from that appearing in other agreements, it provides that China may not engage in any of the specified activities without the agreement of the United States. If long-term arrangements are not agreed, it makes clear that each side will refrain from such activities if either side objects—i.e., until there is mutual agreement between the United States and the P.R.C. Both the United States and the P.R.C. understand this.

All of these guarantees are reciprocal in nature and would apply to Chinese exports to the United States. They are, in substance, identical to those in all our other post-1978 agreements. Unlike the other agreements concluded since 1978, however, this one is with a single nuclear-weapon state, as such states are defined in the Treaty on the Non-Proliferation of Nuclear Weapons (NPT). This agreement does not provide for International Atomic Energy Agency safeguards in the P.R.C. on nuclear material, equipment, or facilities subject to the agreement since they are not required for nuclear-weapon states by either the Atomic Energy Act or the NPT. But neither does the agreement foreclose such safeguards, were China to undertake a voluntary offer with the IAEA as the other nuclear-weapon states have done.

The agreement contains provisions for consultations, exchanges of information, and visits to the sites of materials, facilities, and components subject to the agreement. The agreement also provides for exchanges of views and information on each country's national accounting and control systems and consultations on physical protection measures. The purpose of these exchanges of visits and information is to ensure that the provisions of the agreement are effectively and openly carried out, including the provision that cooperation will be for exclusively peaceful purposes. Those provisions have the duration envisaged in Section 123(a)(1) of the Atomic Energy Act.

Benefits of the Agreement

There are very substantial benefits to be derived from this agreement. The agreement will lay the groundwork for strengthening economic ties between the United States and China and create new opportunities for U.S. companies to participate in China's expanding energy sector. China has begun the development of a major nuclear power program to meet its growing energy needs. The Chinese view nuclear energy as playing a key role in China's industrial development and modernization program. U.S. firms are already involved in other energy projects in China to develop coal, oil, and other energy resources, and we believe that participating in a diversified and well-balanced energy program in China is supportive of U.S. interests.

A most important benefit of peaceful nuclear cooperation between the United States and China is the opportunity it provides for both countries to work together to prevent the spread of nuclear explosives. President Reagan has declared that the nonproliferation of nuclear weapons is a fundamental national security and foreign policy objective of the United States. This consideration was at the top of our agenda during our talks with the Chinese and will remain the paramount concern of the United States. Clearly, cooperation in the peaceful uses of nuclear energy must rest on a foundation of shared views and principles on the necessity of deterring the threat of nuclear proliferation.

Since negotiations began on the proposed agreement, China made significant new statements of its nonproliferation policy which show that China is opposed to the spread of nuclear explosives to additional countries. On January 10, 1984, at the White House, Premier Zhao stated:

> China does not advocate nor encourage proliferation. We do not engage in proliferation ourselves, nor do we help other countries develop nuclear weapons.

Premier Zhao reiterated this statement in February in Beijing and at the sixth National People's Congress in May. The Premier's speech to the National People's Congress is the closest equivalent in China to a presidential "State of the Union" address. The statement was endorsed by the National People's Congress and published as official policy.

In January 1985, the official Chinese press published a statement by Vice Premier Li Peng that China has no present or future intention to help nonnuclear-weapon states develop nuclear weapons and that China's present or future cooperation with other countries is confined to peaceful purposes. The Chinese have made clear to us that when they say that they will not assist other countries to develop nuclear weapons, this also applies to all nuclear explosives. This is a basic Chinese policy which we believe will guide China's nuclear cooperation in the future.

China has also taken important steps to participate in international nonproliferation efforts. It joined the International Atomic Energy Agency in January 1984 and has stated that it requires the application of IAEA safeguards to nuclear exports to non-nuclear-weapon states. In adopting this policy, China is acting in accordance with existing international norms for nuclear trade.

As China undertakes nuclear cooperation with other countries and moves into international nuclear affairs, it is vital that we have a bilateral forum which allows us to work closely with China to maintain and strengthen the international nonproliferation regime. The agreement itself establishes a formal framework for consultations enabling regular exchanges of views and information on matters of mutual interest, including means to prevent the spread of nuclear explosives.

Our contacts with the Chinese have already demonstrated that they appreciate the importance we attach to nonproliferation. We are satisfied that the policies they have adopted are consistent with our own basic views. Formalizing our ties in the peaceful uses of nuclear energy through an agreement for cooperation will provide a means to advance our shared objectives.

We believe the agreement serves the national security and nonproliferation interests of the United States. We believe it deserves the full support of the Congress.

MR. WOLFOWITZ

It is a pleasure for me to join Secretary [of Energy John] Herrington, ACDA Director Adelman, and Ambassador Kennedy to discuss with you the U.S.-P.R.C. agreement on peaceful nuclear cooperation. In my prepared remarks, I would like to stress the importance of this agreement in our overall relationship with the P.R.C.

But first, a word about the road we traveled before the agreement was signed last week. Mr. Adelman's and Ambassador Kennedy's statements explain the importance of this agreement to our nonproliferation goals, and I do not want to go over the same ground.

But I would like to underscore that U.S. nonproliferation concerns were paramount in our negotiations with the Chinese on the agreement. The requirements of U.S. nonproliferation policy and law—and not other foreign policy considerations—were absolute determinants of the shape and content of the agreement which we initialed and signed and of the discussions related to it. Despite the importance we attach to our overall relationship, great though it is, we repeatedly emphasized to the Chinese that the relationship could in no way obviate the need to meet our nonproliferation requirements and the requirements of U.S. law.

Only when our nonproliferation concerns were met—concerns addressed in Mr. Adelman's and Ambassador Kennedy's testimony—were U.S. agencies able to move forward with a recommendation to the President that the agreement be signed. Over the past year and more, many people in our government worked hard on this issue. Discussions with the Chinese continued through diplomatic channels for many months prior to Ambassador Kennedy's June trip to Beijing.

The groundwork was completed during that June visit. But further interagency consultations here, reporting to the President, and the President's own decision to approve were required before the agreement could be signed. We were pleased that these procedures were completed in time for the Li visit, which offered a propitious occasion for a signing ceremony, but we were fully prepared to take more time if that had been necessary.

Now that U.S. Government concerns have been met and the agreement is signed and before Congress, let me turn to the question of what this agreement will mean for bilateral relations between the United States and China.

Implications for U.S.-China Relations

The first images that some in the United States might conjure up are those of pure economic gain for our side: billions of dollars in contracts; massive U.S. equipment exports; aid to the stricken American nuclear power industry; U.S. reactors for the city lights and factories of China.

There is a kernel of truth behind these somewhat exaggerated expectations, but I would submit that dreams of one-sided commercial gain do not constitute the most important positive aspects of our cooperation with China in the peaceful uses of nuclear energy.

Yes, there will be opportunities for American companies to compete for nuclear power business in China. The market is there, and European and Japanese competitors are already active in it. China will look to the outside primarily for assistance in building up its indigenous nuclear power plant manufacturing industry. Over the long run, more than anything, China will want to import technology, modern management methods, and old-fashioned engineering know-how. In these areas—which are vitally important for the safety and efficiency of reactor operation—U.S. companies have a wealth of experience and flexibility, which puts them in a strong competitive position.

Also, there is no doubt that in the first stages of China's nuclear power program—in which three or four nuclear plants will be built, including five to seven reactors—the Chinese industry will want to make major equipment imports. A nuclear cooperation agreement will have to be in force before U.S. companies can apply to the Nuclear Regulatory Commission to ship major reactor components to China.

But beyond its implications for the sale of discrete pieces of equipment for nuclear power reactors in China, the agreement can fill a gap in our relationship with the P.R.C. Once in force, it will become an important support of a general framework of cooperation with China. If we fail to bring it into force, the framework will be that much less coherent and that gap—which you could label "nonproliferation objectives and peaceful cooperation in nuclear energy"—will remain open.

For the past several years, under both Democratic and Republican administrations, the United States has worked to strengthen and broaden political and economic ties with the P.R.C. Seeing a modernizing China as a potential force for peace and stability in East Asia, the United States is committed to assisting China's ongoing modernization effort. The President and other Administration leaders have recognized that, while we and China have our differences, we consider China a friendly country. While not a U.S. ally, neither is China allied with any other power, and it shares some important concerns with us. Holding this basic view of China's position in the world, the United States has sought to regularize our relations.

In areas such as trade, investment, finance, civil aviation, and scientific, technological, and industrial cooperation—to name a few—we have sought to establish a framework of agreements and arrangements consistent with the generally good relations we and China enjoy. In setting up this framework, we and the Chinese have learned a great deal about each other's political and economic systems. Our bilateral agreements offer mutual benefits and mutual obligations. They have been a measure of China's interest in strengthening its ties with us and a test of our commitment to China's modernization.

We think the framework we have built up has not only benefited our bilateral relations but also encouraged China to be a more constructive player in the international arena. From another viewpoint, China's own push to open its economy and society to the outside world after years of isolationism has been an impetus for U.S.-P.R.C. bilateral cooperation. Whatever one's point of view, I think it's fair to say that our framework of cooperation with China and China's opening to the outside are mutually reinforcing and mutually beneficial.

Within the context I've described, the nuclear cooperation agreement will reinforce the Sino-U.S. relationship by furthering both our nonproliferation goals and our cooperation in peaceful uses of nuclear energy. We in the Administration think it is an important agreement—one that deserves the support of the Congress.

To sum up, bringing the present agreement into force will:

• Allow us to maintain constructive consultations with the P.R.C. on nonproliferation issues;
• Give U.S. firms the opportunity to make a significant contribution to the development of China's civil nuclear power industry; and
• Reinforce the overall framework of our relationship with the P.R.C.

---

[1]The complete transcript of the hearings will be published by the committee and will be available from the Superintendent of Documents, U.S. Government Printing Office, Washington, D.C. 20402. ■

NUCLEAR PROLIFERATION: The Current and Future Threat

John H. Glenn

PROLOGUE: *Although the number of nations that openly maintain stockpiles of nuclear weapons has remained constant for nearly 20 years, the delicate fabric of institutional and moral commitments that restrains nuclear proliferation is showing signs of coming unraveled.*

In this essay, John H. Glenn, Democratic senator from Ohio, warns that the world could soon face a nuclear arms race in South Asia and the Middle East. At a time when the international agency responsible for safeguarding nuclear materials is becoming increasingly politicized, more and more nations are gaining access to sensitive technology. Glenn, the principal author of the 1978 Nuclear Nonproliferation Act, which tightened controls on U.S. nuclear exports, argues that the mounting threat of proliferation warrants the highest national attention.

UNFINISHED BUSINESS: NUCLEAR PROLIFERATION

Five nations in the world today overtly manufacture nuclear weapons: the United States, the Soviet Union, Great Britain, France, and China. At least 10 other nations are capable of producing nuclear weapons in a relatively short time; two may already have done so clandestinely. Sixteen other nations are moving toward a nuclear weapons capability, and evidence suggests that there may be military purposes behind the nuclear programs in eight of these countries.

The establishment of Nuclear Emergency Search Teams (NEST) in the United States to investigate threats to detonate nuclear devices or to use nuclear material in some harmful way is testimony to the existence of a terrorist interest in nuclear materials. Nuclear weapons have been designed and tested that can fit into a golf bag.

Thus, while the world's attention has recently been focused on the nuclear arms race between the superpowers, developments are occurring that in the future will put nuclear weapons into the hands of other nations, including some in politically volatile areas of the world. This increases the likelihood of such weapons being used during conflict and threatens us with the specter of terrorist acquisition of portable nuclear explosive devices.

The acquisition of nuclear weapons by one nation tends to encourage proliferation by inducing others to seek a matching nuclear deterrent. This is especially dangerous when the acquiring countries lack the sophisticated command, control, and communications systems necessary to prevent the unintended use of these weapons in times of crisis. The world has been lulled into a false sense of security on this potentially disastrous issue by a natural preoccupation with the activities of existing nuclear weapon states and by the fact that no new *overt* nuclear weapon state has come into existence since 1964. Nevertheless, the threat of proliferation is real and growing, and we should accord it the highest level of attention.

During the past 40 years, a variety of national and international policies and institutions have evolved to curtail the spread of nuclear weapons. Collectively, these are known as the world's nonproliferation regime. Foremost in this regime is the Nuclear Non-Proliferation Treaty (NPT), which went into effect in 1970 and has since been signed by 118 nonweapon states and 3 weapon states, Great Britain, the United States, and the Soviet Union. Two weapon states, France and China, have not signed. The nations adhering to the treaty, together with France, which has said it will act in accordance with the treaty, account for 98 percent of the world's nuclear power capacity, all of the world's exports of enriched uranium, and almost all of the reprocessing capability.

In essence, the Non-Proliferation Treaty promises full access to peaceful nuclear technology, subject to international safeguards, to any country that promises to forgo acquiring nuclear weapons. The treaty bars signatories from helping other countries to acquire or make nuclear weapons and prohibits nonweapon states from acquiring nuclear weapons or using nuclear energy for any military purpose. It requires non-nuclear weapon states to place under international safeguards all their nuclear facilities in which fissionable material—material suitable for use in nuclear weapons—is used; that is, these facilities must be subject to a system of materials accounting and inspection carried out by the International Atomic Energy Agency (IAEA). The safeguards process is essentially a record-keeping, not a policing, activity; the IAEA has no authority to impose sanctions against a nation that diverts fissionable material to military purposes.

In return for these restrictions, the treaty guarantees "the inalienable right of all the parties to the treaty to develop research, production and use of nuclear energy for peaceful purposes without discrimination" and obligates the parties to "facilitate... the fullest possible exchange of equipment, materials and scientific and technological information for the peaceful uses of nuclear energy." The treaty extends this right to acquire and use peaceful nuclear energy even to "peaceful nuclear explosives"—bombs by any other name—for engineering projects and mineral extraction, but restricts possession of explosive devices only to weapon states. Another key article of the treaty requires the nuclear weapon states to "pursue negotiations in good faith on effective measures relating to cessation of the nuclear arms race at an early date and to nuclear disarmament, and on a treaty on general and complete disarmament under strict and effective international control." Adherence to the provisions of the Non-Proliferation Treaty is entirely voluntary. There are no sanctions for violations, and a signatory may withdraw from the treaty on 90-days notice by declaring that its "supreme" interests are jeopardized by extraordinary events "related to the subject matter of the treaty."

Other elements of the nonproliferation regime include: formal and informal agreements among nuclear suppliers to exercise restraint in their exports and to not sell certain kinds of materials or equipment without requiring that safeguards be imposed; alliances and other security arrangements to influence nations to not acquire nuclear weapons; international networks of intelligence gathering and exchange concerning nuclear activities worldwide; and individual national policies, including export laws such as the U.S. Nuclear Nonproliferation Act of 1978, to discourage misuse of nuclear technology. This act is designed to establish tighter criteria for nuclear exports from the United States, to impose controls on the separation and use of plutonium from spent reactor fuel of U.S. origin, and to provide for sanctions against nations that violate safeguards or engage in other actions indicating movement toward a nuclear weapons program.

II

During the past decade, concern has grown worldwide over the issue of horizontal proliferation—the acquisition of nuclear weapons by nations that do not yet have them. This has helped to produce some cooperation among nuclear suppliers to limit voluntarily certain kinds of nuclear trade when proliferation risks are evident. But the extent of cooperation is still inadequate, and major problems remain that could threaten future progress.

Any realistic policy must address two basic elements in horizontal proliferation: the political will and the technical capability of the potential proliferator. West Germany, Japan, Canada, and Sweden have the technical capability to produce nuclear weapons but have chosen not to do so because they believe their security concerns are best met by other means.

Thus, a key factor in preventing horizontal proliferation is to assist nations in meeting their legitimate security needs, thereby reducing their motivation to obtain nuclear weapons. Alliances, economic and military assistance, and the fostering of better international relations—including confidence-building measures between rivals—can all contribute significantly to this sense of security.

In addition, the attitude of the weapon states toward the role of nuclear weapons in their own security can affect the motivation of nonweapon states with security problems. That is, if the nuclear powers react to international tensions by building more nuclear weapons, the connection between security and nuclear weapons is enhanced. On the other hand, the evident reluctance of weapon states to use nuclear weapons in military situations suggests that their usefulness is limited. The latter point is also made by agreements to reduce nuclear arms.

The risk of horizontal proliferation also depends on the technical capability of states to build nuclear weapons. That, in turn, depends on access to fissile material, either plutonium or highly enriched uranium. States that have access to an ongoing supply of such materials essentially have a nuclear arsenal within their grasp, even if they still face some difficult technical problems in the fabrication of bombs and triggering mechanisms. If uranium enrichment (which produces highly enriched uranium and requires no nuclear reactor) and reprocessing technology (which separates plutonium from spent nuclear fuel) become widespread, proliferation can no longer be controlled from the standpoint of technical capability. The problem, therefore, becomes more difficult. For this reason, the supplier nations, including West Germany and France, that formerly demonstrated an indifference to the problem by signing agreements to export reprocessing plants to such nations as Brazil, Pakistan, and South Korea, have since agreed to exercise restraint in transferring these sensitive nuclear technologies. (The Pakistan and South Korea agreements were subsequently cancelled.)

Unfortunately, this does not mean there is agreement to restrict the use of plutonium and highly enriched uranium (particularly the former) in the nuclear reactors of the future. Although a current worldwide glut of uranium and enrichment capacity has eliminated shortages of fuel for nuclear power plants, a number of industrialized and near-industrialized countries are pursuing research and development on a breeder reactor that operates on a uranium oxide-plutonium oxide fuel and can theoretically produce more plutonium than it consumes. Some of these countries are also interested in eventually operating their conventional nuclear reactors with such a mixed-oxide fuel. This threatens to create a "plutonium economy" in these countries, putting tons of plutonium into the commercial sphere and raising the availability of plutonium by theft, black market purchase, or other illegal means. Furthermore, it legitimizes the commercial production and use of weapons material, thereby making it far more difficult to discern the true intent of other states seeking the same material. Because a nuclear bomb can be constructed using only a few kilograms of plutonium, it is not clear that any international safeguard system would be adequate to deal with such plutonium commercialization.

Although the United States can avoid using plutonium as a fuel in most circumstances, other nations are not as rich in alternatives. This raises an important policy issue: to what extent should the United States help other nations carry on research and development programs aimed at producing plutonium for breeders or for conventional reactors? The United States can currently control the reprocessing of U.S.-origin spent fuel outside of the countries belonging to Euratom, an organ of the European Economic Community, and seeks to extend its influence to the decisions of this European consortium as well. But for the United States to refuse to permit reprocessing in a country with good nonproliferation credentials, such as Japan, would provoke hostility, the loss of future fuel enrichment service contracts, and a decline in future U.S. influence over that country's nuclear program. However, for the United States to relax restrictions on reprocessing would be to risk accelerating the emergence of plutonium economies in other nations and to reduce our own national security.

Fortunately, the economics of the breeder reactor, reprocessing, and the recycling of plutonium into conventional reactors now appears to be quite unfavorable. All such programs—including that of the French, the leaders in the field—are being cut back. Hence, more time is available to consider alternatives to advanced nuclear technology and to improve safeguards. But if the alternatives fail, pressures may again increase for the widespread use of plutonium in power reactors. The United States must be prepared with policy contingencies if the existing safeguard system remains inadequate to the task.

III

In addition to horizontal proliferation, the problem of vertical proliferation continues: that is, stockpiles of weapons belonging to the nuclear powers are increasing. The United States and the Soviet Union together reportedly possess more than 50,000 nuclear warheads. At a time when arms control negotiations have broken down, proposals to develop newer and more modern weapons are being favorably received in both Washington and Moscow. This buildup is increasingly unacceptable to the nonweapon states, which insist that the nuclear powers live up to their obligations under Article VI of the Non-Proliferation Treaty, which calls for the nuclear weapon states to pursue genuine arms control agreements. Failure to pursue such agreements was a major issue at the 1980 NPT review conference and is quite likely to be so again at the 1985 conference.

Considerable time would be required, even under favorable diplomatic conditions, for the superpowers to negotiate a *verifiable* treaty involving significant nuclear arms reductions. This has motivated some proliferation experts to search for meaningful near-term arms control objectives that would have a beneficial impact on nonproliferation as well as on U.S.-Soviet relations. A comprehensive ban on nuclear weapons testing is one example of such a measure.

The main stumbling block to a comprehensive test ban in the past has been the issue of verifying compliance. Scientists disagree about the threshold at which underground nuclear explosions can be detected and whether

UNFINISHED BUSINESS: NUCLEAR PROLIFERATION

explosions can be distinguished from seismic events, such as earthquakes. Many now believe that our instrumentation, which will surely improve, is sufficiently sensitive that a test ban would not pose significant risk to our national security. For its part, the Soviet Union has not rejected the possibility of permitting unmanned detection instruments on its territory. U.S. policymakers will have to decide whether the residual risks of signing a test ban treaty exceed the growing risk of failing to check the unraveling of the nonproliferation regime.

In addition to the comprehensive test ban, a *verifiable* agreement by the United States and the Soviet Union to halt or limit the production of separated fissile material (highly enriched uranium or plutonium) would also have a beneficial effect on the climate for both nuclear arms control and nonproliferation. Eventually, all the weapon states would have to join in such an agreement if it were to be fully effective.

IV

Although 121 countries have signed the Non-Proliferation Treaty, a significant number of nations still have not, including some that are known to be considering or actively pursuing a nuclear weapons program and others that are developing unsafeguarded nuclear facilities that could provide fissile material for a future weapons program.

Israel and South Africa reportedly have undeclared nuclear weapons or are producing weapons-grade material. India, which has exploded a fission device, is believed to be maintaining a stockpile of unsafeguarded plutonium and can add to this stockpile at will.

For several years, Pakistan has been engaged in a worldwide effort to purchase or otherwise acquire plans, components, equipment, and technology for the construction of a gas centrifuge nuclear enrichment plant to produce highly enriched uranium. (A. Q. Khan, head of Pakistan's nuclear enrichment project, was accused of stealing plans for a centrifuge facility from a Dutch company. He was convicted in absentia by a Dutch court.) Pakistan, with only one small nuclear power plant, has also built a reprocessing plant and is reportedly working on bomb-triggering mechanisms.

Argentina and Brazil have both been interested in developing capabilities for reprocessing plutonium and for producing highly enriched uranium. Until its recent change of government, Argentina was well on its way to achieving this capability with indigenous, unsafeguarded facilities. The future plans of the Argentine government in this area are unclear. Brazil has an agreement with West Germany that provides for German export of facilities for the full fuel-cycle processing of nuclear fuels, both reprocessing and enrichment (under safeguards). Brazil is developing unsafeguarded facilities as well. Neither Argentina nor Brazil is presently committed to adhering to the Treaty of Tlatelolco, which entered into force in 1968 and is designed to create a nuclear-weapon-free zone in Latin America.

In addition to the above nonsignatory nations, some parties to the Non-Proliferation Treaty have engaged in nuclear activities that raise suspicions about their future intent. These nations include Iraq, Libya, Iran, South

Korea, and Taiwan. Alarmed by Iraqi activities, the Israelis launched an air strike that destroyed a research reactor near Baghdad on June 7, 1981.

The common motives that link these countries are rivalry and insecurity. For example, India produces her "peaceful nuclear explosion" to deter China; Pakistan develops the bomb to deter India. South Africa and Israel may produce nuclear weapons to deter military assaults by hostile forces vastly superior in number; Arab countries such as Iraq and Libya want to counter any Israeli nuclear advantage. Argentina and Brazil vie for political supremacy in South America and may see nuclear weapons capability as enhancing their efforts. South Korea worries about North Korean military superiority and the possible removal of U.S. protection. Taiwan is concerned about its future as China grows in strength and influence.

American diplomacy and policy will have to be flexible in dealing with these diverse situations, and in most cases international cooperation, including coordinated diplomacy, will be required to prevent the present situation from worsening.

V

A review conference is held every five years to examine how the Non-Proliferation Treaty is working and to search for a consensus on ways to improve it. In addition, parties to the treaty are to decide in 1995 on whether or not to extend the treaty. The past two review conferences held in 1975 and 1980 were rancorous affairs, with some parties charging that the supplier states, especially the United States, had not lived up to their obligations under Article IV, which obligates the supplier states to share the benefits of nuclear technology. And, as mentioned earlier, several nations protested that the superpowers had failed to meet their obligations under Article VI to curb their own nuclear arms race.

The nuclear technology issue is exacerbated by the fact that some nations that are not parties to the Non-Proliferation Treaty receive more technical assistance from the IAEA than do parties to the treaty, and that only the United States, Canada, and Australia require all recipients of nuclear trade to satisfy essentially the same safeguard requirements as are required for NPT parties. Because other suppliers are not as meticulous in their trading practices, some NPT signatories have begun to question the value of their nonproliferation commitment. Some have even hinted that unless the supplier nations and the superpowers better fulfill their obligations under Articles IV and VI, some nations may defect from the treaty.

Should the NPT collapse in 1995 or before, a major tool for maintaining the international nonproliferation regime would be lost. On the other hand, as Iraq, Libya, Iran, South Korea, and Taiwan make amply clear, the NPT is not adequate to assure the nuclear suppliers that all signatory countries are sufficiently committed to nonproliferation to allow transfers of sensitive nuclear technology, even with safeguards. Straddling the line between supporting the NPT and strengthening nuclear export controls will require deft maneuvering by the United States and other supplier nations.

UNFINISHED BUSINESS: NUCLEAR PROLIFERATION

VI

The International Atomic Energy Agency has managed a difficult transition from an agency whose primary focus was the promotion of nuclear energy and technical assistance to an agency in which the safeguard function is no longer a subordinate activity. But difficulties remain and are growing. The agency has been greatly politicized during the past decade, with Israel and South Africa under periodic attack for reasons unrelated to their agency obligations. In 1982 the United States walked out of the organization for several months to protest a move to strip the Israelis of their credentials at the International Atomic Energy Agency General Conference that year because of Israel's attack on the Iraqi reactor. The Israeli issue has still not been resolved, and the IAEA General Conference of 1984 voted to postpone the issue of imposing sanctions against Israel for another year.

The agency's 156 inspectors are responsible for monitoring the whereabouts of some 48,000 tons of nuclear material worldwide (including 6.8 tons of separated plutonium and 11 tons of highly enriched uranium) at roughly 320 sites in more than 50 countries. Because of a shortage of qualified inspectors, the IAEA must husband its resources to ensure that the most sensitive facilities are properly safeguarded. (Of the IAEA's 1984 budget of $143 million, $37 million was allocated for safeguards.) In particular, bulk-handling facilities, through which highly enriched uranium and plutonium flow, require continuous monitoring by resident inspectors. In a sufficiently large plant, state-of-the-art measurement techniques do not allow the IAEA, on the basis of measurements alone, to declare that diversions have not occurred; the limit of error on materials unaccounted for may still allow significant quantities of fissile material to escape without detection. To raise the level of confidence, an effective surveillance and detection system must be installed in addition to materials accounting and inspection activities.

Serious doubts exist as to whether the IAEA will ever have sufficient trained manpower to meet its own technical objectives for ensuring the early detection of a diversion of nuclear material. (As mentioned earlier, the IAEA has no police authority or ability to *prevent* diversion.) To raise its public credibility substantially, the agency would have to initiate unannounced inspections, end the secrecy surrounding inspection results, undertake closer observation of nuclear operations using both instruments and human monitors, and refuse to allow inspected states an unlimited veto of chosen inspectors.

The Israeli raid on Iraq's safeguarded Tammuz I reactor was clearly a vote of no confidence in the safeguard system. In September 1980, Iraq temporarily evicted all French nuclear technicians working on the project, saying it could not guarantee their protection during the Iran-Iraq war. Then, in November, Iraq announced it was suspending IAEA inspection of its nuclear facilities until the war was over. Meanwhile, the Iraqi government was refusing a French request to substitute less highly enriched uranium for bomb-grade uranium in the reactor core. The Israeli air raid that destroyed the reactor was the first direct military action ever undertaken to prevent another country from furthering its nuclear weapons capability.

VII

Maintaining effective international nonproliferation norms requires a commitment by nuclear suppliers to a common set of standards. While some progress has occurred in recent years in extending the list of equipment and components that should carry safeguards when transferred, there is still significant disagreement among suppliers on such fundamental questions as whether nuclear trade should be allowed with nonweapon states that have unsafeguarded facilities. The French, in particular, believe that a requirement for comprehensive safeguards is too rigid, while other suppliers, notably the United States, argue that a strict policy enhances the political value of adherence to the treaty.

The problem of maintaining common supplier standards is likely to worsen as so-called "second-tier" suppliers enter the picture. India, China, South Africa, Argentina, Brazil, Spain, and Niger are all gearing up to compete in the world nuclear export market. Unfortunately, the commitment of some of these countries to a strong nonproliferation regime varies from weak to none. Finding ways to bring the export policies of second-tier suppliers into line with accepted practices (perhaps through joint ventures with first-tier suppliers that would preserve uniform standards) will require imaginative policies and persistent diplomacy.

The recently negotiated but unsigned agreement for cooperation between the United States and China warrants special mention. The agreement—whose language has not been made available to date—is currently in limbo while the United States attempts to clarify Chinese pledges not to help nations seeking nuclear assistance if there are proliferation implications. According to press reports, the Chinese may have cooperated with Pakistan in sharing nuclear information useful for weaponmaking. While the U.S.-China agreement and subsequent sales of equipment may help to induce China to share in strengthening the nonproliferation regime, the agreement must be completely unambiguous in terms of the responsibilities of the Chinese to satisfy the letter and the spirit of applicable U.S. legislation, especially the Nuclear Nonproliferation Act. Care must also be exercised that the agreement not be seen as unduly emphasizing the discriminatory nature of the nonproliferation regime. A nuclear agreement with another weapon state that contains overweak safeguards against using exported nuclear material or equipment for weapon purposes would be seen by many nations as another blow to their own commitment not to proliferate, particularly when one of the weapon states (China) has refused to sign the Non-Proliferation Treaty.

VIII

Far more ominous at this point is the prospect, in the near-to-intermediate term, of a nuclear arms race in South Asia and the Middle East. If the Pakistani nuclear program culminates in construction of a weapon—or, especially, a nuclear test explosion—it will be politically difficult for India to stand pat. Whether the initial Indian reaction would be to build a nuclear arsenal, match the test with another of its own, launch a preemptive military strike to knock out the offending nuclear facilities, or simply wait and see what the Pakistanis do next, a Pakistani bomb would have serious repercussions not only in South Asia but in the Middle East and elsewhere.

The United States has been wrestling with this problem for a decade. In 1976 Congress passed the Glenn/Symington amendment to the Foreign Assistance Act, an amendment that requires cutting off economic and military assistance to countries engaged in certain nuclear trading practices and other behavior detrimental to nonproliferation. U.S. aid to Pakistan was ended in 1979 under this provision. It was restored in 1981 after the Soviet invasion of Afghanistan, with a provision that assistance must be suspended again in the event of a Pakistani nuclear test. Additional moves are being considered by Congress to make military assistance to Pakistan contingent on better nuclear behavior by that country.

As Pakistan moves closer to nuclear weapons capability, the United States will be faced with the dilemma of balancing its security interests in South Asia with its wider interest in nonproliferation. Continuing U.S. aid to Pakistan helps to ensure Pakistani cooperation in containing Soviet ambitions in South Asia, and it may give the United States some leverage over future Pakistani actions. However, it sends a poor signal to potential proliferators around the world as to the depth of the U.S. commitment to nonproliferation and, in particular, to the notion that violators of nonproliferation norms should be penalized. The United States must decide at what point its long-term security interests become more threatened by Pakistani nuclear activities than by possible Pakistani noncooperation on Afghanistan.

An equally delicate problem exists in the Middle East, where it is tacitly assumed that Israel has a nuclear capability, stemming from an unsafeguarded research reactor in the Negev that was delivered to Israel by France in 1961. Israel's nuclear program, coupled with the bitter hostility that marks relations among states in that region, has increased incentives for other Middle Eastern nations to acquire nuclear weapons. Shortly after seizing power in 1969, Libyan leader Colonel Muammar Qaddafi reportedly tried unsuccessfully to purchase an atomic bomb from China. He is rumored to have made similar efforts with other states.

Before the revolution that brought the Ayatollah Khomeini to power, the Shah of Iran launched an ambitious nuclear program that would have eventually given Iran a potential weapons capability. The program has since been suspended but could one day be revived. Considering the lack of restraint in the use of chemical weapons in the Iran-Iraq war, one shudders to think what might be happening in the Middle East today if those nations had nuclear weapons. The Israeli preemptive air strike against the Iraqi reactor and the violence of the Iran-Iraq conflict have induced greater caution on the part of nuclear suppliers. Nonetheless, the specter of a future nuclear arms race in the Middle East cannot be dismissed.

In both South Asia and the Middle East, there has been occasional talk of negotiating a nuclear-weapon-free zone, but the prospect of accomplishing such a goal outside the context of a general political settlement does not seem promising. The participants in any proposed nuclear-weapon-free zone tend to demand the inclusion of an excessive number of neighboring states.

IX

The balance sheet on nonproliferation is not encouraging. Although the number of declared nuclear weapon states has remained constant for nearly 20 years, at least 10 nations have moved close to an overt nuclear capability. These nations have built an undeclared stockpile of weapons, constructed or are constructing unsafeguarded facilities to produce fissile material, have an interest in weapons development, or have sought nuclear technology incompatible with a cost-effective program of power generation but compatible with development of a future weapons program. Some of these nations have signed the Non-Proliferation Treaty, but most have not, indicating in both cases that it is futile to rely on the NPT alone for protection against proliferation.

Current international agreements on nuclear trade do not rule out transfers of sensitive technology that are difficult to safeguard. Moreover, the international agency responsible for the safeguard function is becoming increasingly politicized.

Although fine in theory, nuclear-weapon-free zones are difficult to achieve. The most successful attempt—the Treaty of Tlatelolco—is still far from being accepted by the Latin American nations whose endorsement is most needed, namely Cuba, Argentina, and Brazil.

Conceivably, in the next decade we could see open or clandestine nuclear arms races in South Asia and the Middle East, while adherence to the NPT suffers further erosion.

And finally, the superpowers still broadcast a message that equates national security with more nuclear weapons, and new technologies promise to make the future production of fissile material easier, less expensive, and more widespread.

On the other side of the ledger, the limited utility of nuclear weapons is now better understood, and greater sensitivity to proliferation exists now than ever before. Nuclear suppliers are more cooperative in enforcing safeguards than they have been in the past, and pressure on the weapon states to reduce their arsenals is growing. In addition, a combination of energy conservation, alternative technologies, and excess oil supplies has dimmed the attractiveness of technologies that pose a high proliferation risk, such as the breeder reactor and the recycling of plutonium for use in conventional reactors.

Despite these gains, ominous prospects demand that the prevention and control of nuclear proliferation remain among the highest priorities of the United States. ∎

Presidential Determination No. 86-03 of November 25, 1985

Determination Pursuant to Section 620E(e) of the Foreign Assistance Act of 1961, as Amended

Memorandum for the Secretary of State

Pursuant to section 620E(e) of the Foreign Assistance Act of 1961, as amended, 22 U.S.C. 2375(e), I hereby certify that Pakistan does not possess a nuclear explosive device and that the proposed United States assistance program will reduce significantly the risk that Pakistan will possess a nuclear explosive device.

You or your delegatee are authorized and directed to publish this determination and certification in the Federal Register.

Ronald Reagan

THE WHITE HOUSE,
Washington, November 25, 1985

U.S.-China Nuclear Cooperation Agreement

PRESIDENT'S STATEMENT, DEC. 16, 1985[1]

I am pleased to sign into law today S.J. Res. 238, in which the Congress states that it favors the agreement for peaceful nuclear cooperation between the United States and the People's Republic of China, which I transmitted to Congress on July 24, 1985. The agreement will have a significant, positive effect on the relations between the United States and the People's Republic of China and will lead to a continuing dialogue with China on important nuclear energy and nonproliferation matters. It will further U.S. nonproliferation and other foreign policy interests. I, therefore, welcome the Congress' support for the agreement.

Since I submitted the agreement without exempting it from any requirement in Section 123(a) of the Atomic Energy Act, no affirmative legislation was required to permit the agreement to be brought into force after the legally stipulated time periods for congressional review had been completed. The agreement may, therefore, be brought into force at that time in accordance with the procedure set forth in Article 10 of the agreement.

The joint resolution does require a one-time certification and a one-time report before exports to China under the agreement may commence. It assigns exclusively to the President the responsibility to review the matters to be certified to and to decide whether the certification may be made. Three matters must be certified: (1) that the arrangements for visits and exchanges of information made pursuant to Article 8 of the agreement are, as called for by this article itself, designed to be effective in ensuring that nuclear exports under the agreement are used solely for intended peaceful purposes; (2) that, after examining all information available to the U.S. Government, including any additional information that China has provided, nuclear exports to China are not precluded under Section 129(2) of the Atomic Energy Act; and (3) that the obligation to consider favorably a request to carry out activities described in Article 5(2) of the agreement does not prejudice the decision of the United States to approve or disapprove such a request. In addition, the joint resolution requires a report on Chinese nonproliferation policies and practices before exports commence.

The joint resolution also states that U.S. exports are subject to U.S. laws and regulations in effect at the time of export. This is a restatement of existing U.S. law and does not conflict with any obligations undertaken by the United States under the agreement. Finally, the joint resolution contains a section intended to ensure that the provisions in the China agreement that are textually different from provisions of the type contained in other U.S. peaceful nuclear cooperation agreements will not be the starting point for future nuclear cooperation agreement negotiations with other countries.

This joint resolution serves our interests in promoting peaceful nuclear cooperation and a nonproliferation dialogue with China. For this reason, I have decided to sign the joint resolution.

I appreciate the efforts of Senators Lugar and Cranston and Representatives Fascell, Broomfield, Bonker, Solarz, as well as others, in developing a joint resolution text that both the Administration and the Congress could accept.

I understand that an amendment relating to the U.S.-China peaceful nuclear cooperation agreement is currently under consideration in the conference on the continuing resolution. I strongly object to that amendment.

---

[1] Text from Weekly Compilation of Presidential Documents of Dec. 23, 1985.

Presidential Determination No. 87-3 of October 27, 1986

Determination Pursuant to Section 620E(e) of the Foreign Assistance Act of 1961, as Amended

Memorandum for the Honorable George P. Shultz, the Secretary of State

Pursuant to section 620E(e) of the Foreign Assistance Act of 1961, as amended, 22 U.S.C. 2375(e), I hereby certify that Pakistan does not possess a nuclear explosive device and that the proposed United States assistance program will reduce significantly the risk that Pakistan will possess a nuclear explosive device.

You or your delegatee are authorized and directed to publish this determination and certification in the Federal Register.

Ronald Reagan

THE WHITE HOUSE,
Washington, October 27, 1986.

"POSSESSION" OF A NUCLEAR WEAPON

DEFINITION USED BY OFFICE OF THE LEGAL ADVISOR
U.S. STATE DEPARTMENT

"Section 62OE(e) [of the Foreign Assistance Act of 1961] conditions the continuation of major forms of assistance to Pakistan upon an annual Presidential certification in writing "that Pakistan does not possess a nuclear explosive device and that the proposed United States assistance program will reduce significantly the risk that Pakistan will possess a nuclear explosive device." Administration of this provision has been expressly reserved by Executive Order to the President. It is therefore incumbent upon the President each year to review all the pertinent facts available to the United States and to make his best judgment as to whether the conditions for certification are met. He has done so twice thus far, certifying under Section 620E(e)on November 25,1985 and on October 27,1986. The Congress was briefed on the status of Pakistan's nuclear program both before and after each certification through annual classified reports submitted pursuant to Section 735 of the International Security and Development Cooperation Act of 1981 and briefings pursuant to Section 602 of the Nuclear Non-Proliferation Act of 1978.

In assessing the question of "possession" under Section 620E(e), two considerations are key, recognizing that it is the President who must make any ultimate judgment. First, the statutory standard is whether Pakistan possesses a nuclear explosive device, not whether Pakistan is attempting to develop or has developed various relevant capacities. Formulations that would have required certification of the absence of activities relevant for the development of a nuclear explosive device were rejected by the Congress in favor of the current statutory language requiring certification of non-possession. A distinction must therefore be drawn between the ability to achieve possession of a nuclear explosive device, and actual possession of such a device.

Second, a state may possess a nuclear explosive device, and yet maintain it in an unassembled form for safety reasons or to maintain effective command and control over its use or for other purposes. The fact that a state does not have an assembled device would not, therefore, necessarily mean that it does not possess a device under the statutory standard. A judgment concerning possession can only be made upon an evaluation of all relevant facts and circumstances of a particular case."

Source: *House Foreign Affairs Committee, Subcommittee on Asian & Pacific Affairs, Hearings on Foreign Assistance Legislation, Fiscal Years 1988/9, March 5, 1987, pp. 487-8.*

Nonproliferation Agreement With Allies

WHITE HOUSE STATEMENT, APR. 16, 1987[1]

The President is pleased to announce a new policy to limit the proliferation of missiles capable of delivering nuclear weapons. The U.S. Government is adopting this policy today in common with the Governments of Canada, France, the Federal Republic of Germany, Italy, Japan, and the United Kingdom. These nations have long been deeply concerned over the dangers of nuclear proliferation. Acting on this concern, these seven governments have formulated guidelines to control the transfer of equipment and technology that could contribute to nuclear-capable missiles.

This initiative was completed only recently, following several years of diplomatic discussions among these governments. The fact that all seven governments have agreed to common guidelines and to a common annex of items to be controlled serves to prevent commercial advantage or disadvantage for any of the countries. Both the guidelines and its annex will be made available to the public.

The President wishes to stress that it is the continuing aim of the U.S. Government to encourage international cooperation in the peaceful use of modern technology, including in the field of space. The guidelines are not intended to impede this objective. However, such encouragement must be given in ways that are fully consistent with the nonproliferation policies of the U.S. Government.

The United States, and its partners in this important initiative, would welcome the adherence of all states to these guidelines in the interest of international peace and security.

---

[1]Text from Weekly Compilation of Presidential Documents of Apr. 20, 1987. ∎

South Pacific Nuclear Free Zone

by J. Stapleton Roy

Statement before the Subcommittee on Asian and Pacific Affairs of the House Foreign Affairs Committee on June 9, 1987. Also included is the text of a statement made by U.S.S.R. Ambassador to Australia Yevgeniy Samoteykin in Suva, Fiji, on December 15, 1986, upon signing Protocols 2 and 3 of the South Pacific Nuclear Free Zone Treaty and submitted to the subcommittee for the record.

Mr. Roy is Deputy Assistant Secretary for East Asian and Pacific Affairs.[1]

It is a pleasure for me to be here today at this hearing on the South Pacific Nuclear Free Zone Treaty and to explain why the United States decided that it could not, under present circumstances, sign the protocols to the treaty.

In August 1985, 8 of the 13 voting members of the South Pacific Forum, including Australia and New Zealand, signed the treaty of Rarotonga which created the South Pacific nuclear free zone (SPNFZ). The treaty bans its parties from developing, producing, testing, owning, or using nuclear explosive devices or from permitting them into their territories. The treaty also has three protocols which would restrict nuclear activity by the nuclear-weapons states within the South Pacific nuclear free zone.

The treaty zone includes an enormous area of the western Pacific, from Australia and Papua New Guinea on the west and generally bounded by the Equator on the north, the 60th south parallel on the south, and the 115th west parallel on the east. It includes New Zealand, a number of small nation states, territories of the United States (American Samoa and Jarvis Island), France, and the United Kingdom.

The treaty came into effect in December 1986 at which time the protocols were opened for signature by the five nuclear-weapons states.

The question of whether to sign the protocols confronted the United States with a difficult dilemma. On the one hand, the treaty responds to a strong regional interest in nuclear nonproliferation, which we share. Further, the treaty negotiators had crafted an agreement which, if looked at in solely regional terms—and I want to stress that point—sought to accommodate U.S. interests and not to impinge on the U.S. capacity to meet its current security commitments in the Asia-Pacific region.

On the other hand, we had to consider the treaty's relationship to U.S. global security interests and responsibilities. We rely on deterrence to prevent the outbreak of global war or armed conflict between the nuclear powers or their allies, the very circumstances which would make the resort to nuclear weapons most likely. The nuclear capabilities of the Western alliance play a vital role in preserving the stability of this deterrence in the face of destabilizing imbalances in conventional military forces and weapons systems produced by geographic, economic, and political factors in Europe and Asia.

We have opposed proposals for nuclear-weapons-free zones where they clearly would disturb the nuclear deterrent on which the West relies. The growing number of such proposals, if pursued and implemented, would undermine our ability to meet our worldwide security commitments. We could not, therefore, ignore the fact that our adherence to the South Pacific protocols would be used by others to argue for those proposed zones. In short, we were unable to isolate our concern for regional views from larger concerns, and we reluctantly concluded that we could not sign the protocols. We were able, however, to assure the parties to the treaty that U.S. practices and activities in the SPNFZ region are not inconsistent with the treaty or its protocols.

In March of this year, the United Kingdom also decided that it could not sign the protocols. In making its announcement, the United Kingdom stated that it had taken "full account of our (i.e., United Kingdom) security interests in the region and more widely, the views of our allies and the regional states themselves, the texts of the treaty and the protocols and the announced policy of the Soviet Union." Like the United States, the United Kingdom gave assurances to the treaty parties with respect to its activities covered by the protocols. Not surprising, France has not signed the protocols.

The Soviet Union and the People's Republic of China have signed the relevant protocols. However, the Soviets did so with such a strong statement of understandings as to throw into question their intention to abide by the treaty. In particular, the Soviets seem to have reserved the right to consider themselves free from their protocol commitments should a party to the treaty exercise its right, as provided in the treaty, to allow visits by nuclear-armed ships or aircraft. Like other Western nuclear powers, the United States follows a "neither confirm nor deny" policy with respect to the presence or absence of nuclear armaments. Thus, the Soviets in effect reserve the right to decide for themselves the extent to which their adherence to SPNFZ is meaningful. So far, at least, the Soviets have not clarified the meaning or intent of their "understandings."

Understandably, parties to the treaty were disappointed by the U.S. decision not to sign the protocols. They believed that the treaty and its protocols had been drafted in such a way as to permit U.S. signature. We appreciate this. At the same time, their disappointment was tempered by the forthright U.S. statement that our activities in the region are not inconsistent with the protocols. They realize that we are not holding ourselves aloof from the treaty because of an interest in carrying out activities inconsistent with it. I believe also that there is increasing appreciation of the reasons behind the U.S. decision, particularly in light of the lack of any clarification of Soviet intentions with respect to the "understandings" attached to their signature of the protocols.

There is broad understanding of the U.S. decision among our other friends and allies. They appreciate the difficulty of striking an appropriate balance between our interest in arms control and nuclear nonproliferation and the need to maintain a global deterrent in which nuclear capabilities continue to play a central role.

SPNFZ Arrangements

The SPNFZ arrangements are set forth in the 16 articles of the SPNFZ Treaty *per se*, its four annexes, and in three protocols.

The substantive provisions of the treaty itself establish obligations with respect to the following principal matters:

- Renunciation of nuclear explosive devices;
- Application of IAEA [International Atomic Energy Agency] safeguards;
- Prevention of stationing of nuclear explosive devices;
- Prevention of testing of nuclear explosive devices;
- Prevention of dumping of radioactive wastes and other radioactive material; and
- Various related arrangements concerning controls, reports, exchanges of information, and consultations.

The provisions relating to the prevention of stationing of nuclear explosive devices specifically provide that each of the treaty parties remains free to decide for itself on visits, transit, or navigation by foreign ships and aircraft (in its territory, territorial waters, or territorial airspace).

The treaty is open for membership by any member of the South Pacific Forum and entered into force in accordance with its provisions on December 11, 1986, the date of deposit of the eighth instrument of ratification.

The four annexes describe the precise boundaries of the treaty zone, the IAEA safeguards referred to in the main body of the treaty, arrangements for the consultative committee, and the complaints procedure.

The treaty has three Protocols.

- Protocol 1 would require its parties not to manufacture, station, or test any nuclear explosive device in their territories within the zone (for the United States, American Samoa and Jarvis Island). This protocol was open for signature by the United States, the United Kingdom, and France.
- Protocol 2 would require its parties not to contribute to any act that would constitute a violation of the treaty and not to use, or threaten to use, any nuclear explosive device against states party to the treaty. This protocol and Protocol 3 are open to all five nuclear-weapons states for signature.
- Protocol 3 would require its parties not to test any nuclear explosive device within the zone.

Soviet Statement

The Soviet Government, which is a consistent supporter of the creation of nuclear-free zones in various parts of the world as an important measure in the fight for the elimination of nuclear weapons, and wishing to contribute to the efforts of the countries of the South Pacific Forum in that area, has decided to sign Protocols Two and Three to the Treaty on a Nuclear-Free Zone in the Southern Pacific. The Soviet Union proceeds from the premise that the creation of such a zone will serve as an important contribution to forming a reliable security system in the Asian-Pacific Region, will strengthen the international regime of non-proliferation of nuclear weapons, and will contribute towards the attainment of the task of eliminating the nuclear weapons on earth once and for all.

Expressing its readiness to become a guarantor of a nuclear-free zone in the Southern Pacific, the Soviet Union hopes that all the other nuclear powers will show appropriate responsibility in approaching the initiative of the countries of that region and will do their utmost to ensure reliably and guarantee a truly non-nuclear status of the non-nuclear zone.

In signing the Protocols Two and Three to the Treaty on a Nuclear-Free Zone in the Southern part of the Pacific, the Government of the Union of Soviet Socialist Republics considers it necessary to make the following statement:

1. The Soviet Union proceeds from the premise that the transportation of nuclear explosive devices by parties to the treaty anywhere within the limits and outside the limits of the nuclear-free zone in the Southern Pacific is covered by the prohibitions envisaged by point "A" of article three of the treaty, in which the sides commit themselves "not to exercise control over any nuclear explosive devices in any form, anywhere within the limits and outside the limits of the nuclear-free zone.

Soviet Understandings

At the time of their December 1986 signature of Protocols 2 and 3, the Soviets issued a statement which is so vague and sweeping as to cast into doubt whether they intend to bind themselves in any important respect in adhering to the protocols. The full text is attached, and you will note that it seems to say that they reserve the right to consider themselves unbound by Protocol 2 when a state exercises its express rights under the treaty to permit port access or transit by ships or aircraft of nuclear-weapons states.

The Soviet statement could be considered a "reservation" legally conditioning their obligations under a broad range of circumstances. Unless the Soviets clarify their intentions, they may seek to use this statement as a basis for asserting the broadest construction of their rights.

---

[1] The complete transcript of the hearings will be published by the committee and will be available from the Superintendent of Documents, U.S. Government Printing Office, Washington, D.C. 20402. ∎

Pakistan and the Nuclear Issue

by Richard W. Murphy

Statement before the Subcommittees on Asian and Pacific Affairs and on International Economic Policy and Trade of the House Foreign Affairs Committee on July 22, 1987. Ambassador Murphy is Assistant Secretary for Near Eastern and South Asian Affairs.[1]

I appreciate the opportunity to discuss the difficult situation created by the recent filing of criminal charges in two cases involving alleged efforts to procure material for Pakistan's nuclear program in violation of U.S. law. Since 1981, the Congress and the Administration have worked closely together in an effort to pursue *both* our nonproliferation objectives and a range of other national security interests in our relations with Pakistan. This effort has never been easy, but the dilemma we face at this moment is sharper and more serious than perhaps ever before.

U.S. Efforts for Nuclear Restraint in Southern Asia

We believe that our renewed security relationship with Pakistan has allowed us to make an important contribution to the prevention of a nuclear arms race in South Asia in the past 6 years. But we have not solved the problem. Despite our best efforts, Pakistan has proceeded to the threshold of nuclear weapons possession. India remains similarly poised to the brink. This is a critical moment for South Asia, and indeed for our vital global interest in nonproliferation.

The Administration, with the support of the authorizing committees of both Houses, has argued that at this time we must intensify our efforts to produce concrete evidence of Pakistani nuclear restraint. We have undertaken a frank and intense dialogue with Pakistan to this end. While our ultimate goal is a firm commitment such as NPT [Nonproliferation Treaty] adherence by both India and Pakistan, our immediate objective is to achieve some restraint in the nuclear area. Neither Pakistan nor India, whatever their nuclear capabilities, has moved irrevocably across the nuclear threshold. We hope that stability can be reinforced through measures taken by both countries which will build confidence in their parallel declarations of intent not to acquire nuclear weapons. We believe that our continuing economic and security assistance to Pakistan not only underpins our extremely important interests by allowing Pakistan to stand up to Soviet pressure through Afghanistan but also serves to encourage Pakistani nuclear restraint and to undercut any perceived security need for acquisition of a national nuclear deterrent. This policy rationale, in our view, remains valid.

Alleged Violations of U.S. Export Laws

The recent criminal cases have shaken the confidence of many Americans in the soundness of these policies. In discussing this matter and its potential foreign policy implications, I would first stress that we are not in a position at this time to make any conclusive judgments. We are, for the time being, dealing with allegations, as well as with a continuing investigation and a possible criminal prosecution. The evidence remains to be fully evaluated. We must bear in mind the need to avoid anything which might be seen to prejudge the outcome of the judicial process. But the public criminal charge itself raises issues with very significant foreign policy implications. We are prepared to discuss these implications and to take prudent action based on our best understanding of the facts at this time.

The Administration views any violation of U.S. export control laws with the utmost seriousness. Indeed, our actions to date demonstrate our commitment to upholding the law. The State Department has cooperated closely with the Justice Department in its investigation and has urged vigorous prosecution. More generally, the United States continues to work closely with other nuclear suppliers to tighten controls on the export of nuclear-related technology and to block clandestine efforts to circumvent these controls.

We are equally committed to the observance of our responsibilities under the Solarz amendment. Indeed, in response to the events which led to the passage of the Solarz amendment in 1985, we underscored to the Pakistan Government that we would not tolerate any violation of our laws. We have subsequently reiterated to Pakistan officials on a number of occasions the implications of such activities for our assistance relationship.

The Pakistan Government, beginning in 1985, has provided unequivocal assurances, both in public and in private, that it would not engage in illegal procurement activities in the United States. In the wake of the arrest of Mr. Pervez, we have expressed our deep concern and have sought an explanation from the Pakistan Government of what it may know of this matter. We have called attention to earlier statements that we would not tolerate violations of our laws and made clear that actions inconsistent with the assurances we have been given would inevitably have serious consequences for our relationship. We have also informed Pakistan that this case reinforces our concerns about Pakistan's nuclear program and increases the need for steps to demonstrate that Pakistan's nuclear program is "peaceful." The Pakistan Government has denied any knowledge of or connection with this case and has offered its full cooperation in our investigation, including a commitment to take action against any individuals found to be violating Pakistani policy or laws.

As I have said, we are not able at this point to make any firm judgments either on the facts or the legal implications of this matter. But, we can certainly assert that the stakes are very high and that the cost of a miscalculation are great. In this complex situation, we are particularly mindful of several major concerns.

First, we must ensure that, by a failure to respond to events, we do not encourage disrespect for our laws or disregard for our policies in the area of nuclear nonproliferation. Others are watching around the world and will judge our resolve.

Second, neither our nonproliferation objectives nor our other security interests would be well-served were we to lose our continuing ability to influence nuclear decisionmaking in South Asia.

And **finally**, we must be actually mindful of our global security interests and of the importance of these interests of maintaining our support for Pakistan in its vital posture of opposition to the Soviet occupation of Afghanistan. Pakistan is carrying an enormous burden in caring for 3 million Afghan refugees and standing up to Soviet pressure and intimidation. The Pakistanis deserve our continuing strong support, just as much as we believe we deserve their respect for our laws.

U.S. Agenda

Our immediate agenda is threefold.

First, we must gather and evaluate all the information available which may bear on this matter and its foreign policy implications.

Second, we must pursue our diplomatic dialogue with Pakistan with vigor, including taking the Pakistan Government up on its offer to assist in the investigation. Pakistan obviously understands the extreme importance of this matter, as well as of the need to reach a better understanding on the larger nuclear issue of which the procurement question is only a part.

Third, we must consult closely with the Congress as our knowledge of this matter accumulates and our consideration of further steps proceeds.

Let me emphasize this latter point. The Congress is already seized with this issue. Final action remains to be taken in regard to fiscal year 1988 assistance and the Administration's request for renewal of authority to waive provisions of the Symington amendment. There is also a strong congressional interest—which we share—in ensuring that the provisions of the Solarz amendment are addressed promptly, but also carefully and thoroughly. This is a matter on which the Congress and the Administration must move forward together, or together take the responsibility for serious setbacks to important national interests.

This, then, is our dilemma: How to ensure that our laws are upheld, protect our global nonproliferation interests, prevent the outbreak of a nuclear arms race in South Asia, and continue our support for Pakistan in its opposition to the Soviet occupation of Afghanistan. Clearly, the outcome depends to a very large degree on Pakistan's response. We wish to believe the assurances of a good and deserving friend such as Pakistan, but under present circumstances, these assurances must be matched by their actions. Only on that basis can the mutual confidence which has underlain our relationship be fully restored. We hope for the best. Much depends on the success of our diplomatic efforts. We will keep this committee and the Congress fully informed as events unfold over the coming weeks.

---

[1]The complete transcript of the hearings will be published by the committee and will be available from the Superintendent of Documents, U.S. Government Printing Office, Washington, D.C. 20402. ■

U.S.-Japan Nuclear Cooperation Agreement

MESSAGE TO THE CONGRESS, NOV. 9, 1987[1]

I am pleased to transmit to the Congress, pursuant to sections 123 b. and 123 d. of the Atomic Energy Act of 1954, as amended (42 U.S.C. 2153 (b), (d)), the text of a proposed Agreement for Cooperation Between the Government of the United States of America and the Government of Japan Concerning Peaceful Uses of Nuclear Energy, including an implementing agreement pursuant to Article 11 of the proposed agreement. I am also pleased to transmit my written approval, authorization and determination concerning the agreement, and the Nuclear Proliferation Assessment Statement by the Director of the United States Arms Control and Disarmament Agency concerning the agreement. The joint memorandum submitted to me by the Departments of State and Energy, which includes a summary of the provisions of the agreement, the views of the Director of the United States Arms Control and Disarmament Agency and an analysis of the approvals and consents contained in the agreement, including the implementing agreement, and associated subsequent arrangements are also enclosed.

I also enclose for your information the texts of a proposed subsequent arrangement under the United States-Norway Revised Agreement for Cooperation Concerning Peaceful Uses of Nuclear Energy and a proposed subsequent arrangement under the United States-EURATOM [European Atomic Energy Community] Additional Agreement for Cooperation Concerning Peaceful Uses of Atomic Energy. These subsequent arrangements are designed to give effect to certain provisions of the United States-Japan implementing agreement and will enter into force only after the agreement enters into force. They are being processed by the Department of Energy in accordance with the applicable provisions of the Atomic Energy Act of 1954, as amended.

The proposed agreement with Japan, including the implementing agreement, has been negotiated in accordance with the Nuclear Non-Proliferation Act of 1978 (NNPA). In my judgment it meets all statutory requirements. It will supersede our 1968 agreement with Japan and, given the magnitude of our long-standing cooperation with Japan in the peaceful uses of nuclear energy, will represent the most significant achievement to date in our program initiated pursuant to section 404(a) of the NNPA to update all existing agreements for peaceful nuclear cooperation to include the more stringent standards established by that Act.

I believe that the new agreement will strengthen the basis for continued close cooperation between the United States and Japan in the peaceful nuclear area and that it will further the non-proliferation and other foreign policy interests of the United States. The implementing agreement provides Japan advance, long-term consent for reprocessing, transfers, alteration and storage of nuclear material subject to the agreement, provided that the reprocessing and subsequent use of the recovered plutonium meet and continue to meet the criteria set out in U.S. law, including criteria relating to safeguards and physical protection. These arrangements should enable Japan to plan for its long-term energy needs on a more assured, predictable basis, while at the same time embodying the most advanced concepts of physical security and safeguards of any agreement. This step forward in our cooperative relations with Japan will be consistent with the NNPA's injunction to take such actions as are required to confirm the reliability of the United States as a nuclear supplier consistent with non-proliferation goals.

Japan is not only a close ally of the United States but is also a party to the Treaty on the Non-Proliferation of Nuclear Weapons and has long been one of the strongest supporters of the international non-proliferation regime. Moreover, the United States and Japan have a substantial identity of views and intentions with regard to preventing nuclear proliferation and are prepared to work together on measures that will contribute to the prevention of proliferation consistent with the peaceful uses of nuclear energy. An exchange of letters between the United States and Japan, the text of which is included in the agreement package, sets forth in detail our shared views on non-proliferation.

I have considered the views and recommendations of the interested agencies in reviewing the proposed agreement and have determined that its performance will promote, and will not constitute an unreasonable risk to, the common defense and security. Accordingly, I have approved the agreement and authorized its execution and urge that the Congress give it favorable consideration.

I have also found that this agreement meets all applicable requirements of the Atomic Energy Act, as amended, for agreements for peaceful nuclear cooperation, and, therefore, I am transmitting it to the Congress without exempting it from any requirement contained in section 123 a. of that Act. This transmission shall constitute a submittal for purposes of both sections 123 b. and 123 d. of the Atomic Energy Act. The Administration is prepared to begin immediately the consultations with the Senate Foreign Relations and House Foreign Affairs Committees as provided in section 123 b. Upon completion of the 30-day continuous session period provided in section 123 b., the 60-day continuous session period provided for in section 123 d. shall commence.

RONALD REAGAN

---

[1]Text from Weekly Compilation of Presidential Documents of Nov. 16, 1987. ∎

Presidential Determination No. 88–4 of December 17, 1987

Determination Pursuant to Section 620E(e) of the Foreign Assistance Act of 1961, as Amended

Memorandum for the Honorable George P. Shultz, the Secretary of State

Pursuant to Section 620 E(e) of the Foreign Assistance Act of 1961, as amended, 22 U.S.C. 2375(e), I hereby certify that Pakistan does not possess a nuclear explosive device and that the proposed United States assistance program will reduce significantly the risk that Pakistan will possess a nuclear explosive device.

You or your delegatee are authorized and directed to publish this determination and certification in the Federal Register.

Ronald Reagan

THE WHITE HOUSE,
Washington, December 17, 1987.

Continuation of Aid to Pakistan

WHITE HOUSE STATEMENT,
JAN. 15, 1988[1]

The President today signed and sent to Congress waivers to the law that would require a cutoff in aid to Pakistan under the Symington and the Solarz amendments because of activities in the nuclear weapons development area. This waiver action was based on the recognition that disrupting one of the pillars of the U.S. relationship with Pakistan would be counterproductive for the strategic interests of the United States, destabilizing for South Asia, and unlikely to achieve the nonproliferation objectives sought by the sponsors.

The Government of Pakistan is aware of our continuing concern over certain aspects of its nuclear program. Despite these problem areas, there are crucial nonproliferation criteria which Pakistan continues to honor. The United States will insist on the maintenance of these restraints even as we work with Pakistan on progress in the areas of concern.

The President's action is preceded by months of extensive consultations with Congress. We have achieved an understanding on the general approach which is reflected in approval by Congress of a 30-month waiver of the Symington amendment and near-full funding for Pakistan for FY 1988. The Administration pledged to continue pressing Pakistan away from a nuclear weapons option and is obliged to certify annually that Pakistan does not possess nuclear weapons.

The reasons which convinced the Administration to waive the Symington amendment also apply to the Solarz amendment, where the waiver applies only retroactively. The Government of Pakistan has pledged that procedures will be tightened to ensure an end to procurement activities in the United States. We will continue to monitor procurement activities in this country to ensure compliance with Pakistan's new procedures.

There is no diminution in the President's commitment to restraining the spread of nuclear weapons in the Indian subcontinent or elsewhere. We will continue to urge Pakistan and India to discuss measures which might be taken to reduce the threat of a nuclear arms race in South Asia. As arms control negotiations between the United States and the Soviet Union begin to bear fruit and set an example, the Administration will be seeking still further ways to make this commitment effective.

---

[1]Text from Weekly Compilation of Presidential Documents of Jan. 18, 1988. ∎

Presidential Determination No. 88–5 of January 15, 1988

Determination Pursuant to Section 670(a) and Section 620E(d) of the Foreign Assistance Act, as Amended

Memorandum for the Secretary of State

By the authority vested in me as President by the Constitution and statutes of the United States of America, including Sections 620E(d) and Section 670(a) of the Foreign Assistance Act of 1961, as amended ("the Act"), I hereby:

(1) determine pursuant to Section 670(a)(1) of the Act that material, equipment, or technology covered by that provision was to be used by Pakistan in the manufacture of a nuclear explosive device; and,

(2) determine and certify, as a result of the determination in paragraph (1) above and pursuant to Section 670(a)(2) of the Act, that not providing assistance referred to in Section 670(a)(1) of the Act to Pakistan would be seriously prejudicial to the achievement of United States nonproliferation objectives and otherwise jeopardize the common defense and security; and,

(3) determine, pursuant to Section 620E(d) of the Act, that the provision of assistance to Pakistan under the Act through April 1, 1990, is in the national interest of the United States and therefore waive the prohibitions of Section 669 of the Act with respect to that period.

You are hereby authorized and directed to report immediately this determination and certification, together with the statement setting forth specific reasons therefor, to the Speaker of the House of Representatives and to the Chairman of the Committee on Foreign Relations of the Senate.

This determination shall be published in the Federal Register.

Ronald Reagan

THE WHITE HOUSE,
Washington, January 15, 1988.

The Concept of "Timely Warning" in the Nuclear Nonproliferation Act of 1978

By

Leonard Weiss
Staff Director
Senate Committee on Governemental Affairs

Inserted in *The Congressional Record* by
Senator John H. Glenn
March 21, 1988

Introduction

In 1984, the first major shipment was made of plutonium separated from U.S.-origin spent fuel to a non-weapon state (Japan) since passage of the Nuclear Nonproliferation Act of 1978 (NNPA) {1}. Approval of the shipment had been given by the Secretary of Energy, with the concurrence of the Secretary of State, who was required by the NNPA to determine whether the retransfer of this plutonium from France (where the reprocessing of spent fuel took place) to Japan would result in a "significant increase of the risk of proliferation..." in which the "foremost" factor was whether the United States would receive "timely warning" of a diversion of the material.

In accordance with procedures adopted pursuant to the NNPA, the interagency discussions of the Japanese request for approval of the shipment involved the Nuclear Regulatory Commission (NRC). Although the NRC concurred with the finding that the shipment would not result in a "significant increase of the risk of proliferation", the Commission questioned whether the Departments of Energy (DOE) and State had followed Congressional intent in arriving at their conclusion that the "timely warning" test had been met. The NRC's position was summarized by NRC Chairman Nunzio J. Palladino as follows {2}:

> "(T)he Commission's disagreement with DOE's position is focused on whether or not non-technical factors are permitted to be considered in connection with reaching any conclusions on the

existence of timely warning. In the Commission's view, the legislative history of the Nuclear Non-proliferation Act of 1978 (NNPA) indicates that Congress intended timely warning to be essentially a technical matter involving such factors as safeguards measures applied to the material and the technical ease of incorporating the material into a nuclear explosive device. Other, non-technical factors were to be considered relevant only in connection with making the overall statutory finding of no significant increase in the risk of proliferation. A close reading of the statutory language in Section 131 b. of the Atomic Energy Act would seem to support the Commission's interpretation regarding timely warning, particularly since otherwise it would be necessary to consider the same non-technical factors both in connection with the timely warning analysis and in connection with the overall "increase in the risk of proliferation" finding. The attachment to this letter lists the more significant technical factors that the Commission believes affect timely warning, and that should be addressed in a classified supplement to future DOE analyses of subsequent arrangements."

The resolution of this issue will set a precedent with possibly profound future implications for U.S. national security and foreign relations.

The DOE/State conclusion on "timely warning" was not accompanied by a detailed supporting analysis. Rather, as indicated in the NRC letter, the conclusion was claimed to result from the presence of certain favorable political factors surrounding the U.S./Japan relationship. Subsequent inquiry {3} has revealed that DOE and State interpret the NNPA as saying that political factors, such as the nature and condition of the governmental system and nonproliferation policies in a recipient country, independently of the technical capabilities of that country, could be determining factors in judging whether the U.S. would receive "timely warning" of a diversion. Therefore, according to this view, some political factors, which

determine the "inherent risk of proliferation" {4} in a
country, could determine that "timely warning" was
available, and these and other political factors could be
used to determine that there was "no significant increase in
the risk of proliferation" stemming from a proposed
retransfer for reprocessing or return of plutonium.
Further, it is claimed that there was no stated or implied
legislative requirement for a supporting analysis of the
DOE/State "timely warning" conclusion or the weight given to
the latter in relation to other factors in determining
proliferation risk.

It is the purpose of this paper to show that the
DOE/State position is not in keeping with the legislative
history of the NNPA or any other indication of Congressional
intent. Rather, we shall show that; (a) the Congressional
intent was to separate and independently weigh the "timely
warning" test from the set of possibly counterbalancing
political factors listed in the NNPA as being pertinent to
an overall judgment as to whether a proposed retransfer
would result in a significant increase of the risk of
proliferation; and, (b) that Congress meant the "timely
warning" test to compare the time needed by the U.S. to
effectively react to a diversion of nuclear material to the
time needed by the diverting country to produce an explosive
device, the latter time being estimated by technical
assessments only. By this view, a political assessment
based on specific political factors could result in approval
of a retransfer request even if the "timely warning" test
fails, but then the burden is on the political assessment to
show that such political factors override "foremost"
consideration of the technical capabilities of the recipient
country to make a nuclear explosive device quickly from
diverted materials.

I. <u>The Language of the Act</u>

The key paragraph, Section 131b (2) of the Atomic Energy
Act of 1954 (Section 303a of the NNPA of 1978) states that,

> "...the Secretary of Energy may not
> enter into any subsequent arrangement for
> the reprocessing of any such material in
> a facility which has not processed power
> reactor fuel assemblies or been the
> subject of a subsequent arrangement
> therefor prior to the date of enactment

of the Nuclear Non-Proliferation Act of 1978 or for subsequent retransfer to a non-nuclear-weapon state of any plutonium in quantities greater than 500 grams resulting from such reprocessing, unless in his judgment, and that of the Secretary of State, such reprocessing or retransfer will not result in a significant increase of the risk of proliferation beyond that which exists at the time that approval is requested. Among all the factors in making this judgment, foremost consideration will be given to whether or not the reprocessing or retransfer will take place under conditions that will ensure retransfer will take place under conditions that will ensure timely warning to the United States of any diversion well in advance of the time at which the non-nuclear-weapon state could transform the diverted material into a nuclear explosive device...."

This language was originally offered by Senator Glenn to the Administration during negotiations prior to the beginning of markup of the NNPA by the Subcommittee on Arms Control, Oceans, and International Environment of the Senate Foreign Relations Committee on September 14, 1977. It was a substitute for proposed language by the Administration that would have replaced the "timely warning" criterion with consideration of "the probability of timely warning" as one (not "foremost") factor among many in determining whether to approve a retransfer request. We shall examine this markup in more detail later on. For now it suffices to note that the Subcommittee approved the Glenn language and ignored the Administration's proposal.

Following the markup by the full Committee (there were two earlier markups by the Committees on Governmental Affairs and Energy and Natural Resources), the legislation was reported out and a report filed which contained the following statement on the meaning of "timely warning"{5}:

> "...the standard of 'timely warning' ...is strictly a measure of whether <u>warning of a diversion</u> (emphasis added) will be received far enough in advance of the time when the recipient could transform the diverted material into an explosive device to permit an adequate diplomatic response."

The Senate bill language was accepted by the House on the grounds that there were no substantive differences between the Senate bill and one passed by the House some months earlier. Representative Zablocki (D-Wisconsin), the floor manager for the House bill, while offering a resolution on February 23, 1978, directing the Clerk of the House to make certain technical corrections in the NNPA, made the following observation about the Senate amendments {6}: "The House reviewed these and found the amended Senate version to be, in all essential respects, consistent with (the House Bill). Upon reaching this judgment, the House, by unanimous consent then moved to recede and accept (the House Bill) as amended." Indeed, on February 9, 1978, when Representative Zablocki received unanimous consent to bring up the Senate bill and successfully proposed its passage by voice vote, he stated {7}:

> "All of the central elements of the House bill - including the important "timely warning" criterion - were faithfully preserved.... On the critical issue of timely warning, I am pleased to say that the Senate's legislative history was indeed consistent with our own."

The concept of "timely warning" was explained in the House report as follows {8}:

> "'Timely warning' has to do with that interval of time that exists between the detection of a diversion and the subsequent transformation of diverted material into an explosive device."

Despite Representative Zablocki's clear statement, the Senate Report's phrase "warning of a diversion" as opposed to the House Report's "detection of a diversion", along with some additional Senate report language has been used by some in State/DOE to bolster a claim that the intent of the Senate on the meaning of "timely warning" was substantially different from that of the House.

We shall show that such a claim is logically unsupportable.

II. A Precise Reformulation of the Timely Warning Issue

There are four time intervals associated with the notion of "timely warning" to the U.S. of a diversion by country "X". For purposes of explanation, we define them as follows.

Reaction Time: The amount of time needed to fashion an appropriate and effective diplomatic response to prevent diverted material from being converted by country "X" into an explosive device. Reaction time is a function of bilateral and multilateral relationships and, therefore, involves a political assessment.

Conversion Time: The time needed by country "X" to convert diverted material into an explosive device. (Note: Conversion time is a function of the industrial and bomb-making infrastructure in country "X", the nature of the diverted material, and the availability of any technology needed to process the diverted material into weapons-usable form. A technical assessment of country "X"'s capabilities would yield an estimate of conversion time, and no political factors are involved.)

Detection Time: The time between diversion of material and either the later detection of the diversion by the safeguards system or the earlier prediction of diversion through intelligence information. (In the latter case, detection time is a negative quantity, and may depend upon observations of political changes in country "X". Note that if we tacitly assume that the safeguards system works as designed, no political factors enter into an estimate of positive detection time. Quality of safeguards is then measured by the value of positive detection time, with smaller values indicating better safeguards.)

Warning Time: The interval between the time when the U.S. learns a diversion has occurred or may occur and the time at which country "X" is capable of producing a nuclear explosive device following the aforementioned diversion of material. (Thus, warning time = conversion time - detection time. It is important to note that warning time involves political as opposed to technical assessments only when detection time is negative.)

-6-

In terms of the above definitions, the concept of "timely warning" in the NNPA becomes as follows:

<u>Definition</u>: The U.S. has received "timely warning" of a diversion by country "X" when warning time is greater than reaction time.

The only thing remaining in order to show equivalence with the statutory concept is to make the connection between some auxiliary concepts in the Senate report with the terminology in this paper.

The phrase "warning time required" in the Senate report as in,"The amount of warning time required will vary (and cannot be defined in terms of a certain number of weeks or months)...", {9} refers to what is here called "reaction time". Thus, if a multinational response is needed for effective diplomacy, a quicker reaction time can be expected in the event that the diverted material was multinationally owned or came from a multinational plant, since all the parties in that venture would have reason to feel aggrieved by the diversion.

The phrase "time...available" as in "...it will be necessary to determine how much time be actually (sic) available under any specific circumstances," {10} refers to what we are calling here "warning time".

The State/DOE position boils down to the claim that Congress did not intend the "timely warning" criterion to involve, on either side of the inequality in the above definition, a quantity estimated only on the basis of a technical assessment.

Since "reaction time" clearly involves political factors, and "warning time" <u>can</u> involve political factors, there appears, superficially at least, to be some merit to the State/DOE argument. On closer examination, however, the apparent merit vanishes.

We reiterate that "warning time" may involve political factors <u>only</u> when "detection time" is negative. The key observation to make is to note that detection time can be negative only in two situations: 1) Either the U.S. has learned of plans for (or suspects) diversion at a time prior to the time of actual retransfer (in which case the approval of retransfer is denied or revoked and there is no problem), or 2) There is a significant interval of time after the retransfer occurs before a diversion is achieved. In this case it can be argued that the clock marking off warning time could be triggered by observed changes in the political character of the government of country "X". But there is nothing in the Senate or House floor debate or report language or in the statute language that suggests making an assumption of existence of a significant time interval between retransfer and diversion, or equivalently, to assume that a significant change had occurred on the meaning of timely warning by the time the final version of the NNPA was passed by the Senate on Feburary 7, 1978, and by the House two days later without further amendment.

To show this, we provide a detailed history of the Congress' consideration of the timely warning issue during its deliberations on the NNPA.

III. The Senate Legislative Markup Record on Timely Warning

Committee markup records, which are uncorrected and not publicly filed, and therefore not readily available to the rest of the Congress, are usually given little or no weight in legal determinations of congressional intent on legislation. Nonetheless, they may, in conjunction with the committee report on the legislation and the floor debate, give some clue as to the meaning of certain legislative provisions when such meaning is otherwise obscure.

The DOE/State defense of its position on "timely warning" in the NNPA apparently includes a claim that the Congressional interpretation of the statutory language at the time of passage reflected the Carter Administration's view as expressed in a formal communication from the State Department to the Senate Foreign Relations Committee (see {4}). Since the only place in the legislative history of the NNPA where the Administration's position on "timely warning" is substantively discussed by Senators occurs in the Senate Foreign Relations Committee markups {11}, {12}, {13} of the legislation, we consider these (uncorrected) markup records in examining the DOE/State claim.

On September 14, 1977, at the Foreign Relations Subcommittee markup (see {11}) Senator Glenn introduced the language on approvals of retransfers for reprocessing or return of plutonium, including the "timely warning" test, that subsequently was adopted as the statute language. This language was a substitute for a previous formulation identical to that contained in the House bill, H.R. 8638, which passed with a dissenting vote on September 28, 1977,

-8-

the same day the Senate Foreign Relations Committee reported out the NNPA. As indicated earlier, Senator Glenn offered this new language following discussions with and in response to objections by the Executive Branch that the previous formulation on approvals of retransfers was too "restrictive in scope" {14}.

It is important to note the motivation as well as substance of the Administration's position at this point. The Administration was facing a serious problem in that the House and Senate bills had virtually identical provisions that subjected decisions on retransfers for reprocessing or return of plutonium to consideration of a single factor, the timely warning criterion. The Administration was concerned that this single test could be used to block U.S. approvals of any such retransfers and dirupt trade relations with our allies. Accordingly, the Administration had to either try to get the Congress to alter the definition of "timely warning" or broaden the test for approvals of retransfers to include other factors besides timely warning. Thus, in its comments on the marked up version of the NNPA reported by the Governmental Affairs Committee, the Administration said this about the proposed test for retransfer {15}:

> "First, it would jeopardize negotiation of new, strict nuclear cooperation agreements since an overly strict interpretation of the "timely warning" standard could rule out all forms of fuel processing necessary for future fuel cycle activities. Second, timely warning should not be the sole basis for making determinations concerning the acceptability of subsequent arrangements, taking into account the existence of other factors which must be evaluated. Additional factors of importance include the non-proliferation policies of the countries concerned, and the size and scope of the activities involved."

Now, it is interesting that the language actually proposed by the Administration by way of compromise, language that was arrived at following negotiations with Senator Glenn, clearly takes the path of broadening the test for approvals for retransfers, and does not change the definition of "timely warning" but merely attempts to make the determination fuzzy by referring only to the the probability of timely warning being available. The proposed language was as follows {16}.

-9-

"The Administrator may not enter into any subsequent arrangement for the reprocessing of any such material in a facility which has not processed power fuel assemblies or been the subject of a subsequent arrangement therefore prior to the date of enactment of the Act or for subsequent retransfer to a non-nuclear-weapon state of any plutonium in quantities greater than 500 grams resulting from such reprocessing unless in his view such reprocessing to retransfer shall take place under conditions that will safely secure the materials and that are designed to ensure reliable and timely detection of diversion. In making his judgment, the Administrator will take into account such factors as the size and scope of the activities involved, the non-proliferation policies of the countries concerned and the probabilities that the arrangements will provide timely warning to the United States of diversions well in advance of the time at which the non-nuclear-weapon state could transform the diverted material into a nuclear explosive device; and".

Senator Glenn's explanation of the amendment he offered at the Foreign Relations Subcommittee markup left no doubt that it was not his intention to change the meaning of timely warning, but rather to broaden the test for approvals of certain retransfers. To see this, we note that in his statement, Senator Glenn referred approvingly to recent congressional testimony by then NRC Commissioner, Victor Gilinsky, defending the timely warning standard against Administration criticism that it was "unnecessary, unworkable, rigid, and unrealistic" {17}. Senator Glenn went on to say, {18}

"The idea of timely warning is the explicitly stated objective of the so-called blue book safeguards of the IAEA, which polices the Non-Proliferation

Treaty. Under this system, as under the U.S. bilateral safeguards which preceded it, records are kept of all nuclear material going into and coming out of civilian power reactors throughout most of the world, and verified by an international inspectorate. The idea is simply that the disappearance of any of this material will be reported to the international community in plenty of time to allow for appropriate counteraction. Thus timely warning is essential to effective safeguards."

Senator Glenn's references to safeguards and timely warning strongly imply that the timely warning criterion in his amendment could be met only if the reaction time afforded by the safeguards system's detection of a diversion was sufficient "to allow for appropriate counter action" {19}.

This thought was echoed in substance by Representative Bingham (D-NY) in introducing this language on the House floor 14 days later. He said {20}:

"{W}e consider (timely warning) to be an essential to the safeguarding of nuclear facilities. If there is no timely warning, there are no effective safeguards."

At this point in the Senate markup <u>and without challenging Glenn's view</u>, the Chief Administrative spokesman, Ambassador Gerard C. Smith, expressed two Administration concerns explicitly. First, he said {21}:

"May I observe on that Gilinsky quotation that we don't disagree with the concept of timely warning. It is a very appropriate consideration here but we feel it will lead to distortions if it is made the <u>exclusive</u> (emphasis added) consideration."

This statement shows that the Administration understood that "timely warning" was a concept that could stand separately and apart from other considerations in determining how to exercise U.S. consent rights for certain retransfers. Indeed, prior to Senator Glenn's statement, Senator Pell had stated that {22}:

> "The Executive Branch believes that the timely warning standard should not be the sole basis (emphasis added) for measuring an arrangement's acceptability...."

There is no hint in this markup record that the Committee viewed the position of the Administration as seeking to alter the meaning of "timely warning" or how to determine it. On the contrary, the position statement by Senator Pell indicates that the Committee saw the Administration's goal as replacing the timely warning test with a broader one in which the test of "timely warning" was an important factor.

The second concern expressed by the Administration at the markup stemmed from its own confusion between "timely warning" and "reaction time". The House report had stated in essence that the amount of reaction time needed to effectively counter a diversion from a reprocessing plant based on the Purex process was unlikely to be larger than the conversion time to make the bomb {23}. The drafters of that report also tried to provide some guidance for a minimum acceptable amount of reaction time, corresponding to a situation where the diverting country only possessed stored spent fuel and had no reprocessing facility. The effect of this would have been to force the denial of nearly all reprocessing requests since "reaction time" would have been mandated to a level greater than "conversion time" in almost all cases, thereby leading to a failure of the "timely warning" test.

In sum, the administration's second complaint was directed to the fixing a priori of a high "reaction time" guideline that effectively did not allow approval of any reprocessing requests. This lack of flexibility in judging reprocessing requests was viewed by Senator Glenn as having been taken care of in his amendment, which did not mandate a "reaction time" beyond that needed for "effective safeguards", and which allowed other factors (besides "timely warning") to be taken into account in judging whether to approve a request. Indeed, although Ambassador Smith's initial reaction to the Glenn language was that "...it doesn't move enough in the direction of flexibility that I think is necessary..."{24}, the Administration's own proposed language at that point, as we have already seen, gave no hint of altering the meaning of "timely warning" or the factors that would involved its determination. Therefore, when the subcommittee adopted Glenn's language, it had no alternative meaning of "timely warning" before it.

This conclusion was reinforced at the opening of the discussion of the Glenn amendment during the full Committee markup on September 20, 1977. In response to the Chairman's {Senator Frank Church, (D-Idaho)} request for an explanation of the amendment, Senator Glenn replied {25}:

> "The main issue on the timely warning amendment is this. Timely warning really means technical safeguards and making a judgment as to whether approving reprocessing for some country will result in a significant elevation of risk. The question arises as the weight that should be given to technical safeguards as opposed to, say, political or foreign policy considerations.
> My position, as reflected in the language adopted by the subcommittee was that technical safeguards, that is, timely warning, should be given primary consideration in these cases. We should not be able to override that because it seems to me that the technical methods of giving timely warning are so critical to the system of safeguards and protections that we have in this area that they should not be ignored."

Now this quote is from an uncorrected record. In the first paragraph, when Glenn says, "'Timely warning' really means technical safeguards", it should be understood (indeed, cannot be understood any other way) from the context of all that has gone before, that the statement implies "'timely warning' really means <u>effective</u> technical safeguards," where, in the Subcommittee markup, Glenn made it clear that effective technical safeguards meant detection of a diversion by technical means "in time for use to do something about it"{26}.

The second paragraph, in the absence of further elucidation, could have been interpreted as meaning that the absence of "timely warning" can never be overridden by political or foreign policy considerations. A later statement by Glenn {27} indicates that he meant for "timely warning" to be the largest single factor ("it would be given the bulk of the consideration") in judging whether a retransfer would result in a significant increase in the risk of proliferation. This view was not challenged by the Committee during its discussion of "timely warning". Rather, the committee concentrated on those other factors which, in strong combination, could produce a decision in favor of a retransfer even if "timely warning" is not clearly determinable. Senator Glenn turned the general discussion to specifics by suggesting that {28}:

> "...in the report language we put in that there are situations in which other factors, besides timely warning, may induce the Secretary of State to give his approval. I will give a few examples."

Senator Glenn then listed the factors that ended up being mentioned in the Senate report and in his floor statement during debate on the bill. Senator Church summarized the discussion by saying {29}:

> "Clearly what is sought is to give timely warning a very high priority; but at the same time to recognize that there may be circumstances...that will suffice and lead us to grant such a request even though timely warning is not present."

Note that there is no suggestion of any change in the definition or interpretation of timely warning as given earlier by Senator Glenn.

Moreover, Senator Glenn indicated that discussions had been held on his proposed language with members of the House Committee on International Relations (indeed, there was much staff contact on this issue at the time) and that "they are in agreement with this language {30}." What is implied here is that the House members agreed not only with Glenn's language, but also with his interpretation of that language.

At this point, Senator Richard Stone (D-Florida) asked for the Administration's views on this matter. Mr. Philip Farley, the chief Administration spokesman at the full Committee Markup, stated that the Administration's position was set forth in letters to the Senate Foreign Relations Committee dated September 12 and September 19, 1977, and asked that these letters be placed in the record {31}. The letter of September 19th, from Assistant Secretary of State Douglas Bennett to Senator John Sparkman (D-Alabama), contained the substantive details of the Administration's position. The most important paragraph is reproduced below {32}:

> "Agreement has been reached on

-14-

suitable language relating to the timely warning standard to govern U.S. approval of reprocessing with the leadership of the House Committee on International Relations. This language is acceptable to the Administration. While setting forth strict standards, it recognizes that other foreign policy and non-proliferation factors must be considered. It should also be recognized that warning time associated with alternative reprocessing technology is difficult to quantify but does represent a continuum, progressing from a minimum time associated with processes that involve separated plutonium to longer times for processes that involve uranium and most of the fission products present in irradiated spent fuel. Timely warning is a function of a number of factors, including the inherent risk of proliferation in the country concerned, the amount of warning time provided, and the degree of improvement in warning time that alternative reprocessing technology provides relative to other technologies."

We note that the phrase "inherent risk of proliferation", which appears almost gratuitously and with no explanation of its meaning, was never used in any previous Executive Branch communication to the Congress on "timely warning". We also reiterate our comment in note {4} that this phrase or concept was given no substantive acknowledgement in the legislative history of the NNPA beyond its appearance in the September 19th letter.

In discussing the content of this letter, Mr. Farley went into a long and cogent explanation concerning the amount of warning time available to the U.S. under various circumstances involving the retransfer of nuclear materials. But his exlanation does not reflect, in words or implication, any notion that timely warning is a function of "the inherent risk of proliferation" in a country, whatever the meaning of that phrase. Indeed, Mr. Farley's explanation of warning time conforms with the notion that one must consider the worst case possibility of a completely unexpected diversion in determining whether one's warning time is "timely" or not. He said {33}:

> "For many States, clearly achieving the capability to proceed fairly quickly to a nuclear explosives capability is increasingly going to be something which they have. <u>In that case, there will be very strict limits on the amount of warning we can expect</u>" (emphasis added).

Mr. Farley did <u>not</u> say that the "strict limits" he referred to depended on a fuzzy concept like the "inherent risk of proliferation" in a country. He tied those limits only to technological capability. There was no further substantive discussion on this point in the markup because the Executive Branch's explanation of the timely warning language was not viewed as differing from the explanation offered earlier by Senator Glenn.

Thus, the State Department letter of September 19th played no role in changing the congressional view of "timely warning" that had existed from the beginning. The Glenn compromise allowed for "timely warning" not to be the controlling factor in every circumstance where one had to judge whether a given subsequent arrangement would result in a significant increase of risk of proliferation, but the meaning of "timely warning" was unaffected.

The above claim is nailed down for good by considering the House floor statements on timely warning, following the Senate markup.

IV. <u>The House Discussion of the New Language on Timely Warning</u>

The House floor debates clearly show that House members viewed the new language as <u>not</u> altering the relationship of timely warning to effective safeguards, i.e., that timely warning was still to be viewed as having to do with "that interval of time that exists between the detection of a diversion and the subsequent transformation into an explosive device" (see {8}).

In support of this proposition we have already offered a statement by Representative Bingham in introducing the Glenn language on September 28, 1977. Statements by other key participants also are supportive of our claim. For example, Representative Paul Findley (R-Ohio), Ranking Member of the House Committee on International Relations, in two speeches given before and after the final markup of the NNPA in the Senate, showed that his view of the meaning of "timely warning" was unaffected by the Senate action. He stated {34}:

-16-

171

> "Moreover, the definition of an effective safeguard standard - timely warning - will insure that recipient nations cannot manufacture, undetected and overnight, bombs from materials we provide for peaceful purposes."

Representative Findley solidified his view of timely warning in the floor debate on September 28, 1977, with the following discussion of the related concept of "warning time"{35} (recall that timely warning is present when warning time exceeds reaction time):

> "One needs to have warning times that are ample enough to give supplier states or the international community an opportunity to orchestrate an effective response <u>to an act of diversion</u> and to be able to do this, moreover, before the violator is able to transform his stolen material into bombs." (Emphasis added.)

Representative Lagomarsino (R-California) in support of the compromise amendment described it as follows {36}:

> "Specifically, it requires that the reprocessing of U.S.-supplied fuel must occur under conditions that provide timely warning of illicit diversion of bomb-usable material. Without such timely warning, the nuclear safeguards system becomes meaningless. We would discover that the plutonium has been diverted after the bombs have been built. Delayed warning or no warning at all would render deterrence impossible."

Representative Lagomarsino went on to paraphrase the amendment, and describe it further. He said {37}:

> "...the timely warning amendment...will further require the Administrator to give foremost consideration to the question of whether the reprocessing facility and the reprocessed product <u>can be safeguarded so</u>

-17-

as to provide timely warning (emphasis added) to the United States of any diversion well before the time at which a violating (emphasis added) country could transform weapons-useable material into a nuclear explosive device. Such warning time is essential if the international community or the community of supplier states is to have the opportunity for action. And it is only when such an opportunity for action exists, that safeguards can reliably be considered to deter".

Finally, Representative Legget (D-California), while expressing general support for the House bill on the day it passed (September 28, 1977), expressed a number of reservations about the changes in the measure, including "timely warning" {38}. His complaints, however, do not address any perceived change in definition, but address the fact that certain facilities were exempted from immediate application of the timely warning standard. The tenor of his remarks suggest that if he had perceived a change in the definition of timely warning to make it "more flexible", he would have cited this as a problem.

The congressional statements discussed above make clear that the change in wording of the amendment did not alter the intent of Congress to view "timely warning" as a measure of whether effective action was possible <u>after discovery of a diversion</u> (i.e., the worst-case scenario) to deter or prevent the diverting country from fashioning a nuclear explosive device. There is no reference in the House debate to any concept such as the "inherent risk of proliferation" as being part of the "timely warning" test. Indeed, there is no indication that any member of the House saw a copy of the Bennett-to-Sparkman letter that contained this phrase, let alone paid any attention to it. The only Administion communications that appear in the record of the House debate are identical letters {39} dated September 17, 1977 from Secretary of State Cyrus Vance to Representatives Zablocki and Findley approving proposed amendments to be offered by Congressman Bingham and expressing support for the amended bill. There is not only no reference to "inherent risk of proliferation" as an ingredient of "timely warning" in these letters, but one of the letter's recipients, Congressman Findley, <u>in the statement that preceded his placement of the letter in the Congressional Record</u> reiterated his view that "timely warning" was connected to the notion of effective international safeguards. In his words {40}:

-18-

173

> "Moreover, the definition of an effective safeguard standard - timely warning - will insure that recipient nations cannot manufacture, undetected and overnight, bombs from materials we provide for peaceful purposes.
> By requiring safeguards to provide reliable, timely warning of diversion we are not committing to a new standard but are returning to an old truth."

Later, in the same statement, Representative Findley said:

> "Existing safeguards when applied to reactors do provide reliable, timely warning", but that "present safeguards, when applied to reprocessing, do not ...permit timely warning."

He went on to say that:

> "{W}e must devise safeguards that, when applied to reprocessing, will provide reliable, timely warning. Promising technologies exist which, if pursued, may satisfy this standard. This bill, by defining the standard that safeguards must meet intends to stimulate these new technologies."

Congressman Findley then referred to collaboration between the Committee and the Administration "to fashion this safeguard standard", and remarked that "...the president and Secretary of State have urged that this legislation pass Congress during this session - in its present form - without amendment" {41}.

Obviously, it was not Congressman Findley's understanding that the Administration was proposing any substantial alteration of interpretation of "timely warning" from the one he had just laid down.

The conclusion is therefore inescapable that the House did not see the Senate action as changing the meaning of timely warning, but only as broadening the test for determining whehter a subsequent arrangement for reprocessing or return of plutonium would result in a significant increase of the risk of proliferation.

V. Conclusion on the Meaning of Timely Warning

There is no logical alternative to the conclusion that the Congress meant for the "timely warning" criterion to apply to the most difficult or "worst-case" situation, where the U.S. would not suspect in advance that a diversion might occur, but would learn about it after the fact, when the safeguards system had detected it. That is, when detection time is a <u>positive</u> quantity. In this case it follows from the definition that <u>"timely warning" is met only when reaction time is less than conversion time</u>, (which depends only on a technical and not a political assessment). This explains why the legislative history of the NNPA is replete with references to "timely warning" as being associated with what we are here calling "conversion time", and squares the statutory (Senate) language on "timely warning" with the discussion of the concept in the House report.

VI. The Relationship of Timely Warning to Other Factors in Determining Proliferation Risk

The Senate report, after a discussion of factors that are involved in judging whether "timely warning" would be present (i.e., factors entering into an assessment of "conversion time" and "detection time"), launches into a listing of "other factors which may be taken into account in determining whether there will be a significant increase in the risk of proliferation." These are {42}:

1) "whether the nation is firmly committed to effective non-proliferation policies and is genuinely willing to accept conditions which would minimize the risk of proliferation";

2) "whether the nation has a security agreement or other important foreign policy relationship with the U.S.";

3) "the nature and stability of the recipient's government, its military, and security position"; and,

4) "the energy resources available to that nation".

There would have been no reason for the Senate to label these as "other factors" if they already were included in judging whether the "timely warning" test was met. To do otherwise would have meant that the Senate was counting such factors twice in giving guidance to DOE on retransfer requests, in which case these component factors would become the "foremost" factors in practice, a result not in keeping with the clear congressional intent to identify "timely warning" as a separate, "foremost" factor.

We have thus established through examination of the

NNPA, the Senate and House Reports on the legislation, the Senate Markups, and the floor debate, that Congress intended "timely warning to be an important factor (the "foremost" one), separable and apart from specific political considerations in determining whether a proposed subsequent arrangement for reprocessing or retransfer of plutonium will result in a "significant increase of the risk of proliferation."

VII. THE NEED FOR ADEQUATE ANALYSIS OF THE TIMELY WARNING CRITERION BY THE EXECUTIVE BRANCH

The chief sponsor and Senate floor manager of the bill, Senator John Glenn, stated during the floor debate on February 7, 1978, that {42}:

> "It is important to note, however, that the bill requires that foremost consideration be given to the question of timely warning. This implies that the latter will receive the greatest weight among all factors. Although this does not require denial of a request when timely warning is not clearly determinable, the language suggests that in the absence of a clear determination that timely warning will indeed be provided, a strong combination of other factors would be necessary to compensate for this weakness in safeguards."

This statement emphasizes the importance of clearly determining that the "timely warning" test has been met. Since Executive Branch decisions on retransfers were made optionally reviewable by the Congress under the NNPA, it would have made no sense for the Congress, which went through tortuous hours of debate and negotiation with the Executive Branch on this issue, to intend the Executive Branch to make an important, possibly critical, determination on "timely warning" without adequate supporting analysis showing that the test, as laid out by the Congress, had been met. Therefore, an Executive Branch determination, such as in the Japanese plutonium case, in which there is inadequate analysis revealing how the presence of "timely warning" was arrived at, which does not show how "foremost consideration" was given to it, and which suggests that extraneous political factors were the main component in the determination, is directly counter to Congressional intent.

VIII. NOTES

{1}   P.L. 95-242, enacted on March 10, 1978.

{2}   Letter from NRC Chairman Nunzio J. Palladino to DOE Secretary Donald P. Hodel, September 13, 1984.

{3}   Private communication.

{4}   A phrase used without definition or explanation by the Administration in discussing its own position on "timely warning' in a letter dated September 19, 1977, from then Assistant Secretary of State Douglas Bennett to the Chairman of the Senate Foreign Relations Committee, Senator John Sparkman (D-Alabama). It should be noted that this phrase was never mentioned or acknowledged in any way in the extensive House and Senate debates on the floor, during markups, or in hearings.

{5}   Senate Report 95-467, October 3, 1977

{6}   Congressional Record - House, February 23, 1978, p. 1456

{7}   Congressional Record - House, February 9, 1978, p. H918.

{8}   House Report 95-587, August 5, 1977, p. 18.

{9}   See {5}, p. 11.

{10} Ibid.

{11} Stenographic Record of Markup - S. 897, U.S. Senate Subcommittee on Arms Control, Oceans, and International Environment, Committee on Foreign Relations; Alderson Reporting Company, September 14, 1977.

{12} Stenographic Record, Committee Business, U.S. Senate Committee on Foreign Relations; Alderson Reporting Company, September 20, 1977.

{13} Stenographic Record, Committee Business, U.S. Senate Committee on Foreign Relations; Alderson Reporting Company, September 28, 1977.

{14} See {5}, Section on Executive Branch Comments on S. 897 (As reported by Senate Committee on Governmental Affairs), September 12, 1977, with cover letter from Secretary of State Cyrus Vance, p. 42.

{15} See {14}, p.47.

{16} Ibid.

{17} See {11}, p. 14.

{18} Ibid.

{19} Ibid.

{20} Congressional Record - House, September 28, 1977, p. H10280.

{21} See {11}, p. 15.

{22} Ibid., p.11.

{23} See {8}, p. 20.

{24} See {11}, p. 15.

{25} See {12}, p. 45.

{26} See {11}, p. 14.

{27} See {12}, p. 61.

{28} Ibid., p. 60.

{29} Ibid., p. 61.

{30} Ibid., p. 57.

{31} Ibid., p. 62, The letter of September 12th from Secretary Vance to Senator John Sparkman, Chairman of the Senate Foreign Relations Committee, is identical to the cover letter referred to in {14}.

{32} See {5}, p. 59.

{33} Ibid., p. 65.

{34} Congressional Record - House, September 22, 1977, p. H9833.

{35} See {20}, p. H10282.

{36} Congressional Record - House, September 28, 1977, p. H9835. Although this statement was made on September 22, it was made in reference to the new language on "timely warning" that was formally considered by the House on September 28, 1977. (See colloquy between Representatives Lagomarsino and Bingham in Congressional Record - House, September 28, 1977, p. H10280).

{37} Ibid.

{38} See {20}, p. H10282.

{39} See {35}, pp. H9832 and H9834.

{40} See {35}, p. H9833.

{41} See {35}, p. H9834.

{42} See {5}, p. 12.

{43} Congressional Record - Senate, February 7, 1978, p. S1310.

{44} Section 131a (1) of the Atomic Energy Act as amended provides for a 15 day period of notice before a proposed subsequent arrangement goes into effect.

Presidential Determination No. 89-7 of November 18, 1988

Determination Pursuant to Section 620E(e) of the Foreign Assistance Act of 1961, as Amended

Memorandum for the Secretary of State

Pursuant to Section 620E(e) of the Foreign Assistance Act of 1961, as amended, 22 U.S.C. 2375(e), I hereby certify that Pakistan does not possess a nuclear explosive device and that the proposed United States assistance program will reduce significantly the risk that Pakistan will possess a nuclear explosive device.

You or your delegatee are authorized and directed to publish this determination and certification in the Federal Register.

Ronald Reagan

THE WHITE HOUSE,
Washington, November 18, 1988.

U.S., U.S.S.R. Hold Nonproliferation Talks

U.S. STATEMENT, DEC. 15, 1988

The 12th round of U.S.-U.S.S.R. bilateral consultations on nuclear nonproliferation issues were held December 12–15, 1988, in Washington. The consultations covered a wide range of issues, including preparations for the 1990 Nonproliferation Treaty (NPT) review conference, prospects for further strengthening the international nonproliferation regime, enhancement of international safeguards, mutual support for the strengthening of the International Atomic Energy Agency (IAEA), and situations of regional concern from a nuclear proliferation perspective. The American delegation was headed by Ambassador at Large Richard T. Kennedy, and the Soviet delegation was headed by Dr. Boris Semenov, First Deputy Chairman of the State Committee for the Utilization of Atomic Energy.

Secretary of State Shultz opened the first plenary session, expressing appreciation for the valuable contribution that these consultations have made to the task of preventing the spread of nuclear weapons to additional countries and noting the importance of continuing cooperation between the United States and U.S.S.R. to strengthen the nonproliferation regime and the need for continuing discussions of this kind. He noted that the leaders of both countries viewed these consultations with satisfaction.

The consultations were conducted in a business-like and constructive atmosphere, with both sides confirming their interest in preventing proliferation of nuclear explosives and helping other countries enjoy the benefit of the peaceful uses of nuclear energy under effective international safeguards. Both sides affirmed the value of continuing these consultations on a regular basis in the future. ■

PRESIDENT BUSH

Presidential Determination No. 90-1 of October 5, 1989

Determination Pursuant to Section 620E(e) of the Foreign Assistance Act of 1961, as Amended

Memorandum for the Secretary of State

Pursuant to Section 620E(e) of the Foreign Assistance Act of 1961, as amended, 22 U.S.C. 2375(e), I hereby certify that Pakistan does not possess a nuclear explosive device and that the proposed United States assistance program will reduce significantly the risk that Pakistan will possess a nuclear explosive device.

You are authorized and directed to publish this determination and certification in the Federal Register.

THE WHITE HOUSE,
Washington, October 5, 1989.

Soviet-United States Joint Statement on Nonproliferation
June 4, 1990

The United States of America and the Union of Soviet Socialist Republics oppose the proliferation of nuclear weapons, chemical weapons, missiles capable of carrying such weapons, and certain other missiles and missile technologies. The more nations that possess such weapons, the more difficult it will be to realize the desire of people everywhere to achieve effective arms control and disarmament measures and to reduce the threat of war. Weapons proliferation can provoke or intensify insecurity and hostility among nations, and threatens mankind with warfare of unprecedented destructiveness.

Our discussions over the past months point the way to a new era in relations between our two countries. We have taken major steps toward concluding agreements to reduce our own strategic nuclear arsenals, to bring limits on nuclear testing into force, and to reach a global ban on chemical weapons. Together with the nations of Europe, we are taking unprecedented steps to reduce existing conventional weaponry as part of a process of building a lasting structure of European security. The progress we are making and the commitments we have made in these bilateral and multilateral arms control efforts clearly demonstrate that arms reductions can contribute to increased security, even when there have been long-standing and deep-seated differences between countries.

The historic steps we have taken to improve U.S.-Soviet relations and to cooperate in the interests of international stability create the possibility of even closer and more concrete cooperation in the areas of nuclear, chemical, and missile non-proliferation.

With these considerations in mind, The United States and the Soviet Union:

- Declare their commitment to preventing the proliferation of nuclear weapons, chemical weapons, and missiles capable of carrying such weapons and certain other missiles and missile technologies, in particular those subject to the provisions of the Missile Technology Control Regime (MTCR);
- Agree to work closely together and with other members of the international community to develop and to put into action concrete measures against the proliferation of these types of weapons; and
- Call on other nations to join in a renewed commitment to effective non-proliferation measures as a means of securing international peace and stability and as a step toward the effective limitation worldwide of nuclear weapons, chemical weapons, missiles, and missile technology.

The two sides have taken specific actions to advance these commitments.

Nuclear Weapons Non-Proliferation

In order to prevent the proliferation of nuclear weapons, the United States and the Soviet Union:
- Reaffirm their steadfast and long-lasting commitment to prevent the proliferation of nuclear weapons and to strengthen the international nuclear weapons non-proliferation regime;
- Reaffirm their strong support for the Treaty on the Non-Proliferation of Nuclear Weapons (NPT) and agree that it continues to make an invaluable contribution to global and regional security and stability;
- Urge all countries which have not yet done so to adhere to the NPT;
- Urge all NPT parties to implement scrupulously their International Atomic Energy Agency (IAEA) safeguards obligations under the Treaty;
- Affirm their intention to cooperate together and with other Treaty parties to ensure a successful 1990 Review Conference on the Treaty on the Non-Proliferation of Nuclear Weapons which would reaffirm support for the objectives of the Treaty and its importance to international security and stability;

- Support the Treaty for the Prohibition of Nuclear Weapons in Latin America (the Treaty of Tlatelolco) and urge all countries in the region to bring it into force at an early date;
- Reiterate their continuing commitment to strengthening the IAEA, whose unique system of safeguards has contributed to the widespread peaceful use of nuclear energy for social and economic development;
- Support increased international cooperation in the peaceful uses of nuclear energy under IAEA safeguards;
- Call on all non-nuclear-weapons states with unsafeguarded nuclear activities to place these activities under international safeguards;
- Agree on the need for stringent controls over exports of nuclear-related material, equipment and technology, to ensure that they will not be misused for nuclear explosive purposes, and urge all other nations capable of exporting nuclear-related technology to apply similarly strict controls;
- Continue to support efforts to improve and strengthen the international nuclear export control regime;
- Support discussions among states in regions of nuclear proliferation concern for the purpose of achieving concrete steps to reduce the risk of nuclear proliferation, and, in particular, join in calling on the nations of the Middle East, Southern Africa, and South Asia to engage in and pursue such discussions;
- Agree to continue their regular, constructive bilateral consultations on nuclear weapons non-proliferation.

Missile and Missile Technology Non-Proliferation

In order to stem the proliferation of missiles and missile technology, the United States and the Soviet Union:
- Have signed the Treaty between the United States of America and the Union of Soviet Socialist Republics on the Elimination of Their Intermediate-Range and Shorter-Range Missiles, demonstrating that controls on—indeed the elimination of—such missiles can enhance national security;
- Reaffirm their intention that the START Treaty be signed by the end of the year;
- Affirm their support for the objectives of the Missile Technology Control Regime, covering missiles, and certain equipment and technology relating to missiles capable of delivering at least 500 kilograms of payload to a range of at least 300 kilometers and they call on all nations that have not done so to observe the spirit and the guidelines of this regime;
- Are taking measures to restrict missile proliferation on a worldwide basis, including export controls and other internal procedures;
- Have instituted bilateral consultations to exchange information concerning such controls and procedures and identify specific measures to prevent missile proliferation;
- Agree to work to stop missile proliferation, particularly in regions of tension, such as the Middle East;
- To this end, affirm their intent to explore regional initiatives to reduce the threat of missile proliferation, including the possibility of offering their good offices to promote such initiatives;
- Recall that they favor international economic cooperation including cooperation aimed at peaceful space exploration, as long as such cooperation could not contribute to missile proliferation;
- Appeal to all countries—to exporters of missiles and missile technology as well as purchasers—to exercise restraint, and express their willingness to continue their respective dialogues with other countries on the non-proliferation of missiles and missile technology.
- Are resolved, on their part, to continue to work to strengthen such international restraint with respect to missile and missile technology proliferation.

Chemical Weapons Non-proliferation

In order to stem the use and proliferation of chemical weapons, the United States and the Soviet Union:

- Declare that a multilateral, effectively verifiable chemical weapons convention banning the development, production and use of chemical weapons and eliminating all stocks on a global basis is the best long-term solution to the threat to international security posed by the use and spread of chemical weapons, and that non-proliferation measures are considered a step toward achieving such a convention;
- Will intensify their cooperation to expedite the negotiations in Geneva with the view to resolving outstanding issues as soon as possible and to finalizing the draft convention at the earliest date;
- Have instituted bilateral confidence building measures, including chemical weapons data exchange and reciprocal site visits;
- Have just signed a trailblazing agreement on destruction and non-production of chemical weapons and on measures to facilitate the multilateral convention on chemical weapons;
- Commit themselves, in that agreement to take practical measures to encourage all chemical weapons-capable states to become parties to the multilateral convention;
- Having declared their possession of chemical weapons, urge other states possessing chemical weapons to declare their possession, to commit to their destruction, and to begin immediately to address, through research and cooperation, the need for chemical weapons destruction capability;
- State that they themselves will not proliferate chemical weapons;
- Have instituted export controls to stem the proliferation of chemical weapons. These measures are not intended to hinder or discriminate against legitimate peaceful chemical activities;
- Have agreed to conduct bilateral discussions to improve the effectiveness of their respective export controls to stem the proliferation of chemical weapons;
- Conduct regular bilateral consultations to broaden bilateral cooperation, including the reciprocal exchange of information on the problems of chemical weapons proliferation;
- Confirm their intent to pursue political and diplomatic actions, where specific cases give rise to concerns about the production, use or spread of chemical weapons;
- Join with other nations in multilateral efforts to coordinate export controls, exchange information, and broaden international cooperation to stem the proliferation of chemical weapons;
- Reaffirm their support for the 1925 Geneva Protocol banning the use of chemical weapons in violation of international law;
- Are taking steps to strengthen the 1925 Geneva Protocol by:

—Encouraging states that are not parties to accede;

—Confirming their intention to provide active support to the United Nations Secretary General in conducting investigations of reported violations of the Protocol;

—Affirming their intention to consider the imposition of sanctions against violators of the Protocol, including those under Chapter VII of the United Nations Charter;

—Agreeing to consult promptly in the event of a violation of the Protocol to discuss possible bilateral and multilateral actions against the offender, as well as appropriate assistance to the victims of such violation;

- Agree that the presence and further proliferation of chemical weapons in areas of tension, such as the Middle East, is particularly dangerous. The two countries therefore affirm their intent to explore regional initiatives in the Middle East and other areas, including the possibility of offering their good offices to promote such initiatives as:

—Efforts to broaden awareness of the dangers of chemical weapons prolifera-

tion and its negative impact on implementation of the multilateral convention on chemical weapons;
—Bilateral or multilateral efforts to stem chemical weapons proliferation, including the renunciation of the production of chemical weapons;
—Efforts to destroy chemical weapons in advance of the multilateral convention on chemical weapons, as the United States and the Soviet Union are doing.

The United States and the Soviet Union call on all nations of the world that have not already done so to join them in taking comparable, effective measures to stem chemical weapons proliferation.

Soviet-United States Joint Statement on Cooperation in Peaceful Uses of Atomic Energy
June 4, 1990

During the state visit of Mikhail S. Gorbachev, President of the USSR, at the invitation of George Bush, President of the United States, the sides concluded a new U.S.-USSR Agreement on Scientific and Technical Cooperation in the Field of Peaceful Uses of Atomic Energy. This Agreement strengthens the longstanding framework for important research in a number of fields of mutual interest, including controlled thermonuclear fusion, fundamental properties of matter, and civilian nuclear reactor safety.

Recognizing the need to manage responsibly the development and utilization of nuclear power, the two sides have agreed on cooperation in the study of the health and environmental effects of past, present and future nuclear power generation, and in strengthening operational safety practices in civilian nuclear reactors. The sides intend to develop and implement promptly a mutually beneficial joint program of work in these fields under this Agreement. They also agreed to explore the possibilities for cooperation in the management of hazardous and radioactive waste.

FACT SHEET

June 3, 1991

**The White House
Office of the Press Secretary
(Kennebunkport, Maine)
May 29, 1991**

Middle East Arms Control Initiative

Fulfilling the pledge he made in his March 6 address to a joint session of Congress, the President announced today a series of proposals intended to curb the spread of nuclear, chemical and biological weapons in the Middle East, as well as the missiles that that can deliver them. The proposals also seek to restrain destabilizing conventional arms build-ups in the region.

The proposals would apply to the entire Middle East, including Iraq, Iran, Libya, Syria, Egypt, Lebanon, Israel, Jordan, Saudi Arabia, and the other states of the Maghreb and the Gulf Cooperation Council. They reflect our consultations with allies, governments in the region, and key suppliers of arms and technology.

The support of both arms exporters and importers will be essential to the success of the initiative. Since proliferation is a global problem, it must find a global solution. At the same time the current situation in the Middle East poses unique dangers and opportunities. Thus, the President's proposal will concentrate on the Middle East as its starting point, while complementing other initiatives such as those taken by Prime Ministers John Major and Brian Mulroney. It includes the following elements.

<u>Supplier Restraint</u>

The initiative calls on the five major suppliers of conventional arms to meet at senior levels in the near future to discuss the establishment of guidelines for restraints on destabilizing transfers of conventional arms, as well as weapons of mass destruction and associated technology. France has agreed to host the initial meeting. (The United Kingdom, France, the Soviet Union, China, and the United States have supplied the vast majority of the conventional arms exported to the Middle East in the last decade.) At the same time, these guidelines will permit states in the region to acquire the conventional capabilities they legitimately need to deter and defend against military aggression.

US ARMS CONTROL AND DISARMAMENT AGENCY, WASHINGTON, D.C. 20451
OFFICE OF PUBLIC AFFAIRS (202) 647-8677

-- These discussions will be expanded to include other suppliers in order to obtain the broadest possible cooperation. The London Summit of the G-7, to be hosted by the UK in July, will provide an early opportunity to begin to engage other governments.

-- To implement this regime, the suppliers would commit:
-- to observe a general code of responsible arms transfers;
-- to avoid destabilizing transfers; and
-- to establish effective domestic export controls on the end-use of arms or other items to be transferred.

-- The guidelines will include a mechanism for consultations among suppliers, who would:
-- notify one another in advance of certain arms sales;
-- meet regularly to consult on arms transfers;
-- consult on an *ad hoc* basis if a supplier believed guidelines were not being observed; and
-- provide one another with an annual report on transfers.

Missiles

The initiative proposes a freeze on the acquisition, production, and testing of surface-to-surface missiles by states in the region with a view to the ultimate elimination of such missiles from their arsenals.

-- Suppliers would also step up efforts to coordinate export licensing for equipment, technology and services that could be used to manufacture surface-to-surface missiles. Export licenses would be provided only for peaceful end uses.

Nuclear Weapons

The initiative builds on existing institutions and focuses on activities directly related to nuclear weapons capability. The initiative would:

-- Call on regional states to implement a verifiable ban on the production and acquisition of weapons-usable nuclear material (enriched uranium or separated plutonium);

-- Reiterate our call on all states in the region that have not already done so to accede to the Non-Proliferation Treaty;

--Reiterate our call to place all nuclear facilities in the region under International Atomic Energy Agency safeguards; and

--Continue to support the eventual creation of a regional nuclear weapon-free zone.

Chemical Weapons

The proposal will build on the President's recent initiative to achieve early completion of the global Chemical Weapons Convention.

- -- The initiative calls for all states in the region to commit to becoming original parties to the Convention.

- -- Given the history of possession and use of chemical weapons in the region, the initiative also calls for regional states to institute confidence-building Chemical Weapons Convention provisions.

Biological Weapons

As with the approach to chemical weapon controls, the proposals build on an existing global approach. The initiative would:

- -- Call for strengthening the 1972 Biological Weapons Convention (BWC) through full implementation of existing BWC provisions and an improved mechanism for information exchange. These measures will be pursued at the five-year Review Conference of the BWC this September.

- -- Urge regional states to adopt biological weapons confidence-building measures.

This initiative complements our continuing support for the continuation of the UN Security Council embargo against arms transfers to Iraq, as well as the efforts of the UN Special Commission to eliminate Iraq's remaining capabilities to use or produce nuclear, chemical, and biological weapons and the missiles to deliver them.

North Korean Nuclear Weapons Threat

Excerpt from the joint ministerial news conference held by Secretary Baker and other ministers following the third Asia-Pacific Economic Cooperation (APEC) ministerial meeting, Seoul, Korea, November 14, 1991.

Q: According to the report released by the Blue House today, of the conversation between you and President Roh Tae Woo, he said that the two-plus-four formula, which has been suggested, is not applicable to Korea because conditions are essentially different than those which obtain in Europe or Germany.

In your article for *Foreign Affairs*, you suggested that the two Koreas and four other powers should create some kind of forum to work on this problem. Could you explain what you had in mind and how it squares with President Roh's feeling that this does. . . .

Secretary Baker: Yes, I can . . . because what President Roh said—based on what you've just reported to me that he said—squares exactly with our discussion. Let me say that I think—we think—the greatest threat to regional security and stability in this area is the threat of nuclear weapons development by North Korea. It is a threat that we believe needs to be addressed. We're in a period of time and in other parts of the world where we seem to be moving, generally speaking, to a lessening of tensions. There are some increased tensions in places like Yugoslavia, I recognize. But there are generally some lessening of tensions around the world from what existed over the past few years. This issue is one that remains firmly on the agenda, not just of this region, I think, but of the world. We see it as a major regional issue, but we also see it as a global issue.

I think the statements recently by President Bush and President Roh give North Korea an opportunity and a reason to deal with this matter and to deal with it in the manner that most of the international community have been requesting for a long, long time. And I am talking about IAEA safeguards and the like.

I believe that the United States is joined by some other countries in wanting to see the matter dealt with satisfactorily, politically, and diplomatically. I believe that is the position of the Government of Japan based on my talks in Tokyo, although the Government of Japan is represented here, and they can certainly speak for themselves. I believe it is the position of the Soviet Union. I would hope it would be the position of the People's Republic of China, but they are here and they can speak for themselves. It's not up to me to do that. But I don't see—I don't think any country can be sanguine or willing to accept the development of a nuclear weapons capability by North Korea. So we have suggested that those of us who are concerned about this should go about the business of trying to get a satisfactory solution to it, if necessary in a multilateral context. But it is different completely and totally from the two-plus-four mechanism and procedure that we used in connection with the unification of Germany, because we are not talking about it with reference to the solution of the problems between the two Koreas.

It has always been the position of the United States that South Korea should have the lead in that—that we would be helpful where we could. I think there are other countries that would like to be helpful in that regard. That is still our position with respect to questions involving resolution of the underlying problems between the North and the South. But with respect to this question of nuclear capability of the North, we think there is a place for multilateral approach to that. It is my understanding that the Government of South Korea agrees with us based on the discussions I've had with the foreign minister here and with President Roh this morning . . . . ❑

Non-proliferation Efforts Bolstered
President Bush, White House Fact Sheets

President's Statement

Released by the White House, Office of the Press Secretary, Washington, DC, July 13, 1992.

A few weeks ago, [Russian] President Boris Yeltsin and I agreed to the most far-reaching reductions in nuclear weaponry since the dawn of the atomic age. Yet even as our own arsenals diminish, the spread of the capability to produce or acquire weapons of mass destruction and the means to deliver them constitutes a growing threat to US national security interests and world peace. In a world in which regional tensions may unpredictably erupt into war, these weapons could have devastating consequences.

That is why this Administration has fought so hard to stem the proliferation of these terrible weapons. We look back with pride on a solid record of accomplishment. Membership in the nuclear Non-Proliferation Treaty (NPT) has grown. The Missile Technology Control Regime and Australia Group have broadened their membership and expanded their controls against trade useful to the development of missiles and chemical and biological weapons. We have toughened our non-proliferation export controls, and other nations have followed suit. We have seen remarkable progress in building and strengthening regional arms control arrangements in Latin America, the Korean Peninsula, and the Middle East.

Yet we need to do more. The demand for these weapons persists, and new suppliers of key technologies are emerging. Export controls alone cannot create an airtight seal against proliferation. In an era of advancing technology and trade liberalization, we need to employ the full range of political, security, intelligence, and other tools at our disposal. Therefore, I have set forth today a set of principles to guide our non-proliferation efforts in the years ahead and directed a number of steps to supplement our existing efforts. These steps include a decision not to produce plutonium and highly enriched uranium for nuclear explosive purposes and a number of proposals to strengthen international actions against those who contribute to the spread of weapons of mass destruction and the missiles that deliver them.

While these steps will strengthen the barriers against proliferation, success will require hard work and, at times, hard choices. The United States, however, is committed to take a leading role in the international effort to thwart the spread of technologies and weapons that cast a cloud over our future.

Non-proliferation Initiative

Fact sheet issued by the White House, Office of the Press Secretary, Washington, DC, July 13, 1992.

Noting that the potential "spread of the capability to produce or acquire weapons of mass destruction and the means to deliver them constitutes a growing threat to US national security interests," the President today announced a comprehensive initiative to bolster American efforts to stem the spread of these capabilities and to discourage any use of such weapons. The initiative seeks to integrate new and existing policies in an overall framework to guide US non-proliferation policy in the years ahead.

GUIDING PRINCIPLES

First, the United States will build on existing global norms against proliferation and, where possible, strengthen and broaden them.

Second, the United States will focus special efforts on those areas where the dangers of proliferation remain acute, notably the Middle East, the Persian Gulf, South Asia, and the Korean Peninsula.

Third, US non-proliferation policy will seek the broadest possible multilateral support while continuing to show leadership on critical issues.

Fourth, the United States will address the proliferation issue through the entire range of political, diplomatic, economic, intelligence, regional security, export controls, and other tools available.

POLICY OBJECTIVES

Nuclear Materials

Nuclear Materials Production. The United States shall not produce plutonium or highly enriched uranium for nuclear explosive purposes. This step is intended to encourage countries in regions of tension, such as the Middle East and South Asia, to take similar actions, such as those proposed in the May 1991 Middle East arms control initiative. The United States will seek further multilateral support for concrete measures to discourage production or acquisition of weapons-usable nuclear materials in South Asia, the Korean Peninsula, or other areas where they would increase the risk of proliferation.

Multilateral Actions

Compliance With International Non-proliferation Norms. The United States will take into account other countries' performance on key international non-proliferation norms in developing its cooperation and technology transfer relationships and will consult with friends and allies on similar approaches.

Enforcement of International Non-proliferation Norms. The United States will consult with friends and allies on international actions to be taken against serious violations of non-proliferation norms, e.g., the transfer of any weapon of mass destruction or key weapon facilities; violation of safeguards agreements; or confirmed use of nuclear, chemical, or biological weapons. Actions could include UN

Security Council embargoes or inspections, assistance to victims of attacks by such weapons, extradition agreements, or immigration restrictions against individuals who have knowingly contributed to proliferation.

Support for Special Inspections and Weapon Destruction. The United States will examine, in consultation with friends and allies, establishment of multilateral funding efforts to support special inspection regimes where necessary and to help states destroy existing weapon stockpiles.

Harmonization of Export Controls. The United States will promote harmonized non-proliferation export control lists and enforcement, including an agreement among suppliers not to undercut one another's export restraint decisions.

Regional Efforts

Targeted Approaches. The United States will continue to focus special efforts on the dangers of proliferation in South Asia, the Persian Gulf, the Middle East, and the Korean Peninsula, including efforts to achieve confidence-building measures; inspection regimes; and other economic, political, and security-related measures.

Former Soviet Union. The United States will continue to work with authorities from Russia and the other new states toward the following objectives:

- Implementation of all relevant international agreements, such as the Non-Proliferation Treaty, Biological Weapons Convention, and, when opened for signature, the Chemical Weapons Convention;
- Effective internal accounting and physical protection against theft or diversion of nuclear-related materials and equipment;
- Effective export controls on chemical, biological, nuclear, and missile technologies consistent with existing multilateral regimes, including appropriate laws and regulations, as well as education of exporters and customs and enforcement officials;
- Safe and secure dismantlement of nuclear warheads and effective controls over nuclear weapon material;
- Creation of opportunities for weapons scientists and engineers to redirect their talents to peaceful endeavors; and
- Consideration of requests for assistance in dismantling or destroying Russian biological weapons facilities or in converting these facilities to production of vaccines and other pharmaceutical products, provided Russia is in full compliance with the Biological Weapons Convention.

Global Norms

Chemical Weapons Convention (CWC). The United States reaffirms its commitment to see a CWC concluded this year and calls on all nations to commit to become original signatories.

Non-proliferation Treaty [NPT] and Tlatelolco. The United States will seek the indefinite extension of the NPT in 1995 and full entry into force of the Treaty of Tlatelolco by 1993.

International Atomic Energy Agency (IAEA). The United States will work with other nations to strengthen the IAEA and will support needed increases in the safeguards budget.

Biological Weapons Convention (BWC). The United States will continue to urge universal adherence to the Biological Weapons Convention and increased support for the confidence-building measures agreed by the parties at the 1991 review conference.

Missile Technology Control Regime (MTCR). The United States reiterates the call of the MTCR partners for all governments to adopt the MTCR guidelines as part of their national policy.

Intelligence

Non-proliferation Center. The intelligence community, including the newly created non-proliferation center, will increase support for international non-proliferation regimes and seek to enlarge the pool of experienced, well-trained experts committed to the non-proliferation mission.

Existing Non-proliferation Efforts

Fact sheet issued by the White House, Office of the Press Secretary, Washington, DC, July 13, 1992.

Non-Proliferation Treaty. In the past year, China, South Africa, Latvia, Lithuania, Estonia, and other new parties brought NPT membership to 149. France will soon be a party. In the START [Strategic Arms Reduction Treaty] protocol signed in Lisbon, Byelarus, Kazakhstan, and Ukraine agreed to join the NPT as non-nuclear weapon states.

International Atomic Energy Agency. The IAEA confirmed its right to conduct "special inspections" at undeclared nuclear facilities. Argentina and Brazil reversed long-standing positions to adopt full-scope IAEA safeguards. After years of delay, North Korea finally complied with its NPT obligations to ratify an IAEA safeguards agreement and accept IAEA inspections.

Nuclear Suppliers Group (NSG). In April 1992, the 27 NSG members agreed to extend nuclear export controls to dual-use items and to require full-scope IAEA safeguards as a condition of significant new nuclear supply.

Missile Technology Control Regime [MTCR]. The MTCR expanded its membership to 22, updated its export control list, and agreed to extend its focus to any missile intended to deliver weapons of mass destruction. China, Argentina, and Israel have pledged to observe the MTCR guidelines.

Enhanced Proliferation Control Initiative (EPCI). Under EPCI, the United States expanded its export controls to cover all 50 identified chemical weapon precursors, dual-use equipment relevant to chemical and biological weapons production, whole chemical plants, and knowing assistance to chemical or biological weapon or missile programs.

Strengthened National Export Controls. Several countries have strengthened their domestic export control laws and enforcement mechanisms. Several countries have adopted laws or regulations similar to the

Global Protection System Against Ballistic Missiles

Text of joint US-Russian statement released by the Office of the Assistant Secretary/Spokesman, Washington, DC, July 14, 1992.

U.S. and Russian high-level delegations met in Moscow on July 13 and 14 to hold consultations on establishing a Global Protection System [GPS] against ballistic missiles.

The consultations were the result of agreement by Presidents Bush and Yeltsin [of Russia] at the Washington Summit. The two Presidents agreed that our two nations should work together with allies and other interested states in developing a concept for such a Global Protection System as part of an overall strategy to counter the proliferation of ballistic missiles and weapons of mass destruction.

The two Presidents had agreed to explore on a priority basis:

- the potential for sharing ballistic missile early warning information through the establishment of an early warning center;
- the potential for cooperation with participating states in developing ballistic missile defense capabilities and technologies; and
- the development of a legal basis for cooperation, including new treaties

and agreements and possible changes of existing agreements necessary to implement a Global Protection System.

The delegations had good and fruitful discussions on all relevant issues. They agreed that their two nations were entering a radically changed security environment, one characterized by the change in the nature of threats to international security, including the growing threat of proliferation of ballistic missiles and weapons of mass destruction to the world community. They also agreed that they needed to work together and with other interested states to find solutions to these new challenges by exploring the potential benefits of a Global Protection System against ballistic missiles and agreeing that it is important to explore the role of defenses in protecting against limited ballistic missile attacks.

The two sides believed that their discussions had created a promising foundation for future work. In that regard, they decided to set up three working groups in which specialists would carry forward expeditiously the task of developing the concept of a Global Protection System.

- A Global Protection System Concept Working Group would consider the structure, modalities, and functions of a future Global Protection System. It would explore the concept of the GPS and examine the relationship among its principal elements. It would create sub-groups, as appropriate, including sub-groups on analysis and concepts, early warning, and cooperation in the anti-tactical ballistic missile defense field.
- A Technology Cooperation Working Group would consider possible research, development, and testing projects and other forms of technological cooperation that could contribute—in possible cooperation with other states—to the realization of the concept of the Global Protection System. The work of this group should reflect the work of the Concept Working Group.
- A Non-proliferation Working Group would conduct joint assessments of trends in the proliferation of weapons of mass destruction and their means of delivery and would explore ways and means of strengthening current international efforts to prevent such proliferation and would explore future initiatives in this area.

The two sides agreed that the working groups would hold their initial meetings at an early date. They further agreed that the high-level group would have a continuing role as a steering group and would meet periodically to address issues assigned to them by Presidents Bush and Yeltsin in their June 17 statement. The two sides undertook to provide the leadership of the two countries with a report on the status of these efforts at an early date. ❏

EPCI, which restrict assistance by their citizens to nuclear, chemical, biological, or missile programs.

Australia Group. The Australia Group expanded its membership to 22 nations and followed the US lead in EPCI by expanding its export controls to cover the 50 chemical weapon precursors as well as chemical weapons-related dual-use equipment. The Group has just adopted a multilateral control list of biological organisms, toxins, and equipment.

Middle East Arms Control Initiative. In May 1991, the President launched a process among the five leading conventional arms suppliers: the United States, the United Kingdom, France, Russia, and China. In October, the five agreed to observe guidelines of restraint in conventional transfers and to information exchange. In May 1992, the five agreed to interim guidelines for exports related to weapons of mass destruction. Under the Middle East peace process, 23 delegations (including Israel and 12 Arab states) gathered in Washington in May 1992 to discuss regional security and arms control.

United Nations. The UN Special Commission and the IAEA have carried out 39 inspections in Iraq, identified and begun to destroy tens of thousands of chemical munitions, destroyed missile-production equipment and over 150 missiles, revealed an extensive nuclear weapons program, and oversaw destruction of nuclear weapon-related facilities.

Latin America. In addition to adopting full-scope IAEA safeguards, Argentina and Brazil joined with Chile to ban chemical and biological weapons in their countries. ■

g. Statement by President Bush on the Purchase of Highly-Enriched Uranium from the Russian Federation

Over the past year the United States and the former Soviet Union have agreed to cut their strategic nuclear arsenals by two-thirds and to eliminate most of their tactical nuclear weapons, including all ground-launched systems. As a result of these dramatic reductions, thousands of nuclear warheads are being dismantled in Russia and the United States. The United States and Russia are cooperating closely to help ensure the safe and secure transport, storage and dismantlement of former Soviet nuclear weapons.

I am pleased to announce that the Russian Federation and the United States have now also initialed an agreement to ensure that highly-enriched uranium from dismantled nuclear weapons will be used only for peaceful purposes. Our two governments have initialed an agreement, which we expect to sign quickly, providing for the conversion of this material into civilian reactor fuel. We have also agreed to establish measures to ensure that the nonproliferation, physical security, material accounting and control, and environmental requirements covering this material are fully met.

Under the agreement, the United States and Russia would seek within the next twelve months to conclude an implementing contract, establishing the terms of the purchase of weapons-grade uranium by the U.S. Department of Energy and the dilution of that material to reactor-grade uranium for sale as commercial reactor fuel. The contract would also provide for the participation of the U.S. private sector and the use by the Russian Federation of a portion of the proceeds to increase the safety of nuclear reactors in the former Soviet Union.

Abroad, this agreement will help ensure that nuclear-weapons grade material does not fall into the wrong hands, while providing funds to promote economic reforms and the transition to a market-based economy. At home, this agreement will secure long-term supplies of less expensive fuel for U.S. nuclear power stations to the benefit of American consumers, with no adverse impact on American jobs. Thus, this U.S.-Russian agreement illustrates how foreign policy accomplishments can promote our domestic economic well-being while making the world a safer place to live.

US Support for Nuclear Suppliers Group
Secretary Christopher, Press Statement

Secretary Christopher
April 1, 1993

Message from the Secretary to the meeting of the Nuclear Suppliers Group in Lucerne, Switzerland, released by the Office of the Press Secretary/Spokesman, Washington, DC.

The United States welcomes the renewed vigor of the Nuclear Suppliers Group (NSG), which reflects the international community's increased emphasis on nuclear non-proliferation. Over the last 2 years, much has been accomplished in two important plenary meetings and in several working groups. Progress over this period has reinforced the role of the Nuclear Suppliers Group as a fundamental component of the international nuclear non-proliferation regime.

I believe that the plenary in Lucerne will continue the outstanding spirit of cooperation among suppliers demonstrated by recent activities of the group. I also want to express the deep appreciation of the US Government to the Government of Switzerland for hosting this meeting.

The United States has been a strong proponent of requiring full-scope IAEA [International Atomic Energy Agency] safeguards as a condition for significant new nuclear supply commitments. This policy was adopted at last year's plenary, and I urge the group now to amend its guidelines to incorporate this important provision. No non-proliferation principle is more appropriate for the first change to the Nuclear Suppliers Guidelines since they were first published in 1978.

Last year, the NSG also created an important new arrangement to harmonize export controls on nuclear-related dual-use commodities. We are honored to chair the dual-use arrangement for the next year. We are also pleased with the progress of the working groups on institutional and technical matters and expect their work to strengthen the non-proliferation efforts of the Group.

The statement issued by last year's plenary appealed to all nuclear exporting countries to adhere to the Nuclear Suppliers Guidelines. I am pleased that Argentina has adhered to the guidelines and will attend this year's meeting. Other countries have also shown interest in adhering to the guidelines. We hope that all countries will come to share our common non-proliferation objectives. We are committed to working with you in the Nuclear Suppliers Group and elsewhere to achieve a world free of the threat of nuclear proliferation.

Fact Sheet: Non-Proliferation and Export Control Policy

Fact sheet released by the White House, Office of the Press Secretary, Washington, DC, September 27, 1993.

The President today established a framework for U.S. efforts to prevent the proliferation of weapons of mass destruction and the missiles that deliver them. He outlined three major principles to guide our non-proliferation and export control policy.

- Our national security requires us to accord higher priority to non-proliferation and to make it an integral element of our relations with other countries.
- To strengthen U.S. economic growth, democratization abroad, and international stability, we actively seek expanded trade and technology exchange with nations, including former adversaries, that abide by global non-proliferation norms.
- We need to build a new consensus—embracing the executive and legislative branches, industry and the public, and friends abroad—to promote effective non-proliferation efforts and integrate our non-proliferation and economic goals.

The President reaffirmed U.S. support for a strong, effective non-proliferation regime that enjoys broad multilateral support and employs all of the means at our disposal to advance our objectives. Key elements of the policy follow.

Fissile Material

The U.S. will undertake a comprehensive approach to the growing accumulation of fissile material from dismantled nuclear weapons and within civil nuclear programs. Under this approach, the U.S. will:

- Seek to eliminate where possible the accumulation of stockpiles of highly enriched uranium or plutonium and to ensure that, where these materials already exist, they are subject to the highest standards of safety, security, and international accountability;
- Propose a multilateral convention prohibiting the production of highly enriched uranium or plutonium for nuclear explosives purposes or outside of international safeguards;
- Encourage more restrictive regional arrangements to constrain fissile material production in regions of instability and high proliferation risk;
- Submit U.S. fissile material no longer needed for our deterrent to inspection by the International Atomic Energy Agency;
- Pursue the purchase of highly enriched uranium from the former Soviet Union and other countries and its conversion to peaceful use as reactor fuel;
- Explore means to limit the stockpiling of plutonium from civil nuclear programs and seek to minimize the civil use of highly enriched uranium; and
- Initiate a comprehensive review of long-term options for plutonium disposition, taking into account technical, non-proliferation, environmental, budgetary, and economic considerations. Russia and other nations with relevant interests and experience will be invited to participate in this study.

The United States does not encourage the civil use of plutonium and, accordingly, does not itself engage in plutonium reprocessing for either nuclear power or nuclear explosive purposes. The United States, however, will maintain its existing commitments regarding the use of plutonium in civil nuclear programs in Western Europe and Japan.

Export Controls

To be truly effective, export controls should be applied uniformly by all suppliers. The United States will harmonize domestic and multilateral controls to the greatest extent possible. At the same time, the need to lead the international community or overriding national security or foreign policy interests may justify unilateral export controls in specific cases. We will review our unilateral dual-use export controls and policies and eliminate them unless such controls are essential to national security and foreign policy interests.

We will streamline the implementation of U.S. non-proliferation export controls. Our system must be more responsive and efficient and not inhibit legitimate exports that play a key role in American economic strength, while preventing exports that would make a material contribution to the proliferation of weapons of mass destruction and the missiles that deliver them.

Nuclear Proliferation

The U.S. will make every effort to secure the indefinite extension of the Non-Proliferation Treaty in 1995. We will seek to ensure that the International Atomic Energy Agency has the resources needed to implement its vital safeguards responsibilities and will work to strengthen the IAEA's ability to detect clandestine nuclear activities.

Missile Proliferation

We will maintain our strong support for the Missile Technology Control Regime. We will promote the principles of the MTCR Guidelines as a global missile non-proliferation norm and seek to use the MTCR as a mechanism for taking joint action to combat missile proliferation. We will support prudent expansion of the MTCR's membership to include additional countries that subscribe to international non-proliferation standards, enforce effective export controls, and abandon offensive ballistic missile programs. The United States will also promote regional efforts to reduce the demand for missile capabilities.

The United States will continue to oppose missile programs of proliferation concern and will exercise particular restraint in missile-related cooperation. We will continue to retain a strong presumption of denial against exports to any country of complete space launch vehicles or major components.

The United States will not support the development or acquisition of space launch vehicles in countries outside the MTCR.

For MTCR member countries, we will not encourage new space launch vehicle programs which raise questions on both non-proliferation and economic viability grounds. The United States will, however, consider exports of MTCR-controlled items to MTCR member countries for peaceful space launch programs on a case-by-case basis. We will review whether additional constraints or safeguards could reduce the risk of misuse of space launch technology. We will seek adoption by all MTCR partners of policies as vigilant as our own.

Chemical and Biological Weapons

To help deter violations of the Biological Weapons Convention, we will promote new measures to provide increased transparency of activities and facilities that could have biological weapons applications. We call on all nations—including our own—to ratify the Chemical Weapons Convention quickly so that it may enter into force by January 13, 1995. We will work with others to support the international Organization for the Prohibition of Chemical Weapons created by the Convention.

Regional Non-proliferation Initiatives

Non-proliferation will receive greater priority in our diplomacy and will be taken into account in our relations with countries around the world. We will make special efforts to address the proliferation threat in regions of tension such as the Korean Peninsula, the Middle East, and South Asia, including efforts to address the underlying motivations for weapons acquisition and to promote regional confidence-building steps.

In Korea, our goal remains a non-nuclear peninsula. We will make every effort to secure North Korea's full compliance with its non-proliferation commitments and effective implementation of the North-South denuclearization agreement.

In parallel with our efforts to obtain a secure, just, and lasting peace in the Middle East, we will promote dialogue and confidence-building steps to create the basis for a Middle East free of weapons of mass destruction. In the Persian Gulf, we will work with other suppliers to contain Iran's nuclear, missile, and CBW ambitions, while preventing reconstruction of Iraq's activities in these areas. In South Asia, we will encourage India and Pakistan to proceed with multilateral discussions of non-proliferation and security issues, with the goal of capping and eventually rolling back their nuclear and missile capabilities.

In developing our overall approach to Latin America and South Africa, we will take account of the significant non-proliferation progress made in these regions in recent years. We will intensify efforts to ensure that the former Soviet Union, Eastern Europe, and China do not contribute to the spread of weapons of mass destruction and missiles.

Military Planning and Doctrine

We will give proliferation a higher profile in our intelligence collection and analysis and defense planning and ensure that our own force structure and military planning address the potential threat from weapons of mass destruction and missiles around the world.

Conventional Arms Transfers

We will actively seek greater transparency in the area of conventional arms transfers and promote regional confidence-building measures to encourage restraint on such transfers to regions of instability. The U.S. will undertake a comprehensive review of conventional arms transfer policy, taking into account national security, arms control, trade, budgetary and economic competitiveness considerations. ■

THE SECRETARY OF DEFENSE
WASHINGTON, DC 20301-1000

December 9, 1993

MEMORANDUM FROM THE SECRETARY OF DEFENSE

RE: The Defense Counterproliferation Initiative

The proliferation of nuclear and other weapons of mass destruction in the hands of potential adversaries is not a new problem, but with the end of the Cold War and the worldwide spread of technology, it has grown into a serious new threat to our nation's security. In fact, it was first on the list of threats identified in our Bottom-Up Review of defense issues earlier this year.

President Clinton, recognizing the threat these weapons pose, has given the Defense Department a new mission to deal with it. In response, we have developed the Defense Counterproliferation Initiative. This initiative seeks to develop new military capabilities to accompany and augment the continuing diplomatic efforts against proliferation.

I discussed the new dangers and the Defense Counterproliferation Initiative in a recent speech at the National Academy of Sciences. I hope the attached text will be of interest to you.

Remarks By
Honorable Les Aspin
Secretary of Defense
National Academy of Sciences
Committee on International Security and Arms Control
December 7, 1993

Thank you very much, Dr. Alberts, and thank all of you for coming this morning. I'm particularly pleased to be able to talk about this important topic before this audience because I know many of you have thought about this. It's something that's going to take all our best efforts.

The national security requirements of the United States have undergone fundamental change in just a few short years. We won the Cold War. The Soviet threat that dominated our strategy, doctrine, weapons acquisition and force structure for so long is gone. With it has gone the threat of global war. But history did not end with that victory, and neither did threats to the United States, its people and its interests.

As part of the Bottom Up Review we began to think seriously about what threats we really faced in this new era. We came up with four chief threats to the United States. First, a new danger posed by the increased threat of proliferation of nuclear weapons and other weapons of mass destruction. Second, regional dangers posed by the threat of aggression by powers such as Saddam Hussein's Iraq. Third, the danger that democratic and market reforms will fail in the former Soviet Union, Eastern Europe and elsewhere. And finally, we recognize an economic danger to our national security. In the short run our security is protected by a strong military, but in the long run it will be protected by a strong economy.

Of these dangers, the one that most urgently and directly threatens America at home and American interests abroad is the new nuclear danger. The old nuclear danger we faced was thousands of warheads in the Soviet Union. The new nuclear danger we face is perhaps a handful of nuclear devices in the hands of rogue states or even terrorist groups. The engine of this new danger is proliferation.

Let us recall briefly how we dealt with the old nuclear danger -- the nuclear danger of the Cold War era. We had three approaches -- deterrence, arms control and a nonproliferation policy based on prevention. They worked.

Our policy of deterrence was aimed primarily at the Soviet Union. Our aim was to guarantee by the structure and disposition of our own nuclear forces that a nuclear attack on the United States or its allies would bring no profit, and thus deter it.

We sought to stabilize these arsenals through arms control and eventually to shrink them through arms reduction. Our nonproliferation policy was aimed at preventing the spread of nuclear weapons by persuading most nations not to go nuclear, and denying the materials and know-how to make bombs to those who pursued them. And in fact, these weapons did not spread as quickly as many suggested.

But that was then and this is now. And now we face the potential of a greatly increased proliferation problem. This increase is the product of two new developments. The first arises from the break-up of the former Soviet Union. The second concerns the nature of technology diffusion in this new era. Each of these developments profoundly changes the nature of the proliferation problem.

Let's look at the former Soviet Union. The continued existence of the former Soviet Union's arsenal amidst revolutionary change gives rise to four potential proliferation problems.

First, and most obvious, is that nuclear weapons are now deployed on the territory of four states. Before, there was one. The safe and secure transport and dismantlement of these weapons is one of the U.S. Government's highest priorities.

Second, we have the potential for what I call "loose nukes." In a time of profound transition in the former Soviet Union, it is possible that nuclear weapons, or the material or technology to make them could find their way to a nuclear black market.

Third, nuclear and other weapons expertise for hire could go to would-be proliferators.

Fourth, whatever restraint the former Soviet Union exercised over its client states with nuclear ambitions, such as North Korea, is much diminished. Regional power balances have been disrupted and old ethnic conflicts have re-emerged.

The other new development that exacerbates today's proliferation problem is a by-product of growth in world trade and the rising tide of technology everywhere.

The world economy today is characterized by an ever increasing volume of trade leading to ever greater diffusion of technology. Simply put, this will make it harder and harder to detect illicit diversions of materials and technology useful for weapons development.

Moreover, many potential aggressors no longer have to import all the sophisticated technology they need. They are "growing" it at home. The growth of indigenous technology can completely change the nonproliferation equation.

Potential proliferators are sometimes said to be "several decades behind the West." This is not much comfort. If a would-be nuclear nation is four decades behind in 1993 then it is at the same technological level as the United States was in 1953. By 1953, the United States had fission weapons. We were building intercontinental range bombers and were developing intercontinental missiles.

Realize, too, that most of the thermonuclear weapons in the United States arsenal today were designed in the 1960s using computers that were then known as "super computers." These same "super computers" are no more powerful than today's laptop personal computers that you can pick up at the store or order through the catalog.

These new developments tell us a couple of very important things. The first, of course, is that we face a bigger proliferation danger than we've ever faced before. But second, and most important, is that a policy of prevention through denial won't be enough to cope with the potential of tomorrow's proliferators.

In concrete terms, here is where we stand today. More than a score of countries -- many of them hostile to the United States, our friends and our allies -- have now or are developing nuclear, biological and/or chemical weapons -- and the means to deliver them. More than 12 countries have operational ballistic missiles and others have programs to develop them.

Weapons of mass destruction may directly threaten our forces in the field, and in a more subtle way threaten the effective use of those forces. In some ways, in fact, the role of nuclear weapons in the U.S. scheme of things has completely changed.

During the Cold War, our principal adversary had conventional forces in Europe that were numerically superior. For us, nuclear weapons were the equalizer. The threat to use them was present and was used to compensate for our smaller numbers of conventional forces. Today, nuclear weapons can still be the equalizer against superior conventional forces. But today it is the United States that has unmatched conventional military power, and it is our potential adversaries who may attain nuclear weapons. We're the ones who could wind up being the equalizee.

And it's not just nuclear weapons. All the potential threat nations are at least capable of producing biological and chemical agents. They might not have usable weapons yet, and they might not use them if they do. But our commanders will have to assume that U.S. forces are threatened.

So the threat is real and it is upon us today. President Clinton directed the world's attention to it in his speech to the United Nations General Assembly in September. He said, "One of our most urgent priorities must be attacking the proliferation of weapons of mass destruction, whether they are nuclear, chemical, or biological; and the ballistic missiles that can rain them down on populations hundreds of miles away . . . If we do not stem the proliferation of the world's deadliest weapons, no democracy can feel secure."

To respond to the President, we have created the Defense Counterproliferation Initiative. With this initiative, we are making the essential change demanded by this increased threat. We are adding the task of protection to the task of prevention.

In past administrations, the emphasis was on prevention. The policy of nonproliferation combined global diplomacy and regional security efforts with the denial of material and know-how to would-be proliferators. Prevention remains our pre-eminent goal. In North Korea, for example, our goals are still a non-nuclear peninsula and a strong nonproliferation regime.

The Defense Counterproliferation Initiative in no way means we will lesson our nonproliferation efforts. In fact, DoD's work will strengthen prevention. What the Defense Counterproliferation Initiative recognizes, however, is that proliferation may still occur. Thus, we are adding protection as a major policy goal.

The chart shows how the two -- prevention and protection -- combine to make a complete attack on the problem. On the left, we have the policy instruments for prevention. On the right are the steps we take to protect if proliferation occurs. What's new is the emphasis on the right side of the chart where the Defense Department has a special responsibility.

At the heart of the Defense Counterproliferation Initiative, therefore, is a drive to develop new military capabilities to deal with this new threat. It has five elements: One, creation of the new mission by the President; two, changing what we buy to meet the threat; three, planning to fight wars differently; four, changing how we collect intelligence and what intelligence we collect; and finally, five, doing all these thing with our allies.

Let's look at each in turn.

First point; new mission. President Clinton not only recognized the danger of the new threat, he gave us this new mission to cope with it. We have issued defense planning guidance to the services to make sure everyone understands what the President wants. I have organized my own staff to reflect the importance of the new mission with the new position of Assistant Secretary of Defense for Nuclear Security and Counterproliferation.

Second point; what we buy. We are reviewing all relevant programs to see what we can do better. For example, we're looking at improved non-nuclear penetrating munitions to deal with underground installations. Saddam Hussein, you'll recall, was building a lot of underground refuges because normal structures were totally vulnerable to our precision air strikes. We cannot let future Saddams escape attack. We're also working hard on better ways to hunt mobile missiles after our difficulties in finding Scuds during the Gulf War. And of course, we have reoriented the Strategic Defense Initiative into the Ballistic Missile Defense Organization so that it concentrates on responding to theater ballistic missile threats that are here today.

We've also proposed a clarification in the ABM treaty. It would allow us to develop and test a theater missile defense system to meet a real threat without undermining an important agreement. This is an essential element of our counterproliferation strategy.

Third point; how we fight wars. We are developing guidance for dealing with this new threat. We have directed the services to tell us how prepared they are for it. The Chairman of the Joint Chiefs of Staff and our regional commanders in chief -- our CINCs -- are developing a military planning process for dealing with adversaries who have weapons of mass destruction.

And our concerns are by no means limited to the nuclear threat. We have a new Joint Office to oversee all DoD biological defense programs. This is the first time the department has organized its collective expertise to deal with the tough biological defense problems we face.

Fourth point; intelligence. After the war with Iraq, we discovered that Saddam Hussein had a much more extensive nuclear weapons program going than we knew. Moreover, we learned during the war that we had failed to destroy his biological and chemical warfare efforts. We do not want to be caught like that again, so we are working to improve our counterproliferation intelligence.

As a first step, we are pursuing an arrangement with the director of central intelligence to establish a new deputy director for military support in the Intelligence Community's Nonproliferation Center. And we're tripling the number of Defense Department experts assigned to the center. We're looking for intelligence that is useful militarily, not only diplomatically.

Fifth point; international cooperation. Our allies and security partners around the world have as much to be concerned about as we do. We have tabled an initiative with NATO to increase alliance efforts against proliferation of weapons of mass destruction.

We are also cooperating actively with the Japanese on deployment of theater missile defense systems there, and possibly on developing such systems together.

We are paying special attention to the dangerous potential problem of weapons and nuclear material proliferating from the Soviet Union. Under the Nunn-Lugar program, we are helping Russia, Belarus, Ukraine and Kazakhstan with the safe and secure dismantling of their nuclear weapons. And we're helping them improve the security of fissile material in both weapons and civilian nuclear facilities by helping them set up material control and accounting systems.

We are even including Russia in our attempt to reshape export controls on sensitive technology. The control system used to be aimed at the Eastern Bloc. Now we are incorporating former Eastern Bloc countries in our efforts to impede would-be proliferators. The Defense Department can play a constructive role in balancing economics and security here. In this effort, we have been guided by the excellent work conducted by the National Academy of Sciences.

To sum up, we've undertaken a new mission. For many years we planned to counter the weapons of mass destruction of the former Soviet Union. Now, we've recognized a new problem and we're acting to meet it with counterproliferation. At the same time, our initiative complements nonproliferation in three important ways. It promotes consensus on the gravity of the threat, helping to maintain the international nonproliferation effort. It reduces the military utility of weapons of mass destruction, while nonproliferation keeps up the price, making them less attractive to the proliferator. And it reduces the vulnerability of the neighbors of those holding these weapons, further reducing the motive to acquire them in self-defense.

We are in a new era. We have released our Bottom Up Review that provided a blueprint for our conventional forces for the years ahead. Our Defense Counterproliferation Initiative will allow us to deal with the number one threat identified in the BUR, and it will help provide the real strength America needs to meet the dangers we face. The public expects nothing less from its Department of Defense than the right responses to the new world.

Thank you.

#

Responding to the Proliferation Threat

Prevention

Dissuasion
- Emphasizing economic, political, and military costs of proliferation
- Positive/negative security assurance and guarantees
- Security assistance
- Public diplomacy

Denial
- Export controls
- Interdiction
- Disruption of supply networks

Arms Control
- NPT, BWC, CWC, ...
- Nuclear free zones
- CSBMs
- "Rolling back" Argentine missiles, South African nukes, ...
- Inspections and monitoring

International Pressure
- Sanctions
- Isolation
- Publicizing violations
- Intelligence sharing to persuade others of the danger

Protection

Defusing
- Cooperative dismantlement
- Safety and security enhancements
- Stabilizing measures
- CSBMs

Deterrence
- Small nuclear arsenals
- CW
- BW
- "Undeterrables"

Offense
- Underground structures
- SCUD hunting
- Contamination problems

Defense
- TMD
- BW vaccines
- Strategic and tactical warning
- Unconventional delivery, counterterrorism
- NEST
- Border/perimeter control

DoD Shares Interagency Responsibility | Special DoD Responsibility

NATIONAL SECURITY COUNCIL
WASHINGTON, D.C. 20506

February 18, 1994

MEMORANDUM FOR ROBERT GALLUCCI
　　　　　　　　　Assistant Secretary for Political-Military Affairs
　　　　　　　　　Department of State

　　　　　　　　　ASHTON CARTER
　　　　　　　　　Assistant Secretary for Nuclear Security and
　　　　　　　　　　　Counterproliferation
　　　　　　　　　Department of Defense

SUBJECT:　　　　Agreed Definitions

We have agreed to the following definitions and will ask our staff to be consistent in their usage.

　　　Proliferation is the spread of nuclear, biological and chemical capabilities and the missiles to deliver them.

　　　Nonproliferation is the use of the full range of political, economic and military tools to prevent proliferation, reverse it diplomatically or protect our interests against an opponent armed with weapons of mass destruction or missiles, should that prove necessary. Nonproliferation tools include: intelligence, global nonproliferation norms and agreements, diplomacy, export controls, security assurances, defenses and the application of military force.

　　　Counterproliferation refers to the activities of the Department of Defense across the full range of U.S. efforts to combat proliferation, including diplomacy, arms control, export controls, and intelligence collection and analysis, with particular responsibility for assuring that U.S. forces and interests can be protected should they confront an adversary armed with weapons of mass destruction or missiles.

　　　　　　　　　　　　　　Daniel Poneman
　　　　　　　　　　　　　　Special Assistant to the President and
　　　　　　　　　　　　　　　Senior Director for Nonproliferation
　　　　　　　　　　　　　　　and Export Controls

Report on Nonproliferation and Counterproliferation Activities and Programs

May 1994

Office of the Deputy Secretary of Defense

THE DEPUTY SECRETARY OF DEFENSE
WASHINGTON, D.C. 20301-1000

May 1, 1994

Members of Congress:

Section 1605 of the FY94 Defense Authorization Act directs the Department of Defense to lead an interagency study of nonproliferation activities currently underway in Executive Branch agencies. This letter transmits the required report, prepared in a collaborative effort by the Departments of Commerce, Energy, State, and Defense; the Chairman of the Joint Chiefs of Staff, the Intelligence Community, the Arms Control and Disarmament Agency, the Office of Science and Technology Policy, and the National Security Council.

President Clinton has identified countering the proliferation of weapons of mass destruction and their delivery systems as "one of the most urgent priorities." A great deal has been accomplished by this administration toward meeting this challenge, and the study provides a welcome opportunity to report to Congress on current activities, progress that has been made, and opportunities for improvement.

The terms of reference for the study as specified in the authorizing legislation required a thorough review of all activities underway in the relevant agencies that are directly or indirectly related to nonproliferation or to counterproliferation. Our charge was to focus on technologies and programs that contribute to nonproliferation and counterproliferation capabilities.

Our review found that federal agencies have achieved significant progress:

1. Through its Nonproliferation Center, the Intelligence Community has established effective interagency procedures to identify intelligence needs for early detection of nonproliferation threats.

2. The Department of Energy maintains an extraordinarily competent and broad technology base that has the potential to make major contributions to nonproliferation and counterproliferation technologies.

3. The Department of Defense has developed an entirely new approach for focusing counterproliferation programs in the areas of technology and acquisition, intelligence programs, and military planning.

4. The Departments of State and Commerce are working on new, expedited export control procedures to support nonproliferation efforts.

5. The Arms Control and Disarmament Agency has strengthened its capability to coordinate arms control and disarmament research through the Arms Control Research Coordinating Committee and Annual Report to Congress on Arms Control Research.

Many agency programs that are not exclusively directed at proliferation make important contributions to this objective, such as reconnaissance systems, theater missile defense systems, and political reporting. But we also found that agencies have different management practices and procedures that make it difficult to compare easily their proliferation efforts. Thus, this initial study should not be viewed as the final word in identifying gaps or overlaps among agency program efforts. <u>The report does, however, identify fourteen priority areas for additional effort that we believe have the greatest potential for making a contribution to our proliferation technology efforts.</u> Approximately $400 million per year are required to pursue these initiatives. The group assumed that this requirement could be addressed within budget planning ceilings of the agencies for FY96 and later years.

Our effort also identified several areas where additional progress is necessary. First, certain technologies are not currently being pursued adequately; an example is biological agent detectors. Second, generally it has proved easier to develop promising new technology <u>ideas</u> than to <u>field</u> useful new capability. This reflects the absence of a common program structure that enables management and application of resources government-wide to achieve desired ends. It is important to assure that agency efforts are not too fractionated and that a critical mass exists for development and deployment of needed capability. Third, the reorientation of national security programs to the post Cold War world, including to our nonproliferation objectives, is still incomplete. Fourth, our study demonstrates the value of interagency attention and coordination to nonproliferation and counterproliferation technology efforts that are being pursued by several agencies. We describe an ongoing interagency process that can continue the coordination and oversight activity that this Congressionally mandated study has begun.

Sincerely,

John M. Deutch

TABLE OF CONTENTS

EXECUTIVE SUMMARY.. ES-1

1.0 INTRODUCTION...1
    1.1 Report Requirements..1
    1.2 The Threat..2
    1.3 Overall Proliferation Policy..3
    1.4 Scope..4

2.0 SURVEY OF CURRENT PLANS, PROGRAMS AND BUDGETS 7
    2.1 Overview Of Non/Counterproliferation Activities and Programs 7
    2.2 Overview of Nonproliferation and Counterproliferation
         Programs by Functional Area 20
    2.3 Summary of Resources for Nonproliferation and Counterproliferation
         Activities And Programs 26

3.0 NONPROLIFERATION AND COUNTERPROLIFERATION NEEDS
AND CAPABILITY DEVELOPMENT OPPORTUNITIES 27
    3.1 Review Committee Assessment...27
    3.2 Areas for Progress in Non/Counterproliferation 30

4.0 PRIORITIES AND ACTIONS..37

APPENDIX A.   USC Section Requiring Report

APPENDIX B.   Study Participants

APPENDIX C.   Summary of Agency NP/CP Budget Plans

APPENDIX D.   Discussion of Special Topics

APPENDIX E.   Acronyms

EXECUTIVE SUMMARY

1. INTRODUCTION

At least twenty countries—many of them hostile to the United States and its allies—have now or are seeking to develop the capability to produce nuclear, biological and/or chemical weapons of mass destruction and the means to deliver them. More than twelve countries have operational ballistic missiles, and others have programs to develop them.

Weapons of mass destruction may directly threaten US forces in the field and, in a more perplexing way, threaten the effective force employment by requiring dispersal of those forces. Potential adversaries may use weapons of mass destruction to deter US power projection abroad. As President Clinton stated to the United Nations in September 1993, *"If we do not stem the proliferation of the world's deadliest weapons, no democracy can feel secure."*

Because of concern over this threat, the National Defense Authorization Act of 1994 (NDAA 94) required the establishment of an interagency review committee composed of representatives from the Departments of State, Defense, Energy, the Intelligence Community, the Joint Chiefs of Staff and the Arms Control Disarmament Agency and tasked the committee to report on nonproliferation and counterproliferation activities and programs. To ensure comprehensiveness, representatives of other departments and agencies were asked to participate.

In accordance with NDAA 94, this report provides a top-down overview of existing, planned and proposed capabilities and technologies, as well as a description of priorities, programmatic options and other issues. Other than Nunn-Lugar activities, this report specifically excludes activities and programs for dealing with extant weapons of mass destruction and the means to deliver them in the Former Soviet Union (FSU) and China, but does address non/counterproliferation activities and programs for dealing with issues germane to the proliferation of WMD through illicit export of materials, technology, and expertise from FSU states. The report discusses ongoing and planned Agency programs and activities that are unique to the non/counterproliferation problem as well as those that are strongly related. The funding summaries presented for these efforts are estimates. The report focuses on the non/counterproliferation capabilities to support US policy goals.

2. DISCUSSION

a. Findings

The review committee performed an assessment of current and proposed non/counterproliferation activities. The following summarizes the findings of this assessment:

- Current non/counterproliferation programs and activities that are unique to non/counterproliferation are approximately $1 billion in FY95 and those that are strongly related are approximately $3 billion. A substantial Intelligence Community effort is not reflected in these numbers (see classified annex).

- High priority shortfalls in operational capability needed to implement US non/counterproliferation policy have been identified in nine areas, along with technology opportunities that exist for addressing them. The Chairman of the Joint Chiefs of Staff is conducting a six-month study, in conjunction with the Services and combatant commands, of counterproliferation military requirements, including a detailed evaluation of the functions of the Services and missions of the combatant commands.

- Sixteen capability areas for progress have been identified to address current and future national non/counterproliferation needs, 14 of which are believed to be underfunded at present. (See Figure 1).

- Better coordination and communication across Departments and Agencies are needed among the more than 80 different groups and entities at all levels in the Federal Government now engaged in supporting national non/counterproliferation policy.

Non/Counterproliferation Areas for Progress	Recommended Increases in Annual Investment (For FY96 and Later)
• Real time detection and characterization of BW/CW Agents including stand-off capability	$75M
• Underground structures detection and characterization	$75M
• Hard underground target defeat including advanced non-nuclear weapons (lethal or non-lethal) capable of holding counterforce targets at risk with low collateral effects	$40M
• Detection and tracking of shipments and control and accountability for stocks of WMD-related materials and personnel including worldwide WMD and dual-use item tracking	$25M
• Capability to detect, locate and render harmless WMD in US	$10M
• Enhancement of Collection and Analysis of Intelligence	$25M
• Support of Chemical Weapons Convention and Biological Weapons Convention	$10M
• Support of Conclusion of a Verifiable Comprehensive Test Ban Treaty	$10M
• Capability to detect, locate and disarm, with high assurance and in a timely fashion, outside the United States WMD hidden by a hostile state or terrorist in a confined area	$15M
• Passive defense capabilities enabling military operations to continue in contaminated conditions-actual or threatened (low cost, lightweight)	$15M
• Rapid production of protective BW vaccines	$15M
• Detection and interception of low flying/stealthy cruise missiles	$50M
• Transparency and control of foreign fissile material	$15M
• Safe disposition for foreign missile- and WMD-related materials (except fissile material)	$20M
• Intercept capability in boost phase	Adequately funded
• Prompt mobile target kill	Adequately funded

Figure 1.

b. **Ongoing Actions**

Consistent with the findings above, the review committee is taking the following actions:

1. The review committee principals will continue to refine the "order of magnitude" estimates of investment increases for the areas for progress shown in Figure 1 to address them within budget planning ceilings of the agencies for FY96 and later years.

2. The review committee has recommended to the NSC the creation of a Nonproliferation and Counterproliferation Technology Working Group ("The Technology Working Group") within the National Security Council structure. This Technology Working Group would be charged with reviewing all the technology efforts underway in the various agencies that pertain to nonproliferation or counterproliferation. The Technology Working Group would also have authority to set priorities for non/counterproliferation technology efforts in the various agencies and to make specific resource allocation recommendations to the participating agencies, the NSC, the OSTP and the OMB. Moreover, the Technology Working Group would have representation from and a strong connection to the National Science and Technology Council. The Technology Working Group would be comprised of representatives with management, resource allocation, and program planning authority. The existing Research and Development Subcommittee of the Community Non-Proliferation Committee provides a good basis for building the Technology Working Group.

3. Technology development should not take place in a policy vacuum. Accordingly, the Technology Working Group would be integrated with the other working groups addressing important proliferation issues. Overall policy guidance would come from a new NSC-chaired Standing Committee of the IWG on Nonproliferation and Export Controls. This Standing Committee would have broad policy oversight and coordination responsibilities and bring together senior managers from the various agencies responsible for proliferation issues to assure communication and integrated management attention across all nonproliferation and counterproliferation efforts and working groups. A conceptual organization diagram is:

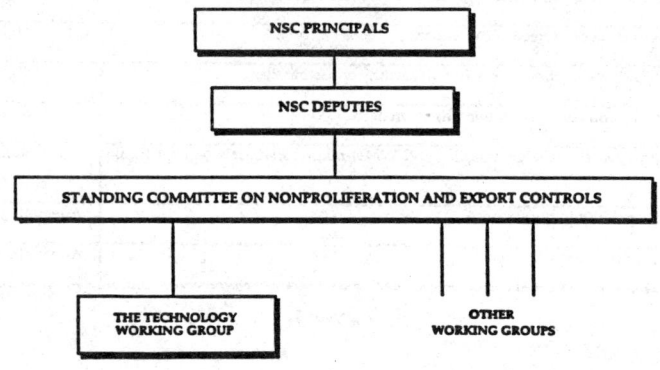

Figure 2.

4. The proposed Technology Working Group and the new Standing Committee on Nonproliferation and Export Controls should have as one of their priorities the continued, careful examination of non/counterproliferation programs to locate and eliminate marginal or unnecessarily redundant activities. This will enhance US capabilities to prevent and defend against proliferation and it could free modest amounts of resources to help fund higher priority areas.

3. SUMMARY

The new consensus on nonproliferation policy that President Clinton called for last September requires, among other things, the creative use of technology and the reallocation of government resources. It is not easy to change the direction of the ship of state--especially when its course for over 45 years was primarily aimed at preparing for threats that have receded, while the problems of proliferation have grown and become more urgent. The actions of this review committee are designed to help steer the new course.

U.S. NON-PROLIFERATION LEGISLATION

THE ATOMIC ENERGY ACT OF 1954 AS AMENDED
EXCERPTS

sec. 1, Declaration
sec. 2, Findings
sec. 3, Purpose
sec. 11, Definitions
sec. 51, Special Nuclear Material
sec. 54, Foreign Distribution of Special Nuclear Materials
sec. 55, Acquisition
sec. 56, Guaranteed Purchase Prices
sec. 57, Prohibition
sec. 58, Review
sec. 61, Source Material
sec. 62, License for Transfers Required
sec. 64, Foreign Distribution of Source Material
sec. 69, Prohibition
sec. 81, Domestic Distribution
sec. 82, Foreign Distribution of Byproduct Material
sec. 83, Ownership and Custody of Certain Byproduct Material and Disposal Sites
sec. 84, Authorities of Commission Respecting Certain Byproduct Materials
sec. 91, Authority
sec. 92, Prohibition
sec. 101, License Required
sec. 102, Utilization and Production Facilities for Industrial or Commercial Purposes
sec. 103, Commercial Licenses
sec. 104, Medical Therapy and Research
sec. 109, Component and Other Parts of Facilities
sec. 111, Exemptions
sec. 121, Effect of International Arrangements
sec. 122, Policies Contained in International Arrangements
sec. 123, Cooperation with Other Nations
sec. 124, International Atomic Pool
sec. 125, Cooperation with Berlin
sec. 126, Export Licensing Procedures
sec. 127, Criteria Governing United States Nuclear Exports
sec. 128, Additional Export Criterion and Procedures
sec. 129, Conduct Resulting in Termination of Nuclear Exports
sec. 130, Congressional Review Procedures
sec. 131, Subsequent Arrangements
[Sec. 132. Authority to Suspend Nuclear Cooperation With Nations Which Have Not Ratified the Convention on the Physical Security of Nuclear Material.]
[Sec. 133. Consultation with the Department of Defense Concerning Certain Exports and Subsequent Arrangements.]
Sec. 134. Further restrictions on exports.

sec. 141, Control of Information Policy
sec. 142, Classification and Declassification of Restricted Data
sec. 143, Dept. of Defense Participation
sec. 144, International Cooperation
sec. 145, Restrictions
sec. 147, Safeguards Information
sec 148, Prohibition Against the Dissemination of Certain Unclassified Information
sec. 149, Fingerprinting for Criminal History
sec. 251, Report to Congress
sec. 301, Joint Committee on Atomic Energy Abolished
sec. 302, Transfers of Certain Functions of the JCAE and Conforming Amendments to Certain Other Laws
sec. 303, Information and Assistance to Congressional Committees

ATOMIC ENERGY ACT OF 1954 [1]

An Act for the development and control of atomic energy.

Be it enacted by the Senate and House of Representatives of the United States of America in Congress assembled,

TITLE I—ATOMIC ENERGY

CHAPTER 1. DECLARATION, FINDINGS, AND PURPOSE

SECTION 1. DECLARATION.—Atomic energy is capable of application for peaceful as well as military purposes. It is therefore declared to be the policy of the United States that—

    a. the development, use, and control of atomic energy shall be directed so as to make the maximum contribution to the general welfare, subject at all times to the paramount objective of making the maximum contribution to the common defense and security; and

---

[1] This Act consists of the Act of August 1, 1946, ch. 724, as amended by the Act of Aug. 30, 1954, ch. 1073 (68 stat. 921) and by subsequent amendments. The Act appears generally in the United States code at 42 U.S.C. 2011 et seq. Bracketed notes are used at the end of each section for the convenience of the reader to indicate the United States Code citation.

b. the development, use, and control of atomic energy shall be directed so as to promote world peace, improve the general welfare, increase the standard of living, and strengthen free competition in private enterprise.

[42 U.S.C. 2011]

SEC. 2. FINDINGS.—The Congress of the United States hereby makes the following findings concerning the development, use, and control of atomic energy:

a. The development, utilization, and control of atomic energy for military and for all other purposes are vital to the common defense and security.

[b. Repealed by Pub. L. 88-489, §1, 78 Stat. 602, Aug. 26, 1964.]

c. The processing and utilization of source, byproduct, and special nuclear material affect interstate and foreign commerce and must be regulated in the national interest.

d. The processing and utilization of source, byproduct, and special nuclear material must be regulated in the national interest and in order to provide for the common defense and security and to protect the health and safety of the public.

e. Source and special nuclear material, production facilities, and utilization facilities are affected with the public interest, and regulation by the United States of the production and utilization of atomic energy and of the facilities used in connection therewith is necessary in the national interest to assure the common defense and security and to protect the health and safety of the public.

f. The necessity for protection against possible interstate damage occurring from the operation of facilities for the production or utilization of source or special nuclear material places the operation of those facilities in interstate commerce for the purposes of this Act.

g. Funds of the United States may be provided for the development and use of atomic energy under conditions which will provide for the common defense and security and promote the general welfare.

[h. Repealed by Pub. L. 88-489, §2, 78 Stat. 602, Aug. 26, 1964.]

i. In order to protect the public and to encourage the development of the atomic energy industry, in the interest of the general welfare and of the common defense and security, the United States may make funds available for a portion of the damages suffered by the public from nuclear incidents, and may limit the liability of those persons liable for such losses.

[42 U.S.C. 2012]

SEC. 3. PURPOSE.—It is the purpose of this Act to effectuate the policies set forth above by providing for—

a. a program of conducting, assisting, and fostering research and development in order to encourage maximum scientific and industrial progress;

b. a program for the dissemination of unclassified scientific and technical information and for the control, dissemination, and declassification of Restricted Data, subject to appropriate safeguards, so as to encourage scientific and industrial progress;

  c. a program for Government control of the possession, use, and production of atomic energy and special nuclear material whether owned by the Government or others, so directed as to make the maximum contribution to the common defense and security and the national welfare, and to provide continued assurance of the Government's ability to enter into and enforce agreements with nations or groups of nations for the control of special nuclear materials and atomic weapons;

  d. a program to encourage widespread participation in the development and utilization of atomic energy for peaceful purposes to the maximum extent consistent with the common defense and security and with the health and safety of the public;

  e. a program of international cooperation to promote the common defense and security and to make available to cooperating nations the benefits of peaceful applications of atomic energy as widely as expanding technology and considerations of the common defense and security will permit; and

  f. a program of administration which will be consistent with the foregoing policies and programs, with international arrangements, and with agreements for cooperation, which will enable the Congress to be currently informed so as to take further legislative action as may be appropriate.

[42 U.S.C. 2013]

CHAPTER 2. DEFINITIONS

SEC. 11. DEFINITION.—The intent of Congress in the definitions as given in this section should be construed from the words or phrases used in the definitions. As used in this Act:

  a. The term "agency of the United States" means the executive branch of the United States, or any Government agency, or the legislative branch of the United States, or any agency, committee, commission, office, or other establishment in the legislative branch, or the judicial branch of the United States, or any office, agency, committee, commission, or other establishment in the judicial branch.

  b. The term "agreement for cooperation" means any agreement with another nation or regional defense organization authorized or permitted by sections 54, 57, 64, 82, 91c., 103, 104, or 144, and made pursuant to section 123.

  c. The term "atomic energy" means all forms of energy released in the course of nuclear fission or nuclear transformation.

  d. The term "atomic weapon" means any device utilizing atomic energy, exclusive of the means for transporting or propelling the device (where such means is a separable and divisible part of the device), the principal purpose of which is for use as, or for development of, a weapon, a weapon prototype, or a weapon test device.

  e. The term "byproduct material" means (1) any radioactive material (except special nuclear material) yielded in or made radioactive by exposure to the radiation incident to the process of producing or utilizing special nuclear material, and (2) the tailings or wastes produced by the extraction or concentration of uranium or thorium from any ore processed primarily for its source material content.

f. The term "Commission" means the Atomic Energy Commission.[1]

g. The term "common defense and security" means the common defense and security of the United States.

h. The term "defense information" means any information in any category determined by any Government agency authorized to classify information, as being information respecting, relating to, or affecting the national defense.

i. The term "design" means (1) specifications, plans, drawings, blueprints, and other items of like nature; (2) the information contained therein; or (3) the research and development data pertinent to the information contained therein.

j. The term "extraordinary nuclear occurrence" means any event causing a discharge or dispersal of source, special nuclear, or byproduct material from its intended place of confinement in amounts offsite, or causing radiation levels offsite, which the Nuclear Regulatory Commission or the Secretary of Energy, as appropriate, determines to be substantial, and which the Nuclear Regulatory Commission or the Secretary of Energy, as appropriate, determines has resulted or will probably result in substantial damages to persons offsite or property offsite. Any determination by the Nuclear Regulatory Commission or the Secretary of Energy, as appropriate, that such an event has, or has not, occurred shall be final and conclusive, and no other official or any court shall have power or jurisdiction to review any such determination. The Nuclear Regulatory Commission or the Secretary of Energy, as appropriate, shall establish criteria in writing setting forth the basis upon which such determination shall be made. As used in this subsection, "offsite" means away from "the location" or the "contract location" as defined in the applicable Nuclear Regulatory Commission or the Secretary of Energy, as appropriate, indemnity agreement, entered into pursuant to section 170.

k. The term "financial protection" means the ability to respond in damages for public liability and to meet the costs of investigating and defending claims and settling suits for such damages.

l. The term "Government agency" means any executive department, commission, independent establishment, corporation, wholly or partly owned by the United States of America which is an instrumentality of the United States, or any board, bureau, division, service, office, officer, authority, administration, or other establishment in the executive branch of the Government.

m. The term "indemnitor" means (1) any insurer with respect to his obligations under a policy of insurance furnished as proof of financial protection; (2) any licensee, contractor or other person

---

[1] The Atomic Energy Commission was abolished and all functions under this section were transferred to the Nuclear Regulatory Commission and the Administrator of the Energy Research and Development Administration by sections 104 and 201 of the Energy Reorganization Act of 1974, Pub. L. 93-438. The Energy Research and Development Administration was terminated and functions vested by law in the Administrator thereof were transferred to the Secretary of Energy (unless otherwise specifically provided) by sections 301(a) and 703 of the Department of Energy Organization Act, Pub. L. 95-91.

For transfer of certain functions from the Nuclear Regulatory Commission to the Chairman thereof, see Reorg. Plan No. 1 of 1980, 45 F.R. 40561, 94 Stat. 3585.

who is obligated under any other form of financial protection, with respect to such obligations; and (3) the Nuclear Regulatory Commission or the Secretary of Energy, as appropriate, with respect to any obligation undertaken by it in an indemnity agreement entered into pursuant to section 170.

n. The term "international arrangement" means any international agreement hereafter approved by the Congress or any treaty during the time such agreement or treaty is in full force and effect, but does not include any agreement for cooperation.

o. The term "Joint Committee" means the Joint Committee on Atomic Energy.[1]

p. The term "licensed activity" means an activity licensed pursuant to this Act and covered by the provisions of section 170 a.

q. The term "nuclear incident" means any occurrence, including an extraordinary nuclear occurrence, within the United States causing, within or outside the United States, bodily injury, sickness, disease, or death, or loss of or damage to property, or loss of use of property, arising out of or resulting from the radioactive, toxic, explosive, or other hazardous properties of source, special nuclear, or byproduct material: *Provided, however,* That as the term is used in section 170 l., it shall include any such occurrence outside the United States: *And provided further,* That as the term is used in section 170 d., it shall include any such occurrence outside the United States if such occurrence involves source, special nuclear, or byproduct material owned by, and used by or under contract with, the United States: *And provided further,* That as the term is used in section 170 c., it shall include any such occurrence outside both the United States and any other nation if such occurrence arises out of or results from the radioactive, toxic, explosive, or other hazardous properties of source, special nuclear, or byproduct material licensed pursuant to chapters 6, 7, 8, and 10 of this Act, which is used on connection with the operation of a licensed stationary production or utilization facility or which moves outside the territorial limits of the United States in transit from one person licensed by the Nuclear Regulatory Commission to another person licensed by the Nuclear Regulatory Commission.

r. The term "operator" means any individual who manipulates the controls of a utilization or production facility.

s. The term "person" means (1) any individual, corporation, partnership, firm, association, trust, estate, public or private institution, group, Government agency other than the Commission, any State or any political subdivision of, or any political entity within a State, any foreign government or nation or any political subdivision of any such government or nation, or other entity; and (2) any legal successor, representative, agent, or agency of the foregoing.

t. The term "person indemnified" means (1) with respect to a nuclear incident occurring within the United States or outside the United States as the term is used in section 170 c., and with re-

---

[1] The Joint Committee on Atomic Energy was abolished by Section 301 of the Atomic Energy Act of 1954, on September 20, 1977. References to the Joint Committee are deemed, on or after Sept. 20, 1977, to refer to the committees of the Senate or House of Representatives which, under the rules of the Senate or House, have jurisdiction over the subject matter with records and files of the Joint Committee being transferred to the respective committees of the House or Senate.

spect to any nuclear incident in connection with the design, development, construction, operation, repair, maintenance, or use of the nuclear ship Savannah, the person with whom an indemnity agreement is executed or who is required to maintain financial protection, and any other person who may be liable for public liability or (2) with respect to any other nuclear incident occurring outside the United States, the person with whom an indemnity agreement is executed and any other person who may be liable for public liability by reason of his activities under any contract with the Secretary of Energy or any project to which indemnification under the provisions of section 170 d., has been extended or under any subcontract, purchase order, or other agreement, of any tier, under any such contract or project.

u. The term "produce," when used in relation to special nuclear material, means (1) to manufacture, make, produce, or refine special nuclear material; (2) to separate special nuclear material from other substances in which such material may be contained; or (3) to make or to produce new special nuclear material.

v. The term "production facility" means (1) any equipment or device determined by rule of the Commission to be capable of the production of special nuclear material in such quantity as to be of significance to the common defense and security, or in such manner as to affect the health and safety of the public; or (2) any important component part especially designed for such equipment or device as determined by the Commission. Except with respect to the export of a uranium enrichment production facility or the construction and operation of a uranium enrichment production facility using Atomic Vapor Laser Isotope Separation technology, such term as used in chapters 10 and 16 shall not include any equipment or device (or important component part especially designed for such equipment or device) capable of separating the isotopes of uranium or enriching uranium in the isotope 235.

w. The term "public liability" means any legal liability arising out of or resulting from a nuclear incident or precautionary evacuation (including all reasonable additional costs incurred by a State, or a political subdivision of a State, in the course of responding to a nuclear incident or a precautionary evacuation), except: (i) claims under State or Federal workmen's compensation acts of employees of persons indemnified who are employed at the site of and in connection with the activity where the nuclear incident occurs; (ii) claims arising out of an act of war; and (iii) whenever used in subsections a., c., and k. of section 170, claims for loss of, or damage to, or loss of use of property which is located at the site of and used in connection with the licensed activity where the nuclear incident occurs. "Public liability" also includes damage to property of persons indemnified: *Provided,* That such property is covered under the terms of the financial protection required, except property which is located at the site of and used in connection with the activity where the nuclear incident occurs.

x. The term "research and development" means (1) theoretical analysis, exploration, or experimentation; or (2) the extension of investigative findings and theories of a scientific or technical nature into practical application for experimental and demonstration purposes, including the experimental production and testing of models, devices, equipment, materials, and processes.

y. The term "Restricted Data" means all data concerning (1) design, manufacture, or utilization of atomic weapons; (2) the production of special nuclear material; or (3) the use of special nuclear material in the production of energy, but shall not include data declassified or removed from the Restricted Data category pursuant to section 142.

z. The term "source material" means (1) uranium, thorium, or any other material which is determined by the Commission pursuant to the provisions of section 61 to be source material; or (2) ores containing one or more of the foregoing materials, in such concentration as the Commission may by regulation determine from time to time.

aa. The term "special nuclear material" means (1) plutonium, uranium enriched in the isotope 233 or in the isotope 235, and any other material which the Commission, pursuant to the provisions of section 51, determines to be special nuclear material, but does not include source material; or (2) any material artifically[1] enriched by any of the foregoing, but does not include source material.

bb. The term "United States" when used in a geographical sense includes all Territories and possessions of the United States, the Canal Zone and Puerto Rico.

cc. The term "utilization facility" means (1) any equipment or device, except an atomic weapon, determined by rule of the Commission to be capable of making use of special nuclear material in such quantity as to be of significance to the common defense and security, or in such manner as to affect the health and safety of the public, or peculiarly adapted for making use of atomic energy in such quantity as to be of significance to the common defense and security, or in such manner as to affect the health and safety of the public; or (2) any important component part especially designed for such equipment or device as determined by the Commission.

dd. The terms "high-level radioactive waste" and "spent nuclear fuel" have the meanings given such terms in section 2 of the Nuclear Waste Policy Act of 1982 (42 U.S.C. 10101).

ee. The term "transuranic waste" means material contaminated with elements that have an atomic number greater than 92, including neptunium, plutonium, americium, and curium, and that are in concentrations greater than 10 nanocuries per gram, or in such other concentrations as the Nuclear Regulatory Commission may prescribe to protect the public health and safety.

ff. The term "nuclear waste activities", as used in section 170, means activities subject to an agreement of indemnification under subsection d. of such section, that the Secretary of Energy is authorized to undertake, under this Act or any other law, involving the storage, handling, transportation, treatment, or disposal of, or research and development on, spent nuclear fuel, high-level radioactive waste, or transuranic waste, including (but not limited to) activities authorized to be carried out under the Waste Isolation

---

[1] So in original. Probably should be "artificially".

Pilot Project under section 213 of Public Law 96-164 (93 Stat. 1265).

gg. The term "precautionary evacuation" means an evacuation of the public within a specified area near a nuclear facility, or the transportation route in the case of an accident involving transportation of source material, special nuclear material, byproduct material, high-level radioactive waste, spent nuclear fuel, or transuranic waste to or from a production or utilization facility, if the evacuation is—

    (1) the result of any event that is not classified as a nuclear incident but that poses imminent danger of bodily injury or property damage from the radiological properties of source material, special nuclear material, byproduct material, high-level radioactive waste, spent nuclear fuel, or transuranic waste, and causes an evacuation; and

    (2) initiated by an official of a State or a political subdivision of a State, who is authorized by State law to initiate such an evacuation and who reasonably determined that such an evacuation was necessary to protect the public health and safety.

hh. The term "public liability action", as used in section 170, means any suit asserting public liability. A public liability action shall be deemed to be an action arising under section 170, and the substantive rules for decision in such action shall be derived from the law of the State in which the nuclear incident involved occurs, unless such law is inconsistent with the provisions of such section.

jj.[1] LEGAL COSTS.—As used in section 170, the term "legal costs" means the costs incurred by a plaintiff or a defendant in initiating, prosecuting, investigating, settling, or defending claims or suits for damage arising under such section.

[42 U.S.C. 2014]

CHAPTER 6. SPECIAL NUCLEAR MATERIAL

SEC. 51. SPECIAL NUCLEAR MATERIAL.—The Commission may determine from time to time that other material is special nuclear material in addition to that specified in the definition as special nuclear material. Before making any such determination, the Commission must find that such material is capable of releasing substantial quantities of atomic energy and must find that the determination that such material is special nuclear material is in the interest of the common defense and security, and the President must have expressly assented in writing to the determination. The Commission's determination, together with the assent of the President, shall be submitted to the Joint Committee and a period of thirty days shall elapse while Congress is in session (in computing such thirty days, there shall be excluded the days on which either House is not in session because of an adjournment for more than three days) before the determination of the Commission may become effective: *Provided, however,* That the Joint Committee, after having received such determination, may by resolution in writing, waive the conditions of or all or any portion of such thirty-day period.

[42 U.S.C. 2071]

SEC. 54. FOREIGN DISTRIBUTION OF SPECIAL NUCLEAR MATERIAL.—a. The Commission is authorized to cooperate with any nation or group of nations by distributing special nuclear material and to distribute such special nuclear material, pursuant to the terms of an agreement for cooperation to which such nation or group of nations is a party and which is made in accordance with section 123. Unless hereafter otherwise authorized by law the Commission shall be compensated for special nuclear material so distributed at not less than the Commission's published charges applicable to the domestic distribution of such material, except that the Commission to assist and encourage research on peaceful uses or for medical therapy may so distribute without charge during any calendar year only a quantity of such material which at the time of transfer does not exceed in value $10,000 in the case of one nation or $50,000 in the case of any group of nations. The Commission may distribute to the International Atomic Energy Agency, or to any group of nations, only such amounts of special nuclear materials and for such period of time as are authorized by Congress: *Provided, however,* That, (i) notwithstanding this provision, the Commission is hereby authorized, subject to the provisions of section 123, to distribute to the Agency five thousand kilograms of contained uranium-235, five hundred grams of uranium-233, and three kilograms of plutonium, together with the amounts of special nuclear material which will match in amount the sum of all quantities of special nuclear materials made available by all other members of the Agency to June 1, 1960; and (ii) notwithstanding the foregoing provisions of this subsection, the Commission may distribute to the International Atomic Energy Agency, or to any group of nations, such other amounts of special nuclear materials and for such other periods of time as are established in writing by the Commission: *Provided, however,* That before they are established by the Commission pursuant to this subdivision (ii), such proposed amounts and periods shall be submitted to the Congress and referred to the Joint Committee and a period of sixty days shall elapse while Congress is in session (in computing such sixty days, there shall be excluded the days on which either House is not in session because of an adjournment of more than three days): *And provided further,* That any such proposed amounts and periods shall not become effective if during such sixty-day period the Congress passes a concurrent resolution stating in substance that it does not favor the proposed action: *And provided further,* That prior to the elapse of the first thirty days of any such sixty-day period the Joint Committee shall submit a report to the Congress of its views and recommendations respecting the proposed amounts and periods and an accompanying proposed concurrent resolution stating in substance that the Congress favors, or does not favor, as the case may be, the proposed amounts or periods. The Commission may agree to repurchase any special nuclear material distributed under a sale arrangement pursuant to this subsection which is not

Sec. 54   ATOMIC ENERGY ACT OF 1954   26

consumed in the course of the activities conducted in accordance with the agreement for cooperation, or any uranium remaining after irradiation of such special nuclear material, at a repurchase price not to exceed the Commission's sale price for comparable special nuclear material or uranium in effect at the time of delivery of such material to the Commission. The Commission may also agree to purchase, consistent with and within the period of the agreement for cooperation, special nuclear material produced in a nuclear reactor located outside the United States through the use of special nuclear material which was leased or sold pursuant to this subsection. Under any such agreement the Commission shall purchase only such material as is delivered to the Commission during any period when there is in effect a guaranteed purchase price for the same material produced in a nuclear reactor by a person licensed under section 104, established by the Commission pursuant to section 56, and the price to be paid shall be the price so established by the Commission and in effect for the same material delivered to the Commission.

b. Notwithstanding the provisions of sections 123, 124, and 125, the Commission is authorized to distribute to any person outside the United States (1) plutonium containing 80 per centum or more by weight of plutonium-238, and (2) other special nuclear material when it has, in accordance with subsection 57 d., exempted certain classes or quantities of such other special nuclear material or kinds of uses or users thereof from the requirements for a license set forth in this chapter. Unless hereafter otherwise authorized by law, the Commission shall be compensated for special nuclear material so distributed at not less than the Commission's published charges applicable to the domestic distribution of such material. The Commission shall not distribute any plutonium containing 80 per centum or more by weight of plutonium-238 to any person under this subsection if, in its opinion, such distribution would be inimical to the common defense and security. The Commission may require such reports regarding the use of material distributed pursuant to the provisions of this subsection as it deems necessary.

c. The Commission is authorized to license or otherwise permit others to distribute special nuclear material to any person outside the United States under the same conditions, except as to charges, as would be applicable if the material were distributed by the Commission.

d. The authority to distribute special nuclear material under this section other than under an export license granted by the Nuclear Regulatory Commission shall extend only to the following small quantities of special nuclear material (in no event more than five hundred grams per year of the uranium isotope 233, the uranium isotope 235, or plutonium contained in special nuclear material to any recipient):

    (1) which are contained in laboratory samples, medical devices, or monitoring or other instruments; or

    (2) the distribution of which is needed to deal with an emergency situation in which time is of the essence.

e. The authority in this section to commit United States funds for any activities pursuant to any subsequent arrangement under section 131 a. (2) (E) shall be subject to the requirements of section 131.

[42 U.S.C. 2074]

SEC. 55. ACQUISITION.—The Commission is authorized, to the extent it deems necessary to effectuate the provisions of this Act, to purchase without regard to the limitations in section 54 or any guaranteed purchase prices established pursuant to section 56, and to take, requisition, condemn, or otherwise acquire any special nuclear material or any interest therein. Any contract of purchase made under this section may be made without regard to the provisions of section 3709 of the Revised Statutes, as amended, upon certification by the Commission that such action is necessary in the interest of the common defense and security, or upon a showing by the Commission that advertising is not reasonably practicable. Partial and advance payments may be made under contracts for such purposes. Just compensation shall be made for any right, property, or interest in property taken, requisitioned, or condemned under this section.[1] *Providing,* That the authority in this section to commit United States funds for any activities pursuant to any subsequent arrangement under section 131 a. (2) (E) shall be subject to the requirements of section 131.

[42 U.S.C. 2075]

SEC. 56. GUARANTEED PURCHASE PRICES.—The Commission shall establish guaranteed purchase prices for plutonium produced in a nuclear reactor by a person licensed under section 104 and delivered to the Commission before January 1, 1971. The Commission shall also establish for such periods of time as it may deem necessary but not to exceed ten years as to any such period, guaranteed purchase prices for uranium enriched in the isotope 233 produced in a nuclear reactor by a person licensed under section 103 or section 104 and delivered to the Commission within the period of the guarantee. Guaranteed purchase prices established under the authority of this section shall not exceed the Commission's determination of the estimated value of plutonium or uranium enriched in the isotope 233 as fuel in nuclear reactors, and such prices shall be established on a nondiscriminatory basis: *Provided,* That the Commission is authorized to establish such guaranteed purchase prices only for such plutonium or uranium enriched in the isotope 233 as the Commission shall determine is produced through the use of special nuclear material which was leased or sold by the Commission pursuant to section 53.

[42 U.S.C. 2076]

SEC. 57. PROHIBITION.—

a. Unless authorized by a general or specific license issued by the Commission, which the Commission is authorized to issue pursuant to section 53, no person may transfer or receive in interstate commerce, transfer, deliver, acquire, own, possess, receive possession of or title to, or import into or export from the United States any special nuclear materials.

---

[1] So in original. Period probably should be a colon.

b. It shall be unlawful for any person to directly or indirectly engage in the production of any special nuclear material outside of the United States except (1) as specifically authorized under an agreement for cooperation made pursuant to section 123, including a specific authorization in a subsequent arrangement under section 131 of this Act, or (2) upon authorization by the Secretary of Energy after a determination that such activity will not be inimical to the interest of the United States: *Provided,* That any such determination by the Secretary of Energy shall be made only with the concurrence of the Department of State and after consultation with the Arms Control and Disarmament Agency, the Nuclear Regulatory Commission, the Department of Commerce, and the Department of Defense. The Secretary of Energy shall, within ninety days after the enactment of the Nuclear Non-Proliferation Act of 1978,[1] establish orderly and expeditious procedures, including provision for necessary administrative actions and inter-agency memoranda of understanding, which are mutually agreeable to the Secretaries of State, Defense, and Commerce, the Director of the Arms Control and Disarmament Agency, and the Nuclear Regulatory Commission for the consideration of requests for authorization under this subsection. Such procedures shall include, at a minimum, explicit direction on the handling of such requests, express deadlines for the solicitation and collection of the views of the consulted agencies (with identified officials responsible for meeting such deadlines), an interagency coordinating authority to monitor the processing of such requests, predetermined procedures for the expeditious handling of intra-agency and inter-agency disagreements and appeals to higher authorities, frequent meetings of inter-agency administrative coordinators to review the status of all pending requests, and similar administrative mechanisms. To the extent practicable, an applicant should be advised of all the information required of the applicant for the entire process for every agency's needs at the beginning of the process. Potentially controversial requests should be identified as quickly as possible so that any required policy decisions or diplomatic consultations can be initiated in a timely manner. An immediate effort should be undertaken to establish quickly any necessary standards and criteria, including the nature of any required assurances or evidentiary showings, for the decision required under this subsection. The processing of any request proposed and filed as of the date of enactment of the Nuclear Non-Proliferation Act of 1978[1] shall not be delayed pending the development and establishment of procedures to implement the requirements of this subsection. Any trade secrets or proprietary information submitted by any person seeking an authorization under this subsection shall be afforded the maximum degree of protection allowable by law: *Provided further,* That the export of component parts as defined in subsection 11 v. (2) or 11 cc. (2) shall be governed by sections 109 and 126 of this Act: *Provided further,* That notwithstanding subsection 402(d) of the Department of Energy Organization Act (Public Law 95-91), the Secretary of Energy and not the Federal Energy Regulatory Commission, shall have sole jurisdiction within the Department of Energy over any matter arising

---

[1] The date of enactment was March 10, 1978.

from any function of the Secretary of Energy in this section, section 54 d., section 64, or section 111 b.

c. The Commission shall not—

(1) distribute any special nuclear material to any person for a use which is not under the jurisdiction of the United States except pursuant to the provisions of section 54; or

(2) distribute any special nuclear material or issue a license pursuant to section 53 to any person within the United States if the Commission finds that the distribution of such special nuclear material or the issuance of such license would be inimical to the common defense and security or would constitute an unreasonable risk to the health and safety of the public.

d. The Commission is authorized to establish classes of special nuclear material and to exempt certain classes or quantities of special nuclear material or kinds of uses or users from the requirements for a license set forth in this section when it makes a finding that the exemption of such classes or quantities of special nuclear material or such kinds of uses or users would not be inimical to the common defense and security and would not constitute an unreasonable risk to the health and safety of the public.

e. Special nuclear material, as defined in section 11, produced in facilities licensed under section 103 or 104 may not be transferred, reprocessed, used, or otherwise made available by any instrumentality of the United States or any other person for nuclear explosive purposes.

[42 U.S.C. 2077]

SEC. 58. REVIEW.—Before the Commission establishes any guaranteed purchase price or guaranteed purchase price period in accordance with the provisions of section 56, or establishes any criteria for the waiver of any charge for the use of special nuclear material licensed and distributed under section 53, the proposed guaranteed purchase price, guaranteed purchase price period, or criteria for the waiver of such charge shall be submitted to the Joint Committee and a period of forty-five days shall elapse while Congress is in session (in computing such forty-five days there shall be excluded the days in which either House is not in session because of adjournment for more than three days): *Provided, however,* That the Joint Committee, after having received the proposed guaranteed purchase price, guaranteed purchase price period, or criteria for the waiver of such charge, may by resolution in writing waive the conditions of, or all or any portion of, such forty-five day period.

[42 U.S.C. 2078]

CHAPTER 7. SOURCE MATERIAL

SEC. 61. SOURCE MATERIAL.—The Commission may determine from time to time that other material is source material in addition to those specified in the definition of source material. Before making such determination, the Commission must find that such material is essential to the production of special nuclear material and must find that the determination that such material is source material is in the interest of the common defense and security, and the President must have expressly assented in writing to the determination. The Commission's determination, together with the assent of the President, shall be submitted to the Joint Committee and a period of thirty days shall elapse while Congress is in session (in computing such thirty days, there shall be excluded the days on which either House is not in session because of an adjournment of more than three days) before the determination of the Commission may become effective: *Provided, however,* That the Joint Committee, after having received such determination, may by resolution in writing waive the conditions of or all or any portion of such thirty-day period.

[42 U.S.C. 2091]

SEC. 62. LICENSE FOR TRANSFERS REQUIRED.—Unless authorized by a general or specific license issued by the Commission, which the Commission is hereby authorized to issue, no person may transfer or receive in interstate commerce, transfer, deliver, receive possession of or title to, or import into or export from the United States any source material after removal from its place of deposit in nature, except that licenses shall not be required for quantities of source material which, in the opinion of the Commission, are unimportant.

[42 U.S.C. 2092]

SEC. 64. FOREIGN DISTRIBUTION OF SOURCE MATERIAL.—The Commission is authorized to cooperate with any nation by distributing source material and to distribute source material pursuant to the terms of an agreement for cooperation to which such nation is a party and which is made in accordance with section 123. The Commission is also authorized to distribute source material outside of the United States upon a determination by the Commission that such activity will not be inimical to the interests of the United States. The authority to distribute source material under this section other than under an export license granted by the Nuclear Regulatory Commission shall in no case extend to quantities of source material in excess of three metric tons per year per recipient.

[42 U.S.C. 2094]

SEC. 69. PROHIBITION.—The Commission shall not license any person to transfer or deliver, receive possession of or title to, or import into or export from the United States any source material if, in the opinion of the Commission, the issuance of a license to such person for such purpose would be inimical to the common defense and security or the health and safety of the public.

[42 U.S.C. 2099]

CHAPTER 8. BYPRODUCT MATERIAL

SEC. 81. DOMESTIC DISTRIBUTION.—No person may transfer or receive in interstate commerce, manufacture, produce, transfer, acquire, own, possess, import, or export any byproduct material, except to the extent authorized by this section, section 82 or section 84. The Commission is authorized to issue general or specific licenses to applicants seeking to use byproduct material for research or development purposes, for medical therapy, industrial uses, agricultural uses, or such other useful applications as may be developed. The Commission may distribute, sell, loan, or lease such byproduct material as it owns to qualified applicants with or without charge: *Provided, however,* That, for byproduct material to be distributed by the Commission for a charge, the Commission shall establish prices on such equitable basis as, in the opinion of the Commission, (a) will provide reasonable compensation to the Government for such material, (b) will not discourage the use of such material or the development of sources of supply of such material independent of the Commission, and (c) will encourage research and development. In distributing such material, the Commission shall give preference to applicants proposing to use such material either in the conduct of research and development or in medical therapy. The Commission shall not permit the distribution of any byproduct material to any licensee, and shall recall or order the recall of any distributed material from any licensee, who is not equipped to observe or who fails to observe such safety standards to protect health as may be established by the Commission or who uses such material in violation of law or regulation of the Commission or in a manner other than as disclosed in the application therefor or approved by the Commission. The Commission is authorized to establish classes of byproduct material and to exempt certain classes or quantities of material or kinds of uses or users from the requirements for a license set forth in this section when it makes a finding that the exemption of such classes or quantities of such material or such kinds of uses or users will not constitute

an unreasonable risk to the common defense and security and to the health and safety of the public.
[42 U.S.C. 2111]

SEC. 82. FOREIGN DISTRIBUTION OF BYPRODUCT MATERIAL.—
a. The Commission is authorized to cooperate with any nation by distributing byproduct material, and to distribute byproduct material, pursuant to the terms of an agreement for cooperation to which such nation is party and which is made in accordance with section 123.

b. The Commission is also authorized to distribute byproduct material to any person outside the United States upon application therefor by such person and demand such charge for such material as would be charged for the material if it were distributed within the United States: *Provided, however,* That the Commission shall not distribute any such material to any person under this section if, in its opinion, such distribution would be inimical to the common defense and security: *And provided further,* That the Commission may require such reports regarding the use of material distributed pursuant to the provisions of this section as it deems necessary.

c. The Commission is authorized to license others to distribute byproduct material to any person outside the United States under the same conditions, except as to charges, as would be applicable if the material were distributed by the Commission.

[42 U.S.C. 2112]

SEC. 83. OWNERSHIP AND CUSTODY OF CERTAIN BYPRODUCT MATERIAL AND DISPOSAL SITES.—
a. Any license issued or renewed after the effective date of this section [1] under section 62 or section 81 for any activity which results in the production of any byproduct material, as defined in section 11 e. (2), shall contain such terms and conditions as the Commission determines to be necessary to assure that, prior to termination of such license—

(1) the licensee will comply with decontamination, decommissioning, and reclamation standards prescribed by the Commission for sites (A) at which ores were processed primarily for their source material content and (B) at which such byproduct material is deposited, and

(2) ownership of any byproduct material, as defined in section 11 e. (2), which resulted from such licensed activity shall be transferred to (A) the United States or (B) in the State in which such activity occurred if such State exercises the option under subsection b. (1) to acquire land used for the disposal of byproduct material.

Any license which is in effect on the effective date of this section [1] and which is subsequently terminated without renewal shall comply with paragraphs (1) and (2) upon termination.

(b)(1)(A)[2] The Commission shall require by rule, regulation, or order that prior to the termination of any license which is issued after the effective date of this section [1], title to the land, including any interests therein (other than land owned by the United States

---
[1] The effective date was 3 years after Nov. 8, 1978. See Pub. L. 95-604, § 202(b).
[2] So in original. Probably should be "b. (1)(A)".

or by a State) which is used for the disposal of any byproduct material, as defined by section 11 e. (2), pursuant to such license shall be transferred to—
    (i) the United States, or
    (ii) the State in which such land is located, at the option of such State,
unless the Commission determines prior to such termination that transfer of title to such land and such byproduct material is not necessary or desirable to protect the public health, safety, or welfare or to minimize or eliminate danger to life or property. Such determination shall be made in accordance with section 181 of this Act. Notwithstanding any other provision of law or any such determination, such property and materials shall be maintained pursuant to a license issued by the Commission pursuant to section 81 of this Act in such manner as will protect the public health, safety, and the environment.

    (B) If the Commission determines by order that use of the surface or subsurface estates, or both, of the land transferred to the United States or to a State under subparagraph (A) would not endanger the public health, safety, welfare, or environment, the Commission, pursuant to such regulations as it may prescribe, shall permit the use of the surface or subsurface estates, or both, of such land in a manner consistent with the provisions of this section. If the Commission permits such use of such land, it shall provide the person who transferred such land with the right of first refusal with respect to such use of such land.

    (2) If transfer to the United States of title to such byproduct material and such land is required under this section, the Secretary of Energy or any Federal agency designated by the President shall, following the Commission's determination of compliance under subsection c., assume title and custody of such byproduct material and land transferred as provided in this subsection. Such Secretary or Federal agency shall maintain such material and land in such manner as will protect the public health and safety and the environment. Such custody may be transferred to another officer or instrumentality of the United States only upon approval of the President.

    (3) If transfer to a State of title to such byproduct material is required in accordance with this subsection, such State shall, following the Commission's determination of compliance under subsection d., assume title and custody of such byproduct material and land transferred as provided in this subsection. Such State shall maintain such material and land in such manner as will protect the public health, safety, and the environment.

    (4) In the case of any such license under section 62, which was in effect on the effective date of this section,[1] the Commission may require, before the termination of such license, such transfer of land and interests therein (as described in paragraph (1) of this subsection) to the United States or a State in which such land is located, at the option of such State, as may be necessary to protect the public health, welfare, and the environment from any effects associated with such byproduct material. In exercising the author-

---

[1] The effective date was 3 years after Nov. 8, 1978. See Pub. L. 95-604, § 202(b).

Sec. 84 ATOMIC ENERGY ACT OF 1954

ity of this paragraph, the Commission shall take into consideration the status of the ownership of such land and interests therein and the ability of the licensee to transfer title and custody thereof to the United States or a State.

(5) The Commission may, pursuant to a license, or by rule or order, require the Secretary or other Federal agency or State having custody of such property and materials to undertake such monitoring, maintenance, and emergency measures as are necessary to protect the public health and safety and such other actions as the Commission deems necessary to comply with the standard promulgated pursuant to section 84 of this Act. The Secretary or such other Federal agency is authorized to carry out maintenance, monitoring, and emergency measures, but shall take no other action pursuant to such license, rule or order, with respect to such property and materials unless expressly authorized by Congress after the date of enactment of this Act.[1]

(6) The transfer of title to land or byproduct materials, as defined in section 11 e. (2), to a State or the United States pursuant to this subsection shall not relieve any licensee of liability for any fraudulent or negligent acts done prior to such transfer.

(7) Material and land transferred to the United States or a State in accordance with this subsection shall be transferred without cost to the United States or a State (other than administrative and legal costs incurred in carrying out such transfer). Subject to the provisions of paragraph (1)(B) of this subsection, the United States or a State shall not transfer title to material or property acquired under this subsection to any person, unless such transfer is in the same manner as provided under section 104(h) of the Uranium Mill Tailings Radiation Control Act of 1978.

(8) The provisions of this subsection respecting transfer of title and custody to land shall not apply in the case of lands held in trust by the United States for any Indian tribe or lands owned by such Indian tribe subject to a restriction against alienation imposed by the United States. In the case of such lands which are used for the disposal of byproduct material, as defined in section 11 e. (2), the licensee shall be required to enter into such arrangements with the Commission as may be appropriate to assure the long-term maintenance and monitoring of such lands by the United States.

c. Upon termination on[2] any license to which this section applies, the Commission shall determine whether or not the licensee has complied with all applicable standards and requirements under such license.

[42 U.S.C. 2113]

SEC. 84. AUTHORITIES OF COMMISSION RESPECTING CERTAIN BYPRODUCT MATERIAL.—

a. The Commission shall insure that the management of any byproduct material, as defined in section 11 e. (2), is carried out in such manner as—

(1) the Commission deems appropriate to protect the public health and safety and the environment from radiological and nonradiological hazards associated with the processing and

---

[1] The date of enactment probably refers to Nov. 8, 1978.
[2] So in original. Probably should be "of".

with the possession and transfer of such material, taking into account the risk to the public health, safety, and the environment, with due consideration of the economic costs and such other factors as the Commission determines to be appropriate,,[1]

(2) conforms with applicable general standards promulgated by the Administrator of the Environmental Protection Agency under section 275, and

(3) conforms to general requirements established by the Commission, with the concurrence of the Administrator, which are, to the maximum extent practicable, at least comparable to requirements applicable to the possession, transfer, and disposal of similar hazardous material regulated by the Administrator under the Solid Waste Disposal Act, as amended.

b. In carrying out its authority under this section, the Commission is authorized to—

(1) by rule, regulation, or order require persons, officers, or instrumentalities exempted from licensing under section 81 of this Act to conduct monitoring, perform remedial work, and to comply with such other measures as it may deem necessary or desirable to protect health or to minimize danger to life or property, and in connection with the disposal or storage of such byproduct material; and

(2) make such studies and inspections and to conduct such monitoring as may be necessary.

Any violation by any person other than the United States or any officer or employee of the United States or a State of any rule, regulation, or order or licensing provision, of the Commission established under this section or section 83 shall be subject to a civil penalty in the same manner and in the same amount as violations subject to a civil penalty under section 234. Nothing in this section affects any authority of the Commission under any other provision of this Act.

c. In the case of sites at which ores are processed primarily for their source material content or which are used for the disposal of byproduct material as defined in section 11 e. (2), a licensee may propose alternatives to specific requirements adopted and enforced by the Commission under this Act. Such alternative proposals may take into account local or regional conditions including geology, topography, hydrology and meteorology. The Commission may treat such alternatives as satisfying Commission requirements if the Commission determines that such alternatives will achieve a level of stabilization and containment of the sites concerned, and a level of protection for public health, safety, and the environment from radiological and nonradiological hazards associated with such sites, which is equivalent to, to the extent practicable, or more stringent than the level which would be achieved by standards and requirements adopted and enforced by the Commission for the same purpose and any final standards promulgated by the Administrator of the Environmental Protection Agency in accordance with section 275.

[42 U.S.C. 2114]

---

[1] Two commas in original.

CHAPTER 9. MILITARY APPLICATION OF ATOMIC ENERGY

SEC. 91. AUTHORITY.—
  a. The Commission is authorized to—
    (1) conduct experiments and do research and development work in the military application of atomic energy;
    (2) engage in the production of atomic weapons, or atomic weapon parts, except that such activities shall be carried on only to the extent that the express consent and direction of the President of the United States has been obtained, which consent and direction shall be obtained at least once each year;
    (3) provide for safe storage, processing, transportation, and disposal of hazardous waste (including radioactive waste) resulting from nuclear materials production, weapons production and surveillance programs, and naval nuclear propulsion programs;
    (4) carry out research on and development of technologies needed for the effective negotiation and verification of international agreements on control of special nuclear materials and nuclear weapons; and
    (5) under applicable law (other than this paragraph) and consistent with other missions of the Department of Energy, make transfers of federally owned or originated technology to State and local governments, private industry, and universities or other nonprofit organizations so that the prospects for commercialization of such technology are enhanced.
  b. The President from time to time may direct the Commission (1) to deliver such quantities of special nuclear material or atomic weapons to the Department of Defense for such use as he deems necessary in the interest of national defense, or (2) to authorize the Department of Defense to manufacture, produce, or acquire any atomic weapon or utilization facility for military purposes: *Provided, however,* That such authorization shall not extend to the production of special nuclear material other than that incidental to the operation of such utilization facilities.
  c. The President may authorize the Commission or the Department of Defense, with the assistance of the other, to cooperate with another nation, and, notwithstanding the provisions of section 57, 62, or 81, to transfer by sale, lease, or loan to that nation, in accordance with terms and conditions of a program approved by the President—
    (1) nonnuclear parts of atomic weapons provided that such nation has made substantial progress in the development of atomic weapons, and other nonnuclear parts of atomic weapons systems involving Restricted Data provided that such transfer will not contribute significantly to that nation's atomic weapon design, development, or fabrication capability; for the purpose of improving that nation's state of training and operational readiness;
    (2) utilization facilities for military applications; and
    (3) source, byproduct, or special nuclear material for research on, development of, production of, or use in utilization facilities for military applications; and

(4) source, byproduct, or special nuclear material for research on, development of, or use in atomic weapons: *Provided, however,* That the transfer of such material to that nation is necessary to improve its atomic weapon design, development, or fabrication capability: *And provided further,* That such nation has substantial progress in the development of atomic weapons,

whenever the President determines that the proposed cooperation and each proposed transfer arrangement for the nonnuclear parts of atomic weapons and atomic weapons systems, utilization facilities or source, byproduct, or special nuclear material will promote and will not constitute an unreasonable risk to the common defense and security, while such other nation is participating with the United States pursuant to an international arrangement by substantial and material contributions to the mutual defense and security: *Provided, however,* That the cooperation is undertaken pursuant to an agreement entered into in accordance with section 123: *And provided further,* That if an agreement for cooperation arranged pursuant to this subsection provides for transfer of utilization facilities for military applications the Commission, or the Department of Defense with respect to cooperation it has been authorized to undertake, may authorize any person to transfer such utilization facilities for military applications in accordance with the terms and conditions of this subsection and of the agreement for cooperation.

[42 U.S.C. 2121]

SEC. 92. PROHIBITION.—It shall be unlawful, except as provided in section 91, for any person to transfer or receive in interstate or foreign commerce, manufacture, produce, transfer, acquire, possess, import, or export any atomic weapon. Nothing in this section shall be deemed to modify the provisions of subsection 31 a. or section 101.

[42 U.S.C. 2122]

CHAPTER 10. ATOMIC ENERGY LICENSES

SEC. 101. LICENSE REQUIRED.—It shall be unlawful, except as provided in section 91, for any person within the United States to transfer or receive in interstate commerce, manufacture, produce, transfer, acquire, possess, use, import, or export any utilization or production facility except under and in accordance with a license issued by the Commission pursuant to section 103 or 104.

[42 U.S.C. 2131]

SEC. 102. UTILIZATION AND PRODUCTION FACILITIES FOR INDUSTRIAL OR COMMERCIAL PURPOSES.—

a. Except as provided in subsections b. and c., or otherwise specifically authorized by law, any license hereafter issued for a utilization or production facility for industrial or commercial purposes shall be issued pursuant to section 103.

b. Any license hereafter issued for a utilization or production facility for industrial or commercial purposes, the construction or operation of which was licensed pursuant to subsection 104 b. prior to enactment into law of this subsection, shall be issued under subsection 104 b.

c. Any license for a utilization or production facility for industrial or commercial purposes constructed or operated under an arrangement with the Commission entered into under the Cooperative Power Reactor Demonstration Program shall, except as otherwise specifically required by applicable law, be issued under subsection 104 b.

[42 U.S.C. 2132]

SEC. 103. COMMERCIAL LICENSES.—

a. The Commission is authorized to issue licenses to persons applying therefor to transfer or receive in interstate commerce, manufacture, produce, transfer, acquire, possess, use, import, or export under the terms of an agreement for cooperation arranged pursuant to section 123, utilization or production facilities for industrial or commercial purposes. Such licenses shall be issued in accordance with the provisions of chapter 16 and subject to such conditions as the Commission may by rule or regulation establish to effectuate the purposes and provisions of this Act.

b. The Commission shall issue such licenses on a non-exclusive basis to persons applying therefor (1) whose proposed activities will serve a useful purpose proportionate to the quantities of special nuclear material or source material to be utilized; (2) who are equipped to observe and who agree to observe such safety standards to protect health and to minimize danger to life or property as the Commission may by rule establish; and (3) who agree to make available to the Commission such technical information and data concerning activities under such licenses as the Commission may determine necessary to promote the common defense and security and to protect the health and safety of the public. All such information may be used by the Commission only for the purposes of the common defense and security and to protect the health and safety of the public.

c. Each such license shall be issued for a specified period, as determined by the Commission, depending on the type of activity to be licensed, but not exceeding forty years, and may be renewed upon the expiration of such period.

d. No license under this section may be given to any person or activities which are not under or within the jurisdiction of the United States, except for the export of production or utilization facilities under terms of an agreement for cooperation arranged pursuant to section 123, or except under the provisions of section 109. No license may be issued to an alien or any any[1] corporation or other entity if the Commission knows or has reason to believe it is owned, controlled, or dominated by an alien, a foreign corporation, or a foreign government. In any event, no license may be issued to any person within the United States if, in the opinion of the Commission, the issuance of a license to such person would be

---

[1] So in original. The second "any" probably should be deleted.

inimical to the common defense and security or to the health and safety of the public.

f.[1] Each license issued for a utilization facility under this section or section 104 b. shall require as a condition thereof that in case of any accident which could result in an unplanned release of quantities of fission products in excess of allowable limits for normal operation established by the Commission, the licensee shall immediately so notify the Commission. Violation of the condition prescribed by this subsection may, in the Commission's discretion, constitute grounds for license revocation. In accordance with section 187 of this Act, the Commission shall promptly amend each license for a utilization facility issued under this section or section 104 b. which is in effect on the date of enactment of this subsection[2] to include the provisions required under this subsection.
[42 U.S.C. 2133]

SEC. 104. MEDICAL THERAPY AND RESEARCH AND DEVELOPMENT.—

a. The Commission is authorized to issue licenses to persons applying therefor for utilization facilities for use in medical therapy. In issuing such licenses the Commission is directed to permit the widest amount of effective medical therapy possible with the amount of special nuclear material available for such purposes and to impose the minimum amount of regulation consistent with its obligations under this Act to promote the common defense and security and to protect the health and safety of the public.

b. As provided for in subsection 102 b. or 102 c., or where specifically authorized by law, the Commission is authorized to issue licenses under this subsection to persons applying therefor for utilization and production facilities for industrial and commercial purposes. In issuing licenses under this subsection, the Commission shall impose the minimum amount of such regulations and terms of license as will permit the Commission to fulfill its obligations under this Act.

c. The Commission is authorized to issue licenses to persons applying therefor for utilization and production facilities useful in the conduct of research and development activities of the types specified in section 31 and which are not facilities of the type specified in subsection 104 b. The Commission is directed to impose only such minimum amount of regulation of the licensee as the Commission finds will permit the Commission to fulfill its obligations under this Act to promote the common defense and security and to protect the health and safety of the public and will permit the conduct of widespread and diverse research and development.

d. No license under this section may be given to any person for activities which are not under or within the jurisdiction of the United States, except for the export of production or utilization facilities under terms of an agreement for cooperation arranged pursuant to section 123 or except under the provisions of section 109. No license may be issued to any corporation or other entity if the Commission knows or has reason to believe it is owned, controlled, or dominated by an alien, a foreign corporation, or a foreign gov-

---
[1] No subsection e. in original.
[2] The date of enactment was June 30, 1980.

ernment. In any event, no license may be issued to any person within the United States if, in the opinion of the Commission, the issuance of a license to such person would be inimical to the common defense and security or to the health and safety of the public.
[42 U.S.C. 2134]

SEC. 109. COMPONENT AND OTHER PARTS OF FACILITIES.—
a. With respect to those utilization and production facilities which are so determined by the Commission pursuant to subsection 11 v. (2) or 11 cc. (2) the Commission may issue general licenses for domestic activities required to be licensed under section 101, if the Commission determines in writing that such general licensing will not constitute an unreasonable risk to the common defense and security.

b. After consulting with the Secretaries of State, Energy, and Commerce and the Director, the Commission is authorized and directed to determine which component parts as defined in subsection 11 v. (2) or 11 cc. (2) and which other items or substances are especially relevant from the standpoint of export control because of their significance for nuclear explosive purposes. Except as provided in section 126 b. (2), no such component, substance, or item which is so determined by the Commission shall be exported unless the Commission issues a general or specific license for its export after finding, based on a reasonable judgment of the assurances provided and other information available to the Federal Government, including the Commission, that the following criteria or their equivalent are met: (1) IAEA safeguards as required by Article III (2) of the Treaty will be applied with respect to such component, substance, or item; (2) no such component, substance, or item will be used for any nuclear explosive device or for research on or development of any nuclear explosive device; and (3) no such component, substance, or item will be retransferred to the jurisdiction of any other nation or group of nations unless the prior consent of the United States is obtained for such retransfer; and after determining in writing that the issuance of each such general or specific license or category of licenses will not be inimical to the common defense and security: *Provided,* That a specific license shall not be required for an export pursuant to this section if the component, item or substance is covered by a facility license issued pursuant to section 126 of this Act.

c. The Commission shall not issue an export license under the authority of subsection b. if it is advised by the executive branch, in accordance with the procedures established under subsection 126 a., that the export would be inimical to the common defense and security of the United States.
[42 U.S.C. 2139]

SEC. 111. [LICENSING BY NUCLEAR REGULATORY COMMISSION OF DISTRIBUTION OF CERTAIN MATERIALS BY DEPARTMENT OF

ENERGY.—][1] a. The Nuclear Regulatory Commission is authorized to license the distribution of special nuclear material, source material, and byproduct material by the Department of Energy pursuant to section 54, 64, and 82 of this Act, respectively, in accordance with the same procedures established by law for the export licensing of such material by any person: *Provided,* That nothing in this section shall require the licensing of the distribution of byproduct material by the Department of Energy under section 82 of this Act.

b. The Department of Energy shall not distribute any special nuclear material or source material under section 54 or 64 of this Act other than under an export license issued by the Nuclear Regulatory Commission until (1) the Department has obtained the concurrence of the Department of State and has consulted with the Arms Control and Disarmament Agency, the Nuclear Regulatory Commission, and the Department of Defense under mutually agreed procedures which shall be established within not more than ninety days after the date of enactment of this provision [2] and (2) the Department finds based on a reasonable judgment of the assurances provided and the information available to the United States Government, that the criteria in section 127 of this Act or their equivalent and any applicable criteria in subsection 128 are met, and that the proposed distribution would not be inimical to the common defense and security.

[42 U.S.C. 2141]

CHAPTER 11. INTERNATIONAL ACTIVITIES

SEC. 121. EFFECT OF INTERNATIONAL ARRANGEMENTS.—Any provision of this Act or any action of the Commission to the extent and during the time that it conflicts with the provisions of any international arrangement made after the date of enactment of this Act shall be deemed to be of no force or effect.

[42 U.S.C. 2151]

SEC. 122. POLICIES CONTAINED IN INTERNATIONAL ARRANGEMENTS.—In the performance of its functions under this Act, the Commission shall give maximum effect to the policies contained in any international arrangement made after the date of enactment of this Act.

[42 U.S.C. 2152]

SEC. 123. COOPERATION WITH OTHER NATIONS.—
No cooperation with any nation, group of nations or regional defense organization pursuant to section 53, 54 a., 57, 64, 82, 91, 103, 104, or 144 shall be undertaken until—
    a. the proposed agreement for cooperation has been submitted to the President, which proposed arrangement shall include the terms, conditions, duration, nature, and scope of the cooperation; and shall include the following requirements:
        (1) a guaranty by the cooperating party that safeguards as set forth in the agreement for cooperation

---

[1] No section heading in original.
[2] The date of enactment was March 10, 1978.

will be maintained with respect to all nuclear materials and equipment transferred pursuant thereto, and with respect to all special nuclear material used in or produced through the use of such nuclear materials and equipment, so long as the material or equipment remains under the jurisdiction or control of the cooperating party, irrespective of the duration of other provisions in the agreement or whether the agreement is terminated or suspended for any reason;

(2) in the case of non-nuclear-weapon states, a requirement, as a condition of continued United States nuclear supply under the agreement for cooperation, that IAEA safeguards be maintained with respect to all nuclear materials in all peaceful nuclear activities within the territory of such state, under its jurisdiction, or carried out under its control anywhere;

(3) except in the case of those agreements for cooperation arranged pursuant to subsection 91 c., a guaranty by the cooperating party that no nuclear materials and equipment or sensitive nuclear technology to be transferred pursuant to such agreement, and no special nuclear material produced through the use of any nuclear materials and equipment or sensitive nuclear technology transferred pursuant to such agreement, will be used for any nuclear explosive device, or for research on or development of any nuclear explosive device, or for any other military purpose;

(4) except in the case of those agreements for cooperation arranged pursuant to subsection 91 c. and agreements for cooperation with nuclear-weapon states, a stipulation that the United States shall have the right to require the return of any nuclear materials and equipment transferred pursuant thereto and any special nuclear material produced through the use thereof if the cooperating party detonates a nuclear explosive device or terminates or abrogates an agreement providing for IAEA safeguards;

(5) a guaranty by the cooperating party that any material or any Restricted Data transferred pursuant to the agreement for cooperation and, except in the case of agreements arranged pursuant to subsection 91 c., 144 b., or 144 c., any production or utilization facility transferred pursuant to the agreement for cooperation or any special nuclear material produced through the use of any such facility or through the use of any material transferred pursuant to the agreement, will not be transferred to unauthorized persons or beyond the jurisdiction or control of the cooperating party without the consent of the United States;

(6) a guaranty by the cooperating party that adequate physical security will be maintained with respect to any nuclear material transferred pursuant to such agreement and with respect to any special nuclear material used in or produced through the use of

any material, production facility, or utilization facility transferred pursuant to such agreement;

(7) except in the case of agreements for cooperation arranged pursuant to subsection 91 c., 144 b. or 144 c., a guaranty by the cooperating party that no material transferred pursuant to the agreement for cooperation and no material used in or produced through the use of any material, production facility, or utilization facility transferred pursuant to the agreement for cooperation will be reprocessed, enriched or (in the case of plutonium, uranium 233, or uranium enriched to greater than twenty percent in the isotope 235, or other nuclear materials which have been irradiated) otherwise altered in form or content without the prior approval of the United States;

(8) except in the case of agreements for cooperation arranged pursuant to subsection 91 c., 144 b. or 144 c., a guaranty by the cooperating party that no plutonium, no uranium 233, and no uranium enriched to greater than twenty percent in the isotope 235, transferred pursuant to the agreement for cooperation, or recovered from any source or special nuclear material so transferred or from any source or special nuclear material used in any production facility or utilization facility transferred pursuant to the agreement for cooperation, will be stored in any facility that has not been approved in advance by the United States; and

(9) except in the case of agreements for cooperation arranged pursuant to subsection 91 c., 144 b., or 144 c., a guaranty by the cooperating party that any special nuclear material, production facility, or utilization facility produced or constructed under the jurisdiction of the cooperating party by or through the use of any sensitive nuclear technology transferred pursuant to such agreement for cooperation will be subject to all the requirements specified in this subsection.

The President may exempt a proposed agreement for cooperation (except an agreement arranged pursuant to subsection 91 c., 144 b., or 144 c.) from any of the requirements of the foregoing sentence if he determines that inclusion of any such requirement would be seriously prejudicial to the achievement of United States non-proliferation objectives or otherwise jeopardize the common defense and security. Except in the case of those agreements for cooperation arranged pursuant to subsection 91 c., 144 b., or 144 c., any proposed agreement for cooperation shall be negotiated by the Secretary of State, with the technical assistance and concurrence of the Secretary of Energy and in consultation with the Director of the Arms Control and Disarmament Agency ("the Director"); and after consultation with the Commission shall be submitted to the President jointly by the Secretary of State and the Secretary of Energy accompanied by the views and recommendations of the Secretary of State, the Secretary of Energy, the Nuclear Regulatory Commission, and the Director, who shall also provide to the President an unclassified Nuclear Proliferation Assessment Statement (A) which shall analyze the consistency of the text of the proposed agreement for cooperation with all the requirements of this Act, with specific attention to whether the proposed agreement is consistent with each of the criteria set forth in this subsection, and (B) regarding the adequacy of the safeguards and other control mechanisms and the peaceful use assurances contained in the agreement for cooperation to ensure that any assistance furnished thereunder will not be used to further any military or nuclear explosive purpose. In the case of those agreements for cooperation arranged pursuant to subsection 91 c., 144 b., or 144 c., any proposed agreement for cooperation shall be submitted to the President by the Secretary of Energy or, in the case of those agreements for cooperation arranged pursuant to subsection 91 c. or 144 b. which are to be implemented by the Department of Defense, by the Secretary of Defense;

b. the President has submitted text of the proposed agreement for cooperation, together with the accompanying unclassified Nuclear Proliferation Assessment Statement, to the Committee on Foreign Relations of the Senate and the Committee on Foreign Affairs of the House of Representatives, the President has consulted with such Committees for a period of not less than thirty days of continuous session (as defined in section 130 g. of this Act) concerning the consistency of the terms of the proposed agreement with all the requirements of this Act, and the President has approved and authorized the execution of the proposed agreement for cooperation and has made a determination in writing that the performance of the proposed agreement will promote, and will not constitute an unreasonable risk to, the common defense and security;

c. the proposed agreement for cooperation (if not an agreement subject to subsection d.) together with the approval and determination of the President, has been submitted to the Committee on International Relations of the House of Representatives [1] and the Committee on Foreign Relations of the Senate for a period of thirty days of continuous session (as defined in subsection 130 g.): *Provided, however,* That these committees, after having received such agreement for cooperation, may by resolution in writing waive the conditions of all or any portion of such thirty-day period; and

d. the proposed agreement for cooperation (if arranged pursuant to subsection 91 c., 144 b., or 144 c., or if entailing implementation of section 53, 54 a., 103, or 104 in relation to a reactor that may be capable of producing more than five thermal megawatts or special nuclear material

---

[1] The name of the Committee on International Relations of the House of Representatives was changed to Committee on Foreign Affairs on Feb. 5, 1979, by House Resolution 89, 96th Congress.

for use in connection therewith) has been submitted to the Congress, together with the approval and determination of the President, for a period of sixty days of continuous session (as defined in subsection 130 g. of this Act) and referred to the Committee on International Relations of the House of Representatives [1] and the Committee on Foreign Relations of the Senate, and in addition, in the case of a proposed agreement for cooperation arranged pursuant to subsection 91 c., 144 b., or 144 c., the Committee on Armed Services of the House of Representatives and the Committee on Armed Services of the Senate, but such proposed agreement for cooperation shall not become effective if during such sixty-day period the Congress adopts, and there is enacted, a joint resolution stating in substance that the Congress does not favor the proposed agreement for cooperation: *Provided,* That the sixty-day period shall not begin until a Nuclear Proliferation Assessment Statement prepared by the Director of the Arms Control and Disarmament Agency, when required by subsection 123 a., has been submitted to the Congress: *Provided further,* That an agreement for cooperation exempted by the President pursuant to subsection a. from any requirement contained in that subsection shall not become effective unless the Congress adopts, and there is enacted, a joint resolution stating that the Congress does favor such agreement. During the sixty-day period the Committee on Foreign Affairs of the House of Representatives and the Committee on Foreign Relations of the Senate shall each hold hearings on the proposed agreement for cooperation and submit a report to their respective bodies recommending whether it should be approved or disapproved. Any such proposed agreement for cooperation shall be considered pursuant to the procedures set forth in section 130 i. of this Act.

Following submission of a proposed agreement for cooperation (except an agreement for cooperation arranged pursuant to subsection 91 c., 144 b., or 144c.) to the Committee on International Relations of the House of Representatives [1] and the Committee on Foreign Relations of the Senate, the Nuclear Regulatory Commission, the Department of State, the Department of Energy, the Arms Control and Disarmament Agency, and the Department of Defense shall, upon the request of either of those committees, promptly furnish to those committees their views as to whether the safeguards and other controls contained therein provide an adequate framework to ensure that any exports as contemplated by such agreement will not be inimical to or constitute an unreasonable risk to the common defense and security.

If, after the date of enactment of the Nuclear Non-Proliferation Act of 1978,[2] the Congress fails to disapprove a proposed agreement for cooperation which exempts the recipient nation from the

---

[1] The name of the Committee on International Relations of the House of Representatives was changed to Committee on Foreign Affairs on Feb. 5, 1979, by House Resolution 89, 96th Congress.
[2] The date of enactment was March 10, 1978.

requirement set forth in subsection 123 a. (2), such failure to act shall constitute a failure to adopt a resolution of disapproval pursuant to subsection 128 b. (3) for purposes of the Commission's consideration of applications and requests under section 126 a. (2) and there shall be no congressional review pursuant to section 128 of any subsequent license or authorization with respect to that state until the first such license or authorization which is issued after twelve months from the elapse of the sixty-day period in which the agreement for cooperation in question is reviewed by the Congress.

[42 U.S.C. 2153]

SEC. 124. INTERNATIONAL ATOMIC POOL.—The President is authorized to enter into an international arrangement with a group of nations providing for international cooperation in the nonmilitary applications of atomic energy and he may thereafter cooperate with that group of nations pursuant to sections 54 a., 57, 64, 82, 103, 104, or 144 a.: *Provided, however,* That the cooperation is undertaken pursuant to an agreement for cooperation entered into in accordance with section 123.

[42 U.S.C. 2154]

SEC. 125. COOPERATION WITH BERLIN.—The President may authorize the Commission to enter into agreements for cooperation with the Federal Republic of Germany in accordance with section 123, on behalf of Berlin, which for the purposes of this Act comprises those areas over which the Berlin Senate exercises jurisdiction (the United States, British, and French sectors) and the Commission may thereafter cooperate with Berlin pursuant to sections 54 a., 57, 64, 82, 103, or 104: *Provided,* That the guaranties required by section 123 shall be made by Berlin with the approval of the allied commandants.

[42 U.S.C. 2153]

SEC. 126. EXPORT LICENSING PROCEDURES.—

a. No license may be issued by the Nuclear Regulatory Commission (the "Commission") for the export of any production or utilization facility, or any source material or special nuclear material, including distributions of any material by the Department of Energy under section 54, 64, or 82, for which a license is required or requested, and no exemption from any requirement for such an export license may be granted by the Commission, as the case may be, until—

(1) the Commission has been notified by the Secretary of State that it is the judgment of the executive branch that the proposed export or exemption will not be inimical to the common defense and security, or that any export in the category to which the proposed export belongs would not be inimical to the common defense and security because it lacks significance for nuclear explosive purposes. The Secretary of State shall, within ninety days after the enactment of this section,[1] establish orderly and expeditious procedures, including provision for necessary administrative actions and inter-agency memoranda of understanding, which are mutually agreeable to the Sec-

---

[1] The date of enactment was March 10, 1978.

retaries of Energy, Defense, and Commerce, the Director of the Arms Control and Disarmament Agency, and the Nuclear Regulatory Commission for the preparation of the executive branch judgment on export applications under this section. Such procedures shall include, at a minimum, explicit direction on the handling of such applications, express deadlines for the solicitation and collection of the views of the consulted agencies (with identified officials responsible for meeting such deadlines), an inter-agency coordinating authority to monitor the processing of such applications, predetermined procedures for the expeditious handling of intra-agency and inter-agency disagreements and appeals to higher authorities, frequent meetings of inter-agency administrative coordinators to review the status of all pending applications, and similar administrative mechanisms. To the extent practicable, an applicant should be advised of all the information required of the applicant for the entire process for every agency's needs at the beginning of the process. Potentially controversial applications should be identified as quickly as possible so that any required policy decisions or diplomatic consultations con [1] be initiated in a timely manner. An immediate effort should be undertaken to establish quickly any necessary standards and criteria, including the nature of any required assurances or evidentiary showings, for the decisions required under this section. The processing of any export application proposed and filed as of the date of enactment of this section [2] shall not be delayed pending the development and establishment of procedures to implement the requirements of this section. The executive branch judgment shall be completed in not more than sixty days from receipt of the application or request, unless the Secretary of State in his discretion specifically authorizes additional time for consideration of the application or request because it is in the national interest to allow such additional time. The Secretary shall notify the Committee on Foreign Relations of the Senate and the Committee on International Relations of the House of Representatives [3] of any such authorization. In submitting any such judgment, the Secretary of State shall specifically address the extent to which the export criteria then in effect are met and the extent to which the cooperating party has adhered to the provisions of the applicable agreement for cooperation. In the event he considers it warranted, the Secretary may also address the following additional factors, among others:

(A) whether issuing the license or granting the exemption will materially advance the non-proliferation policy of the United States by encouraging the recipient nation to adhere to the Treaty, or to participate in the undertakings contemplated by section 403 or 404(a) of the Nuclear Non-Proliferation Act of 1978;

[1] So in original. Probably should be "can".
[2] The date of enactment was March 10, 1978.
[3] The name of the Committee on International Relations of the House of Representatives was changed to Committee on Foreign Affairs on Feb. 5, 1979, by House Resolution 89, 96th Congress.

(B) whether failure to issue the license or grant the exemption would otherwise be seriously prejudicial to the non-proliferation objectives of the United States; and

(C) whether the recipient nation or group of nations has agreed that conditions substantially identical to the export criteria set forth in section 127 of this Act will be applied by another nuclear supplier nation or group of nations to the proposed United States export, and whether, in the Secretary's judgment those conditions will be implemented in a manner acceptable to the United States.

The Secretary of State shall provide appropriate data and recommendations, subject to requests for additional data and recommendations, as required by the Commission or the Secretary of Energy, as the case may be; and

(2) the Commission finds, based on a reasonable judgment of the assurances provided and other information available to the Federal Government, including the Commission, that the criteria in section 127 of this Act or their equivalent, and any other applicable statutory requirements, are met: *Provided,* That continued cooperation under an agreement for cooperation as authorized in accordance with section 124 of this Act shall not be prevented by failure to meet the provisions of paragraph (4) or (5) of section 127 for a period of thirty days after enactment of this section,[1] and for a period of twenty-three months thereafter if the Secretary of State notifies the Commission that the nation or group of nations bound by the relevant agreement has agreed to negotiations as called for in section 404(a) of the Nuclear Non-Proliferation Act of 1978; however, nothing in this subsection shall be deemed to relinquish any rights which the United States may have under agreements for cooperation in force on the date of enactment of this section[1]: *Provided, further,* That if, upon the expiration of such twenty-four month period, the President determines that failure to continue cooperation with any group of nations which has been exempted pursuant to the above proviso from the provisions of paragraph (4) or (5) of section 127 of this Act, but which has not yet agreed to comply with those provisions would be seriously prejudicial to the achievement of United States non-proliferation objectives or otherwise jeopardize the common defense and security, he may, after notifying the Congress of his determination, extend by Executive order the duration of the above proviso for a period of twelve months, and may further extend the duration of such proviso by one year increments annually thereafter if he again makes such determination and so notifies the Congress. In the event that the Committee on International Relations of the House of Representatives[2] or the Committee on Foreign Relations of the Senate reports a joint resolution to take any action with respect to any such extension, such joint resolution will be considered in the House or Senate, as the case may be, under pro-

---
[1] The date of enactment was March 10, 1978.
[2] The name of the Committee on International Relations of the House of Representatives was changed to Committee on Foreign Affairs on Feb. 5, 1979, by House Resolution 89, 96th Congress.

cedures identical to those provided for the consideration of resolutions pursuant to section 130 of this Act: *And additionally provided,* That the Commission is authorized to (A) make a single finding under this subsection for more than a single application or request, where the applications or requests involve exports to the same country, in the same general time frame, of similar significance for nuclear explosive purposes and under reasonably similar circumstances and (B) make a finding under this subsection that there is no material changed circumstance associated with a new application or request from those existing at the time of the last application or request for an export to the same country, where the prior application or request was approved by the Commission using all applicable procedures of this section, and such finding of no material changed circumstance shall be deemed to satisfy the requirement of this paragraph for findings of the Commission. The decision not to make any such finding in lieu of the findings which would otherwise be required to be made under this paragraph shall not be subject to judicial review: *And provided further,* That nothing contained in this section is intended to require the Commission independently to conduct or prohibit the Commission from independently conducting country or site specific visitations in the Commission's consideration of the application of IAEA safeguards.

b. (1) Timely consideration shall be given by the Commission to requests for export licenses and exemptions and such requests shall be granted upon a determination that all applicable statutory requirements have been met.

(2) If, after receiving the executive branch judgment that the issuance of a proposed export license will not be inimical to the common defense and security, the Commission does not issue the proposed license on a timely basis because it is unable to make the statutory determinations required under this Act, the Commission shall publicly issue its decision to that effect, and shall submit the license application to the President. The Commission's decision shall include an explanation of the basis for the decision and any dissenting or separate views. If, after receiving the proposed license application and reviewing the Commission's decision, the President determines that withholding the proposed export would be seriously prejudicial to the achievement of United States non-proliferation objectives, or would otherwise jeopardize the common defense and security, the proposed export may be authorized by Executive order: *Provided,* That prior to any such export, the President shall submit the Executive order, together with his explanation of why, in light of the Commission's decision, the export should nonetheless be made, to the Congress for a period of sixty days of continuous session (as defined in subsection 130 g.) and shall be referred to the Committee on International Relations of the House of Representatives [1] and the Committee on Foreign Relations of the Senate, but any such proposed export shall not occur if during such sixty-day period the Congress adopts a concurrent resolution stat-

---

[1] The name of the Committee on International Relations of the House of Representatives was changed to Committee on Foreign Affairs on Feb. 5, 1979, by House Resolution 89, 96th Congress.

ing in substance that it does not favor the proposed export. Any such Executive order shall be considered pursuant to the procedures set forth in section 130 of this Act for the consideration of Presidential submissions: *And provided further,* That the procedures established pursuant to subsection (b) of section 304 of the Nuclear Non-Proliferation Act of 1978 shall provide that the Commission shall immediately initiate review of any application for a license under this section and to the maximum extent feasible shall expeditiously process the application concurrently with the executive branch reviews, while awaiting the final executive branch judgment. In initiating its review, the Commission may identify a set of concerns and requests for information associated with the projected issuance of such license and shall transmit such concerns and requests to the executive branch which shall address such concerns and requests in its written communications with the Commission. Such procedures shall also provide that if the Commission has not completed action on the application within sixty days after the receipt of an executive branch judgment that the proposed export or exemption is not inimical to the common defense and security or that any export in the category to which the proposed export belongs would not be inimical to the common defense and security because it lacks significance for nuclear explosive purposes, the Commission shall inform the applicant in writing of the reason for delay and provide follow-up reports as appropriate. If the Commission has not completed action by the end of an additional sixty days (a total of one hundred and twenty days from receipt of the executive branch judgment), the President may authorize the proposed export by Executive order, upon a finding that further delay would be excessive and upon making the findings required for such Presidential authorizations under this subsection, and subject to the Congressional review procedures set forth herein. However, if the Commission has commenced procedures for public participation regarding the proposed export under regulations promulgated pursuant to subsection (b) of section 304 of the Nuclear Non-Proliferation Act of 1978, or—within sixty days after receipt of the executive branch judgment on the proposed export—the Commission has identified and transmitted to the executive branch a set of additional concerns or requests for information, the President may not authorize the proposed export until sixty days after public proceedings are completed or sixty days after a full executive branch response to the Commission's additional concerns or requests has been made consistent with subsection a. (1) of this section: *Provided further,* That nothing in this section shall affect the right of the Commission to obtain data and recommendations from the Secretary of State at any time as provided in subsection a. (1) of this section.

c. In the event that the House of Representatives or the Senate passes a joint resolution which would adopt one or more additional export criteria, or would modify any existing export criteria under this Act, any such joint resolution shall be referred in the other House to the Committee on Foreign Relations of the Senate or the Committee on International Relations of the House of Representatives,[1] as the case may be, and shall be considered by the other House under applicable procedures provided for the consideration of resolutions pursuant to section 130 of this Act.

[42 U.S.C. 2155]

SEC. 127. CRITERIA GOVERNING UNITED STATES NUCLEAR EXPORTS.—

The United States adopts the following criteria which, in addition to other requirements of law, will govern exports for peaceful nuclear uses from the United States of source material, special nuclear material, production or utilization facilities, and any sensitive nuclear technology:

(1) IAEA safeguards as required by Article III(2) of the Treaty will be applied with respect to any such material or facilities proposed to be exported, to any such material or facilities previously exported and subject to the applicable agreement for cooperation, and to any special nuclear material used in or produced through the use thereof.

(2) No such material, facilities, or sensitive nuclear technology proposed to be exported or previously exported and subject to the applicable agreement for cooperation, and no special nuclear material produced through the use of such materials, facilities, or sensitive nuclear technology, will be used for any nuclear explosive device or for research on or development of any nuclear explosive device.

(3) Adequate physical security measures will be maintained with respect to such material or facilities proposed to be exported and to any special nuclear material used in or produced through the use thereof. Following the effective date of any regulations promulgated by the Commission pursuant to section 304(d) of the Nuclear Non-Proliferation Act of 1978, physical security measures shall be deemed adequate if such measures provide a level of protection equivalent to that required by the applicable regulations.

(4) No such materials, facilities, or sensitive nuclear technology proposed to be exported, and no special nuclear material produced through the use of such material, will be retransferred to the jurisdiction of any other nation or group of nations unless the prior approval of the United States is obtained for such retransfer. In addition to other requirements of law, the United States may approve such retransfer only if the nation or group of nations designated to receive such retransfer agrees that it shall be subject to the conditions required by this section.

(5) No such material proposed to be exported and no special nuclear material produced through the use of such material will be reprocessed, and no irradiated fuel elements containing such material removed from a reactor shall be altered in form or content, unless the prior approval of the United States is obtained for such reprocessing or alteration.

---

[1] The name of the Committee on International Relations of the House of Representatives was changed to Committee on Foreign Affairs on Feb. 5, 1979, by House Resolution 89, 96th Congress.

(6) No such sensitive nuclear technology shall be exported unless the foregoing conditions shall be applied to any nuclear material or equipment which is produced or constructed under the jurisdiction of the recipient nation or group of nations by or through the use of any such exported sensitive nuclear technology.

[42 U.S.C. 2156]

SEC. 128. ADDITIONAL EXPORT CRITERION AND PROCEDURES.—

a. (1) As a condition of continued United States export of source material, special nuclear material, production or utilization facilities, and any sensitive nuclear technology to non-nuclear-weapon states, no such export shall be made unless IAEA safeguards are maintained with respect to all peaceful nuclear activities in, under the jurisdiction of, or carried out under the control of such state at the time of the export.

(2) The President shall seek to achieve adherence to the foregoing criterion by recipient non-nuclear-weapon states.

b. The criterion set forth in subsection a. shall be applied as an export criterion with respect to any application for the export of materials, facilities, or technology specified in subsection a. which is filed after eighteen months from the date of enactment of this section,[1] or for any such application under which the first export would occur at least twenty-four months after the date of enactment of this section,[1] except as provided in the following paragraphs:

(1) if the Commission or the Department of Energy, as the case may be, is notified that the President has determined that failure to approve an export to which this subsection applies because such criterion has not yet been met would be seriously prejudicial to the achievement of United States non-proliferation objectives or otherwise jeopardize the common defense and security, the license or authorization may be issued subject to other applicable requirements of law: *Provided,* That no such export of any production or utilization facility or of any source or special nuclear material (intended for use as fuel in any production or utilization facility) which has been licensed or authorized pursuant to this subsection shall be made to any non-nuclear-weapon state which has failed to meet such criterion until the first such license or authorization with respect to such state is submitted to the Congress (together with a detailed assessment of the reasons underlying the President's determination, the judgment of the executive branch required under section 126 of this Act, and any Commission opinion and views) for a period of sixty days of continuous session (as defined in subsection 130 g. of this Act) and referred to the Committee on International Relations of the House of Representatives[2] and the Committee on Foreign Relations of the Senate, but such export shall not occur if during such sixty-day period the Congress adopts a concurrent resolution stating in sub-

---

[1] The date of enactment was March 10, 1978.
[2] The name of the Committee on International Relations of the House of Representatives was changed to Committee on Foreign Affairs on Feb. 5, 1979, by House Resolution 89, 96th Congress.

stance that the Congress does not favor the proposed export. Any such license or authorization shall be considered pursuant to the procedures set forth in section 130 of this Act for the consideration of Presidential submissions.

(2) If the Congress adopts a resolution of disapproval pursuant to paragraph (1), no further export of materials, facilities, or technology specified in subsection a. shall be permitted for the remainder of that Congress, unless such state meets the criterion or the President notifies the Congress that he has determined that significant progress has been made in achieving adherence to such criterion by such state or that United States foreign policy interests dictate reconsideration and the Congress, pursuant to the procedure of paragraph (1), does not adopt a concurrent resolution stating in substance that it disagrees with the President's determination.

(3) If the Congress does not adopt a resolution of disapproval with respect to a license or authorization submitted pursuant to paragraph (1), the criterion set forth in subsection a. shall not be applied as an export criterion with respect to exports of materials, facilities and technology specified in subsection a. to that state: *Provided,* That the first license or authorization with respect to that state which is issued pursuant to this paragraph after twelve months from the elapse of the sixty-day period specified in paragraph (1), and the first such license or authorization which is issued after each twelve-month period thereafter, shall be submitted to the Congress for review pursuant to the procedures specified in paragraph (1): *Provided further.*[1] That if the Congress adopts a resolution of disapproval during any review period provided for by this paragraph, the provisions of paragraph (2) shall apply with respect to further exports to such state.

[42 U.S.C. 2157]

SEC. 129. CONDUCT RESULTING IN TERMINATION OF NUCLEAR EXPORTS.—

No nuclear materials and equipment or sensitive nuclear technology shall be exported to—

(1) any non-nuclear-weapon state that is found by the President to have, at any time after the effective date of this section,[2]

(A) detonated a nuclear explosive device; or

(B) terminated or abrogated IAEA safeguards; or

(C) materially violated an IAEA safeguards agreement; or

(D) engaged in activities involving source or special nuclear material and having direct significance for the manufacture or acquisition of nuclear explosive devices, and has failed to take steps which, in the President's judgment, represent sufficient progress toward terminating such activities; or

---
[1] Period in original. Probably should be comma.
[2] The effective date was March 10, 1978.

(2) any nation or group of nations that is found by the President to have, at any time after the effective date of this section, [1]

(A) materially violated an agreement for cooperation with the United States, or, with respect to material or equipment not supplied under an agreement for cooperation, materially violated the terms under which such material or equipment was supplied or the terms of any commitments obtained with respect thereto pursuant to section 402(a) of the Nuclear Non-Proliferation Act of 1978; or

(B) assisted, encouraged, or induced any non-nuclear-weapon state to engage in activities involving source or special nuclear material and having direct significance for the manufacture or acquisition of nuclear explosive devices, and has failed to take steps which, in the President's judgment, represent sufficient progress toward terminating such assistance, encouragement, or inducement; or

(C) entered into an agreement after the date of enactment of this section [1] for the transfer of reprocessing equipment, materials, or technology to the sovereign control of a non-nuclear-weapon state except in connection with an international fuel cycle evaluation in which the United States is a participant or pursuant to a subsequent international agreement or understanding to which the United States subscribes;

unless the President determines that cessation of such exports would be seriously prejudicial to the achievement of United States non-proliferation objectives or otherwise jeopardize the common defense and security: *Provided,* That prior to the effective date of any such determination, the President's determination, together with a report containing the reasons for his determination, shall be submitted to the Congress and referred to the Committee on International Relations of the House of Representatives [2] and the Committee on Foreign Relations of the Senate for a period of sixty days of continuous session (as defined in subsection 130 g. of this Act), but any such determination shall not become effective if during such sixty-day period the Congress adopts a concurrent resolution stating in substance that it does not favor the determination. Any such determination shall be considered pursuant to the procedures set forth in section 130 of this Act for the consideration of Presidential submissions.

[42 U.S.C. 2158]

SEC. 130. CONGRESSIONAL REVIEW PROCEDURES.—

a. Not later than forty-five days of continuous session of Congress after the date of transmittal to the Congress of any submission of the President required by subsection 126 a. (2), 126 b. (2), 128 b., 129, 131 a. (3), or 131 f. (1)(A) of this Act, the Committee on Foreign Relations of the Senate and the Committee on International Relations of the House of Representatives,[2] shall each sub-

---

[1] The date of enactment was March 10, 1978.
[2] The name of the Committee on International Relations of the House of Representatives was changed to Committee on Foreign Affairs on Feb. 5, 1979, by House Resolution 89, 96th Congress.

Sec. 130 ATOMIC ENERGY ACT OF 1954 62

mit a report to its respective House on its views and recommendations respecting such Presidential submission together with a resolution, as defined in subsection f., stating in substance that the Congress approves or disapproves such submission, as the case may be: *Provided,* That if any such committee has not reported such a resolution at the end of such forty-five day period, such committee shall be deemed to be discharged from further consideration of such submission. If no such resolution has been reported at the end of such period, the first resolution, as defined in subsection f., which is introduced within five days thereafter within such House shall be placed on the appropriate calendar of such House.

b. When the relevant committee of committees have reported such a resolution (or have been discharged from further consideration of such a resolution pursuant to subsection a.) or when a resolution has been introduced and placed on the appropriate calendar pursuant to subsection a., as the case may be, it is at any time thereafter in order (even though a previous motion to the same effect has been disagreed to) for any Member of the respective House to move to proceed to the consideration of the resolution. The motion is highly privileged and is not debatable. The motion shall not be subject to amendment, or to a motion to postpone, or to a motion to proceed to the consideration of other business. A motion to reconsider the vote by which the motion is agreed to or disagreed to shall not be in order. If a motion to proceed to the consideration of the resolution is agreed to, the resolution shall remain the unfinished business of the respective House until disposed of.

c. Debate on the resolution, and on all debatable motions and appeals in connection therewith, shall be limited to not more than ten hours, which shall be divided equally between individuals favoring and individuals opposing the resolution. A motion further to limit debate is in order and not debatable. An amendment to a motion to postpone, or a motion to recommit the resolution, or a motion to proceed to the consideration of other business is not in order. A motion to reconsider the vote by which the resolution is agreed to or disagreed to shall not be in order. No amendment to any concurrent resolution pursuant to the procedures of this section is in order except as provided in subsection d.

d. Immediately following (1) the conclusion of the debate on such concurrent resolution, (2) a single quorum call at the conclusion of debate if requested in accordance with the rules of the appropriate House, and (3) the consideration of an amendment introduced by the Majority Leader or his designee to insert the phrase, "does not" in lieu of the word "does" if the resolution under consideration is a concurrent resolution of approval, the vote on final approval of the resolution shall occur.

e. Appeals from the decisions of the Chair relating to the application of the rules of the Senate or the House of Representatives, as the case may be, to the procedure relating to such a resolution shall be decided without debate.

f. For the purposes of subsections a. through e. of this section, the term "resolution" means a concurrent resolution of the Congress, the matter after the resolving clause of which is as follows: "That the Congress (does or does not) favor the   transmitted to the Congress by the President on   , ", the blank spaces therein to be appropriately filled, and the affirmative or negative phrase within the parenthetical to be appropriately selected.

g. (1) Except as provided in paragraph (2), for the purposes of this section—

(A) continuity of session is broken only by an adjournment of Congress sine die; and

(B) the days on which either House is not in session because of an adjournment of more than three days to a day certain are excluded in the computation of any period of time in which Congress is in continuous session.

(2) For purposes of this section insofar as it applies to section 123—

(A) continuity of session is broken only by an adjournment of Congress sine die at the end of a Congress; and

(B) the days on which either House is not in session because of an adjournment of more than three days are excluded in the computation of any period of time in which Congress is in continuous session.

h. This section is enacted by Congress—

(1) as an exercise of the rulemaking power of the Senate and the House of Representatives, respectively, and as such they are deemed a part of the rules of each House, respectively, but applicable only with respect to the procedure to be followed in that House in the case of resolutions described by subsection f. of this section; and they supersede other rules only to the extent that they are inconsistent therewith; and

(2) with full recognition of the constitutional right of either House to change the rules (so far as relating to the procedure of that House) at any time, in the same manner and to the same extent as in the case of any other rule of that House.

i. (1) For the purposes of this subsection, the term "joint resolution" means a joint resolution, the matter after the resolving clause of which is as follows: "That the Congress (does or does not) favor the proposed agreement for cooperation transmitted to the Congress by the President on   .", with the date of the transmission of the proposed agreement for cooperation inserted in the blank, and the affirmative or negative phrase within the parenthetical appropriately selected.

(2) On the day on which a proposed agreement for cooperation is submitted to the House of Representatives and the Senate under section 123 d., a joint resolution with respect to such agreement for cooperation shall be introduced (by request) in the House by the chairman of the Committee on Foreign Affairs, for himself and the ranking minority member of the Committee, or by Members of the House designated by the chairman and ranking minority member; and shall be introduced (by request) in the Senate by the majority leader of the Senate, for himself and the minority leader of the Senate, or by Members of the Senate designated by the majority leader and minority leader of the Senate. If either House is not in session on the day on which such an agreement for cooperation is submitted, the joint resolution shall be introduced in that House, as provided in the preceding sentence, on the first day thereafter on which that House is in session.

(3) All joint resolutions introduced in the House of Representatives shall be referred to the appropriate committee or committees, and all joint resolutions introduced in the Senate shall be referred to the Committee on Foreign Relations and in addition, in the case of a proposed agreement for cooperation arranged pursuant to section 91 c., 144 b., or 144 c., the Committee on Armed Services.

(4) If the committee of either House to which a joint resolution has been referred has not reported it at the end of 45 days after its introduction, the committee shall be discharged from further consideration of the joint resolution or of any other joint resolution introduced with respect to the same matter; except that, in the case of a joint resolution which has been referred to more than one committee, if before the end of that 45-day period one such committee has reported the joint resolution, any other committee to which the joint resolution was referred shall be discharged from further consideration of the joint resolution or of any other joint resolution introduced with respect to the same matter.

(5) A joint resolution under this subsection shall be considered in the Senate in accordance with the provisions of section 601(b)(4) of the International Security Assistance and Arms Export Control Act of 1976. For the purpose of expediting the consideration and passage of joint resolutions reported or discharged pursuant to the provisions of this subsection, it shall be in order for the Committee on Rules of the House of Representatives to present for consideration a resolution of the House of Representatives providing procedures for the immediate consideration of a joint resolution under this subsection which may be similar, if applicable, to the procedures set forth in section 601(b)(4) of the International Security Assistance and Arms Export Control Act of 1976.

(6) In the case of a joint resolution described in paragraph (1), if prior to the passage by one House of a joint resolution of that House, that House receives a joint resolution with respect to the same matter from the other House, then—

(A) the procedure in that House shall be the same as if no joint resolution had been received from the other House; but

(B) the vote on final passage shall be on the joint resolution of the other House.

[42 U.S.C. 2159]

SEC. 131. SUBSEQUENT ARRANGEMENTS.—

a. (1) Prior to entering into any proposed subsequent arrangement under an agreement for cooperation (other than an agreement for cooperation arranged pursuant to subsection 91 c., 144 b., or 144 c. of this Act), the Secretary of Energy shall obtain the concurrence of the Secretary of State and shall consult with the Director, the Commission, and the Secretary of Defense: *Provided,* That the Secretary of State shall have the leading role in any negotiations of a policy nature pertaining to any proposed subsequent arrangement regarding arrangements for the storage or disposition of irradiated fuel elements or approvals for the transfer, for which prior approval is required under an agreement for cooperation, by a recipient of source or special nuclear material, production or utilization facilities, or nuclear technology. Notice of any proposed subsequent arrangement shall be published in the Federal Register, together with the written determination of the Secretary of Energy that such arrangement will not be inimical to the common defense and security, and such proposed subsequent arrangement shall not take effect before fifteen days after publication. Whenever the Director declares that he intends to prepare a Nuclear Proliferation Assessment Statement pursuant to paragraph (2) of this subsection, notice of the proposed subsequent arrangement which is the subject of the Director's declaration shall not be published until after the receipt by the Secretary of Energy of such Statement or the expiration of the time authorized by subsection c. for the preparation of such Statement, whichever occurs first.

(2) If in the Director's view a proposed subsequent arrangement might significantly contribute to proliferation, he may prepare an unclassified Nuclear Proliferation Assessment Statement with regard to such proposed subsequent arrangement regarding the adequacy of the safeguards and other control mechanisms and the application of the peaceful use assurances of the relevant agreement to ensure that assistance to be furnished pursuant to the subsequent arrangement will not be used to further any military or nuclear explosive purpose. For the purposes of this section, the term "subsequent arrangements" means arrangements entered into by any agency or department of the United States Government with respect to cooperation with any nation or group of nations (but not purely private or domestic arrangements) involving—

(A) contracts for the furnishing of nuclear materials and equipment;

(B) approvals for the transfer, for which prior approval is required under an agreement for cooperation, by a recipient of any source or special nuclear material, production or utilization facility, or nuclear technology;

(C) authorization for the distribution of nuclear materials and equipment pursuant to this Act which is not subject to the procedures set forth in section 111 b., section 126, or section 109 b.;

(D) arrangements for physical security;

(E) arrangements for the storage or disposition of irradiated fuel elements;

(F) arrangements for the application of safeguards with respect to nuclear materials and equipment; or

(G) any other arrangement which the President finds to be important from the standpoint of preventing proliferation.

(3) The United States will give timely consideration to all requests for prior approval, when required by this Act, for the reprocessing of material proposed to be exported, previously exported and subject to the applicable agreement for cooperation, or special nuclear material produced through the use of such material or a production or utilization facility transferred pursuant to such agreement for cooperation, or to the altering of irradiated fuel elements containing such material, and additionally, to the maximum extent feasible, will attempt to expedite such consideration when the terms and conditions for such actions are set forth in such agreement for cooperation or in some other international agreement executed by the United States and subject to congressional review procedures comparable to those set forth in section 123 of this Act.

Sec. 131 ATOMIC ENERGY ACT OF 1954 66

(4) All other statutory requirements under other sections of this Act for the approval or conduct of any arrangement subject to this subsection shall continue to apply and any other such requirements for prior approval or conditions for entering such arrangements shall also be satisfied before the arrangement takes effect pursuant to subsection a. (1).

b. With regard to any special nuclear material exported by the United States or produced through the use of any nuclear materials and equipment or sensitive nuclear technology exported by the United States—

(1) the Secretary of Energy may not enter into any subsequent arrangement for the retransfer of any such material to a third country for reprocessing, for the reprocessing of any such material, or for the subsequent retransfer of any plutonium in quantities greater than 500 grams resulting from the reprocessing of any such material, until he has provided the Committee on International Relations of the House of Representatives[1] and the Committee on Foreign Relations of the Senate with a report containing his reasons for entering into such arrangement and a period of 15 days of continuous session (as defined in subsection 130 g. of this Act) has elapsed: *Provided, however,* That if in the view of the President an emergency exists due to unforeseen circumstances requiring immediate entry into a subsequent arrangement, such period shall consist of fifteen calendar days;

(2) the Secretary of Energy may not enter into any subsequent arrangement for the reprocessing of any such material in a facility which has not processed power reactor fuel assemblies or been the subject of a subsequent arrangement therefor prior to the date of enactment of the Nuclear Non-Proliferation Act of 1978[2] or for subsequent retransfer to a non-nuclear-weapon state of any plutonium in quantities greater than 500 grams resulting from such reprocessing, unless in his judgment, and that of the Secretary of State, such reprocessing or retransfer will not result in a significant increase of the risk of proliferation beyond that which exists at the time that approval is requested. Among all the factors in making this judgment, foremost consideration will be given to whether or not the reprocessing or retransfer will take place under conditions that will ensure timely warning to the United States of any diversion well in advance of the time at which the non-nuclear-weapon state could transform the diverted material into a nuclear explosive device; and

(3) the Secretary of Energy shall attempt to ensure, in entering into any subsequent arrangement for the reprocessing of any such material in any facility that has processed power reactor fuel assemblies or been the subject of a subsequent arrangement therefor prior to the date of enactment of the Nuclear Non-Proliferation Act of 1978,[2] or for the subsequent retransfer to any non-nuclear-weapon state of any plutonium in quantities greater than 500 grams resulting from such reprocessing, that such reprocessing or retransfer shall take place under conditions comparable to those which in his

---

[1] The name of the Committee on International Relations of the House of Representatives was changed to Committee on Foreign Affairs on Feb. 5, 1979, by House Resolution 89, 96th Congress.
[2] The date of enactment was March 10, 1978.

view, and that of the Secretary of State, satisfy the standards set forth in paragraph (2).

c. The Secretary of Energy shall, within ninety days after the enactment of this section, establish orderly and expeditious procedures, including provision for necessary administrative actions and inter-agency memoranda of understanding, which are mutually agreeable to the Secretaries of State, Defense, and Commerce, the Director of the Arms Control and Disarmament Agency, and the Nuclear Regulatory Commission for the consideration of requests for subsequent arrangements under this section. Such procedures shall include, at a minimum, explicit direction on the handling of such requests, express deadlines for the solicitation and collection of the views of the consulted agencies (with identified officials responsible for meeting such deadlines), an inter-agency coordinating authority to monitor the processing of such requests, predetermined procedures for the expeditious handling of intra-agency and inter-agency disagreements and appeals to higher authorities, frequent meetings of inter-agency administrative coordinators to review the status of all pending requests, and similar administrative mechanisms. To the extent practicable, an applicant should be advised of all the information required of the applicant for the entire process for every agency's needs at the beginning of the process. Potentially controversial requests should be identified as quickly as possible so that any required policy decisions or diplomatic consultations can be initiated in a timely manner. An immediate effort should be undertaken to establish quickly any necessary standards and criteria, including the nature of any required assurance or evidentiary showings, for the decisions required under this section. Further, such procedures shall specify that if he intends to prepare a Nuclear Proliferation Assessment Statement, the Director shall so declare in his response to the Department of Energy. If the Director declares that he intends to prepare such a Statement, he shall do so within sixty days of his receipt of a copy of the proposed subsequent arrangement (during which time the Secretary of Energy may not enter into the subsequent arrangement), unless pursuant to the Director's request, the President waives the sixty-day requirement and notifies the Committee on International Relations of the House of Representatives [1] and the Committee on Foreign Relations of the Senate of such waiver and the justification therefor. The processing of any subsequent arrangement proposed and filed as of the date of enactment of this section [2] shall not be delayed pending the development and establishment of procedures to implement the requirements of this section.

d. Nothing in this section is intended to prohibit, permanently or unconditionally, the reprocessing of spent fuel owned by a foreign nation which fuel has been supplied by the United States, to preclude the United States from full participation in the International Nuclear Fuel Cycle Evaluation provided for in section 105 of the Nuclear Non-Proliferation Act of 1978; to in any way limit the presentation or consideration in that evaluation of any nuclear

---

[1] The name of the Committee on International Relations of the House of Representatives was changed to Committee on Foreign Affairs on Feb. 5, 1979, by House Resolution 89, 96th Congress.
[2] The date of enactment was March 10, 1978.

fuel cycle by the United States or any other participation; nor to prejudice open and objective consideration of the results of the evaluation.

e. Notwithstanding subsection 402(d) of the Department of Energy Organization Act (Public Law 95–91), the Secretary of Energy, and not the Federal Energy Regulatory Commission, shall have sole jurisdiction within the Department of Energy over any matter arising from any function of the Secretary of Energy in this section.

f. (1) With regard to any subsequent arrangement under subsection a. (2) (E) (for the storage or disposition of irradiated fuel elements), where such arrangement involves a direct or indirect commitment of the United States for the storage or other disposition, interim or permanent, of any foreign spent nuclear fuel in the United States, the Secretary of Energy may not enter into any such subsequent arrangements, unless:

(A)(i) Such commitment of the United States has been submitted to the Congress for a period of sixty days of continuous session (as defined in subsection 130 g. of this Act) and has been referred to the Committee on International Relations of the House of Representatives and the Committee on Foreign Relations of the Senate, but any such commitment shall not become effective if during such sixty-day period the Congress adopts a concurrent resolution stating in substance that it does not favor the commitment, any such commitment to be considered pursuant to the procedures set forth in section 130 of this Act for the consideration of Presidential submissions; or (ii) if the President has submitted a detailed generic plan for such disposition or storage in the United States to the Congress for a period of sixty days of continuous session (as defined in subsection 130 g. of this Act), which plan has been referred to the Committee on International Relations of the House of Representatives and the Committee on Foreign Relations of the Senate and has not been disapproved during such sixty-day period by the adoption of a concurrent resolution stating in substance that Congress does not favor the plan; and the commitment is subject to the terms of an effective plan. Any such plan shall be considered pursuant to the procedures set forth in section 130 of this Act for the consideration of Presidential submission;

(B) The Secretary of Energy has complied with subsection a.; and

(C) The Secretary of Energy has complied, or in the arrangement will comply with all other statutory requirements of this Act, under sections 54 and 55 and any other applicable sections, and any other requirements of law.

(2) Subsection [1] (1) shall not apply to the storage or other disposition in the United States of limited quantities of foreign spent nuclear fuel if the President determines that (A) a commitment under section 54 or 55 of this Act of the United States for storage or other disposition of such limited quantities in the United States is required by an emergency situation, (B) it is in the national interest to take such immediate action, and (C) he notifies the Com-

---

[1] So in original. Probably should be "paragraph".

mittees on International Relations and Science and Technology of the House of Representatives [1] and the Committees on Foreign Relations and Energy and Natural Resources of the Senate of the determination and action, with a detailed explanation and justification thereof, as soon as possible.

(3) Any plan submitted by the President under subsection f. (1) shall include a detailed discussion, with detailed information, and any supporting documentation thereof, relating to policy objectives, technical description, geographic information, cost data and justifications, legal and regulatory considerations, environmental impact information and any related international agreements, arrangements or understandings.

(4) For the purposes of this subsection, the term "foreign spent nuclear fuel" shall include any nuclear fuel irradiated in any nuclear power reactor located outside of the United States and operated by any foreign legal entity, government or nongovernment, regardless of the legal ownership or other control of the fuel or the reactor and regardless of the origin or licensing of the fuel or reactor, but not including fuel irradiated in a research reactor.

[42 U.S.C. 2160]

SEC. 132. AUTHORITY TO SUSPEND NUCLEAR COOPERATION WITH NATIONS WHICH HAVE NOT RATIFIED THE CONVENTION ON THE PHYSICAL SECURITY OF NUCLEAR MATERIAL.—

"The President may suspend nuclear cooperation under this Act with any nation or group of nations which has not ratified the Convention on the Physical Security of Nuclear Material."

[42 U.S.C. 2160b]

SEC. 133. CONSULTATION WITH THE DEPARTMENT OF DEFENSE CONCERNING CERTAIN EXPORTS AND SUBSEQUENT ARRANGEMENTS.—

a. In addition to other applicable requirements—

(1) a license may be issued by the Nuclear Regulatory Commission under this Act for the export of special nuclear material described in subsection b.; and

(2) approval may be granted by the Secretary of Energy under section 131 of this Act for the transfer of special nuclear material described in subsection b.;

only after the Secretary of Defense has been consulted on whether the physical protection of that material during the export or transfer will be adequate to deter theft, sabotage, and other acts of international terrorism which would result in the diversion of that material. If, in the view of the Secretary of Defense based on all available intelligence information, the export or transfer might be subject to a genuine terrorist threat, the Secretary shall provide to the Nuclear Regulatory Commission or the Secretary of Energy, as appropriate, his written assessment of the risk and a description of the actions the Secretary of Defense considers necessary to upgrade physical protection measures.

---

[1] The name of the Committee on International Relations of the House of Representatives was changed to Committee on Foreign Affairs on Feb. 5, 1979, by House Resolution 89, 96th Congress. The name of the Committee on Science and Technology of the House of Representatives was changed to the Committee on Science, Space, and Technology on January 6, 1987, by House Resolution 5, 100th Congress.

b. Subsection a. applies to the export or transfer of more than 2 kilograms of plutonium or more than 20 kilograms of uranium enriched to more than 20 percent in the isotope 233 or the isotope 235.

[42 U.S.C. 2160c]

SEC. 134. FURTHER RESTRICTIONS ON EXPORTS.—
a. The Commission may issue a license for the export of highly enriched uranium to be used as a fuel or target in a nuclear research or test reactor only if, in addition to any other requirement of this Act, the Commission determines that—
(1) there is no alternative nuclear reactor fuel or target enriched in the isotope 235 to a lesser percent than the proposed export, that can be used in that reactor;
(2) the proposed recipient of that uranium has provided assurances that, whenever an alternative nuclear reactor fuel or target can be used in that reactor, it will use that alternative in lieu of highly enriched uranium; and
(3) the United States Government is actively developing an alternative nuclear reactor fuel or target that can be used in that reactor.
b. As used in this section—
(1) the term "alternative nuclear reactor fuel or target" means a nuclear reactor fuel or target which is enriched to less than 20 percent in the isotope U-235;
(2) the term "highly enriched uranium" means uranium enriched to 20 percent or more in the isotope U-235; and
(3) a fuel or target "can be used" in a nuclear research or test reactor if—
(A) the fuel or target has been qualified by the Reduced Enrichment Research and Test Reactor Program of the Department of Energy, and
(B) use of the fuel or target will permit the large majority of ongoing and planned experiments and isotope production to be conducted in the reactor without a large percentage increase in the total cost of operating the reactor.

[42 U.S.C. 2160d]

CHAPTER 12. CONTROL OF INFORMATION

SEC. 141. POLICY.—It shall be the policy of the Commission to control the dissemination and declassification of Restricted Data in such a manner as to assure the common defense and security. Consistent with such policy, the Commission shall be guided by the following principles:
a. Until effective and enforceable international safeguards against the use of atomic energy for destructive purposes have been established by an international arrangement, there shall be no exchange of Restricted Data with other nations except as authorized by section 144; and
b. The dissemination of scientific and technical information relating to atomic energy should be permitted and encouraged so as to provide that free interchange of ideas and criticism which is es-

sential to scientific and industrial progress and public understanding and to enlarge the fund of technical information.
[42 U.S.C. 2161]

SEC. 142. CLASSIFICATION AND DECLASSIFICATION OF RESTRICTED DATA.—

a. The Commission shall from time to time determine the data, within the definition of Restricted Data, which can be published without undue risk of the common defense and security and shall thereupon cause such data to be declassified and removed from the category of Restricted Data.

b. The Commission shall maintain a continuous review of Restricted Data and of any Classification Guides issued for the guidance of those in the atomic energy program with respect to the areas of Restricted Data which have been declassified in order to determine which information may be declassified and removed from the category of Restricted Data without undue risk to the common defense and security.

c. In the case of Restricted Data which the Commission and the Department of Defense jointly determine to relate primarily to the military utilization of atomic weapons, the determination that such data may be published without constituting an unreasonable risk to the common defense and security shall be made by the Commission and the Department of Defense jointly, and if the Commission and the Department of Defense do not agree, the determination shall be made by the President.

d. The Commission shall remove from the Restricted Data category such data as the Commission and the Department of Defense jointly determine relates primarily to the military utilization of atomic weapons and which the Commission and Department of Defense jointly determine can be adequately safeguarded as defense information: *Provided, however,* That no such data so removed from the Restricted Data category shall be transmitted or otherwise made available to any nation or regional defense organization, while such data remains defense information, except pursuant to an agreement for cooperation entered into in accordance with subsection 144 b.

e. The Commission shall remove from the Restricted Data category such information concerning the atomic energy programs of other nations as the Commission and the Director of Central Intelligence jointly determine to be necessary to carry out the provisions of section 102(d) of the National Security Act of 1947, as amended, and can be adequately safeguarded as defense information.

f. Notwithstanding any other law, the President may publicly release Restricted Data regarding the nuclear weapons stockpile of the United States if the United States and member states of the Commonwealth of Independent States reach reciprocal agreement on the release of such data.

[42 U.S.C. 2162]

SEC. 143. DEPARTMENT OF DEFENSE PARTICIPATION.—The Commission may authorize any of its employees, or employees of any contractor, prospective contractor, licensee or prospective licensee of the Commission or any other person authorized access to Restricted Data by the Commission under subsections 145 b. and 145

c. to permit any employee of an agency of the Department of Defense or of its contractors, or any member of the Armed Forces to have access to Restricted Data required in the performance of his duties and so certified by the head of the appropriate agency of the Department of Defense or his designee: *Provided, however,* That the head of the appropriate agency of the Department of Defense or his designee has determined, in accordance with the established personnel security procedures and standards of such agency, that permitting the member or employee to have access to such Restricted Data will not endanger the common defense and security: *And provided further,* That the Secretary of Defense finds that the established personnel and other security procedures and standards of such agency are adequate and in reasonable conformity to the standards established by the Commission under section 145.

[42 U.S.C. 2163]

SEC. 144. INTERNATIONAL COOPERATION.—
a. The President may authorize the Commission to cooperate with another nation and to communicate to that nation Restricted Data on—
(1) refining, purification, and subsequent treatment of source material;
(2) civilian reactor development;
(3) production of special nuclear material;
(4) health and safety;
(5) industrial and other applications of atomic energy for peaceful purposes; and
(6) research and development relating to the foregoing:
Provided, however, That no such cooperation shall involve the communication of Restricted Data relating to the design or fabrication of atomic weapons: *And provided further,* That the cooperation is undertaken pursuant to an agreement for cooperation entered into in accordance with section 123, or is undertaken pursuant to an agreement existing on the effective date of this Act.[1]

b. The President may authorize the Department of Defense, with the assistance of the Commission, to cooperate with another nation or with a regional defense organization to which the United States is a party, and to communicate to that nation or organization such Restricted Data (including design information) as is necessary to—
(1) the development of defense plans;
(2) the training of personnel in the employment of and defense against atomic weapons and other military applications of atomic energy;
(3) the evaluation of the capabilities of potential enemies in the employment of atomic weapons and other military applications of atomic energy; and
(4) the development of compatible delivery systems for atomic weapons;
whenever the President determines that the proposed cooperation and the proposed communication of the Restricted Data will promote and will not constitute an unreasonable risk to the common

---
[1] The effective date was Aug. 30, 1954.

defense and security, while such other nation or organization is participating with the United States pursuant to an international arrangement by substantial and material contributions to the mutual defense and security: *Provided, however,* That the cooperation is undertaken pursuant to an agreement entered into in accordance with section 123.

c. In addition to the cooperation authorized in subsections 144 a. and 144 b., the President may authorize the Commission, with the assistance of the Department of Defense, to cooperate with another nation and—

(1) to exchange with that nation Restricted Data concerning atomic weapons: *Provided,* That communication of such Restricted Data to that nation is necessary to improve its atomic weapon design, development, or fabrication capability and provided that nation has made substantial progress in the development of atomic weapons; and

(2) to communicate or exchange with that nation Restricted Data concerning research, development, or design, of military reactors,

whenever the President determines that the proposed cooperation and the communication of the proposed Restricted Data will promote and will not constitute an unreasonable risk to the common defense and security, while such other nation is participating with the United States pursuant to an international arrangement by substantial and material contributions to the mutual defense and security: *Provided, however,* That the cooperation is undertaken pursuant to an agreement entered into in accordance with section 123.

d. The President may authorize any agency of the United States to communicate in accordance with the terms and conditions of an agreement for cooperation arranged pursuant to subsection 144 a., b., or c., such Restricted Data as is determined to be transmissible under the agreement for cooperation involved.

[42 U.S.C. 2164]

SEC. 145. RESTRICTIONS.—

a. No arrangement shall be made under section 31, no contract shall be made or continued in effect under section 41, and no license shall be issued under section 103 or 104, unless the person with whom such arrangement is made, the contractor or prospective contractor, or the prospective licensee agrees in writing not to permit any individual to have access to Restricted Data until the Civil Service Commission [1] shall have made an investigation and report to the Commission on the character, associations, and loyalty of such individual, and the Commission shall have determined that permitting such person to have access to Restricted Data will not endanger the common defense and security.

b. Except as authorized by the Commission or the General Manager upon a determination by the Commission or General Manager that such action is clearly consistent with the national in-

---

[1] Reorg. Plan No. 2 of 1978, §102, 43 F.R. 36037, 92 Stat. 3783, transferred all functions vested by statute in the United States Civil Service Commission to the Director of the Office of Personnel Management (except as otherwise specified), effective Jan. 1, 1979, as provided by section 1-102 of Ex. Ord. No. 12107, Dec. 28, 1978, 44 F.R. 1055.

terest, no individual shall be employed by the Commission noshall the Commission permit any individual to have access to Restricted Data until the Civil Service Commission [1] shall have made an investigation and report to the Commission on the character, associations, and loyalty of such individual, and the Commission shall have determined that permitting such person to have access to Restricted Data will not endanger the common defense and security.

  c. In lieu of the investigation and report to be made by the Civil Service Commission [1] pursuant to subsection b. of this section, the Commission may accept an investigation and report on the character, associations, and loyalty of an individual made by another Government agency which conducts personnel security investigations, provided that a security clearance has been granted to such individual by another Government agency based on such investigation and report.

  d. In the event an investigation made pursuant to subsection a. and b. of this section develops any data reflecting that the individual who is the subject of the investigation is of questionable loyalty, the Civil Service Commission [1] shall refer the matter to the Federal Bureau of Investigation for the conduct of a full field investigation, the results of which shall be furnished to the Civil Service Commission [1] for its information and appropriate action.

  e. If the President deems it to be in the national interest he may from time to time determine that investigations of any group or class which are required by subsections a., b., and c. of this section be made by the Federal Bureau of Investigation.

  f. Notwithstanding the provisions of subsections a., b., and c., of this section, a majority of the members of the Commission shall certify those specific positions which are of a high degree of importance or sensitivity, and upon such certification, the investigation and reports required by such provisions shall be made by the Federal Bureau of Investigation.

  g. The Commission shall establish standards and specifications in writing as to the scope and extent of investigations, the reports of which will be utilized by the Commission in making the determination, pursuant to subsections a., b., and c., of this section, that permitting a person access to restricted data will not endanger the common defense and security. Such standards and specifications shall be based on the location and class or kind of work to be done, and shall, among other considerations, take into account the degree of importance to the common defense and security of the restricted data to which access will be permitted.

  h. Whenever the Congress declares that a state of war exists, or in the event of a national disaster due to enemy attack, the Commission is authorized during the state of war or period of national disaster due to enemy attack to employ individuals and to permit individuals access to Restricted Data pending the investigation report, and determination required by section 145 b., to the extent that and so long as the Commission finds that such action is

---

[1] Reorg. Plan No. 2 of 1978, §102, 43 F.R. 36037, 92 Stat. 3783, transferred all functions vested by statute in the United States Civil Service Commission to the Director of the Office of Personnel Management (except as otherwise specified), effective Jan. 1, 1979, as provided by section 1-102 of Ex. Ord. No. 12107, Dec. 28, 1978, 44 F.R. 1055.

required to prevent impairment of its activities in furtherance of the common defense and security.
[42 U.S.C. 2165]

SEC. 147. SAFEGUARDS INFORMATION.—
a. In addition to any other authority or requirement regarding protection from disclosure of information, and subject to subsection (b)(3) of section 552 of title 5 of the United States Code, the Commission shall prescribe such regulations, after notice and opportunity for public comment, or issue such orders, as necessary to prohibit the unauthorized disclosure of safeguards information which specifically identifies a licensee's or applicant's detailed—
    (1) control and accounting procedures or security measures (including security plans, procedures, and equipment) for the physical protection of special nuclear material, by whomever possessed, whether in transit or at fixed sites, in quantities determined by the Commission to be significant to the public health and safety or the common defense and security;
    (2) security measures (including security plans, procedures, and equipment) for the physical protection of source material or byproduct material, by whomever possessed, whether in transit or at fixed sites, in quantities determined by the Commission to be significant to the public health and safety or the common defense and security; or
    (3) security measures (including security plans, procedures, and equipment) for the physical protection of and the location of certain plant equipment vital to the safety of production or utilization facilities involving nuclear materials covered by paragraphs (1) and (2)[1]
if the unauthorized disclosure of such information could reasonably be expected to have a significant adverse effect on the health and safety of the public or the common defense and security by significantly increasing the likelihood of theft, diversion, or sabotage of such material or such facility. The Commission shall exercise the authority of this subsection—
    (A) so as to apply the minimum restrictions needed to protect the health and safety of the public or the common defense and security, and
    (B) upon a determination that the unauthorized disclosure of such information could reasonably be expected to have a significant adverse effect on the health and safety of the public or the common defense and security by significantly increasing

---

[1] So in original. Probably should be followed by a semicolon.

Sec. 147   ATOMIC ENERGY ACT OF 1954

the likelihood of theft, diversion, or sabotage of such material or such facility.
Nothing in this Act shall authorize the Commission to prohibit the public disclosure of information pertaining to the routes and quantities of shipments of source material, by-product material, high level nuclear waste, or irradiated nuclear reactor fuel. Any person, whether or not a licensee of the Commission, who violates any regulation adopted under this section shall be subject to the civil monetary penalties of section 234 of this Act. Nothing in this section shall be construed to authorize the withholding of information from the duly authorized committees of the Congress.

b. For the purposes of section 223 of this Act, any regulations or orders prescribed or issued by the Commission under this section shall also be deemed to be prescribed or issued under section 161 b. of this Act.

c. Any determination by the Commission concerning the applicability of this section shall be subject to judicial review pursuant to subsection (a)(4)(B) of section 552 of title 5 of the United States Code.

d. Upon prescribing or issuing any regulation or order under subsection a. of this section, the Commission shall submit to Congress a report that:

(1) specifically identifies the type of information the Commission intends to protect from disclosure under the regulation or order;

(2) specifically states the Commission's justification for determining that unauthorized disclosure of the information to be protected from disclosure under the regulation or order could reasonably be expected to have a significant adverse effect on the health and safety of the public or the common defense and security by significantly increasing the likelihood of theft, diversion, or sabotage of such material or such facility, as specified under subsection (a) of this section; and

(3) provides justification, including proposed alternative regulations or orders, that the regulation or order applies only the minimum restrictions needed to protect the health and safety of the public or the common defense and security.

e. In addition to the reports required under subsection d. of this section, the Commission shall submit to Congress on a quarterly basis a report detailing the Commission's application during that period of every regulation or order prescribed or issued under this section. In particular, the report shall:

(1) identify any information protected from disclosure pursuant to such regulation or order;

(2) specifically state the Commission's justification for determining that unauthorized disclosure of the information protected from disclosure under such regulation or order could reasonably be expected to have a significant adverse effect on the health and safety of the public or the common defense and security by significantly increasing the likelihood of theft, diversion or sabotage of such material or such facility, as specified under subsection a. of this section; and

(3) provide justification that the Commission has applied such regulation or order so as to protect from disclosure only

the minimum amount of information necessary to protect the health and safety of the public or the common defense and security.

[42 U.S.C. 2167]

SEC. 148. PROHIBITION AGAINST THE DISSEMINATION OF CERTAIN UNCLASSIFIED INFORMATION.—

a. (1) In addition to any other authority or requirement regarding protection from dissemination of information, and subject to section 552(b)(3) of title 5, United States Code, the Secretary, with respect to atomic energy defense programs, of Energy (hereinafter in this section referred to as the "Secretary") shall prescribe such regulations, after notice and opportunity for public comment thereon, or issue such orders as may be necessary to prohibit the unauthorized dissemination of unclassified information pertaining to—

(A) the design of production facilities or utilization facilities;

(B) security measures (including security plans, procedures, and equipment) for the physical protection of (i) production or utilization facilities, (ii) nuclear material contained in such facilities, or (iii) nuclear material in transit; or

(C) the design, manufacture, or utilization of any atomic weapon or component if the design, manufacture, or utilization of such weapon or component was contained in any information declassified or removed from the Restricted Data category by the Secretary (or the head of the predecessor agency of the Department of Energy) pursuant to section 142.

(2) The Secretary may prescribe regulations or issue orders under paragraph (1) to prohibit the dissemination of any information described in such paragraph only if and to the extent that the Secretary determines that the unauthorized dissemination of such information could reasonably be expected to have a significant adverse effect on the health and safety of the public or the common defense and security by significantly increasing the likelihood of (A) illegal production of nuclear weapons, or (B) theft, diversion, or sabotage of nuclear materials, equipment, or facilities.

(3) In making a determination under paragraph (2), the Secretary may consider what the likelihood of an illegal production, theft, diversion, or sabotage referred to in such paragraph would be if the information proposed to be prohibited from dissemination under this section were at no time available for dissemination.

(4) The Secretary shall exercise his authority under this subsection to prohibit the dissemination of any information described in subsection a. (1)—

(A) so as to apply the minimum restrictions needed to protect the health and safety of the public or the common defense and security; and

(B) upon a determination that the unauthorized dissemination of such information could reasonably be expected to result in a significant adverse effect on the health and safety of the public or the common defense and security by significantly increasing the likelihood of (i) illegal production of nuclear weapons, or (ii) theft, diversion, or sabotage of nuclear materials, equipment, or facilities.

Sec. 149 ATOMIC ENERGY ACT OF 1954

(5) Nothing in this section shall be construed to authorize the Secretary to authorize the withholding of information from the appropriate committees of the Congress.

b. (1) Any person who violates any regulation or order of the Secretary issued under this section with respect to the unauthorized dissemination of information shall be subject to a civil penalty, to be imposed by the Secretary, of not to exceed $100,000 for each such violation. The Secretary may compromise, mitigate, or remit any penalty imposed under this subsection.

(2) The provisions of subsections b. and c. of section 234 of this Act shall be applicable with respect to the imposition of civil penalties by the Secretary under this section in the same manner that such provisions are applicable to the imposition of civil penalties by the Commission under subsection a. of such section.

c. For the purposes of section 223 of this Act, any regulation prescribed or order issued by the Secretary under this section shall also be deemed to be prescribed or issued under section 161 b. of this Act.

d. Any determination by the Secretary concerning the applicability of this section shall be subject to judicial review pursuant to section 552(a)(4)(B) of title 5, United States Code.

e. The Secretary shall prepare on a quarterly basis a report to be made available upon the request of any interested person, detailing the Secretary's application during that period of each regulation or order prescribed or issued under this section. In particular, such report shall—

(1) identify any information protected from disclosure pursuant to such regulation or order;

(2) specifically state the Secretary's justification for determining that unauthorized dissemination of the information protected from disclosure under such regulation or order could reasonably be expected to have a significant adverse effect on the health and safety of the public or the common defense and security by significantly increasing the likelihood of illegal production of nuclear weapons, or theft, diversion, or sabotage of nuclear materials, equipment, or facilities, as specified under subsection a.; and

(3) provide justification that the Secretary has applied such regulation or order so as to protect from disclosure only the minimum amount of information necessary to protect the health and safety of the public or the common defense and security.

[42 U.S.C. 2168]

SEC. 149. FINGERPRINTING FOR CRIMINAL HISTORY RECORD CHECKS.—

a. The Nuclear Regulatory Commission (in this section referred to as the "Commission") shall require each licensee or applicant for a license to operate a utilization facility under section 103 or 104 b. to fingerprint each individual who is permitted unescorted access to the facility or is permitted access to safeguards information under section 147. All fingerprints obtained by a licensee or applicant as required in the preceding sentence shall be submitted to the Attorney General of the United States through the Commission for identification and a criminal history records check. The costs of any identification and records check conducted pursuant to the preceding sentence shall be paid by the licensee or applicant. Notwithstanding any other provision of law, the Attorney General may provide all the results of the search of the Commission, and, in accordance with regulations prescribed under this section, the Commission may provide such results to the licensee or applicant submitting such fingerprints.

b. The Commission, by rule, may relieve persons from the obligations imposed by this section, upon specified terms, conditions, and periods, if the Commission finds that such action is consistent with its obligations to promote the common defense and security and to protect the health and safety of the public.

c. For purposes of administering this section, the Commission shall prescribe, subject to public notice and comment, regulations—

(1) to implement procedures for the taking of fingerprints;

(2) to establish the conditions for use of information received from the Attorney General, in order—

(A) to limit the redissemination of such information;

(B) to ensure that such information is used solely for the purpose of determining whether an individual shall be permitted unescorted access to the facility of a licensee or applicant or shall be permitted access to safeguards information under section 147;

(C) to ensure that no final determination may be made solely on the basis of information provided under this section involving—

(i) an arrest more than 1 year old for which there is no information of the disposition of the case; or

(ii) an arrest that resulted in dismissal of the charge or an acquittal; and

(D) to protect individuals subject to fingerprinting under this section from misuse of the criminal history records; and

(3) to provide each individual subject to fingerprinting under this section with the right to complete, correct, and explain information contained in the criminal history records prior to any final adverse determination.

d. (1) The Commission may establish and collect fees to process fingerprints and criminal history records under this section.

(2) Notwithstanding section 3302(b) of title 31, United States Code, and to the extent approved in appropriation Acts—

(A) a portion of the amounts collected under this subsection in any fiscal year may be retained and used by the Commission to carry out this section; and

(B) the remaining portion of the amounts collected under this subsection in such fiscal year may be transferred periodically to the Attorney General and used by the Attorney General to carry out this section.

(3) Any amount made available for use under paragraph (2) shall remain available until expended.

[42 U.S.C. 2169]

SEC. 251. REPORT TO CONGRESS.[1]—The Commission shall submit to the Congress, in January of each year, a report concerning the activities of the Commission. The Commission shall include in such report, and shall at such other times as it deems desirable submit to the Congress, such recommendations for additional legislation as the Commission deems necessary or desirable.[2]
[42 U.S.C. 2016]

CHAPTER 20. JOINT COMMITTEE ON ATOMIC ENERGY ABOLISHED; FUNCTIONS AND RESPONSIBILITIES REASSIGNED

SEC. 301. JOINT COMMITTEE ON ATOMIC ENERGY ABOLISHED.—
a. The Joint Committee on Atomic Energy is abolished.
b. Any reference in any rule, resolution, or order of the Senate or the House of Representatives or in any law, regulation, or Executive order to the Joint Committee on Atomic Energy shall, on and after the date of enactment of this section,[2] be considered as referring to the committees of the Senate and the House of Representatives which, under the rules of the Senate and the House, have jurisdiction over the subject matter of such reference.
c. All records, data, charts, and files of the Joint Committee on Atomic Energy are transferred to the committees of the Senate and House of Representatives which, under the rules of the Senate and the House, have jurisdiction over the subject matters to which such records, data, charts, and files relate. In the event that any record, data, chart, or file shall be within the jurisdiction of more than one committee, duplicate copies shall be provided upon request.
[42 U.S.C. 2258]

SEC. 302. TRANSFERS OF CERTAIN FUNCTIONS OF THE JOINT COMMITTEE ON ATOMIC ENERGY AND CONFORMING AMENDMENTS TO CERTAIN OTHER LAWS.—

a. Effective on the date of enactment of this section,[1] chapter 17 of this Act is repealed.

b. Section 103 of the Atomic Energy Community Act of 1955, as amended, is repealed.

c. Section 3 of the Congressional Budget and Impoundment Control Act of 1974 is amended by—
  (1) striking the subsection designation "(a)"; and
  (2) repealing subsection (b).

d. Section 252(a)(3) of the Legislative Reorganization Act of 1970 is repealed.

SEC. 303. INFORMATION AND ASSISTANCE TO CONGRESSIONAL COMMITTEES.—

a. The Secretary of Energy and the Nuclear Regulatory Commission shall keep the committees of the Senate and the House of Representatives which, under the rules of the Senate and the House, have jurisdiction over the functions of the Secretary or the Commission, fully and currently informed with respect to the activities of the Secretary and the Commission.

b. The Department of Defense and Department of State shall keep the committees of the Senate and the House of Representatives which, under the rules of the Senate and the House, have jurisdiction over national security considerations of nuclear energy, fully and currently informed with respect to such matters within the Department of Defense and Department of State relating to national security considerations of nuclear technology which are within the jurisdiction of such committees.

c. Any Government agency shall furnish any information requested by the committees of the Senate and the House of Representatives which, under the rules of the Senate and the House, have jurisdiction over the development, utilization, or application of nuclear energy, with respect to the activities or responsibilities of such agency in the field of nuclear energy which are within the jurisdiction of such committees.

d. The committees of the Senate and the House of Representatives which, under the rules of the Senate and the House, have jurisdiction over the development, utilization, or application of nuclear energy, are authorized to utilize the services, information, facilities, and personnel of any Government agency which has activities or responsibilities in the field of nuclear energy which are within the jurisdiction of such committees: *Provided, however,* That any utilization of personnel by such committees shall be on a reimbursable basis and shall require, with respect to committees of the Senate, the prior written consent of the Committee on Rules and Administration, and with respect to committees of the House of Representatives, the prior written consent of the Committee on House Administration.

[42 U.S.C. 2259]

---

[1] The date of enactment was Sept. 20, 1977.

FOREIGN ASSISTANCE ACT OF 1961 (P.L. 87-195) Sec. 620E

Sec. 620E.[764] **Assistance to Pakistan.**—(a) The Congress recognizes that Soviet Forces occupying Afghanistan pose a security threat to Pakistan. The Congress also recognizes that an independent and democratic Pakistan with continued friendly ties with the United States is in the interest of both nations. The Congress finds that United States assistance will help Pakistan maintain its independence. Assistance to Pakistan is intended to benefit the people of Pakistan by helping them meet the burdens imposed by the presence of Soviet forces in Afghanistan and by promoting economic development. In authorizing assistance to Pakistan, it is the intent of Congress to promote the expeditious restoration of full civil liberties and representative government in Pakistan. The Congress further recognizes that it is in the mutual interest of Pakistan and the United States to avoid the profoundly destabilizing effects of the

---

[764] 22 U.S.C. 2375. Sec. 620E was added by sec. 736 of the International Security and Development Cooperation Act of 1981 (Public Law 97-113; 95 Stat. 1561). The President exercised his authority under subsec. (d) on Feb. 11, 1982.

Sec. 620F FOREIGN ASSISTANCE ACT OF 1961 (P.L. 87-195)

proliferation of nuclear explosive devices or the capacity to manufacture or otherwise acquire nuclear devices.

(b) The United States reaffirms the commitment made in its 1959 bilateral agreement with Pakistan relating to aggression from a Communist or Communist-dominated state.

(c) Security assistance for Pakistan shall be made available in order to assist Pakistan in dealing with the threat to its security posed by the Soviet presence in Afghanistan. The United States will take appropriate steps to ensure that defense articles provided by the United States to Pakistan are used for defensive purposes.

(d) The President may waive the prohibitions of section 669 of this Act at any time during the period beginning on the date of enactment of this section and ending on September 30, 1994,[765] to provide assistance to Pakistan during that period if he determines that to do so is in the national interest of the United States.[766]

(e)[767] No assistance shall be furnished to Pakistan and no military equipment or technology shall be sold or transferred to Pakistan, pursuant to the authorities contained in this Act or any other Act, unless the President shall have certified in writing to the Speaker of the House of Representatives and the chairman of the Committee on Foreign Relations of the Senate, during the fiscal year in which assistance is to be furnished or military equipment or technology is to be sold or transferred, that Pakistan does not possess a nuclear explosive device and that the proposed United States assistance program will reduce significantly the risk that Pakistan will possess a nuclear explosive device.

SEC. 620F.[768] NUCLEAR NON-PROLIFERATION POLICY IN SOUTH ASIA.

(a) FINDINGS.—The Congress finds that—

---

[765] Sec. 536(a) of the Foreign Operations, Export Financing, and Related Programs Appropriations Act, 1994 (Public Law 103-87; 107 Stat. 955), amended "September 30, 1993" to read "September 30, 1994".

Sec. 536(b) of that Act, furthermore, provided the following:

"(b) None of the funds appropriated in this Act shall be obligated or expended for Pakistan except as provided through the regular notification procedures of the Committees on Appropriations.".

[766] The President determined "that provision of assistance to Pakistan under the Act through April 1, 1991, is in the national interest of the United States, and therefore waive[d] the prohibitions of section 669 of the Act (22 U.S.C. 2429) with respect to that period." (Presidential Determination 90-15 of March 28, 1990; 55 F.R. 17417). The President has not waived this prohibition since 1990. See also the next note.

[767] Subsec. (e) was added by sec. 902 of the International Security and Development Cooperation Act of 1985 (Public Law 99-83; 99 Stat. 268). Presidential Determinations No. 86-3 of November 25, 1985; No. 87-3 of October 27, 1986; No. 88-4 of December 17, 1987; 89-7 of November 18, 1988; and 90-1 of October 5, 1989, 54 F.R. 43797; certified that Pakistan does not have a nuclear explosive device and that U.S. assistance would reduce significantly the risk that Pakistan will possess a nuclear explosive device. The President has not certified for fiscal years 1991-1994.

[768] 22 U.S.C. 2376. Added by sec. 585(a) of the Foreign Operations, Export Financing, and Related Programs Appropriations Act, 1993 (Public Law 102-391; 106 Stat. 1688).

Sec. 585(b) of that Act further provided:

"(b) REPORT ON SOUTH ASIAN NUCLEAR PROGRAMS.—Not later than six months after the enactment of this Act, the President shall submit a report with respect to the People's Republic of China, Pakistan, and India in writing to the Committees on Appropriations, the Speaker of the House of Representatives, the chairman of the Committee on Foreign Relations of the Senate, on those country's nuclear and ballistic missile programs, including, but not limited to—

"(1) a determination as to whether that country possesses a nuclear explosive device or whether it possesses all the components necessary for the assembly of such a device;

"(2) a complete report on the status of that country's missile development program, foreign assistance to that program, and foreign sales of missiles or missile components to that country and steps which the United States has taken in response to such sales; and

Continued

(1) the proliferation of weapons of mass destruction remains one of the most serious threats to international peace and stability;

(2) South Asia, in particular, is an area where the threat of a regional nuclear exchange remains high due to continued Indo-Pakistani tensions over issues such as Kashmir;

(3) to date, United States efforts to halt proliferation in South Asia have failed;

(4) although global disarmament is a desirable goal which should be vigorously pursued, both regional and sub-regional security arrangements can serve to decrease tensions and promote non-proliferation in certain areas;

(5) thus far, there has been some success on a regional basis, such as the South Pacific Nuclear Weapons Free Zone and the Treaty of Tlatelolco in Latin America;

(6) in particular, in Latin America, the Treaty of Tlatelolco has been signed by all the nuclear powers;

(7) a critical part of this treaty is Protocol II which prohibits nuclear attacks by nuclear weapons states on signatories to the treaty;

(8) in 1991, a proposal was made for a regional conference on non-proliferation in South Asia which would include Pakistan, India, the People's Republic of China, the Soviet Union, and the United States; and

(9) thus far, Pakistan, China, Russia, and the United States have expressed interest in attending such a conference, whereas India has refused to attend.

(b) POLICY.—It is the sense of the Congress that the President should pursue a policy which seeks a regional negotiated solution to the issue of nuclear non-proliferation in South Asia at the earliest possible time, including a protocol to be signed by all nuclear weapons states, prohibiting nuclear attacks by nuclear weapons states on countries in the region. Such a policy should have as its ultimate goal concurrent accession by Pakistan and India to the Nuclear Non-Proliferation Treaty, and should also include as needed a phased approach to that goal through a series of agreements among the parties on nuclear issues, such as the agreement reached by Pakistan and India not to attack one another's nuclear facilities.

(c) REPORT ON PROGRESS TOWARD REGIONAL NON-PROLIFERATION.—Not later than April 1, 1993, and every six months thereafter, the President shall submit a report to the Committees on Appropriations, the Speaker of the House of Representatives, and the chairman of the Committee on Foreign Relations of the Senate, on nuclear proliferation in South Asia, including efforts taken by the United States to achieve a regional agreement on nuclear non-proliferation, and including a comprehensive list of the obstacles to concluding such a regional agreement.

"(3) a report on whether that country has agreed to fully adhere, and is adhering, to all peaceful nuclear cooperation agreements with the United States and has formally agreed to place all United States-supplied nuclear materials under international safeguards in perpetuity.".

Sec. 669 FOREIGN ASSISTANCE ACT OF 1961 (P.L. 87-195)

Sec. 669.[963] **Nuclear Enrichment Transfers.**—(a) Except as provided in subsection (b), no funds authorized to be appropriated by this Act or the Arms Export Control Act may be used for the purpose of providing economic assistance (including assistance under chapter 4 or part II), providing military[964] assistance or grant military education and training, providing assistance under chapter 6 of part II,[965] or extending military credits or making guarantees, to any country which, on or after the date of enactment of the International Security Assistance Act of 1977, delivers nuclear enrichment equipment, materials, or technology to any other country, or receives such equipment, materials, or technology from any other country, unless before such delivery—

(1) the supplying country and receiving country have reached agreement to place all such equipment, materials, or technology, upon delivery, under multilateral auspices and management when available; and

(2) the recipient country has entered into an agreement with the International Atomic Energy Agency to place all such equipment, materials, technology, and all nuclear fuel and facilities in such country under the safeguards system of such Agency.

(b)(1) Notwithstanding subsection (a) of this section, the President may furnish assistance which would otherwise be prohibited under such subsection if he determines and certifies in writing to the Speaker of the House of Representatives and the Committee on Foreign Relations of the Senate that—

(A) the termination of such assistance would have a serious adverse effect on vital United States interests; and

(B) he has received reliable assurances that the country in question will not acquire or develop nuclear weapons or assist other nations in doing so.

Such certification shall set forth the reasons supporting such determination in each particular case.[966]

(2)[967] (A) A certification under paragraph (1) of this subsection shall take effect on the date on which the certification is received by the Congress. However, if, within 30 calendar days after receiving this certification, the Congress adopts a concurrent resolution stating in substance that the Congress disapproves the furnishing of assistance pursuant to the certification, then upon the adoption of that resolution the certification shall cease to be effective and all deliveries of assistance furnished under the authority of that certification shall be suspended immediately.

---

[963] 22 U.S.C. 2429. Sec. 669, as added by sec. 305 of Public Law 94-329, was amended and restated by sec. 12 of the International Security Assistance Act of 1977 (Public Law 95-92; 91 Stat. 620).

[964] Sec. 10(b)(4) of the International Security Assistance Act of 1978 (Public Law 95-384; 92 Stat. 735), added the parenthetical phrase and struck the words "or security supporting" which previously appeared at this point.

[965] The reference to chapter 6 of part II was added by sec. 12(c)(3) of the International Security Assistance Act of 1978 (Public Law 95-384; 92 Stat. 737).

[966] Sec. 735 of the International Security and Development Cooperation Act of 1981 (Public Law 97-113; 95 Stat. 1561) required an annual report from the President beginning with fiscal year 1983 on the nuclear programs and related activities of any country for which a waiver of secs. 669 or 670 is in effect. See page 494 for the complete text of sec. 735.

[967] Par. (2) was amended and restated by sec. 737(b) of the International Security and Development Cooperation Act of 1981 (Public Law 97-113; 95 Stat. 1562). It formerly read as follows:

"(2) Any joint resolution which would terminate or restrict assistance described in subsection (a) with respect to a country to which the prohibition in such subsection applies shall, if introduced within thirty days after the transmittal of a certification under paragraph (1) of this subsection with respect to such country, be considered in the Senate in accordance with the provisions of section 601(b) of the International Security Assistance and Arms Export Control Act of 1976.".

(B) Any concurrent resolution under this paragraph shall be considered in the Senate in accordance with the provisions of section 601(b) of the International Security Assistance and Arms Export Control Act of 1976.

(C) For the purpose of expediting the consideration and adoption of concurrent resolutions under this paragraph, a motion to proceed to the consideration of any such resolution after it has been reported by the appropriate committee shall be treated as highly privileged in the House of Representatives.

Sec. 670.[968] **Nuclear Reprocessing Transfers, Illegal Exports for Nuclear Explosive Devices, Transfers of Nuclear Explosive Devices, and Nuclear Detonations.**—(a)(1) Except as provided in paragraph (2) of this subsection, no funds authorized to be appropriated by this Act or the Arms Export Control Act may be used for the purpose of providing economic assistance (including assistance under chapter 4 of part II), providing military assistance or grant military education and training, providing assistance under chapter 6 of part II, or extending military credits or making guarantees, to any country which (A)[969] on or after the date of enactment of the International Security Assistance Act of 1977 delivers nuclear reprocessing equipment, materials, or technology to any other country or receives such equipment, materials, or technology from any other country (except for the transfer of reprocessing technology associated with the investigation, under international evaluation programs in which the United States participates, of technologies which are alternatives to pure plutonium reprocessing), or (B)[969] is a non-nuclear-weapon state which, on or after the date of enactment of the International Security and Development Cooperation Act of 1985, exports illegally (or attempts to export illegally) from the United States any material, equipment, or technology which would contribute significantly to the ability of such country to manufacture a nuclear explosive device, if the President determines that the material, equipment, or technology was to be used by such country in the manufacture of a nuclear explosive device. For purposes of clause (B), an export (or attempted export) by a person who is an agent of, or is otherwise acting on behalf of or in the interests of, a country shall be considered to be an export (or attempted export) by that country.

(2) Notwithstanding paragraph (1) of this subsection, the President may furnish assistance which would otherwise be prohibited under that paragraph if he determines and certifies in writing to the Speaker of the House of Representatives and the Committee on

---

[968] 22 U.S.C. 2429a. Sec. 670, as added by sec. 12 of Public Law 95-92 (91 Stat. 620), was amended and restated by sec. 737(c) of the International Security and Development Cooperation Act of 1981 (Public Law 97-113; 95 Stat. 1562).

Sec. 737(a) of Public Law 97-113 also provided the following:

"Sec. 737. (a) The Congress finds that any transfer of a nuclear explosive device to a non-nuclear-weapon state or, in the case of a non-nuclear-weapon state, any receipt or detonation of a nuclear explosive device would cause grave damage to bilateral relations between the United States and that country.".

The language in the caption of sec. 670: "Illegal Exports for Nuclear Explosive Devices", was added by sec. 1204(b) of the International Security and Development Cooperation Act of 1985 (Public Law 99-83; 99 Stat. 277).

[969] Subpar. (B) and the designation for subpar. (A) were added by sec. 1204(a) (1), (2), and (3) of the International Security and Development Cooperation Act of 1985 (Public Law 99-83; 99 Stat. 277).

Sec. 670 FOREIGN ASSISTANCE ACT OF 1961 (P.L. 87-195)

Foreign Relations of the Senate that the termination of such assistance would be seriously prejudicial to the achievement of United States nonproliferation objectives or otherwise jeopardize the common defense and security. The President shall transmit with such certification a statement setting forth the specific reasons therefor.[966]

(3)(A) A certification under paragraph (2) of this subsection shall take effect on the date on which the certification is received by the Congress. However, if, within 30 calendar days after receiving this certification, the Congress adopts a concurrent resolution stating in substance that the Congress disapproves the furnishing of assistance pursuant to the certification, then upon the adoption of that resolution the certification shall cease to be effective and all deliveries of assistance furnished under the authority of that certification shall be suspended immediately.

(B) Any concurrent resolution under this paragraph shall be considered in the Senate in accordance with the provisions of section 601(b) of the International Security Assistance and Arms Export Control Act of 1976.

(C) For the purpose of expediting the consideration and adoption of concurrent resolutions under this paragraph, a motion to proceed to the consideration of any such resolution after it has been reported by the appropriate committee shall be treated as highly privileged in the House of Representatives.

(b)(1) Except as provided in paragraphs (2) and (3) of this subsection, no funds authorized to be appropriated by this Act or the Arms Export Control Act may be used for the purpose of providing economic assistance (including assistance under chapter 4 of part II), providing military assistance or grant military education and training, providing assistance under chapter 6 of part II, or extending military credits or making guarantees, to any country which on or after the date of enactment of the International Security Assistance Act of 1977—

(A) transfers a nuclear explosive device to a non-nuclear-weapon state, or

(B) is a non-nuclear-weapon state and either—

(i) receives a nuclear explosive device, or

(ii) detonates a nuclear explosive device.

(2)(A) Notwithstanding paragraph (1) of this subsection, the President may, for a period of not more than 30 days of continuous session, furnish assistance which would otherwise be prohibited under paragraph (1) of this subsection if, before furnishing such assistance, the President transmits to the Speaker of the House of Representatives, and to the Chairman of the Committee on Foreign Relations of the Senate, a certification that he has determined that an immediate termination of assistance to that country would be detrimental to the national security of the United States. Not more than one such certification may be transmitted for a country with respect to the same detonation, transfer, or receipt of a nuclear explosive device.

(B) If the President transmits a certification to the Congress under subparagraph (A), a joint resolution which would permit the President to exercise the waiver authority of paragraph (3) of this subsection shall, if introduced in either House within 30 days of continuous session after the Congress receives this certification, be considered in the Senate and House of Representatives in accordance with subparagraphs (C) and (D) of this paragraph.

(C) Any joint resolution under this paragraph shall be considered in the Senate in accordance with the provisions of section 601(b) of the International Security Assistance and Arms Export Control Act of 1976.

(D) For the purpose of expediting the consideration and adoption of joint resolution under this paragraph, a motion to proceed to the consideration of such a joint resolution after it has been reported by the appropriate committee shall be treated as highly privileged in the House of Representatives.

(E) For purposes of this paragraph, the term "joint resolution" means a joint resolution the matter after the resolving clause of which is as follows: "That the Congress having received on ——— a certification by the President under section 670(b)(2) of the Foreign Assistance Act of 1961 with respect to   , the Congress hereby authorizes the President to exercise the waiver authority contained in section 670(b)(3) of that Act.", with the date of receipt of the certification inserted in the first blank and the name of the country inserted in the second blank.

(3) Notwithstanding paragraph (1) of this subsection, if the Congress enacts a joint resolution under paragraph (2) of this subsection, the President may furnish assistance which would otherwise be prohibited under paragraph (1) if he determines and certifies in writing to the Speaker of the House of Representatives and the Committee on Foreign Relations of the Senate that the termination of such assistance would be seriously prejudicial to the achievement of United States nonproliferation objectives or otherwise jeopardize the common defense and security. The President shall transmit with such certification a statement setting forth the specific reasons therefor.

(4) For purposes of this subsection, continuity of session is broken only by an adjournment of Congress sine die and the days on which either House is not in session because of an adjournment of more than three days to a day certain are excluded in the computation of any period of time in which Congress is in continuous session.

(c) As used in this section, the term "non-nuclear-weapon state" means any country which is not a nuclear-weapon state, as defined in article IX(3) of the Treaty on the Non-Proliferation of Nuclear Weapons.

ATOMIC WEAPONS AND SPECIAL NUCLEAR MATERIALS REWARDS ACT

An Act to provide rewards for information concerning the illegal introduction into the United States, or the illegal manufacture or acquisition in the United States, of special nuclear material and atomic weapons.

Be it enacted by the Senate and House of Representatives of the United States of America in Congress assembled, That:

"Sec. 2. Any person who furnishes original information to the United States—

"(a) leading to the finding or other acquisition by the United States of special nuclear material or an atomic weapon which has been introduced into the United States or manufactured or acquired therein contrary to the laws of the United States, or

"(b) with respect to the introduction or attempted introduction into the United States or the manufacture or acquisition or attempted manufacture or acquisition of, or a conspiracy to introduce into the United States or to manufacture or acquire, special nuclear material or an atomic weapon contrary to the laws of the United States, or

"(c) with respect to the export or attempted export, or a conspiracy to export, special nuclear material or an atomic weapon from the United States contrary to the laws of the United States,

shall be rewarded by the payment of an amount not to exceed $500,000.

"Sec. 3. The Attorney General shall determine whether a person furnishing information to the United States is entitled to a reward and the amount to be paid pursuant to section 2. Before making a reward under this section the Attorney General shall advise and consult with the Atomic Energy Commission. A reward of $50,000 or more may not be made without the approval of the President.".

Sec. 4. If the information leading to an award under section 3 is furnished by an alien, the Secretary of State, the Attorney General, and the Director of Central Intelligence, acting jointly, may determine that the entry of such alien into the United States is in the public interest and, in that event, such alien and the members of his immediate family may receive immigrant visas and may be admitted to the United States for permanent residence, notwithstanding the requirements of the Immigration and Nationality Act.

ATOMIC WEAPONS AND SPECIAL NUCLEAR MATERIALS REWARDS ACT

"Sec. 5. (a) The Attorney General is authorized to hold such hearings and make, promulgate, issue, rescind, and amend such rules and regulations as may be necessary to carry out the purposes of this Act.

"(b) A determination made by the Attorney General under section 3 of this Act shall be final and conclusive and no court shall have power or jurisdiction to review it.".

(c) Section 6 of the Act [16] is amended by deleting the words "Awards Board" and by substituting in lieu thereof the words "Attorney General".

Sec. 6. Any awards granted under section 3 of this Act shall be certified by the Awards Board and, together with the approval of the President in those cases where such approval is required, transmitted to the Director of Central Intelligence for payment out of funds appropriated or available for the administration of the National Security Act of 1947, as amended.[45]

Sec. 7. As used in this Act—

(a) The term "atomic energy" means all forms of energy released in the course of nuclear fission or nuclear transformation.

(b) The term "atomic weapon" means any device utilizing atomic energy, exclusive of the means for transporting or propelling the device (where such means is a separable and divisible part of the device), the principal purpose of which is for use as, or for development of, a weapon, a weapon prototype, or a weapon test device.

(c) The term "special nuclear material" means plutonium, or uranium enriched in the isotope 233 or in the isotope 235, or any other material which is found to be special nuclear material pursuant to the provisions of the Atomic Energy Act of 1954.[46]

(d) The term "United States," when used in a geographical sense, includes Puerto Rico, all Territories and possessions of the United States and the Canal Zone; except that in section 4, the term "United States" when so used shall have the meaning given to it in the Immigration and Nationality Act.

Approved July 15, 1955.

---

45. 5 U.S.C.A. §§ 1, 171–171j, 171k–171n, 181—1, 181—2, 181a, 182, 182a, 411a, 411b, 421a, 421b, 626–626d; 50 U.S.C.A. §§ 401–405.

46. 5 U.S.C.A. §§ 1031, 1032; 42 U.S.C.A. § 2011 et seq.

International Atomic Energy Agency Participation Act of 1957, as amended

Partial text of Public Law 85-177 [H.R. 8992], 71 Stat. 453, approved August 28, 1957; as amended by Public Law 85-795, 72 Stat. 959, approved August 28, 1958; Public Law 89-348, 79 Stat. 1310, approved November 8, 1965; and by Public Law 96-465 [H.R. 6790], 94 Stat. 2071 at 2161, approved October 17, 1980

AN ACT To provide for the appointment of representatives of the United States in the organs of the International Atomic Energy Agency, and to make other provisions with respect to the participation of the United States in that Agency, and for other purposes.

Be it enacted by the Senate and House of Representatives of the United States of America in Congress assembled, That this Act may be cited as the "International Atomic Energy Agency Participation Act of 1957".

Sec. 2.[1] (a) The President, by and with the advice and consent of the Senate, shall appoint a representative and a deputy representative of the United States to the International Atomic Energy Agency (hereinafter referred to as the "Agency"), who shall hold office at the pleasure of the President. Such representative and deputy representative shall represent the United States on the Board of Governors of the Agency, may represent the United States at the General Conference, and may serve ex officio as United States representative on any organ of that Agency, and shall perform such other functions in connection with the participation of the United States in the Agency as the President may from time to time direct.

(b) The President, by and with the advice and consent of the Senate, may appoint or designate from time to time to attend a specified session or specified sessions of the General Conference of the Agency a representative of the United States and such number of alternates as he may determine consistent with the rules of procedure of the General Conference.

(c) The President may also appoint or designate from time to time such other persons as he may deem necessary to represent the United States in the organs of the Agency. The President may designate any officer of the United States Government, whose appointment is subject to confirmation by the Senate, to act, without additional compensation, for temporary periods as the representative of the United States on the Board of Governors or to the General Conference of the Agency in the absence or disability of the representative and deputy representative appointed under section 2(a) or in lieu of such representatives in connection with a specified subject matter.

(d) All persons appointed or designated in pursuance of authority contained in this section shall receive compensation at rates deter-

---

[1] 22 U.S.C. 2021.

mined by the President upon the basis of duties to be performed but not in excess of rates authorized by sections 401, 402, and 403 of the Foreign Service Act of 1980 by chiefs of mission, members of the Senior Foreign Service, and Foreign Service officers occupying positions of equivalent importance, except that no Member of the Senate or House of Representatives or officer of the United States who is designated under subsection (b) or subsection (c) of this section as a delegate or representative of the United States or as an alternate to attend any specified session or specified sessions of the General Conference shall be entitled to receive such compensation.[2] Any person who receives compensation pursuant to the provisions of this subsection may be granted allowances and benefits not to exceed those received under the Foreign Service Act of 1980 by chiefs of mission, members of the Senior Foreign Service and Foreign Service officers occupying positions of equivalent importance.[3]

Sec. 3.[4] The participation of the United States in the International Atomic Energy Agency shall be consistent with and in furtherance of the purposes of the Agency set forth in its statute and the policy concerning the development, use, and control of atomic energy set forth in the Atomic Energy Act of 1954, as amended. [The President shall, from time to time as occasion may require, but not less than once each year, make reports to the Congress on the activities of the International Atomic Energy Agency and on the participation of the United States therein.][5] In addition to any other requirements of law, the Department of State and the Atomic Energy Commission shall keep the Joint Committee on Atomic Energy, the House Committee on Foreign Affairs, and the Senate Committee on Foreign Relations, as appropriate, currently informed with respect to the activities of the Agency and the participation of the United States therein.

Sec. 4.[6] The representatives provided for in section 2 hereof, when representing the United States in the organs of the Agency, shall, at all times, act in accordance with the instructions of the President, and such representatives shall, in accordance with such instructions, cast any and all votes under the statute of the International Atomic Energy Agency.

Sec. 5.[7] There is hereby authorized to be appropriated annually to the Department of State, out of any money in the Treasury not otherwise appropriated, such sums as may be necessary for the payment by the United States of its share of the expenses of the International Atomic Energy Agency as apportioned by the Agency in accordance with paragraph (D) of article XIV of the statute of the Agency, and for all necessary salaries and expenses of the rep-

---

[2] References in this subsection to sections of the Foreign Service Act of 1980 and to the Senior Foreign Service were inserted by sec. 2206(a)(7) of Public Law 94-465 (94 Stat. 2161), effective Feb. 15, 1981. These replaced a reference to secs. 411 and 412 of the Foreign Service Act of 1946.
[3] The references to the Foreign Service Act of 1980 and to the Senior Foreign Service were inserted by sec. 2206(a)(7) of Public Law 96-465 (94 Stat. 2161), effective Feb. 15, 1981.
[4] 22 U.S.C. 2022.
[5] Public Law 89-348 (79 Stat. 1310, sec. I(20), amended Public Law 85-177 by repealing the requirement of a report to the Congress by the President not less than once each year on the activities of the International Atomic Energy Agency and on the participation of the United States therein.
[6] 22 U.S.C. 2023.
[7] 22 U.S.C. 2024.

resentatives provided for in section 2 hereof and of their appropriate staffs, including personal services without regard to the civil service laws and the Classification Act of 1949, as amended; travel expenses without regard to the Standardized Government Travel Regulations, as amended, the Travel Expense Act of 1949, as amended, and section 10 of the Act of March 3, 1933, as amended; salaries as authorized by the Foreign Service Act of 1980,[8] or as authorized by the Atomic Energy Act of 1954, as amended, and expenses and allowances of personnel and dependents as authorized by the Foreign Service Act of 1980;[8] services as authorized by sec. 15 of the Act of Aug. 2, 1946 (5 U.S.C. 55a);[9] translating and other services, by contract; hire of passenger motor vehicles and other local transportation; printing and binding without regard to section II of the Act of March 1, 1919 (44 U.S.C. 111); official functions and courtesies; such sums as may be necessary to defray the expenses of United States participation in the Preparatory Commission for the Agency, established pursuant to annex I of the statute of the Agency; and such other expenses as may be authorized by the Secretary of State.

Sec. 6.[10] (a)[11] Notwithstanding any other provision of law, Executive order or regulation, a Federal employee who, with the approval of the Federal agency, or the head of the department by which he is employed, leaves his position to enter the employ of the Agency shall not be considered for the purposes of the Civil Service Retirement Act, as amended, and the Federal Employees' Group Life Insurance Act of 1954, as amended, as separated from his Federal position during such employment with the Agency but not to extend beyond the first three consecutive years of his entering the employ of the Agency: *Provided,* (1) That he shall pay to the Civil Service Commission[12] within ninety days from the date he is separated without prejudice from the Agency all necessary deductions and agency contributions for coverage under the Civil Service Retirement Act for the period of his employment by the Agency, and (2) That all deductions and agency contributions necessary for continued coverage under the Federal Employees' Group Life Insurance Act of 1954, as amended, shall be made during the term of his employment with the International Atomic Energy Agency. If such employee, within three years from the date of his employment with the Agency, and within ninety days from the date he is separated without prejudice from the Agency, applies to be restored to his Federal position, he shall within thirty days of such application be restored to such position or to a position of like seniority, status and pay.

---

[8] Reference to the Foreign Service Act of 1980 was inserted in lieu of a reference to the Foreign Service Act of 1946 by sec. 2206(a)(7) of Public Law 96–465 (94 Stat. 2162), effective Feb. 15, 1981.
[9] Public Law 89–554 (80 Stat. 416) codified sec. 15 of the Act of Aug. 2, 1946, as 5 U.S.C. 3109.
[10] 22 U.S.C. 2025.
[11] Sec. 7 of Public Law 85–795 (72 Stat. 959), approved Aug. 28, 1958, repealed sec. 6(a), "except that it shall be considered to remain in effect with respect to any employee subject thereto who is serving as an employee of the International Atomic Energy Agency on the date of enactment of this Act and who does not make the election referred to in sec. 6 and for the purposes of any rights and benefits vested thereunder prior to such date.".
[12] The Office of Personnel Management was substituted for the Civil Service Commission pursuant to sec. 102 of Reorganization Plan No. 2 of 1978.

314

(b) Notwithstanding any other provision of law, Executive order or regulation, any Presidential appointee or elected officer who leaves his position to enter, or who within ninety days after the termination of his position enters, the employ of the Agency, shall be entitled to the coverage and benefits of the Civil Service Retirement Act, as amended, and the Federal Employees' Group Life Insurance Act of 1954, as amended, but not beyond the earlier of either the termination of his employment with the Agency or the expiration of three years from the date he entered employment with the Agency: *Provided,* (1) That he shall pay to the Civil Service Commission [12] within ninety days from the date he is separated without prejudice from the Agency all necessary deductions and agency contributions for coverage under the Civil Service Retirement Act for the period of his employment by the agency and (2) That all deductions and agency contributions necessary for continued coverage under the Federal Employees' Group Life Insurance Act of 1954, as amended, shall be made during the term of his employment with the Agency.

(c) The President is authorized to prescribe such regulations as may be necessary to carry out the provisions of this section and to protect the retirement, insurance and such other civil service rights and privileges as the President may find appropriate.

* * * * * * *

Sec. 8.[13] In the event of an amendment to the Statute of the Agency being adopted in accordance with article XVIII-C of the Statute to which the Senate by formal vote shall refuse its advice and consent, upon notification by the Senate to the President of such refusal to advise and consent, all further authority under section [14] 2, 3, 4, and 5 of this Act, as amended, shall terminate: *Provided, however,* That the Secretary of State, under such regulations as the President shall promulgate, shall have the necessary authority to complete the prompt and orderly settlement of obligations and commitments to the Agency already incurred and pay salaries, allowances, travel expenses, and other expenses required for a prompt and orderly termination of United States participation in the Agency: *And provided further,* That the representative and the deputy representative of the United States to the Agency, and such other officers or employees representing the United States in the Agency, under such regulations as the President shall promulgate, shall retain their authority under this Act for such time as may be necessary to complete the settlement of matters arising out of the United States participation in the Agency.

---

[13] 22 U.S.C. 2026.
[14] Should read "sections".

EURATOM Cooperation Act of 1958, as amended

Public Law 85-846 [S. 4273], 72 Stat. 1084, approved August 28, 1958; as amended by Public Law 87-206, 75 Stat. 479, approved September 6, 1961; Public Law 88-394, 78 Stat. 376, approved August 1, 1964; Public Law 90-190, 81 Stat. 578, approved December 14, 1967; and by Public Law 93-88, 87 Stat. 296, approved August 14, 1973

AN ACT To provide for cooperation with the European Atomic Energy Community.

Be it enacted by the Senate and House of Representatives of the United States of America in Congress assembled, That this Act may be cited as the "EURATOM Cooperation Act of 1958".

Sec. 2.[1] As used in this Act—

(a) "The Community" means the European Atomic Energy Community (EURATOM).

(b) The "Commission" means the Atomic Energy Commission, as established by the Atomic Energy Act of 1954, as amended.

(c) "Joint program" means the cooperative program established by the Community and the United States and carried out in accordance with the provisions of an agreement for cooperation entered into pursuant to the provisions of section 123 of the Atomic Energy Act of 1954, as amended, to bring into operation in the territory of the members of the Community powerplants using nuclear reactors of types selected by the Commission and the Community, having as a goal a total installed capacity of approximately one million kilowatts of electricity by December 31, 1963, except that two reactors may be selected to be in operation by December 31, 1965.

(d) All other terms used in this Act shall have the same meaning as terms described in section 11 of the Atomic Energy Act of 1954, as amended.

Sec. 3.[2] There is hereby authorized to be appropriated to the Commission, in accordance with the provisions of section 261(a)(2) of the Atomic Energy Act of 1954, as amended, the sum of $3,000,000 [3] as an initial authorization for fiscal year 1959 for use in a cooperative program of research and development in connection with the types of reactors selected by the Commission and the Community under the joint program. The Commission may enter into contracts for such periods as it deems necessary, but in no event to exceed five years, for the purpose of conducting the research and development program authorized by this section: *Provided,* That the Community authorizes an equivalent amount for use in the cooperative program of research and development.

---

[1] 42 U.S.C. 2291.
[2] 42 U.S.C. 2292.
[3] Sec. 109 of Public Law 86-50, sec. 109 of Public Law 87-701, sec. 103 of Public Law 88-72, sec. 101(a) of Public Law 88-332, and sec. 101 of Public Law 89-32 authorized appropriation of an additional $7,000,000, $5,000,000, $7,500,000, $3,000,000, and $3,000,000, respectively.

Sec. 4.[4] The Commission is authorized, within limits of amounts which may hereafter be authorized to be appropriated in accordance with the provisions of section 261(a)(2) of the Atomic Energy Act of 1954, as amended, to make guarantee contracts which shall in the aggregate not exceed a total contingent liability of $90,000,000 designed to assure that the charges to an operator of a reactor constructed under the joint program for fabricating, processing, and transporting fuel will be no greater than would result under the fuel fabricating and fuel life guarantees which the Commission shall establish for such reactor. Within the limits of such amounts, the Commission is authorized to make contracts under this section, without regard to the provisions of sections 3679 and 3709 of the Revised Statutes, as amended, for such period of time as it determines to be necessary: *Provided, however,* That no such contracts may extend for a period longer than that necessary to cover fuel loaded into a reactor constructed under the joint program during the first ten years of the reactor operation or prior to December 31, 1973 (or December 31, 1975, for not more than two reactors selected under section 2(c)), whichever is earlier. In establishing criteria for the selection of projects and in entering into such guarantee contracts, the Commission shall be guided by, but not limited to, the following principles:

(a) The Commission shall encourage a strong and competitive atomic equipment manufacturing industry in the United States designed to provide diversified sources of supply for reactor parts and reactor fuel elements under the joint program;

(b) The guarantee shall be consistent with the provisions of this Act and of Attachment A to the Memorandum of Understanding between the Government of the United States and the Community, signed in Brussels on May 29, 1958, and in Washington, District of Columbia, on June 12, 1958, and transmitted to Congress on June 23, 1958;

(c) [5] The Commission shall establish and publish criteria for computing the maximum fuel element charge and minimum fuel element life to be guaranteed by the manufacturer as a basis for inviting and evaluating proposals.

(d) The guarantee by the manufacturer shall be as favorable as any other guarantee offered by the manufacturer for any comparable fuel element within a reasonable time period; and

(e) The Commission shall obtain a royalty-free, nonexclusive, irrevocable license for governmental purposes to any patents on inventions or discoveries made or conceived by the manufacturer in the course of development or fabrication of fuel elements during the period covered by the Commission's guarantee.

Sec. 5.[6] Pursuant to the provisions of section 54 of the Atomic Energy Act of 1954, as amended, there is hereby authorized for sale or lease to the Community—

---

[4] 42 U.S.C. 2293.
[5] Public Law 87-206 (75 Stat. 475), amended sec. 4(c). Prior to amendment it read: "The commission shall establish and publish minimum levels of fuel element cost and life to be guaranteed by the manufacturer as a basis for inviting and evaluating proposals.".
[6] 42 U.S.C. 2294. Sec. 13 of Public Law 90-190 (81 Stat. 575) amended sec. 5 by substituting a new section. Sec. 5 previously read as follows:

Continued

an amount of contained uranium 235 which does not exceed that necessary to support the fuel cycle of power reactors located within the Community having a total installed capacity of thirty-five thousand megawatts of electric energy, together with twenty-five thousand kilograms of contained uranium 235 for other purposes; [7]

one thousand five hundred kilograms of plutonium; and thirty kilograms of uranium 233;
in accordance with the provisions of an agreement or agreements for cooperation between the Government of the United States and the Community entered into pursuant to the provisions of section 123 of the Atomic Energy Act of 1954, as amended: *Provided,* That the Government of the United States obtains the equivalent of a first lien of any such material sold to the Community for which payment is not made in full at the time of transfer. The Commission may enter into contracts to provide, after December 31, 1968, for the producing or enriching of all, or part of, the above-mentioned contained uranium 235 pursuant to the provisions of subsection 161 v. (B) of said Act, as amended in lieu of sale or lease thereof.

Sec. 6.[8] (a) The Atomic Energy Commission is authorized to purchase or otherwise acquire from the Community special nuclear material or any interest therein from reactors constructed under the joint program in accordance with the terms of an agreement for cooperation entered into pursuant to the provisions of section 123 of the Atomic Energy Act of 1954, as amended: *Provided,* That neither plutonium nor uranium 233 nor any interest therein shall be acquired under this section in excess of the total quantities authorized by law. The Commission is hereby authorized to acquire from the Community pursuant to this section up to four thousand one hundred kilograms of plutonium for use only for peaceful purposes.

(b) Any contract made under the provisions of this section to acquire plutonium or any interest therein may be at such prices and for such period of time as the Commission may deem necessary: *Provided,* That with respect to plutonium produced in any reactor constructed under the joint program, no such contract shall be for a period greater than ten years of operation of such reactors or December 31, 1973 (or December 31, 1975, for not more than two reactors selected under section 2(c)), whichever is earlier: *And provided further,* That no such contract shall provide for compensation or the payment of a purchase price in excess of the Commission's es-

---

"Sec. 5. Pursuant to the provisions of section 54 of the Atomic Energy Act of 1954, as amended, there is hereby authorized for sale or lease to the Community:
"Seventy thousand kilograms of contained uranium 235
"Five hundred kilograms of plutonium
"Thirty kilograms of uranium 233
"In accordance with the provisions of an agreement or agreements for cooperation between the Government of the United States and the Community entered into pursuant to the provisions of section 123 of the Atomic Energy Act of 1954 as amended: *Provided,* That the Government of the United States obtains the equivalent of a first lien of any such material sold to the Community for which payment is not made in full at the time of transfer.".
Sec. 5 had earlier been amended by Public Law 88-394 (78 Stat. 376), sec. 5, and by Public Law 87-206 (75 Stat. 475), sec. 19.

[7] Public Law 93-88 (87 Stat. 296), amended this paragraph. Previously, it read "two hundred fifteen thousand kilograms of contained uranium 235;".
[8] 42 U.S.C. 2295.

tablished price in effect at the time of delivery to the Commission for such fuel material as fuel in a nuclear reactor.

(c) Any contract made under the provisions of this section to acquire uranium enriched in the isotope uranium 235 may be at such price and for such period of time as the Commission may deem necessary: *Provided,* That no such contract shall be for a period of time extending beyond the terminal date of the agreement for cooperation with the Community or provide for the acquisition of uranium enriched in the isotope U-235 in excess of the quantities of such material that have been distributed to the Community by the Commission less the quantity consumed in the nuclear reactors involved in the joint program: *And provided further,* That no such contract shall provide for compensation or the payment of a purchase price in excess of the Atomic Energy Commission's established charges for such material in effect at the time delivery is made to the Commission.

(d) Any contract made under this section for the purchase of special nuclear material or any interest therein may be made without regard to the provisions of section 3679 of the Revised Statutes, as amended.

(e) Any contract made under this section may be made without regard to section 3709 of the Revised Statutes, as amended, upon certification by the Commission that such action is necessary in the interest of the common defense and security, or upon a showing by the Commission that advertising is not reasonably practicable.

Sec. 7.[9] The Government of the United States of America shall not be liable for any damages or third party liability arising out of or resulting from the joint program: *Provided however,* That nothing in this section shall deprive any person of any rights under section 170 of the Atomic Energy Act of 1954, as amended. *And provided further,* That nothing in this section shall apply to arrangements made by the Commission under a research and development program authorized in section 3.[10] The Government of the United States shall take such steps as may be necessary, including appropriate disclaimer or indemnity arrangements, in order to carry out the provisions of this section.

---

[9] 42 U.S.C. 2296.
[10] The proviso was added by Public Law 87-206 (75 Stat. 475).

EURATOM Resolution

Senate Concurrent Resolution 116, 85th Congress, 2d Session, passed August 23, 1958

Whereas the United States of America has instituted a program of international cooperation to make available to cooperating nations the benefits of peaceful applications of atomic energy; and

Whereas the United States of America and the European Atomic Energy Community (EURATOM) have entered into an agreement providing for cooperation in programs designed to advance the peaceful application of atomic energy: Therefore be it

Resolved by the Senate (the House of Representatives concurring), That pursuant to the provisions of section 11(l) and 124 of the Atomic Energy Act of 1954, as amended, the agreement between the Government of the United States of America and the European Atomic Energy Community (EURATOM), signed at Brussels on May 29, 1958, and at Washington on June 19, 1958, concerning cooperation between the parties in programs for the advancement of the peaceful application of atomic energy, be and hereby is approved. This resolution does not constitute approval or disapproval of the memorandum of understanding, or any other agreements which have not been formally approved or authorized by the Congress.

PUBLIC LAW 95-118 [H.R. 5262]; Oct. 3, 1977

INTERNATIONAL BANK FOR RECONSTRUCTION AND DEVELOPMENT

For Legislative History of Act, see p. 2670

An Act to provide for increased participation by the United States in the International Bank for Reconstruction and Development, the International Development Association, the International Finance Corporation, the Asian Development Bank and the Asian Development Fund, and for other purposes.

Be it enacted by the Senate and House of Representatives of the United States of America in Congress assembled,

International financial institutions. U.S. participation, increase.

TITLE I—PURPOSE AND POLICY; DECLARATION OF CONGRESSIONAL INTENT IN RESPECT TO CONTINUED PARTICIPATION OF THE UNITED STATES GOVERNMENT IN INTERNATIONAL FINANCIAL INSTITUTIONS FOSTERING ECONOMIC DEVELOPMENT IN LESS DEVELOPED COUNTRIES

TITLE VII—HUMAN RIGHTS

SEC. 701. (a) The United States Government, in connection with its voice and vote in the International Bank for Reconstruction and Development, the International Development Association, the International Finance Corporation, the Inter-American Development Bank, the African Development Fund, and the Asian Development Bank, shall advance the cause of human rights, including by seeking to channel assistance toward countries other than those whose governments engage in—

Assistance policies. 22 USC 262d.

(1) a consistent pattern of gross violations of internationally recognized human rights, such as torture or cruel, inhumane, or degrading treatment or punishment, prolonged detention without charges, or other flagrant denial to life, liberty, and the security of person; or

(2) provide refuge to individuals committing acts of international terrorism by hijacking aircraft.

(b) Further, the Secretary of the Treasury shall instruct each Executive Director of the above institutions to consider in carrying out his duties:

(1) specific actions by either the executive branch or the Congress as a whole on individual bilateral assistance programs because of human rights considerations;

(2) the extent to which the economic assistance provided by the above institutions directly benefit the needy people in the recipient country;

(3) whether the recipient country has detonated a nuclear device or is not a State Party to the Treaty on Nonproliferation of Nuclear Weapons or both; and

(4) in relation to assistance for the Socialist Republic of Vietnam, the People's Democratic Republic of Laos, and Democratic Kampuchea (Cambodia), the responsiveness of the governments of such countries in providing a more substantial accounting of Americans missing in action.

PUBLIC LAW 95-143 [H.R. 6415]; OCT. 26, 1977

EXPORT-IMPORT BANK ACT OF 1945

For Legislative History of Act, see p. 3126

An Act to extend and amend the Export-Import Bank Act of 1945.

Be it enacted by the Senate and House of Representatives of the United States of America in Congress assembled,

Export-Import Bank Act of 1945, amendments. Export financing, international agreements. 12 USC 635. Human rights.

SECTION 1. Section 2(b)(1)(A) of the Export-Import Bank Act of 1945 is amended by inserting before the period at the end of the third sentence the following: "and shall, in cooperation with other appropriate United States Government agencies, seek to reach international agreements to reduce government subsidized export financing".

SEC. 2. The last sentence of section 2(b)(1)(B) of the Export-Import Bank Act of 1945 is amended by inserting before the period at the end thereof the following: ", and shall also take into account, in consultation with the Secretary of State, the observance of and respect for human rights in the country to receive the exports supported by a loan or financial guarantee and the effect such exports may have on human rights in such country".

SEC. 3. (a) The first sentence of section 2(b)(3) of the Export-Import Bank Act of 1945 is amended—

(1) by inserting "(i)" immediately after "No loan or financial guarantee or combination thereof";

(2) by striking out "shall be finally approved by the Board of Directors of the Bank, and no loan or financial guarantee or combination thereof" and inserting in lieu thereof ", (ii) in an amount"; and

(3) by inserting immediately after "Union of Soviet Socialist Republics" the following: ", or (iii) for the export of technology, fuel, equipment, materials, or goods or services to be used in the construction, alteration, operation, or maintenance of nuclear power, enrichment, reprocessing, research, or heavy water production facilities,".

Nuclear safeguards, violations. Report to congressional committees and Board of Directors.

(b) Section 2(b) of the Export-Import Bank Act of 1945 is amended by redesignating paragraphs (4) through (6) as paragraphs (5) through (7), respectively, and by inserting immediately after paragraph (3) the following new paragraph:

"(4) The Secretary of State shall report to the appropriate committees of Congress and to the Board of Directors of the Export-Import Bank if he determines that any country that has agreed to International Atomic Energy Agency nuclear safeguards materially violates, abrogates, or terminates, after the date of enactment of this paragraph, such safeguards or that any country that has entered into an agreement for cooperation concerning the civil use of nuclear energy with the United States materially violates, abrogates, or terminates, after the date of enactment of this paragraph, any guarantee or other undertaking to the United States made in such agreement or that any country that is not a nuclear-weapons state (as defined in article IX(3) of the Treaty on the Non-Proliferation of Nuclear Weapons) detonates, after the date of enactment of this paragraph, a nuclear explosive device. The Secretary shall specify which country or countries he has determined to have so acted, and the Board shall not give approval to guarantee, insure, or extend credit, or participate

Exports, credit support, limitation. Presidential determination, report to Congress.

91 STAT. 1210

in the extension of credit in support of United States exports to such country unless the President determines that it is in the national interest for the Bank to guarantee, insure, or extend credit, or participate in the extension of credit in support of United States exports to such country and such determination has been reported to the Congress not less than twenty-five days of continuous session of the Congress prior to the date of such approval. For the purpose of the preceding sentence, continuity of a session of the Congress shall be considered as broken only by an adjournment of the Congress sine die, and the days on which either House is not in session because of an adjournment of more than three days to a day certain shall be excluded in the computation of the twenty-five day period referred to in such sentence.".

(c) The first sentence of section 2(b)(5) of the Export-Import Bank Act of 1945, as redesignated by subsection (b), is amended—

(1) by striking out "or" immediately after "the United States."; and

(2) by inserting before the period at the end thereof the following: ". or (C) the purchase of any liquid metal fast breeder nuclear reactor or any nuclear fuel reprocessing facility".

SEC. 4. Section 8 of the Export-Import Bank Act of 1945 is amended by striking out "June 30" and inserting in lieu thereof "September 30".

Approved October 26, 1977.

Nuclear Non-Proliferation Act of 1978

Partial text of Public Law 95-242 [H.R. 8638], 92 Stat. 120, approved March 10, 1978; as amended by Public Law 99-661 [National Defense Authorization Act for Fiscal Year 1987; S. 2638], 100 Stat. 3816, approved November 11, 1986

AN ACT To provide for more efficient and effective control over the proliferation of nuclear explosive capability.

Be it enacted by the Senate and House of Representatives of the United States of America in Congress assembled, That this Act may be cited as the "Nuclear Non-Proliferation Act of 1978."

STATEMENT OF POLICY

SEC. 2.[1] The Congress finds and declares that the proliferation of nuclear explosive devices or of the direct capability to manufacture or otherwise acquire such devices poses a grave threat to the security interests of the United States and to continued international progress toward world peace and development. Recent events emphasize the urgency of this threat and the imperative need to increase the effectiveness of international safeguards and controls on peaceful nuclear activities to prevent proliferation. Accordingly, it is the policy of the United States to—

(a) actively pursue through international initiatives mechanisms for fuel supply assurances and the establishment of more effective international controls over the transfer and use of nuclear materials and equipment and nuclear technology for peaceful purposes in order to prevent proliferation, including the establishment of common international sanctions;

(b) take such actions as are required to confirm the reliability of the United States in meeting its commitments to supply nuclear reactors and fuel to nations which adhere to effective non-proliferation policies by establishing procedures to facilitate the timely processing of requests for subsequent arrangements and export licenses;

---

[1] 22 U.S.C. 3201.

(c) strongly encourage nations which have not ratified the Treaty on the Non-Proliferation of Nuclear Weapons to do so at the earliest possible date; [2] and

(d) cooperate with foreign nations in identifying and adapting suitable technologies for energy production and, in particular, to identify alternative options to nuclear power in aiding such nations to meet their energy needs, consistent with the economic and material resources of those nations and environmental protection.

STATEMENT OF PURPOSE

SEC. 3.[3] It is the purpose of this Act to promote the policies set forth above by—

(a) establishing a more effective framework for international cooperation to meet the energy needs of all nations and to ensure that the worldwide development of peaceful nuclear activities and the export by any nation of nuclear materials and equipment and nuclear technology intended for use in peaceful nuclear activities do not contribute to proliferation;

(b) authorizing the United States to take such actions as are required to ensure that it will act reliably in meeting its commitment to supply nuclear reactors and fuel to nations which adhere to effective non-proliferation policies;

(c) providing incentives to the other nations of the world to join in such international cooperative efforts and to ratify the Treaty; and

(d) ensuring effective controls by the United States over its exports of nuclear materials and equipment and of nuclear technology.

DEFINITIONS

SEC. 4.[4] (a) As used in this Act, the term—

(1) "Commission" means the Nuclear Regulatory Commission;

(2) "Director" means the Director of the Arms Control and Disarmament Agency;

(3) "IAEA" means International Atomic Energy Agency;

(4) "nuclear materials and equipment" means source material, special nuclear material, production facilities, utilization facilities, and components, items or substances determined to have significance for nuclear explosive purposes pursuant to subsection 109 b. of the 1954 Act;

(5) "physical security measures" means measures to reasonably ensure that source or special nuclear material will only be used for authorized purpose and to prevent theft and sabotage;

---

[2] This policy was reiterated by Congress in sec. 507 of the International Development Cooperation Act of 1979 (Public Law 96-53; 93 Stat. 378) (see *Legislation on Foreign Relations Through 1992*, vol. I, page 520). Sec. 507(b), which was repealed in 1981, also called for a report (submitted to Congress on November 19, 1979) from the Secretary of State, on steps taken by the Department of State to encourage nations which are not parties to the treaty to become parties.
[3] 22 U.S.C. 3202.
[4] 22 U.S.C. 3203.

(6) "sensitive nuclear technology" means any information (including information incorporated in a production or utilization facility or important component part thereof) which is not available to the public and which is important to the design, construction, fabrication, operation or maintenance of a uranium enrichment or nuclear fuel reprocessing facility or a facility for the production of heavy water, but shall not include Restricted Data controlled pursuant to chapter 12 of the 1954 Act;

(7) "1954 Act" means the Atomic Energy Act of 1954, as amended; and

(8) "the Treaty" means the Treaty on the Non-Proliferation of Nuclear Weapons.[5]

(b) All other terms used in this Act not defined in this section shall have the meanings ascribed to them by the 1954 Act, the Energy Reorganization Act of 1974, and the Treaty.

TITLE I—UNITED STATES INITIATIVES TO PROVIDE ADEQUATE NUCLEAR FUEL SUPPLY

POLICY

SEC. 101.[6] The United States, as a matter of national policy, shall take such actions and institute such measures as may be necessary and feasible to assure other nations and groups of nations that may seek to utilize the benefits of atomic energy for peaceful purposes that it will provide a reliable supply of nuclear fuel to those nations and groups of nations which adhere to policies designed to prevent proliferation. Such nuclear fuel shall be provided under agreements entered into pursuant to section 161 of the 1954 Act or as otherwise authorized by law. The United States shall ensure that it will have available the capacity on a long-term basis to enter into new fuel supply commitments consistent with its nonproliferation policies and domestic energy needs. The Commission shall, on a timely basis, authorize the export of nuclear materials and equipment when all the applicable statutory requirements are met.

URANIUM ENRICHMENT CAPACITY

SEC. 102.[7] The Secretary of Energy is directed to initiate construction planning and design, construction, and operation activities for expansion of uranium enrichment capacity, as elsewhere provided by law. Further the Secretary as well as the Nuclear Regulatory Commission, the Secretary of State, and the Director of the Arms Control and Disarmament Agency are directed to establish and implement procedures which will ensure to the maximum extent feasible, consistent with this Act, orderly processing of subsequent arrangements and export licenses with minimum time delay.

---

[5] See *Legislation on Foreign Relations Through 1988*, vol. V, sec. L, for text of treaty.
[6] 22 U.S.C. 3221.
[7] 22 U.S.C. 3222.

REPORT

SEC. 103. The President shall promptly undertake a study to determine the need for additional United States enrichment capacity to meet domestic and foreign needs and to promote United States nonproliferation objectives abroad. The President shall report to the Congress on the results of this study within twelve months after the date of enactment of this Act.

INTERNATIONAL UNDERTAKINGS

SEC. 104.[8] (a) Consistent with section 105 of this Act, the President shall institute prompt discussions with other nations and groups of nations, including both supplier and recipient nations, to develop international approaches for meeting future worldwide nuclear fuel needs. In particular, the President is authorized and urged to seek to negotiate as soon as practicable with nations possessing nuclear fuel production facilities or source material, and such other nations and groups of nations, such as the IAEA, as may be deemed appropriate, with a view toward the timely establishment of binding international undertakings providing for—

(1) the establishment of an international nuclear fuel authority (INFA) with responsibility for providing agreed upon fuel services and allocating agreed upon quantities of fuel resources to ensure fuel supply on reasonable terms in accordance with agreements between INFA and supplier and recipient nations;

(2) a set of conditions consistent with subsection (d) under which international fuel assurances under INFA auspices will be provided to recipient nations, including conditions which will ensure that the transferred materials will not be used for nuclear explosive devices;

(3) devising, consistent with the policy goals set forth in section 403 of this Act, feasible and environmentally sound approaches for the siting, development, and management under effective international auspices and inspection of facilities for the provision of nuclear fuel services, including the storage of special nuclear material;

(4) the establishment of repositories for the storage of spent nuclear reactor fuel under effective international auspices and inspection;

(5) the establishment of arrangements under which nations placing spent fuel in such repositories would receive appropriate compensation for the energy content of such spent fuel if recovery of such energy content is deemed necessary or desirable; and

(6) sanctions for violation of the provisions of or for abrogation of such binding international undertakings.

(b) The President shall submit to Congress not later than six months after the date of enactment of this Act proposals for initial fuel assurances, including creation of an interim stockpile of uranium enriched to less than 20 percent in the uranium isotope 235 (low-enriched uranium) to be available for transfer pursuant to a

---

[8] 22 U.S.C. 3223.

sales arrangement to nations which adhere to strict policies designed to prevent proliferation when and if necessary to ensure continuity of nuclear fuel supply to such nations. Such submission shall include proposals for the transfer of low-enriched uranium up to an amount sufficient to produce 100,000 MWe years of power from light water nuclear reactors, and shall also include proposals for seeking contributions from other supplier nations to such an interim stockpile pending the establishment of INFA.

(c) The President shall, in the report required by section 103, also address the desirability of and options for foreign participation, including investment, in new United States uranium enrichment facilities. This report shall also address the arrangements that would be required to implement such participation and the commitments that would be required as a condition of such participation. This report shall be accompanied by any proposed legislation to implement these arrangements.

(d) The fuel assurances contemplated by this section shall be for the benefit of nations that adhere to policies designated to prevent proliferation. In negotiating the binding international undertakings called for in this section, the President shall, in particular, seek to ensure that the benefits of such undertakings are available to non-nuclear-weapon states only if such states accept IAEA safeguards on all their peaceful nuclear activities, do not manufacture or otherwise acquire any nuclear explosive device, do not establish any new enrichment or reprocessing facilities under their de facto or de jure control, and place any such existing facilities under effective international auspices and inspection.

(e) The report required by section 601 shall include information on the progress made in any negotiations pursuant to this section.

(f)(1) The President may not enter into any binding international undertaking negotiated pursuant to subsection (a) which is not a treaty until such time as such proposed undertaking has been submitted to the Congress and has been approved by concurrent resolution.

(2) The proposals prepared pursuant to subsection (b) shall be submitted to the Congress as part of an annual authorization Act for the Department of Energy.

REEVALUATION OF NUCLEAR FUEL CYCLE

SEC. 105.[9] The President shall take immediate initiatives to invite all nuclear supplier and recipient nations to reevaluate all aspects of the nuclear fuel cycle, with emphasis on alternatives to an economy based on the separation of pure plutonium or the presence of high enriched uranium, methods to deal with spent fuel storage, and methods to improve the safeguards for existing nuclear technology. The President shall, in the first report required by section 601, detail the progress of such international reevaluation.

---

[9] 22 U.S.C. 3224.

TITLE II—UNITED STATES INITIATIVES TO STRENGTHEN THE INTERNATIONAL SAFEGUARDS SYSTEM

POLICY

SEC. 201.[10] The United States is committed to continued strong support for the principles of the Treaty on the Non-Proliferation of Nuclear Weapons, to a strengthened and more effective International Atomic Energy Agency and to a comprehensive safeguards system administered by the Agency to deter proliferation. Accordingly, the United States shall seek to act with other nations to—

(a) continue to strengthen the safeguards program of the IAEA and, in order to implement this section, contribute funds, technical resources, and other support to assist the IAEA in effectively implementing safeguards;

(b) ensure that the IAEA has the resources to carry out the provisions of article XII of the Statute of the IAEA;

(c) improve the IAEA safeguards system (including accountability) to ensure—

  (1) the timely detection of a possible diversion of sources of special nuclear materials which could be used for nuclear explosive devices;

  (2) the timely dissemination of information regarding such diversion; and

  (3) the timely implementation of internationally agreed procedures in the event of such diversion;

(d) ensure that the IAEA receives on a timely basis the data needed for it to administer an effective and comprehensive international safeguards program and that the IAEA provides timely notice to the world community of any evidence of a violation of any safeguards agreement to which it is a party; and

(e) encourage the IAEA, to the maximum degree consistent with the Statute, to provide nations which supply nuclear materials and equipment with the data needed to assure such nations of adherence to bilateral commitments applicable to such supply.

TRAINING PROGRAM

SEC. 202.[11] The Department of Energy, in consultation with the Commission, shall establish and operate a safeguards and physical security training program to be made available to persons from nations and groups of nations which have developed or acquired, or may be expected to develop or acquire, nuclear materials and equipment for use for peaceful purposes. Any such program shall include training in the most advanced safeguards and physical security techniques and technology, consistent with the national security interests of the United States.

---

[10] 22 U.S.C. 3241.
[11] 22 U.S.C. 3242.

NEGOTIATIONS

SEC. 203.[12] The United States shall seek to negotiate with other nations and groups of nations to—
  (1) adopt general principles and procedures, including common international sanctions, to be followed in the event that a nation violates any material obligation with respect to the peaceful use of nuclear materials and equipment or nuclear technology, or in the event that any nation violates the principles of the Treaty, including the detonation by a non-nuclear-weapon state of a nuclear explosive device; and
  (2) establish international procedures to be followed in the event of diversion, theft, or sabotage of nuclear materials or sabotage of nuclear facilities, and for recovering nuclear materials that have been lost or stolen, or obtained or used by a nation or by any person or group in contravention of the principles of the Treaty.

TITLE III—EXPORT ORGANIZATION AND CRITERIA

* * * * * * *

EXPORT LICENSING PROCEDURES

SEC. 304. (a)[13] * * *
  (b)[14] Within one hundred and twenty days of the date of enactment of this Act, the Commission shall, after consultations with the Secretary of State, promulgate regulations establishing procedures (1) for the granting, suspending, revoking, or amending of any nuclear export license or exemption pursuant to its statutory authority; (2) for public participation in nuclear export licensing proceedings when the Commission finds that such participation will be in the public interest and will assist the Commission in making the statutory determinations required by the 1954 Act, including such public hearings and access to information as the Commission deems appropriate: *Provided,* That judicial review as to any such finding shall be limited to the determination of whether such finding was arbitrary and capricious; (3) for a public written Commission opinion accompanied by the dissenting or separate views of any Commissioner, in those proceedings where one or more Commissioners have dissenting or separate views on the issuance of an export license; and (4) for public notice of Commission proceedings and decisions, and for recording of minutes and votes of the Commission: *Provided further,* That until the regulations required by this subsection have been promulgated, the Commission shall implement the provisions of this Act under temporary procedures established by the Commission.
  (c)[14] The procedures to be established pursuant to subsection (b) shall constitute the exclusive basis for hearings in nuclear export licensing proceedings before the Commission and, notwithstanding

---
[12] 22 U.S.C. 3243.
[13] Subsec. (a) added a new sec. 126 to the 1954 Act regarding export licensing procedures. For text of sec. 126, see page 337.
[14] 42 U.S.C. 2155a.

nuclear explosives devices for any purpose, except as permitted by Article V, the Treaty;

(2) IAEA safeguards will be applied to all peaceful nuclear activities in, under the jurisdiction of, or under the control of any non-nuclear-weapon state;

(3) adequate physical security measure will be established and maintained by any nation or group of nations on all of its nuclear activities;

(4) no nuclear materials and equipment and no nuclear technology intended for peaceful purposes in, under the jurisdiction of, or under the control of any nation or group of nations shall be transferred to the jurisdiction of any other nation or group of nations which does not agree to stringent undertakings meeting the objectives of this section; and

(5) no nation or group of nations will assist, encourage, or induce any non-nuclear-weapon state to manufacture or otherwise acquire any nuclear explosive device.

(b)(1) No source or special nuclear material within the territory of any nation or group of nations, under its jurisdiction, or under its control anywhere will be enriched (as described in paragraph aa. (2) of section 11 of the 1954 Act) or reprocessed, no irradiated fuel elements containing such material which are to be removed from a reactor will be altered in form or content, and no fabrication or stockpiling involving plutonium, uranium 233, or uranium enriched to greater than 20 percent in the isotope 235 shall be performed except in a facility under effective international auspices and inspection, and any such irradiated fuel elements shall be transferred to such a facility as soon as practicable after removal from a reactor consistent with safety requirements. Such facilities shall be limited in number to the greatest extent feasible and shall be carefully sited and managed so as to minimize the proliferation and environmental risks associated with such facilities. In addition, there shall be conditions to limit the access of non-nuclear-weapon states other than the host country to sensitive nuclear technology associated with such facilities.

(2) Any facilities within the territory of any nation or group of nations, under its jurisdiction, or under its control anywhere for the necessary short-term storage of fuel elements containing plutonium, uranium 233, or uranium enriched to greater than 20 percent in the isotope 235 prior to placement in a reactor or of irradiated fuel elements prior to transfer as required in subparagraph (1) shall be placed under effective international auspices and inspection.

(c) Adequate physical security measures will be established and maintained with respect to all nuclear activities within the territory of each nation and group of nations, under its jurisdiction, or under its control anywhere, and with respect to any international shipment of significant quantities of source or special nuclear material or irradiated source or special nuclear material, which shall also be conducted under international safeguards.

(d) Nothing in this section shall be interpreted to require international control or supervision of any United States military activities.

Sec. 404   NUCLEAR NON-PROLIFERATION (P.L. 95-242)

RENEGOTIATION OF AGREEMENTS FOR COOPERATION

SEC. 404.[20] (a) The President shall initiate a program immediately to renegotiate agreements for cooperation in effect on the date of enactment of this Act, or otherwise to obtain the agreement of parties to such agreements for cooperation to the undertakings that would be required for new agreements under the 1954 Act. To the extent that an agreement for cooperation in effect on the date of enactment of this Act with a cooperating party contains provisions equivalent to any or all of the criteria set forth in section 127 of the 1954 Act with respect to materials and equipment transferred pursuant thereto or with respect to any special nuclear material used in or produced through the use of any such material or equipment, any renegotiated agreement with that cooperating party shall continue to contain an equivalent provision with respect to such transferred materials and equipment and such special nuclear material. To the extent that an agreement for cooperation in effect on the date of enactment of this Act with a cooperating party does not contain provisions with respect to any nuclear materials and equipment which have previously been transferred under an agreement for cooperation with the United States and which are under the jurisdiction or control of the cooperating party and with respect to any special nuclear material which is used in or produced through the use thereof and which is under the jurisdiction or control of the cooperating party, which are equivalent to any or all of those required for new and amended agreements for cooperation under section 123 a. of the 1954 Act, the President shall vigorously seek to obtain the application of such provisions with respect to such nuclear materials and equipment and such special nuclear material. Nothing in this Act or in the 1954 Act shall be deemed to relinquish any rights which the United States may have under any agreement for cooperation in force on the date of enactment of this Act.

(b) The President shall annually review each of requirements (1) through (9) set forth for inclusion in agreements for cooperation under section 123 a. of the 1954 Act and the export policy goals set forth in section 401 to determine whether it is in the interest of United States non-proliferation objectives for any such requirements or export policies which are not already being applied as export criteria to be enacted as additional export criteria.

(c) If the President proposed enactment of any such requirements or export policies as additional export criteria or to take any other action with respect to such requirements or export policy goals for the purpose of encouraging adherence by nations and groups of nations to such requirements and policies, he shall submit such a proposal together with an explanation thereof to the Congress.

(d) If the Committee on Foreign Relations of the Senate or the Committee on International Relations of the House of Representatives, after reviewing the President's annual report or any proposed legislation, determines that it is in the interest of the United States non-proliferation objectives to take any action with respect to such requirements or export policy goals, it shall report a joint

---

[20] 42 U.S.C. 2153c.

resolution to implement such determination. Any joint resolution so reported shall be considered in the Senate and the House of Representatives, respectively, under applicable procedures provided for the consideration of resolutions pursuant to subsection 130 b. through g. of the 1954 Act.

AUTHORITY TO CONTINUE AGREEMENTS

SEC. 405.[21] (a) The amendments to section 123 of the 1954 Act made by this Act shall not affect the authority to continue cooperation pursuant to agreements for cooperation entered into prior to the date of enactment of this Act.

Nothing in this Act shall affect the authority to include dispute settlement provisions, including arbitration, in any agreement made pursuant to an Agreement for Cooperation.

REVIEW

SEC. 406.[22] No court or regulatory body shall have any jurisdiction under any law to compel the performance of or to review the adequacy of the performance of any Nuclear Proliferation Assessment Statement called for in this Act or in the 1954 Act.

PROTECTION OF THE ENVIRONMENT

SEC. 407.[23] The President shall endeavor to provide in any agreement entered into pursuant to section 123 of the 1954 Act for cooperation between the parties in protecting the international environment from radioactive, chemical or thermal contamination arising from peaceful nuclear activities.

TITLE V—UNITED STATES ASSISTANCE TO DEVELOPING COUNTRIES

POLICY; REPORT

SEC. 501.[24] The United States shall endeavor to cooperate with other nations, international institutions, and private organizations in establishing programs to assist in the development of non-nuclear energy resources, to cooperate with both developing and industrialized nations in protecting the international environment from contamination arising from both nuclear and non-nuclear energy activities, and shall seek to cooperate with and aid developing countries in meeting their energy needs through the development of such resources and the application of non-nuclear technologies consistent with the economic factors, the material resources of those countries, and environmental protection. The United States

---

[21] 42 U.S.C. 2153d.
[22] 42 U.S.C. 2160a.
[23] 42 U.S.C. 2153e. Sec. 1913 of Public Law 95-630 (92 Stat. 3727) provided:
"SEC. 1913. No environmental rule, regulation, or procedure shall become effective with regard to exports subject to the provisions of 22 U.S.C. 3201 et seq., the Nuclear Non-Proliferation Act of 1978, until such time as the President has reported to Congress on the progress achieved pursuant to section 407 of the Act (42 U.S.C. 2153e) entitled 'Protection of the Environment' which requires the President to seek to provide, in agreements required under the Act, for cooperation between the parties in protecting the environment from radioactive, chemical or thermal contaminations arising from peaceful nuclear activities.".
[24] 42 U.S.C. 3261.

shall additionally seek to encourage other industrialized nations and groups of nations to make commitments for similar cooperation and aid to developing countries. The President shall report annually to Congress on the level of other nations' and groups of nations' commitments under such program and the relation of any such commitments to United States efforts under this title. In cooperating with and providing such assistance to developing countries, the United States shall give priority to parties to the Treaty.

PROGRAMS

SEC. 502.[25] (a) The United States shall initiate a program, consistent with the aims of section 501, to cooperate with developing countries for the purpose of—
    (1) meeting the energy needs required for the development of such countries;
    (2) reducing the dependence of such countries on petroleum fuels, with emphasis given to utilizing solar and other renewable energy resources; and
    (3) expanding the energy alternatives to such countries.

(b) Such program shall include cooperation in evaluating the energy alternatives of developing countries, facilitating international trade in energy commodities, developing energy resources, and applying suitable energy technologies. The program shall include both general and country-specific energy assessments and cooperative projects in resource exploration and production, training, research and development.

(c) As an integral part of such program, the Department of Energy, under the general policy guidance of the Department of State and in cooperation with the Agency for International Development and other Federal agencies as appropriate, shall initiate, as soon as practicable, a program for the exchange of United States scientists, technicians, and energy experts with those of developing countries to implement the purposes of this section.

(d) For the purposes of carrying out this section, there is authorized to be appropriated such sums as are contained in annual authorization Acts for the Department of Energy, including such sums which have been authorized for such purposes under previous legislation.

(e) Under the direction of the President, the Secretary of State shall ensure the coordination of the activities authorized by this title with other related activities of the United States conducted abroad, including the programs authorized by sections 103(c), 106(a)(2), and 119 of the Foreign Assistance Act of 1961.[26]

REPORT

SEC. 503.[27] Not later than twelve months after the date of enactment of this Act, the President shall report to the Congress on the

---

[25] 42 U.S.C. 3262.
[26] For text, see *Legislation on Foreign Relations Through 1992*, vol. I. Sec. 119 of the Foreign Assistance Act of 1961 was repealed in 1980.
[27] 42 U.S.C. 3262 note.

feasibility of expanding the cooperative activities established pursuant to section 502(c) into an international cooperative effort to include a scientific peace corps designed to encourage large numbers of technically trained volunteers to live and work in developing countries for varying periods of time for the purpose of engaging in projects to aid in meeting the energy needs of such countries through the search for and utilization of indigenous energy resources and the application of suitable technology, including the widespread utilization of renewable and unconventional energy technologies. Such report shall also include a discussion of other mechanisms to conduct a coordinated international effort to develop, demonstrate, and encourage the utilization of such technologies in developing countries.

TITLE VI—EXECUTIVE REPORTING

REPORTS OF THE PRESIDENT

SEC. 601.[28] (a) The President shall review all activities of Government departments and agencies relating to preventing proliferation and shall make a report to Congress in January of 1979 and annually in January of each year thereafter on the Government's efforts to prevent proliferation. This report shall include but not be limited to—

(1) a description of the progress made toward—

(A) negotiating the initiatives contemplated in sections 104 and 105 of this Act;

(B) negotiating the international arrangements or other mutual undertakings contemplated in section 403 of this Act;

(C) encouraging non-nuclear-weapon states that are not party to the Treaty to adhere to the Treaty or, pending such adherence, to enter into comparable agreements with respect to safeguards and to foreswear the development of any nuclear explosive devices, and discouraging nuclear exports to non-nuclear-weapon states which have not taken such steps;

(D) strengthening the safeguards of the IAEA as contemplated in section 201 of this Act; and

(E) renegotiating agreements for cooperation as contemplated in section 404(a) of this Act;

(2) an assessment of the impact of the progress described in paragraph (1) on the non-proliferation policy of the United States; an explanation of the precise reasons why progress has not been made on any particular point and recommendations with respect to appropriate measures to encourage progress; and a statement of what legislative modifications, if any, are necessary in his judgment to achieve the non-proliferation policy of the United States;

(3) a determination as to which non-nuclear-weapon states with which the United States has an agreement for cooperation in effect or under negotiation, if any, have—

---

[28] 22 U.S.C. 3231.

Sec. 602 NUCLEAR NON-PROLIFERATION (P.L. 95-242) 400

(A) detonated a nuclear device; or
(B) refused to accept the safeguards of the IAEA on all of their peaceful nuclear activities; or
(C) refused to give specific assurances that they will not manufacture or otherwise acquire any nuclear explosive device; or
(D) engaged in activities involving source or special nuclear material and having direct significance for the manufacture or acquisition of nuclear explosive devices;
(4) an assessment of whether any of the policies set forth in this Act have, on balance, been counterproductive from the standpoint of preventing proliferation; and
(5) a description of the progress made toward establishing procedures to facilitate the timely processing of requests for subsequent arrangements and export licenses in order to enhance the reliability of the United States in meeting its commitments to supply nuclear reactors and fuel to nations which adhere to effective non-proliferation policies.
(b) In the first report required by this section, the President shall analyze each civil agreement for cooperation negotiated pursuant to section 123 of the 1954 Act, and shall discuss the scope and adequacy of the requirements and obligations relating to safeguards and other controls therein.

ADDITIONAL REPORTS

SEC. 602.[29] (a) The annual reports to the Congress by the Commission and the Department of Energy which are otherwise required by law shall also include views and recommendations regarding the policies and actions of the United States to prevent proliferation which are the statutory responsibility of those agencies. The Department's report shall include a detailed analysis of the proliferation implications of advanced enrichment and reprocessing techniques, advanced reactors, and alternative nuclear fuel cycles. This part of the report shall include a comprehensive version which includes any relevant classified information and a summary unclassified version.
(b) The reporting requirements of this title are in addition to and not in lieu of any other reporting requirements under applicable law.
(c) The Department of State, the Department of Defense,[30] the Arms Control and Disarmament Agency, the Department of Commerce, the Department of Energy, and the Commission shall keep the Committees on Foreign Relations and Governmental Affairs of the Senate and the Committee on International Relations of the House of Representatives fully and currently informed with respect to their activities to carry out the purposes and policies of this Act and to otherwise prevent proliferation, and with respect to the current activities of foreign nations which are of significance from the proliferation standpoint.

---

[29] 22 U.S.C. 3282.
[30] The reference to the "Department of Defense" was added by Public Law 99-661 (100 Stat. 4004).

(d) Any classified portions of the reports required by this Act shall be submitted to the Senate Foreign Relations Committee and the House International Relations Committee.

(e) Three years after enactment of this Act, the Comptroller General shall complete a study and report to the Congress on the implementation and impact of this Act on the nuclear non-proliferation policies, purposes, and objectives of this Act. The Secretaries of State, Energy, Defense, and Commerce and the Commission and the Director shall cooperate with the Comptroller General in the conduct of the study. The report shall contain such recommendations as the Comptroller General deems necessary to support the nuclear non-proliferation policies, purposes, and objectives of this Act.

(f)[31] (1) The Secretary of Defense shall have access, on a timely basis, to all information regarding nuclear proliferation matters which the Secretary of State or the Secretary of Energy has or is entitled to have. Such access shall include access to all communications, materials, documents, and records relating to nuclear proliferation matters.

(2) This subsection does not apply to any intradepartmental document of the Department of State or the Department of Energy, or any portion of such document, that is solely concerned with internal, confidential advice on policy concerning the conduct of interagency deliberations on nuclear proliferation matters.

SAVING CLAUSE

SEC. 603.[32] (a) All orders, determinations, rules, regulations, permits, contracts, agreements, certificates, licenses, and privileges—

(1) which have been issued, made, granted, or allowed to become effective in the exercise of functions which are the subject of this Act, by (i) any agency or officer, or part thereof, in exercising the functions which are affected by this Act, or (ii) any court of competent jurisdiction, and

(2) which are in effect at the time this Act takes effect,

shall continue in effect according to their terms until modified, terminated, superseded, set aside, or repealed as the case may be, by the parties thereto or by any court of competent jurisdiction.

(b) Nothing in this Act shall affect the procedures or requirements applicable to agreements for cooperation entered into pursuant to section 91 c., 144 b., or 144 c. of the 1954 Act or arrangements pursuant thereto as it was in effect immediately prior to the date of enactment of this Act.

(c) Except where otherwise provided, the provisions of this Act shall take effect immediately upon enactment regardless of any requirement for the promulgation of regulations to implement such provisions.

---

[31] Subsec. (f) was added by sec. 1370 of Public Law 99-661 (100 Stat. 4004).
[32] 42 U.S.C. 2153f.

Export Administration Act of 1979 [1]

Public Law 96-72 [S. 737], 93 Stat. 503, approved September 29, 1979; as amended by Public Law 96-533 [International Security and Development Cooperation Act of 1980; H.R. 6942], 94 Stat. 3131 at 3157, approved December 16, 1980; Public Law 97-145 [Export Administration Act of 1981; H.R. 3567], 95 Stat. 1727, approved December 29, 1981; Public Law 98-108 [H.R. 3962], 97 Stat. 744, approved October 1, 1983; Public Law 98-207 [H.R. 4476], 97 Stat. 1391, approved December 5, 1983; Public Law 98-222 [H.R. 4956], 98 Stat. 36, approved February 29, 1984; Public Law 99-64 [Export Administration Amendments Act of 1985; S. 883], 99 Stat. 120, approved July 12, 1985; Public Law 99-399 [Omnibus Diplomatic Security and Antiterrorism Act of 1986; H.R. 4151], 100 Stat. 853, approved August 27, 1986; Public Law 99-633 [S. 2245], 100 Stat. 3522, approved November 7, 1986; Public Law 100-418 [Omnibus Trade and Competitiveness Act of 1988; H.R. 4848], 102 Stat. 1107, approved August 23, 1988; Public Law 100-449 [United States-Canada Free-Trade Agreement Implementation Act of 1988; H.R. 5090], 102 Stat. 1851, approved September 28, 1988; and by Public Law 101-222 [Anti-Terrorism and Arms Export Amendments Act of 1989; H.R. 91], 103 Stat. 1892, approved December 12, 1989

> NOTE.—The Export Administration Act of 1979 replaced the Export Administration Act of 1969, as amended, which expired on Sept. 30, 1979. The Export Administration Act of 1979 was comprehensively amended by the Export Administration Amendments Act of 1985 [Public Law 99-64; 99 Stat. 120]. The current text of the Act is reproduced below.

AN ACT To provide authority to regulate exports, to improve the efficiency of export regulation, and to minimize interference with the ability to engage in commerce.

EFFECT ON OTHER ACTS

SEC. 17.[61] (a) IN GENERAL.—Except as otherwise provided in this Act, nothing contained in this Act shall be construed to modify, repeal, supersede, or otherwise affect the provisions of any other laws authorizing control over exports of any commodity.

(b) COORDINATION OF CONTROLS.—The authority granted to the President under this Act shall be exercised in such manner as to achieve effective coordination with the authority exercised under section 38 of the Arms Export Control Act (22 U.S.C. 2778).

(c) CIVIL AIRCRAFT EQUIPMENT.—Notwithstanding any other provision of law, any product (1) which is standard equipment certified by the Federal Aviation Administration, in civil aircraft and is an integral part of such aircraft, and (2) which is to be exported to a country other than a controlled country, shall be subject to export controls exclusively under this Act. Any such product shall not be subject to controls under section 38(b)(2) of the Arms Export Control Act.

(d) NONPROLIFERATION CONTROLS.—(1) Nothing in section 5 or 6 of this Act shall be construed to supersede the procedures published by the President pursuant to section 309(c) of the Nuclear Non-Proliferation Act of 1978.

(2) With respect to any export license application which, under the procedures published by the President pursuant to section 309(c) of the Nuclear Non-Proliferation Act of 1978, is referred to the Subgroup on Nuclear Export Coordination or other interagency group, the provisions of section 10 of this Act shall apply with respect to such license application only to the extent that they are consistent with such published procedures, except that if the processing of any such application under such procedures is not completed within 180 days after the receipt of the application by the Secretary, the applicant shall have the rights of appeal and court action provided in section 10(j) of this Act.

(e) TERMINATION OF OTHER AUTHORITY.—On October 1, 1979, the Mutual Defense Assistance Control Act of 1951 (22 U.S.C. 1611-1613d), is superseded.

Export of Nuclear Material

(1) U.S. Exports of Low-Enriched Uranium Fuel

Public Law 96-280 [S.J. Res. 89], 94 Stat. 550, approved June 18, 1980

JOINT RESOLUTION Permitting the supply of additional low enriched uranium fuel under international agreements for cooperation in the civil uses of nuclear energy, and for other purposes.

Whereas the Nuclear Non-Proliferation Act of 1978 urges the United States to provide a reliable supply of nuclear fuel to those nations which adhere to policies designed to prevent the proliferation of nuclear weapons; and

Whereas the United States, in order to achieve the goals of that Act should be able to continue to supply low-enriched uranium fuel to nations that have entered into good faith negotiations as called for in section 404(a) of the Act; and

Whereas pending such negotiations, limitations now contained in certain agreements for cooperation on the amount of low-enriched uranium which may be supplied thereunder are insufficient to permit adequate assurance of supplies: Now, therefore, be it.

Resolved by the Senate and House of Representatives of the United States of America in Congress assembled,

SECTION 1.[1] Limits contained in agreements for cooperation on the amount of low-enriched uranium which may be transferred by or exported from the United States pursuant thereto shall not be construed to preclude transfer or export of amounts of low-enriched uranium in excess of such limits to nations which are parties to the Treaty on the Non-Proliferation of Nuclear Weapons.

SEC. 2.[1] (a) The terms used in this joint resolution shall have the meanings ascribed to them by the Atomic Energy Act of 1954 and by the Nuclear Non-Proliferation Act of 1978.

(b) The term "low-enriched uranium" means uranium enriched to less than 20 per centum in the isotope 235.

---

[1] 42 U.S.C. 2153c note.

PUBLIC LAW 97-351 [H.R. 5228]; October 18, 1982

CONVENTION ON THE PHYSICAL PROTECTION OF NUCLEAR MATERIAL IMPLEMENTATION ACT OF 1982

For Legislative History of Act, see p. 3229

An Act to amend title 18 of the United States Code to implement the Convention on the Physical Protection of Nuclear Material, and for other purposes.

Be it enacted by the Senate and House of Representatives of the United States of America in Congress assembled,

Convention on the Physical Protection of Nuclear Material Implementation Act of 1982. 18 USC 831 note.

SHORT TITLE

SECTION 1. This Act may be cited as the "Convention on the Physical Protection of Nuclear Material Implementation Act of 1982".

IMPLEMENTATION OF CONVENTION AND PROHIBITION OF RELATED OFFENSES

SEC. 2. (a) Chapter 39 of title 18 of the United States Code is amended by inserting after the table of sections at the beginning of such chapter the following new section:

"**§ 831. Prohibited transactions involving nuclear materials**

18 USC 831.

"(a) Whoever, if one of the circumstances described in subsection (c) of this section occurs—

"(1) without lawful authority, intentionally receives, possesses, uses, transfers, alters, disposes of, or disperses any nuclear material and—

"(A) thereby knowingly causes the death of or serious bodily injury to any person or substantial damage to property; or

"(B) knows that circumstances exist which are likely to cause the death of or serious bodily injury to any person or substantial damage to property;

"(2) with intent to deprive another of nuclear material, knowingly—

"(A) takes and carries away nuclear material of another without authority;

"(B) makes an unauthorized use, disposition, or transfer, of nuclear material belonging to another; or

"(C) uses fraud and thereby obtains nuclear material belonging to another;

"(3) knowingly—

"(A) uses force; or

"(B) threatens or places another in fear that any person other than the actor will imminently be subject to bodily injury;

and thereby takes nuclear material belonging to another from the person or presence of any other;

"(4) intentionally intimidates any person and thereby obtains nuclear material belonging to another;

"(5) with intent to compel any person, international organization, or governmental entity to do or refrain from doing any act, knowingly threatens to engage in conduct described in paragraph (2)(A) or (3) of this subsection;

"(6) knowingly threatens to use nuclear material to cause death or serious bodily injury to any person or substantial damage to property under circumstances in which the threat may reasonably be understood as an expression of serious purposes;

"(7) attempts to commit an offense under paragraph (1), (2), (3), or (4) of this subsection; or

"(8) is a party to a conspiracy of two or more persons to commit an offense under paragraph (1), (2), (3), or (4) of this subsection, if any of the parties intentionally engages in any conduct in furtherance of such offense;

shall be punished as provided in subsection (b) of this section.

"(b) The punishment for an offense under—

"(1) paragraphs (1) through (7) of subsection (a) of this section is—

"(A) a fine of not more than $250,000; and
"(B) imprisonment—

"(i) for any term of years or for life (I) if, while committing the offense, the offender knowingly causes the death of any person; or (II) if, while committing an offense under paragraph (1) or (3) of subsection (a) of this section, the offender, under circumstances manifesting extreme indifference to the life of an individual, knowingly engages in any conduct and thereby recklessly causes the death of or serious bodily injury to any person; and

"(ii) for not more than 20 years in any other case; and

"(2) paragraph (8) of subsection (a) of this section is—

"(A) a fine of not more than $250,000; and
"(B) imprisonment—

"(i) for not more than 20 years if the offense which is the object of the conspiracy is punishable under paragraph (1)(B)(i); and

"(ii) for not more than 10 years in any other case.

"(c) The circumstances referred to in subsection (a) of this section are that—

"(1) the offense is committed in the United States or the special maritime and territorial jurisdiction of the United States, or the special aircraft jurisdiction of the United States (as defined in section 101 of the Federal Aviation Act of 1958 (49 U.S.C. 1301));

"(2) the defendant is a national of the United States, as defined in section 101 of the Immigration and Nationality Act (8 U.S.C. 1101);

"(3) at the time of the offense the nuclear material is in use, storage, or transport, for peaceful purposes, and after the conduct required for the offense occurs the defendant is found in the United States, even if the conduct required for the offense occurs outside the United States; or

"(4) the conduct required for the offense occurs with respect to the carriage of a consignment of nuclear material for peaceful purposes by any means of transportation intended to go beyond the territory of the state where the shipment originates beginning with the departure from a facility of the shipper in that state and ending with the arrival at a facility of the receiver within the state of ultimate destination and either of such states is the United States.

"(d) The Attorney General may request assistance from the Secretary of Defense under chapter 18 of title 10 in the enforcement of this section and the Secretary of Defense may provide such assistance in accordance with chapter 18 of title 10, except that the Secretary of Defense may provide such assistance through any Department of Defense personnel. 10 USC 371 et seq.

"(e)(1) The Attorney General may also request assistance from the Secretary of Defense under this subsection in the enforcement of this section. Notwithstanding section 1385 of this title, the Secretary of Defense may, in accordance with other applicable law, provide such assistance to the Attorney General if— 18 USC 1385.

"(A) an emergency situation exists (as jointly determined by the Attorney General and the Secretary of Defense in their discretion); and

"(B) the provision of such assistance will not adversely affect the military preparedness of the United States (as determined by the Secretary of Defense in such Secretary's discretion).

"(3) As used in this subsection, the term 'emergency situation' means a circumstance— "Emergency situation."

"(A) that poses a serious threat to the interests of the United States; and

"(B) in which—

"(i) enforcement of the law would be seriously impaired if the assistance were not provided; and

"(ii) civilian law enforcement personnel are not capable of enforcing the law.

"(4) Assistance under this section may include—

"(A) use of personnel of the Department of Defense to arrest persons and conduct searches and seizures with respect to violations of this section; and

"(B) such other activity as is incidental to the enforcement of this section, or to the protection of persons or property from conduct that violates this section.

"(5) The Secretary of Defense may require reimbursement as a condition of assistance under this section.

"(6) The Attorney General may delegate the Attorney General's function under this subsection only to a Deputy, Associate, or Assistant Attorney General.

"(f) As used in this section— Definitions.

"(1) the term 'nuclear material' means material containing any—

"(A) plutonium with an isotopic concentration not in excess of 80 percent plutonium 238;

"(B) uranium not in the form of ore or ore residue that contains the mixture of isotopes as occurring in nature;

"(C) uranium that contains the isotope 233 or 235 or both in such amount that the abundance ratio of the sum of those isotopes to the isotope 238 is greater than the ratio of the isotope 235 to the isotope 238 occurring in nature; or

"(D) uranium 233;

"(2) the term 'international organization' means a public international organization designated as such pursuant to section 1 of the International Organizations Immunities Act (22

U.S.C. 288) or a public organization created pursuant to treaty or other agreement under international law as an instrument through or by which two or more foreign governments engage in some aspect of their conduct of international affairs;

"(3) the term 'serious bodily injury' means bodily injury which involves—

"(A) a substantial risk of death;
"(B) extreme physical pain;
"(C) protracted and obvious disfigurement; or
"(D) protracted loss or impairment of the function of a bodily member, organ, or mental faculty; and

"(4) the term 'bodily injury' means—

"(A) a cut, abrasion, bruise, burn, or disfigurement;
"(B) physical pain;
"(C) illness;
"(D) impairment of a function of a bodily member, organ, or mental faculty; or
"(E) any other injury to the body, no matter how temporary.".

(b) The table of sections for chapter 39 of title 18 of the United States Code is amended by striking out the items relating to sections 831 through 835 and inserting in lieu thereof the following:

"831. Prohibited transactions involving nuclear materials.".

AMENDMENT TO DEFINITION OF INTERNATIONAL ORGANIZATIONS USED IN DEFINING OFFENSES AGAINST INTERNATIONALLY PROTECTED PERSONS

SEC. 3. Section 1116(b)(5) of title 18 of the United States Code is amended by inserting before the period the following: "or a public organization created pursuant to treaty or other agreement under international law as an instrument through or by which two or more foreign governments engage in some aspect of their conduct of international affairs".

Approved October 18, 1982.

LEGISLATIVE HISTORY—H.R. 5228 (S. 1446):

HOUSE REPORT No. 97-624 (Comm. on the Judiciary).
CONGRESSIONAL RECORD, Vol. 128 (1982):
    July 19, 20, considered and passed House.
    Sept. 14, considered and passed Senate, amended.
    Sept. 28, House concurred in Senate amendment No. 1; disagreed to certain amendments; concurred in others with amendments.
    Oct. 1, Senate concurred in House amendments and receded from its disagreements.
WEEKLY COMPILATION OF PRESIDENTIAL DOCUMENTS, Vol. 18, No. 42 (1982):
    Oct. 19, Presidential statement.

Nuclear Waste Policy Act of 1982

Partial text of Public Law 97-425 [H.R. 3809], 96 Stat. 2201, approved January 7, 1983

AN ACT To provide for the development of repositories for the disposal of high-level radioactive waste and spent nuclear fuel, to establish a program of research, development, and demonstration regarding the disposal of high-level radioactive waste and spent nuclear fuel, and for other purposes.

Be it enacted by the Senate and House of Representatives of the United States of America in Congress assembled,

* * * * * * *

TECHNICAL ASSISTANCE TO NON-NUCLEAR WEAPON STATES IN THE FIELD OF SPENT FUEL STORAGE AND DISPOSAL

SEC. 223.[1] (a) It shall be the policy of the United States to cooperate with and provide technical assistance to non-nuclear weapon states in the field of spent fuel storage and disposal.

(b)(1) Within 90 days of enactment of this Act, the Secretary and the Commission shall publish a joint notice in the Federal Register stating that the United States is prepared to cooperate with and provide technical assistance to non-nuclear weapon states in the fields of at-reactor spent fuel storage; away-from-reactor spent fuel storage; monitored, retrievable spent fuel storage; geologic disposal of spent fuel; and the health, safety, and environmental regulation of such activities. The notice shall summarize the resources that can be made available for international cooperation and assistance in these fields through existing programs of the Department and the Commission, including the availability of: (i) data from past or ongoing research and development projects; (ii) consultations with expert Department or Commission personnel or contractors; and (iii) liaison with private business entities and organizations working in these fields.

(2) The joint notice described in the preceding subparagraph shall be updated and reissued annually for 5 succeeding years.

(c) Following publication of the annual joint notice referred to in paragraph (2), the Secretary of State shall inform the governments of non-nuclear weapon states and, as feasible, the organizations operating nuclear powerplants in such states, that the United States is prepared to cooperate with and provide technical assistance to non-nuclear weapon states in the fields of spent fuel storage and disposal, as set forth in the joint notice. The Secretary of State shall also solicit expressions of interest from non-nuclear weapon state governments and non-nuclear weapon state nuclear power reactor operators concerning their participation in expanded United States cooperation and technical assistance programs in these fields. The Secretary of State shall transmit any such expressions of interest to the Department and the Commission.

(d) With his budget presentation materials for the Department and the Commission for fiscal years 1984 through 1989, the President shall include funding requests for an expanded program of cooperation and technical assistance with non-nuclear weapon states in the fields of spent fuel storage and disposal as appropriate in light of expressions of interest in such cooperation and assistance on the part of non-nuclear weapon state governments and non-nuclear weapon state power reactor operators.

(e) For the purposes of this subsection, the term "non-nuclear weapon state" shall have the same meaning as that set forth in article IX of the Treaty on the Non-Proliferation of Nuclear Weapons (21 U.S.C. 438).[2]

(f) Nothing in this subsection shall authorize the Department or the Commission to take any action not authorized under existing law.

PUBLIC LAW 99-183 [S.J. Res. 238]; December 16, 1985

AGREEMENT FOR NUCLEAR COOPERATION BETWEEN THE UNITED STATES AND CHINA

Joint Resolution relating to the approval and implementation of the proposed agreement for nuclear cooperation between the United States and the People's Republic of China.

Energy.

Resolved by the Senate and House of Representatives of the United States of America in Congress assembled, That (a)(1) the Congress does favor the Agreement for Cooperation Between the Government of the United States of America and the Government of the People's Republic of China Concerning Peaceful Uses of Nuclear Energy, done on July 23, 1985 (hereafter in this joint resolution referred to as the "Agreement").

Ante, p. 159.

(2) Notwithstanding section 123 of the Atomic Energy Act of 1954, the Agreement becomes effective in accordance with the provisions of this joint resolution and other applicable provisions of law.

Exports.

(b) Notwithstanding any other provision of law or any international agreement, no license may be issued for export to the People's Republic of China of any nuclear material, facilities, or components subject to the Agreement, and no approval for the transfer or retransfer to the People's Republic of China of any nuclear material, facilities, or components subject to the Agreement shall be given—

    (1) until the expiration of a period of thirty days of continuous session of Congress after the President has certified to the Congress that—

        (A) the reciprocal arrangements made pursuant to Article 8 of the Agreement have been designed to be effective in ensuring that any nuclear material, facilities, or components provided under the Agreement shall be utilized solely for intended peaceful purposes as set forth in the Agreement;

        (B) the Government of the People's Republic of China has provided additional information concerning its nuclear nonproliferation policies and that, based on this and all other information available to the United States Government, the People's Republic of China is not in violation of paragraph

42 USC 2158.

        (2) of section 129 of the Atomic Energy Act of 1954; and

        (C) the obligation to consider favorably a request to carry out activities described in Article 5(2) of the Agreement shall not prejudice the decision of the United States to approve or disapprove such a request; and

President of U.S. Report.

    (2) until the President has submitted to the Speaker of the House of Representatives and the chairman of the Committee on Foreign Relations of the Senate a report detailing the history and current developments in the nonproliferation policies and practices of the People's Republic of China.

The report described in paragraph (2) shall be submitted in unclassified form with a classified addendum.

99 STAT. 1174

Dec. 16   U.S.—CHINA NUCLEAR AGREEMENT   P.L. 99-183

(c) Each proposed export pursuant to the Agreement shall be subject to United States laws and regulations in effect at the time of each such export.

Exports.

(d) Nothing in the Agreement or this joint resolution may be construed as providing a precedent or other basis for the negotiation or renegotiation of any other agreement for nuclear cooperation.

(e) For purposes of subsection (b)—
   (1) the continuity of a session of Congress is broken only by adjournment of the Congress sine die at the end of a Congress; and
   (2) the days on which either House is not in session because of an adjournment of more than three days to a day certain are excluded in the computation of the period indicated.

Approved December 16, 1985.

Diplomatic Security and Anti-Terrorism [1]

Anti-Terrorism Act of 1987

Partial text of Public Law 100-204 [Foreign Relations Authorization Act, Fiscal Years 1988 and 1989; H.R. 1777], 101 Stat. 1406, approved December 22, 1987

AN ACT To authorize appropriations for fiscal years 1988 and 1989 for the Department of State, the U.S. Information Agency, the Voice of America, the Board for International Broadcasting, and for other purposes.

Be it enacted by the Senate and House of Representatives of the United States of America in Congress assembled,

* * * * * *

TITLE VI—INTERNATIONAL NUCLEAR TERRORISM

SEC. 601.[39] ACTIONS TO COMBAT INTERNATIONAL NUCLEAR TERRORISM.

(a) ACTIONS TO BE TAKEN BY THE PRESIDENT.—The Congress hereby directs the President—

(1) to seek universal adherence to the Convention on the Physical Protection of Nuclear Material;

(2) to—

(A) conduct a review, enlisting the participation of all relevant departments and agencies of the Government, to determine whether the recommendations on Physical Protection of Nuclear Material published by the International Atomic Energy Agency are adequate to deter theft, sabotage, and the use of nuclear facilities and materials in acts of international terrorism, and

(B) transmit the results of this review to the Director-General of the International Atomic Energy Agency;

(3) to take, in concert with United States allies and other countries, such steps as may be necessary—

(A) to keep to a minimum the amount of weapons-grade nuclear material in international transit, and

(B) to ensure that when any such material is transported internationally, it is under the most effective means for adequately protecting it from acts or attempted acts of sabotage or theft by terrorist groups or nations; and

(4) to seek agreement in the United Nations Security Council to establish—

(A) an effective regime of international sanctions against any nation or subnational group which conducts or sponsors acts of international nuclear terrorism, and

(B) measures for coordinating responses to all acts of international nuclear terrorism, including measures for the recovery of stolen nuclear material and the clean-up of nuclear releases.

(b) REPORTS TO THE CONGRESS.—The President shall report to the Congress annually, in the reports required by section 601 of the Nuclear Non-Proliferation Act of 1978 (22 U.S.C. 3281), on the progress made during the preceding year in achieving the objectives described in this section.

* * * * * * *

SEC. 604. REVIEW OF PHYSICAL SECURITY STANDARDS.

(a) REVIEWS.—The Secretary of Energy, the Secretary of Defense, the Secretary of State, the Director of the Arms Controls and Disarmament Agency, and the Nuclear Regulatory Commission shall each review the adequacy of the physical security standards currently applicable with respect to the shipment and storage (outside the United States) of plutonium, and uranium enriched to more than 20 percent in the isotope 233 or the isotope 235, which is subject to United States prior consent rights, with special attention to protection against risks of seizure or other terrorist acts.

---

[39] 22 U.S.C. 2244.

(b) REPORTS.—Not later than 6 months after the date of enactment of this Act, the Secretary of Energy, the Secretary of Defense, the Secretary of State, the Director of the Arms Control and Disarmament Agency, and the Nuclear Regulatory Commission shall each submit a written report to the Committee on Foreign Affairs of the House of Representatives and the Committee on Foreign Relations of the Senate setting forth the results of the review conducted pursuant to this section, together with appropriate recommendations.

SEC. 605. INTERNATIONAL REVIEW OF THE NUCLEAR TERRORISM PROBLEM.

The Congress strongly urges the President to seek a comprehensive review of the problem of nuclear terrorism by an international conference.

* * * * * * *

TITLE VII—MULTILATERAL COOPERATION TO COMBAT INTERNATIONAL TERRORISM

SEC. 701. INTERNATIONAL ANTITERRORISM COMMITTEE.

(a) FINDINGS.—The Congress finds that—

(1) international terrorism is and remains a serious threat to the peace and security of free, democratic nations;

(2) the challenge of terrorism can only by met effectively by concerted action on the part of all responsible nations;

(3) the major developed democracies evidenced their commitment to cooperation in the fight against terrorism by the 1978 Bonn Economic Summit Declaration on Terrorism; and

(4) that commitment was renewed and strengthened at the 1986 Tokyo Economic Summit and expressed in a joint statement on terrorism.

(b) INTERNATIONAL ANTITERRORISM COMMITTEE—The Congress hereby directs the President to continue to seek the establishment of an international committee, to be known as the International Antiterrorism Committee. As a first step in establishing such committee, the President should propose to the North Atlantic Treaty Organization the establishment of a standing political committee to examine all aspects of international terrorism, review opportunities for cooperation, and make recommendations to member nations. After the establishment of this committee, the President should invite such other countries who may choose to participate. The purpose of the International Antiterrorism Committee should be to focus the attention and secure the cooperation of the governments and the public of the participating countries and of other countries on the problems and responses to international terrorism (including nuclear terrorism), by serving as a forum at both the political and law enforcement levels.

NATIONAL DEFENSE AUTHORIZATION ACT FOR FISCAL YEAR 1994 (P.L. 103-160)
(Excerpts)

SEC. 1163. SENSE OF CONGRESS REGARDING UNITED STATES POLICY ON PLUTONIUM.

(a) FINDING.—The Congress finds that reprocessing spent nuclear fuel referred to in subsection (c) to recover plutonium may pose serious environmental hazards and increase the risk of proliferation of weapons-usable plutonium.

(b) SENSE OF CONGRESS.—It is the sense of the Congress that the President should take action to encourage the reduction or cessation of the reprocessing of spent nuclear fuel referred to in subsection (c) to recover plutonium until the environmental and proliferation concerns related to such reprocessing are resolved.

(c) COVERED SPENT NUCLEAR FUEL.—The spent nuclear fuel referred to in subsections (a) and (b) is spent nuclear fuel used in a commercial nuclear power reactor by the Government of a foreign country or by a foreign-owned or foreign-controlled entity.

TITLE XII—COOPERATIVE THREAT REDUCTION WITH STATES OF FORMER SOVIET UNION

SEC. 1201. SHORT TITLE.

This title may be cited as the "Cooperative Threat Reduction Act of 1993".

SEC. 1202. FINDINGS ON COOPERATIVE THREAT REDUCTION.

The Congress finds that it is in the national security interest of the United States for the United States to do the following:

(1) Facilitate, on a priority basis, the transportation, storage, safeguarding, and elimination of nuclear and other weapons of the independent states of the former Soviet Union, including—

(A) the safe and secure storage of fissile materials derived from the elimination of nuclear weapons;

(B) the dismantlement of (i) intercontinental ballistic missiles and launchers for such missiles, (ii) submarine-launched ballistic missiles and launchers for such missiles, and (iii) heavy bombers; and

(C) the elimination of chemical, biological and other weapons capabilities.

(2) Facilitate, on a priority basis, the prevention of proliferation of weapons (and components of weapons) of mass destruction and destabilizing conventional weapons of the independent states of the former Soviet Union and the establishment of verifiable safeguards against the proliferation of such weapons and components.

(3) Facilitate, on a priority basis, the prevention of diversion of weapons-related scientific expertise of the independent states of the former Soviet Union to terrorist groups or third countries.

(4) Support (A) the demilitarization of the defense-related industry and equipment of the independent states of the former Soviet Union, and (B) the conversion of such industry and equipment to civilian purposes and uses.

(5) Expand military-to-military and defense contacts between the United States and the independent states of the former Soviet Union.

SEC. 1203. AUTHORITY FOR PROGRAMS TO FACILITATE COOPERATIVE THREAT REDUCTION.

(a) IN GENERAL.—Notwithstanding any other provision of law, the President may conduct programs described in subsection (b) to assist the independent states of the former Soviet Union in the demilitarization of the former Soviet Union. Any such program may be carried out only to the extent that the President determines that the program will directly contribute to the national security interests of the United States.

(b) AUTHORIZED PROGRAMS.—The programs referred to in subsection (a) are the following:

(1) Programs to facilitate the elimination, and the safe and secure transportation and storage, of nuclear, chemical, and other weapons and their delivery vehicles.

(2) Programs to facilitate the safe and secure storage of fissile materials derived from the elimination of nuclear weapons.

(3) Programs to prevent the proliferation of weapons, weapons components, and weapons-related technology and expertise.

(4) Programs to expand military-to-military and defense contacts.

(5) Programs to facilitate the demilitarization of defense industries and the conversion of military technologies and capabilities into civilian activities.

(6) Programs to assist in the environmental restoration of former military sites and installations when such restoration is necessary to the demilitarization or conversion programs authorized in paragraph (5).

(7) Programs to provide housing for former military personnel of the former Soviet Union released from military service in connection with the dismantlement of strategic nuclear weapons, when provision of such housing is necessary for dismantlement of strategic nuclear weapons and when no other funds are available for such housing.

(8) Other programs as described in section 212(b) of the Soviet Nuclear Threat Reduction Act of 1991 (title II of Public Law 102–228; 22 U.S.C. 2551 note) and section 1412(b) of the

Former Soviet Union Demilitarization Act of 1992 (title XIV of Public Law 102-484; 22 U.S.C. 5901 et seq.).

(c) UNITED STATES PARTICIPATION.—The programs described in subsection (b) should, to the extent feasible, draw upon United States technology and expertise, especially from the private sector of the United States.

(d) RESTRICTIONS.—Assistance authorized by subsection (a) may not be provided to any independent state of the former Soviet Union for any year unless the President certifies to Congress for that year that the proposed recipient state is committed to each of the following:

(1) Making substantial investment of its resources for dismantling or destroying its weapons of mass destruction, if such state has an obligation under a treaty or other agreement to destroy or dismantle any such weapons.

(2) Foregoing any military modernization program that exceeds legitimate defense requirements and foregoing the replacement of destroyed weapons of mass destruction.

(3) Foregoing any use in new nuclear weapons of fissionable or other components of destroyed nuclear weapons.

(4) Facilitating United States verification of any weapons destruction carried out under this title, section 1412(b) of the Former Soviet Union Demilitarization Act of 1992 (title XIV of Public Law 102-484; 22 U.S.C. 590(b)), or section 212(b) of the Soviet Nuclear Threat Reduction Act of 1991 (title II of Public Law 102-228; 22 U.S.C. 2551 note).

(5) Complying with all relevant arms control agreements.

(6) Observing internationally recognized human rights, including the protection of minorities.

TITLE XVI—ARMS CONTROL MATTERS

Subtitle A—Programs in Support of the Prevention and Control of Proliferation of Weapons of Mass Destruction

SEC. 1601. STUDY OF GLOBAL PROLIFERATION OF STRATEGIC AND ADVANCED CONVENTIONAL MILITARY WEAPONS AND RELATED EQUIPMENT AND TECHNOLOGY.

(a) STUDY.—The President shall conduct a study of (1) the factors that contribute to the proliferation of strategic and advanced conventional military weapons and related equipment and technologies, and (2) the policy options that are available to the United States to inhibit such proliferation.

(b) CONDUCT OF STUDY.—In carrying out the study the President shall do the following:

(1) Identify those factors contributing to global weapons proliferation which can be most effectively regulated.

(2) Identify and assess policy approaches available to the United States to discourage the transfer of strategic and advanced conventional military weapons and related equipment and technology.

(3) Assess the effectiveness of current multilateral efforts to control the transfer of such military weapons and equipment and such technology.

(4) Identify and examine methods by which the United States could reinforce these multilateral efforts to discourage the transfer of such weapons and equipment and such tech-

nology, including placing conditions on assistance provided by the United States to other nations.

(5) Identify the circumstances under which United States national security interests might best be served by a transfer of conventional military weapons and related equipment and technology, and specifically assess whether such circumstances exist when such a transfer is made to an allied country which, with the United States, has mutual national security interests to be served by such a transfer.

(6) Assess the effect on the United States economy and the national technology and industrial base (as defined by section 2491(1) of title 10, United States Code) which might result from potential changes in United States policy controlling the transfer of such military weapons and related equipment and the technology.

(c) ADVISORY BOARD.—(1) Within 15 days after the date of the enactment of this Act, the President shall establish an Advisory Board on Arms Proliferation Policy. The advisory board shall be composed of 5 members. The President shall appoint the members from among persons in private life who are noted for their stature and expertise in matters covered by the study required under subsection (a) and shall ensure, in making the appointments, that the advisory board is composed of members from diverse backgrounds. The President shall designate one of the members as chairman of the advisory board.

(2) The President is encouraged—

(A) to obtain the advice of the advisory board regarding the matters studied pursuant to subsection (a) and to consider that advice in carrying out the study; and

(B) to ensure that the advisory board is informed in a timely manner and on a continuing basis of the results of policy reviews carried out under the study by persons outside the board.

(3) The members of the advisory board shall receive no pay for serving on the advisory board. However, the members shall be allowed travel expenses and per diem in accordance with the regulations referred to in paragraph (6).

(4) Upon request of the chairman of the advisory board, the Secretary of Defense or the head of any other Federal department or agency may detail, without reimbursement for costs, any of the personnel of the department or agency to the advisory board to assist the board in carrying out its duties.

(5) The Secretary of Defense shall designate a federally funded research and development center with expertise in the matters covered by the study required under subsection (a) to provide the advisory board with such support services as the advisory board may need to carry out its duties.

(6) Except as otherwise provided in this section, the provisions of the Federal Advisory Committee Act (5 U.S.C. App.), and the regulations prescribed by the Administrator of General Services pursuant to that Act, shall apply to the advisory board. Subsections (e) and (f) of section 10 of such Act do not apply to the advisory board.

(7) The advisory board shall terminate 30 days after the date on which the President submits the final report of the advisory board to Congress pursuant to subsection (d)(2)(B).

(d) REPORTS.—(1) The Advisory Board on Arms Proliferation Policy shall submit to the President, not later than May 15, 1994, a report containing its findings, conclusions, and recommendations on the matters covered by the study carried out pursuant to subsection (a).

(2) The President shall submit to Congress, not later than June 1, 1994—

(A) a report on the study carried out pursuant to subsection (a), including the President's findings and conclusions regarding the matters considered in the study; and

(B) the report of the Advisory Board on Arms Proliferation Policy received under paragraph (1), together with the comments, if any, of the President on that report.

SEC. 1602. EXTENSION OF EXISTING AUTHORITIES.

(a) EXTENSION TO FISCAL YEAR 1994.—Section 1505 of the National Defense Authorization Act for Fiscal Year 1993 (22 U.S.C. 5859a) is amended by striking out "fiscal year 1993" in subsections (a), (d)(1), and (e) and inserting in lieu thereof "fiscal year 1994".

(b) FUNDING.—Subsection (d)(3) of such section is amended—

(1) by striking out "40,000,000" and inserting in lieu thereof "$25,000,000, including funds used for activities of the On-Site Inspection Agency in support of the United Nations Special Commission on Iraq"; and

(2) by striking out the second sentence.

(c) REPEAL OF NOTICE-AND-WAIT REQUIREMENT.—Subsection (d) of such section is further amended by striking out paragraph (4).

SEC. 1603. STUDIES RELATING TO UNITED STATES COUNTERPROLIFERATION POLICY.

(a) AUTHORIZATION TO CONDUCT STUDIES.—During fiscal year 1994, the Secretary of Defense may conduct studies and analysis programs in support of counterproliferation policy of the United States.

(b) COUNTERPROLIFERATION STUDIES.—Studies and analysis programs under this section may include programs intended to explore defense policy issues that might be involved in efforts to prevent and counter the proliferation of weapons of mass destruction and their delivery systems. Such efforts include—

(1) enhancing United States military capabilities to deter and respond to terrorism, theft, and proliferation involving weapons of mass destruction;

(2) cooperating in international programs to enhance military capabilities to deter and respond to terrorism, theft, and proliferation involving weapons of mass destruction; and

(3) otherwise contributing to Department of Defense capabilities to deter, identify, monitor, and respond to such terrorism, theft, and proliferation involving weapons of mass destruction.

(c) DESIGNATION OF COORDINATOR.—The Under Secretary of Defense for Policy, subject to the supervision and control of the Secretary of Defense, shall coordinate the policy studies and analysis of the Department of Defense on countering proliferation of weapons of mass destruction and their delivery systems.

(d) FUNDS.—Funds for programs authorized in this section shall be derived from amounts made available to the Department of Defense for fiscal year 1994 or from balances in working capital accounts of the Department of Defense. The total amount expended for fiscal year 1994 to carry out studies and analysis programs under subsection (a) may not exceed $6,000,000.

(e) RESTRICTION.—None of the funds referred to in subsection (d) shall be available for the purposes stated in this section until 15 days after the date on which the Secretary of Defense submits to the appropriate congressional committees a report setting forth—

    (1) a description of all of the activities within the Department of Defense that are being carried out or are to be carried out for the purposes stated in this section;

    (2) the plan for coordinating and integrating those activities within the Department of Defense;

    (3) the plan for coordinating and integrating those activities with those of other Federal agencies; and

    (4) the sources of the funds to be used for such purposes.

(f) REPORT.—Not later than April 30 of each year, and not later than October 30 of each year, the Secretary of Defense shall submit to the appropriate congressional committees a report on the activities carried out under subsection (a). Each report shall set forth for the six-month period ending on the last day of the month preceding the month in which the report is due the following:

    (1) A description of the studies and analysis carried out.

    (2) The amounts spent for such studies and analysis.

    (3) The organizations that conducted the studies and analysis.

    (4) An explanation of the extent to which such studies and analysis contributes to the counterproliferation policy of the United States and United States military capabilities to deter and respond to terrorism, theft, and proliferation involving weapons of mass destruction.

    (5) A description of the measures being taken to ensure that such studies and analysis within the Department of Defense is managed effectively and coordinated comprehensively.

SEC. 1604. SENSE OF CONGRESS REGARDING UNITED STATES CAPABILITIES TO PREVENT AND COUNTER WEAPONS PROLIFERATION.

It is the sense of Congress that—

    (1) the United States should have the ability to counter effectively potential threats to United States interests that arise from the proliferation of such weapons;

    (2) the Department of Defense, the Department of State, the Department of Energy, the Arms Control and Disarmament Agency, and the intelligence community have important roles, as well as unique capabilities and expertise, in preventing the proliferation of weapons of mass destruction and dealing with the consequences of any proliferation of such weapons, including capabilities and expertise regarding—

        (A) detection and monitoring of proliferation of weapons of mass destruction;

        (B) development of effective export control regimes;

(C) interdiction and destruction of weapons of mass destruction and related weapons material; and

(D) carrying out international monitoring and inspection regimes that relate to proliferation of such weapons and material;

(3) the Department of Defense, the Department of Energy, and the intelligence community have unique capabilities and expertise that contribute directly to the ability of the United States to implement United States policy to counter effectively the threats that arise from the proliferation of weapons of mass destruction, including capabilities and expertise regarding—

(A) responses to terrorism, theft, or accidents involving weapons of mass destruction;

(B) conduct of intrusive international inspections for verification of arms control treaties;

(C) direct and discrete counterproliferation actions that require use of force; and

(D) development and deployment of active military countermeasures and protective measures against threats resulting from arms proliferation, including defenses against ballistic missile attacks; and

(4) the United States should continue to maintain and improve its capabilities to identify, monitor, and respond to the proliferation of weapons of mass destruction and delivery systems for such weapons.

SEC. 1605. JOINT COMMITTEE FOR REVIEW OF PROLIFERATION PROGRAMS OF THE UNITED STATES.

(a) ESTABLISHMENT.—(1) There is hereby established a Non-Proliferation Program Review Committee composed of the following members:

(A) The Secretary of Defense.
(B) The Secretary of State.
(C) The Secretary of Energy.
(D) The Director of Central Intelligence.
(E) The Director of the United States Arms Control and Disarmament Agency.
(F) The Chairman of the Joint Chiefs of Staff.

(2) The Secretary of Defense shall chair the committee.

(3) A member of the committee may designate a representative to perform routinely the duties of the member. A representative shall be in a position of Deputy Assistant Secretary or a position equivalent to or above the level of Deputy Assistant Secretary. A representative of the Chairman of the Joint Chiefs of Staff shall be a person in a grade equivalent to that of Deputy Assistant Secretary of Defense.

(4) The Secretary of Defense may delegate to the Under Secretary of Defense for Acquisition and Technology the performance of the duties of the Chairman of the committee.

(5) The members of the committee shall first meet not later than 30 days after the date of the enactment of this Act. Upon designation of working level officials and representatives, the members of the committee shall jointly notify the appropriate committees of Congress that the committee has been constituted. The notification shall

identify the representatives designated pursuant to paragraph (3) and the working level officials of the committee.

(b) PURPOSES OF THE COMMITTEE.—The purposes of the committee are as follows:

(1) To optimize funding for, and ensure the development and deployment of—

(A) highly effective technologies and capabilities for the detection, monitoring, collection, processing, analysis, and dissemination of information in support of United States nonproliferation policy; and

(B) disabling technologies in support of such policy.

(2) To identify and eliminate undesirable redundancies or uncoordinated efforts in the development and deployment of such technologies and capabilities.

(c) DUTIES.—The committee shall—

(1) identify and review existing and proposed capabilities (including counterproliferation capabilities) and technologies for support of United States nonproliferation policy with regard to—

(A) intelligence;
(B) battlefield surveillance;
(C) passive defenses;
(D) active defenses;
(E) counterforce capabilities;
(F) inspection support; and
(G) support of export control programs;

(2) as part of the review pursuant to paragraph (1), review all directed energy and laser programs for detecting, characterizing, or interdicting weapons of mass destruction, their delivery platforms, or other orbiting platforms with a view to the elimination of redundancy and the optimization of funding for the systems not eliminated;

(3) review the programs (including the crisis management program) developed by the Department of State to counter terrorism involving weapons of mass destruction and their delivery systems;

(4) prescribe requirements and priorities for the development and deployment of highly effective capabilities and technologies to support fully the nonproliferation policy of the United States;

(5) identify deficiencies in existing capabilities and technologies;

(6) formulate near-term, mid-term, and long-term programmatic options for meeting requirements established by the committee and eliminating deficiencies identified by the committee; and

(7) in carrying out the other duties of the committee, ensure that all types of counterproliferation actions are considered.

(d) ACCESS TO INFORMATION.—The committee shall have access to information on all programs, projects, and activities of the Department of Defense, the Department of State, the Department of Energy, the intelligence community, and the Arms Control and Disarmament Agency that are pertinent to the purposes and duties of the committee.

(e) BUDGET RECOMMENDATIONS.—The committee may submit to the officials referred to in subsection (a) any recommendation regarding existing or planned budgets as the committee considers appropriate to encourage funding for capabilities and technologies at the level necessary to support United States nonproliferation policy.

(f) TERMINATION OF COMMITTEE.—The committee shall cease to exist six months after the date on which the report of the Secretary of Defense under section 1605 is submitted to Congress.

SEC. 1606. REPORT ON NONPROLIFERATION AND COUNTERPROLIFERATION ACTIVITIES AND PROGRAMS.

(a) REPORT REQUIRED.—Not later than May 1, 1994, the Secretary of Defense shall submit to Congress a report on the findings of the committee on nonproliferation activities established by section 1604.

(b) CONTENT OF REPORT.—The report shall include the following matters:

(1) A complete list, by program, of the existing, planned, and proposed capabilities and technologies reviewed by the committee, including all directed energy and laser programs reviewed pursuant to section 1604(c)(2).

(2) A complete description of the requirements and priorities established by the committee.

(3) A comprehensive discussion of the near-term, mid-term, and long-term programmatic options formulated by the committee for meeting requirements prescribed by the committee and eliminating deficiencies identified by the committee, including the annual funding requirements and completion dates established for each such option.

(4) An explanation of the recommendations made pursuant to section 1604(e) and a full discussion of the actions taken on such recommendations, including the actions taken to implement the recommendations.

(5) A discussion of the existing and planned capabilities of the Department of Defense—

(A) to detect and monitor clandestine programs for the acquisition or production of weapons of mass destruction;

(B) to respond to terrorism or accidents involving such weapons and thefts of materials related to any weapon of mass destruction; and

(C) to assist in the interdiction and destruction of weapons of mass destruction, related weapons materials, and advanced conventional weapons.

(6) A description of—

(A) the extent to which the Secretary of Defense has incorporated nonproliferation and counterproliferation missions into the overall missions of the unified combatant commands; and

(B) how the special operations command established pursuant to section 167(a) of title 10, United States Code, might support the commanders of the other unified combatant commands and the commanders of the specified combatant commands in the performance of such overall missions.

(c) FORMS OF REPORT.—The report shall be submitted in both unclassified and classified forms, as appropriate.

SEC. 1607. DEFINITIONS.

For purposes of this subtitle:
(1) The term "appropriate congressional committees" means—
(A) the Committee on Armed Services, the Committee on Appropriations, the Committee on Foreign Relations, and the Select Committee on Intelligence of the Senate; and
(B) the Committee on Armed Services, the Committee on Appropriations, the Committee on Foreign Affairs, and the Permanent Select Committee on Intelligence of the House of Representatives.
(2) The term "intelligence community" has the meaning given such term in section 3 of the National Security Act of 1947 (50 U.S.C. 401a).

Subtitle B—International Nonproliferation Activities

SEC. 1611. NUCLEAR NONPROLIFERATION.

(a) FINDINGS.—The Congress finds the following:
(1) The United States has been seeking to contain the spread of nuclear weapons technology and materials.
(2) With the end of the Cold War and the breakup of the Soviet Union, the proliferation of nuclear weapons is now a leading military threat to the national security of the United States and its allies.
(3) The United Nations Security Council declared on January 31, 1992, that "proliferation of all weapons of mass destruction constitutes a threat to international peace and security" and committed to taking appropriate action to prevent proliferation from occurring.
(4) Aside from the five declared nuclear weapon states, a number of other nations have or are pursuing nuclear weapons capabilities.
(5) The IAEA is a valuable international institution to counter proliferation, but the effectiveness of its system to safeguard nuclear materials may be adversely affected by financial constraints.
(6) The Nuclear Non-Proliferation Treaty codifies world consensus against further nuclear proliferation and is scheduled for review and extension in 1995.
(7) The Nuclear Nonproliferation Act of 1978 declared that the United States is committed to continued strong support for the Nuclear Non-Proliferation Treaty and to a strengthened and more effective IAEA, and established that it is United States policy to establish more effective controls over the transfer of nuclear equipment, materials, and technology.

(b) COMPREHENSIVE NUCLEAR NONPROLIFERATION POLICY.—In order to end nuclear proliferation and reduce current nuclear arsenals and supplies of weapons-usable nuclear materials, it should be the policy of the United States to pursue a comprehensive policy to end the further spread of nuclear weapons capability, roll back nuclear proliferation where it has occurred, and prevent the use of nuclear weapons anywhere in the world, with the following additional objectives:

(1) Successful conclusion of all pending nuclear arms control and disarmament agreements with all the republics of the former Soviet Union and their secure implementation.

(2) Full participation by all the republics of the former Soviet Union in all multilateral nuclear nonproliferation efforts and acceptance of IAEA safeguards on all their nuclear facilities.

(3) Strengthening of United States and international support to the IAEA so that the IAEA has the technical, financial, and political resources to verify that countries are complying with their nonproliferation commitments.

(4) Strengthening of nuclear export controls in the United States and other nuclear supplier nations, impose sanctions on individuals, companies, and countries which contribute to nuclear proliferation, and provide increased public information on nuclear export licenses approved in the United States.

(5) Reduction in incentives for countries to pursue the acquisition of nuclear weapons by seeking to reduce regional tensions and to strengthen regional security agreements, and encourage the United Nations Security Council to increase its role in enforcing international nuclear nonproliferation agreements.

(6) Support for the indefinite extension of the Nuclear Non-Proliferation Treaty at the 1995 conference to review and extend that treaty and seek to ensure that all countries sign the treaty or participate in a comparable international regime for monitoring and safeguarding nuclear facilities and materials.

(7) Reaching agreement with the Russian Federation to end the production of new types of nuclear warheads.

(8) Pursuing, once the START I treaty and the START II treaty are ratified by all parties, a multilateral agreement to significantly reduce the strategic nuclear arsenals of the United States and the Russian Federation to below the levels of the START II treaty, with lower levels for the United Kingdom, France, and the People's Republic of China.

(9) Reaching immediate agreement with the Russian Federation to halt permanently the production of fissile material for weapons purposes, and working to achieve worldwide agreements to—

(A) end in the shortest possible time the production of weapons-usable fissile material;

(B) place existing stockpiles of such materials under bilateral or international controls; and

(C) require countries to place all of their nuclear facilities dedicated to peaceful purposes under IAEA safeguards.

(10) Strengthening IAEA safeguards to more effectively verify that countries are complying with their nonproliferation commitments and provide the IAEA with the political, technical, and financial support necessary to implement the necessary safeguard reforms.

(11) Conclusion of a multilateral comprehensive nuclear test ban treaty.

(c) REQUIREMENTS FOR IMPLEMENTATION OF POLICY.—(1) Not later than 180 days after the date of the enactment of this Act, the President shall submit to the Congress a report, in unclassified form, with a classified appendix if necessary, on the actions the United States has taken and the actions the United States plans to take during the succeeding 12-month period to implement each of the policy objectives set forth in this section.

(2) Not later than 180 days after the date of the enactment of this Act, the President shall submit to the Congress a report in unclassified form, with a classified appendix if necessary, which—

(A) addresses the implications of the adoption by the United States of a policy of no-first-use of nuclear weapons;

(B) addresses the implications of an agreement with the other nuclear weapons states to adopt such a policy; and

(C) addresses the implications of a verifiable bilateral agreement with the Russian Federation under which both countries withdraw from their arsenals and dismantle all tactical nuclear weapons, and seek to extend to all nuclear weapons states this zero option for tactical nuclear weapons.

(d) DEFINITIONS.—For purposes of this section:

(1) The term "IAEA" means the International Atomic Energy Agency.

(2) The term "IAEA safeguards" means the safeguards set forth in an agreement between a country and the IAEA, as authorized by Article III(A)(5) of the Statute of the International Atomic Energy Agency.

(3) The term "non-nuclear weapon state" means any country that is not a nuclear weapon state.

(4) The term "Nuclear Non-Proliferation Treaty" means the Treaty on the Non-Proliferation of Nuclear Weapons, signed at Washington, London, and Moscow on July 1, 1968.

(5) The term "nuclear weapon state" means any country that is a nuclear-weapon state, as defined by Article IX(3) of the Treaty on the Non-Proliferation of Nuclear Weapons, signed at Washington, London, and Moscow on July 1, 1968.

(6) The term "weapons-usable fissile materials" means highly enriched uranium and separated or reprocessed plutonium.

(7) The term "policy of no first use of nuclear weapons" means a commitment not to initiate the use of nuclear weapons.

(8) The term "START II treaty" means the Treaty on Further Reductions and Limitations of Strategic Offensive Arms, signed by the United States and the Russian Federation on January 3, 1993.

SEC. 1612. CONDITION ON ASSISTANCE TO RUSSIA FOR CONSTRUCTION OF PLUTONIUM STORAGE FACILITY.

(a) LIMITATION.—Until a certification under subsection (b) is made, no funds may be obligated or expended by the United States for the purpose of assisting the Ministry of Atomic Energy of Russia to construct a storage facility for surplus plutonium from dismantled weapons.

(b) CERTIFICATION OF RUSSIA'S COMMITMENT TO HALT CHEMICAL SEPARATION OF WEAPON-GRADE PLUTONIUM.—The prohibition in subsection (a) shall cease to apply upon a certification by the President to Congress that Russia—

(1) is committed to halting the chemical separation of weapon-grade plutonium from spent nuclear fuel; and

(2) is taking all practical steps to halt such separation at the earliest possible date.

(c) SENSE OF CONGRESS ON PLUTONIUM POLICY.—It is the sense of Congress that a key objective of the United States with respect to the nonproliferation of nuclear weapons should be to obtain a clear and unequivocal commitment from the Government of Russia that it will (1) cease all production and separation of weapon-grade plutonium, and (2) halt chemical separation of plutonium produced in civil nuclear power reactors.

(d) REPORT.—Not later than June 1, 1994, the President shall submit to Congress a report on the status of efforts by the United States to secure the commitments and achieve the objective described in subsections (b) and (c). The President shall include in the report a discussion of the status of joint efforts by the United States and Russia to replace any remaining Russian plutonium production reactors with alternative power sources or to convert such reactors to operation with alternative fuels that would permit their operation without generating weapon-grade plutonium.

SEC. 1613. NORTH KOREA AND THE TREATY ON THE NON-PROLIFERATION OF NUCLEAR WEAPONS.

(a) FINDINGS.—The Congress finds the following:

(1) The Treaty on the Non-Proliferation of Nuclear Weapons, to which 156 states are party, is the cornerstone of the international nuclear nonproliferation regime.

(2) Any nonnuclear weapon state that is a party to the Treaty on the Non-Proliferation of Nuclear Weapons is obligated to accept International Atomic Energy Agency safeguards on all source or special fissionable material that is within its territory, under its jurisdiction, or carried out under its control anywhere.

(3) The International Atomic Energy Agency is permitted to conduct inspections in a nonnuclear weapon state that is a party to the Treaty at any site, whether or not declared by that state, to ensure that all source or special fissionable material in that state is under safeguards.

(4) North Korea acceded to the Treaty on the Non-Proliferation of Nuclear Weapons as a nonnuclear weapons state in December 1985.

(5) North Korea, after acceding to that treaty, refused until 1992 to accept International Atomic Energy Agency safeguards as required under the treaty.

(6) Inspections of North Korea's nuclear materials by the International Atomic Energy Agency suggested discrepancies in North Korea's declarations regarding special nuclear materials.

(7) North Korea has not given a scientifically satisfactory explanation for those discrepancies.

(8) North Korea refused to provide International Atomic Energy Agency inspectors with full access to two sites for the

purposes of verifying its compliance with the Treaty on the Non-Proliferation of Nuclear Weapons.

(9) When called upon by the International Atomic Energy Agency to provide such full access as required by the Treaty, North Korea announced its intention to withdraw from the Treaty, effective after the required three months notice.

(10) After intensive negotiations with the United States, North Korea agreed to suspend its intention to withdraw from the Treaty on the Non-Proliferation of Nuclear Weapons and begin consultations with the International Atomic Energy Agency on providing access to its suspect sites.

(11) In an attempt to persuade North Korea to abandon its nuclear weapons program, the United States has offered to discuss with North Korea specific incentives that could be provided for North Korea once (A) outstanding inspection issues between North Korea and the International Atomic Energy Agency are resolved, and (B) progress is made in bilateral talks between North Korea and South Korea.

(b) CONGRESSIONAL STATEMENTS.—The Congress—

(1) notes that the continued refusal of North Korea nearly eight years after ratification of the Treaty on the Non-Proliferation of Nuclear Weapons to fully accept International Atomic Energy Agency safeguards raises serious questions regarding a possible North Korean nuclear weapons program;

(2) notes that possession by North Korea of nuclear weapons (A) would threaten peace and stability in Asia, (B) would jeopardize the existing nuclear non-proliferation regime, and (C) would undermine the goal of the United States to extend the Treaty on the Non-Proliferation of Nuclear Weapons at the 1995 review conference;

(3) urges continued pressure from the President, United States allies, and the United Nations Security Council on North Korea to adhere to the Treaty and provide full access to the International Atomic Energy Agency in the shortest time possible;

(4) urges the President, United States allies, and the United Nations Security Council to press for continued talks between North Korea and South Korea on denuclearization of the Korean peninsula;

(5) urges that no trade, financial, or other economic benefits be provided to North Korea by the United States or United States allies until North Korea has (A) provided full access to the International Atomic Energy Agency, (B) satisfactorily explained any discrepancies in its declarations of bomb-grade material, and (C) fully demonstrated that it does not have or seek a nuclear weapons capability; and

(6) calls on the President and the international community to take steps to strengthen the international nuclear non-proliferation regime.

SEC. 1614. SENSE OF CONGRESS RELATING TO THE PROLIFERATION OF SPACE LAUNCH VEHICLE TECHNOLOGIES.

(a) FINDINGS.—The Congress finds the following:

(1) The United States has joined with other nations in the Missile Technology Control Regime (MTCR), which restricts the

transfer of missiles or equipment or technology that could contribute to the design, development, or production of missiles capable of delivering weapons of mass destruction.

(2) Missile technology is indistinguishable from, and interchangeable with, space launch vehicle technology.

(3) Transfers of missile technology or space launch vehicle technology cannot be safeguarded in a manner that would provide timely warning of diversion for military purposes.

(4) It has been United States policy since agreeing to the guidelines of the Missile Technology Control Regime to treat the sale or transfer of space launch vehicle technology as restrictively as the sale or transfer of missile technology.

(5) Previous congressional action on missile proliferation, notably title XVII of the National Defense Authorization Act for Fiscal Year 1991 (Public Law 101–510; 104 Stat. 1738), has explicitly supported the policy described in paragraph (4) through such actions as the statutory definition of the term "missile" to mean "a category I system as defined in the MTCR Annex, and any other unmanned delivery system of similar capability, as well as the specially designed production facilities for these systems".

(6) There is strong evidence that emerging national space launch programs in the Third World are not economically viable.

(7) The United States has been successful in dissuading other countries from pursuing space launch vehicle programs in part by offering to cooperate with those countries in other areas of space science and technology.

(8) The United States has successfully dissuaded other MTCR adherents, and countries who have agreed to abide by MTCR guidelines, from providing assistance to emerging national space launch programs in the Third World.

(b) STRICT INTERPRETATION OF MTCR.—The Congress supports the strict interpretation by the United States of the Missile Technology Control Regime concerning—

(1) the inability to distinguish space launch vehicle technology from missile technology under the regime; and

(2) the inability to safeguard space launch vehicle technology in a manner that would provide timely warning of the diversion of such technology to military purposes.

(c) SENSE OF CONGRESS.—It is the sense of Congress that the United States Government and the governments of other nations adhering to the Missile Technology Control Regime should be recognized by the international community for—

(1) the success of those governments in restricting the export of space launch vehicle technology and of missile technology; and

(2) the significant contribution made by the imposition of such restrictions to reducing the proliferation of missile technology capable of being used to deliver weapons of mass destruction.

(d) DEFINITION.—For purposes of this section, the term "Missile Technology Control Regime" or "MTCR" means the policy statement, between the United States, the United Kingdom, the Federal Repub-

lic of Germany, France, Italy, Canada, and Japan, announced on
April 16, 1987, to restrict sensitive missile-relevant transfers based
on the MTCR Annex, and any amendments thereto.

PUBLIC LAW 103-236—APR. 30, 1994   108 STAT. 491

FOREIGN RELATIONS AUTHORIZATION ACT, FISCAL YEARS 1994 AND 1995

TITLE VII—ARMS CONTROL

PART A—ARMS CONTROL AND NONPROLIFERATION ACT OF 1994

Arms Control and Nonproliferation Act of 1994.

SEC. 701. SHORT TITLE; REFERENCES IN PART; TABLE OF CONTENTS.

(a) SHORT TITLE.—This part may be cited as the "Arms Control and Nonproliferation Act of 1994".

(b) REFERENCES IN PART.—Except as specifically provided in this part, whenever in this part an amendment or repeal is expressed as an amendment to or repeal of a provision, the reference shall be deemed to be made to the Arms Control and Disarmament Act.

SEC. 702. CONGRESSIONAL DECLARATIONS; PURPOSE.

(a) CONGRESSIONAL DECLARATIONS.—The Congress declares that—

(1) a fundamental goal of the United States, particularly in the wake of the highly turbulent and uncertain international situation fostered by the end of the Cold War, the disintegration of the Soviet Union and the resulting emergence of fifteen new independent states, and the revolutionary changes in Eastern Europe, is to prevent the proliferation of nuclear weapons and their means of delivery and of advanced conventional armaments, to eliminate chemical and biological weapons, and to reduce and limit the large numbers of nuclear weapons in the former Soviet Union, as well as to prevent regional conflicts and conventional arms races; and

(2) an ultimate goal of the United States continues to be a world in which the use of force is subordinated to the rule of law and international change is achieved peacefully without the danger and burden of destabilizing and costly armaments.

(b) PURPOSE.—The purpose of this part is—

(1) to strengthen the United States Arms Control and Disarmament Agency; and

(2) to improve congressional oversight of the arms control, nonproliferation, and disarmament activities of the United States Arms Control and Disarmament Agency, and of the Agency's operating budget.

SEC. 703. PURPOSES.

Section 2 (22 U.S.C. 2551) is amended in the text following the third undesignated paragraph by striking paragraphs (a), (b), (c), and (d) and by inserting the following new paragraphs:

"(1) The preparation for and management of United States participation in international negotiations and implementation fora in the arms control and disarmament field.

"(2) When directed by the President, the preparation for, and management of, United States participation in international negotiations and implementation fora in the nonproliferation field.

"(3) The conduct, support, and coordination of research for arms control, nonproliferation, and disarmament policy formulation.

"(4) The preparation for, operation of, or, as appropriate, direction of, United States participation in such control systems as may become part of United States arms control, nonproliferation, and disarmament activities.

"(5) The dissemination and coordination of public information concerning arms control, nonproliferation, and disarmament.".

SEC. 704. REPEALS.

The following provisions of law are hereby repealed:
(1) Subsections (b) and (c) of section 36 (22 U.S.C. 2576), relating to arms control impact information and analysis.
(2) Section 38 (22 U.S.C. 2578), relating to reports on Standing Consultative Commission activities.
(3) Section 52 (22 U.S.C. 2592), relating to reports on adherence to and compliance with agreements.

SEC. 705. DIRECTOR.

Section 22 (22 U.S.C. 2562) is amended to read as follows:

"DIRECTOR

President.

"SEC. 22. (a) APPOINTMENT.—The Agency shall be headed by a Director appointed by the President, by and with the advice and consent of the Senate. No person serving on active duty as a commissioned officer of the Armed Forces of the United States may be appointed Director.

"(b) DUTIES.—(1) The Director shall serve as the principal adviser to the Secretary of State, the National Security Council, and the President and other executive branch Government officials on matters relating to arms control, nonproliferation, and disarmament. In carrying out his duties under this Act, the Director, under the direction of the President and the Secretary of State, shall have primary responsibility within the Government for matters relating to arms control and disarmament, and, whenever directed by the President, primary responsibility within the Government for matters relating to nonproliferation.

"(2) The Director shall attend all meetings of the National Security Council involving weapons procurement, arms sales, consideration of the defense budget, and all arms control, nonproliferation, and disarmament matters.".

SEC. 706. BUREAUS, OFFICES, AND DIVISIONS.

Section 25 (22 U.S.C. 2565) is amended to read as follows:

"BUREAUS, OFFICES, AND DIVISIONS

"SEC. 25. The Director may establish within the Agency such bureaus, offices, and divisions as he may determine to be necessary

PUBLIC LAW 103-236—APR. 30, 1994   108 STAT. 525

(5) the term "the Treaty" means the Treaty on the Non-Proliferation of Nuclear Weapons, signed at Washington, London, and Moscow on July 1, 1968; and

(6) the terms "IAEA safeguards", "non-nuclear-weapon state", "nuclear explosive device", and "special nuclear material" have the meanings given those terms in section 830 of this Act.

PART D—TERMINATION

22 USC 3201 note.

SEC. 851. TERMINATION UPON ENACTMENT OF NEXT FOREIGN RELATIONS ACT.

On the date of enactment of the first Foreign Relations Authorization Act that is enacted after the enactment of this Act, the provisions of parts A and B of this title shall cease to be effective, the amendments made by those parts shall be repealed, and any provision of law repealed by those parts shall be reenacted.

to discharge his responsibilities pursuant to this Act, including a bureau of intelligence and information support and an office to perform legal services for the Agency.".

SEC. 707. SCIENTIFIC AND POLICY ADVISORY COMMITTEE.

Section 26 (22 U.S.C. 2566) is amended to read as follows:

"SCIENTIFIC AND POLICY ADVISORY COMMITTEE

"SEC. 26. (a) ESTABLISHMENT.—(1) The President may appoint a Scientific and Policy Advisory Committee (in this section referred to as the 'Committee') of not to exceed 15 members, not less than eight of whom shall be scientists.

"(2) The members of the Committee shall be appointed as follows: President.

"(A) One member, who shall be a person of renown and distinction, shall be appointed by the President, by and with the advice and consent of the Senate, as Chairman of the Committee.

"(B) Fourteen other members shall be appointed by the President.

"(3) The Committee shall meet at least twice each year.

"(b) FUNCTION.—It shall be the responsibility of the Committee to advise the President, the Secretary of State, and the Director respecting scientific, technical, and policy matters affecting arms control, nonproliferation, and disarmament.

"(c) REIMBURSEMENT OF EXPENSES.—The members of the Committee may receive reimbursement of expenses only in accordance with the provisions applicable to the reimbursement of experts and consultants under section 41(d) of this Act.

"(d) TERMINATION.—The Committee shall terminate two years after the date of enactment of the Arms Control and Nonproliferation Act of 1994.

"(e) DEFINITION.—As used in this section, the term 'scientist' means an individual who has a demonstrated knowledge and technical expertise with respect to arms control, nonproliferation, and disarmament matters and who has distinguished himself or herself in any of the fields of physics, chemistry, mathematics, biology, or engineering, including weapons engineering.".

SEC. 708. PRESIDENTIAL SPECIAL REPRESENTATIVES.

(a) IN GENERAL.—Section 27 (22 U.S.C. 2567) is amended to read as follows:

"PRESIDENTIAL SPECIAL REPRESENTATIVES

"SEC. 27. The President may appoint, by and with the advice and consent of the Senate, Special Representatives of the President for arms control, nonproliferation, and disarmament matters. Each Presidential Special Representative shall hold the rank of ambassador. One such Representative may serve in the Agency as Chief Science Advisor. Presidential Special Representatives appointed under this section shall perform their duties and exercise their powers under the direction of the President and the Secretary of State, acting through the Director. The Agency shall be the Government agency responsible for providing administrative support, including funding, staff, and office space, to all Presidential Special Representatives.".

(b) CONFORMING AMENDMENT.—Section 5315 of title 5, United States Code, is amended by striking:

"Special Representatives for Arms Control and Disarmament Negotiations, United States Arms Control and Disarmament Agency (2)."
and inserting:

"Special Representatives of the President for arms control, nonproliferation, and disarmament matters, United States Arms Control and Disarmament Agency.".

SEC. 709. POLICY FORMULATION.

Section 33 (22 U.S.C. 2573) is amended to read as follows:

"POLICY FORMULATION

"SEC. 33. (a) FORMULATION.—The Director shall prepare for the President, the Secretary of State, and the heads of such other Government agencies as the President may determine, recommendations and advice concerning United States arms control, nonproliferation, and disarmament policy.

"(b) PROHIBITION.—No action shall be taken pursuant to this or any other Act that would obligate the United States to reduce or limit the Armed Forces or armaments of the United States in a militarily significant manner, except pursuant to the treaty-making power of the President set forth in Article II, Section 2, Clause 2 of the Constitution or unless authorized by the enactment of further affirmative legislation by the Congress of the United States.".

SEC. 710. NEGOTIATION MANAGEMENT.

Section 34 (22 U.S.C. 2574) is amended to read as follows:

"NEGOTIATION MANAGEMENT

"SEC. 34. (a) RESPONSIBILITIES.—The Director, under the direction of the President and the Secretary of State, shall have primary responsibility for the preparation, conduct, and management of United States participation in all international negotiations and implementation fora in the field of arms control and disarmament and shall have primary responsibility, whenever directed by the President, for the preparation, conduct, and management of United States participation in international negotiations and implementation fora in the field of nonproliferation. In furtherance of these responsibilities, Special Representatives of the President appointed pursuant to section 27, shall, as directed by the President, serve as the United States Government representatives to international organizations, conferences, and activities relating to the field of nonproliferation, such as the preparations for and conduct of the review relating to the Treaty on the Non-Proliferation of Nuclear Weapons.

"(b) FUNCTIONS WITH RESPECT TO THE UNITED STATES INFORMATION AGENCY.—The Director shall perform functions pursuant to section 2(c) of the Reorganization Plan 8 of 1953 with respect to providing to the United States Information Agency official United States positions and policy on arms control, nonproliferation, and disarmament matters for dissemination abroad.

"(c) AUTHORITY.—The Director is authorized—

PUBLIC LAW 103-236—APR. 30, 1994   108 STAT. 495

"(1) for the purpose of conducting negotiations concerning arms control, nonproliferation, or disarmament or for the purpose of exercising any other authority given him by this Act—
"(A) to consult and communicate with, or to direct the consultation and communication with, representatives of other nations or of international organizations, and
"(B) to communicate in the name of the Secretary of State with diplomatic representatives of the United States in the United States or abroad;
"(2) to formulate plans and make preparations for the establishment, operation, and funding of inspections and control systems which may become part of the United States arms control, nonproliferation, and disarmament activities; and
"(3) as authorized by law, to put into effect, direct, or otherwise assume United States responsibility for such systems.".

SEC. 711. REPORT ON MEASURES TO COORDINATE RESEARCH AND DEVELOPMENT.   President.

Not later than December 31, 1994, the President shall submit to the Congress a report prepared by the Director of the United States Arms Control and Disarmament Agency, in coordination with the Secretary of State, the Secretary of Defense, the Secretary of Energy, the Chairman of the Joint Chiefs of Staff, and the Director of Central Intelligence, with respect to the procedures established pursuant to section 35 of the Arms Control and Disarmament Act (22 U.S.C. 2575) for the effective coordination of research and development on arms control, nonproliferation, and disarmament among all departments and agencies of the executive branch of Government.

SEC. 712. VERIFICATION OF COMPLIANCE.

Section 37 (22 U.S.C. 2577) is amended to read as follows:

"VERIFICATION OF COMPLIANCE

"SEC. 37. (a) IN GENERAL.—In order to ensure that arms control, nonproliferation, and disarmament agreements can be adequately verified, the Director shall report to Congress, on a timely basis, or upon request by an appropriate committee of the Congress—   Reports.
"(1) in the case of any arms control, nonproliferation, or disarmament agreement that has been concluded by the United States, the determination of the Director as to the degree to which the components of such agreement can be verified;
"(2) in the case of any arms control, nonproliferation, or disarmament agreement that has entered into force, any significant degradation or alteration in the capacity of the United States to verify compliance of the components of such agreement;
"(3) the amount and percentage of research funds expended by the Agency for the purpose of analyzing issues relating to arms control, nonproliferation, and disarmament verification; and
"(4) the number of professional personnel assigned to arms control verification on a full-time basis by each Government agency.
"(b) STANDARD FOR VERIFICATION OF COMPLIANCE.—In making determinations under paragraphs (1) and (2) of subsection (a), the

Director shall assume that all measures of concealment not expressly prohibited could be employed and that standard practices could be altered so as to impede verification.

"(c) RULE OF CONSTRUCTION.—Except as otherwise provided for by law, nothing in this section may be construed as requiring the disclosure of sensitive information relating to intelligence sources or methods or persons employed in the verification of compliance with arms control, nonproliferation, and disarmament agreements.

"(d) PARTICIPATION OF THE AGENCY.—In order to ensure adherence of the United States to obligations or commitments undertaken in arms control, nonproliferation, and disarmament agreements, and in order for the Director to make the assessment required by section 51(a)(5), the Director, or the Director's designee, shall participate in all interagency groups or organizations within the executive branch of Government that assess, analyze, or review United States planned or ongoing policies, programs, or actions that have a direct bearing on United States adherence to obligations undertaken in arms control, nonproliferation, or disarmament agreements.".

SEC. 713. NEGOTIATING RECORDS.

(a) IN GENERAL.—The Arms Control and Disarmament Act is amended by inserting after section 37 the following:

"NEGOTIATING RECORDS

"SEC. 38. (a) PREPARATION OF RECORDS.—The Director shall establish and maintain records for each arms control, nonproliferation, and disarmament agreement to which the United States is a party and which was under negotiation or in force on or after January 1, 1990, which shall include classified and unclassified materials such as instructions and guidance, position papers, reporting cables and memoranda of conversation, working papers, draft texts of the agreement, diplomatic notes, notes verbal, and other internal and external correspondence.

"(b) NEGOTIATING AND IMPLEMENTATION RECORDS.—In particular, the Director shall establish and maintain a negotiating and implementation record for each such agreement, which shall be comprehensive and detailed, and shall document all communications between the parties with respect to such agreement. Such records shall be maintained both in hard copy and magnetic media.

"(c) PARTICIPATION OF AGENCY PERSONNEL.—In order to implement effectively this section, the Director shall ensure that Agency personnel participate throughout the negotiation and implementation phases of all arms control, nonproliferation, and disarmament agreements.".

(b) REPORT REQUIRED.—Not later than January 31, 1995, the Director of the United States Arms Control and Disarmament Agency shall submit to the Speaker of the House of Representatives and to the chairman of the Committee on Foreign Relations of the Senate a detailed report describing the actions he has undertaken to implement section 38 of the Arms Control and Disarmament Act.

PUBLIC LAW 103-236—APR. 30, 1994   108 STAT. 497

SEC. 714. AUTHORITIES WITH RESPECT TO NONPROLIFERATION MATTERS.

(a) AMENDMENTS TO THE ARMS EXPORT CONTROL ACT.—(1) Section 38(a)(2) of the Arms Export Control Act (22 U.S.C. 2778(a)(2)) is amended to read as follows:

"(2) Decisions on issuing export licenses under this section shall be made in coordination with the Director of the United States Arms Control and Disarmament Agency, taking into account the Director's assessment as to whether the export of an article would contribute to an arms race, aid in the development of weapons of mass destruction, support international terrorism, increase the possibility of outbreak or escalation of conflict, or prejudice the development of bilateral or multilateral arms control or nonproliferation agreements or other arrangements. The Director of the Arms Control and Disarmament Agency is authorized, whenever the Director determines that the issuance of an export license under this section would be detrimental to the national security of the United States, to recommend to the President that such export license be disapproved.".

(2) Section 42(a) of such Act (22 U.S.C. 2791(a)) is amended—
    (A) in the second sentence, by redesignating clauses (1), (2), and (3) as clauses (A), (B), and (C), respectively;
    (B) by inserting "(1)" immediately after "(a)";
    (C) by amending clause (C) (as redesignated) to read as follows: "(C) the assessment of the Director of the United States Arms Control and Disarmament Agency as to whether, and the extent to which, such sale might contribute to an arms race, aid in the development of weapons of mass destruction, support international terrorism, increase the possibility of outbreak or escalation of conflict, or prejudice the development of bilateral or multilateral arms control or nonproliferation agreements or other arrangements."; and
    (D) by adding at the end the following:

"(2) Any proposed sale made pursuant to this Act shall be approved only after consultation with the Director of the United States Arms Control and Disarmament Agency. The Director of the Arms Control and Disarmament Agency is authorized, whenever the Director determines that a sale under this section would be detrimental to the national security of the United States, to recommend to the President that such sale be disapproved.".

(3) Section 71(a) of such Act (22 U.S.C. 2797(a)) is amended by inserting ", the Director of the Arms Control and Disarmament Agency," after "the Secretary of Defense".

(4) Section 71(b)(1) of such Act (22 U.S.C. 2797(b)(1)) is amended by inserting "and the Director of the United States Arms Control and Disarmament Agency" after "Secretary of Defense".

(5) Section 71(b)(2) of such Act (22 U.S.C. 2797(b)(2)) is amended—
    (A) by striking "and the Secretary of Commerce" and inserting ", the Secretary of Commerce, and the Director of the United States Arms Control and Disarmament Agency"; and
    (B) by inserting "or the Director" after "relevant Secretary".

(6) Section 71(c) of such Act (22 U.S.C. 2797(c)) is amended by inserting "with the Director of the United States Arms Control and Disarmament Agency," after "Director of Central Intelligence,".

(7) Section 73(d) of such Act (22 U.S.C. 2797(d)) is amended by striking "and the Secretary of Commerce," and inserting ",

the Secretary of Commerce, and the Director of the United States Arms Control and Disarmament Agency,".

(b) AMENDMENT TO THE NUCLEAR NON-PROLIFERATION ACT.—Section 309(c) of the Nuclear Non-Proliferation Act of 1978 (42 U.S.C. 2139a(c)) is amended in the second sentence by striking out ", as required,".

SEC. 715. APPOINTMENT AND COMPENSATION OF PERSONNEL.

Section 41(b) of the Arms Control and Disarmament Act (22 U.S.C. 2581(b)) is amended by striking "except that during the 2-year" and all that follows through the end thereof and inserting "except that the Director may, to the extent the Director determines necessary to the discharge of his responsibilities, appoint and fix the compensation of employees possessing specialized technical expertise without regard to the provisions of title 5, United States Code, governing appointments in the competitive service and the provisions of chapter 51 and subchapter III of chapter 53 of such title relating to classification and General Schedule pay rates, if the Director ensures that—

"(1) any employee who is appointed under this exception is not paid at a rate—

"(A) in excess of the rate payable for positions of equivalent difficulty or responsibility, or

"(B) exceeding the maximum rate payable for grade 15 of the General Schedule; and

"(2) the number of employees appointed under this exception shall not exceed 10 percent of the Agency's full-time-equivalent ceiling.".

SEC. 716. SECURITY REQUIREMENTS.

Section 45(a) (22 U.S.C. 2585) is amended in the third sentence—

(1) by inserting "or employed directly from other Government agencies" after "persons detailed from other Government agencies"; and

(2) by striking "by the Department of Defense or the Department of State" and inserting "by such agencies".

SEC. 717. REPORTS.

(a) IN GENERAL.—Title IV of the Arms Control and Disarmament Act is amended—

(1) by striking sections 49 and 50;

(2) by redesignating sections 51 and 53 as sections 49 and 50, respectively; and

(3) by inserting after section 50 (as redesignated by paragraph (2)) the following new sections:

"ANNUAL REPORT TO CONGRESS

"SEC. 51. (a) IN GENERAL.—Not later than January 31 of each year, the President shall submit to the Speaker of the House of Representatives and to the chairman of the Committee on Foreign Relations of the Senate a report prepared by the Director, in consultation with the Secretary of State, the Secretary of Defense, the Secretary of Energy, the Chairman of the Joint Chiefs of Staff, and the Director of Central Intelligence, on the status of United States policy and actions with respect to arms control, nonproliferation, and disarmament. Such report shall include—

"(1) a detailed statement concerning the arms control and disarmament objectives of the executive branch of Government for the forthcoming year;

"(2) a detailed statement concerning the nonproliferation objectives of the executive branch of Government for the forthcoming year;

"(3) a detailed assessment of the status of any ongoing arms control or disarmament negotiations, including a comprehensive description of negotiations or other activities during the preceding year and an appraisal of the status and prospects for the forthcoming year;

"(4) a detailed assessment of the status of any ongoing nonproliferation negotiations or other activities, including a comprehensive description of the negotiations or other activities during the preceding year and an appraisal of the status and prospects for the forthcoming year;

"(5) a detailed assessment of adherence of the United States to obligations undertaken in arms control, nonproliferation, and disarmament agreements, including information on the policies and organization of each relevant agency or department of the United States to ensure adherence to such obligations, a description of national security programs with a direct bearing on questions of adherence to such obligations and of steps being taken to ensure adherence, and a compilation of any substantive questions raised during the preceding year and any corrective action taken; and

"(6) a detailed assessment of the adherence of other nations to obligations undertaken in all arms control, nonproliferation, and disarmament agreements to which the United States is a participating state, including information on actions taken by each nation with regard to the size, structure, and disposition of its military forces in order to comply with arms control, nonproliferation, or disarmament agreements, and shall include, in the case of each agreement about which compliance questions exist—

"(A) a description of each significant issue raised and efforts made and contemplated with the other participating state to seek resolution of the difficulty;

"(B) an assessment of damage, if any, to the United States security and other interests; and

"(C) recommendations as to any steps that should be considered to redress any damage to United States national security and to reduce compliance problems.

"(b) CLASSIFICATION OF THE REPORT.—The report required by this section shall be submitted in unclassified form, with classified annexes, as appropriate.

"PUBLIC ANNUAL REPORT ON WORLD MILITARY EXPENDITURES AND ARMS TRANSFERS

"SEC. 52. Not later than December 31 of each year, the Director shall publish an unclassified report on world military expenditures and arms transfers. Such report shall provide detailed, comprehensive, and statistical information regarding military expenditures, arms transfers, armed forces, and related economic data for each country of the world. In addition, such report shall include pertinent in-depth analyses as well as highlights with respect to arms transfers and proliferation trends and initiatives affecting such developments.".

22 USC 2551 note.

(b) REPORT ON REVITALIZATION OF ACDA.—Not later than December 31, 1995, the Director of the United States Arms Control and Disarmament Agency shall submit to the Speaker of the House of Representatives and the chairman of the Committee on Foreign Relations of the Senate a detailed report describing the actions that have been taken and that are underway to revitalize the United States Arms Control and Disarmament Agency pursuant to the provisions of this part and the amendments made by this part.

SEC. 718. FUNDING.

(a) IN GENERAL.—Title IV of the Arms Control and Disarmament Act, as amended by section 717, is further amended by adding at the end the following:

"REQUIREMENT FOR AUTHORIZATION OF APPROPRIATIONS

22 USC 2593c.

"SEC. 53. (a) LIMITATION ON OBLIGATION AND EXPENDITURE OF FUNDS.—Notwithstanding any other provision of law, for the fiscal year 1994 and for each subsequent year, any funds appropriated for the Agency shall not be available for obligation or expenditure—

"(1) unless such funds are appropriated pursuant to an authorization of appropriations; or

"(2) in excess of the authorized level of appropriations.

"(b) SUBSEQUENT AUTHORIZATION.—The limitation under subsection (a) shall not apply to the extent that an authorization of appropriations is enacted after such funds are appropriated.

"(c) APPLICATION.—The provisions of this section—

"(1) may not be superseded, except by a provision of law which specifically repeals, modifies, or supersedes the provisions of this section; and

"(2) shall not apply to, or affect in any manner, permanent appropriations, trust funds, and other similar accounts which are authorized by law and administered by the Agency.

"TRANSFERS AND REPROGRAMMINGS

22 USC 2593d.

"SEC. 54. (a) TRANSFER OF FUNDS.—Funds appropriated for the purpose of carrying out this Act may be allocated or transferred to any agency for such purpose. Such funds shall be available for obligation and expenditure in accordance with the authorities of this Act or in accordance with the authorities governing the activities of the agencies to which such funds are allocated or transferred.

"(b) LIMITATION.—Not more than 12 percent of any appropriation made for the purpose of carrying out this Act shall be obligated or reserved during the last month of the fiscal year.".

"(c) CONGRESSIONAL NOTIFICATION OF CERTAIN REPROGRAMMINGS.—Unless the Committee on Foreign Affairs of the House of Representatives and the Committee on Foreign Relations of the Senate are notified at least 15 days in advance of the proposed reprogramming, funds appropriated to carry out this Act (other than funds to carry out title V) shall not be available for obligation or expenditure through any reprogramming of funds that—

"(1) would create or eliminate a program, project, or activity;
"(2) would increase funds or personnel by any means for any program, project, or activity for which funds have been denied or restricted by the Congress;
"(3) would relocate an office or employees;
"(4) would reorganize offices, programs, projects, or activities;
"(5) would involve contracting out functions which had been performed by Federal employees; or
"(6) would involve a reprogramming in excess of $1,000,000 or 10 percent (whichever is less) and would—
"(A) augment existing programs, projects, or activities,
"(B) reduce by 10 percent or more the funding for any existing program, project, activity, or personnel approved by the Congress, or
"(C) result from any general savings from a reduction in personnel that would result in a change in existing programs, activities, or projects approved by the Congress.
"(d) LIMITATION ON END-OF-YEAR REPROGRAMMINGS.—Funds appropriated to carry out this Act (other than funds to carry out title V) shall not be available for obligation or expenditure through any reprogramming described in paragraph (1) during the last 15 days in which such funds are available for obligation or expenditure (as the case may be) unless the notification required by that paragraph was submitted before that 15-day period.".

SEC. 719. CONFORMING AMENDMENTS.

(a) Section 2 (22 U.S.C. 2551) is amended—
(1) in the second undesignated paragraph, by inserting ", nonproliferation," after "Arms control"; and
(2) in the second and third undesignated paragraphs, by inserting ", nonproliferation," after "arms control" each place it appears.
(b) Section 28 (22 U.S.C. 2568) is amended—
(1) in the first sentence, by striking "field of arms control and disarmament" and inserting "fields of arms control, nonproliferation, and disarmament"; and
(2) in the second sentence, by inserting ", nonproliferation," after "arms control".
(c) Section 31 (22 U.S.C. 2571) is amended—
(1) in the text above paragraph (a), by striking "field of arms control and disarmament" each of the three places it appears and inserting "fields of arms control, nonproliferation, and disarmament";
(2) in the first sentence, by inserting "and nonproliferation" after disarmament; and
(3) in the fourth sentence, by inserting ", nonproliferation," after "arms control" each of the eight places it appears.
(d) Section 35 (22 U.S.C. 2575) is amended by inserting ", nonproliferation," after "arms control".
(e) Section 36 (22 U.S.C. 2576) is amended—
(1) by amending the section heading to read as follows:
"ARMS CONTROL INFORMATION";
(2) by striking "(a)"; and
(3) by inserting ", nonproliferation," after "arms control" each of the two places it appears.

TITLE VIII—NUCLEAR PROLIFERATION PREVENTION ACT

Nuclear Proliferation Prevention Act of 1994.

SEC. 801. SHORT TITLE.

22 USC 3201 note.

This title may be cited as the "Nuclear Proliferation Prevention Act of 1994".

PART A—REPORTING ON NUCLEAR EXPORTS

SEC. 811. REPORTS TO CONGRESS.

Section 601(a) of the Nuclear Non-Proliferation Act of 1978 (22 U.S.C. 3281(a)) is amended—
 (1) in paragraph (4), by striking "and" after the semicolon;
 (2) in paragraph (5), by striking the period and inserting a semicolon; and
 (3) by adding after paragraph (5) the following:
 "(6) a description of the implementation of nuclear and nuclear-related dual-use export controls in the preceding calendar year, including a summary by type of commodity and destination of—
  "(A) all transactions for which—
   "(i) an export license was issued for any good controlled under section 309(c) of this Act;
   "(ii) an export license was issued under section 109 b. of the 1954 Act;
   "(iii) approvals were issued under the Export Administration Act of 1979, or section 109 b.(3) of the 1954 Act, for the retransfer of any item, technical data, component, or substance; or
   "(iv) authorizations were made as required by section 57 b.(2) of the 1954 Act to engage, directly or indirectly, in the production of special nuclear material;
  "(B) each instance in which—
   "(i) a sanction has been imposed under section 821(a) or section 824 of the Nuclear Proliferation Prevention Act of 1994 or section 102(b)(1) of the Arms Export Control Act;

"(ii) sales or leases have been denied under section 3(f) of the Arms Export Control Act or transactions prohibited by reason of acts relating to proliferation of nuclear explosive devices as described in section 40(d) of that Act;

"(iii) a sanction has not been imposed by reason of section 821(c)(2) of the Nuclear Proliferation Prevention Act of 1994 or the imposition of a sanction has been delayed under section 102(b)(4) of the Arms Export Control Act; or

"(iv) a waiver of a sanction has been made under—
"(I) section 821(f) or section 824 of the Nuclear Proliferation Prevention Act of 1994,
"(II) section 620E(d) of the Foreign Assistance Act of 1961, or paragraph (5) or (6)(B) of section 102(b) of the Arms Export Control Act,
"(III) section 40(g) of the Arms Export Control Act with respect to the last sentence of section 40(d) of that Act, or
"(IV) section 614 of the Foreign Assistance Act of 1961 with respect to section 620E of that Act or section 3(f), the last sentence of section 40(d), or 102(b)(1) of the Arms Export Control Act; and

"(C) the progress of those independent states of the former Soviet Union that are non-nuclear-weapon states and of the Baltic states towards achieving the objective of applying full scope safeguards to all their peaceful nuclear activities.

Portions of the information required by paragraph (6) may be submitted in classified form, as necessary. Any such information that may not be published or disclosed under section 12(c)(1) of the Export Administration Act of 1979 shall be submitted as confidential.".

PART B—SANCTIONS FOR NUCLEAR PROLIFERATION

SEC. 821. IMPOSITION OF PROCUREMENT SANCTION ON PERSONS ENGAGING IN EXPORT ACTIVITIES THAT CONTRIBUTE TO PROLIFERATION.

(a) DETERMINATION BY THE PRESIDENT.—

(1) IN GENERAL.—Except as provided in subsection (b)(2), the President shall impose the sanction described in subsection (c) if the President determines in writing that, on or after the effective date of this part, a foreign person or a United States person has materially and with requisite knowledge contributed, through the export from the United States or any other country of any goods or technology (as defined in section 830(2)), to the efforts by any individual, group, or non-nuclear-weapon state to acquire unsafeguarded special nuclear material or to use, develop, produce, stockpile, or otherwise acquire any nuclear explosive device.

(2) PERSONS AGAINST WHICH THE SANCTION IS TO BE IMPOSED.—The sanction shall be imposed pursuant to paragraph (1) on—

22 USC 3201 note.

(A) the foreign person or United States person with respect to which the President makes the determination described in that paragraph;

(B) any successor entity to that foreign person or United States person;

(C) any foreign person or United States person that is a parent or subsidiary of that person if that parent or subsidiary materially and with requisite knowledge assisted in the activities which were the basis of that determination; and

(D) any foreign person or United States person that is an affiliate of that person if that affiliate materially and with requisite knowledge assisted in the activities which were the basis of that determination and if that affiliate is controlled in fact by that person.

(3) OTHER SANCTIONS AVAILABLE.—The sanction which is required to be imposed for activities described in this subsection is in addition to any other sanction which may be imposed for the same activities under any other provision of law.

(4) DEFINITION.—For purposes of this subsection, the term "requisite knowledge" means situations in which a person "knows", as "knowing" is defined in section 104 of the Foreign Corrupt Practices Act of 1977 (15 U.S.C. 78dd-2).

(b) CONSULTATION WITH AND ACTIONS BY FOREIGN GOVERNMENT OF JURISDICTION.—

(1) CONSULTATIONS.—If the President makes a determination described in subsection (a)(1) with respect to a foreign person, the Congress urges the President to initiate consultations immediately with the government with primary jurisdiction over that foreign person with respect to the imposition of the sanction pursuant to this section.

(2) ACTIONS BY GOVERNMENT OF JURISDICTION.—In order to pursue such consultations with that government, the President may delay imposition of the sanction pursuant to this section for up to 90 days. Following these consultations, the President shall impose the sanction unless the President determines and certifies in writing to the Congress that that government has taken specific and effective actions, including appropriate penalties, to terminate the involvement of the foreign person in the activities described in subsection (a)(1). The President may delay the imposition of the sanction for up to an additional 90 days if the President determines and certifies in writing to the Congress that that government is in the process of taking the actions described in the preceding sentence.

President.

(3) REPORT TO CONGRESS.—Not later than 90 days after making a determination under subsection (a)(1), the President shall submit to the Committee on Foreign Relations and the Committee on Governmental Affairs of the Senate and the Committee on Foreign Affairs of the House of Representatives a report on the status of consultations with the appropriate government under this subsection, and the basis for any determination under paragraph (2) of this subsection that such government has taken specific corrective actions.

President.

(c) SANCTION.—

(1) DESCRIPTION OF SANCTION.—The sanction to be imposed pursuant to subsection (a)(1) is, except as provided in paragraph

(2) of this subsection, that the United States Government shall not procure, or enter into any contract for the procurement of, any goods or services from any person described in subsection (a)(2).

(2) EXCEPTIONS.—The President shall not be required to apply or maintain the sanction under this section—

(A) in the case of procurement of defense articles or defense services—

(i) under existing contracts or subcontracts, including the exercise of options for production quantities to satisfy requirements essential to the national security of the United States;

(ii) if the President determines in writing that the person or other entity to which the sanction would otherwise be applied is a sole source supplier of the defense articles or services, that the defense articles or services are essential, and that alternative sources are not readily or reasonably available; or

(iii) if the President determines in writing that such articles or services are essential to the national security under defense coproduction agreements;

(B) to products or services provided under contracts entered into before the date on which the President publishes his intention to impose the sanction;

(C) to—

(i) spare parts which are essential to United States products or production;

(ii) component parts, but not finished products, essential to United States products or production; or

(iii) routine servicing and maintenance of products, to the extent that alternative sources are not readily or reasonably available;

(D) to information and technology essential to United States products or production; or

(E) to medical or other humanitarian items.

(d) ADVISORY OPINIONS.—Upon the request of any person, the Secretary of State may, in consultation with the Secretary of Defense, issue in writing an advisory opinion to that person as to whether a proposed activity by that person would subject that person to the sanction under this section. Any person who relies in good faith on such an advisory opinion which states that the proposed activity would not subject a person to such sanction, and any person who thereafter engages in such activity, may not be made subject to such sanction on account of such activity.

(e) TERMINATION OF THE SANCTION.—The sanction imposed pursuant to this section shall apply for a period of at least 12 months following the imposition of the sanction and shall cease to apply thereafter only if the President determines and certifies in writing to the Congress that—

(1) reliable information indicates that the foreign person or United States person with respect to which the determination was made under subsection (a)(1) has ceased to aid or abet any individual, group, or non-nuclear-weapon state in its efforts to acquire unsafeguarded special nuclear material or any nuclear explosive device, as described in that subsection; and

(2) the President has received reliable assurances from the foreign person or United States person, as the case may

be, that such person will not, in the future, aid or abet any individual, group, or non-nuclear-weapon state in its efforts to acquire unsafeguarded special nuclear material or any nuclear explosive device, as described in subsection (a)(1).

(f) WAIVER.—

(1) CRITERION FOR WAIVER.—The President may waive the application of the sanction imposed on any person pursuant to this section, after the end of the 12-month period beginning on the date on which that sanction was imposed on that person, if the President determines and certifies in writing to the Congress that the continued imposition of the sanction would have a serious adverse effect on vital United States interests.

(2) NOTIFICATION OF AND REPORT TO CONGRESS.—If the President decides to exercise the waiver authority provided in paragraph (1), the President shall so notify the Congress not less than 20 days before the waiver takes effect. Such notification shall include a report fully articulating the rationale and circumstances which led the President to exercise the waiver authority.

SEC. 822. ELIGIBILITY FOR ASSISTANCE.

(a) AMENDMENTS TO THE ARMS EXPORT CONTROL ACT.—

(1) PROHIBITION.—Section 3 of the Arms Export Control Act (22 U.S.C. 2753) is amended by adding at the end the following new subsection:

"(f) No sales or leases shall be made to any country that the President has determined is in material breach of its binding commitments to the United States under international treaties or agreements concerning the nonproliferation of nuclear explosive devices (as defined in section 830(4) of the Nuclear Proliferation Prevention Act of 1994) and unsafeguarded special nuclear material (as defined in section 830(8) of that Act).".

(2) DEFINITION OF SUPPORT FOR INTERNATIONAL TERRORISM.—Section 40 of such Act (22 U.S.C. 2780) is amended—

(A) in subsection (d), by adding at the end the following new sentence: "For purposes of this subsection, such acts shall include all activities that the Secretary determines willfully aid or abet the international proliferation of nuclear explosive devices to individuals or groups or willfully aid or abet an individual or groups in acquiring unsafeguarded special nuclear material."; and

(B) in subsection (l)—

(i) in paragraph (2), by striking "and" after the semicolon;

(ii) in paragraph (3), by striking the period at the end and inserting a semicolon; and

(iii) by adding at the end the following:

"(4) the term 'nuclear explosive device' has the meaning given that term in section 830(4) of the Nuclear Proliferation Prevention Act of 1994; and

"(5) the term 'unsafeguarded special nuclear material' has the meaning given that term in section 830(8) of the Nuclear Proliferation Prevention Act of 1994.".

(b) FOREIGN ASSISTANCE ACT OF 1961.—

(1) PRESIDENTIAL DETERMINATION 82-7.—Notwithstanding any other provision of law, Presidential Determination No. 82-7 of February 10, 1982, made pursuant to section 670(a)(2)

of the Foreign Assistance Act of 1961, shall have no force or effect with respect to any grounds for the prohibition of assistance under section 102(a)(1) of the Arms Export Control Act arising on or after the effective date of this part.

(2) AMENDMENT.—Section 620E(d) of the Foreign Assistance Act of 1961 (22 U.S.C. 2375(d)) is amended to read as follows:

"(d) The President may waive the prohibitions of section 101 of the Arms Export Control Act with respect to any grounds for the prohibition of assistance under that section arising before the effective date of part B of the Nuclear Proliferation Prevention Act of 1994 to provide assistance to Pakistan if he determines that to do so is in the national interest of the United States.".

SEC. 823. ROLE OF INTERNATIONAL FINANCIAL INSTITUTIONS.

(a) IN GENERAL.—The Secretary of the Treasury shall instruct the United States executive director to each of the international financial institutions described in section 701(a) of the International Financial Institutions Act (22 U.S.C. 262d(a)) to use the voice and vote of the United States to oppose any use of the institution's funds to promote the acquisition of unsafeguarded special nuclear material or the development, stockpiling, or use of any nuclear explosive device by any non-nuclear-weapon state.

(b) DUTIES OF UNITED STATES EXECUTIVE DIRECTORS.—Section 701(b)(3) of the International Financial Institutions Act (22 U.S.C. 262d(b)(3)) is amended to read as follows:

"(3) whether the recipient country—

"(A) is seeking to acquire unsafeguarded special nuclear material (as defined in section 830(8) of the Nuclear Proliferation Prevention Act of 1994) or a nuclear explosive device (as defined in section 830(4) of that Act);

"(B) is not a State Party to the Treaty on the Non-Proliferation of Nuclear Weapons; or

"(C) has detonated a nuclear explosive device; and".

SEC. 824. PROHIBITION ON ASSISTING NUCLEAR PROLIFERATION THROUGH THE PROVISION OF FINANCING.

(a) PROHIBITED ACTIVITY DEFINED.—For purposes of this section, the term "prohibited activity" means the act of knowingly, materially, and directly contributing or attempting to contribute, through the provision of financing, to—

(1) the acquisition of unsafeguarded special nuclear material; or

(2) the use, development, production, stockpiling, or other acquisition of any nuclear explosive device,

by any individual, group, or non-nuclear-weapon state.

(b) PROHIBITION.—To the extent that the United States has jurisdiction to prohibit such activity by such person, no United States person and no foreign person may engage in any prohibited activity.

(c) PRESIDENTIAL DETERMINATION AND ORDER WITH RESPECT TO UNITED STATES AND FOREIGN PERSONS.—If the President determines, in writing after opportunity for a hearing on the record, that a United States person or a foreign person has engaged in a prohibited activity (without regard to whether subsection (b) applies), the President shall, by order, impose the sanctions described in subsection (d) on such person.

(d) SANCTIONS.—The following sanctions shall be imposed pursuant to any order issued under subsection (c) with respect to any United States person or any foreign person:
  (1) BAN ON DEALINGS IN GOVERNMENT FINANCE.—
    (A) DESIGNATION AS PRIMARY DEALER.—Neither the Board of Governors of the Federal Reserve System nor the Federal Reserve Bank of New York may designate, or permit the continuation of any prior designation of, the person as a primary dealer in United States Government debt instruments.
    (B) SERVICE AS DEPOSITARY.—The person may not serve as a depositary for United States Government funds.
  (2) RESTRICTIONS ON OPERATIONS.—The person may not, directly or indirectly—
    (A) commence any line of business in the United States in which the person was not engaged as of the date of the order; or
    (B) conduct business from any location in the United States at which the person did not conduct business as of the date of the order.
(e) JUDICIAL REVIEW.—Any determination of the President under subsection (c) shall be subject to judicial review in accordance with chapter 7 of part I of title 5, United States Code.
(f) CONSULTATION WITH AND ACTIONS BY FOREIGN GOVERNMENT OF JURISDICTION.—
  (1) CONSULTATIONS.—If the President makes a determination under subsection (c) with respect to a foreign person, the Congress urges the President to initiate consultations immediately with any appropriate foreign government with respect to the imposition of any sanction pursuant to this section.
  (2) ACTIONS BY GOVERNMENT OF JURISDICTION.—
    (A) SUSPENSION OF PERIOD FOR IMPOSING SANCTIONS.—In order to pursue consultations described in paragraph (1) with any government referred to in such paragraph, the President may delay, for up to 90 days, the effective date of an order under subsection (c) imposing any sanction.
    (B) COORDINATION WITH ACTIVITIES OF FOREIGN GOVERNMENT.—Following consultations described in paragraph (1), the order issued by the President under subsection (c) imposing any sanction on a foreign person shall take effect unless the President determines, and certifies in writing to the Congress, that the government referred to in paragraph (1) has taken specific and effective actions, including the imposition of appropriate penalties, to terminate the involvement of the foreign person in any prohibited activity.
    (C) EXTENSION OF PERIOD.—After the end of the period described in subparagraph (A), the President may delay, for up to an additional 90 days, the effective date of an order issued under subsection (b) imposing any sanction on a foreign person if the President determines, and certifies in writing to the Congress, that the appropriate foreign government is in the process of taking actions described in subparagraph (B).
  (3) REPORT TO CONGRESS.—Before the end of the 90-day period beginning on the date on which an order is issued

under subsection (c), the President shall submit to the Congress a report on—
> (A) the status of consultations under this subsection with the government referred to in paragraph (1); and
> (B) the basis for any determination under paragraph (2) that such government has taken specific corrective actions.

(g) TERMINATION OF THE SANCTIONS.—Any sanction imposed on any person pursuant to an order issued under subsection (c) shall—
> (1) remain in effect for a period of not less than 12 months; and
> (2) cease to apply after the end of such 12-month period only if the President determines, and certifies in writing to the Congress, that—
>> (A) the person has ceased to engage in any prohibited activity; and
>> (B) the President has received reliable assurances from such person that the person will not, in the future, engage in any prohibited activity.

(h) WAIVER.—The President may waive the continued application of any sanction imposed on any person pursuant to an order issued under subsection (c) if the President determines, and certifies in writing to the Congress, that the continued imposition of the sanction would have a serious adverse effect on the safety and soundness of the domestic or international financial system or on domestic or international payments systems.

(i) ENFORCEMENT ACTION.—The Attorney General may bring an action in an appropriate district court of the United States for injunctive and other appropriate relief with respect to—
> (1) any violation of subsection (b); or
> (2) any order issued pursuant to subsection (c).

(j) KNOWINGLY DEFINED.—
> (1) IN GENERAL.—For purposes of this section, the term "knowingly" means the state of mind of a person with respect to conduct, a circumstance, or a result in which—
>> (A) such person is aware that such person is engaging in such conduct, that such circumstance exists, or that such result is substantially certain to occur; or
>> (B) such person has a firm belief that such circumstance exists or that such result is substantially certain to occur.
>
> (2) KNOWLEDGE OF THE EXISTENCE OF A PARTICULAR CIRCUMSTANCE.—If knowledge of the existence of a particular circumstance is required for an offense, such knowledge is established if a person is aware of a high probability of the existence of such circumstance, unless the person actually believes that such circumstance does not exist.

(k) SCOPE OF APPLICATION.—This section shall apply with respect to prohibited activities which occur on or after the date this part takes effect.

SEC. 825. EXPORT-IMPORT BANK.

Section 2(b)(4) of the Export-Import Bank Act of 1945 (12 U.S.C. 635(b)(4)) is amended in the first sentence by inserting after "device" the following: "(as defined in section 830(4) of the Nuclear Proliferation Prevention Act of 1994), or that any country

PUBLIC LAW 103-236—APR. 30, 1994   108 STAT. 515

has willfully aided or abetted any non-nuclear-weapon state (as defined in section 830(5) of that Act) to acquire any such nuclear explosive device or to acquire unsafeguarded special nuclear material (as defined in section 830(8) of that Act).".

SEC. 826. AMENDMENT TO THE ARMS EXPORT CONTROL ACT.

(a) IN GENERAL.—The Arms Export Control Act is amended by adding at the end the following new chapter:

"CHAPTER 10—NUCLEAR NONPROLIFERATION CONTROLS

"SEC. 101. NUCLEAR ENRICHMENT TRANSFERS.   22 USC 2799aa.

"(a) PROHIBITIONS; SAFEGUARDS AND MANAGEMENT.—Except as provided in subsection (b) of this section, no funds made available to carry out the Foreign Assistance Act of 1961 or this Act may be used for the purpose of providing economic assistance (including assistance under chapter 4 of part II of the Foreign Assistance Act of 1961), providing military assistance or grant military education and training, providing assistance under chapter 6 of part II of that Act, or extending military credits or making guarantees, to any country which the President determines delivers nuclear enrichment equipment, materials, or technology to any other country on or after August 4, 1977, or receives such equipment, materials, or technology from any other country on or after August 4, 1977, unless before such delivery—

"(1) the supplying country and receiving country have reached agreement to place all such equipment, materials, or technology, upon delivery, under multilateral auspices and management when available; and

"(2) the recipient country has entered into an agreement with the International Atomic Energy Agency to place all such equipment, materials, technology, and all nuclear fuel and facilities in such country under the safeguards system of such Agency.

"(b) CERTIFICATION BY PRESIDENT OF NECESSITY OF CONTINUED ASSISTANCE; DISAPPROVAL BY CONGRESS.—(1) Notwithstanding subsection (a) of this section, the President may furnish assistance which would otherwise be prohibited under such subsection if he determines and certifies in writing to the Speaker of the House of Representatives and the Committee on Foreign Relations of the Senate that—

"(A) the termination of such assistance would have a serious adverse effect on vital United States interests; and

"(B) he has received reliable assurances that the country in question will not acquire or develop nuclear weapons or assist other nations in doing so.

Such certification shall set forth the reasons supporting such determination in each particular case.

"(2)(A) A certification under paragraph (1) of this subsection shall take effect on the date on which the certification is received by the Congress. However, if, within thirty calendar days after receiving this certification, the Congress enacts a joint resolution stating in substance that the Congress disapproves the furnishing of assistance pursuant to the certification, then upon the enactment of that resolution the certification shall cease to be effective and all deliveries of assistance furnished under the authority of that certification shall be suspended immediately.

"(B) Any joint resolution under this paragraph shall be considered in the Senate in accordance with the provisions of section 601(b) of the International Security Assistance and Arms Export Control Act of 1976.

President.
22 USC
2799aa-1.

"SEC. 102. NUCLEAR REPROCESSING TRANSFERS, ILLEGAL EXPORTS FOR NUCLEAR EXPLOSIVE DEVICES, TRANSFERS OF NUCLEAR EXPLOSIVE DEVICES, AND NUCLEAR DETONATIONS.

"(a) PROHIBITIONS ON ASSISTANCE TO COUNTRIES INVOLVED IN TRANSFER OF NUCLEAR REPROCESSING EQUIPMENT, MATERIALS, OR TECHNOLOGY; EXCEPTIONS; PROCEDURES APPLICABLE.—(1) Except as provided in paragraph (2) of this subsection, no funds made available to carry out the Foreign Assistance Act of 1961 or this Act may be used for the purpose of providing economic assistance (including assistance under chapter 4 of part II of the Foreign Assistance Act of 1961), providing military assistance or grant military education and training, providing assistance under chapter 6 of part II of that Act, or extending military credits or making guarantees, to any country which the President determines—

"(A) delivers nuclear reprocessing equipment, materials, or technology to any other country on or after August 4, 1977, or receives such equipment, materials, or technology from any other country on or after August 4, 1977 (except for the transfer of reprocessing technology associated with the investigation, under international evaluation programs in which the United States participates, of technologies which are alternatives to pure plutonium reprocessing), or

"(B) is a non-nuclear-weapon state which, on or after August 8, 1985, exports illegally (or attempts to export illegally) from the United States any material, equipment, or technology which would contribute significantly to the ability of such country to manufacture a nuclear explosive device, if the President determines that the material, equipment, or technology was to be used by such country in the manufacture of a nuclear explosive device.

For purposes of clause (B), an export (or attempted export) by a person who is an agent of, or is otherwise acting on behalf of or in the interests of, a country shall be considered to be an export (or attempted export) by that country.

"(2) Notwithstanding paragraph (1) of this subsection, the President in any fiscal year may furnish assistance which would otherwise be prohibited under that paragraph if he determines and certifies in writing during that fiscal year to the Speaker of the House of Representatives and the Committee on Foreign Relations of the Senate that the termination of such assistance would be seriously prejudicial to the achievement of United States nonproliferation objectives or otherwise jeopardize the common defense and security. The President shall transmit with such certification a statement setting forth the specific reasons therefor.

"(3)(A) A certification under paragraph (2) of this subsection shall take effect on the date on which the certification is received by the Congress. However, if, within 30 calendar days after receiving this certification, the Congress enacts a joint resolution stating in substance that the Congress disapproves the furnishing of assistance pursuant to the certification, then upon the enactment of that resolution the certification shall cease to be effective and all deliveries of assistance furnished under the authority of that certification shall be suspended immediately.

"(B) Any joint resolution under this paragraph shall be considered in the Senate in accordance with the provisions of section 601(b) of the International Security Assistance and Arms Export Control Act of 1976.

"(b) PROHIBITIONS ON ASSISTANCE TO COUNTRIES INVOLVED IN TRANSFER OR USE OF NUCLEAR EXPLOSIVE DEVICES; EXCEPTIONS; PROCEDURES APPLICABLE.—(1) Except as provided in paragraphs (4), (5), and (6), in the event that the President determines that any country, after the effective date of part B of the Nuclear Proliferation Prevention Act of 1994—

"(A) transfers to a non-nuclear-weapon state a nuclear explosive device,

"(B) is a non-nuclear-weapon state and either—

"(i) receives a nuclear explosive device, or

"(ii) detonates a nuclear explosive device,

"(C) transfers to a non-nuclear-weapon state any design information or component which is determined by the President to be important to, and known by the transferring country to be intended by the recipient state for use in, the development or manufacture of any nuclear explosive device, or

"(D) is a non-nuclear-weapon state and seeks and receives any design information or component which is determined by the President to be important to, and intended by the recipient state for use in, the development or manufacture of any nuclear explosive device,

then the President shall forthwith report in writing his determination to the Congress and shall forthwith impose the sanctions described in paragraph (2) against that country.

"(2) The sanctions referred to in paragraph (1) are as follows:

"(A) The United States Government shall terminate assistance to that country under the Foreign Assistance Act of 1961, except for humanitarian assistance or food or other agricultural commodities.

"(B) The United States Government shall terminate—

"(i) sales to that country under this Act of any defense articles, defense services, or design and construction services, and

"(ii) licenses for the export to that country of any item on the United States Munitions List.

"(C) The United States Government shall terminate all foreign military financing for that country under this Act.

"(D) The United States Government shall deny to that country any credit, credit guarantees, or other financial assistance by any department, agency, or instrumentality of the United States Government, except that the sanction of this subparagraph shall not apply—

"(i) to any transaction subject to the reporting requirements of title V of the National Security Act of 1947 (relating to congressional oversight of intelligence activities), or

"(ii) to humanitarian assistance.

"(E) The United States Government shall oppose, in accordance with section 701 of the International Financial Institutions

Act (22 U.S.C. 262d), the extension of any loan or financial or technical assistance to that country by any international financial institution.

"(F) The United States Government shall prohibit any United States bank from making any loan or providing any credit to the government of that country, except for loans or credits for the purpose of purchasing food or other agricultural commodities.

"(G) The authorities of section 6 of the Export Administration Act of 1979 shall be used to prohibit exports to that country of specific goods and technology (excluding food and other agricultural commodities), except that such prohibition shall not apply to any transaction subject to the reporting requirements of title V of the National Security Act of 1947 (relating to congressional oversight of intelligence activities).

"(3) As used in this subsection—

"(A) the term 'design information' means specific information that relates to the design of a nuclear explosive device and that is not available to the public; and

"(B) the term 'component' means a specific component of a nuclear explosive device.

"(4)(A) Notwithstanding paragraph (1) of this subsection, the President may, for a period of not more than 30 days of continuous session, delay the imposition of sanctions which would otherwise be required under paragraph (1)(A) or (1)(B) of this subsection if the President first transmits to the Speaker of the House of Representatives, and to the chairman of the Committee on Foreign Relations of the Senate, a certification that he has determined that an immediate imposition of sanctions on that country would be detrimental to the national security of the United States. Not more than one such certification may be transmitted for a country with respect to the same detonation, transfer, or receipt of a nuclear explosive device.

"(B) If the President transmits a certification to the Congress under subparagraph (A), a joint resolution which would permit the President to exercise the waiver authority of paragraph (5) of this subsection shall, if introduced in either House within thirty days of continuous session after the Congress receives this certification, be considered in the Senate in accordance with subparagraph (C) of this paragraph.

"(C) Any joint resolution under this paragraph shall be considered in the Senate in accordance with the provisions of section 601(b) of the International Security Assistance and Arms Export Control Act of 1976.

"(D) For purposes of this paragraph, the term "joint resolution" means a joint resolution the matter after the resolving clause of which is as follows: "That the Congress having received on ___ a certification by the President under section 102(b)(4) of the Arms Export Control Act with respect to ___, the Congress hereby authorizes the President to exercise the waiver authority contained in section 102(b)(5) of that Act.", with the date of receipt of the certification inserted in the first blank and the name of the country inserted in the second blank.

"(5) Notwithstanding paragraph (1) of this subsection, if the Congress enacts a joint resolution under paragraph (4) of this subsection, the President may waive any sanction which would otherwise be required under paragraph (1)(A) or (1)(B) if he deter-

PUBLIC LAW 103-236—APR. 30, 1994   108 STAT. 519

mines and certifies in writing to the Speaker of the House of Representatives and the Committee on Foreign Relations of the Senate that the imposition of such sanction would be seriously prejudicial to the achievement of United States nonproliferation objectives or otherwise jeopardize the common defense and security. The President shall transmit with such certification a statement setting forth the specific reasons therefor.

"(6)(A) In the event the President is required to impose sanctions against a country under paragraph (1)(C) or (1)(D), the President shall forthwith so inform such country and shall impose the required sanctions beginning 30 days after submitting to the Congress the report required by paragraph (1) unless, and to the extent that, there is enacted during the 30-day period a law prohibiting the imposition of such sanctions.

"(B) Notwithstanding any other provision of law, the sanctions which are required to be imposed against a country under paragraph (1)(C) or (1)(D) shall not apply if the President determines and certifies in writing to the Committee on Foreign Relations and the Committee on Governmental Affairs of the Senate and the Committee on Foreign Affairs of the House of Representatives that the application of such sanctions against such country would have a serious adverse effect on vital United States interests. The President shall transmit with such certification a statement setting forth the specific reasons therefor.

"(7) For purposes of this subsection, continuity of session is broken only by an adjournment of Congress sine die and the days on which either House is not in session because of an adjournment of more than three days to a day certain are excluded in the computation of any period of time in which Congress is in continuous session.

"(8) The President may not delegate or transfer his power, authority, or discretion to make or modify determinations under this subsection.

"(c) NON-NUCLEAR-WEAPON STATE DEFINED.—As used in this section, the term 'non-nuclear-weapon state' means any country which is not a nuclear-weapon state, as defined in Article IX(3) of the Treaty on the Non-Proliferation of Nuclear Weapons.

"SEC. 103. DEFINITION OF NUCLEAR EXPLOSIVE DEVICE.   22 USC
                                                                 2799aa-2.
"As used in this chapter, the term 'nuclear explosive device' has the meaning given that term in section 830(4) of the Nuclear Proliferation Prevention Act of 1994.".

(b) REPEALS.—Sections 669 and 670 of the Foreign Assistance Act of 1961 are hereby repealed.   22 USC 2429,
                                                                 2429a.
(c) REFERENCES IN LAW.—Any reference in law as of the date of enactment of this Act to section 669 or 670 of the Foreign Assistance Act of 1961 shall, after such date, be deemed to be a reference to section 101 or 102, as the case may be, of the Arms Export Control Act.

SEC. 827. REWARD.

Section 36(a) of the State Department Basic Authorities Act of 1956 (22 U.S.C. 2708(a)) is amended—
    (1) by redesignating paragraphs (1) through (3) as subparagraphs (A) through (C), respectively;
    (2) by inserting "(1)" after "(a)"; and
    (3) by adding at the end the following:

"(2) For purposes of this subsection, the term 'act of international terrorism' includes any act substantially contributing to the acquisition of unsafeguarded special nuclear material (as defined in section 830(8) of the Nuclear Proliferation Prevention Act of 1994) or any nuclear explosive device (as defined in section 830(4) of that Act) by an individual, group, or non-nuclear-weapon state (as defined in section 830(5) of that Act).".

SEC. 828. REPORTS.

(a) CONTENT OF ACDA ANNUAL REPORT.—Section 51(a) of the Arms Control and Disarmament Act, as inserted by this Act, is amended—

(1) by striking "and" at the end of paragraph (5);

(2) by striking the period at the end of paragraph (6) and inserting "; and";

(3) by adding after paragraph (6) the following new paragraph:

"(7) a discussion of any material noncompliance by foreign governments with their binding commitments to the United States with respect to the prevention of the spread of nuclear explosive devices (as defined in section 830(4) of the Nuclear Proliferation Prevention Act of 1994) by non-nuclear-weapon states (as defined in section 830(5) of that Act) or the acquisition by such states of unsafeguarded special nuclear material (as defined in section 830(8) of that Act), including—

"(A) a net assessment of the aggregate military significance of all such violations;

"(B) a statement of the compliance policy of the United States with respect to violations of those commitments; and

"(C) what actions, if any, the President has taken or proposes to take to bring any nation committing such a violation into compliance with those commitments."; and

(4) by adding at the end the following new subsection:

"(c) REPORTING CONSECUTIVE NONCOMPLIANCE.—If the President in consecutive reports submitted to the Congress under this section reports that any designated nation is not in full compliance with its binding nonproliferation commitments to the United States, then the President shall include in the second such report an assessment of what actions are necessary to compensate for such violations.".

(b) REPORTING ON DEMARCHES.—(1) It is the sense of the Congress that the Department of State should, in the course of implementing its reporting responsibilities under section 602(c) of the Nuclear Non-Proliferation Act of 1978, include a summary of demarches that the United States has issued or received from foreign governments with respect to activities which are of significance from the proliferation standpoint.

(2) For purposes of this section, the term "demarche" means any official communication by one government to another, by written or oral means, intended by the originating government to express—

(A) a concern over a past, present, or possible future action or activity of the recipient government, or of a person within the jurisdiction of that government, contributing to the global spread of unsafeguarded special nuclear material or of nuclear explosive devices;

(B) a request for the recipient government to counter such action or activity; or

(C) both the concern and request described in subparagraphs (A) and (B).

SEC. 829. TECHNICAL CORRECTION.

Section 133 b. of the Atomic Energy Act of 1954 (42 U.S.C. 2160c) is amended by striking "20 kilograms" and inserting "5 kilograms".

SEC. 830. DEFINITIONS.

For purposes of this part—

(1) the term "foreign person" means—

(A) an individual who is not a citizen of the United States or an alien admitted for permanent residence to the United States; or

(B) a corporation, partnership, or other nongovernment entity which is created or organized under the laws of a foreign country or which has its principal place of business outside the United States;

(2) the term "goods or technology" means—

(A) nuclear materials and equipment and sensitive nuclear technology (as such terms are defined in section 4 of the Nuclear Non-Proliferation Act of 1978), all export items designated by the President pursuant to section 309(c) of the Nuclear Non-Proliferation Act of 1978, and all technical assistance requiring authorization under section 57 b. of the Atomic Energy Act of 1954, and

(B) in the case of exports from a country other than the United States, any goods or technology that, if exported from the United States, would be goods or technology described in subparagraph (A);

(3) the term "IAEA safeguards" means the safeguards set forth in an agreement between a country and the International Atomic Energy Agency, as authorized by Article III(A)(5) of the Statute of the International Atomic Energy Agency;

(4) the term "nuclear explosive device" means any device, whether assembled or disassembled, that is designed to produce an instantaneous release of an amount of nuclear energy from special nuclear material that is greater than the amount of energy that would be released from the detonation of one pound of trinitrotoluene (TNT);

(5) the term "non-nuclear-weapon state" means any country which is not a nuclear-weapon state, as defined by Article IX (3) of the Treaty on the Non-Proliferation of Nuclear Weapons, signed at Washington, London, and Moscow on July 1, 1968;

(6) the term "special nuclear material" has the meaning given that term in section 11 aa. of the Atomic Energy Act of 1954 (42 U.S.C. 2014aa);

(7) the term "United States person" means—

(A) an individual who is a citizen of the United States or an alien admitted for permanent residence to the United States; or

(B) a corporation, partnership, or other nongovernment entity which is not a foreign person; and

(8) the term "unsafeguarded special nuclear material" means special nuclear material which is held in violation of

108 STAT. 522   PUBLIC LAW 103-236—APR. 30, 1994

IAEA safeguards or not subject to IAEA safeguards (excluding any quantity of material that could, if it were exported from the United States, be exported under a general license issued by the Nuclear Regulatory Commission).

SEC. 831. EFFECTIVE DATE.

The provisions of this part, and the amendments made by this part, shall take effect 60 days after the date of the enactment of this Act.

22 USC 3201 note.

PART C—INTERNATIONAL ATOMIC ENERGY AGENCY

SEC. 841. BILATERAL AND MULTILATERAL INITIATIVES.

It is the sense of the Congress that in order to maintain and enhance international confidence in the effectiveness of IAEA safeguards and in other multilateral undertakings to halt the global proliferation of nuclear weapons, the United States should seek to negotiate with other nations and groups of nations, including the IAEA Board of Governors and the Nuclear Suppliers Group, to—

(1) build international support for the principle that nuclear supply relationships must require purchasing nations to agree to full-scope international safeguards;

(2) encourage each nuclear-weapon state within the meaning of the Treaty to undertake a comprehensive review of its own procedures for declassifying information relating to the design or production of nuclear explosive devices and to investigate any measures that would reduce the risk of such information contributing to nuclear weapons proliferation;

(3) encourage the deferral of efforts to produce weapons-grade nuclear material for large-scale commercial uses until such time as safeguards are developed that can detect, on a timely and reliable basis, the diversion of significant quantities of such material for nuclear explosive purposes;

(4) pursue greater financial support for the implementation and improvement of safeguards from all IAEA member nations with significant nuclear programs, particularly from those nations that are currently using or planning to use weapons-grade nuclear material for commercial purposes;

(5) arrange for the timely payment of annual financial contributions by all members of the IAEA, including the United States;

(6) pursue the elimination of international commerce in highly enriched uranium for use in research reactors while encouraging multilateral cooperation to develop and to use low-enriched alternative nuclear fuels;

(7) oppose efforts by non-nuclear-weapon states to develop or use unsafeguarded nuclear fuels for purposes of naval propulsion;

(8) pursue an international open skies arrangement that would authorize the IAEA to operate surveillance aircraft and would facilitate IAEA access to satellite information for safeguards verification purposes;

(9) develop an institutional means for IAEA member nations to share intelligence material with the IAEA on possible

safeguards violations without compromising national security or intelligence sources or methods;

(10) require any exporter of a sensitive nuclear facility or sensitive nuclear technology to a non-nuclear-weapon state to notify the IAEA prior to export and to require safeguards over that facility or technology, regardless of its destination; and

(11) seek agreement among the parties to the Treaty to apply IAEA safeguards in perpetuity and to establish new limits on the right to withdraw from the Treaty.

SEC. 842. IAEA INTERNAL REFORMS.

In order to promote the early adoption of reforms in the implementation of the safeguards responsibilities of the IAEA, the Congress urges the President to negotiate with other nations and groups of nations, including the IAEA Board of Governors and the Nuclear Suppliers Group, to—

(1) improve the access of the IAEA within nuclear facilities that are capable of producing, processing, or fabricating special nuclear material suitable for use in a nuclear explosive device;

(2)(A) facilitate the IAEA's efforts to meet and to maintain its own goals for detecting the diversion of nuclear materials and equipment, giving particular attention to facilities in which there are bulk quantities of plutonium; and

(B) if it is not technically feasible for the IAEA to meet those detection goals in a particular facility, require the IAEA to declare publicly that it is unable to do so;

(3) enable the IAEA to issue fines for violations of safeguards procedures, to pay rewards for information on possible safeguards violations, and to establish a "hot line" for the reporting of such violations and other illicit uses of weapons-grade nuclear material;

(4) establish safeguards at facilities engaged in the manufacture of equipment or material that is especially designated or prepared for the processing, use, or production of special fissionable material or, in the case of non-nuclear-weapon states, of any nuclear explosive device;

(5) establish safeguards over nuclear research and development activities and facilities;

(6) implement special inspections of undeclared nuclear facilities, as provided for under existing safeguards procedures, and seek authority for the IAEA to conduct challenge inspections on demand at suspected nuclear sites;

(7) expand the scope of safeguards to include tritium, uranium concentrates, and nuclear waste containing special fissionable material, and increase the scope of such safeguards on heavy water;

(8) revise downward the IAEA's official minimum amounts of nuclear material ("significant quantity") needed to make a nuclear explosive device and establish these amounts as national rather than facility standards;

(9) expand the use of full-time resident IAEA inspectors at sensitive fuel cycle facilities;

(10) promote the use of near real time material accountancy in the conduct of safeguards at facilities that use, produce, or store significant quantities of special fissionable material;

108 STAT. 524   PUBLIC LAW 103-236—APR. 30, 1994

(11) develop with other IAEA member nations an agreement on procedures to expedite approvals of visa applications by IAEA inspectors;

(12) provide the IAEA the additional funds, technical assistance, and political support necessary to carry out the goals set forth in this subsection; and

Public information.
(13) make public the annual safeguards implementation report of the IAEA, establishing a public registry of commodities in international nuclear commerce, including dual-use goods, and creating a public repository of current nuclear trade control laws, agreements, regulations, and enforcement and judicial actions by IAEA member nations.

President.
SEC. 843. REPORTING REQUIREMENT.

(a) REPORT REQUIRED.—The President shall, in the report required by section 601(a) of the Nuclear Non-Proliferation Act of 1978, describe—

(1) the steps he has taken to implement sections 841 and 842, and

(2) the progress that has been made and the obstacles that have been encountered in seeking to meet the objectives set forth in sections 841 and 842.

(b) CONTENTS OF REPORT.—Each report under paragraph (1) shall describe—

(1) the bilateral and multilateral initiatives that the President has taken during the period since the enactment of this Act in pursuit of each of the objectives set forth in sections 841 and 842;

(2) any obstacles that have been encountered in the pursuit of those initiatives;

(3) any additional initiatives that have been proposed by other countries or international organizations to strengthen the implementation of IAEA safeguards;

(4) all activities of the Federal Government in support of the objectives set forth in sections 841 and 842;

(5) any recommendations of the President on additional measures to enhance the effectiveness of IAEA safeguards; and

(6) any initiatives that the President plans to take in support of each of the objectives set forth in sections 841 and 842.

SEC. 844. DEFINITIONS.

As used in this part—

(1) the term "highly enriched uranium" means uranium enriched to 20 percent or more in the isotope U-235;

(2) the term "IAEA" means the International Atomic Energy Agency;

(3) the term "near real time material accountancy" means a method of accounting for the location, quantity, and disposition of special fissionable material at facilities that store or process such material, in which verification of peaceful use is continuously achieved by means of frequent physical inventories and the use of in-process instrumentation;

(4) the term "special fissionable material" has the meaning given that term by Article XX(1) of the Statute of the International Atomic Energy Agency, done at the Headquarters of the United Nations on October 26, 1956;

INTERNATIONAL TREATIES AGREEMENTS AND LAWS

Treaty on the Non-Proliferation of Nuclear Weapons (NPT)

The States concluding this Treaty, hereinafter referred to as the 'Parties to the Treaty',

Considering the devastation that would be visited upon all mankind by a nuclear war and the consequent need to make every effort to avert the danger of such a war and to take measures to safeguard the security of peoples,

Believing that the proliferation of nuclear weapons would seriously enhance the danger of nuclear war,

In conformity with resolutions of the United Nations General Assembly calling for the conclusion of an agreement on the prevention of wider dissemination of nuclear weapons,

Undertaking to co-operate in facilitating the application of International Atomic Energy Agency safeguards on peaceful nuclear activities,

Expressing their support for research, development and other efforts to further the application, within the framework of the International Atomic Energy Agency safeguards system, of the principle of safeguarding effectively the flow of source and special fissionable materials by use of instruments and other techniques at certain strategic points,

Affirming the principle that the benefits of peaceful applications of nuclear technology, including any technological by-products which may be derived by nuclear-weapon States from the development of nuclear explosive devices, should be available for peaceful purposes to all Parties to the Treaty, whether nuclear-weapon or non-nuclear-weapon States,

Convinced that, in furtherance of this principle, all Parties to the Treaty are entitled to participate in the fullest possible exchange of scientific information for, and to contribute alone or in co-operation with other States to, the further development of the applications of atomic energy for peaceful purposes,

Declaring their intention to achieve at the earliest possible date the cessation of the nuclear arms race and to undertake effective measures in the direction of nuclear disarmament,

Urging the co-operation of all States in the attainment of this objective,

Recalling the determination expressed by the Parties to the 1963 Treaty banning nuclear weapons tests in the atmosphere, in outer space and under water in its Preamble to seek to achieve the discontinuance of all test explosions of nuclear weapons for all time and to continue negotiations to this end,

Desiring to further the easing of international tension and the strengthening of trust between States in order to facilitate the cessation of the manufacture of nuclear weapons, the liquidation of all their existing stockpiles, and the elimination from national arsenals of nuclear weapons and the means of their delivery pursuant to a Treaty on general and complete disarmament under strict and effective international control,

Recalling that, in accordance with the Charter of the United Nations, States must refrain in their international relations from the threat or use of force against the territorial integrity or political independence of any State or in any other manner inconsistent with the Purposes of the United Nations and that the establishment and maintenance of international peace and security are to be promoted with the least diversion for armaments of the world's human and economic resources,

Have agreed as follows:

Article I

Each nuclear-weapon State Party to the Treaty undertakes not to transfer to any recipient whatsoever nuclear weapons or other nuclear explosive devices or control over such weapons or explosive devices directly, or indirectly; and not in any way to assist, encourage, or induce any non-nuclear-weapon State to manufacture or otherwise acquire nuclear weapons or other nuclear explosive devices, or control over such weapons or explosive devices.

Article II

Each non-nuclear-weapon State Party to the Treaty undertakes not to receive the transfer from any transferor whatsoever of nuclear weapons or other nuclear explosive devices or of control over such weapons or explosive devices directly, or indirectly; not to manufacture or otherwise acquire nuclear weapons or other nuclear explosive devices; and not to seek or receive any assistance in the manufacture of nuclear weapons or other nuclear explosive devices.

Article III

1. Each non-nuclear-weapon State Party to the Treaty undertakes to accept safeguards, as set forth in an agreement to be negotiated and concluded with the International Atomic Energy Agency in accordance with the Statute of the International Atomic Energy Agency and the Agency's safeguards system, for the

NON-PROLIFERATION TREATY

exclusive purpose of verification of the fulfilment of its obligations assumed under this Treaty with a view to preventing diversion of nuclear energy from peaceful uses to nuclear weapons or other nuclear explosive devices. Procedures for the safeguards required by this Article shall be followed with respect to source or special fissionable material whether it is being produced, processed or used in any principal nuclear facility or is outside any such facility. The safeguards required by this Article shall be applied on all source or special fissionable material in all peaceful nuclear activities within the territory of such State, under its jurisdiction, or carried out under its control anywhere.

2. Each State Party to the Treaty undertakes not to provide:
   (a) source or special fissionable material, or
   (b) equipment or material especially designed or prepared for the processing, use or production of special fissionable material, to any non-nuclear-weapon State for peaceful purposes, unless the source or special fissionable material shall be subject to the safeguards required by this Article.
3. The safeguards required by this Article shall be implemented in a manner designed to comply with Article IV of this Treaty, and to avoid hampering the economic or technological development of the Parties or international co-operation in the field of peaceful nuclear activities, including the international exchange of nuclear material and equipment for the processing, use or production of nuclear material for peaceful purposes in accordance with the provisions of this Article and the principle of safeguarding set forth in the Preamble of the Treaty.
4. Non-nuclear-weapon States Party to the Treaty shall conclude agreements with the International Atomic Energy Agency to meet the requirements of this Article either individually or together with other States in accordance with the Statute of the International Atomic Energy Agency. Negotiation of such agreements shall commence within 180 days from the original entry into force of this Treaty. For States depositing their instruments of ratification or accession after the 180-day period, negotiation of such agreements shall commence not later than the date of such deposit. Such agreements shall enter into force not later than eighteen months after the date of initiation of negotiations.

Article IV

1. Nothing in this Treaty shall be interpreted as affecting the inalienable right of all the Parties to the Treaty to develop research, production and use of nuclear energy for peaceful purposes without discrimination and in conformity with Articles I and II of this Treaty.
2. All the Parties to the Treaty undertake to facilitate, and have the right to participate in, the fullest possible exchange of equipment, materials and scientific and technological information for the peaceful uses of nuclear energy. Parties to the Treaty in a position to do so shall also co-operate in contributing alone or together with other States or international organisations to the further development of the applications of nuclear energy for peaceful purposes, especially in the territories of non-nuclear-weapon States Party to the Treaty, with due consideration for the needs of the developing areas of the world.

Article V

Each Party to the Treaty undertakes to take appropriate measures to ensure that, in accordance with this Treaty, under appropriate international observation and through appropriate international procedures, potential benefits from any peaceful applications of nuclear explosions will be made available to non-nuclear-weapon States Party to the Treaty on a non-discriminatory basis and that the charge to such Parties for the explosive devices used will be as low as possible and exclude any charge for research and development. Non-nuclear-weapon States Party to the Treaty shall be able to obtain such benefits, pursuant to a special international agreement or agreements, through an appropriate international body with adequate representation of non-nuclear-weapon States. Negotiations on this subject shall commence as soon as possible after the Treaty enters into force. Non-nuclear-weapon States Party to the Treaty so desiring may also obtain such benefits pursuant to bilateral agreements.

Article VI

Each of the Parties to the Treaty undertakes to pursue negotiations in good faith on effective measures relating to cessation of the nuclear arms race at an early date and to nuclear disarmament, and on a treaty on general and complete disarmament under strict and effective international control.

Article VII

Nothing in this Treaty affects the right of any group of States to conclude regional treaties in order to assure the total absence of nuclear weapons in their respective territories.

Article VIII

1. Any Party to the Treaty may propose amendments to this Treaty. The text of any proposed amendment shall be submitted to the Depository Governments which shall circulate it to all Parties to the Treaty. Thereupon, if requested to do so by one-third or more of the Parties to the Treaty, the Depository Governments shall convene a conference, to which they shall invite all the Parties to the Treaty, to consider such an amendment.
2. Any amendment to this Treaty must be approved by a majority of the votes of all the Parties to the Treaty, including the votes of all nuclear-weapon States Party to the Treaty and all other Parties which, on the date the amendment is circulated, are members of the Board of Governors of the International Atomic Energy Agency. The amendment shall enter into force for each Party that deposits its instrument of ratification of the amendment upon the deposit of such instruments of ratification by a majority of all the Parties, including the instruments of ratification of all nuclear-weapon States Party to the Treaty and all other Parties which, on the date the amendment is circulated, are members of the Board of Governors of the International Atomic Energy Agency. Thereafter, it shall enter into force for any other Party upon the deposit of its instrument of ratification of the amendment.
3. Five years after the entry into force of this Treaty, a conference of Parties to the Treaty shall be held in Geneva, Switzerland, in order to review the operation of this Treaty with a view to assuring that the purposes of the Preamble and the provisions of the Treaty are being realised. At intervals of five years thereafter, a majority of the Parties to the Treaty may obtain, by submitting a proposal to this effect to the Depository Governments, the convening of further conferences with the same objective of reviewing the operation of the Treaty.

Article IX

1. This Treaty shall be open to all States for signature. Any State which does not sign the Treaty before its entry into force in accordance with paragraph 3 of this Article may accede to it at any time.
2. This Treaty shall be subject to ratification by signatory States. Instruments of ratification and instruments of accession shall be deposited with the Government of the United Kingdom of Great Britain and Northern Ireland, the Union of Soviet Socialist Republics and the United States of America, which are hereby designated the Depository Governments.
3. This Treaty shall enter into force after its ratification by the States, the Governments of which are designated Depositories of the Treaty, and forty other States signatory to this Treaty and the deposit of their instruments of ratification. For the purposes of this Treaty, a nuclear-weapon State is one which has manufactured and exploded a nuclear weapon or other nuclear explosive device prior to 1 January 1967.
4. For States whose instruments of ratification or accession are deposited subsequent to the entry into force of this Treaty, it shall enter into force on the date of the deposit of their instruments of ratification or accession.
5. The Depository Governments shall promptly inform all signatory and acceding States of the date of each signature, the date of deposit of each instrument of ratification or of accession, the date of the entry into force of this Treaty, and the date of receipt of any requests for convening a conference or other notices.
6. This Treaty shall be registered by the Depository Governments pursuant to Article 102 of the Charter of the United Nations.

Article X

1. Each Party shall in exercising its national sovereignty have the right to withdraw from the Treaty if it decides that extraordinary events, related to the subject matter of this Treaty, have jeopardised the supreme interests of its country. It shall give notice of such withdrawal to all other Parties to the Treaty and to the United Nations Security Council three months in advance. Such notice shall include a statement of the extraordinary events it regards as having jeopardised its supreme interests.
2. Twenty-five years after the entry into force of the Treaty, a conference shall be convened to decide whether the Treaty shall continue in force indefinitely, or shall be extended for an additional fixed period or periods. This decision shall be taken by a majority of the Parties to the Treaty.

Article XI

This Treaty, the English, Russian, French, Spanish and Chinese texts of which are equally authentic, shall be deposited in the archives of the Depository Governments. Duly certified copies of this Treaty shall be transmitted by the Depository Governments to the Governments of the signatory and acceding States.

IN WITNESS WHEREOF the undersigned, duly authorized, have signed this Treaty.

A-4　　　　　　　　　　　　NON-PROLIFERATION TREATY

DONE in triplicate, at the cities of London, Moscow and Washington, the first day of July, one thousand nine hundred and sixty-eight.

List of Parties to the NPT

Afghanistan	Hungary	St. Lucia
Albania	Iceland	St. Vincent and the Grenadines
Antigua and Barbuda	Indonesia	San Marino
Australia	Iran, Islamic Republic of	Sao Tome and Principe
Austria	Iraq	Saudi Arabia
Azerbaijan	Ireland	Senegal
Bahamas	Italy	Seychelles
Bahrain	Jamaica	Sierra Leone
Bangladesh	Japan	Singapore
Barbados	Jordan	Slovenia
Belgium	Kenya	Solomon Islands
Belize	Kiribati	Somalia
Benin	Korea, Democratic People's	South Africa
Bhutan	Republic of[2]	Spain
Bolivia	Korea, Republic of	Sri Lanka
Botswana	Kuwait	Sudan
Brunei	Lao People's Democratic Republic	Suriname
Bulgaria	Latvia	Swaziland
Burkina Faso	Lebanon	Sweden
Burundi	Lesotho	Switzerland
Cambodia	Liberia	Syrian Arab Republic
Cameroon	Libyan Arab Jamahiriya	Taiwan, Province of China
Canada	Liechtenstein	Tanzania, United Republic of
Cape Verde	Lithuania	Thailand
Central African Republic	Luxembourg	Togo
Chad	Madagascar	Tonga
China, People's Republic of	Malawi	Trinidad and Tobago
Colombia	Malaysia	Tunisia
Congo	Maldives	Turkey
Costa Rica	Mali	Tuvalu
Côte d'Ivoire	Malta	Uganda
Cyprus	Mauritius	United Kingdom
Czechoslovakia[1]	Mexico	United States of America
Denmark	Mongolia	Uruguay
Dominica	Morocco	Uzbekistan
Dominican Republic	Mozambique	Venezuela
Ecuador	Myanmar	Viet Nam
Equatorial Guinea	Namibia	Western Samoa
Egypt	Nauru	Yemen
El Salvador	Nepal	Yugoslavia
Estonia	Netherlands	Zaire
Ethiopia	New Zealand	Zambia
Fiji	Nicaragua	Zimbabwe
Finland	Niger	
France	Nigeria	The following former states of the Soviet Union have indicated an intention to accede to the NPT, but have either not yet done so or are in the process of doing so:
Gabon	Norway	
Gambia	Panama	
Germany	Papua New Guinea	
Ghana	Paraguay	
Greece	Peru	Armenia
Grenada	Philippines	Belarus
Guatemala	Poland	Kazakhstan
Guinea	Portugal	Kirgizstan
Guinea-Bissau	Qatar	Moldova
Haiti	Romania	Tajikistan
Holy See	Russian Federation	Turkimenistan
Honduras	Rwanda	Ukraine

[1] As of 1 January 1993, Czechoslovakia became two separate states, the Czech Republic and the Slovak Republic.
[2] On 12 March 1993, the Democratic People's Republic of Korea announced its intention to withdraw from the NPT. Under Article X.1, three months notice of this must be given.

376

Participation in the

Review Conferences of the Parties to the Treaty on the

Non-Proliferation of Nuclear Weapons

Bruce Unger
Department of International Relations
Randolph-Macon College
June 28, 1993

There have been four Review Conferences of the Parties to the Treaty on the Non-proliferation of Nuclear Weapons, each with its own Rules of Procedure. These four sets of Rules of Procedure have contained similar provisions governing participation.[1]

At each Conference, the Rules of Procedure have used a nation's relationship to the Non-proliferation Treaty (NPT) to define the level of participation. States which have ratified or otherwise acceded to the NPT are entitled to full participation. Full participation confers the rights to attend all meetings, to submit official Conference documents, to have the floor, and to participate in the adoption of decisions. Signatory states which have yet to ratify or accede may attend with all rights accept taking part in the formal decision making process. Other states eligible to sign or ratify the NPT, but which have yet to do so, may apply for observer status. Observer states may attend open meetings and may submit documents. However, such documents lack official standing. The Third and Fourth Review Conferences extended observer status to national liberation organizations which enjoyed such status in the United Nations General Assembly.[2] Finally, the Rules of Procedure at all Review Conferences provided for the participation of various international and regional organizations.

---

[1]The rules governing participation are found in: NPT/CONF/20, 9 May 1975, Rules 1 and 44, pp. 1, 11; NPT/CONF.II/15, 13 August 1980, Rules 1 and 44, pp. 1, 11; NPT/CONF.III/41, 9 September 1985, Rules 1 and 44, pp. 1 and 11; NPT/CONF.IV/1, 2 May 1990, Annex IV, Rules 1 and 44, pp. 14, 25, 26.

[2]NPT/CONF.III/41, Rule 44,2(b), p. 11; NPT/CONF.IV/1, Rule 44,2(b), p.26.

In May, 1993, the First Session of the Preparatory Committee for the 1995 Conference had before it a Conference Room Paper, prepared by the Secretariat at the request of the NPT Depositaries, which contained Draft Rules of Procedure. This document drew heavily from the Rules of Procedure of the Fourth Review Conference. The Draft Rules contained one recommended change in the Rules of Procedure that affect participation: the deletion of the provisions for signatory states which have yet to ratify the NPT. The rationale was simple. There now are no states in that category.[3] No action was taken on the Draft Rules during the First Session of the Prepartory Committee.

---

[3]NPT/CONF.1995/PC.1/CRP.1, 7 May 1993, Rule 44, pp. 16-18.

Participation in NPT Review Conferences

	\multicolumn{4}{c}{Review Conference}			
	First	Second	Third	Fourth

Full Participant = x   Signatory = s   Observer = o
Non-national Actor = n

	First	Second	Third	Fourth
Afghanistan			x	
Algeria	o	o	o	o
Argentina	o	o	o	o
Australia	x	x	x	x
Austria	x	x	x	x
Bahrain			o	x
Bangladesh		x	x	x
Belgium	x	x	x	x
Bhutan			x	x
Bolivia	x		x	x
Brazil	o	o	o	o
Brunei Darussalam			x	x
Bulgaria	x	x	x	x
Burundi		x	x	
Byelorussia				o
Cameroon		x	x	x
Canada	x	x	x	x
Chile		o	o	o
China				o
Colombia			s	x
Congo		x		
Costa Rica		x		x
Cote d'Ivoire		x	x	x
Cuba	o	o	o	o
Cyprus	x	x	x	x
Czech and Slovak Federal Republic	x	x	x	x
Denmark	x	x	x	x
Ecuador	x	x	x	x
Egypt	s	s	x	x
Ethiopia	x	x	x	x
Finland	x	x	x	x
France				o
Gabon	x	x		
German Democratic Republic	x	x	x	x
Germany, Federal Republic of	x	x	x	x
Ghana	x	x	x	x
Greece	x	x	x	x

Participation in NPT Review Conferences
Continued

	Review Conference			
	First	Second	Third	Fourth
Guatemala			x	
Holy See	x	x	x	x
Honduras	x	x	x	x
Hungary	x	x	x	x
Iceland	x	x	x	x
Indonesia		x	x	x
Iran	x	x	x	x
Iraq	x(a)	x	x	x
Ireland	x	x	x	x
Israel	o	o	o	o
Italy	x	x	x	x
Jamaica	x			x
Japan	s	x	x	x
Jordan	x	x	x	x
Kenya		x	x	x
Korea, North				x
Korea, South		x	x	x
Kuwait			s	x
Lebanon	x	x	x	
Liberia	x			
Libya	x	x	x	x
Liechtenstein		x	x	x
Luxembourg	x	x	x	x
Malaysia		x	x	x
Maldives			x	
Malta		x	x	x
Mauritius	x		x	
Mexico	x	x	x	x
Mongolia	x	x	x	x
Morocco	x	x	x	x
Mozambique		o		
Myanmar				o
Nauru			x	
Nepal	x		x	
Netherlands	x	x	x	x
New Zealand	x	x	x	x
Nicaragua	x	x	x	x
Nigeria	x	x	x	x
Norway	x	x	x	x
Oman				o
Pakistan			o	o
Panama	s	x	x	
Papua New Guinea			x	

Participation in NPT Review Conferences
Continued

	Review Conference			
	First	Second	Third	Fourth
Peru	x	x	x	x
Philippines	x	x	x	x
Poland	x	x	x	x
Portugal		x	x	x
Qatar				x
Romania	x	x	x	x
Rwanda			x	
San Marino	x	x	x	x
Sao Tome and Principe				x
Saudi Arabia				x
Senegal	x	x	x	x
Seychelles			x	
Sierra Leone		x		
Singapore				x
Somalia		x	x	x
South Africa	o			
Spain	o	o	o	x
Sri Lanka		x	x	x
Sudan	x	x	x	x
Sweden	x	x	x	x
Switzerland	s	x	x	x
Syria	x	x	x	x
Tanzania		o	o	o
Thailand	x	x	x	x
Trinidad and Tobago	s			
Tunisia	x	x	x	x
Turkey	s	x	x	x
Uganda			x	x
Ukraine				o
USSR	x	x	x	x
United Arab Emirates		o		
United Kingdom	x	x	x	x
USA	x	x	x	x
Uruguay	x	x	x	x
Venezuela	s	x	x	x
Viet Nam			x	x
Yemen, Aden (b)		x	x	
Yemen Arab Republic (b)			s	
Yemen, Republic of (b)				x
Yugoslavia	x	x	x	x
Zaire	x	x	x	
Zambia		o		
Zimbabwe				o

Participation in NPT Review Conferences
Continued

	Review Conference			
	First	Second	Third	Fourth
CEC (c)				n
IAEA	n	n	n	n
League of Arab States	n	n	n	n
OPANAL (d)	n	n	n	n
OAU			n	
PLO			n	n
United Nations	n	n	n	n

Sources: NPT/CONF/35/I, 30 May 1975, pp. 4-5;
NPT/CONF.II/22/I, 7 September 1980, pp. 4-5;
NPT/CONF.III/64/I, 25 September 1985, pp. 6-7;
NPT/CONF.IV/45/I, 4 October 1990, pp. 6-7.

(a) Although a party to the NPT, Iraq attended the first Review Conference as an observer at its own request. See: NPT/Conf/35/I, p. 4n.

(b) The People's Democratic Republic of Yemen (Aden) and the Yemen Arab Republic merged to form the Republic of Yemen in 1990.

(c) The Commission of the European Communities.

(d) Agency for the Prohibition of Nuclear Weapons in Latin America.

Selected Citations on Participation in NPT Review Conferences

First Review Conference

Donna Kramer. The Nuclear Non-proliferation Treaty Review Conference. Prologue: The Review Conference of 1980. Epilogue: The Review Conference of 1975. CRS Report No. 80-65S. March 28, 1980, pp. 20-23.

Bruce Unger. "The Nuclear Non-proliferation Treaty Review Conference." World Affairs, 139, 2 (Fall, 1976), pp. 94, 110, 111.

Second Review Conference

Charles Gellner. Security Issues, Including SALT II, in the Second Review Conference on the Nuclear Nonproliferation Treaty (NPT). CRS Report. November, 1980, pp. 4-5.

Donna Kramer. Nuclear Non-proliferation Treaty Review Conference of 1980. CRS Issue Brief IB80071. September 29, 1980, pp. 6-7.

Third Review Conference

Ambassador Lewis Dunn. Prepared Statement. U.S. Congress. Senate. Committee on Governmental Affairs. Subcommittee on Energy, Nuclear Proliferation, and Government Processes. Hearing. Third Non-proliferation Treaty Review Conference and 29th Regular Session of the General Conference of the International Atomic Energy Agency. 99th Congress, 1st Session. S. Hrg. 99-488. November 20, 1985, pp. 41-42.

Fourth Review Conference

David Fischer and Harald Muller. "The Fourth Review of the Non-proliferation Treaty." In: SIPRI Yearbook 1991: World Armaments and Disarmament. New York: Oxford University Press, 1991, pp. 555-556.

Treaty Banning Nuclear Weapon Tests in the Atmosphere, in Outer Space and Under Water [Partial Test Ban Treaty]

The Governments of the United States of America, the United Kingdom of Great Britain and Northern Ireland, and the Union of Soviet Socialist Republics, hereinafter referred to as the 'Original Parties',

Proclaiming as their principal aim the speediest possible achievement of an agreement on general and complete disarmament under strict international control in accordance with the objectives of the United Nations which would put an end to the armaments race and eliminate the incentive to the production and testing of all kinds of weapons, including nuclear weapons.

Seeking to achieve the discontinuance of all test explosions of nuclear weapons for all time, determined to continue negotiations to this end, and desiring to put an end to the contamination of man's environment by radioactive substances,

Have agreed as follows;

Article I

1. Each of the Parties to this Treaty undertake to prohibit, to prevent, and not to carry out any nuclear weapon test explosion, or any other nuclear explosion, at any place under its jurisdiction or control:
   (a) in the atmosphere, beyond its limits, including outer space; or under water, including territorial waters or high seas; or
   (b) in any other environment if such explosion causes radioactive debris to be present outside the territorial limits of the State under whose jurisdiction or control such explosion is conducted. It is understood in this connection that the provisions of this subparagraph are without prejudice to the conclusion of a treaty resulting in the permanent banning of all nuclear test explosions, including all such explosions underground, the conclusion of which, as the Parties have stated in the Preamble to this Treaty, they seek to achieve.
2. Each of the Parties to this Treaty undertakes furthermore to refrain from causing, encouraging, or in any way participating in, the carrying out of any nuclear weapon test explosion, or any other nuclear explosion, anywhere which would take place in any of the environments described, or have the effect referred to, in paragraph 1 of this Article.

Article II

1. Any Party may propose amendments to this Treaty. The text of any proposed amendments shall be submitted to the Depositary Governments which shall circulate it to all Parties to this Treaty. Thereafter, if requested to do so by one-third or more of the Parties, the Depositary Governments shall convene a conference, to which they shall invite all the Parties, to consider such amendment.
2. Any amendment to this Treaty must be approved by a majority of the votes of all the Parties to this Treaty, including the votes of all of the Original Parties. The amendment shall enter into force for all Parties upon the deposit of instruments of ratification by a majority of all the Parties, including the instruments of ratification of all the Original Parties.

Article III

1. This Treaty shall be open to all States for signature. Any State which does not sign this Treaty before its entry into force in accordance with paragraph 3 of this Article may accede to it at any time.
2. This Treaty shall be subject to ratification by signatory States. Instruments of ratification and instruments of accession shall be deposited with the Governments of the Original Parties — the United States of America, the United Kingdom of Great Britain and Northern Ireland, and the Union of Soviet Socialist Republics — which are hereby designated the Depositary Governments.
3. This Treaty shall enter into force after its ratification by all the Original Parties and the deposit of their instruments of ratification.
4. For States whose instruments of ratification or accession are deposited subsequent to the entry into force of this Treaty, it shall enter into force on the date of the deposit of their instruments of ratification or accession.
5. The Depositary Governments shall promptly inform all signatory and acceding States of the date of each signature, the date of deposit of each instrument of ratification of and accession to this Treaty, the date of its entry into force, and the date of receipt of any requests for conferences or other notices.
6. This Treaty shall be registered by the Depositary Governments pursuant to Article 102 of the Charter of the United Nations.

Article IV

This Treaty shall be of unlimited duration.
Each Party shall in exercising its national sovereignty have the right to withdraw from the Treaty if it decides that extraordinary events, related to the subject matter of this Treaty, have jeopardized the supreme interests of its country. It shall give notice of such withdrawal to all other Parties to the Treaty three months in advance.

Article V

This Treaty, of which the English and Russian texts are equally authentic, shall be deposited in the archives of the Depositary Governments. Duly certified copies of this Treaty shall be transmitted by the Depositary Governments to the Governments of the signatory and acceding States.

IN WITNESS WHEREOF the undersigned, duly authorized, have signed this Treaty.

DONE in triplicate at the city of Moscow the fifth day of August, one thousand nine hundred and sixty-three.

Signatories and Parties to the Treaty Banning Nuclear Weapon Tests in the Atmosphere, in Outer Space and Under Water

Afghanistan	Equatorial Guinea	Madagascar	Sierra Leone
Algeria	Ethiopia	Malawi	Singapore
Antigua and Barbuda	Fiji	Malaysia	Somalia
Argentina	Finland	Mali	South Africa
Australia	Gabon	Malta	Spain
Austria	Gambia	Mauritania	Sri Lanka
Bahamas	Germany	Mauritius	Sudan
Bangladesh	Ghana	Mexico	Swaziland
Belarus	Greece	Mongolia	Sweden
Belgium	Guatemala	Morocco	Switzerland
Benin	Guinea-Bissau	Myanmar [formerly Burma]	Syria
Bhutan	Haiti	Nepal	Taiwan, Province of China
Bolivia	Honduras	Netherlands	Tanzania, United Republic of
Botswana	Hungary	New Zealand	Thailand
Brazil	Iceland	Nicaragua	Togo
Bulgaria	India	Niger	Tonga
Burkina Faso	Indonesia	Nigeria	Trinidad and Tobago
Burundi	Iran, Islamic Republic of	Norway	Tunisia
Cameroon	Iraq	Pakistan	Turkey
Canada	Ireland	Panama	Uganda
Cape Verde	Israel	Papua New Guinea	Ukraine
Central African Republic	Italy	Paraguay	United Kingdom
Chad	Jamaica	Peru	United States of America
Chile	Japan	Philippines	Uruguay
Colombia	Jordan	Poland	Venezuela
Costa Rica	Kenya	Portugal	Yemen
Côte d'Ivoire	Korea, Republic of	Romania	Yugoslavia
Cyprus	Kuwait	Russian Federation	Zaire
Czechoslovakia[1]	Lao People's Democratic Republic	Rwanda	Zambia
Denmark	Lebanon	Samoa	
Dominican Republic	Liberia	San Marino	
Ecuador	Libyan Arab Jamahiriya	Senegal	
Egypt	Luxembourg	Seychelles	
El Salvador			

1 As of 1 Jaury 1993, Czechoslovakia became two separate states, the Czech Republic and the Slovak Republic.

Treaty for the Prohibition of Nuclear Weapons in Latin America
[Treaty of Tlatelolco]

OPENED FOR SIGNATURE AT MEXICO CITY: 14 February 1967
ENTERED INTO FORCE: For each Government individually
THE DEPOSITORY GOVERNMENT: Mexico

PREAMBLE

In the name of their peoples and faithfully interpreting their desires and aspirations, the Governments of the States which sign the Treaty for the Prohibition of Nuclear Weapons in Latin America,

Desiring to contribute, so far as lies in their power, towards ending the armaments race, especially in the field of nuclear weapons, and towards strengthening a world at peace, based on the sovereign equality of States, mutual respect and good neighbourliness,

Recalling that the United Nations General Assembly, in its Resolution 808 (IX), adopted unanimously as one of the three points of a co-ordinated programme of disarmament 'the total prohibition of the use and manufacture of nuclear weapons and weapons of mass destruction of every type',

Recalling that militarily denuclearized zones are not an end in themselves but rather a means for achieving general and complete disarmament at a later stage,

Recalling United Nations General Assembly Resolution 1911 (XVIII), which established that the measures that should be agreed upon for the denuclearization of Latin America should be taken 'in the light of the principles of the Charter of the United Nations and of regional agreements',

Recalling United Nations General Assembly Resolution 2028 (XX), which established the principle of an acceptable balance of mutual responsibilities and duties for the nuclear and non-nuclear powers, and

Recalling that the Charter of the Organization of American States proclaims that it is an essential purpose of the Organization to strengthen the peace and security of the hemisphere,

Convinced:

That the incalculable destructive power of nuclear weapons has made it imperative that the legal prohibition of war should be strictly observed in practice if the survival of civilization and of mankind itself is to be assured,

That nuclear weapons, whose terrible effects are suffered, indiscriminately and inexorably, by military forces and civilian population alike, constitute, through the persistence of the radioactivity they release, an attack on the integrity of the human species and ultimately may even render the whole earth uninhabitable,

That general and complete disarmament under effective international control is a vital matter which all the peoples of the world equally demand,

That the proliferation of nuclear weapons, which seems inevitable unless States, in the exercise of their sovereign rights, impose restrictions on themselves in order to prevent it, would make any agreement on disarmament enormously difficult and would increase the danger of the outbreak of a nuclear conflagration,

That the establishment of militarily denuclearized zones is closely linked with the maintenance of peace and security in the respective regions,

That the military denuclearization of vast geographical zones, adopted by the sovereign decision of the States comprised therein, will exercise a beneficial influence on other regions where similar conditions exist,

That the privileged situation of the signatory States, whose territories are wholly free from nuclear weapons, imposes upon them the inescapable duty of preserving that situation both in their own interests and for the good of mankind,

That the existence of nuclear weapons in any country of Latin America would make it a target for possible nuclear attacks and would inevitably set off, throughout the region, a ruinous race in nuclear weapons which would involve the unjustifiable diversion, for warlike purposes, of the limited resources required for economic and social development,

That the foregoing reasons, together with the traditional peace-loving outlook of Latin America, give rise to an inescapable necessity that nuclear energy should be used in that region exclusively for peaceful purposes, and that the Latin American countries should use their right to the greatest and most equitable possible access to this new source of energy in order to expedite the economic and social development of their peoples,

Convinced finally:

That the military denuclearization of Latin America — being understood to mean the undertaking entered into internationally in this Treaty to keep their territories forever free from nuclear weapons — will constitute a measure which will spare their peoples from the squandering of their limited resources on nuclear armaments and will protect them against possible nuclear attacks on their territories, and will also constitute a significant contribution towards preventing the proliferation of nuclear weapons and a powerful factor for general and complete disarmament, and

That Latin America, faithful to its tradition of universality, must not only endeavour to banish from its homelands the scourge of a nuclear war, but must also strive to promote the well-being and advancement of its peoples, at the same time co-operating in the fulfilment of the ideas of mankind, that is to say, in the consolidation of a permanent peace based on equal rights, economic fairness and social justice for all, in accordance with the principles and purposes set forth in the Charter of the United Nations and in the Charter of the Organization of American States,

Have agreed as follows:

OBLIGATIONS
Article 1

1. The Contracting Parties hereby undertake to use exclusively for peaceful purposes the nuclear material and facilities which are under their jurisdiction, and to prohibit and prevent in their respective territories:
   (a) The testing, use, manufacture, production or acquisition by any means whatsoever of any nuclear weapons, by the Parties themselves, directly or indirectly, on behalf of anyone else or in any other way, and
   (b) The receipt, storage, installation, deployment and any form of possession of any nuclear weapons, directly or indirectly, by the Parties themselves, by anyone on their behalf or in any other way.
2. The Contracting Parties also undertake to refrain from engaging in, encouraging or authorizing, directly or indirectly, or in any way participating in the testing, use, manufacture, production, possession or control of any nuclear weapon.

DEFINITION OF THE CONTRACTING PARTIES
Article 2

For the purposes of this Treaty, the Contracting Parties are those for whom the Treaty is in force.

DEFINITION OF TERRITORY
Article 3

For the purposes of this Treaty, the term 'territory' shall include the territorial sea, air space and any other space over which the State exercises sovereignty in accordance with its own legislation.

ZONE OF APPLICATION
Article 4

1. The zone of application of this Treaty is the whole of the territories for which the Treaty is in force.
2. Upon fulfilment of the requirements of article 28, paragraph 1, the zone of application of this Treaty shall also be that which is situated in the western hemisphere within the following limits (except the continental part of the territory of the United States of America and its territorial waters): starting at a point located at 35° north latitude, 75° west longitude; from this point directly southward to a point at 30° north latitude, 50° west longitude; from there, directly eastward to a point at 30° north latitude, 50° west longitude; from there, along a loxodromic line to a point at 5° north latitude, 20° west longitude; from there, directly southward to a point at 60° south latitude, 20° west longitude; from there, directly westward to a point at 60° south latitude, 115° west longitude; from there, directly northward to a point at 0 latitude, 115° west longitude; from there along a loxodromic line to a point at 35° north latitude, 150° west longitude; from there, directly eastward to a point at 36° north latitude, 75° west longitude.

DEFINITION OF NUCLEAR WEAPONS
Article 5

For the purposes of this Treaty, a nuclear weapon is any device which is capable of releasing nuclear energy in an uncontrolled manner and which has a group of characteristics that are appropriate for use for warlike purposes. An instrument that may be used for the transport or propulsion of the device is not included in this definition if it is separable from the device and not an indivisible part thereof.

MEETING OF SIGNATORIES
Article 6

At the request of any of the signatory States or if the Agency established by article 7 should so decide, a meeting of all the signatories may be convoked to consider in common questions which may affect the very essence of this instrument, including possible amendments to it. In either case, the meeting will be convoked by the General Secretary.

ORGANIZATION
Article 7

1. In order to ensure compliance with the obligations of this Treaty, the Contracting Parties hereby establish an international organization to be known as the Agency for the Prohibition of Nuclear Weapons in Latin America, hereinafter referred to as 'the Agency'. Only the Contracting Parties shall be affected by its decisions.
2. The Agency shall be responsible for the holding of periodic or extraordinary consultations among Member States on matters relating to the purposes, measures and procedures set forth in this Treaty and to the supervision of compliance with the obligations arising therefrom.
3. The Contracting Parties agree to extend to the Agency full and prompt co-operation in accordance with the provisions of this Treaty, of any agreements they may conclude with the Agency and of any agreements the Agency may conclude with any other international organization or body.
4. The headquarters of the Agency shall be in Mexico City.

ORGANS
Article 8

1. There are hereby established as principal organs of the Agency a General Conference, a Council and a Secretariat.
2. Such subsidiary organs as are considered necessary by the General Conference may be established within the purview of this Treaty.

THE GENERAL CONFERENCE
Article 9

1. The General Conference, the supreme organ of the Agency, shall be composed of all the Contracting Parties; it shall hold regular sessions every two years, and may also hold special sessions whenever this Treaty so provides or, in the opinion of the Council, the circumstances so require.
2. The General Conference:
    (a) May consider and decide on any matters or questions covered by this Treaty, within the limits thereof, including those referring to powers and functions of any organ provided for in this Treaty;
    (b) Shall establish procedures for the control system to ensure observance of this Treaty in accordance with its provisions;
    (c) Shall elect the Members of the Council and the General Secretary;
    (d) May remove the General Secretary from office if the proper functioning of the Agency so requires;
    (e) Shall receive and consider the biennial and special reports submitted by the Council and the General Secretary;
    (f) Shall initiate and consider studies designed to facilitate the optimum fulfilment of the aims of this Treaty, without prejudice to the power of the General Secretary independently to carry out similar studies for submission to and consideration by the Conference;
    (g) Shall be the organ competent to authorize the conclusion of agreements with Governments and other international organisations and bodies.
3. The General Conference shall adopt the Agency's budget and fix the scale of financial contributions to be paid by Member States, taking into account the systems and criteria used for the same purpose by the United Nations.
4. The General Conference shall elect its officers for each session and may establish such subsidiary organs as it deems necessary for the performance of its functions.
5. Each Member of the Agency shall have one vote. The decisions of the General Conference shall be taken by a two-thirds majority of the Members present and voting in the case of matters relating to the control system and measures referred to in article 20, the admission of new Members, the election or removal of the General Secretary, adoption of the budget and matters related thereto. Decisions on other matters, as well as procedural questions and also determination of which questions must be decided by a two-thirds majority, shall be taken by a simple majority of the Members present and voting

6. The General Conference shall adopt its own rules of procedure.

THE COUNCIL
Article 10

1. The Council shall be composed of five Members of the Agency elected by the General Conference from among the Contracting Parties, due account being taken of equitable geographic distribution.
2. The Members of the Council shall be elected for a term of four years. However, in the first election three will be elected for two years. Outgoing Members may not be re-elected for the following period unless the limited number of States for which the Treaty is in force so requires.
3. Each Member of the Council shall have one representative.
4. The Council shall be so organized as to be able to function continuously.
5. In addition to the functions conferred upon it by this Treaty and to those which may be assigned to it by the General Conference, the Council shall, through the General Secretary, ensure the proper operation of the control system in accordance with the provisions of this Treaty and with the decisions adopted by the General Conference.
6. The Council shall submit an annual report on its work to the General Conference as well as such special reports as it deems necessary or which the General Conference requests of it.
7. The Council shall elect its officers for each session.
8. The decisions of the Council shall be taken by a simple majority of its Members present and voting.
9. The Council shall adopt its own rules of procedure.

THE SECRETARIAT
Article 11

1. The Secretariat shall consist of a General Secretary, who shall be the chief administrative officer of the Agency, and of such staff as the Agency may require. The term of office of the General Secretary shall be four years and he may be re-elected for a single additional term. The General Secretary may not be a national of the country in which the Agency has its headquarters. In case the office of General Secretary becomes vacant, a new election shall be held to fill the office for the remainder of the term.
2. The staff of the Secretariat shall be appointed by the General Secretary, in accordance with rules laid down by the General Conference.
3. In addition to the functions conferred upon him by this Treaty and to those which may be assigned to him by the General Conference, the General Secretary shall ensure, as provided by article 10, paragraph 5, the proper operation of the control system established by this Treaty, in accordance with the provisions of the Treaty and the decisions taken by the General Conference.
4. The General Secretary shall act in that capacity in all meetings of the General Conference and of the Council and shall make an annual report to both bodies on the work of the Agency and any special reports requested by the General Conference or the Council or which the General Secretary may deem desirable.
5. The General Secretary shall establish the procedures for distributing to all Contracting Parties information received by the Agency from governmental sources and such information from non-governmental sources as may be of interest to the Agency.
6. In the performance of their duties the General Secretary and the staff shall not seek or receive instructions from any Government or from any other authority external to the Agency and shall refrain from any action which might reflect on their position as international officials responsible only to the Agency; subject to their responsibility to the Agency, they shall not disclose any industrial secrets or other confidential information coming to their knowledge by reason of their official duties in the Agency.
7. Each of the Contracting Parties undertakes to respect the exclusively international character of the responsibilities of the General Secretary and the staff and not to seek the influence them in the discharge of their responsibilities.

CONTROL SYSTEM
Article 12

1. For the purpose of verifying compliance with the obligations entered into by the Contracting Parties in accordance with article 1, a control system shall be established which shall be put into effect in accordance with the provisions of articles 13-18 of this Treaty.
2. The control system shall be used in particular for the purpose of verifying:
    (a) That devices, services and facilities intended for peaceful uses of nuclear energy are not used in the testing or manufacture of nuclear weapons;

(b) That none of the activities prohibited in article 1 of this Treaty are carried out in the territory of the Contracting Parties with nuclear materials or weapons introduced from abroad; and

(c) That explosions for peaceful purposes are compatible with article 18 of this Treaty.

IAEA SAFEGUARDS
Article 13

Each Contracting Party shall negotiate multilateral or bilateral agreements with the International Atomic Energy Agency for the application of its safeguards to its nuclear activities. Each Contracting Party shall initiate negotiations within a period of 180 days after the date of the deposit of its instrument of ratification of this Treaty. These agreements shall enter into force, for each Party, not later than eighteen months after the date of the initiation of such negotiations except in case of unforeseen circumstances or *Force Majeure*.

REPORTS OF THE PARTIES
Article 14

1. The Contracting Parties shall submit to the Agency and to the International Atomic Energy Agency, for their information, semi-annual reports stating that no activity prohibited under this Treaty has occurred in their respective territories.
2. The Contracting Parties shall simultaneously transmit to the Agency a copy of any report they may submit to the International Atomic Energy Agency which relates to matters that are the subject of this Treaty and to the application of safeguards.
3. The Contracting Parties shall also transmit to the Organization of American States, for its information, any reports that may be of interest to it, in accordance with the obligations established by the Inter-American System.

SPECIAL REPORTS REQUESTED BY THE GENERAL SECRETARY
Article 15

1. With the authorization of the Council, the General Secretary may request any of the Contracting Parties to provide the Agency with complementary or supplementary information regarding any event or circumstance connected with compliance with this Treaty, explaining his reasons. The Contracting Parties undertake to co-operate promptly and fully with the General Secretary.
2. The General Secretary shall inform the Council and the Contracting Parties forthwith of such requests and of the respective replies.

SPECIAL INSPECTIONS
Article 16

1. The International Atomic Energy Agency and the Council established by this Treaty have the power of carrying out special inspections in the following cases:
   (a) In the case of the International Atomic Energy Agency, in accordance with the agreements referred to in article 13 of this Treaty;
   (b) In the case of the Council:
      (i) When so requested, the reasons for the request being stated, by any Party which suspects that some activity prohibited by this Treaty has been carried out or is about to be carried out, either in the territory of any other Party or in any other place on such latter Party's behalf, the Council shall immediately arrange for such an inspection in accordance with article 10, paragraph 5;
      (ii) When requested by any Party which has been suspected of or charged with having violated this Treaty, the Council shall immediately arrange for the special inspection requested in accordance with article 10, paragraph 5. The above request will be made to the Council through the General Secretary.
2. The costs and expenses of any special inspection carried out under paragraph 1, subparagraph (b), sections (i) and (ii) shall be borne by the requesting Party or Parties, except where the Council concludes on the basis of the report on the special inspection that, in view of the circumstances existing in the case, such costs and expenses should be borne by the Agency.
3. The General Conference shall formulate the procedures for the organization and execution of the special inspections carried out in accordance with paragraph 1, subparagraph (b), sections (i) and (ii) of this article.
4. The Contracting Parties undertake to grant the inspectors carrying out such special inspections full and free access to all places and all information which may be necessary for the performance of their duties and which are directly and intimately connected with the suspicion of violation of this Treaty. If so requested

by the authorities of the Contracting Party in whose territory the inspection is carried out, the inspectors designated by the General Conference shall be accompanied by representatives of said authorities, provided that this does not in any way delay or hinder the work of the inspectors.
5. The Council shall immediately transmit to all the Parties, through the General Secretary, a copy of any report resulting from special inspections.
6. Similarly, the Council shall send through the General Secretary to the Secretary-General of the United Nations, for transmission to the United Nations Security Council and General Assembly, and to the Council of the Organization of American States, for its information, a copy of any report resulting from any special inspection carried out in accordance with paragraph 1, subparagraph (b), sections (i) and (ii) of this article.
7. The Council may decide, or any Contracting Party may request, the convening of a special session of the General Conference for the purpose of considering the reports resulting from any special inspection. In such a case, the General Secretary shall take immediate steps to convene the special session requested.
8. The General Conference, convened in special session under this article, may make recommendations to the Contracting Parties and submit reports to the Secretary-General of the United Nations to be transmitted to the United Nations Security Council and the General Assembly.

USE OF NUCLEAR ENERGY FOR PEACEFUL PURPOSES
Article 17

Nothing in the provisions of this Treaty shall prejudice the rights of the Contracting Parties, in conformity with this Treaty, to use nuclear energy for peaceful purposes, in particular for their economic development and social progress.

EXPLOSIONS FOR PEACEFUL PURPOSES
Article 18

1. The Contracting Parties may carry out explosions of nuclear devices for peaceful purposes — including explosions which involve devices similar to those used in nuclear weapons — or collaborate with third parties for the same purpose, provided that they do so in accordance with the provisions of this article and the other articles of the Treaty, particularly articles 1 and 5.
2. Contracting Parties intending to carry out, or to co-operate in carrying out, such an explosion shall notify the Agency and the International Atomic Energy Agency, as far in advance as the circumstances require, of the date of the explosion and shall at the same time provide the following information:
   (a) The nature of the nuclear device and the source from which it was obtained;
   (b) The place and purpose of the planned explosion;
   (c) The procedures which will be followed in order to comply with paragraph 3 of this article;
   (d) The expected force of the device, and
   (e) The fullest possible information on any possible radioactive fall-out that may result from the explosion or explosions, and measures which will be taken to avoid danger to the population, flora, fauna and territories of any other Party or Parties.
3. The General Secretary and the technical personnel designated by the Council and the International Atomic Energy Agency may observe all the preparations, including the explosion of the device, and shall have unrestricted access to any area in the vicinity of the site of the explosion in order to ascertain whether the device and the procedures followed during the explosion are in conformity with the information supplied under paragraph 2 of this article and the other provisions of this Treaty.
4. The Contracting Parties may accept the collaboration of third parties for the purpose set forth in paragraph 1 of the present article, in accordance with paragraphs 2 and 3 thereof.

RELATIONS WITH OTHER INTERNATIONAL ORGANIZATIONS
Article 19

1. The Agency may conclude such agreements with the International Atomic Energy Agency as are authorized by the General Conference and as it considers likely to facilitate the efficient operation of the control system established by this Treaty.
2. The Agency may also enter into relations with any international organization or body, especially any which may be established in the future to supervise disarmament or measures for the control of armaments in any part of the world.
3. The Contracting Parties may, if they see fit, request the advice of the Inter-American Nuclear Energy Commission on all technical matters connected with the application of this Treaty with which the Commission is competent to deal under its Statute.

MEASURES IN THE EVENT OF VIOLATION OF THE TREATY
Article 20

1. The General Conference shall take note of all cases in which, in its opinion, any Contracting Party is not complying fully with its obligations under this Treaty and shall draw the matter to the attention of the Party concerned, making such recommendations as it deems appropriate.
2. If, in its opinion, such non-compliance constitutes a violation of this Treaty which might endanger peace and security, the General Conference shall report thereon simultaneously to the United Nations Security Council and the General Assembly through the Secretary-General of the United Nations, and to the Council of the Organization of American States. The General Conference shall likewise report to the International Atomic Energy Agency for such purposes as are relevant in accordance with its Statute.

UNITED NATIONS AND ORGANIZATION OF AMERICAN STATES
Article 21

None of the provisions of this Treaty shall be construed as impairing the rights and obligations of the Parties under the Charter of the United Nations or, in the case of States Members of the Organization of American States, under existing regional treaties.

PRIVILEGES AND IMMUNITIES
Article 22

1. The Agency shall enjoy in the territory of each of the Contracting Parties such legal capacity and such privileges and immunities as may be necessary for the exercise of its functions and the fulfilment of its purposes.
2. Representatives of the Contracting Parties accredited to the Agency and officials of the Agency shall similarly enjoy such privileges and immunities as are necessary for the performance of their functions.
3. The Agency may conclude agreement with the Contracting Parties with a view to determining the details of the application of paragraphs 1 and 2 of this article.

NOTIFICATION OF OTHER AGREEMENTS
Article 23

Once this Treaty has entered into force, the Secretariat shall be notified immediately of any international agreement concluded by any of the Contracting Parties on matters with which this Treaty is concerned; the Secretariat shall register it and notify the other Contracting Parties.

SETTLEMENT OF DISPUTES
Article 24

Unless the Parties concerned agree on another mode of peaceful settlement, any question or dispute concerning the interpretation or application of this Treaty which is not settled shall be referred to the International Court of Justice with the prior consent of the Parties to the controversy.

SIGNATURE
Article 25

1. This Treaty shall be open indefinitely for signature by:
   (a) All the Latin American Republics, and
   (b) All other sovereign States situated in their entirety south of latitude 35° north in the western hemisphere; and, except as provided in paragraph 2 of this article, all such States which become sovereign, when they have been admitted by the General Conference.
2. The General Conference shall not take any decision regarding the admission of a political entity part or all of whose territory is the subject, prior to the date when this Treaty is opened for signature, of a dispute or claim between an extra-continental country and one or more Latin American States, so long as the dispute has not been settled by peaceful means.

RATIFICATION AND DEPOSIT
Article 26

1. This Treaty shall be subject to ratification by signatory State in accordance with their respective constitutional procedures.
2. This Treaty and the instrument of ratification shall be deposited with the Government of the Mexican United States, which is hereby designated the Depositary Government.

3. The Depositary Government shall send certified copies of this Treaty to the Governments of signatory States and shall notify them of the deposit of each instrument of ratification.

RESERVATIONS
Article 27

This treaty shall not be subject to reservations.

ENTRY INTO FORCE
Article 28

1. Subject to the provisions of paragraph 2 of this article, this Treaty shall enter into force among the States that have ratified it as soon as the following requirements have been met:
    (a) Deposit of the instruments of ratification of this Treaty with the Depositary Government by the Governments of the States mentioned in article 25 which are in existence on the date when this Treaty is opened for signature and which are not affected by the provisions of article 25, paragraph 2;
    (b) Signature and ratification of Additional Protocol I annexed to this Treaty by all extra-continental or continental States having *de jure* or *de facto* international responsibility for territories situated in the zone of application of the Treaty;
    (c) Signature and ratification of the Additional Protocol II annexed to this Treaty by all powers possessing nuclear weapons;
    (d) Conclusion of bilateral or multilateral agreement on the application of the Safeguards System of the International Atomic Energy Agency in accordance with article 13 of this Treaty.
2. All signatory States shall have the imprescriptible right to waive, wholly or in part, the requirements laid down in the preceding paragraph. They may do so by means of a declaration which shall be annexed to their respective instrument of ratification and which may be formulated at the time of deposit of the instrument or subsequently. For those States which exercise this right, this Treaty shall enter into force upon deposit of the declaration, or as soon as those requirements have been met which have not been expressly waived.
3. As soon as this Treaty has entered into force in accordance with the provisions of paragraph 2 for eleven States, the Depositary Government shall convene a preliminary meeting of those States in order that the Agency may be set up and commence its work.
4. After the entry into force of this Treaty for all the countries of the zone, the rise of a new power possessing nuclear weapons shall have the effect of suspending the execution of this Treaty for those countries which have ratified it without waiving requirements of paragraph 1, subparagraph (c) of this article, and which request such suspension; the Treaty shall remain suspended until the new power, on its own initiative or upon request by the General Conference, ratifies the annexed Additional Protocol II.

AMENDMENTS
Article 29

1. Any Contracting Party may propose amendments to this Treaty and shall submit its proposals to the Council through the General Secretary, who shall transmit them to all the other Contracting Parties and, in addition, to all other signatories in accordance with article 6. The Council, through the General Secretary, shall immediately following the meeting of signatories convene a special session of the General Conference to examine the proposals made, for the adoption of which a two-thirds majority of the Contracting Parties present and voting shall be required.
2. Amendments adopted shall enter into force as soon as the requirements set forth in article 28 of this Treaty have been complied with.

DURATION AND DENUNCIATION
Article 30

1. This Treaty shall be of a permanent nature and shall remain in force indefinitely, but any Party may denounce it by notifying the General Secretary of the Agency if, in the opinion of the denouncing State, there have arisen or may arise circumstances connected with the content of this Treaty or of the annexed Additional Protocols I and II which affect its supreme interests or the peace and security of one or more Contracting Parties.
2. The denunciation shall take effect three months after the delivery to the General Secretary of the Agency of the notification by the Government of the signatory State concerned. The General Secretary shall immediately communicate such notification to the other Contracting Parties and to the Secretary-General

of the United Nations for the information of the United Nations Security Council and the General Assembly. He shall also communicate it to the Secretary-General of the Organization of American States.

AUTHENTIC TEXTS AND REGISTRATION
Article 31

This Treaty, of which the Spanish, Chinese, English, French, Portuguese and Russian texts are equally authentic, shall be registered by the Depositary Government in accordance with article 102 of the United Nations Charter. The Depositary Government shall notify the Secretary-General of the United Nations of the signatures, ratifications and amendments relating to this Treaty and shall communicate them to the Secretary-General of the Organization of American States for its information.

Transitional Article

Denunciation of the declaration referred to in article 28, paragraph 2, shall be subject to the same procedures as the denunciation of this Treaty, except that it will take effect on the date of delivery of the respective notification.

IN WITNESS THEREOF the undersigned Plenipotentiaries, having deposited their full powers, found in good and due form, sign this Treaty on behalf of their respective Governments.

DONE at Mexico, Distrito Federal, on the Fourteenth day of February, one thousand nine hundred and sixty-seven.

ADDITIONAL PROTOCOL I

The undersigned Plenipotentiaries, furnished with full powers by their respective Governments,

Convinced that the Treaty for the Prohibition of Nuclear Weapons in Latin America, negotiated and signed in accordance with the recommendations of the General Assembly of the United Nations in Resolution 1911 (XVIII) of 27 November 1963, represents an important step towards ensuring the non-proliferation of nuclear weapons,

Aware that the non-proliferation of nuclear weapons is not an end in itself but, rather, a means of achieving general and complete disarmament at a later stage, and

Desiring to contribute, so far as lies in their power, towards ending the armaments race, especially in the field of nuclear weapons, and towards strengthening a world peace, based on mutual respect and sovereign equality of States,

Have agreed as follows:

Article 1

To undertake to apply the statute of denuclearization in respect of warlike purposes as defined in articles 1, 3, 5 and 13 of the Treaty for the Prohibition of Nuclear Weapons in Latin America in territories for which, *de jure* or *de facto*, they are internationally responsible and which lie within the limits of the geographical zone established in that Treaty.

Article 2

The duration of this Protocol shall be the same as that of the Treaty for the Prohibition of Nuclear Weapons in Latin America of which this Protocol is an annex, and the provisions regarding ratification and denunciation contained in the Treaty shall be applicable to it.

Article 3

This Protocol shall enter into force, for the States which have ratified it, on the date of the deposit of their respective instruments of ratification.

IN WITNESS WHEREOF the undersigned Plenipotentiaries, having deposited their full powers, found in good and due form, sign this Protocol on behalf of their respective Governments.

ADDITIONAL PROTOCOL II

The undersigned Plenipotentiaries, furnished with full powers by their respective Governments,

Convinced that the Treaty for the Prohibition of Nuclear Weapons in Latin America, negotiated and signed in accordance with the recommendations of the General Assembly of the United Nations in Resolution 1911 (XVIII) of 27 November 1963, represents an important step towards ensuring the non-proliferation of nuclear weapons.

Aware that the non-proliferation of nuclear weapons is not an end in itself but, rather, a means of achieving general and complete disarmament at a later stage, and

Desiring to contribute, so far as lies in their power, towards ending the armaments race, especially in the field of nuclear weapons, and towards promoting and strengthening a world at peace, based on mutual respect and sovereign equality of States,

Have agreed as follows:

Article 1

The statute of denuclearization of Latin America in respect of warlike purposes, as defined, delimited and set forth in the Treaty for the Prohibition of Nuclear Weapons in Latin America of which this instrument is an annex, shall be fully respected by the Parties to this Protocol in all its express aims and provisions.

Article 2

The Governments represented by the undersigned Plenipotentiaries undertake, therefore, not to contribute in any way to the performance of acts involving a violation of the obligations of article 1 of the Treaty in the territories to which the Treaty applies in accordance with article 4 thereof.

Article 3

The Governments represented by the undersigned Plenipotentiaries also undertake not to use or threaten to use nuclear weapons against the Contracting Parties of the Treaty for the Prohibition of Nuclear Weapons in Latin America.

Article 4

The duration of this Protocol shall be the same as that of the Treaty for the Prohibition of Nuclear Weapons in Latin America of which this Protocol is an annex, and the definitions of territory and nuclear weapons set forth in articles 3 and 5 of the Treaty shall be applicable to this Protocol, as well as the provisions regarding ratification, reservations, denunciation, authentic texts and registration contained in articles 26, 27, 30 and 31 of the Treaty.

Article 5

This Protocol shall enter into force, for the States which have ratified it, on the date of the deposit of their respective instrument of ratification.

IN WITNESS WHEREOF, the undersigned Plenipotentiaries, having deposited their full powers, found to be in good and due form, hereby sign this Additional Protocol on behalf of their respective Governments.

Signatories and Parties to the Treaty of Tlatelolco

Antigua and Barbuda
Argentina*
Bahamas
Barbados
Bolivia
Brazil*
Chile*
Colombia
Costa Rica
Dominica
Dominican Republic
Ecuador
El Salvador
Grenada
Guatemala
Haiti
Honduras
Jamaica
Mexico
Nicaragua
Panama
Paraguay
Peru
Suriname
Trinidad and Tobago
Uruguay
Venezuela

Additional Protocol I
France
Netherlands
United Kingdom
United States of America

Additional Protocol II
People's Republic of China
France
Russian Federation
United Kingdom
United States of America

* Not full parties.
   Cuba has indicated an intention to accede if Argentina, Brazil and Chile become full parties.

South Pacific Nuclear Free Zone Treaty [Treaty of Rarotonga]

Preamble

The Parties to this Treaty

United in their commitment to a world at peace,

Gravely concerned that the continuing nuclear arms race presents the risk of nuclear war which would have devastating consequences for all people,

Convinced that all countries have an obligation to make every effort to achieve the goal of eliminating nuclear weapons, the terror which they hold for humankind and the threat which they pose to life on earth,

Believing that regional arms control measures can contribute to global efforts to reverse the nuclear arms race and promote the national security of each country in the region and the common security of all,

Determined to ensure, so far as lies within their power, that the bounty and beauty of the land and sea in their region shall remain the heritage of their peoples and their descendants in perpetuity to be enjoyed by all in peace,

Reaffirming the importance of the Treaty on the Non-Proliferation of Nuclear Weapons (NPT) in preventing the proliferation of nuclear weapons and in contributing to world security,

Noting, in particular, that Article VII of the NPT recognises the right of any group of States to conclude regional treaties in order to assure the total absence of nuclear weapons in their respective territories,

Noting that the prohibitions of emplantation and emplacement of nuclear weapons on the sea-bed and the ocean floor and in the subsoil thereof contained in the Treaty on the Prohibition of the Emplacement of Nuclear Weapons and Other Weapons of Mass Destruction on the Sea-Bed and the Ocean Floor and in the Subsoil Thereof apply in the South Pacific,

Noting also that the prohibition of testing of nuclear weapons in the atmosphere or under water, including territorial waters or high seas, contained in the Treaty Banning Nuclear Weapon Tests in the Atmosphere, in Outer Space and under Water applies in the South Pacific,

Determined to keep the region free of environmental pollution by radioactive wastes and other radioactive matter,

Guided by the decision of the Fifteenth South Pacific Forum at Tuvalu that a nuclear free zone should be established in the region at the earliest possible opportunity in accordance with the principles set out in the communique of that meeting,

Have agreed as follows:

Article 1

Usage of terms

For the purposes of this Treaty and its Protocols:
(a) 'South Pacific Nuclear Free Zone' means the areas described in Annex 1 as illustrated by the map attached to that Annex;
(b) 'territory' means internal waters, territorial sea and archipelagic waters, the sea-bed and subsoil beneath, the land territory and the airspace above them;
   (c) 'nuclear explosive device' means any nuclear weapon or other explosive device capable of releasing nuclear energy, irrespective of the purpose for which it could be used. The term includes such a weapon or device in unassembled and partly assembled forms, but, does not include the means of transport or delivery of such a weapon or device if separable from and not an indivisible part of it;
   (d) 'stationing' means emplantation, emplacement, transportation on land or inland waters, stockpiling, storage, installation and deployment.

Article 2

Application of the Treaty
1. Except where otherwise specified, this Treaty and its Protocols shall apply to territory within the South Pacific Nuclear Free Zone.
2. Nothing in this Treaty shall prejudice or in any way affect the rights, or the exercise of the right, of any State under international law with regard to freedom of the seas.

Article 3
Renunciation of nuclear explosive devices
Each Party undertakes:
(a) not to manufacture or otherwise acquire, possess or have control over any nuclear explosive device by any means anywhere inside or outside the South Pacific Nuclear Free Zone;
(b) not to seek or receive any assistance in the manufacture or acquisition of any nuclear explosive device;
(c) not to take any action to assist or encourage the manufacture or acquisition of any nuclear explosive device by any State.

Article 4
Peaceful nuclear activities
Each Party undertakes:
(a) not to provide source or special fissionable material, or equipment or material especially designed or prepared for the processing, use or production of special fissionable material for peaceful purposes to:
  (i) any non-nuclear-weapon State unless subject to the safeguards required by Article III.1 of the NPT, or
  (ii) any nuclear-weapon State unless subject to applicable safeguards agreement with the International Atomic Energy Agency (IAEA).
  Any such provision shall be in accordance with strict non-proliferation measures to provide assurance of exclusively peaceful non-explosive use;
(b) to support the continued effectiveness of the international non-proliferation system based on the NPT and the IAEA safeguards system.

Article 5
Prevention of stationing of nuclear explosive devices
1. Each Party undertakes to prevent in its territory the stationing of any nuclear explosive device.
2. Each Party in the exercise of it sovereign right remains free to decide for itself whether to allow visit by foreign ships and aircraft to its ports and airfields, transit of its airspace by foreign aircraft, and navigation by foreign ships in its territorial sea or archipelagic waters in a manner not covered by the rights of innocent passage, archipelagic sea lane passage or transit passage of straits.

Article 6
Prevention of testing of nuclear explosive devices
Each Party undertakes:
(a) to prevent in its territory the testing of any nuclear explosive device;
(b) not to take any action to assist or encourage the testing of any nuclear explosive device by any State.

Article 7
Prevention of dumping
1. Each Party undertakes:
   (a) not to dump radioactive wastes and other radioactive matter at sea anywhere within the South Pacific Nuclear Free Zone;
   (b) to prevent the dumping of radioactive wastes and other radioactive matter by anyone in its territorial sea;
   (c) not to take any action to assist or encourage the dumping by anyone of radioactive wastes and other radioactive matter at sea anywhere within the South Pacific Nuclear Free Zone;
   (d) to support the conclusion as soon as possible of the proposed Convention relating to the protection of the natural resources and environment of the South Pacific region and its Protocol for the prevention of pollution of the South Pacific region by dumping, with the aim of precluding dumping at sea of radioactive wastes and other radioactive matter by anyone anywhere in the region.
2. Paragraphs 1 (a) and 1 (b) of this Article shall not apply to areas of the South Pacific Nuclear Free Zone in respect of which such a Convention and Protocol have entered into force.

Article 8
Control system
1. The Parties hereby establish a control system for the purpose of verifying compliance with their obligations under this Treaty.
2. The control system shall comprise:

(a) reports and exchange of information as provided for in Article 9;
(b) consultations as provided for in Article 10 and Annex 4 (1);
(c) the application to peaceful nuclear activities of safeguards by the IAEA as provided for in Annex 2;
(d) a complaints procedure as provided for in Annex 4.

Article 9
Reports and exchanges of information
1. Each Party shall report to the Director of the South Pacific Bureau for Economic Co-operation (the Director) as soon as possible any significant event within its jurisdiction affecting the implementation of this Treaty. The Director shall circulate such reports promptly to all Parties.
2. The Parties shall endeavour to keep each other informed on matters arising under or in relation to this Treaty. They may exchange information by communicating it to the Director, who shall circulate it to all Parties.
3. The Director shall report annually to the South Pacific Forum on the status of this Treaty and matters arising under or in relation to it, incorporating reports and communications made under paragraphs 1 and 2 of this Article and matters arising under Articles 8 (2) (d) and 10 and Annex 2 (4).

Article 10
Consultations and review
Without prejudice to the conduct of consultations among Parties by other means, the Director, at the request of any Party, shall convene a meeting of the Consultative Committee established by Annex 3 for consultation and co-operation on any matter arising in relation to this Treaty or for reviewing its operation.

Article 11
Amendment
The Consultative Committee shall consider proposals for amendment of the provisions of this Treaty proposed by any Party and circulated by the Director to all Parties not less than three months prior to the convening of the Consultative Committee for this purpose. Any proposal agreed upon by consensus by the Consultative Committee shall be communicated to the Director, who shall circulate it for acceptance to all Parties. An amendment shall enter into force thirty days after receipt by the depository of acceptances from all Parties.

Article 12
Signature and ratification
1. This Treaty shall be open for signature by any Member of the South Pacific Forum.
2. This Treaty shall be subject to ratification. Instruments of ratification shall be deposited with the Director who is hereby designated depository of this Treaty and its Protocols.
3. If a member of the South Pacific Forum whose territory is outside the South Pacific Nuclear Free Zone becomes a Party to this Treaty, Annex 1 shall be deemed to be amended so far as is required to enclose at least the territory of that Party within the boundaries of the South Pacific Nuclear Free Zone. The delineation of any area added pursuant to this paragraph shall be approved by the South Pacific Forum.

Article 13
Withdrawal
1. This Treaty is of a permanent nature and shall remain in force indefinitely, provided that in the event of a violation by any Party of a provision of this Treaty essential to the achievement of the objectives of the Treaty or of the spirit of the Treaty, every other Party shall have the right to withdraw from the Treaty.
2. Withdrawal shall be effected by giving notice twelve months in advance to the Director who shall circulate such notice to all other Parties.

Article 14
Reservations
This Treaty shall not be subject to reservations.

Article 15
Entry into force
1. This Treaty shall enter into force on the date of deposit of the eighth instrument of ratification.
2. For a signatory which ratifies this Treaty after the date of deposit of the eighth instrument of ratification, the Treaty shall enter into force on the date of deposit of its instrument of ratification.

Article 16
Depository functions

The depository shall register this Treaty and its Protocols pursuant to Article 102 of the Charter of the United Nations and shall transmit certified copies of the Treaty and its Protocols to all Members of the South Pacific Forum and all States eligible to become Party to the Protocols to the Treaty and shall notify them of signatures and ratifications of the Treaty and it Protocols.

IN WITNESS WHEREOF the undersigned, being duly authorised by their Government, have signed this Treaty.

DONE at , this day of , One thousand nine hundred and eighty-[five], in a single original in the English language.

ANNEX 1
South Pacific Nuclear Free Zone

A. The area bounded by a line—
   (1) commencing at the point of intersection of the Equator by the maritime boundary between Indonesia and Papua New Guinea;
   (2) running thence northerly along that maritime boundary to its intersection by the outer limit of the exclusive economic zone of Papua New Guinea;
   (3) thence generally north-easterly and south-easterly along that outer limit to its intersection by the Equator;
   (4) thence east along the Equator to it intersection by the meridian of Longitude 163 degrees East;
   (5) thence north along that meridian to its intersection by the parallel of Latitude 3 degrees North;
   (6) thence east along that parallel to its intersection by the meridian of Longitude 171 degrees East;
   (7) thence north along that meridian to its intersection by the parallel of Latitude 4 degrees North;
   (8) thence east along that parallel to its intersection by the meridian of Longitude 180 degrees East;
   (9) thence south along that meridian to its intersection by the Equator;
   (10) thence east along the Equator to its intersection by the meridian of Longitude 165 degrees West;
   (11) thence north along that meridian to its intersection by the parallel of Latitude 5 degrees 30 minutes North;
   (12) thence east along that parallel to its intersection by the meridian of Longitude 154 degrees West;
   (13) thence south along that meridian to its intersection by the Equator;
   (14) thence east along the Equator to its intersection by the meridian of Longitude 115 degrees West;
   (15) thence south along that meridian to its intersection by the parallel of Latitude 60 degrees South;
   (16) thence west along that parallel to its intersection by the meridian of Longitude 115 degrees East;
   (17) thence north along that meridian to its southernmost intersection by the outer limit of the territorial sea of Australia;
   (18) thence generally northerly and easterly along the outer limit of the territorial sea of Australia to its intersection by the meridian of Longitude 136 degrees 45 minutes East;
   (19) thence north-easterly along the geodesic to the point of Latitude 10 degrees 50 minutes South, Longitude 139 degrees 12 minutes East;
   (20) thence north-easterly along the maritime boundary between Indonesia and Papua New Guinea to where it joins the land border between those two countries;
   (21) thence generally northerly along that land border to where it joints the maritime boundary between Indonesia and Papua New Guinea, on the northern coastline of Papua New Guinea; and
   (22) thence generally northerly along that boundary to the point of commencement.
B. The areas within the outer limits of the territorial seas of all Australian islands lying westward of the area described in paragraph A and north of Latitude 60 degrees South, provided that any such areas shall cease to be part of the South Pacific Nuclear Free Zone upon receipt by the depository of written notice from the Government of Australia stating that the areas have become subject to another treaty having an object and purpose substantially the same as that of this Treaty.

ANNEX 2
IAEA Safeguards

1. The safeguards referred to in Article 8 shall in respect of each Party be applied by the IAEA as set forth in an agreement negotiated and concluded with the IAEA on all source or special fissionable material in all peaceful nuclear activities within the territory of the Party, under its jurisdiction or carried out under its control anywhere.

2. The agreement referred to in paragraph 1 shall be, or shall be equivalent in its scope and effect to, an agreement required in connection with the NPT on the basis of the material reproduced in document INFCIRC/153 (Corrected) of the IAEA. Each Party shall take all appropriate steps to ensure that such an agreement is in force for it not later than eighteen months after the date of entry into force for that Party of this Treaty.
3. For the purposes of this Treaty, the safeguards referred to in paragraph 1 shall have as their purpose the verification of the non-diversion of nuclear material from peaceful nuclear activities to nuclear explosive devices.
4. Each Party agrees upon the request of any other Party to transmit to that Party and to the Director for the information of all Parties a copy of the overall conclusions of the most recent report by the IAEA on its inspection activities in the territory of the Party concerned, and to advise the Director promptly of any subsequent findings of the Board of Governors of the IAEA in relation to those conclusions for the information of all Parties.

ANNEX 3
Consultative Committee

1. There is hereby established a Consultative Committee which shall be convened by the Director from time to time pursuant to Articles 10 and 11 and Annex 4 (2). The Consultative Committee shall be constituted of representatives of the Parties, each Party being entitled to appoint one representative who may be accompanied by advisers. Unless otherwise agreed, the Consultative Committee shall be chaired at any given meeting by the representative of the Party which last hosted the meeting of Heads of Government of Members of the South Pacific Forum. A quorum shall be constituted by representatives of half the Parties. Subject to the provisions of Article 11, decisions of the Consultative Committee shall be taken by consensus or, failing consensus, by a two-thirds majority of those present and voting. The Consultative Committee shall adopt such other rules of procedure as it sees fit.
2. The costs of the Consultative Committee, including the cost of special inspections pursuant to Annex 4, shall be borne by the South Pacific Bureau for Economic Co-operation. It may seek special funding should this be required.

ANNEX 4
Complaints Procedure

1. A Party which considers that there are grounds for a complaint that another Party is in breach of its obligations under this Treaty shall, before bringing such a complaint to the Director, bring the subject-matter of the Complaint to the attention of the Party complained of and shall allow the latter reasonable opportunity to provide it with an explanation and to resolve the matter.
2. If the matter is not so resolved, the complainant Party may bring the complaint to the Director with a request that the Consultative Committee be convened to consider it. Complaints shall be supported by an account of evidence of breach of obligations known to the complainant Party. Upon receipt of a complaint the Director shall convene the Consultative Committee as quickly as possible to consider it.
3. The Consultative Committee, taking account of effort made under paragraph 1, shall afford the Party complained of a reasonable opportunity to provide it with an explanation of the matter.
4. If, after considering any explanation given to it by the representatives of the Party complained of, the Consultative Committee decides that there is sufficient substance in the complaint to warrant a special inspection in the territory of that Party or elsewhere, the Consultative Committee shall direct that such special inspection be made as quickly as possible by a special inspection team of three suitably qualified special inspectors appointed by the Consultative Committee in consultation with the complained of and complainant Parties, provided that no national of either Party shall serve on the special inspection team. If so requested by the Party complained of, the special inspection team shall be accompanied by representatives of that Party. Neither the right of consultation on the appointment of special inspectors, nor the right to accompany special inspectors, shall delay the work of the special inspection team.
5. In making a special inspection, special inspectors shall be subject to the direction only of the Consultative Committee and shall comply with such directives concerning tasks, objectives, confidentiality and procedures as may be decided upon by it. Directives shall take account of the legitimate interests of the Party complained of in complying with its other international obligations and commitments and shall not duplicate safeguards procedures to be undertaken by the IAEA pursuant to agreements referred to in Annex 2(1). The special inspectors shall discharge their duties with due respect for the laws of the Party complained of.

6. Each Party shall give to special inspectors full and free access to all information and places within its territory which may be relevant to enable the special inspectors to implement the directives given to them by the Consultative Committee.
7. The Party complained of shall take all appropriate steps to facilitate the special inspection, and shall grant to special inspectors privileges and immunities necessary for the performance of their functions, including inviolability for all papers and documents and immunity from arrest, detention and legal process for acts done and words spoken and written, for the purpose of the special inspection.
8. The special inspectors shall report in writing as quickly as possible to the Consultative Committee, outlining their activities, setting out relevant facts and information as ascertained by them, with supporting evidence and documentation as appropriate, and stating their conclusions. The Consultative Committee shall report fully to all Members of the South Pacific Forum, giving its decision as to whether the Party complained of is in breach of its obligations under this Treaty.
9. If the Consultative Committee has decided that the Party complained of is in breach of its obligations under this Treaty, or that the above provisions have not been complied with, or at any time at the request of either the complainant or complained of Party, the Parties shall meet promptly at a meeting of the South Pacific Forum.

PROTOCOL 1

The Parties to this Protocol

Noting the South Pacific Nuclear Free Zone Treaty (the Treaty)

Have agreed as follows:

Article 1

Each Party undertakes to apply, in respect of the territories for which it is internationally responsible situated within the South Pacific Nuclear Free Zone, the prohibitions contained in Articles 3, 5 and 6, in so far as they relate to the manufacture, stationing and testing of any nuclear explosive device within those territories, and the safeguards specified in Article 8 (2) (c) and Annex 2 of the Treaty.

Article 2

Each Party may, by written notification to the depository, indicate its acceptance from the date of such notification of any alteration to its obligations under this Protocol brought about by the entry into force of an amendment to the Treaty pursuant to Article 11 of the Treaty.

Article 3

This Protocol shall be open for signature by France, the United Kingdom of Great Britain and Northern Ireland and the United States of America.

Article 4

This Protocol shall be subject to ratification.

Article 5

This Protocol shall enter into force for each State on the date of its deposit with the depository of its instrument of ratification.

IN WITNESS WHEREOF the undersigned, being duly authorised by their Governments, have signed this Protocol.

DONE at   , this   day of   , One thousand nine hundred and eighty-[five], in a single original in the English language.

PROTOCOL 2

The Parties to this Protocol

Noting the South Pacific Nuclear Free Zone Treaty (the Treaty)

Have agreed as follows:

Article 1

Each Party undertakes not to contribute to any act which constitutes a violation of the Treaty or it Protocols by Parties to them.

Article 2

Each Party further undertakes not to use or threaten to use any nuclear explosive device against:
(a) Parties to the Treaty; or
(b) any territory within the South Pacific Nuclear Free Zone for which a State that has become a Party to Protocol I is internationally responsible.

Article 3

Each Party may, by written notification to the depository, indicate its acceptance from the date of such notification of any alteration to its obligations under this Protocol brought about by the entry into force of an amendment to the Treaty pursuant to Article 11 of the Treaty or by the extension of the South Pacific Nuclear Free Zone pursuant to Article 12 (3) of the Treaty.

Article 4

This Protocol shall be open for signature by France, the People's Republic of China, the Union of Soviet Socialist Republics, the United Kingdom of Great Britain and Northern Ireland and the United States of America.

Article 5
This Protocol shall be subject to ratification.

Article 6
This Protocol shall enter into force for each State on the date of its deposit with the depository of its instrument of ratification.

IN WITNESS WHEREOF the undersigned, being duly authorised by their Governments, have signed this Protocol.

DONE at   , this   day of   , One thousand nine hundred and eighty-[five], in a single original in the English language.

PROTOCOL 3

The Parties to this Protocol

Noting the South Pacific Nuclear Free Zone Treaty (the Treaty)

Have agreed as follows:

Article 1
Each party undertakes not to test any nuclear explosive device anywhere within the South Pacific Nuclear Free Zone.

Article 2
Each Party may, by written notification to the depository, indicate its acceptance from the date of such notification of any alteration to its obligation under this Protocol brought about by the entry into force of an amendment to the Treaty pursuant to Article 11 of the Treaty or by the extension of the South Pacific Nuclear Free Zone pursuant to Article 12 (3) of the Treaty.

Article 3
This Protocol shall be open for signature by France, the People's Republic of China, the Union of Soviet Socialist Republics, the United Kingdom of Great Britain and Northern Ireland and the United States of America.

Article 4
This Protocol shall be subject to ratification.

Signatories and Parties to the Treaty of Rarotonga

Australia
Cook Islands
Fiji
Kiribati
Nauru
New Zealand
Niue
Papua New Guinea
Samoa
Solomon Islands
Tuvalu

Protocol 1

Protocol 2
China, People's Republic of
Russian Federation

Protocol 3
China, People's Republic of
Russian Federation

Convention on the Physical Protection of Nuclear Material

(Signed at Vienna and New York on 3 March 1980. Entered into force on 8 February 1987.
Depositary: IAEA Director General)

The states parties to this convention,

Recognizing the right of all States to develop and apply nuclear energy for peaceful purposes and their legitimate interests in the potential benefits to be derived from the peaceful application of nuclear energy,

Convinced of the need for facilitating international co-operation in the peaceful application of nuclear energy,

Desiring to avert the potential dangers posed by the unlawful taking and use of nuclear material,

Convinced that offences relating to nuclear material are a matter of grave concern and that there is an urgent need to adopt appropriate and effective measures to ensure the prevention, detection and punishment of such offences,

Aware of the need for international co-operation to establish, in conformity with the national law of each State Party and with this Convention, effective measures for the physical protection of nuclear material,

Convinced that this Convention should facilitate the safe transfer of nuclear material,

Stressing also the importance of the physical protection of nuclear material in domestic use, storage and transport,

Recognizing the importance of effective physical protection of nuclear material used for military purposes, and understanding that such material is and will continue to be accorded stringent physical protection,

Have agreed as follows:

Article 1

For the purposes of this Convention:
(a) 'nuclear material' means plutonium except that with isotopic concentration exceeding 80% in plutonium-238; uranium-233; uranium enriched in the isotope 235 or 233; uranium containing the mixture of isotopes as occurring in nature other than in the form of ore or ore-residue; any material containing one or more of the foregoing;
(b) 'uranium enriched in the isotope 235 or 233' means uranium containing the isotope 235 or 233 or both in an amount such that the abundance ratio of the sum of these isotopes to the isotope 238 is greater than the ratio of the isotope 235 to the isotope 238 occurring in nature;
(c) 'international nuclear transport' means the carriage of a consignment of nuclear material by any means of transportation intended to go beyond the territory of the State where the shipment originates beginning with the departure from a facility of the shipper in that State and ending with the arrival at a facility of the receiver within the State of ultimate destination.

Article 2

1. This Convention shall apply to nuclear material used for peaceful purposes while in international nuclear transport.
2. With the exception of articles 3 and 4 and paragraph 3 of article 5, this Convention shall also apply to nuclear material used for peaceful purposes while in domestic use, storage and transport.
3. Apart from the commitments expressly undertaken by States Parties in the articles covered by paragraph 2 with respect to nuclear material used for peaceful purposes while in domestic use, storage and transport, nothing in this Convention shall be interpreted as affecting the sovereign rights of a State regarding the domestic use, storage and transport of such nuclear material.

Article 3

Each State Party shall take appropriate steps within the framework of its national law and consistent with international law to ensure as far as practicable that, during international nuclear transport, nuclear material within its territory, or on board a ship or aircraft under its jurisdiction insofar as such ship or aircraft is engaged in the transport to or from the State, is protected at the levels described in Annex I.

Article 4

1. Each State Party shall not export or authorize the export of nuclear material unless the State Party has received assurances that such material will be protected during the international nuclear transport at the levels described in Annex I.

2. Each State Party shall not import or authorize the import of nuclear material from a State not party to this Convention unless the State Party has received assurances that such material will during the international nuclear transport be protected at the levels described in Annex I.
3. A State Party shall not allow the transit through its territory by land or internal waterways or through its airports or seaports of nuclear material between States that are not parties to this Convention unless the State Party has received assurances as far as practicable that this nuclear material will be protected during international nuclear transport at the levels described in Annex I.
4. Each State Party shall apply within the framework of its national law the levels of physical protection described in Annex I to nuclear material being transported from a part of that State to another part of the same State through international waters or airspace.
5. The State Party responsible for receiving assurances that the nuclear material will be protected at the levels described in Annex I according to paragraphs 1 to 3 shall identify and inform in advance States which the nuclear material is expected to transit by land or international waterways, or whose airports or seaports it is expected to enter.
6. The responsibility for obtaining assurances referred to in paragraph 1 may be transferred, by mutual agreement, to the State Party involved in the transport as the importing State.
7. Nothing in this article shall be interpreted as in any way affecting the territorial sovereignty and jurisdiction of a State, including that over its airspace and territorial sea.

Article 5

1. States Parties shall identify and make known to each other directly or through the International Atomic Energy Agency their central authority and point of contact having responsibility for physical protection of nuclear material and for co-ordinating recovery and response operations in the event of any unauthorized removal, use or alteration of nuclear material or in the event of credible threat thereof.
2. In the case of theft, robbery or any other unlawful taking of nuclear material or of credible threat thereof, States Parties shall, in accordance with their national law, provide co-operation and assistance to the maximum feasible extent in the recovery and protection of such material to any State that so requests. In particular:
   (a) a State Party shall take appropriate steps to inform as soon as possible other States, which appear to it to be concerned, of any theft, robbery or other unlawful taking of nuclear material or credible threat thereof and to inform, where appropriate, international organizations;
   (b) as appropriate, the States Parties concerned shall exchange information with each other or international organizations with a view to protecting threatened nuclear material, verifying the integrity of the shipping container, or recovering unlawfully taken nuclear material and shall:
      (i) co-ordinate their efforts through diplomatic and other agreed channels;
      (ii) render assistance, if requested;
      (iii) ensure the return of nuclear material stolen or missing as a consequence of the above-mentioned events.
   The means of implementation of this co-operation shall be determined by the States Parties concerned.
3. States Parties shall co-operate and consult as appropriate, with each other directly or through international organizations, with a view to obtaining guidance on the design, maintenance and improvement of systems of physical protection of nuclear material in international transport.

Article 6

1. States Parties shall take appropriate measures consistent with their national law to protect the confidentiality of any information which they receive in confidence by virtue of the provisions of this Convention from another State Party or through participation in an activity carried out for the implementation of this Convention. If States Parties provide information to international organizations in confidence, steps shall be taken to ensure that the confidentiality of such information is protected.
2. States Parties shall not be required by this Convention to provide any information which they are not permitted to communicate pursuant to national law or which would jeopardize the security of the State concerned or the physical protection of nuclear material.

Article 7

1. The intentional commission of:
   (a) an act without lawful authority which constitutes the receipt, possession, use, transfer, alteration, disposal or dispersal of nuclear material and which causes or is likely to cause death or serious injury to any person or substantial damage to property;
   (b) a theft or robbery of nuclear material;

(c) an embezzlement or fraudulent obtaining of nuclear material;
(d) an act constituting a demand for nuclear material by threat or use of force or by any other form of intimidation;
(e) a threat:
  (i) to use nuclear material to cause death or serious injury to any person or substantial property damage, or
  (ii) to commit an offence described in sub-paragraph (b) in order to compel a natural or legal person, international organization or State to do or to refrain from doing any act;
(f) an attempt to commit any offence described in paragraphs (a), (b) or (c); and
(g) an act which constitutes participation in any offence described in paragraphs (a) to (f) shall be made a punishable offence by each State Party under its national law.

2. Each State Party shall make the offences described in this article punishable by appropriate penalties which take into account their grave nature.

Article 8

1. Each State Party shall take such measures as may be necessary to establish its jurisdiction over the offences set forth in article 7 in the following cases:
   (a) when the offence is committed in the territory of that State or on board a ship or aircraft registered in that State;
   (b) when the alleged offender is a national of that State.
2. Each State Party shall likewise take such measures as may be necessary to establish its jurisdiction over these offences in cases where the alleged offender is present in its territory and it does not extradite him pursuant to article 11 to any of the States mentioned in paragraph 1.
3. This Convention does not exclude any criminal jurisdiction exercised in accordance with national law.
4. In addition to the States Parties mentioned in paragraphs 1 and 2, each State Party may, consistent with international law, establish its jurisdiction over the offences set forth in article 7 when it is involved in international nuclear transport as the exporting or importing state.

Article 9

Upon being satisfied that the circumstances so warrant, the State Party in whose territory the alleged offender is present shall take appropriate measures, including detention, under its national law to ensure his presence for the purpose of prosecution or extradition. Measures taken according to this article shall be notified without delay to the States required to establish jurisdiction pursuant to article 8, and where appropriate, all other States concerned.

Article 10

The State Party in whose territory the alleged offender is present shall, if it does not extradite him, submit, without exception whatsoever and without undue delay, the case to its competent authorities for the purpose of prosecution, through proceedings in accordance with the laws of that State.

Article 11

1. The offences in article 7 shall be deemed to be included as extraditable offences in any extradition treaty existing between State Parties. States Parties undertake to include those offences as extraditable offences in every future extradition treaty to be concluded between them.
2. If a State Party which makes extradition conditional on the existence of a treaty receives a request for extradition from another State Party with which it has no extradition treaty, it may at its option consider this Convention as the legal basis for extradition in respect of those offences. Extradition shall be subject to the other conditions provided by the law of the requested State.
3. States Parties which do not make extradition conditional on the existence of a treaty shall recognize those offences as extraditable offences between themselves subject to the conditions provided by the law of the requested State.
4. Each of the offences shall be treated, for the purpose of extradition between States Parties, as if it had been committed not only in the place in which it occurred but also in the territories of the States Parties required to establish their jurisdiction in accordance with paragraph 1 of article 8.

Article 12

Any person regarding whom proceedings are being carried out in connection with any of the offences set forth in article 7 shall be guaranteed fair treatment at all stages of the proceedings.

Article 13
1. States Parties shall afford one another the greatest measure of assistance in connection with criminal proceedings brought in respect of the offences set forth in article 7, including the supply of evidence at their disposal necessary for the proceedings. The law of the State requested shall apply in all cases.
2. The provisions of paragraph 1 shall not affect obligations under any other treaty, bilateral or multilateral, which governs or will govern, in whole or in part, mutual assistance in criminal matters.

Article 14
1. Each State Party shall inform the depositary of its laws and regulations which give effect to this Convention. The depositary shall communicate such information periodically to all States Parties.
2. The State Party where an alleged offender is prosecuted shall, wherever practicable, first communicate the final outcome of the proceedings to the States directly concerned. The State Party shall also communicate the final outcome to the depositary who shall inform all States.
3. Where an offence involves nuclear material used for peaceful purposes in domestic use, storage or transport, and both the alleged offender and the nuclear material remain in the territory of the State Party in which the offence was committed, nothing in this Convention shall be interpreted as requiring that State Party to provide information concerning criminal proceedings arising out of such an offence.

Article 15
The Annexes constitute an integral part of this Convention.

Article 16
1. A conference of States Parties shall be convened by the depositary five years after the entry into force of this Convention to review the implementation of the Convention and its adequacy as concerns the preamble, the whole of the operative part and the annexes in the light of the then prevailing situation.
2. At intervals of not less than five years thereafter, the majority of States Parties may obtain, by submitting a proposal to this effect to the depositary, the convening of further conferences with the same objective.

Article 17
1. In the event of a dispute between two or more States Parties concerning the interpretation or application of this Convention, such States Parties shall consult with a view to the settlement of the dispute by negotiation, or by any other peaceful means of settling disputes acceptable to all parties to the dispute.
2. Any dispute of this character which cannot be settled in the manner prescribed in paragraph 1 shall, at the request of any party to such dispute, be submitted to arbitration or referred to the International Court of Justice for decision. Where a dispute is submitted to arbitration, if, within six months from the date of the request, the parties to the dispute are unable to agree on the organization of the arbitration, a party may request the President of the International Court of Justice or the Secretary-General of the United Nations to appoint one or more arbitrators. In case of conflicting requests by the parties to the dispute, the request to the Secretary-General of the United Nations shall have priority.
3. Each State Party may at the time of signature, ratification, acceptance or approval of this Convention or accession thereto declare that it does not consider itself bound by either or both of the dispute settlement procedures provided for in paragraph 2. The other States Parties shall not be bound by a dispute settlement procedure provided for in paragraph 2, with respect to a State Party which has made a reservation to that procedure.
4. Any State Party which has made a reservation in accordance with paragraph 3 may at any time withdraw that reservation by notification to the depositary.

Article 18
1. This Convention shall be open for signature by all States at the Headquarters of the International Atomic Energy Agency in Vienna and at the Headquarters of the United Nations in New York from 3 March 1980 until its entry into force.
2. This Convention is subject to ratification, acceptance or approval by the signatory States.
3. After its entry into force, this Convention will be open for accession by all States.
4. (a) This Convention shall be open for signature or accession by international organizations and regional organizations of an integrated or other nature, provided that any such organization is constituted by sovereign States and has competence in respect of the negotiation, conclusion and application of international agreements in matters covered by this Convention.
   (b) In matters within their competence, such organizations shall, on their own behalf, exercise the rights and fulfil the responsibilities which this Convention attributes to States Parties.

(c) When becoming party to this Convention such an organization shall communicate to the depositary a declaration indicating which States are members thereof and which articles of this Convention do not apply to it.
(d) Such an organization shall not hold any vote additional to those of its Member States.
5. Instruments of ratification, acceptance, approval or accession shall be deposited with the depositary.

Article 19

1. This Convention shall enter into force on the thirtieth day following the date of deposit of the twenty-first instrument of ratification, acceptance or approval with the depositary.
2. For each State ratifying, accepting, approving or acceding to the Convention after the date of deposit of the twenty-first instrument of ratification, acceptance or approval, the Convention shall enter into force on the thirtieth day after the deposit by such State of its instrument of ratification, acceptance, approval or accession.

Article 20

1. Without prejudice to article 16 a State Party may propose amendments to this Convention. The proposed amendment shall be submitted to the depositary who shall circulate it immediately to all States Parties. If a majority of States Parties request the depositary to convene a conference to consider the proposed amendments, the depositary shall invite all States Parties to attend such a conference to begin not sooner than thirty days after the invitations are issued. Any amendment adopted at the conference by a two-thirds majority of all States Parties shall be promptly circulated by the depositary to all States Parties.
2. The amendment shall enter into force for each State Party that deposits its instrument of ratification, acceptance or approval of the amendment on the thirtieth day after the date on which two thirds of the States Parties have deposited their instruments of ratification, acceptance or approval with the depositary. Thereafter, the amendment shall enter into force for any other State Party on the day on which that State Party deposits its instrument of ratification, acceptance or approval of the amendment.

Article 21

1. Any State Party may denounce this Convention by written notification to the depositary.
2. Denunciation shall take effect one hundred and eighty days following the date on which notification is received by the depositary.

Article 22

The depositary shall promptly notify all States of:
(a) each signature of this Convention;
(b) each deposit of an instrument of ratification, acceptance, approval or accession;
(c) any reservation or withdrawal in accordance with article 17.
(d) any communication made by an organization in accordance with paragraph 4 (c) of article 18;
(e) the entry into force of this Convention;
(f) the entry into force of any amendment to this Convention; and
(g) any denunciation made under article 21.

Article 23

The original of this Convention, of which the Arabic, Chinese, English, French, Russian and Spanish texts are equally authentic, shall be deposited with the Director General of the International Atomic Energy Agency who shall send certified copies thereof to all States.

ANNEX I

Levels of physical protection to be applied to international transport of nuclear material as categorized in Annex II.

1. Levels of physical protection for nuclear material during storage incidental to international nuclear transport include:
   (a) For Category III materials, storage within an area to which access is controlled;
   (b) For Category II materials, storage within an area under constant surveillance by guards or electronic devices, surrounded by a physical barrier with a limited number of points of entry under appropriate control or any area with an equivalent level of physical protection;
   (c) For Category I material, storage within a protected area as defined for Category II above, to which, in addition, access is restricted to persons whose trustworthiness has been determined, and which is under surveillance by guards who are in close communication with appropriate response forces. Specific measures taken in this context should have as their object the detection and prevention of any assault, unauthorized access or unauthorized removal of material.
2. Levels of physical protection for nuclear material during international transport include:
   (a) For Category II and III materials, transportation shall take place under special precautions including prior arrangements among sender, receiver, and carrier, and prior agreement between natural or legal persons subject to the jurisdiction and regulation of exporting and importing States, specifying time, place and procedures for transferring transport responsibility;
   (b) For Category I materials, transportation shall take place under special precautions identified above for transportation of Category II and III materials, and in addition, under constant surveillance by escorts and under conditions which assure close communication with appropriate response forces.
   (c) For natural uranium other than in the form of ore or ore-residue, transportation protection for quantities exceeding 500 kilograms uranium shall include advance notification of shipment specifying mode of transport, expected time of arrival and confirmation of receipt of shipment.

Material	Form	Category I	Category II	Category III[c]
Plutonium[a]	Unirradiated[b]	2kg or more	Less than 2kg but more than 500g	500g or less but more than 15g
Uranium-235	Unirradiated[b] uranium enriched to 20% U-235 or more	5kg or more	Less than 5kg but more than 1 kg	1kg or less but more than 15g
	uranium enriched to 10% U-235 or but less than 20%		10 kg or more	Less than 10kg but more than 1kg
	uranium enriched above natural, but less than 10% U-235			10 kg or more
Uranium-233	Unirradiated[b]	2kg or more	Less than 2kg but more than 500g	500g or less but more than 15g
Irradiated fuel			Depleted or natural uranium, thorium or low-enriched fuel (less than 10% fissile content)[d,e]	

Notes:
a   All plutonium except that with isotopic concentration exceeding 80% in plutonium-238.
b   Material not irradiated in a reactor or material irradiated in a reactor but with a radiation level equal to or less than 100 rads/hour at one metre unshielded.
c   Quantities not falling in Category III and natural uranium should be protected in accordance with prudent management practice.
d   Although this level of protection is recommended, it would be open to States, upon evaluation of the specific circumstances, to assign a different category of physical protection.
e   Other fuel which by virtue of its original fissile material content is classified as Category I or II before irradiation may be reduced one category level while the radiation level from the fuel exceeds 100 rads/hour at one metre unshielded.

Signatories to the Convention on the Physical Protection of Nuclear Material

Argentina
Australia
Austria
Belgium
Brazil
Bulgaria
Canada
China, People's Republic of
Czechoslovakia
Denmark
Finland
France
Germany
Greece
Guatemala
Hungary
Indonesia
Ireland
Italy
Japan
Korea, Republic of
Liechtenstein
Luxembourg
Mexico
Mongolia
Netherlands
Norway
Paraguay
Philippines
Poland
Portugal
Russian Federation
Spain
Sweden
Switzerland
Turkey
United Kingdom
United States of America
Yugoslavia

The following have signed but not ratified the Convention:

Dominican Republic
Ecuador
Haiti
Israel
Morocco
Niger
Panama
Romania
South Africa

UN Security Council Resolution on Security Assurances to Non-Nuclear Weapon States

Adopted at New York on 19 June 1968

The Security Council,

Noting with appreciation the desire of a large number of States to subscribe to the Treaty on the Non-Proliferation of Nuclear Weapons, and thereby to undertake not to receive the transfer from any transferor whatsoever of nuclear weapons or other nuclear explosive devices or of control over such weapons or explosive devices directly or indirectly, not to manufacture or otherwise acquire nuclear weapons or other nuclear explosive devices, and not to seek or receive any assistance in the manufacture of nuclear weapons or other nuclear explosive devices,

Taking into consideration the concern of certain of these States that, in conjunction with their adherence to the Treaty on the Non-Proliferation of Nuclear Weapons, appropriate measures be undertaken to safeguard their security,

Bearing in mind that any aggression accompanied by the use of nuclear weapons would endanger the peace and security of all States,

1. *Recognizes* that aggression with nuclear weapons or the threat of such aggression against a non-nuclear-weapon State would create a situation in which the Security Council, and above all its nuclear-weapon State permanent members, would have to act immediately in accordance with their obligations under the United Nations Charter;
2. *Welcomes* the intention expressed by certain States that they will provide or support immediate assistance, in accordance with the Charter, to any non-nuclear-weapon State Party to the Treaty on the Non-Proliferation of Nuclear Weapons that is a victim of an act or an object of a threat of aggression in which nuclear weapons are used;
3. *Reaffirms* in particular the inherent right, recognized under Article 51 of the Charter, of individual and collective self-defense if an armed attack occurs against a Member of the United Nations, until the Security Council has taken measures necessary to maintain international peace and security.

Source: UN document S/RES/255 (1968) in Resolutions and Decisions of the Security Council 1968, Security Council Official Records: Twenty-third year (United Nations, New York, 1970)

THE STRUCTURE AND CONTENT OF AGREEMENTS BETWEEN THE AGENCY AND STATES REQUIRED IN CONNECTION WITH THE TREATY ON THE NON-PROLIFERATION OF NUCLEAR WEAPONS

(Text taken from IAEA Information Circular No. 153 (INFCIRC/153), dated June 1972)

PART I

BASIC UNDERTAKING

1. The Agreement should contain, in accordance with Article III.1 of the Treaty on the Non-Proliferation of Nuclear Weapons, an undertaking by the State to accept safeguards, in accordance with the terms of the Agreement, on all source or special fissionable material in all peaceful nuclear activities within its territory, under its jurisdiction or carried out under its control anywhere, for the exclusive purpose of verifying that such material is not diverted to nuclear weapons or other nuclear explosive devices.

APPLICATION OF SAFEGUARDS

2. The Agreement should provide for the Agency's right and obligation to ensure that safeguards will be applied, in accordance with the terms of the Agreement, on all source or special fissionable material in all peaceful nuclear activities within the territory of the State, under its jurisdiction or carried out under its control anywhere, for the exclusive purpose of verifying that such material is not diverted to nuclear weapons or other nuclear explosive devices.

CO-OPERATION BETWEEN THE AGENCY AND THE STATE

3. The Agreement should provide that the Agency and the State shall co-operate to facilitate the implementation of the safeguards provided for therein.

IMPLEMENTATION OF SAFEGUARDS

4. The Agreement should provide that safeguards shall be implemented in a manner designed:
   (a) To avoid hampering the economic and technological development of the State or international co-operation in the field of peaceful nuclear activities, including international exchange of *nuclear material*;
   (b) To avoid undue interference in the State's peaceful nuclear activities, and in particular in the operation of *facilities*; and
   (c) To be consistent with prudent management practices required for the economic and safe conduct of nuclear activities.
5. The Agreement should provide that the Agency shall take every precaution to protect commercial and industrial secrets and other confidential information coming to its knowledge in the implementation of the Agreement. The Agency shall not publish or communicate to any State, organization or person any information obtained by it in connection with the implementation of the Agreement, except that specific information relating to such implementation in the State may be given to the Board of Governors and to such Agency staff members as require such knowledge by reason of their official duties in connection with safeguards, but only to the extent necessary for the Agency to fulfil its responsibilities in implementing the Agreement. Summarized information on *nuclear material* being safeguarded by the Agency under the Agreement may be published upon decision of the Board if the states directly concerned agree.
6. The Agreement should provide that in implementing safeguards pursuant thereto the Agency shall take full account of technological developments in the field of safeguards, and shall make every effort to ensure optimum cost-effectiveness and the application of the principle of safeguarding effectively the flow of *nuclear material* subject to safeguards under the Agreement by use of instruments and other techniques at certain *strategic points* to the extent that present or future technology permits. In order to ensure optimum cost-effectiveness, use should be made, for example, of such means as:
   (a) Containment as a means of defining *material balance points* for accounting purposes;
   (b) Statistical techniques and random sampling in evaluating the flow of *nuclear material*; and
   (c) Concentration of verification procedures on those stages in the nuclear fuel cycle involving the production, processing, use or storage of *nuclear material* from which nuclear weapons or other nuclear explosive devices could readily be made, and minimization of verification procedures in respect of other *nuclear material* on condition that this does not hamper the Agency in applying safeguards under the Agreement.

NATIONAL SYSTEM OF ACCOUNTING FOR AND CONTROL OF NUCLEAR MATERIAL

7. The Agreement should provide that the State shall establish and maintain a system of accounting for and control of all *nuclear material* subject to safeguards under the Agreement, and that such safeguards shall be applied in such a manner as to enable the Agency to verify, in ascertaining that there has been no diversion of *nuclear material* from peaceful uses to nuclear weapons or other nuclear explosive devices, findings of the State's system. The Agency's verification shall include, inter alia, independent measurements and observations conducted by the Agency in accordance with the procedures specified in Part II below. The Agency, in its verification, shall take due account of the technical effectiveness of the State's system.

PROVISION OF INFORMATION TO THE AGENCY

8. The Agreement should provide that to ensure the effective implementation of safeguards thereunder the Agency shall be provided, in accordance with the provisions set out in Part II below, with information concerning *nuclear material* subject to safeguards under the Agreement and the features of *facilities* relevant to safeguarding such material. The Agency shall require only the minimum amount of information and data consistent with carrying out its responsibilities under the Agreement. Information pertaining to *facilities* shall be the minimum necessary for safeguarding *nuclear material* subject to safeguards under the Agreement. In examining design information, the Agency shall, at the request of the State, be prepared to examine on premises of the State design information which the State regards as being of particular sensitivity. Such information would not have to be physically transmitted to the Agency provided that it remained available for ready further examination by the Agency on premises of the State.

AGENCY INSPECTORS

9. The Agreement should provide that the State shall take the necessary steps to ensure that Agency inspectors can effectively discharge their functions under the Agreement. The Agency shall secure the consent of the State to the designation of Agency inspectors to that State. If the State, either upon proposal of a designation or at any other time after a designation has been made, objects to the designation, the Agency shall propose to the State an alternative designation or designations. The repeated refusal of a State to accept the designation of Agency inspectors which would impede the inspections conducted under the Agreement would be considered by the Board upon referral by the Director General with a view to appropriate action. The visits and activities of Agency Inspectors shall be so arranged as to reduce to a minimum the possible inconvenience and disturbance to the State and to the peaceful nuclear activities inspected, as well as to ensure protection of industrial secrets or any other confidential information coming to the inspectors' knowledge.

PRIVILEGES AND IMMUNITIES

10. The Agreement should specify the privileges and immunities which shall be granted to the Agency and its staff in respect of their functions under the Agreement. In the case of a State party to the Agreement on the Privileges and Immunities of the Agency, the provisions thereof, as in force for such State, shall apply. In the case of other States, the privileges and immunities granted should be such as to ensure that:

    (a) The Agency and it staff will be in a position to discharge their functions under the Agreement effectively; and

    (b) No such State will be placed thereby in a more favourable position than States part to the Agreement on the Privileges and Immunities of the Agency.

TERMINATION OF SAFEGUARDS

Consumption or dilution of nuclear material

11. The Agreement should provide that safeguards shall terminate on *nuclear material* subject to safeguards thereunder upon determination by the Agency that it has been consumed, or has been diluted in such a way that it is no longer usable for any nuclear activity relevant from the point of view of safeguards, or has become practicably irrecoverable.

Transfer of nuclear material out of the State

12. The Agreement should provide, with respect to *nuclear material* subject to safeguards thereunder, for notification of transfers of such material out of the State, in accordance with the provisions set out in paragraphs 92-94 below. The Agency shall terminate safeguards under the Agreement on *nuclear material* when the recipient State has assumed responsibility therefore, as provided for in paragraph 91. The Agency shall maintain records indicating each transfer and, where applicable, the re-application of safeguards to the transferred *nuclear material*.

Provisions relating to nuclear material to be used in non-nuclear activities

13. The Agreement should provide that if the State wishes to use *nuclear material* subject to safeguards thereunder in non-nuclear activities, such as the production of alloys or ceramics, it shall agree with the Agency on the circumstances under which the safeguards on such *nuclear material* may be terminated.

NON-APPLICATION OF SAFEGUARDS TO NUCLEAR MATERIAL TO BE USED IN NON-PEACEFUL ACTIVITIES

14. The Agreement should provide that if the State intends to exercise its discretion to use *nuclear material* which is required to be safeguarded thereunder in a nuclear activity which does not require the application of safeguards under the Agreement, the following procedures will apply:

    (a) The State shall inform the Agency of the activity, making it clear:

        (i) That the use of the *nuclear material* is a non-prescribed military activity will not be in conflict with an undertaking the State may have given and in respect of which Agency safeguards apply, that the *nuclear material* will be used only in a peaceful nuclear activity; and

        (ii) That during the period of non-application of safeguards the *nuclear material* will not be used for the production of nuclear weapons or other nuclear explosive devices;

    (b) The State and the Agency shall make an arrangement so that, only while the *nuclear material* is in such an activity, the safeguards provided for in the Agreement will not be applied. The arrangement shall identify, to the extent possible, the period or circumstances during which safeguards will not be applied. In any event, the safeguards provided for in the Agreement shall again apply as soon as the *nuclear material* is reintroduced into a peaceful nuclear activity. The Agency shall be kept informed of the total quantity and composition of such unsafeguarded *nuclear material* in the State and of any exports of such material; and

(c) Each arrangement shall be made in agreement with the Agency. The Agency's agreement shall be given as promptly as possible; it shall only relate to the temporary and procedural provisions, reporting arrangements, etc., but shall not involve any approval or classified knowledge of the military activity or relate to the use of the *nuclear material* therein.

FINANCE

15. The Agreement should contain one of the following sets of provisions:

    (a) An agreement with a Member of the Agency should provide that each party thereto shall bear the expenses it incurs in implementing its responsibilities thereunder. However, if the State or persons under its jurisdiction incur extraordinary expenses as a result of a specific request by the Agency, the Agency shall reimburse such expenses provided that it has agreed in advance to do so. In any case the Agency shall bear the cost of any additional measuring or sampling which inspectors may request; or

    (b) An agreement with a party not a Member of the Agency should in application of the provisions of Article XIV.C of the Statute, provide that the party shall reimburse fully to the Agency the safeguards expenses the Agency incurs thereunder. However, if the party or persons under its jurisdiction incur extraordinary expenses as a result of a specific request by the Agency, the Agency shall reimburse such expenses provided that it has agreed in advance to do so.

THIRD PARTY LIABILITY FOR NUCLEAR DAMAGE

16. The Agreement should provide that the State shall ensure that any protection against third party liability in respect of nuclear damage, including any insurance or other financial security, which may be available under its laws or regulations shall apply to the Agency and its officials for the purpose of the implementation of the Agreement, in the same way as that protection applies to nationals of the State.

INTERNATIONAL RESPONSIBILITY

17. The Agreement should provide that any claim by one party thereto against the other in respect of any damage, other than damage arising out of a nuclear incident, resulting from the implementation of safeguards under the Agreement, shall be settled in accordance with international law.

MEASURES IN RELATION TO VERIFICATION OF NON-DIVERSION

18. The Agreement should provide that if the Board, upon report of the Director General decides that an action by the State is essential and urgent in order to ensure verification that *nuclear material* subject to safeguards under the Agreement is not diverted to nuclear weapons or other nuclear explosive devices the Board shall be able to call upon the State to take the required action without delay, irrespective of whether procedures for the settlement of a dispute have been invoked.

19. The Agreement should provide that if the Board upon examination of relevant information reported to it by the Director General finds that the Agency is not able to verify that there has been no diversion of *nuclear material* required to be safeguarded under the Agreement to nuclear weapons or other nuclear explosive devices, it may make the reports provided for in paragraph C of Article XII of the Statute and may also take, where applicable, the other measures provided for in that paragraph. In taking such action the Board shall take account of the degree of assurance provided by the safeguards measures that have been applied and shall afford the State ever reasonable opportunity to furnish the Board with any necessary reassurance.

INTERPRETATION AND APPLICATION OF THE AGREEMENT AND SETTLEMENT OF DISPUTES

20. The Agreement should provide that the parties thereto shall, at the request of either, consult about any question arising out of the interpretation or application thereof.

21. The Agreement should provide that the State shall have the right to request that any question arising out of the interpretation or application thereof be considered by the Board; and that the State shall be invited by the Board to participate in the discussion of any such question by the Board.

22. The Agreement should provide that any dispute arising out of the interpretation or application thereof except a dispute with regard to a finding by the Board under paragraph 19 above or an action taken by the Board pursuant to such a finding which is not settled by negotiation or another procedure agreed to by the parties should, on the request of either party, be submitted to an arbitral tribunal composed as follows: each party would designate one arbitrator, and the two arbitrators so designated would elect a third, who would be the Chairman. If, within 30 days of the request for arbitration, either party has not designated an arbitrator, either party to the dispute may request the president of the International Court of Justice to appoint an arbitrator. The same procedure would apply if, within 30 days of the designation or appointment of the second arbitrator, the third arbitrator had not been elected. A majority of the members of the arbitral tribunal would constitute a quorum, and all decisions would require the concurrence of two arbitrators. The arbitral procedure would be fixed by the tribunal. The decisions of the tribunal would be binding on both parties.

FINAL CLAUSES

Amendment of the Agreement

23. The Agreement should provide that the parties thereto shall, at the request of either of them, consult each other on amendment of the Agreement. All amendments shall require the agreement of both parties. It might additionally be provided, if convenient to the State, that the agreement of the parties on amendments to Part II of the Agreement could be achieved by recourse to a simplified procedure. The Director General shall promptly inform all Member States of any amendment to the Agreement.

Suspension of application of Agency safeguards under other agreements

24. Where applicable and where the State desires such a provision to appear, the Agreement should provide that the application or Agency safeguards in the State under other safeguards agreements with the Agency shall be suspended while the Agreement is in force. If the State has received assistance from the Agency for a project, the State's undertaking in the Project Agreement not to use items subject thereto in such a way as to further any military purpose shall continue to apply.

Entry into force and duration

25. The Agreement should provide that it shall enter into force on the date on which the Agency receives from the State written notification that the statutory and constitutional requirements for entry into force have been met. The Director General shall promptly inform all Member States of the entry into force.

26. The Agreement should provide for it to remain in force as long as the State is party to the Treaty on the Non-Proliferation of Nuclear Weapons.

PART II

INTRODUCTION

27. The Agreement should provide that the purpose of Part II thereof is to specify the procedures to be applied for the implementation of the safeguards provisions of Part I.

OBJECTIVE OF SAFEGUARDS

28. The Agreement should provide that the objective of safeguards is the timely detection of diversion of significant quantities of *nuclear material* from peaceful nuclear activities to the manufacture of nuclear weapons or of other nuclear explosive devices or for purposes unknown, and deterrence of such diversion by the risk of early detection.

29. To this end the Agreement should provide for the use of material accountancy as a safeguards measure of fundamental importance, with containment and surveillance as important complementary measures.

30. The Agreement should provide that the technical conclusion of the Agency's verification activities shall be a statement, in respect of each *material balance area*, of the amount of *material unaccounted for* over a specific period, giving the limits of accuracy of the amounts stated.

NATIONAL SYSTEM OF ACCOUNTING FOR AND CONTROL OF NUCLEAR MATERIAL

31. The Agreement should provide that pursuant to paragraph 7 above the Agency, in carrying out its verification activities, shall make full use of the State's system of accounting for and control of all *nuclear material* subject to safeguards under the Agreement, and shall avoid unnecessary duplication of the State's accounting and control activities.

32. The Agreement should provide that the State's system of accounting for and control of all *nuclear material* subject to safeguards under the Agreement shall be based on a structure of material balance areas, and shall make provision as appropriate and specified in the Subsidiary Arrangements for the establishment of such measures as:

    (a) A measurement system for the determination of the quantities of *nuclear material* received, produced, shipped, lost or otherwise removed from inventory, and the quantities on inventory;

    (b) The evaluation of precision and accuracy of measurements and the estimation of measurement uncertainty;

    (c) Procedures for identifying, reviewing and evaluating differences in shipper/receiver measurements;

    (d) Procedures for taking a *physical inventory*.

    (e) Procedures for the evaluation of accumulations of unmeasured inventory and unmeasured losses;

    (f) A system of records and reports showing, for each *material balance area*, the inventory of *nuclear material* and the changes in that inventory including receipts into and transfers out of the *material balance area*;

    (g) Provisions to ensure that the accounting procedures and arrangements are being operated correctly; and

    (h) Procedures for the submission of reports to the Agency in accordance with paragraphs 59-69 below.

STARTING POINT OF SAFEGUARDS

33. The Agreement should provide that safeguards shall not apply thereunder to material in mining or ore processing activities.

34. The Agreement should provide that:

    (a) When any material containing uranium or thorium which has not reached the stage of the nuclear fuel cycle described in sub-paragraph (c) below is directly or indirectly exported to a non-nuclear-weapon State, the State shall inform the Agency of its quantity, composition and destination, unless the material is exported for specifically non-nuclear purposes;

(b) When any material containing uranium or thorium which has not reached the stage of the nuclear fuel cycle described in sub-paragraph (c) below is imported, the State shall inform the Agency of its quantity and composition, unless the material is imported for specifically non-nuclear purposes; and

(c) When any *nuclear material* of a composition and purity suitable for fuel fabrication or for being isotopically enriched leaves the plant or the process stage in which it has been produced, or when such *nuclear materials*, or any other *nuclear material* produced at a later stage in the nuclear fuel cycle, is imported into the State, the *nuclear material* shall become subject to the other safeguards procedures specified in the Agreement.

TERMINATION OF SAFEGUARDS

35. The Agreement should provide that safeguards shall terminate on *nuclear material* subject to safeguards thereunder under the conditions set forth in paragraph 11 above. Where the conditions of that paragraph are not met, but the State considers that the recover of safeguarded *nuclear material* from residues is not for the time being practicable or desirable, the Agency and the State shall consult on the appropriate safeguards measures to be applied. It should further be provided that safeguards shall terminate on *nuclear material* subject to safeguards under the Agreement under the conditions set forth in paragraph 13 above, provided that the State and the Agency agree that such *nuclear material* is practicably irrecoverable.

EXEMPTIONS FROM SAFEGUARDS

36. The Agreement should provide that the Agency shall, at the request of the State, exempt *nuclear material* from safeguards, as follows:

    (a) Special fissionable material, when it is used in gram quantities or less as a sensing component in instruments;

    (b) *Nuclear material*, when it is used in non-nuclear activities in accordance with paragraph 13 above, if such *nuclear material* is recoverable; and

    (c) Plutonium with an isotopic concentration of plutonium-238 exceeding 80%.

37. The Agreement should provide that *nuclear material* that would otherwise be subject to safeguards shall be exempted from safeguards at the request of the State, provided that *nuclear material* so exempted in the State may not at any time exceed:

    (a) One kilogram in total of special fissionable material, which may consist of one of more of the following:

        (i) Plutonium;

        (ii) Uranium with an *enrichment* of 0.2 (20%) and above, taken account of by multiplying its weight by its *enrichment*; and

        (iii) Uranium with an *enrichment* below 0.2 (20%) and above that of natural uranium, taken account of by multiplying its weight five times the square of its *enrichment*;

    (b) Ten metric tons in total of natural uranium and depleted uranium with an *enrichment* above 0.005 (0.5%);

    (c) Twenty metric tons of depleted uranium with a *enrichment* of 0.005 (0.5%) or below; and

    (d) Twenty metric tons of thorium;

    or such greater amounts as may be specified by the Board of Governors for uniform application.

38. The Agreement should provide that if exempted *nuclear material* is to be processed or stored together with safeguarded *nuclear material*, provision should be made for the re-application of safeguards thereto.

SUBSIDIARY ARRANGEMENTS

39. The Agreement should provide that the Agency and the State shall make Subsidiary Arrangements which shall specify in detail, to the extent necessary to permit the Agency to fulfil its responsibilities under the Agreement in an effective and efficient manner, how the procedures laid down in the Agreement are to be applied. Provision should be made for the possibility of an extension or change of the Subsidiary Arrangements by agreement between the Agency and the State without amendment of the Agreement.

40. It should be provided that the Subsidiary Arrangements shall enter into force at the same time as, or as soon as possible after, the entry into force of the Agreement. The State and the Agency shall make ever effort to achieve their entry into force within 90 days of the entry into force of the Agreement, a later date being acceptable only with the agreement of both parties. The State shall provide the Agency promptly with the information required for completing the Subsidiary Arrangements. The Agreement should also provide that, upon its entry into force, the Agency shall be entitled to apply the procedures laid down therein in respect of the *nuclear material* listed in the inventory provided for in paragraph 41 below.

INVENTORY

41. The Agreement should provide that, on the basis of the initial report referred to in paragraph 62 below, the Agency shall establish a unified inventory of all *nuclear material* in the State subject to safeguards under the Agreement, irrespective of its origin, and maintain this inventory on the basis of subsequent reports and of the results of its verification activities. Copies of the inventory shall be made available to the State at agreed intervals.

DESIGN INFORMATION

General

42. Pursuant to paragraph 8 above, the Agreement should stipulate that design information in respect of existing *facilities* shall be provided to the Agency during the discussion of the Subsidiary Arrangements, and that the time limits for the provision of such information in respect of new *facilities* shall be specified in the Subsidiary Arrangements. It should further be stipulated that such information shall be provided as early as possible before *nuclear material* is introduced into a new *facility*.
43. The Agreement should specify that the design information in respect of each *facility* to be made available to the Agency shall include, when applicable:
    (a) Identification of the *facility*, stating its general character, purpose, nominal capacity and geographic location, and the name and address to be used for routine business purposes;
    (b) Description of the general arrangement of the *facility* with reference, to the extent feasible, to the form, location and flow of *nuclear material* and to the general layout of important items of equipment which use, produce or process *nuclear material*;
    (c) Description of features of the *facility* relating to material accountancy, containment and surveillance; and
    (d) Description of the existing and proposed procedures at the *facility* for *nuclear material* accountancy and control, with special reference to *material balance points* established by the operator, measurements of flow and procedures for *physical inventory* taking.
44. The Agreement should further provide that other information relevant to the application of safeguards shall be made available to the Agency in respect of each *facility*, in particular on organizational responsibility for material accountancy and control. It should also be provided that the State shall make available to the Agency supplementary information on the health and safety procedures which the Agency shall observe and with which the inspectors shall comply at the *facility*.
45. The Agreement should stipulate that design information in respect of a modification relevant for safeguards purposes shall be provided for examination sufficiently in advance for the safeguards procedures to be adjusted when necessary.

Purposes of examination of design information

46. The Agreement should provide that the design information made available to the Agency shall be used for the following purposes:
    (a) To identify the features of *facility* and *nuclear material* relevant to the application of safeguards to *nuclear material* in sufficient detail to facilitate verification;
    (b) To determine *material balance points* to be used for Agency accounting purposes and to select those *strategic points* which are *key measurement points* and which will be used to determine the *nuclear material* flows and inventories; in determining such *material balance points* the Agency shall, inter alia, use the following criteria:
        (i) The size of the *material balance area* should be related to the accuracy with which the material balance can be established;
        (ii) In determining the *material balance area* advantage should be taken of any opportunity to use containment and surveillance to help ensure the completeness of flow measurements and thereby simplify the application of safeguards and concentrate measurement efforts at *key measurement points*;
        (iii) A number of *material balance points* in use at a *facility* or at distinct sites may be combined in one *material balance area* to be used for Agency accounting purposes when the Agency determines that this is consistent with its verification requirements; and
        (iv) If the State so requests, a special *material balance area* around a process step involving commercially sensitive information may be established;
    (c) To establish the nominal timing and procedures for taking of *physical inventory* for Agency accounting purposes;
    (d) To establish the records and reports requirements and records evaluation procedures;
    (e) To establish requirements and procedures for verification of the quantity and location of *nuclear material*; and
    (f) To select appropriate combinations of containment and surveillance methods and techniques and the *strategic points* at which they are are to be applied.
    It should further be provided that the results of the examination of the design information shall be included in the Subsidiary Arrangements.

Re-examination of design information

47. The Agreement should provide that design information shall be re-examined in the light of changes in operating conditions, of developments in safeguards technology or of experience in the application of verification procedures, with a view to modifying the action the Agency has taken pursuant to paragraph 46 above.

Verification of design information

48. The Agreement should provide that the Agency, in co-operation with the State, may send inspectors to *facilities* to verify the design information provided to the Agency pursuant to paragraphs 42-45 above for the purposes stated in paragraph 46.

INFORMATION IN RESPECT OF NUCLEAR MATERIAL OUTSIDE FACILITIES

49. The Agreement should provide that the following information concerning *nuclear material* customarily used outside *facilities* shall be provided as applicable to the Agency:
    (a) General description of the use of the *nuclear material*, its geographic location, and the user's name and address for routine business purposes; and
    (b) General description of the existing and proposed procedures for *nuclear material* accountancy and control, including organizations responsibility for material accountancy and control.

    The Agreement should further provide that the Agency shall be informed on a timely basis of any change in the information provided to it under this paragraph.

50. The Agreement should provide that the information made available to the Agency in respect of *nuclear material* customarily used outside *facilities* may be used, to the extent relevant, for the purposes set out in sub-paragraphs 46(b)-(f) above.

RECORDS SYSTEM
General

51. The Agreement should provide that in establishing a national system of accounting for and control of *nuclear material* as referred to in paragraph 7 above, the State shall arrange that records are kept in respect of each *material balance area*. Provision should also be made that the Subsidiary Arrangements shall describe the records to be kept in respect of each *material balance area*.

52. The Agreement should provide that the State shall make arrangements to facilitate the examination of records by inspectors, particularly if the records are not kept in English, French, Russia or Spanish.

53. The Agreement should provide that the records shall be retained for at least five years.

54. The Agreement should provide that the records shall consist, as appropriate, of:
    (a) Accounting records of all *nuclear material* subject to safeguards under the Agreement; and
    (b) Operating records for *facilities* containing such *nuclear material*.

55. The Agreement should provide that the system of measurements on which the records used for the preparation of reports are based shall either conform to the latest international standards or be equivalent in quality to such standards.

Accounting records

56. The Agreement should provide that the accounting records shall set forth the following in respect of each *material balance area*:
    (a) All *inventory changes*, so as to permit a determination of the *book inventory* at any time;
    (b) All measurement results that are used for determination of the *physical inventory*; and
    (c) All *adjustments* and *corrections* that have been made in respect of *inventory changes*, *book inventories* and *physical inventories*.

57. The Agreement should provide that for all *inventory changes* and *physical inventories* the records shall show, in respect of each *batch* of *nuclear material*: material identification, *batch data* and *source data*. Provision should further be included that records shall account for uranium, thorium and plutonium separately in each *batch* of *nuclear material*. Furthermore, the date of the *inventory change* and, when appropriate, the originating *material balance area* and the receiving *material balance area* or the recipient, shall be indicated for each *inventory change*.

Operating records

58. The Agreement should provide that the operating records shall set forth as appropriate in respect of each *material balance area*:
    (a) Those operating data which are used to establish changes in the quantities and composition of *nuclear material*;
    (b) The data obtained from the calibration of tanks and instruments and from sampling and analyses, the procedures to control the quality of measurements and the derived estimates of random and systematic error;
    (c) The description of the sequence of the actions taken in preparing for, and in taking, a *physical inventory* in order to ensure that it is correct and complete; and
    (d) The description of the actions taken in order to ascertain the cause and magnitude of any accidental or unmeasured loss that might occur.

REPORTS SYSTEM
General

59. The Agreement should specify that the State shall provide the Agency with reports as detailed in paragraphs 60-69 below in respect of *nuclear material* subject to safeguards thereunder.

60. The Agreement should provide that reports shall be made in English, French, Russian or Spanish, except as otherwise specified in the Subsidiary Arrangements.

61. The Agreement should provide that reports shall be based on the records kept in accordance with paragraphs 51-58 above and shall consist, as appropriate, of accounting reports and special reports.

Accounting reports

62. The Agreement should stipulate that the Agency shall be provided with a initial report on all *nuclear material* which is to be subject to safeguards thereunder. It should also be provided that the initial report shall be dispatched by the State to the Agency within 30 days of the last day of the calendar month in which the Agreement enters into force, and shall reflect the situation as of the last day of that month.

63. The Agreement should stipulate that for each *material balance area* the State shall provide the Agency with the following accounting reports:

    (a) *inventory change* reports showing changes in the inventory of *nuclear material*. The reports shall be dispatched as soon as possible and in any event within 30 days after the end of the month in which the *inventory changes* occurred or were established; and

    (b) Material balance reports showing the material balance based on a *physical inventory* of *nuclear material* actually present in the *material balance area*. The report shall be dispatched as soon as possible and in any event within 30 days after the *physical inventory* has been taken. The reports shall be based on data available as of the date of reporting and may be corrected at a later date as required.

64. The Agreement should provide that *inventory change* reports shall specify identification and *batch data* for each *batch* of *nuclear material*, the date of the *inventory change* and, as appropriate, the originating *material balance area* and the receiving *material balance area* or the recipient. These reports shall be accompanied by concise notes:

    (a) Explaining the *inventory changes*, on the basis of the operating data contained in the operating records provided for under sub-paragraph 58(a) above; and

    (b) Describing, as specified in the Subsidiary Arrangements, the anticipated operational programme, particularly the taking of a *physical inventory*.

65. The Agreement should provide that the State shall report each *inventory change*, *adjustment* and *correction* either periodically in a consolidated list or individually. The *inventory changes* shall be reported in terms of *batches*; small amounts, such as analytical samples, as specified in the Subsidiary Arrangements, may be combined and reported as one *inventory change*.

66. The Agreement should stipulate that the Agency shall provide the State with semi-annual statements of *book inventory* of *nuclear material* subject to safeguards, for each *material balance area*, as based on the *inventory change* reports for the period covered by each such statement.

67. The Agreement should specify that the material balance reports shall include the following entries, unless otherwise agreed by the Agency and the State:

    (a) Beginning *physical inventory*;
    (b) *inventory changes* (first increases, then decreases);
    (c) Ending *book inventory*;
    (d) *shipper/receiver differences*;
    (e) Adjusted ending *book inventory*;
    (f) Ending *physical inventory*; and
    (g) *material accounted for*.

    A statement of the *physical inventory*, listing all *batches* separately and specifying material identification and *batch data* for each *batch*, shall be attached to each material balance report.

Special reports

68. The Agreement should provide that the State shall make special reports without delay:

    (a) If any unusual incident or circumstances lead the State to believe that there is or may have been loss of *nuclear material* that exceeds the limits to be specified for this purpose in the Subsidiary Arrangements; or

    (b) If the containment has unexpectedly changed from that specified in the Subsidiary Arrangements to the extent that unauthorized removal of *nuclear material* has become possible.

Amplification and clarification of reports

69. The Agreement should provide that at the Agency's request the State shall supply amplifications or clarifications of any report, in so far as relevant for the purpose of safeguards.

INSPECTIONS

General

70. The Agreement should stipulate that the Agency shall have the right to make inspections as provided for in paragraphs 71-82 below.

Purposes of inspections

71. The Agreement should provide that the Agency may make ad hoc inspections in order to:

    (a) Verify the information contained in the initial report on the *nuclear material* subject to safeguards under the Agreement;

(b) Identify and verify changes in the situation which have occurred since the date of the initial report; and
(c) Identify, and if possible verify the quantity and composition of, *nuclear material* in accordance with paragraphs 93 and 96 below, before its transfer out of or upon its transfer into the State.

72. The Agreement should provide that the Agency may make routine inspections in order to:
    (a) Verify that reports are consistent with records;
    (b) Verify the location, identity, quantity and composition of all *nuclear material* subject to safeguards under the Agreement; and
    (c) Verify information on the possible causes of *material unaccounted for, shipper/receiver differences* and uncertainties in the *book inventory*.

73. The Agreement should provide that the Agency may make special inspections subject to the procedures laid down in paragraph 77 below:
    (a) In order to verify the information contained in special reports; or
    (b) If the Agency considers that information made available by the State, including explanations from the State and information obtained from routine inspections, is not adequate for the Agency to fulfil its responsibilities under the Agreement.

    An inspection shall be deemed to be special when it is either additional to the routine inspection effort provided for in paragraphs 78-82 below, or involves access to information or locations in addition to the access specified in paragraph 76 for ad hoc and routine inspections, or both.

Scope of inspections

74. The Agreement should provide that for the purposes stated in paragraphs 71-73 above the Agency may:
    (a) Examine the records kept pursuant to paragraphs 51-58;
    (b) Make independent measurements of all *nuclear material* subject to safeguards under the Agreement;
    (c) Verify the functioning and calibration of instruments and other measuring and control equipment;
    (d) Apply and make use of surveillance and containment measures;
    and
    (e) Use other objective methods which have been demonstrated to be technically feasible.

75. It should further be provided that within the scope of paragraph 74 above the Agency shall be enabled:
    (a) To observe that samples at *key measurement points* for material balance accounting are taken in accordance with procedures which produce representative samples, to observe the treatment and analysis of the samples and to obtain duplicates of such samples;
    (b) To observe that the measurements of *nuclear material* at *key measurement points* for material balance accounting are representative, and to observe the calibration of the instruments and equipment involved;
    (c) To make arrangements with the State that, if necessary:
        (i) Additional measurements are made and additional samples taken for the Agency's use;
        (ii) The Agency's standard analytical samples are analysed;
        (iii) Appropriate absolute standards are used in calibrating instruments and other equipment; and
    (d) To arrange to use its own equipment for independent measurement and surveillance, and if so agreed and specified in the Subsidiary Arrangements, to arrange to install such equipment;
    (e) To apply its seals and other identifying and tamper-indicating devices to containments, if so agreed and specified in the Subsidiary Arrangements; and
    (f) To make arrangements with the State for the shipping of samples taken for the Agency's use.

Access for inspections

76. The Agreement should provide that:
    (a) For the purposes specified in sub-paragraphs 71(a) and (b) above and until such time as the *strategic points* have been specified in the Subsidiary Arrangements, the Agency's inspectors shall have access to any location where the initial report or any inspections carried out in connection with it indicate that *nuclear material* is present;
    (b) For the purposes specified in sub-paragraph 71(c) above the inspectors shall have access to any location of which the Agency has been notified in accordance with sub-paragraphs 92(c) or 95(c) below;
    (c) For the purposes specified in paragraph 72 above the Agency's inspectors shall have access only to the *strategic points* specified in the Subsidiary Arrangements and to the records maintained pursuant to paragraphs 51-58; and
    (d) In the event of the State concluding that any unusual circumstances require extended limitations on access by the Agency, the State and the Agency shall promptly make arrangements with a view to enabling the Agency to discharge its safeguards responsibilities in the light of these limitations. The Director General shall report each such arrangement to the Board.

77. The Agreement should provide that in circumstances which may lead to special inspections for the purposes specified in paragraph 73 above the State and the Agency shall consult forthwith. As a result of such consultations the Agency may make inspections in addition to the routine inspection effort provided for in paragraphs 78-82 below, and may obtain access

in agreement with the State to information or locations in addition to the access specified in paragraph 76 above for ad hoc and routine inspections. Any disagreement concerning the need for additional access shall be resolved in accordance with paragraphs 21 and 22; in case action by the State is essential and urgent, paragraph 18 above shall apply.

Frequency and intensity of routine inspections

78. The Agreement should provide that the number, intensity, duration and timing of routine inspections shall be kept to the minimum consistent with the effective implementation of the safeguards procedures set forth therein, and that the Agency shall make the optimum and most economical use of available inspection resources.

79. The Agreement should provide that in the case of *facilities* and *material balance area* outside *facilities* with a content or *annual throughput*, whichever is greater, of *nuclear material* not exceeding five *effective kilograms*, routine inspections shall not exceed one per year. For other *facilities* the number, intensity, duration, timing and mode of inspections shall be determined on the basis that in the maximum or limiting case the inspection regime shall be no more intensive than is necessary and sufficient to maintain continuity of knowledge of the flow and inventory of *nuclear material*.

80. The Agreement should provide that the maximum routine inspection effort in respect of *facilities* with a content or *annual throughput* of *nuclear material* exceeding five *effective kilograms* shall be determined as follows:

    (a) For reactors and sealed stores, the maximum total of routine inspection per year shall be determined by allowing one sixth of a *man-year of inspection* for each such *facility* in the State;

    (b) For other *facilities* involving plutonium or uranium enriched to more than 5%, the maximum total of routine inspection per year shall be determined by allowing for each such *facility* $30 \times \sqrt{E}$ man-days of inspection per year, where E is the inventory or *annual throughput* of *nuclear material*, whichever is greater, expressed in *effective kilograms*. The maximum established for any such *facility* shall not, however, be less than 1.5 *man-years of inspection*; and

    (c) For all other *facilities*, the maximum total of routine inspection per year shall be determined by allowing for each such *facility* one third of a *man-year of inspection* plus $0.4 \times E$ man-days of inspection per year, where E is the inventory or *annual throughput* of *nuclear material*, whichever is greater, expressed in *effective kilograms*.

    The Agreement should further provide that the Agency and the State may agree to amend the maximum figures specified in this paragraph upon determination by the Board that such amendment is reasonable.

81. Subject to paragraphs 78-80 above the criteria to be used for determining the actual number, intensity, duration, timing and mode of routine inspections of any *facility* shall include:

    (a) The form of *nuclear material*, in particular, whether the material is in bulk form or contained in a number of separate items; its chemical composition and, in the case of uranium, whether it is of low or high *enrichment*; and its accessibility;

    (b) The effectiveness of the State's accounting and control system, including the extent to which the operators of *facilities* are functionally independent of the State's accounting and control system; the extent to which the measures specified in paragraph 32 above have been implemented by the State; the promptness of reports submitted to the Agency; their consistency with the Agency's independent verification; and the amount and accuracy of the *material unaccounted for*, as verified by the Agency;

    (c) Characteristics of the State's nuclear fuel cycle, in particular, the number and types of *facilities* containing *nuclear material* subject to safeguards, the characteristics of such *facilities* relevant to safeguards, notably the degree of containment; the extent to which the design of such *facilities* facilitates verification of the flow and inventory of *nuclear material*; and the extent to which information from different *material balance points* can be correlated;

    (d) International interdependence, in particular, the extent to which *nuclear material* is received from or sent to other States for use or processing; any verification activity by the Agency in connection therewith; and the extent to which the State's nuclear activities are interrelated with those of other States; and

    (e) Technical developments in the field of safeguards, including the use of statistical techniques and random sampling in evaluating the flow of *nuclear material*.

82. The Agreement should provide for consultation between the Agency and the State if the latter considers that the inspection effort is being deployed with undue concentration on particular *facilities*.

Notice of inspections

83. The Agreement should provide that the Agency shall give advance notice to the State before arrival of inspectors at *facilities* or *material balance points* outside *facilities*, as follows:

    (a) For ad hoc inspections pursuant to sub-paragraph 71(c) above, at least 24 hours; for those pursuant to sub-paragraphs 71(a) and (b), as well as the activities provided for in paragraph 48, at least one week;

    (b) For special inspections pursuant to paragraph 73 above, as promptly as possible after the Agency and the State have consulted as provided for in paragraph 77, it being understood that notification of arrival normally will constitute part of the consultations; and

    (c) For routine inspections pursuant to paragraph 72 above, at least 24 hours in respect of the *facilities* referred to in sub-paragraph 80(b) and sealed stores containing plutonium or uranium enriched to more than 5%, and one week in all other cases.

Such notice of inspections shall include the names of the inspectors and shall indicate the *facilities* and the *material balance area* outside *facilities* to be visited and the periods during which they will be visited. If the inspectors are to arrive from outside the State the Agency shall also give advance notice of the place and time of their arrival in the State.

84. However, the Agreement should also provide that, as a supplementary measure, the Agency may carry out without advance notification a portion of the routine inspections pursuant to paragraph 80 above in accordance with the principle of random sampling. In performing any unannounced inspections, the Agency shall fully take into account any operational programme provided by the State pursuant to paragraph 64(b). Moreover, whenever practicable, and on the basis of the operational programme, it shall advise the State periodically of its general programme of announced and unannounced inspections, specifying the general periods when inspections are foreseen. In carrying out any unannounced inspections, the Agency shall make every effort to minimize any practical difficulties for *facility* operators and the State, bearing in mind the relevant provisions of paragraphs 44 above and 89 below. Similarly the State shall make every effort to facilitate the task of the inspectors.

Designation of inspectors

85. The Agreement should provide that:
    (a) The Director General shall inform the State in writing of the name, qualifications, nationality, grade and such other particulars as may be relevant, of each Agency official he proposes for designation as a inspector for the State;
    (b) The State shall inform the Director General within 30 days of the receipt of such a proposal whether it accepts the proposal;
    (c) The Director General may designate each official who has been accepted by the State as one of the inspectors for the State, and shall inform the State of such designations; and
    (d) The Director General, acting in response to a request by the State or on his own initiative, shall immediately inform the State of the withdrawal of the designation of any official as an inspector for the State.

    The Agreement should also provide, however, that in respect of inspectors needed for the purposes stated in paragraph 48 above and to carry out ad hoc inspections pursuant to sub-paragraphs 71(a) and (b) the designation procedures shall be completed if possible within 30 days after the entry into force of the Agreement. If such designation appears impossible within this time limit, inspectors for such purposes shall be designated on a temporary basis.

86. The Agreement should provide that the State shall grant or renew as quickly as possible appropriate visas, where required, for each inspector designated for the State.

Conduct and visits of inspectors

87. The Agreement should provide that inspectors, in exercising their functions under paragraphs 48 and 71-75 above, shall carry out their activities in a manner designed to avoid hampering or delaying the construction, commissioning or operation of *facilities* or affecting their safety. In particular inspectors shall not operate any *facility* themselves or direct the staff of a *facility* to carry out any operation. If inspectors consider that in pursuance of paragraphs 74 and 75, particular operations in a *facility* should be carried out by the operator, they shall make a request therefor.

88. When inspectors require services available in the State, including the use of equipment, in connection with the performance of inspections, the State shall facilitate the procurement of such services and the use of such equipment by inspectors.

89. The Agreement should provide that the State shall have the right to have inspectors accompanied during their inspections by representatives of the State, provided that inspectors shall not thereby be delayed or otherwise impeded in the exercise of their functions.

STATEMENTS ON THE AGENCY'S VERIFICATION ACTIVITIES

90. The Agreement should provide that the Agency shall inform the State of:
    (a) The results of inspections, at intervals to be specified in the Subsidiary Arrangements; and
    (b) The conclusions it has drawn from its verification activities in the State, in particular by means of statements in respect of each *material balance area*, which shall be made as soon as possible after a *physical inventory* has been taken and verified by the Agency and a material balance has been struck.

INTERNATIONAL TRANSFERS

General

91. The Agreement should provide that *nuclear material* subject or required to be subject to safeguards thereunder which is transferred internationally shall, for purposes of the Agreement, be regarded as being the responsibility of the State:
    (a) In the case of import, from the time that such responsibility ceases to lie with the exporting State, and no later than the time at which the *nuclear material* reaches its destination; and
    (b) In the case of export, up to the time at which the recipient State assumes such responsibility, and no later than the time at which the *nuclear material* reaches its destination.

The Agreement should provide that the States concerned shall make suitable arrangements to determine the point at which the transfer of responsibility will take place. No State shall be deemed to have such responsibility for *nuclear material* merely by reason of the fact that the *nuclear material* is in transit on or over its territory or territorial waters, or that it is being transported under its flag or in its aircraft.

Transfers out of the State

92. The Agreement should provide that any intended transfer out of the State of safeguarded *nuclear material* in a amount exceeding one *effective kilogram* or by successive shipments to the same State within a period of three months each of less than one *effective kilogram* but exceeding in total one *effective kilogram*, shall be notified to the Agency after the conclusion of the contractual arrangements leading to the transfer and normally at least two weeks before the *nuclear material* is to be prepared for shipping. The Agency and the State may agree on different procedures for advance notification. The notification shall specify:

    (a) The identification and, if possible, the expected quantity and composition of the *nuclear material* to be transferred, and the *material balance area* from which it will come;
    (b) The State for which the *nuclear material* is destined;
    (c) The dates on and locations at which the *nuclear material* is to be prepared for shipping;
    (d) The approximate dates of dispatch and arrival of the *nuclear material*; and
    (e) At what point of the transfer the recipient State will assume responsibility for the *nuclear material*, and the probable date on which this point will be reached.

93. The Agreement should further provide that the purpose of this notification shall be to enable the Agency if necessary to identify, and if possible verify the quantity and composition of, *nuclear material* subject to safeguards under the Agreement before it is transferred out of the State and, if the Agency so wishes or the State so requests, to affix seals to the *nuclear material* when it has been prepared for shipping. However, the transfer of the *nuclear material* shall not be delayed in any way by any action taken or contemplated by the Agency pursuant to this notification.

94. The Agreement should provide that, if the *nuclear material* will not be subject to Agency safeguards in the recipient State, the exporting State shall make arrangements for the Agency to receive, within three months of the time when the recipient State accepts responsibility for the *nuclear material* from the exporting State, confirmation by the recipient State of the transfer.

Transfers into the State

95. The Agreement should provide that the expected transfer into the State of *nuclear material* required to be subject to safeguards in an amount greater than one *effective kilogram*, or by successive shipments from the same State within a period of three months each of less than one *effective kilogram* but exceeding in total one *effective kilogram*, shall be notified to the Agency as much in advance as possible of the expected arrival of the *nuclear material*, and in any case not later than the date on which the recipient State assumes responsibility therefor. The Agency and the State may agree on different procedures for advance notification. The notification shall specify:

    (a) The identification and, if possible, the expected quantity and composition of the *nuclear material*;
    (b) At what point of the transfer responsibility for the *nuclear material* will be assumed by the State for the purposes of the Agreement, and the probable date on which this point will be reached; and
    (c) The expected date of arrival, the location to which the *nuclear material* is to be delivered and the date on which it is intended that the *nuclear material* should be unpacked.

96. The Agreement should provide that the purpose of this notification shall be to enable the Agency if necessary to identify, and if possible verify the quantity and composition of, *nuclear material* subject to safeguards which has been transferred into the State, by means of inspection of the consignment at the time it is unpacked. However, unpacking shall not be delayed by any action taken or contemplated by the Agency pursuant to this notification.

Special reports

97. The Agreement should provide that in the case of international transfers a special report as envisaged in paragraph 68 above shall be made if any unusual incident or circumstances lead the State to believe that there is or may have been loss of *nuclear material*, including the occurrence of significant delay during the transfer.

DEFINITIONS

98. "Adjustment" means an entry into an accounting record or a report showing a *shipper/receiver difference* or *material unaccounted for*.

99. "Annual throughput" means, for the purposes of paragraphs 79 and 80 above, the amount of *nuclear material* transferred annually out of a *facility* working at nominal capacity.

100. "Batch" means a portion of *nuclear material* handled as a unit for accounting purposes at a *key measurement point* and for which the composition and quantity are defined by a single set of specifications or measurements. The *nuclear material* may be in bulk form or contained in a number of separate items.

101. "Batch data" means the total weight of each element of *nuclear material* and, in the case of plutonium and uranium, the isotopic composition when appropriate. The units of account shall be as follows:

    (a) Grams of contained plutonium;

(b) Grams of total uranium and grams of contained uranium-235 plus uranium-233 for uranium enriched in these isotopes; and

(c) Kilograms of contained thorium, natural uranium or depleted uranium.

For reporting purposes the weights of individual items in the *batch* shall be added together before rounding to the nearest unit.

102. "Book inventory" of a *material balance area* means the algebraic sum of the most recent *physical inventory* of that *material balance area* and of all *inventory changes* that have occurred since that *physical inventory* was taken.

103. "Correction" means an entry into a accounting record or a report to rectify an identified mistake or to reflect an improved measurement of a quantity previously entered into the record or report. Each correction must identify the entry to which it pertains.

104. "Effective kilogram" means a special unit used in safeguarding *nuclear material*. The quantity in "effective kilograms" is obtained by taking:

(a) For plutonium, its weight in kilograms;

(b) For uranium with an *enrichment* of 0.01 (1%) and above, its weight in kilograms multiplied by the square of its *enrichment*;

(c) For uranium with an *enrichment* below 0.01 (1%) and above 0.005 (0.5%), its weight in kilograms multiplied by 0.0001; and

(d) For depleted uranium with an *enrichment* of 0.005 (0.5%) or below, and for thorium, its weight in kilograms multiplied by 0.00005.

105. "Enrichment" means the ratio of the combined weight of the isotopes uranium-233 and uranium-235 to that of the total uranium in question.

106. "Facility" means:

(a) A reactor, a critical facility, a conversion plant, a fabrication plant, a reprocessing plant, an isotope separation plant or a separate storage installation; or

(b) Any location where *nuclear material* in amounts greater than one *effective kilogram* is customarily used.

107. "Inventory change" means an increase or decrease, in terms of BATCHES, of *nuclear material* in a *material balance area* such a change shall involve one of the following:

(a) Increases:

(i) Import;

(ii) Domestic receipt: receipts from other *material balance points*, receipts from a non-safeguarded (non-peaceful) activity or receipts at the starting point of safeguards;

(iii) Nuclear production: production of special fissionable material in a reactor; and

(iv) De-exemption: reapplication of safeguards on *nuclear material* previously exempted therefrom on account of its use or quantity.

(b) Decreases:

(i) Export;

(ii) Domestic shipment: shipments to other *material balance points* or shipments for a non-safeguarded (non-peaceful) activity;

(iii) Nuclear loss: loss of *nuclear material* due to its transformation into other element(s) or isotope(s) as a result of nuclear reactions;

(iv) Measured discard: *nuclear material* which has been measured, or estimated on the basis of measurements, and disposed of in such a way that it is not suitable for further nuclear use;

(v) Retained waste: *nuclear material* generated from processing or from an operational accident, which is deemed to be unrecoverable for the time being but which is stored;

(vi) Exemption: exemption of *nuclear material* from safeguards on account of its use or quantity; and

(vii) Other loss: for example, accidental loss (that is, irretrievable and inadvertent loss of *nuclear material* as the result of an operational accident) or theft.

108. "Key measurement point" means a location where *nuclear material* appears in such a form that it may be measured to determine material flow or inventory. "Key measurement points" thus include, but are not limited to, the inputs and outputs (including measured discards) and storages in *material balance points*.

109. "Man-year of inspection" means, for the purposes of paragraph 80 above, 300 man-days of inspection, a man-day being a day during which a single inspector has access to a *facility* at any time for a total of not more than eight hours.

110. "Material balance area" means an area in or outside of a *facility* such that:

(a) The quantity of *nuclear material* in each transfer into or out of each "material balance area" can be determined; and

(b) The *physical inventory* of *nuclear material* in each "material balance area" can be determined when necessary, in accordance with specified procedures, in order that the material balance for Agency safeguards purposes can be established.

111. "Material unaccounted for" means the difference between *book inventory* and *physical inventory*.

IAEA Model Safeguards Agreement

112. "Nuclear material" means any source or any special fissionable material as defined in Article XX of the Statute. The term source material shall not be interpreted as applying to ore or ore residue. Any determination by the Board under Article XX of the Statute after the entry into force of this Agreement which adds to the materials considered to be source material or special fissionable material shall have effect under this Agreement only upon acceptance by the State.
113. "Physical inventory" means the sum of all the measured or derived estimates of *batch* quantities of *nuclear material* on hand at a given time within a *material balance area*, obtained in accordance with specified procedures.
114. "Shipper/receiver difference" means the difference between the quantity of *nuclear material* in a *batch* as stated by the shipping *material balance area* and as measured at the receiving *material balance area*.
115. "Source data" means those data, recorded during measurement or calibration or used to derive empirical relationships, which identify *nuclear material* and provide *batch data*. "Source data" may include, for example, weight of compounds, conversion factors to determine weight of element, specific gravity, element concentration, isotopic ratios, relationship between volume and manometer readings and relationship between plutonium produced and power generated.
116. "Strategic point" means a location selected during examination of design information where, under normal conditions and when combined with the information from all "strategic points" taken together, the information necessary and sufficient for the implementation of safeguards measures is obtained and verified; a "strategic point" may include any location where key measurements related to material balance accountancy are made and where containment and surveillance measures are executed.

Guidelines for Nuclear Transfers

(Text reproduced from INFCIRC/254)

(Agreed at London on 21 September 1977)

1. The following fundamental principles for safeguards and export controls should apply to nuclear transfers to any non-nuclear-weapon State for peaceful purposes. In this connection, suppliers have defined an export trigger list and agreed on common criteria for technology transfers.

Prohibition on nuclear explosives

2. Suppliers should authorize transfer of items identified in the trigger list only upon formal governmental assurances from recipients explicitly excluding uses which would result in any nuclear explosive device.

Physical protection

3. (a) All nuclear materials and facilities identified by the agreed trigger list should be placed under effective physical protection to prevent unauthorized use and handling. The levels of physical protection to be ensured in relation to the type of materials, equipment and facilities, have been agreed by suppliers, taking account of international recommendations.

   (b) The implementation of measures of physical protection in the recipient country is the responsibility of the Government of that country. However, in order to implement the terms agreed upon amongst suppliers, the levels of physical protection on which these matters have to be based should be the subject of an agreement between supplier and recipient.

   (c) In each case special arrangements should be made for a clear definition of responsibilities for the transport of trigger list items.

Safeguards

4. Suppliers should transfer trigger list items only when covered by IAEA safeguards, with duration and coverage provisions in conformance with the GOV/1621 guidelines. Exceptions should be made only after consultation with the parties to this understanding.

5. Suppliers will jointly reconsider their common safeguards requirements, whenever appropriate.

Safeguards triggered by the transfer of certain technology

6. (a) The requirements of paragraphs 2, 3 and 4 above should also apply to facilities for reprocessing, enrichment, or heavy-water production, utilizing technology directly transferred by the supplier or derived from transferred facilities, or major critical components thereof.

   (b) The transfer of such facilities, or major critical components thereof, or related technology, should require an undertaking (1) that IAEA safeguards apply to any facilities of the same type, (i.e. if the design, construction or operating processes are based on the same or similar physical or chemical processes, as defined in the trigger list) constructed during an agreed period in the recipient country and (2) that there should at all times be in effect a safeguards agreement permitting the IAEA to apply Agency safeguards with respect to such facilities identified by the recipient, or by the supplier in consultation with the recipient, as using transferred technology.

Special controls on sensitive exports

7. Suppliers should exercise restraint in the transfer of sensitive facilities, technology and weapons-usable materials. If enrichment or reprocessing facilities, equipment or technology are to be transferred, suppliers should encourage recipients to accept, as an alternative to national plants, supplier involvement and/or other appropriate multinational participation in resulting facilities. Suppliers should also promote international (including IAEA) activities concerned with multinational regional fuel cycle centres.

Special controls on export of enrichment facilities, equipment and technology.

8. For a transfer of an enrichment facility, or technology therefor, the recipient nation should agree that neither the transferred facility, nor any facility based on such technology, will be designed or operated for the production of greater than 20% enriched uranium without the consent of the supplier nation, of which the IAEA should be advised.

Controls on supplied or derived weapons-usable material

9. Suppliers recognize the importance, in order to advance the objectives of these Guidelines and to provide opportunities further to reduce the risks of proliferation, of including in agreements on supply of nuclear materials or of facilities which produce weapons-usable material, provisions calling for mutual agreement between the supplier and the recipient on arrangements for reprocessing, storage, alteration, use, transfer or re-transfer of any weapons-usable material involved. Suppliers should endeavour to include such provisions whenever appropriate and practicable.

Controls on retransfer

10. (a) Suppliers should transfer trigger list items, including technology defined under paragraph 6, only upon the recipient's

assurance that in the case of:
(1) retransfer of such items, or
(2) transfer of trigger list items derived from facilities originally transferred by the supplier, or with the help of equipment or technology originally transferred by the supplier; the recipient of the retransfer or transfer will have provided the same assurances as those required by the supplier for the original transfer.
(b) In addition the supplier's consent should be required for: (1) any retransfer of the facilities, major critical components, or technology described in paragraph 6; (2) any transfer of facilities or major critical components derived from those items; (3) any retransfer of heavy water or weapons-usable material.

Supporting activities

Physical security

11. Suppliers should promote international co-operation on the exchange of physical security information, protection of nuclear materials in transit, and recovery of stolen nuclear materials and equipment.

Support for effective IAEA safeguards

12. Suppliers should make special efforts in support of effective implementation of IAEA safeguards. Suppliers should also support the Agency's efforts to assist Member States in the improvement of their national systems of accounting and control of nuclear material and to increase the technical effectiveness of safeguards.

Similarly, they should make every effort to support the IAEA in increasing further the adequacy of safeguards in the light of technical developments and the rapidly growing number of nuclear facilities, and to support appropriate initiatives aimed at improving the effectiveness of IAEA safeguards.

Sensitive plant design features

13. Suppliers should encourage the designers and makers of sensitive equipment to construct it in such a way as to facilitate the application of safeguards.

Consultations

14. (a) Suppliers should maintain contact and consult through regular channels on matters connected with the implementation of these Guidelines.
(b) Suppliers should consult, as each deems appropriate, with other Governments concerned on specific sensitive cases, to ensure that any transfer does not contribute to risks of conflict or instability.
(c) In the event that one or more suppliers believe that there has been a violation of supplier/recipient understandings resulting from these Guidelines, particularly in the case of an explosion of a nuclear device, or illegal termination or violation of IAEA safeguards by a recipient, suppliers should consult promptly through diplomatic channels in order to determine and assess the reality and extent of the alleged violation.

Pending the early outcome of such consultations, suppliers will not act in a manner that could prejudice any measure that may be adopted by other suppliers concerning their current contacts with that recipient.

Upon the findings of such consultations, the suppliers, bearing in mind Article XII of the IAEA Statute, should agree on an appropriate response and possible action which could include the termination of nuclear transfers to that recipient.

15. In considering transfers, each supplier should exercise prudence having regard to all the circumstances of each case, including any risk that technology transfers not covered by paragraph 6, or subsequent retransfers, might result in unsafeguarded nuclear materials.

16. Unanimous consent is required for any changes in these Guidelines, including any which might result from the reconsideration mentioned in paragraph 5.

ANNEX A. TRIGGER LIST REFERRED TO IN GUIDELINES

PART A. Material and equipment

1. Source or special fissionable material as defined in Article XX of the Statute of the International Atomic Energy Agency; provided that items specified in subparagraph (a) below, and exports of source or special fissionable material to a given recipient country, within a period of 12 months, below the limits specified in subparagraph (b) below, shall not be included:

   (a) Plutonium with an isotopic concentration of plutonium-238 exceeding 80%.
   Special fissionable material when used in gram quantities or less as a sensing component in instruments; and
   Source material which the Government is satisfied is to be used only in non-nuclear activities, such as the production of alloys or ceramics;

   (b) Special fissionable material   50 effective grams;
   Natural uranium   500 kilograms;
   Depleted uranium   1000 kilograms;
   and
   Thorium   1000 kilograms.

2.1. Reactors and equipment therefor:

2.1.1. Nuclear reactors capable of operation so as to maintain a controlled self-sustaining fission chain reaction, excluding zero energy reactors, the latter being defined as reactors with a designed maximum rate of production of plutonium not exceeding 100 grams per year.

2.1.2. Reactor pressure vessels:
Metal vessels, as complete units or as major shop-fabricated parts therefor, which are especially designed or prepared to contain the core of a nuclear reactor as defined in paragraph 2.1.1. above and are capable of withstanding the operating pressure of the primary coolant.

2.1.3. Reactor fuel charging and discharging machines: Manipulative equipment especially designed or prepared for inserting or removing fuel in a nuclear reactor as defined in paragraph 2.1.1. above capable of on-load operation or employing technically sophisticated positioning or alignment features to allow complex off-load fuelling operations such as those in which direct viewing of or access to the fuel is not normally available.

2.1.4. Reactor control rods:
Rods especially designed or prepared for the control of the reaction rate in a nuclear reactor as defined in paragraph 2.1.1. above.

2.1.5. Reactor pressure tubes:
Tubes which are especially designed or prepared to contain fuel elements and the primary coolant in a reactor as defined in paragraph 2.1.1. above at an operating pressure in excess of 50 atmospheres.

2.1.6. Zirconium tubes:
Zirconium metal and alloys in the form of tubes or assemblies of tubes, and in quantities exceeding 500 kg per year, especially designed or prepared for use in a reactor as defined in paragraph 2.1.1. above, and in which the relationship of hafnium to zirconium is less than 1:500 parts by weight.

2.1.7. Primary coolant pumps:
Pumps especially designed or prepared for circulating liquid metal as primary coolant for nuclear reactors as defined in paragraph 2.1.1 above.

2.2. Non-nuclear materials for reactors:

2.2.1. Deuterium and heavy water:
Deuterium and any deuterium compound in which the ratio of deuterium to hydrogen exceeds 1:5000 for use in a nuclear reactor as defined in paragraph 2.1.1 above in quantities exceeding 200 kg of deuterium atoms for any one recipient country in any period of 12 months.

2.2.2. Nuclear grade graphite:
Graphite having a purity level better than 5 parts per million boron equivalent and with a density greater than 1.50 grams per cubic centimetre in quantities exceeding 30 metric tons for any one recipient country in any period of 12 months.

2.3.1. Plants for the reprocessing of irradiated fuel elements, and equipment especially designed or prepared therefor.

2.4.1. Plants for the fabrication of fuel elements.

2.5.1. Equipment, other than analytical instruments, especially designed or prepared for the separation of isotopes of uranium.

2.6.1. Plants for the production of heavy water, deuterium and deuterium compounds and equipment especially designed or prepared therefor.

Clarifications of certain of the items on the above list are annexed.

PART B. Common criteria for technology transfers under paragraph 6 of the Guidelines

1. "Technology" means technical data in physical form designated by the supplying country as important to the design, construction, operation, or maintenance of enrichment, reprocessing, or heavy water production facilities or major critical components thereof, but excluding data available to the public, for example, in published books and periodicals, or that which has been made available internationally without restrictions upon its further dissemination.

2. "Major critical components" are:
   (a) in the case of an isotope separation plant of the gaseous diffusion type; *diffusion barrier*;
   (b) in the case of an isotope separation plant of the gas centrifuge type: *gas centrifuge assemblies, corrosion-resistant to UF_6*;
   (c) in the case of an isotope separation plant of the jet nozzle type: *the nozzle units*;
   (d) in the case of an isotope plant of the vortex type: *the vortex units*.

3. For facilities covered by paragraph 6 of the Guidelines for which no major critical component is described in paragraph 2 above, if a supplier nation should transfer in the aggregate a significant fraction of the items essential to the operation of such a facility, together with the knowhow for construction and operation of that facility, that transfer should be deemed to be a transfer of "facilities or major critical components thereof".

4. The definitions in the preceding paragraphs are solely for the purposes of paragraph 6 of the Guidelines and this Part B, which differ from those applicable to Part A of this trigger list, which should not be interpreted as limited by such definition.

5. For the purposes of implementing paragraph 6 of the Guidelines, the following facilities should be deemed to be "of the same type (i.e. if their design, construction or operating processes are based on the same or similar physical or chemical processes)":

Where the technology transferred is such as to make possible the construction in the recipient State of a facility of the following type, or major critical components thereof:	The following will be deemed to be facilities of the same type:
(a) an isotope separation plant of the gaseous diffusion type	any other isotope separation plant using the gaseous diffusion process
(b) an isotope separation plant of the gas centrifuge type	any other isotope separation plant using the gas centrifuge process
(c) an isotope separation plant of the jet nozzle type	any other isotope separation plant using the jet nozzle process
(d) an isotope separation plant of the vortex type	any other isotope separation plant using the vortex process
(e) a fuel reprocessing plant using the solvent extraction process	any other fuel reprocessing plant using the solvent extraction process
(f) a heavy water plant using the exchange process	any other heavy water plant using the exchange process
(g) a heavy water plant using the electrolytic process	any other heavy water plant using the electrolytic process
(h) a heavy water plant using the hydrogen distillation process	any other heavy water plant using the hydrogen distillation process

Note: In the case of reprocessing, enrichment, and heavy water facilities whose design, construction, or operation processes are based on physical or chemical processes other than those enumerated above, a similar approach would be applied to define facilities "of the same type", and a need to define major critical components of such facilities might arise.

6. The reference in paragraph 6(b) of the Guidelines to "any facilities of the same type constructed during an agreed period in the recipient's country" is understood to refer to such facilities (or major critical components thereof), the first operation of which commences within a period of at least 20 years from the date of the first operation of (1) a facility which has been transferred or incorporates transferred major critical components or of (2) a facility of the same type built after the transfer of technology. It is understood that during that period there would be a conclusive presumption that any facility of the same type utilized transferred technology. But the agreed period is not intended to limit the duration of the safeguards imposed or the duration of the right to identify facilities as being constructed or operated on the basis of or by the use of transferred technology in accordance with paragraph 6(b) (2) of the Guidelines.

Annex.

Clarifications of items on the trigger list

A. Complete nuclear reactors

(Item 2.1.1. of the trigger list)

1. A "nuclear reactor" basically includes the items within or attached directly to the reactor vessel, the equipment which controls the level of power in the core, and the components which normally contain or come in direct contact with or control the primary coolant of the reactor core.

2. The export of the whole set of major items within this boundary will take place only in accordance with the procedures of

the Guidelines. Those individual items within this functionally defined boundary which will be exported only in accordance with the procedures of the Guidelines are listed in paragraphs 2.1.1. to 2.1.5.

The Government reserves to itself the right to apply the procedures of the Guidelines to other items within the functionally defined boundary.

3. It is not intended to exclude reactors which could reasonably be capable of modification to produce significantly more than 100 grams of plutonium per year. Reactors designed for sustained operation at significant power levels, regardless of their capacity for plutonium production, are not considered as "zero energy reactors".

B. Pressure vessels

(Item 2.1.2. of the trigger list)

4. A top plate for a reactor pressure vessel is covered by item 2.1.1. as a major shop-fabricated part of a pressure vessel.

5. Reactor internals (e.g. support columns and plates for the core and other vessel internals, control rod guide tubes, thermal shields, baffles, core grid plates, diffuser plates, etc.) are normally supplied by the reactor supplier. In some cases, certain internal support components are included in the fabrication of the pressure vessel. These items are sufficiently critical to the safety and reliability of the operation of the reactor (and, therefore, to the guarantees and liability of the reactor supplier), so that their supply, outside the basic supply arrangement for the reactor itself, would not be common practice. Therefore, although the separate supply of these unique, especially designed and prepared, critical, large and expensive items would not necessarily be considered as falling outside the area of concern, such a mode of supply is considered unlikely.

C. Reactor control rods

(Item 2.1.4 of the trigger list)

6. This item includes, in addition to the neutron absorbing part, the support or suspension structures therefor if supplied separately.

D. Fuel reprocessing plants

(Item 2.3.1 of the trigger list)

7. A "plant for the reprocessing of irradiated fuel elements" includes the equipment and components which normally come in direct contact with and directly control the irradiated fuel and the major nuclear material and fission product processing streams. The export of the whole set of major items within this boundary will take place only in accordance with the procedures of the Guidelines. In the present state of technology the following items of equipment are considered to fall within the meaning of the phrase "and equipment especially designed or prepared therefor":

   (a) Irradiated fuel element chopping machines: remotely operated equipment especially designed or prepared for use in a reprocessing plant as identified above and intended to cut, chop or shear irradiated nuclear fuel assemblies, bundles or rods; and

   (b) Critically safe tanks (e.g. small diameter, annular or slab tanks) especially designed or prepared for use in a reprocessing plant as identified above, intended for dissolution of irradiated nuclear fuel and which are capable of withstanding hot, highly corrosive liquid, and which can be remotely loaded and maintained;

8. The Government reserves to itself the right to apply the procedures of the Guidelines to other items within the functionally defined boundary.

E. Fuel fabrication plants

(Item 2.4.1 of the trigger list)

9. A "plant for the fabrication of fuel elements" includes the equipment:

   (a) Which normally comes in direct contact with, or directly processes, or controls, the production flow of nuclear material, or

   (b) Which seals the nuclear material within the cladding.

10. The export of the whole set of items for the foregoing operations will take place only in accordance with the procedures of the Guidelines. The Government will also give consideration to application of the procedures of the Guidelines to individual items intended for any of the foregoing operations, as well as for other fuel fabrication operations such as checking the integrity of the cladding or the seal, and the finish treatment to the sealed fuel.

F. Isotope separation plant equipment

(Item 2.5.1 of the trigger list)

11. "Equipment, other than analytical instruments, especially designed or prepared for the separation of isotopes or uranium" includes each of the major items of equipment especially designed or prepared for the separation process. Such items include:

- gaseous diffusion barriers,
- gaseous diffuser housings,
- gas centrifuge assemblies, corrosion-resistant to UF_6,
- jet nozzle separation units,
- vortex separation units,
- large UF_6, corrosion-resistant axial or centrifugal compressors,
- special compressor seals for such compressors.

Table: Categorization of Nuclear Material

Material	Form	Category I	Category II	Category III
1. Plutonium[a]	Unirradiated[b]	2kg or more	Less than 2kg but more than 500g	500g or less[c]
2. Uranium-235	Unirradiated[b]			
	— uranium enriched to 20% ^{235}U or more	5kg or more	Less than 5kg but more than 1kg	1kg or less[c]
	— uranium enriched to 10% ^{235}U but less than 20%		10kg or more	Less than 10kg[e]
	— uranium enriched above natural, but less than 10% ^{235}U[d]			10kg or more
3. Uranium-233	Unirradiated[b]	2kg or more	Less than 2kg but more than 500g	500g or less[c]
4. Irradiated fuel			Depleted or natural uranium, thorium or low-enriched fuel (less than 10% fissile content)[e,f]	

a As identified in the trigger list.
b Material not irradiated in a reactor or material irradiated in a reactor but with a radiation level equal to or less than 100 rads/hour at one metre unshielded.
c Less than a radiologically significant quantity should be exempted.
d Natural uranium, depleted uranium and thorium and quantities of uranium enriched to less than 10% not falling in Category III should be protected in accordance with prudent management practice.
e Although this level of protection is recommended, it would be open to States, upon evaluation of the specific circumstances, to assign a different category of physical protection.
f Other fuel which by virtue of its original fissile material content is classified as Category I or II before irradiation may be reduced one category level while the radiation level from the fuel exceeds 100 rads/hour at one metre unshielded.

ANNEX B. CRITERIA FOR LEVELS OF PHYSICAL PROTECTION

1. The purpose of physical protection of nuclear materials is to prevent unauthorized use and handling of these materials. Paragraph 3 (a) of the Guidelines document calls for agreement among suppliers on the levels of protection to be ensured in relation to the type of materials, and equipment and facilities containing these materials, taking account of international recommendations.
2. Paragraph 3 (b) of the Guidelines document states that implementation of measures of physical protection in the recipient country is the responsibility of the Government of that country. However, the levels of physical protection on which these measures have to be based should be the subject of an agreement between supplier and recipient. In this context these requirements should apply to all States.
3. The document INFCIRC/225 of the International Atomic Energy Agency entitled "The Physical Protection of Nuclear Material" and similar documents which from time to time are prepared by international groups of experts and updated as appropriate to account for changes in the state of the art and state of knowledge with regard to physical protection of nuclear material are a useful basis for guiding recipient States in designing a system of physical protection measures and procedures.
4. The categorization of nuclear material presented in the attached table or as it may be updated from time to time by mutual agreement of suppliers shall serve as the agreed basis for designating specific levels of physical protection in relation to the type of materials, and equipment and facilities containing these materials, pursuant to paragraph 3 (a) and 3 (b) of the Guidelines document.
5. The agreed levels of physical protection to be ensured by the competent national authorities in the use, storage and transportation of the materials listed in the attached table shall as a minimum include protection characteristics as follows:

Category III
Use and storage within an area to which access is controlled.

Transportation under special precautions including prior arrangements among sender, recipient and carrier, and prior agreement between entities subject to the jurisdiction and regulation of supplier and recipient States, respectively, in case of international transport specifying time, place and procedures for transferring transport responsibility.

Category II
Use and Storage within a protected area to which access is controlled, i.e. an area under constant surveillance by guards or electronic devices surrounded by a physical barrier with a limited number of points of entry under appropriate control, or any area with an equivalent level of physical protection.

Transportation under special precautions including prior arrangements among sender, recipient and carrier, and prior agreement between entities subject to the jurisdiction and regulation of supplier and recipient States, respectively, in case of international transport, specifying time, place and procedures for transferring transport responsibility.

Category I
Materials in this Category shall be protected with highly reliable systems against unauthorized use as follows:

Use and Storage within a highly protected area, i.e. a protected area as defined for Category II above, to which, in addition, access is restricted to persons whose trustworthiness has been determined, and which is under surveillance by guards who are in close communication with appropriate response forces. Specific measures taken in this context should have as their objective the detection and prevention of any assault, unauthorized access or unauthorized removal of material.

Transportation under specific precautions as identified above for transportation of Category II and III materials and, in addition, under constant surveillance by escorts and under conditions which assure close communication with appropriate response forces.

6. Suppliers should request identification by recipients of those agencies or authorities having responsibility for ensuring that levels of protection are adequately met and having responsibility for internally co-ordinating response/recovery operations in the event of unauthorized use or handling of protected materials. Suppliers and recipients should also designate points of contact within their national authorities to co-operate on matters of out-of-country transportation and other matter of mutual concern.

FACT SHEET

January 24, 1994

MULTILATERAL NUCLEAR EXPORT CONTROL REGIMES

Zangger (NPT Exporters) Committee

The Zangger Committee presently consists of 29 states (see attached list) and was formed in the early 1970s to establish guidelines for the export control provisions of the NPT (Article III(2)). The list of controlled items -- called the "trigger list" because their export triggers safeguards -- consists of nuclear material and "especially designed or prepared" (EDP) material, equipment, and facilities (i.e., not dual-use items) normally used in peaceful nuclear programs. These are items, such as plutonium and highly-enriched uranium (HEU), reactors, reprocessing and enrichment plants, and EDP equipment for such facilities, which if misused could contribute to a nuclear explosive program.

The trigger list has been updated substantially since it was first adopted in 1974 to provide more specification in key areas of the nuclear fuel-cycle, i.e. enrichment, reprocessing, and heavy water production. The major Zangger Committee requirements for exports of trigger list items are that they 1) not be used for nuclear explosives, 2) be subject to IAEA safeguards in the recipient non-nuclear weapon state, and 3) not be reexported unless they are subject to safeguards in the new recipient state.

The Committee meets twice a year in Vienna. The current Chairman is Fritz Schmidt, a senior official in the Austrian Federal Chancellory, and the Committee Secretary is an officer in the United Kingdom Mission in Vienna. Claude Zangger of Switzerland was the Committee's first Chairman and served almost 20 years until his retirement in 1989. The Committee has continued to be named after him in honor of his long service. New members are admitted by invitation and accept the "understandings" of the Committee through a confidential exchange of notes with all existing members. Most of the obligations accepted by Committee members have become a part of the public record through communications to the IAEA Director General and subsequent publication in the Agency's Information Circular (INFCIRC) 209 series.

US ARMS CONTROL AND DISARMAMENT AGENCY, WASHINGTON, D.C. 20451
OFFICE OF PUBLIC INFORMATION (1-800-581-ACDA)

Nuclear Suppliers Group (NSG)

Following the 1974 nuclear explosion by India, the United States proposed the formation of a Nuclear Suppliers Group (NSG) and initially approached 6 other major supplier states. The primary purpose was to expand beyond the controls of the Zangger Committee and to involve the key non-NPT supplier, France. The NSG grew to 15 countries by early 1978 when its guidelines and control list were published. Currently the membership totals 28, including France (see attached list).

The major features of the NSG Guidelines that go beyond those of Zangger are requirements for 1) an agreement between the IAEA and the recipient state requiring the application of safeguards on all fissionable materials in its current and peaceful activities ("full-scope IAEA safeguards"), 2) physical protection against unauthorized use of transferred materials and facilities, and 3) restraint in the transfer of sensitive facilities, technology, and weapons-usable materials, i.e., exports that could contribute to the acquisition of plutonium or HEU by a state of proliferation concern. The Guidelines also call for consultations among members on specific sensitive cases to ensure that transfers do not contribute to risks of conflict and instability.

The NSG did not meet throughout the 1980s, but suppliers consulted regularly on a bilateral basis. The NSG resumed meeting multilaterally in March 1991 in The Hague; annual plenaries were also held in 1992 and 1993 in Warsaw and Lucerne, Switzerland. These meetings led to a strengthening of the NSG regime through an upgrade of its fuel-cycle control list and through adoption of an arrangement for controlling nuclear-related dual-use items (i.e., those with both nuclear and non-nuclear applications). In 1993, the NSG incorporated the full-scope IAEA safeguards supply condition, a long-time goal of U.S. nonproliferation efforts, into its guidelines.

The new dual-use control arrangement contains its own Guidelines prohibiting the transfer of controlled items for use in a non-nuclear weapon state in a nuclear explosive activity or an unsafeguarded nuclear fuel-cycle activity, or when there is an unacceptable risk of diversion to such an activity. To reduce the risk of diversion, the Guidelines require recipients to provide assurances 1) specifying how transferred items will be used, 2) stating that they will not be used for proscribed activities, and 3) stating that the suppliers consent will be obtained before any retransfers of the items.

The British chaired the NSG in the 1970s, but this responsibility will likely continue to rotate depending on venue. The current chair is Switzerland, and Spain will chair in 1994 and Finland in 1995. There is no NSG Secretariat, although Japan is the point of contact for the dual-use arrangement. The first 15 NSG members were admitted by invitation, and they exchanged bilateral notes accepting the guidelines and control list and communicated these commitments to the IAEA Director General. Due to inactivity during the 1980s, there was no formal action taken on enlarging the group, but several additional states adhered to the NSG Guidelines by sending a letter to the DG and have since been accepted as members. The NSG has now adopted procedural arrangements for formally accepting new members.

The NSG Guidelines are published by the IAEA in its Information Circular series. INFCIRC/254/Rev. 1/Part 1 contains the original Guidelines as amended, and 254/Rev. 1/Part 2 contains the dual-use arrangement.

MEMBERSHIP OF ZANGGER COMMITTEE AND NUCLEAR SUPPLIERS GROUP

	Zangger Committee	NSG
Australia	x	x
Austria	x	x
Belgium	x	x
Bulgaria	x	x
Canada	x	x
Czech Republic	x	x
Denmark	x	x
France	x	x
Finland	x	x
FRG	x	x
Greece	x	x
Hungary	x	x
Ireland	x	x
Italy	x	x
Japan	x	x
Luxembourg	x	x
Netherlands	x	x
Norway	x	x
Poland	x	x
Portugal	x	x
Romania	x	x
Russia	x	x
Slovak Republic	x	x
South Africa	x	
Spain	x	x
Sweden	x	x
Switzerland	x	x
UK	x	x
US	x	x

*Argentina has adhered to the NSG Guidelines and was an observer at the 1993 NSG plenary meeting.

FACT SHEET

May 17, 1993

THE MISSILE TECHNOLOGY CONTROL REGIME

In April 1987, the United States and its six major trading partners (Canada, the former West Germany, France, Italy, Japan, and the United Kingdom) created the Missile Technology Regime (MTCR) to restrict the proliferation of missiles and related technology.

The MTCR, the only multilateral missile nonproliferation regime, is neither an international agreement nor a treaty. It is a voluntary arrangement among countries which share a common interest in arresting missile proliferation. The regime consists of common export policy guidelines applied to a common list of controlled items which each MTCR member implements in accordance with its national legislation. The purpose of the regime is to limit the spread of missiles and unmanned air vehicles/delivery systems capable of carrying a 500 kilogram payload at least 300 kilometers. In January 1993, MTCR Partners announced that the Guidelines had been extended to cover delivery systems intended to carry all types of weapons of mass destruction (chemical and biological as well as nuclear).

The MTCR Annex of controlled items is divided into two sections (Category I and Category II) and includes equipment and technology, both military and dual-use, that are relevant to missile development, production, and operation.

Category I - According to the MTCR Guidelines, exports of Category I items are subject to a strong presumption of denial and are rarely licensed for export. Category I items include complete missile systems (ballistic missiles, space launch vehicles and sounding rockets); unmanned air-vehicle systems such as cruise missiles, target and reconnaissance drones; specially designed production facilities for these systems; and certain complete subsystems such as rocket engines or stages, reentry vehicles, guidance sets, thrust vector controls and warhead safing, arming, fuzing, and firing mechanisms. Transfers of production facilities for Category I items are flatly prohibited.

US ARMS CONTROL AND DISARMAMENT AGENCY, WASHINGTON, D.C. 20451
OFFICE OF PUBLIC AFFAIRS   (202) 647-8677

Category II - The MTCR Guidelines permit licensing of Category II (dual-use) items as long as they are not destined for end-use in the development of a missile of MTCR range/payload capability. Category II items cover a wide range of parts, components and subsystems such as propellants, structure materials, test equipment and facilities, and flight instruments. These items may be exported at the discretion of the MTCR Partner Government, on a case by case basis, for acceptable end uses. They may also be exported under government-to-government assurances which provide that they not be used on a missile system capable of delivering a 500 kilogram payload to a range of least 300 kilometers.

The present MTCR Partners are:

Australia	Greece	Norway
Austria	Ireland	Portugal
Belgium	Iceland	Spain
Canada	Italy	Sweden
Denmark	Japan	Switzerland
Finland	Luxembourg	United Kingdom
France	Netherlands	United States
Germany	New Zealand	

As of March 1993, Argentina and Hungary had been admitted to the MTCR, contingent on completing certain technical procedures. The Guidelines remain open to all nations to implement, whether or not they become formal members of the MTCR, and all governments are encouraged to do so.

The MTCR Partners recognize that the technology used in ballistic missiles is virtually identical to that used in space launch vehicles and that there are several countries whose missile or space launch vehicle projects would enable them to export missile technology. MTCR Guidelines have been designed not to impede national space programs or international cooperation in such programs as long as such programs could not contribute to delivery systems for weapons of mass destruction. Bilateral discussions concerning the MTCR have been held with many of these countries and they may seek to join the MTCR once they have established a commitment to the principles of nonproliferation and a record of effective export controls.

REVISIONS TO MTCR GUIDELINES

<u>Missile Technology Control Regime</u>

The United States Government has, after careful consideration and subject to its international treaty obligations, decided that, when considering the transfer of equipment and technology related to missiles, it will act in accordance with the attached Guidelines beginning on January 7, 1993. These Guidelines replace those adopted on April 16, 1987.

<u>Guidelines for Sensitive Missile-Relevant Transfers</u>

1. The purpose of these Guidelines is to limit the risks of proliferation of weapons of mass destruction (i.e. nuclear, chemical and biological weapons), by controlling transfers that could make a contribution to delivery systems (other than manned aircraft) for such weapons. The Guidelines are not designed to impede national space programs or international cooperation in such programs as long as such programs could not contribute to delivery systems for weapons of mass destruction. These Guidelines, including the attached Annex, form the basis for controlling transfers to any destination beyond the Government's jurisdiction or control of all delivery systems (other than manned aircraft) capable of delivering weapons of mass destruction, and of equipment and technology relevant to missiles whose performance in terms of payload and range exceeds stated parameters. Restraint will be exercised in the consideration of all transfers of items contained within the Annex and all such transfers will be considered on a case-by-case basis. The Government will implement the Guidelines in accordance with national legislation.

2. The Annex consists of two categories of items, which term includes equipment and technology. Category I items, all of which are in Annex Items 1 and 2, are those items of greatest sensitivity. If a Category I item is included in a system, that system will also be considered as Category I, except when the incorporated item cannot be separated, removed or duplicated. Particular restraint will be exercised in the consideration of Category I transfers regardless of their purpose, and there will be a strong presumption to deny such transfers. Particular restraint will also be exercised in the consideration of transfers of any items in the Annex, or of any missiles (whether or not in the Annex), if the Government judges, on the basis of all available, persuasive information, evaluated according to factors including those in paragraph 3, that they are intended to be used for the delivery of weapons of mass destruction, and there will be a strong presumption to deny such transfers. Until further notice, the transfer of Category I production facilities will not be authorized. The transfer of other Category I items will be authorized only or rare occasions and where the Government (A) obtains binding government-to-government undertakings embodying the assurances from the recipient government called for in paragraph 5 of these Guidelines and (B) assumes

responsibility for taking all steps necessary to ensure that the item is put only to its stated end-use. It is understood that the decision to transfer remains the sole and sovereign judgment of the United States Government.

3. In the evaluation of transfer applications for Annex items, the following factors will be taken into account:

    A. Concerns about the proliferation of weapons of mass destruction;

    B. The capabilities and objectives of the missile and space programs of the recipient state;

    C. The significance of the transfer in terms of the potential development of delivery systems (other than manned aircraft) for weapons of mass destruction;

    D. The assessment of the end-use of the transfers, including the relevant assurances of the recipient states referred to in sub-paragraphs 5.A and 5.B below;

    E. The applicability of relevant multilateral agreements.

4. The transfer of design and production technology directly associated with any items in the Annex will be subject to as great a degree of scrutiny and control as will the equipment itself, to the extent permitted by national legislation.

5. Where the transfer could contribute to a delivery system for weapons of mass destruction, the Government will authorize transfers of items in the Annex only on receipt of appropriate assurances from the government of the recipient state that:

    A. The items will be used only for the purpose stated and that such use will not be modified nor the items modified or replicated without the prior consent of the United States Government;

    B. Neither the items nor replicas nor derivatives thereof will be retransferred without the consent of the United States Government.

6. In furtherance of the effective operation of the Guidelines, the United States Government will, as necessary and appropriate, exchange relevant information with other governments applying the same Guidelines.

7. The adherence of all States to these Guidelines in the interest of international peace and security would be welcome.

MEETING OF ADHERENTS TO THE NUCLEAR SUPPLIERS GUIDELINES
WARSAW, MARCH 31 - APRIL 3, 1992

Statement on full scope safeguards

(1) At their meeting in Warsaw on April 3, 1992, the Adherents
to the Nuclear Suppliers Guidelines,

- desiring to contribute to an effective non-
-proliferation regime, and to the widest possible
implementation of the objectives of the Treaty
on the Non-Proliferation of Nuclear Weapons,
- seeking to promote international co-operation in
the research, development and safe use of nuclear
energy for peaceful purposes,

have adopted the following policy on full scope safeguards
as a condition of future nuclear supplies:

(a) The transfer of nuclear facilities, equipment,
components, material and technology as referred
to in the export trigger list of the Guidelines for
Nuclear Transfers (see INFCIRC/254), should not be
authorised to a non-nuclear-weapon State unless that
State has brought into force an agreement with the IAEA
requiring the application of safeguards on all source
and special fissionable material in its current and
future peaceful nuclear activities.

(b) Transfers covered by paragraph (a) to a non-nuclear-weapon State without such a safeguards agreement should only be authorised in exceptional cases when they are deemed essential for the safe operation of existing facilities and if safeguards are applied to those facilities. Suppliers should inform and, if appropriate, consult in the event that they intend to authorise or to deny such transfers.

(c) This policy does not apply to existing agreements and contracts; however, adherents to the Guidelines underline the importance of making all supplies in conformity with it.

(d) Additional conditions of supply may be applied as a matter of national policy.

(2) The Adherents to the Nuclear Suppliers Guidelines appeal to all states which export nuclear facilities, equipment, components, material or technology to adopt the same policy.

(3) The Adherents to the Nuclear Suppliers Guidelines invited the Chairman of the meeting to communicate this statement to the Director-General of the IAEA for information of member states.

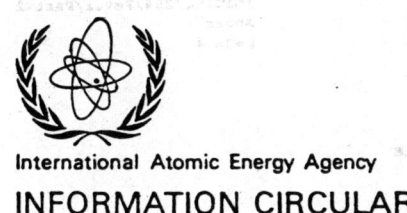

International Atomic Energy Agency

INFORMATION CIRCULAR

INF

INFCIRC/254/Rev.1/Part 2
July 1992

GENERAL Distr.
Original: ENGLISH, FRENCH
RUSSIAN and SPANISH

**COMMUNICATIONS RECEIVED FROM CERTAIN MEMBER STATES
REGARDING GUIDELINES FOR THE EXPORT OF NUCLEAR
MATERIAL, EQUIPMENT AND TECHNOLOGY**

<u>Nuclear-related Dual-use Transfers</u>

1. The Director General has received notes verbales dated 15 May 1992 from the Resident Representatives to the Agency of Australia, Austria, Belgium, Bulgaria, Canada, Czech and Slovak Federal Republic, Denmark, Finland, France, Germany, Greece, Hungary, Ireland, Italy, Japan, Luxembourg, Netherlands, Norway, Poland, Portugal, Romania, Russian Federation, Spain, Sweden, Switzerland, the United Kingdom of Great Britain and Northern Ireland, and the United States of America relating to the export of nuclear material, equipment and technology.

2. The purpose of the notes verbales is to provide information on those Governments' Guidelines for Transfers of Nuclear-related Dual-use Equipment, Material and related Technology.

3. In the light of the wish expressed at the end of each note verbale, the text of the notes verbales is annexed hereto.

INFCIRC/254/Rev.1/Part 2
Annex
page 1

NOTE VERBALE

The Permanent Mission of [Member State] presents its compliments to the Director General of the International Atomic Energy Agency and has the honour to provide information on its Government's nuclear export policies and practices.

The Government of [Member State] has decided that, when considering the transfer of nuclear-related dual-use equipment, material and related technology, it will act in accordance with the provisions of the attached documents.

In reaching this decision, the Government of [Member State] is fully aware of the need to contribute to economic development while avoiding contributing in any way to the dangers of a proliferation of nuclear weapons or other nuclear explosive devices, and of the need to remove non-proliferation assurances from the field of commercial competition.

The Government of [Member State], so far as trade within the European Community is concerned, will implement these documents in the light of its commitments as a Member State of that Community.[*/]

[*/] Paragraph in the notes verbales from the members of the European Community.

GUIDELINES FOR TRANSFERS OF NUCLEAR-RELATED DUAL-USE EQUIPMENT, MATERIAL AND RELATED TECHNOLOGY

OBJECTIVE

1. With the objective of averting the proliferation of nuclear weapons, suppliers have had under consideration procedures in relation to the transfer of certain equipment, material, and related technology that could make a major contribution to a "nuclear explosive activity" or an "unsafeguarded nuclear fuel-cycle activity." In this connection, suppliers have agreed on the following principles, common definitions, and an export control list of equipment, material, and related technology. The Guidelines are not designed to impede international cooperation as long as such cooperation will not contribute to a nuclear explosive activity or an unsafeguarded nuclear fuel-cycle activity. Suppliers intend to implement the Guidelines in accordance with national legislation and relevant international commitments.

BASIC PRINCIPLE

2. Suppliers should not authorize transfers of equipment, material, or related technology identified in the Annex:

   -- for use in a non-nuclear-weapon state in a nuclear explosive activity or an unsafeguarded nuclear fuel cycle activity, or

   -- in general, when there is an unacceptable risk of diversion to such an activity, or when the transfers are contrary to the objective of averting the proliferation of nuclear weapons.

EXPLANATION OF TERMS

3. (a) "Nuclear explosive activity" includes research on or development, design, manufacture, construction, testing or maintenance of any nuclear explosive device or components or subsystems of such a device.

   (b) "Unsafeguarded nuclear fuel-cycle activity" includes research on or development, design, manufacture, construction, operation or maintenance of any reactor, critical facility, conversion plant, fabrication plant, reprocessing plant, plant for the separation of isotopes of source or special fissionable material, or separate storage installation, where there is no obligation to accept International Atomic Energy Agency (IAEA) safeguards at the relevant facility or installation, existing or future, when it contains any source or special fissionable material; or of any heavy water production plant where there is no obligation to accept IAEA safeguards on any nuclear material produced by or used in connection with any heavy water produced therefrom; or where any such obligation is not met.

ESTABLISHMENT OF EXPORT LICENSING PROCEDURES

4. Suppliers should establish export licensing procedures for the transfer of equipment, material, and related technology identified in the Annex. These procedures should include enforcement measures for violations. In considering whether to authorize such transfers, suppliers should exercise prudence in order to carry out the Basic Principle and should take relevant factors into account, including:

   (a) Whether the recipient state is a party to the Nuclear Non-Proliferation Treaty (NPT) or to the Treaty for the Prohibition of Nuclear Weapons in Latin America (Treaty of Tlatelolco), or to a similar international legally-binding nuclear non-proliferation agreement, and has an IAEA safeguards agreement in force applicable to all its peaceful nuclear activities;

   (b) Whether any recipient state that is not party to the NPT, Treaty of Tlatelolco, or a similar international legally-binding nuclear non-proliferation agreement has any facilities or installations listed in paragraph 3(b) above that are operational or being designed or constructed that are not, or will not be, subject to IAEA safeguards;

   (c) Whether the equipment, material, or related technology to be transferred is appropriate for the stated end-use and whether that stated end-use is appropriate for the end-user;

   (d) Whether the equipment, material, or related technology to be transferred is to be used in research on or development, design, manufacture, construction, operation, or maintenance of any reprocessing or enrichment facility;

   (e) Whether governmental actions, statements, and policies of the recipient state are supportive of nuclear non-proliferation and whether the recipient state is in compliance with its international obligations in the field of nonproliferation;

   (f) Whether the recipients have been engaged in clandestine or illegal procurement activities; and

   (g) Whether a transfer has not been authorized to the end-user or whether the end-user has diverted for purposes inconsistent with the Guidelines any transfer previously authorized.

CONDITIONS FOR TRANSFERS

5. In the process of determining that the transfer will not pose any unacceptable risk of diversion, in accordance with the Basic Principle and to meet the objectives of the Guidelines, the supplier should obtain, before authorizing the transfer and in a manner consistent with its national law and practices, the following:

    (a) a statement from the end-user specifying the uses and end-use locations of the proposed transfers; and

    (b) an assurance explicitly stating that the proposed transfer or any replica thereof will not be used in any nuclear explosive activity or unsafeguarded nuclear fuel-cycle activity.

CONSENT RIGHTS OVER RETRANSFERS

6. Before authorizing the transfer of equipment, material, or related technology identified in the Annex to a country not adhering to the Guidelines, suppliers should obtain assurances that their consent will be secured, in a manner consistent with their national law and practices, prior to any retransfer to a third country of the equipment, material, or related technology, or any replica thereof.

CONCLUDING PROVISIONS

7. The supplier reserves to itself discretion as to the application of the Guidelines to other items of significance in addition to those identified in the Annex, and as to the application of other conditions for transfer that it may consider necessary in addition to those provided for in paragraph 5 of the Guidelines.

8. In furtherance of the effective implementation of the Guidelines, suppliers should, as necessary and appropriate, exchange relevant information and consult with other states adhering to the Guidelines.

9. In the interest of international peace and security, the adherence of all states to the Guidelines would be welcome.

PROGRAMME FOR PROMOTING NUCLEAR NON-PROLIFERATION

Number 18   **NEWSBRIEF**   **Summer 1992**

List of contents of Annex

Industrial Equipment
Spin-forming and flow-forming machines
'Numerical control units' - machine tools
Dimensional inspection systems
Vacuum induction furnaces
Isostatic presses
Robots and end effectors
Vibration test equipment
Furnaces -- arc remelt, electron beam, and plasma

Materials
Aluminum, high strength
Beryllium
Bismuth, high purity
Boron, isotopically enriched in boron-10
Calcium, high purity
Chlorine trifluoride
Crucibles made of materials resistant to liquid actinide metals
Fibrous and filamentary materials
Hafnium
Lithium, isotopically enriched in lithium-6
Magnesium, high purity
Maraging steel, high strength
Radium
Titanium alloys
Tungsten
Zirconium

Uranium Isotope Separation Equipment and Components
Electrolytic cells for fluorine production
Rotor and bellows equipment
Centrifugal multiplane balancing machines
Filament winding machines
Frequency changers
Lasers, laser amplifiers and oscillators
Mass spectrometers and mass spectrometer ion sources
Pressure measuring instruments, corrosion-resistant
Valves, corrosion resistant
Superconducting solenoidal electromagnets
Vacuum pumps
Direct current high-power supplies, 100 V or greater
High voltage direct current power supplies. 20,000 V or greater
Electromagnetic isotope separators

Heavy Water Production Plant Related Equipment (other than trigger list items)
Specialized packing for water separation
Pumps for potassium amide/liquid ammonia
Water-hydrogen sulfide exchange tray columns
Hydrogen-cryogenic distillation columns
Ammonia converters or synthesis reactors

Implosion Systems Development Equipment
Flash X-ray equipment
Multistage light gas guns/high velocity guns
Mechanical rotating mirror cameras
Electronic streak and framing cameras and tubes
Specialized instrumentation for hydrodynamic experiments

Explosives and Related Equipment
Detonators and multipoint initiation systems
Electronic components for firing sets
Switching devices
Capacitors
Firing sets and equivalent high-current pulsers, for controlled detonators
High explosives relevant to nuclear weapons

Nuclear Testing Equipment and Components
Oscilloscopes
Photomultiplier tubes
Pulse generators, high speed

Other
Neutron generator systems
General nuclear related equipment
Remote manipulators
Radiation shielding windows
Radiation-hardened TV cameras
Tritium, tritium compounds and mixtures
Tritium facilities or plants and components therefor
Platinized carbon catalysts
Helium-3
Alpha-emitting radionuclides

[Note: This is a summary of a more detailed list entitled "List of Nuclear-Related Dual-Use Equipment and Materials and Related Technology," which appears as an annex to the International Atomic Energy Agency's INFCIRC/254/Rev. 1/Part 2, July 1992.]

APPENDICES

1. UNSC resolution 687 of 3 April 1991 (excerpts)

The Security Council,

Recalling its resolutions 660 (1990), 661 (1990), 662 (1990), 664 (1990), 665 (1990), 666 (1990), 667 (1990), 669 (1990), 670 (1990), 674 (1990), 677 (1990), 678 (1990) and 686 (1991),

(...)

Conscious also of the statements by Iraq threatening to use weapons in violation of its obligations under the Geneva Protocol for the Prohibition of the Use in War of Asphyxiating, Poisonous or Other Gases, and of Bacteriological Methods of Warfare, signed at Geneva on 17 June 1925, and of its prior use of chemical weapons and affirming that grave consequences would follow any further use by Iraq of such weapons,

Recalling that Iraq has subscribed to the Declaration adopted by all States participating in the Conference of States Parties to the 1925 Geneva Protocol and Other Interested States, held at Paris from 7 to 11 January 1989, establishing the objective of universal elimination of chemical and biological weapons,

Recalling further that Iraq has signed the Convention on the Prohibition of the Development, Production and Stockpiling of Bacteriological (Biological) and Toxin Weapons and on Their Destruction, of 10 April 1972,

Noting the importance of Iraq ratifying this Convention,

Noting moreover the importance of all States adhering to this Convention and encouraging its forthcoming Review Conference to reinforce the authority, efficiency and universal scope of the Convention,

Stressing the importance of an early conclusion by the Conference on Disarmament of its work on a Convention on the Universal Prohibition of Chemical Weapons and of universal adherence thereto,

Aware of the use by Iraq of ballistic missiles in unprovoked attacks and therefore of the need to take specific measures in regard to such missiles located in Iraq,

Concerned by the reports in the hands of Member States that Iraq has attempted to acquire materials for a nuclear-weapons programme contrary to its obligations under the Treaty on the Non-Proliferation of Nuclear Weapons of 1 July 1968,

Recalling the objective of the establishment of a nuclear-weapon-free zone in the region of the Middle East,

Conscious of the threat which all weapons of mass destruction pose to peace and security in the area and of the need to work towards the establishment in the Middle East of a zone free of such weapons,

Conscious also of the objective of achieving balanced and comprehensive control of armaments in the region,

Conscious further of the importance of achieving the objectives noted above using all available means, including a dialogue among the States of the region,

(...)

(...)

C

7. *Invites* Iraq to reaffirm unconditionally its obligations under the Geneva Protocol for the Prohibition of the Use in War of Asphyxiating, Poisonous or Other Gases, and of Bacteriological Methods of Warfare, signed at Geneva on 17 June 1925, and to ratify the Convention on the Prohibition of the Development, Production and Stockpiling of Bacteriological (Biological) and Toxin Weapons and on Their Destruction, of 10 April 1972;

8. *Decides* that Iraq shall unconditionally accept the destruction, removal, or rendering harmless, under international supervision, of:
a) all chemical and biological weapons and all stocks of agents and all related subsystems and components and all research, development, support and manufacturing facilities;
b) all ballistic missiles with a range greater than 150 kilometres and related major parts, and repair and production facilities;

9. *Decides*, for the implementation of paragraph 8 above, the following:
a) Iraq shall submit to the Secretary-General, within fifteen days of the adoption of this resolution, a declaration of the locations, amounts and types of all items specified in paragraph 8 and agree to urgent, on-site inspection as specified below;
b) the Secretary-General, in consultation with the appropriate Governments and, where appropriate, with the Director-General of the World Health Organization (WHO), within 45 days of the passage of this resolution, shall develop, and submit to the Council for approval, a plan calling for the completion of the following acts within 45 days of such approval:
i) the forming of a Special Commission, which shall carry out immediate on-site inspection of Iraq's biological, chemical and missile capabilities, based on Iraq's declarations and the designation of any additional locations by the Special Commission itself;
ii) the yielding by Iraq of possession to the Special Commission for destruction, removal or rendering harmless, taking into account the requirements of public safety, of all items specified under paragraph 8 (a) above including items at the additional locations designated by the Special Commission under paragraph 9 (b) (i) above and the destruction by Iraq, under supervision of the Special Commission, of all its missile capabilities including launchers as specified under paragraph 8 (b) above;
iii) the provision by the Special Commission of the assistance and cooperation to the Director-General of the International Atomic Energy Agency (IAEA) required in paragraphs 12 and 13 below;

10. *Decides* that Iraq shall unconditionally undertake not to use, develop, construct or acquire any of the items specified in paragraphs 8 and 9 above and requests the Secretary-General, in consultation with the Special Commission, to develop a plan for the future ongoing monitoring and verification of Iraq's compliance with this paragraph, to be submitted to the Council for approval within 120 days of the passage of this resolution;

11. *Invites* Iraq to reaffirm unconditionally its obligations under the Treaty on the Non-Proliferation of Nuclear Weapons, of 1 July 1968;

12. *Decides* that Iraq shall unconditionally agree not to acquire or develop nuclear weapons or nuclear-weapons-usable material or any subsystems or components or any research, development, support or manufacturing facilities related to the above; to submit to the Secretary-General and the Director-General of the International Atomic Energy Agency (IAEA) within 15 days of the adoption of this resolution a declaration of the locations, amounts, and types of all items specified above; to place all of its nuclear-weapons-usable materials under the exclusive control, for custody and removal, of the IAEA, with the assistance and cooperation of the Special Commission as provided for in the plan of the Secretary-General discussed in paragraph 9 (b) above; to accept, in accordance with the arrangements provided for in paragraph 13 below, urgent on-site inspection and the destruction, removal, or rendering harmless as appropriate of all items specified above; and to accept the plan discussed in paragraph 13 below for the future ongoing monitoring and verification of its compliance with these undertakings;

13. *Requests* the Director-General of the International Atomic Energy Agency (IAEA) through the Secretary-General, with the assistance and cooperation of the Special Commission as provided for in the plan of the Secretary-General in paragraph 9 (b) above, to carry out immediate on-site inspection of Iraq's nuclear capabilities based on Iraq's declarations and the designation of any additional locations by the Special Commission; to develop a plan for submission to the Security Council within 45 days calling for the destruction, removal, or rendering harmless as appropriate of all items listed in paragraph 12 above; to carry out the plan within 45 days following approval by the Security Council; and to develop a plan, taking into account the rights and obligations of Iraq under the Treaty on the Non-Proliferation of Nuclear Weapons, of 1 July 1968, for the future ongoing monitoring and verification of Iraq's compliance with paragraph 12 above, including an inventory of all nuclear material in Iraq subject to the Agency's verification and inspections to confirm that IAEA safeguards cover all relevant nuclear activities in Iraq, to be submitted to the Council for approval within 120 days of the passage of this resolution;

14. *Takes note* that the actions to be taken by Iraq in paragraphs 8, 9, 10, 11, 12 and 13 of this resolution represent steps towards the goal of establishing in the Middle East a zone free from weapons of mass destruction and all missiles for their delivery and the objective of a global ban on chemical weapons;

(...)

UN Security Council Declaration on Disarmament, Arms Control and Weapons of Mass Destruction, 31 January 1992

(Text reproduced from S/PV.3046)

The members of the Council, while fully conscious of the responsibilities of other organs of the United Nations in the fields of disarmament, arms control and non-proliferation, reaffirm the crucial contribution which progress in these areas can make to the maintenance of international peace and security. They express their commitment to take concrete steps to enhance the effectiveness of the United Nations in these areas.

The members of the Council underline the need for all Member States to fulfil their obligations in relation to arms control and disarmament; to prevent the proliferation in all its aspects of all weapons of mass destruction; to avoid excessive and destabilizing accumulations and transfers of arms; and to resolve peacefully in accordance with the Charter any problems concerning these matters threatening or disrupting the maintenance of regional and global stability. They emphasize the importance of the early ratification and implementation by the States concerned of all international and regional arms control arrangements, especially the START and CFE Treaties.

The proliferation of all weapons of mass destruction constitutes a threat to international peace and security. The members of the Council commit themselves to working to prevent the spread of technology related to the research for or production of such weapons and to take appropriate action to that end.

On nuclear proliferation, they note the importance of the decision of many countries to adhere to the Non-Proliferation Treaty and emphasize the integral role in the implementation of that Treaty of fully effective IAEA safeguards, as well as the importance of effective export controls. The members of the Council will take appropriate measures in the case of any violations notified to them by the IAEA.

On chemical weapons, they support the efforts of the Geneva Conference with a view to reaching agreement on the conclusion, by the end of 1992, of a universal convention, including a verification regime, to prohibit chemical weapons.

[Source: *PPNN Newsbrief, Spring 1992*, p. 15.]

Commonwealth of Independent States

Declaration on Nuclear Arms*

22 December 1991

Byelorussia, Kazakhstan, the Russian Federation and Ukraine, called henceforth Member States,

CONFIRMING their adherence to the non-proliferation of nuclear armaments;

STRIVING for the elimination of all nuclear armaments, and

WISHING to strengthen international stability, have agreed on the following:

Article 1

The nuclear armaments that are part of the unified strategic armed forces insure the collective security of all members of the Commonwealth of Independent States (CIS).

Article 2

The Member States of this Agreement confirm the obligation not to be the first to use nuclear weapons.

Article 3

The Member States of this Agreement are jointly drawing up a policy on nuclear matters.

---

*   Translation by the Tass Press Agency, published in the Newsbrief of the Programme for Promoting Nuclear Non-Proliferation (PPNN), Winter 1991/92. Reproduced in the Bulletin by kind permission of Mr. John Simpson (PPNN), Mountbatten Centre for International Studies, University of Southhampton, United Kingdom.

Source: *Nuclear Law Bulletin 49*, June 1992, 102-103.

Article 4

Until nuclear weapons have been completely eliminated on the territory of the Republic of Byelorussia and Ukraine, decisions on the need to use them are taken, by agreement with the heads of the Member States of the Agreement, by the R.S.F.S.R. [Russian Soviet Federated Socialist Republic] President, on the basis of procedures drawn up jointly by the Member States.

Article 5

1. The Republics of Byelorussia and Ukraine undertake to join the 1968 Nuclear Non-Proliferation Treaty as non-nuclear states and to conclude with the International Atomic Energy Agency the appropriate safeguard agreements.

2. The Member States of this Agreement undertake not to transfer to anyone nuclear weapons or other triggering devices and technologies, or control over such nuclear triggering devices, either directly or indirectly, as well as not in any way to help, encourage and prompt any state not possessing nuclear weapons to produce nuclear weapons or other nuclear triggering devices, and also control over such weapons or triggering devices.

3. The provisions of paragraph 2 of this Article do not stand in the way of transferring nuclear weapons from Byelorussia, Kazakhstan and Ukraine to R.S.F.S.R. territory with a view to destroying them.

Article 6

The Members States of this Agreement, in accordance with the international treaty, will assist in the eliminating of nuclear weapons. By July 1, 1992 Byelorussia, Kazakhstan and Ukraine will insure the withdrawal of tactical nuclear weapons to central factory premises for dismantling under joint supervision.

Article 7

The Governments of Byelorussia, Kazakhstan, the Russian Federation and Ukraine undertake to submit a treaty on strategic offensive arms to the Supreme Soviets of their states.

Article 8

This agreement requires ratification. It will come into force on the 30th day after the handing over of all ratification papers to the government of the R.S.F.S.R. for safekeeping.

Mutual Defense Treaty between the Republic of Korea and the United States of America

Signed at Washington October 1, 1953
Entered into force November 18, 1954

The Parties to this Treaty,

Reaffirming their desire to live in peace with all governments, and desiring to strengthen the fabric of peace in the Pacific area,

Desiring to declare publicly and formally their common determination to defend themselves against external armed attack so that no potential aggressor could be under the illusion that either of them stand alone in the Pacific area,

Desiring further to strengthen their efforts for collective defense for the preservation of peace and security pending the development of a more comprehensive and effective system of regional security in the Pacific area,

Have agreed as follows:

ARTICLE 1

The Parties undertake to settle any international disputes in which they may be involved by peaceful means in such a manner that international peace and security and justice are not endangered and to refrain in their international relations from the threat or use of force in any manner inconsistent with the purpose of the United Nations, or obligations assumed by any Party toward the United Nations.

ARTICLE 2

The Parties will consult together whenever, in the opinion of either of them, the political independence or security of either of the Parties is threatened by external armed attack. Seperately and jointly, by self-help and mutual aid, the Parties will maintain and develop appropriate means to deter armed attack and will take suitable measures in consultation and agreement to implement this Treaty to further its purpose.

ARTICLE 3

Each party recognizes that an armed attack in the Pacific area on either of the Parties in territories now under their respective administrative control of the other, would be dangerous to its own peace and safety and declares that it would act to meet the common danger in accordance with its constitutional processes.

ARTICLE 4

The Republic of Korea grants, and the Unites States of America accepts, the right to dispose United States land, air and sea forces in and about the territory of the Republic of Korea as determined by mutual agreement.

ARTICLE 5

This Treaty shall be ratified by the United States of America and the Republic of Korea in accordance with their respective constitutional processes and will come into force when instrument of ratification thereof have been exchanged by them at Washington.

ARTICLE 6

This Treaty shall remain in force indefinitely. Either Party may terminate it one year after notice has been given to the other party.

IN WITNESS WHEREOF the undersigned plenipotentiaries have signed this Treaty.

DONE in duplicate at Washington, in the Korean and English languages, this first day of October 1953.

FOR THE REPUBLIC OF KOREA:
/s/Y. T. Pyun

FOR THE UNITED STATES OF AMERICA:
/s/John Foster Dulles

Joint Declaration of the Denuclearization of the Korean Peninsula

To enter into force as of February 19, 1992

The South and the North, desiring to eliminate the danger of nuclear war through denuclearization of the Korean peninsula, and thus to create an environment and conditions favorable for peace and peaceful unification of our country and contribute to peace and security in Asia and the world, declare as follows:

1. The South and the North shall not test, manufacture, produce, receive, possess, store, deploy or use nuclear weapons.

2. The South and the North shall use nuclear energy solely for peaceful purposes.

3. The South and the North shall not possess nuclear reprocessing and uranium enrichment facilities.

4. The South and the North, in order to verify the denuclearization of the Korean peninsula, shall conduct inspections of the objects selected by the other side and agreed upon between the two sides, in accordance with procedures and methods to be determined by a South-North joint nuclear control commission.

5. The South and the North, in order to implement this joint declaration, shall establish and operate a South-North joint nuclear control commission within one (1) month of the effectuation of this joint declaration.

6. This Joint Declaration shall enter into force as of the day the South and the North exchange notifications of completion of the procedures for the entry into force of this declaration.

January 20, 1992

Chung Won-shik
Prime Minister of the
Republic of Korea

Yon Hyong-muk
Premier of the
Administration Council of
the Democratic People's
Republic of Korea

Chief delegate
of the South
delegation to the
South-North
High-level Talks

Head
of the North
delegation to the
South-North
High-level Talks

AGREED FRAMEWORK BETWEEN THE UNITED STATES OF AMERICA AND THE DEMOCRATIC PEOPLE'S REPUBLIC OF KOREA

Geneva, October 23, 1994

Delegations of the Governments of the United States of America (U.S.) and the Democratic People's Republic of Korea (DPRK) held talks in Geneva from September 23 to October 23, 1994 to negotiate an overall resolution of the nuclear issue on the Korean Peninsula.

Both sides reaffirmed the importance of attaining the objectives contained in the August 12, 1994 Agreed Statement between the U.S. and the DPRK and upholding the principles of the June 11, 1993 Joint Statement of the U.S. and the DPRK to achieve peace and security on a nuclear-free Korean peninsula. The U.S. and the DPRK decided to take the following actions for the resolution of the nuclear issue:

I. Both sides will cooperate to replace the DPRK's graphite-moderated reactors and related facilities with light-water reactor (LWR) power plants.

    1) In accordance with the October 20, 1994 letter of assurances from the U.S. President, the U.S. will undertake to make arrangements for the provision to the DPRK of a LWR project with a total generating capacity of approximately 2,000 MW(e) by a target date of 2003.

- The U.S. will organize under its leadership an international consortium to finance and supply the LWR project to be provided to the DPRK. The U.S., representing the international consortium, will serve as the principle point of contact with the DPRK for the LWR project.

- The U.S., representing the consortium, will make best efforts to secure the conclusion of a supply contract with the DPRK within six months of the date of this Document for the provision of the LWR project. Contract talks will begin as soon as possible after the date of this Document.

- As necessary, the U.S. and the DPRK will conclude a bilateral agreement for cooperation in the field of peaceful uses of nuclear energy.

2) In accordance with the October 20, 1994 letter of assurances from the U.S. President, the U.S., representing the consortium, will make arrange-

ments to offset the energy foregone due to the freeze of the DPRK's graphite-moderated reactors and related facilities, pending completion of the first LWR unit.

- Alternative energy will be provided in the form of heavy oil for heating and electricity production.

- Deliveries of heavy oil will begin within three months of the date of the Document and will reach a rate of 500,000 tons annually, in accordance with an agreed schedule of deliveries.

3) Upon receipt of the U.S. assurances for the provision of LWR's and for the arrangements for interim energy alternatives, the DPRK will freeze its graphite-moderated reactors and related facilities and will eventually dismantle these reactors and related facilities.

- The freeze on the DPRK's graphite-moderated reactors and related facilities will be fully implemented within one month of the date of this Document. During this one-month period, and throughout the freeze, the International Atomic Energy Agency (IAEA) will be allowed to monitor this freeze, and the DPRK will provide full cooperation to the IAEA for this purpose.

- Dismantlement of the DPRK's graphite-moderated reactors and related facilities will be completed when the LWR project is completed.

- The U.S. and the DPRK will cooperated in finding a method to store safely the spent fuel from the 5 MW(e) experimental reactor during the construction of the LWR project, and to dispose of the fuel in a safe manner that does not involve reprocessing in the DPRK.

4) As soon as possible after the date of this Document U.S. and DPRK experts will hold two sets of experts talks.

- At one set of talks, experts will discuss issues related to alternative energy and the replacement of the graphite-moderated reactor program with the LWR project.

- At the other set of talks, experts will discuss specific arrangements for spent fuel storage and ultimate disposition.

II. The two sides will move toward full normalization of political and economic relations.

1) Within three months of the date of this Document, both sides will reduce barriers to trade and investment, including restrictions on telecommunications services and financial transactions.

2) Each side will open a liaison office in the other's capital following resolution of consular and other technical issues through expert level discussions.

3) As progress is made on issues of concern to each side, the U.S. and the DPRK will upgrade bilateral relations to the Ambassadorial level.

III. Both sides will work together for peace and security on a nuclear-free Korean peninsula.

1) The U.S. will provide formal assurances to the DPRK, against the threat or use of nuclear weapons by the U.S.

2) The DPRK will engage in North-South dialogue, as this Agreed Framework will help create an atmosphere that promotes such dialogue.

IV. Both sides will work together to strengthen the international nonproliferation regime.

1) The DPRK will remain a party to the Treaty on the Non-Proliferation of Nuclear Weapons (NPT) and will allow implementation of its safeguards agreement under the Treaty.

2) Upon conclusion of the supply contract for the provision of the LWR project, ad hoc and routine inspections will resume under the DPRK's safeguards agreement with the IAEA with respect to the facilities not subject to the freeze. Pending conclusion of the supply contract, inspections required by the IAEA for the continuity of safeguards will continue at the facilities not subject to the freeze.

3) When a significant portion of the LWR project is complete but before delivery of key nuclear components, the DPRK will come into full compliance with its safeguards agreement with the IAEA (INFCIRC/403), including taking all steps that may be deemed necessary by the IAEA, following consultations with the Agency with regard to verifying the accuracy and completeness of the DPRK's initial report on all nuclear material in the DPRK.

TECHNICAL ASPECTS

Glossary

Aerodynamic enrichment method	A process of uranium enrichment that is based on centrifugal effects of a fast moving uranium hexafluoride gas in very small curved-wall chambers.
Alpha particle	A charged particle emitted from the nucleus of an atom, having a mass and charge equal in magnitude to a helium nucleus.
Americium	Transuranic element with atomic number 95. Americium-241, an alpha and gamma emitter, is a decay product of plutonium-241.
Atomic bomb	A bomb whose energy comes from the fission of uranium or plutonium.
Atomic number	The number of protons in the atomic nucleus of an element.
Beryllium metal	A highly toxic steel-grey metal, possessing a low neutron absorption cross-section and high melting point, which can be used in nuclear reactors as a moderator or reflector. In nuclear weapons, beryllium surrounds the fissile material and reflects neutrons back into the nuclear reaction, considerably reducing the amount of fissile material required. Beryllium is also used in guidance systems and other parts for aircraft, missiles or space vehicles.
Beta decay	Radioactive decay involving the emission of a beta particle. This is a charged particle with the mass and charge equal to that of an electron or positron.
Blanket	A layer of fertile material, such as uranium-238 or thorium-232, placed around the core of a reactor. During operation of the reactor, additional fissile material is produced in the blanket.
Boiling water reactor	A light-water nuclear reactor in which steam is produced in the reactor and passed directly to the turbogenerator.
Burn-up	The percentage of heavy metal atoms fissioned or the thermal energy produced per mass of fuel (usually measured in Megawatt days per tonne, MWd/t).
Calutron	(*CALifornia University CycloTRON*). An electromagnetic uranium enrichment machine. Used in the Manhattan Project to produce HEU for the Hiroshima bomb and developed in the Iraqi bomb programme. Alpha machines are the first stage, producing LEU, from natural uranium; beta machines are the second stage, producing HEU from the output of the alpha machines.

Source: David Albright, Frans Berkhout, and William Walker, *World Inventory of Plutonium and Highly Enriched Uranium, 1992* (New York: Oxford University Press, 1993), xiii- xxv

GLOSSARY

CANDU	(Canadian deuterium–uranium reactor.) The most widely used type of heavy water reactor. The CANDU reactor uses natural uranium as a fuel and heavy water as a moderator and a coolant.
Cascade	A connected series of enrichment machines, material from one being passed to another for further enrichment.
Centrifuge	See ultracentrifuge.
Chain reaction	The continuing process of nuclear fissioning in which the neutrons released from a fission trigger at least one other nuclear fission. In a nuclear weapon an extremely rapid, multiplying chain reaction causes the explosive release of energy. In a reactor, the pace of the chain reaction is controlled and sustained.
Chemical enrichment	This method of uranium isotope separation depends on a slight tendency of uranium-235 and uranium-238 to concentrate in different molecules when uranium compounds are continuously brought into contact. Catalysts are used to speed up the chemical exchange.
Chemical processing	Chemical treatment of materials to separate specific usable constituents.
Cladding	The material which encases the nuclear fuel, reducing the risk of radioactive materials leaking from the fuel.
Coolant	A substance circulated through a nuclear reactor to remove or transfer heat. The most common coolants are carbon dioxide, water and heavy water.
Core	The central portion of a nuclear reactor containing the fuel elements and usually the moderator. Also the central portion of a nuclear weapon containing highly enriched uranium or plutonium.
Critical mass	The minimum mass required to sustain a chain reaction. The exact mass varies with many factors such as the particular isotope present, its concentration and chemical form, the geometrical arrangement of the material and its density. When fissile materials are compressed by high explosives in implosion-type atomic weapons, the critical mass needed for a nuclear explosion is reduced.
Depleted uranium	Uranium with a smaller percentage of uranium-235 than the 0.7 per cent found in natural uranium. It is a by-product of the uranium enrichment process, during which uranium-235 is culled from one batch of uranium, thereby depleting it, and added to another batch to increase its concentration of uranium-235.
Diversion	The deliberate removal of fissionable material in civil fuel cycles for other uses.
Draw-down	A policy of consuming stocks of nuclear material.
Dry storage	Storage of irradiated nuclear fuel in a gas (either air or an inert gas) environment.
Enrichment	The process of increasing the concentration of one isotope of a given element (in the case of uranium, increasing the concentration of uranium-235).
Facilities list	The list of nuclear facilities declared by states parties to the Treaty on the Non-Proliferation of Nuclear Weapons to the IAEA that may be subject to safeguards. In non-nuclear weapon states this includes all nuclear facilities, in nuclear weapon states it includes only facilities designated by the state.
Facility attachment	The detailed plan for applying safeguards at a particular plant. This usually defines the material balance areas, and indicates the strategic points to which the IAEA inspector may have access during inspections and at which safeguards instruments may be installed.
Fast breeder reactor	A nuclear reactor in which fuel is irradiated with high-energy neutrons and which produces more fissile material than it consumes, a process known as breeding. Fissile material is produced both in the reactor's core and through neutron capture in fertile material placed around the core (blanket).
Feed stock	Material introduced into a facility at the start of the process, such as uranium hexafluoride in an enrichment plant.
Fertile	Material composed of atoms which readily absorb neutrons to produce fissionable materials. One such element is uranium-238, which becomes plutonium-239 after it absorbs a neutron. Fertile material alone cannot sustain a chain reaction.
Fission	The process by which a neutron strikes a nucleus and splits it into fragments or 'fission products'. During the process of nuclear fission, several neutrons are emitted at high speed and radiation is released.
Fissionable material	Material, whose nuclei can be induced to fission by a neutron.
Fissile material	Material composed of atoms which fission when irradiated by slow or 'thermal' neutrons. Uranium-235 and plutonium-239 are the most common examples of fissile materials.
Fuel element	Engineered bundle of nuclear fuel pins.
Fuel pin	Single rod of basic chain-reacting material, including both fissile and fertile materials.

GLOSSARY

Fusion	The formation of a heavier nucleus from two lighter ones (usually hydrogen isotopes), with the attendant release of energy (as in a hydrogen bomb).
Gamma radiation	High-energy electromagnetic radiation emitted from nuclei as a result of nuclear reactions and decay.
Gas centrifuge process	A method of isotope separation in which heavy gaseous atoms or molecules are separated from light ones by centrifugal force and an induced counter-current flow in the swirling gas.
Gas-cooled reactor	A nuclear reactor employing a gas (usually CO_2) as a coolant, rather than water or liquid metal.
Gaseous diffusion	A method of isotope separation based on the fact that gas atoms or molecules with different masses will diffuse through a porous barrier (or membrane) at different rates. The method is used to separate uranium-235 from uranium-238. It requires large plants and significant amounts of electric power.
Gas-graphite reactor	A nuclear reactor in which a gas is the coolant and graphite is the moderator.
Graphite	One of the two elemental forms of carbon, used as a moderator in some thermal reactor types (Magnox, RBMK).
Heavy water	Water containing significantly more than the natural proportion (1 in 6500) of heavy hydrogen (deuterium) atoms to ordinary hydrogen atoms. (Hydrogen atoms have one proton, deuterium atoms have one proton and one neutron.) Heavy water is used as a moderator in some reactors because it slows down neutrons more effectively and absorbs them less (than light, or normal, water) making it possible to fission natural uranium and sustain a chain reaction.
Heavy water reactor	A reactor that uses heavy water as its moderator and natural uranium as fuel. See CANDU.
Highly enriched uranium	Uranium in which the percentage of uranium-235 nuclei has been increased from the natural level of 0.7 per cent to some level greater than 20 per cent, usually around 90 per cent.
Hot cells	Lead-shielded rooms with remote handling equipment for examining and processing radioactive materials. In particular, hot cells can be used for examining spent reactor fuel.
Hydrogen bomb	A nuclear weapon that derives its energy largely from fusion. Also known as a thermonuclear bomb.
Irradiation	Exposure to a radioactive source; usually in the case of materials being placed in an operating nuclear reactor.
Isotope	Atoms having the same number of protons, but a different number of neutrons. Two isotopes of the same atom are chemically similar and are therefore difficult to separate by ordinary chemical means. Isotopes can have very different nuclear properties, however. For example, one isotope may spontaneously fission readily, while another isotope of the same atom may not fission at all. An isotope is specified by its atomic mass number (the number of protons plus neutrons) following the symbol denoting the chemical element (e.g., uranium-235 is an isotope of uranium).
Kilogram	A metric weight equivalent to 2.2 pounds.
Kiloton	The energy of a nuclear explosion that is equivalent to an explosion of 1000 tonnes of TNT.
Laser enrichment method	A still experimental process of uranium enrichment in which lasers are used to separate uranium isotopes.
Light water	Ordinary water (H_2O), as distinguished from heavy water (D_2O).
Light water reactor	A reactor that uses ordinary water as moderator and coolant and low-enriched uranium as fuel.
Light water-cooled, graphite-moderated reactor	Russian Chernobyl-type reactor cooled by water and moderated with graphite.
Low-enriched uranium	Uranium in which the percentage of uranium-235 nuclei has been increased from the natural level of 0.7 per cent up to 20 per cent, usually 3 to 5 per cent. With the increased level of fissile material, low-enriched uranium can sustain a chain reaction when immersed in light water and is used as fuel in light-water reactors.
Magnox fuel	Uranium metal fuel clad with magnesium oxide (magnox).
Magnox reactor	Gas-cooled, graphite-moderated reactor built principally in the UK and France.
Maraging steel	Special hardened steel used in the fabrication of centrifuge rotors and rocket motors.
Mass number	The number of protons and neutrons in the atomic nucleus. Elements may occur in forms displaying a range of mass numbers—i.e., plutonium-238, -239, -240, -241, -242.
Medium-enriched uranium	Uranium in which the percentage of uranium-235 nuclei has been increased from the natural level of 0.7 per cent to between 20 and 50 per cent. (Potentially usable for nuclear weapons, but very large quantities are needed.)
Megawatt	One million watts-electric (MWe): used in reference to a nuclear power plant, one million watts of electricity. One million watts-thermal (MWth): one million watts of heat.

GLOSSARY

Metric tonne	1000 kilograms. A metric weight equivalent to 2200 pounds or 1.1 tons.
Milling	A process in the uranium fuel cycle by which ore containing only a very small percentage of uranium oxide (U_3O_8) is converted into material containing a high percentage (80 per cent) of U_3O_8, often referred to as yellowcake.
Mixed-oxide fuel	Nuclear fuel containing both uranium and plutonium. Most fissions in the fuel will be of plutonium nuclei.
Moderator	A component (usually water, heavy water, or graphite) of some nuclear reactor types that slows neutrons, thereby increasing their chances of fissioning fertile material.
Natural uranium	Uranium as found in nature, containing 0.72 per cent of uranium-235, 99.27 per cent of uranium-238 and a trace of uranium-234.
Neutron	An uncharged elementary particle, with a mass slightly greater than that of a proton, found in the nucleus of every atom heavier than hydrogen. Nuclear fission is caused when a nucleus is irradiated with neutrons. Fissions may be caused by relatively low energy (thermal) neutrons, or by high energy (fast) neutrons. Fission reactors are therefore classed as either 'fast reactors' or 'thermal reactors'.
Nuclear energy	The energy liberated by a nuclear reaction (fission or fusion) or by spontaneous radioactivity.
Nuclear fuel	Basic chain-reacting material, including both fissile and fertile materials. Commonly used nuclear fuels are natural uranium and low-enriched uranium; high-enriched uranium and plutonium are used in some reactors.
Nuclear fuel cycle	The set of chemical and physical operations needed to prepare nuclear material for use in reactors and to dispose of or recycle the material after its removal from the reactor. Existing fuel cycles begin with uranium as the natural resource and create plutonium as a by-product. Some future fuel cycles may rely on thorium and produce the fissionable isotope uranium-233.
Nuclear fuel element	A rod, tube, plate or other mechanical shape or form into which nuclear fuel is fabricated for use in a reactor.
Nuclear fuel fabrication plant	A facility where the nuclear material (e.g., enriched or natural uranium) is fabricated into fuel elements to be inserted into a reactor.
Nuclear power plant	Any device that converts nuclear energy into useful power. In a nuclear electric power plant, heat produced by a reactor is used to produce steam to drive a turbine that in turn drives an electricity generator.
Nuclear reactor	A heat engine configured to sustain a controlled nuclear chain reaction when fuelled with fissionable materials. Reactors are of three general types: electric power reactors, plutonium production reactors and research reactors.
Nuclear waste	The radioactive by-products formed by fission and other nuclear processes in a reactor. Most nuclear waste is initially contained in spent fuel. If this material is reprocessed, new categories of waste result.
Nuclear weapons	A collective term for atomic bombs and hydrogen bombs. Weapons based on a nuclear explosion. The term is generally used throughout the text to mean atomic bombs only, unless used with reference to the nuclear weapon states (all five of which have both atomic and hydrogen weapons).
Nucleus	The part of an atom containing protons and neutrons.
On-load refuelling	Re-fuelling of nuclear reactors under power (i.e., Magnox and CANDU reactors).
Pit	The shaped core of a nuclear weapon containing fissile material, a tamper and a reflector.
Plutonium-239 (^{239}Pu)	A fissile isotope generated artificially when uranium-238, through irradiation, captures an extra neutron. It is one of the two fissile materials that have been used for the core of nuclear weapons, the other being uranium-235.
Plutonium-240 (^{240}Pu)	An isotope produced in reactors when a ^{239}Pu atom absorbs a neutron instead of fissioning. Its presence complicates the construction of nuclear explosives because of its high neutron emission and its high heat output.
Plutonium recycle	The re-use of separated plutonium as fuel in nuclear reactors.
Pond storage	Storage of irradiated fuel under water.
Power reactor	A reactor designed to produce electricity as distinguished from reactors used primarily for research or for producing radiation or fissionable materials.
Primary	The fission explosive detonated first in a thermonuclear warhead containing two or more stages (secondaries).
Production reactor	A reactor designed primarily for large-scale production of plutonium-239 by neutron irradiation of uranium-238.
Proton	A positively-charged nuclear particle, one of the two principal components of nuclei, with a mass similar to a neutron.
Radioactivity	The spontaneous disintegration of an unstable atomic nucleus resulting in the emission of sub-atomic particles.
Radioisotope	A radioactive isotope.

GLOSSARY

Reprocessing	Chemical treatment of spent nuclear fuel to separate the plutonium and uranium from unwanted radioactive waste by-products and (under present plans) from each other. Spent fuel is handled in batches known as 'campaigns'.
Research reactor	A reactor primarily designed to supply neutrons for experimental purposes. It may also be used for training, materials testing and production of radioisotopes.
Safeguards	Technical and inspection measures for verifying that nuclear materials are not being diverted from civil to other uses.
Secondary	See primary.
Separative work	A measure of the effort required in an enrichment facility to separate uranium of a given uranium-235 content into two fractions; one with a higher percentage and one with a lower percentage of uranium-235. The unit of separative work is the kilogram separative work unit (kg SWU), or separative work unit (SWU) for short. The initial material is called the 'feed'. The fraction with a higher proportion of uranium-235 is called the 'product', the other is called the 'tails'.
Significant quantity	The approximate amount of nuclear material (not just fissile material) which the IAEA considers a state would need to manufacture its first nuclear explosive. Eight kilograms of plutonium are considered significant and 25 kilograms of weapon-grade uranium are significant.
Solvent extraction	Technique for separating plutonium, uranium and fission products in a reprocessing plant using solvents.
Spent fuel	Fuel elements that have been removed from the reactor after use because they contain too little fissile and fertile material and too high a concentration of unwanted radioactive by-products to sustain reactor operation. Spent fuel is both thermally and radioactively hot.
Tails	The waste stream of an enrichment facility that contains depleted uranium. It is expressed as a percentage of the uranium-235 content and called 'tails assay'.
Thermal reactor	See neutron.
Thermal recycle	See plutonium recycle.
Thermonuclear bomb	A hydrogen bomb.
Thorium-232	A fertile material.
Tritium	The heaviest hydrogen isotope, containing one proton and two neutrons in the nucleus, produced typically by bombarding lithium-6 with neutrons. In a fission weapon, tritium is used with deuterium in a fusion process known as 'boosting' to produce excess neutrons, which set off additional fissions in the core. In this way, tritium can either reduce the amount of fissile material required, or multiply (i.e., boost) the weapon's destructive power many times. In fusion reactions, tritium and deuterium bond at very high temperatures, releasing a neutron with 14 million electron-volts of energy.
Uranium	A radioactive element with the atomic number 92 and, as found in natural ores, an average atomic weight of 238. The two principal natural isotopes are uranium-235 (0.72 per cent of natural uranium), which is fissionable, and uranium-238 (99.27 per cent of natural uranium), which is fertile.
Uranium-233 (^{233}U)	A fissionable isotope bred in fertile thorium-232. Like plutonium-239 it is theoretically an excellent material for nuclear weapons, but is not known to have been used for this purpose except in research programmes. Can be used as reactor fuel.
Uranium-235 (^{235}U)	The only naturally occurring fissionable isotope. Natural uranium contains 0.72 per cent ^{235}U; light water reactors use about 3 to 5 per cent and weapon-grade uranium has more than 90 per cent ^{235}U.
Uranium-238 (^{238}U)	A fertile material. Natural uranium is composed of approximately 99.3 per cent ^{238}U.
Uranium dioxide (UO_2)	Purified uranium. The form of natural uranium used in heavy water reactors. Also the form of uranium used to fabricate enriched uranium fuel elements.
Uranium oxide (U_3O_8)	The most common oxide of uranium found in typical ores. U_3O_8 is extracted from the ore during the milling process. The ore typically contains only 0.1 per cent U_3O_8; yellowcake, the product of the milling process, contains about 80 per cent U_3O_8.
Uranium hexafluoride (UF_6)	A volatile compound of uranium and fluorine. UF_6 is a solid at atmospheric pressure and room temperature, but can be transformed into gas by heating. UF_6 gas (alone, or in combination with hydrogen or helium) is the feed stock in most uranium enrichment processes and is sometimes produced as an intermediate product in the process of purifying yellowcake to produce uranium oxide.
Vessel	The part of a reactor that contains the nuclear fuel.
Weapon-grade material	Nuclear material of the type most suitable for nuclear weapons, i.e., uranium enriched to over 90 per cent ^{235}U or plutonium that is primarily ^{239}Pu.
Yellowcake	A concentrate produced during the milling process that contains about 80 per cent uranium oxide (U_3O_8). In preparation for uranium enrichment, the yellowcake is converted to

Yield	The total energy released in a nuclear explosion. It is usually expressed in equivalent tons of TNT (the quantity of TNT required to produce a corresponding amount of energy).
Zirconium	A greyish-white lustrous metal which is commonly used in an alloy form (i.e., zircalloy) to encase fuel rods in nuclear reactors.

Sources: Congressional Research Service, *Nuclear Proliferation Factbook* (US Government Printing Office: Washington, DC, 1977); Energy Research & Development Administration, *U.S. Nuclear Power Export Activities* (National Technical Information Service: Springfield, Va., 1976); Fischer, D. and Szasz, P., ed. J. Goldblat, SIPRI, *Safeguarding the Atom: a Critical Appraisal* (Taylor and Francis: London, 1985); Nero, A. V. *A Guidebook to Nuclear Reactors* (University of California Press: Berkeley, Calif., 1979); Nuclear Energy Policy Study Group, *Nuclear Power: Issues and Choices* (Ballinger: Cambridge, Mass, 1977); Office of Technology Assessment, *Nuclear Proliferation and Safeguards* (Office of Technology Assessment: Washington, DC, 1977); *Nuclear Power in an Age of Uncertainty* (Office of Technology Assessment: Washington, DC, 1984); Spector, L. S., *Nuclear Ambitions* (Westview Press: Boulder, Colo, 1990); Wohlstetter, A., *Swords from Plowshares: The Military Potential of Civilian Nuclear Energy* (The University of Chicago Press: Chicago, Ill., 1977); United Nations Association of the USA, *Nuclear Proliferation: A Citizen's Guide to Policy Choices* (UNA-USA: New York, 1983).

Abbreviations, acronyms and conventions

Acronyms and abbreviations

AGR	Advanced gas-cooled reactor
APM	Atelier Pilote Marcoule
ATR	Advanced thermal reactor
AVLIS	Atomic Vapor Laser Isotope Separation Project (USA)
BARC	Bhabha Atomic Research Centre (India)
BNFL	British Nuclear Fuels plc
BWR	Boiling water reactor
CANDU	Canadian deuterium–uranium reactor
CEA	Commissariat à l'Énergie Atomique (France)
CETEX	Army Technological Centre (Brazil)
CIA	US Central Intelligence Agency
CIS	Commonwealth of Independent States
CNEA	National Atomic Energy Commission (Argentina)
CNEN	National Nuclear Energy Commission (Brazil)
Cogema	Compagnie Générale des Matières Nucléaires
DATR	Demonstration ATR
DAE	Department of Atomic Energy (India)
DFBR	Demonstration FBR
DFR	Dounreay Demonstration Fast Reactor (UK)
DNPDE	Dounreay Nuclear Power Development Establishment
DOE	Department of Energy (USA)
DWK	Deutsche Gesellschaft für Wiederaufarbeitung von Kernbrennstoffe
EC	European Community
EdF	Électricité de France
EMIS	Electromagnetic isotope separation
ENEL	Ente Nazionale per l'Energia Elettrica
Euratom	European Atomic Energy Community
FBR	Fast breeder reactor
FBTR	Fast Breeder Test Reactor
FFTF	Fast Flux Test Facility (Hanford, USA)
GCR	Gas-cooled, graphite-moderated reactor
HEP	Head-end plant
HEU	Highly enriched uranium
HTR	High-temperature reactor
HWR	Heavy water-cooled and -moderated reactor
IAEA	International Atomic Energy Agency
INEL	Idaho National Engineering Laboratory
INF	Intermediate-range nuclear forces
IPEN	Institute of Energy and Nuclear Research (Brazil)
IPS	International Plutonium Storage
JNFS	Japan Nuclear Fuel Services Company
KfK	Kernforschungszentrum Karlsruhe

KNK	Kompakte Natriumgekühlte Kernreaktoranlage
LEU	Low-enriched uranium
LWGR	Light water-cooled, graphite-moderated reactor
LWR	Light water reactor
Magnox	Magnesium oxide
MAPI	Ministry of Atomic Power and Industry (former USSR)
MAPS	Madras Atomic Power Station (India)
MITI	Ministry of International Trade and Industry (Japan)
MOX	Mixed-oxide (uranium and plutonium)
MTR	Materials Test Reactor
MZFR	Mehrzweckforschungsreaktor
NAPS	Narora Atomic Power Station (India)
NEA	Nuclear Energy Agency, OECD
NERSA	Groupement Central Nucléaire Européen à Neutrons Rapides
NFS	Nuclear Fuel Services
NPT	Treaty on the Non-Proliferation of Nuclear Weapons
NNWS	Non-nuclear weapon state
NRDC	Natural Resources Defense Council (USA)
NWS	Nuclear weapon state
OECD	Organization for Economic Cooperation and Development
PCM	Plutonium contaminated materials
PFDF	Plutonium Fuel Development Facility
PFFF	Plutonium Fuel Fabrication Facility
PFBR	Prototype fast breeder reactor
PPPF	Plutonium Fuel Production Facility (Tokai, Japan)
PFR	Prototype Fast Reactor (UK)
PNC	Power Reactor and Nuclear Fuel Development Corporation (Japan)
PREFRE	Power Reactor Fuel Reprocessing (India)
PUREX	Plutonium uranium extraction
PWR	Pressurized water reactor
R&D	Research and development
RAPS 1	Rajasthan Atomic Power Station 1 (India)
RBMK	High-power, channel-type reactor (former USSR)
RepU	Reprocessed uranium
RERTR	Reduced Enrichment for Research and Test Reactors
RWE	Rheinische-Westfälische Elektrizitätswerk AG
SAGSI	Standing Advisory Group on Safeguards Implementation (IAEA)
SAP	Service de l'Atelier Pilote
SBK	Schnell-Brüter Kernkraftwerkgesellschaft mbH
START	Strategic Arms Reduction Talks
SWU	Separative work units
THORP	Thermal Oxide Reprocessing Plant (UK)
TOP	Traitement d'Oxydes Pilote
TOR	Traitement d'Oxydes Rapides
TRR	Taiwan Research Reactor
UCOR	Uranium Enrichment Corporation (South Africa)
UKAEA	United Kingdom Atomic Energy Authority
Urenco	Uranium Enrichment Company
VAK	Versuchsatomkraftwerk Kahl
VDEW	Vereinigung Deutscher Elektrizitätswerke
VVER	Water-water power reactor
WAK	Wiederaufarbeitungsanlage Karlsruhe
WGU	Weapon-grade uranium
ZPPR	Zero Power Plutonium Reactor (Idaho, USA)

Conventions

g	Gram
GWdth	Gigawatt-days of thermal energy
GWe	Gigawatt-electric
GWe (net)	Gigawatt-electric not including power consumed by the power station itself
kg	Kilogram
kWh	Kilowatt-hour
km	Kilometre
mg	Milligram
MW	Megawatt
MWd/t	Megawatt-days per tonne of fuel
MWe	Megawatt-electric
MWth	Megawatt-thermal
MWde	Megawatt-days of electrical energy
MWdth	Megawatt-days of thermal energy
SWU	Kilogram separative work unit
t	Tonne
TWhe	Terawatt-hour of electric energy
..	Data not available or not applicable
–	Nil or a negligible figure

GLOSSARY

Boiling-water reactor (BWR) -- A light-water reactor which employs a direct cycle; the water coolant that passes through the reactor is converted to high pressure steam that flows directly through the turbine.

Breeder reactor -- A nuclear reactor that produces more fissile material than it consumes. In fast breeder reactors, high-energy (fast) neutrons produce most of the fissions, while in thermal breeder reactors, fissions are principally caused by low-energy (thermal) neutrons.

Burner reactor -- A reactor which consumes fissile material without replacing it; also called a destruction reactor.

Control rods -- Rods containing neutron-absorbing material; an important form of control for any reactor.

Coolant -- The medium in a nuclear reactor which absorbs heat from the reactor core where fission occurs and heat is produced and transfers it to heat exchange systems which convert the heat into steam.

Criticality -- A condition where the number of neutrons (or fissions) in a chain reacting system is the same from one generation to the next.

Enrichment -- The process of increasing the concentration of one isotope of a given element; usually the isotope of interest is U^{235}.

Fast reactor -- A nuclear reactor in which nearly all the neutrons liberated in fission have high energies and so, if no moderator is present in the reactor core or reflector, the majority of fissions are produced by fast neutrons. If a fertile species is present in the fast reactor core or in the blanket surrounding the core, it will be converted into fissile material by neutron capture. When the fissile nuclide produced is identical with that used to maintain the fission chain, the reactor is called a breeder.

Fissile isotope -- An isotope that will split, or fission, into two (or more) lighter elements plus extra neutrons when it absorbs a neutron. The fission process and the fissile isotopes are the source of energy in nuclear weapons and nuclear reactors.

Fresh fuel -- Reactor fuel that has not been irradiated in a nuclear reactor.

Fuel assembly -- A grouping of fuel elements which is not taken apart during the charging and discharging of a reactor core.

Source: Sarah S. Doyle, Rufus H. Shumate, and Joseph A. Yager, *Evaluation of Means of Disposing of Fissile Material from Dismantled Former Soviet Nuclear Weapons* (McLean, Va.: SAIC, 11 January 1993),

Fuel cycle -- The sequence of processing, manufacturing, and transportation steps involved in producing fuel for a nuclear reactor, and in processing fuel discharged from the reactor. The uranium fuel cycle includes uranium mining and milling, conversion to uranium hexafluoride (UF_6), isotopic enrichment, fuel fabrication, reprocessing, recycling to recovered fissile isotopes, and disposal of radioactive wastes.

Fuel element -- The smallest structurally discrete part of a reactor which has fuel as its principal constituent.

Fuel fabrication plant -- A facility in which the nuclear material (e.g., uranium or plutonium) is fabricated into fuel elements to be inserted into a reactor.

Half-Life -- The time required for the activity of a given radioactive species to decrease to half of its initial value due to radioactive decay. The half-life is a characteristic property of each radioactive species and is independent of its amount or condition. The half-life of tritium is 12.3 years.

Heavy metal -- In connection with fission reactors, the fuel materials uranium, plutonium, thorium, and their reaction products.

Heavy-water -- Water with a relatively high proportion of hydrogen in the isotopic form of deuterium.

Heavy-water reactor (HWR) -- A nuclear reactor which uses heavy-water (deuterium) for moderation and cooling.

Highly-enriched uranium (HEU) -- Uranium enriched in U^{235} or U^{233} to concentrations above 20%; enrichments of 90% and more are used in weapons.

Isotopes -- Atoms of the same chemical element whose nuclei contain different numbers of neutrons and hence have different masses, even though chemically identical. Isotopes are specified by their atomic mass number, that is, the total number of protons plus neutrons, and a symbol denoting the chemical element, e.g., U^{235} for uranium-235.

Isotopic composition -- The percentage of isotopes in a material, e.g., natural uranium contains 99.28% U^{238} and 0.72% U^{235}.

Light-water reactor (LWR) -- A nuclear reactor that uses ordinary water for cooling and moderation.

Light-water graphite-moderated reactor (LWGR) -- A reactor that uses ordinary water for cooling and graphite for moderation. In the former Soviet Union this type of reactor is often referred to as RBMK. Since the Hanford N Reactor in the United States was shut down, the

26 LWGRs in the former Soviet Union are the only ones operating in the world.

Low-enriched uranium (LEU) -- Uranium enriched in U^{233} or U^{235}, with concentrations less than 20%; enrichment of 3-5% is common in light-water reactor fuel.

Mixed Oxide (MOX) -- A mixture of uranium dioxide and plutonium dioxide.

Mixed Oxide Fuel -- Nuclear reactor fuel composed of plutonium and uranium in oxide form. The plutonium replaces some of the fissile uranium, thus reducing the need for uranium ore and enrichment.

Natural uranium -- Uranium that has not been enriched; it consists of 99.3% U^{238}, 0.7% U^{235}, and traces of U^{234}.

Once-through -- A nuclear fuel "cycle" in which spent nuclear fuel is stored indefinitely or disposed of after being used only once; it is not recycled.

Plutonium (Pu) -- A heavy, radioactive man-made metallic element. Its most important isotope is fissionable Pu-239, produced by neutron irradiation of U^{238}. It can be used in reactor fuel and in nuclear explosive devices.

Plutonium-239 (Pu^{239}) -- A fissile isotope created as a result of capture of a neutron by U^{238}. Plutonium used in nuclear weapons is generally 93% Pu^{239}.

Plutonium-240 (Pu^{240}) -- A fissile isotope whose presence complicates the construction of nuclear explosives because of its high rate of spontaneous fission. It is produced in reactors when a Pu^{239} atom absorbs a neutron instead of fissioning.

Plutonium dioxide (PuO_2) -- A chemical form of plutonium used in mixed-oxide fuels; much safer to handle than plutonium metal.

Pressurized-water reactor (PWR) -- A light-water moderated and cooled reactor that employs an indirect cycle; the cooling water that passes through the reactor is kept under high pressure to keep it from boiling, but it heats water in a secondary loop that produces steam that drives the turbine.

Radioactive -- Having the ability to decay spontaneously, thereby changing to another nuclide.

Radioactive decay -- The process by which a nucleus of one type transforms into another, accompanied by emission of radiation.

Recycle -- The reuse of unburned uranium and plutonium in fresh fuel after chemical separation from fission products in spent fuel.

Reactor core -- The central portion of a nuclear reactor, containing the fuel elements and the control rods. It is in this region that the nuclear reactions occur, with the exception of those caused outside the core by escaping radiation or radioactivity.

Reactor-grade plutonium -- Plutonium that contains more than 7 percent of the isotope plutonium-240. It is created in most power reactors under normal operating conditions.

Reprocessing -- The chemical dissolution of irradiated fuel and separation into waste and fuel fractions; may also include conversion to particular chemical and physical forms.

Separative work unit (SWU) -- A measure of the amount of effort required to enrich uranium; measured in units of mass (kilograms or tons).

Spent fuel -- Nuclear fuel removed from a reactor following irradiation. Spent fuel is both physically and radioactively hot.

Thermal reactor -- A reactor in which the fission chain reaction is sustained by low-energy (thermal) neutrons.

Thorium-232 (Th^{232}) -- A fertile, naturally occurring isotope from which the fissile isotope U^{233} can be bred.

Uranium -- A radioactive element of atomic number 92. Naturally occurring uranium is a mixture of 99.28 percent U^{238}, 0.715 percent U^{235}, and 0.0058 percent U^{234}.

Uranium-233 (U^{233}) -- A fissile isotope bred by fertile Thorium-232. It has qualities similar to Pu^{239}.

Uranium-235 (U^{235}) -- The only naturally-occurring fissile isotope, which makes up 0.7% of natural uranium. Reactor-grade uranium generally enriched to about 3% U^{235}. Weapons-grade uranium enriched to about 90% U^{235}.

Uranium oxide (U_3O_8) -- Natural uranium concentrated at the mine. Usually known as yellowcake.

Weapons-grade plutonium -- Plutonium that contains less than 7 percent of plutonium-240, an isotope that complicates the design of nuclear weapons.

TECHNICAL ASPECTS

FUEL CYCLE

A3   Nuclear Devices and the Nuclear Fuel Cycle

A3.1   Introduction

The purpose of this Appendix is to provide a primer on nuclear devices and the nuclear fuel cycle to support the discussion in the main sections of the paper. The neutron-induced fission of uranium or plutonium nuclei into lighter nuclei provides the energy to power all nuclear reactors and drive nuclear explosive devices for weapons. Yet, there are crucial differences in operation between these two classes of nuclear devices and among the major categories within each class. This Appendix briefly describes the operating principles and the characteristics of nuclear weapons in the U.S. and Soviet inventories as well as of the reactors and other nuclear fuel cycle components for civilian use. Weapons materials production is reviewed in Appendix A4.

Nuclear Materials, Reactors, and Explosive Devices[1-3]

Fissionable Materials. The elements thorium, uranium, and plutonium have isotopes that can be obtained in sufficient quantity to fuel fission devices. Of these, the isotopes ^{232}Th, ^{235}U, and ^{238}U occur in nature; but ^{233}U and ^{239}Pu do not. All five isotopes (as well as many artificial ones) can be fissioned by "fast" neutrons, i.e., with energies of Mev, producing 2.5 to 3 neutrons per fission. For ^{238}U, ^{232}Th and most other isotopes, the fission cross section goes to zero at low neutron energy. However, for a few isotopes, notably ^{235}U, ^{233}U, and ^{239}Pu, the fission cross section increases by more than an order of magnitude at low neutron energy. Thus, "slow" or "thermalized" neutrons can induce a fission reaction and play a special role in nuclear reactors. Natural uranium contains 99.285% ^{238}U and only 0.715% of the ^{235}U which is slow-neutron fissionable. Therefore, isotopic enrichment of natural uranium is important to obtain higher concentrations. Even so, the abundant isotope, ^{238}U, is also useful since it can be employed to produce ^{239}Pu by a neutron-gamma reaction followed by a radioactive decay chain. That is,

$$n + {}^{238}U \longrightarrow {}^{239}U \longrightarrow {}^{239}Np \longrightarrow {}^{239}Pu$$

Similarly, slow-neutron-fissionable ^{233}U can be produced using abundant ^{232}Th.

$$n + {}^{232}Th \longrightarrow {}^{233}Th \longrightarrow {}^{233}Pa \longrightarrow {}^{233}U$$

Of the three slow-neutron-fissionable isotopes, ^{233}U has the highest cross section. Thus, it would be the first choice for reactors were it available. But given the natural abundances, the ^{235}U fuel cycle was the obvious starting place. It was also natural to turn to the use of ^{239}Pu for nuclear weapons and for reactors as well, because both its fast and slow neutron cross sections are somewhat higher than those of ^{235}U. Nevertheless, the ^{232}Th-^{233}U cycle also has been used.

Criticality. To achieve a chain reaction in the core, at least one of the neutrons released by fission of a nucleus must, on average, cause fission of another nucleus before the neutron is absorbed in a nonfission process or leaves

Source: L. Charles Hebel, *Limiting and Reducing Inventories of Fissionable Weapons Materials* (Stanford: Center for International Security and Arms Control, November 1991), 107-31

the core. The critical mass is that amount of fissionable material that can just sustain a chain reaction under given conditions. Not all the neutrons present in a reactor are those "promptly" emitted in a fission reaction. A significant fraction may be "delayed" neutrons arising from radioactive decay of fission products and their daughters, which have accumulated from previous fissions. Thus, it is important to distinguish between "prompt criticality," which arises from prompt neutrons alone, and "delayed criticality," in which delayed neutrons contribute a significant fraction of the fissions.

A nuclear explosive device uses high explosives to compress or otherwise change the core from its normal subcritical configuration into a highly prompt-critical configuration. Then, the number of fast neutrons grows exponentially for a fraction of a microsecond until the fission energy released disassembles the core and stops the chain reaction. In contrast with a nuclear explosive device, a reactor core can be maintained stably for long time periods in a delayed-critical condition. A fraction of the radioactive decays in a reactor core occur in the range of a tenth of a second to minutes. The associated population of delayed neutrons makes it possible to achieve stable conditions by sensing the reactivity fluctuations and using feedback control, as discussed below.

Achieving and sustaining criticality of a core depends on each isotope, through its neutron cross section, and on several characteristics of the core and its surroundings, which may be selected and/or controlled. Five may be singled out for emphasis:

1. The core density, which depends on the composition of the fissionable material (e.g., metallic, oxide, carbide) and its phase; the density may vary temporally in a device and, in a composite core structure, can also vary spatially;

2. The core geometry, which is often of cylindrical or spherical symmetry and which can be hollow or solid;

3. The presence of neutron-absorbing isotopes in the core, those produced by the fission process and which can poison the chain reaction, as well as materials like Cadmium and Boron which have high neutron capture cross sections and may be introduced intentionally for control purposes;

4. The presence of neutron-reflecting materials, which return some of the neutrons that escape the core and, thus, increase the fraction of neutrons that produce fission; and

5. The presence of moderators, which slow down the neutrons through elastic collisions before such neutrons induce fission, to take advantage of the increased fission cross section in certain isotopes for slow neutrons. Some substances function as both reflectors and moderators.

Typical moderators in use are water, graphite, deuterium (heavy water), helium, and beryllium. The neutron absorption of moderators must be low and, therefore, the substances must be very pure. The figure of merit is the moderating ratio, which is the logarithmic energy decrement per collision divided by the absorption cross section. The moderating ratio of heavy water is highest by far, with graphite and beryllium in the middle, and helium and (ordinary) water lower but adequate for practical applications in reactors.

Reactor Classification. Reactors are classified in two broad categories. In thermal reactors, the energy release arises from low velocity neutrons that cause fission of ^{235}U or ^{239}Pu. Many neutrons from fission or decay escape the fuel rods. These neutrons are slowed to near thermal velocity by the moderator and diffuse back into the rods to induce additional fissions. In fast reactors, the second category, most of the fissions arise from neutrons with energy in the Mev range, typically using ^{239}Pu with ^{238}U (or ^{233}U with ^{232}Th) for fuel.

Because of the time scale associated with delayed neutrons, it is possible to achieve stable control of the reactivity fluctuations in a reactor by a mechanism that detects changes and adjusts a neutron absorber or reflector to compensate. One type of control device is a rod of neutron-absorbing material that can be moved into or out of the core; another type is an adjustable neutron reflector that can return a fraction of the neutrons that have leaked from the core. In either case an operator moves the devices to achieve a delayed critical condition that just sustains a chain reaction. For thermal reactors the fraction of delayed neutrons is such as to permit straightforward control system design. Also, as the core of a thermal reactor heats up, the effective fission cross section decreases, enhancing stability. In fast reactors, the fraction of delayed neutrons is typically smaller, the reactor core more compact, and the fast-fission cross section temperature independent—making reactor control more complex although quite feasible.

The production of new fissionable material during the nuclear reaction is an important source of energy in a reactor. The net fissionable isotope production per unit fission, including losses, is expressed by the conversion ratio, CR. For typical reactors moderated with light water, CR is about 0.6 while for deuterium- and graphite-moderated reactors CR is somewhat higher. However, one can achieve a value of CR greater than one, a breeder reactor, which produces more fissionable material than it consumes during its operation. Breeding in a thermal reactor is possible using the $^{232}Th-^{232}U$ cycle. However, the cross sections favor a fast neutron breeder using the $^{238}U-^{239}U$ cycle. Reprocessing spent fuel would recover the fissionable material for recycle.

Modern Nuclear Weapons and the Role of Tritium[2-7]

The World War II weapon *Little Boy* was a gun-type device of high-enriched uranium (HEU), in which two subcritical sections of the core were brought together by high explosive (HE) using a gunbarrel arrangement. *Little Boy* produced a nuclear yield of about 12 kilotons (measured in HE equivalent). The other weapon known as *Fat Man* was an implosion-type device with a spherical plutonium core of about 8 kg, surrounded by HE formed into explosive lenses. When they were detonated at many "points" essentially simultaneously, a highly symmetric shock wave achieved high compression and criticality of the core, producing a nuclear yield of about 20 kilotons. Since the original World War II antiques, many improvements in materials, components, and design, verified by extensive testing, have resulted in nuclear explosive devices that require significantly less fissionable material, are smaller and lighter, yet produce much greater yield. Today's nuclear explosive devices have yields from a few hundred tons to many megatons and weigh from about 100 lbs to several tonnes.

Even in *Fat Man* the core was surrounded with a "tamper" which consists of a shell of material that increases the yield in two ways. First, it reflects back into the core many neutrons that otherwise would have escaped, so that they can give rise to additional fissions which increase the yield. Second, a tamper may retard the disassembly of the core, maintaining it in a supercritical condition longer. Early tampers used natural or depleted uranium. Later, better neutron reflectors (e.g., Be) were added. References 1 and 6 provide critical mass data that illustrates the benefit of a good neutron-reflecting tamper. For example, the critical mass of a shell of metallic Pu is listed as 4.5 to 5 kg versus 8.6 kg with a uranium tamper, and that of metallic 94% ^{235}U is 13 to 15 kg versus 26.6 kg with a uranium tamper.

Two key developments soon transformed weapon design. One was the introduction of tritium (T) which can undergo fusion ignition with deuterium (D) at the temperatures achieved in a nuclear explosive device. In the D-T reaction, one 14 Mev neutron is released per 5 mass units, compared to the fission reaction in which 200 Mev is released per 240 mass units with an average of 2.3 neutrons in the Mev range. Thus, the D-T reaction gives 3.4 times more energy per unit mass than fission. The energy release per se is less important than the fusion neutrons, which cause additional fission in plutonium or uranium and greatly boost the yield of the device. Such "boosted" nuclear devices typically are smaller and use less fissionable material than would otherwise be required. Also, a provision to adjust the amount of the gas can enable selectable yield in the warhead.

In a single stage implosion-type device the introduction of D-T in the core can boost the energy yield of the device by an order of magnitude, e.g., from the 20 kilotons of *Fat Man* to a hundred kilotons or more. Further, by designing the device to permit the escape of a significant fraction of the 14 Mev neutrons, a so-called "enhanced radiation" weapon can be created. *NWDv18* describes several single stage nuclear weapons. The early W19 warhead for the Army's 280mm atomic canon was a gun-type, all- ^{235}U device that relied on pure fission. The more practical W33 warhead (1955) for the 8-inch artillery shell was again an all-^{235}U gun-type device weighing about 250 lbs with yields of 5 to 10 Kilotons. By comparison, in the modern W79 warhead (1980) for the 8-inch artillery shell which displaced the W33, a plutonium implosion device with a D-T boost achieves several kilotons yield (selectable) in about 215 lbs.

The second key development was the two stage device in which x-rays from one nuclear explosion, called the "primary" stage, initiates the compression of an another "secondary" core in the weapon. The radiation-induced pressure caused by the primary explosion can be much greater than that achievable with ordinary HE. Thus, the compression of the secondary stage is greater and the yield per mass of fissionable material much higher than possible in a single stage. A two stage device can be achieved with pure fission, i.e., without boosting. The largest such device reportedly had a yield of about 500 kilotons.

However, fusion ignition can readily be achieved in the secondary stage of a device whose first stage is a primary core of plutonium, ^{235}U, or a combination of the two. The secondary stage typically uses 15 to 30 kg of ^{235}U. The yield of such a secondary can be several orders of magnitude greater than that of a boosted primary; explosions with yields of tens of megatons have been announced. Moreover, once the secondary is ignited, it is a copious source of fast neutrons, so much so that yet additional yield can be gained by encasing the device in depleted uranium because ^{238}U undergoes fast neutron fission. Early thermonuclear devices typically used ^{6}LiD to supply the tritium through an in-situ neutron reaction with the ^{6}Li, which is initiated inside the weapon by the fission neutrons. This avoids the need to store tritium bottles in the warhead, which must be replenished periodically due to the radioactive decay of the tritium. However, the use of tritium gas in the primary core of a two stage device can significantly decrease the amount of fissionable material needed to ignite the secondary, resulting in lighter, more compact warheads whose characteristics offset the inconvenience of periodic tritium gas refill.

NWDv1[8] describes several ^{6}LiD fueled devices. The B43 warhead (1961) was a 1 MT bomb of about 2,000 lbs. The B53 bomb and the related W53 Titan ICBM warhead (1962) were whoppers of about 8,000 lbs with 9 MT yields; according to NWDv1, this design used ^{235}U for in both primary core and the secondary. Later, more compact warheads used plutonium primary cores with a tritium bottle for high yield-to-weight ratio. For example, The B61 bomb (1968) has a selectable yield in the 100 to 500KT range and weighs 700 to 800 lbs. A yet more efficient design, the W68 (1971) for Poseidon, achieves a 40 to 50 KT yield in a compact warhead of 376 lb. Showing yet further improvement, the W76 warhead (1978) for Trident achieves a 100 KT yield with a weight of 362 lbs.

In the publicly available literature, e.g., NWDv1,[8] one can see a trend beginning in the early 1960s to use more plutonium and less HEU in warhead designs. This trend parallels the change of emphasis from big gravity bombs and huge single missile warheads in the 1950s and early 1960s to successively smaller RVs for MIRV-ed missiles. NWDv2,[9] NWDv4[10] and other published assessments[11] show that the number of weapons in the U.S. stockpile peaked around 1965, and the peak in total weapon yield occurred even earlier. The numerical decline in the nuclear weapon stockpile from 1965 to 1985 is perhaps 15 to 25%. Yet, throughout most of that period, the amount of weapons-grade plutonium increased significantly, reflecting the design trends noted above.

Thus, while tritium is not essential for nuclear weapons, its use together with design improvements has lead to a large increase in yield-to-weight ratio. NWDv1[12] shows a log-log plot of yield-to-weight ratio for 33 weapons that entered the inventory from the mid 1940s to the mid 1980s. Early devices gave ratios of yield-to-weight (weapon) of about 0.005 to 0.01% kilotons of yield per kilogram. By the mid-1980s, the ratio had reached 0.05 to 0.1% for tactical weapons of 10 to 20 KT yield and 1% to 2% in larger strategic weapons of 200 KT to several MT yield. Over the period, weapon size had shrunk dramatically.

A less obvious impact of tritium use is on device safety. It is paramount that a device be a dud if the HE is accidentally detonated in a fire or an inadvertent impact. That is, if any one point of the high explosive detonates, the asymmetric implosion should cause no nuclear yield. A number of devices used mechanical schemes for safing. As commented above, the use of tritium in the primaries of weapons permits the designer to attain useful yields with less fissionable material than otherwise needed. This has the consequence of significantly increasing the margin of safety for asymmetric implosions, in many cases doing away with the need for ancillary mechanical contrivances.

Were tritium production for weapons to cease, a shortage of tritium would tend to reduce weapon yields overall and, in time, would impact the viability of boosted primaries. Section 3.4 notes several options in the short term for stretching the supply of tritium and minimizing the impact on the weapons inventory. Section 6.2 notes that given time (and resources), weapon redesign could partially offset the effects by introducing more fissionable material to compensate for less tritium—hardly a desirable outcome in view of the massive testing program which undoubtedly would be required.

Finally, tritium is used in the "zipper," a small plasma-driven device to produce a burst of neutrons. As the implosion takes place, the injection of neutrons from a zipper at the moment of optimal criticality begins the chain reaction at a time that results in maximum yield from the device. This points to a constraint with plutonium. Some isotopes, notably ^{240}Pu, undergo radioactive decay that is accompanied by the release of a neutron. If such isotopes are present in sufficient quantity with the ^{239}Pu, the neutrons from decay may initiate the chain reaction after the core has become prompt-critical but before the compression has reached an optimum density. This pre-initiation is a random phenomenon and can result in an unpredictable (lower) yield. Thus, the percentage of ^{240}Pu in weapon materials must be limited, which has given rise to various "grades" of plutonium. So-called weapons-grade nominally has 6% ^{240}Pu, super-weapons-grade 3%, fuel-grade 7 to 19%, and reactor-grade >19%.

Section 1.2 and Appendix A2 estimate the nuclear materials that could be made surplus as a result of prospective arms control. The publicly available literature suggests that modern nuclear explosive devices employ some 4 to 6 kg of weapons-grade plutonium in a primary core and about 15 to 25 Kg of HEU in a secondary. Thus, for the purpose of estimates, this paper adopts the following, admittedly oversimplified model of weapons in the inventory: (1) single stage weapons with a Pu core of 4.5 to 5 kg; (2) two stage weapons with a Pu primary of 4.5 to 5 kg and a secondary core of 20 to 25 kg HEU. This nominal value for plutonium is consistent with the information in Section 3.1 of the estimated amount of weapons-grade Pu divided by the estimated number of nuclear warheads. The corresponding comparison for HEU is less definitive.

A3.2 Types of Nuclear Reactors

This section discusses nuclear reactors in two broad classes: thermal reactors, which depend upon a moderator to thermalize the neutrons in order to take advantage of the large fission cross section of ^{235}U or ^{239}Pu at low neutron energy; and fast reactors, which depend upon the fast neutron fission cross sections and breed ^{239}Pu with ^{238}U (or ^{233}U with ^{232}Th).

Thermal Reactors[1,13]

Light Water Moderated Reactors (PWRs and BWRs). The civilian reactor market in the US, Europe, and other nations is dominated by the light-water-moderated reactor (LWR). A modern LWR operates with LEU, typically 3% to 3.5%, and comes in two variations: (a) pressurized water reactors (PWRs), which employ a secondary steam circuit to drive the turbines; and (b) boiling water reactors (BWRs), which use only a single water-steam circuit. As of late 1989, the U.S. had about 109 large LWRs in operation, the U.S.S.R. about 24 large PWRs.

The LWR fuel consists of pellets of sintered UO_2 of low enrichment sealed inside long zircalloy tubes which are arranged in large fuel rod assemblies. Alternatively, the fuel pellets could be made of mixed U-Pu oxide. Typically, 1/3 of the fuel assemblies in an LWR are replaced during the annual shutdown—namely, those assemblies that have the highest burn-up and, thus, which have the least fissionable material remaining and have acquired the most neutron-absorbing artificial isotopes. As a rule-of-thumb, about 900 kg fissionable is required in the fresh fuel assembly for a 1,000 MW_{el} LWR; in comparison, the spent fuel assembly still retains about 390 kg of fissionable material.[1]

The characteristics of the ordinary water moderator results in a "tightly coupled" core that operates neutronically as a single unit. Compared to heavy water- or graphite-moderated reactors, this type of core is not as flexible for production of weapons-grade materials, especially since the reactor must be shut down for batch refueling. But LWRs could be used for such a purpose if needed. An LWR can readily be controlled. Loss of coolant, however, would cause a severe accident, so a complex emergency core cooling system is added to the basic water-steam system to cope with possible emergencies. Commercial LWRs currently range to more than a 1,200 MW$_{el}$ with thermal efficiencies limited to about 33% by the water-steam pressure characteristics.

The original design in the U.S. evolved from one developed by the U.S. Navy for submarines and surface ships. Several factors—the desire for a compact power plant, a need to operate for long periods at sea without refueling, and an ability accommodate a wide range of operating conditions—dictated use of an undermoderated, high power density HEU core. Currently, some 165 reactors are used on naval vessels—about 35 on ballistic missile submarines, about 95 on attack submarines, and the remainder on surface vessels. Also, the Navy has about nine more at land bases for development and test programs and for training crews.

<u>Heavy Water Moderated Reactors (HWRs and PHWRs)</u>. Heavy water is the best of the moderators in terms of its neutron economy, as was discussed in Section 3.1. The control characteristics of a HWR can be excellent. Heavy water has such low neutron absorption that an HWR can even be designed to sustain a chain reaction with natural uranium, which could permit plutonium production without requiring uranium enrichment. The U.S. has operated HWRs for many years at Savannah River, GA, for production of weapons-grade plutonium and tritium. The Canadian AEC developed a technology for operating such a reactor with pressure tubes for the fuel and coolant, i.e., a PHWR, which separates the coolant from the moderator and which gives fairly good thermal efficiency. This PHWR under the name CANDU (CANadian Deuterium uranium) has been deployed in Canada and marketed overseas in sizes up to 600 MW$_{el}$.

Compared to an LWR, a HWR has a relatively larger core with more widely spaced fuel rods to allow for moderation. HWRs have been in use since the earliest days of nuclear energy, although heavy water itself is a major production challenge. A HWR offers great flexibility of operation. Online removal and replacement of fuel rods can be carried out while the reactor is in operation, and different types and constitutions of fuel rods can be placed in various regions of the core. In the CANDU, the core lies on its side; two fuel charge machines, one on either end of the core, insert/replace the small fuel rod bundles on a programmed schedule or as required by the operator.

The CANDU units have proved popular in a number of developing nations because reactor control is fairly straightforward and the size range fits the needs of their electrical power grids. Because of the capability to refuel online in a semicontinuous fashion, the IAEA and the Canadian AEC developed a special safeguards regime that the Canadian government requires be implemented as a condition of sale. (See Section 3.)

<u>Liquid Cooled Graphite Moderated Reactors (LGRs)</u>. The design approach of LGRs has not varied a great deal since this type of reactor was developed in the early days of nuclear energy, although many technological improvements have been introduced, and the practical size has increased a great deal. The typical design is rectangular comprising many large blocks of pure graphite, which are

penetrated by control rods and by long fuel assemblies through which water is circulated as a coolant. Graphite is intermediate between ordinary and heavy water in its neutron moderation characteristics with the result that a typical LGR is relatively larger than an LWR of the same power rating. The large graphite mass can serve effectively as an heat sink although a thermal instability can exist, as discussed below.

The typical LGR is neutronically large. That is, the neutron migration length is small compared to the overall core dimensions, a situation that results in a loosely coupled core. Various regions of a core can be configured quite independently of other regions; for example, in a large unit of 1200 MW_{el} as many as 12 to 24 distinct regions of the core can be configured and reconfigured with rods inserted and removed while the reactor operates. This characteristic offers great flexibility for production reactors although it complicates the trimming of the characteristics by the operator.

The U.K., the US, and the U.S.S.R. have employed LGRs for many years to produce weapons-grade plutonium. As discussed in Appendix A4, the U.S. operated 9 LGRs at Hanford, WA, all of which are now shut down; the U.S.S.R. acknowledges 13, of which 5 are said to be shut down. The U.S.S.R. also operates about 15 RBMK-type LGRs of 1000 MW_{el} or more, like those at Chernobyl, for civilian power production. In the RBMK, the fuel rod bundles are vertical, and a machine on top of the core conducts the fuel removal and replacement. This online refueling capability complicates somewhat the safeguards regime that would be required in the U.S.S.R. in conjunction with a cutoff of fissionable material production for weapons.

Due to the graphite moderator, an LGR uses less enrichment than is typical of LWRs. Slightly enriched uranium (SEU) at about 1% ^{235}U was used for the fuel/target rods for the Hanford N-Reactor, and the Soviet RBMKs use 1.8 to 2.4%. However, depending on the enrichment and the control rod configuration, an LGR can exhibit a tendency to local temperature instability that complicates control. That is, an LGR has a positive void coefficient—which means that reactivity increases if a steam bubble develops in the water coolant—and the moderator temperature coefficient of reactivity is also positive. In addition, reactors with graphite blocks that have been in place for a long time without thermal annealing have exhibited localized thermal releases, which produced graphite fires that were hard to extinguish. Thus, LGRs have seen limited deployment for civilian applications except in the U.S.S.R. The Soviet military production reactors are reported to be similar to the civilian RBMKs only smaller.

<u>High Temperature Gas Cooled Reactors (HTGRs)</u>. The thermal efficiency of water-moderated reactors is limited by the temperature to which the coolant can be raised, i.e., by pressurization. The HTGR employs helium gas as a coolant, permitting high temperatures and thermal efficiency approaching 40%. Typical designs of a commercial unit use hexagonal blocks of graphite as the moderator, each block with small coated pellets combining fissionable and fertile material,

typically HEU for the fissionable component and thorium for the fertile component. The total core mass is a good deal higher than for water-moderated reactors because of the relatively larger mass of graphite required for thermalization. For civilian applications long burn-up of the pellets results in fairly efficient use of the fissionable material even without reprocessing. Because of their excellent thermal efficiency and their inherent safety features if the helium coolant is inadvertently lost, HTGRs are a candidate for next-generation power reactors.

Fast Reactors[1,13]

As discussed in Section A3.1 the neutronics of fast reactors is quite favorable for breeding plutonium using the ^{238}U-^{239}Pu cycle; a CR of 1.4 is achievable. The typical designs use a core with fuel rods containing ^{239}Pu or uranium enriched to >20% ^{235}U in the central portion of the rod. For efficient breeding, the fertile ^{238}U is placed at either end of the rod and in a "blanket" of rods surrounding the core. Fast neutrons that leak from the central regions of the core are captured in the ^{238}U blankets, thereby breeding more ^{239}Pu that is recovered periodically by reprocessing the fuel.

The core of a fast breeder requires a more highly enriched fuel than a thermal reactor because of the lower fast neutron cross section. This leads to compact core designs that operate at high power density, requiring an efficient coolant. Liquid metal, in particular liquid sodium, has been the coolant of choice for most of the nations' programs because of its low neutron absorption, low moderation, and good thermal conduction. However, the use of such a coolant has required the solution of practical engineering problems and has resulted in relatively high reactor costs. Also, considerable investment is required for the reprocessing step to close a breeder fuel cycle. Nevertheless, HEU represents a feasible alternative fuel to start a breeder cycle.

Fast breeder development has been pursued for many years by the U.S, U.K., France, F.R.G., Japan, and the U.S.S.R. France has an active program centered on the Super-Phenix reactor and the related fuel-cycle facilities. Japan is actively engaged in development, construction and test of fast breeder prototypes. In the U.S., the only working prototype is located at the Idaho Falls reservation, and there are no plans for additional prototypes in the near future. The U.S.S.R. on the other hand, is constructing a series of prototype breeders in the several hundred megawatt range. The possibility of a future fast breeder fuel cycle must be considered in evaluating a safeguards regime for the civilian nuclear fuel cycle, as discussed in Section 5 and Appendix A5.

A3.3 The Components of the Nuclear Fuel cycle
The Front End of the Fuel Cycle[1]

Mining, Extraction, and Conversion. Natural uranium is found in about 4 ppm of the earth's surface, but the fissionable isotope ^{235}U occurs only in low concentration, about 0.7%. Much of the natural uranium is widespread in low grade ores that are not economical to process at the current level of demand. In the U.S., the principal deposits are located in the Colorado Plateau covering portions of several states. Other large deposits occur in Eastern Europe, Africa, the Soviet Union, China, and Australia. The ore is mined in both open pit and underground operations. Subsequent extraction at the mill consists of crushing the ore, followed by chemical dissolution and physical separation of the uranium portion, and finally consolidation of the product, U_3O_8, called "yellowcake." After milling, the yellowcake typically is converted to uranium hexafluoride, UF_6, which is readily volatilized for enrichment and is suitable for storage.

Uranium mines in the U.S. and U.S.S.R. are in many, widely dispersed locations. In 1979, 362 underground and open pit mines were still operating in the U.S. By 1983, that number is reported to have declined to 110 due to reduced demand. The number of uranium mills, which process and concentrate the ore, are much fewer in number. The larger mills, numbering some two dozen in the U.S., are recognizable their large piles of leached ore tailings. Perhaps another 15 to 20 mills of smaller scale in the U.S. recover uranium by solution mining or as a by-product of other mining operations, e.g., phosphate extraction.

Isotope Enrichment.[14] The means for isotope separation depend upon small differences in physical properties that are due to the slight differences in mass among the isotopes. Three methods—thermal diffusion, centrifuge and jet nozzle, and laser-induced separation—are useful for production-scale separation of fissionable isotopes and, thus, for enrichment of uranium. The method originally used in the U.S. in the early 1940s employed magnetic isotope separation accomplished with a great many mass spectrometers, called Calutrons.[15] Because of the inefficiency of that process, a huge plant was required and a prodigious amount of electricity was used to produce enough HEU for the first nuclear weapons. The method was displaced by thermal diffusion and passed into the history books until the recent revelation of the attempted use of Calutrons by Iraq, brought to light in 1991 in the aftermath of the Persian Gulf War.

Production-scale plants can be used to produce two classes of output: (1) SEU or LEU for ordinary reactor fuel, or (2) HEU for weapons or for naval and certain research reactors. Since a typical enrichment plant can produce a few tonnes of HEU per month, enough for many nuclear weapons, such plants pose significant safeguards issues. The technologies are described below. The U.S. plants are outlined in Section A4, and their safeguards issues are discussed in Sections 2 and 3. Section 3 also includes a discussion of safeguards for the European centrifuge facilities.

Separative Work measures the work expended in achieving the separation into tails and product. The Separative Work Unit (SWU) is the amount of work per unit mass of product at a particular product assay, typically referenced to a 0.2% tails assay; a more useful unit is the MSWU per 1,000 kilogram (or metric tonne) of product. A useful table of values for concentrations ranging from 0.20% to 98.0% is given in NWDv2.[14]

Thermal Diffusion — The earliest practical enrichment technology, which was employed at Oak Ridge starting in the mid 1940s and later in the U.S.S.R., depends on the slightly different diffusion rates of gaseous $^{235}UF_6$ and $^{238}UF_6$ through special porous barriers under high pressure. Since each stage in a thermal diffusion process achieves a slight change in the mass ratio of the isotopic constituents, a countercurrent recycle cascade uses thousands of successive stages in each of which a number of units are connected in parallel. Due to conservation of mass, the largest number of units per stage are required at ^{235}U concentrations close to the natural abundance of the feed (0.7%), with successively less units in parallel as the enrichment increases or decreases from that value. Below the natural abundance of the starting material, a stripping or "bottoming" section recovers ^{235}U down to a residual concentration of 0.2 to 0.25% in the tailings. The stages in the enriching section raise the concentration to about 3 to 3.5% ^{235}U for commercial LWRs. For HEU additional stages in a "topping cycle" raise the ^{235}U concentration to the 93.5% used for weapons or the 97.3% used for U.S. naval reactor fuel. Typical thermal diffusion plants are massive, occupying thousands of acres, and are prodigious users of electricity. The three plants in the U.S. are aging and expensive to maintain and operate; the plant at Oak Ridge, TN, has been shut down since 1985.

Centrifuge and Jet Nozzle — Another practical method depends on slightly different rates of separation of the isotopes in an high speed gas centrifuge[16] or gasses expanding at high pressure in a jet nozzle or helikon structure. Gas centrifuge technology became practical at production scale in the 1970s with development of precision long-life bearings and special high strength steel to withstand the centrifugal force. Each unit in a modern gas centrifuge stage achieves a much greater change in the ratio of the constituents than can be obtained in the thermal diffusion process, but the throughput per unit is much smaller. Compared to their diffusion counterparts, centrifuge plants are smaller for a given throughput, typically covering hundreds of acres, and use 100 to 400 kwh/SWU compared to 2,400 kwh/SWU. Centrifuge plants in the MSWU range are online in several European nations, and the U.S.S.R. reportedly has 10 plants of about 1 MSWU each operating or under construction. In the U.S., the DOE built the initial part of a centrifuge plant but now emphasizes laser enrichment technology for future facilities.

Atomic Vapor Laser Isotope Separation (AVLIS) — The DOE laboratories developed a new separation method driven by high power lasers that are tuned to particular spectral lines of the different isotopes in an atomic vapor. The details of the AVLIS technology remain classified, but some aspects are public information. A feed stream of uranium metal vapor is irradiated by photons from high power organic dye lasers to selectively excite/ionize the ^{235}U atoms in the vapor stream. The ions are removed from the vapor by electric fields and collected. The separation per stage is sufficiently effective that care must be taken to avoid criticality problems in the collected product. Further development is underway to improve laser reliability at high pulse rate and high energy density. In addition to AVLIS, the DOE laboratories and contractors have explored other molecular vapor and plasma separation processes that are apparently technically feasible for uranium and plutonium isotope separation.

Relative to the mature methods discussed above, laser enrichment appears to be capable of a larger change in the isotopic mass fraction per stage and has much more modest power requirements, estimated at 65 kwh/SWU. Thus, it may become possible to construct and operate a cost-effective laser enrichment plant for production-scale quantities of LEU, and eventually for HEU, in a plant of smaller size and a smaller capital investment than with the conventional methods. However, the initial use at a commercial-scale considered by the DOE is to remove the undesirable ^{240}Pu isotope to create weapons-grade material from fuel-grade or even reactor-grade plutonium. Later, the technology may lend itself to a topping enrichment cycle in a small plant, i.e., a process to convert LEU to HEU.

A pilot-scale laser enrichment demonstration plant to upgrade plutonium has been put in operation at the Lawrence Livermore National Laboratory. The DOE has proposed to build a large-scale plutonium separation plant of about 1 MSWU equivalent at the Idaho Falls reservation. Conceivably, the AVLIS technology may become the technology of choice to produce LEU efficiently in a plant of ordinary industrial size. As discussed in Section 3, these possibilities would complicate the task of discovering covert enrichment facilities. Therefore, while laser enrichment is still a specialized high technology and not yet in widespread deployment, it already has important arms control implications.

Heavy Water Production. Deuterium, Symbol D, is a stable isotope of Hydrogen. Heavy water, D_2O, exists in natural water in low concentration, about one part in 6500. The production of heavy water depends on the slight differences of D_2O and H_2O in distillation and chemical exchange processes to obtain the reactor-grade concentration of 99.75%. The U.S. and Canada have used several chemical or electrochemical schemes. For example, the U.S. facility at Savannah River, GA, uses dual-temperature hydrogen sulfide extraction combined with distillation. Sales of the CANDU reactor to a number of countries is supported by Canadian exports of heavy water under IAEA safeguards. A few heavy water production plants exist in nonnuclear-weapon states under safeguards. Yet some states, notably India and Argentina, have plants outside the IAEA safeguards regime.

Fuel Fabrication.[16] Following enrichment, the UF_6 is converted to the solid oxide, UO_2. As an option plutonium oxide can be added in low concentration to obtain a mixed oxide, either by adding and mixing separately prepared powders of the two oxides or by co-precipitating them. In either case the oxide is compressed into pellets which are loaded into fuel rods. The rods, in turn, are grouped into fuel assemblies for transportation and use in the reactor. Thus, at this stage the uranium typically exists only as LEU. In contrast, the plutonium in mixed U-Pu oxides could be separated by conventional chemical techniques rather than isotopic separation and, thus, would pose a different safeguards and security issue than merely LEU, as discussed in Section 3.2.

The Back End of the Fuel Cycle[1]

Reprocessing and Recycle.[16,17] After use in a reactor, the fuel is highly radioactive from the variety of fission products and transuranic elements produced. The fuel also contains unconsumed ^{235}U and a significant amount of fissionable plutonium produced from neutron transmutation of ^{238}U, the abundant and uranium isotope which is the diluent. For example, the fuel discharged from a 1000 MW_{el} LWR exposed to a average burn-up of 33 MW_{th}-days per kg would still contain about 390 kg of fissionable material, compared to 900 kg in the usual fresh fuel charge. Chemical reprocessing is used in the military fuel cycle to recover the plutonium and recycle the ^{235}U. For widespread commercial use, however, such recycle is far from economic compared to direct disposal of the spent fuel and would raise significant nonproliferation issues.

At a reprocessing plant the spent fuel rods are disassembled from the bundles and chopped into small pieces. These are dissolved in nitric acid, and the Purex process is used to perform the chemical extraction. A thick-walled separation facility or "canyon" is almost entirely a remote operation due to the intense radiation. An organic solvent is used to separate the nitrates of uranium, plutonium, and neptunium from the fission products cesium and strontium. Further treatments isolate the separated streams of uranyl nitrate, plutonium oxide and neptunium nitrate. (For details, see Reference 16.)

The uranyl nitrate is calcined into uranium oxide powder and shipped either back to an enrichment plant for mixing with fresh feed or to a plant for processing into metal. The plutonium oxide is processed to obtain PuF_4 which is reduced to metallic plutonium and fabricated into weapon components. Most of the other materials are stored as nuclear waste in various forms. The Purex process was developed by the U.S.A.E.C. in the 1940s and has become the industry standard. Many refinements in technology have been introduced over the years to reduce radiation exposure of employees and to increase the overall process efficiency. The U.S. has operated chemical separation plants capable of more than 2,000 tonnes/yr of spent fuel at Hanford, WA, and Savannah River, GA, and a 950 tonnes/yr plant near Idaho Falls, ID.[18] The U.S.S.R. is reported to have several plants of similar capacities. Large separation plants also exist in China, the U.K., and France. Small- to medium-scale reprocessing facilities for experimental purposes currently exist in a number of other nations.

Waste Management. Wastes are generated in abundance and variety at every stage of the fuel cycle. Much of the waste involves a low level of radioactivity and typically is handled by a province, state, or regional body, depending on the nation. Much of the waste from reprocessing, and of course the spent fuel itself, involves a high level of radioactivity, and its disposal is the focus of much public debate in the U.S. and elsewhere. This paper is not the place to examine waste management issues in any detail. One should note that reprocessing for the civilian fuel cycle is the norm only for a few European nations and Japan and, to some extent, the U.S.S.R. Most other nations, including the U.S., store the spent fuel in large water pools for cooling, planning to dispose of the spent fuel itself in licensed geologic repositories. Yet, the permanent safe disposal of the spent fuel (or the high level waste from reprocessing) remains to be demonstrated to the satisfaction of the public or their elected representatives.

Critical Fuel Cycle Processes for Arms Control

The parts of the fuel cycle of most concern are those where high enriched uranium can be produced or diverted, or where plutonium is available—not only weapons-grade plutonium but also fuel- or reactor-grade, as discussed below. The discussion here expands on that of the preceding sections for those steps that raise issues for arms control and nonproliferation.

To separate ^{235}U from natural uranium, the initial technology, the Calutron, was quickly superseded. However, the revelation in mid-1991 of Iraq's attempted use of Calutrons prompts reconsideration of the nuclear proliferation potential of that forgotten method.[15] Advances in particle accelerator technology since the 1940s, especially high current ion sources and better beam steering and control at high current densities, would result in more efficient Calutron devices. Also, a modern application could start from LEU of 3.5 to 4% ^{235}U, which would improve the overall efficiency and reduce the requirements for producing modest amounts of HEU. Perhaps, enough could be produced for a nuclear weapon per year, albeit in a large industrial-scale facility requiring significant electrical power.

Except for the inefficient Calutron process, the technology for isotope separation required the application of sophisticated technology and engineering. In any case, the effort entailed a large capital investment in plant and several years of construction. It would be difficult if not impossible for a nation to hide such a project, and the construction period would allow time for diplomatic efforts. Thus, the use of LEU for commercial LWR fuel was not only very feasible but also strategic—the ^{238}U served to "denature" the fissionable ^{235}U by posing the enrichment barrier.

The combination of high technology, large capital requirements, and diplomatic arm-twisting restrained the spread of enrichment plants for many years. The U.S. policy to allow open sale of LEU also helped deter competitors from arising. However, around 1970, the U.S.A.E.C. temporarily closed its books on the sales of LEU, and shortly thereafter, several European nations started building their own enrichment plants using the centrifuge approach. Somewhat later, South Africa built a plant to support its nuclear industry. In the late 1980s, Brazil, with help from European suppliers, gained the capability for producing HEU after almost two decades of effort developing centrifuge technology. In mid-1991, the IAEA inspections conducted after the Persian Gulf War revealed that Iraq was well along the way to implementing centrifuge enrichment. Yet, barriers inherent in the conventional isotope separation technologies are still formidable.

However, laser enrichment appears capable of achieving a much higher degree of enrichment per stage. Notwithstanding the sophistication of laser technology, in time it may enable production-scale enrichment capability on a more modest physical scale than the conventional enrichment technologies. Thus, the existing nonproliferation regime must learn to cope with laser enrichment technology or risk collapse. Sections 3 takes into account the possibility of covert HEU production with laser enrichment.

While isotopic dilution has been and may continue to be an effective tool to denature uranium, no such technical fix is possible for plutonium. Most of the plutonium isotopes are fast-neutron fissile with critical masses that are only a little greater than that for ^{239}Pu. Reference 1 lists the critical masses for mixtures of ^{239}Pu and ^{240}Pu in the alpha-phase metallic form surrounded by a thick uranium or beryllium reflector, as a function of the volume fraction of the contaminating ^{240}Pu isotope. For pure ^{239}Pu, the critical mass is listed as 4.4 kg; for 10% ^{240}Pu, 5.0 kg; for 30%, 6.7 kg. Reference 6 gives additional critical mass information for other configurations and materials.

However, plutonium that contains a significant fraction of ^{240}Pu or ^{242}Pu is far less desirable for a nuclear explosive than is nearly pure ^{239}Pu. As discussed in Section A3.1, neutrons that are randomly emitted by the other Pu isotopes lead to pre-initiation of the weapon, which results in a lower and unpredictable weapon yield. Yet, the yield of such a nonoptimal device, a dud in relative terms, might be a kiloton or more. Even if the starting material were highly radioactive, the resources of a state or even of a determined subnational group could obtain material in a matter of weeks that would hardly be ideal for a nuclear weapon but would cause great concern.

In nonnuclear-weapon states the materials from which enough plutonium for one or more weapons could be separated by chemical processes—e.g., at a mixed oxide fuel fabrication plant, at a reprocessing plant, or in transportation between plants—pose issues of safeguards and security. However, the diversion of such material at civilian facilities would be of little interest to nuclear weapon states with production plants and stockpiles of weapons-grade material. But if such states entered into an agreement to cutoff production and reduce their nuclear arsenals, then their civilian fuel-cycle facilities also would have to come under full-scale safeguards. The safeguards regime would not only be concerned for declared facilities but also for possible covert facilities.

In the early 1970s, many nations planned a large number of nuclear power plants—projections of over 1000 worldwide by the 1980s were commonplace—and had concerns about the assurance of their supply of uranium for the long term. A number of nations planned to reprocess the spent fuel from their civilian reactors and recycle the fissionable materials. After chemical separation, the recovered uranium could be recycled via an enrichment plant. The plutonium could be stored or recycled, at first into thermal reactors and later into fast (breeder) reactors. But by the late 1970s, the large projected number of power reactors was clearly groundless. Also, the world supply of uranium would last for many decades at a favorable price for the number of nuclear power plants that were likely. By the 1980s, uranium was a glut on the world market.

Moreover, the operation of prototype full-scale breeder and reprocessing facilities demonstrated that they involved much higher costs than proponents had projected during the 1960s and 1970s. Reprocessing and recycle requires a major investment in plant and trained personnel. The overall fuel cycle cost of reprocessing and recycle for thermal reactors is far from economic on an incremental cost basis. The equivalent break-even cost of uranium ore currently is some 7-15 times higher than the current market price. This cost estimate depends sensitively on assumptions about the discount rate, capital cost, operating efficiency, effective capacity, operating cost, and the lifetime of the facilities. Even where the reprocessing plants exist, the sunk-cost economics of thermal recycle is marginal if reprocessing experience is appraised realistically. The economics of a fast reactor cycle is harder to estimate since several aspects of the technology are far less mature at commercial scale. Some present estimates show that uranium ore would have to cost 2.5 to 6 times the current market price for a fast breeder cycle to become cost-effective on economics alone.

Thus, the realities of fuel-cycle economics and the concerns about nonproliferation have reinforced a "once-through" fuel cycle, i.e., one without any reprocessing and with direct disposal of the plutonium-bearing spent fuel. Indeed, Germany announced in mid-1991 that it was canceling its breeder plans, and even France has curtailed its aggressive program. The Soviet breeder program has been cut back from earlier plans to deploy several operating liquid-metal-cooled reactors of commercial scale in the 1990s; only one 600 Mw fast breeder is in operation at Beloyarski, near Kyshtym. As of mid-1991, Japan remains as the one major nation aggressively pursuing a Pu-based, fast breeder effort.

Appendix A3 Notes and References

1. (APS) "Report of the APS Study Group on Nuclear Fuel Cycles and Waste Management," *Rev. Mod. Phys.* Vol. 50, No. 1, Part II (Jan. 1978). See Ch.3, "Primer on the Nuclear Fuel Cycle."
2. John S. Foster, "Nuclear Weapons," *Encyclopedia Americana*, 20; see also articles by Hans Bethe and Edward Teller on various aspects of nuclear weapon technology.
3. (NAS1) "The Nuclear Weapons Complex: Management for Health, Safety, and the Environment" by The Committee to Provide Interim Oversite of the DOE Nuclear Weapons Complex, National Research Council (National Academy Press, December 1989) See Appendix C on "Criticality."
4. J. Carson Mark, "Nuclear Weapons," *Nuclear Proliferation and Safeguards* (Preager, NY 1977).
5. NAS1, op. cit., Appendix E "The Physics of Nuclear Weapons Design."
6. H. Paxton, Los Alamos, "Critical Mass Data," *LAMS-3067* (Los Alamos Scientific Laboratory, 1964); and H. Paxton et al., "Critical Dimensions of Systems Containing ^{235}U, ^{239}Pu, and ^{233}U," *TID-7028*, (Oak Ridge National Laboratory, 1964).
7. For a history, see R. Rhodes, *The Making of the Atomic Bomb*, (Simon & Schuster, 1986).
8. (NWDv1) T. Cochran, W. Arkin, R. Norris, and M. Hoenig, "Nuclear Weapons Databook", Vol. I, U.S. *Nuclear Forces and Capabilities* (Ballinger, 1984).
9. (NWDv2) T. Cochran, W. Arkin, R. Norris, and M. Hoenig, *Nuclear Weapons Databook*, Vol. II "U.S. Nuclear Warhead Production" (Ballinger, 1987). See also, (NWDv3) T. Cochran, W. Arkin, R. Norris, and M. Hoenig, "Nuclear Weapons Databook," Vol. III *U.S. Nuclear Warhead Facility Profiles* (Ballinger, 1987).
10. (NWDv4) T. Cochran, W. Arkin, R. Norris, and J. Sands, "Nuclear Weapons Databook," Vol. IV *Soviet Nuclear Weapons* (Ballinger, 1989).
11. Testimony of R. Wagner, Assistant to the Sec. of Defense (Atomic Energy) before the House Appropriations Committee, 1985 (*EWDA*, Part 6, p.118). See also testimony of C. Weinberger, Sec. of Defense, before the Senate Armed Services Committee, Hearings on the FY85 DOD Budget, Part 1, p. 123. See the discussion in the "Nuclear Weapons Databook," Vol. IV.
12. NWDv1, op. cit., p. 36.
13. APS, op. cit., Chapter 8 "Advanced Fuel Cycles."
14. NWDv2, op. cit., pp. 82-90 and Chapter 5. Note the table of conversions on p. 127.
15. For information and background see D. Albright and M. Hibbs, "Iraq's Nuclear Hide-and-Seek," *Bulletin of the Atomic Scientists*, September 1991, pp. 14-23.
16. APS, op.cit., Chapter 4 "Reprocessing and Recycle."
17. NAS1, op. cit., Appendix D "Plutonium."
18. NAS1, op.cit., See especially Appendix B on "The DOE Nuclear Weapons Complex."

A4 The Military Nuclear Fuel Cycle and Facilities

The process flow from uranium ore to weapons-grade plutonium, HEU and tritium (plus waste products) is briefly reviewed in this appendix for the U.S. and Soviet military production complexes. Because of the meager public information on Soviet production facilities and operations, Section 3 uses the U.S. production complex as a generic model to assess the feasibility and verification issues of a four-step control framework compared to other approaches.[1-3] This appendix provides support for that assessment.

A4.1. The U.S. Production Complex

For the Department of Energy (DOE) production complex extensive information is summarized in a report by a National Academy of Sciences Committee, *The Nuclear Weapons Complex*,[4] (*NAS1*), as well as in the *Nuclear Weapons Databook, Vol. II, US Nuclear Warhead Production*[5] (*NWDv2*) and in *Vol. III, US Nuclear Warhead Facility Profiles*[6] (*NWDv3*) with references to the original sources. Figure A4-1 shows a functional diagram of the fissionable materials flows for the DOE complex. A few facilities outlined below may not be directly involved in a production cutoff but conceivably could be sites in which to hide covert production facilities and activities, as discussed in Section 3.3.

Hanford, WA

<u>Production Reactors</u>. The original eight graphite-moderated production reactors (designated B, D, F, H, DR, C, KE, and KW) have been shut down, and decommissioning is in progress or has been completed. Only the N-Reactor could potentially be operable. This reactor is a 4,000 MW_{th} graphite channel design that started operation in late 1963 and could produce about 750 Kg. per year of weapons-grade Pu at the design capacity factor of 60%. Currently, the N-Reactor is in cold shut down following a review of safety issues related to the aging of the facility and the adequacy of its safety systems. In addition to the dedicated production reactors, the site also contains the Fast Flux Test Facility (FFTF) which is a 400 MW_{th} sodium-cooled fast reactor originally designed to support breeder reactor R&D and currently used for testing a variety of fuels and materials.

<u>Chemical Separation Plant</u>. Four separation plants (designated T, B, U, and REDOX) have been shut down for many years. The PUREX plant was operated from 1955 to 1972 and then was reactivated in 1983 to recover plutonium from the irradiated fuel from the N-Reactor. The maximum capacity is 2,300 MT/yr.

<u>Support Facilities</u>. (1) UO_3 Plant for conversion of uranium nitrate from the separation plant to uranium oxide for shipment; (2) a Fuel Fabrication Facility for fabrication of reactor elements from SEU Billets, and The Plutonium Finishing Plant for Pu processing and scrap recovery; (3) waste facilities for fractionation, encapsulation, storage, and decontamination.

Savannah River, SC

Production Reactors. Five heavy-water-moderated production reactors (designated R, P, L, K, and C) were constructed in the 1950s, capable of operation nominally at about 2,000-2,200 MW$_{th}$ for production of plutonium and about 2,400 MW$_{th}$ for production of tritium. Three remain operable. Recently, these reactors were forced to operate at reduced power and then temporarily shut down following a review of safety issues.

Chemical Separation Plant. Two large separation facilities (designated F and H) recover and separate plutonium, neptunium (for ^{238}Pu production) and uranium from irradiated targets using the PUREX process or its modifications; the nominal capacity of the F facility is 2,700 MT/yr. Also, the site has a tritium facility for processing the Al-^{6}Li targets and separating, purifying and packaging tritium.

Support Facilities. (1) Fuel & Target Fabrication Facility, to fabricate driver fuel assemblies of high-enriched uranium alloys, with target assemblies either of depleted uranium for plutonium production or of aluminum-lithium alloy for tritium production; (2) Heavy Water Plant first operated in 1952 with a original capacity of 450 to 480 MT/yr, which was partially dismantled in stages and units retired to a capacity of only 90 MT/yr when operation was terminated in 1982; (3) miscellaneous tanks and other facilities to store/dispose of the nuclear wastes.

Idaho Falls, ID

Reactors. A variety of experimental reactors are located at the Idaho National Engineering Laboratory. The Advanced Test Reactor (ATR) at 250MW$_{th}$, and perhaps the Experimental Breeder Reactor (EBR-II) at 62.5MW$_{th}$ with its associated reprocessing facility, are potentially pertinent to a cutoff. Also, the Navy maintains a training center for submarine crews with several reactors of modest capability.

Chemical Separation Plant. A separation plant (ICPP) is in operation to recover HEU from the spent fuel from the Navy submarine reactors. The current capacity is about 950 MT/yr, which is projected to double in the 1990s.

Waste Facilities. (1) ICPP Waste Storage and Calcining Facilities, to store and process high-level waste from the separation facility; Fluorinel Dissolution Process and Storage Facility (FAST) to receive, store, and perform head-end chemical dissolution of a variety of Navy Fuels; (3) CPP Fuel Storage Facility, a water-filled basin for spent fuel from EBR-II, the Naval reactors, and experimental programs.

Oak Ridge, TN

Gaseous Diffusion Enrichment Plant. The large plant at ORNL is housed in five buildings and has a capability of 7.7 million SWU/year. The plant is restricted to a maximum enrichment of about 4% and has been placed on stand-by.

Centrifuge Demonstration Facility. A small facility, to demonstrate the SET III technology planned for installation at Portmouth, is shut down.

Y-12 Plant. The plant has extensive facilities for material processing and component fabrication for the weapons production complex and for civilian DOE R&D programs. Also, the Lithium Enrichment Facility is on stand-by ORNL

Paducah, KY

Gaseous Diffusion Enrichment Plant. This large plant with 11.3 million SWU /year is optimized for stripping from natural uranium or intermediate tails (0.3-0.7%) from other plants and acts as the bottom stage to feed the ORNL and Portsmouth plants. The normal output is 0.9-1% enrichment.

Portsmouth, OH

Gaseous Diffusion Enrichment Plant. This large plant with 8.3 million SWU/year is the only U.S. enrichment plant in which to produce intermediate-EU and HEU (93.5% ^{235}U). The plant has only periodic operation at present.

Centrifuge Enrichment Plant. The plant was canceled after 1st process building was completed and the first train of 0.144 million SWU/year was tested.

Livermore. CA

Special Isotope Separation Laboratory. Based on the AVLIS technology developed at LLNL, a prototype facility scheduled for operation beginning in 1988.

Fernald, OH

Feed Materials Production Center. As a main input the gaseous UF_6 is converted first to the "green salt" UF_4 and then to metallic form. The plant has extensive facilities for processing a variety of uranium feed materials, including ore concentrates and recycle scrap for other DOE operations, that consist of depleted or slightly enriched uranium. The output can make several forms for distribution to the Ashtabula, Hanford, Savannah River, Paducah and Portmouth facilities.

Ashtabula, OH

Extrusion Plant. This small plant extrudes uranium tubes and billets using depleted or slightly enriched ingots from the Fernald, OH, facility.

Mound Facility, Miamisburg, OH

Tritium Recovery Facility. This is a small facility for recovery of tritium from nuclear weapons components.

A4.2. The Soviet Production Complex

The Soviet production complex is regarded as comparable to that of the U.S., based on what meager literature is publicly available about Soviet nuclear materials production plus rough estimates of total plutonium and HEU based on information about Soviet weapon systems. Until recently, the principal source of public information was the *Nuclear Weapons Databook, Vol. IV, Soviet Nuclear Weapons*[7] (*NWDv4*). Several of the Soviet production reactors are of a heavy-water-moderated type of several hundred megawatts capacity, presumably similar in operation to those at the U.S. Savannah River facility. Several other Soviet production reactors are of a graphite-moderated type also having a capacity of several hundred megawatts, similar to but smaller than the large Soviet commercial RBMK-type reactors discussed in Appendix A3.

In 1989, the DOE congressional testimony[8] cited 14 reactors dedicated to production of weapons-grade plutonium. On October 25, 1989, Soviet officials[9] acknowledged 13 such reactors still in production at that time. Five of these, located in a closed area called Chelyabinsk-40 near Kyshtym in the Ural mountains, were the subject of a mid 1989 visit[10] by a party of U.S. congressional members and two physicists. Information in *NWDv4* on the Chelyabinsk-40 complex, including pictures taken by the French SPOT satellite, has been updated by a Fact Sheet[10] released after the 1989 visit and a more complete description[11] published in May 1991 by the two physics in the party.

NWDv4 briefly summarizes[12,13] the public information prior to the mid-1989 visit: "Plutonium production for weapons takes place at at least four sites: the Kyshtym complex . . . Dodonovo, on the Yenisey river just north of Krasnoyarsk in Siberia; The 'Siberian Plant' reported to be located near Troitsk or Tomsk; and Beloyarskiy, near Sverdlovsk just north of Kyshtym. . . . Kyshtym and Dodonovo are believed to be sites of dedicated plutonium production reactors. The Siberian Plant and Beloyarskiy are dual purpose reactors used for the production of plutonium and electricity. Nothing further is known about the Dodonovo facility other than that it is probably the site of Soviet tritium production. . . . There can be little doubt that the primary function of the Siberian power station [completed in 1958] is the production of plutonium for weapons . . . In 1964 it was reported that the station had exceeded its design capacity of 600 MW_{el}. . . . Beloyarskiy is the site of two graphite-moderated, channel reactors which began operation in 1964 and 1967 respectively. These reactors are reportedly used periodically to fulfill shortfalls in plutonium production."

The change in the picture after the 1989 visit and the present state of confusion about the number of production reactors can be gained by comparing the above citation from *NWDv4* to the more recent summary in Reference 11; for example: "Prior to 1987, there were 14 production reactors at these sites. Between 1987 and December 31, 1989, seven were shut down. That leaves a single heavy-water reactor operating at Chelyabinsk-40 and three reactors, also believed to be of the heavy-water type, at Dodonovo, as well as three graphite reactors at Tomsk. The Soviets announced in October 1989 that they planned to shut down all plutonium-producing reactors by the year 2000—presumably including the three Tomsk reactors. But this leaves ambiguous the status of the four heavy-water reactors, which are believed to be dedicated to tritium production."[11]

The Chelyabinsk-40 and Tomsk facilities include a large chemical separation plant—presumably using a process like PUREX discussed in the US literature—a fuel fabrication plant, plus facilities for storing spent fuel and high level waste from reprocessing. Also, a 600 Megawatt liquid-metal-cooled fast breeder reactor is in operation at Beloyarski, near Kyshtym.[11] This breeder, like three others planned/under construction at an earlier time, was slated for operation on plutonium-based fuel but is said to be operating on HEU at present. The Fact Sheet points out that in 1978 the Kyshtym chemical separation facility shifted from processing military production reactor fuel to processing fuel from Soviet 440 MWe LWRs (VVER-type) and naval reactors. Also, the literature[7,11] implies possible chemical separation plants at sites other than those at Kyshtym and Tomsk.

Reference 11 provides a brief account of production reactors at two other sites: the Siberian Atomic Power Station located near Tomsk, sometimes referred to as Tomsk-7; and facilities at a site near Dodonovo, a Siberian town close to Krasnoyarsk. Also, the commercial RBMK-type reactors conduct on-line refueling, as discussed in Appendix A3. Thus, they could lend themselves to the short burnup requirements of weapons-grade plutonium production, i.e., to minimize ^{240}Pu contamination. Whether these commercial reactors coming online since the mid-1970s have been used extensively for such a purpose is not well known based on the public literature; NWDv4 makes a rough estimate of their possible production.[14] For the total Soviet production of weapons-grade plutonium, Reference 11 makes an estimate using "assumptions based on intelligent guesses," which is stated to be on the order of 115 to 140 tonnes.

In addition, the U.S.S.R. has several large facilities for uranium enrichment. NWDv4 gives a brief description of the history of the Soviet uranium mining and enrichment and identifies a major enrichment facility located at Verkhniy-Neyvinskiy in the Ural mountains and the likelihood of another of a similar type, referred to as the "Siberian Plant," now thought to be near Tomsk.[16] NWDv4 suggests that both plants are the gaseous diffusion type of 7-10 MSWU/yr capacity, which have operated for many years. The 1989 Fact Sheet[10] names a third site for enrichment at Angarsk and implies that the Soviets are shifting enrichment from gaseous diffusion to centrifuge technology. The total capacity of the latter type is reported to be about 10 MSWU/yr at perhaps 1 MSWU/yr per plant, presumably to support the growing number of large commercial LWRs. About 24 such reactors are online for electricity production as of mid 1989. Beyond this sketchy account, public information on the location, capacity, and total production of Soviet enrichment facilities is unavailable.

497

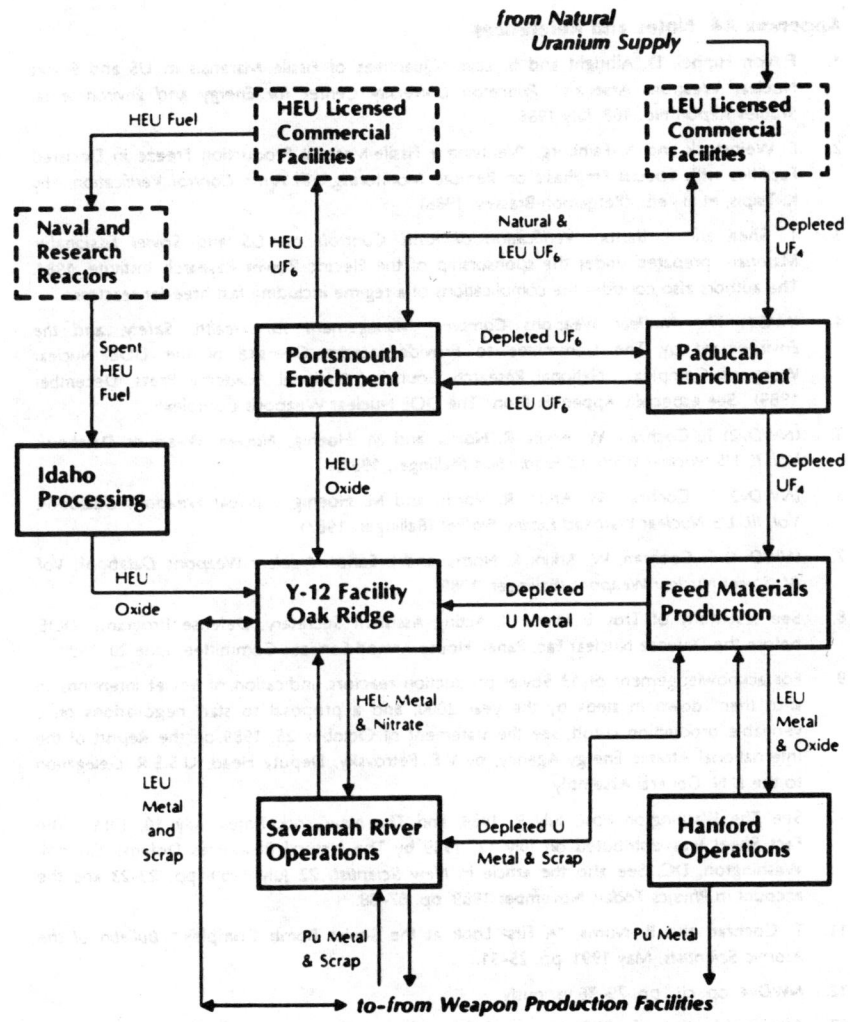

Figure A4-1   Flows of Fissionable Materials in the DOE Production Complex

Appendix A4 Notes and References

1. F. von Hippel, D. Albright and B. Levi, "Quantities of Fissile Materials in US and Soviet Nuclear Weapons Arsenals," *Princeton University Center for Energy and Environmental Studies Report* No. 168, July 1986.
2. E. Weinstock and A. Fainberg, "Verifying a Fissile-Material Production Freeze in Declared Facilities with Special Emphasis on Remote Monitoring," in *Arms Control Verification*, by K. Tsipis, et al., ed., (Pergamon-Brassey, 1986)
3. T. Shea and J. Barton, *Verification of Arms Controls on US and Soviet Fissionable Materials*, prepared under the sponsorship of the Electric Power Research Institute, 1984. The authors also consider the complications of a regime including fast breeder reactors.
4. (NAS1) *The Nuclear Weapons Complex: Management for Health, Safety, and the Environment* by The Committee to Provide Interim Oversite of the DOE Nuclear Weapons Complex, National Research Council (National Academy Press, December 1989). See especially Appendix B on "The DOE Nuclear Weapons Complex"
5. (NWDv2) T. Cochran, W. Arkin, R. Norris, and M. Hoenig, *Nuclear Weapons Databook, Vol. II, US Nuclear Warhead Production* (Ballinger, 1987).
6. (NWDv3) T. Cochran, W. Arkin, R. Norris, and M. Hoenig, *Nuclear Weapons Databook, Vol. III, US Nuclear Warhead Facility Profiles* (Ballinger, 1987)
7. (NWDv4) T. Cochran, W. Arkin, R. Norris, and J. Sands, *Nuclear Weapons Databook, Vol. IV, Soviet Nuclear Weapons* (Ballinger, 1989)
8. See testimony of Troy E. Wade II, Acting Assistant Secretary, Defense Programs, DOE, before the Defense Nuclear Fac. Panel, House Armed Services Committee, June 20, 1989
9. For acknowledgement of 13 Soviet production reactors, indication of Soviet intentions to shut them down in steps by the year 2000, and a proposal to start negotiations on a verifiable production cutoff, see the statement of October 25, 1989 on the Report of the International Atomic Energy Agency, by V.F. Petrovsky, Deputy Head, U.S.S.R. Delegation to the U.N. General Assembly.
10. See *The Washington Post*, July 9, 1989, and *The New York Times*, July 10, 1989. The Fact Sheet was distributed on July 12, 1989 by The Natural Resources Defense Council, Washington, DC. See also the article in *New Scientist*, 22 July 1989. pp. 22-23 and the account in *Physics Today*, November 1989, pp. 87-88.
11. T. Cochran and R. Norris, "A First Look at the Soviet Bomb Complex," *Bulletin of the Atomic Scientists*, May 1991, pp. 25-31.
12. NWDv4, op. cit., pp. 79-86 variously
13. After publication of NWDv4, one of the authors learned that the "Siberian" plant is at Tomsk and that the small commercial graphite-moderated reactor at Beloyarskiy is not part of the regular production complex. (T. Cochran - Private Comm.)
14. NWDv4, op. cit., pp. 86
15. NWDv4, op. cit., pp. 90-94

controls agreed upon by the superpowers could impact the effectiveness of the present nonproliferation regime.

The history of proposals by the superpowers to control their fissile weapons resources reflects an unfortunate pattern. Starting with the Baruch Plan in the mid-1940s, U.S. proposals were dismissed by the Soviets as unwarranted interference in their internal affairs or merely legalized espionage. Early proposals sometimes were linked to other initiatives, such as the U.S. proposals for a test ban, and the Soviet proposals for comprehensive disarmament. Yet, the proposals often contained useful elements. On several occasions, the UN/IAEA was proposed as a repository for fissile weapons materials, usually in conjunction with a phase-down or cutoff of materials production. The following list illustrates some notable proposals by governments, private individuals, and groups:[8]

- Dec. 1953   Eisenhower "Atoms for Peace" address features ". . . contribution of uranium and other fissionable material to the UN/IAEA . . . ."[9]
- Mar. 1956   Address followed up in a letter (Eisenhower to Bulganin) proposes a verified fissionable materials production cutoff.
- Mar. 1957   U.S. Proposal to the U.N. General Assembly features future fissile materials production for nonweapons only;[10] U.S. links proposal to Test Ban;[11] U.S.S.R. insists on larger disarmament package.[12]
- July 1957   France proposes detailed production cutoff.[13]
- 1958-1959   Production cutoff becomes the centerpiece of U.S. initiatives.[14] U.S.S.R. proposes General Comprehensive Disarmament.[15]
- Sep. 1960   Eisenhower proposes to the U.N. General Assembly transferring 30 tons of ^{235}U to peaceful uses plus a progressive weapons-material production shutdown.
- Sep. 1961   Kennedy proposes a ban on fissionable weapon material production as part of disarmament plan.[16] Other initiatives are emphasized.
- Mar. 1962   Rusk proposes transfer of 50 tons of ^{235}U to peaceful uses.
- Aug. 1962   U.K. makes detailed technical proposal involving verification of past weapons-material production.[17]
- 1963-1964   After Limited Test Ban Treaty (LTBT) signature, U.S. proposes "unequal" transfers of ^{235}U (40 tons vs. 60 tons).
- Jan. 1964   Johnson announces unilateral cuts (25% of ^{235}U and shutdown of four production reactors).
- Apr. 1964   U.S., U.K., and U.S.S.R. jointly announce reductions in rates of fissionable weapons-material production.[18]

- 1965 U.S. adds "demonstrated destruction" of nuclear weapons to earlier proposals on cutoff and transfers.

- Aug. 1966 Ms. Myrdal (Sweden) proposes all nations cease producing fissionable materials for weapons by July 1, 1967.

- Dec. 1967 U.S. and U.K. offer to accept IAEA inspection of all their civilian nuclear reactors.[19]

- 1966-1968 Nonproliferation Treaty (NPT) negotiated. (Signed July 1968 and came into force in 1970.)[20]

- 1969 U.S. formally proposes[21] placing nuclear production facilities under IAEA safeguards; U.S.S.R. rejects proposal.

- 1978 U.N. special session on disarmament. U.S. internal debate on cutoff; other nations propose cutoff. U.S. Congress passes the Nuclear Nonproliferation Act.

- 1979-1982 "Freeze Movement" endorses a production cutoff. U.S. silent, but does not remove cutoff proposal from the table. U.S.S.R. links progress with weapons destruction.[22] Several third-country[23,24] and other initiatives.[25]

- 1982 Gromyko in U.N. special session[26] supports a cutoff as ". . . one of several initial . . ." stages, but U.S. ignores the initiative; U.S.S.R. accepts IAEA safeguards on civilian nuclear facilities.[27]

- 1984-1989 Academy-sponsored multinational scientific initiatives.[28] Active interest by nuclear-power groups;[29] Private discussions among U.S. and Soviet scientists.[30]

- 1989 Gorbachev announces U.S.S.R. will cease of production[31] of HEU and will shut down two Pu production reactors.[32] At the U.N., the U.S.S.R. announces a schedule to shut down all such production and proposes preparation for negotiations.[33] U.S. administration ignores proposal.

- 1990 U.S. Congress passes a provision in the Defense Authorization Bill for FY91 urging the administration to begin negotiations on a Pu-HEU production cutoff and on warhead dismantlement.[35]

- 1991 The Persian Gulf war exposes Iraq's covert attempt to develop nuclear weapons capability, in violation of its NPT obligations. South Africa joins the NPT. France and China announce their intent to become NPT members.

This brief summary shows that, while far apart originally, the positions of the U.S. and the Soviet government on fissionable weapon materials appear to have moved closer together. Indeed, the U.S. has not produced HEU for weapon purposes since 1964 and has not removed from the table its broad 1969 proposal[21]

Research reactors: country-by-country listing (Algeria-Czech Republic)

In this section, the research reactors are listed alphabetically, by country and by status (indicated by a symbol, the key to which is below).

Key to Symbols

● Operable   ★ Under construction   ○ Planned   ▫ Shut down   ø Cancelled or indefinitely deferred

Name	Status	Type	Steady power, kW	Application	Owner/operator	Date of criticality
ALGERIA						
ARR-1	●	Pool	1 000.000	Research	Haut Commissariat a la Recherche	04/89
NUR	●	Pool	1 000.000	Research	Unite de Recherche en Genie	03/89
ALG-1	○	Pool	500.000	Research		
ARGENTINA						
RA-0	●	Tank	0.010	Training	UN Cordoba/CNEA	00/65
RA-1	●	Tank	60.000	Research	CNEA	01/58
RA-2	●	Critical assembly	0.030	Critical assembly	CNEA	07/66
RA-3	●	Pool	4500	Research	CNEA	08/68
RA-4	●	Homogeneous(s)	0.001	Training	Rosario National University	00/72
RA-6	●	Tank	500.000	Research	Centro Atomico Bariloche	09/82
RA-9	○	Pool	22 000.000	Research	CNEA	
AUSTRALIA						
HIFAR	●	Heavy water	10 000.000	Research	Australian Nuclear Science and Technology Organisation	01/58
Moata	●	Argonaut	100.000	Research	Australian Nuclear Science & Technology Organisation	04/61
AUSTRIA						
Astra	●	Pool	10000	Research	Oesterreichisches Forschungzentrum Seibersdorf GmbH	09/60
RIG-Graz	●	Argonaut	10.000	Training and research	Reaktorinstitut, Verein zur Föderung der Strahlenforschung	05/65
Sar-Graz	●	Argonaut	10.000	Training	Reaktorinstitut, Verein zur Föderung der Strahlenforschung	05/65
Triga II Vienna	●	Pool	250.000	Research	Atominstitute	03/62
BANGLADESH						
Triga Mk II, Bangladesh	●	Triga Mk II	3 000	Research	Bangladesh Atomic Energy Commission	09/86
BELGIUM						
BR-02	●	Pool	0.500	Critical assembly	SCK/CEN	12/59
BR-1	●	Graphite	4 000.000	Research	SCK/CEN	05/56
BR-2	●	Tank	100 000.000	Test	SCK/CEN	06/61
BR-3	●	PWR	40 900.000	Electricity production	SCK/CEN	08/62
Thetis RR-BN-1	●	Pool	250	Research	University of Ghent	04/67
Venus	●	Tank	0.500	Critical assembly	SCK/CEN	00/64
BRAZIL						
Argonaut Reactor	●	Argonaut	0.200	Training	Instituto de Engenharia Nuclear	02/65
IEA-R1	●	Pool	2 000.000	Research	IPEN-CNEN/SP	09/85
IPEN/MB-01	●	Critical assembly	0.1	Critical assembly	IPEN-CNEN/SP	11/88
IPR-R1	●	Triga Mk I	100.000	Training and research	Comissao Nacional de Energia Nuclear	11/60
BULGARIA						
IRT Sofia	●	Pool	2 000.000	Research	Institute for Nuclear Research and Energy	09/61
CANADA						
MNR	●	Pool	5 000.000	Research	McMaster University	04/59
NRU	●	Heavy water	135 000.000	Research	AECL	11/57
Slowpoke, Alberta	●		20.000	Research	University of Alberta	04/77
Slowpoke, Saskatchewan	●		20.000	Research	Saskatchewan Research Council	03/81
Slowpoke-2, Halifax	●		20.000	Research	Dalhousie University	07/76
Slowpoke-2, Montreal	●		20.000	Training	Ecole Polytechnique de Montreal	05/76
Slowpoke-2, Ottowa	●		20.000	Research	AECL	05/71
Slowpoke-2, RMC	●	Pool	20.000	Training and research	Royal Military College	09/85
Slowpoke-2, University of Toronto	●	HEU - light water - Beryllium	20.000	Training and research	University of Toronto Slowpoke Reactor Facility	03/76
Slowpoke-4	●		2 000.000	Prototype	AECL	07/87
ZED-2	●	Tank	0.200	Research	AECL	09/60
Maple, Canada	★	Tank in pool	10 000.000	Isotope production	AECL	01/95
NRX	▫	Heavy water	42 000.000	Research	AECL	07/47
PTR	▫	Pool	0.100	Research	AECL	11/57
Slowpoke-2, Nordion	▫	Pool	20.000	Research	Nordion International Inc	06/84
WR-1	▫	Pressure tube	60 000.000	Research	AECL	11/65
CHILE						
La Reina, Rech-1	●	Pool	5000	Research	Comision Chilena de Energia Nuclear	10/74
Rech-2	●	Pool	10000	Research	Comision Chilena de Energia Nuclear	09/89
CHINA						
HFETR	●	Tank	125 000.000	Test	Southwest Research Institute	12/79
HFETR critical	●	Critical assembly		Critical assembly	Southwest Research Institute	00/79
HWRR-II	●	Heavy water	15 000.000	Research	Institute of Atomic Energy	09/58
LTHR	●	Heating	5 000.000	Prototype	Institute of Nuclear Energy	07/89
MNSR IAE	●	Tank in pool	27.000	Research	Institute of Atomic Energy	03/84
MNSR-SD	●	Tank in pool	27.000	Research	Shan Dong Geology Bureau	00/89
MNSR-SZ	●	Tank in pool	27.000	Research	Shenzhen University	00/88
PPR Pulsing	●	Pool	1 000.000	Research	Southwest Research Institute	06/90
SPR	●	Pool	3 500.000	Research	Institute of Atomic Energy	12/64
SPRR-300	●	Pool	3 000.000	Research	Southwest Research Institute	06/79
Tsinghua	●	Pool - two cores	2,800.000	Research	Institute of Nuclear Energy	10/64
Zero power fast reactor	●	Critical fast		Research	Southwest Research Institute	00/76
COLOMBIA						
IAN-R1	●	Pool	30	Research	Instituto de Ciencias Nucleares y Energias Alternativas	01/65
CUBA						
CU-1	○	Critical assembly	.	Training		
CZECH REPUBLIC						
LR-0	●	Pool	5.000	Critical assembly	Nuclear Research Institute Rez plc	12/82
LWR-15 Rez	●	Pool	10.000	Research	Nuclear Research Institute Rez plc	09/57
SR-0	●	Pool	1.000	Research	Skoda National Corporations	00/70
VR-1 Sparrow	●	Pool	10.000	Training	FJFI-Faculty of Nuclear Sciences and Physical Engineering	12/90
VR-1B	ø	Pool	100.000	Training		

Research reactors: country-by-country listing (Denmark-India)

Name	Status	Type	Steady power, kW	Application	Owner/operator	Date of criticality
DENMARK						
DR-1	●	Homogeneous(l)	2	Training	Riso National Laboratory	08/57
DR-3	●	Heavy water	10000	Test	Riso National Laboratory	01/60
DR-2	◘	Tank	5 000.000	Research	Riso National Laboratory	12/58
EGYPT						
ETRR-1	●	Tank	2 000.000	Research	Atomic Energy Authority	02/61
ETRR-2	○		20 000.000	Research		
FINLAND						
FIR-1	●	Triga Mk II	250	Research	Technical Research Centre	03/62
SCA	◘	Critical assembly		Critical assembly	Technical Research Centre	07/63
FRANCE						
Cabri	●	Pool	25 000.000	Test	CEN Cadarache	00/63
Eole	●	Tank in pool	0.100	Critical assembly	CEN Cadarache	12/65
Harmonie	●	Tank	1.000	Research	CEN Cadarache	08/65
High Flux Reactor	●	Heavy water	57 000	Research	Institut Laue Langevin	01/71
Isis	●	Pool	700.000	Research	CEN Saclay	04/66
Masurca	●	Critical fast	3.000	Critical assembly	CEA Cadarache	12/66
Minerve	●	Pool	0.100	Critical assembly	CEN Cadarache	09/59
Orphee	●	Pool	14 000.000	Research	CEN Saclay	12/80
Osiris	●	Pool	70 000.000	Research	CEN Saclay	09/66
Phebus	●	Pool	40 000.000	Test	CEN Cadarache	08/78
Phenix	●	LMFBR	563 000.000	Prototype	CEN Direction des Reacteurs Nucléaires	08/73
Pile Azur	●	Critical assembly	0.100	Critical assembly	Technicatome	04/62
Prototype Advanced Boiler	●		120 000.000	Electricity production	Technicatome/CEN Cadarache	11/75
Scarabee N	●	Pool	100 000.000	Test	CEN Cadarache	00/82
Silene	●	Homogeneous(l)	1.000	Research	CEN Valduc	00/74
Siloe	●	Pool	35 000.000	Research	CEN Grenoble	03/63
Siloette	●	Pool	100.000	Research	CEN Grenoble	02/64
Strasbourg-Cronenbourg	●	Argonaut	100.000	Training	University of Strasbourg	11/66
Ulysse	●	Argonaut	100.000	Training	INSTN Saclay	07/61
Cesar	◘	Critical assembly	10.000	Critical assembly	CEN Cadarache	12/64
EL 3	◘	Heavy water	18 000.000	Test	CEA	00/57
EL 4	◘		26 700.000	Prototype	EdF	12/66
Marius	◘	Critical assembly	0.400	Training	CEN Cadarache	01/60
Melusine	◘	Pool	8 000.000	Research	CEA Grenoble	07/58
Mirene	◘	Homogeneous(l)		Test	CEN Valduc	00/75
Nereide	◘	Pool	500.000	Research	CEA	09/60
Rapsodie	◘	LMFBR	40 000.000	Test	CEN Cadarache	01/67
Triton	◘	Pool	6 500.000	Research	CEA	06/59
GERMANY						
AKR	●	Homogeneous(s)	0.002	Training	Technical University of Dresden	07/78
BER-2	●	Pool	10000	Research	Hahn-Meitner Institut	04/91
FMRB	●	Pool	1000	Research	Physikalisch Technische Bundanst	10/67
FRG-1	●	Pool	5000	Research	GKSS-Forschungszentrum	10/58
FRG-2	●	Pool	15000	Test	GKSS-Forschungszentrum	03/63
FRJ-2	●	Heavy water	23 000.000	Research	KFA Juelich	11/62
FRM	●	Pool	4000	Research	Technische Universitat München	10/57
KNK II	●	Sodium fast neutron	5800	Electricity production	KFK Karlsruhe	00/71
RAKE	●	Tank	0.010	Research	Central Institute for Nuclear Research	10/69
RFR	●	Tank	10 000.000	Research	Central Institute for Nuclear Research	12/57
RRR	●	Argonaut		Research	Central Institute for Nuclear Research	12 62
Sur 100 Hannover 12/71	●	Homogeneous(s)		Training	Institut fuer Kerntechnik und Zerstoerungsfreie Pruefverfahren	
Sur Aachen	●	Homogeneous(s)	0.001	Training	Institut fuer Elekinsche Anlagen und Energiewirtschaft	09/66
Sur Berlin	●	Homogeneous(s)	0.001	Training	Institut fuer Energietechnik Technical University of Berlin	07/63
Sur Furtwangen	●	Homogeneous(s)		Training	Fachhochschule Furtwangen	06/73
Sur Hamburg	●	Homogeneous(s)	0.001	Training	Fachhochschule Hamburg	01/65
Sur Karlsruhe	●	Homogeneous(s)	0.0001	Training	Fortbildungszentrum für Technik und Umwelt (FTU)	03/66
Sur Kiel	●	Homogeneous(s)	0.001	Training	Fachhochschule Kiel	03/66
Sur Stuttgart	●	Homogeneous(s)	0.001	Training	Institut fuer Kernenergetik und Energiesysteme	04/64
Sur Ulm	●	Homogeneous(s)		Training	Institut fuer Kerntechnik	12/65
Triga Heidelberg II	●	Triga Mk I	250.000	Research, training and isotope production	Deutsches Krebsforschungszentrum	09/77
Triga, Mainz	●	Triga Mk II	100	Research	Institut fuer Kernchemie	08/65
Triga-I Hannover	●	Triga Mk I	250.000	Research	Abteilung fuer Nuklearmedizin	01/73
ZLFR	●	Tank	44000	Training	Technische Hochschule Zittau	07/79
FR2	◘	Tank	44000	Test	KfK Karlsruhe	03/61
FRF-2	◘	Triga converter	1 000.000	Research	J Wolfgang Goethe Universitat	10/77
FRN	◘	Triga Mk III	1 000.000	Research	GSF-Forschungszentrum für Umwelt und Gesundheit	00/72
Sneak	◘	Critical assembly	1	Critical assembly	KfK Karlsruhe	-12/66
Stark	◘	Argonaut	0.01	Research	KfK Karlsruhe	01/63
Sur Bremen	◘	Homogeneous(s)	0.0001	Research	Hochschule Bremen	10/67
Sur Darmstadt	◘	Homogeneous(s)		Training	Technische Hochschule Darmstadt	09/63
Trigs Heidelberg I	◘	Triga Mk I	250.000	Research, training and isotope production	Institute of Nuclear Medicine, Heidelberg	08/66
Sur Munich	●	Homogeneous(s)		Training	Technische Universitat München	02/62
GREECE						
Democritus, GRR-1	●	Pool	5 000.000	Research	Greek Atomic Energy Commission	07/61
NTU	●	Subcritical		Critical assembly	National Technical University	00/70
HUNGARY						
Nuclear Training Reactor	●	Pool	100.000	Training	Technical University of Budapest	05-71
WWR-SR10	●	Tank	10 000.000	Research	Central Research Institute for Physics	03/59
ZR-6M	●	Critical assembly		Critical assembly	Central Research Institute for Physics	11/72
INDIA						
Apsara	●	Pool	1 000.000	Research	Bhabha Atomic Research Centre	08/56
Cirus	●	Heavy water tank	40 000.000	Research	Bhabha Atomic Research Centre	07/60
Dhruva	●	Heavy water tank	100 000.000	Research	Bhabha Atomic Research Centre	08/85
FBTR	●	LMFBR	40 000.000	Test	Indira Gandhi Centre For Atomic Research	10/85
Purnima II	●	Homogeneous(l)	0.005	Critical assembly	Bhabha Atomic Research Centre	05/84
Kamini	●	U 233 fuel	30.000		Indira Ghand Centre for Atomic Research	11/92
Purnima	●	Fast neutron		Critical assembly	Bhabha Atomic Research Centre	05/72
Zerlina	◘	Tank	0.100	Critical assembly	Bhabha Atomic Research Centre	01/61

Research reactors: country-by-country listing (Indonesia-Netherlands)

Name	Status	Type	Steady power, kW	Application	Owner/operator	Date of criticality
INDONESIA						
MPR-30	●	Pool	30 000.000	Test		07/87
PPNY-Batan	●	Triga Mk II	100.000	Research isotope production	Yogyakarta Nuclear Research Centre - Batan	01/79
RSG G A Siwabessy (RSG-GAS)	●	Pool	30 000.000	Test and isotope production	PRSG Batan	07/87
Triga II, Bandung	●	Triga Mk II	1 000.000	Research, training and isotope production	Research Centre for Nuclear Techniques	10/64
IRAN						
NRC RR	●	Pool	5 000.000	Research	Nuclear Research Centre	11/67
ZPR	●	Critical assembly		Critical assembly	Atomic Energy Organisation of Iran	00/90
IRAQ						
IRT-5000	◘	Pool	5 000.000	Research	Nuclear Research Centre	00/67
Tammuz-2	◘	Pool	500.000	Research	Nuclear Research Centre	03/87
ISRAEL						
IRR-1	●	Pool	5 000.000	Research	Israel Atomic Energy Commission	06/60
IRR-2	◘	Heavy water	26 000.000	Test		12/63
ITALY						
AGN 201, Constanza	●	Homogeneous(s)	0.020	Training	University of Palermo	02/60
Lena, Pavia	●	Triga Mk II	250.000	Research	University of Pavia	11/65
RSV Tapiro	●	Fast neutron	5	Research	ENEA	04/71
SM-1	●	Subcritical		Research	University of Pavia	00/61
Triga, RC-1	●	Triga Mk II	1 000.000	Research	ENEA	06/60
L-54 M	◘	Homogeneous(l)	50.000	Training	ENEA	11/59
Rana	◘	Pool	10.000	Research	ENEA	02/65
RB-1	◘	Critical graphite	20.010	Research	ENEA	07/62
RB-3	◘	Heavy water zero power	0.100	Research	ENEA	08/71
Ritmo, RC-4	◘	Pool	0.010	Critical assembly	ENEA	07/65
Rospo 2	◘	Pool	0.2	Critical assembly	ENEA	00/63
RTS-1	◘	Pool	5 000.000	Research	Cresam	04/63
Struttura Sottocritica	◘	Subcritical		Research	School of Nuclear Physics	00/62
Pec	C	Fast neutron	120 000.000	Prototype	ENEA	00/89
JAMAICA						
UWI CNS Slowpoke	●	Tank in pool	20	Research	Centre for Nuclear Sciences University of the West Indies	03/84
JAPAN						
DCA	●	Critical assembly	1	Critical assembly	PNC Oarai Engineering Center	12/69
FCA	●	Fast Critical Assembly	2.000	Critical assembly	Tokai Research Establishment Japan Atomic Energy Research Institute	04/67
JMTR	●	Tank	50 000.000	Test	Oarai Research Establishment	04/68
JMTRC	●	Pool	0.100	Critical assembly	Oarai Research Establishment	10/65
Joyo	●	LMFBR	100000	Research	PNC Oarai Engineering Centre	04/77
JRR-2	●	Heavy water	10 000.000	Research	Tokai Research Establishment Japan Atomic Energy Research Institute	10/60
JRR-3 (M)	●	Pool	20 000.000	Research	Tokai Research Establishment Japan Atomic Energy Research Institute	
JRR-4	●	Pool	3 500.000	Research	Tokai Research Establishment Japan Atomic Energy Research Institute	
KUCA	●	Dual core (solid/liquid mod)	0.100	Critical assembly	Research Reactor Institute, Kyoto University	08/74
KUR	●	Tank	5 000.000	Research	Research Reactor Institute, Kyoto University	06/64
NAIG	●	Tank	0.200	Critical assembly	NAIG Nuclear Research Laboratory	12/63
NSRR	●	Triga ACPR	300.000	Research	Tokai Research Establishment Japan Atomic Energy Research Institute	
TCA	●	Critical assembly	0.200	Critical assembly	Tokai Research Establishment Japan Atomic Energy Research Institute	
Triga II, Rikkyo	●	Triga Mk II	100.000	Research	Institute for Atomic Energy	12/61
TTR-1	●	Pool	100.000	Research	Research and Development Centre, Toshiba Corporation	03/62
UTR Kinki	●	Modified Argonaut	0.001	Training and research	Kinki University Atomic Energy Research Institute	11/61
VHTRC	●	Critical assembly	0.010	Critical assembly	Tokai Research Establishment Japan Atomic Energy Research Institute	01/61
Yayoi	●	Fast neutron	2	Research	University of Tokyo	
HTTR	★	HTGR	30 000	Research	Japan Atomic Energy Research Institute	04/71
HTR	●	Pool	100	Research	Hitachi	12/61
MITRR Musashi	◘	Triga Mk II	100.000	Research	Musashi Institute of Technology	01/63
PEOPLE'S DEM REP OF KOREA						
IRT DPRK	●	Pool	8 000.000	Research	State Comm for Atomic Energy	08/65
REPUBLIC OF KOREA						
AGN-201 Suwon	●	Homogeneous(s)	0.001	Training and research	Kyung Hee University	12/82
Triga Mk II, Seoul	●	Triga Mk II	250.000	Training	KAERI	03/62
Triga Mk III, Seoul	●	Triga Mk III	2 000.000	Research	KAERI	05/72
KMRR (Korea Multipurpose Res Reactor)	★	Open Pool	30 000.000	Research and isotope production	KAERI	12/94
MTR	◘		30 000.000	Test		00/91
REPUBLIC OF LATVIA						
IRT	●	Pool	5000	Research	Nuclear Research Center Latvian Academy of Science	09/61
LIBYA						
IRT-1	●	Pool	10 000.000	Research	Tajoura Nuclear Research Centre	03/83
MALAYSIA						
Triga, Puspati	●	Triga Mk II	1000	Research	Nuclear Energy Unit, Ministry of Science, Technology and the Environment	06/82
MEXICO						
Chicago Modelo 9000	●	Subcritical		Training	University Autonoma de Zacatecas	05/69
Triga Mk II	●	Triga Mk III	1000	Research	ININ	11/68
Sur-100, Unam	◘	Homogeneous(s)		Training	UNAM	09/72
MOROCCO						
MA-R1	★	Triga Mk I	100.000	Research	CNESTN	00/92
NETHERLANDS						
HOR	●	Pool	2 000.000	Research	Interfacultair Reactor Institute, Technische Universiteit Delft	04/63
HRF High FLux Reactor	●	Tank	45.000	Test	Joint Research Centre	11/61

● Operable; ★ Under construction; ○ Planned; ◘ Shutdown; ● Cancelled or Indefinitely deferred; ▲ Decommissioned

Research reactors: country-by-country listing (Norway-Taiwan)

Name	Status	Type	Steady power, kW	Application	Owner/operator	Date of criticality
LFR	●	Argonaut	30.000	Research	ECN	09/60
Bam	⊃	Pool	100.000	Research	Institute for Atomic Sciences	04/63
NORWAY						
Halden	●	Heavy water	25 000.000	Research	IFE	06/59
Jeep II	●	Tank	2000	Research	Institutt for energiteknikk	12/66
PAKISTAN						
Parr-1	●	Pool	9 000.000	Research	Pinstech	12/65
PERU						
PER-2	●	Pool	10000	Research and isotope production		IPEN
11/88						
RP-0	●	Critical assembly	0.001	Training	IPEN	07/78
PHILIPPINES						
PRR-1	●	Triga converter	3000	Research	Philippine Nuclear Research Institute	08/63
POLAND						
Agata	●	Pool	0.1	Critical assembly	Institute of Atomic Energy	05/73
EWA	●	Tank	10000	Test	Institute of Atomic Energy	06/58
Maria	●	Pool	30000	Test	Institute of Atomic Energy	12/74
Anna	⊃	Critical assembly	0.100	Critical assembly	Institute of Atomic Energy	00/83
Maryla	⊃	Pool	100.000	Research	Institute of Nuclear Research	02/67
PORTUGAL						
RPI (Reactor Portugues de Investigacao)	●	Pool	1 000.000	Research	INETI	04/61
ROMANIA						
Triga ACPR	●	Triga dual core	14 000.000	Test	Institute for Nuclear Power Reactors	11/79
RP-01	⊃	Tank		Critical assembly		
RUSSIA						
Argus	●	Homogeneous(l)	50.000	Research	Kurchatov Institute	12/81
BOR-60	●	Fast neutron	12 000.000	Electricity production	MAEP	12/69
BR-10	●	Fast neutron	5 000.000	Electricity production	Institute of Physics, Obninsk	06/58
F-1	●	Graphite	24.000	Research	Kurchatov Institute	12/46
IBR-30	●	Fast neutron	30.000	Research	Institute of Nuclear Research	00/69
IIN-3M	●	Homogeneous(l)	10.000	Research	Kurchatov Institute	00/72
IR-8	●	Pool	8 000.000	Research	Kurchatov Institute	08/81
IRT-A	●	Pool	2 500.000	Research	Moscow Institute of Physical Engineering	05/67
IRT-O, Tomsk	●	Pool	6.000	Research	Institute for Nuclear Physics	08/67
IRT-MEPhI	●	Open Pool	2500	Research	Moscow Engineering Physics Institute	05/67
IRT-T	●	Pool	6 000.000	Research	Institute of Nuclear Physics	08/67
IVV-2M	●	Pool	15 000.000	Research	AESC of the USSR	04/66
MiR.M1	●	Pool	100 000.000	Test	RIAR	12/66
MR	●	Channels/pool	40 000.000	Research	Kurchatov Institute	12/63
RBT-10/1	●	Pool	10 000.000	Test	RIAR	12/83
RBT-10/2	●	Pool	10 000.000	Test	RIAR	12/84
RBT-6	●	Pool	6 000.000	Test	RIAR	10/75
SM-2	●	Pressurized	100 000.000	Test and isotope production	RIAR	12/66
WWR-CM-20	●	Tank	20 000.000	Research	Tashkent Nuclear Physics Institute	09/59
WWR-K	●	Tank	10 000.000	Research	Institute of Nuclear Physics	10/57
WWR-M, Gatchina	●	Tank	18 000.000	Research	Petersburg Nuclear Physics Institute	12/59
WWR-TS	●	Tank	12 000.000	Research	Ministry of Chem Industry	10/64
PIK	*	High flux	100 000.000	Research	Petersburg Nuclear Physics Institute	
Sphinx	*	Channel	200 000.000	Test		
IFR	⊃	Fast neutron	6.000	Critical assembly	Institute of Physics, Dubna	12/60
IRT-M Moscow	⊃	Pool	8 000.000	Research	Kurchatov Institute	11/57
IRT-M, Minsk	⊃	Pool	4 000.000	Research	Institute of Nuclear Power, Minsk	04/62
RFT	⊃	Pool	20 000.000	Test	Kurchatov Institute	00/52
Romashka	⊃	Homogeneous(s)	40.000	Research		08/64
SBR-2	⊃	Fast neutron	200.000	Research	State Committee for Atomic Energy	00/56
TR	⊃	Heavy water	2.500.000	Research	Institute of Theoretical and Experimental Physics	04/49
WWR-2	⊃	Tank	3 000.000	Research	Kurchatov Institute	07/53
IRT-M, Tbilisi	●	Pool	5 000.000	Research	Institute of Physics of the Georgian Academy of Sciences, Tbilisi	10/50
SLOVENIA						
Ljubljana	●	Triga Mk II	250.000	Research	Jozef Stefan Institute	05/66
REPUBLIC OF SOUTH AFRICA						
Safari-1	●	Tank	20000	Research	Atomic Energy Corporation of South Africa	03/65
SPAIN						
JEN-1	●	Pool	2 000.000	Research	Junta de Energia Nuclear	10/58
ARBi	⊃	Argonaut	10.000	Training		06/62
ARGOS	⊃	Argonaut	1.000	Training		06/61
Coral-1	⊃	Critical assembly		Research	Junta de Energia Nuclear	03/68
SWEDEN						
R-2	●	Tank	50 000.000	Test	Studsvik Nuclear AB	05/60
R-2 0	●	Pool	1 000.000	Research	Studsvik Nuclear AB	06/60
Kritz	▲	Critical assembly		Critical assembly	Studsvik EcoSafe	10/69
SWITZERLAND						
AGN 201 P	●	Homogeneous(s)	0.020	Training	Geneva University	06/58
AGN-211 P	●	Homogeneous(s)	2.000	Training	Institute for Physics	08/59
Crocus	●	Critical assembly	0.001	Training	Nuclear Energy Laboratory	00/70
Proteus	●	Critical assembly	1	Research	Paul Scherrer Institute	01/68
Saphir	●	Pool	10000	Research	Paul Scherrer Institute	04/57
Diorit	⊃	Tank	30000	Research	Paul Scherrer Institute	00/60
SYRIA						
SYR 1	⊃	Pool	10 000.000	Research		00/90
TAIWAN						
Thar	●	Argonaut	10.000	Research	Nuclear Science and Technology Development Centre	04/74
Ther	●	Pool	2 800.000	Research	Institute of Nuclear Energy Research	00/54
THMER	●	Mobile educational		Training	Nuclear Science and Technology Development Centre	11/75
Thor	●	Triga converter	1 000.000	Research	Nuclear Science and Technology Development Centre	04/61
WBRL	●	Homogeneous(l)	100.000	Research	Institute of Nuclear Energy Research	08/76
ZPRL	●	Pool	10.000	Research	Institute of Nuclear Energy Research	02/71

Research reactors: country-by-country listing (Thailand-USA)

Name	Status	Type	Steady power, kW	Application	Owner/operator	Date of criticality
TRR	⊐	Heavy water	40 000.000	Test	Institute of Nuclear Energy Research	01/73
THAILAND						
TRR-1/M1	●	Triga Mk III	2 000.000	Research	Office of Atomic Energy for Peace	10/62
TURKEY						
ITU-TRR	●	Triga Mk II	250	Training and research	Istanbul Technical University	03/79
TR-2	●	Pool	5 000	Research	Cekmece Nuclear Research and Training Centre	12/81
TR-1	⊐	Pool	1.000	Research		01/62
UK						
Dimple	●	Heavy water	0.1	Research	AEA Technology	00/62
ICI Triga Reactor	●	Triga Mk I	250	Research	ICI Chemicals and Polymers Ltd	08/71
Imperial College Reactor	●	Pool	100	Training	Imperial College of Science Technology and Medicine	04/65
Jason	●	Argonaut	10.000	Training	Royal Naval College	09/59
Neptune	●	Tank	0.100	Critical assembly	Rolls Royce and Associates	03/63
Nestor	●	Argonaut	30	Research	AEA Technology	00/61
UTR-300	●	Argonaut	300	Training and research	Scottish Universities Research and Reactor Centre, University of Glasgow	06/63
Viper	●	Fast burst	2.000	Test	AWE Aldermaston	00/67
Vulcan, STF	●	Tank		Research	Rolls Royce and Associates/Ministry of Defence	07/87
Bepo	⊐	Graphite	6500	Research	AEA Technology	07/48
Berkeley Zero Energy	⊐	Graphite	1.000	Research	Nuclear Electric	04/66
Daphne	⊐	Heavy water	0.1	Research	AEA Technology	00/62
Dido	⊐	Heavy water	25500	Test	AEA Technology	11/56
DMTR	⊐	Heavy water	25000	Test	AEA Technology	05/58
Dragon	⊐	Helium cooled	20000	Test	AEA Technology	00/64
Gleep	⊐	Graphite	50	Research	AEA Technology	08/47
Hazel	⊐	Homogeneous(l)		Critical assembly	AEA Technology	00/57
Hector	⊐	Zero power	0.1	Research	AEA Technology	03/63
Hector, graphite	⊐	Graphite	0.1	Research	AEA Technology	03/63
Herald	⊐	Pool	5 000.000	Research	AWE Aldermaston	00/60
Hero	⊐	Graphite	3	Critical assembly	AEA Technology	06/62
Horace	⊐	Critical assembly	0.010	Critical assembly	Ministry of Defence	05/58
Juno	⊐	Critical assembly	0.1	Critical assembly	AEA Technology	03/64
Lido	⊐	Pool	300	Research	AEA Technology	09/56
Pluto	⊐	Heavy water	25500	Test	AEA Technology	10/57
Universities Research Reactor	⊐	Argonaut	300	Training	Universities of Liverpool and Manchester	07/64
Vera	⊐	Critical fast	0.100	Research	Ministry of Defence	00/61
Vulcan, DSMP	⊐	Tank		Research	Rolls Royce and Associates/Ministry of Defence	00/61
Zebra	⊐	Zero power fast		Research	AEA Technology	12/62
Zenith I	⊐	Graphite	0.5	Research	AEA Technology	12/59
Zenith II	⊐	Graphite	1	Research	AEA Technology	03/72
Zephyr	⊐	Critical fast	0.002	Critical assembly	AEA Technology	01/54
Zeus	⊐	Critical fast	0.1	Critical assembly	AEA Technology	00/55
OMC UTR-B	▲	Argonaut	100.000	Training	Queen Mary College	08/64
UKRAINE						
WWR-M	●	Tank	10 000.000	Research	Institute for Nuclear Research, Kiev	12/60
URUGUAY						
RU-1	⊐	Pool	1.000	Training		04/78
USA						
ACRR Annular Core	●	Pool	2 000.000	Research	Sandia Laboratories	06/67
AFRRI	●	Triga Mk F	1 000.000	Research	AFRRI	00/63
AFSR	●	Fast neutron	1.000	Research	Argonne National Laboratory	00/59
AGN-201, Idaho State University	●	Homogeneous(s)	0.005	Training	Idaho State University	00/67
AGN-201, Texas A & M	●	Homogeneous(s)	0.005	Training	Texas A & M University	00/57
AGN-201, University of New Mexico	●	Homogeneous(s)	0.005	Training	University of New Mexico	00/66
AGN-211, University of Oklahoma	●	Homogeneous(s)	0.100	Training	University of Oklahoma	02/59
APRFR	●	Fast burst	10.000	Research	US Army	00/68
ARMF	●	Pool	100.000	Critical assembly	EG&G Idaho	10/60
ARRR Aerotest	●	Triga converter	250	Research	Aerotest Operations	07/64
ATR	●	Tank	250 000.000	Test	EG&G Idaho	07/67
ATRC	●	Tank	5.000	Critical assembly	EG&G Idaho	00/64
Big Ten	●	Critical assembly		Critical assembly	Los Alamos Scientific Laboratory	00/72
BMRR	●	Tank	3 000.000	Research	Brookhaven National Laboratory	03/59
BMRR SUNY Buffalo	●	Pool	2000	Research	State University of New York, Buffalo	05/64
CFRMF	●	Pool	100.000	Research	EG&G Idaho	12/62
Comet	●	Critical assembly		Critical assembly	Los Alamos Scientific Laboratory	00/52
D1G Destroyer Prototype	●	Pressurized		Prototype	GE	00/62
Dow Triga	●	Triga Mk I	300.000	Research	Dow Chemical Co	07/67
EBR II	●		62 500.000	Electricity production	Argonne National Laboratory	09/61
FFTF	●	Fast neutron	400 000.000	Test	Westinghouse Hanford	00/80
Flattop	●	Critical assembly		Critical assembly	Los Alamos Scientific Laboratory	00/57
Ford Nuclear Reactor	●	Pool	2 000.000	Research	University of Michigan	09/57
GA-Triga F	●	Triga Mk F	1500	Test and research	General Atomics	07/60
GA-Triga I	●	Triga Mk I	250	Test and research	General Atomics	05/58
Godiva	●	Critical assembly		Critical assembly	Los Alamos Scientific Laboratory	00/67
GSTR Geological Survey	●	Triga Mk I	1 000.000	Research	US Geological Survey	02/69
GTRR, Georgia Tech	●	Heavy water	5 000.000	Research	Georgia Institute of Technology	12/64
HFBR	●	Heavy water	60 000.000	Test	Brookhaven National Laboratory	10/65
HFIR	●	Tank	850.000	Test	Martin Marietta Energy Systems	08/65
Honeycomb	●	Critical assembly		Critical assembly	Los Alamos Scientific Laboratory	00/60
HST Rocky Flats	●	Critical assembly		Critical assembly	Rockwell International	00/65
Jezebel	●	Critical assembly		Critical assembly	Los Alamos Scientific Laboratory	00/54
Kansas State University	●	Triga Mk II	250	Training	Kansas State University	10/62
Mars	●	Critical assembly		Critical assembly	Los Alamos Scientific Laboratory	00/74
MCZPR	●	Pool	0.001	Training	Manhattan College	03/64
MITR-II	●	Tank	5 000.000	Research	Massachusetts Institute of Technology	07/58
MURR	●	Tank in pool	10 000.000	Research	University of Missouri	10/66
MUTR, University of Maryland	●	Triga converter	250.000	Training	University of Maryland	12/60
NBSR	●	Heavy water	20 000.000	Research	National Bureau of Standards	12/67
NRAD	●	Triga	250.000	Research	Argonne National Laboratory - West	10/77
NRF	●	Triga Mk I	1 000.000	Research	Westinghouse Hanford	03/77
NSCR, Texas A & M	●	Triga converter	1 000.000	Research	Texas Engineering Experiment Station	01/62

● Operable; ★ Under construction; ○ Planned; ⊐ Shutdown; ⊘ Cancelled or indefinitely deferred; ▲ Decommissioned

Research reactors: country-by-country listing (USA)

Name	Status	Type	Steady power, kW	Application	Owner/operator	Date of criticality
					Texas A & M University System	
NTR	●	Tank	100,000	Research	GE	11/57
Nuclear Test Gauge	●	Subcritical		Research	E I Dupont de Nemours & Co	11/58
Omega West Reactor	●	Tank	8,000,000	Test	Los Alamos Scientific Laboratory	07/56
OSTR, Oregon State University	●	Triga Mk II	1,000,000	Research	Oregon State University	00/67
OSURR, Ohio State University	●	Pool	10,000	Training	Ohio State University	03/61
Parka	●	Critical assembly		Critical assembly	Los Alamos Scientific Laboratory	00/63
Penn State Breazeale Reactor	●	Triga Mk III	1,000,000	Research	Pennsylvania State University	08/55
PNL-CML	●	Homogeneous(l)		Critical assembly	Battelle Memorial Institute	00/61
Pulstar, North Carolina State University	●	Pool	1000	Research	North Carolina State University	00/72
PUR-1	●	Pool	1	Training	Purdue University	01/62
RCF	●	Critical assembly	0.1	Training and research	Rensselaer Polytechnic Institute	01/64
Reed Reactor Facility	●	Triga Mk I	250	Research	Reed Institute	07/68
RINSC	●	Pool	2,000,000	Research	Rhode Island Atomic Energy Commission	07/64
S1C Submarine Prototype	●	Pressurized		Prototype	GE	00/59
S1W	●	Pressurized		Prototype	Westinghouse Electric	00/53
S3G Submarine Prototype	●	Pressurized		Prototype	GE	00/58
S5G	●	Pressurized		Prototype	Westinghouse Electric	00/65
Solution System	●	Critical assembly		Critical assembly	Rockwell International	00/65
SPR II	●	Fast burst	9,000	Research	Sandia Laboratories	03/67
SPR III	●	Fast burst	9,000	Research	Sandia Laboratories	08/75
SR-305	●	Graphite	0.050	Critical assembly	Westinghouse Savannah River Company (WSRC)	00/53
Tank Reservoir	●	Critical assembly		Critical assembly	Rockwell International	00/65
Treat	●	Graphite pulse	80	Research	Argonne National Laboratory	02/59
Triga Cornell	●	Triga Mk II	500,000	Research	Cornell University	00/62
Triga Reactor Dept of Veterans Affairs	●	Triga Mk I	20,000	Research	Omaha V A Medical Centre	06/59
Triga, University of Utah	●	Triga Mk I	100,000	Research	University of Utah	10/75
TSR-2	●	Tank	1,000,000	Research	Pacific Northwest Laboratories	03/60
UCI Nuclear Reactor Irvine	●	Triga Mk I	250,000	Research	University of California, Irvine	11/69
UCSB L-77	●	Homogeneous(l)	10,000	Training	University of California, Santa Barbara	01/75
UFTR, University of Florida	●	Modified Argonaut	100	Training and research	University of Florida	05/59
UI-Lopra	●	Triga Mk III	10	Training	University of Illinois	12/71
UI-Triga Mk II	●	Triga Mk II	1500	Research	University of Illinois	07/69
ULR	●	Pool	1000	Research	University of Massachusetts - Lowell	01/75
UMRR	●	Pool	200,000	Research	University of Missouri, Rolla	12/61
University of Arizona Triga	●	Triga Mk I	100,000	Research	University of Arizona	12/58
UT-Triga	●	Triga Mk II	1,100,000	Research	University of Texas Nuclear Engineering Teaching Laboratory	03/92
UTR-10	●	Argonaut	10,000	Training	Iowa State University	10/59
UVAR	●	Pool	2000	Research	University of Virginia	06/80
UWNR, University of Wisconsin	●	Triga conversion	1,000,000	Research	University of Wisconsin	03/61
Vertical Split Table	●	Critical assembly		Critical assembly	Rockwell International	00/65
WP1	●	Pool	10,000	Training	Worcester Polytechnic Institute	12/59
WSUR	●	Triga converter	1,000,000	Research	Washington State University	03/61
Zero Power Reactor	●	Tank	500,000	Training	Cornell University	00/62
ZPPR	●		1,000	Critical assembly	Argonne National Laboratory	04/69
ZPR, Zero PWR Reactor	●	Tank		Training	Cornell University	00/62
SNRS	○	Triga	1,000,000	Research	McClellan Air Force Base	10/89
Advanced Neutron Source	○	Ultra high flux	270,000,000	Research		
ACPR Annular Core	□		600,000	Test	Sandia Laboratories	06/67
AF NETF	□	Tank	10,000,000	Test	US Air Force	00/59
AGN 201, Argonne	□	Homogeneous(s)		Training	Argonne National Laboratory	00/57
AGN-201 Catholic University	□	Homogeneous(s)		Training	Catholic University of America	11/57
AGN-201, California Polytechnic	□	Homogeneous(s)		Training	California Polytechnic	00/73
AGN-201, Colorado State University	□	Homogeneous(s)		Training	Colorado State University	00/57
AGN-201, Memphis State University	□	Homogeneous(s)		Training	Memphis State University	00/77
AGN-201, New York University	□	Homogeneous(s)		Training	New York University	06/68
AGN-201, Polytechnic Inst of New York	□	Homogeneous(s)		Training	Polytechnic Institute of New York	00/67
AGN-201, Tuskegee University	□	Homogeneous(s)		Training	Tuskegee University	00/74
AGN-201, University of Delaware	□	Homogeneous(s)		Training	University of Delaware	00/58
AGN-211, Rice University	□	Homogeneous(s)		Training	Rice University	00/59
AGN-211, West Virginia	□	Homogeneous(s)		Training	West Virginia University	00/59
ALRR Ames	□	Heavy water	5,000,000	Research	Ames Laboratory	00/63
AMMRC	□		5,000,000	Research	Army Material and Mechanical Research Centre	00/60
APFA-III	□	Critical assembly	1	Critical assembly	General Atomics	00/67
ARR(L-54)	□	Homogeneous(l)	75,000	Research	Armour Research Foundation	00/56
Astr. Aerospace Systems	□	Tank	10,000,000	Test	General Dynamics/Convair	00/54
ATSR	□	Pool	10,000	Research	Argonne National Laboratory	00/57
BAWTR	□	Pool	6,000,000	Test	B&W	00/64
BGRR	□	Graphite	20,000,000	Test	Brookhaven National Laboratory	00/50
Borax-1	□		1,400,000	Research	Argonne National Laboratory	00/53
Borax-2	□		5,500,000	Research	Argonne National Laboratory	00/54
Borax-3	□		5,500,000	Research	Argonne National Laboratory	00/54
Borax-4	□		5,500,000	Research	Argonne National Laboratory	00/54
Borax-5	□		20,000,000	Research	Argonne National Laboratory	00/62
Brigham Young University	□	Homogeneous(s)		Training	Brigham Young University	09/67
BRR	□	Pool	2,000,000	Research	Battelle Columbus Laboratory	00/56
BRR UC Berkeley	□	Triga Mk III	1,000,000	Research	Berkeley	00/66
BRTR, University of Kansas	□	Pool	10,000	Training	University of Kansas	06/61
BSR	□	Pool	2,000,000	Research	Martin Marietta Energy Systems	12/50
Cavalier	□	Pool	0.1	Training	University of Virginia	00/74
Chicago Pile 2	□	Graphite pile	2,000	Research	Argonne National Laboratory	00/43
Chicago Pile 3	□	Heavy water	300,000	Research	Argonne National Laboratory	00/44
Chicago Pile 5	□	Heavy water	5,000,000	Research	Argonne National Laboratory	02/54
Cintichem Nuclear Reactor	□	Pool	5,000,000	Research	Cintichem Inc	09/61
Clementine	□		25,000	Test	Los Alamos Scientific Laboratory	00/46
CP-1, Chicago Pile 1	□	Graphite pile	0.200	Critical assembly	University of Chicago	12/42
CP-11	□	Argonaut		Training	—	00/57
CX-10	□	Critical assembly	1,000	Critical assembly	GSW	00/58
Demo Reactor	□	Pool	10,000	Training	Oak Ridge National Laboratory	00/69
DORF	□	Triga Mk F	250,000	Research	Harry Diamond Laboratory	00/61
EAEP	□	Pool	10,000	Training	Oak Ridge National Laboratory	00/63
EBR-I	□	Sodium fast neutron	1,400,000	Prototype	Argonne National Laboratory	12/51
ETR	□	Tank	175,000,000	Test	EG&G Idaho	09/57
FRAN	□	Prompt burst		Research	Lawrence Livermore Laboratory	00/67
FS-1	□	Critical assembly	1,000	Critical assembly	Brookhaven National Laboratory	00/67

Research reactors: country-by-country listing (USA-Vietnam)

Name	Status	Type	Steady power, kW	Application	Owner/operator	Date of criticality
GA-Triga III	◘	Triga Mk III	1500	Research	General Atomics	00/66
Gas Cavity Reactor	◘	Gas cavity reactor	2,200.000	Prototype	GE	00/60
GETR	◘	Tank	50 000.000	Test	GE	00/58
HOTCE	◘	Critical assembly		Critical assembly	GE	00/56
HPRR	◘	Other	10.000	Research	Martin Marietta Energy Systems	00/62
HTLTR	◘	Graphite	2.000	Research	Pacific Northwest Laboratory	00/67
HTR USA	◘	Graphite		Research	United Nuclear	00/44
HTRE-1	◘	Air cooled	20 000.000	Prototype	GE	00/56
HTRE-2	◘	Air cooled	14 000.000	Prototype	GE	00/57
HTRE-3	◘	Air cooled	32 000.000	Prototype	GE	00/58
HWCTR	◘	Heavy water	61 000.000	Test	E I Dupont de Nemours	03/62
Hydro	◘	Critical assembly		Test	Los Alamos Scientific Laboratory	00/56
Hypo	◘	Homogeneous(l)	6.000	Research	Los Alamos Scientific Laboratory	00/44
IRL	◘	Pool	5 000.000	Research	Industrial Reactor Laboratories	00/58
Janus	◘	Tank	200.000	Research	Argonne National Laboratory	00/64
Juggernaut	◘	Argonaut	250.000	Research	Argonne National Laboratory	01/62
KEWB	◘	Homogeneous(l)		Test	Atomics International	00/56
Kinglet	◘	Homogeneous(l)		Test	Los Alamos Scientific Laboratory	00/72
Kiwi	◘			Test	Los Alamos Scientific Laboratory	00/65
Kukla	◘	Prompt burst		Research	Lawrence Livermore Laboratory	00/59
L-47	◘	Homogeneous(l)		Training	Atomics International	00/57
L-54 Walter Reed	◘	Homogeneous(l)	50.000	Research	Walter Reed Army Institute	09/62
L-77	◘	Homogeneous(l)	10.000	Training	Rockwell	00/59
L-77, Rockwell	◘	Homogeneous(l)	0.010	Training	Rockwell	00/60
L-77, University of Nevada	◘	Homogeneous(l)		Training	University of Nevada	00/63
L-77, University of Wyoming	◘	Homogeneous(l)		Training	University of Wyoming	00/59
L-85, Nuclear Examination	◘	Homogeneous(l)	3 000.000	Research	Rockwell	04/52
Lattice Test Reactor	◘	Heavy water	0.500	Research	E I Dupont de Nemours	01/67
LITR	◘	Tank	3 000.000	Research	Martin Marietta Energy Systems	00/50
LIWB	◘	Homogeneous(l)	0.500	Research	Lawrence Livermore Laboratory	00/53
LPR-USA	◘	Pool	1 000.000	Research	B&W	09/58
LPTR	◘	Tank	3 000.000	Research	Lawrence Livermore Laboratory	12/57
Ltr. Ground Test Reactor	◘	Pool	10 000.000	Test	General Dynamics/Convair	00/54
ML-1	◘	Nitrogen cooled	3,300.000	Prototype	Aerojet General Nucleonics	00/61
MTR USA	◘	Tank	40 000.000	Test	Phillips Petroleum	00/52
Naval Research Reactor	◘	Pool	1 000.000	Research	Naval Research Laboratory	00/56
Oak Ridge Graphite	◘	Graphite	3,500.000	Research and isotope production	Martin Marietta Energy Systems	00/43
Oak Ridge Research	◘	Tank in pool	30 000.000	Research	Martin Marietta Energy Systems	03/58
OMRE	◘	Organic	12 000.000	Prototype	Atomics International	00/57
Pawling Research Reactor	◘	Heavy water		Research	United Nuclear	00/58
PBMUR	◘	Pool	100.000	Research	National Aeronautics and Space Administration	00/61
PCA	◘	Pool	10.000	Critical assembly	Martin Marietta Energy Systems	08/58
PCTR	◘	Pool	0.100	Research	Pacific Northwest Laboratory	00/55
PDP	◘	Heavy water	0.500	Research	E I Dupont de Nemours	10/53
Phrenic	◘	Pool	100.000	Research	Brookhaven National Laboratory	00/65
Plumbrook Reactor	◘	Tank	60 000.000	Test	National Aeronautics and Space Administration	00/61
Power Burst Facility	◘	Tank	26 000.000	Test	EG&G Idaho	09/72
PRCF	◘	Critical assembly		Critical assembly	Battelle Memorial Institute	00/60
RER Lockheed	◘	Pool	3 000.000	Research	Lockheed Aircraft Corp	00/58
RRR, Mississippi State University	◘	Pool	10.000	Training	Mississippi State University	00/59
Schizo	◘	Pool	100.000	Research	Brookhaven National Laboratory	00/58
SEFOR	◘	Fast neutron	20000	Research	University of Arkansas (Mechanical Engineering Department)	00/69
SER	◘	Tank	5 000.000	Test	Sandia Laboratories	00/61
SL-1	◘	BWR	3 000.000	Prototype	C-E	00/58
Snaptran-1	◘			Test	Los Alamos Scientific Laboratory	00/65
Snaptran-2	◘			Test	Phillips Petroleum	00/65
Snaptran-3	◘			Test	Phillips Petroleum	00/64
Spert-1	◘	Tank		Test	Phillips Petroleum	00/55
Spert-2	◘	Pool		Test	Phillips Petroleum	00/60
Spert-3	◘			Test	Phillips Petroleum	00/58
Spert-4	◘	Pool		Test	Phillips Petroleum	00/62
SPR, Stanford University	◘	Pool	10.000	Training	Stanford University	12/59
Standard Pile	◘	Graphite pile	10.000	Research	E I Dupont de Nemours	07/53
Stir	◘	Pool	1 000.000	Test	Atomics International	00/61
Super Kukla	◘	Prompt burst		Test	Lawrence Livermore Laboratory	00/64
Supo	◘	Homogeneous(l)	25.000	Test	Los Alamos Scientific Laboratory	00/49
Suzie	◘	Pool		Test	GE	00/51
Triga Mk F, Northrop	◘	Triga Mk F	1 000.000	Research	Northrop	00/63
Triga Mk II Columbia University	◘	Triga Mk II	250.000	Research	Columbia University	00/77
Triga, Puerto Rico Nuclear Center	◘	Triga converter	2 000.000	Research	Puerto Rico Nuclear Centre	00/72
TSR-1	◘	Tank in pool	500.000	Research	Martin Marietta Energy Systems	00/54
TSR-II	◘	Tank	1 000.000	Research	Martin Marietta Energy Systems	03/60
TTR-2	◘	Pool	0.100	Research	Pacific Northwest Laboratory	00/55
UCLA R1	◘	Argonaut	100.000	Training	University of California, Los Angeles	10/60
UI-Triga Mk I	◘	Triga Mk I	100	Training	University of Illinois	01/60
UT-Triga, University of Texas	◘	Triga Mk I	250.000	Research	University of Texas	00/63
UTR-1	◘	Argonaut		Training	American Standard Co	00/58
UWNR, University of Washington	◘	Argonaut	100	Training	University of Washington	04/61
VPI	◘	Argonaut	100.000	Training	Virginia Polytechnic Institute	12/59
WNTR	◘	Tank	1.000	Training	Westinghouse Electric	00/72
WTR	◘	Pool	60 000.000	Test	Westinghouse Electric	00/59
ZPR-6	◘	Critical assembly		Critical assembly	Argonne National Laboratory	00/63
ZPR-9	◘	Critical fast		Critical assembly	Argonne National Laboratory	00/67
ATUTR	●			Research		00/92
AGN-201, Georgia Tech	●	Homogeneous(s)	0.0001	Research	Georgia Institute of Technology	01/68
Loft	▲	Tank	50 000.000	Test	EG&G Idaho	02/78
R-3, North Carolina State University	▲	Pool	10	Training	North Carolina State University	00/60
Triga Mk I, Michigan State University	▲	Triga Mk I	250.000	Research	Michigan State University	03/69

VENEZUELA

Name	Status	Type	Steady power, kW	Application	Owner/operator	Date of criticality
RV-1	●	Pool	3000	Research	Instituto Venezolano de Investigaciones Científicas (IVIC)	07/60

VIETNAM

Name	Status	Type	Steady power, kW	Application	Owner/operator	Date of criticality
Dalat	●	Pool	500	Research	Dalat Nuclear Research Institute	11/83

● Operable; ★ Under construction; ○ Planned; ◘ Shutdown; ● Cancelled or indefinitely deferred; ▲ Decommissioned

Research reactors: country-by-country listing (former Yugoslavia-Zaire)

Name	Status	Type	Steady power, kW	Application	Owner/operator	Date of criticality
former YUGOSLAVIA						
R-B	●●	Heavy water		Critical assembly	Boris Kidric Institute	04/58
RA	●●	Heavy water	6 500.000	Research	Boris Kidric Institute	12/59
ZAIRE						
Trico	●	Triga Mk II	1000	Research	CREN K	00/59

ABBREVIATIONS

Operators

AECL – Atomic Energy of Canada
B&W – Babcock & Wilcox (USA)
C-E – Combustion Engineering (USA)
CEA – Commissariat a l'Energie Atomique (F)
CEGB – Central Electricity Generating Board (UK)
CNEA – Comision Nacional de Energia Atomica (RA)
CNEN – Commissao Nacional de Energia Nuclear (BR)
ECN – Netherlands Energy Research Foundation (NL)
EdF – Electricite de France
EIR – now Paul Scherrer Institute (CH)
ENEA – Comitato Nazionale per la Ricerca e per lo Sviluppo dell l'Energia Nucleare e delle Energie Alternative (I)
GE – General Electric (USA)
IFE – Institut for Energiteknikk (NO)
ININ – Institute Nacionale de Investigaciones Nucleares (MX)
IPEN – Instituto Peruano de Energia Nucleare (PER)
KAERI – Korea Atomic Energy Research Institute (K)
KWU – now the KWU division of Siemens (D)
LNETI – Laboratoria Nacional de Engenharia e Technologia Industrial (POR)
MAEP – Ministry of Atomic Energy and Industry
OECD – Organisation for Economic Co-operation and Development
PNC – Power Reactor and Nuclear Fuel Development Corporation (J)
SCK/CEN – Studiecentrum voor Kernenergie/Centre d'Etude de l'Energie Nucleaire (B)
UKAEA – UK Atomic Energy Authority

WORLD NUCLEAR INDUSTRY HANDBOOK 1994

Fuel cycle facilities:

This section contains general information on fuel cycle facilities worldwide, excluding cancelled plant. The plants are listed by type, then by country. The information given covers status (indicated by a symbol, the key to which is listed below); last year's production; capacity; operator; feed, products and process (where applicable); date of commercial operation, and date of shutdown (where applicable). The assistance of the Uranium Institute in providing some of the data is gratefully acknowledged.

Key to symbols
● Operable ★ Under construction ○ Planned ⌧ Shut down or on stand-by

Uranium ore processing

	Status	Capacity	1992 production	Operator	Feed	Product	Process	Date of comm'l operation	Date of shut down
ARGENTINA									
Faustina	●			CNEA	Phosphoric acid	U3O8	DEPA/TOPO		
Ownership: 100% Freeport Uranium Recovery Corporation									
La Estela	●	20 tU/y	19 tU	CNEA	Ore	U3O8	H/IX	/86	
Open pit mine. Heap leach.									
Los Gigantes	●	80 tU/y	38 tU	CNEA	Ore	U3O8	H/IX	/82	
Open pit mine. Heap leach. Production facilities owned by Sanchez Granel Ingeniera and product sold to CNEA									
San Rafael	●	120 tU/y	77 tU	CNEA	Ore	U3O8	H/IX	/70	
Open pit mine, heap leach									
Sierra Pintada	○	500 tU/y		CNEA	Ore	U3O8	A/IX	/92	
Open pit mine, conventional mill. Financing problems causing delays									
Los Adobes	⌧	55 tU/y	0	CNEA	Ore	U3O8	H/IX		/85
Ownership: 100% CNEA									
Malargue	⌧	70 tU/y		CNEA	Ore	U3O8	A/IX/SX	/55	/87
Open pit mine, conventional mill									
AUSTRALIA									
Nabarlek	●	1145 tU/y	360 tU	Queensland	Ore	U3O8	A+H/SX	/79	
Although milling of the high grade ore from the original orebody has been completed, a new orebody has been announced which is expected to enable production to continue for several years									
Olympic Dam	●	1600 tU/y	1370 tU3O8	WMC	Ore	U3O8	A/SX	08/88	
Ownership: 100% WMC (Olympic Dam Corp) Pty Ltd. WMC (ODC) is a wholly-owned subsidiary of Western Mining. WMC(ODC) the operator, is a wholly-owned subsidiary of Western Mining. Initial capacity of 1500tU/y came on stream August 1988. Plant will be expanded depending on growth in the uranium market. Olympic Dam produces chiefly copper, with uranium, gold and silver.									
Ranger	●	3000 tU/y	3080 tU/y	ERA	Ore	U3O8	A/SX	11/81	
Ownership: North Broken Hill-PEKO 65.09%, 9.91% public shareholders; 10.00% JAURD (Japanese Australia Uranium Resources Development Company Limited); 6.25% Rheinbraun; 4.00% Urangesellschaft; Interoran 2.50%; Cogema 1.25%; OKG 1.00%									
Yeelirrie	○	2500 tU/y		Western Mining	Ore	U3O8	Basic leach		
Ownership: 90% Western Mining; 10% Urangesellschaft Australia Pty Ltd. Project on hold awaiting a change in the Australian three-mines policy. Ore body has been explored but not developed.									
BELGIUM									
Puurs and Engis	●	50 tU/y	46 tU	PRT	Phosphoric acid	U3O8	DEPA/TOPO	/80	
Ownership: 100% Societe de Prayon Rupel SA. All production is allocated to Synatom									
BRAZIL									
Pocos de Caldas	●	420 tU/y	55 tU	UB	Ore	U3O8	A/SX	12/81	
Urânio do Brasil is a subsidiary of the new, state-owned Industrias Nucleares do Brasil, which replaces the former Nuclebras									
BULGARIA									
Buchovo	●	600 tU/y		Redki Metali	Ore	U3O8	Drying		
Eleshniza	●	380 tU/y	90 tU/y	Redki Metali	Ore	U3O8	Stripping		12/95
Both these mills serve the Plovdiv mine.									
CANADA									
Cluff Mining	●	1500	800	Amok	Ore	U3O8	A/SX	00/81	
Ownership: 80% Amok Ltd, 20% Cameco Corporation.									
Denison/Elliot Lake	●	2700 tU/y	1400 tU	Denison Mines	Ore	U3O8	A/IX	06/57	
Ownership: 100% Denison Mines Ltd									
Elliot Lake/Panel	●	1000 tU/y	0 tU	Rio Algom	Ore	U3O8	A/IX	/79	07/93
Ownership: 100% Rio Algom									
Elliot Lake/Stanleigh	●	700 tU/y	700 tU	Rio Algom	Ore	U3O8	A/IX	/83	
Key Lake	●	4600 tU/y	5100 tU/y	Key Lake Mining	Ore	U3O8	A/SX	/83	
Ownership: 66.67% Cameco; 33.33% UEM									
Rabbit Lake	●	4600 tU/y	2160 tU	Cameco	Ore	U3O8	A/SX/UP	01/75	
Ownership: 66.67% Cameco; 33.33% UEM									
McArthur River				Cameco	Ore	U3O8			
Ownership: 53.991% Cameco; 29.775% UEM; 9.063% Interuranium; 7.171% Cogema. McArthur River is a uranium exploration property.									
Cigar Lake	○			Cigar Lake Min	Ore	U3O8			
Ownership: 48.75% Cameco - Corporation; 32.625% Cogema Canada Ltd; 12.875% Idemitsu Uranium Exploration Canada Ltd; 3.75% Corona Grande Exploration Corporation; 2.00% Korea Electric Power Corp. Current status pre-feasibility testing. Start of underground test mine construction 10/88.									
Dawn Lake	○			Cameco	Ore	U3O8			
Ownership: 50.076% CAMECO; 20.115% Cogema; 17.989% Power Reactor and Nuclear Fuel Development Corp (Japan); 7.5% Nuclear Electric (UK); 4.32% Korea Electric Power									

Fuel cycle facilities: (uranium ore processing)

	Status	Capacity	1992 production	Operator	Feed	Product	Process	Date of comm'l operation	Date of shut down
Corp. Dawn Lake is a uranium exploration property.									
Kiggavik and Sissons Schultz South	○			Uran Can	Ore	U3O8			
Ownership: Urangesellschaft Canada 79%; Daewoo (Korea) 1%. CEGBC Canada Ltd 20% Project in feasibility study stage and is located in Northwest Territories									
McClean Lake	○			Minatco	Ore	U3O8			
Ownership: 50% Canadian Occidental; 50% Inco. These companies have an agreement with Minatco under which Minatco will earn a one-third interest in the project by spending CDN$23 million on feasibility and becoming the project operator									
Midwest Joint Venture	○	1633 tU3O8/y		Denison Mines	Ore	U3O8	A/SX	01/94	
Ownership: Denison Mines 45%; Bow Valley Industries Ltd 20%; Uranerz 20%; 20% OURD (Canada) Co Ltd									
Beaverlodge	⊃	0		Eldorado Nuc	Ore	U3O8			06/82
The owner/operator, Eldorado Nuclear, is currently (mid-1988) merging with the Saskatchewan Mining and Development Corporation									
Calgary	⊃	60 tU/y	0	ESI	Phosphoric acid	U3O8	DEPA/TOPO	/63	
Ownership: 51% ESI; 49% Urangesellschaft Canada									
Elliot Lake/Quirke	⊃	2000 tU/y	1070 tU	Rio Algom	Ore	U3O8	A/IX	/68	07/93
CHINA									
Hengyang, Hunan	●	1100 tU/y		CNNC	Ore	U3O8	A/IX	/62	
Hengjian, Jiangxi	●			CNNC	Ore	U3O8	A/IX		
These are understood to be the two main mills in China, but at least seven other uranium processing centres have been reported, including Zhuzhou, Shao Kuan, Guizhou, Urumqi, Huxian, Yining, Quinlong. The total ore processing capacity for China has been estimated at 3000 tU/y. The production in 1992 has been put at 955 tU.									
CZECH REPUBLIC									
Rozna	●	600 tU/y	470 tU/y	Diamo	Ore	U3O8	A/SX		
Straz	●	800 tU/y	800 tU/y	Diamo	Ore	U3O8	A/SX	/94	
FRANCE									
Bertholène	●	70 tU/y	65 tU	Cogema	Ore	Loaded resins		/82	01/94
Ownership: 99% TCM; 1% Cogema. Process: Static acid leach in vats and ion exchange resins. (loaded resins are trucked to Le Cherbois (Jouac) for elution and U3O8 production									
Herault Mining Division	●	1000 tU/y	885 tU	Cogema	Ore	U3O8	A/SX	01/81	
La Crouzille Mining Division	●	1000 tU/y	805 tU	Cogema	Ore	U3O8	A/SX		07/96
Ownership: 100% Cogema									
Le Bernardan, Le Cherbois	●	550 tU/y	432 tU	Cogema	Ore	U3O8	A/SX	05/79	
Ownership: 99% TCM; 1% Cogema.									
Le Cellier	●	300 tU/y		MOKTA	Ore	U3O8	A	/77	
Ownership: 100% Cogema									
Mailhac/Bernadan	●	500 tU/y		Dong Trieu	Ore	U3O8	A/SX	/79	
St Pierre-du-Cantal	●	100 tU/y		SCUMRA	Ore	U3O8	A/IX	/78	
Inguiniel, Calardieu	⊃		0	SIMURA	Ore	U3O8			
Ownership: 51.69% MOKTA; 48.31% private interests. Deposits now exhausted									
St Pierre (Cantal)	⊃	100 tU/y	0	SCUMRA	Ore	U3O8	A/RIP	/77	/84
Ownership: 94.2% Total Compagnie Miniere; 5.8% private interests									
GABON									
Mounana	●	1100 tU/y	846 tU	COMUF	Ore	U3O8	A/SX	/82	
Ownership: 38.98% MOKTA; 24.75% Gabon government; 18.81% Cogema; 12.99% Pechiney; 3.47% COGEI; 1.00% Gabon public									
GERMANY									
Ellweiler	⊃	125 tU/y	0 tU	Gew Brunhilde	Ore	U3O8	A/IX		/89
HUNGARY									
Cserkut	●	700 tU/y	430 tU/y	Mecsekuran	Ore	U3O8	H+A/SX		
INDIA									
Jaduguda	●	200 tU/y	115 tU	U Corp India	Ore	U3O8	A/IX	/68	
Ownership: 100% Uranium Corporation of India Ltd									
Mosaboni	●		15 tU	U Corp India	Copper by product	U3O8			
Rakha	●		15 tU	U Corp India	Copper by product	U3O8			
Surda	●		15 tU	U Corp India	Copper by product	U3O8			
JAPAN									
Ningyo-Toge	⊃	50 tU/y	0	PNC	Ore	U3O8	A/SX		
NIURES	⊃	10 kgU/y		MMA	Seawater	U3O8	Adsorb/Elute	04/86	03/88
Nio Institute for Uranium Recovery from Seawater decommissioned in March 1990									
KAZAKHSTAN									
Aktou, Shevchenko	●	1000 tU/y	400 tU/y		Ore	U3O8	P2O5		
Stepnogorsk	●	3000 tU/y	800 tU/y		Ore	U3O8	A/IX		
KYRGYSTAN									
Kara Balta	●	3600 tU/y	1100 tU/y	Kara Balta Ore Mining Comb	Ore	U3O8	I/IX		
Capacity currently being reduced by 50% to 1800 tU/y.									

WORLD NUCLEAR INDUSTRY HANDBOOK 1994

Fuel cycle facilities: (uranium ore processing)

	Status	Capacity	1992 production	Operator	Feed	Product	Process	Date of comm'l operation	Date of shut down
MEXICO									
Los Amoles	⊐	200 tU/y		CFM	Ore	U3O8	H/SX		
Peña Blanca	⊐	200 tU/y	0	CFM	Ore	U3O8	A/SX		
MOROCCO									
Sah	●	470 tU/y		OCP	Phosphoric acid	U3O8	DEPA/TOPO	/86	
Jorf Lasfar	●	370 tU/y		OCP	Phosphoric acid	U3O8	DEPA/TOPO	/71	
Nador	○	185 tU/y		OCP	Phosphoric acid	U3O8	DEPA/TOPO		
NAMIBIA									
Rossing Mine	●	4000 tU/y	2500 tU	Rossing	Ore	U3O8	A/SX	/76	/18
Ownership: 41.35% Rio Tinto Zinc Corp Ltd; 10.00% Total Compagnie Minière; 10.00% Rio Algom Ltd; 10.10% Industrial Development Corp of South Africa; 5.00% Urangesellschaft; 3.37% Namibian Government; 2.30% General Mining and Finance.									
NIGER									
Akouta	●	2300 tU/y	2000 tU	COMINAK	Ore	U3O8	A/SX	/78	
Ownership: 34% Cogema; 31% Office National des Ressources Minières; 25% Overseas Uranium Resources Development Company; 10% Empresa Nacional del Uranio SA									
Arlit (acid)	●	2000 tU/y	1000 tU	SOMAIR	Ore	U3O8	A/SX	01/71	
Arlit as a whole is owned: 36.80% Office National des Ressources Minières, 37.48 Cogema, 19.36% CFM; 6.54% Urangesellschaft.									
Arlit (heap)	●	2000 tU/y	1000	SOMAIR	Ore	U3O8	A/SX	02/71	
Arlit as a whole is owned: 35.59% Office National des Ressources Minières, 37.48 Cogema, 19.36% CFM, 6.54% Urangesellschaft.									
PAKISTAN									
Dera Ghazi Khan	●	30 tU/y	23 tU	PAEC	Ore	U3O8	A/SX	85	
Issa Khel	○			PAEC	Ore	U3O8			
PORTUGAL									
Urgeirica (acid)	●	140 tU/y		ENU	Ore	U3O8	A.SX	51	
Urgeirica (heap)	●	15 tU/y		ENU	Ore	U3O8	H	51	
Urgeirica (in situ)	●	15 tU/y		ENU	Ore	U3O8	I	51	
Nisa (acid)	○	170 tU/y		ENU	Ore	U3O8	A/SX	90	
Nisa (heap)	○	30 tU/y		ENU	Ore	U3O8	H	90	
ROMANIA									
Brasov	●	900 tU/y	120 tU/y	Unknown	Ore	U3O8	A/SX		
RUSSIA									
Krasnokamensk, Priargunsk	●	4000 tU/y	2640 tU/y	Priargunsky	Ore	U3O8	K/P/IX		
SOUTH AFRICA, REPUBLIC OF									
Buffelsfontein	●	400 tU/y	356 tU	Buffelsfontein	Ore	U3O8	A/SX	/57	
GENCOR administers the operations of Buffelsfontein Gold Mining Company Ltd									
Hartebeestfontein	●	350 tU/y	320 tU	HGMC	Ore	U3O8	A/IX	56	
Anglovaal Ltd administers the operations of Hartebeestfontein Gold Mining Company Ltd									
Metallurgical Scheme	●	450 tU/y	423 tU	FREEGOLD	Ore	U3O8	A/SX	/77	
A central uranium recovery facility serving several mines									
Palabora	●	150 tU/y	115 tU	PMC	Ore	U3O8	A/SX	/71	
Ownership: 38.9% Rio Tinto Zinc Corp; 18.9% Anglo-American Corp; 8.7% De Beers; 32.5% other interests									
Vaal Reefs	●	1500 tU/y	1374 tU	Vaal Reefs	Ore	U3O8	A/IX	06/53	
Vaal Reefs Exploration and Mining Company Ltd is administered by Anglo American Corp of South Africa Ltd.									
Western Areas	●	200 tU/y	192 tU	Western Areas	Ore	U3O8		/82	
Western Areas Gold Mining Company Ltd is administered by Johannesburg Consolidated Investment Company Ltd									
Afrikander Lease	⊐	300 tU/y	0		Ore	U3O8	A/SX	/82	
Beisa	⊐	450 tU/y	0		Ore	U3O8	A/SX	/84	
Blyvooruitzicht	⊐	500 tU/y	0	Blyvooruitzicht	Ore	U3O8	IX	/67	12/84
Chemwes	⊐	500 tU/y	0 tU	Chemwes	Ore	U3O8	A/CIX/SX	/79	/88
Chemwes ceased uranium production in the fourth quarter of 1988. GENCOR administers the operations of Chemwes Ltd									
Driefontein	⊐	500 tU/y	0 tU	Driefontein Con	Ore	U3O8	A/SX	/58	/88
Uranium produced as a by-product of gold. Uranium production ceased in the third quarter of 1988. Plant has been converted to a gold recovery facility. Gold Fields of South Africa administers the operations of Driefontein Consolidated Ltd									
East Rand	⊐	250 tU/y	0	ERGO	Reclaimed tailings	U3O8	A/IX	03/78	02/91
Harmony	⊐	150 tU/y	0	Harmony	Ore	U3O8	A/IX/SX	/55	01/88
Rand Mines Ltd administers the operations of the Harmony Gold Mining Company Ltd									
Joint Metall Sch	⊐	500 tU/y	0	Anglo-American	Ore	U3O8	A/SX	/77	07/93
West Rand Cons	⊐	500 tU/y	0 tU	GENGOLD	Ore	U3O8	A/SX	10/52	08/61
Ceased production in August 1992. Surface structures now demolished and land sold to private developer.									
Western Deep Levels	⊐	300 tU/y	0	Anglo-American	Ore	U3O8	A/SX		07/93

● Operable ★ Under construction ○ Planned ⊐ Shut down or on stand-by   NUCLEAR ENGINEERING INTERNATIONAL

Fuel cycle facilities: (uranium ore processing)

	Status	Capacity	1992 production	Operator	Feed	Product	Process	Date of comm'l operation	Date of shut down
SPAIN									
Saelices el Chico	●	190 tU/y	210 tU	ENUSA	Ore	U3O8	H/SX	05/75	
Quercus	○	615 tU/y		ENUSA	Ore	U3O8	H+A/SX	/92	
TADJIKISTAN									
Chkalovsk	○	2000 tU/y	1200 tU/y	Vostokredmet	Ore	U3O8	I/IX		
TUNISIA									
Gabes	○			ICM	Phosphoric acid	U3O8	DEPA/TOPO	/93	
Ownership: 100% Tunisian government									
UKRAINE									
Zholtye Vody	●	2000 tU/y	600 tU/y		Ore	U3O8	A/SX		
USA									
Ambrosia Lake, Mine Water	●		62 tU	Quivira	Mine water	U3O8			
Ownership: 100% Quivira Mining Company.									
Bill Smith	●	30 tU/y	29 tU	Rio Algom Inc	Ore	U3O8	I		
Pilot plant operating. Rio Algom has agreed to buy Bill Smith from Kerr McGee									
Blanding	●	3000 tU/y	1150 tU	EFN	Ore	U3O8	Acid leach	05/80	
Bruni	●	330 tU/y		URI	Ore	U3O8	I	/77	
Ownership: 50% Uranium Resources Inc; 50% Coastal Uranium									
Canon City	●	330 tU/y	0	Cotter	Ore	U3O8	Acid leach	05/58	
Ownership: 100% Cotter Corporation. Mill placed on standby in January 1987. Production allocated to Commonwealth Edison									
Crow-Butte	●	10 tU/y	8 tU	Ferret	Ore	U3O8	I	/90	
Ownership: 65% Ferret Exploration Company; 25% Uranerz; 10% Korea Electric Power Corp. Pilot plant operating									
Donaldsonville	●	175 tU/y		Freeport	Phosphoric acid	U3O8	D2EHPA/ TOPO	/81	
The Uncle Sam plant provides drying and finishing processes for the Donaldsonville plant, which was put on stand-by in Oct '89 but restarted operations on 1 Jan '91.									
Freeport			19 tU	Rhone-Poulenc	Ore	U3O8	By-product		
Highland	●	450 tU/y	308 tU	Power	Ore	U3O8	I	/88	
Highland is operated by Everest Minerals Corp, a wholly-owned subsidiary of Everest Exploration Company Inc									
Highland Uranium Project	●		1083000 lbU3O8	PRI	Ore	U3O8	I		01/88
Hobson Central Processing Plant	●	400 tU/y	0 tU	Everest	Ore	U3O8	I	/79	
Ownership: 100% Everest Exploration Inc. Hobson is the processing centre for Mount Lucas, Las Palmas, Tex-1 and Gruy-7B									
Jeffrey City				US Energy	Mine only	Mine only		/88	
Acquired from Western Nuclear early 1988. Ore toll milled at Pathfinder's Shirley Basin									
Kanab North				EFN	Mine only	Mine only			
Joint venture with Swiss utilities									
La Sal		500 tU/y		Rio Algom	Ore	U3O8	K/DP	/72	
McBryde				Caithness	Ore	U3O8	I		
Ownership: 100% Caithness Mining. In restoration									
Mount Taylor			80 tU	Chevron	Mine only	Mine only		03/85	
Ownership: 100% Chevron Resources. Mine reactivated in 1985. Ore being processed at Homestake mill									
Panna Maria	●	960 tU/y	600 tU	Chevron	Ore	U3O8	A/SX	02/79	
Ownership: 100% Chevron Resources. Put back into operation in 1986									
Pigeon	●			EFN	Mine only	Mine only			
Joint venture with Swiss utilities									
Rhode Ranch	●	580 tU/y	580 tU	Chevron	Mine only	Mine only	Open pit	03/88	
Ownership: 55% Chevron; 45% Total Minerals. Ore is shipped to the Panna Maria mill									
Sahuarita				Anamax	Copper leach liquors	U3O8		/80	
Schwartzwalder			0	Cotter	Mine only	Mine only		06/66	
Closed since early 1987. Cotter maintains an exploration programme to develop additional reserves									
Shirley Basin		1000 tU/y	154 tU	Pathfinder	Ore	U3O8	A/IX		
Shirley Basin, Texaco		700 tU/y		Texaco	Ore	U3O8	A/SX		/86
Uncle Sam	●	310 tU/y	350 tU	Freeport	Phosphoric acid	U3O8	D2EHPA/TOPO		/78
Ownership: 100% Freeport Uranium Recovery Corp. Uranium is produced as a by-product.									
White Mesa	●	2100 tU/y	1400 tU	UMETCO	Ore	U3O8	A/SX	/81	
Ownership: 70% UMETCO Minerals Corporation; 30% Energy Fuels Nuclear. Vanadium ore processing also conducted.									
Alta Mesa	*	385 tU/y		Total Min	Solution	U3O8	I		
Kingsville Dome				URI	Ore	U3O8	I	/88	
Ownership: 100% Uranium Resources Inc									
Arizona 1	○			EFN	Mine only	Mine only			
Joint venture with Swiss utilities									
Canyon	○			EFN	Mine only	Mine only			
Ownership: 60% EFN; 40% Uranerz									
Green Mountain				US Energy	Mine only	Mine only			
Hermit	○			EFN	Mine only	Mine only			
Joint venture with Swiss utilities									
Juniper Ridge	○			Agip Mining	Ore	U3O8		/89	
Ownership: 100% Agip Mining									

Fuel cycle facilities: (uranium ore processing)

	Status	Capacity	1992 production	Operator	Feed	Product	Process	Date of comm't operation	Date of shut down
Peach	○			ANC	Ore	U3O8			
Undeveloped ore deposit									
Pinenut	○			EFN	Mine only	Mine only			
Joint venture with Swiss utilities									
Powder River				Rio Algom Inc	Ore	U3O8	In situ leach		
Ownership: 100% Kerr McGee Corp. Facility is currently at the pilot plant stage									
Ambrosia Lake, Conventional	⊐		0	Quivra	Ore	U3O8			
Ownership: 100% Quivra Mining Company. Placed on standby in 1985									
Bartow	⊐		0	UG USA	Phosphoric acid	U3O8	DEPA/TOPO		
Bear Creek	⊐		0	Rocky Mountain	Ore	U3O8			12/85
Ownership: 50% Rocky Mountain Energy Company; 50% Mono Power									
Benavides	⊐		0	URI	Ore	U3O8	I		
Ownership: 100% Uranium Resources Inc. Currently in restoration									
Bingham Canyon	⊐	50 tU/y	0 tU	EFN	Copper leach liquors	U3O8	RIP columns	/80	03/89
Bison Basin	⊐		0	Ogle/Western	Ore	U3O8	I		
Ownership: 50% Ogle Petroleum Company; 50% Western Fuel Inc. Facility is wholly owned by Duke Power. Facility currently in restoration following its closure in 1983									
Bluewater	⊐		0	Anaconda	Ore	U3O8			03/82
Ownership: 100% Anaconda Copper Company									
Burns Ranch	⊐	15 tU/y		USX	Ore	U3O8	I		
Restoration in progress									
Christensen Ranch	⊐	230 tU	0 tU	Malapai	Solution	U3O8		04/89	02/90
Ownership: 100% Malapai Resources Company. Operations are temporarily suspended. Facility operated and managed by TOTAL Minerals Corporation									
Church Rock	⊐	1000 tU/y	0	UNC	Ore	U3O8	A/SX		/86
Ownership: 100% United Nuclear Corporation. Facility on standby									
Clay West	⊐	40 tU/y	0	USX	Ore	U3O8	I	/75	/87
Ownership: 50% USX; 50% Niagara Mohawk Uranium. Mined out in 1987. Restoration in progress									
Conquista	⊐		0	Conoco	Ore	U3O8			/82
Ownership: 66.7% Conoco Inc; 33.3% Pioneer Nuclear									
Delta	⊐	10 tU/y	0	Brush Wellman	Beryllium ores	U3O8		/80	
Ownership: 100% Brush Wellman. Decommissioned									
El Mesquite/Holiday/O'Hern	⊐	150 tU	0 tU	Malapai	Solution	U3O8	I	01/81	02/90
Facility operated and managed by TOTAL Minerals Corporation. Currently on standby and in restoration									
Falls City	⊐		0	Solution Engg	Ore	U3O8			
Ownership: 100% Solution Engineering Inc. Facility placed on standby in February 1982									
Farmland	⊐	250 tU/y	0	Uranges	Phosphoric acid	U3O8	DEPA/TOPO		
Ownership: 100% Urangesellschaft. On standby since 1982. Purchased from Westinghouse in 1985									
Ford	⊐	500 tU/y	0	Dawn Mining	Ore	U3O8	A/SX		/86
Gardinier	⊐			Gardinier	Phosphoric acid	U3O8	DEPA/TOPO		
Ownership: 100% Gardinier									
Gas Hills Mill	⊐		0	ANC	Ore	U3O8			
Gas Hills, Federal	⊐	500 tU/y	0	Fed American	Ore	U3O8	A/IX+SX		/86
Gas Hills, UMETCO	⊐		0	UMETCO	Ore	U3O8			/84
Ownership: 100% UMETCO Minerals Corporation. Open pit mine, conventional heap leach. Placed on standby in 1984. Final reclamation has started									
Grants, Anaconda	⊐	3000 tU/y	0	Anaconda	Ore	U3O8	A/RIP		/86
Grants, Churchrock	⊐	4000 tU/y	0	Rio Algom Inc	Ore	U3O8	A/SX		/86
Hack 1, 2, 3	⊐		0	EFN	Mine only	Mine only			
Restoration in progress. Joint venture with Swiss utilities									
Irigaray	⊐	190 tU/y	0 tU	Malapai	Solution	U3O8	I	/88	02/90
Ownership: 100% Malapai Resources Company. Operations are temporarily suspended. Facility operated and managed by TOTAL Minerals Corporation									
L-Bar Uranium Mine and Mill	⊐	1000 tU/y	0	RTZ, Kennecott	Ore	U3O8	A/SX	/77	05/81
During 1986 the mine and mill were demolished, the shaft sealed and the mine flooded. The tailings pond was reclaimed during 1989									
Lisbon	⊐	410 tU/y	0 tU	Rio Algom	Ore	U3O8			/88
Ownership: 100% Rio Algom Corporation									
Lucky Mc	⊐	1000 tU/y	0 tU	Pathfinder	Ore	U3O8	A/IX	/86	03/88
Ownership: 80% Cogema; 20% Pathfinder Mines Corporation									
Maybell	⊐		0	UMETCO	Ore	U3O8			
Ownership: 100% UMETCO Minerals Corporation. Final reclamation has started									
Midnite	⊐		0	Dawn Mining	Mine only	Mine only			
Ownership: 51% Newmont Mining Corporation; 49% Midnite Mining Inc									
Mount Lucas	⊐	400 tU/y	0	Everest	In situ leach satellite	na		/84	/88
Restoration in progress									
Natrona County	⊐	500 tU/y	0	UMETCO	Ore	U3O8	A/IX+SX		/86
Final reclamation has started									
Palangana	⊐		0	Chevron	Ore	U3O8	I		
Petrotomics	⊐		0	Getty Oil	Ore	U3O8			/85
Ownership: 100% Getty Oil Company									
Powder River Basin, Bear	⊐	400 tU/y	0	Bear Creek	Ore	U3O8	A/SX		
Powder River Basin, Exxon	⊐	1500 tU/y	0	Exxon	Ore	U3O8	A/SX		/86
Red Desert	⊐	350 tU/y	0	Mineral Explor	Ore	U3O8			/86
Ruby Ranch	⊐		0	Santa Fe Mining	Ore	U3O8	I		
Ownership: 100% Santa Fe Mining									
Sherwood	⊐		0	Western Nuclear	Ore	U3O8			
Ownership: 100% Western Nuclear Inc. Open pit mine, conventional mill									
Shootering Canyon	⊐	400 tU/y	0	Plateau	Ore	U3O8			
Ownership: 100% Plateau Resources Company, which is a subsidiary of Consumers Power. The facility is currently on standby									
Split Rock	⊐		0	Western Nuclear	Ore	U3O8			
Ownership: 100% Western Nuclear Inc. Decommissioning in progress									
Tampa	⊐	200 tU/y	0	Gardinier	Phosphoric acid	U3O8	DEPA/TOPO		/83

128   ● Operable   ★ Under construction   ○ Planned   ⊐ Shut down or on stand-by   NUCLEAR ENGINEERING INTERNATIONAL

Fuel cycle facilities: (uranium ore processing, uranium refining & conversion)

	Status	Capacity	1992 production	Operator	Feed	Product	Process	Date of comm'l operation	Date of shut down
Tex-1	◻		0	Everest	In situ leach satellite	na		/87	03/90
Trevino	◻	150 tU/y	0	Conoco	Ore	U3O8	I	/81	/85
Ownership: 100% Conoco Inc									
UNC Recovery	◻		0	UNC	Phosphoric acid	U3O8	DEPA/TOPO		
Ownership: 100% UNC Recovery Corporation, which has now been dismantled									
Uravan	◻	1000 tU/y	0	UMETCO	Ore	U3O8	A/IX		/86
Ownership: 100% UMETCO Minerals Corporation, which is a subsidiary of Union Carbide. Final reclamation underway									
Wellpinit	◻	200 tU/y	0	Western Nuclear	Ore	U3O8	A/IX		/86
Las Palmas	◻		0	Everest	In situ leach satellite	na		/81	/84
Restoration in progress									
Moab	◻	800 tU/y	0	Atlas	Ore	U3O8	A+K	01/56	03/84
Ownership: 100% Atlas Corporation.									
UZBEKISTAN									
Navoi	●	4000 tU/y	1850 tU/y		Ore	U3O8	I/A/JX		
YUGOSLAVIA									
Zirovski vrh	●	120 tU/y	57 tU	RUZV	Ore	U3O8	A/SX	01/85	
Ownership: 100% Republic of Slovenia									
Bor-Prahovo	○				Phosphoric acid	U3O8	DEPA/TOPO		

Uranium refining & conversion

	Status	Capacity	1992 production	Operator	Feed	Product	Process	Date of comm'l operation	Date of shut down
ARGENTINA									
Cordoba (phase 1)	●	55 tU/y		CNEA	U3O8	UO2		/57	
Built with indigenous technology									
Cordoba (phase 2)	✱	150 tU/y		CNEA	U3O8	UO2			
Built with RBU of FR Germany									
Ezeuza	○	150 tU/y		CNEA	U3O8	UO2			
BRAZIL									
Sao Paulo	●	90 tU/y		IPEN	U3O8	UF6		/84	
Resende	○	500 tU/y		INB	U3O8	UF6			
CANADA									
Blind River	●	18000 tU/y	5914 tU	Cameco	U3O8	UO3	Nitric acid	/83	
Port Hope (UF6)	●	10500 tU/y		Cameco	UO3	UF6	Fluorination	/84	
Port Hope (UO2)	●	2700 tU/y		Cameco	UO3	UO2		/84	
FRANCE									
Malvesi	●	14000 tU/y	11000 tU	Comurhex	U3O8	UF4+U	Wet	/59	
Pierrelatte (Comurhex) Nat U	●	14000 tU/y	11000 tU	Comurhex	UF4	UF6	Wet	/61	
Pierrelatte (Comurhex) Repu	●	350 tU/y	300 tU	Comurhex	Reprocessed uranium	UF6	Wet	/76	
INDIA									
Hyderabad	●	250 tU/y		DAE	U3O8	UO2		/71	
Trombay	●			DAE	U3O8	U		/60	
JAPAN									
Ningyo-Toge (trioxide)	●	6 tU/y		PNC	UO3	UF6		/82	
Ningyo-Toge (yellowcake)	●	200 tU/y		PNC	U3O8	UF6		/82	
KOREA, REPUBLIC OF									
Taejeon (UO2)	●	200 tU/y		KNFC	UF6	UO2	AUC	01/90	
RUSSIA									
Angarsk, Irkutsk	●			Electrol CC					
Tomsk 7	●			Sibkhimkombinat					
SOUTH AFRICA, REPUBLIC OF									
Valindaba	●	700 tU/y		UCOR	U3O8	UF6		/86	
TURKEY									
CNRC Nuclear Fuel Pilot Plant	●	1 tU/y	40 kgU	CNRC	U3O8	UO2	D/SX/ADU	10/86	
UNITED KINGDOM									
Springfields (UF6)	✱	6000 tU/y		BNFL	U3O8	UF6		00/93	
Springfields (UO2)	✱	710 tU/y		BNFL	UF6	U		01/95	

Fuel cycle facilities: (uranium refining & conversion/enrichment)

	Status	Capacity	1992 production	Operator	Feed	Product	Process	Date of comm'l operation	Date of shut down
USA									
Metropolis Works	●	12700 tU/y		Allied	U3O8	UF6	DFV	/59	
Sequoyah Fuels Conversion Facility	⊓	9090 tU/y		Sequoyah Fuels	Dry powder & wet slurry	UF6	Wet	05/70	11/92
Sequoyah Fuels Reduction Facility	⊓	3400 tUF4/y		Sequoyah Fuels	Depleted UF6	Depleted UF4	Vapour phase	07/87	07/93

Enrichment

	Status	Capacity	1992 production	Operator	Feed	Product	Process	Date of comm'l operation	Date of shut down
ARGENTINA									
Pilcaniyeu (phase 1)	●	20000 swu/y		CNEA	na	na	Diffusion		
Pilcaniyeu (phase 2)	✱	100000 swu/y		CNEA	na	na	Diffusion	/90	
BRAZIL									
Resende Jet Nozzle Plant	✱	10000 swu/y		Nuclei	UF6	UF6	Jet nozzle		
Resende ownership includes INB (75%), Steag (15%) and Interatom (10%)									
Sorocaba	O			IPEN	na	na	Centrifuge		
CHINA									
Lanchow	●	200000 swu/y		Unknown	na	na	Diffusion	/80	
An additional 200000 swu/y enrichment plant is reportedly planned, to be built by Minatom of Russia, with construction scheduled to start in 1994.									
FRANCE									
Georges Besse Plant	●	10800000 swu/y		Eurodif	na	na	Diffusion	/79	
GERMANY									
Gronau	●	530000 swu/y		Urenco D	na	na	Centrifuge	08/85	
Capacity expected to expand to 1 000 000swu/y									
JAPAN									
Hyuga	●	2000 swu/y		Asahi	na	na	Chemical	12/86	
Ningyo-Toge (Demo)	●	200000 swu/y		PNC	na	na	Centrifuge	/89	
Ningyo-Toge (Pilot)	●	50000 swu/y		PNC	na	na	Centrifuge	/82	
Rokkasho-Mura (phase 1)	●	600000 swu/y		JNFL	na	na	Centrifuge	03/92	
450 000 swu/y is complete - the remaining 150 000 swu/y of the first phase is due to be completed in 1994.									
Rokkasho-Mura (phase 2)	✱	900000 swu/y		JNFL	na	na	Centrifuge	12/92	
JNFL is planning to expand enrichment capacity by 150 000 swu each year and to complete the first stage of construction work (600 000 swu/y) by fiscal 1994, eventually reaching the 1 500 000 swu/y goal for the whole Rokkasho-Mura plant.									
NETHERLANDS									
Almelo	●	1200000 swu/y	1200000 swu	Urenco N	na	na	Centrifuge	/81	
PAKISTAN									
Kahuta	●	5000 swu/y		PAEC	na	na	Centrifuge	/84	
Will be expanded to about 15 000swu/y									
RUSSIA									
Angarsk, Irkutsk	●			Electrochem Comb			Centrifuge		
Krasnoyarsk-45, Krasnoyarsk	●			Sibkhimstroy			Centrifuge	/64	
Tomsk 7, Tomsk	●			Sibkhimkombinat			Centrifuge		
Has been used for REPU.									
Sverdlovsk-44, Ekateringburg	●	3000000 swu/y		Electrochem Comb			Centrifuge		
Total Russian enrichment capacity is around 14 million swu/y and total 1992 production was 7 million swu/y.									
SOUTH AFRICA, REPUBLIC OF									
Valindaba (Pelindaba East)	●	300000 swu/y		UCOR	na	na	Helikon	/82	
UNITED KINGDOM									
Urenco (Capenhurst)	●	850000 swu/y	850000 swu	Urenco	na	na	Centrifuge	11/76	
USA									
Paducah Gaseous Diffusion Plant	●	11300000 swu/y	5400000 swu	USEC	na	na	Diffusion	12/54	
Martin Marietta Energy Systems Inc operates the plant.									
Portsmouth Gaseous Diffusion Plant	●	7900000 swu/y	6100000 swu	USEC	na	na	Diffusion	11/55	
Claiborne Parish, LA	O	1500000 swu/y		LES	na	na	Centrifuge	/98	
LES (Louisiana Energy Services) is proposing to construct this plant in three phases over five years.									
Oak Ridge	⊓	7700000 swu/y	0	Exxon	na	na	Diffusion	/45	

● Operable ✱ Under construction O Planned ⊓ Shut down or on stand-by

Fuel cycle facilities: (fuel fabrication)

Fuel fabrication

	Status	Capacity	1992 production	Operator	Feed	Product	Process	Date of comm't operation	Date of shut down
ARGENTINA									
Ezeiza	●	300 tHM/y		CNEA	na	PHWR	na	/82	
BELGIUM									
Dessel, Belgonucleaire	●	35 tHM/y	35 tHM	BN	na	LWR/MOX	na	01/85	
Dessel, FBFC	●	400 tHM/y		FBFC	na	PWR			
BRAZIL									
Resende	●	100 tHM/y	16 tHM	INB	Pellets, UO2	PWR	na	11/81	
CANADA									
Peterborough, Ont Assembly only	●	1000 tHM/y		GE Canada	na	PHWR	na	/67	
Port Hope: Zircatec	●	1200 tHM/y		Zircatec	na	PHWR	na	/56	
Toronto Pellets only	●	1050 tHM/y		GE Canada	na	PHWR	na	/67	
Moncton	⊃	250 tHM/y	0	C-E	na	PHWR	na		
CHINA									
Yibin Capacity scheduled to reach 150tU/y by 1995	●				na	LWR	na	/87	
FRANCE									
Cadarache	●	15 tHM/y		Cogema	na	FBR/LWR MOX		na	
Melox	●	120 tHM/y		Melox	na	LWR MOX	na	/95	
GERMANY									
Hanau (RBU)	●	720 tHM/y		RBU	na	BWR;PWR	na	/85	
Lingen	●	300 tHM/y		ANF	na	BWR;PWR	na		
Siemens, Brennelementwerke Hanau	●	25 tHM/y	22 tHM	Siemens	na	FBR/LWR MOX	na		
Hanau MOX plant Start-up delayed due to licensing problems	●	120 tHM/y			na	BWR/PWR MOX			
INDIA									
Hyderabad (HWR) (Phase 1)	●	300 tHM/y		DAE	na	PHWR	na	/71	
Hyderabad (LWR)	●	25 tHM/y		DAE	na	BWR	na		
Nuclear Fuel Complex	●	600 tHM/y		NFC	Yellow cake	PHWR fuel	ADU Route	12/95	
Hyderabad (HWR) (Phase 2) Construction started 04/93.	⊃	600 tHM/y		DAE	na	PHWR	na	/95	
ITALY									
Bosco-Marengo	●	200 tHM/y	0 tHM	Fab Nucl	na	BWR & PWR fuel bundle	na	05/74	
Saluggia	●	60 tHM/y		ENEA	na	HWR;LWR	na	/86	
JAPAN									
Kumatori	●	265 tHM/y		NFI	na	BWR;PWR	na	/76	
Tokai (NFI)	●	200 tHM/y	60 tU	NFI	na	BWR;PWR;ATR;FBR;HTR	na	/80	
Tokai-Mura (MNF)	●	440 tHM/y		MNF	na	PWR	na	01/82	
Tokai-Mura (PFFF)	●	9 tHM/y		PNC	na	ATR MOX	na	/72	
Tokai-Mura (PFFF-FBR)	●	1 tHM/y		PNC	na	FBR MOX	na	/72	
Tokai-Mura (PFPF-FBR)	●	4 tHM/y		PNC	na	FBR MOX	na	/88	
Yokosuka	●	640 tHM/y		JNF	na	BWR	na	01/70	
Tokai-Mura (PFPF-LWR/ATR)	●	35 tHM/y		PNC	na	LWR/ATR MOX	na	/91	
KAZAKHSTAN									
Ust Kamenogorsk, Ulbinski Combine Provides 80% of total ex-USSR requirement for pellets.	●				UF6	UO2	ADU reconversion		
Ust Kamenogorsk, Ulbinski Combine Pellets for RBMK and VVER.	●	2650 t/y				VVER/RBMK pellets	Pelletising		
KOREA, REPUBLIC OF									
Taejeon (Fuel Fab)	●	200 tHM/y		KNFC	na	PWR	na	01/89	

Fuel cycle facilities: (fuel fabrication/away from reactor storage)

	Status	Capacity	1992 production	Operator	Feed	Product	Process	Date of comm'l operation	Date of shut down
MEXICO									
PPFC	●	2 tHM/y	0	ININ	UO2	BWR Fuel Bundles	na		10/93
PAKISTAN									
Chashma	●			PAEC	na	PHWR	na	/86	
RUSSIA									
Chelyabinsk, Paket	●	300 kg/y(10-12FAs)	100 kg/y(4FAs)			FBR fuel			
Being reconstructed to supply 40 FA/y (1t MOX) FBR fuel for the BN-600 FBR.									
Elektrostal, Moscow Region	●	700 t/y	230 t/y	Atommash		VVER-440 fuel assemblies			
Elektrostal, Moscow Region	●	570 t/y	570 t/y			RBMK fuel assemblies			
Elektrostal, Moscow Region	●	20 t/y				FBR fuel assemblies			
Elektrostal, Moscow Region	●	15 t/y				FBR blanket			
Novosibirsk, Siberia	●	1000 t/y	210 t/y			VVER-1000 elements			
Chelyabinsk	★			Mayak		MOX fuel for FBRs			
Considering addition of a pilot plant for VVER-1000 MOX fuel.									
Krasnoyarsk, Siberia	○					MOX for VVERs			
SPAIN									
Juzbado	●	200 tHM/y	180 tHM	ENUSA	na	BWR;PWR	na	06/85	
SWEDEN									
Vasteras	●	400 tUO2/y		ABB Atom	na	BWR;PWR	na	/71	
UNITED KINGDOM									
Dounreay (Research Reactor Fuel 1)	●	500 elements/y	200 elements/y	AEA Technology	U/Al alloy	Research reactor fuel	na	/59	
Springfields (Magnox)	●	1300 tHM/y		BNFL	na	Magnox	na	/60	
Dounreay (Research Reactor Fuel 3)	●	500 elements/y		AEA Technology	Silicide	Research reactor fuel	na		01/93
Springfields (AGR)	★	330 tHM/y		BNFL	na	AGR	na	00/95	
Springfields (PWR)	●	200 tHM/y		BNFL	na	PWR	na	/00/95	
Dounreay (Research Reactor Fuel 2)	○	500 elements/y		AEA Technology	UAlx	Research reactor fuel	na		12/92
Sellafield MDF (LWR MOX fuel fab)	★	8tHM/y		BNFL	Pu and U oxides	LWR MOX			/94
Sellafield (LWR MOX fuel fab)	○	120 tHM/y		BNFL	Pu and U oxides	LWR MOX	na	12/97	
Sellafield (FBR MOX fuel fab)	▢	6 tHM/y	0	BNFL	na	FBR MOX	na	01/70	01/88
USA									
Columbia Plant	●	1500 tHM/y		West	na	PWR	ADU, IDR	/69	
Commercial Nuclear Fuel Plant	●	400 tHM/y	232 t	BWFC	na	PWR	na	01/70	
Hematite	●	300 tHM/y	275 tHM/y	ABB CENF	na	PWR	na	01/74	
UO2 powder, pelletizing									
Richland	●	700 tHM/y		SPC	uF6	BWR;PWR	na		
Wilmington	●	1100 tHM/y		GE	na	BWR	na	/82	
Windsor	●	300 tHM/y	275 tHM/y	ABB CENF	na	PWR	na	01/69	
Manufactures fuel assembly structural components and sends to Hematite Missouri plant for assembly into final configured fuel assemblies									
Apollo	▢	360 tHM/y	0 tHM	B&W	na	UO2 powder and pellets	na		
Currently shut down. Active decontamination and soil characterization underway. Facility being deconstructed in 1992.									

Away from reactor storage

	Status	Capacity	1992 production	Operator	Feed	Product	Process	Date of comm'l operation	Date of shut down
ARGENTINA									
Ezeiza	★			CNEA	PHWR	na	Pool		
BELGIUM									
Mol	▢	370 tHM		Eurochemic	LWR	na	Pool		
BULGARIA									
Kozloduy	★	600 tHM			LWR	na	Pool		
CZECH REPUBLIC									
Jaslovske Bohunice	●	600 tHM	429 tHM	NPP Bohunice	PWR	na	Pool	11/87	
FINLAND									
KPA Store, Olkiluoto	●	1270 t		TVO	LWR	na	Pool	09/87	
FRANCE									
Cascad	●	180 tHM		CEA	HWR	na	Dry vault	/87	

● Operable ★ Under construction ○ Planned ▢ Shut down or on stand-by

Fuel cycle facilities: (away from reactor storage/reprocessing)

	Status	Capacity	1992 production	Operator	Feed	Product	Process	Date of comm'l operation	Date of shut down
GERMANY									
Gorleben	●	1500 tHM		GNS	LWR	na	Dry cask	/84	
Karlsruhe	●	55 tHM		KfK	LWR	na	Pool	/71	
Ahaus	★	1500 tHM		GNS	LWR	na	Dry cask	/90	
Greifswald	●	550 tHM		EWNC	VVER-40	na	Pool	/85	
JAPAN									
Tokai-Mura	●	237 tHM		PNC	LWR/ATR	na	Pool	/77	
Tokai-Mura (phase 1)	●	97 tHM		PNC	LWR	na	Pool	/85	
Rokkasho-Mura	★	3000 tHM		JNF	LWR	na	Pool	04/96	
Tokai-Mura (phase 2)	○	140 tHM		PNC	LWR	na	Pool		
RUSSIA									
Chelyabinsk, South Urals	●				VVER-440	na	Pool		
Storage facility associated with the RT-1 reprocessing facility for VVER-440 fuel.									
Krasnoyarsk, Siberia	●	6000 tHM			VVER-1000 fuel	na	Pool		
Current capacity 3000 tHM. Currently reported to be storing 1000 tHM. This pool is for fuel awaiting reprocessing in the RT-2 plant, which has not yet started up. Each RBMK in the ex-USSR has 2000tHM spent fuel storage capacity. The intention is not to reprocess RBMK fuel.									
SWEDEN									
CLAB	●	5000 tHM	250 tHM	SKB	LWR	na	Pool	07/85	
UNITED KINGDOM									
Sellafield (AGR)	●	3000 tHM		BNFL	AGR	na	Pool	01/81	
Sellafield (Magnox)	●	3500 tHM		BNFL	Magnox	na	Pool	01/85	
Sellafield (Oxide)	●	5000 tHM		BNFL	LWR spent fuel	na	Pool	01/64	
Wylfa	●	700 tHM		Nuc Elec	Magnox	na	Dry vault	09/79	
USA									
Idaho Falls	●			DOE Idaho	LWR	na	Dry		
Morris	●	750 MTU		GE	LWR	na	Pool		
Barnwell	⊃	400 tHM	0	AGNS	LWR	na	Pool	.80	

Underground repository

	Status	Capacity	1992 production	Operator	Feed	Product	Process	Date of comm'l operation	Date of shut down
SWEDEN									
SFR	●	60000 cubic m	3000 cubic m	SKB	LLW/ILW	na	na	04/88	

Reprocessing

	Status	Capacity	1992 production	Operator	Feed	Product	Process	Date of comm'l operation	Date of shut down
ARGENTINA									
Ezeiza	★	5 tHM/y		CNEA	Oxide	U:Pu	Purex	'89	
BELGIUM									
Mol	⊃	100 tHM/y	0	Eurochemic	Oxide	U:Pu	Purex	/74	
BRAZIL									
Sao Paulo	●			IPEN	Oxide	U:Pu	Purex		
FRANCE									
La Hague (UP2 400)	●	400 tHM/y	220 tHM	Cogema	Oxide;LWR MOX;FBR MOX	U:Pu	Purex	/76	
Will be replaced by UP2 800 in 1994.									
La Hague (UP3)	●	800 tHM/y	448 tHM	Cogema	Oxide	U:Pu	Purex	/90	
Marcoule	●	400 tHM/y	410	Cogema	U metal	U:Pu	Purex	/58	
Now for gas cooled reactor fuel only									
La Hague (UP2 800)	★	800 tHM/y		Cogema	Oxide;MOX	U:Pu	Purex	01/94	
Will replace UP2 400.									
GERMANY									
WAK	⊃	40 tHM/y	19 tHM	KfK	Oxide	U:Pu	Purex	09/71	12/90
WAK is operated by Wiederaufarbeitungsanlage Karlsruhe Betriebsgesellschaft mbh and owned by KfK									
INDIA									
Kalpakkam (phase 1)	●	125 tHM/y		DAE	Oxide	U:Pu	Purex	/86	
Tarapur	●	100 tHM/y		DAE	Oxide	U:Pu	Purex	/77	
Trombay	●	50 tHM/y		DAE	Oxide	U:Pu	Purex	/85	
Kalpakkam (phase 2)	★	1000 tHM/y		DAE	Oxide	U:Pu	Purex		

Fuel cycle facilities: (reprocessing, heavy water production)

	Status	Capacity	1992 production	Operator	Feed	Product	Process	Date of comm'l operation	Date of shut down
ITALY									
Saluggia	●	10 tHM/y		ENEA	Oxide	U:Pu	Purex	/83	
JAPAN									
Rokkasho-Mura	★	800 tHM/y		JNF	Oxide	U:Pu	Purex	01/00	
RUSSIA									
RT-1, Chelyabinsk, South Urals	●	400 tHM/y	120 tHM	Mayak	VVER-440	U:Pu	Aqueous extraction using tributyl phosphate	/71	
The site also includes a 500t/h vitrification facility.									
RT-2, Krasnoyarsk	★	3000 tHM/y		Sibkhimstroy	VVER-1000 spent fuel	U:Pu			
The plan is to bring this plant on stream in two lines of about 1500 tHM/y each, but current construction progress remains uncertain.									
Tomsk, Siberia	●			Sibkhimkombinat					
Production reactor fuel only.									
UNITED KINGDOM									
Dounreay Reprocessing Plant	●	8 tHM/y	2 tHM/y	AEA Technology	U/Al alloy	H	Purex	01/80	
Sellafield (Magnox)	●	1500 tHM/y		BNFL	U metal	U:Pu	Purex	01/64	
Sellafield (Thorp)	★	850 tHM/y		BNFL	Oxide	U:Pu	Purex	/93	
Throughput expected to be 7000tHM over the first ten years of operation									
USA									
Idaho Falls	●			DOE Idaho	LWR	U:Pu	Purex		
Rockwell Hanford	●	2400 tHM/y		Rockwell	Oxide	U:Pu	Purex		
Savannah River Site	●	2700 tHM/y		DOE-SR	Oxide	U:Pu	Purex	/54	
Barnwell	⊃	1500 tHM/y	0	AGNS	LWR	U:Pu	Purex	/83	
West Valley	⊃	300 tHM/y	0	NFS	Oxide	U:Pu	Purex	/66	

Heavy water production

	Status	Capacity	1992 production	Operator	Feed	Product	Process	Date of comm'l operation	Date of shut down
ARGENTINA									
Arroyito (phase 1)	★	100 t/y		CNEA	na	D2O	MHAE	/88	
Arroyito (phase 2)	★	150 t/y		CNEA	na	D2O	MHAE	/89	
Arroyito (phase 3)	★	200 t/y		CNEA	na	D2O	MHAE	/90	
Atucha	●			CNEA	na	D2O	nk		
CANADA									
Bruce Heavy Water Plant B	●	106 kg/h	695 t	Ont Hyd	H2O	D2O	GS	01/81	
Bruce Heavy Water Plant A	⊃	106 kg/h	0	Ont Hyd	H2O	D2O	GS	01/73	06/84
Glace Bay	⊃	250 t/y	0	AECL	H2O	D2O	GS		
INDIA									
Baroda	●	67 t/y		DAE	na	D2O	MHAE	/80	
Kota	●	100 t/y		DAE	na	D2O	GS	/81	
Nangal	●	14 t/y		DAE	na	D2O	E/D	/62	
Talcher (phase 1)	●	62 t/y		DAE	na	D2O	MHAE	/80	
Tuticorin	●	71 t/y		DAE	na	D2O	MHAE	/78	
Manuguru	★	185 t/y		DAE	na	D2O	VD		
Thal-Vaishet	●	110 t/y		DAE	na	D2O	VD		
Talcher (phase 2)	O	72 t/y		DAE	na	D2O	MHAE	/90	
USA									
Savannah River Site	●	190 t/y		DOE-SR	na	D2O	GS	/52	

Zirconium metal production

	Status	Capacity	1992 production	Operator	Feed	Product	Process	Date of comm'l operation	Date of shut down
ARGENTINA									
Ezeiza	●			CNEA	na	S;l	na	/81	
Pilcaniyeu	★			CNEA	na	r	na	/90	
BRAZIL									
Sao Paulo	★	5 t/y		IPEN	na	r	na	/86	

● Operable   ★ Under construction   O Planned   ⊃ Shut down or on stand-by   NUCLEAR ENGINEERING INTERNATIONAL

Fuel cycle facilities: (heavy water production/zirconium metal production)

	Status	Capacity	1992 production	Operator	Feed	Product	Process	Date of comm'l operation	Date of shut down
CANADA									
Port Hope, Eldorado	◯	300 t/y	0	Eldorado Nuc	na	I	na	/76	
FRANCE									
Jarrie	●	2000 t/y		CEZUS	na	r	na	/82	
Montreuil Juigne	●			CEZUS	na	Tubes and bars		na	
Rugles	●			CEZUS	na	Flat products	na		
Ugine	●			CEZUS	na	Melting and forging		na	
INDIA									
Hyderabad	●	210 t/y		DAE	na	S,I	na	/72	
Palayakayal	◯	300 t/y		DAE	Zircon sand	unknown			
JAPAN									
Nagahama	●	300 t/y		CEZUS	na	Tubes	na	/89	
USA									
Albany	●	2000 t/y		Tel Wah Chang	na	S,I	na	/76	
Western Zirconium Plant	●			West	Zircon Sand	Metal		/80	
Akron	◯	500 t/y	0	Amax	na	I	na	/76	

Zirconium tubing production

	Status	Capacity	1992 production	Operator	Feed	Product	Process	Date of comm'l operation	Date of shut down
ARGENTINA									
San Carlos de Bariloche	◯			CNEA	Zirconium metal	nk	na	/90	
CANADA									
Arnprior	●	1600 km/y		GE Canada	Zirconium metal	Zy-2,Zy-4	na	/81	
Cobourg	●	760 t/y		Zircatec	Zirconium metal	PWR, BWR, PHWR	na	/81	
FRANCE									
Paimboeuf	●	4000 km/y		Zircotube	Zirconium metal	Zy-4	Tube pilgering	04/80	
GERMANY									
Duisburg	●	1400 t/y		Nuklearrohr	Zirconium metal	nk	na	/81	
Hellenthal	●	350 t/y		Mannesmann	Zirconium metal	nk	na	/81	
INDIA									
Hyderabad (HWR) (Phase 1)	●	80 t/y		DAE	Zr sponge	Zr/2/Zr-Nb	na	/72	
Hyderabad (HWR) (Phase 2)	◯	80 t/y		DAE	Zr sponge	Zr/2/PHWR	na	/72	
JAPAN									
Amagasaki	●	350 t/y		Sumitomo	Zirconium metal	nk	na	/81	
Kobe	●	500 t/y		Kobe Steel	Zirconium metal	nk	na	/81	
Okegawa	●	900000 m/y	500000 m	Mitsubishi Mat	Zirconium metal	nk	na	/74	
RUSSIA									
Glazov, Udmurtia	●	6000 t/y (2000 t/y)	2000 km/y		Zirconium alloy tube				
SWEDEN									
Sandviken	●	1200 t/y		Sandvik	Zirconium sponge	na	na	/65	
USA									
Allens Park	●	500 t/y		Nikko	Zirconium metal	nk	na	/81	
Kennewick	●	2200 t/y		Sandvik Spec M	Zirconium metal	Zy-2,Zy-4	na	/81	
Specialty Metals Plant	●	13000000 ft/y		West	Zirconium metal	nk	na	/68	
Wilmington	●			GE	Zirconium sponge	na	na		

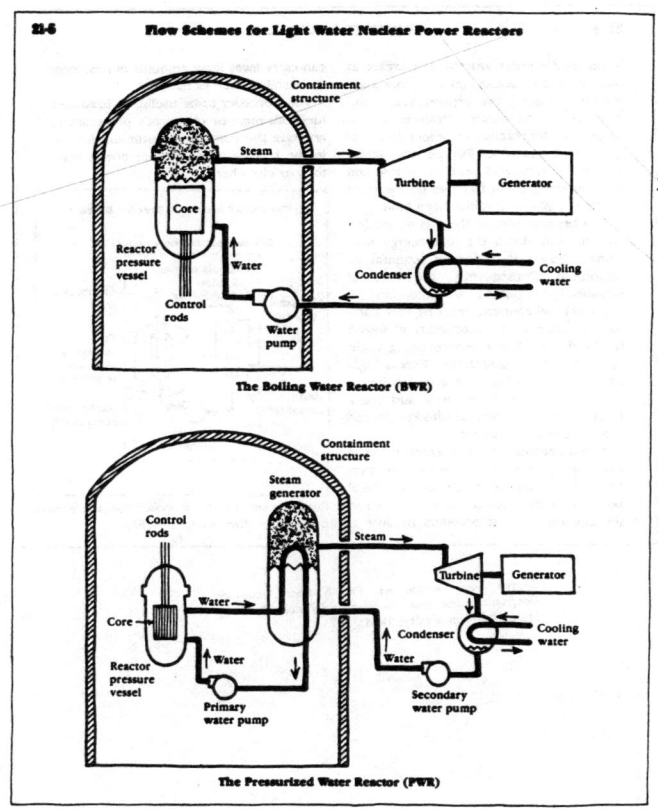

Source: Jack Dennis, ed., *The Nuclear Almanac: Confronting the Atom in War and Peace* (Reading, Mass.: Addison-Wesley, 1984), 392

21-8 BREEDER REACTORS

A nuclear breeder reactor can create at least as much nuclear fuel as it consumes, thereby reducing the dependence of nuclear power on secure resources of uranium. Breeder reactors are under commercial development in Europe and Japan, where the supply of uranium is low and uranium-enrichment facilities on the scale of the U.S. plants have not been built.

In a breeder reactor there is no moderator to slow down the high-energy neutrons released in fission of uranium or plutonium. Consequently, the core of uranium-235 (U-235) or plutonium-239 (Pu-239) fuel elements must be very compact to increase the probability of fission to the degree that a self-sustaining chain reaction can be maintained. Excess high-energy neutrons from the core irradiate a blanket of fertile U-238 rods and transmute some of the material into Pu-239 and other plutonium isotopes.

A fast-neutron breeder reactor has a very high power density in its core, perhaps five times as much as in typical power reactors. Liquid sodium is used as the coolant in most breeders because it can carry away large amounts of heat from the small volume of material.

For a breeder to be useful, its irradiated fuel rods must be chemically processed to separate the converted plutonium for use in the reactor core, in other power reactors, or elsewhere.

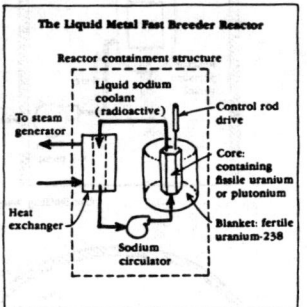

Configuration of fuel and coolant flow in the liquid metal fast breeder reactor (LMFBR).

Source: Jack Dennis, ed., *The Nuclear Almanac: Confronting the Atom in War and Peace* (Reading, Mass.: Addison-Wesley, 1984), 397

523

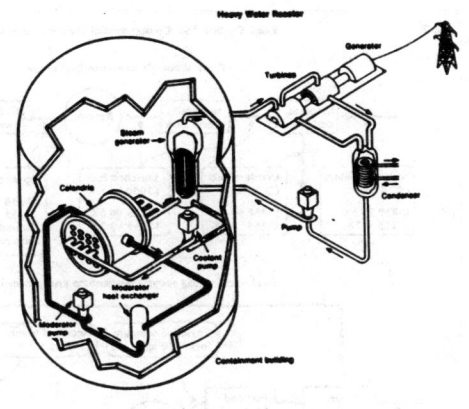

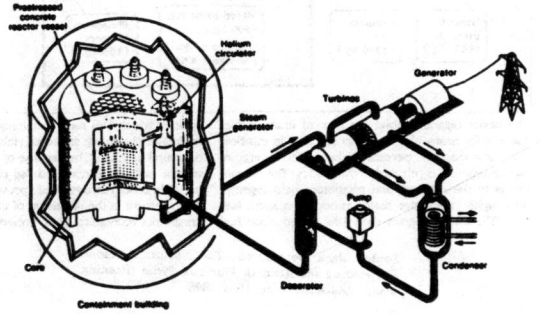

Source: U.S. Congress, Office of Technology Assessment, *Nuclear Power in an Age of Uncertainty* (Washington, D.C.: GPO, 1984), 98

21-7 Fuel Cycles for Commercial Power Reactors

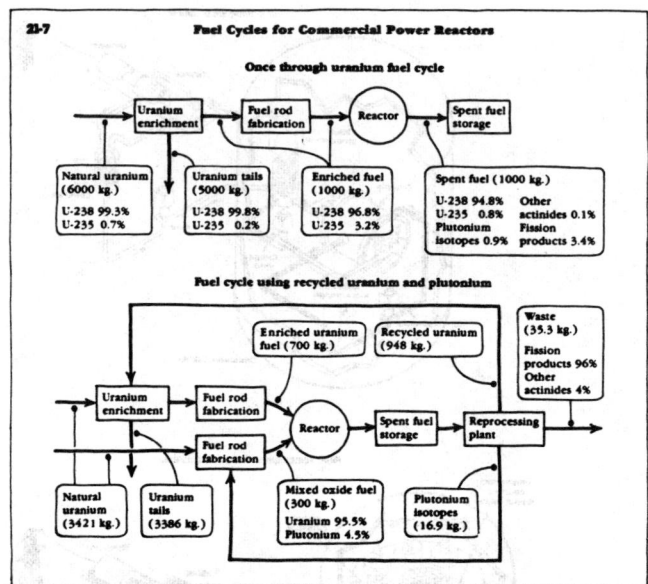

The upper diagram shows the flow of uranium fuel material for nearly all U.S. power reactors. In this flow chart, less than one percent of the nuclear energy of natural uranium is released in the reactor. The remainder is in the uranium and plutonium held together with highly radioactive fission products in spent fuel rods. The lower diagram shows the mixed oxide fuel cycle in which fuel rods containing a mixture of uranium and plutonium are used, yielding a reduced use of natural uranium. The expense of reprocessing spent reactor fuel has discouraged use of this process. The use of breeder reactors would provide a much greater improvement in the utilization of uranium, but breeders are not economical given present uranium supplies.

Source: Jack Dennis, ed., *The Nuclear Almanac: Confronting the Atom in War and Peace* (Reading, Mass.: Addison-Wesley, 1984), 395

Figure 6. Nuclear fuel cycles: (*a*) once-through, (*b*) uranium recycle, (*c*) uranium plus plutonium recycle, (*d*) in a FBR

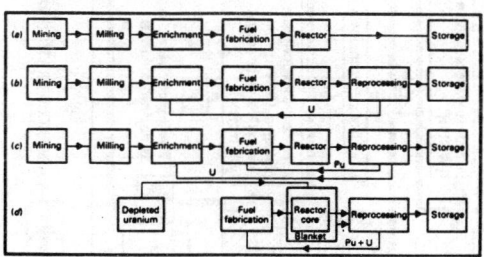

Source: SIPRI, *Nuclear Energy and Nuclear Weapons Proliferation* (London: Taylor & Francis, 1979), 388)

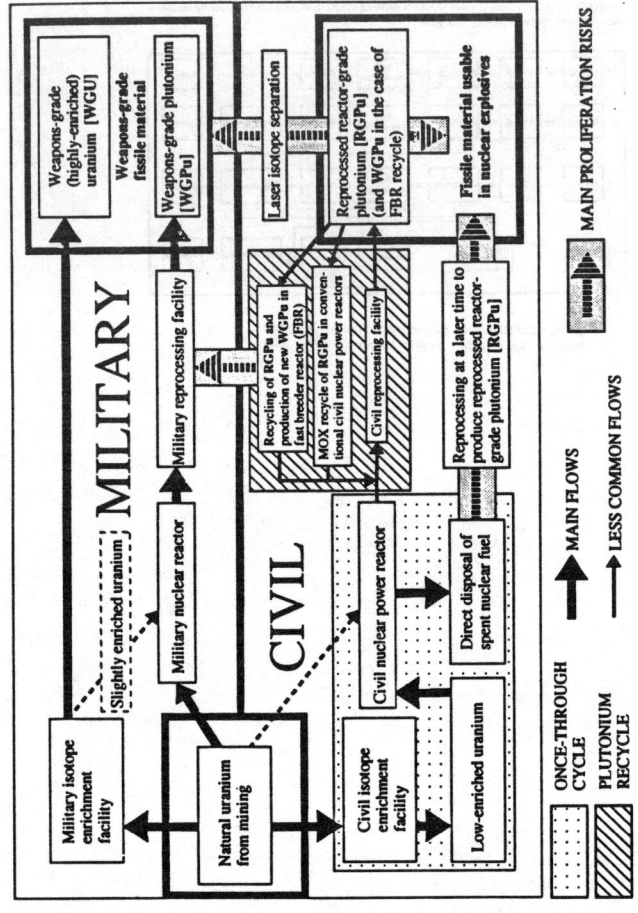

Figure 2.1. Schematic diagram of flows of fissile material in the civil and military nuclear establishment

Source: Johan Swahn, *The Long-Term Nuclear Explosives Predicament* (Goeteborg, Sweden: Chalmers University of Technology, 1992), 21

Table 12. Summary of the diversion points in the LWR fuel cycle

Facility	Material	Is the material useful to the national diverter?	Is the material useful to the non-state adversary?
Mine Mill Conversion facility	Natural uranium (0.7 per cent U-235) as ore (0.2 per cent uranium) U_3O_8 UF_6	Yes, but only as feed for a dedicated facility (plutonium production reactor or enrichment plant)	No (but criminals might engage in black market in these materials)
Enrichment plant	Low enriched uranium (3 per cent U-235 as	Yes, but only as feed for a dedicated enrichment plant	No (criminals might engage in black market in these materials)
Transportation to reactor Temporary storage at reactor	UF_6 UO_2 UO_2 in fuel assemblies	Nation would eventually have to replace fuel	
Reactor spent fuel storage	Pu—about 0.8 per cent in highly radio-active spent fuel	Yes; dedicated reprocessing facility required	No except yes for large, very well financed, technically competent group with a secure base of operations and a few members willing to risk radiation injury
Reprocessing plant Transport to fuel fabrication plant Input area to fuel fabrication plant	Pure $Pu(NO_3)_4$ or pure PuO_2	Yes; nation would probably convert material to metallic plutonium	Yes; if $Pu(NO_3)_4$, simple conversion to PuO_2 required. If PuO_2, material directly usable in explosive
Plutonium fuel fabrication plant	PuO_2 (3 per cent to 7 per cent) mixed with over 90 per cent UO_2	Yes, chemical separation of Pu from mixture only a minor obstacle. Logistics of diverting 100 to 200 kg of material for one explosive troublesome	Yes, but chemical separation a time consuming operation. Logistics of stealing or diverting 100 to 300 kg of material for one explosive cause problems
Transport to reactor Temporary storage at reactor	About 1 per cent Pu as PuO_2 mixed with UO_2 in fuel assemblies	Yes, as above. (nation would eventually have to replace fuel)	Yes, but chemical separation a time consuming operation. Logistics of stealing complete fuel assemblies present significant obstacle

Source: SIPRI, *Nuclear Energy and Nuclear Weapons Proliferation* (London: Taylor & Francis, 1979), 403)

Table 13. Number of shipments in the nuclear fuel cycle projected to the year 2000

	Shipments per year in		
	1980	1990	2000
Fuel	670	2 500	5 400
Spent fuel	2 000	6 400	12 000
Plutonium	20	143	438
Wastes and fission products	630	2 450	5 500

Source: SIPRI, *Nuclear Energy and Nuclear Weapons Proliferation* (London: Taylor & Francis, 1979), 406)

5
Uranium Enrichment

marine reactors. The depleted uranium (the enrichment plant "*tails*") is fabricated into components (e.g., tampers) of nuclear warheads and into targets for the plutonium production reactors. Because of its high density it is used in a variety of other military and commercial applications including antitank bullets and ballast.

From World War II to the present, a number of very different processes have been developed for enriching uranium (and other multi-isotope elements, as well). Early attempts at separating uranium isotopes employed the electromagnetic process (the Calutron), thermal diffusion, gaseous diffusion, and the gas centrifuge. Today, gaseous diffusion and the gas centrifuge dominate uranium enrichment worldwide. Both enrich a gaseous feed of uranium hexafluoride (UF_6) molecules of uranium atoms compounded with fluorine. Coming into use, with varying degrees of acceptance, are several other isotope separation methods: laser isotope separation, plasma separation, chemical enrichment, and aerodynamic processes.

Enrichment Concepts

Two of the most important concepts underlying operation of all enrichment plants are *material balance* and *separative work*.

Material Balance

Uranium is neither created nor destroyed in the enrichment process. Material balance implies that the amount of uranium that enters an enrichment plant (as the feed stream) equals the amount that leaves. It leaves in two streams—one containing enriched *product* with a U-235 concentration greater than the feed, and the other containing depleted uranium *tails* with a lesser U-235 concentration. Despite shifts in the concentration of the uranium isotopes (e.g. U-235), the amount of each isotope entering the plant in the feed equals the amount leaving in the product and tails streams.

Suppose, for example, a customer orders 50,000 kg of 3 percent enriched uranium (containing 1500 kg U-235) and the plant operates with a tails assay of 0.2 percent. To do its job the plant requires a feed of 274,000 kg of natural uranium (containing about 1950 kg U-235) and, along with the desired product, produces a tails stream containing 224,000 kg depleted uranium (containing 450 kg U-235). The amount of material in and out of the plant balances; that is, *feed is equal to product plus tails* both for the total amount of uranium (274,000 kg = 50,000 kg + 224,000 kg) and for the amount of U-235 (1950 kg = 1500 kg + 450 kg).

The second column of Table 5.1 gives the quantity of feed needed per kilogram of product for the product assays contained in the first column and for a tails assay of 0.2 percent. Other situations may be calculated directly.[7]

Uranium Enrichment

Naturally occurring uranium contains only 0.711 percent (by weight) of the fissile isotope U-235 along with 99.3 percent of non-fissile U-238 and trace amounts of U-234. Enrichment processes concentrate the U-235. Enriched uranium is used for a wide range of applications. Enriched to about 1 percent U-235, it fuels plutonium production reactors (e.g., the N-Reactor); to about 3 to 4 percent, it fuels commercial light water power reactors; to about 20 percent or greater, it fuels research and test reactors; to about 93.5 percent, it is used in U.S. nuclear warheads; and to 97.3 percent, it fuels U.S. submarine reactors.

---

[6] Savannah River is planning to fabricate highly enriched production reactor fuel from U_3O_8 by powder metallurgy.

[7] Material balance. At equilibrium, the outflow of product P and tails T from the cascade must equal the inflow of feed. Thus, for all uranium, $F = P + T$, and for the U-235 alone, $x_f F = x_p P + x_t T$, so that the ratio of feed to product for given U-235 fractions is:

$$F/P = (x_p - x_t)/(x_f - x_t).$$

where
x_p = assay of the product, weight fraction of U-235.
x_f = assay of the feed (normally 0.00711), weight fraction of U-235, and
x_t = assay of the cascade tails, weight fraction of U-235.

Source: Thomas B. Cochran et al., *Nuclear Weapons Databook*, vol. 2, *U.S. Nuclear Warhead Production* (Cambridge, Mass.: Ballinger, 1987), 125-35

5
Uranium Enrichment

Separative Work

Separative work measures the effort expended in separating the feed into product and tails. Enrichment demands effort: the larger the concentration of U-235 in the product and the smaller the concentration in the tails, the greater the effort required. The amount of separative work is expressed quantitatively in kilogram separative work units (kg SWUs or simply SWUs). The separative work performed by an enrichment plant (or smaller enrichment unit such as a single gas centrifuge machine) is proportional to the quantity of feed (kilograms) and independent of "assay" (the concentration of U-235). In many plants the capital investment is proportional to the separative work capacity, and the annual operating costs are proportional to the amount of separative work done. Enrichment services are sold in dollars per SWU; the DOE price to commercial customers in 1984 ranged from $138 to $149 per SWU.

The separative work used by the enrichment plant may also be determined from Table 5.1. The third column shows that the enrichment of natural uranium to 3 percent at tails assay of 0.2 percent requires 4.306 kg SWU per kilogram of product. Thus the production of 50,000 kg of 3 percent enriched uranium requires about 215,300 SWU.

Similarly, one can determine how much 93 percent enriched uranium the customer could have acquired for the same number of SWUs. According to Table 5.1, 235.55 SWU are expended per kilogram of 93 percent product at 0.2 percent tails assay, and 181.605 kg of natural uranium feed are required. Consequently, the expenditure of 215,300 SWUs produces only 914 kg of 93 percent enriched uranium and requires about 166,000 kg of feed.

SWU requirements in other situations may be calculated directly.[8]

Enrichment Terminology

Below, a number of terms commonly used in describing the design, construction, and operation of an enrichment plant are discussed.

Stage

The basic separating unit in an enrichment plant is a *stage*. A stage, for example, could be a single porous gaseous diffusion barrier, a single gas centrifuge, or a number of either connected in parallel. An entering stream of natural uranium with a U-235 assay $x = 0.00711$ (or, more generally, uranium with any fraction x of U-235 and $1 - x$ of U-238) divides into two streams leaving the stage: an enriched (or *heads*) stream with a U-235 fraction y and a depleted (or *tails*) stream with fraction z. (y is greater than x and z is less than x.) (See Figure 5.3.)

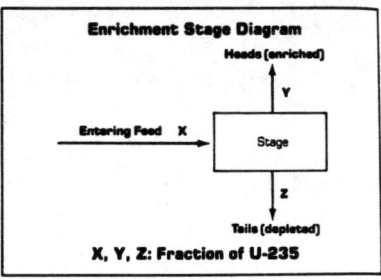

Figure 5.3 Enrichment stage diagram

Separation Factor

The elementary separation factor of a single stage measures the degree of separation achieved in the enriched stream relative to the depleted stream. In the enriched stream the atom fraction of U-235 is equal to y, the atom fraction of U-238 is $1 - y$, and the *abundance ratio* of U-235 to U-238 is defined as $y/(1 - y)$. Similarly, in the depleted stream, the abundance ratio is given by $z/(1 - z)$. The *separation factor* of the stage is defined as the abundance ratio of the enriched stream divided by the abundance ratio of the depleted stream. A separation factor of one means that no separation has occurred. For a separation factor just slightly greater than one (e.g., 1.0043, typical of a gaseous diffusion stage), many stages are usually required to achieve the desired degree of separation.

Cascade

Because the stage separation factor is usually small, stages are connected in series to form a *cascade* in order to achieve the desired separation of U-235 between the product (enriched) and tails (depleted) streams.

The cascade illustrated in Figure 5.4 is "tapered," with the number of parallel-connected units in each stage (proportional to the stage capacity) decreasing as the product and waste ends are approached. The separative work capacity of the cascade is the sum of the separative capacities (SWU/yr) of the individual stages.

The gas centrifuge plant designed by Urenco provides a typical example of an enrichment cascade.[9] It is composed of tens of thousands of identical centrifuge machines. When these are configured for enriching natural uranium to 3 percent U-235 with 0.2 percent tails,

---

8 The separative work per unit of product may be computed from:
$S/P = [V(x_p) - V(x_t)] - (F/P)[V(x_f) - V(x_t)]$,
where
$V(x) = (2x-1) \ln[x/(1-x)]$,
and $V(x_p)$, $V(x_t)$ and $V(x_f)$ are the values of $V(x)$ at the assays of product, cascade tails and feed, respectively.

For derivation of these formulae see AEC, *Gaseous Diffusion Plant Operations* (Oak Ridge Operations Office, Report No. ORO-684, 1972).

9 IAEA *International Nuclear Fuel Cycle Evaluation*, Volume 2, (Vienna, 1980), p. 54.

5
Uranium Enrichment

Table 5.1
Enriching Services[a]

Product Assay (wt. % U-235)	0.2 Percent Tails Assay Standard Table of Enriching Services		Product Assay (wt. % U-235)	0.2 Percent Tails Assay Standard Table of Enriching Services	
	Feed Component (Normal) (kg U Feed/kg U Product)	Separative Work Component (kg SWU/kg U Product)		Feed Component (Normal) (kg U Feed/kg U Product)	Separative Work Component (kg SWU/kg U Product)
0.20	0.000	0.000	2.60	4.697	3.441
0.25	0.098	-0.100	2.80	5.088	3.871
0.30	0.196	-0.158	3.00	5.479	4.306
0.35	0.294	-0.189	3.20	5.871	4.746
0.38	0.352	-0.197	3.40	6.262	5.191
0.40	0.391	-0.198	3.60	6.654	5.638
0.42	0.431	-0.197	3.80	7.045	6.090
0.44	0.470	-0.194	4.00	7.436	6.544
0.46	0.509	-0.189	4.50	8.415	7.690
0.48	0.548	-0.182	5.00	9.393	8.851
0.50	0.587	-0.173	5.50	10.372	10.022
0.52	0.626	-0.163	6.00	11.350	11.203
0.54	0.665	-0.151	7.00	13.307	13.587
0.56	0.705	-0.137	8.00	15.264	15.995
0.58	0.744	-0.123	9.00	17.221	18.422
0.60	0.783	-0.107	10.00	19.178	20.863
0.65	0.881	-0.062	12.00	23.092	25.762
0.70	0.978	-0.012	14.00	27.006	30.737
0.711 (Normal)	1.000	0.000	16.00	30.920	35.719
0.75	1.076	0.044	18.00	34.834	40.724
0.80	1.174	0.104	20.00	38.728	45.747
0.85	1.272	0.168	25.00	48.532	58.369
0.90	1.370	0.236	30.00	58.317	71.064
0.95	1.468	0.307	35.00	68.102	83.816
1.00	1.566	0.380	40.00	77.887	96.616
1.10	1.761	0.535	50.00	97.456	122.344
1.20	1.957	0.698	60.00	117.025	148.235
1.30	2.156	0.868	70.00	136.595	174.302
1.40	2.348	1.045	80.00	156.164	200.605
1.50	2.544	1.227	85.00	165.949	213.892
1.60	2.740	1.413	90.00	175.734	227.341
1.70	2.935	1.603	92.00	179.648	232.796
1.80	3.131	1.797	93.00	181.605	235.550
1.90	3.327	1.994	94.00	183.562	238.328
2.00	3.523	2.194	96.00	187.476	244.642
2.20	3.914	2.602	98.00	191.389	269.982
2.40	4.305	3.018			

[a] The equation for S/P in the table is based on the separation of a binary mixture—for example, U-235 and U-238. Natural uranium, however, contains a third isotope, U-235, assaying about 0.0055 percent by weight. The uranium enrichment plants enrich U-235 along with U-235. At U-235 assays greater than about 94 percent, there is sufficient U-234 present in the isotopic mixture being processed to require a "minor isotope" correction. Table 5.1 incorporates such a correction on the separative work component for product assays above 94 percent U-235. For example, at a product assay of 98 percent U-235, the tabulated separative work per unit product is about 8 percent higher than the value obtained from the equation above for a pure U-235, U-238 mixture.

Source: U.S. AEC, Gaseous Diffusion Plant Operations (Oak Ridge Operations Office, Report No. ORO-684, 1972), p. 37.

they are arranged into twelve stages with an overall annual capacity of 1.0 million SWU. If the cascade was reconfigured to produce highly enriched uranium (by increasing the number of stages with fewer centrifuges per stage), the SWU capacity of the cascade would still be 1.0 million SWU, but the product flow rate would be decreased and fewer kilograms of product would be produced per year.

Enriching and Stripping Sections
In Figure 5.4, feed entering near the center of the cascade is enriched to the desired product composition in the enriching section. The *stripping section* increases the

5
Gaseous Diffusion Process

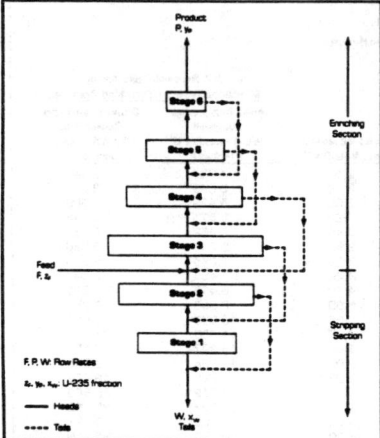

Figure 5.4 Cascade diagram: Countercurrent Recycle Cascade

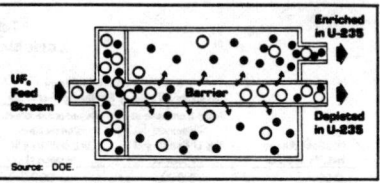

Figure 5.5 Schematic diagram of a diffuser in a gaseous diffusion plant.

recovery of U-235 from the feed by decreasing the fraction of U-235 in the tails. The sole purpose of the stripping section is to reduce the amount of feed required to make a given amount of product.[10]

The number of stages in a cascade depends on the elementary separation factor for each stage. This separation factor may be rewritten as the product of the *heads separation factor* (the abundance ratio of the enriched stream divided by the abundance ratio of the feed stream) and the *tails separation factor* (the abundance ratio of the feed stream divided by the abundance ratio of the depleted stream). For example, in a so-called "symmetrical gaseous diffusion stage," the heads and tails separation factors are equal, each with a value of 1.0021. As material moves up through the enriching section, the heads separation factor is compounded. This determines the number of stages needed for the desired enrichment. Likewise, compounding the tails separation factor in the stripping section reduces the U-235 concentration from the feed assay to the desired concentration in the tails, thus determining the number of stages in this section.

Ideal Cascade

Figure 5.4 shows a *countercurrent recycle cascade*. The tails from each stage feed into the input stream of the preceding stage making it a *symmetrical cascade*. This cascade is *ideal* if the U-235 concentration is the same in all streams that merge together. The flow between stages in an ideal cascade is minimum, making for lowest cost of operation. At each stage, the streams moving away from the ends of the cascade—the tails stream in the enriching section and the heads stream in the stripping section—are known as *reflux* (because they flow back toward the center). In an ideal cascade, the ratio of the heads flow rate to feed flow rate at each stage (known as *cut theta*) is just slightly less than one half. Other flow arrangements require different "cuts."

The ideal cascade is tapered, and the width of each stage (i.e., the number of units) is proportional to the heads flow rate from the stage. The cascade is widest at the feed point, and as the product end is approached, the U-235 concentration increases and the flow rate drops. The separative work performed by an ideal cascade is proportional to the total "interstage flow," the sum of heads and tails flows emerging from all stages.

At startup, an operating cascade must be run without withdrawal of enriched product for a period of time known as the *equilibrium time*. This practice builds up the plant's *working inventory* of U-235. The period may amount to several months of normal production.

Enrichment Processes
Gaseous Diffusion Process

Gaseous diffusion is the technology principally in use worldwide for enriching uranium (see Table 5.2). Each stage of a cascade consists of compressors, heat exchangers, and a diffuser that houses membranes. In the enrichment process, a feed of UF_6 gas is compressed and flows past the diffuser's porous membrane barrier (see Figure 5.5). Some of the gas molecules contain U-235, others contain U-238. The molecules with U-235 pass preferentially through the membrane micropores to form an enriched product. Stages have capacities of several thousand SWUs per year, and a plant may consist of several thousand stages. The power consumption of a gaseous diffusion plant (GDP) is about 2400 kwh/SWU. This is five to twenty times greater than consumption for a gas centrifuge plant. While gaseous diffusion is an established enrichment technology, most countries construct-

5
Gaseous Diffusion Process

Table 5.2
Worldwide Uranium Enrichment Capacity: Existing and Planned
(in millions of SWU/yr)

Supplier	Existing Capacity Process	1985	Planned Capacity 1990	1995	Production FY 1983
United States					
Oak Ridge, TN	diffusion	7.9	0.0[a]	[7.9][b]	
Paducah, KY	diffusion	11.4	11.4	11.4	
Portsmouth, OH	diffusion	8.0	8.0	8.0	
AVLIS Plant	AVLIS	0.0	0.0	[13.2][b]	0.0
Subtotal U.S.		27.3	19.4	19.4-29.4[b]	12.0
France					
Eurodiff	diffusion	10.8	10.8	10.8	5.5
Cogema	laser	0.0	0.0	1.0[c]	0.0
West Germany, Netherlands, United Kingdom					
Urenco	centrifuge	1.0	2.0	3	0.6-0.8
Soviet Union					
domestic	?	?	?	?	
export	diffusion	3.0	2-3	2-3	2-3
Japan	centrifuge	0.05	0.2	1-2	?
South Africa	helicon	0.03	0.3	0.3	?
Brazil	jet-nozzle	0.01	0.1	0.2	?
	centrifuge labscale[d]		?	?	0.0
Australia	centrifuge	0.0	0.0	1.0	0.0
Pakistan	centrifuge	0.0	0.005	0.0	
TOTAL		42	45-46	59	

a Oak Ridge GDP placed on standby at end of FY 1985. DOE plans (1985) to bring Oak Ridge back into service in 1991.
b DOE plans to replace one GDP (probably Oak Ridge) with a plant based on AVLIS technology in the mid-1990s. This plant will probably be constructed in increments with a final capacity of 10 million SWU.
c *Nuclear Fuel* (17 June 1985): 3-4.
d Leonard S. Spector, *Nuclear Proliferation Today* (New York: Vintage Books, 1984), p. 272.

Source: Based on statement of Robert Civiak in HSTC Energy Conservation and Power, Serial No. 98-116, 21 October 1983 and 1 March 1984, p. 124.

ing or planning new facilities are choosing more energy efficient processes.

In a simple gaseous diffusion stage, the porous diffusion barrier has micropores 10 nanometers in diameter (1 nm is one billionth of a meter), smaller than the mean free path of the molecules. About half of the feed gas passes through the barrier to the low pressure side, where the gas is slightly richer in U-235 than the feed. The selective passage of U-235-containing molecules through the barrier is due to their slightly greater mean speed than heavier molecules containing U-238. The lighter molecules strike the barrier at greater frequency and pass through more often.

The separation factor for a gaseous diffusion stage equals the ratio of the mean speeds of the lighter and heavier molecules. It has the value 1.0043.[11] This small separation factor requires, in practice, many stages connected in series to form a cascade in order to achieve the

[11] The separation factor is defined as the ratio of the fraction of U-235 to the fraction of U-238 in the enriched UF_6 divided by the corresponding ratio in the depleted gas. Since at fixed temperature the mean speed of a molecule is inversely proportional to the square root of its mass, the separation factor is found by taking the square root of the ratio of the mass of a UF_6 molecule of U-238 (352 mass units) to the mass of a UF_6 molecule of U-235 (349 mass units): separation factor = square root of 352/349 = 1.0043.

5
Gas Centrifuge Process

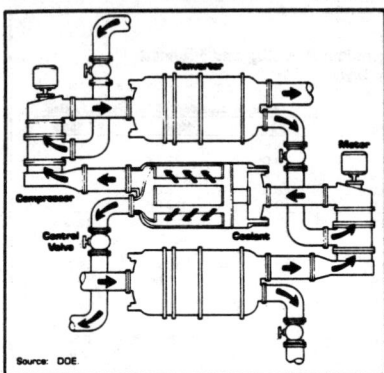

Figure 5.6 Gaseous diffusion stage arrangement in a cascade

desired degree of enrichment. In each stage of a gaseous diffusion cascade (see Figure 5.6) compressors take partially depleted gas from the next higher stage and partially enriched gas from the next lower stage as the feed. This entering stream is compressed and cooled before passage through the diffusion barrier.

Gas Centrifuge Process

In the centrifuge process a feed of uranium hexafluoride (UF_6) gas is enriched in a rapidly rotating cylinder. Separation of uranium isotopes is brought about by the combined effects of a centrifugal force field and countercurrent circulation. Each stage of a gas centrifuge enrichment plant consists of one or more high speed machines connected in parallel, with pipes and valves.

The first gram quantities of uranium enriched by gas centrifuge were obtained in 1941 at the University of Virginia by I.W. Beams. During World War II development was carried out by Westinghouse and Standard Oil of New Jersey, but the project was discontinued in favor of other processes. During and after the war, the German engineer G. Zippe devised a simple method of inducing countercurrent flow by internal scoops and baffles. He produced a small and mechanically simple machine. Larger and more complex centrifuges were developed by others. The centrifuge process is a mature technology in Europe at the Urenco plant and is coming into increased use in other countries (see Table 5.2). From 1977 until 1985, when construction of the Portsmouth GCEP was cancelled in favor of atomic vapor laser isotope separation, it was the leading technology for new U.S. enrichment capacity.

A gas centrifuge machine consists of a long, thin vertical cylinder made from strong material (fiberglass, aluminum, steel, graphite fiber) rotating at high speed about its axis in an evacuated casing. Urenco centrifuges are reported to have a peripheral speed of 400 m/s. Rotors of the U.S. Set V advanced gas centrifuges (AGC) were designed with high strength materials able to sustain even higher speeds.

UF_6 gas introduced into the cylinder (see Figure 5.7) is set into rotation. Centrifugal acceleration increases the outer rim concentration of the heavier U-238 hexafluoride molecules relative to the lighter U-235 molecules.[12] This radial separation of the uranium isotopes is greatly enhanced by a countercurrent flow induced in the UF_6 gas along the vertical axis of the rotating cylinder (see Figure 5.7). The effects of the radial separation and the axial flow combine to produce a large isotopic separation along the central axis. Depleted uranium is removed from one end of the cylinder and enriched uranium from the other.[13]

The "heavy" stream enriched in U-238 moves downward near the rim (see Figure 5.7) while the "light" stream enriched in U-235 moves upward along the central axis. The U-235 gradient induced by this flow increases upward along the axis. The section of the cylinder above the central feed point serves as an enriching section, and UF_6 enriched in U-235 is scooped out at the top from the light stream. The section of the rotating cylinder below the feed point is the stripping section, and depleted UF_6 is scooped out at the bottom from the heavy stream.

Separation factors of 1.2 to 1.5 or higher can be achieved for the centrifuge.[14] While single stage separation factors are substantially larger than in a gaseous diffusion cascade, the throughput of material is much smaller. Consequently a large-capacity centrifuge plant requires a large number of machines connected in parallel to obtain the necessary flow. Furthermore, a single stage will not suffice; several must be connected to form a cascade.

Separative work capacity ranges from 5 SWU/yr for European machines to 200 SWU/yr for U.S. Set III machines at Portsmouth. U.S. Set V machines, in advanced stages of development when the Portsmouth GCEP plant was cancelled in 1985, were designed for separative work capacities of about 600 SWU/yr. Urenco cascades comprise tens of thousands of centrifuges in some twelve stages with overall capacity of 1.0 to 2.2 million SWU/yr. The first U.S. processing building at Portsmouth was to have 5760 Set III machines with a capacity

---

12 At the rim, the ratio of the concentration of U-238 to the concentration of U-235 is greater than this same ratio evaluated at the axis by the factor exp ($\Delta M v_r^2/2RT$), where ΔM is the isotopic mass difference of U-238 and U-235 (3 atomic mass units), v_r is the velocity at the rim, R is the gas constant, and T is the absolute temperature. For v_r = 500 meters/sec and T = 300°K, the ratio of concentrations at the rim is 1.162 times the ratio at the axis. In addition, the gas pressure at the rim is 46 million times the gas pressure on the axis.

13 The countercurrent flow may be induced in a number of ways: (1) by a series of scoops and baffles (as in Figure 5.7) that remain stationary while the cylinder rotates, (2) by heating one end of the centrifuge and cooling the other, or (3) by pumps external to the machine.

14 DOE United States Gas Centrifuge Program for Uranium Enrichment, UCC-ND 1977, Rev. 2 6/81; Stanley Whitley, Reviews of Modern Physics 56, 1 (January 1984): 67-97. Most of the unclassified information on centrifuge operation dates from the 1960s.

5
AVLIS

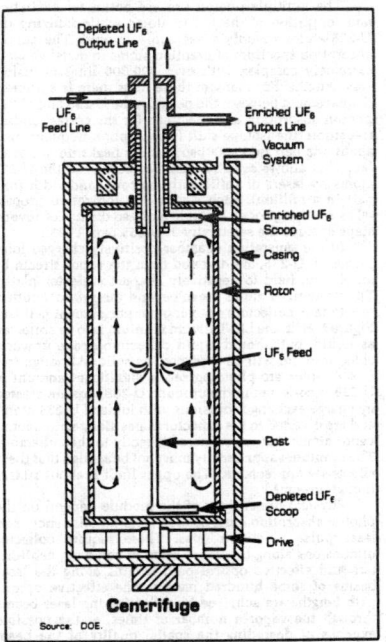

Figure 5.7 Illustration of a Centrifuge Enrichment Stage. Natural UF_6 feed enters along the axis of the centrifuge and enriched product is withdrawn at the top near the rim.

of 1.1 million SWU/yr.[15] Power consumption in a gas centrifuge plant ranges from 100 to 400 kwh/SWU, substantially less than for a gaseous diffusion plant.

The degree of enrichment in a single machine depends on several factors: the mass difference of the isotopes being separated, the peripheral speed of the rotor, and the length of the centrifuge. Other things being equal, the separative capacity of a centrifuge is proportional to its length.

Increasing the length and the peripheral speed increases both its separation factor and its separative capacity.[16] Strength limitations restrict the peripheral speed to some 400 m/s for aluminum alloy, 500 m/s for glass fiber, and 700 m/s for carbon fiber-epoxy resin composite. Titanium and steel alloys and the composite materials have brought major increases in strength.[17] U.S. advanced gas centrifuge Set V machines (600 SWU/yr) are made of new high strength rotor materials, permitting greatly increased rotational speeds.[18]

A centrifuge rotor may go into resonant vibrations as it spins through critical speeds ("criticals") where the rotational frequency equals the natural frequency of vibration of the rotor. As the length (Z) increases, flexural (longitudinal) vibrations become a hazard because the larger the ratio Z/d of rotor length to diameter (d) the smaller the critical speed at which these modes occur. Avoidance of flexural resonances can be achieved with Z/d of about 7 and a peripheral speed less than 400 m/s using an aluminum, steel, or titanium rotor.[19] Subcritical operation with greater length to diameter ratios requires a material with a higher "modulus of flexure."[20] The U.S. Set V machines were probably designed with "criticals" at higher speeds than for Set III machines. The estimated Z/d ratio is about 20 for both.

Atomic Vapor Laser Isotope Separation (AVLIS)

In the AVLIS enrichment process, a stream of uranium metal vapor feed is irradiated by visible light from organic dye lasers to selectively excite and ionize U-235 atoms. The ions are swept out of the vapor by electric fields into an enriched product stream that is deposited on solid or liquid collectors. Technical uncertainties in the development of the AVLIS process are associated with laser reliability at high pulse rate and high energy density, optical propagation of laser pulses in multistage setups, and reliability of the atomic vapor collector system. Power consumption is estimated at 65 kwh/SWU. The AVLIS process is under development in the United States, United Kingdom, France, Italy, Japan, and Israel. In the United States, the AVLIS process is currently being developed at Lawrence Livermore National Laboratory.[21]

An AVLIS plant may consist of a single module or a multicell array. It may be used to enrich natural uranium or strip depleted tails. According to DOE, the AVLIS process can be configured to operate at any tails assay.[22] The separative capacity of the AVLIS module used by DOE in its advanced enrichment selection process (1985) was

---

15 *Nuclear Fuel,* (27 February 1984), p. 3; (6 June 1983), p. 9.
16 For rotor length Z, diameter d, and peripheral speed v, the separative capacity is proportional to v⁴Z and the separation factor is proportional to v²Z/d. Whitley, *Reviews of Modern Physics* (January 1984); 69-70.
17 *Ibid.,* p. 84.
18 DOE Uranium Enrichment 1983 Annual Report, ORO-842 (undated), p. 10. For the same feed density and Z/d ratios, the peripheral speed for Set V machines is greater than for Set III machines (200 SWU) by a factor of (600/200)¹/⁴ = 1.3.
19 Whitley, *Reviews of Modern Physics:* 78.
20 *Ibid.*
21 *Nuclear Fuel* (12 March 1984): 2. In the United States, the AVLIS process was originally developed at LLNL and by Jersey Nuclear-Avco Isotopes (JNAI). The JNAI program was canceled. See H.A. Bethe, *Science* (30 July 1982): 398; *Physics Today* (November 1982): 70. In April 1982, the LLNL AVLIS process was selected by DOE over other advanced isotope separation (AIS) processes (MLIS and PSP) for continued development for uranium enrichment; *Nuclear Fuel* (28 February 1983): 4; DOE, Press Release, 5 June 1985; *Nuclear Fuel* (17 June 1985): 9 ff.
22 HSTC, Serial No. 90-116, 21 October 1983, 1 March 1984, p. 238. It has also been stated that the technology is designed for 0.047 percent tails; HAC, FY 1985 DOE, Part 6, p. 987.

5
AVLIS

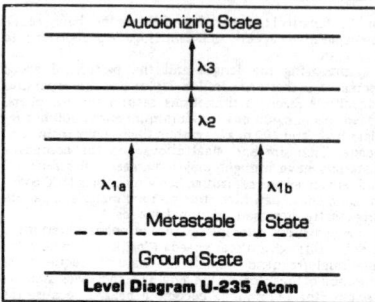

Figure 5.8 Energy level diagram of U-235 atom showing states consecutively excited by visible photons from tunable dye lasers in AVLIS process.

870,000 SWU/yr.[23]

In 1985, DOE selected the AVLIS process over the advanced gas centrifuge (AGC) to provide new enrichment capacity in the mid-1990s and beyond. The LLNL AVLIS process was also selected earlier for the plutonium special isotope separation (SIS) program to enrich plutonium in the isotope Pu-239.

In the LLNL AVLIS process[24] a supersonic beam of uranium vapor atoms is produced by bombarding liquid uranium metal feed with a beam from an electron gun and is then cooled by expansion. The vapor beam enters a separation chamber system into which four distinct wavelengths of visible (red-orange) light from tunable dye lasers is directed. The tunable dye lasers are pumped by high-repetition-rate copper-vapor lasers that emit green light. The green light does not degrade the organic dye. Many stages of copper-vapor laser amplification are required, and large modularized copper-vapor lasers have been tested at Livermore.

Atoms of U-235 in the ground state are selectively excited by absorption of a sequence of visible photons from tunable dye lasers operating at three wavelengths λ_{1a}, λ_2, and λ_3 (see Figure 5.8). Atoms of U-235 cooled to the lowest metastable state are first excited by a fourth laser of wavelength λ_{1b} and then by light of wavelengths λ_2 and λ_3. In both cases the last photon absorbed puts the U-235 atom into an autoionizing excited state that quickly decays into an ionized (positively charged) uranium atom and an electron. The total energy supplied to each atom is in excess of 6.13 electron volts (eV), the ionization energy of U-235.

The multiple photon process optimizes excitation and ionization of the U-235 atoms while ionizing the U-238 atoms by only a negligible amount. The atomic absorption spectrum of uranium atoms in metal vapor is extremely complex with over 300,000 lines at visible wavelengths. For many of these lines there is sufficient displacement between the peaks in the U-235 and U-238 photon absorption cross-sections for the corresponding transition (the isotope shift in absorption frequencies is about one part in 50,000) so that the peaks do not overlap. This allows selective photoexcitation of the U-235 atoms by lasers of sufficiently narrow bandwidth (one part in a million). Each step in the ionization process takes advantage of an isotopic shift, so the use of several steps ensures the selectivity of U-235 over U-238.

In the separation chamber positively charged ions, primarily U-235, are diverted from the vapor stream by an electric field to negatively charged collector plates. The un-ionized atoms move beyond the product collectors to tails collectors or to another enrichment cell (see Figure 5.9). In the LLNL design uranium is to be collected as liquid, but, should liquid collection prove unworkable, uranium will be recovered as solid. Although few U-238 atoms are photoionized, a significant amount of U-238 is collected in the product. U-238 ions are created by charge exchange collisions with ionized U-235 atoms and are diverted to the collector plates along with neutral vapor atoms that are scattered directly to the collectors. The uranium vapor density must not be so high that these effects are appreciable. (The upper limit is about 10 trillion atoms/cm^3.)

Physical dimensions of the module depend on the photon absorption cross-section (photon efficiency) and laser pulse repetition rates. These require collector dimensions along the vapor beam of some ten centimeters and effective optical path lengths along the laser beams of some hundred meters. The effective optical path lengths are achieved by reflecting the laser beams through the vapor a number of times, at the possible expense of degrading the spatial quality of the beam because of diffraction and inhomogeneities in the index of refraction.

Research on plutonium laser isotope separation based on the AVLIS process is being conducted at Livermore using the same laser systems that are used for enriching uranium. However, for plutonium enrichment the "unwanted" isotopes—Pu-240 and Pu-242—are ionized and swept out of the vapor beam, while for uranium enrichment the desired isotope U-235 is ionized by the laser light.[25] The separator-collector technologies used in the two applications of AVLIS differ, due to the high toxicity of plutonium and to differences in critical mass and other physical properties of plutonium and uranium. DOE plans to operate a special isotope separation (SIS)

---

[23] DOE, Process Evaluation Board, "Uranium Enrichment Technology and Assessment," 15 May 1985; reproduced in *Nuclear Fuel* (17 June 1985): 18.
[24] DOE, Report of the Energy Research and Advisory Board (ERAB) Study Group on Advanced Isotope Separation, November 1980, p. 29 ff (hereafter Study Group): "Laser Enrichment—No Easy Path to Proliferation," *Nuclear Engineering International* (April 1980): 13; *Physics Today* (July 1979): 17.
[25] HAC, FY 1986 EWDA, Part 7, p. 676.

MLIS/PSP

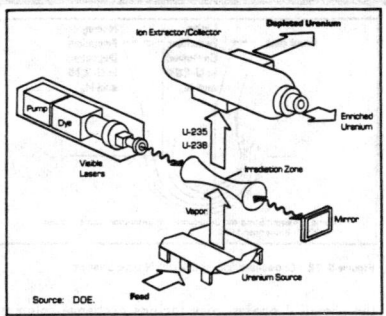

Figure 5.9 Illustration of the Atomic Vapor Laser Isotope Separation Process

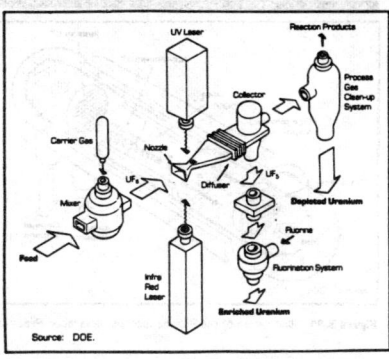

Figure 5.10 Illustration of the Molecular Laser Isotope Separation Process

plant for plutonium enrichment at Hanford in the 1990s using the AVLIS process.

Molecular Vapor Laser Isotope Separation[26]

In the molecular vapor laser isotope separation process (MLIS) lasers are used to select molecules containing U-235 from a gas feed of UF_6. Specifically, fluorine atoms are selectively photodissociated from UF_6 molecules containing U-235. The resulting enriched stream of UF_5 condenses and is filtered out of the gas as a solid.

The MLIS process was developed at Los Alamos National Laboratory for both uranium and plutonium enrichment (the latter using a feed of PuF_6).[27] Although DOE selected AVLIS technology over MLIS for a future plutonium enrichment plant, MLIS research continues on a small scale at LANL and the non-fissile isotopes Pu-240 and Pu-242 are being separated for weapons research.

Although individual MLIS enrichment units have a large separation factor, an MLIS enrichment plant is conceived as a staged system to achieve flexibility. Components in a unit include an expansion nozzle, a compressor, and infrared and ultraviolet lasers. Technical uncertainties in MLIS development concern laser performance at high repetition rates and high intensity. The estimated power consumption of an MLIS plant is about 77 kwh/SWU.

In the MLIS process, the UF_6 feed together with a carrier gas of nitrogen or argon is first cooled by rapidly expanding it through a nozzle (see Figure 5.10). The supersonic gas which emerges from the nozzle is irradiated by a carbon dioxide (CO_2) infrared laser that selectively excites vibrational modes in molecules containing U-235.[28] An ultraviolet laser light (from a xenon chloride excimer laser) is then used to dissociate fluorine atoms from the excited gas molecules, producing an enriched product stream of UF_5 that precipitates out of the gas flow as a fine powder. The gas stream is recompressed through a diffuser where the UF_5 powder is filtered out. The resulting tails stream of depleted UF_6 is pumped to another stage for further processing, and the UF_5 may be refluorinated for further enrichment.

Plasma Separation Process

In the plasma separation process (PSP) uranium metal vapor is ionized and injected into a high vacuum chamber containing a uniform axial magnetic field, produced by a superconducting coil (see Figure 5.11). Radiofrequency energy is introduced by an electric field superimposed perpendicular to the magnetic field and tuned to oscillate at a frequency of 127 kilohertz, the "cyclotron resonance frequency" of the U-235 ions. In the vacuum chamber, U-235 ions selectively absorb the radio-frequency energy. As a result, their orbits increase

---

26 DOE, ERAB, Study Group, pp. 31-32.
27 At the end of April 1982 DOE selected the AVLIS uranium enrichment technology over MLIS for full-scale engineering development; *Inside Energy* (7 May 1982). In August 1983, AVLIS was also chosen over MLIS for a plutonium enrichment plant.
28 UF_6 molecules have an octahedral structure with the uranium atom at the center and the six fluorine atoms at the corners. The molecule can vibrate in six modes, but only two involve motion of the uranium atom. Each of these two exhibits an isotopic shift, vibrating at slightly different frequencies, depending on whether the atom at the center is U-235 or U-238. Of these two, the mode in which the uranium atom and two opposite fluorine atoms move up and down perpendicular to the plane of the other four fluorine atoms (the "infrared-active stretching fundamental") is important for the MLIS process. Vibration of this mode in UF_6 gas molecules is strongly excited by infrared light of about 16,000 nm (1 nm is one billionth of a meter) from a carbon dioxide (CO_2) laser (also an H_2 Raman laser, CF_4 laser, or tunable semiconductor laser). Because of the isotopic shift, molecules with U-235 atoms may be selectively set into vibration without disturbing molecules with U-238 atoms. This excitation is followed by dissociation with an ultraviolet laser at 308 nm to form UF_5. The energy of the ultraviolet laser is insufficient to dissociate the unexcited UF_6. Benedict, et al., *Nuclear Chemical Engineering*, p. 919; Jack P. Aldridge, et al., "Measurement and analysis of the infrared-active stretching fundamental (ν_3) of UF_6," *Journal of Chem. Phys.* (1 July 1985): 34-38, provides a rigorous treatment of MLIS-related UF_6 spectroscopy.

5

Other Processes

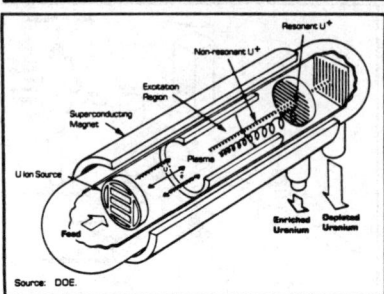

Figure 5.11 Illustration of the Plasma Isotope Separation Process

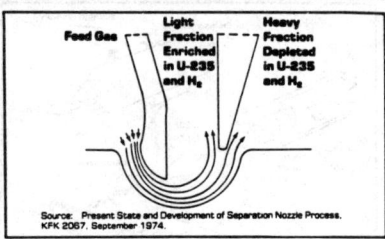

Figure 5.12 Cross-section of the Jet Nozzle System

in diameter until the U-235 ions intersect collector plates aligned parallel to the magnetic field. The product on the collector plates is enriched in U-235, while the U-238 ions, with small diameter orbits, pass through to the tails plate.[29]

The success of the PSP is based on a 1 percent difference between the cyclotron resonance frequencies at which U-235 and U-238 ions spiral about the field lines in a uniform magnetic field.[30] Components of a PSP enrichment unit include an ion source, a superconducting magnet, a radio-frequency oscillator, and a collector system. Power consumption is about 221 kwh/SWU.[31]

PSP has been under development by TRW, Inc. since 1976. It was a candidate (along with AVLIS and MLIS) in DOE's advanced isotope separation program until AVLIS was selected in 1982 for further development. Currently, TRW's PSP process is being developed by DOE Defense Programs to remove "unwanted" uranium-236 (and U-234 and U-238) that builds up in irradiated fuel during operation of the Savannah River production reactors. A PSP plant is scheduled to operate at Savannah River in the late 1980s.

Chemical Enrichment

Chemical enrichment of uranium depends on an exchange reaction between two chemical species in two different phases. At phase equilibrium there is a difference in uranium isotopic composition in the two phases. One phase may be stationary, or the two phases may move in countercurrent flow. The separation factor, depending on the phases used, ranges from 1.0013 to 1.0030.

Components of an enrichment unit, depending on the chemical phases, may include exchange columns, packed towers, mixer settlers, pumps, and piping.

Chemical enrichment is a maturing technology. France leads in industrial development. Demonstration on a laboratory scale is occurring in the United States and Japan. The French ion exchange enrichment process, called Chemex, has moved into the pilot stage with a 1/10-scale (1000 SWU/yr) plant scheduled to start up at Pierrelatte in September 1984.[32] The Chemex process uses trivalent uranium for the aqueous phase, with tetravalent uranium in a lighter organic phase. Chemex exchange is instantaneous and is reported to have a very high separation factor, four times that for other reactions.

The French Pierrelatte pilot plant will have "a few" pulse columns 10 meters high and 380 millimeters in diameter. As conceived, a commercial Chemex plant would have twenty exchange columns per cascade, arranged in modules of two vertical cascades, with columns 25 to 30 meters high and 1.2 to 1.6 cm in diameter. Each cascade would be capable of producing 250,000 SWU/yr, and an industrial module would have a capacity of 500,000 SWU/yr.

Aerodynamic Processes

Two aerodynamic processes have been developed to an industrial scale: the Becker jet nozzle process developed at Karlsruhe, West Germany, and the helikon process developed in Valindaba, South Africa.

In both the jet nozzle process (see Figure 5.12) and the helikon process, a mixture of UF_6 gas and hydrogen gas flows at high speed in a sharply curved path. The resulting centrifugal acceleration partially separates the lighter and heavier uranium isotopes.[33] The helikon uses an advanced vortex system to separate isotopes.

For the jet nozzle process an enrichment stage—a single nozzle or several nozzles connected in parallel—

---

29 DOE, ERAB, Study Group, p. 32.
30 Singly charged ions of mass M moving in a uniform magnetic field of strength B spiral about the direction of the field at a frequency given by the expression, $f = 1.52 \times 10^3$ B/M, where B is magnetic field strength in gauss and M is in atomic mass units (AMU). The difference in ion mass of 3 AMU between U-238 and U-235 results in the 1 percent difference in their cyclotron frequencies. The radiofrequency field oscillating in phase with the motion of the ionized U-235 atoms increases their orbital radius without affecting the U-238 atoms.
31 DOE, ERAB, Study Group, p. 18.
32 Nucleonics Week (7 June 1984): 11.
33 See Allan S. Krass, Peter Boskma, Boelie Elzen and Will A.Smit, *Uranium Enrichment and Nuclear Weapons Proliferation* London: Taylor and Francis, 1983), p. 136; Benedict et al., *Nuclear Chemical Engineering*, p. 817.

has a separation factor of about 1.015. For the helikon, a module is the basic unit and the separation factor is on the order of 1.025. Currently jet nozzles with openings ranging from 25 to 100 microns are being used on the laboratory scale or being designed for pilot plants.[34] A commercial-size jet nozzle plant for LEU production would have about 450 stages. Power consumption is estimated to be 3000 to 5000 kwh/SWU for both aerodynamic processes, larger than for gaseous diffusion.

Both jet-nozzle and helikon processes are maturing technologies. A jet-nozzle pilot plant with a capacity of 10,000 SWU/yr is scheduled to operate in Brazil in 1985-89.[35] The plant in Brazil is being constructed by West Germany. Eventual expansion to 200,000 SWU/yr is planned. A helikon plant with a capacity in excess of 30,000 SWU/yr is operating in South Africa (see Table 5.2).

Table 2.1. Important enrichment technique property ratings according to their contribution to proliferation sensitivity

	Separation factor	Equilibrium time and inventory	Size of dedicated facility	Ease of batch recycle	Reflux chemistry and criticality problems
Gaseous diffusion	3	3	3	3	1
Centrifuge	2	1	1	1	1
Aerodynamic					
Nozzle	3	1	2	2	1
Helikon	3	1	2	1	1
Chemical					
Solvent extraction	3	3	3	3	2
Ion exchange	3	3	3	3	2
Laser					
Molecular (MLIS)	1	1	1	1	1
Atomic (AVLIS)	1	1	2	3	3
Electromagnetic					
Calutron	1	1	3	2	3
Ion cyclotron resonance	1	1	2	2	3

Table 2.2. Technological thresholds to proliferation

	Threshold		
Strategy	Low	Intermediate	High
Misuse of existing facility	Centrifuge	Gaseous diffusion	Chemical exchange
	Helikon	Jet nozzle	
	MLIS	AVLIS	
	Plasma	Calutron	
Construction of dedicated facility		Centrifuge	Gaseous diffusion
		Helikon	Chemical exchange
		MLIS	AVLIS
			Plasma
			Jet nozzle
			Calutron

Source: Allan S. Krass et al., <u>Uranium Enrichment and Nuclear Weapon Proliferation</u> (New York: Taylor and Francis, 1983), 19

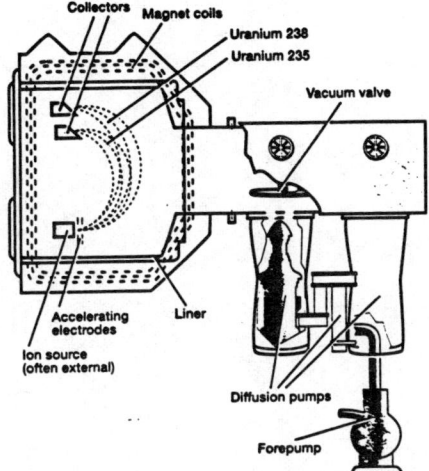

Figure 2.2. A schematic drawing of a calutron (from Albright & Hibbs (1991B, p. 19))

Source: Johan Swahn, *The Long-Term Nuclear Explosives Predicament* (Goeteborg, Sweden: Chalmers University of Technology, 1992), 26

TECHNICAL ASPECTS

PLUTONIUM

1 PLUTONIUM AND ITS PRODUCTION

The world faces a crucial problem. What should be done with the huge, and increasing, stockpile of plutonium created by the civilian reprocessing of spent reactor fuel and by the dismantling of nuclear weapons as disarmament agreements lead to considerable reductions in the American and ex-Soviet nuclear arsenals? Until the end of the Cold War, civil and military stocks of plutonium (named after Pluto, the mythical God of Hell) were regarded as distinct, but as plutonium is removed from nuclear weapons and transferred to the civilian sector the distinction disappears.

The problem with plutonium is its nature. Plutonium is man-made in nuclear reactors; only traces occur naturally. It is an exceedingly toxic material — the inhalation of just a minute particle can cause lung cancer, the ingestion of plutonium can cause bone and liver cancer. The half-life of plutonium is about 24,000 years, so that for all intents and purposes it remains permanently in the environment. Contaminated areas would be uninhabitable until decontaminated. Perhaps, most important, plutonium can be used to make nuclear weapons. Preventing the further spread of nuclear weapons has become a main foreign policy goal of many powers, enhanced by the discovery that Iraq, although a party to the Nuclear Non-Proliferation Treaty (NPT), was developing nuclear weapons.

Fundamental to the control of nuclear-weapon proliferation is the control of plutonium supplies; the more plutonium there is in the world the more difficult this becomes. This difficulty is considerably enhanced, to say the least, by the small quantity of plutonium needed to make a nuclear weapon. No more than ten kilograms of plutonium metal — about the size of an orange — is enough. To protect plutonium against the theft of kilogram quantities is virtually impossible when tonnes of the material exist. Moreover, as more plutonium becomes available the risk of nuclear terrorism increases.

Apart from its possible use as a future fuel in fast reactors or, combined with uranium, as a possible mixed-oxide fuel for 'conventional' (or thermal) reactors, plutonium has no peaceful uses other than in the power source for satellites and, in minute amounts, in heart pacemakers. An understanding of the technical nature of plutonium and the method of its production is critical to any adequate analysis of the political issues. This chapter broadly provides such background information and some of the consequences for political decisions.

Nuclear fission and plutonium production

All atoms can be thought of as consisting of a nucleus around which electrons travel in elliptical orbits, like planets travelling around the Sun. If an atom was magnified to the size of a house the nucleus would be smaller than a pinhead inside it. The nucleus of an atom contains nucleons — protons and neutrons — occupying a small volume at the centre of the atom. All the nuclei of a given element (it may be gold, silver, lead, tin, and so on) contain the same number of protons, called the atomic number. The atomic number of plutonium (Pu) is 94; that of uranium (U) is 92. The orbits of the electrons, compared with the size of the nucleus, are large so that the atom is mostly empty space. The number of electrons orbiting the nucleus is equal to the number of protons within the nucleus.

Although each nucleus of the atoms of an element contains the same number of protons, the number of neutrons in the nuclei of the atoms of a given element may differ. The element is then said to have a number of isotopes. For example, ordinary uranium (which is the heaviest naturally occurring element in the periodic table of elements), as dug out of the ground, consists of a mixture of two isotopes. Both isotopes have the same atomic number (92) as the atoms of both contain 92 protons, but the nuclei of one isotope contains 143 neutrons and those of the other contain 146 neutrons. These two isotopes are referred to as uranium-235, shortened to U-235, and uranium-238, or U-238. The numbers 235 and 238 (mass numbers) are the total numbers of nucleons (i.e., protons plus neutrons in each isotope). The isotope U-235 is of crucial interest to both the designers of nuclear reactors and the designers of nuclear weapons because it is the only fissile element in nature; thus it is relatively easy to make the nucleus of an atom of U-235 undergo fission. All that is necessary is to allow it to capture (i.e., absorb) a neutron.

When a U-235 nucleus captures a neutron, a nucleus of the isotope U-236 is formed (the new nucleus has 92 protons and is, therefore, still uranium, but it has 143+1, or 144 neutrons which makes it U-236). A U-236 nucleus is extremely unstable, so unstable that it rapidly splits (i.e., fissions) into two fragments. Each fragment is in fact a nucleus of an atom of an element with an atomic number around the middle of the periodic table; they are called fission products. Typical fission products, which are

Source: Frank Barnaby, *The Plutonium Legacy:
Nuclear Proliferation Out of Control?* (Oxford: Oxford
Research Group, Current Decision Report no. 12
(April 1993), 1-6

normally radioactive isotopes (known as radioisotopes), include strontium-90, caesium-137, iodine-131, and so on.

In addition to the fission products, two or three neutrons are given off during the fission process. The total sum of the masses of the fission products plus the masses of the two or three neutrons is invariably slightly less than the mass of the U-236 nucleus. This mass difference appears as energy accompanying the fission process. The amount of energy (E) produced is given by Einstein's famous formula $E = mc^2$, where m is the mass difference and c is the velocity of light.

Although the mass difference m is very small for each individual fission, the velocity of light squared is large and, therefore, a relatively large amount of energy is released during fission. The complete fissioning of one gram of U-235 would produce about 23,000 kilowatt-hours of heat, equivalent to burning about 3 tonnes of coal.

The neutrons emitted during the fission process are able to initiate further fissions in neighbouring U-235 nuclei. Provided that one of the two or three neutrons emitted during a fission event can be made to fission another nucleus, a self-sustaining process (a fission chain reaction) can be produced. Energy is then generated for as long as the chain reaction continues.

In a nuclear-power reactor, the energy produced by a relatively slow, controlled fission chain reaction is normally used to boil water to produce steam. The steam is then used to drive a turbine to generate electricity. In a nuclear weapon the fission chain reaction is not controlled and is incredibly fast, so that it can produce a large amount of energy in a very short time. A massive explosion results.

A crucial difference between U-235 and U-238 is that a nucleus of U-235 will undergo fission when *any* neutron, whether it is moving very fast or very slowly, is captured by it, but a neutron can cause a U-238 nucleus to fission only if it is travelling faster than a certain speed. Generally speaking, the neutrons given off when a U-235 nucleus undergoes fission are not travelling fast enough to produce fission in U-238 nuclei. Nuclear weapons can, therefore, be made from U-235 but not from U-238.

Isotopes which undergo fission after capturing either a slow or a fast neutron are known as fissile materials. As we have seen, U-235 is a fissile material; Pu-239 is another. U-238 is not. Natural uranium contains mostly U-238; only 0.7 per cent is U-235. Nuclear reactors are normally fuelled with uranium. Some of the U-238 nuclei in the fuel elements will capture neutrons from the fission of U-235: when a uranium-238 nucleus captures a fission neutron a nucleus of U-239 is produced. U-239 will undergo radioactive decay first to neptunium (with 93 protons) and then to Pu-239 (with 94 protons). Consequently, as uranium fuel is used up in a nuclear reactor, Pu-239 steadily accumulates in the fuel elements as an inevitable by-product. Pu-239, like U-235, is a fissile material used to fabricate nuclear weapons.

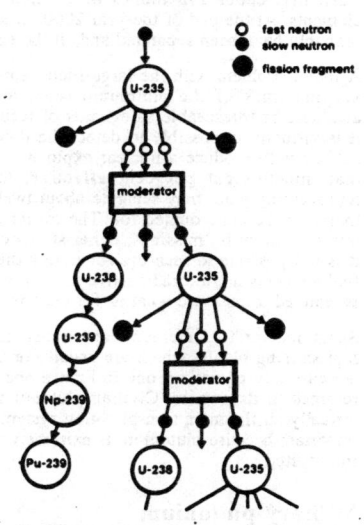

The chain reaction. This shows the fission of U-235 and the subsequent capture of neutrons by U-238 leading to the production of plutonium.

Enrichment

For use as fuel in most nuclear-power reactors, the amount of U-235 in uranium is increased from its natural concentration of 0.7 per cent to a concentration of 3 or 4 per cent. For use in nuclear weapons the concentration of U-235 is normally increased to very high levels. Nuclear-weapon designers prefer their uranium to contain at least 90 per cent U-235.

The process of increasing the concentration of U-235 in natural uranium is known as uranium enrichment. Because U-235 and U-238 isotopes are chemically identical, it is necessary to use a physical method to separate them: this is now normally done by spinning a gaseous uranium compound in a series of high-speed centrifuges. The heavier U-238 molecules are thrown to the side of the cylindrical centrifuge and the lighter U-235 molecules are concentrated around the centre. The gas enriched in U-235 can then be drawn off.

Civilian plutonium

As previously stated, plutonium is a man-made element; only insignificant traces are found in nature. The first plutonium was produced fifty years ago in a cyclotron, by E.O. Lawrence at Berkeley, California, when only milligram quantities were produced; significant amounts of plutonium are produced only in nuclear reactors. The first reactor started up on 2 December, 1942. When removed from the reactor, a fuel element contains unused uranium, plutonium and fission products. These three substances can be chemically separated from each other in a plant, called a reprocessing plant.

The total amount of plutonium in the world today is about 1000 tonnes. Of this total, about 260 tonnes was produced for military purposes and about 740 tonnes was produced in civilian nuclear reactors. Civilian plutonium is contained in fuel elements in reactors; spent reactor fuel elements in stores waiting for reprocessing or disposal; reprocessing plants; and in civilian plutonium stores. Today, there are about 420 civilian nuclear-power reactors operating in twenty-nine countries,[1] producing about forty-six tonnes of plutonium a year. Another seventy-six nuclear-power reactors are under construction. When these are operating they will produce a total of about ten tonnes of plutonium a year. Taking into account the reactors which are shut down, the rate of plutonium production in the year 2000 will be about 50 tonnes a year.

Currently, about 135 tonnes of civilian plutonium have been separated from spent reactor fuel elements. At the end of the year 2000, according to current plans, some 300 tonnes of plutonium will probably have been separated and, at the end of 2010, some 550 tonnes will have been separated.

A major problem with the large-scale reprocessing of plutonium in civilian plants is the difficulty of keeping track of the plutonium separated from spent reactor fuel elements. Even with the best available or foreseeable safeguards of technology, when thousands of kilograms are separated a year it is virtually impossible to detect the diversion (for example, the theft) of an amount of plutonium sufficient to produce a nuclear explosive. Safeguards at reprocessing plants are unlikely to be better than ninety-eight per cent effective, and probably significantly worse. A large commercial reprocessing plant may separate about twelve tonnes of plutonium a year. About 240 kilograms may, therefore, be unaccounted for. The owners of the plant will simply not know whether or not some of this plutonium is 'missing', either stolen or lost. Plutonium remains unaccounted for mainly because it is not possible to measure accurately the amount of plutonium put into the plant (the spent reactor fuel elements are too radioactive to handle) and because the plant itself is so radioactive that it cannot be entered to measure what is, for example, in the pipework.

Spent reactor fuel elements are transported from the countries owning nuclear-power reactors to reprocessing plants, which are usually in another country (only three commercial reprocessing plants are currently operating, one in France and two in the UK). After reprocessing, plutonium is normally returned to its owners. Civilian plutonium will, therefore, be increasingly transported worldwide on virtually all the main transportation systems — road, rail, sea and air. This increasing transportation is important because plutonium is extremely vulnerable to theft or accidental loss at sea while it is being transported.

Military plutonium

Military plutonium, normally produced in special plutonium-production reactors, is contained in nuclear weapons and in military reserve stocks. As American and ex-Soviet nuclear arsenals are reduced, plutonium is being removed from nuclear weapons and put into stores.

Military plutonium is owned by the nuclear-weapon powers — Russia, China, France, the UK and the USA. In addition, Israel and India have produced significant amounts of plutonium for nuclear weapons. The amounts of military plutonium in these countries is as follows: the ex-Soviet Union, about 125 tonnes; the USA, about 97 tonnes; the UK, about 2.8 tonnes; France, about 6 tonnes; and China, about 2.5 tonnes. Israel has accumulated approximately 600 kilograms of military plutonium and India has approximately 290 kilograms.[2]

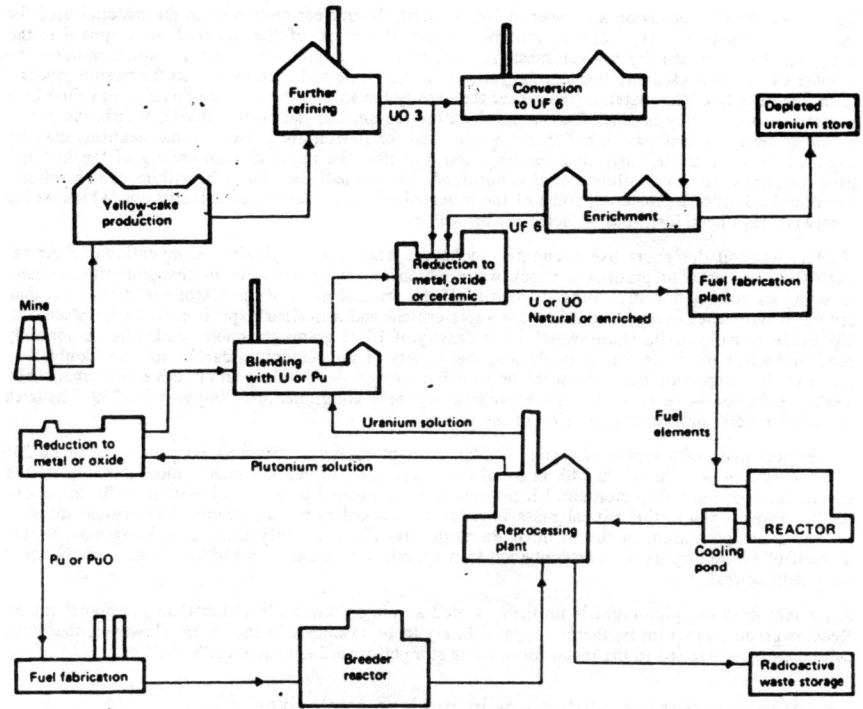

The nuclear fuel cycle. These industrial plants are rarely located exclusively in one country, often necessitating transport of radioactive material.

Reactor-grade plutonium

The isotopic composition of the plutonium produced in reactors operated for different purposes varies. The plutonium produced specifically for military purposes is rich in the isotope Pu-239, typically containing more than 93 per cent of Pu-239.

Plutonium is also produced in nuclear-power reactors when they are operated to produce electricity in the most economical way; this form is known as reactor-grade plutonium. Because it is subjected to longer irradiation in the reactor it typically contains significant amounts of each of a number of plutonium isotopes. A nucleus of Pu-239 in the fuel element of a nuclear-power reactor may capture one of the neutrons produced during fission. If it does, it becomes Pu-240. In turn, a Pu-240 nucleus may capture a neutron and become Pu-241, and so on; as time goes on, therefore, the amounts of Pu-240, Pu-241 and Pu-242 increase. Reactor-grade plutonium typically contains approximately sixty per cent Pu-239, twenty-five per cent Pu-240 (in military plutonium the amount is typically seven per cent), ten per cent Pu-241 and a few per cent Pu-242.

Critical masses

The smallest amount of fissile material in which a self-sustaining chain reaction is just sustained is known as the critical mass. The critical mass is that from which just as many neutrons escape per unit time as are released by fission. If this mass of material is increased the number of neutrons produced by fission builds up, and considerably more fissions occur in each successive generation of fission. A 'super-critical' mass is created and a nuclear explosion takes place. In a super-critical mass the rate of production of fission neutrons exceeds all neutron losses and a rapid and uncontrollable increase in the number of neutrons within the mass occurs.

The critical mass depends on a number of factors: first, the nuclear properties of the material used for the fission, whether it is U-235 or Pu-239; second, the shape of the material — a sphere is the optimum shape because for a given mass the surface area is minimised which, in turn, minimises the number of neutrons escaping through the surface per unit time and thereby lost to the fission process; third, the density of the material (the higher the density the shorter the average distance travelled by a neutron before causing another fission and therefore the smaller the critical mass); fourth, the purity of the material (if materials other than the one used for fission are present, some neutrons may be captured by their nuclei instead of causing fission); fifth, the physical surrounding of the material used for fission (if the fissile material is surrounded by a medium such as beryllium, which reflects neutrons back into the material, some of the reflected neutrons may be used for fission which would otherwise have been lost, thus reducing the critical mass).

Nuclear-weapon designers use a cunning technique known as implosion. Conventional chemical explosives are used to produce a shock wave which uniformly compresses the plutonium sphere, reducing its volume and increasing its density. If the original mass of the plutonium is just less than critical it will, after compression, become super-critical and a nuclear explosion will take place. Pu-239 in the so-called delta phase, which has a density of 15.92 grams per cubic centimetre, is normally used in nuclear weapons. Using implosion, the density of the plutonium can be roughly doubled so that a nuclear explosion could, with the best modern design — including an effective, but practicable, neutron reflector — be achieved with approximately three kilograms of delta-phase Pu-239. The trick is to obtain very uniform compression of the sphere.

The critical mass of a sphere of typical reactor-grade plutonium, containing sixty per cent of Pu-239 and twenty-five per cent of Pu-240, in metal form is roughly fifteen kilograms (more than double the critical mass of military plutonium).[3] If the sphere is surrounded by a natural uranium reflector, about ten centimetres thick, the critical mass is reduced to about seven kilograms. The critical mass of reactor-grade plutonium in the form of Pu-oxide crystals is roughly thirty-five kilograms. If this amount of plutonium oxide was contained in a spherical container, its radius would be only about nine centimetres.

After reprocessing, plutonium is normally stored as plutonium oxide rather than plutonium metal. Reactor-grade plutonium is, therefore, most likely to be available in this form. However, the oxide can be easily converted to the metal form, using straightforward chemical methods.

Use of reactor-grade plutonium in nuclear explosives

Can reactor-grade plutonium be used to produce effective nuclear explosions? This is an important question because, if it can, countries operating nuclear-power reactors for peaceful purposes have access to plutonium that could be used to produce nuclear weapons. As the quantity of reactor-grade plutonium in the world increases, it becomes easier for a country to acquire it illegally and produce nuclear weapons. It also becomes easier for terrorists to acquire it.

The presence of Pu-240 is undoubtedly a nuisance for nuclear-weapon designers. The main problem with using reactor-grade plutonium as a nuclear weapon is that the spontaneous fission rate of Pu-240 is much greater than that of Pu-239; in a kilogram of reactor-grade plutonium the average time between spontaneous fissions is less than a micro-second (a millionth of a second). This means that very fast implosion techniques (see below) would be necessary in a nuclear device made from reactor-grade plutonium to prevent pre-detonation, which leads to uncertain explosive yields.

Spontaneous fission produces a neutron background in a sphere of military plutonium used in a typical nuclear weapon of about one neutron every two or three micro-seconds. With a mean time of a few micro-seconds between neutrons — a very much longer time than the duration of the fission chain reaction — radial compression rates of a few millimetres per micro-second will prevent pre-detonation. Implosion techniques can achieve this without much difficulty. However, for reactor-grade plutonium the mean time between neutrons is a small fraction of a micro-second; extremely fast assembly would be needed to achieve super-criticality. Implosion technologies to provide the very high shock velocities and compression needed to prevent pre-detonation are available but probably not to a sub-national group, at least in the foreseeable future.

In spite of this, it is often still said that civilian plutonium cannot be used in nuclear weapons. Amory Lovins explains that this incorrect view is based on the following assumptions:
- that reactor-grade plutonium is far more hazardous than weapons-grade plutonium to people handling it;

- that a nuclear explosive device made from reactor-grade plutonium is much more likely to explode unintentionally;
- that such a device, if it explodes at all, will not explode violently enough to do much damage, nor to accomplish the main aims of the makers; and
- that its explosive yield is too unpredictable to be acceptable to its makers.

Lovins concludes that 'each of these assumptions contains, in certain circumstances, an element of truth' but, he adds, 'each is generally, or can by plausible counter-measures be rendered, false. Their implication that reactor-grade plutonium is not very dangerous is wishful thinking, and causes the proliferation risks of civil nuclear activities to be gravely underestimated'.[4]

That reactor-grade plutonium can be used to produce a nuclear weapon has been shown in the USA, where such devices have been built *and tested*.[5] The fact that a non-nuclear-weapon state could fabricate nuclear weapons from reactor-grade plutonium has been discussed in detail by Victor Gilinsky, an American Nuclear Regulatory Commissioner: 'So far as reactor-grade plutonium is concerned, the fact is that it is possible to use this material for nuclear warheads at all levels of technical sophistication. In other words, countries less advanced than the major industrial powers but, nevertheless, possessing nuclear power programs can make very respectable weapons... Of course, when reactor-grade plutonium is used there may be a penalty in performance that is considerable or insignificant, depending on the weapon design. But, whatever we might once have thought, we now know that even simple designs, albeit with some uncertainties in yield, can serve as effective, highly powerful weapons — reliably in the kiloton range'.[6]

A country operating a nuclear-power reactor could acquire military-grade plutonium by removing reactor fuel elements at an appropriate (i.e., earlier) time. For the most economical generation of electricity, fuel elements are normally left in a nuclear-power reactor for about four years, by which time the plutonium will be reactor grade. However, if some of the fuel elements are removed after a few months, the plutonium will be of military grade because only a relatively small percentage of Pu-240 and higher isotopes will have been produced.

References

1. International Atomic Energy Agency 'Nuclear power status around the world', *IAEA Bulletin*, Volume 33, Number 3, 1991.
2. Albright, D., Berkhout, F. and Walker, W. *World Inventory of Plutonium and Highly Enriched Uranium*, Oxford University Press, Oxford, 1993.
3. Carson, Mark J. *Reactor-Grade Plutonium's Explosive Properties*, Nuclear Control Institute, Washington, August 1990.
4. Lovins, Amory B. 'Nuclear weapons and power-reactor plutonium', *Nature*, 28 February 1980, and typographical corrections, 13 March 1980.
5. Gilette, R. *Impure Plutonium Used in 1962 A-test*, Los Angeles Times, 16 September, 1977.
6. Gilinsky, V. *Plutonium, Proliferation, and Policy*, Massachusetts Institute of Technology, report S-14-76, 1 November, 1976.

NPT/95 — NPT AT THE CROSSROADS
Issues Bearing on Extending and Strengthening the Treaty

NUCLEAR CONTROL INSTITUTE

Reactor-Grade Plutonium's Explosive Properties

J. Carson Mark
Consultant, Nuclear Control Institute

Fourth in a series of papers on issues bearing on extending and strengthening the Nuclear Non-Proliferation Treaty.

J. Carson Mark served as head of the Theoretical Division of Los Alamos National Laboratory and has served on the U.S. Nuclear Regulatory Commission Advisory Committee on Reactor Safeguards and on the Science Advisory Board of the U.S. Air Force.

August 1990

These comments relate to the question of whether a terrorist organization or a threshold state could make use of plutonium recovered from light water reactor fuel to construct a nuclear explosive device having a significantly damaging yield. Three aspects of this question will be discussed separately:

I. Criticality Properties of Reactor-grade Plutonium;
II. Effects of Predetonation on Yield Distribution;
III. Some of the Problems Confronting a Terrorist Organization.

Finally, several conclusions are noted in IV.

This paper is being written at this time because questions appear to persist in some non-proliferation policy circles about whether a bomb really could be made from reactor-grade plutonium of especially high burnup and whether the task is too daunting for a threshold state or terrorist group, even if it is technically feasible.

This paper is derived from information in the public domain. It is appropriate, therefore, to make the information and its significance available to policymakers and members of the public who are concerned about preventing the spread of nuclear explosives.

The question of whether terrorists could build nuclear weapons was also examined by this author and four colleagues in a paper prepared in 1986 for a task force on nuclear terrorism.[1]

I. Criticality Properties of Reactor-grade Plutonium

The original implosion assembly system used in the Trinity test in 1945 was capable of obtaining 20 kilotons from weapons-grade plutonium. In the weapons tests conducted in 1948 it was shown that an assembly system of the same size could also handle U-235 effectively. From the discussion below it may be seen that such an assembly system would be capable of bringing reactor-grade plutonium of any degree of burnup to a state in which it could provide yields in the multi-kiloton range. The original implosion system had a diameter of less than 5 feet, including an outer aerodynamic case. Thus, it does not (as was recently suggested) require a "device of the dimensions of a fair sized room" to handle reactor grade plutonium. Moreover, it is well known that the design of the first implosion system was quite conservative, and that there are a number of straightforward improvements which could be implemented to reduce the size of the device on the basis of laboratory-type experiments without having to resort to nuclear tests.

Discussion

In addition to the isotope Pu-239 the plutonium extracted from spent LWR fuel may contain appreciable fractions of other plutonium isotopes formed as a result of successive neutron capture or n-2n reactions. At very low burnup levels the fractional amounts of the secondary isotopes are very small. At a level of a few thousand megawatt-days per metric ton (MWD/MT), for example, the fraction of Pu-240 may be a few percent of the total plutonium, with the fraction of Pu-241 being approximately an order of magnitude smaller, and that of Pu-242 an order of magnitude smaller still. At higher burnups these fractional amounts increase so that at a very high level (≈50,000 MWD/MT or so—about as high as current interest appears to extend) a pattern of the following general sort could be approached:

(Pu-239: Pu-240: Pu-241: Pu-242) = (.40: .30: .15: .15).

Other plutonium isotopes would also be present, but in relatively small amounts. The most prominent of these would be Pu-238, which could reach a level of a few percent in very high burnup material. This would not have a significant effect on critical masses. But because of its relatively short half-lives for alpha decay and spontaneous

NUCLEAR CONTROL INSTITUTE

Nuclear Control Institute, established in 1981, is an independent policy research center concerned with problems of nuclear proliferation. It develops strategies for preventing the spread and reversing the growth of nuclear arms.

Nuclear Control Institute
1000 Connecticut Avenue, N.W.
Suite 704
Washington, D.C. 20036
202-822-8444/Fax: 202-452-0892

NUCLEAR CONTROL INSTITUTE

fission, the amount of Pu-238 might need to be taken into account in determining the alpha activity or neutron source in plutonium from highly exposed reactor fuel.

Each of the plutonium isotopes is sufficiently fissionable that the separated isotope in metal form could provide a bare critical mass, so that a bare critical assembly could be made with plutonium metal no matter what its isotopic composition might be. The odd isotopes (Pu-239 and 241) are both "fissile"—that is, fission may be induced in them by neutrons of any energy, whether slow or fast. Their fission cross sections differ in detail but are similar enough that their bare critical masses are nearly equal, being about 15 kg in δ-phase metal (ρ = 15.6 g/cc). The isotope Pu-238 is "fissionable"—that is, only neutrons with energy above some threshold can induce fission. However, the Pu-238 threshold is at some quite low energy and its fission cross section above about 0.5 MeV is larger than that of Pu-239. In spite of producing fewer neutrons per fission (2.75 vs. 3.0) the bare critical mass of Pu-238 in δ-phase metal is also ≈15 kg.

> ... [a Trinity-type device] would be capable of bringing reactor-grade plutonium of any degree of burn-up to a state in which it could provide yields in the multi-ton range.

For Pu-240 the fission threshold is at a few hundred kilovolts; but above 1 MeV the fission cross section, though smaller than that for Pu-239, is larger than that for U-235. The number of neutrons per fission (≈3) is the same as that for Pu-239, 241, and 242. The bare critical mass of Pu-240 in δ-phase metal is about 40 kg. This is smaller than that for 94% U-235 in uranium metal at normal density (ρ = 18.7 g/cc), which is ≈52 kg. Thus Pu-240 is a significantly more effective fissionable material than 94% U-235 in a metal system. It should be noted, however, that this relative superiority would not carry over to the same extent for these materials in the form of oxides. In PuO_2 or U-235 O_2 the average energy of the neutrons is reduced appreciably by their scattering on oxygen. In a Pu-240 O_2 system, therefore, some fraction of the neutrons in the spectrum applicable to a metal system will be moved to energies near or below the Pu-240 threshold where the Pu-240 fission cross section is poor, whereas the fission cross section of U-235 holds up for such lower neutron energies.

At energies above 1 MeV, the fission cross section of the isotope Pu-242 is quite similar to that of Pu-240, but it is a less effective fissionable material because its fission threshold is about a hundred keV higher. The bare critical mass of Pu-242 in δ-phase metal has been calculated to be ≈177 kg. To bring this more in line with the other isotopes, one can think of replacing the Pu-242 component with a new component consisting of a 50-50 mixture of Pu-242 and Pu-241, with the material taken from the Pu-241 fraction since there is enough of that to supply what's necessary even at the extreme high burnup level considered. The fission cross section of this new component, which is the average of the cross sections of Pu-241 and Pu-242, is quite similar to that of Pu-240 in the range of energies above 1 MeV, and considerably larger at lower energies where the Pu-240 and 242 cross sections fall away, while that for Pu-241 does not. Thus, the material of the new component is superior to Pu-240, which in turn is superior to U-235. At all burnup levels, then, the critical mass of reactor-grade plutonium is intermediate between that of Pu-239 and U-235.

By the use of a reflector a few inches thick, the critical mass of all these materials can be reduced by a factor of two, or so, below the bare critical mass; and, at least provided the reflector is of some heavy metal so as not to moderate the neutrons to an important extent, the relative ranking of the critical masses will be preserved.

II. Effects of Predetonation on Yield Distribution

One week after the first fission explosion on July 16, 1945, Robert Oppenheimer wrote to General Leslie Groves' deputy and described the expectations concerning the use of the Trinity device in combat.[2] He said: "... The possibility that the first combat plutonium Fat Man will give a less than optimal performance is about 12 per cent. There is about a 6 per cent chance that the energy release will be under 5000 tons, and about a 2 per cent chance that it will be under 1000 tons. It should not be much less than 1000 tons unless there is an actual malfunctioning of some of the components." One week later General Groves wrote to the Chief of Staff: "There is a definite possibility, 12 per cent rising to 20 per cent, as we increase our rate of production at the Hanford Engineer Works, with the type of weapon tested that the blast will be smaller due to detonation in advance of the optimum time. But in any event, the explosion should be on the order of thousands of tons."

Evidently both Oppenheimer and Groves were referring to what will be identified in the following discussion as the "fizzle yield"; that is, the smallest nuclear yield this particular device would provide. They do not state a value for this yield; but in view of their saying "it should not be much less than 1000 tons" it may be presumed that they were thinking of some value like 700 tons, or so. The effect of using reactor-grade plutonium in this assembly instead of the high purity plutonium used in 1945 would be to increase the probability that the yield realized would fall short of the levels mentioned by Oppenheimer, but it would not greatly change the actual value of the fizzle yield—which would always be equaled, or exceeded.

In the following discussion some indication is given of the differences between plutonium and highly enriched uranium with respect to pre-detonation and fizzle yields.

Discussion

In any supercritical system, the number of neutrons, the rate of fission, and the level of energy generated increase exponentially—that is, they all vary with time in a way which may be written as $e^{\alpha t}$. The value of the time constant α, which is zero in a system which is just critical and in which the neutron population remains constant, may be as large as one, or a few, times 10^8/sec in a highly supercritical metal system of U-235 or Pu-239. Obviously, the value of α increases with the degree of supercriticality (since a smaller fraction of the neutrons escape without causing a fission), with the density of the fissile material (since, with the atoms closer together, the distance and time for a neutron to cause a fission is reduced), with the average neutron velocity (which is higher in metal than in oxide, for example), and with the factors which favor small critical masses.

Independent of the value of alpha, nothing of much consequence occurs in a supercritical system containing only fissile material in the core until the energy level becomes high enough to vaporize all that material. Only then do pressures build up which can force a disassembly or halt the motion which may be driving the assembly towards a more supercritical condition. At about that point the core begins to expand, and its density starts to drop, and the value of alpha (as also the degree of super-criticality, and the rate of increase of the neutron population and energy generation) begin to decrease rapidly toward zero (at which point the system is critical and the neutron population and the energy generation rate are at, or near, their maximum) and on to negative values (where the neutrons rapidly leak away, the energy generation rate falls off, and the reaction is over). Typically, most of the energy from the reaction is developed during this disassembly phase.

> ... a bare critical assembly could be made with plutonium metal no matter what its isotopic composition might be.

As indicated by Robert Serber in the "Los Alamos Primer" of April 1943[3], on the basis of an approximate calculation valid only for a small degree of supercriticality, in any particular system the efficiency of the reaction (the fraction of the fissile material actually consumed) will be proportional to the third power of alpha at the time the motion of disassembly first gets well under way. In a core with a mass of 10 kg, or so, this stage will be reached when the value of $\alpha \cdot t$ is somewhere between 40 and 45, where t is measured from the time the chain reaction is initiated. If the system is highly supercritical when the chain starts, so that $\alpha = 10^8$/sec, say, then the time for $\alpha \cdot t$ to reach a value ≈ 45

will be extremely short, and there could be rather little change in the degree of supercriticality (or alpha) during this time. However, had the chain started much earlier in the assembly process, when the value of alpha was much smaller, there could have been an appreciable change in alpha during this incubation period—while the 45 generations (as they might be called) were being accumulated. In such a case one would consider the $\int \alpha \cdot dt$ (rather than $\alpha \cdot t$) taken from the time the chain started till $\int \alpha \cdot dt = 45$, and the explosion alpha would be the value applying at the end of that period. Clearly, the smallest possible explosion alpha will be that resulting from a chain which started just as the system reached critical (and alpha reached zero) in the course of its assembly. The yield resulting from this situation will be the smallest possible, and has been referred to as the "fizzle" yield.

Oppenheimer's breakdown of probabilities may be rephrased in the following way, namely: that, with the implosion assembly system and the high grade of plutonium being used, the probability was 0.88 that a device would survive long enough without a chain being initiated that it would provide the nominal yield; about 0.94 that it would survive long enough that the yield would be greater than 5 kilotons (one quarter of the nominal); about 0.98 that it would survive long enough to provide a yield in excess of one kiloton. Only in 0.02 of all firings would a chain be initiated so early that the energy release would be between the fizzle yield and one kiloton. Were one to change only the strength of the neutron source (which arises from spontaneous fission and alpha-n reactions) while keeping the mass and reactivity of the fissile material and everything else the same, these probabilities would change. Were the neutron source twice as large, for example, the probability of realizing the nominal yield would be only $(0.88)^2$, u.s.w. In particular, for sources 10, 20, 30, and 40 times larger than the one which applied at Trinity these probabilities (and the fraction initiated very close to critical) would be as shown in the following Table.

Source:	Yield: Nominal	above 5 kt	above 1 kt	Fizzle to 1 kt
Trinity	.88	.94	.98	.02
10 X "	.28	.54	.82	.18
20 X "	.08	.29	.67	.33
30 X "	.02	.16	.55	.45
40 X "	.006	.08	.45	.55

The largest of the sources above is most probably larger than that in the most heavily exposed plutonium considered earlier. It will be seen that as the neutron source is increased from a low level to a very high level the distribution of yields realized changes from one in which the nominal yield is the typical yield and very severe predetonation is rare, to one in which the nominal yield is rare (though never completely excluded) and the typical yields are in a band from one to a few times larger than the fizzle yield.

With the improved data and greatly improved calculation capability which have become available in the meantime, the particular values quoted by Oppenheimer in 1945 would no doubt require some revision. The substitution of a somewhat larger mass of reactor-grade plutonium for the high-grade plutonium employed in the Trinity device would also lead to some changes, both in the nominal yield and the fizzle yield. However, the general pattern pictured above would continue to apply: in the same assembly system some mass of reactor plutonium of any grade would (since this asssembly system was capable of making effective use of U-235, which is a less reactive material than reactor-grade plutonium) have a nominal yield of ≈10kT or more, and an associated fizzle yield of a few percent of its nominal yield—which is to say, some hundreds of tons. Under heavy predetonation the yields realized would most frequently fall in the range of one to a few times the fizzle yield—never less, but occasionally many times larger. Though almost all of these yields are much smaller than the nominal yield, they would nevertheless constitute quite damaging explosions, and are not reasonably dismissed as "duds" as has sometimes been suggested.

> *By the use of a reflector a few inches thick, the critical mass of all these materials can be reduced by a factor of two, or so, below the bare critical mass....*

As a final comment concerning fizzle yields it may be noted that the more rapidly the criticality (or alpha) of the fissile material increases after it first becomes critical the larger the value of alpha at the moment when $\int \alpha \cdot dt = 45$. If, for example, we assume that alpha increases linearly with time, so that $\alpha = k \cdot t$, then, when $\int \alpha \cdot dt = 45$, we have $t = \sqrt{(90/k)}$ and $\alpha = \sqrt{(90 \cdot k)}$—which is larger, the larger k may be. Since the efficiency of the fizzle explosion varies as the cube of this value of alpha, the faster the assembly proceeds the larger the fizzle yield of a given mass of fissile material. From the fact that the Trinity assembly was a very conservative design, it would seem likely that straightforward ways could be found to realize a faster-moving implosion, which could have the effect of increasing fizzle yields to higher levels than those applying above.

On the other hand, since the time interval from first critical to complete assembly might be something like 50 times longer in a gun-assembly system than in an implosion —so that the slope of the alpha-curve (the value of k, above) would be much smaller—not only would initiation be essentially guaranteed early in the assembly process even by the neutron source in very high-grade plutonium, but the value of alpha at the earliest possible explosion time would be smaller by a factor of something like √50, and the fizzle yield would be reduced by a large factor. Thus, not even the best weapons-grade plutonium is of any interest in connection with a gun-type assembly system.

> **The effect of using reactor-grade plutonium ... would not greatly change the actual value of the fizzle yield—which would always be equaled or exceeded.**

These considerations come out quite differently in connection with highly enriched uranium because the neutron source from spontaneous fission in such material is smaller than that in even the best grades of plutonium by a factor of more than a thousand. In the relatively slow-moving gun-type device one might wish to assemble a couple of critical masses, or so, which would imply bringing together something like 50 kg of 94% U-235, since the critical mass with a reflector can be about half the bare critical mass of 52 kg. The fizzle yield of such a system would, again, be some uninteresting low value; but, with the very low neutron source which could be realized in this material, the probability of initiating a chain at a very early stage of the assembly process may be small enough to ignore. Indeed, Luis Alvarez, a scientist with the Manhattan Project during its war years, has said:[4] "With modern weapons-grade uranium the background neutron rate is so low that terrorists, if they had such material, would have a good chance of setting off a high-yield explosion simply by dropping one half of the material on to the other half." What he meant by "high-yield" or "good chance" are not explained; but his mere statement calls attention to the fact that highly enriched uranium is in a class by itself.

III. Some of the Problems Confronting a Terrorist Organization

• Technical Personnel.
Competence and thorough understanding will be required in a wide range of technical specialties. These include: shock hydrodynamics, critical assemblies, chemistry, metallurgy, machining, electrical circuits, explosives, health physics, and others. At least several people who can work as a team will be needed. These will have to be carefully selected to ensure that all necessary skills are covered, but they need not have been previously engaged in designing or building nuclear weapons.
• Costs.
In addition to support for the personnel over a period adequate for planning, preparation and execution, a considerable variety of specialized equipment and instrumentation will be required, all or most of which can be obtained through commercial sources.
• Hazards.
Radiation, criticality, the handling of noxious materials and explosives all present potential hazards which will have to be foreseen and provided against.
• Detection.
Assuming the operation is contrary to the wishes of the local national authorities the organization must exercise all necessary precautions to avoid detection of their activities. They would no doubt be faced by a massive search operation employing the most sensitive detection equipment available once it should be known that someone had acquired a supply of material suitable for use as an explosive.
• Acquisition.
Very early in its planning and equipment procurement phase the organization will need information concerning the physical form and chemical state of the fissile material it will have to work with. This will be necessary before they can decide just what equipment they will need. The isotopic content of the material could be determined by straightforward means. The actual acquisition of the material would probably be the responsibility of a separate task force for which the problems and hazards would be those set by the safeguards and security authorities.

IV. Conclusions

1. Taking "weapon" to signify an object suitable for stockpile by a military organization, then heavily irradiated reactor plutonium would not be attractive for an arsenal of pure fission devices. For that purpose one would wish to have a set of warheads with a reliable known yield. One would also wish to have objects which could be turned out in a production-line fashion. However, for a terrorist organization acting alone or on behalf of a rogue state, with interests focused on the possible use of one, or a very few, devices, these considerations might be weighed quite differently. In addition, radiation exposures associated with fabrication which might be unacceptable for a sustained activity might not be troublesome for a one-shot operation.

2. It has been suggested that the fact that the U.S. appears to have made only one experiment using reactor-grade plutonium and has not chosen to adopt it for regular weapons production indicates that such material is of little worth. That is not the correct interpretation. There is, of course, no question but that weapons-grade material is preferable from a design standpoint; and if, as for the U.S., one has the option and is paying for the plutonium anyway, one chooses the most advantageous. So would the terrorist if he had a choice. But if he can't get weapons-grade material he would take whatever he can get, should any be open to him.

3. The technical problems confronting a terrorist organization considering the use of reactor-grade plutonium are not different in kind from those involved in using weapons-grade plutonium, but only in degree. For example, it is of great importance to avoid the inhalation of plutonium dust or vapor; but the provisions which would be adequate for weapons-grade material would require little, if any, modification to be acceptable for reactor-grade material. The hazards and difficulties associated with assembling a device would be less if highly enriched uranium were used.

The technical problems confronting a terrorist organization considering the use of reactor-grade plutonium are not different in kind from those involved in using weapons-grade plutonium, but only in degree.

4. The method of coping with the problems and difficulties of making an explosive device with reactor-grade plutonium is entirely in the hands of the terrorist organization. The information necessary to meet the needs is available, and can be assembled by a properly chosen team of specialists. It cannot be said whether or not they would conclude that the effort involved is within their reach, or "worthwhile", since that depends on many factors known only to them. It can be said that the only point on which established authorities can influence their decision is on that of the acquisition of material. Whether that should be more or less difficult, and whether or not the fact of their successful acquisition would be known rapidly and with assurance, could be important in this respect.

5. Assuming they do not also have access to a supply of highly enriched uranium, and assuming that the working group in question has been specifically formed to produce a first device in as short a time as possible with a high degree of confidence in obtaining a significant nuclear yield, the amount of material they would have to acquire could scarcely be as small as 5 kg, though it might not have to be very much larger than 10 kg. Even for a working group with the time and the means of conducting an extended series of non-nuclear assembly experiments—circumstances more likely to apply to a group engaged in a national effort by some Nth country than to a terrorist group—an amount of at least several kilograms would be necessary.

6. It has been suggested that rather than trying for an explosive device a terrorist organization might merely set out to disperse a quantity of reactor-grade plutonium in some highly populated location. This would bypass many of the difficult technical problems involved in producing an explosive device; and in this case reactor-grade plutonium, being several times more noxious than weapons-grade, could be the material of choice. However, it is not fully clear what objective would be realized by actually going through with such an action which could not be met as well, or better, by a well-publicized and credible threat. Here, again, the main line of defense available to the authorities is to ensure that the acquisition of such material is difficult, and that they have the means of assuring themselves rapidly whether or not the material claimed to be available is missing.

7. Finally, if methods of separating plutonium isotopes using laser technology (already receiving serious consideration in the U.S.) should, in the future, come within the reach of many industrial states, then stocks of reactor-grade plutonium would present a much more direct access to proliferation of nuclear weapons than they may appear to do at present.

ENDNOTES

1. J. Carson Mark, Theodore Taylor, Eugene Eyster, William Maraman and Jacob Wechsler, "Can Terrorists Build Nuclear Weapons?", in *Preventing Nuclear Terrorism: The Report and Papers of the International Task Force on Prevention of Nuclear Terrorism*, Leventhal and Alexander, eds., Lexington Books, 1987, pp. 55-65.

2. Quoted by Albert Wohlstetter in *Foreign Policy*; 25, winter, 1976-77; p. 160.

3. R. Serber, "The Los Alamos Primer", Report L.A. 1, April, 1943. (Declassified in 1965.)

4. Luis W. Alvarez, *Adventures of a Physicist*, Basic Books, New York, 1987, p. 125.

Permission to quote or to reprint is granted in advance, provided that acknowledgement is made as to the source and that the Nuclear Control Institute is notified as to the form and use made of the material.

Table I.2. Plutonium production in various types of reactor

Type of reactor	Irradiation level of heavy metal (MWd/kg)	Average enrichment (% U-235)	Initial fuel inventory (kg/MW(e))		Pu-239 production (g/MW(e) yr)
			Core (natural U)	Blanket (depleted U)	
BWR	17	2	434	–	250
PWR	22.6	2.3	365	–	255
AGR	–	1.6	620	–	100
HWR (CANDU)	6	0.711	143	–	490
HTGR (USA)	54.5	~93	326	–	–
SGHWR	15.5	1.8	520	–	150
FBR (UK)	~70	–	9.5 (depleted U) 2.8 (Pu)[a]	16.9 (depleted U)	2850 (core Pu)[b] 409 (blanket Pu)[b]

[a] Plutonium composition is 57 per cent Pu-239, 24 per cent Pu-240, 14 per cent Pu-241 and 5 per cent Pu-242.
[b] Total of 2 980 kg/yr containing 58 per cent Pu-239, 28 per cent Pu-240, 9 per cent Pu-241 and 5 per cent Pu-242.

Sources: See References [2] and [3].

Figure 8.7. Improving the proliferation resistance of the plutonium cycle

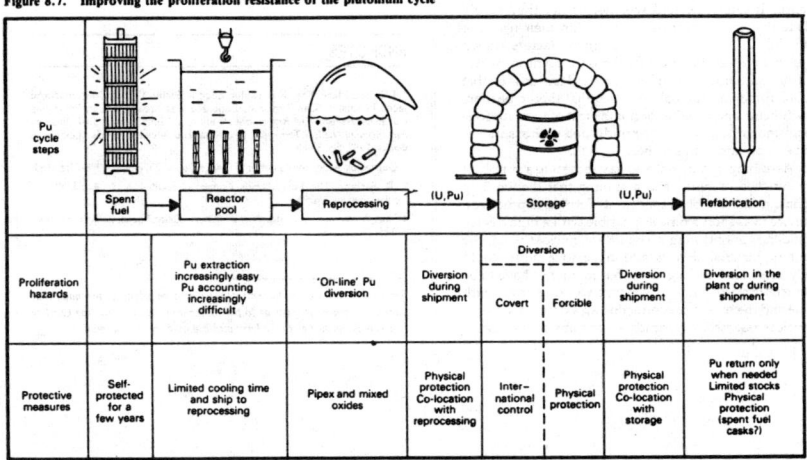

Source: SIPRI, *Nuclear Energy and Nuclear Weapons Proliferation* (London: Taylor & Francis, 1979), ...)

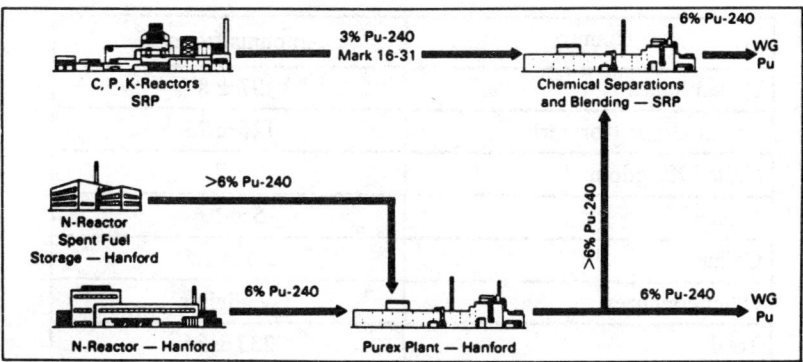

Figure 3.2 Current methods for producing weapon-grade plutonium (1984)

Table 3.5
Weapon-Grade Plutonium from Reactor Production and Blending

FY	Hanford Weapon-Grade Separated[a] (kg)	Savannah River Weapon-Grade Separated[a] (kg)	Savannah River Supergrade Separated[a] (kg)	Fuel-Grade Required[a] (kg)		Weapon-Grade by Blending (kg)	Total Weapon-Grade (kg)
				Annual	Cumulative		
1982		700[d]	360[d]	180	180	540	1240
1983		240[d]	700[d]	350	530	1050	1290
1984	910[b]	0	1085	540	1070	1590	2500
1985	1050[b]	0	1055	530	1600	1585	2635
1986	650[c]	0	1345	670	2270	2015	2665
1987	650[c]	0	1635	820	3090	2455	3105
1988	650[c]	0	1570	785	3875	2355	3005
1989	650[c]	0	1525	760	4635	2285	2935
1990	650[c]	0	1435	720	5355	2155	2805

a Allows for 6-month cooling period of discharged fuel before processing.
b PUREX separated only 6 percent Pu-240 plutonium in FY 1984 (from 1046 MT uranium) and in FY 1985 (from 1200 MT uranium), culling out all of the 6 percent Pu-240 plutonium in storage and processing fuel from current production.
c Assumes N-Reactor operation at 4000 MW$_t$ and 52 percent capacity factor.
d Assumes 20 percent of the plutonium production in FY 1981 and 50 percent of the production in FY 1982 is supergrade.
e This assumes blending with 12 percent (average) Pu-240 plutonium and gives an upper bound to fuel-grade requirements. Blending with 9 percent Pu-240 plutonium, for example, requires 50 percent less fuel-grade plutonium.

Thomas B. Cochran et al., *Nuclear Weapons Databook*, vol. 2, *U.S. Nuclear Warhead Production* (Cambridge, Mass.: Ballinger, 1987), 66

Country	Amounts [tonnes]
United States	97 ± 8
Soviet Union (former)	125 ± 25
United Kingdom	3.7
France	5 ± 1.6
China	2.5 ± 1.5
Other countries	negligible
Total	233 ± 36

Table 5.9. An estimate of the global amounts of WGPu

Country	Amounts [tonnes]
United States	600
Soviet Union (former)	500
United Kingdom, France, China	not available
Other countries	negligible
Total	1100

Table 5.10. An estimate of global amounts of WGU.

Source: Johan Swahn, *The Long-Term Nuclear Explosives Predicament* (Goeteborg, Sweden: Chalmers University of Technology, 1992), 122

Table 1: Summary table of world plutonium stocks and surpluses (Pu^{tot}, tonnes, end of 1990)

	Nuclear Weapon States	Non-Nuclear Weapon States	non-NPT countries[a]	Total
Weapons In weapons[b]	260	0	0.8	260
Civil In irradiated fuel	296[c] (366)[d]	218[c] (148)[d]	17	531
Recycled in MOX	31[e]	18[f]	0	49
Stored as oxide	64[g]	8[h]	0.3	72
Total (by ownership)	651	244	18	912
Total (by location)	(721)	(174)	18	912

Notes:
a. Includes Israel, India, Pakistan, Brazil, Argentina and Taiwan
b. Includes associated stocks. Italics denote larger error margins than in the rest of the table.
c. Includes an estimated 5 tonnes of plutonium contained in East European and Finnish spent fuel sent to Chelyabinsk under 'take-back' arrangements (adjacent figure of 218 tonnes in the next column excludes this amount).
d. Figures in brackets take account of an estimated 70 tonnes of foreign plutonium held in store in France and the United Kingdom in spent fuel or as separated plutonium. (adjacent figure of 148 tonnes in the next column excludes this amount).
e. Comprises 25.3 tonnes of civil plutonium recycled in fast reactors and other R&D facilities (5 tonnes in UK, 12.5 in France, 0.5 in the former USSR, and 6.7 tonnes in the USA - the last figure includes material imported from the UK), and 5.8 tonnes of plutonium recycled in thermal reactors in France. 4.5 tonnes of foreign-owned plutonium in Superphénix fuel is not included under this column, but in the adjacent column.
f. Comprises 4.5 and 2.5 tonnes of plutonium recycled in Japanese and German fast reactors respectively, 4.5 tonnes of plutonium owned by Italian, German and Dutch utilities loaded into Superphénix, and 6.5 tonnes of plutonium recycled in German, Swiss and Belgian thermal reactors.
g. Includes 2 tonnes of plutonium separated at Sellafield and La Hague, but not yet returned to owners in NNWS.
h. Comprises 27.8 tonnes of plutonium separated from NNWS fuel, less 18 tonnes of recycled material, less 2 tonnes held in store (see note g).

Source: D Albright, F Berkhout and W Walker, World Inventory of Plutonium and Highly-Enriched Uranium 1992, OUP/SIPRI, 1992 forthcoming, table 12.3.

Source: Frans Berkhout et al., "Disposition of Separated Plutonium," *Science & Global Security* 3 (1993): 163

Table 2: Commercial reprocessing plants around the world

Country	Location	Owner/Operator	Facility	Fuel	Capacity (tHM/yr)	Operated
United Kingdom	Sellafield	BNF plc	B205	metal	1500	1964-2010?
			B204/205	oxide	300	1969-1973
			THORP	oxide	700	1992/3-
	Thurso	UKAEA	DNPDE	oxide (MTR)	<1	1959-
				oxide (FBR)	7	1980-1997?
France	Marcoule	Cogema	UP1	metal	400	1958-2000?
	La Hague	Cogema	UP2	metal + oxide	400	1966-1987 (metal)
						1976-1990 (oxide)
	La Hague	Cogema	UP3	oxide	800	1990-
	La Hague	Cogema	UP2-800	oxide	800	1993-
United States	West Valley	Nuclear Fuel Services	West Valley	oxide	300	1966-72
Russia[a]	Chelyabinsk-40	Minatom RF	Mayak	oxide	600	1978-
Japan	Tokai-mura	PNC	Tokai	oxide	90	1981-
	Rokkasho-mura	JNFS	Rokkasho	oxide	800	2002?-
India	Tarapur	DAE	PREFRE	oxide	30-150	1982-
	Kalpakkam	DAE		oxide	100-200	1993/4?-
Germany	Karlsruhe	KfK/DWK	WAK	oxide	35	1971-1990
Belgium	Mol	Eurochemic	Mol	oxide	30	1966-1974

Notes:
a. Construction was begun on another plant at Krasnoyarsk in Siberia (Dodonovo-27), but halted when about 30 percent complete. We assume the plant will not be completed.

Source: Frans Berkhout et al., Disposition of Separated Plutonium (Princeton: The Center for Energy and Environmental Studies, September 1992, p. 17

Table 3: Plutonium fuel fabrication facilities

Country	Facility	Operator	Operated	Fuel type	Capacity (tMOX/yr)
Operating facilities					
France	Cadarache/ATPu	CEA	1970-1989	FBR	15
United Kingdom	Sellafield/B?	BNF plc	1970-1989	FBR	4
Japan	Tokai/PFFF	PNC	1972-	FBR + ATR	1(FBR) + 9(ATR)
Belgium	Dessel/DEMOX	BN	1973-	FBR + LWR	35
Germany	Hanau/BEW1	Siemens	1974-1992?	FBR + LWR	25-30
Japan	Tokai/PFPF	PNC	1988-	FBR	5
Russia[a]	Chelyabinsk-40 "Granat"	MAPI/ Minatom RF	1988-	FBR	35-40kgMOX
Russia[a]	Chelyabinsk-40 "Paket"	MAPI/ Minatom RF	1988-	FBR	35-40kgMOX
France	Cadarache/CFCa	Cogema	1990-	FBR + LWR	10(FBR) + 15(LWR)
Planned facilities					
Germany	Hanau /BEW2	Siemens	1992?-	LWR	80-120
Japan	Tokai/PFPF	PNC	1993/4	ATR	40
United Kingdom	Sellafield/MDF	BNFL	1993-	LWR	8
France	Marcoule /Melox	Cogema	1996-	LWR	115
Belgium	Dessel 2	BN	mid-1990s?	LWR	35
Russia[a]	Chelyabinsk-40	Minatom RF?	mid-1990s?	FBR	25-30
United Kingdom	Sellafield/SMP	BNFL	1997/8?	LWR	50-70
Japan	Rokkasho-mura	JNFS?	late-1990s?	LWR	100?
Russia[a]	Chelyabinsk-40	Minatom RF?	late-1990s?	VVER	100-300??

Notes:

a. All Russian plants are referred to in: V.N. Solonin, "Utilization of Nuclear Materials Released as the Result of Nuclear Disarmament", paper given to the International Symposium on *Conversion of Nuclear Weapons for Peaceful Purposes*, Rome, 15-17 June 1992.

Source: Frans Berkhout et al., *Disposition of Separated Plutonium* (Princeton: The Center for Energy and Environmental Studies, September 1992, p. 17

Table 5: Isotopic concentration and physical characteristics of plutonium

Isotope (half-life)	Reactor-grade[a] (Percent)		Weapon-grade[b] (Percent)	Decay heat (kW/t)	Neutron Emission Rate[c] ($s^{-1} kg^{-1}$)	Delayed Neutron Fraction[d] (thermal)	Relative radiation hazard[e]
	Spent LEU fuel	Spent MOX fuel					
Pu-238 (87.7 yrs)	1.3	2.3	0.012	560	2.6E6		540
Pu-239 (24,100 yrs)	60.3	38.1	93.8	1.9	22	0.0021	1
Pu-240 (6,560 yrs)	24.3	32.7	5.8	6.8	0.91E6		31
Pu-241 (14.4 yrs)	8.3	17.3	0.23	4.2	49	0.0049	10
Pu-242 (376,000yrs)	4.7	8.3	0.022	0.1	1.7E6		26
Am-241 (430 yrs)	0.8	1.3	0.12	114	1200		2,600
Radiation hazard relative to Pu-239	18	28	4.3				
Maximum storage of separated Pu[f]	8 years	7 years	No limit				
Decay heat (kW/t) of Pu after 10 years storage	13.2	22.6	3				
Neutron Emission Rate ($s^{-1}kg^{-1}$)	3.3E5	5.0E5	0.53E5				

Notes:
a. OECD/NEA, *Plutonium Fuel: an assessment*, Paris, 1989, Table 12A.
b. Weapon material stored for 10 years. Source: N J Nicholas, K L Coop and R J Estep, *Capability and Limitation Study of DDT Passive-Active Neutron Waste Assay Instrument*, Los Alamos National Laboratory, LA-12237-MS, 1992.
c. F von Hippel and R Sagdeev, *Reversing the Arms Race*, Gordon and Breech Science Publishers, New York, 1990, p 315.
d. The proportion of neutrons yielded per fission of the isotope which are delayed neutrons. Source: G.R. Keepin, *Physics of Nuclear Kinetics*, Adison-Wesley, Reading, 1965, p 102.
e. Based on the relative magnitudes of the summed X-ray, gamma and neutron surface doses for a one kilogramme sphere of pure nuclide. The total dose for Pu-239 is 12.1 milliSieverts/hr. Source: OECD/NEA, op cit, Table 3.
f. Fuel irradiated in a PWR to 33 GWd/t and stored for 10 years.
g. The period of time separated plutonium could be stored before becoming unacceptable at the new MOX fabrication facilities. Assuming plutonium separated after 10 years fuel storage and a maximum Am-241 concentration of 2.5 percent.

Source: Frans Berkhout et al., *Disposition of Separated Plutonium* (Princeton: The Center for Energy and Environmental Studies, September 1992, p. 25

Table A1: Estimated plutonium discharged and separated from power reactor fuel (Putot, tonnes)

		through 1990		1991-2000		through 2000
	Plutonium discharged from reactors	Plutonium separated	Percentage of total plutonium separated	Plutonium discharged from reactors	Plutonium separated	Cumulative percentage of total plutonium separated
Countries reprocessing fuel						
Belgium	11.5	1.2	10%	10	4	24%
Bulgaria, Czechoslovakia, Hungary, GDR and Finland[a]	23.7	5?	21%	38	0?	8%
CIS	78.1	20?	26%	78	157	15%?
France	82.2[b]	23.6[b]	29%[c]	105	45	38%
Germany	38.8	15.8[d]	41%	45[e]	34	60%
India	3.5	0.1-0.3	3-9%	10	27	15%?
Italy	5.6	2.6	46%	<1	2	74%
Japan	57.4	6.4	11%	83	54	43%
Netherlands	2.4	0.7	29%	1	1	47%
Spain	9.7[f]	0		17	1.5	6%
Switzerland	9.2	1.1	12%	7	9	63%
United Kingdom	53.1	42.5	80%	30	25	80%
United States	176.0	1.5	1%	180	0	<0.5%
Countries not reprocessing fuel						
Canada	53.6	0		60	0	
Rep. of Korea	8.4	0		23	0	
Sweden	20.7	0[g]		22	0	
Taiwan	7.6	0		11	0	
Rest of the world[h]	12.1	0		16	0	
Total	653.6	120.6	18	737	192.5	23%

Source: Frans Berkhout et al., Disposition of Separated Plutonium (Princeton: The Center for Energy and Environmental Studies, September 1992, p. A1

Table A1 contd.

Notes:

a. The two TVO BWRs in Finland is counted under this category.
b. Includes 4.2 tonnes of plutonium discharged from the Spanish Vandellos 1 Magnox reactor supplied by France together with fuel under a 'take back' arrangement under which France retains ownership of plutonium.
c. Counting only reactors operating in France, the proportion of plutonium separated would be 25 percent (19.5 tonnes separated out of 78.2 tonnes discharged).
d. Includes some 0.5 tPu^{tot} separated from Swedish spent fuel at La Hague and coming into German ownership under a swap arrangement in 1990.
e. This includes 230 tonnes of fuel due to be discharged from decommissioned reactors in the former GDR, containing an estimated 900 kg of plutonium.
f. This does not include Vandellos 1 plutonium discharges (see note a).
g. Some 57 tonnes of Swedish fuel have been reprocessed at La Hague, but the separated plutonium has been swapped with German utilities (see note c).
h. Includes Argentina, Brazil, China, Cuba, Mexico, Pakistan, Romania, South Africa and Yugoslavia.

Table A5: Projection of separated plutonium balances in 2000 (Pu^{tot}, tonnes)

	Plutonium separated (1991-2000)	Plutonium use Fast reactors (1991-2000)	Plutonium use Thermal reactors (1991-2000)	Plutonium balance (1991-2000)	Plutonium balance (cumulative, see Table A2)
Belgium	4	0	3.9	0.1	1
Bulgaria, Czech, Hungary and Finland	0?	0	0	0?	
CIS	15?	0	0	15?	40?
France	45	3.9	27	14.1	19.3
Germany	32	0	28.2	3.8	12.2
India	27	0?	0	27	27
Italy	2	0	0	2	0.8
Japan	49	6.5	5.7	36.8	38.7
Netherlands	1	0	0	1	1.3
Spain	1.5	0	0	1.5	1.5
Switzerland	8	0	5.7	2.3	2.4
United Kingdom	25	0	0	25	62.5
United States	0	0	0	0	-5.2
Total	184.5	10.4	70.5	103.6	176.5

Note:
Figures have been left with four significant figures not to denote precision, but to show fully the results of the assumptions used here.

Source: Frans Berkhout et al, Disposition of Separated Plutonium (Princeton: The Center for Energy and Environmental Studies, September 1992, p. A5

Table Two
SEPARATED CIVIL PLUTONIUM - PROJECTED 2000

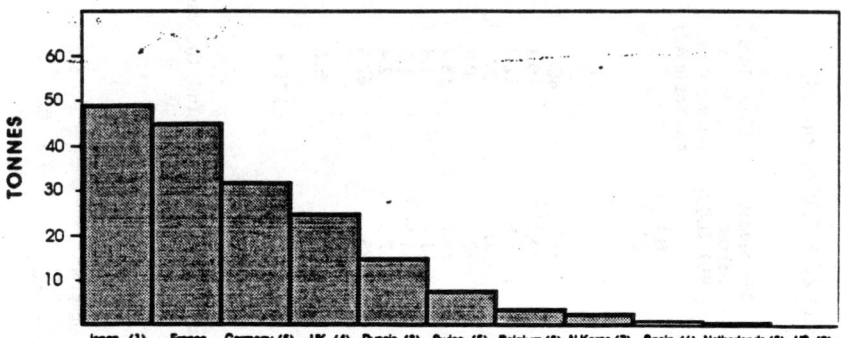

Japan (1)   France   Germany (5)   UK (4)   Russia (3)   Swiss (5)   Belgium (5)   N.Korea (7)   Spain (6)   Netherlands (5)   US (2)

Notes

1 - assumes completion of full contracts with THORP, UP-3. Does not include reprocessing of Magnox fuel at B205 facility. Total plutonium discharged from reactors from 1991 - 2000 is 83 tonnes (source Hippel et al., Disposition of Separated Plutonium). Also does not include carry over from pre-1991, of 6.4 tonnes total separated and 1.4 'surplus' in March 1993.

Also note the figures for Japan from 2000 - 2010, would include the operation of Rokkasho-mura plant, with capacity to separate about 8 tonnes plutonium per year. Thus cumulative total for 1991-2010 would be 113 tonnes. Demand would be in the region of 5.7 tonnes plutonium loaded as MOX in two LWR's, and 6.5 tonnes as FBR/ATR - MOX by 2000.(source: Hippel et al) Even with an expansion by a factor of four for consumption by 2010, which on current projections seems unlikely, demand would consume 48 tonnes or 35% of supply. Thus even on the most optimistic demand figures, Japan will be left with 65 tonnes plutonium surplus to civil requirements by 2010.

2 - Is carry over stocks from end of civil reprocessing in 1970's. Assumed no commercial reprocessing startup.

3 - assumes operation of Chelyabinsk reprocessing plant, not including start-up of RT-2 facility.

4 - assumes commissioning of THORP plant.

5 - assumes completion of full contracts with THORP and UP-3

6 - assumes completion of full contracts for reprocessing of Magnox fuel, at La Hague and Sellafield.

7 - figures are maximum, based upon projected start-up times of reactors and Yongbyon reprocessing plant

8 - No figures are provided for South Korea as the country does not as yet have access to reprocessing, current stocks within spent fuel would be approximately 31.4 tonnes plutonium in 2000.

Source: *The Plutonium Trade: A Troubling New Era of Proliferation?* (Greenpeace International, 1 March 1993), 5

Table One
SEPARATED MILITARY PLUTONIUM TO 1990

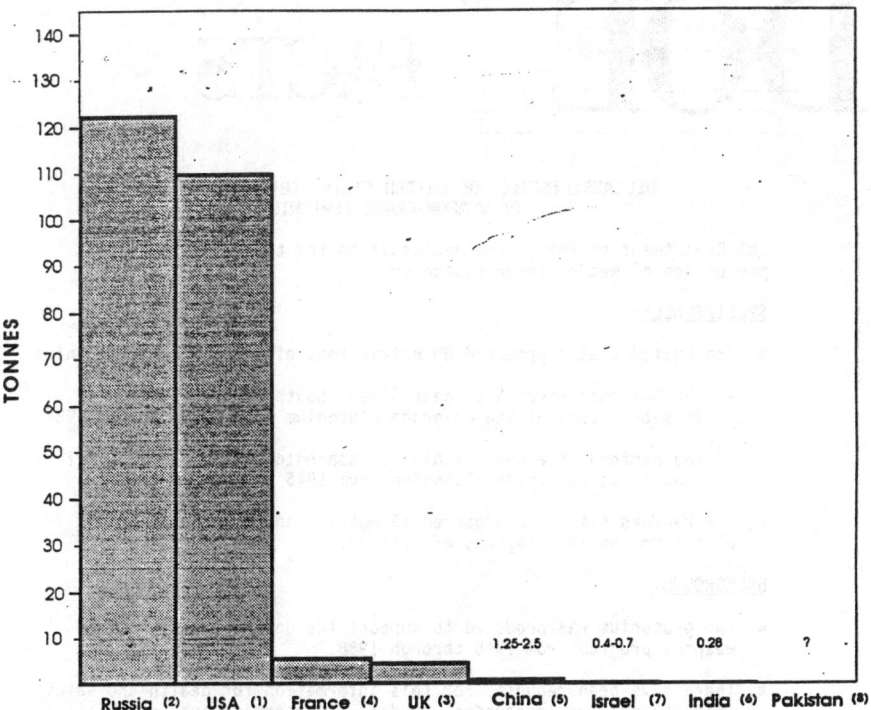

All figures were reported in Plutonium: Deadly Gold of the Nuclear Age, September 1992, International Physicians for the Prevention of Nuclear War (IPPNW), and Institute for Energy and Environmental Research (IEER).

Notes

1 - uncertainty of +/- 5-10%; source Cochran, TB; Arkin, WM; Norris, RS; Hoenig, MM; in Nuclear Weapons Databook, Vol:II, US Nuclear Warhead Production.
2 - less estimated 6 tonnes for tritium production, uncertainty of approximately +/- 16%; figures from Russian/Soviet nuclear warhead production, Cochran, TB and Norris, RS. Nuclear Weapons Databook Working papers, NWD, 92-4, NRDC, Washington 1992.
3 - cited in Plutonium: Deadly Gold of the Nuclear Age, opcit.
4 - source Barrilot, B. The manufacture of nuclear weapons in France, 1991, Documentation and Research Centre for Peace and Conflicts, Lyon, France;
5 - uses a basis of 5 kg per warhead, with between 250-350 weapons deployed. Error factor is estimated at two, therefore warhead range is between 250 and 500. Range of plutonium is therefore between 1,250 kg and 2,500 kg. source: Fieldhouse, RW; Chinese nuclear weapons: a current and historical overview. Nuclear Weapons Databook Working Paper, NRDC, March 1991; cited in Plutonium: Deadly Gold of the Nuclear Age.
6 - Albright, D. Reprocessing and programs in Argentina, Brazil, India, Israel, and South Africa: nuclear explosive materials production. Working paper, Federation of American Scientists, Washington, DC. 1988.
7 - Plutonium: Deadly Gold of the Nuclear Age, opcit.
8 - Operation of New Labs reprocessing plant, estimated to be able to separate 10-20kg of plutonium each year. Spector, L. and Smith, JR. Nuclear Ambitions, Boulder: Westview Press, 1990.

Source: *The Plutonium Trade: A Troubling New Era of Proliferation?* (Greenpeace International, 1 March 1993), 5

DOE FACTS

DECLASSIFICATION OF UNITED STATES TOTAL PRODUCTION OF WEAPON-GRADE PLUTONIUM

The Department of Energy has declassified the total United States production of weapon-grade plutonium.

SPECIFICALLY:

- The United States produced 89 metric tons of weapon-grade plutonium.
  - The Savannah River Site near Aiken, South Carolina, produced 36 metric tons of weapon-grade plutonium from 1953 through 1988.
  - The Hanford site near Richland, Washington, produced 53 metric tons of weapon-grade plutonium from 1945 through 1987.
- The Hanford site also produced 13 metric tons of reactor-grade plutonium and 13 kilograms of tritium.

BACKGROUND:

- The plutonium was produced to support the United States nuclear weapons program from 1945 through 1988.
- There have been requests for this information for health and safety calculations for independent studies to determine public radiation dosages.
- The Congressional Office of Technology Assessment has also suggested the release of this information.

BENEFITS:

- As part of the Secretary's Openness Initiative, the Department is declassifying the information concerning the total United States plutonium production. As a result of this declassification, the public will have information that is important to the current debate over proper management and ultimate disposition of plutonium.

(MORE)

U.S. Department of Energy
Office of Public Affairs
Contact: Sam Grizzle
(202) 586-5806

Source: Department of Energy, "Openness Press Conference", 7 December 1993.

Page 2

- Citizens will also be better informed about U.S. plutonium production activities which have had significant environmental impact at production and separation facilities.

- Release of previously secret information should also encourage other nations to declassify similar information.

- This information is also useful to historians of the nuclear age.

- This information is also useful in health studies of workers and the communities and related activities as it shows the magnitude of production.

WHO ARE THE KEY STAKEHOLDERS?:

- <u>The Public</u>: The public living near the site is, and has been, concerned with the health and safety issues relating to plutonium production.

- <u>Environmentalists</u>: With the declassification, those interested in determining the total magnitude of the production effort and its impact will have important information.

- <u>Freedom of Information Act Requesters</u>: The Department of Energy has received Freedom of Information Act requests concerning plutonium production and this information, until today, has been denied.

- <u>Historians and Researchers</u>: This information will be available for historical summaries and will end speculation on the subject of the magnitude of production.

- <u>Health Researchers</u>: This declassification will permit greater public review of information of potential value for epidemiologic or other health studies regarding workers and the community.

(MORE)

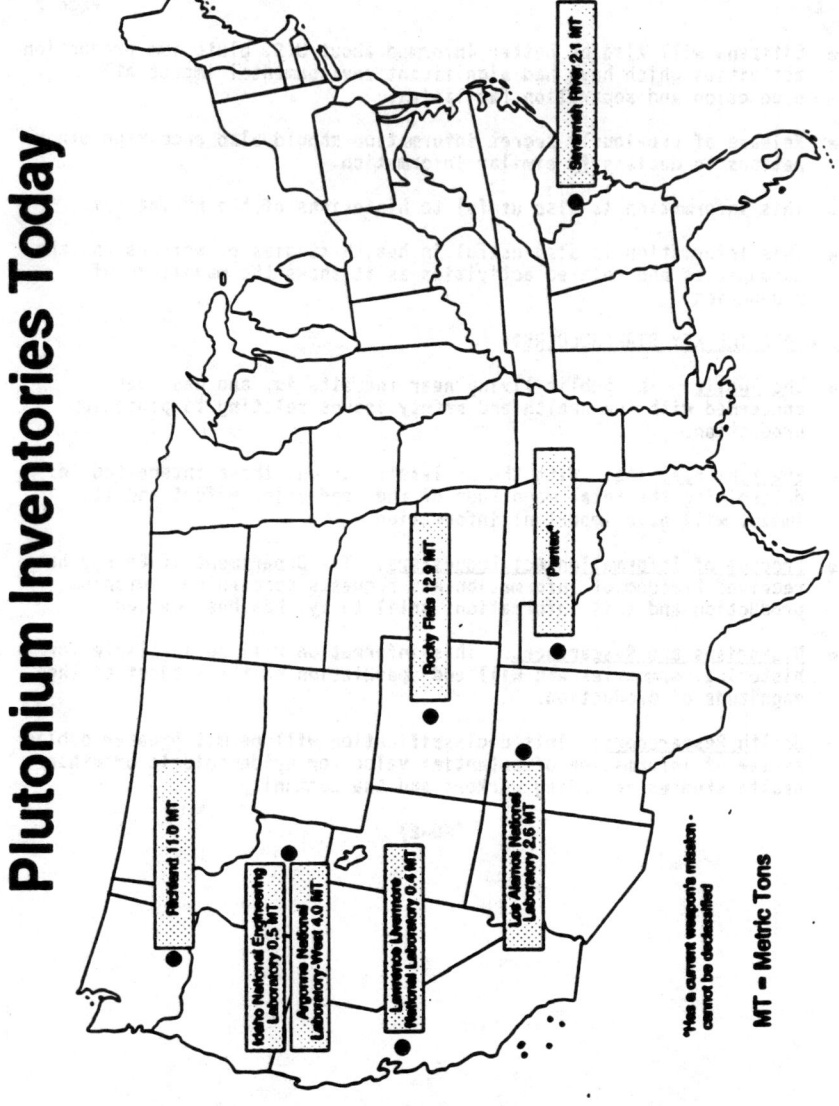

DECLASSIFICATION OF TODAY'S PLUTONIUM INVENTORY AT SAVANNAH RIVER SITE NEAR AIKEN, SOUTH CAROLINA

The Department of Energy has declassified the total inventory of plutonium at the Savannah River Site.

SPECIFICALLY:

- The total quantity of plutonium currently at Savannah River is 2.1 metric tons. This amounts to:

    0.5 metric tons of metals, sources, standards, etc.

    1.3 metric tons of compounds.

    0.3 metric tons of irradiated materials.

BACKGROUND:

- The material is stored in different forms including metal, oxide, liquid, and process residues.

- The Department of Energy is cooperating with independent studies conducted by the State of South Carolina and the Centers for Disease Control and Prevention to estimate offsite radiation and chemical releases from Savannah River and to measure potential health effects upon the workforce.

- This declassified information will permit more open discussions with environmental, health and safety interests and local Governments. While other information does remain classified, we will be working with stakeholders to establish priorities for additional declassifications.

- We are actively studying the proposed declassification of the Savannah River historical plutonium annual production to determine any nonproliferation implications.

(MORE)

U.S. Department of Energy
Office of Public Affairs
Contact: Sam Grizzle
(202) 586-5806

■ *U.S. Department of Energy* ● *Office of the Press Secretary* ● *Washington, DC 20585* ■

BENEFITS:

- As part of the Secretary's Openness Initiative, the Department is declassifying the information concerning the plutonium inventory and its form at the Savannah River Site. As a result of this declassification, the public will have information that is important to the current debate over proper management and ultimate disposition of plutonium.

- This information is useful in health studies and related activities regarding workers and the community.

- Release of previously secret information should also encourage other nations to declassify similar information.

WHO ARE THE KEY STAKEHOLDERS?:

- <u>The General Public</u>: The public living near the site is, and has been, concerned with health and safety issues relating to the inventories of plutonium at Savannah River.

- <u>Environmentalists</u>. With this declassification, those interested in environmental oversight of the plutonium related activities at Savannah River will have more information relating to this function.

- <u>Freedom of Information Act Requesters</u>. The Department of Energy has received Freedom of Information Act requests concerning Savannah River plutonium inventories and this information, until today, has been denied to the requesters.

- <u>Health Researchers.</u> This declassification will permit greater public review of information of potential value for epidemiologic or other health studies, such as those carried out by the Centers for Disease Control and Prevention for workers and the community.

(MORE)

QUESTIONS AND ANSWERS

Q. Why is plutonium stored at Savannah River?

A. During the past 40 years, the Savannah River Site produced plutonium to meet national security requirements. The Savannah River Site is not currently producing any plutonium, although a significant amount of plutonium in various forms remains at the site. Consideration is being given to possible processing of the materials to place them in a form suitable for long-term storage.

Q. Is this plutonium stored safely?

A. Yes. Plutonium at the Savannah River site is carefully stored in secure vaults with ventilation and filtration systems. This plutonium is stored in metal and oxide forms. Additional processing, however, may be required to prepare the material for long-term storage. Part of this processing effort would involve repackaging the material into containers suitable for long-term storage and monitoring. During these operations the principal hazards are to operations personnel. The direct radiation from handling plutonium increases with time due to the buildup of decay products. The potential for exposure to airborne and respirable particles of plutonium depends on how often the material is handled and the probability of releasing plutonium oxide particles from containers unsuitable for long-term storage.

Q. How many weapons pits are stored at Savannah River?

A. The number of pits in storage at Savannah River is currently classified, but the plutonium in the pits is included in the total inventory that was released today. This information has been identified by the Secretary to be studied for possible future declassification.

(MORE)

U.S. Department of Energy • Office of the Press Secretary • Washington, DC 20585

Page 2

Q. If you are declassifying the Savannah River Site inventories, what about Pantex?

A. The total quantity of plutonium at Pantex remains classified due to a proliferation concern that the amount of plutonium in a nuclear weapon could be determined by correlating the number of dismantlements being released to the public, to future increases in the plutonium inventory.

# DOE FACTS

DECLASSIFICATION OF TODAY'S PLUTONIUM INVENTORY AT ROCKY FLATS PLANT NEAR DENVER, COLORADO

The Department of Energy has declassified the total plutonium inventory at the Rocky Flats Plant.

SPECIFICALLY:

- **Current total inventory of plutonium at Rocky Flats is 12.9 metric tons.** This amounts to:

  6.6 metric tons of metal.

  3.2 metric tons of compounds.

  3.1 metric tons of mixtures, etc.

BACKGROUND:

- The current total inventory of plutonium at Rocky Flats does not include material that will be recovered during decontamination of buildings and equipment or material in waste.

- This declassified information will permit more open discussions with environmental, safety and health interests and local Governments.

- The Department of Energy is cooperating with independent studies conducted by the Colorado Department of Health to estimate offsite radiation and chemical releases from Rocky Flats and to measure potential health effects upon the plant's workforce.

- We will be working with stakeholders to establish priorities for additional declassifications.

(MORE)

U.S. Department of Energy
Office of Public Affairs
Contact: Sam Grizzle
(202) 586-5806

BENEFIT:

- As part of the Secretary's Openness Initiative, the Department is declassifying the information concerning the plutonium inventory and its form at the Rocky Flats Plant. As a result of this declassification, the public will have information that is important to the current debate over proper management and ultimate disposition of plutonium.

- This information is useful in health studies and related activities concerning workers and the community.

- Release of previously secret information should also encourage other nations to declassify similar information.

WHO ARE THE KEY STAKEHOLDERS?:

- <u>Regulators</u>. Rocky Flats Program Unit of the Colorado Department of Health and the Colorado Department of Health Director.

- <u>The Public</u>. The public living near the plant is, and has been, concerned with the health and safety issues relating to the inventories of plutonium at the Rocky Flats Plant. This includes the general public and Rocky Flats employees.

- <u>Environmental, Safety and Health Interests</u>. Sierra Club, Greenpeace, Rocky Mountain Peace Center, Defense Nuclear Facilities Safety Board, Colorado Council on Rocky Flats, Rocky Flats Cleanup Commission, Rocky Flats Local Impacts Initiative, and the Citizens Advisory Board.

- <u>Health Researchers.</u> This declassification will permit greater public review of information of potential value for epidemiologic or other health studies regarding workers and the public.

(MORE)

QUESTIONS AND ANSWERS

Q. Will this plutonium be removed from Colorado?

A. The movement of plutonium from Rocky Flats is currently being addressed in a programmatic environmental impact statement for reconfiguration of the nuclear weapons complex. The Department of Energy held public scoping meetings in several locations across the country in September and October 1993. The environmental impact statement is expected to be final, following public comment, in late 1994.

Q. What are the medical impacts of the plutonium released offsite?

A. On October 21, 1993, the State of Colorado's Health Advisory Panel announced the findings of Phase I of a comprehensive health study of Rocky Flats. According to the panel's news release, "Phase I studies indicate that community exposures from past contaminant releases from Rocky Flats are small." The news release also states, "Preliminary estimates of health risk from these releases are small. In the areas of greatest impact, the risks are less than one chance of excess cancer in 100,000."

On November 24, 1993, the Colorado Department of Health announced it has received $500,000 from the National Institute of Occupational Safety and Health for the first year of a study of cancer incidence and mortality among workers at the Rocky Flats Plant who have been exposed to radioactive materials and chemicals. The state study is projected to take 5 years and cost an estimated $2.5 million.

(MORE)

Q. What is the Department of Energy doing to safeguard and monitor this plutonium?

A. Plutonium is stored with rigorous safeguards and safety measures subject to independent oversight.

The results of the Rocky Flats Plant's extensive environmental monitoring program are shared and compared each month with the state and neighboring communities in a public meeting. Radiation doses to the public from plant operations are typically below any regulatory limit and less than are received from naturally occurring radiation sources in the Denver metropolitan area.

Q. The Department of Energy Rocky Flats Office issued a news release in early July 1993 indicating the plutonium inventory was 10 or 11 metric tons, but today's release indicates 12.9 metric tons. What is the difference?

A. The 12.9 metric tons figure is the official inventory. In order to be able to provide an unclassified figure in July, the amount was approximated.

 **FACTS**

DECLASSIFICATION OF TODAY'S PLUTONIUM INVENTORY AT ARGONNE NATIONAL LABORATORY-WEST NEAR IDAHO FALLS, IDAHO

The Department of Energy has declassified the total inventory of plutonium at the Argonne National Laboratory-West.

SPECIFICALLY:

- The total quantity of plutonium currently at Argonne National Laboratory-West is 4.0 metric tons. This amounts to:
    - 3.8 metric tons of unirradiated fuel elements, zero power physics reactor plates, and experimental capsules.
    - 0.1 metric tons of oxide and metal.
    - 0.1 metric tons of irradiated fuel elements and scrap.

- In the past, information was declassified concerning the inventory of 0.5 metric tons of plutonium in irradiated fuel elements at the Idaho National Engineering Laboratory near Idaho Falls, Idaho.

BACKGROUND:

- The material is in different forms including metal, compounds, and scrap.

- The Department of Energy is cooperating in independent studies conducted by the State of Idaho and the Centers for Disease Control and Prevention to estimate offsite radiation and chemical releases from Argonne National Laboratory-West and the Idaho National Engineering Laboratory and to measure potential health effects upon facility work forces.

- This declassified information will permit more open discussions with environmental, safety and health interests and local Governments. While other information does remain classified, we will be working with stakeholders to establish priorities for additional declassifications.

(MORE)

U.S. Department of Energy
Office of Public Affairs
Contact: Sam Grizzle
(202) 586-5806

■ U.S. Department of Energy ● Office of the Press Secretary ● Washington, DC 20585 ■

BENEFITS:

- As part of the Secretary's Openness Initiative, the Department is declassifying the information concerning the plutonium inventory at the Argonne National Laboratory-West. As a result of this declassification, the public will have information that is important in the current debate over the proper management and ultimate disposition of plutonium.

- Release of previously secret information should also encourage other nations to declassify similar information.

- Will permit openness with the public on matters pertaining to public health and safety and the cleanup, storage, and disposal of nuclear materials.

- This information is useful in health studies and related activities concerning workers and the community.

WHO ARE THE KEY STAKEHOLDERS?:

- <u>The Public</u>. The public living near the site is, and has been, concerned with the health and safety issues relating to the inventories of plutonium at the Argonne National Laboratory-West and the Idaho National Engineering Laboratory.

- <u>Environmental, Safety and Health Interests</u>. Environmental Defense Institute and Snake River Alliance.

- <u>Regulators</u>. This information will assist State regulators in performing their functions.

 **FACTS**

DECLASSIFICATION OF TODAY'S PLUTONIUM INVENTORY AT LOS ALAMOS NATIONAL LABORATORY NEAR LOS ALAMOS, NEW MEXICO AND PLUTONIUM INVENTORY AT LAWRENCE LIVERMORE NATIONAL LABORATORY NEAR LIVERMORE, CALIFORNIA

The Department of Energy has declassified the total inventory of plutonium at the Los Alamos National Laboratory and the Lawrence Livermore National Laboratory.

SPECIFICALLY:

- The total quantity of plutonium currently at the Los Alamos National Laboratory is 2.6 metric tons.

- The total quantity of plutonium currently at the Lawrence Livermore National Laboratory is 0.4 metric tons.

BACKGROUND:

- The material is in different forms including metal, compounds, and scrap.

- This information will permit more open discussions with environmental, safety and health interests and local Governments. While other information does remain classified, we will be working with stakeholders to establish priorities for additional declassifications.

BENEFITS:

- As part of the Secretary's Openness Initiative, the Department is declassifying the information concerning the plutonium inventory and its form at the Los Alamos National Laboratory and the Lawrence Livermore National Laboratory. As a result of this declassification, the public will have information that is important in the current debate over the proper management and ultimate disposition of plutonium.

(MORE)

U.S. Department of Energy
Office of Public Affairs
Contact: Sam Grizzle
(202) 586-5806

- Release of previously secret information should also encourage other nations to declassify similar information.

- Will permit openness with the public on matters pertaining to public health and safety and the cleanup, storage, and disposal of nuclear materials.

- This information is useful in health studies and related activities concerning workers and the community.

WHO ARE THE KEY STAKEHOLDERS?:

- **The Public.** The public living near the site is, and has been, concerned with health and safety issues relating to the inventories of plutonium at the Los Alamos National Laboratory and the Lawrence Livermore National Laboratory.

- **Regulators.** The State and Federal regulators of the two laboratories will have use for the declassified information for health and safety issues resulting from the inventories of plutonium at both laboratories.

- **Environmentalists.** With this declassification, those interested in the environmental issues and oversight of the plutonium related activities at the Los Alamos National Laboratory and the Lawrence Livermore National Laboratory will have more information relating to this function.

- **Health Researchers.** This declassification will permit greater public review of information of potential value for epidemiologic or other health issues regarding workers and the community.

DOE FACTS

DECLASSIFICATION OF TODAY'S PLUTONIUM INVENTORY AT THE HANFORD SITE NEAR RICHLAND, WASHINGTON

The Department of Energy has declassified the total plutonium inventory at the Hanford Site.

SPECIFICALLY:

- The total quantity of plutonium currently at Hanford is 11.0 metric tons. This amounts to:

    4.0 metric tons in N-reactor fuel.

    3.2 metric tons in Fast Flux Test Facility Fuel.

    3.8 metric tons in form of metal, oxide, and scrap.

    The inventory consists of reactor-grade plutonium except for approximately 0.2 metric tons of weapon-grade plutonium contained in the N-reactor fuel.

BACKGROUND:

- Hanford produced weapon-grade plutonium for the Nations nuclear weapon stockpile. Also, Hanford produced reactor-grade plutonium for use as experimental reactor fuel. Much of the reactor-grade plutonium is still at Hanford.

- The material is stored in various forms including metal, oxide, fuel elements, and scrap.

BENEFITS:

- As part of the Secretary's Openness Initiative, the Department is declassifying the information concerning the plutonium inventory at the Hanford Site. As a result of this declassification, the public will have information that is important to the current debate over proper management and ultimate disposition of plutonium.

- Release of previously secret information should also encourage other nations to declassify similar information.

(MORE)

U.S. Department of Energy
Office of Public Affairs
Contact: Sam Grizzle
(202) 586-5806

Page 2

- Will permit unclassified discussions of plutonium inventory data relevant to worker and public health and safety issues with State regulators, the Centers for Disease Control and Prevention, the Environmental Protection Agency, and other stakeholders.

- Will permit open public debate on policy issues pertaining to cleanup, storage, and disposal of nuclear materials.

- This information is useful in health studies and related activities concerning workers and the community.

WHO ARE THE KEY STAKEHOLDERS?:

- The Public. The public living near the site is, and has been, concerned with the health and safety issues relating to the inventories of plutonium at the Hanford Site.

- Environmentalists. With this declassification, those interested in environmental oversight of the plutonium related activities at Hanford will have information relating to this function. Those interested include the Hanford Education Action League, Tribal interests, Nuclear Safety Campaign, and Heart of America Northwest.

- Health Researchers. This declassification will permit greater public review of information of potential value for epidemiologic or other health studies regarding workers and the public by interested researchers such as the Centers for Disease Control and Prevention.

- Regulators. This information will assist State regulators in performing their functions.

(MORE)

 FACTS

QUESTIONS AND ANSWERS

Q. Of what value is this information?

A. State regulators and the Environmental Protection Agency will be able to receive total quantities and some breakdown, on an unclassified basis. Local environmental groups will be able to better oversee plutonium related activities that have an impact on public health and safety. Environmental impact statements for spent fuel disposal and other activities may be carried out in a more open fashion.

Q. What is the Department of Energy doing to safeguard and monitor this plutonium?

A. Plutonium is stored with rigorous safeguards and safety measures subject to independent oversight.

The results of Hanford's extensive environmental monitoring program are made public. Radiation doses to the public from Hanford operations are typically below any regulatory limit and less than are received from naturally occurring radiation sources in the local metropolitan area.

● U.S. Department of Energy ● Office of the Press Secretary ● Washington, DC 20585 ●

DECLASSIFICATION OF TOTAL PLUTONIUM PRODUCTION AT THE HANFORD SITE NEAR RICHLAND, WASHINGTON

The Department of Energy has declassified the remaining secret information regarding the total plutonium quantities produced or processed at the Hanford Site.

SPECIFICALLY:

- Today's declassification, combined with the information declassified in September 1992, allows the public release of Hanford's total production of 53 metric tons of weapon-grade plutonium and 13 kilograms of tritium. It also declassifies that part of N-reactor's plutonium production which was weapon-grade, i.e., 2.5 metric tons.

- In addition, Hanford produced 13 metric tons of reactor-grade plutonium.

BACKGROUND:

- Hanford plutonium production had been classified to protect the Nation's nuclear weapons production capabilities and, in some cases, to protect nuclear weapon design information. With the current world situation and the cessation of nuclear weapons production, this information is no longer a national security issue.

- The Department of Energy is cooperating with the independent Hanford Environmental Dose Reconstruction study conducted by the Centers for Disease Control and Prevention to estimate offsite radiation releases from Hanford.

BENEFITS:

- Better informed citizens will be able to participate more effectively in discussions about past activities and their impact on the Hanford Region.

(MORE)

U.S. Department of Energy
Office of Public Affairs
Contact: Sam Grizzle
(202) 586-5806

- Release of previously secret information should also encourage other nations to declassify similar information.

- As part of the Secretary's Openness Initiative, the Department is declassifying the total quantities of weapon-grade plutonium production at the Hanford Site, as well as today's plutonium inventory. As a result of this declassification, the public will have information that is important in the current debate over the proper management and ultimate disposition of plutonium.

- Will facilitate open review of documents containing information relating to potential worker and community health effects, as well as environmental impacts, resulting from Hanford operations.

- Will permit more open public debate on policy issues pertaining to cleanup, storage, and disposal of nuclear materials.

WHO ARE THE KEY STAKEHOLDERS?:

- The Public. The public living near the site is, and has been, concerned with the health and safety issues relating to the production of plutonium at the Hanford Site.

- Environmentalists. With this declassification, those interested in migration of radioactivity off the site can use this information in their calculations. Those interested include the Hanford Education Action League; Tribal interests; the Hanford Environmental Dose Reconstruction Project; Heart of America; the States of Washington, Oregon, and Idaho; the Centers for Disease Control and Prevention; and the Environmental Protection Agency.

(MORE)

- **Freedom of Information Act Requesters**. The Department of Energy has received Freedom of Information Act requests concerning Hanford plutonium production and this information, until today, has been denied.

- **Historians and Researchers**. There has been speculation on the Hanford plutonium production by those interested in the subject. This declassification will end the speculation.

- **Health Researchers.** This declassification will permit greater public review of information of potential value for epidemiologic or other health studies and will facilitate the Centers for Disease Control and Prevention studies regarding workers and this community.

- **State Regulators.** This information will assist State regulators in performing their functions.

 FACTS

ADDITIONAL INFORMATION CONCERNING
UNDERGROUND NUCLEAR WEAPON TEST OF REACTOR-GRADE PLUTONIUM

The Department of Energy is providing additional information related to a 1962 underground nuclear test at the Nevada Test Site that used reactor-grade plutonium in the nuclear explosive.

SPECIFICALLY:

- A successful test was conducted in 1962, which used reactor-grade plutonium in the nuclear explosive in place of weapon-grade plutonium.

- The yield was less than 20 kilotons.

BACKGROUND:

- This test was conducted to obtain nuclear design information concerning the feasibility of using reactor-grade plutonium as the nuclear explosive material.

- The test confirmed that reactor-grade plutonium could be used to make a nuclear explosive. This fact was declassified in July 1977.

- The release of additional information was deemed important to enhance public awareness of nuclear proliferation issues associated with reactor-grade plutonium that can be separated during reprocessing of spent commercial reactor fuel.

- The United States maintains an extensive nuclear test data base and predictive capabilities. This information, combined with the results of this low yield test, reveals that weapons can be constructed with reactor-grade plutonium.

(More)

U.S. Department of Energy
Office of Public Affairs
Contact: Sam Grizzle
(202) 586-5806

- Prior to the 1970's, there were only two terms in use to define plutonium grades: weapon-grade (no more than 7 percent Pu-240) and reactor-grade (greater than 7 percent Pu-240). In the early 1970's, the term fuel-grade (approximately 7 percent to 19 percent Pu-240) came into use, which shifted the reactor-grade definition to 19 percent or greater Pu-240.

BENEFITS:

- As part of the Secretary of Energy's Openness Initiative, the Department of Energy is providing additional information regarding a 1962 underground nuclear test that used reactor-grade plutonium. As a result, the American public will have information that is important to the current debate over nonproliferation issues associated with reactor-grade plutonium that can be separated during spent fuel reprocessing and the importance of international safeguards. The release of this information should encourage other nations to declassify similar test information.

- This information will be useful in the international arena in defining the nonproliferation regime for separated reactor-grade plutonium. It will be useful in confirming and underpinning the requirements for international safeguards.

- This information will correct erroneous statements made elsewhere about the potential use of reactor-grade fuel for nuclear weapons.

WHO ARE THE KEY STAKEHOLDERS?:

- The Public. This information will be useful to nonproliferation public interest groups who are debating nuclear proliferation issues.

- Public Interest Organizations. Stakeholders include environmental, safety and health groups, historians, archivists, researchers, scientists, and industrial workers, as well as State and Federal personnel. Those interested in oversight of nuclear weapons testing related activities will have additional information regarding the nuclear test of reactor-grade plutonium. Public interest organizations which have expressed such an interest include (but are not limited to): Energy Research Foundation, Environmental Information Network, Friends of the Earth, Greenpeace, Institute for Science and International Security, League of Women Voters, Military Production Network, National Association of Atomic

(More)

Page 3

Veterans, National Security Archive, Natural Resources Defense Council, Nevada Desert Experience, Nuclear Control Institute, Physicians for Social Responsibility, Plutonium Challenge, Sierra Club, University of Sussex/England, and the Western States Legal Foundation.

- **Environmentalists**. With this declassification, those interested in environmental oversight of plutonium related activities will have additional information regarding the utility of reactor-grade plutonium. Those interested include Greenpeace, Institute for Science and International Security, Nuclear Control Institute and the University of Sussex, England.

(More)

QUESTIONS AND ANSWERS

Q. Why wasn't the exact yield of the event released?

A. Revelation of the yield was determined to be of value to certain proliferants.

Q. What was the quantity of reactor-grade plutonium used in the test?

A. In this circumstance, specific information would be of benefit to certain proliferants and is not releasable.

Q. What is the grade of plutonium used in U.S. nuclear weapons?

A. The United States uses weapon-grade plutonium. Weapon-grade plutonium is defined as plutonium containing no more than 7 percent plutonium-240.

Q. Why is weapon-grade plutonium better than reactor-grade plutonium in weapons?

A. Reactor-grade plutonium is significantly more radioactive which complicates its use in nuclear weapons.

Q. If this was a successful test as you indicate, why didn't the United States use reactor-grade plutonium in nuclear weapons?

A. Reactor-grade plutonium is significantly more radioactive which complicates the design, manufacture and stockpiling of weapons. Use of reactor-grade plutonium would require large expenditures for remote manufacturing facilities to minimize radiation exposure to workers. Reactor-grade plutonium use in weapons would cause concern over radiation exposure to military service personnel. In any event, Public Law 97-415 prohibits United States defense use of plutonium produced in licensed facilities, i.e., commercial reactors.

(More)

U.S. Department of Energy • Office of the Press Secretary • Washington, DC 20585

Q. What was the source of the reactor-grade plutonium?

A. The plutonium was provided by the United Kingdom under the 1958 United States/United Kingdom Mutual Defense Agreement.

Q. What was the actual plutonium isotopic composition used in this test?

A. It is the policy not to reveal the actual isotopic composition of plutonium used in specific weapons or tests to prevent releasing information which may be of assistance to proliferants.

TECHNICAL ASPECTS

NUCLEAR WEAPONS

11-1 PRINCIPAL PLANTS OF THE U.S. NUCLEAR WEAPONS INDUSTRY

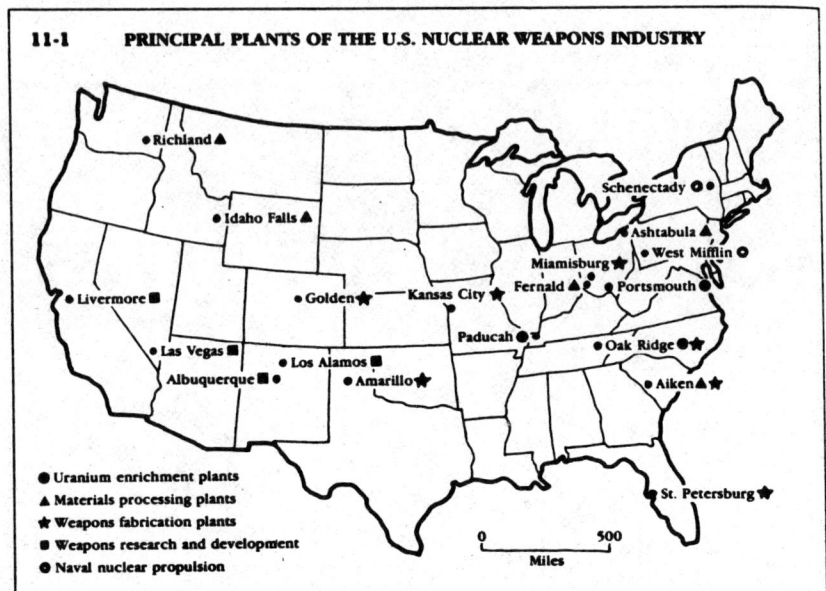

Source: Jack Dennis, ed., *The Nuclear Almanac: Confronting the Atom in War and Peace* (Reading, Mass.: Addison-Wesley, 1984), 208

Glossary of Terms

Actinides	The series of heavy radioactive metallic elements of increasing atomic number from actinium (89) through hahnium (105).
Advanced Gas Centrifuge (AGC)	High speed, high-efficiency gas centrifuge for enriching uranium hexafluoride.
Advanced Isotope Separation (AIS)	Processes under development for enriching uranium, including Molecular Laser Isotope Separation (MLIS), Atomic Vapor Laser Isotope Separation (AVLIS), the Plasma Separation Process (PSP), and the Advanced Gas Centrifuge (AGC).
Airburst	The explosion of a nuclear weapon in the air at height greater than the maximum radius of the fireball.
Alpha particle	A positively charged particle, made up of two neutrons and two protons, emitted by certain radioactive nuclei. The nucleus of He-4 atom.
Anti-submarine warfare (ASW)	Methods of warfare utilizing specialized sensors, data processing techniques, weapons platforms, and weapons intended to search for, identify, and destroy submarines.
Anti-ballistic missile (ABM)	A defense missile used to intercept and destroy an attacking strategic ballistic missile.
Aqueous phase	In solvent extraction, the water-containing layer, as differentiated from the organic phase.
Arming	As applied to weapons and ammunition, the changing from a safe condition to a state of readiness for initiation.
Arms control	The process of limiting or reducing arms to lessen the risk of conflict and to reduce the consequences of a conflict should it occur.
Arms control agreement verification	The collection, processing, and reporting of data indicating testing or employment of proscribed weapon systems, including country of origin and location, weapon and payload identification, and event type.
ATMX	The designation assigned to a special railcar used to transport nuclear weapons. Only series 500 and 600 ATMX cars are nuclear weapons transporting railcars.
Atomic bomb	An explosive device whose energy comes from the fissioning of uranium or plutonium. A fission bomb, as distinguised from a hydrogen bomb.
Atomic demolition munition (ADM)	Nuclear device designed to be detonated on or below the surface, or under water, to block, deny, and/or canalize enemy forces.
Atomic number	The number of protons in an atomic nucleus.
Atomic weight	The mass of an atom expressed in atomic mass units (amu), usually relative to carbon-12, which is defined to have a mass of 12 amu. Approximately, the sum of the number of neutrons and protons in the nucleus.
Ballistic missile	A missile that follows a ballistic trajectory, relying only on gravity and aerodynamic drag when its thrust is terminated.
Ballistic missile defense (BMD)	A defensive system designed to destroy incoming ballistic missiles or their warheads. Usually conceived as structured in several different layers that attack missiles in any of their trajectory phases: boost phase, post-boost phase, midcourse phase, and terminal (or reentry) phase.
Beryllium	Element with atomic number 4 and atomic weights between 6 and 11. Used in nuclear weapons as a neutron reflector and a neutron source.

Source: Thomas B. Cochran et al., *Nuclear Weapons Databook*, vol. 2, *U.S. Nuclear Warhead Production* (Cambridge, Mass.: Ballinger, 1987), 194-212

Glossary of Terms

Beta particle	An electron or positron emitted by an atomic nucleus during radioactive decay.
Blanket	A layer of assemblies containing fertile material, such as uranium-238 or thorium-232, surrounding the core of a nuclear reactor, for the purpose of absorbing escaping neutrons.
Blast	The pressure pulse (shock wave) in air initiated by the expansion of the hot gases produced by an explosion.
Blast yield	That portion of the total energy of a nuclear explosion that is manifested as a blast (or shock) wave.
Boosted fission weapon	A nuclear weapon in which neutrons produced by thermonuclear reactions serve to enhance the fission process. The thermonuclear energy represents only a small fraction of the total explosion energy.
Burnup	The precentage of fuel atoms fissioned during operation of a nuclear reactor. Also, the energy produced by a nuclear reactor, usually expressed as Mwd per MT of fuel.
Byproduct material	Any radioactive material (except special nuclear material) yielded in or made radioactive by exposure to the radiation incident to the production or utilization of special nuclear material.
Chain reaction	A series of reactions in fissionable material in which neutrons that are the product of fission reactions induce subsequent fissions.
Cladding	The material forming the outer layer of a nuclear fuel element. May be aluminum, steel, or Zircalloy, an alloy of zirconium.
Command disable system	A system incorporating command and control features that destroys a weapon's ability to achieve a significant nuclear yield.
Component	Any operational, experimental, or research-related part, subsection, design, or material used in the manufacture or utilization of a nuclear weapon, nuclear explosive device, or nuclear weapon test assembly.
Control rods	Rods of neutron absorbing material that are inserted into the core of a nuclear reactor to control its operation.
Conversion ratio	The ratio of the number of atoms of new fissile materials produced in a reactor to the number of atoms of fissile material consumed. This ratio is usually less than unity.
Crater	The pit, depression, or cavity formed in the surface of the earth by a surface or underground explosion. Crater formation can occur by vaporization of the surface material, by the scouring effect of air blast, by throwout of disturbed material, or by subsidence. In general, changes from one process to the next occur with increasing depth of burst. The *apparent crater* is the depression which is seen after the burst; it is smaller than the true crater, which is covered with a layer of loose earth, rock, etcetera. In a deep underground burst when there is no rupture of the surface, the resulting cavity (a sealed pocked of smoke and gas) is called a *camouflet*.
Critical facility	A research facility that contains nuclear material and can sustain a chain reaction but produces no power and requires no cooling. Its core is designed for great flexibility and uses fuel that can be repositioned and varied to investigate different reactor concepts and core configurations.
Critical mass	The least mass of fissionable material that will allow a self-sustaining nuclear chain reactor. The critical mass depends on the type of fissionable isotope, its chemical form, geometrical arrangement, and density.

Glossary of Terms

Critical nuclear weapons design information (CNWDI)	That TOP SECRET Restricted Data or SECRET Restricted Data revealing the theory of operation or design of the components of a thermonuclear or implosion-type fission bomb, warhead, demolition munition, or test device. Specially excluded is information concerning arming, fuzing, and firing systems; limited life components; and total contained quantity of fissionable, fusionable, and high explosive materials by type. Among these excluded items are the components which Service personnel set, maintain, operate, test or replace.	Deuterium	A hydrogen isotope (atomic weight 2) with one proton and one neutron in the nucleus. Represented by letter D or by H-2. Used as a thermonuclear fuel constituent and as a neutron moderator (in the form of heavy water) in nuclear reactors.
		Disablement	The rendering of a nuclear weapon incapable of achieving a nuclear yield for some specified period of time. Not included in disablement are the prevention of the recovery of active nuclear material and preventing the obtainment of classified design information.
Cruise missile	A low-flying, air-breathing, guided missile that, like an aircraft, relies on propulsion to balance drag and aerodynamic lift to balance gravity.	Electromagnetic pulse (EMP)	A sharp pulse of radio-frequency (long wavelength) electromagnetic radiation produced when a nuclear explosion occurs in an unsymmetrical environment, especially at or near the earth's surface or at high altitudes. It is caused by Compton-recoil electrons and by photoelectrons. The intense electric and magnetic fields can damage unprotected electrical and electronic equipment over a large area.
Cryogenic	Relating to the production of very low temperatures.		
Curie (Ci)	A unit of radioactivity; the activity of a quantity of any radioactive nuclide undergoing 37 thousand million disintegrations per second.		
Custody	1. As defined in the AEC-DOD Stockpile Agreement, custody is the responsibility for the control of transfer and movement of, and access to, weapons and components. Custody also includes the maintenance of accountability for weapons and components. 2. As used within the individual Military Services, custody is the guardianship and safekeeping of nuclear weapons and their components and of source and special nuclear material. Custody may or may not include accountability.	Electron-volt	A unit of energy. 22.5 billion trillion electron-volts equal one kilowatt-hour.
		Enhanced radiation weapon	A nuclear explosive device designed to maximize nuclear radiation effects and reduce blast and thermal effects.
		Enrichment	Increasing the concentration of one isotope of an element relative to the other isotopes. For example, uranium-235 relative to uranium-238 or plutonium-239 relative to plutonium-240.
		Feed material	A nuclear material introduced at the start of a process or operation (e.g., uranium hexafluoride (UF_6) as the feed to an enrichment process or uranium metal as the feed to a fuel fabrication process).
Depleted uranium	Uranium having a concentration of U-235 smaller than found in nature (0.711 percent).		
Detonator	A device containing a sensitive explosive intended to produce a detonation wave for detonating a high explosive element.	Fertile isotope	An isotope that is converted into a fissile isotope, either directly or after a brief decay process, by absorbing a neutron. For example,

Glossary of Terms

Fireball The luminous sphere of hot gases produced by a nuclear explosion. [preceded by: fertile U-238 captures a neutron to form U-239, which subsequently decays to fissile Pu-239.]

Firing system The system of components in a nuclear weapon that converts (if necessary), stores, and releases electrical energy to detonate the weapon when commanded by the fuzing system.

Fissile material An isotope that readily fissions after absorbing a slow neutron, emitting 2 to 3 neutrons. Fissile materials are U-235, U-233, Pu-239, and Pu-241.

Fission The splitting of the nucleus of a heavy atom following absorption of a neutron into two lighter nuclei, accompanied by the release of neutrons, X-rays, gamma rays, and kinetic energy of the fission products.

Fissionable material A material that will undergo nuclear fission. Includes fissile materials, but also isotopes such as U-238 that are fissioned only by fast neutrons.

Fission products The product nuclei resulting from the fission of a heavy nucleus (e.g., uranium-235 or plutonium-239). These are distinguished from the *direct fission products* or *fission fragments* that are formed by the actual splitting of the heavy-element nucleus. The fission fragments are radioactive and decay into daughter products. The complex mixture of fission products thus formed contains about 200 different isotopes of over thirty elements.

Fission weapon A nuclear warhead whose material is uranium or plutonium that is brought to a critical mass under pressure from a chemical explosive detonation to create an explosion that produces blast, thermal radiation, and nuclear radiation. The complete fission of one pound of fissionable material would have a yield equivalent to 8000 tons of TNT. Commonly known as atomic bomb.

Fission yield The amount of energy released by fission in a thermonuclear (fusion) explosion as distinct from that released by fusion.

Formerly Restricted Data (FRD) Information removed from the Restricted Data category upon a joint determination by the Department of Energy (or antecedent agencies) and Department of Defense that such information relates primarily to the military utilization of atomic weapons and that such information can be adequately safeguarded as classified defense information. (Section 142d, Atomic Energy Act of 1954, as amended.)

Fuel cycle The set of chemical and physical operations needed to prepare nuclear material for use in reactors and to dispose of or recycle the material after its removal from the reactor.

Fuel element A rod, tube, or other form into which nuclear fuel is fabricated for use in a reactor.

Fuel fabrication plant A facility where the nuclear material (e.g., enriched or natural uranium) is fabricated into fuel elements for a reactor.

Fuel processing plant A plant where irradiated fuel elements are dissolved, waste materials removed, and reusable materials are recovered.

Fusion The process in which two light nuclei atoms, especially isotopes of hydrogen, combine to form a heavier nucleus with the release of a substantial amount of energy. Extremely high temperatures, resulting in highly energetic, fast-moving nuclei, are required to initiate fusion reactions.

Fusion weapon Nuclear warhead containing fusion materials (e.g., deuterium and tritium) that are brought to critical density and temperature conditions by use of a primary fission reaction (thermonuclear) in order to initiate and sustain a rapid fusion process, which in turn creates an explosion that

Glossary of Terms

	produces blast, thermal radiation, and nuclear radiation. Commonly known as hydrogen bomb or thermonuclear weapon.
Fuze	A union of one or more subassemblies or major components that, when combined with other major assemblies as required (such as bomb, power supply, etc.), is capable either in itself or in conjunction with a firing set of controlling the electrical or mechanical arming and firing of a weapon.
Fuzing system	The system of components in a nuclear weapon that determines the time and place to detonate the weapon.
Gamma ray	High-energy electromagnetic radiation emitted by nuclei during nuclear reactions or radioactive decay.
Gaseous diffusion	An isotope separation process used for enriching uranium in uranium-235 based on the fact that the lighter isotopes of a gas diffuse through a porous barrier at a greater rate than the heavier isotopes.
Gas centrifuge	A rotating cylinder that can be used for enrichment of uranium hexafluoride gas. The heavier uranium isotope U-238 tends to concentrate at the walls of the rotating centrifuge, leaving uranium enriched in U-235 near the center.
Gun-type weapon	A device in which two or more pieces of fissionable material, each less than a critical mass, are brought together very rapidly so as to form a supercritical mass that can explode as the result of a rapidly expanding fission chain.
Half-life	The time in which one half of a quantity of identical radioactive atoms decays.
Heavy metal	The fuel materials, including uranium, plutonium and thorium, with atomic numbers of 90 and above.
Heavy water	Water containing significantly more than the natural proportion (1 part in 6500) of deuterium atoms (as D_2O) to ordinary hydrogen atoms (as H_2O).
Heavy water reactor	A nuclear reactor that uses heavy water as moderator and/or coolant.
Helium	Element (symbol He) with atomic number 2 and atomic weights between 3 and 8.
Highly enriched uranium (HEU)	Uranium that is enriched in U-235 to above 20 percent, usually 90 percent or greater.
High-level waste (HLW)	The highly radioactive waste containing fission products that is discharged from a nuclear fuel processing plant.
Homogenous core	A reactor core composed of only one type of fuel assembly.
Igloo	An earth-covered structure of concrete and/or steel designed for the storage of ammunition and explosives.
Implosion weapon	A weapon in which a quantity of fissionable material, less than a critical mass at ordinary pressure, has its volume suddenly reduced by compression (a step accomplished by using chemical explosives) so that it becomes supercritical, producing a nuclear explosion.
Inertial confinement fusion (ICF)	A concept for attaining the density and temperature condition that will produce nuclear fusion by use of lasers or particle beams to compress and heat small pellets of fusion fuel. The energy released is in the form of fast neutrons, X-rays, charged particles, and debris.
Initial operational capability (IOC)	The date when the first combat missile unit is equipped and trained, and logistic support established to permit performance of combat missions in the field. An initial operational capability date is associated with each new missile system as a target date for delivery of combat equipment,

Glossary of Terms

Intercontinental ballistic missile (ICBM)	A land-based rocket-propelled vehicle capable of delivering a warhead over intercontinental distances. Once rocket propulsion is terminated an ICBM travels on a ballistic trajectory. Repair parts, maintenance equipment, and publications, plus supply of trained personnel.
Intermediate-range ballistic missile (IRBM)	A ballistic missile, with a range capability from about 1500 to 3000 nautical miles.
Ion exchange	Chemical methods of recovering products or removing impurities from solutions involving the exchange of ions between the solution and an insoluble resin. Used in uranium milling to recover uranium from acid leach liquors and in fuel processing for final product decontamination and the separation of certain fission products from high level waste. For the separation of metals, ion exchange is preferable over solvent extraction for small quantities or low concentrations.
Irradiation	Exposure to neutrons in a nuclear reactor. More generally, exposure to any source of radiation.
Isotopes	Atoms of the same chemical element having different numbers of neutrons in their nucleus. An isotope is specified by its atomic number and a symbol denoting the chemical element (e.g., U-235 for uranium with 235 neutrons and protons).
Joint test assembly (JTA)	Warheads and bombs employed in test projects. JTAs are non-nuclear test configurations with appropriate instrumentation installed. *Joint test assembly, pre-build* Instrumented warheads on bombs assembled alongside war reserve weapons. The nuclear explosive package is excluded, with instrumentation substituted that will allow subsystem evaluation at a later time during weapon evaluation. *Joint test assembly, rebuild* Weapons randomly selected from War Reserve stockpile in which the nuclear explosive package is removed and instrumentation substituted prior to evaluation.
Joint test subassembly (JTS)	The instrumented package substituted for the nuclear explosive package.
Kiloton (Kt)	The energy of a nuclear explositon that is equivalent to the explosion of 1000 tons of trinitrotoluene (TNT) high explosive.
Laser	A device that produces a coherent, intense, and collimated beam of electromagnetic radiation of well-determined wavelength, through a physical process known as stimulated emission.
Laser isotope separation (LIS)	An enrichment process in which desired isotopes are separated by differentially exciting a vapor or gas with a finely tuned laser. Used to separate U-235 from U-238 and Pu-240 and Pu-244 from Pu-239.
Light-water reactor	A nuclear reactor that uses ordinary water as moderator and coolant.
Liquid-metal fast breeder reactor	A nuclear reactor that uses a liquid metal (e.g., sodium) for cooling, operates with high-energy (fast) neutrons, and produces more fissionable material than it consumes.
Lithium	Element with atomic number 3 and atomic weight between 5 and 9. As thermonuclear fuel constituent, it is usually compounded with deuterium.
Low-enriched uranium	Uranium enriched in U-235 to less than 20 percent, usually 2 to 4 percent.
Mean free path	The average path distance a particle (neutron or photon) travels before undergoing a specified reaction (with a nucleus or electron) in matter.

Glossary of Terms

Megaton (Mt) — A measure of the explosive yield of a nuclear weapon equivalent to one million tons of trinitrotoluene (TNT) high explosive. Equal approximately to one thousand million calories or 4.2 thousand million million joules.

Megawatt thermal (Mw$_t$) — A measure of the rate of heat production (power output) in a nuclear reactor equal to one million watts.

Megawatt-day (Mwd) — A measure of thermal energy production in a nuclear reactor. One Mwd is equal to 86.4 thousand million joules.

Military characteristics — Those characteristics of equipment upon which depend its ability to perform desired military functions. Military characteristics include physical and operational characteristics but not technical characteristics.

"Mod" designator number — Modifications made to the major assembly design of a weapon system. Mod-0 is the first version of a weapon design, with subsequent modifications of the weapon design numbered consecutively.

Moderator — A material (e.g., water, heavy water, or graphite) in the core of a nuclear reactor that slows neutrons by elastic collision, thus increasing their chance of absorption by a fissile nucleus.

Metric Ton (MT) — 1000 kilograms, or 2205 pounds.

Multiple independently targetable reentry vehicle (MIRV) — Multiple reentry vehicles carried by a ballistic missile, each of which can be directed to a separate and arbitrarily located target.

Multiplication Factor (k) — A quantity that describes the degree to which a chain reacting system can sustain operation. k is equal to the ratio of the number of neutrons in a given generation to the number in the preceding generation. When k is equal to unity, the fission chain reaction is self-sustaining and the reactor is "critical"; for k less than unity, the chain reaction dies out and the reactor is "subcritical"; for k greater than unity the reaction grows and is "supercritical."

National Security Information — A category of information classified under Executive Order 12356, "National Security Information."

Natural uranium — Uranium as found in nature, containing about 0.711 percent of U-235, 99.3 percent of U-238, and a trace of U-234.

Neutron flux — A measure of the intensity of neutron radiation equal to the product of neutron density and velocity. Expressed as the number of neutrons per square centimeter per second.

Neutron generator — A high-voltage vacuum tube used in contemporary nuclear weapons to furnish neutrons at a precise instant to begin fission reactions in fissile cores.

Nuclear component — A part of a nuclear weapon that contains fissionable or fusionable material.

Nuclear device — Nuclear fission or fission and fusion materials, together with the arming, fuzing, firing, chemical explosive, canister, and diagnostic measurement equipment, that have not reached the development status of an operational weapon.

Nuclear radiation — Particle and electromagnetic radiation emitted from atomic nuclei in various nuclear processes. The important nuclear radiations, from the weapons effects standpoint, are alpha and beta particles, gamma rays, and neutrons. X-rays are not nuclear radiations since they do not originate in atomic nuclei.

Nuclear reactor — A device in which a controlled, self-sustaining nuclear reaction can be maintained with provisions for cooling to remove generated heat. Types include power reactors, research and test reactors, and production reactors.

Nuclear waste — The radioactive by-products formed by fission and other nu-

Glossary of Terms

	clear processes in a reactor. Separated from spent fuel in a processing plant.	Pipeline	Refers to the quantity of an item required in the supply system to maintain an uninterrupted replacement flow.
Nuclear weapon	A device that releases nuclear energy in an explosive matter as the result of nuclear reactions involving the fission or fusion of atomic nuclei, or both.	Pit	The components of a warhead located within the inner boundary of the high explosive assembly but not including safing materials.
Nuclear weapons effects	Effects associated with the explosion of a nuclear weapon, including blast, heat, X-rays, prompt nuclear radiation, and electromagnetic pulse.	Plutonium	A heavy, man-made, radioactive metallic element (symbol Pu). The most important isotopes are Pu-238 and Pu-239.
Nuclear winter	Global effects of nuclear war resulting in the lowering of land surface temperatures to near freezing or below due to the spread of massive amounts of smoke from fires and dust through the atmosphere screening out the sun's energy.	Plutonium-239	A fissile isotope produced by neutron capture in uranium-238. It is used in the core of nuclear weapons.
		Plutonium-240	An isotope of plutonium, produced in reactors by neutron capture in Pu-239. Because of its high rate of spontaneous fission, its presence increases the chance of preinitiation and affects the design and operation of nuclear explosive devices.
One-point detonation	A detonation of high explosive which is initiated at a single point. This type of detonation may be intentionally initiated in certain self-destruct systems.		
One-point safe	The probability that the detonation of the high explosive of a nuclear weapon by initiation at any one point has a chance of no greater than one in a million of producing a nuclear yield in excess of 4-pounds TNT equivalent. It is a term to describe the degree of safety in a nuclear weapon.	Preinitiation	The initiation of the fission chain reaction in the active material of a nuclear weapon at any time earlier than at which either the designed or the maximum compression or degree of assembly is attained.
		Primary	The fission trigger or first stage of a multistage thermonuclear weapon or device.
Oralloy	Abbreviation for Oak Ridge Alloy. Highly enriched uranium metal, typically 93.5 percent U-235, used in nuclear weapons.	Production	The conversion of raw materials into products and/or components through a series of manufacturing processes. It includes functions of production engineering, controlling, quality assurance, and the determination of resources requirements.
Organic phase	In solvent extraction processes (e.g., PUREX) for fuel processing, the solvent (organic) containing layer, as differentiated from the aqueous phase.		
Permissive action link (PAL)	A device included in or attached to a nuclear weapon system to preclude arming and/or launching until the insertion of a prescribed discrete code or combination.	Production reactor	A nuclear reactor that is designed primarily for the production of plutonium, tritium, and other isotopes by neutron irradiation of selected target materials.

Glossary of Terms

PUREX	Abbreviation for Plutonium U[R]anium E[X]traction. A solvent extraction process commonly used in fuel processing that individually separates the uranium, neptunium, and plutonium from the accompanying fission products contained in the irradiated fuel.
Quality assurance (QC)	A continuing program of test and evaluation to determine whether weapons materiel is of satisfactory quality, to determine the degree of conformance to design intent, and to determine the status of functional stockpile readiness through the use of periodic inspection reports and other checks.
Radioactivity	The spontaneous disintegration of an unstable atomic nucleus resulting in the emission of either alpha or beta particles, gamma rays, or neutrons.
Reactor core	The central portion of a nuclear reactor containing the fuel elements.
Reclama	A request to duly constituted authority to reconsider its decision or its proposed action.
Recycle	The reuse of unburned uranium and plutonium in fresh fuel after separation from fission products in spent fuel at a reprocessing plant.
Reentry vehicle (RV)	That portion of a ballistic missile which carries the nuclear warhead. It is called a reentry vehicle because it reenters the earth's atmosphere in the terminal portion of the missile trajectory.
Reflector	A layer of material immediately surrounding a reactor core which scatters back or deflects into the core many neutrons that would otherwise escape. Also, in nuclear warheads. Common reflector materials are graphite, beryllium, and natural uranium.
Reprocessing	The chemical treatment of spent reactor fuel to separate the plutonium and uranium from the fission products and from each other.
Research and development (R&D) phases	The phases through which R&D effort passes in its evolution from initial inception to mature technology are: (1) basic research, (2) applied research, (3) exploratory development, (4) advanced development, and (5) engineering development.
Research reactor	A nuclear reactor that is designed primarily for training and research.
Resonance capture	An inelastic nuclear collision that occurs because of the strong tendency for a nucleus to capture incident particles or photons of electromagnetic radiation having particular (resonant) energies.
Restricted Data (RD)	All data (information) concerning: (a) design, manufacture, or utilization of atomic weapons; (b) the production of special nuclear material; or (c) the use of special nuclear material in the production of energy, but shall not include data declassified or removed from the restricted data category pursuant to Section 142 of the Atomic Energy Act. (Section 11w, Atomic Energy Act of 1954, as amended.)
Safing	As applied to weapons and ammunition, the changing from a state of readiness for initiation to a safe condition.
Salt cake	The damp solid formed when the liquid fraction of the high-level waste is removed through the use of an evaporation crystallizer.
Scrap	Rejected nuclear material removed from the process stream. Often requires separation from contaminants or chemical treatment to return the material to a state acceptable for subsequent processing.
Separative work	A measure of the effort required in an enrichment plant or unit to separate uranium of a given U-235 content into two fractions, one having a higher percentage and one having a lower percent-

Glossary of Terms

	age of U-235. The unit of separative work is the kilogram separative work unit (kg SWU).
Solvent extraction	Chemical methods of recovering metals based on their preferential solubility in solvents immiscible in water. Used in uranium milling to separate uranium from leach liquor and in fuel processing to separate plutonium and uranium from fission products.
Source material	As defined under the Atomic Energy Act, ores containing uranium or thorium.
Special isotope separation (SIS) plant	DOE facility using the atomic vapor laser isotope separation (AVLIS) process (or molecular laser isotope separation (MLIS) process) to enrich plutonium in the isotope Pu-239.
Special nuclear material (SNM)	As defined under the Atomic Energy Act, plutonium, uranium-233, and uranium enriched in the isotope U-233 or the isotope U-235. SNM does not include source material such as natural uranium or thorium.
Spent fuel	Fuel elements that have been removed from the reactor because they contain too little fissile material and too high a concentration of radioactive fission products. They are highly radioactive.
Stimulated emission	Physical process by which an excited molecule is induced by incident radiation to emit radiation at an identical frequency and in phase with the incident radiation.
Stockpile	Nuclear storage. Also, the total number of nuclear weapons which a nation maintains in storage at all locations and potentially available for deployment.
Stockpile to target sequence	1. The order of events involved in removing a nuclear weapon from storage, and assembling, testing, transporting, and delivering it on the target. 2. A document that defines the logistical and employment concepts and related physical environments involved in the delivery of a nuclear weapon from the stockpile to the target. It may also define the logistical flow involved in moving nuclear weapons to and from the stockpile for quality assurance testing, modification and retrofit, and the recycling of limited life components.
Strategic forces	Nuclear weapons and delivery systems designed for nuclear attack against strategic targets or for active defense agains such an attack. Bombers, missile systems, and strategic interceptors. Commonly refers to offensive weapons in the United States and Soviet Union that can deliver a nuclear strike on each other or a third party.
Stripping	In uranium enrichment, the process of enriching the tails of an enrichment plant or previous enrichment stage. In the PUREX solvent extraction process, the transfer of product from the organic phase back into the aqueous phase.
Subcritical	An assembly containing an insufficient quantity of fissile fuel to sustain a fission reaction.
Submarine-launched ballistic missile (SLBM)	A ballistic missile carried in and capable of being launched from a submarine.
Tactical nuclear weapons	Nuclear capable devices assigned to support the conduct of battles and deployed close to likely areas of military engagement.
Tails	The depleted stream of an enrichment plant or stage after the enriched product is removed. Expressed as percent of U-235 content. Also, applies to the depleted stream from uranium milling.
Tamper	A heavy, dense material surrounding the fissionable material in an atomic weapon, for the purpose of holding the supercritical assembly together longer by its

Glossary of Terms

	inertia, and also for the purpose of reflecting neutrons, thus increasing the fission rate of the active material.
Target	Material irradiated with neutrons in a production reactor in order to produce plutonium-239, tritium, uranium-236, plutonium-238, or other desired isotopes.
Thermal neutrons	Low-energy, low-speed neutrons in thermal equilibrium with their surroundings. Frequently, neutrons with speed of 2200 m/s.
Thermal reactor	A reactor in which the fission chain reaction is sustained by low-energy (thermal) neutrons which have been moderated to thermal energy in order to increase reaction probabilities.
Thermonuclear weapon	A nuclear weapon (also referred to as hydrogen weapon) in which the main contribution to the explosive energy results from fusion of light nuclei, such as deuterium and tritium. The high temperatures required for such fusion reactions are obtained by means of an initial fission explosion.
Thorium-232	A naturally occurring isotope from which the fissile isotope U-233 can be bred by neutron capture.
Transuranic (TRU) elements	Elements with atomic number greater than uranium (atomic number 92). They include neptunium, plutonium, americium, and curium.
Tritium	An isotope of hydrogen, with an atomic number 1, atomic weight of 3, and a nucleus composed of one proton and two neutrons. Tritium decays by beta decay, with a half-life of 12.3 years. It can be produced by lithium-6 bombardment in nuclear reactors or in the fusion fuel of thermonuclear weapons. Represented by T or H-3.
Uranium-233	A fissile isotope bred by neutron capture in thorium-232. It is similar in weapons use to Pu-239.
Uranium-235	The only naturally occurring fissile isotope. Natural uranium has 0.7 percent of U-235. Reactors use natural or enriched uranium as fuel. Weapons use uranium enriched to about 93.5 percent U-235.
Uranium-238	A fertile isotope from wich Pu-239 can be bred. It comprises 99.3 percent of natural uranium.
Uranium hexafluoride	A volatile compound of uranium and fluorine that is a white crystalline solid at room temperature and atmospheric pressure but vaporizes upon heating, at 56.6 degrees C. Feedstock in gaseous diffusion, gas centrifuge, and other enrichment processes.
Uranium milling	The process by which uranium ore containing only a very small percentage of uranium oxide (U_3O_8) is converted into material containing a high percentage (80 percent) of U_3O_8, often referred to as yellowcake.
Uranium ore concentrate	U_3O_8, often referred to as yellowcake.
Vitrification	The solidification process in which high level waste is melted with a frit to form a glass.
Warhead	That part of a missile, projectile, torpedo, rocket, or other munition which contains either the nuclear or the thermonuclear system, high explosive system, chemical or biological agents, or inert materials, intended to inflict damage.
War reserve (nuclear)	Nuclear weapons materiel stockpiled in the custody of the Department of Energy or transferred to the custody of the Department of Defense and intended for employment in the event of war.
Weapons grade (or weapon-grade)	Nuclear material considered most suitable for a nuclear weapon. Uranium enriched to about 93% U-235 (Oralloy) or plutonium with greater than about 93%

Glossary of Terms

	Pu-239. Weapons can be fabricated from lower grade material.
Wooden bomb	A concept which pictures a weapon as being completely reliable and having an infinite shelf life while at the same time requiring no special handling, storage, or surveillance.
X-rays	Intermediate energy electromagnetic radiation, typically emitted during atomic transitions, having wavelength shorter than 10 billionths of a meter. Differentiated from more energetic and shorter wavelength gamma rays, which originate in the nucleus.
X-ray laser	A laser producing a beam of coherent x-rays. A device driven by a nuclear explosion to produce a burst of coherent X-ray radiation before the device is vaporized by the fireball.
Yellowcake	The product of the uranium milling process, containing about 80 percent U_3O_8. Loosely, U_3O_8 itself.
Yield	The energy released in a nuclear explosion, expressed usually as the number of tons of TNT releasing the same amount of energy. The total yield is manifested as nuclear radiation, thermal radiation, and blast energy, the actual distribution being dependent upon the medium in which the explosion occurs, the type of weapon, and the time after detonation.
Yield-to-weight ratio	The ratio of the yield to the mass of a nuclear warhead. Expressed as Kt per kg or Mt per kg.
Yield-to-volume ratio	The ratio of the yield to the volume of a nuclear warhead.

Glossary of Abbreviations and Acronyms

A

AASM	Advanced Air-Surface Missile System
AAU	Argonne Associated Universities
ABM	Anti-Ballistic Missile
ADM	Atomic Demolition Munition
AEC	Atomic Energy Commission
AF	Air Force
AFB	Air Force Base
AFGL	Air Force Geophysics Laboratory
AFS	Air Force Station
AFSC	Air Force Systems Command
AFRRI	Armed Forces Radiobiology Research Institute
AFWL	Air Force Weapons Laboratory
AGC	Advanced Gas Centrifuge
AIS	Advanced Isotope Separation
Al	Aluminum
ALO	Albuquerque Operations Office
Am	Americium
AMAC	Aircraft Monitor and Control
AMC	Army Materiel Command
AMCCOM	Army armament Munitions and Chemical C[O]mmand
AMU	Atomic Mass Unit
ANCA	Army Nuclear and Chemical Agency
ANL	Argonne National Laboratory
Ar	Argon
ARES	Advanced Research EMP Simulator
ARHCO	Atlantic Richfield Hanford C[O]mpany
ARSTAF	A[R]my S[TAF]f
ASD	Aeronautical Systems Division
ASDP	Assistant Secretary for Defense Programs
ASN (R,E & S)	Assistant Secretary of the Navy (Research, Engineering, and Systems)
ASROC	Anti-Submarine R[OC]ket
ASTD (AE)	Assistant to the Secretary of Defense (Atomic Energy)
ASW	Anti-Submarine Warfare
ATB	Advanced Technology Bomber ("Stealth")
ATF-1	Advanced Toroidal Facility-1
AVLIS	Atomic Vapor Laser Isotope Separation
AWST	Aviation Week and Space Technology (magazine)

B

B	Bomb
BCSR	Boeing Computer Services, Richland, Inc.
Be	Beryllium
BeO	Beryllium Oxide
BMD	Ballistic Missile Defense
BNL	Brookhaven National Laboratory
BOAR	Bureau of Ordnance Atomic Rocket
BPET	Breeder Processing Engineering Test
BWIP	Basalt Waste Isolation Project
BWR	Boiling Water Reactor

C

CARL	Comparative Animal Research Laboratory

Glossary of Abbreviations and Acronyms

CCD	Counter[C]urrent Decantation	DNA	Defense Nuclear Agency
Cf	Californium	DOD	Department of Defense
CFMO	Central Scrap Management Office	DOE	Department of Energy
		DPS	Decision Package Sets
CFX	Californium Multiplia	DRAAG	Design Review And Acceptance Group
CG	Consolidated Guidance		
CGN	Nuclear powered cruiser	DRP	Defense Review Panel
Ci	Curie	DSARC	Defense Systems Acquisition Review Council
Cm	Curium		
CND	Campaign for Nuclear Disarmament	DSCS	Defense Satellite Communications System
CNO	Chief of Naval Operations	D-T	Deuterium-Tritium
CO_2	Carbon Dioxide	DU	Depleted Uranium
COE	Chief Of Engineers	DWPF	Defense Waste Processing Facility
CPDF	Centrifuge Plant Demonstration Facility		
		E	
CSA	Chief of Staff of the Army	EBR	Experimental Breeder Reactor
CUP	Cascade Upgrade Program	EBT-B	Elmo Bumpy Torus-B
CVN	Nuclear-powered aircraft carrier	ECF	Expended Core Facility
CY	Calendar Year	EG&G	(Formerly) Edgerton, Germeshausen, and Grier, Inc.
D		EMP	Electro[M]agnetic Pulse
D	Deuterium	EMPSAC	EMP Simulator for Aircraft
D_2O	Deuterium Oxide ("heavy water")	ENICO	Exxon Nuclear Idaho C[O]mpany
		EOD	Explosive Ordnance Disposal
DARCOM	Army Material Development And Readiness C[OM]mand	EPA	Environmental Protection Agency
DARPA	Defense Advanced Research Projects Agency	ER	Enhanced Radiation
		ERAB	Energy Research Advisory Board
DCNO	Deputy Chief of Naval Operations	ERDA	Energy Research and Development Administration
DCP	Development Concept Paper		
DCSLOG	Deputy Chief of Staff for L[OG]istics	ESD	Electronic Systems Division
		ETR	Eastern Test Range
DCSOPS	Deputy Chief of Staff for Operations and Plans; or in the Air Force Deputy Chief of Staff, Operations, Plans and Readiness	eV	Electron Volt
		EWD	Energy and Water Development
		EWDA	Energy and Water Development Appropriation Subcommittee
DCSRDA	Deputy Chief of Staff, Research, Development, and Acquisition		
		F	
DEIS	Draft Environmental Impact Statement	F	Fuel-grade; or Fluorine
DG	Defense Guidance	FBM	Fleet Ballistic Missile

Glossary of Abbreviations and Acronyms

FCDNA	Field Command Defense Nuclear Agency	HEHF	Hanford Environmental Health Foundation
FEIS	Final Environmental Impact Statement	HEU	Highly Enriched Uranium
		HLOS	Horizontal Line Of Sight
FEMA	Federal Emergency Management Agency	HLW	High Level Waste
		HP	Horse[P]ower
FFTF	Fast Flux Test Facility	HPD	Horizontal Polarized Dipole
FMEF	Fuels and Materials Examination Facility	HQ	Head[Q]uarters
		HQMC	Head[Q]uarters, Marine Corps
FMPC	Feed Materials Production Center	HSTC	House Science and Technology Committee
FPU	First Production Unit		
FRD	Formerly Restricted Data	HTGR	High Temperature Gas Reactor
FTE	Full-Time Equivalents	HTRE	Heat Transfer Reactor Experiment
FY	Fiscal Year		
		HUMINT	H[UM]an I[NT]elligence
G		HWR	Heavy Water Reactor
g	Gram		
		I	
GAO	General Accounting Office	ICBM	Intercontinental Ballistic Missile
GCEP	Gas Centrifuge Enrichment Plant	ICPP	Idaho Chemical Processing Plant
GDP	Gaseous Diffusion Plant	ID	Inside Diameter
GE	General Electric Company	IFPF	Idaho Fuels Processing Facility (Now ICPP)
GLCM	Ground-Launched Cruise Missile		
		IG	Inspector General
GOCO	Government Owned-Contractor Operated	IHE	Insensitive High Explosive
		INC	Insertable Nuclear Component
GS	Dual-Temperature Water-Hydrogen Sulfide Exchange	INEL	Idaho National Engineering Laboratory
GSA	General Services Administration		
		INFCE	International Nuclear Fuel Cycle Evaluation
H			
H	Hydrogen	IOC	Initial Operational Capability
H_2O	Hydrogen Oxide ("Water")	IPNS	Intense Pulsed Neutron Source
HAC	House Appropriations Committee (see Chapter One, footnote 9)	IRBM	Intermediate-Range Ballistic Missile
HASC	House Armed Services Committee (see Chapter One, footnote 9)	ISPM	International Solar Polar Mission
		ISX-B	Impurity Studies Experiment-B
HEAF	High Explosive Application Facility		
		J	
He	Helium	JAIEG	Joint Atomic Information Exchange Group
HE	High Explosive		
HEDL	Hanford Engineering Development Laboratory	JAJ	J.A. Jones Construction Service Company

Glossary of Abbreviations and Acronyms

JCAE	Joint Committee on Atomic Energy	LMFBR	Liquid Metal Fast Breeder Reactor
JCS	Joint Chiefs of Staff	LoADS	Low Altitude Defense System
JEC	Joint Economic Committee	LSI	Large Scale Integrated
JLRSA	Joint Long-Range Strategic Appraisal	LWBR	Light Water Breeder Reactor
JNACC	Joint Nuclear Accident Coordinating Center	**M**	
JPAM	Joint Program Assessment Memorandum	M	Meter; million (10^6)
		MC	Military Characteristics
JSAM	Joint Strategic Assessment Memorandum	MED	Manhattan Engineer District
		MENS	Mission Element Needs Statement
JSCP	Joint Strategic Capability Plan	MeV	Million Electron Volts
JSPD	Joint Strategic Planning Document	MFTF-B	Mirror Fusion Test Facility-B
		MIR	Major Impact Report
JSPS	Joint Strategic Planning System	MIRV	Multiple Independently targetable Reentry Vehicle
JTA	Joint Test Assembly		
JTCAMS	Joint Ta[C]tic[A]l Missile System	Mk	Mark
K		MLC	Military Liaison Committee
K	Kilo- (1000)	MLIS	Molecular Laser Isotope Separation
KEH	Kaiser Engineers Hanford Company	MM	Minute[M]an
Kg	Kilogram	MMP	Materials Management Plan
KJ	Kilo[J]oule	MRS	Monitored Retrieval Storage
KMR	Kwajalein Missile Range	MSWU	Million Separative Work Units
Kt	Kilotons	Mt	Megaton
Kwh	Kilowatt-hour	MT	Metric Ton
		MTU	Metric Ton Uranium
L		Mw	Megawatt
LAMPF	Los Alamos Meson Physics Facility (Now Clinton P. Anderson Meson Physics Facility)	Mwd	Megawatt-day
		Mw_e	Megawatt (electric)
		Mw_t	Megawatt (thermal)
LANL	Los Alamos National Laboratory		
LBL	Lawrence Berkeley Laboratory	**N**	
LCTF	Large Coil Test Facility	N	Neutron
Li	Lithium	NASAP	Nonproliferation Alternative Systems Assessment Program
Lithco	Lithium Corporation of America		
LIS	Laser Isotope Separation	NATO	North Atlantic Treaty Organization
LLNL	Lawrence Livermore National Laboratory	NAVMAT	N[AV]al M[AT]eriel
LLW	Low Level Waste	NBC	Nuclear Biological and Chemical

Glossary of Abbreviations and Acronyms

NDB	Nuclear Depth Bomb	OD	Outside Diameter
NDEW	Nuclear-Driven Directed Energy Weapons	ODCSOPS	Office of the Deputy Chief of Staff for Operation[S] and Plans
NDRC	National Defense Research Council	OJCS	Office of the Joint Chiefs of Staff
NDT	Non[D]estructive Testing	OMA	Office of Military Application
NERP	(Oak Ridge) National Environmental Research Park	OMB	Office of Management and Budget
NFS	Nuclear Fuel Services	ONEST	Overseas Nuclear Emergency Search Team
nm	Nanometer (10^{-9} meter)	ORAU	Oak Ridge Associated Universities
NMC	Naval Material Command		
NMMSS	Nuclear Materials Management and Safeguard[S]	ORGDC	Oak Ridge Gaseous Diffusion Complex
NNPP	Naval Nuclear Propulsion Program	ORGDP	Oak Ridge Gaseous Diffusion Plant
Np	Neptunium	ORNL	Oak Ridge National Laboratory
NPR	New Production Reactor	OSD	Office of the Secretary of Defense
NR	Nuclear powered Research submarine	OSRD	Office of Scientific Research and Development
NRC	Nuclear Regulatory Commission	OUSDRE	Office of the Under Secretary of Defense for Research and Engineering
NRDC	Natural Resources Defense Council, Inc.		
NRL	Naval Research Laboratory	**P**	
NSC	National Security Council	PAL	Permissive Action Link
NSDD	National Security Decision Directive	PBFA	Particle Beam Fusion Accelerator
NSDM	National Security Decision Memorandum	PD	Presidential Directive
NTRS	National Reactor Testing Station (Now INEL)	PDM	Program Decision Memorandum
		PFM	Process Facility Modification
NTS	Nevada Test Site	PHOTINT	P[HO]tographic I[NT]elligence
NUMEC	Nuclear Materials Equipment Corporation	PNL	Pacific Northwest Laboratory
NVO	Nevada Operations Office	POG	Program Officers Group
NWCF	New Waste Calcining Facility	PPBS	Planning, Programming, and Budgeting System
NWDG	Nuclear Weapons Development Guidance	PSP	Plasma Separation Process
NWEF	Naval Weapons Evaluation Facility	PSR	Proton Storage Rin
		Pu	Plutonium
NWSM	Nuclear Weapons Stockpile Memorandum	PuLIS	Plutonium Laser Isotope Separation
O		PUREX	Plutonium U[R]anium E[X]traction
O	Oxygen	PWR	Pressurized Water Reactor

210 Nuclear Weapons Databook, Volume II

Glossary of Abbreviations and Acronyms

R

R		Republican
R&D		Research and Development
RBOF		Receiving Basin for Offsite Fuel
RD&T		Research, Development and Testing
RDT&E		Research, Development, Testing and Evaluation
REEC		Reynolds Electrical and Engineering Company
RHO		Rockwell Hanford Operations
RMI		Reactive Metals, Inc.
RRR		Reduced-Residual-Radioactivity
RTG		Thermoelectric Generator
RV		Reentry Vehicle

S

S	Second
SAC	Strategic Air Command; or Senate Appropriations Committee (see Chapter One, footnote 9)
SADM	Special Atomic Demolition Munition
SAF	Secure Automated Fabrication
SAGA	Studies, Analysis and Gaming Agency
SAMTO	Space And Missile Test Organization
SASC	Senate Armed Services Committee (see Chapter One, footnote 9)
SECDEF	S[EC]retary of D[EF]ense
SEU	Slightly Enriched Uranium
SICBM	Small ICBM
SIGINT	S[IG]nals I[NT]elligence
SIS	Special Isotope Separation
SLBM	Submarine-Launched Ballistic Missile
SNL	Sandia National Laboratories
SNLA	Sandia National Laboratories at Albuquerque
SNLL	Sandia National Laboratories at Livermore
SNM	Special Nuclear Material
SOW	Stand[O]ff Weapon
SR	Savannah River
SRAM	Short-Range Attack Missile
SRL	Savannah River Laboratory
SRO	Savannah River Operations office
SRP	Savannah River Plant
SSBN	Nuclear-powered ballistic missile submarine
SSN	Nuclear-powered attack submarine
STL	Simulation Technology Laboratory
STS	Stockpile-to-Target Sequence
SUBROC	S[UB]marine R[OC]ket
SWU	Separative Work Unit

T

T	Tritium; Tera- (10^{12})
TAN	Test Area North
TASM	Tactical Air-to-Surface Missile, or Tomahawk Anti-Ship Missile
TBP	Tri[B]utyl Phosphate
TFTR	Tokamak Fusion Test Reactor
TRADOC	T[RA]ning And D[O]ctrine Command
TREAT	Transient Reactor Test Facility
TRU	T[R]ans[U]ranic waste
TTR	Tonopah Test Range
Tw	Terawatt (10^{12} watts)

U

U	Uranium
UCCND	Union Carbide Corporation, Nuclear Division
UF_4	Uranium tetra[F]luoride
UF_6	Uranium hexa[F]luoride
UO_2	Uranium Dioxide
UO_3	Uranium Trioxide
U_3O_8	Uranium Oxide ("yellowcake")
UK	United Kingdom
UNH	Uranyl Nitrate Hexahydrate, $UO_2(NO_3)_2 \cdot 6H_2O$

Glossary of Abbreviations and Acronyms

UNI	United Nuclear Industries, Inc.	WCF	Waste Calcining Facility
U.S.	United States	WEC	Westinghouse Electric Corporation
USACDA	United States Arms Control and Disarmament Agency	WHC	Westinghouse Hanford Company
USD(P)	Under Secretary of Defense, Policy	WIPP	Waste Isolation Pilot Plant
USDRE	Under Secretary of Defense for Research and Engineering	WPPSS	Washington Public Power Supply System
U.S.S.R.	Union of Soviet Socialist Republics	WSCR	Weapon Design and Cost Report
		WTR	Western Test Range
V		**Y**	
VLA	Vertical-Launch ASROC	Yr	Year
VLSI	Very Large Scale Integrated		
VPD	Vertical Polarized Dipole	**Z**	
		ZPPR	Zero Power Plutonium Reactor
W		ZPR	Zero Power Reactor
W	Warhead, or Weapon-grade		

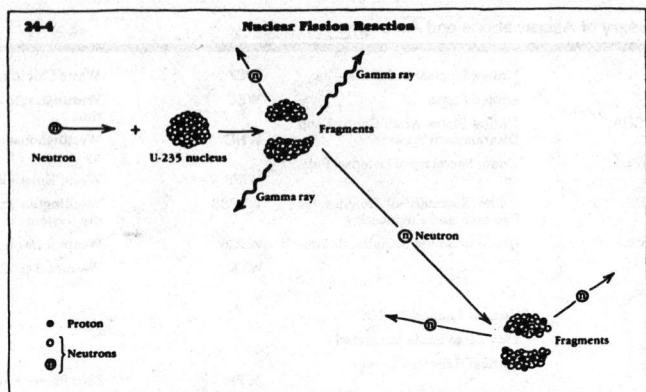

24-4 Nuclear Fission Reaction

A neutron striking a uranium-235 (U-235) nucleus may cause it to split into two roughly equal fragments—yielding energy in gamma rays and in the motion of the fragments. Several neutrons are released that may go on to cause further fissions of U-235 nuclei. The fission fragments are themselves unstable and shoot off beta rays, gamma rays, and sometimes a neutron as they transmute into stable nuclides.

Source: Jack Dennis, ed., *The Nuclear Almanac: Confronting the Atom in War and Peace* (Reading, Mass.: Addison-Wesley, 1984), 456

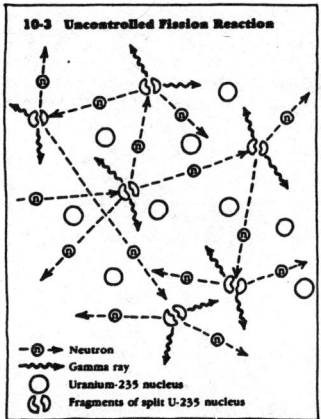

10-3 Uncontrolled Fission Reaction

In an uncontrolled chain reaction, neutrons split uranium-235 nuclei, yielding fission fragments, gamma rays, and two or more neutrons which can multiply the number of nuclei split in each succeeding generation. Each generation takes just one-tenth of a billionth of a second.

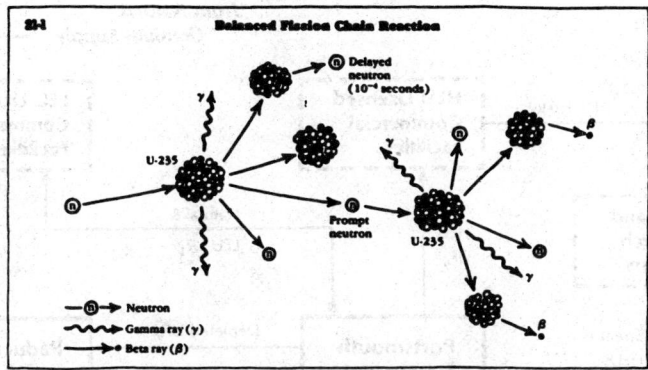

In a power reactor the objective is to maintain a balanced chain reaction—one in which neutrons are being produced and consumed at the same rate. About half of the neutrons released in fission are required to sustain the reaction by splitting more uranium atoms. The excess neutrons are mostly absorbed into other materials present in the reactor core. It is possible to maintain the fragile balance by using neutron-absorbing control rods only because a small fraction of the neutrons from fission are released, not immediately, but a fraction of a millisecond after the fission event.

Source: Jack Dennis, ed., *The Nuclear Almanac: Confronting the Atom in War and Peace* (Reading, Mass.: Addison-Wesley, 1984), 198

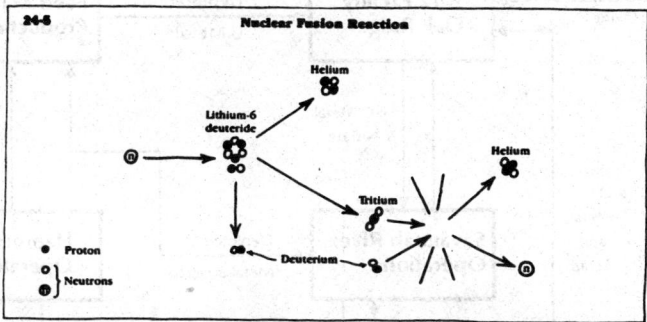

Lithium deuteride is a solid material made up of lithium and deuterium (heavy hydrogen). Molecules of this compound, which contain the light isotope lithium-6, can be used to supply tritium and deuterium for nuclear fusion. Upon absorbing a neutron, a lithium-6 nucleus will split into tritium and helium. Under conditions of very high temperature and pressure, the helium and deuterium nuclei will fuse together, releasing their nuclear energy.

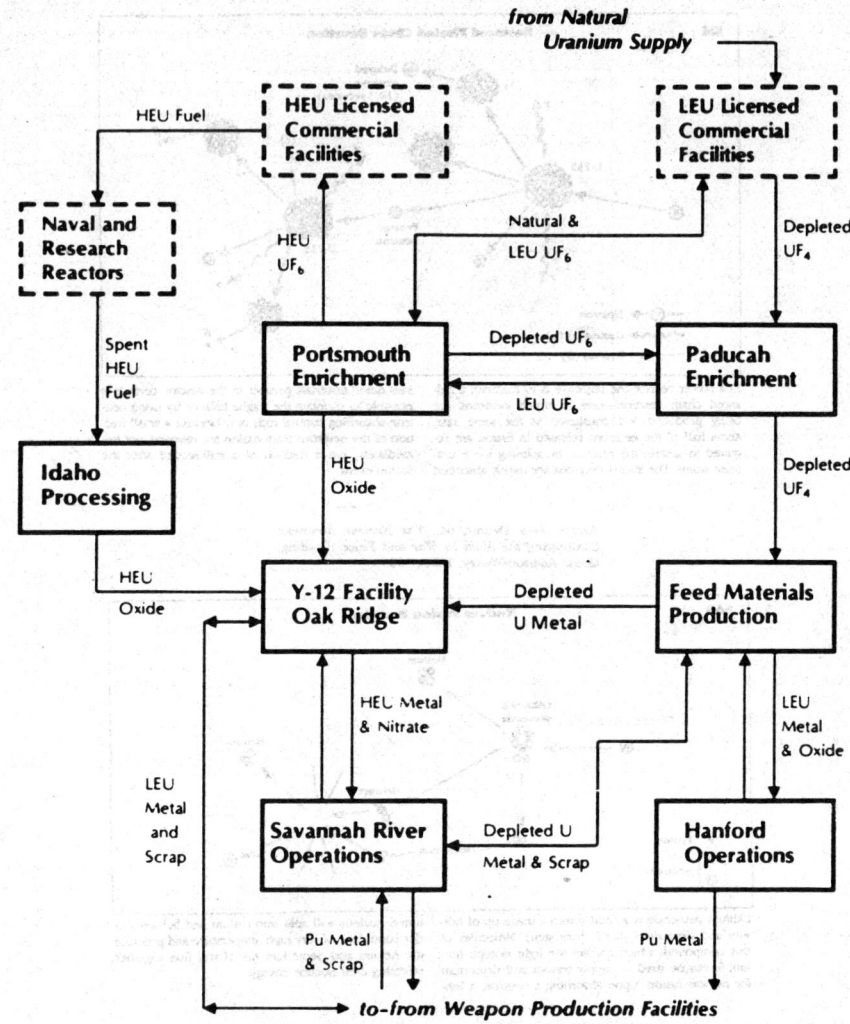

Figure A4-1   Flows of Fissionable Materials in the DOE Production Complex

Source: L. Charles Hebel, Limiting and Reducing Inventories of *Fissionable Weapons Materials* (Stanford: Center for International Security and Arms Control, November 1991), 130

Figure 7.1. The critical masses of uranium and plutonium as functions of fissile content

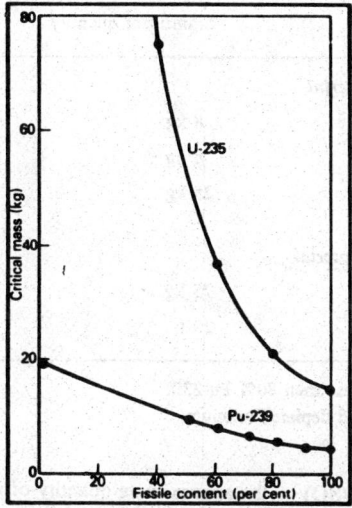

Note: The two metals are in the form of spheres enclosed in thick neutron reflectors of natural uranium. The rapid increase in its critical mass makes isotopically dilute uranium unusable as a bomb. This is not so for plutonium, making it a greater proliferation hazard.

Table I.3. Critical masses of various fissile materials

Enrichment (% of U-235 or Pu-239)	Critical mass (kg) in metal form						
	Uranium-235		Plutonium		Uranium-233	
	Without reflector	With Be reflector	Without reflector	With Be reflector	Without reflector	With Be reflector
0	–	–	–	–	–	–
10	–	~1300	–	–	–	–
20	–	~250	–	–	–	–
30	–	–	–	–	–	–
40	–	75	–	–	–	–
50	145	50	–	9.6	–	–
60	105	37	–	7.8	–	–
70	82	–	23	6.7	–	–
80	66	21	–	5.6	–	–
90	54	–	–	5.0	–	–
100	50	15	15	4.4	17	4 to 5

Sources: See references [3] and [4].

Source: SIPRI, *Nuclear Energy and Nuclear Weapons Proliferation* (London: Taylor & Francis, 1979), 115)

TABLE III. SIGNIFICANT QUANTITIES

Material	Significant quantity	Safeguards apply to:
Direct-use nuclear material		
Pu[a]	8 kg	Total element
U-233	8 kg	Total isotope
U (U-235 $\geq$ 20%)	25 kg	U-235 contained
Indirect-use nuclear material		
U (U-235 < 20%)[b]	75 kg	U-235 contained
Th	20 t	Total element

[a] For Pu containing less than 80% Pu-238.
[b] Including natural and depleted uranium.

107. Significant quantity (SQ) — the approximate quantity of nuclear material in respect of which, taking into account any conversion process involved, the possibility of manufacturing a nuclear explosive device cannot be excluded. Significant quantity values currently in use are given in Table III. They are used, inter alia, to select accountancy verification goals (see No. 122). Significant quantities should not be confused with critical masses; the former take into account unavoidable losses of conversion and manufacturing processes.

Source: IAEA Safeguards Glossary, 1987 Edition, p. 24.

Types of uranium	Composition (%)	
	^{235}U	^{238}U
Natural uranium	0.7	99.3
Slightly-enriched uranium	1.0-1.8	≈98.5
Low-enriched uranium	3	97
Weapon-grade uranium (WGU)	93.5	6.5

Table 2.1. Composition of different qualities of uranium

Type of Plutonium	Composition (%)				
	^{238}Pu	^{239}Pu	^{240}Pu	^{241}Pu	^{242}Pu
Super-grade plutonium	-	99	1	-	-
Weapon-grade plutonium (WGPu)	-	93.5	6	0.5	-
Fuel-grade plutonium	≈7-19% ^{240}Pu				
Reactor-grade plutonium (RGPu)	1.4	56.5	23.4	13.9	4.8
MOX-grade plutonium	2	42	31	14	11
Fast breeder reactor blanket plutonium	-	96	4	-	-

Table 2.2. Composition of different qualities of plutonium[66]

Fissile material		Density (g·cm^{-3})	Approximate critical masses (kg)		
			Bare sphere	With 5-10 cm natural uranium shell	With 5-10 cm beryllium shell
WGU		18.8	52	25-20	22-15
WGPu	α–phase	19.5	11	7-5	6-4
	δ–phase	15.8	17	12-7	9-5
RGPu	α–phase	19.4	12	no estimate	no estimate
	δ–phase	15.7	20	no estimate	no estimate
^{233}U		18.5	16	7.5-6.5	7.5-6.5

Table 3.1. Critical masses of important types of fissile material[8]

Technology level	Weapons-grade plutonium [kg]	Weapons-grade uranium [kg]	Reactor-grade plutonium [kg]
Manhattan project	6	60	–
Present-day technology	3	20	4

Table 6.1. Estimates of the amounts of fissile material necessary for the construction of nuclear explosives

Source: Johan Swahn, *The Long-Term Nuclear Explosives Predicament* (Goeteborg, Sweden: Chalmers University of Technology, 1992), 40

10-5 HOW NUCLEAR WEAPONS WORK

A fission bomb works by assembling a supercritical mass of fissionable material—uranium-235 or plutonium-239 in which a massive chain reaction occurs. This must be done very quickly or the initial energy release will blow the bomb apart before the chain reaction has gotten well started. Two methods have been used to assemble a supercritical mass. The gun mechanism was used in the uranium bomb exploded over Hiroshima: two subcritical pieces of uranium are brought together by an explosive charge inside a cylindrical tube much like the barrel of a gun. Although it was simple in concept, such bombs were cumbersome and heavy. In addition, the gun mechanism would not work in a plutonium bomb because sufficiently pure Pu-239 is nearly impossible to produce—plutonium-240 and other contaminants continually emit neutrons that would give a premature start to the chain reaction before full supercritical assembly was achieved. The solution to these difficulties is the implosion technique, now the preferred method. A sphere or shell of fissionable material is compressed by the focussed blast of surrounding chemical explosive. The pressure of some millions of pounds per square inch forces the fissionable material into a smaller volume, hence a higher density, increasing strongly the chance a neutron will split another nucleus before it escapes. The assembly becomes supercritical. A precisely timed burst from an electronic neutron source triggers a massive chain reaction ensuring a high-yield nuclear explosion. The plutonium or uranium may be surrounded by a tamper, a shell of material—beryllium or uranium-238, for example—that "reflects" a portion of the neutrons escaping from the core. Use of a tamper significantly reduces the amount of fissionable material required to make a nuclear weapon.

A thermonuclear bomb uses a fission explosion to create the temperature and pressure required to ignite a fusion reaction in a mass of lithium deuteride. In a typical thermonuclear weapon, high-energy neutrons arising from the fusion reaction go on to split uranium-238 nuclei in a final surrounding mantle, adding to the destructive force of the explosion. In a "neutron bomb" the U-238 mantle is omitted, permitting the fast neutrons to escape into the surroundings.

A thermonuclear weapon is sufficiently complex that extensive testing would seem essential to develop a practical military weapon. Since the end of World War II digital computers have played an essential role in the design of nuclear weapons—solving the complex equations that describe the physical phenomena of a nuclear explosion and providing knowledge equivalent to that obtained from many test explosions. It all began with John von Neumann and the Institute for Advanced Studies (IAS) computer at Princeton. Now, the most powerful computers available are used at the Livermore and Los Alamos National Laboratories to develop designs of nuclear weapons.

Source: Jack Dennis, ed., *The Nuclear Almanac: Confronting the Atomic War and Peace* (Reading, Mass.: Addison-Wesley, 1984), 202

Table 6A.2. Estimated number of nuclear explosions 16 July 1945–5 August 1963 (the signing of the Partial Test Ban Treaty)

a = atmospheric; u = underground

Year	USA a	USA u	USSR a	USSR u	UK a	UK u	France a	France u	Total
1945	3	0							3
1946	2[a]	0							2
1947	0	0							0
1948	3	0							3
1949	0	0	1	0					1
1950	0	0	0	0					0
1951	15	1	2	0					18
1952	10	0	0	0	1	0			11
1953	11	0	4	0	2	0			17
1954	6	0	7	0	0	0			13
1955	17[a]	1	5[a]	0	0	0			23
1956	18	0	9	0	6	0			33
1957	27	5	15[a]	0	7	0			54
1958	62[b]	15	29	0	5	0			111
1949–58, exact years not available			18						18
1959	0	0	0	0	0	0			0[d]
1960	0	0	0	0	0	0	3	0	3[d]
1961	0	10	50[a]	1[c]	0	0	1	1	63[d]
1962	39[a]	57	43	1[c]	0	2	0	1	143
1 Jan.– 5 Aug. 1963	4	25	0	0	0	0	0	2	31
Total	217	114	183[e] (214)[f]	2[c]	21	2	4	4	547 (576)[f]

[a] One of these tests was carried out under water.

[b] Two of these tests were carried out under water.

[c] Soviet information released in Sep. 1990 did not confirm whether these were underground or atmospheric tests.

[d] The UK, the USA and the USSR observed a moratorium on testing, Nov. 1958–Sep. 1961.

[e] The total figure for Soviet atmospheric tests includes the 18 additional tests conducted in the period 1949–58, the exact years for which are not available.

[f] The totals in brackets include the (probably atmospheric) explosions revealed by Soviet authorities in Sep. 1990, the exact years for which have still not been announced. See *SIPRI Yearbook 1991*, p. 41. If the two tests in 1961 and 1962 (see note c) were atmospheric tests, this figure should read 216, under the column for atmospheric tests.

Source: *SIPRI Yearbook 1993: World Armaments and Disarmament* (New York: Oxford University Press, 1992), 256.

Table 6A.3. Estimated number of nuclear explosions 6 August 1963–31 December 1992

a = atmospheric; u = underground

Year	USA[a] a	USA[a] u	USSR a	USSR u	UK[a] a	UK[a] u	France a	France u	China a	China u	India a	India u	Total
6 Aug.–31 Dec. 1963	0	15	0	0	0	0	0	1					16
1964	0	38	0	6	0	1	0	3	1	0			49
1965	0	36	0	10	0	1	0	4	1	0			52
1966	0	43	0	15	0	0	6	1	3	0			68
1967	0	34	0	17	0	0	3	0	2	0			56
1968	0	45[b]	0	15	0	0	5	0	1	0			66
1969	0	38	0	16	0	0	0	0	1	1			56
1970	0	35	0	17	0	0	8	0	1	0			61
1971	0	17	0	19	0	0	6	0	1	0			43
1972	0	18	0	22	0	0	3	0	2	0			45
1973	0	16[c]	0	14	0	0	5	0	1	0			36
1974	0	14	0	18	0	1	8	0	1	0	0	1	43
1975	0	20	0	15	0	0	0	2	0	1	0	0	38
1976	0	18	0	17	0	1	0	4	3	1	0	0	44
1977	0	19	0	18	0	0	0	8[d]	1	0	0	0	46
1978	0	17	0	27	0	2	0	8	2	1	0	0	57
1979	0	15	0	29	0	1	0	9	1	0	0	0	55
1980	0	14	0	21	0	3	0	13	1	0	0	0	52
1981	0	16	0	22	0	1	0	12	0	0	0	0	51
1982	0	18	0	32	0	1	0	6	0	1	0	0	58
1983	0	17	0	27	0	1	0	9	0	2	0	0	56
1984	0	17	0	29	0	2	0	8	0	2	0	0	58
1985	0	17	0	9[e]	0	1	0	8	0	0	0	0	35
1986	0	14	0	0[e]	0	1	0	8	0	0	0	0	23
1987	0	14	0	23	0	1	0	8	0	1	0	0	47
1988	0	14	0	17	0	0	0	8	0	1	0	0	40
1989	0	11	0	7	0	1	0	8	0	0	0	0	27
1990	0	8	0	1	0	1	0	6	0	2	0	0	18
1991	0	7	0	0	0	1	0	6	0	0	0	0	14
1992	0	6	0	0	0	0	0	0	0	2	0	0	8
Total	0	611	0	463 (500)[f]	0	21	44	140	23	15	0	1	1 318 (1 355)[f]

[a] See note a, table 6A.4.

[b] Five devices used simultaneously in the same test are counted here as one explosion.

[c] Three devices used simultaneously in the same test are counted here as one explosion.

[d] Two of these tests may have been conducted in 1975 or 1976.

[e] The USSR observed a unilateral moratorium on testing, Aug. 1985–Feb. 1987.

[f] The totals in brackets include the explosions revealed by the Soviet authorities in Sep. 1990, the exact years for which have still not been announced. See *SIPRI Yearbook 1991*, p. 41.

Table 6A.4. Estimated number of nuclear explosions 16 July 1945–31 December 1992

USA[a]	USSR[b]	UK[a]	France	China	India	Total
942	648 (715)	44	192	38	1	1 865 (1 931)[b]

[a] All British tests from 1962 have been conducted jointly with the United States at the Nevada Test Site. Therefore, the number of US tests is actually higher than indicated here.

[b] The figures in brackets for the former Soviet Union include additional tests announced by the Soviet authorities in Sep. 1990 for the period 1949–90. See *SIPRI Yearbook 1991*, p. 41.

Source: *SIPRI Yearbook 1993: World Armaments and Disarmament* (New York: Oxford University Press, 1992), 257.

270

GENERAL PRINCIPLES OF NUCLEAR EXPLOSIONS

CHARACTERISTICS OF NUCLEAR EXPLOSIONS

INTRODUCTION

1.01 An explosion, in general, results from the very rapid release of a large amount of energy within a limited space. This is true for a conventional "high explosive," such as TNT, as well as for a nuclear (or atomic) explosion,[1] although the energy is produced in quite different ways (§ 1.10). The sudden liberation of energy causes a considerable increase of temperature and pressure, so that all the materials present are converted into hot, compressed gases. Since these gases are at very high temperatures and pressures, they expand rapidly and thus initiate a pressure wave, called a "shock wave," in the surrounding medium—air, water, or earth. The characteristic of a shock wave is that there is a sudden increase of pressure at the front, with a gradual decrease behind it, as shown in Fig. 1.01. A shock wave in air is generally referred to as a "blast wave" because it resembles and is accompanied by a very strong wind. In water or in the ground, however, the term "shock" is used, because the effect is like that of a sudden impact.

1.02 Nuclear weapons are similar to those of more conventional types in so far as their destructive action is due mainly to blast or shock. On the other hand, there are several basic differences between nuclear and high-explosive weapons. In the first place, nuclear explosions can be many thousands (or millions) of times more powerful than the largest conventional detonations. Second, a fairly large proportion of the energy in a nuclear explosion is emitted in the form of light and heat, generally referred to as "thermal radiation." It is capable of causing skin burns and of starting fires at considerable

---

[1] The terms "nuclear" and "atomic" may be used interchangeably as far as such weapons and explosions are concerned, but "nuclear" is preferred for the reason given in § 1.10.

Source: Samuel Glasstone, The Effects of Nuclear Weapons. United States Department of Defense, 1962, pp. 1-12.

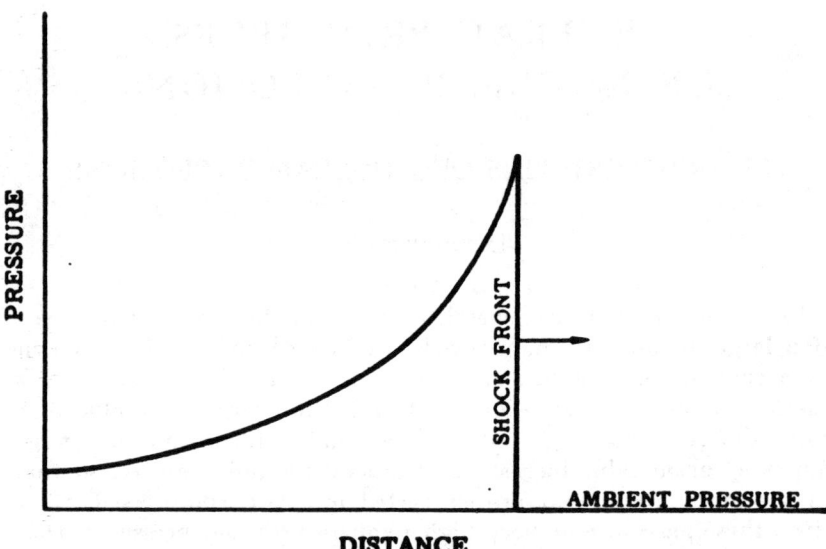

Figure 1.01. Variation of pressure (in excess of ambient) with distance in a shock wave.

distances. Third, the nuclear explosion is accompanied by highly-penetrating and harmful invisible rays, called the "initial nuclear radiation." Finally, the substances remaining after a nuclear explosion are radioactive, emitting similar radiations over an extended period of time. This is known as the "residual nuclear radiation" or "residual radioactivity" (Fig. 1.02).

1.03 It is because of these fundamental differences between a nuclear and a conventional explosion, including the tremendously greater power of the former, that the effects of nuclear weapons require special consideration. In this connection, a knowledge and understanding of the mechanical and the various radiation phenomena associated with a nuclear explosion are of vital importance.

1.04 The purpose of this book is to describe the different forms in which the energy of a nuclear explosion are released, to explain how they are propagated, and to show how they may affect men and materials. Where numerical values are given for specific observed effects, it should be kept in mind that there are inevitable uncertainties associated with the data, for at least two reasons. In the first place, there are inherent difficulties in making exact measurements of weapons effects. The results are often dependent on circumstances which are difficult, if not impossible, to control, even in a test and

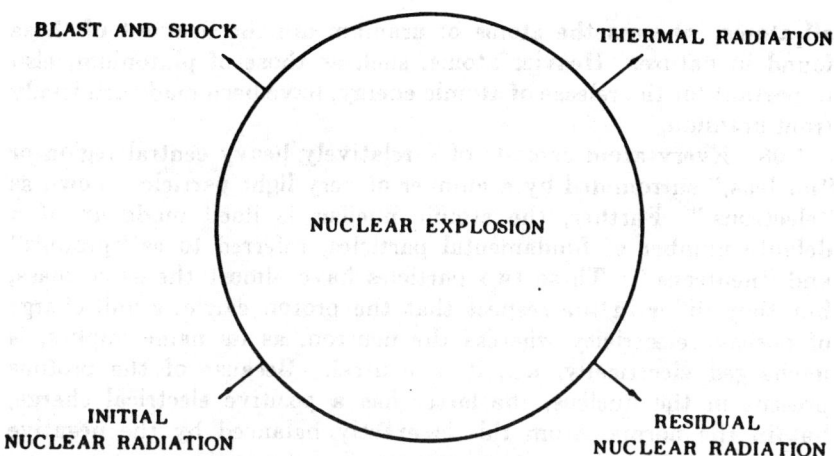

Figure 1.02. Effects of a nuclear explosion.

certainly cannot be predicted in the event of an attack. Furthermore, two weapons having the same yield of explosive energy may have different quantitative effects because of differences in composition and design.

1.05 It is hoped, nevertheless, that the information contained in this volume, which is the best available, may be of assistance to those responsible for defense planning and in making preparations to deal with the emergencies that may arise from nuclear warfare. In addition, architects and engineers may be able to utilize the data in the design of structures having increased resistance to damage by blast, shock, and fire, and which provide shielding against nuclear radiations.

Atomic Structure and Isotopes

1.06 All substances are made up from one or more of about 90 different kinds of simple materials known as "elements." Among the common elements are the gases hydrogen, oxygen, and nitrogen; the solid nonmetals carbon, sulfur, and phosphorus; and various metals, such as iron, copper, and zinc. A less familiar element, which has attained prominence in recent years because of its use as a source of atomic (or nuclear) energy, is uranium, normally a solid metal.

1.07 The smallest part of any element that can exist, while still retaining the characteristics of the element, is called an "atom" of that element. Thus, there are atoms of hydrogen, of iron, of uranium, and so on, for all the elements. The hydrogen atom is the lightest of all atoms, whereas the atoms of uranium are the heaviest of those found in nature. Heavier atoms, such as those of plutonium, also important for the release of atomic energy, have been made artificially from uranium.

1.08 Every atom consists of a relatively heavy central region or "nucleus," surrounded by a number of very light particles known as "electrons." Further, the atomic nucleus is itself made up of a definite number of fundamental particles, referred to as "protons" and "neutrons." These two particles have almost the same mass, but they differ in the respect that the proton carries a unit charge of positive electricity whereas the neutron, as its name implies, is uncharged electrically, i.e., it is neutral. Because of the protons present in the nucleus, the latter has a positive electrical charge, but in the normal atom this is exactly balanced by the negative charge carried by the electrons surrounding the nucleus.

1.09 The essential difference between atoms of different elements lies in the number of protons (or positive charges) in the nucleus; this is called the "atomic number" of the element. Hydrogen atoms, for example, contain only one proton, helium atoms have two protons, uranium atoms have 92 protons, and plutonium atoms 94 protons. Although all the nuclei of a given element contain the same number of protons, they may have different numbers of neutrons. The resulting atomic species, which have identical atomic numbers but which differ in their masses, are called "isotopes" of the particular element. All but about 20 of the elements occur in nature in two or more isotopic forms, and many other isotopes, which are unstable, i.e., radioactive, have been obtained in various ways.

Release of Nuclear Energy: Fission and Fusion Reactions

1.10 As stated in § 1.01, an explosion is caused by the very rapid release of a large amount of energy. In the case of a conventional explosion, this energy arises from chemical reactions; these involve a rearrangement among the atoms, e.g., of hydrogen, carbon, oxygen, and nitrogen, present in the chemical high-explosive material. In a nuclear explosion, on the other hand, the energy is produced as a result of the formation of different atomic nuclei by the redistribution of the protons and neutrons within the interacting nuclei. What is commonly referred to as atomic energy is thus, strictly, nuclear energy, since it results from particular nuclear interactions. It is for the same reason, too, that atomic weapons are preferably called "nuclear weapons." The forces between the protons and neutrons within atomic nuclei are tremendously greater than those between the atoms; consequently, nuclear energy is of a much higher order of magnitude than conventional (or chemical) energy when equal masses are considered.

1.11 Many nuclear processes are known, but not all of these are accompanied by the release of energy. There is a definite equivalence between mass and energy, and when a decrease of mass occurs in a nuclear reaction there is an accompanying release of a certain amount of energy related to the decrease in mass. These mass changes are really a reflection of the difference in the forces in the various nuclei. It is a basic law of nature that the conversion of any system in which the constituents are held together by weaker forces into one in which the forces are stronger must be accompanied by the release of energy, and a corresponding decrease in mass.

1.12 In addition to the necessity for the nuclear process to be one in which there is a net decrease in mass, the release of nuclear energy in amounts sufficient to cause an explosion requires that the reaction should be able to reproduce itself once it has been started. Two kinds of nuclear interactions can satisfy the conditions for the production of large amounts of energy in a short time. They are known as "fission" and "fusion." The former process takes place with some of the heaviest (high atomic number) nuclei, whereas the latter, at the other extreme, involves some of the lightest (low atomic number) nuclei.

1.13 The materials used to produce nuclear explosions by fission are certain isotopes of the elements uranium and plutonium. Uranium as found in nature consists of two isotopes, namely uranium-235 and uranium-238; the former, which is by far the less abundant, is the readily fissionable species used in nuclear weapons. The element plutonium does not occur naturally, and the fissionable isotope plutonium-239 is made artificially. When a free (or unattached) neutron enters the nucleus of a fissionable atom, it can cause the nucleus to split into two smaller parts. This is the fission process, which is accompanied by the release of a large amount of energy. The smaller (or lighter) nuclei which result are called the "fission products." The complete fission of 1 pound of uranium or of plutonium releases as much energy as the explosion of 8,000 tons of TNT.

1.14 In nuclear fusion, a pair of light nuclei unite (or fuse) together, to form a nucleus of a heavier atom. An example is the fusion of the hydrogen isotope known as deuterium or "heavy hydrogen." Under suitable conditions, two deuterium nuclei may combine to form the nucleus of a heavier element, helium, with the release of energy.

1.15 Nuclear fusion reactions can be brought about by means of very high temperatures, and they are thus referred to as "thermonuclear processes." The actual quantity of energy liberated, for a given mass of material, depends on the particular isotope (or isotopes) involved in the nuclear fusion reaction. As an example, the fusion of all the nuclei present in 1 pound of the hydrogen isotope deuterium would release roughly the same amount of energy as the explosion of 26,000 tons of TNT.

1.16 In certain fusion processes, among nuclei of the hydrogen isotopes, neutrons of high energy are liberated (see § 1.68). These can cause fission in the most abundant isotope (uranium-238) in ordinary uranium as well as in uranium-235. Consequently, association of the appropriate fusion reactions with natural uranium can result in an extensive utilization of the latter for the release of energy. A device in which fission and fusion (thermonuclear) reactions are combined can therefore produce an explosion of great power. On the average, in weapons of this type, roughly equal amounts of explosive energy result from fission and from fusion.

1.17 A distinction is sometimes made between atomic weapons in which the energy arises from fission, on the one hand, and hydrogen (or thermonuclear) weapons, involving fusion, on the other hand. In each case, however, the explosive energy results from nuclear reactions, so that they may both be correctly described as nuclear (or atomic) weapons. In this book, therefore, the general terms "nuclear bomb" and "nuclear weapon" will be used, irrespective of the type of nuclear reaction producing the energy of the explosion.

Energy Yield of a Nuclear Explosion

1.18 The power of a nuclear weapon is expressed in terms of the energy release (or yield) when it explodes compared with the energy liberated by the explosion of TNT. Thus, a 1-kiloton nuclear weapon is one which produces the same amount of energy in an explosion as does 1 kiloton (or 1,000 tons) of TNT. Similarly, a 1-megaton weapon would have the energy equivalent of 1 million tons (or 1,000 kilotons) of TNT. The earliest nuclear bombs, such as those dropped over Japan in 1945, and those used in the tests at Bikini in 1946, released roughly the same quantity of energy as 20,000 tons (or 20 kilotons) of TNT. Since that time, much more powerful weapons, with energy yields in the megaton range, have been developed.

1.19 From the statement in § 1.13 that the fission of 1 pound of uranium or plutonium will release the same amount of energy as

8,000 tons of TNT, it is evident that in a 20-kiloton nuclear weapon 2.5 pounds of material undergo fission. However, the actual weight of uranium or plutonium in such a weapon is greater than this amount. In other words, in a fission weapon, only part of the nuclear material suffers fission. The efficiency is thus said to be less than 100 percent.

Thermal Radiation

1.20 It has been mentioned that one important difference between nuclear and conventional (or chemical) explosions is the appearance of an appreciable proportion of the energy as thermal radiation in the former case. The basic reason for this difference is that, weight for weight, the energy produced in a nuclear explosion is millions of times as great as that in a chemical explosion. Consequently, the temperatures reached in the former case are much higher than in the latter, namely, tens of millions of degrees in a nuclear explosion compared with a few thousands in a conventional explosion. As a result of this great difference in temperature, the distribution of the explosion energy is quite different in the two cases.

1.21 Broadly speaking, the energy may be divided into three categories: kinetic (or external) energy, i.e., energy of motion of electrons, atoms, and molecules as a whole; internal energy of these particles; and thermal radiation energy. The proportion of thermal energy increases rapidly with increasing temperature. At the moderate temperatures attained in a chemical explosion, the amount of thermal radiation is comparatively small, and so essentially all the energy released at the time of the explosion appears as kinetic and internal energy. This is almost entirely converted into blast and shock, in the manner described in § 1.01. Because of the very much higher temperatures in a nuclear explosion, however, a considerable proportion of the energy released is present as thermal radiation which is ultimately emitted as intense heat and light rays. The manner in which this takes place is described later (§ 1.73 *et seq.*). Blast and shock are also produced as in a conventional explosion.

Distribution of Energy in Nuclear Explosions

1.22 The fraction of the explosion yield received as thermal energy at a distance from the burst point depends on the nature of the weapon and particularly on the environment of the explosion. For a detonation in the atmosphere below an altitude of about 100,000 feet, it ranges from about 30 to 40 percent. For purposes of illustration it will be assumed here that 35 percent of the explosion energy is received as thermal energy. In this event, about 50 percent of the fission energy will be utilized in the production of blast and shock (Fig. 1.22). At higher altitudes, where there is less air with which the energy of the exploding weapon can interact, the proportion of the fission energy converted into blast is decreased, whereas the thermal radiation is increased. On the other hand, at the other extreme of a completely confined underground explosion of a nuclear weapon, little or no thermal radiation escapes.

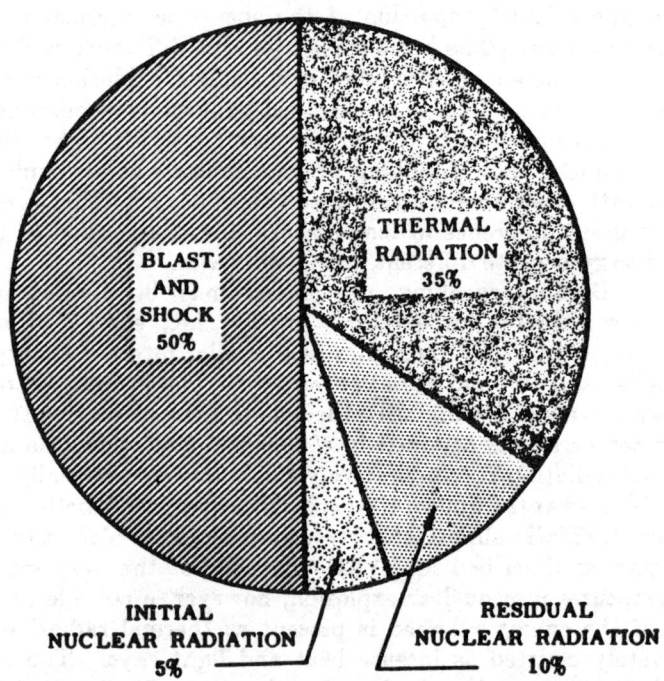

Figure 1.22. Distribution of energy in a typical air burst of a fission weapon in air at an altitude below 100,000 feet.

1.23 In addition to the 85 percent of the fission energy which is converted into blast, shock, and thermal radiation, the remaining 15 percent is released as various nuclear radiations. Of this, some 5 percent constitutes the initial nuclear radiations produced within a minute or so of the explosion. The final 10 percent of the total fission explosion energy represents that of the residual (or delayed) nuclear radiation which is emitted over a period of time. This is due almost entirely to the radioactivity of the fission products present in the weapon residues (or debris) after the explosion. In a thermonuclear device, in which only about half of the total energy arises from fission (§ 1.16), the residual nuclear radiation carries only 5 percent of the energy released in the explosion. It should be noted that there are no nuclear radiations from a conventional explosion since the nuclei are unaffected in the chemical reactions which take place.

1.24 Since about 10 percent of the total fission energy is released in the form of residual nuclear radiation some time after the detonation, this is not included when the energy yield of a nuclear explosion is stated, e.g., in terms of the TNT equivalent as in § 1.18. Hence, in a pure fission weapon the explosion energy is about 90 percent of the total fission energy, and in a thermonuclear device it is, on the average, about 95 percent of the total energy of the fission and fusion reactions.

1.25 The initial nuclear radiations consist mainly of "gamma rays," which are electromagnetic radiations of high energy (see § 1.69) originating in atomic nuclei, and neutrons. These radiations, especially gamma rays, can travel great distances through air and can penetrate considerable thicknesses of material. Although they can neither be seen nor felt by human beings, except in very large doses which produce a tingling sensation, gamma rays and neutrons can produce harmful effects even at a distance from their source. Consequently, the initial nuclear radiations are an important aspect of nuclear explosions.

1.26 The delayed nuclear radiations, as mentioned earlier, arise from the fission products which, in the course of their radioactive decay, emit gamma rays and another type of nuclear radiation called "beta particles." The latter are identical with electrons, i.e., subatomic particles carrying a negative electric charge (§ 1.08), moving with high speed. Beta particles, which are also invisible, are much less penetrating than gamma rays, but like the latter they represent a potential hazard.

1.27 The spontaneous emission of beta particles and gamma rays from radioactive substances, such as the fission products, is a gradual process. It takes place over a period of time, at a rate depending upon the nature of the material and upon the amount present. Because of the continuous decay, the quantity of radioactive material and the rate of emission of radiation decrease steadily. This means that the residual nuclear radiation, due mainly to the fission products, is most intense soon after the explosion but diminishes in the course of time.

279

Types of Nuclear Explosions

1.28 The immediate phenomena associated with a nuclear explosion, as well as the effects of shock and blast, and thermal and nuclear radiations, vary with the location of the point of burst in relation to the surface of the earth. For descriptive purposes five types of burst are distinguished, although many variations and intermediate situations can arise in practice. The main types, which will be defined below, are (1) air burst, (2) high-altitude burst, (3) underwater burst, (4) underground burst, and (5) surface burst.

1.29 Almost immediately after a nuclear explosion, the weapon residues incorporate material from the surrounding medium and form an intensely hot and luminous mass, roughly spherical in shape, called the "fireball." An "air burst" is defined as one in which the weapon is exploded in the air at an altitude below 100,000 feet, but at such a height that the fireball (at roughly maximum brilliance in its later stages) does not touch the surface of the earth. For example, in the explosion of a 1-megaton weapon the fireball may grow until it is nearly 5,800 feet (1.1 mile) across at maximum brilliance. This means that, in this particular case, the explosion must occur at least 2,900 feet above the earth's surface if it is to be called an air burst.

1.30 The quantitative aspects of an air burst will be dependent upon the actual height of the explosion, as well as upon its energy yield, but the general phenomena are much the same in all cases. Nearly all of the shock energy appears as air blast, although some is generally also transmitted into the ground. The thermal radiation will travel large distances through the air and will be of sufficient intensity to cause moderately severe burns of exposed skin as far away as 12 miles from a 1-megaton explosion, on a fairly clear day. The warmth may be felt at a distance of 75 miles. For air bursts of higher energy yields, the corresponding distances will, of course, be greater. Since the thermal radiation is largely stopped by ordinary opaque materials, buildings and clothing can provide protection.

1.31 The initial nuclear radiations from an air burst will also penetrate a long way in air, although the intensity falls off fairly rapidly at increasing distances from the explosion. The nuclear radiations are not easily absorbed, and fairly thick layers of materials, preferably of high density, are needed to reduce their intensity to harmless proportions. For example, at a distance of 1 mile from the air burst of a 1-megaton nuclear weapon, an individual would probably need the protection of about 1 foot of steel or 4 feet of concrete to be relatively safe from the effects of the initial nuclear radiations. However, at this distance the blast effect would be so great that only specially designed blast-resistant structures would survive.

280

1.32 In the event of a high or moderately high air burst, the fission products remaining after the nuclear explosion will be spread out over a large area. The residual nuclear radiations arising from these products will be of minor immediate consequence on the ground. On the other hand, if the burst occurs nearer the earth's surface, the fission products may fuse with particles of earth, part of which will soon fall to the ground at points close to the explosion. This dirt and other debris will be contaminated with radioactive material and will, consequently, represent a possible danger to living organisms.

1.33 A "high-altitude burst" is defined as one in which the explosion takes place at an altitude in excess of 100,000 feet. Above this level, the air density is so low that the interaction of the weapon energy with the surroundings is markedly different from that at lower altitudes and, moreover, varies with the altitude. The absence of relatively dense air causes the fireball characteristics in a high-altitude explosion to differ from those of an air burst. For example, the fraction of the energy of fission converted into blast and shock is less and decreases with increasing altitude. A larger proportion of the explosion energy is then in the form of thermal radiation. It has been estimated that at great heights, where the density of the air is extremely low, more than 50 percent of the fission energy might appear as thermal radiation at some distance from the exploding weapon.

1.34 In contrast to thermal radiation, the fraction of the explosion energy emitted as nuclear radiations is independent of the height of burst. However, the attenuation of the initial nuclear radiations with increasing distance from the explosion is determined by the total amount of air through which the radiation travels. This means that, for a given explosion energy yield, more initial nuclear radiation will be received at the same slant distance on the earth's surface from a high-altitude detonation than from a moderately high air burst. On the other hand, in a high-altitude nuclear explosion the fission products will be widely dispersed in the stratosphere, so that there is no immediate hazard on the surface from the residual nuclear radiations.

1.35 If a nuclear explosion occurs under such conditions that its center is beneath the ground or under the surface of water, the situation is described as an "underground burst" or an "underwater burst," respectively. Since some of the effects of these two types of explosions are similar, they will be considered here together as subsurface bursts. In a subsurface burst, most of the shock energy of the explosion appears as underground or underwater shock, but a certain proportion, which is less the greater the depth of the burst, escapes and produces air blast. Much of the thermal radiation and of the initial nuclear radiations will be absorbed within a short distance of the explosion. The energy of the absorbed radiations will merely contribute to the heating of the ground or body of water. Depending upon the depth of the explosion, some of the thermal and nuclear radiations will escape, but the intensities will be less than for an air burst. However, the residual nuclear radiations now become of considerable significance, since large quantities of earth or water in the vicinity of the explosion will be contaminated with radioactive fission products.

1.36 A "surface burst" is regarded as one which occurs either at or slightly above the actual surface of the land or water. Provided the distance above the surface is not great, the phenomena are essentially the same as for a burst occurring on the surface. As the height of burst increases up to a point where the fireball (at maximum brilliance in its later stages) no longer touches the land or water, there is a transition zone in which the behavior is intermediate between that of a true surface burst and of an air burst. In surface bursts, the air blast and ground (or water) shock are produced in varying proportions depending on the energy of the explosion and the height of burst.

1.37 Although the five types of burst have been considered as being fairly distinct, there is actually no clear line of demarcation between them. It will be apparent that, as the height of the explosion is decreased, a high-altitude burst will become an air burst, and an air burst will become a surface burst. Similarly, a surface burst merges into a subsurface explosion at a shallow depth, when part of the fireball actually breaks through the surface of the land or water. It is nevertheless a matter of convenience, as will be seen in later chapters, to divide nuclear explosions into the five general types defined above.

UNITED NATIONS, 1968

GENERAL CHARACTERISTICS OF NUCLEAR EXPLOSIONS

1. The yield of a nuclear weapon is expressed in terms of the energy released when it is exploded, compared with the energy liberated by the explosion of the chemical explosive trinitrotoluene (TNT). The biggest bombs ever made from conventional explosive contained the equivalent of about 10 tons of TNT. A one-kiloton nuclear weapon produces the same amount of energy as 1,000 tons of TNT. Correspondingly, a one-megaton weapon would release energy equivalent to 1 million tons (or 1,000 kilotons) of TNT. Using powerful rockets, any such weapons could be delivered, in less than an hour, between any two points on earth. Nuclear explosions of more than fifty megatons have already occurred and even larger ones are possible, since there appears to be no upper limit to the yield of a nuclear weapon except in terms of practicable size and weight.

In the atmosphere

2. When a nuclear weapon is exploded in the atmosphere, 50 per cent of its total energy is released as blast and shock, 35 per cent as thermal radiation and 15 per cent as nuclear radiation (see figure IX). These proportions vary according to whether the explosion is carried out in the atmosphere, or at altitudes greater than 100,000 feet, or underground. At high altitudes, the proportion of

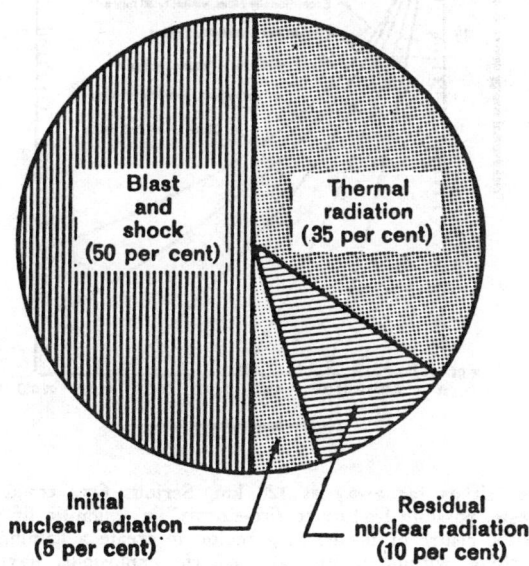

FIGURE IX. DISTRIBUTION OF ENERGY IN AN AIR-BURST OF A FISSION WEAPON AT AN ALTITUDE OF LESS THAN 100,000 FEET

energy converted into blast would be decreased while the proportion of intense thermal radiation would be increased; in the underground case, no thermal radiation would escape. A nuclear explosion thus differs characteristically from an explosion caused by conventional explosives, not only in that its explosive power is several orders of magnitude greater than for a conventional explosive of the same mass, but also in so far as it results in effects from thermal and nuclear radiation.

3. The blast effects and associated overpressures from any particular nuclear explosion depend on the power of the weapon exploded and the altitude at which the explosion occurs (tables 1 and 2). The thermal radiation travels through the atmosphere at the speed of light and to distances depending on visibility through the atmosphere at the time of the explosion (see figure X). It can be of sufficient intensity from a one-megaton explosion on a fairly clear day to cause moderately severe burns on exposed skin over a radius of twenty kilometres (table 3). The

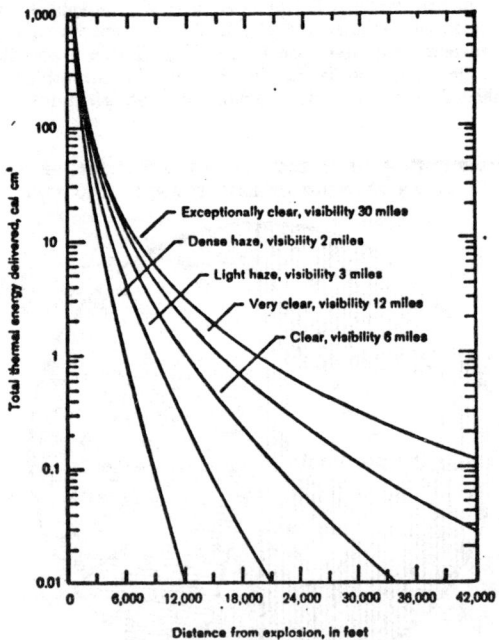

FIGURE X. TOTAL THERMAL ENERGY DELIVERED, AS A FUNCTION OF DISTANCE FROM A 20-KILOTON NUCLEAR BOMB, FOR DIFFERENT ATMOSPHERIC VISIBILITIES

heat might be felt as far away as 120 km. Serious fires could be started in cities and forests, possibly leading to fire-storms, i.e., gigantic fires in which air is sucked into the centre of the burning region to create a flaming funnel which destroys everything within it. For atmospheric explosions, having an energy greater than one megaton, these distances would be even greater. It has been estimated that on a clear day, a ten-megaton bomb exploded at an altitude of fifty kilometres would scorch the earth's surface over an area with a radius of some seventy kilometres. The thermal energy received per unit area, at a specified distance from a nuclear explosion, is usually expressed in calories per square centimetre.

TABLE 1. DAMAGE RANGES FOR 20-KILOTON TYPICAL AIR-BURST AT HEIGHT OF ABOUT 600 METRES

Peak wind velocity (mph)	Positive phase duration (sec)	Peak dynamic pressure (psi)	Peak over-pressure (psi)	Range from ground zero (miles)	Damage description
				2	Light damage to window frames and doors, moderate plaster damage out to about 4 miles; glass breakage possible out to 8 miles
70	0.95	0.09	2.0	10 (1,000 ft: 1.8)	Fine kindling fuels: ignited
79	0.94	0.12	2.3	9 (1.6)	Wood-frame buildings: moderate damage; Smoke stacks: slight damage
93	0.92	0.17	2.7	8 (1.4)	
112	0.90	0.27	3.2	7 (1.2)	Wood-frame buildings: severe damage; Radio and TV transmitting towers: moderate damage; Wall-bearing, brick building (apartment house type): moderate damage
139	0.86	0.42	4.2	6 (1.0)	Wall-bearing, brick buildings (apartment house type): severe damage; Telephone and power lines: limit of significant damage
190	0.80	0.80	6.0	5 (0.8)	Multi-story, wall-bearing buildings (monumental type): moderate damage; Light steel-frame, industrial buildings: moderate damage
291	0.72	1.50	10.0	4 (0.6)	Multi-story, wall-bearing buildings (monumental type): severe damage; Light steel-frame industrial buildings: severe damage; Highway and RR truss bridges: moderate damage
431	0.63	3.90	16.3	3 (0.4)	Multi-story, steel-frame building (office type): severe damage; Transportation vehicles: moderate damage; Multi-story, blast-resistant designed, reinforced-concrete building: moderate damage
459	0.54	7.60	32.5	2 (0.2)	Multi-story, reinforced-concrete, frame building (office type): severe damage; Multi-story, blast-resistant designed, reinforced-concrete buildings: severe damage; All other (above ground) structures: severely damaged or destroyed
260	0.44	3.70	30.0	1	
				0	Ground zero for 20 kiloton air burst

TABLE 2. DAMAGE RANGES FOR 1-MEGATON TYPICAL AIR-BURST AT HEIGHT OF ABOUT 2,000 METRES

Peak wind velocity (mph)	Positive phase duration (sec)	Peak dynamic pressure (psi)	Peak over-pressure (psi)	Range from ground zero (miles)	Damage
				10	Light damage to window frames and doors, moderate plaster damage out to about 15 miles; glass breakage possible out to 30 miles
44	3.45	0.036	1.2		
				9	
51	3.45	0.049	1.4		Fine kindling fuels: ignited
				8	
60	3.44	0.072	1.7		
				7	
72	3.43	0.11	2.1		Smokestacks: slight damage
				6	
98	3.40	0.16	2.6		Wood-frame buildings: moderate damage
					Radio and TV transmitting towers: moderate damage
				5	Wood-frame buildings: severe damage
117	3.24	0.28	3.5		Telephone and power lines: limit of significant damage
					Wall-bearing, brick buildings (apartment house type): moderate damage
				4	Wall-bearing, brick buildings (apartment house type): severe damage
177	3.02	0.60	5.5		Light steel-frame, industrial buildings: moderate damage
					Light steel-frame, industrial buildings: severe damage
					Multi-story, wall-bearing buildings (monumental type): moderate damage
				3	Multi-story, wall-bearing buildings (monumental type): severe damage
276	2.69	1.40	9.4		Highway and RR truss bridges: moderate damage
					Multi-story, steel-frame building (office type): severe damage
				2	Transportation vehicles: moderate damage
464	2.25	6.22	10.0		Multi-story, reinforced-concrete frame buildings (office type): severe damage
					Multi-story, blast-resistant designed, reinforced-concrete buildings: moderate
307	1.75	3.60	27.0	1	Multi-story, blast-resistant designed, reinforced-concrete buildings: severe
					All other (above ground) structures: severely damaged or destroyed
				0	Ground zero for 1 megaton air burst

TABLE 3. RANGES, IN KILOMETRES FROM GROUND-ZERO, AT WHICH FIRST- AND SECOND-DEGREE BURNS WOULD BE INFLICTED BY EXPLOSIONS OF VARIOUS MAGNITUDES IN THE ATMOSPHERE*

Degree of burn	Distance in km from effective explosion				
	1 kt	10 kt	100 kt	1 Mt	10 Mt
First-degree burn (reddening of skin)	1.12	3	8.5	22.4	48
Second-degree burn (blistering of skin)	0.8	2.4	6.4	18	38.4

* In the case of surface explosions, the corresponding distances would be approximately ⅘ those for an aerial explosion of the same effectiveness.

4. Figure XI shows the area over which blast and thermal radiation effects would occur for typical ten-kiloton, one-megaton and ten-megaton explosions in the atmosphere. Within the circle in which overpressure amounts to 0.35 kg/cm² most normal buildings would be completely destroyed. For blast overpressure of 0.07 kg/cm² window frames, doors and walls would be only slightly damaged. Within the central zone of heavy damage there would be great danger of fires and individuals would be exposed to effects of nuclear and thermal radiation as well as blast.

INITIAL NUCLEAR RADIATION

5. The nuclear radiation from a nuclear explosion, occurring in the atmosphere, may be further considered as consisting of one third initial radiation, i.e., produced within a minute or so of the explosion, and two thirds residual or delayed nuclear radiation, i.e., emitted over a much longer period of time. The initial radiation may cause radiation sickness or death in human beings, depending on the dose of radiation received (table 4). A radiation dose of 100 rads[a] does not usually have harmful consequences for an exposed organism. A dose of 200 rads may produce some blood changes while a dose of 1,000 rads will cause illness within four hours and death within two or three weeks. Doses of 400 to 500 rads will cause radiation sickness and a 50 per cent expectation of death. These dose estimates apply to acute gamma[b] radiation; the same effects would be produced by lower doses of neutrons (see also table 5).

6. The initial nuclear radiation from an explosion in the atmosphere also travels a long way in air, although the intensity falls off fairly rapidly with increasing distance from the explosion. Unlike thermal radiation, nuclear radiation passes easily through most physical barriers. Heavy layers of materials are needed to reduce the intensity of nuclear radiation to harmless proportions; e.g., at a distance of 1.5 kilometres from a one-megaton weapon, burst in the atmosphere, an individual would need the protection of about 30 cm of steel or 130 cm of concrete to be relatively safe from the effects of initial nuclear radiation. On the other hand, any opaque object such as buildings or protective clothing interposed between the nuclear explosion and exposed skin would provide protection against thermal radiation. This would remain true even if the building were subsequently destroyed by blast, since the main thermal radiation would have passed before the arrival of the blast wave.

[a] Rad: A unit of absorbed dose of radiation; it represents the absorption of 100 ergs of nuclear (or ionizing) radiation per gramme of the absorbing material or tissue. An erg is a unit of work. It is the work done when a unit force of one dyne moves a body through one centimetre in the direction of action of the force.
[b] Gamma rays (or radiations) are electromagnetic radiations of high energy originating in atomic nuclei and accompanying many nuclear reactions, for example, fission and radio-activity.

TABLE 4. SUMMARY OF CLINICAL EFFECTS OF ACUTE IONIZING RADIATION DOSES

	0 to 100 rads — subclinical range	100 to 1,000 rads — therapeutic range (i.e., range in which therapy may be effective)				Over 1,000 rads — lethal range	
Range		100 to 200 rads	200 to 600 rads	600 to 1,000 rads	1,000 to 5,000 rads	Over 5,000 rads
		Clinical surveillance	Therapy effective	Therapy promising	Therapy palliative	
Incidence of vomiting	None	100 rads: 5 per cent 200 rads: 50 per cent	300 rads: 100 per cent	100 per cent	100 per cent	
Delay time	—	3 hours	2 hours	1 hour	30 minutes	
Leading organ	None	Haematopoietic tissue			Gastrointestinal tract	Central nervous system
Characteristic signs	None	Moderate leukopenia	Severe leukopenia; purpura; haemorrhage; infection; epilation above 300 rads		Diarrhoea; fever; disturbance of electrolyte balance	Convulsions; tremor; ataxia; lethargy
Critical period post-exposure	—	—	4 to 6 weeks		5 to 14 days	1 to 48 hours
Therapy	Reassurance	Reassurance; haematologic surveillance	Blood transfusion; antibiotics	Consider bone marrow transplantation	Maintenance of electrolyte balance	Sedatives
Prognosis	Excellent	Excellent	Good	Guarded	Hopeless	
Convalescent period	None	Several weeks	1 to 12 months	Long		
Incidence of death	None	None	0 to 80 per cent (variable)	80 to 100 per cent (variable)	90 to 100 per cent	
Death occurs within	—	—	2 months		2 weeks	2 days
Cause of death	—	—	Haemorrhage; infection		Circulatory collapse	Respiratory failure; brain oedema

FIGURE XI. ENVIRONMENTAL VARIATIONS DUE TO BLAST AND THERMAL RADIATION FOR 10 KT, 1-MT AND 10-MT EXPLOSIONS IN THE ATMOSPHERE

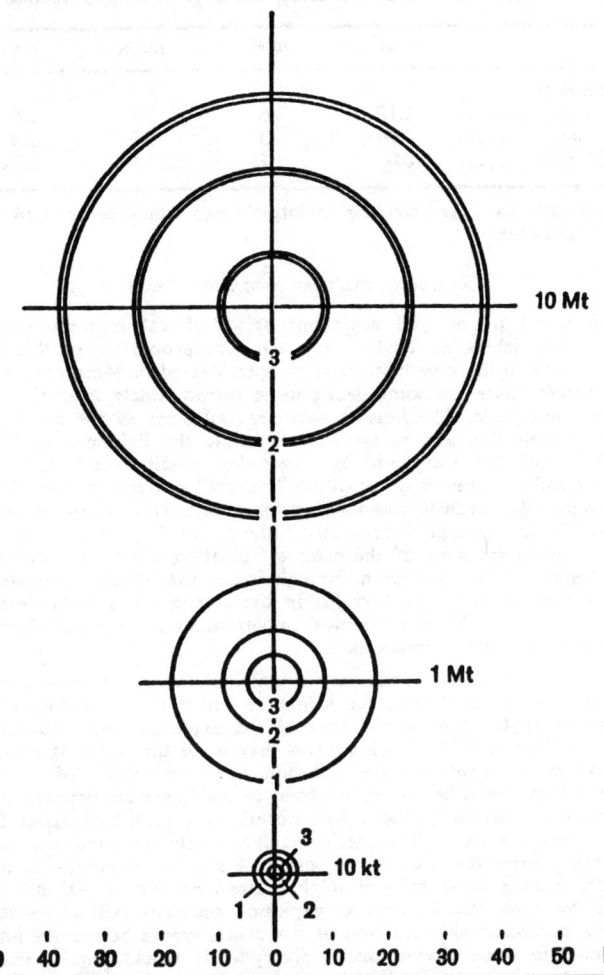

No	Effects	10 kt		1 Mt		10 Mt	
		Range (km)	Area (km^2)	Range (km)	Area (km^2)	Range (km)	Area (km^2)
1	Second degree burns..,	2.4	18.1	18	1018	38.4	4362
2	Overpressure 0.07 kG/cm^2	1.6	8.0	8.8	243	19.2	1158
3	Overpressure 0.35 kG/cm^2	1.2	4.5	4.5	63.6	14.7	680

TABLE 5. RANGES, IN KILOMETRES FROM GROUND-ZERO, WITHIN WHICH AN ATMOSPHERIC EXPLOSION WILL PRODUCE GIVEN DOSES OF INITIAL NUCLEAR RADIATION*

	1 kt	10 kt	100 kt	1 Mt	10 Mt
Radiation dose					
100 rads	1.12	1.6	2.1	2.9	3.8
500 rads	0.96	1.3	1.8	2.4	3.4
1,000 rads	0.8	1.12	1.6	2.24	3.2

* Distances for corresponding radiation doses would be reduced in the case of surface explosions.

Residual nuclear radiation (fall-out)

7. Residual or delayed radiation[e] arises almost entirely from the radio-activity of the debris left by the explosion. The proportion of this radiation may vary according to the type of nuclear weapon exploded. Meteorological and gravitational forces cause the bomb debris to be spread widely through the atmosphere over the countryside. The heavier particles fall close to the scene of the explosion, descending like a mild sand-storm, while the lighter particles are carried downwind. Both the heavy and light particles contain fused fission products and are highly radio-active; they constitute "fall-out" containing some fission products which remain dangerously radio-active for a relatively short period of time and some which will remain dangerously radio-active for many years. The former category contributes most of the external radiation after the initial burst; it also contributes to internal radiation through iodine-131 which when absorbed in the body is concentrated in the thyroid. In the second (long-lived) category, strontium-90 and caesium-137 are the most important fission products leading to radio-active contamination of human diets.

8. Relatively local fall-out may contaminate very extensive areas, depending on the size of the explosion, the height at which the explosion takes place, the wind pattern in the area at the time of the explosion and rain-out through the atmosphere (figure XII). Such an area may be of the order of some fifty square kilometres for a twenty-kiloton explosion, near the surface of the earth. In this case the debris would be largely confined to the lower atmosphere and about half of it would be removed, chiefly by rainfall, in a period of about three or four weeks, although some of the particles might circle the earth one or more times before being deposited. For an explosion of say ten megatons at the surface of the earth, intense local fall-out might extend as far as 500-600 km from the point of the explosion. If such an explosion occurred well above the surface of the earth, a considerable fraction of the debris would be carried into the stratosphere and, in these circumstances, some debris would require months or even years to return to earth. By that time a large proportion of the radio-active atoms produced by the explosion would have decayed.

9. In one particular incident, when a fifteen-megaton device was detonated in a nuclear test on a coral island, the resulting fall-out seriously contaminated an elongated area extending approximately 530 km downwind and varying in width up to nearly 100 km. In addition, there was a severely contaminated region upwind extending some thirty kilometres from the point of detonation. A total area of some 18,000 sq. km. was contaminated to such an extent that survival would

---

[e] Some delayed radiation may arise from radio-activity produced in materials in soil or structures as a result of nuclear reactions, following the capture of neutrons in such materials, after a nuclear explosion. This is known as induced XIII shows the estimated exposures that would have been received by individuals, radio-activity.

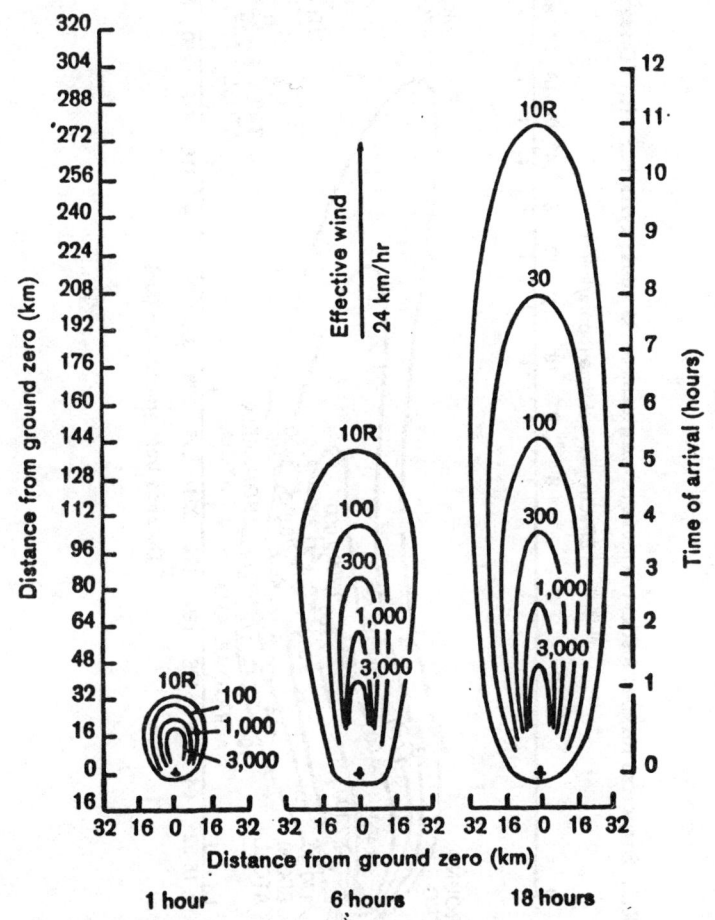

FIGURE XII. TOTAL-EXPOSURE CONTOURS FROM EARLY FALL-OUT AT 1, 6 AND 18 HOURS AFTER SURFACE-BURST WITH 1-MEGATON FISSION YIELD (24 KM/HR EFFECTIVE WIND SPEED). EXPOSURES IN ROENTGENS (R). ONE ROENTGEN OF GAMMA RADIATION CORRESPONDS TO THE ABSORPTION OF ABOUT 87 ERGS PER GRAMME OF AIR

have depended on evacuation of the area or taking protective measures. Figure remaining unprotected in the open, at various locations ninety-six hours following the explosion. Since an exposure of 700 rads spread over a period of ninety-six hours would probably prove fatal in a majority of cases, it follows that, for this particular explosion, there was sufficient radio-activity in a downwind belt of 270 km × 56 km to have threatened the lives of nearly all persons who remained in the area unprotected for at least ninety-six hours. At greater distances there would have been many cases of sickness resulting in temporary incapacity.

10. Residual radiation, liberated by the decay of nuclear debris, may cause an increase of several hundred times the radiation normally present as background radiation in any area and may seriously inhibit or even prevent local rescue and

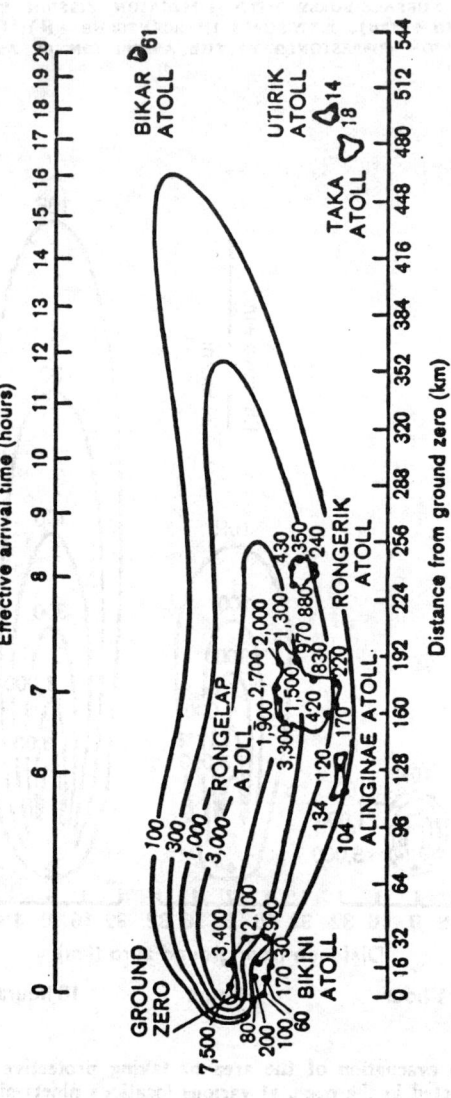

FIGURE XIII. ESTIMATED TOTAL-EXPOSURE CONTOURS IN ROENTGENS AT 96 HOURS AFTER THE BRAVO TEST EXPLOSION

relief operations. Apart from the direct hazard of such additional radiation to human beings, there is an indirect hazard from heavy fall-out contamination of soil, plant life and water supplies, through subsequent ingestion of contaminated food supplies. In the incident reported in the previous paragraph, the people exposed at Rongelap, particularly children, also received high doses of radiation to the thyroid due to internal radiation from ingested radio-iodine. Water supplies may well be rendered temporarily unusable. These direct and indirect hazards add to the immediate physical disaster of a nuclear explosion by producing radiation sickness and death for sections of the population who, being on the periphery of the immediate damage area, would otherwise have appeared to survive the explosion. In fact the human casualties may be caused at distances where the immediate physical effects of the explosion are totally absent.

11. It can be calculated that a hypothetical nuclear attack of 10,000 megatons in ground-bursts could, in the course of sixty days, destroy 80 per cent of the population of the United States, if unprotected, while an attack of 20,000 megatons could cover the entire country with radio-active fall-out, killing 95 per cent of the unprotected population. Similarly in the Soviet Union, which has an area greater than that of the United States, a 10,000 megaton blow could wipe out 75 per cent of the population, whereas a 20,000 megaton attack could increase the population losses to around 90 per cent.

12. Fall-out from nuclear explosions still provides a major contribution to the radio-active contamination of our natural environment. The rate at which it is deposited over the world depends on a number of factors, including the total amount of radio-active material remaining in the stratosphere. Any injection of nuclear debris into the stratosphere, as a result of high-yield nuclear explosions, is followed after a period of time by a rise in fall-out rates roughly proportional to the amount injected. In the absence of further atmospheric nuclear tests, depletion of the stratosphere progressively takes place and the rate of fall-out decreases accordingly. The global rates of deposition have been well documented in a series of publications by the United Nations Scientific Committee on the Effects of Atomic Radiation. These relate to studies from the beginning of nuclear tests and continue through the years of public concern about long-term radiation hazards, beginning with the intensive nuclear weapon testing in the atmosphere in the 1950s, and including the intensive atmospheric testing in 1961/1962, immediately before the nuclear test ban treaty of 1963. Although that treaty sought to prohibit any further nuclear weapon testing in the atmosphere, some further testing in the atmosphere has been carried out by two countries which did not sign the test ban treaty. However, the United Nations Scientific Committee reported in 1966 that the atmospheric tests in central Asia up to that year contributed negligibly to the risk of radiation, as compared with that already existing from the previous injection of nuclear debris into the stratosphere.

Underwater explosions

13. In explosion under water, as in the case of a nuclear explosion in the atmosphere, a fire-ball is again formed and the rapid expansion of hot gases initiates a shock wave. But the fire-ball is much smaller, and remains visible only until the bubble of constituent hot high-pressure gases and steam reaches the surface of the water. The shock wave causes a spray dome to rise over the point of burst, with time of rise and height of dome depending on the energy yield of the explosion and the depth of detonation. Details of underwater nuclear explosions carried out in the Pacific in 1946 and 1958 are given in annex III, reference 1.

14. Thermal radiation emitted from the fire-ball while under water would be absorbed by the surrounding water. So, too, is the initial nuclear radiation although, as soon as the fire-ball reaches the surface, gamma radiation from fission

products in the water column and the subsequent radio-active cloud acts as initial nuclear radiation. The water fall-out from the cloud, and the "base surge" (spray rising from water surface), would be responsible for delayed or residual nuclear radiation. Thus, since in this case the "initial" nuclear radiation merges continuously with that produced over a period of time, it is less meaningful to make the same kind of distinction between initial and residual radiation as applies in the case of an explosion in the atmosphere.

15. After an underwater nuclear explosion, most of the radio-activity remaining in the water and on the bottom would be found initially in the vicinity of the explosion. Table 6 shows the rate of spread of radio-active material and the decrease in dose rate, following the shallow underwater explosion in the Pacific in 1946. For detonations in deep water some activity may be left on the surface to diffuse rapidly downward and outward, thus reducing the radio-activity level to safe limits for personnel.

16. Radio-activity falling back from the high airborne cloud on to the sea extends downward much farther than "base surge" contamination or that transported by the water. The fall-out debris quickly mixes with the water and, since the water absorbs (or attenuates) the radiation to a considerable extent, the radio-active hazard is much less than would result from the same fall-out over land. The radio-active material is gradually transported to other locations by prevailing currents and, if these are known, the path of the contaminated water can be predicted.

TABLE 6. DIMENSIONS AND DOSE RATE IN CONTAMINATED WATER AFTER THE 20 KT UNDERWATER EXPLOSION AT BIKINI, 1946

Time after explosion (hours)	Mean diameter of contaminated area (km)	Maximum dose rate (rads per hr)
4	7.3	3.1
38	7.6	0.42
62	12.0	0.21
86	13.6	0.042
100	15.2	0.025
130	18.4	0.008
200	20.8	0.0004

Source: United Nations. Effects of the Possible Use of Nuclear Weapons and the Security and Economic Implications for States of the Acquisition and Further Development of These Weapons. Report of the Secretary General. 1968.

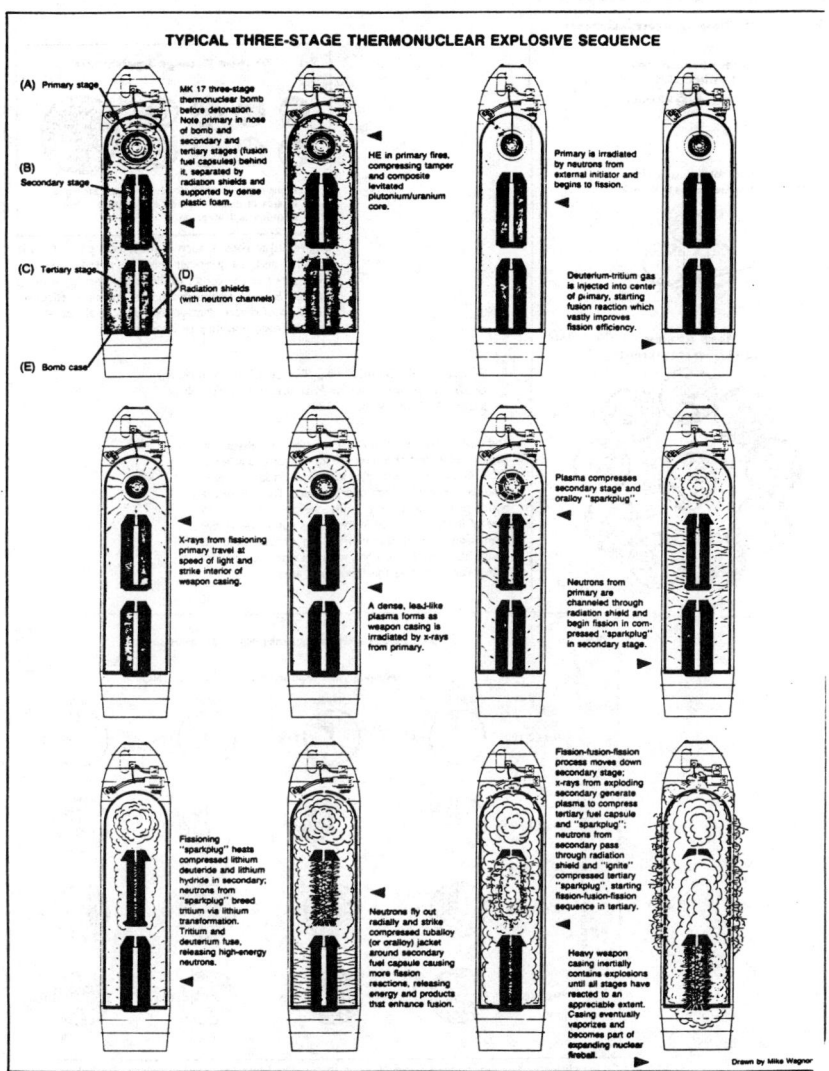

Source: Chuck Hansen, *U.S. Nuclear Weapons: The Secret History* (New York: Orion Books, 1988), 22

9-2 Nuclear Weapon Destructiveness

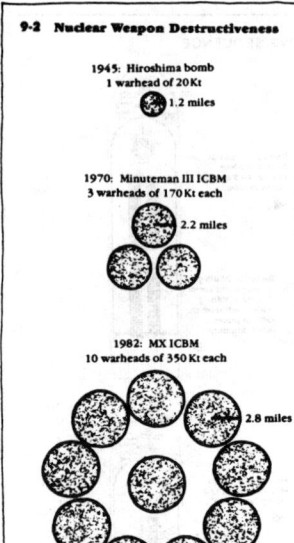

1945: Hiroshima bomb
1 warhead of 20 Kt
1.2 miles

1970: Minuteman III ICBM
3 warheads of 170 Kt each
2.2 miles

1982: MX ICBM
10 warheads of 350 Kt each
2.8 miles

7-1 Weapon Damage Equivalents

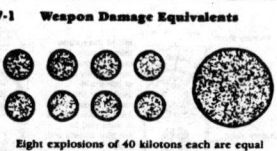

Eight explosions of 40 kilotons each are equal in area of damage to one explosion of 1000 kilotons or 1 megaton.

High-yield warheads, such as those of the U.S. Titan II missiles and many Soviet missiles, overdamage and even vaporize the center of the target, thereby wasting energy. Several smaller warheads are more effective. The area of severe damage increases by about 60 percent for each doubling of weapon yield.

Source: Jack Dennis, ed., *The Nuclear Almanac: Confronting the Atom in War and Peace* (Reading, Mass.: Addison-Wesley, 1984),

The destructiveness of nuclear weapons increases with larger yields and through use of multiple warheads. Each circle indicates the area subjected to three pounds per square inch overpressure. The Hiroshima bomb produced three pounds overpressure over an area of four square miles. Produced some twenty-five years later, one Minuteman III can destroy over ten times that area; the new MX with ten warheads can destroy over fifty times the Hiroshima area.

7-2 Kill Probabilities Against Hard Targets

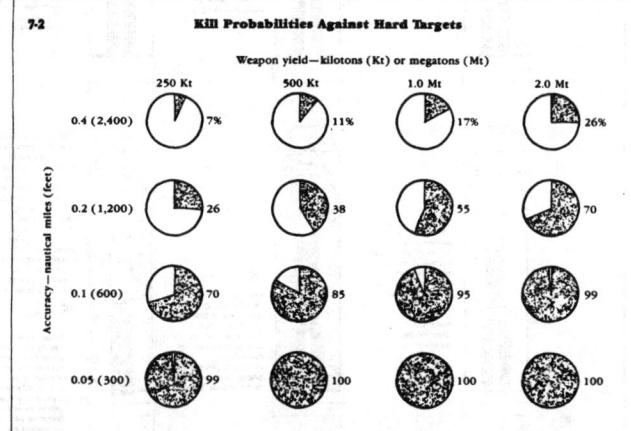

Getting closer to a target is much more effective than using bigger nuclear warheads, particularly for hardened targets such as missile silos. These kill probabilities are for targets designed to withstand 2,000 pounds per square inch of blast wave overpressure.

Doubling the yield improves the kill probability, but doubling the accuracy does much better. Additional factors such as missile reliability are not considered in these estimates.

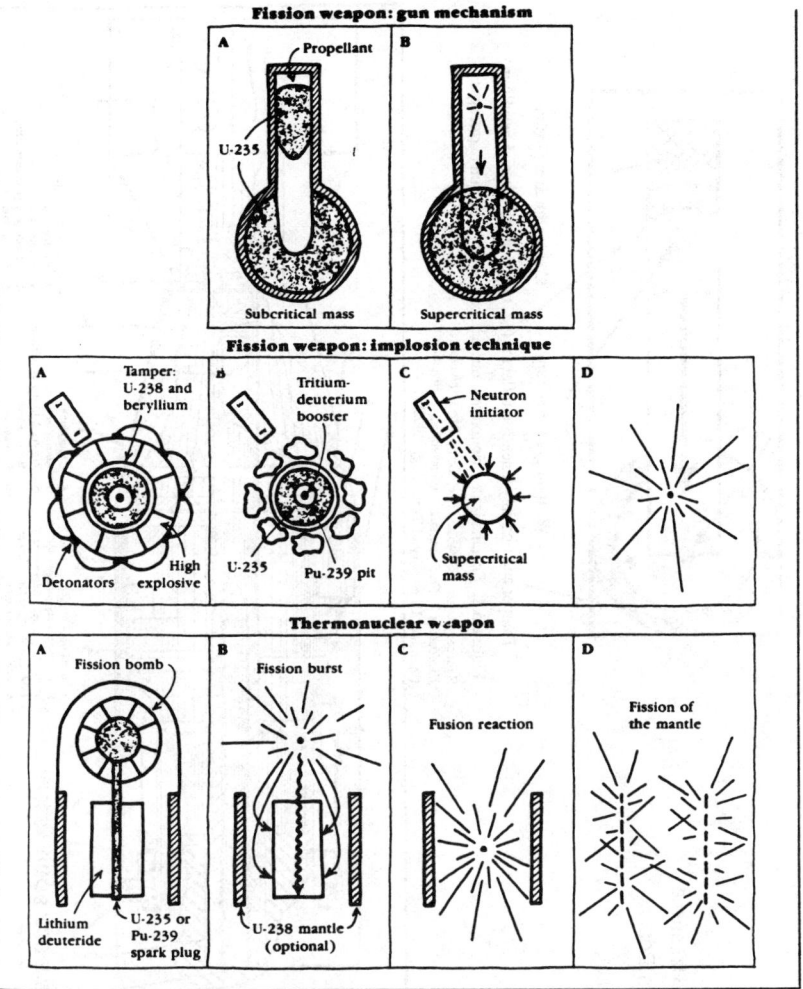

The gun principle used in the Hiroshima bomb; the implosion principle for detonating a fission bomb; the stages of a thermonuclear explosion.

Source: Jack Dennis, ed., *The Nuclear Almanac: Confronting the Atom in War and Peace* (Reading, Mass.: Addison-Wesley, 1984),

Model of Hiroshima Uranium Bomb

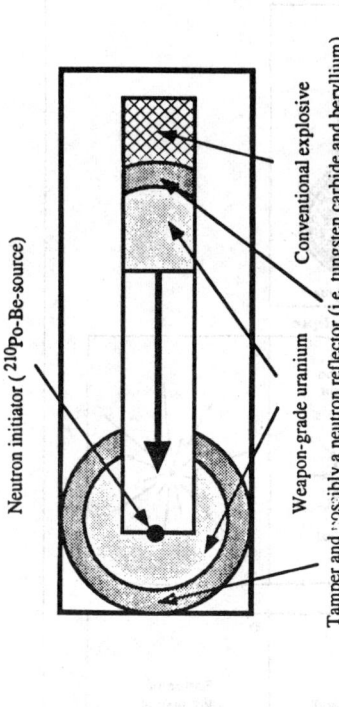

Figure 3.1. Schematic description of a nuclear explosive of the gun barrel type

Source: Johan Swahn, *The Long-Term Nuclear Explosives Predicament* (Goeteborg, Sweden: Chalmers University of Technology, 1992).

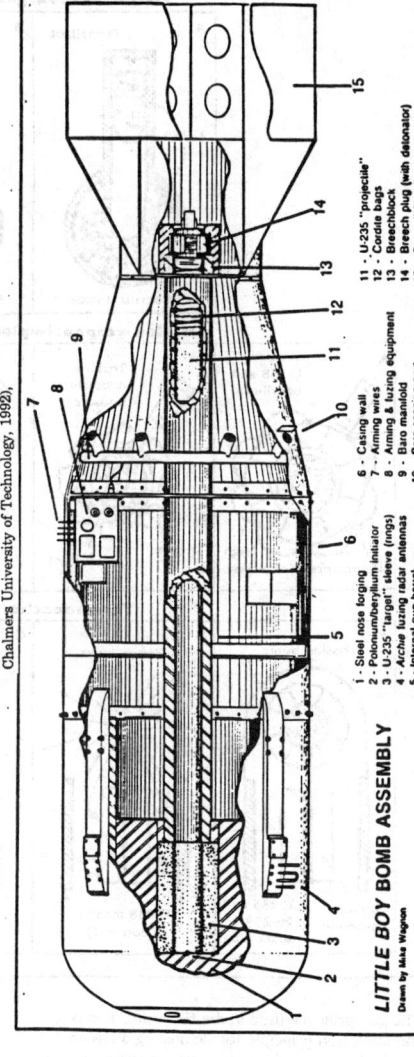

LITTLE BOY BOMB ASSEMBLY
Drawn by Mike Wagnon

1 - Steel nose forging
2 - Polonium/beryllium initiator
3 - U-235 "target" sleeve (rings)
4 - Archie fuzing radar antennas
5 - Internal gun barrel
6 - Casing wall
7 - Arming wires
8 - Arming & fuzing equipment
9 - Baro manifold
10 - Baro sensing port
11 - U-235 "projectile"
12 - Cordite bags
13 - Breechblock
14 - Breech plug (with detonator)
15 - Box tail fins

Source: Chuck Hansen, *U.S. Nuclear Weapons: The Secret History* (New York: Orion Books, 1988), 121

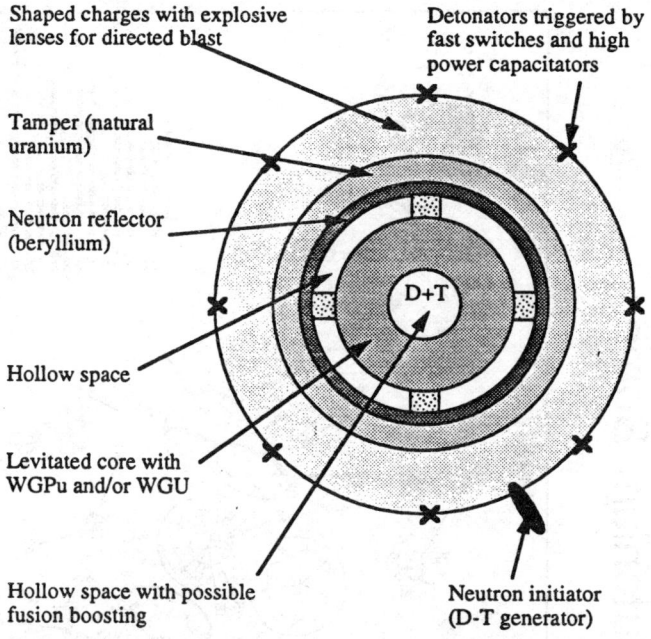

Figure 3.2. Schematic description of a nuclear explosive of the implosion type

Source: Johan Swahn, *The Long-Term Nuclear Explosives Predicament* (Goeteborg, Sweden: Chalmers University of Technology, 1992),

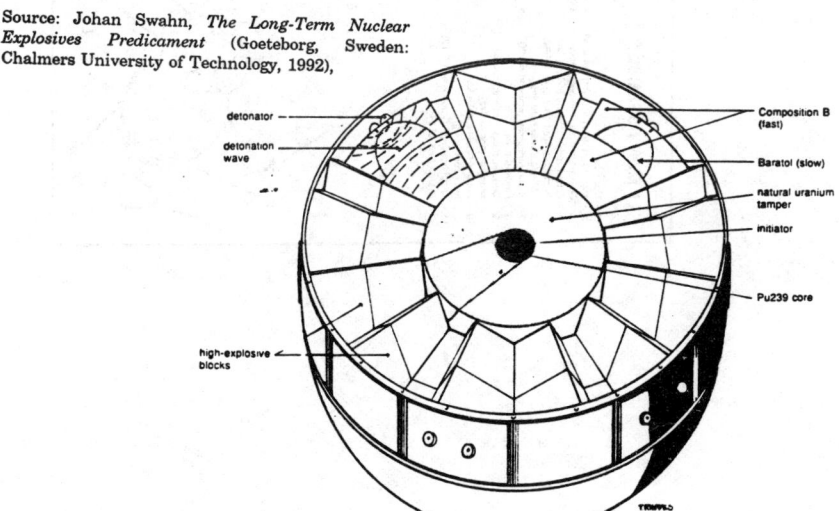

Source: Richard Rhodes, *The Making of the Atomic Bomb* (New York: Simon and Schuster, 1986),

Model of Nagasaki Plutonium Bomb

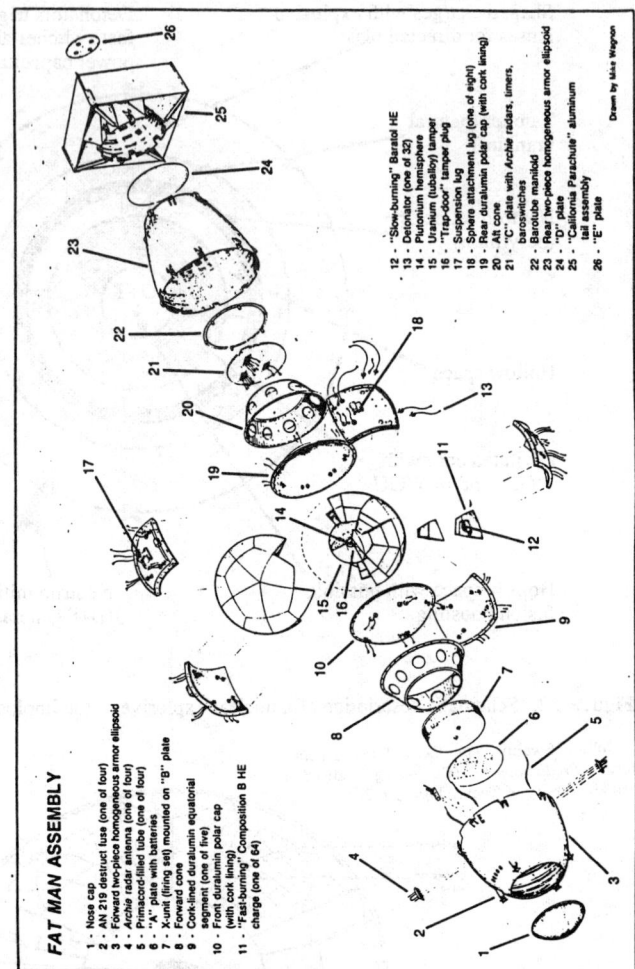

655

Photo 4.1, taken by former Israeli nuclear technician Mordechai Vanunu, is said to be a cutaway model of an Israeli atomic bomb. Dark metal sphere (front left) represents the plutonium core of the bomb. This would be enclosed by the silvery metal pieces (rear left), which screw together, making a second larger sphere. The silvery metal pieces are thought to represent a beryllium reflector/tamper, intended to compress the smaller sphere of plutonium during detonation and enhance yield. The silvery sphere would then be surrounded by high explosives, represented by the dark hemisphere (rear right).
© *London Sunday Times*.

Source: Leonard S. Spector, *The Undeclared Bomb*, (Cambridge: Ballinger Publishing, 1988), 194.

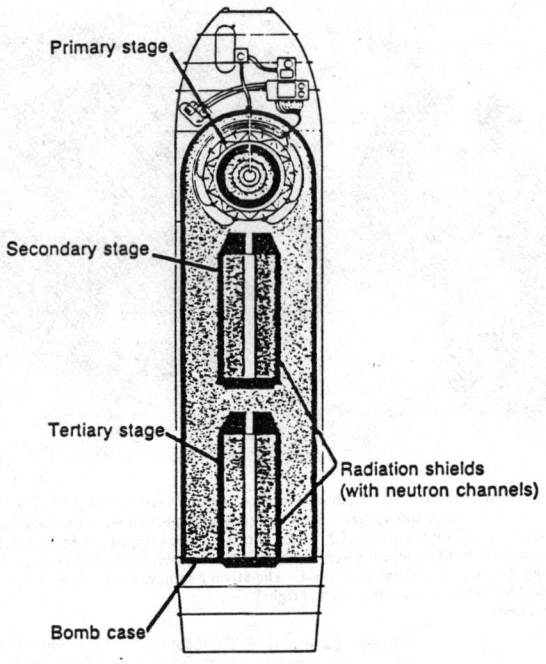

Figure 3.3. Schematic drawing of a fusion nuclear explosive (from Hansen (1988, p. 22))

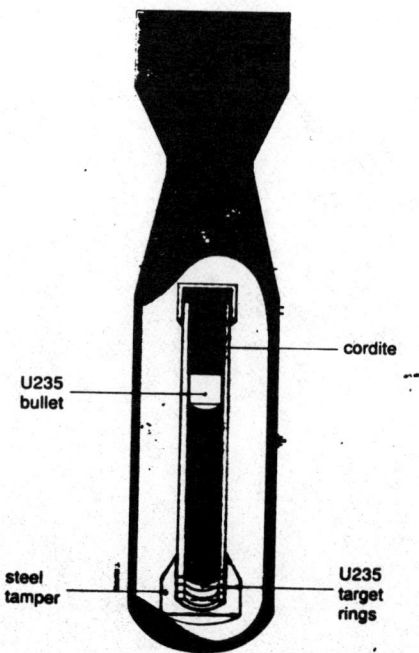

16-5 Test Sites and Seismic Stations

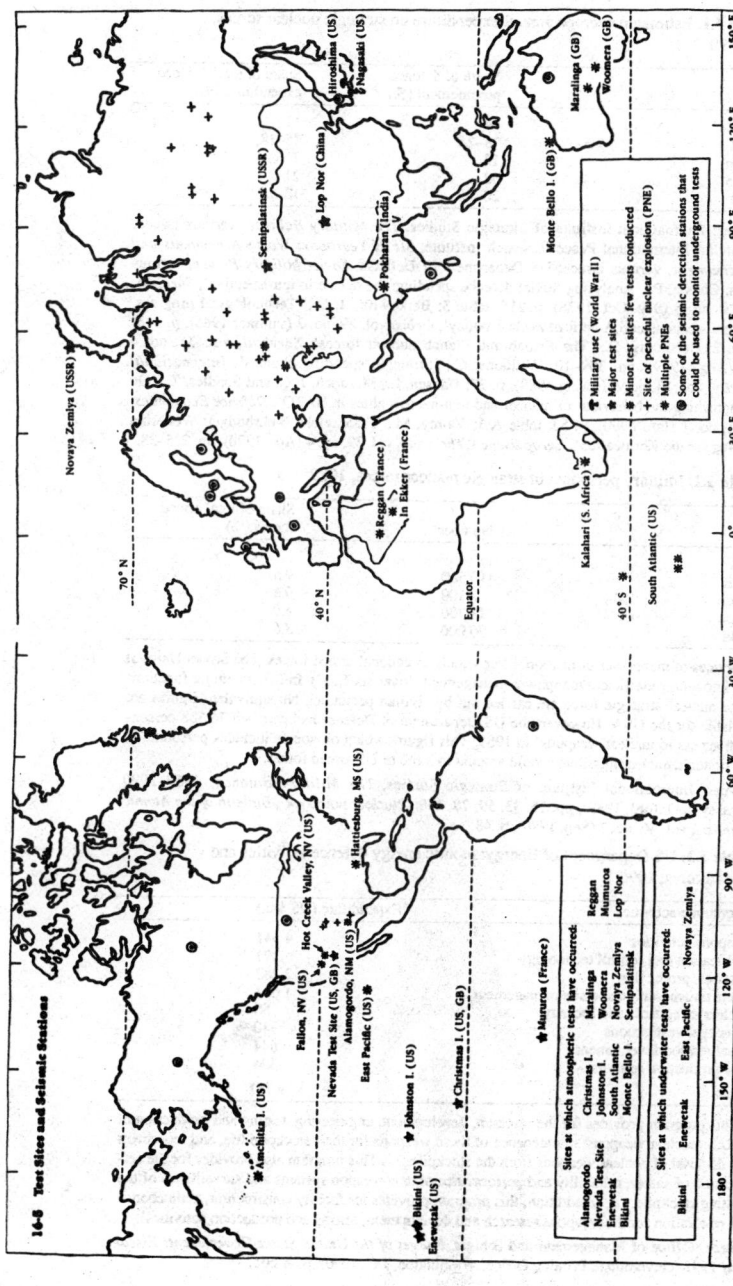

The locations of nuclear explosions encircle the globe and include places within the Soviet Union but away from the usual weapon test sites, where the detonations are presumed to be peaceful nuclear explosions. The site indicated in South Africa was reportedly prepared for a nuclear test but was not used, perhaps because of international pressure. Also shown are some of the more sensitive seismic detection stations used to monitor underground tests. There are other networks of seismic stations in France and in the Soviet Union.

Source: Jack Dennis, ed., *The Nuclear Almanac: Confronting the Atom in War and Peace* (Reading, Mass.: Addison-Wesley, 1984).

Table 3.1. Estimated average annual expenditure on strategic nuclear forces, 1970-90

	Share of defence procurement (%)	Share of total defence expenditure (%)
USA	14	11
USSR	18-25	15-18
Britain	12	7
France	32	21
China	20-25	12-15

Sources: International Institute of Strategic Studies, *The Military Balance*, various issues; Stockholm International Peace Research Institute, *SIPRI Yearbook: World Armaments and Disarmament*, various issues; US Department of Defense, *Soviet Military Power*, various issues; Cockle, P., 'Analysing Soviet defence spending: the debate in retrospective', *Survival*, vol. 20, no. 5 (Sep./Oct. 1978), p. 215, table 3; Berkowitz, B. D., 'Technological progress,' strategic weapons and American nuclear policy', *Orbis*, vol. 29, no. 2 (summer 1985), p. 248, figure 2; Heisbourg, F., 'The British and French nuclear forces', *Survival*, vol. 31, no. 4 (July/Aug. 1989), pp. 309-10; Williams, C., 'Strategic spending choices', *International Security*, vol. 13, no. 4 (spring 1989), p. 27; Hansen, L., Murdoch, J. C. and Sandler, T., 'On distinguishing the behaviour of nuclear and non-nuclear allies in NATO', *Defence Economics*, vol. 1, no. 1 (Jan. 1990), p. 53, table A.1; Valmy, M., 'Frankreichs Wehrbudget: Weiterhin Vorrang für die Kernwaffen', *Europäische Wehrkunde*, vol. 39, no. 4 (Apr. 1990), pp. 225-28.

Table 3.2. Military personnel in strategic nuclear forces, 1989

	Number[a]	Share of total armed forces (%)
USA	..	..
USSR	410 500	9.6
Britain	2 100	0.6
France	18 700	4.0
China	90 000	3.0

[a] Practices of manpower utilization differ widely in national armed forces. The Soviet Union is well known for inefficient manpower management ('over-staffing'). In Britain, major functions in the nuclear strategic force are carried out by civilian personnel. No equivalent figures are available for the USA. However, the US Department of Defense had certified 76 588 persons 'with access to nuclear weapons' in 1989. This figure, which obviously includes personnel in sub-strategic nuclear missions, would amount to 3.6% of US armed forces.

Sources: International Institute of Strategic Studies, *The Military Balance, 1989-1990* (Brassey's: Oxford, 1989), pp. 16, 33, 59, 78, 146; 'Nuclear notebook', *Bulletin of the Atomic Scientists*, vol. 46, no. 7 (Sep. 1990), p. 48.

Table 3.3. US Department of Energy: atomic energy defence activities and expenditures, 1990

Programme activities	Expenditure (US $m.)
Weapons activities[a]	4 541
Verification and control technology	171
Materials production	2 287
Waste transportation and site management	1 684
Nuclear safeguards and security	88
Security investigations	40
Naval reactor development	644
New production reactors	304
Total	**9 761**

[a] 'This program provides for the research, development, engineering, testing and production of all U.S. nuclear weapons; maintenance of these weapons for their stockpile life, and retirement and disposal of nuclear weapons from the stockpile.... This program also provides for the certification of safety, reliability and performance of new weapon systems and surveillance of the existing stockpile.... In addition, this program provides for facility construction, maintenance and restoration for the weapons research and development, testing and production activities'.

Source: Office of Management and Budget, *Budget of the United States Government: Fiscal Year 1991* (Government Printing Office: Washington, DC, 1990), p. A-661.

Source: Regina Cowen Carp, ed., *Security without Nuclear Weapons? Different Perspectives on Non-Nuclear Security* (New York: Oxford University Press, 1992),

Table 1.2
U.S. Nuclear Warhead Production 1945–85

Warhead Designator[a]	Delivery System	Laboratory[c]	Phase 3[d] Development Engineering	Phase 4 Production Engineering	Phase 5 First Production	Phase 6 Quantity Production Begin[e]	Phase 6 Quantity Production (complete)	Phase 7 Retirement Begin[e]	Phase 7 Retirement (complete)	Cancelled	Number Built[f]
FM	Bomb	LANL	6/43			8/45	12/48	3/49	7/49		20
LB[g]	Bomb	LANL	6/43			8/45	2/50	1/51	1/51		5
Mk-III(B3)	Bomb	LANL	8/45			4/47	4/49	3/50	12/50		120
Mk-IV(B4)	Bomb	LANL	8/45			3/49	5/51	7/52	5/53		550
Mk-5(B5)	Bomb	LANL	5/48			5/52	7/53	6/57	1/63		140
Mk-5(W5)	REGULUS I	LANL	5/48			2/53	6/53	7/61	1/63		35
	MATADOR										65
Mk-6(B6)	Bomb	LANL	1/51			7/51	4/54	6/57	1/61		1100
MK-7(B7)	Bomb	LANL	11/50			8/52	6/58	11/62	6/67		470
Mk-7(W7)	CORPORAL	LANL	11/50			7/53	5/58	8/60	5/67		300
	BETTY (Mk-90 Depth Bomb)										225
	BOAR Bomb										225
	HONEST JOHN										300
	ADM-B										300
Mk-8(B8)[*]	Bomb (Impact Fuse)	LANL	3/50			2/52	5/53	5/57	8/57		40
Mk-8(W8)[*]	REGULUS I	LANL	3/50				Cancelled			5/55	0
Mk-9(S9)[*]	280mm howitzer	LANL	10/50			4/52	11/53	5/57	5/57		80
TX-10(B10)[*]	Bomb (Air Burst Else)	LANL	5/51				Cancelled in Favor of B12			5/52	0
Mk-11(B11)[*]	Bomb (Navy Mk-91)	LANL/DOD	10/51			7/53	Cancelled	?	?	5/55	40
Mk-12(B12)	Bomb	LANL	9/52			12/54	2/57	7/58	7/62		250
Mk-12(W12)	TALOS/TADM?	LANL	12/54				Cancelled in Favor of W30			11/55	0
TX-13(B13)	Bomb	LANL	8/54				Cancelled in Favor of B18			8/54	0
TX-13(W13)	SNARK/NAVAJO	LANL	8/54				Cancelled			9/54	0
EC14[**g]	TN Bomb	LANL	8/52			2/54	9/54	9/54	10/54		5
Mk-15(B15)[**]	TN Bomb	LANL	10/53			4/55	2/57	8/61	4/65		1200
Mk-15(W15)[**]	SNARK/REDSTONE	LANL	8/55				Cancelled in Favor of W39			1/56	5
EC16[***]	TN Bomb	LANL	6/52			3/54	3/54	4/54	4/54		5
EC17[**]	TN Bomb	LANL	10/53			5/54	9/54	10/54	11/54		5
Mk-17(B17)[**]	TN Bomb	LANL	10/53			10/54	11/55	11/56	10/57		200
Mk-18(B18)	Super Oralloy Bomb	LANL	8/52			7/53	2/55	1/56	4/56		90
S19	280mm howitzer	LANL/DOD	4/53			3/56	Cancelled	?	?		80
B20	TN Bomb	LANL	?				Cancelled in Favor of B15	8/54			0
B21	TN Bomb	LANL	5/54			12/55	7/56	6/57	11/57		275
B22	TN Bomb	LANL	8/53				Cancelled in Favor of B21			4/54	0
S23[*]	16-inch naval gun	LANL/DOD	8/53			12/56	?	10/62	10/62		50
EC24	TN Bomb	LANL	10/53			4/54	9/54	10/54	11/54		10
B24	TN Bomb	LANL	10/53			10/54	11/55	9/56	10/56		105
EC25	GENIE	LANL	11/54			11/56	12/56	7/57	7/57		20
W25	GENIE	LANL	11/54	12/56		5/57	5/60	8/61	12/84		3150
B26	TN Bomb	LANL	5/54				Cancelled in Favor of B21				0
B27	TN Bomb (Mk-101)	LLNL	9/55	3/57		11/58	3/60	11/62	7/64		700
W27	REGULUS II	LLNL	9/55	3/58		9/58	6/59	8/62	7/65		25
B28I	TN Bomb/(Navy Mk-113)	LANL	8/54	1/57		8/58	5/66	1/64	active		4500
W28I	HOUND DOG	LANL	8/54	1/57		8/58	5/66	1/64			600
	MACE										100
B29	TN Bomb	LANL	9/54				Cancelled in Favor B15/39			8/55	0
W30I	TALOS	LANL	4/55	3/57		2/59	1/65	1/62	3/79		300
	TADM										300
W31	HONEST JOHN	LANL	12/54	3/57		10/58	12/61	7/67	active		1650
	NIKE HERCULES								active		2550
	ADM										300
S32[*]	240mm howitzer	LANL/DOD					Cancelled in Favor of W48			5/55	0
S33[*]	8-inch howitzer	LANL/DOD	12/54			1/57	1/65	FY83	active		1000
W34	LULU/Mk-101 depth bmb)	LANL	4/55	1/57		6/58	9/62	7/64	9/77		2000
	HOTPOINT (Mk-105 bomb)										600
	ASTOR (Mk-45 torpedo)										600
W35	ATLAS	LANL	7/56				Cancelled in Favor of W49			12/57	0
	TITAN										0
	THOR										0
	JUPITER										0
B36	TN Bomb	LANL	8/54	5/55		4/56	6/58	8/61	1/62		940
W37	NIKE HERCULES	LANL	4/56				Cancelled in Favor of W31			10/56	0
W38	ATLAS E/F	LLNL	2/59	11/59		5/61	1/63	1/65	5/65		110
	TITAN I										70
B39	TN Bomb	LANL	8/55	3/56		2/57	3/58	1/62	11/66		700
W39	SNARK	LANL	1/56	3/56		4/58	7/58	8/62	9/65		30
	REDSTONE										60
W40	BOMARC	LANL	5/58	2/58		9/59	5/62	10/63	11/72		350
	LA CROSSE										400
B41	TN Bomb	LLNL	2/57	10/58		9/60	6/62	11/63	7/76		500
W41	Unnamed ICBM	LLNL	11/58				Cancelled			7/57	0
W42	HAWK	LLNL	5/57				Cancelled			6/61	0
	FALCON										0
	SPARROW										0
	EAGLE										0
B43	TN Bomb/(Navy Mk-112)	LANL	10/58	2/59		4/61	10/65	12/72	active		1000
W44	ASROC	LANL	11/58	8/59		5/61	3/68	5/74	active		574
W45	MADM (Mod 3)	LLNL	11/58	10/59		1/62	6/66	7/67	FY84		350
	LITTLE JOHN										500
	TERRIER										750
	BULLPUP B										100
B46	TN Bomb	LANL	7/57				Cancelled in Favor of B53			10/58	0
W46	TITAN II	LANL	7/57				Cancelled in Favor of W53			10/58	0
EC47	POLARIS A1	LLNL	8/57			4/60	6/60	6/60	6/60		300
W47I	POLARIS A1/A2	LLNL	8/57	11/58		6/60	7/64	7/61	11/74		1060
W48I	155mm howitzer	LLNL	7/57	1/61		10/63	3/68	8/65	active		1060

Thomas B. Cochran et al., *Nuclear Weapons Databook*, vol. 2, *U.S. Nuclear Warhead Production* (Cambridge, Mass.: Ballinger, 1987), 10-11

Table 1.2
U.S. Nuclear Warhead Production 1945–85

Warhead Designator[a]	Delivery System	Laboratory[b]	Phase 3[c] Development Engineering	Phase 4 Production Engineering	Phase 5 First Production	Phase 6 Quantity Production Begin[d]	Phase 6 Quantity Production Completed	Phase 7 Retirement Begin[e]	Phase 7 Retirement Completed	Cancelled	Number Built[f]
W49	THOR	LANL	12/57	1/58		9/58	1/61	2/62	6/75		35
	JUPITER										30
	ATLAS D										30
W50	PERSHING I	LANL	8/58	6/61		3/63	12/65	4/73	active		280
W51	DAVY CROCKETT	LLNL	6/58				Cancelled in Favor of W54			1/59	0
	FALCON										0
W52	SERGEANT	LANL	5/60	7/61		5/62	4/66	3/74	8/78		300
B53	TN Bomb	LANL	12/58	7/60		8/62	6/65	7/67	active		340
W53	TITAN II	LANL	10/60	5/61		12/62	12/63	10/69	active		60
W54	FALCON	LANL	1/59	8/59		4/61	2/65	7/67	4/72		1000
	DAVY CROCKETT										400
B54	Special ADM	LANL	8/60	6/62		8/64	6/66	FY67	active		260
W55	SUBROC	LLNL	3/59	11/61		6/64[l]	4/74	FY83	active		285
W56[j]	MINUTEMAN I/II	LANL	12/60	9/61		3/63	5/69	9/66	active		1000
B57	ASW Depth Bomb/Bomb	LANL	1/60	1/61		1/63	5/67	6/75	active		3100
W58	POLARIS A3	LLNL	9/60	11/62		3/64	6/67	9/68	4/82		1400
W59	MINUTEMAN I	LANL	12/60	1/61		6/62	7/63	12/64	6/69		150
W60	TYPHON	LLNL	10/61				Cancelled			3/64	0
B61-0,-1	TN Bomb	LANL	1/63	5/65	10/66	1/68[n]	4/71		active		2600
B61-2	TN Bomb	LANL	8/71	6/72[n]	3/75	6/75	1/77		active		
B61-3	TN Bomb	LANL	4/72[n]	12/76	5/79	10/79			active		
B61-4	TN Bomb	LANL	4/72[n]	12/76	5/79	8/79			active		
B61-5	TN Bomb	LANL	6/75	6/75	6/77	9/77	9/79				
B61-6	TN Bomb	LANL	4/84								
B61-7	TN Bomb (Modified B61-1)	LANL	5/7?	3/82	6/85	9/85					
B61-8	TN Bomb	LANL	4/84								
W62	MINUTEMAN III (MK-12)	LANL	6/64	3/67	3/70	3/70	6/76	4/80			1725
W63 (ER)	LANCE	LLNL	7/64				Cancelled in Favor of W70			1166	0
W64 (ER)	LANCE	LANL	7/64				Cancelled in Favor of W63			9/64	0
W65 (ER)	SPRINT	LLNL	10/65				Cancelled in Favor of W66			1/68	0
W66 (ER)	SPRINT	LANL	1/68[n]	1/72	6/74	10/74	3/75	FY85	8/85		70
W67	MINUTEMAN III	LANL	6/66				Cancelled			12/67	0
	POSEIDON										
W68	POSEIDON	LLNL	12/66	5/68	5/70	12/70	6/75	9/77	active		5220
W69	SRAM	LANL	1/67	1/68	10/71	2/72	9/76		active		1200
W70-0-1-2	LANCE	LLNL	4/69[n]	12/70	6/73	6/73	7/77[n]	7/79	active		902
W70-3 (ER)	LANCE	LANL	4/76	4/76[n]	5/81	8/81	2/83		active		380
W[*]71	SPARTAN	LLNL	3/68	1/72	7/74	10/74	7/75	inactive	storage		30
W72	WALLEYE	LLNL	5/69	5/69	8/70	9/70	4/72	7/79	9/79		300
W73	CONDOR	LANL	7/68				Cancelled			9/70	0
W74	155mm howitzer	LANL	3/70				Cancelled			6/73	0
W75	8-inch howitzer	LLNL	6/71				Cancelled			6/73	0
W76	TRIDENT I	LANL	5/73	11/75	6/78[o]	11/78			active		3000
B77	TN Bomb	LANL	5/74				Cancelled			12/77	0
W78	MINUTEMAN III (Mk-12A)	LANL	7/74	3/77[p]	8/79	9/79	10/82		active		1000
W79 (ER)	8-inch howitzer	LANL	1/75	3/77[p]	7/81	9/81	?10/83		active		325
W79 (non-ER)	8-inch howitzer	LLNL					8/86		active		225
W80-0	SLCM	LANL	6/76	3/82	12/83	3/84			active		100
W80-1	ALCM	LANL	6/76	1/79	1/81	2/82			active		1200
W81	STANDARD2	LLNL	10/77								0
W82 (ER)	155mm howitzer	LANL	2/78				Cancelled			10/83	0
W82 (non-ER)	155mm howitzer	LLNL		5/86							
B83	TN Bomb	LANL	1/79	9/80	6/83	9/83			active		500
W84	GLCM	LLNL	9/78	12/80	6/83	9/83			active		160
W85 AB/SB	PERSHING II	LANL	5/79	9/80	2/83	5/83			active		120
W86 EP	PERSHING II	LANL	5/79				Cancelled			9/80	0
W87	MX/PEACEKEEPER	LLNL	2/82	10/83	4/86	7/86					0
W88	TRIDENT II	LANL	3/84		?4/89	?/89					0
Wxx											
									TOTAL		60262

* Gun Assembly Weapons. All others are implosion weapons.
** First Thermonuclear designs.
a Warhead has more than one mod or yield option. Retirement (Phase 7) begins for certain mod(s)/yield(s) prior to the completion of other mod(s)/yield(s) of the same warhead.
 All current nuclear warheads are designated either "B" or "W" followed by a number. Gravity bombs are designated with a "B". Warheads with other applications, for example for missiles, use the designation "W". Prior to the 1960s nuclear warheads were assigned "Mark" ("Mk") numbers. Other designations in the Table include "FM" for FATMAN, "LB" for LITTLE BOY, "TX" for a few experimental (but cancelled) warheads, "EC" for Emergency Capability, and "S" for some atomic artillery shells.
b LANL: Los Alamos National Laboratory; LLNL: Lawrence Livermore National Laboratory. LANL/DOD cosponsors for several gun assembly warheads.
c Month, year. For a description of Phases see Chapter Four.
d The W25 was the first warhead developed under the 1953 DOD/AEC Agreement.
e There is frequently some ambiguity in defining when the retirement of a warhead begins. The start of Phase 7 may indicate the date when retirements of warheads for quality assurance sampling began, or it may indicate the date when all of the warheads of that type were removed from the stockpile for dismantlement.
f Authors estimates.
g Replaced by B17.
h Replaced by B17.
i Original 1/58. Withdrawn 3/58 and Reaccepted 8/58.
j Ibid.
k Original FPU 8/59. Withdrawn 8/59 and Reaccepted 9/59.
l Originally FPU 1/64. Withdrawn 4/64 and Reaccepted 6/64. SUBROC was produced in two runs. The original production run was completed in 3/68. The second Phase 4 authorization date was 3/70. Phase 5 began 2/72 and Phase 6 began 5/72, and was completed 4/74.
m Originally began Phase 6 1/67. Withdrawn 5/67 and Reaccepted 1/68.
n Phase 4 activities were suspended in 6/73 and reauthorized in 1/74.
o Phase 3 activities were rescheduled in 11/74 as a result of a 17-month slip in the commencement of Phase 6.
p Ibid.
q Development efforts on the W65 before cancellation could be considered applicable to the W66 program.
r Originally began Phase 6 on 6/70, withdrawn 9/70 and reaccepted 12/70.
 Development of the W63 before cancellation could be considered applicable to the W70 program. The original Phase 3 was 11/68, which was suspended in 1/68 and reinstated in 4/69.
 Production completed for W70-2. Other mods presumed to be completed earlier.
 Phase 4 activities for the W70-3 (and W79) were suspended 30 September 1977 and reinstated 1 November 1978.
 Phase 5 date represents partial build only.
 Phase 4 was first authorized 11/75, suspended 2/76 and reauthorized 3/77.
 Phase 4 activities for the W79 (and W70-3) were suspended 30 September 1977 and reinstated 1 November 1978.

Sources: DOE, Table B. "Cumulative History of Weapons Programs Key Dates and Time Spans," 31 December 1984. Table C. "Cumulative History of LANL/DOD and EC Programs and Weapons Programs Suspended or Cancelled," 31 December 1983. Letter from Col. Virgil D. Kempton, DOE Office of Military Application, to Robert S. Norris, 21 February 1986.

Table 1.8
Nuclear Warheads in Full Scale Production and Research and Development
(1985-1990s)

WARHEADS IN PRODUCTION

Number	Description and Date[a]	Est. Total	Est./Year
B61-3	Tactical Bomb (10/79)	1000	125
B61-4	Tactical Bomb (05/79)[b]	1000	125
W76	TRIDENT I (06/78)	3200	320 [c]
W79	8-inch Artillery (07/81)	625 [d]	100
W80-1	Air-Launched Cruise (01/81)[e]	3100	350
W80-0	Sea-Launched Cruise (03/84)	750	90
B83	Strategic Bomb (06/83)[f]	3000	425
W84	Ground-Launched Cruise (06/83)	500	125
W85	PERSHING II (02/83)	125	60
W87	MX Missile (04/86)[g]	525-1050	175-350

WARHEADS IN R&D

Number	Description
W81	STANDARD-2 Surface-to-Air Missile
W82	155mm Artillery Fired Atomic Projectile (Production period 1989-92 to produce approximately 300)
W88	TRIDENT II (First deliveries FY 1989)
Wxx	SEA LANCE Antisubmarine Warfare/Standoff Weapon (ASW/SOW)[h]
Wxx	Antisubmarine Warfare/Vertical-Launch ASROC (ASW/VLA)[i]
Wxx	Antisubmarine Warfare/Nuclear Depth/Strike Bomb (ASW/ND/SB)[j]
Wxx	Tactical Follow-on Missile[k]
Wxx	SRAM II (Phase 2 scheduled for completion May 1986)
Wxx	Small Intercontinental Ballistic Missile (SICBM) (Phase 2 scheduled for completion March 1986)
Wxx	Ballistic Missile Defense (BMD)—Nuclear Option
Wxx	Tactical Air-to-Surface Missile (TASM)
Wxx	Earth Penetrator Weapon (EPW)

a Date indicates First Production Unit.
b B61-3,4 are to replace older Navy B43s, B57s, and older Air Force tactical bombs: HASC, FY 1986 DOE, pp. 56, 67.
c The rate is not constant. For the first five years the rate was probably around 400 per year for the twelve LAFAYETTE/FRANKLIN and first two OHIO class SSBNs, all of which deployed between October 1979 and the summer of 1983. The rate is probably around 240 per year for the last five years for the next six OHIO class SSBNs. The First W76 warhead for the TRIDENT I SLBM was produced in June of 1978 and is likely to be produced until 1988. Approximately 3200 are needed initially for six FRANKLIN, six LAFAYETTE, and the first eight OHIO class SSBNs. Under current plans eventually the force of 20 TRIDENT SSBNs carrying 480 TRIDENT II SLBMs would have a mix of lighter weight (212 lb for the Mk-4 reentry body), lower yield (100 Kt) W76 warheads with heavier ("substantially less than 500 pounds" for the Mk-5 reentry body), higher yield (475 Kt) W88 warheads. The quote is from HAC, FY 1986 EWDA, Part 7, p. 290. On mixing the two warheads, see HAC, FY 1985 DOD, Part 6, p. 111; HAC FY 1985 EWDA, Part 7, p. 414; AWST (3 September 1984):

d 299; Aerospace Daily (13 March 1985): 65-66. On the yield, see AWST (17 January 1983): 26; AWST (5 March 1984): 17; SAC, FY 1984 DOD, Part 1, p. 475.
d Production of the enhanced radiation version of the W79 was halted by Congress in October 1984. The W79 will complete production in FY 1986.
e The W80-1 will also be used for the Advanced Cruise Missile.
f The B83 Strategic Bomb is replacing the B28, B43, and B53.
g The first ten MX ICBMs are scheduled to be operational in December 1986. Production of the 300 Kt W87 warhead will begin during spring/summer of 1986 and if one hundred missiles are deployed slightly over 1000 warheads would be produced during a three year period. At the end of 1985 Congress limited the number of MX missiles to be deployed to 50.
h To replace the W55 SUBROC warhead. Phase 3 is expected to begin by August 1986.
i To replace the W44 ASROC warhead.
j To replace B57 nuclear depth bomb, and some B61 mods for the Navy.
k Formerly called JTCAMS.

Thomas B. Cochran et al., *Nuclear Weapons Databook*, vol. 2, *U.S. Nuclear Warhead Production* (Cambridge, Mass.: Ballinger, 1987), 22

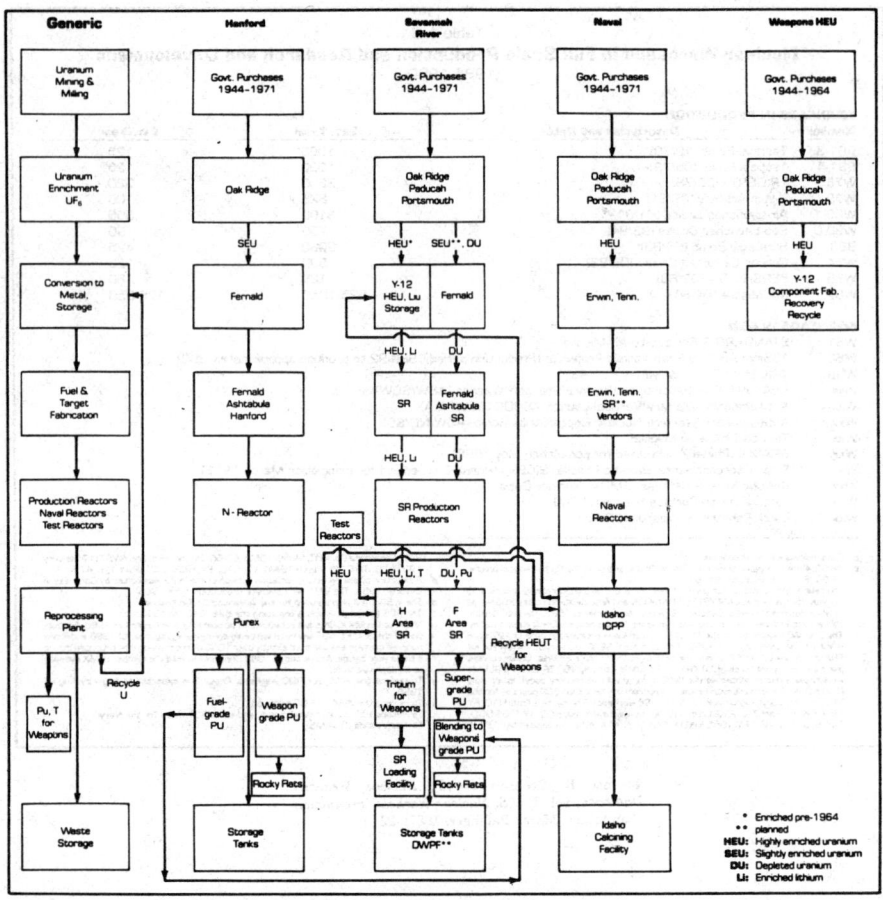

Figure 3.3 Nuclear weapons production and naval propulsion fuel cycles

Thomas B. Cochran et al., *Nuclear Weapons Databook*, vol. 2, *U.S. Nuclear Warhead Production* (Cambridge, Mass.: Ballinger, 1987), 68

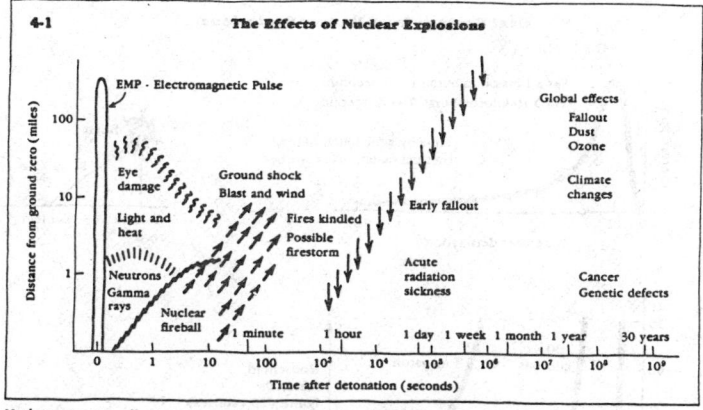

Nuclear weapons effects are extensive in space and time. In addition to the blast and heat that cause the most severe immediate damage, and the radioactive fallout downwind from a surface burst, there are the electromagnetic pulse, which instantly disrupts electronic equipment perhaps hundreds of miles away, and potential genetic damage expressed in future generations of beings.

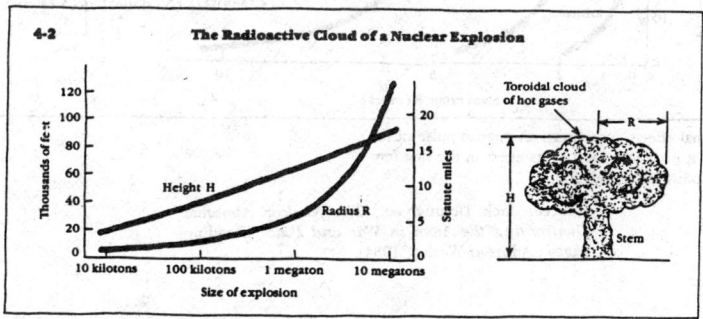

The mushroom cloud of a nuclear explosion reaches its full height in just a few minutes. Here the height and radius are estimated for 10 minutes after a surface or low-altitude burst.

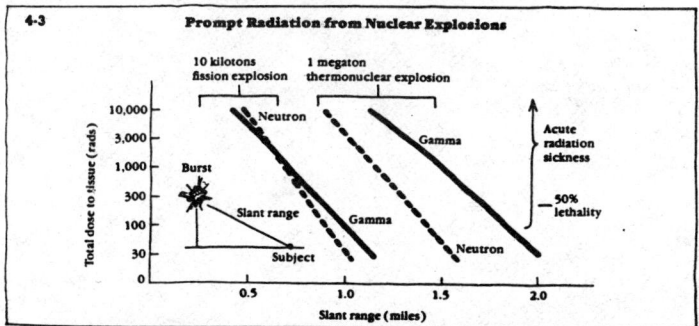

All forms of ionizing radiation are produced, but the forms that travel far enough through air to have significant effects are gamma rays and neutrons. These are produced in an instantaneous burst followed by a rapid decrease, so practically all prompt radiation occurs in less than one second.

Source: Jack Dennis, ed., *The Nuclear Almanac: Confronting the Atom in War and Peace* (Reading, Mass.: Addison-Wesley, 1984).

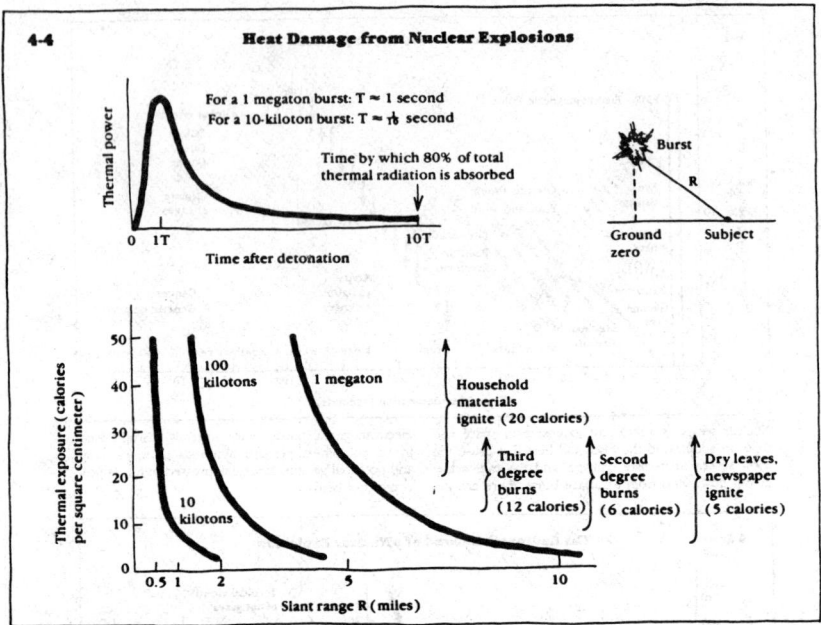

4-4 Heat Damage from Nuclear Explosions

The thermal effects come from an intense pulse of radiation that produces most of its effect in the first few seconds following detonation.

Source: Jack Dennis, ed., *The Nuclear Almanac: Confronting the Atom in War and Peace* (Reading, Mass.: Addison-Wesley, 1984),

4-6 Air Blast and Wind from Nuclear Explosions

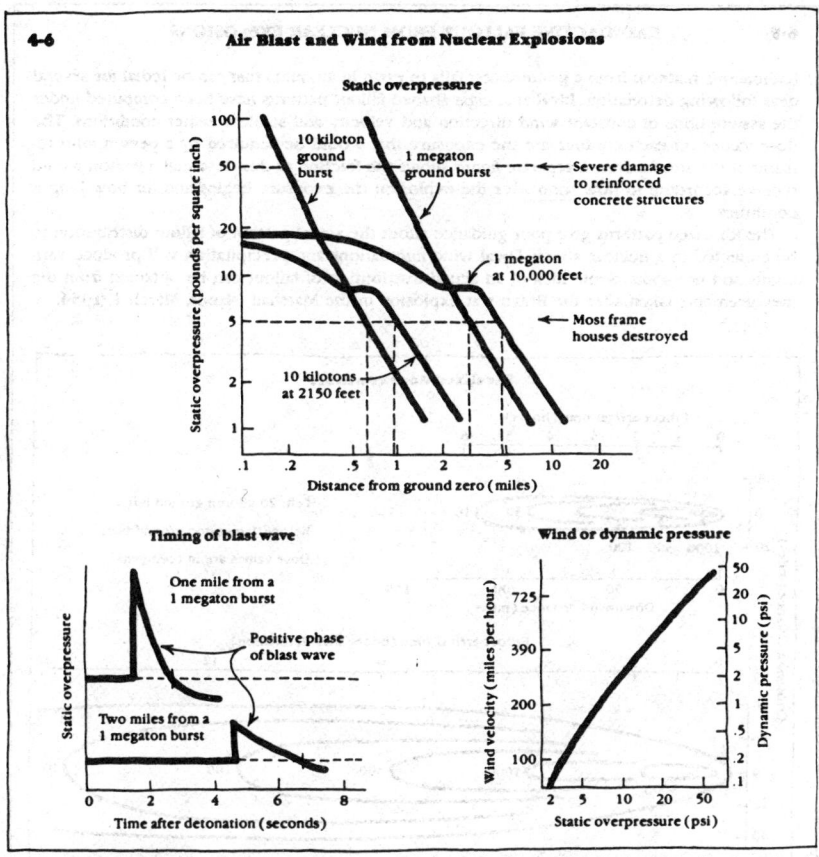

The height of a nuclear explosion above the surface has an important effect on the blast wave produced. For an airburst, the blast wave and its reflection from the ground combine to produce a higher overpressure than for a groundburst. For each value of static overpressure there is a corresponding dynamic pressure, first experienced as a fierce wind blowing outward from the explosion.

Source: Jack Dennis, ed., *The Nuclear Almanac: Confronting the Atom in War and Peace* (Reading. Mass.: Addison-Wesley, 1984),

4-9 RADIOACTIVE FALLOUT FROM NUCLEAR EXPLOSIONS

Radioactive material from a groundburst falls to earth in amounts that can be lethal for several days following detonation. Idealized, cigar-shaped fallout patterns have been computed under the assumptions of constant wind direction and velocity and stable weather conditions. The dose values on each contour are the exposure that would be acquired by a person who remains at the site forever. A separate figure shows the fraction of this dose that a person would receive according to how soon after the explosion the exposure begins and for how long it continues.

The idealized patterns give poor guidance about the actual pattern of fallout distribution to be expected in a nuclear attack. Local wind fluctuations and precipitation will produce variations and hot spots. Some idea of an actual distribution of fallout can be obtained from the measurements taken after the Bravo test explosion in the Marshall Islands, March 1, 1954.

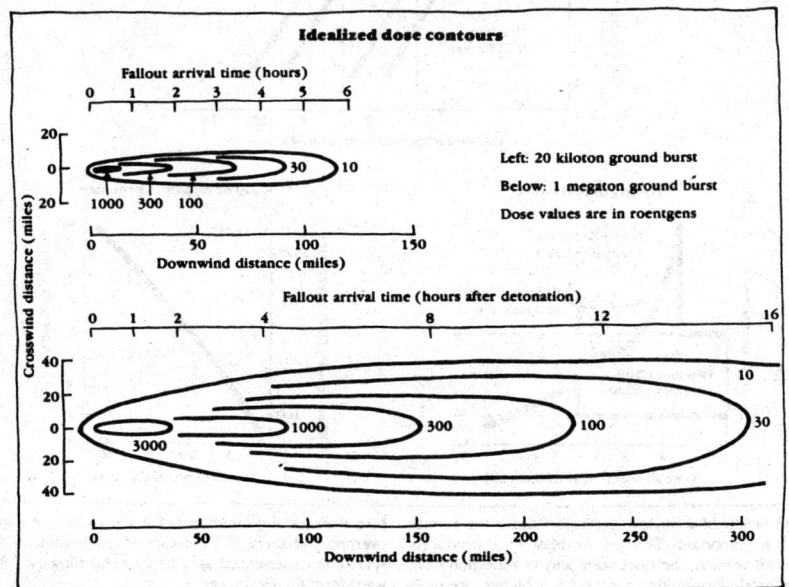

Idealized fallout patterns for 20-kiloton and one-megaton nuclear explosions occurring at ground level with a 20-mile-per-hour wind.

Source: Jack Dennis, ed., *The Nuclear Almanac: Confronting the Atom in War and Peace* (Reading, Mass.: Addison-Wesley, 1984),

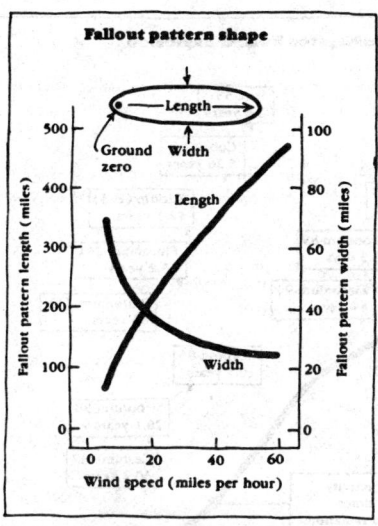

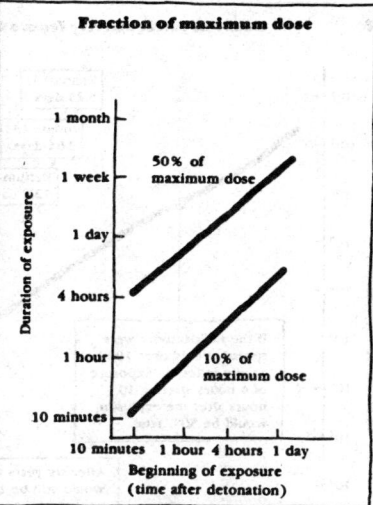

Curves giving length and width of the 100-rad contour computed for a one-megaton groundburst with various wind speeds.

These curves show how the dose received by a subject depends on when exposure begins and how long it continues.

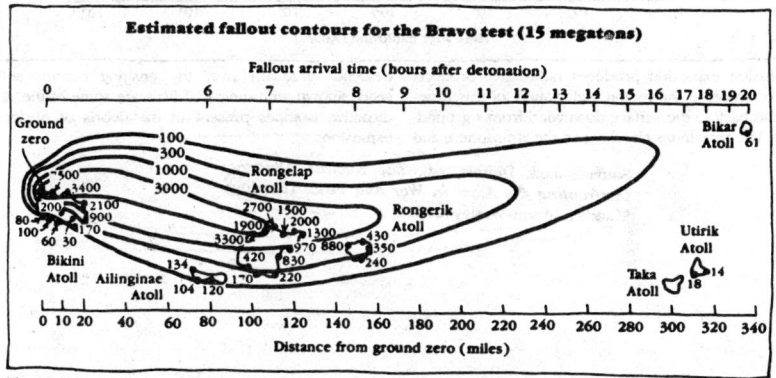

The labeled sites give accumulated doses in rads measured 96 hours after detonation.

Source: Jack Dennis, ed., *The Nuclear Almanac: Confronting the Atom in War and Peace* (Reading, Mass.: Addison-Wesley, 1984),

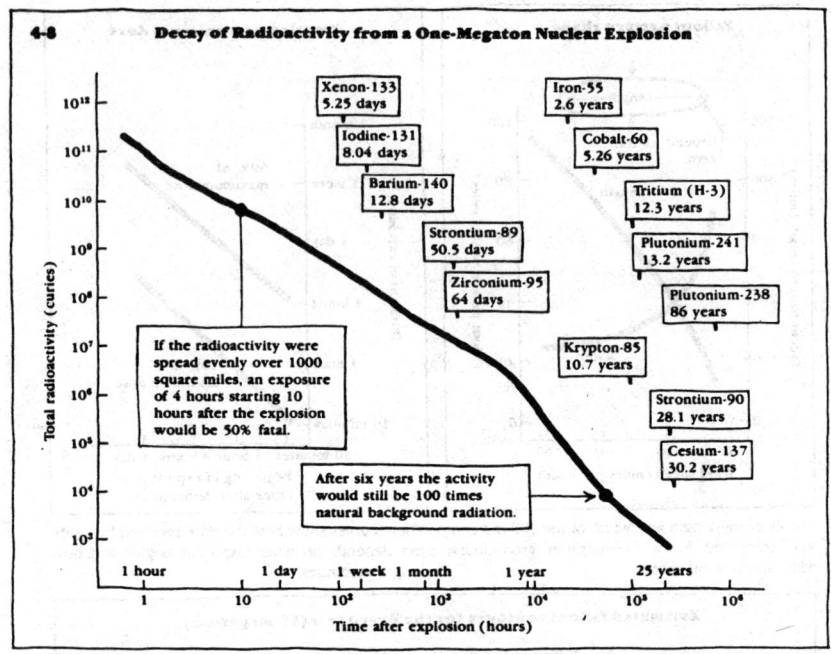

Any fission explosion produces radioactive products in proportion to the fission yield. Much of this material falls back to the surface downwind from a groundburst. The remainder circulates in the atmosphere and descends gradually over the ensuing months and years. Shown with their half lives are some of the radioactive isotopes present in the debris of nuclear explosions.

Source: Jack Dennis, ed., *The Nuclear Almanac: Confronting the Atom in War and Peace* (Reading, Mass.: Addison-Wesley, 1984),

5-4 INFLUENCE OF DURATION OF EXPOSURE

Effect	Required Dose (rems) If Delivered Over One Week	If Delivered Over One Month
Threshold for radiation sickness	150	200
Five percent may die	250	350
Fifty percent may die	450	600

It does not matter much whether a dose of radiation is received as intense radiation for several hours or at a slower rate over several weeks. What matters is the total accumulated dose.

5-5 SHORT-TERM EFFECTS OF ACUTE RADIATION EXPOSURE

Acute Dose (roentgens)	Probable Effects
0 to 50	No obvious effects, except possible minor blood changes.
80 to 120	Vomiting and nausea for about one day in five to 10 percent of exposed persons; fatigue but no serious disability.
130 to 170	Vomiting and nausea for about one day, followed by other symptoms of radiation sickness in about 25 percent of persons; no deaths.
180 to 220	Vomiting and nausea for about one day, followed by other symptoms of radiation sickness in about 50 percent of persons; no deaths.
270 to 330	Vomiting and nausea in nearly all persons on first day, followed by other symptoms of radiation sickness; about 20 percent deaths within two to six weeks after exposure; survivors convalescent for about six months.
400 to 500	Vomiting and nausea in all persons on first day, followed by other symptoms of radiation sickness; about 50 percent deaths within one month; survivors convalescent for about six months.
550 to 750	Vomiting and nausea in all persons within four hours after exposure, followed by other symptoms of radiation sickness; up to 100 percent deaths; few survivors convalescent for six months.
1000	Vomiting and nausea in all persons within one to two hours; probably no survivors.
5000	Incapacitation almost immediately; all persons dead in one week.

A summary of the major features of radiation sickness showing the typical course of the sickness for different levels of exposure.

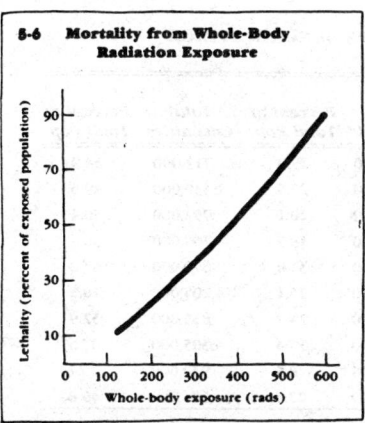

5-6 Mortality from Whole-Body Radiation Exposure

The curve is steep. The difference between survival without medical care and certain death is the difference between doses of 100 and 800 rads. It would be very difficult to identify the victims who should be treated.

Source: Jack Dennis, ed., *The Nuclear Almanac: Confronting the Atom in War and Peace* (Reading, Mass.: Addison-Wesley, 1984),

5-2 CASUALTIES FROM A ONE-MEGATON ATTACK ON DETROIT

Distance from Blast	Population in Zone	Blast Fatalities	Burn Casualties as a Percent of Persons Exposed to Fireball			
			High Visibility (10 miles)		Low Visibility (2 miles)	
0 to 1.7 miles	70,000	70,000				
1.7 to 2.7 miles	250,000	130,000	Deaths	100 %	Deaths	100 %
2.7 to 4.7 miles	400,000	20,000	Deaths	100 %	Injuries:	
					Severe	13 %
					Minor	87 %
4.7 to 7.5 miles	600,000	0	Deaths	43 %	Unharmed	100 %
			Injuries:			
			Severe	50 %		
			Minor	7 %		

Estimated blast and burn casualties for a hypothetical one-megaton ground detonation on Detroit. Note that the number of burn casualties from exposure to the fireball varies enormously with atmospheric conditions. If the attack occurred on a clear summer day, some 25 percent of the population might be exposed, resulting in 190,000 fatalities and 75,000 injuries.

5-9 PROMPT DEATHS AND INJURIES FROM A NUCLEAR ATTACK ON U.S. CITIES

City	Census Population, 1970	Killed	Percent of Total Pop.	Injured	Percent of Total Pop.	Total Casualties	Percent of Total Pop.
Atlanta	1,298,000	363,000	28.0	350,000	27.0	713,000	54.9
Boston	2,884,000	695,000	24.1	735,000	25.5	1,430,000	49.6
Cleveland	1,890,000	572,000	30.3	380,000	20.1	952,000	50.4
Dallas	2,087,000	345,000	16.5	415,000	19.9	760,000	36.4
Kansas City	1,027,000	352,000	34.3	318,000	31.0	670,000	65.2
Los Angeles	8,664,000	2,033,000	23.5	2,172,000	25.1	4,205,000	48.5
Minneapolis	1,577,000	443,000	28.1	392,000	24.9	835,000	52.9
New York	16,323,000	1,667,000	10.2	2,838,000	17.4	4,505,000	27.6
San Francisco	3,613,000	624,000	17.3	306,000	8.5	930,000	25.7
Seattle	1,213,000	332,000	27.4	272,000	22.4	604,000	49.8

These figures show the devastation that would be wrought by a single one-megaton nuclear weapon exploded over an American city. The numbers of casualties were calculated by the U.S. Arms Control and Disarmament Agency using census data; they measure the effects of blast, heat, and prompt radiation, but not fallout. If the attack were to occur during working hours when "downtown" populations are much higher, or if a firestorm were to follow, the numbers of casualties would be much greater.

Source: Jack Dennis, ed., *The Nuclear Almanac: Confronting the Atom in War and Peace* (Reading, Mass.: Addison-Wesley, 1984),

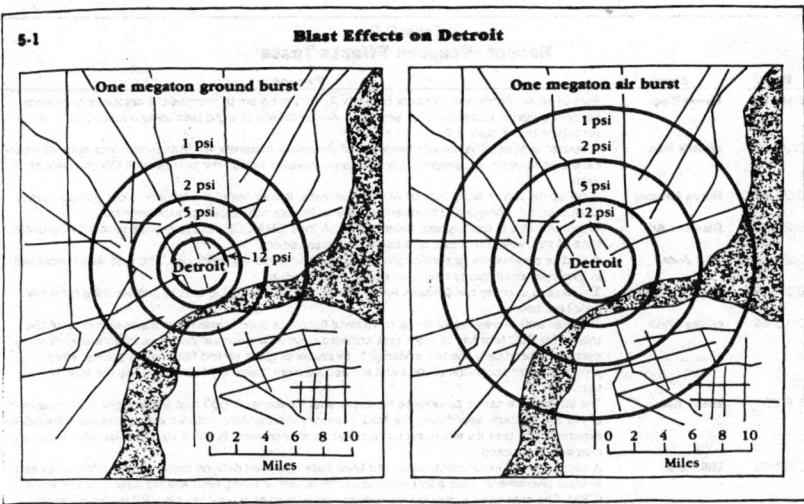

5-1 Blast Effects on Detroit

This pair of maps shows the effect of burst height on the blast effects of a nuclear explosion. The circles are labeled with the blast overpressure in pounds per square inch (psi). At the optimum altitude of burst, the direct and ground-reflected blast waves combine to push the 5-psi circle more than a mile farther out. Inside the 5-psi circle, most buildings would be destroyed.

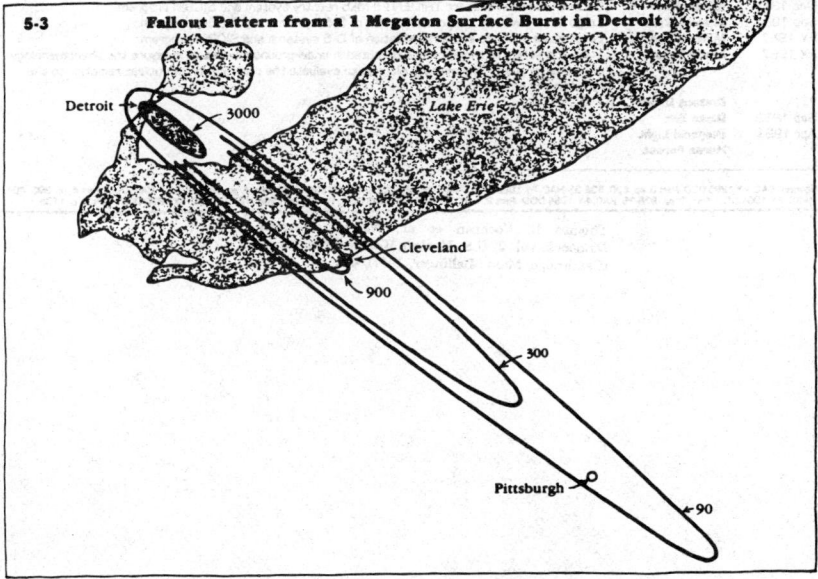

5-3 Fallout Pattern from a 1 Megaton Surface Burst in Detroit

The idealized pattern of fallout following a one-megaton surface burst in Detroit is shown for a uniform northwest wind of 15 miles per hour. The contours show the locations where the indicated radiation dose (in rems) would be received during seven days of exposure without shielding. A dose of 400 to 500 rems is roughly 50 percent lethal.

Source: Jack Dennis, ed., *The Nuclear Almanac: Confronting the Atom in War and Peace* (Reading, Mass.: Addison-Wesley, 1984),

Table 2.9
Recent Weapons Effects Tests

Date	Event	Purpose
06/24/80	**Huron King**	Part of an Air Force and National Security Agency program to improve the database on nuclear hardening design techniques for satellites. A vertical line of sight test using a small DSCS III prototype (see Figure 2.24).
10/31/80	**Miners Iron**	A test to evaluate the nuclear hardness of candidate materials for MX components such as motor cases, ablative nozzle, propellant and external booster parts. The test used 2000 channels of data.
09/23/82	**Huron Landing**	A horizontal line of sight test on MX components. It was one of the largest, most complex tests DNA ever did, using 3000 channels of data to assess 400 separate experiments.
09/23/82	**Diamond Ace**	The first event in the **Distant Arbor** series. A joint DNA/DOE test to provide detailed diagnostic data of the radiation output of a low-yield nuclear device.
05/26/83	**Mini Jade**	A test to obtain data to predict ground motion and cratering prediction. The test was conducted in a hemispherical cavity having an eleven meter radius.
09/21/83	**Midnight Zephyr**	The second event in the **Distant Arbor** series. A joint DNA/DOE test to provide data for a low yield test bed.
02/15/84	**Midas Myth**	The first test in a series of three to validate hardness specifications for major elements of the triad. This 800 foot line of sight test provided data on the nuclear hardness of strategic reentry systems, specifically the MX's Mark 21. First use of glass strand fiber optics cables, which provide clearer reception of data and are secure from "tapping," thus improving the level of security.
04/6/85	**Misty Rain**	The second in a series to validate hardness specifications. A 900 foot line of sight test in support of the MX system, specifically the MK21 reentry vehicle. Also included was a satellite vulnerability experiment to test its electronics in a radiation environment. Some X-ray laser lethality testing was also conducted.
10/09/85	**Mill Yard**	A second cavity experiment, similar to **Mini Jade**, obtained data on cratering phenomenology and airblast phenomena. Also addressed issues on superhardening silos and the basing of the small ICBM. The shot used a very low yield device detonated at ground level in a 22 meter diameter hemispherical cavity.
10/09/85	**Diamond Beech**	Third and final proof test for low yield test bed.
04/10/86	**Mighty Oak**	The final test to validate hardness specifications for the Mark-21 reentry vehicle for the MX missile and the first validation test for the TRIDENT II (D-5) reentry system. X-ray laser lethality experiments were also conducted. Test malfunctioned. Yield was 1.3 Kt. Former tests in the series were **Midas Myth** and **Misty Rain**.
Scheduled		
Dec 1986	**Middle Note**	Second validation test for TRIDENT II Mk5 reentry system and SICBM program.
Sep 1987	**Mission Cyber**	Large scale event to support validation of D-5 systems and SICBM program.
FY 1987	**Mineral Quarry**	Large scale event to support validation of D-5 systems and SICBM program.
FY 1987	**Misty Echo**	Third of a series of three events executed in underground cavities to measure the phenomenology of nuclear craters. The event is planned to evaluate the contribution of nuclear radiation to the formation of a crater.
?	**Distant Drum**	
Sep 1989	**Disko Elm**	
Apr 1991	**Diagonal Light**	
?	**Huron Forest**	

Sources: SAC, FY 1985 DOD, Part 3, pp. 530, 532-33; HAC, FY 1985 DOD, Part 5, pp. 552-53; HASC, FY 1985 DOD, Part 4, pp. 992; HAC, FY 1984 DOD, Part 4, pp. 395, 404; HASC, FY 1984 DOD, Part 5, pp. 976-78; SAC, FY 1984 DOD, Part 2, p. 803; HASC, FY 1983 DOD, Part 5, pp. 1202, 1212; HASC, FY 1982 DOD, Part 4, p. 1166.

Thomas B. Cochran et al., *Nuclear Weapons Databook*, vol. 2, *U.S. Nuclear Warhead Production* (Cambridge, Mass.: Ballinger, 1987), 47

INTELLIGENCE BRIEFS ON PROLIFERATION: COMPARISON BETWEEN PUBLIC RUSSIAN AND U.S. ASSESSMENTS

This table compares recent public assessments of the weapons proliferation threat prepared by Russian and U.S. intelligence agencies. On January 28, 1993, the Russian Foreign Intelligence Service (F.I.S.) released an unclassified report entitled, *A New Challenge After the Cold War: Proliferation of Weapons of Mass Destruction*. The Foreign Broadcast Information Service translated this report into English (see JPRS, TND-93-007, 3/5/93), which Sen. John Glenn released at a hearing of the Senate Governmental Affairs Committee on February 24, 1993. The C.I.A. views were compiled from public testimony at this hearing of the Director of Central Intelligence, James Woolsey, and the Director of the Nonproliferation Center, Gordon Oehler. Abbreviations: NW = nuclear weapon; CW = chemical weapon; BW = biological weapon; WMD = weapons of mass destruction; Pu = plutonium; HEU = highly enriched uranium; IAEA = International Atomic Energy Agency; NPT = Nuclear Non-Proliferation Treaty; CIS = Commonwealth of Independent States; MTCR = Missile Technology Control Regime; FSU = former Soviet Union; ALCM = Air-Launched Cruise Missile; SLCM = Submarine-Launched Cruise Missile. (Table prepared by Maren Leed.)

Country	C.I.A.	RUSSIAN F.I.S.
ALGERIA	Nuclear: deals with China appear consistent with NPT	Nuclear: Chinese heavy water reactor to be inaugurated this year · resulting Pu could be enough for weapon in six years
	Chemical: not discussed	Chemical: no reliable data, believe research was terminated by mid-1992
	Biological: not discussed	Biological: no reliable data, believe research was terminated by mid-1992
	Delivery Systems: not discussed	Delivery Systems: has limited stocks of Frog 4s and 7s
ARGENTINA	Nuclear: not discussed	Nuclear: no information on military programs underway · has technological potential for rapid creation of nuclear explosive device if political decision is made
	Chemical: not discussed	Chemical: no reliable data
	Biological: not discussed	Biological: no reliable data
	Delivery Systems: cooperating in dismantling Condor program	Delivery Systems: Condor program terminated, now under control of civilian space agency
BELARUS	Nuclear: has SS-25s under Russian control	Nuclear: not discussed
	Chemical: not discussed	Chemical: not discussed
	Biological: not discussed	Biological: not discussed
	Delivery Systems: not discussed	Delivery Systems: not discussed
BRAZIL	Nuclear: not discussed	Nuclear: "a major advanced program of research of a military-applied nature"; no evidence of weapons · parallel secret program run by military · can enrich uranium to 5%, eventually to 20% · has reprocessing lab with 5 kg Pu/year capacity · all main technological processes for closed fuel cycle have been developed and tested · could rapidly make a NW upon political decision

	Chemical: not discussed	Chemical: has scientific and technological capabilities which could be reoriented
	Biological: not discussed	Biological: has scientific and technological capabilities which could be reoriented
	Delivery Systems: not discussed	Delivery Systems: Sonda rockets could be used as ballistic missiles · developing Orbita and SS ballistic missiles with ranges of 150-1200km · expanding cooperation with China on liquid-fuel components, control and guidance systems · trying to recruit CIS scientists
CHILE	Nuclear: not discussed	Nuclear: no NWs; has neither the technical or financial capabilities for NW program
	Chemical: not discussed	Chemical: may have stockpiles, has special storage facilities, aerial bombs and cannon-launched projectiles · troops trained for chemical protection
	Biological: not discussed	Biological: no information
	Delivery Systems: not discussed	Delivery Systems: not discussed
CHINA	Nuclear: acceded to NPT last year · looking to modernize NW programs; nuclear energy cooperation with Russia · "there has been compliance with NPT" but "that doesn't mean that our concerns about Chinese sales of nuclear technologies go away ..." · is "biggest supplier of nuclear technologies to Iran": some could be diverted into a NW program; negotiating to sell two power reactors; sold electromagnetic isotope separation unit (calutron) · may be "aggressively attempting to recruit CIS scientists" · "biggest cooperator" with Pakistan, Pakistan's bomb may be Chinese design: "Beijing prior to joining the Non-Proliferation Treaty... probably provided some NW-related assistance to Islamabad that may have included training, may have included equipment." · "unclear whether Beijing has broken off contact with elements associated with Pakistan's weapons programs" · "further proliferation out of China ... [is] front and center as our concern"	Nuclear: (also see Algeria section) · has bilateral nuclear agreement with Egypt · has since 1960's helped North Korean to build an infrastructure for nuclear energy development · reportedly signed nuclear cooperation agreement with Libya in February 1992
	Chemical: concerned about transfers to Middle East; has signed CW Convention	Chemical: selling arsenic to Pakistan, yet no private firms in Pakistan use arsenic
	Biological: may have germ warfare program	Biological: not discussed

		Delivery Systems: press reports on sale to Pakistan of "some sort of" equipment related to M-11; CIA can provide classified details · developing and producing ICBMs · continues to obtain missile technology from Russia and Ukraine, is pursuing agreements "covering increasingly more sensitive areas" · probable reexporter of sensitive technologies controlled in West · missile transfers to Middle East a concern · selling whole missile systems as well as production technology to Persian Gulf states that have later armed them with weapons of mass destruction	Delivery Systems: a "source for the proliferation of missile technologies in Third World countries" · helping Brazil with assimilation of techniques for producing liquid-fuel components · helping Egypt to modify Sakr plant, modify Scud Bs and surface-to-surface missiles · selling missile technology to Brazil and Pakistan
EGYPT	Nuclear: not discussed		Nuclear: no information on a military program, no weapons in the foreseeable future
	Chemical: not discussed		Chemical: has scientific and technical base capable of weapons production from local and imported raw material · able to produce nerve and blister agents · no known efforts to obtain munitions
	Biological: has a program		Biological: has research program, may be cooperating with US labs · US naval-medical lab operating in Egypt
	Delivery Systems: is developing and producing missiles		Delivery Systems: has Scud B, Frog 7 launchers, Sakr short-range missiles · Scuds, Frogs capable of CW delivery · 1990 agreement signed with China to help modernize Sakr plant, modify Scud Bs and three surface-to-surface missiles
INDIA	Nuclear: "nuclear arms race" now underway in South Asia offers "the most probable prospect" for the use of such weapons · has capability to assemble small number of weapons very quickly · interested in developing thermonuclear bombs · CIA can provide classified details		Nuclear: among nations that "unofficially possess" NWs; has "advanced program of military-applied research" · cites belief of specialists that India will soon begin exporting heavy-water reactors · large potential production capability and experimental base · could reprocess unsafeguarded Pu "for the creation of a powerful arsenal of nuclear weapons"
	Chemical: capable of developing weapons		Chemical: troops are armed with CWs and CW defenses, train in CW conditions · has highly developed industry capable of producing both for domestic and exporting needs
	Biological: capable of developing weapons		Biological: no BWs but has "considerable potential" in biotechnology; five military centers involved in "developments in the military-biological area"; civilian research is "primarily ... defensive"

	Delivery Systems: pursuing advanced computer technology probably for long-range nuclear ballistic missiles · interest in space-launch vehicle technology "troubling" because of applicability to ICBMs · buying cryogenic engines from Russia -- possible violation of MTCR	**Delivery Systems:** has large number of aircraft capable of delivering WMD · Privthi missile successfully tested · Agni missile modifications accelerated · experimental design work being done on ALCMs
IRAN	**Nuclear:** has basic technology, is a "country of concern"; CIA can provide classified details · nuclear cooperation talks with Russia · actively pursuing NWs although a party to NPT -- its commitment to the NPT is "very dubious" · principally supplied by China, currently negotiating to buy two reactors · probably 8-10 years away from NWs, or sooner with foreign help	**Nuclear:** doesn't possess NWs but has military applied research program · unlikely to acquire weapons this century without scientific and technical assistance · three inhibiting factors (1) weakened by war, (2) insufficient industrial base, (3) dependence on foreign science and technology
	Chemical: has active program capable of manufacturing hundreds of tons of agent a year · primarily choking and blister agents, may have nerve agent stockpile	**Chemical:** has mustard gas and sarin · partially dependent on imports for source chemicals · CW munitions mostly 155 mm artillery shells, 120 mm mines, chemical aerial bombs
	Biological: has capability for a program · if not already producing probably will be shortly	**Biological:** has a 3-year old program, may have small stocks of agents
	Delivery Systems: has extended-range Scud Cs from North Korea · recently bought diesel subs and advanced aircraft from Russia · has anti-ship cruise missiles · has fighter aircraft, long-range fighter bombers · improving military capabilities by buying advanced conventional weapons that are "formidable challenge" to U.S. military operations	**Delivery Systems:** has Scud Bs from Syria and North Korea, Chinese Silkworms, six of its own short-range (40-130 km) missiles · pursuing 200 km ballistic missile · problems with personnel shortages, technology, scarce source material, financing
IRAQ	**Nuclear:** has basic technology · maintains key non-fissile materials and equipment	**Nuclear:** doesn't have bomb because it lacks a "sufficient quantity of special fissionable material" · production capacity "put out of action"
	Chemical: has stockpile of agents and munitions · 150,000 filled and unfilled weapons, 5000 tons of chemicals declared to UN · retains production equipment	**Chemical:** As of 6/1/91 had 341,000 CW munitions, 750 tonnes of VX, mustard gases · Iraqis cooperating with efforts to destroy stocks within a year
	Biological: program is of "greatest immediate concern" · pre-War "advanced capability" not seriously degraded · easiest to conceal	**Biological:** reports unconfirmed · lack of information though situation is being examined

	Delivery Systems: has "grossly understated" missile holdings to UN · retains missiles, support equipment and propellant · capable of firing Scuds	Delivery Systems: declared ballistic missiles have been destroyed · 200 Scud-class missiles being hidden, possibly in other Arab countries · pursuing missile production capability
ISRAEL	Nuclear: not discussed; CIA can provide classified details·	Nuclear: has weapons and delivery systems · has capacity to manufacture 5-10 weapons/year · potential Pu production capability up to 40 kg/year at unsafeguarded reprocessing plant · may have 100-200 NWs, "up to 20" of which could have been produced between 1970-1980 · has technological potential for continued design improvements · has patented a laser method to enrich uranium; has developed a magnetic isotope separation method · "interest in the development of thermonuclear weapons cannot be ruled out"
	Chemical: not discussed	Chemical: has manufactured its own stock · can produce nerve and blister agents, "all types" of toxic substances · has large-scale, active research program
	Biological: not discussed	Biological: no direct evidence of BWs, but has general biological research program with potential military applications · cooperating with US DoD labs on BW defenses
	Delivery Systems: developing and producing missiles	Delivery Systems: stockpile of most modern missile potential in Near and Middle East, a majority of which is domestically produced · has more than 100 Lance missiles · produces MAR 290s and 350s, Jericho 1s, 2s and 2Bs, ranging 750-1300 km · Ofek satellite program ongoing · Shavit missile capable of nuclear payload, 4500 km range · pursuing SLCM based on Tomahawks · source of proliferation of missile technologies in Middle East
KAZAKHSTAN	Nuclear: has SS-18s under Russian control	Nuclear: not discussed
	Chemical: not discussed	Chemical: not discussed
	Biological: not discussed	Biological: not discussed
	Delivery Systems: has "bombers with bomber weapons active" under Russian control	Delivery Systems: not discussed
LIBYA	Nuclear: reference to Qaddafi statement about a quest for the bomb	Nuclear: no information on presence of NWs · has research program · available engineering, science and technology base would not allow for creation of NWs in foreseeable future

	Chemical: has stockpiled CWs · is constructing a second CW production plant	Chemical: has 70-80 tonnes of CW stocks · has produced sarin, mustard gas, phosgene in limited quantities insufficient for large-scale combat · international pressure has resulted in reduction of production, beginning of dismantlement · no information on destruction of equipment, 50 tonne stock of mustard gas · production may be continuing at new plants
	Biological: not discussed	Biological: is engaged in initial testing, is pursuing cooperative programs with other Arab countries
	Delivery Systems: has "apparently agreed" to buy "missiles" from North Korea and is trying to import other missile technology · has anti-ship cruise missiles	Delivery Systems: has Frogs and Scuds that can't carry nuclear payloads · trying to buy longer-range ballistic missiles, particularly CSS-2 missiles from China, others from Brazil · has pursued domestic production capability
NORTH KOREA	Nuclear: believe is hiding weapons-related activities · possibly manufactured enough fissile material for one NW · two reactors at Yongbyon built for Pu production, not electric power	Nuclear: doesn't possess NWs although it has an advanced program · transparency increasing but can't conclude NW program has been abandoned
	Chemical: no evidence of CW exports · has CW stockpiles	Chemical: has CW program and an "adequate" industrial base · notes North Korean denial of possession of CWs
	Biological: no evidence of BW exports · has BW research program	Biological: has BW program for anthrax, cholera, bubonic plague, smallpox · BWs being tested on island territories
	Delivery Systems: has sold extended-range Scud Cs to Syria, Iran; "has apparently agreed" to sell "missiles" to Libya · has sold "whole systems and production technology" to several Gulf states · is "most grave current concern," willing to sell anything to anyone with money · developing and actively marketing new 1000 km range missile · leaders in production of long-range artillery	Delivery Systems: has Frog 5s and 7s, Scud Bs and Cs · is upgrading Scuds, reexporting them to Near and Middle East · testing Nodong 1 intermediate-range missile · has national missile industry that can produce CW/NW delivery systems · selling missile technologies in Middle East

 **FACTS**

DECLASSIFICATION OF PRE-1961 PACIFIC NUCLEAR TEST YIELDS

The Department of Energy and the Department of Defense have jointly declassified the yields of all nuclear tests conducted in the Pacific prior to the 1958-1961 moratorium.

SPECIFICALLY:

- Attached is a listing of the dates and yields.

BACKGROUND:

- The yields of tests now declassified were part of Operations Greenhouse, Redwing, and Hardtack I conducted from 1951 to 1958. The yields of tests during Operation Crossroads conducted in 1946 at Bikini; Operation Sandstone (1948) at Enewetak; Operation Ivy (1952) at Enewetak; and Operation Castle (1954) at Bikini and Enewetak had been previously declassified. All told, 21 of the 66 tests conducted at Bikini and Enewetak had been previously declassified. With the declassification of the remaining 45 test yields and the declassification of the three high altitude tests Teak, Orange, and Yucca, all tests conducted in the Pacific prior to the 1958-61 moratorium have been declassified.

- In 1992 the Minister of Foreign Affairs, Republic of Marshall Islands, requested declassification of test yields conducted at Bikini and Enewetak.

- Some of these nuclear test yields may have been inadvertently released from Government control, and estimates were previously published by citizen groups.

BENEFITS:

- The declassified yields can now be publicly used in environmental studies of nuclear testing at Bikini and Enewetak, as well as studies of worldwide fallout.

- Release of previously secret information should also encourage other nuclear nations to declassify similar information.

(MORE)

U.S. Department of Energy
Office of Public Affairs
Contact: Sam Grizzle
(202) 586-5806

Source: Department of Energy, "Openness Press Conference", 7 December 1993.

WHO ARE THE KEY STAKEHOLDERS?:

- **Environmentalists**. With this declassification, those interested in worldwide fallout will have better unclassified information for their calculations.

- **Historians and Researchers**. There have been a number of requests for information by those interested in this subject. This declassification will provide them with information to complete their projects.

- **Health Researchers.** This declassification will permit greater public review of information of potential value for epidemiologic or other health studies regarding workers and the community.

- **Freedom of Information Act Requestors.** With this declassification, a number of documents which were classified only because they contained the yields of these tests can now be declassified. Forty-three Freedom of Information Act requests have concerned the weapons testing program in the Pacific.

Attachment

UNITED STATES
DEPARTMENT OF ENERGY

LIST OF DECLASSIFIED YIELDS OF TESTS CONDUCTED IN THE PACIFIC PRIOR TO 1958-1961 MORATORIUM

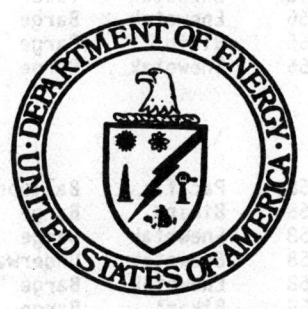

LIST OF DECLASSIFIED YIELDS OF TESTS CONDUCTED IN PACIFIC PRIOR TO 1958-61 MORATORIUM

Name	Date	Location	Type	Yield (in kilotons)
Operation Greenhouse				
Dog	4/07/51	Enewetak	Tower	81
George	5/08/51	Enewetak	Tower	225
Item	5/24/51	Enewetak	Tower	45.5
Operation Redwing				
Cherokee	5/20/56	Bikini	Airdrop	3800
Yuma	5/27/56	Enewetak	Tower	0.19
Erie	5/30/56	Enewetak	Tower	14.9
Flathead	6/11/56	Bikini	Barge	365
Blackfoot	6/11/56	Enewetak	Tower	8
Kickapoo	6/13/56	Enewetak	Tower	1.49
Osage	6/16/56	Enewetak	Airdrop	1.7
Inca	6/21/56	Enewetak	Tower	15.2
Dakota	6/25/56	Bikini	Barge	1100
Mohawk	7/02/56	Enewetak	Tower	360
Apache	7/08/56	Enewetak	Barge	1850
Navajo	7/10/56	Bikini	Barge	4500
Huron	7/21/56	Enewetak	Barge	250
Operation Hardtack I				
Yucca	4/28/58	Pacific	Balloon	1.7
Fir	5/11/58	Bikini	Barge	1360
Butternut	5/11/58	Enewetak	Barge	81
Wahoo	5/16/58	Enewetak	Underwater	9
Holly	5/20/58	Enewetak	Barge	5.9
Nutmeg	5/21/58	Bikini	Barge	25.1
Yellowwood	5/26/58	Enewetak	Barge	330
Magnolia	5/26/58	Enewetak	Barge	57
Tobacco	5/30/58	Enewetak	Barge	11.6
Sycamore	5/31/58	Bikini	Barge	92
Rose	6/02/58	Enewetak	Barge	15
Umbrella	6/08/58	Enewetak	Underwater	8
Maple	6/10/58	Bikini	Barge	·213

CONTINUED

Name	Date	Location	Type	Yield
Aspen	6/14/58	Bikini	Barge	319
Walnut	6/14/58	Enewetak	Barge	1450
Linden	6/18/58	Enewetak	Barge	11
Redwood	6/27/58	Bikini	Barge	412
Elder	6/27/58	Enewetak	Barge	880
Hickory	6/29/58	Bikini	Barge	14
Sequoia	7/01/58	Enewetak	Barge	5.2
Cedar	7/02/58	Bikini	Barge	220
Dogwood	7/05/58	Enewetak	Barge	397
Poplar	7/12/58	Bikini	Barge	9300
Scaevola	7/14/58	Enewetak	Barge	0*
Pisonia	7/17/58	Enewetak	Barge	255
Juniper	7/22/58	Bikini	Barge	65
Olive	7/22/58	Enewetak	Barge	202
Pine	7/26/58	Enewetak	Barge	2000
Teak	8/01/58	Johnston	Rocket	3800
Quince	8/06/58	Enewetak	Surface	0**
Orange	8/12/58	Johnston	Rocket	3800
Fig	8/18/58	Enewetak	Surface	0.02

*safety experiment

**weapons related, yield was not up to expectation

(MORE)

DOE FACTS

QUESTIONS AND ANSWERS

Q. What is meant by Pacific pre-moratorium tests?

A. These are nuclear tests that were conducted in the Pacific Ocean testing areas prior to October 31, 1958. From November 1958 to August 1961, the United States did not conduct any nuclear weapon tests, as part of a moratorium on testing which was also observed by the United Kingdom and the Former Soviet Union. The Former Soviet Union resumed testing September 1, 1961. With this declassification, all remaining, previously classified, yields of tests conducted in the Pacific prior to the 1958-1961 moratorium are now being released.

Q. Are all pre-1961 atmospheric test yields declassified?

A. Yes.

Q. If tests were for weapons design purposes, can you say what the weapons were?

A. No, in most instances the association of specific tests with specific weapons is classified to protect nuclear weapon design capabilities.

Q. Have the island residents been compensated?

A. Yes. The United States has paid $25,000 to each individual with a radiation-related medical condition. In 1977, the United States also paid $1,000 to each resident on Utrik Atoll. In addition, a Nuclear Claims Tribunal now has jurisdiction to compensate claims related to nuclear tests.

Q. What were the health effects from these tests?

A. The United States has operated a medical surveillance program for the exposed population for the last 36 years. Data from this program have been and continue to be used to study potential relationships between the testing program and subsequent health effects. The Department of Energy is committed to sharing this information for independent analysis and building scientific consensus.

(MORE)

Q. How does this information affect worldwide fallout estimates?

A. We hope this information will be useful to independent researchers interested in worldwide fallout. It is worth noting that the United States has already done extensive monitoring over the years to document contributions to worldwide fallout levels from other nations testing nuclear weapons.

Q. The Bulletin of Atomic Scientists has already reported many of these yields. Is this really a declassification?

A. Yes, it is a declassification and represents an official release of data that had previously been classified. Some of these yields may have been inadvertently released from Government control and estimates were previously published by citizen groups.

 **FACTS**

DECLASSIFICATION OF UNANNOUNCED NUCLEAR TESTS AT THE NEVADA TEST SITE

The Department of Energy has declassified the total number of tests conducted at the Nevada Test Site including all previously unannounced tests. Nuclear weapon tests are defined by the Threshold Test Ban Treaty as follows:

- The term "underground nuclear weapon test," hereinafter "test," means either a single underground nuclear explosion conducted at a test site, or two or more underground nuclear explosions conducted at a test site within an area delineated by a circle having a diameter of two kilometers and conducted within a total period of time of 0.1 second. The yield of a test is the aggregate yield of all explosions in the test.

- The term "explosion" means the release of nuclear energy from an explosive canister.

- The term "explosive canister" means, with respect to every explosion, the container or covering for one or more nuclear explosives.

SPECIFICALLY:

- **There were 925 nuclear tests at the Nevada Test Site of which 204 were previously unannounced.**

- **The total number of tests conducted by the U.S. worldwide is 1,051.**

- These tests include a number of locations other than the Nevada Test Site which were previously announced; e.g., other sites in the United States as well as in the Pacific and Atlantic Oceans.

- Additional aspects related to these tests such as specific yields, number of devices, etc., will be reviewed for future release and further review will be carried out to refine the accuracy of the historical test information.

(MORE)

U.S. Department of Energy
Office of Public Affairs
Contact: Sam Grizzle
(202) 586-5806

Source: Department of Energy, "Openness Press Conference", 7 December 1993.

BACKGROUND:

- Both underground and atmospheric tests have been conducted at the Nevada Test Site since 1951. In the past, 204 of the underground tests were not announced and their existence was classified to inhibit Soviet monitoring of United States activities.

- With the end of the Cold War era and the Administration's renewed emphasis on openness in Government, the Department of Energy considers release of this information important to more fully inform the public of the U.S. nuclear testing program.

- Historically, all tests in which radioactivity was detected offsite were announced. However, some of the unannounced tests released small quantities of radioactivity onsite. Information on these releases is provided in the attachment.

- The precise geographical locations of all tests at the Nevada Test Site are available upon request for environmental restoration studies.

- Considerable data pertaining to fallout studies is already available to the public.

BENEFITS:

- The public will have access to a broad range of test-related data.

- This information is useful in health studies regarding workers and the community.

- Release of this information should also encourage other nuclear weapon nations to declassify similar information.

WHO ARE THE KEY STAKEHOLDERS?:

- Environmentalists. This declassified information will assist in studies related to the migration of radioactivity.

- Freedom of Information Act Requesters. The Department of Energy has also received a number of Freedom of Information Act requests for unannounced test information which, until today, has been denied.

(MORE)

Page 3

- <u>Historians and Researchers.</u> There has been speculation on the number of unannounced tests by those interested in the subject. This declassification will end the speculation.

- <u>Health Researchers.</u> This declassification will permit greater public review of information of potential value for epidemiologic or other health studies regarding workers and the community.

- A summary report on the testing information is attached. In addition, a detailed report is available which includes additional information regarding the depth of burial, exact time of the tests, sponsors of the tests, etc.

Attachment

(MORE)

UNITED STATES
DEPARTMENT OF ENERGY

SUMMARY LIST
OF PREVIOUSLY
UNANNOUNCED TESTS

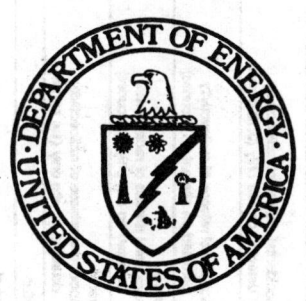

United States Nuclear Tests -- By Date

Event Name	Date (GCT)	Location	Type	Purpose	Yield Range
Operation Nibilck					
Carp Accidental release of radioactivity detected on site only (570 curies)	09/27/63	NTS*	Shaft	Weapons Related	Less than 20 kt
Narraguagus	09/27/63	NTS	Shaft	Weapons Related	Less than 20 kt
Mullet	10/17/63	NTS	Shaft	Weapons Related	Less than 20 kt
Tuna Accidental release of radioactivity detected on site only (0.12 curies)	12/20/63	NTS	Shaft	Weapons Related	Less than 20 kt
Club Accidental release of radioactivity detected on site only (1.2 curies)	01/30/64	NTS	Shaft	Weapons Related	Less than 20 kt
Solendon Accidental release of radioactivity detected on site only (9.6 curies)	02/12/64	NTS	Shaft	Weapons Related	Less than 20 kt
Bunker Accidental release of radioactivity detected on site only (1.4 curies)	02/13/64	NTS	Shaft	Weapons Related	Less than 20 kt
Bonefish	02/18/64	NTS	Shaft	Weapons Related	Less than 20 kt
Mackerel	02/18/64	NTS	Shaft	Weapons Related	Less than 20 kt
Handicap Accidental release of radioactivity detected on site only (300 curies)	03/12/64	NTS	Shaft	Weapons Related	Less than 20 kt
Bogey Accidental release of radioactivity detected on site only (6.9 curies)	04/17/64	NTS	Shaft	Weapons Related	Less than 20 kt

*NTS = Nevada Test Site

Date Prepared: November 15, 1993

United States Nuclear Tests -- By Date

Event Name	Date (GCT)	Location	Type	Purpose	Yield Range
Operation Niblick -- Continued					
Driver Accidental release of radioactivity detected on site only (37 curies)	05/07/64	NTS	Shaft	Weapons Related	Less than 20 kt
Bitterling	06/12/64	NTS	Shaft	Weapons Related	Less than 20 kt
Duffer	06/18/64	NTS	Shaft	Weapons Related	Less than 20 kt
Operation Whetstone					
Links Accidental release of radioactivity detected on site only (less than 6.7 curies)	07/23/64	NTS	Shaft	Weapons Related	Less than 20 kt
Trogon	07/24/64	NTS	Shaft	Weapons Related	Less than 20 kt
Player	08/27/64	NTS	Shaft	Weapons Related	Less than 20 kt
Spoon	09/11/64	NTS	Shaft	Weapons Related	Less than 20 kt
Courser	09/25/64	NTS	Shaft	Joint US-UK	Less than 20 kt
Garden	10/23/64	NTS	Shaft	Weapons Related	Less than 20 kt
Cassowary	12/16/64	NTS	Shaft	Weapons Related	Less than 20 kt
Tern Accidental release of radioactivity detected on site only (170 curies)	01/29/65	NTS	Shaft	Weapons Related	Less than 20 kt
Seersucker Accidental release of radioactivity detected on site only (1.3 curies)	02/19/65	NTS	Shaft	Weapons Related	Less than 20 kt
Suede	03/20/65	NTS	Shaft	Weapons Related	Less than 20 kt
Chenille Accidental release of radioactivity detected on site only (0.93 curies)	04/22/65	NTS	Shaft	Weapons Related	Less than 20 kt

Date Prepared: November 15, 1993

United States Nuclear Tests -- By Date

Event Name	Date (GCT)	Location	Type	Purpose	Yield Range
Operation Whetstone - Continued					
Muscovy	04/23/65	NTS	Shaft	Weapons Related	Less than 20 kt
Organdy	06/11/65	NTS	Shaft	Weapons Related	Less than 20 kt
Operation Flintlock					
Izzer	07/16/65	NTS	Shaft	Weapons Related	Less than 20 kt
Pongee Accidental release of radioactivity detected on site only (6.4 curies)	07/22/65	NTS	Shaft	Weapons Related	Less than 20 kt
Ticking	08/21/65	NTS	Shaft	Weapons Related	Less than 20 kt
Kermet Accidental release of radioactivity detected on site only (less than 5.5 curies)	11/23/65	NTS	Shaft	Weapons Related	Less than 20 kt
Sienna	01/18/66	NTS	Shaft	Weapons Related	Less than 20 kt
Reo Accidental release of radioactivity detected on site only (10 curies)	01/22/66	NTS	Shaft	Weapons Related	Less than 20 kt
Ochre	04/29/66	NTS	Shaft	Weapons Related	Less than 20 kt
Operation Latchkey					
Tangerine	08/12/66	NTS	Shaft	Weapons Related	Less than 20 kt
Khaki	10/15/66	NTS	Shaft	Weapons Related	Less than 20 kt
Vigil Accidental release of radioactivity detected on site only (1.4 millicuries)	11/22/66	NTS	Shaft	Weapons Related	Less than 20 kt
Sidecar Accidental release of radioactivity detected on site only (41 millicuries)	12/13/66	NTS	Shaft	Weapons Related	Less than 20 kt

Date Prepared: November 15, 1993

United States Nuclear Tests -- By Date

Event Name	Date (GCT)	Location	Type	Purpose	Yield Range
Operation Latchkey -- Continued					
Rivet I	01/18/67	NTS	Shaft	Weapons Related	Less than 20 kt
Rivet II Accidental release of radioactivity detected on site only (58 millicuries)	01/26/67	NTS	Shaft	Weapons Related	Less than 20 kt
Mushroom Accidental release of radioactivity detected on site only (0.36 curies)	03/03/67	NTS	Shaft	Weapons Related	Less than 20 kt
Fizz	03/10/67	NTS	Shaft	Weapons Related	Less than 20 kt
Oakland	04/04/67	NTS	Shaft	Weapons Related	Less than 20 kt
Hellman Accidental release of radioactivity detected on site only (31 millicuries)	04/06/67	NTS	Shaft	Weapons Related	Less than 20 kt
Absinthe	05/26/67	NTS	Shaft	Weapons Related	Less than 20 kt
Operation Crosstie					
Vito	07/14/67	NTS	Shaft	Weapons Related	Less than 20 kt
Gibson	08/04/67	NTS	Shaft	Weapons Related	Less than 20 kt
Lexington	08/24/67	NTS	Shaft	Weapons Related	Less than 20 kt
Gilroy	09/15/67	NTS	Shaft	Weapons Related	Less than 20 kt
Cognac Accidental release of radioactivity detected on site only (64 millicuries)	10/25/67	NTS	Shaft	Weapons Related	Less than 20 kt
Worth	10/25/67	NTS	Shaft	Weapons Related	Less than 20 kt
Polka	12/06/67	NTS	Shaft	Weapons Related	Less than 20 kt

Date Prepared: November 15, 1993

United States Nuclear Tests -- By Date

Operation Crosstie -- Continued

Event Name	Date (GCT)	Location	Type	Purpose	Yield Range
Brush Accidental release of radioactivity detected on site only (20 microcuries)	01/24/68	NTS	Shaft	Weapons Related	Less than 20 kt
Mallet	01/31/68	NTS	Shaft	Weapons Related	Less than 20 kt
Torch	02/21/68	NTS	Shaft	Weapons Related	Less than 20 kt
Russet Accidental release of radioactivity detected on site only (29 curies)	03/05/68	NTS	Shaft	Weapons Related	Less than 20 kt
Bevel	04/04/68	NTS	Shaft	Weapons Related	Less than 20 kt
Hatchet	05/03/68	NTS	Shaft	Weapons Related	Less than 20 kt
Crock	05/08/68	NTS	Shaft	Weapons Related	Less than 20 kt
Adze Accidental release of radioactivity detected on site only (7 millicuries)	05/28/68	NTS	Shaft	Weapons Related	Less than 20 kt
Wembley	06/05/68	NTS	Shaft	Weapons Related	Less than 20 kt
Funnel Accidental release of radioactivity detected on site only (20 microcuries)	06/25/68	NTS	Shaft	Weapons Related	Less than 20 kt
Sevilla Accidental release of radioactivity detected on site only (4 millicuries)	06/25/68	NTS	Shaft	Weapons Related	Less than 20 kt

Operation Bowline

Event Name	Date (GCT)	Location	Type	Purpose	Yield Range
Spud	07/17/68	NTS	Shaft	Weapons Related	Less than 20 kt
Imp Accidental release of radioactivity detected on site only (4,200 curies)	08/09/68	NTS	Shaft	Weapons Related	Less than 20 kt

United States Nuclear Tests -- By Date

Event Name	Date (GCT)	Location	Type	Purpose	Yield Range
Operation Bowline -- Continued					
Rack	08/15/68	NTS	Shaft	Weapons Related	Less than 20 kt
Welder	10/03/68	NTS	Shaft	Weapons Related	Less than 20 kt
Vat	10/10/68	NTS	Shaft	Weapons Related	Less than 20 kt
Hula Accidental release of radioactivity detected on site only (60 millicuries)	10/29/68	NTS	Shaft	Weapons Related	Less than 20 kt
Bit	10/31/68	NTS	Shaft	Weapons Related	Less than 20 kt
File	10/31/68	NTS	Shaft	Weapons Related	Less than 20 kt
Auger	11/15/68	NTS	Shaft	Weapons Related	Less than 20 kt
Bay Leaf	12/12/68	NTS	Shaft	Weapons Related	Less than 20 kt
Scissors Accidental release of radioactivity detected on site only (130 microcuries)	12/12/68	NTS	Shaft	Weapons Related	Less than 20 kt
Shave	01/22/69	NTS	Shaft	Weapons Related	Less than 20 kt
Biggin	01/30/69	NTS	Shaft	Weapons Related	Less than 20 kt
Nipper	02/04/69	NTS	Shaft	Weapons Related	Less than 20 kt
Winch	02/04/69	NTS	Shaft	Weapons Related	Less than 20 kt
Valise	03/18/69	NTS	Shaft	Weapons Related	Less than 20 kt
Chatty	03/18/69	NTS	Shaft	Weapons Related	Less than 20 kt
Gourd	04/24/69	NTS	Shaft	Weapons Related	Less than 20 kt
Aliment	05/15/69	NTS	Shaft	Weapons Related	Less than 20 kt
Ipecac Accidental release of radioactivity detected on site only (trace)	05/27/69	NTS	Shaft	Weapons Related	Less than 20 kt

Date Prepared: November 15, 1993

United States Nuclear Tests -- By Date

Event Name	Date (GCT)	Location	Type	Purpose	Yield Range
Operation Bowline -- Continued					
Bowl	06/26/69	NTS	Shaft	Weapons Related	Less than 20 kt
Operation Mandrel					
Horehound	08/27/69	NTS	Shaft	Weapons Related	Less than 20 kt
Kyack Accidental release of radioactivity detected on site only (510 curies)	09/20/69	NTS	Shaft	Weapons Related	Less than 20 kt
Seaweed Accidental release of radioactivity detected on site only (50 nanocuries)	10/01/69	NTS	Shaft	Weapons Related	Less than 20 kt
Seaweed B Accidental release of radioactivity detected on site only (200 nanocuries)	10/16/69	NTS	Shaft	Weapons Related	Less than 20 kt
Planer	11/21/69	NTS	Shaft	Weapons Related	Less than 20 kt
Cuantro	12/10/69	NTS	Shaft	Weapons Related	Less than 20 kt
Tun Accidental release of radioactivity detected on site only (72 curies)	12/10/69	NTS	Shaft	Weapons Related	Less than 20 kt
Belen	02/04/70	NTS	Shaft	Weapons Related	20 to 200 kt
Piton A Accidental release of radioactivity detected on site only (25,000 curies)	05/28/70	NTS	Shaft	Weapons Related	Less than 20 kt
Piton	05/28/70	NTS	Shaft	Weapons Related	Less than 20 kt
Operation Emery					
Scree Accidental release of radioactivity detected on site only (11 curies)	10/13/70	NTS	Shaft	Weapons Related	Less than 20 kt

Date Prepared: November 15, 1993

United States Nuclear Tests -- By Date

Event Name	Date (GCT)	Location	Type	Purpose	Yield Range
Operation Emery -- Continued					
Truchas Accidental release of radioactivity detected on site only (3 curies)	10/28/70	NTS	Shaft	Weapons Related	Less than 20 kt
Penasco	11/19/70	NTS	Shaft	Weapons Related	Less than 20 kt
Corazon	12/03/70	NTS	Shaft	Weapons Related	Less than 20 kt
Canjilon	12/16/70	NTS	Shaft	Weapons Related	Less than 20 kt
Dexter	06/23/71	NTS	Shaft	Weapons Related	Less than 20 kt
Operation Grommet					
Bracken	07/09/71	NTS	Shaft	Weapons Related	Less than 20 kt
Apodaca	07/21/71	NTS	Shaft	Weapons Related	Less than 20 kt
Barranca	08/04/71	NTS	Shaft	Weapons Related	Less than 20 kt
Nama	08/05/71	NTS	Shaft	Weapons Related	Less than 20 kt
Baltic	08/06/71	NTS	Shaft	Weapons Related	Less than 20 kt
Frijoles	09/22/71	NTS	Shaft	Weapons Related	Less than 20 kt
Chantilly	09/29/71	NTS	Shaft	Weapons Related	Less than 20 kt
Lagoon	10/14/71	NTS	Shaft	Weapons Related	Less than 20 kt
Parnassia	11/30/71	NTS	Shaft	Weapons Related	Less than 20 kt
Hospah	12/14/71	NTS	Shaft	Weapons Related	Less than 20 kt
Yerba	12/14/71	NTS	Shaft	Weapons Related	Less than 20 kt
Mescalero	01/05/72	NTS	Shaft	Weapons Related	Less than 20 kt
Cowles	02/03/72	NTS	Shaft	Weapons Related	Less than 20 kt
Dianthus	02/17/72	NTS	Shaft	Weapons Related	Less than 20 kt

Date Prepared: November 15, 1993

United States Nuclear Tests -- By Date

Event Name	Date (GCT)	Location	Type	Purpose	Yield Range
Operation Grommet -- Continued					
Sappho	03/23/72	NTS	Shaft	Weapons Related	Less than 20 kt
Onaja	03/30/72	NTS	Shaft	Weapons Related	Less than 20 kt
Jicarilla	04/19/92	NTS	Shaft	Weapons Related	Less than 20 kt
Kara	05/11/72	NTS	Shaft	Weapons Related	Less than 20 kt
Merida	06/07/72	NTS	Shaft	Weapons Related	Less than 20 kt
Capitan	06/28/72	NTS	Shaft	Weapons Related	Less than 20 kt
Haplopappus	06/28/72	NTS	Shaft	Weapons Related	Less than 20 kt
Tajique	06/28/72	NTS	Shaft	Weapons Related	Less than 20 kt
Operation Toggle					
Atarque	07/25/72	NTS	Shaft	Weapons Related	Less than 20 kt
Cuchillo	08/09/72	NTS	Shaft	Weapons Related	Less than 20 kt
Akbar	11/09/72	NTS	Shaft	Weapons Related	Less than 20 kt
Arsenate	11/09/72	NTS	Shaft	Weapons Related	Less than 20 kt
Canna	11/17/72	NTS	Shaft	Weapons Related	Less than 20 kt
Tuloso	12/12/72	NTS	Shaft	Weapons Related	Less than 20 kt
Solanum	12/14/72	NTS	Shaft	Weapons Related	Less than 20 kt
Alumroot	02/14/73	NTS	Shaft	Weapons Related	Less than 20 kt
Gazook	03/23/73	NTS	Shaft	Weapons Related	Less than 20 kt
Natoma	04/05/73	NTS	Shaft	Weapons Related	Less than 20 kt
Colmor	04/26/73	NTS	Shaft	Weapons Related	Less than 20 kt
Mesita	05/09/73	NTS	Shaft	Weapons Related	Less than 20 kt
Cabresto	05/24/73	NTS	Shaft	Weapons Related	Less than 20 kt

Date Prepared: November 15, 1993

United States Nuclear Tests -- By Date

Event Name	Date (GCT)	Location	Type	Purpose	Yield Range
Operation Toggle -- Continued					
Kashan	05/24/73	NTS	Shaft	Weapons Related	Less than 20 kt
Potrillo	06/21/73	NTS	Shaft	Weapons Related	20 to 200 kt
Silene	06/28/73	NTS	Shaft	Weapons Related	Less than 20 kt
Operation Arbor					
Polygonum	10/02/73	NTS	Shaft	Weapons Related	Less than 20 kt
Waller	10/02/73	NTS	Shaft	Weapons Related	Less than 20 kt
Pajara	12/12/73	NTS	Shaft	Weapons Related	Less than 20 kt
Seafoam	12/13/73	NTS	Shaft	Weapons Related	Less than 20 kt
Elida	12/19/73	NTS	Shaft	Weapons Related	Less than 20 kt
Spar	12/19/73	NTS	Shaft	Weapons Related	Less than 20 kt
Pinedrops	01/10/74	NTS	Shaft	Weapons Related	Less than 20 kt
Hulsea	03/14/74	NTS	Shaft	Weapons Related	Less than 20 kt
Sapello	04/12/74	NTS	Shaft	Weapons Related	Less than 20 kt
Portrero	04/23/74	NTS	Shaft	Weapons Related	Less than 20 kt
Plomo	05/01/74	NTS	Shaft	Weapons Related	Less than 20 kt
Jib	05/08/74	NTS	Shaft	Weapons Related	Less than 20 kt
Grove	05/22/74	NTS	Shaft	Weapons Related	Less than 20 kt
Jara	06/06/74	NTS	Shaft	Weapons Related	Less than 20 kt
Operation Bedrock					
Crestlake	07/18/74	NTS	Shaft	Weapons Related	Less than 20 kt
Pratt	09/25/74	NTS	Shaft	Weapons Related	Less than 20 kt
Trumbull	09/26/74	NTS	Shaft	Weapons Related	Less than 20 kt

Date Prepared: November 15, 1993

United States Nuclear Tests -- By Date

Event Name	Date (GCT)	Location	Type	Purpose	Yield Range
Operation Bedrock -- Continued					
Estaca	10/17/74	NTS	Shaft	Weapons Related	Less than 20 kt
Temescal	11/02/74	NTS	Shaft	Weapons Related	Less than 20 kt
Puddle	11/26/74	NTS	Shaft	Weapons Related	Less than 20 kt
Keel	12/16/74	NTS	Shaft	Weapons Related	Less than 20 kt
Portola	02/06/75	NTS	Shaft	Weapons Related	Less than 20 kt
Teleme	02/06/75	NTS	Shaft	Weapons Related	Less than 20 kt
Bilge	02/19/75	NTS	Shaft	Weapons Related	Less than 20 kt
Alviso	06/11/75	NTS	Shaft	Weapons Related	Less than 20 kt
Futtock	06/18/75	NTS	Shaft	Weapons Related	Less than 20 kt
Operation Anvil					
Deck	11/18/75	NTS	Shaft	Weapons Related	Less than 20 kt
Shallows	02/26/76	NTS	Shaft	Weapons Related	Less than 20 kt
Rivoli	05/20/76	NTS	Shaft	Weapons Related	Less than 20 kt
Operation Fulcrum					
Gouda	10/06/76	NTS	Shaft	Weapons Related	Less than 20 kt
Sprit	11/10/76	NTS	Shaft	Weapons Related	Less than 20 kt
Sutter	12/21/76	NTS	Shaft	Weapons Related	Less than 20 kt
Oarlock	02/16/77	NTS	Shaft	Weapons Related	Less than 20 kt
Dofino	03/08/77	NTS	Shaft	Weapons Related	Less than 20 kt
Forefoot	06/02/77	NTS	Shaft	Weapons Related	Less than 20 kt
Carnelian	07/28/77	NTS	Shaft	Weapons Related	Less than 20 kt
Flotost	08/16/77	NTS	Shaft	Weapons Related	Less than 20 kt

Date Prepared: November 15, 1993

United States Nuclear Tests — By Date

Event Name	Date (GCT)	Location	Type	Purpose	Yield Range
Operation Fulcrum — Continued					
Gruyere	08/16/77	NTS	Shaft	Weapons Related	Less than 20 kt
Scupper	08/19/77	NTS	Shaft	Weapons Related	Less than 20 kt
Operation Cresset					
Rib	12/14/77	NTS	Shaft	Weapons Related	Less than 20 kt
Karab	03/16/78	NTS	Shaft	Weapons Related	Less than 20 kt
Topmast	03/23/78	NTS	Shaft	Weapons Related	Less than 20 kt
Asco	04/25/78	NTS	Shaft	Weapons Related	Less than 20 kt
Jackpots	06/01/78	NTS	Shaft	Weapons Related	Less than 20 kt
Satz	07/07/78	NTS	Shaft	Weapons Related	Less than 20 kt
Cremino	09/27/78	NTS	Shaft	Weapons Related	Less than 20 kt
Operation Quicksilver					
Concentration	12/01/78	NTS	Shaft	Weapons Related	Less than 20 kt
Freezeout	05/11/79	NTS	Shaft	Weapons Related	Less than 20 kt
Operation Phalanx					
Jarlsberg	08/27/83	NTS	Shaft	Weapons Related	Less than 20 kt
Branco	09/21/83	NTS	Shaft	Weapons Related	Less than 20 kt
Navata	09/29/83	NTS	Shaft	Weapons Related	Less than 20 kt
Operation Fusileer					
Muggins	12/09/83	NTS	Shaft	Weapons Related	Less than 20 kt
Orkney	05/02/84	NTS	Shaft	Weapons Related	Less than 20 kt
Bellow	05/16/84	NTS	Shaft	Weapons Related	Less than 20 kt

Date Prepared: November 15, 1993

United States Nuclear Tests -- By Date

Event Name	Date (GCT)	Location	Type	Purpose	Yield Range
Operation Fusileer -- Continued					
Normanna	07/12/84	NTS	Shaft	Weapons Related	Less than 20 kt
Wexford	08/30/84	NTS	Shaft	Weapons Related	Less than 20 kt
Operation Grenadier					
Vermejo	10/02/84	NTS	Shaft	Weapons Related	Less than 20 kt
Minero	12/20/84	NTS	Shaft	Weapons Related	Less than 20 kt
Cebrero	08/14/85	NTS	Shaft	Weapons Related	Less than 20 kt
Operation Charioteer					
Abo	10/30/85	NTS	Shaft	Weapons Related	Less than 20 kt
Mogollon	04/20/86	NTS	Shaft	Weapons Related	Less than 20 kt
Galveston	09/04/86	NTS	Shaft	Weapons Related	Less than 20 kt
Operation Touchstone					
Harlingen	08/23/88	NTS	Shaft	Weapons Related	Less than 20 kt
Operation Cornerstone					
Monahans	11/09/88	NTS	Shaft	Weapons Related	Less than 20 kt
Kawich A	12/09/88	NTS	Shaft	Weapons Related	Less than 20 kt
Operation Aqueduct					
Bowie	04/06/90	NTS	Shaft	Weapons Related	Less than 20 kt

Date Prepared: November 15, 1993

(MORE)

QUESTIONS AND ANSWERS

Q. Why didn't the Department of Energy announce these tests to begin with?

A. As a matter of past policy, the United States did not announce all of its underground nuclear tests in order to inhibit Soviet monitoring of United States activities.

Q. Why aren't the exact yields of these nuclear tests released?

A. With the announcement of each test, a yield range is provided. Exact yields are not provided in order to protect nuclear weapon design capabilities.

Q. Does this reveal all the nuclear detonations at the test site?

A. This declassifies all nuclear tests conducted at the Nevada Test Site. However, some of these tests had multiple explosives resulting in multiple nuclear detonations which are being reviewed for potential declassification.

Q. Offsite, how much radiation was released by these tests?

A. None. All offsite releases of radiation at the Nevada Test Site were announced at the time the releases occurred. Documented information on all releases at the Nevada Test Site has been made available to the public.

(MORE)

Q. Onsite, how much radiation did employees receive from these tests?

A. It would be most unusual for employees to have received radiation from an underground test since forward areas are completely evacuated before the conduct of the actual tests. Furthermore, all employees and other personnel are required to wear individual radiation monitors while at the Nevada Test Site. Data from these monitors is recorded and retained as a permanent record to assure the health and safety of employees and other personnel.

Q. On all tests, was all offsite radiation made public? If yes, where is this information?

A. Yes, it has been made public. This information is available through the Nevada Operations Office's Coordination and Information Center in Las Vegas, Nevada. It is also available from the National Technical Information Service, U.S. Department of Commerce, 5285 Port Royal Road, Springfield, Virginia 22161.

Q. Does the Department of Energy now classify any information pertaining to offsite contamination from nuclear tests?

A. No, it is all unclassified.

Q. Did these tests contaminate underground water?

A. Although there has been some localized contamination of groundwater in the immediate vicinities of tests, we believe there has been very little movement of that water. Test site employees obtain their drinking water from several wells on the site. Site wells are monitored regularly and radioactive contaminants have never been found in test site drinking water.

(MORE)

Q. What were the significant contaminants to the environment from these 204 tests?

A. As with all underground nuclear tests, localized pockets of fission products resulting from the detonation are fused and confined underground in the immediate vicinity of the detonation. There was no significant environmental contamination at the surface of the ground. Virtually all of the radiation was in the form of short-lived noble gases that quickly dissipated in the air. None of the releases were detected off the Nevada Test Site, and there were no lasting environmental impacts, even in the immediate areas of the tests.

NUCLEAR NOTEBOOK

KNOWN NUCLEAR TESTS WORLDWIDE, 1945–1993

Officials in the United States, Russia, Britain, and France have released a great deal of new information about their nuclear testing programs since last year's update ("Nuclear Notebook," April 1993).

United States. On December 7, 1993, U.S. Energy Secretary Hazel O'Leary divulged that there had been 204 "secret"—or unannounced—tests from 1963 to 1990. Of the 204 tests, 111 were known previously, having been detected through seismic monitoring and other means. The new U.S. total of 1,051 includes 24 joint tests with Britain, but not the bombs dropped on Hiroshima and Nagasaki.

Soviet Union. Various Russian, Kazakh, and U.S. documents have helped break down the 715 Soviet tests (including peaceful nuclear explosions, or PNEs) by date, type, location, and purpose. Some of the material is contradictory, so further revisions to the table are possible.

Our current best estimate is that, by type, there have been 204 Soviet tests in the atmosphere, 508 underground, and three underwater. By location, 496 tests were conducted in Kazakhstan, 214 in Russia, and five in three other republics. Within Kazakhstan, 470 tests were conducted at the Semipalatinsk test site, 354 of them underground. At the Russian Novaya Zemlya test site, there have been 132 tests, 87 in the atmosphere, three underwater, and 42 underground.

There is also new information about four nuclear anti-ballistic missile (ABM) tests conducted in September and October 1961.

Two of the tests exploded near the Kapustin Yar ballistic missile launch site, southeast of the Russian city of Volgograd (then Stalingrad). The first was fired on September 6, 1961, five days after the Soviets had broken the moratorium. The 25-kiloton blast exploded at an altitude of around 50,000 feet. The second explosion, an estimated 200-kiloton blast, detonated on October 6, 1961 at an altitude of 100,000–200,000 feet.

Later that month, two rockets—probably fired from Kapustin Yar—flew eastward toward Sary Shagan in southwest Kazakhstan, where nuclear detonations of less than 5 kilotons each went off at high altitudes. The first test, on October 21, 1961, exploded at a height of 160 miles. The second test occurred on October 27, 1961, and exploded at an altitude of 80 miles. Although Sary Shagan conducted work on strategic air defense and anti-satellite systems, the height of these explosions suggests an ABM application.

The Soviet Union's extensive PNE program, which began in January 1965, had conducted 116 PNEs by September 1988. In comparison, the United States conducted 27 PNEs between 1961 and 1973.

The Soviets used these explosions primarily to support the oil, gas, and mineral industries. Thirty-nine explosions were used in the deep seismic sounding program (seismic waves, generated by one or more nuclear detonations, are recorded and analyzed to understand geological features at great depths). North of the Caspian Sea, 36 PNEs were conducted to create underground storage cavities, mainly for gas condensate. An additional 21 were done to help extract gas and oil, and five were exploded to extinguish burning gas or oil wells. One nuclear explosion was used to help build a canal linking the northern Kara Sea to the Caspian Sea via the Pechora and Kama rivers. Other excavation projects created reservoirs. Most of the PNEs—81, to be precise—were conducted in

October 1952: "Mike," the first thermonuclear test.

Russia. There were 30 in Kazakhstan, two each in Ukraine and Uzbekistan, and one in Turkmenistan.

Britain. In October 1993, the British published the yields of the nine "Grapple" tests conducted at Christmas and Malden Islands from May 1957 to September 1958. Three tests used fission devices, four were successful two-stage thermonuclear tests, and two were unsuccessful.

Prime Minister Harold Macmillan said the initial test on May 15, 1957, "was the successful explosion of the first British H-bomb." In fact, it was not successful, producing a yield of only 300 kilotons. After another try on June 19—this time with a 200-kiloton yield—adjustments were made, and a successful two-stage hydrogen bomb test with a 1.8-megaton yield was accomplished on November 8 that year. One test of a "fall-back" bomb—in case the H-bomb didn't work—used a fission device. That test on May 31, 1957, produced a surprisingly high yield, 720 kilotons.

The yields of the 12 atmospheric tests conducted in Australia from 1952 to 1957 were known already. But one of the secret tests revealed by Secretary O'Leary was a joint U.S.-British test, raising to 24 the number of British underground tests conducted at the Nevada Test Site since 1962.

France. In December, the French Commissariat à l'Energie Atomique said that France had conducted 204 tests, including 12 safety tests. Seventeen were conducted in Algeria, and 175 in

Estimated megatonnage expended in the atmosphere		
United States	141 megatons	(July 16, 1945–November 4, 1962)
Soviet Union	257 megatons	(August 29, 1949–December 25, 1962)
Britain	8 megatons	(October 3, 1952–September 23, 1958)
France	10 megatons	(February 13, 1960–September 15, 1974)
China	22 megatons	(October 16, 1964–October 16, 1980)
TOTAL	438 megatons	

NUCLEAR NOTEBOOK

the Pacific—41 in the atmosphere from 1966 to 1974, and 134 underground from 1975 to 1991. The 12 safety tests are not specified by year in the table because the precise dates are not known, although five are thought to have taken place between 1966 and 1974.

The five declared nuclear powers have acknowledged 2,031 nuclear tests that have taken place since 1945. By location, 942 tests have been conducted in the United States, 496 in Kazakhstan, 302 in the Pacific and Australia, and 214 in Russia. All 39 Chinese tests were held in the far northwest corner of the country, at Lop Nur.

Tests have occurred atop towers, on barges, suspended from balloons, dropped from aircraft, after lifting by rockets (to heights of 300 miles), on the earth's surface, underwater (to depths of 2,000 feet), and underground in vertical shafts (to depths of more than 8,000 feet) and in horizontal tunnels.

About 25 percent of the tests were conducted in the atmosphere. The 511 atmospheric tests totaled some 438 megatons—equal to 29,000 Hiroshima-sized bombs. More than half of that megatonnage was concentrated in a 16-month period from September 1961 to December 1962.

It's worth noting that a "test" and an "explosion" may not necessarily be synonymous, depending on the nation. The United States, for example, defines an underground test as either a single explosion or two or more explosions fired within 0.1 second of each another within a circular area 2 kilometers in diameter. The announced yield is the cumulative total of all the devices. Multiple devices were sometimes placed in the same shaft (known as a "string of pearls") and fired in rapid succession. The definition was developed in the 1990 Protocol to the Threshold Test Ban Treaty with the Soviet Union.

Nuclear Notebook is prepared by Robert S. Norris of the Natural Resources Defense Council and William M. Arkin. Inquiries should be directed to NRDC, 1350 New York Avenue, N.W., Suite 300, Washington, D.C. 20005 (202-783-7800).

	U.S.		S.U.		Britain		France		China		
Year	A	U	A	U	A	U	A	U	A	U	Total
1945	1	0	0	0	0	0	0	0	0	0	1
1946	2	0	0	0	0	0	0	0	0	0	2
1947	0	0	0	0	0	0	0	0	0	0	0
1948	3	0	0	0	0	0	0	0	0	0	3
1949	0	0	1	0	0	0	0	0	0	0	1
1950	0	0	0	0	0	0	0	0	0	0	0
1951	15	1	2	0	0	0	0	0	0	0	18
1952	10	0	0	0	1	0	0	0	0	0	11
1953	11	0	5	0	2	0	0	0	0	0	18
1954	6	0	9	0	0	0	0	0	0	0	15
1955	17	1	6	0	0	0	0	0	0	0	24
1956	18	0	8	0	6	0	0	0	0	0	32
1957	27	5	18	0	7	0	0	0	0	0	57
1958	62	15	35	0	5	0	0	0	0	0	117
1959	0	0	0	0	0	0	0	0	0	0	0
1960	0	0	0	0	0	0	3	0	0	0	3
1961	0	10	52	1	0	0	1	2	0	0	66
1962	39	57	71	1	0	2*	0	1	0	0	171
1963	4	43	0	0	0	0	0	3	0	0	50
1964	0	45	0	10	0	2	0	3	1	0	61
1965	0	38	0	10/4**	0	1	0	4	1	0	58
1966	0	48	0	16/2	0	0	5	0	3	0	74
1967	0	42	0	16/1	0	0	3	0	2	0	64
1968	0	55	0	14/4	0	0	5	0	1	0	79
1969	0	46	0	14/4	0	0	0	0	1	1	66
1970	0	38	0	11/3	0	0	8	0	1	0	61
1971	0	24	0	16/7	0	0	5	0	1	0	53
1972	0	26	0	17/8	0	0	3	0	2	0	56
1973	0	24	0	12/5	0	0	5	0	1	0	47
1974	0	22	0	17/4	0	1	7	0	1	0	53†
1975	0	22	0	17/2	0	0	0	2	0	1	44
1976	0	20	0	18/3	0	1	0	4	3	1	50
1977	0	20	0	18/5	0	0	0	8	1	0	52
1978	0	19	0	22/7	0	2	0	8	2	1	61
1979	0	15	0	24/8	0	1	0	9	1	0	58
1980	0	14	0	20/5	0	3	0	13	1	0	56
1981	0	16	0	16/5	0	1	0	12	0	0	50
1982	0	18	0	12/9	0	1	0	9	0	1	50
1983	0	18	0	19/9	0	1	0	9	0	2	58
1984	0	18	0	18/11	0	2	0	8	0	2	59
1985	0	17	0	10/2	0	1	0	8	0	0	38
1986	0	14	0	0	0	1	0	8	0	0	23
1987	0	14	0	20/6	0	1	0	8	0	1	50
1988	0	15	0	14/2	0	0	0	8	0	1	40
1989	0	11	0	8	0	1	0	8	0	0	28
1990	0	8	0	1	0	1	0	6	0	2	18
1991	0	7	0	0	0	1	0	6	0	0	14
1992	0	6	0	0	0	0	0	0	0	2	8
1993	0	0	0	0	0	0	0	0	0	1	1
Total	215	812	207	508	21	24	45	147***	23	16	2,031†

A=atmospheric; U=underground. *All British underground tests were conducted in the United States. **Number after the "/" represents Soviet peaceful nuclear explosions. ***12 French safety tests not identified by date are not included here; however, they have been added to the grand total. †Includes one underground explosion by India on May 17, 1974.

TECHNICAL ASPECTS

DISPOSAL

Integrating Uranium from Weapons into the Civil Fuel Cycle

Thomas L. Neff[a]

Under a recently-approved agreement, Russia will sell perhaps 500 tonnes of highly enriched uranium (HEU) recovered from its dismantled nuclear weapons to the US Department of Energy over the next twenty years. Blended with natural or depleted uranium to produce low-enriched uranium for reactor fuel, this HEU could displace power consumption in the electricity-intensive gaseous diffusion plants of the US. The sale of the HEU could be done in a way that minimizes uranium market disruptions and benefits both the US and Russia.

INTRODUCTION

Since the birth of the nuclear age, Western nations have made strenuous efforts to separate civil and military uses of the atom. In recent years, this barrier has been eroded from the civil commercial side, resulting in the further proliferation of nuclear weapons and weapons capabilities. Most recently, the collapse of the former Soviet Union and the fading of the Cold War threaten to erode the historic barrier from the other side, with the potential for spread of materials or know-how from weapons programs.

In hindsight, it is clear that the separation between military and commercial uses was essentially institutional and geopolitical, not technical in nature, and was largely an artifice of the West; the Soviet Union did not make such a distinction. With the erosion of the barrier in the West, and the collapse of the Soviet Union, it will be necessary to reconstruct nuclear security regimes. In

---

a. Center for International Studies, Massachusetts Institute of Technology, Cambridge, Massachusetts

A version of this article was initially presented at the Uranium Institute Annual Symposium on 10 September 1992, and was also published by NUKEM in October 1992. The article presented is printed here with permission of NUKEM.

doing so, economic forces—perhaps the ultimate power in the collapsed Union—will play an essential role. The challenge is to align technical and commercial forces in the direction of non-proliferation and global security.

To do so, we must find solutions that—to the extent possible—internalize economic incentives. There are such incentives: massive investments in military programs have produced products that have commercial value. And even where this is not the case, where there are costs to demobilization and cleanup, there are savings to be realized from tackling civil and military nuclear problems in tandem. In short, we need a new structure of security and commercial imperatives and incentives that are *both* security and commercially driven.

Nuclear arms reductions—involving both highly enriched uranium and plutonium— will be a costly process; at the same time, nations are spending large amounts on civil nuclear fuel cycle activities. Would it be possible to find ways to reduce the total combined cost to society of both of these?

As we will show here, the answer is yes, but the mechanisms may not have the simple implications that commercial players may think. For example, some in the civil industry appear to believe that government actions to dismantle warheads—at taxpayer expense—will automatically result in cheap or even free uranium and enrichment derived from the highly enriched uranium (HEU) extracted from nuclear warheads. This is not the case: the products of HEU would need to be sold for substantial amounts to pay for the costs of dismantlement. What can be done is to find an overall cost-minimizing strategy that is good for everyone.

HIGHLY ENRICHED URANIUM[*]

The way to do this for HEU was proposed by the author more than a year ago[†] as a way to enhance financial and political mechanisms for the safe dismantlement of former Soviet nuclear weapons; the strategy was subsequently developed in consultation with the US and Russian governments. In effect, HEU from either US or former Soviet warheads can be used to displace power consumption in the electricity-intensive gaseous diffusion plants that still form the backbone of Western nuclear fuel supply. An agreement incorporating this idea was finally given initial approval by both the Russian and US govern-

---
[*] The presentation at the Uranium Institute from which this article derives also included discussions of plutonium disposition.
[†] *New York Times*, 24 October 1991 (Op Ed).

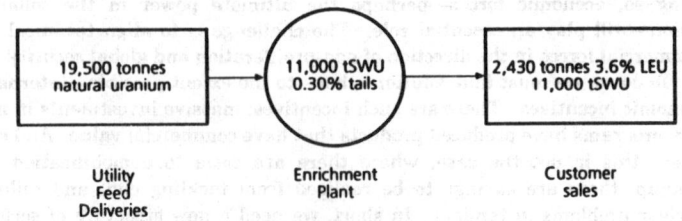

Figure 1: The basic operation of the US enrichment enterprise.

ments in September 1992, providing for the use of perhaps 500 tonnes of Russian HEU by the US Department of Energy (DOE) enrichment enterprise, or its successor, over the next twenty years.

Figure 1 shows the basic operation of the US enrichment enterprise without HEU or other complications. Each year, under existing contracts, utilities deliver about 19,500 metric tonnes of natural uranium to DOE. At a transaction tails assay of 0.30 percent, DOE supplies about 11 million kilograms-SWU and delivers about 2,400 metric tonnes of low-enriched product (at an average assay of about 3.6 percent U-235) to utilities for fabrication into reactor fuel. Matters have actually been a bit more complicated than this as DOE has been forced to find ways to reduce its costs. But the basic example here is correct.

Now suppose that one can provide some of the product delivered to utilities by blending down HEU (say at 93.5 percent U-235) with natural or depleted uranium to make low-enriched uranium (LEU). As is shown at the top of figure 2, ten tonnes of HEU can be blended with natural uranium to make about 321 tonnes of LEU, or about 13 percent of DOE deliveries. This avoids the production of about 1.45 million SWU, which would otherwise require consumption of about 3.6 billion kilowatt-hours of electricity. If the avoided cost to DOE were $50 per SWU, this would mean a savings of about $70 million, equivalent to about $7,000 per kilogram of HEU.

From this sum we must deduct the cost of converting, transporting and blending HEU into LEU. Estimates of this cost are still quite uncertain but probably lie between $2,000 and $3,000 per kilogram of HEU. We will assume a cost of $2,500, in which case, the net value of the HEU for this direct commercial use would be about $4,500 per kilogram.

However, this picture is not complete. Under their contracts with DOE, utilities would be delivering about 2,300 tonnes of natural uranium that

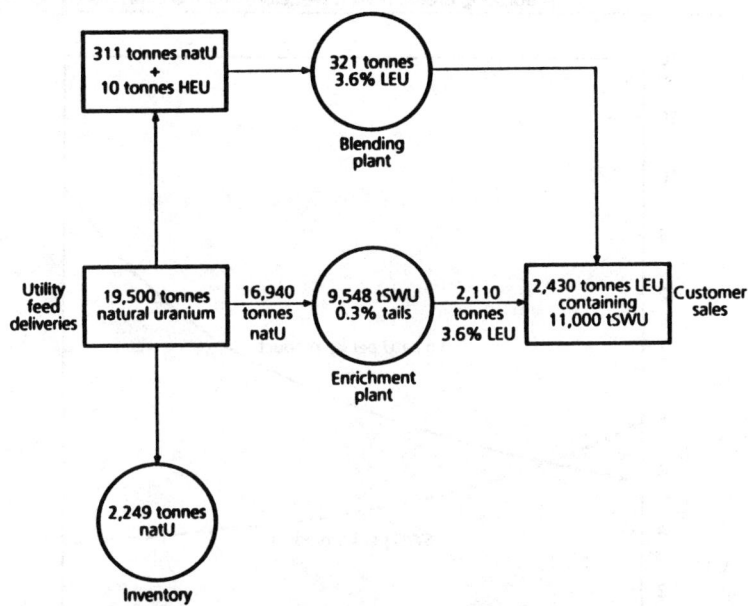

Figure 2: Blending natural uranium and HEU with no overfeed; displacing 1,452 tonnes SWU.

would be displaced by the use of HEU (note that only a small amount of feed is required for blending). In figure 2, we have assumed that this material is simply put into DOE inventory.

But there is a better use for this feed, one that significantly increases the amount that might be paid for the HEU. If the "surplus" feed is used to "overfeed" the enrichment cascades, it can further reduce the number of SWU that must be generated and the power that must be purchased. Overfeeding consists of operating the gaseous diffusion plants at a tails assay higher than the contract level of 0.30 percent. Such overfeeding will increase the amount of natural-uranium feed used to produce a kilogram of product and reduce the amount of separative-work units required (see figure 3). Calculation shows that all of the "surplus" feed delivered by utilities can be absorbed by operating the DOE plants at 0.355 percent tails assay.

What is the value of this overfeeding, and what does it mean for the amount that might be paid for HEU? As figure 4 shows, the combination of

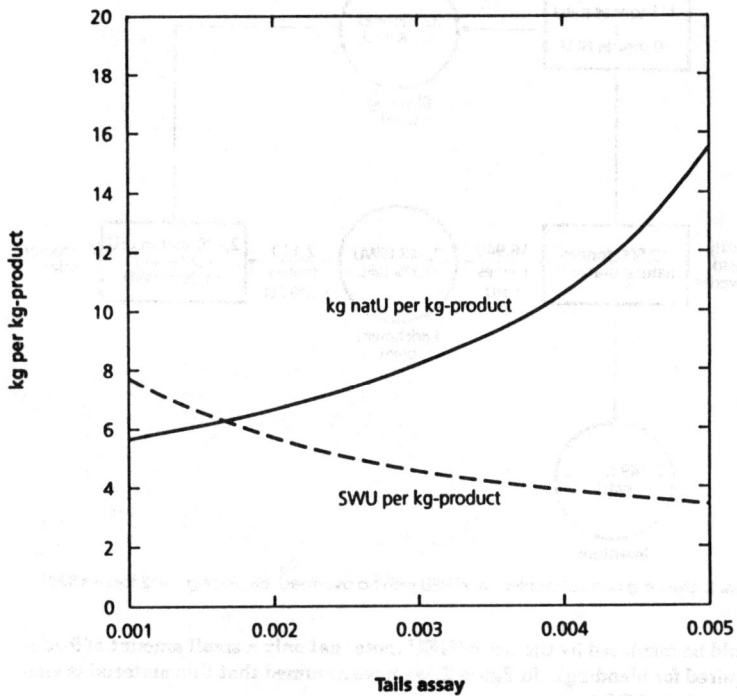

Figure 3: Kilograms of natural-uranium feed and kilograms of separative work units required per kilogram of 3.6 percent LEU for different enrichment-tails assays.

overfeeding and blending possible with an HEU purchase results in avoidance of nearly 2.4 million SWU, about a million more than results just from blending alone. With our assumed avoided cost of $50 per SWU, overfeed results in a savings of an additional $45 million dollars, or about $4,500 per kilogram of HEU. Note that this is a pure savings since no HEU conversion costs are involved. The overfeed savings is thus just as large as the direct savings from HEU blending.

We summarize the SWU savings from these two sources, and the financial implications, in table 1. The total savings from using 10 tonnes HEU (with associated overfeed and net of conversion and blending costs) is more than $90

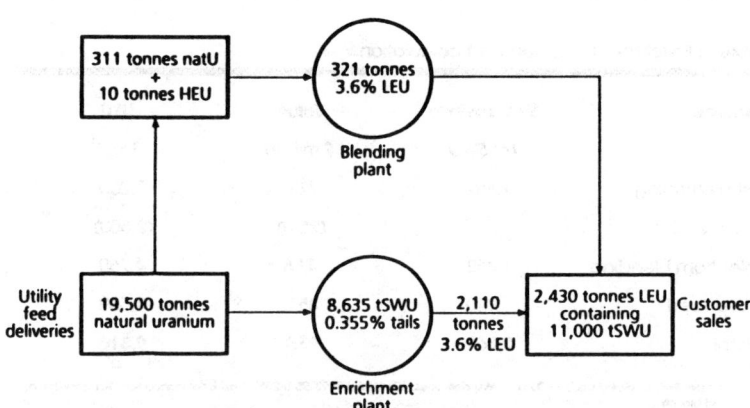

Figure 4: Blending natural uranium and HEU with overfeed, displacing 2,362 tonnes SWU.

million dollars, or $9,000 per kilogram of HEU. This money can be used by Russia to finance dismantlement, with surpluses used for other purposes, such as reactor safety improvements.

It is the present US intention to purchase HEU from Russia with the money saved in the enrichment activity. That is, it must be "budget-neutral" and based on avoided cost. In practice, the calculation of avoided cost is not an obvious matter, being wrapped up in arcane matters of government accounting as well as direct power costs. Our $50 per SWU value may be slightly high, or significantly low, depending on how one does the accounting. DOE (or the Office of Management and the Budget) may also use other formulas for estimating avoided cost. Similarly, the actual cost of converting and blending HEU may be less or greater than assumed here.

However, it is essential for fuel market participants to understand that half or more of the value of the HEU comes from displaced uranium feed and that use of deliveries for overfeeding—or at least payment for the uranium resulting from displacement—is central to economic feasibility. The direct blending of HEU provides less than half the value, as illustrated in table 1. Thus the proposed deal cannot succeed commercially without the overfeeding of surplus uranium by the enrichment enterprise.

Those who see the HEU deal as resulting in freeing up of uranium and increased supply in the market are thus mistaken. If uranium were displaced into the market, the economic and policy realities of the US-Russian deal would not permit it to take place in the first place.

Table 1: Enrichment avoided cost calculation.[a]

Source	SWU savings mt SWU	Value $ million	HEU $ kg^{-1}
HEU blending	1,452	72.6	7,260
less cost		(25.0)	(2,500)
Net from blending	1,452	47.6	4,760
Overfeed	910	45.5	4,550
Total	2,362	93.1	9,310

a. $50 per SWU avoided cost; 11,000 mt SWU deliveries; 10 mt HEU @ 93.5% U-235. Cost is for conversion, transportation, and blending.

As may be seen from table 1, the amounts paid for Russian HEU, under our assumption of $50 per SWU avoided cost, would be equivalent to sale of the products of HEU for $50 per SWU and $7.80 per pound of uranium oxide (about $45 million for 2,300 tonnes natural uranium as overfeed). Russia could blend down its own HEU and sell it in the open market, but the impact of large amounts of such sales (especially in a thin enrichment market) would quite likely be to drive prices below those that might be obtained from DOE, based on avoided cost (if avoided cost for enrichment is at the level assumed, or higher).

Russia and the US have common interest in reducing the market impacts of weapons dismantlement, to avoid cannibalizing their own regular sales of uranium and enrichment services and further depressing their remaining industries and employment in them.

What is interesting about the HEU deal is that it is possible to combine disposition of Russian military HEU with commercial imperatives of the DOE civil enrichment enterprise in such a way as to benefit both parties. That this can occur with no market impact is truly remarkable. It is also remarkable that use of HEU on an avoided cost basis would not change the competitive structure of the enrichment supply industry, since DOE costs would not change appreciably.

If the volumes of HEU grow very large, it becomes more difficult, but not technically or economically impossible, to use the combination of blending and overfeed to reduce costs. To do this at 30 tonnes HEU per year, it would be necessary to increase tails assay in figure 3 to about 0.46 percent U-235 and to reduce actual SWU production to about 5.5 million SWU per year. DOE enrichment plants have operated at such tails assays in the past, but the reduced demand on the enrichment plants could eventually require closing Portsmouth or Paducah. If DOE were to expand SWU sales, or stockpile excess feed, it would be feasible to absorb even larger amounts of HEU.

Dismantling the Bomb and Managing the Nuclear Materials

Nuclear warhead storage bunkers

PHOTO BY ROBERT DEL TREDICI

U.S. Congress

Office of
Technology
Assessment

Summary | 1

During the Cold War, both the United States and the Soviet Union built and maintained large stockpiles of nuclear weapons. Over the past 2 years, the leaders of these nations have pledged to withdraw tactical weapons and sharply reduce the size of the strategic weapons arsenal. Both nations have begun to retire thousands of weapons and to dismantle the nuclear warheads—the part of the weapon that contains its massive destructive power. Reducing the nuclear arsenals of both nations presents a unique opportunity and a challenge. The opportunity is to eliminate large numbers of warheads and reduce the threat of nuclear war. The challenge is to devise feasible and practical means of dismantling them and managing the constituent nuclear materials without causing new environmental, safety, or security problems. Still needed are decisions, policies, and plans to guide both the short- and the long-term goals of this effort.

Treaty agreements, such as the Intermediate Range Nuclear Forces (INF) and the Strategic Arms Reduction (START) treaties, negotiated to date require that weapons be retired from deployed status and that the means of delivering them be removed or destroyed. They do not require that warheads be dismantled or that warhead parts and materials be destroyed. However, the United States has undertaken to remove certain weapons from the stockpile, return warheads to the facilities that assembled them, dismantle the warheads, and store or dispose of their components, parts, and key nuclear materials. Substantial disassembly work is ongoing. The specific plans and schedules, however, are not available to the general public. Nor is the ultimate scope of this effort.

> "Successful dismantlement and disposition of the weapons materials may be the single most important public health, environmental, and social challenge we face."
>
> **Public health expert participating at OTA panel meeting**

> "Current dismantlement can either be done well and set a foundation for future progress, or it can be done badly, leaving so much unaccounted for, so much room for uncertainty, so much inequity that it will set back, if not destroy, future possibilities."
>
> **Local citizen's group reviewer of OTA report**

2 | Dismantling the Bomb and Managing the Nuclear Materials

The Office of Technology Assessment (OTA) has analyzed the present U.S. approach to this undertaking and concludes that current Federal efforts are insufficient to the challenge because they are scattered and lack uniform objectives; they are not based on a clear mission; the public distrusts the responsible Federal agencies, and fears that the environmental and health impacts may be no better than past performance; and there has been little informed public debate to establish national goals. In essence, the Nation has no coordinated, comprehensive national policy on nuclear warhead dismantlement, and current overall management of the task is weak.

Neither the United States nor Russia has developed a technically and politically feasible plan to dismantle warheads and dispose of the nuclear materials from them. Policies for nuclear warhead dismantlement and materials control are important to both U.S. and international security. While recent pronouncements and agreements by national leaders may set goals for reduction of the weapons stockpile, they do not, by themselves, eliminate nuclear weapons. Although nuclear weapons can be rendered less threatening by destroying the means of delivering them (as recently negotiated treaties require), destroying warheads and their constituent nuclear materials safely and effectively is a very difficult task. Many of the most dangerous materials will need careful management for generations.

OTA's analysis of the dismantlement program makes clear that eliminating these warheads—or even destroying a portion of the stockpile of nuclear weapons that have been amassed—will be neither simple nor painless. The difficulties of weapons retirement and warhead dismantlement should not be underestimated. Plans for long-term storage or disposition of nuclear materials must be resolved, and difficult decisions regarding these matters must be made at the highest levels of government.

THE CHALLENGE

Tens of thousands of nuclear weapons are still deployed in the United States, Russia, and other nations (i.e., ready for use or deliverable). Others, although not deployed, are part of what is called —in the United States—the "reserve" stockpile, meaning they are maintained as "backups" for deployed weapons. Still other weapons are removed from both the active stockpile and the inactive reserve, and "retired." The warhead portions of the retired weapons are eventually returned to a Weapons Complex plant for dismantlement.[1]

The Strategic Arms Reduction Treaty, START II, which awaits ratification, provides for some warheads that are presently deployed to be separated from delivery vehicles or otherwise placed in a status in which they are not deliverable or ready for use. START II does not impose any requirements to actually dismantle the warheads that are removed from deployed status. Neither START agreement calls for dismantling any warheads that are now in the reserve stockpile or that may be added to it in the future.

Potential political instability in the former Soviet Union raises concern that control over some weapons will diminish and they will fall into the hands of revolutionary regimes or terrorist groups. The potential proliferation of nuclear weapons poses a serious threat to international security. There is also the possibility that a weapon may detonate accidentally or pose other types of safety problems. Accidental explosions are a concern if groups with limited technical capability and resources have control of these weapons.

---

[1] Dismantlement means the removal of all nonnuclear components, including the chemical high explosive that surrounds the nuclear materials. Dismantlement also includes waste management and disposal of other parts and materials. It does not, however, include destruction of the key nuclear materials or even of the major nuclear subassemblies.

For these and other reasons, the criteria against which options for dismantlement, storage, and disposition of components from nuclear warheads must be assessed differ significantly from those that applied to warhead production. In the past, national security was accorded much more prominent attention than environmental risks. Today, however, there is a need for responsible stewardship of the long-lived nuclear materials that are bequeathed to future generations, and safeguards will be required to protect the safety and health of the public and of the workers who carry out dismantlement.

New technologies may offer solutions or partial solutions to some of the problems associated with either safe disposal or utilization of materials whose radioactive half-lives are measured in many thousands of years. Yet few proven technologies are readily available. Nonproliferation concerns will affect decisions about technologies because of the pressure to come up with options that reduce the risks of nuclear materials being easily diverted into new warheads.

Dismantlement of nuclear warheads is proceeding at a time when trust of government in general, and DOE in particular, is--at best--fragile. The culture of secrecy and insularity embraced by the Department of Energy (DOE) and its predecessor agencies has had a corrosive effect on relations between the Department and the communities neighboring nuclear weapons facilities. The United States begins with the handicap of widespread public mistrust of its own institutions charged with these responsibilities because of their previous failures to safeguard the environment and health. Thus, one of the first tasks is to rebuild institutional credibility.

To do this, the priorities and characteristics of the institutions that supported warhead production will have to be carefully rethought. Greater attention to environmental, safety, and health impacts is essential. If the United States is to successfully carry out nuclear warhead dismantlement and materials management and disposition, and to engage in cooperative efforts with Russia, new institutional capabilities and management approaches are essential. These institutions will be expected to devote much more attention to the environmental impacts of proposed ways of handling nuclear materials than was given when warhead production was the primary concern.

THE OFFICE OF TECHNOLOGY ASSESSMENT STUDY

This study addresses the challenge of eliminating thousands of nuclear warheads. It traces the U.S. process within the responsible Federal agencies, with particular attention to factors that may affect realization of the national goal of safe and secure stockpile reduction in a manner that protects human health and the environment. The report also reviews related work in Russia, focusing on the ability of the United States to influence a safe, secure, and environmentally sound process there.

If the United States wishes to develop and implement policies leading to substantial nuclear arms reduction worldwide, as well as to substantial reduction of the nuclear materials with which to make new warheads, certain actions are important and probably more urgent than generally realized. This report discusses the following major activities involved in the unprecedented enterprise to achieve nuclear stockpile reduction:

- the process for retiring weapons from active deployment in the military and returning their nuclear warheads to the facilities that manufactured them; and dismantlement of the warheads, and subsequent handling of the parts and materials from them; and
- the storage, control, and ultimate disposition of key nuclear materials (plutonium and highly enriched uranium) from the warheads.

4 | Dismantling the Bomb and Managing the Nuclear Materials

Box 1-A—Key Findings

- Ongoing Federal programs and plans within the Departments of Defense and Energy for retirement and dismantlement of nuclear weapons are currently treated as a short-term modification of existing practice rather than a change in focus from past missions of production and stockpile maintenance.
- Numbers of weapons in the active stockpile, and numbers to be retired and dismantled, are contained in classified documents not available to the general public. Existing and pending international agreements do not require that any warheads be dismantled, only that they be removed from delivery systems. The nation's massive nuclear stockpile is now partly dismantled, partly in temporary storage, partly in transition, and partly deployed.
- Environmental, safety, and health problems continue in the operation of the DOE Weapons Complex, and certain aspects of current dismantlement activities—the use of old facilities, additional sources and generation of waste, and slow adoption of modern health and safety practices—may affect the success of dismantlement programs.
- A continuing lack of public credibility may have a major impact on progress in dismantlement and on implementing key operational decisions. Public interest groups have obtained a legitimate voice in influencing DOE operations through environmental legislation and their political power. Despite new public participation initiatives, the major DOE sites have yet to ensure adequate communication with the public, to understand public concerns, or to involve the public in critical decisions.
- It is likely that significant portions of the highly enriched uranium and plutonium recovered from dismantled warheads will need to be stored for decades regardless of the ultimate disposition option chosen for them. Significant time will be required for making disposition decisions and formulating policies; for planning, designing, funding, building, and testing even the most available technology; for gaining regulatory and public acceptance; and for actually processing quantities of materials.
- The use of surplus plutonium from weapons as fuel for U.S. commercial reactors is unlikely because of economic factors, the concerns of U.S. utilities about regulatory constraints and public acceptance, and the need to evaluate U.S. policies that discourage commercial plutonium use.
- If the policies articulated urge expeditious processing or conversion of plutonium to less weapons-usable forms, it may be best to pursue the most available near-term technologies. OTA finds that a process to immobilize it directly in some form such as vitrified glass or, with appropriate poisons, to decrease its proliferation risk and a Government-built and operated dedicated light-water reactor that uses mixed plutonium and uranium fuels are two such near-term technologies.
- It is impossible to fission plutonium completely (and thus "destroy" all of it), but certain new developments may be able to convert it to different radionuclides at a much more efficient rate than existing technologies. However, the research required to develop such advanced reactors and converters would be costly, and would require times on the order of decades.
- The U.S. program to assist Russia with nuclear warhead dismantlement has initiated important cooperative work but has not addressed the broader issues of mutual goals and interests in stockpile and materials reduction or control, nor has it had a significant effect on Russian dismantlement.
- The United States has not verified specific warhead dismantlement activities and accomplishments in Russia, and has no direct cooperative process for developing accurate information about Russian dismantlement status and capabilities.
- Efforts to integrate U.S. warhead dismantlement plans with programs to assist Russia have not received substantive attention. There is little linkage between Russian economic, environmental, or social needs and U.S. programs to assist and encourage Russian dismantlement or related activities.
- While the United States views expeditious Russian warhead dismantlement and materials disposition as vital to its national security, Russia's agenda is dominated by economic and political issues that could relegate dismantlement to a low priority.

The following sections summarize the status of ongoing dismantlement activities, OTA's findings, and an analysis of the policy issues involved and the initiatives proposed.[2] The key OTA findings listed in box 1-A summarize the major points discussed in this report. The findings address U.S. warhead dismantlement and materials management, and U.S. cooperation with Russia regarding the disposition of weapons in the former Soviet Union.

Box 1-B lists issues related to the process of nuclear warhead dismantlement and materials management. These issues are presented in the form of questions and relate to the major decisions that the United States will have to make to facilitate dismantlement both here and in the former Soviet Union.

Finally, box 1-C presents the key policy initiatives developed by OTA in this report. These initiatives are intended to offer possible approaches to improve Government programs and enhance their chances of success. They could be adopted either through legislative initiatives or by the Administration with congressional encouragement. The options can be pursued either individually or as a group. They are presented in the order in which they are discussed in chapter 7.

DISMANTLEMENT OF NUCLEAR WARHEADS

■ Status

According to a long-standing administrative procedure for management and control of nuclear weapons within Federal agencies and the military services, dismantlement begins with a presidential decision approving the annual Nuclear Weapons Stockpile Plan. Retired weapons are then transferred to a military base within the continental United States, where the warhead is usually separated from the delivery system and returned to the DOE facility that assembled it. DOE retains custody until it is dismantled and its components have been disposed of. In recent years, thousands of U.S. nuclear weapons have been put on retirement status: many of these have been returned to DOE for dismantlement; others are in storage at military bases, waiting their turn in the dismantlement process. In FY 1993, the United States expects to dismantle about 1,400 warheads, but plans for the total number of weapons to be retired and disassembled, as well as the future size of a reduced warhead stockpile, are not available for public release.

Warheads returned from the Department of Defense (DOD) to the Department of Energy for dismantlement are transported to the DOE Pantex Plant near Amarillo, Texas, where they were built. Several Department facilities are currently engaged in warhead dismantlement and related work, with major activities centered at Pantex, Y-12 (in Oak Ridge, Tennessee), and Savannah River (in Aiken, South Carolina). At Pantex, plutonium pits (the primary explosive parts) are removed from warheads, placed in containers, and stored in bunkers. Other parts and wastes are characterized, stored, and disposed of in a variety of ways. Nuclear warhead "secondaries" and highly enriched uranium (HEU) are shipped to the Y-12 Plant at Oak Ridge for further storage or disassembly. Tritium gas canisters are shipped to the Savannah River Plant for storage or processing.

The United States has recently announced that it will no longer produce weapons-grade plutonium or highly enriched uranium for warheads. In practice, these activities ceased some years ago, and production facilities have not been operating. Thus, the United States plans to store some of the materials extracted from disassembled warheads

---

[2] The analyses in this report are based on unclassified information. Thus, certain data such as weapons types, numbers of weapons, retirement schedules, warhead designs, materials shapes, and some processes are discussed only in general terms. OTA did have access to classified information in the course of the study and has prepared a classified annex to this report, which contains more detailed information regarding the nuclear weapons stockpile, future plans with respect to nuclear weapons, and related data.

6 | Dismantling the Bomb and Managing the Nuclear Materials

Box 1-B—Issues Related to Weapons Dismantlement and Materials Management

U.S. WEAPONS DISMANTLEMENT AND MATERIALS MANAGEMENT

Policy and Strategy

How many U.S. warheads are to be retired and dismantled?

How much weapons-grade plutonium and highly enriched uranium (HEU) from already dismantled weapons and from weapons planned for dismantlement will not be required for stockpile purposes, and can thus be declared surplus?

Should information about numbers of weapons to be dismantled and amounts of surplus materials from dismantled weapons be made public?

Should surplus plutonium pits from U.S. warheads be stored indefinitely or disposed of as waste?

Should surplus HEU from U.S. warheads be stored indefinitely or converted for use in commercial power reactors?

Should U.S. surplus materials be made amenable to monitoring or inspection under a bilateral arrangement with Russia?

Operations and Management

When will dismantlement of retired weapons or weapons planned to be retired be completed?

What additional measures should be taken to manage the dismantlement mission so as to protect the environment, as well as public and worker health and safety?

How long should plutonium pits from dismantled warheads be retained in temporary storage at Pantex—and the HEU from dismantled warheads in storage at Y-12?

What type of processing facility is needed to maintain the plutonium pits?

What type of facilities are needed for long-term storage of plutonium and HEU (pending some future use or disposal), and where could such facilities be located?

What type of technologies should be used if plutonium is deemed to be a waste, and what facilities are needed to implement disposal plans?

Should the surplus materials from dismantled warheads be stored separately from materials needed for weapons stockpile requirements?

To what extent can and should operational information be made available to the public, and how can public participation best be ensured?

Through what process will a site or sites be chosen for facilities required to carry out ultimate disposition options including long-term storage, conversion to fuel, or disposal as waste?

Organizational Structure

Should responsibility for management and disposition of surplus materials from warheads be retained in the Department of Energy's Defense Programs, or given to a new organization within DOE or another existing agency, or should a new organization be created for this purpose?

How should the transition be made between the present organizational structure and a potential future one?

How can external oversight and enforcement be strengthened—what agencies should be engaged, and what mechanisms should be developed?

RUSSIA'S NUCLEAR WEAPONS DISMANTLEMENT AND MATERIALS MANAGEMENT

How can the United States best encourage and aid Russia in dismantling warheads, and in the management and disposition of materials from them, and how should those efforts be structured?

Should the United States propose or enter into reciprocal arrangements with Russia involving information exchange, transparency, and inspections?

Should the United States encourage or promote any role by an international organization with respect to Russian weapons and nuclear materials?

Should the United States enter into joint study projects or provide technical assistance to Russia for processes leading to ultimate disposition of plutonium?

---

for possible future military use. The facilities that were used to recycle old warhead parts such as plutonium pits have been shut down, largely for environmental and safety reasons.

Plutonium pits from recently dismantled warheads are being stored at the Pantex Plant, where warhead disassembly takes place. DOE is running out of storage space for plutonium pits at Pantex and wants to change the storage configuration in existing bunkers to accommodate more pits, but the specific plan has not been approved yet. HEU from disassembled warheads is now being stored at the Y-12 facility, and there are no current plans to store it elsewhere.

■ Findings

The Nation's massive nuclear stockpile is now partly dismantled, partly in temporary storage, partly in transition, and partly deployed. Whereas past dismantlement activities were geared to maintaining the weapons stockpile, present and future activities are intended to permanently reduce it. Since fewer new weapons will be made, most of the materials recovered from dismantled warheads will no longer be recycled for use in other weapons. More plutonium and HEU will have to be stored and managed for long periods of time, and international factors may have significant impacts on materials management decisions. Yet, Federal programs and plans within DOD and DOE for retirement and dismantlement of nuclear weapons are currently treated as a short-term modification of existing practice, rather than a change in focus from the past missions of production and stockpile maintenance.

Existing and pending international agreements require only the removal of warheads from delivery systems. Preparation for long-term institutional custody of warheads and their nuclear materials lacks direction. DOE does not have comprehensive and accurate estimates of the total current or future annual costs of this enterprise, but available information indicates that DOE expenditures for dismantlement activities at all sites could be approaching $1 billion annually.

Thus far, there have been few if any serious problems with respect to dismantlement, but some process difficulties and logistical problems have caused schedule changes. One potential stumbling block is the storage of plutonium pits from warheads. Although DOE has stated that it needs to change the storage configuration in its World War II-vintage bunkers at Pantex to accommodate the anticipated number of pits coming from warheads, it has not yet produced the documentation required for approval. The State of Texas, community groups, and other experts have found DOE's environmental analysis to be deficient and have objected to the fact that DOE originally restricted access to the associated safety review. In addition, some citizen groups in Texas are concerned that although DOE says the pits will remain in "temporary storage" for 6 to 10 years, Pantex could turn into a de facto long-term storage site, and the pits may

8 | Dismantling the Bomb and Managing the Nuclear Materials

Box 1-C—Summary of Policy Initiatives

Congress could implement—or the Administration could undertake to implement—the following policy initiatives:

Initiative 1—A National Dismantlement Policy

Develop and announce a national policy that sets goals for warhead dismantment and materials management, and specifies the amount of plutonium and highly enriched uranium from dismantd warheads that will not be needed to support future stockpile requirements.

Initiative 2—Strengthening DOE Management

Implement a DOE management system that gives priority to protecting the environment, health, and safety; expand and strengthen external oversight of DOE dismantment and materials management activities by independent outside entities.

Initiative 3—Nuclear Materials Storage

Establish an interagency task force that includes Federal agencies with expertise in regulatory, international, and public involvement matters to recommend a plan for safe, secure storage of nuclear materials, and to develop a process acceptable to the interested public for siting new or modified storage facilities.

Initiative 4—Nuclear Materials Disposition

Create a national commission to recommend goals, policies, and programs for ultimate disposition of surplus plutonium and HEU from warheads, and to provide a basis for developing an ultimate disposition policy for these materials.

Initiative 5—A New Materials Management Organization

Create a new organization outside DOE to manage surplus materials from warheads, or establish a new organization for this purpose within DOE or some other existing agency.

Initiative 6—Information Access

Review and possibly revise the existing legal basis for restricting access to information in light of today's post-Cold War national security objectives, and accelerate efforts to increase access to information relevant to warhead dismantment and materials disposition.

Initiative 7—Cooperation with Russia

Strengthen the relationship between U.S. assistance to Russia for materials disposition and other programs in which assistance is desired by Russia; develop a means for joint assessment of plutonium disposition technologies; and negotiate mutual disclosure of information and reciprocal materials monitoring arrangements.

---

deteriorate before alternative storage arrangements are available.

Another stumbling block is DOE's poor record with respect to environmental and safety matters at its Nuclear Weapons Complex in the past, which has led to concerns among the interested public and affected communities about future DOE activities at those sites. Recent process difficulties during dismantlement at Pantex have caused the public to continue to question health and safety practices. Lack of public trust and credibility could adversely affect prospects for successful conduct of dismantlement and materials management activities.

While DOE is working on improvements to its environmental, health, and safety programs at the

Dismantlement means more than putting weapons under wraps like these "extinct" bombs at the National Atomic Museum in Albuquerque.

Nuclear Weapons Complex, current dismantlement activities still face problems, such as the use of old facilities, waste generation, and the slow adoption of modern worker health and safety practices. DOE's lack of public credibility could also have a negative impact on prospects for making key operational decisions regarding dismantlement and management of materials from warheads. Despite DOE's efforts to develop better public participation initiatives, the major dismantlement sites have yet to ensure adequate communications with the public, address public concerns, or involve the public in making decisions about dismantlement and materials management that could affect surrounding communities. In addition, considerable work remains to develop a national consensus around dismantlement goals and to ensure the protection of human safety, environmental integrity, and international security.

■ Policy Issues and Initiatives

Although present efforts to dismantle warheads and manage warhead materials are being treated by DOD and DOE as business as usual, these activities should be viewed as constituting a new mission with different challenges than in the past. Failure to effectively carry out the new mission here could adversely affect similar efforts abroad, with harmful consequences for international security and the global environment.

A NATIONAL DISMANTLEMENT POLICY

To define the new mission, and guide the agencies in implementing it, the Nation could establish a policy that sets forth the long-term goals and rationale for dismantlement. As part of that policy, decisions about the number of weapons to be retired and dismantled, as well as the time frame for dismantlement, would be made public. The Administration will also have to decide on the amount of plutonium and HEU currently available from dismantled warheads that is not needed to support nuclear weapons stockpile requirements and could be declared surplus to military needs. To aid this process, Congress could direct that an unclassified report containing such information be prepared and updated annually. This initiative would facilitate understanding of the rationale and goals of dismantlement; help ensure the public that future actions are consistent both with safety and protection of human health and the environment, and with U.S. strategic needs; and signal the international community that the United States is serious in its intent to dismantle warheads.

STRENGTHENING DOE MANAGEMENT

Although DOE is attempting to establish new guidelines for protecting the environment, health, and safety in its dismantlement and nuclear materials management activities, these matters require continuing attention. It is critical for DOE to develop a management system at all levels of its organization that is strongly committed to environmental, safety, and health improvements, and that effectively integrates this commitment into its operations. To help ensure that this occurs, external oversight of DOE's dismantlement and materials management program and plans should be strengthened. One way to accomplish this is for Congress to provide the Defense Nuclear Facilities Safety Board with the necessary re-

10 | Dismantling the Bomb and Managing the Nuclear Materials

sources and personnel (and any additional authority required) for this purpose. To assure communities around the sites that activities are being conducted properly, the Board—as well as DOE—could provide greater opportunity for public involvement than in the past. In addition, the Occupational Safety and Health Administration (OSHA) could be given jurisdiction over DOE worker health and safety.

In general, Congress could insist that DOE upgrade and strengthen its management systems to adopt and maintain high standards of worker health and safety, public health, and environmental protection.

MANAGEMENT OF NUCLEAR MATERIALS
■ Status

The two principal nuclear materials in warheads are plutonium and highly enriched uranium. Together or separately, they can be made into new warheads; thus there is a need to keep these materials safe and secured. Because of their radioactive half-lives, these materials will continue to pose some level of risk to human health and the environment for many thousands of years. OTA has thus focused on plutonium and HEU, although the disposition and disposal of many other materials from dismantled warheads are of concern.

A few hundred tons of plutonium and more than a thousand tons of HEU (exact numbers are classified) were produced worldwide for warheads. Today, this stockpile exists either in intact warheads or weapons, in forms ready to be made into warheads, or as pits and other forms removed from retired weapons. The United States and Russia have by far the largest portion of these materials. Both plutonium and uranium are also found in various forms and quantities in the nuclear industry worldwide, along with other

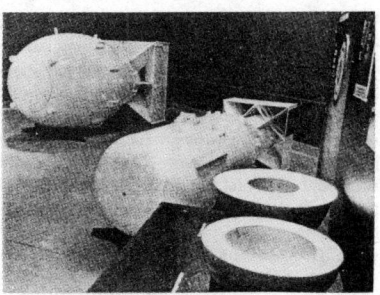

Models of World War II nuclear weapons Fat Man and Little Boy at the Bradbury Science Museum in Los Alamos, New Mexico. Conventional explosive hemispheres that surround the plutonium pit in a nuclear warhead are shown in the foreground.

industries that use nuclear materials. Some weapons-grade HEU is used in naval and research reactor fuel. Some plutonium that has been separated from commercial spent fuel could also be used in warheads even though it was not made for such use.

Nuclear materials taken from dismantled U.S. warheads, including plutonium pits placed in the bunkers at the Pantex Plant and HEU housed at the Oak Ridge Y-12 Plant, are considered to be in temporary or interim storage. Although DOE has stated its intention to store plutonium pits in temporary bunkers at Pantex for the next 6 to 10 years, it has not announced any plans to provide safe storage for the pits beyond that time. DOE also has not indicated its long-term storage plans for HEU.

Long-term or permanent solutions to the disposition[3] of these materials await policy decisions by the President and Congress. DOE has not declared any of this material to be surplus. However, recent DOE-sponsored studies have

---

[3] In this report, the term "disposition" means the spectrum of possibilities about what to do with these materials beyond weaponry—first to store them in a safe, secure facility; perhaps to destroy some portions if technically feasible and practical; perhaps to utilize them to produce civilian energy, if security is adequate and if the technology and economics prove sound; and finally to dispose of them as waste if technology and national policies permit.

focused on options for plutonium disposition through the use of various fuels containing plutonium in existing or advanced nuclear reactors. Within these reactors the plutonium would be irradiated and some of it converted to other radionuclides and fission products, possibly with the generation of electricity. Other studies have addressed plutonium storage for moderate to long-range time frames and techniques for turning plutonium into a form suitable for disposal as waste. Debate over these options is based largely on whether plutonium is viewed as a valuable asset whose beneficial uses are to be explored or a major liability to be disposed of in the safest and most secure way.

It is extremely difficult to convert significant amounts of plutonium into a substance that would be nonradioactive or harmless to health and the environment. Existing reactor technologies can be used to consume it as fuel, that is, to irradiate it and transform portions of it over time. Mixed-oxide (plutonium and uranium) fueled reactors are an example of existing technology that may be modified or adapted for plutonium disposition. Advanced reactor or converter technologies could be developed to achieve a large degree of plutonium transformation (and perhaps also to produce energy). However, available information indicates that their development would require significant time and resources, and it is uncertain how effective they would be. Alternatively plutonium could be disposed of more directly by using available technologies to embed it in other materials that make it difficult to recover (such as vitrified waste).

Some processing of nuclear materials is required to convert them into forms appropriate for many of the disposition options that have been proposed, including preparing them for disposal as waste. Processing of plutonium and uranium has historically raised environmental and public health concerns, as well as concerns about occupational health and safety. Regardless of the technology or disposition approach selected, radioactive waste will be generated and require long-term management.

■ Findings

Storage of plutonium and HEU from dismantled warheads will be required for one to several decades, regardless of what choices are made for ultimate disposition of these materials. DOE will present some approaches for a long-term storage facility as part of its Weapons Complex reconfiguration (in conjunction with the preparation of a Programmatic Environmental Impact Statement under the National Environmental Policy Act), and there are expected to be opportunities for public comment in that process.

Since the Administration has not made an official determination as to whether any plutonium and HEU from warheads will be declared surplus (e.g., not needed for future weapons), as yet there has been no comprehensive Federal planning process for the ultimate disposition or management of surplus materials. Discussions in and out of Government of plutonium disposition reveal little support for the use of surplus U.S. plutonium from warheads as fuel for U.S. commercial reactors. Some factors contributing to the lack of enthusiasm for this option are concerns of U.S. utilities about regulatory, public acceptance, and economic issues, as well as the fact that the United States has in the past discouraged commercial plutonium use because of proliferation concerns. DOE and certain private firms have expressed interest in the construction of special plutonium-fueled reactors at Federal sites to eliminate portions of weapons plutonium while also generating electricity.

Decisions about the fate of plutonium from U.S. weapons could influence similar decisions in Russia and other nations that may be planning to use plutonium in reactors. To reduce the world stockpile of plutonium that is readily available for weapons, actions need to be taken to discourage future production and to facilitate controlling the

12 | Dismantling the Bomb and Managing the Nuclear Materials

existing materials and making them unusable for weapons.

With respect to HEU from U.S. warheads, it is unlikely that this material will ever be considered waste. Technology is available to convert it for use as reactor fuel. However, current plans for introducing uranium extracted from Russian warheads into commercial U.S. power plants will probably precede any similar program for U.S. material. Thus, storage of HEU for several decades is a likely outcome, and safe, secure means for long-term storage must be planned.

■ Policy Issues and Initiatives

Eventually, the United States will have to decide what it ultimately wants to do with the stored plutonium and highly enriched uranium from its dismantled warheads. If none of it is declared surplus, presumably the plan would call for storage for an indefinite period or until it is needed for weapons. If some of the nuclear material from warheads is declared surplus, possible disposition options would include storing it indefinitely, converting it for use in existing or future reactors, or disposing of it as waste (not likely for uranium).

NUCLEAR MATERIALS STORAGE

Regardless of the ultimate disposition of plutonium and HEU from warheads, safe storage of these materials for several decades will have to be planned as soon as possible. There are many controversial and difficult issues that will take much time and effort to resolve. These include finding the most effective way to ensure safe and secure long-term storage of these materials, determining how such facilities should be regulated, and considering whether and how storage facilities can be made amenable to any bilateral or international inspections that may be agreed to in the future. Gaining public acceptance for the location of any new or modified facilities will be difficult. Because some of the issues that need to be addressed are not within the purview or expertise of DOE, it may not be desirable to confine the planning process to DOE. A broader planning process involving government agencies in addition to DOE could help identify, anticipate, and resolve key issues.

One way to provide such a process is for Congress or the President to establish an interagency task force to make recommendations about the best way to achieve safe and secure storage. The task force can also examine the feasibility and consequences of storing surplus plutonium and highly enriched uranium separately from materials reserved for stockpile requirements, and determine what type of arrangement would facilitate potential bilateral or international inspections. Also, because settling upon a suitable and acceptable location for nuclear materials storage will be a problem, the task force should consult with the public and attempt to develop a facility siting process that is agreeable to the potentially affected communities.

NUCLEAR MATERIALS DISPOSITION

In the longer term, a process will be needed to determine the ultimate disposition of surplus plutonium and HEU from warheads. So far, discussions of options have been carried on largely by technical experts and there is no consensus about most matters.

National policy on these issues is just beginning to be discussed, and the criteria against which options can be evaluated are only beginning to be considered. To help determine how nuclear materials are to be dealt with over the long term, a means should be developed to provide the President and Congress with a comprehensive basis for making the policy decisions necessary before long-term disposition of U.S. nuclear materials can begin. A preliminary step might be to obtain a broad range of governmental and nongovernmental views about what national policies, and the key criteria for evaluating them, should be. One mechanism for doing this is for the President or Congress to create a national commission that would evaluate the technical, institutional, and economic issues, and recommend goals, policies, and programs relevant to the ultimate disposition of nuclear materials from warheads.

A NEW MATERIALS MANAGEMENT ORGANIZATION

Whatever the outcome of decisions about storage and ultimate disposition of surplus plutonium and HEU, the present organization charged with this responsibility (DOE's Office of Defense Programs (DP)) may not be well suited to carry out the new nonmilitary mission of managing materials from warheads. Historically, its activities have been subject to minimal regulation, its operations have been conducted in secret, and it has not sought or welcomed public involvement or been concerned about the international implications of its actions. Its priorities continue to be maintaining the warhead stockpile.

In contrast, the mission of storing and dealing with surplus materials is essentially civilian in nature, and potentially subject to extensive domestic regulation and to scrutiny by the international community. It may be best to have an organization that is structured from the start to do this job in a way that gives priority to ensuring safety and protecting human health and the environment, operating in an open manner, involving the public more effectively, responding to public concerns, and being constantly aware of the international implications of its activities. Such an organization could be created within DOE. Alternatively, Congress could create an organization outside DOE (perhaps in some existing agency) to carry out activities related to the disposition of surplus nuclear materials from dismantled warheads.

INFORMATION ACCESS

∎ Status

The institutional framework for making decisions about nuclear warhead dismantlement and materials disposition is essentially the same as it was throughout the Cold War. The decisionmaking structure has historically been characterized by lack of regulation or outside oversight, restricted public access to information, and little if any public involvement. Current restrictions on access to information relevant to nuclear warhead dismantlement and materials disposition are based on legislative requirements generally intended to protect national security during the Cold War.

∎ Findings

The executive branch has undertaken some reviews of various Federal agency procedures related to classification and declassification of information, but those efforts are typically slow and may not address public concerns about the lack of information access in warhead dismantlement and materials management matters, particularly with respect to environmental, health, and safety issues.

Many of the restrictions on information enacted to meet the Cold War situation may no longer be necessary to preserve national security, although certain types of information about warhead design and manufacture must still be withheld because of potential terrorist activities and other security concerns. However, a great deal of information relevant to warhead dismantlement and materials management could be made more accessible, particularly data having to do with the environment, health, and safety.

∎ Policy Issues and Initiatives

In light of the increased authority of the States and of the public in activities at the Nuclear Weapons Complex, DOE will have to plan and conduct its dismantlement and materials management activities in a more open manner that will permit more public involvement. To facilitate public access to relevant information, legislative and administrative restrictions on information access should be evaluated to determine what changes are needed to suit the new circumstances of the post-Cold War era and enhance public

14 | Dismantling the Bomb and Managing the Nuclear Materials

involvement. Although the Administration is reviewing some of these matters, more attention could be devoted to efforts to revise current standards and procedures for access to information specifically related to warhead dismantlement and materials management. Also, Congress could review the Atomic Energy Act and other pertinent laws, or request that the Administration conduct such a review, and recommend changes to facilitate public access to appropriate data relevant to nuclear warhead dismantlement and materials management.

COOPERATION WITH RUSSIA

■ Status

Russia has announced plans to retire and dismantle a substantial portion of its nuclear weapons stockpile over the next decade or more. The United States has pledged several hundred million dollars for technical assistance in this connection, but only a small portion has been spent.

The Russians have indicated that a lack of storage for their nuclear materials, especially plutonium, is impeding their ability to dismantle warheads. After a series of discussions, the United States and Russia have agreed that Russia will design its own storage facility for special nuclear materials from warheads, with design assistance from the United States provided through the U.S. Army Corps of Engineers. The Russians plan to begin site preparation for this storage facility within a year, but many political, technical, and financial obstacles could hinder its successful completion in the near term.

U.S.-Russian agreements have also been reached on U.S. provision of, or assistance with, specific items such as armored blankets, warhead storage containers, emergency response systems, and secure rail cars to enhance the safe transport of weapons. However, these efforts have not had any significant effect yet on Russian warhead dismantlement—an objective that requires continuous emphasis at the highest levels of U.S. Government and by the several agencies designated to conduct the Russian assistance program.

With respect to the HEU from Russian weapons, the United States and Russia entered into an agreement in February 1993 (subject to terms not yet finalized) whereby 500 metric tons of the material would be converted to low-enriched uranium (LEU) in Russian facilities and then purchased by the United States. At least 10 metric tons would have to be converted in each of the first five years and 30 metric tons in each of the following years (for a total of 20 years). A final purchase agreement has yet to be executed, however.

An implementing agreement would specify price, certain conditions, and a method of sharing proceeds among other former Soviet republics. The contract is intended to provide for participation by both the U.S. private sector and Russian enterprises; it is also intended to establish "transparency measures" for materials control and accounting.

■ Findings

While the United States views expeditious Russian warhead dismantlement and materials disposition as vital to its national security, Russia's agenda is dominated by economic and political issues that could diminish the priority given to dismantlement. U.S. efforts to assist Russia with nuclear warhead dismantlement have initiated an important cooperative process but have not yet had a significant effect on the Russian dismantlement program. And they have not been carried out in a manner that addresses the broader issues of mutual goals and interests in stockpile reduction and materials management.

The U.S. purchase of Russian HEU from warheads is nearing final agreement and will contribute to a reduction of the materials available for new nuclear weapons there. However, it will be decades before large portions of the total Russian inventory of this material are converted and transferred to the United States, and therefore a significant risk of diversion will remain. The United States appears to have entered into this agreement without a fully articulated analysis of what further steps might be taken to improve the management and control of warhead materials to prevent their diversion.

The United States has not verified specific warhead dismantlement activities and accomplishments in Russia, and has no direct cooperative process for developing accurate information about Russian dismantlement status and capabilities. Further, the United States has not established a policy or approach to mutual dismantlement verification, warhead materials storage, or other materials management and control activities (including possible future production of warhead materials).

Efforts to integrate U.S. warhead dismantlement progress and plans with programs to assist Russia have not received adequate attention. There is also little linkage between Russian economic, environmental, or social needs and U.S. programs to assist or encourage Russian dismantlement and other related activities.

■ **Policy Issues and Initiatives**

The United States needs a plan for helping Russia's dismantlement and materials management process to proceed safely and without allowing warheads or warhead materials to get into the wrong hands. An important aspect of the plan is to increase coordination between the agencies responsible for U.S. materials management and disposition programs and those responsible for U.S. policy toward Russia. This is important because the United States must develop policies that utilize U.S. experience in its programs to assist Russia.

Because many problems and needs in Russia are unrelated to dismantlement, it is also important at this time to strengthen the link between U.S. assistance in nuclear materials disposition programs and other programs in which assistance is desired by Russia. It would help if there were cooperative efforts between the two nations in these matters.

To carry cooperative efforts further, an arrangement could be worked out with Russia whereby the United States would fund a 2-year joint study of materials disposition scenarios to be conducted by a U.S.-Russian multidisciplinary team based in Russia. To help ensure that dismantlement and materials disposition are proceeding safely and securely, the United States could also develop and negotiate with Russia an initiative for mutual disclosure of the amounts of weapons plutonium and highly enriched uranium possessed by each country.

An important issue is whether any storage or processing facilities used in connection with warhead dismantlement and materials management should be subject to international monitoring, inspections, or even control. In that regard, it remains to be seen whether the United States can realistically expect to verify, either directly or through international agencies, Russia's compliance with a specified rate of dismantlement—and its controlled storage of special nuclear material— without some reciprocal interest by Russia in verifying U.S. progress along the same lines. A high-level governmental process is needed to consider and address means to achieve reciprocal arrangements to verify the amounts and monitor the status of these materials in the future.

CONCLUSION

Reducing the nuclear weapons stockpile will not be simple, painless, or inexpensive. Although the work of retiring and disassembling weapons that are outdated or no longer needed in the stockpile is under way, the next critical steps in the process are uncertain because no national policy exists to guide future dismantlement and materials management activities in the United States. In addition, the United States has not developed an effective strategy for encouraging and assisting Russia in its efforts to safely dismantle its warheads, and to safely and securely manage the materials from them.

It is important that warhead dismantlement and materials management be conducted successfully both here and abroad. Failure to do the job right in the United States could create risks of accidents, dangers to workers, and harm to the environment and populations. In Russia, all of these risks exist, but there are also risks that the weapons or materials could be diverted and fall into the wrong hands.

Yet, the existing approach by the United States to both U.S. and Russian dismantlement is insufficient. As yet, the Nation has no coordinated, comprehensive policy on this subject and there has been little informed public debate on the establishment of national goals.

The prospects for successfully carrying out dismantlement and materials management activities in the future—and perhaps assisting Russia in similar efforts—can be improved if leadership is provided now at the highest levels of government. Policy guidance will be needed from these levels. To provide such guidance, the Federal Government will first have to articulate a national policy on dismantlement—a policy that sets the objectives and rationale for permanent stockpile reduction.

In sum, the challenge ahead requires planning and decisions in the near term if it is to be successful in the long term. The process deserves consistent and enduring talent, dedication, and resources, as well as astute management.

Executive Summary

Management and Disposition of Excess Weapons Plutonium

Committee on International Security and Arms Control

National Academy of Sciences

NATIONAL ACADEMY PRESS
Washington, D.C. 1994

NOTICE: This report has been reviewed by a group other than the authors according to procedures approved by the President of the National Academy of Sciences.

The National Academy of Sciences is a private, nonprofit, self-perpetuating society of distinguished scholars engaged in scientific and engineering research, dedicated to the furtherance of science and technology and to their use for the general welfare. Upon the authority of the charter granted to it by the Congress in 1863, the Academy has a mandate that requires it to advise the federal government on scientific and technical matters. Dr. Bruce M. Alberts is president of the National Academy of Sciences.

The National Academy of Engineering was established in 1964, under the charter of the National Academy of Sciences, as a parallel organization of outstanding engineers. It is autonomous in its administration and in the selection of its members, sharing with the National Academy of Sciences the responsibility for advising the federal government. The National Academy of Engineering also sponsors engineering programs aimed at meeting national needs, encourages education and research, and recognizes the superior achievement of engineers. Dr. Robert M. White is president of the National Academy of Engineering.

The Institute of Medicine was established in 1970 by the National Academy of Sciences to secure the services of eminent members of appropriate professions in the examination of policy matters pertaining to the health of the public. The Institute acts under the responsibility given to the National Academy of Sciences by its congressional charter to be an adviser to the federal government and, upon its own initiative, to identify issues of medical care, research, and education. Dr. Kenneth I. Shine is president of the Institute of Medicine.

The Committee on International Security and Arms Control is a standing committee of the National Academy of Sciences. Its membership includes members of all three bodies.

The National Research Council was organized by the National Academy of Sciences in 1916 to associate the broad community of science and technology with the Academy's purposes of furthering knowledge and advising the federal government. Functioning in accordance with general policies determined by the Academy, the Council has become the principal operating agency of both the National Academy of Sciences and the National Academy of Engineering in providing services to the government, the public, and the scientific and engineering communities. The Council is administered jointly by both Academies and the Institute of Medicine. Dr. Bruce M. Alberts and Dr. Robert M. White are chairman and vice-chairman, respectively, of the National Research Council.

This project was made possible with funding support from the Department of Energy, the John D. and Catherine T. MacArthur Foundation, and National Research Council funds. The MacArthur Foundation and the Carnegie Corporation of New York provide core support for the work of the Committee on International Security and Arms Control, including projects such as this.

This Executive Summary is available in limited quantities from the Committee on International Security and Arms Control, 2101 Constitution Avenue N.W., Washington, DC 20418.

The complete volume of *Management and Disposition of Excess Weapons Plutonium*, upon which this Executive Summary is based, is available for sale from the National Academy Press, 2101 Constitution Avenue N.W., Washington, DC 20418.

Copyright © 1994 by the National Academy of Sciences. All rights reserved.

Printed in the United States of America

COMMITTEE ON INTERNATIONAL SECURITY AND ARMS CONTROL

JOHN P. HOLDREN *(Chair)*, Class of 1935 Professor of Energy, University of California-Berkeley
CATHERINE MCARDLE KELLEHER *(Vice Chair)*, Senior Fellow, Foreign Policy Studies Program, The Brookings Institution
WOLFGANG K.H. PANOFSKY *(Plutonium Study Chair)*, Professor and Director Emeritus, Stanford Linear Accelerator Center, Stanford University
JOHN D. BALDESCHWIELER, Division of Chemistry and Chemical Engineering, California Institute of Technology
PAUL M. DOTY, Department of Biochemistry and Molecular Biology; and Director Emeritus, Center for Science and International Affairs, Harvard University
ALEXANDER H. FLAX, President Emeritus, Institute for Defense Analyses; and Senior Fellow, National Academy of Engineering
RICHARD L. GARWIN, IBM Fellow Emeritus, Thomas J. Watson Research Center, IBM Corporation
DAVID C. JONES, General (retired), U.S. Air Force
SPURGEON M. KEENY, JR., President, Arms Control Association
JOSHUA LEDERBERG, University Professor, The Rockefeller University
MICHAEL M. MAY, Director Emeritus, Lawrence Livermore National Laboratory
C. KUMAR N. PATEL, Vice Chancellor, Research, University of California-Los Angeles
JONATHAN D. POLLACK, Corporate Research Manager for International Policy, The RAND Corporation
JOHN D. STEINBRUNER, Director, Foreign Policy Studies Program, The Brookings Institution
ROBERT H. WERTHEIM, Rear Admiral (retired), U.S. Navy
JEROME B. WIESNER *(Consultant to the Chair)*, Institute Professor, Massachusetts Institute of Technology

Staff

JAMES WYNGAARDEN, ex officio, Foreign Secretary, National Academy of Sciences
JO L. HUSBANDS, Director
MATTHEW BUNN, Plutonium Study Director
LA'FAYE LEWIS-OLIVER, Administrative Assistant
MONICA OLIVA, Research Assistant
LOIS E. PETERSON, Research Associate

PANEL ON REACTOR-RELATED OPTIONS FOR THE DISPOSITION OF EXCESS WEAPONS PLUTONIUM

JOHN P. HOLDREN *(Chair)*, Class of 1935 Professor of Energy, University of California-Berkeley

JOHN AHEARNE, Executive Director, Sigma Xi, The Scientific Research Society

ROBERT BUDNITZ, President, Future Resources Associates

RICHARD L. GARWIN, IBM Fellow Emeritus, Thomas J. Watson Research Center, IBM Corporation

MICHAEL M. MAY, Director Emeritus, Lawrence Livermore National Laboratory

THOMAS PIGFORD, Professor of Nuclear Engineering, University of California-Berkeley

JOHN TAYLOR, Vice President, Nuclear Power Division, Electric Power Research Institute

Staff

MATTHEW BUNN, Plutonium Study Director
LA'FAYE LEWIS-OLIVER, Administrative Assistant
MONICA OLIVA, Research Assistant
LOIS E. PETERSON, Research Associate

Preface

With the end of the Cold War, the United States and the nations of the former Soviet Union are engaged in arms reductions on an unprecedented scale. What to do with the materials from the tens of thousands of nuclear weapons to be dismantled has become a pressing problem for international security. This study results from a request to the National Academy of Sciences' Committee on International Security and Arms Control (CISAC) by General Brent Scowcroft, then the National Security Adviser to President Bush. Scowcroft asked for a full-scale study of the management and disposition options for plutonium after hearing a CISAC briefing on its discussions in March 1992 with a counterpart group from the Russian Academy of Sciences. The Clinton administration confirmed CISAC's mandate in January 1993.

The formal U.S. government sponsor of the report is the Office of Nuclear Energy of the Department of Energy (DOE). Additional support for the project is being provided by the John D. and Catherine T. MacArthur Foundation and National Research Council funds. The MacArthur Foundation and the Carnegie Corporation of New York provide core support for CISAC, including its policy reports.

CISAC is a standing committee of the academy, unlike most National Research Council committees, which are formed to conduct a particular study and then dissolved. Established in 1980 to bring the scientific and technical capabilities of the academy to bear on problems of international security, CISAC's members include distinguished scientists, engineers, and policy experts. CISAC's objectives are to (1) engage similar organizations in other countries in discussions of international security and arms control policy; (2) develop recommendations and other initiatives on scientific and technical issues related to international security and arms control; and (3) respond to requests for analysis and information from the government. John P. Holdren (Class of 1935 Professor of Energy, University of California-Berkeley) serves

vi   PREFACE

as chair, with Catherine McArdle Kelleher (Senior Fellow, The Brookings Institution) as vice-chair.

CISAC's former chair, Wolfgang K.H. Panofsky (Professor and Director Emeritus, Stanford Linear Accelerator Center, Stanford University), chairs the plutonium study project. With the exception of Joshua Lederberg, who was unable to participate in the project, all members of CISAC took part in the study and have unanimously endorsed this report.

In carrying out its study, CISAC focused on the substantial security risks posed by these excess nuclear weapons and materials. The committee examined the stages of the reductions process, beginning with dismantlement of nuclear weapons, continuing through intermediate storage of the fissile materials from those weapons, and ending with long-term disposition of those materials. The committee focused specifically on the political and institutional context of these steps, both nationally and internationally. The committee has attempted to evaluate the consequences of each step for enduring, stable nuclear arms reductions and for improving the prospects for nuclear nonproliferation.

One important set of options would introduce the plutonium into nuclear reactors or into the waste stream from nuclear reactors. In order to supplement the committee's technical expertise for examining these options, CISAC formed a small Panel on Reactor-Related Options for the Disposition of Excess Weapons Plutonium, headed by John P. Holdren, to evaluate and make recommendations to the committee. The panel report, which is being published as a companion volume, was subject to a separate peer review by the National Academy of Sciences.

The study proved to be a huge undertaking, demanding hundreds of hours of research, discussion, and drafting from committee and panel members who were operating under a tight schedule to produce the report in time to be most valuable for U.S. policymaking. The committee and the panel received dozens of briefings from U.S. government and private experts, visited sites in the U.S. nuclear weapons production complex, and traveled to Russia, where they met with major figures involved in formulating that country's policy on disposition.

The CISAC staff provided invaluable assistance throughout the course of the study. Study Director Matthew Bunn, who supported both the committee and the panel reports, deserves special recognition. Not only did he draft much of the full committee report, and portions of the panel report, he also coordinated the effort and did research on key issues that greatly enriched the study. Mr. Bunn produced prodigious quantities of work in amazingly short time and made major intellectual contributions to the study's development. It could not have been completed without him.

CISAC's staff director, Jo Husbands, also deserves recognition. She provided crucial guidance and support throughout the study, with unfailing intelligence and unflappable good humor. She also kept the committee's other projects on track while the study was under way. Lois Peterson and Monica Oliva, CISAC's research associate and research assistant, respectively, labored long and hard to provide both substantive and administrative assistance, including much of the work of preparing the manuscript for publication. La'Faye Lewis-Oliver, CISAC's Administrative Assistant, provided essential administrative support throughout the process.

The issue of management and disposition of plutonium from arms reductions has a long history and a voluminous literature, stretching back almost to the beginning of the nuclear age. In recent years, these issues have been studied by a wide variety of groups and individuals in the United States, including those associated with the Department of Energy and other agencies of the U.S. government, the Office of Technology Assessment, the Natural Resources Defense Council, the Federation of American Scientists, the Center for Science and International Affairs at Harvard University, the Institute for Energy and Environmental Research, several Department of Energy laboratories, and a variety of private companies. Groups and individuals in Russia, Europe, Japan, and elsewhere have also examined the problem. In carrying out its study, CISAC benefited greatly from this substantial body of prior work, and extensive communications with many of those involved in it, for which the committee is profoundly grateful.

In addition, CISAC was fortunate to receive help from many parts of the Department of Energy. Staff members from DOE headquarters and facilities, including Hanford, Savannah River, Los Alamos, and Lawrence Livermore, generously gave time to help clarify and resolve technical issues, as well as providing access to relevant experts and materials. The Idaho National Engineering Laboratory merits particular recognition for its significant effort, without charge to the academy, to analyze several aspects of the reactor disposition options, such as nonfertile reactor fuels. Without this assistance, it would have been impossible for the committee to examine these issues in the depth required, with the time and personnel at its disposal.

Finally, but not least, CISAC received invaluable assistance from William G. Sutcliffe of Lawrence Livermore National Laboratory, who served as an unpaid consultant and an informal liaison to DOE for the project. His contacts and his own extensive knowledge of both the substance and the policy process for these issues were often indispensable.

There are no easy answers to the problems posed by the fissile materials that are part of the legacy of the Cold War arms competition between the United States and the former Soviet Union. As the committee makes clear in its study, the issues it addresses and the options it outlines and evaluates will

viii   *PREFACE*

be of critical importance to the future prospects for nonproliferation and arms reduction. Action is urgently needed, and the study is a road map to assist policymakers as they make these difficult choices. In CISAC's words, "The existence of this surplus material constitutes a clear and present danger to national and international security. None of the options yet identified for managing this material can eliminate this danger; all they can do is to reduce the risks."

Bruce Alberts
President, National Academy of Sciences

Contents

Executive Summary
    Principal Recommendations, 1
    Criteria and Context, 3
    The Proposed Weapons and Fissile Materials Regime, 7
    Intermediate Storage, 10
    Long-term Disposition, 12
    The Institutional Framework, 18

Recommendations
    Declarations and Dismantlement, 21
    Intermediate Storage, 22
    Disposition, 23
    Total Plutonium Inventories, 26

Appendix: Table of Contents of the Main Report, 29

Executive Summary

Under the first and second Strategic Arms Reduction Treaties (START I and II) and unilateral pledges made by Presidents Bush, Gorbachev, and Yeltsin, many thousands of U.S. and Russian nuclear weapons are slated to be retired within the next decade. As a result, 50 or more metric tons of plutonium on each side are expected to become surplus to military needs, along with hundreds of tons of highly enriched uranium (HEU). These two materials are the essential ingredients of nuclear weapons, and limits on access to them are the primary technical barrier to acquisition of nuclear weapons capability in the world today. Several kilograms of plutonium, or several times that amount of HEU, are sufficient to make a nuclear weapon.

The existence of this surplus material constitutes a clear and present danger to national and international security. None of the options yet identified for managing this material can eliminate this danger; all they can do is to reduce the risks. Moreover, none of the options for long-term disposition of excess weapons plutonium can be expected to substantially reduce the inventories of excess plutonium from nuclear weapons for at least a decade.

PRINCIPAL RECOMMENDATIONS

Our study of this problem leads us to the following four principal recommendations:

1. *A New Weapons and Fissile Materials Regime.* We recommend that the United States work to reach agreement with Russia on a new, reciprocal regime that would include:

   (a) declarations of stockpiles of nuclear weapons and all fissile materials;
   (b) cooperative measures to clarify and confirm those declarations;

2 EXECUTIVE SUMMARY

  (c) an agreed halt to the production of fissile materials for weapons; and
  (d) agreed, monitored net reductions from these stockpiles.

Monitoring of warhead dismantlement and commitment of excess fissile materials to non-weapons use or disposal, initially under bilateral and later under international safeguards, would be integral parts of this regime, as would some form of monitoring of whatever warhead assembly continues.

2. *Safeguarded Storage.* We recommend that the United States and Russia pursue a reciprocal regime of secure, internationally monitored storage of fissile material, with the aim of ensuring that the inventory in storage can be withdrawn only for non-weapons purposes.

3. *Long-Term Plutonium Disposition.* We recommend that the United States and Russia pursue long-term plutonium disposition options that:

  (a) minimize the time during which the plutonium is stored in forms readily usable for nuclear weapons;
  (b) preserve material safeguards and security during the disposition process, seeking to maintain the same high standards of security and accounting applied to stored nuclear weapons;
  (c) result in a form from which the plutonium would be as difficult to recover for weapons use as the larger and growing quantity of plutonium in commercial spent fuel; and
  (d) meet high standards of protection for public and worker health and for the environment.

The two most promising alternatives for achieving these aims are:

- fabrication and use as fuel, without reprocessing, in existing or modified nuclear reactors; or
- vitrification in combination with high-level radioactive waste.

A third option, burial of the excess plutonium in deep boreholes, has until now been less thoroughly studied than have the first two options, but could turn out to be comparably attractive.

4. *All Fissile Material.* We recommend that the United States pursue new international arrangements to improve safeguards and physical security over all forms of plutonium and HEU worldwide. In particular, new cooperative efforts to improve security and accounting for all fissile materials in the former Soviet Union should be an urgent priority.

Because plutonium in spent fuel or glass logs incorporating high-level wastes still entails a risk of weapons use, and because the barrier to such use diminishes with time as the radioactivity decays, consideration of further steps to reduce the long-term proliferation risks of such materials is required, regardless of what option is chosen for disposition of weapons plutonium. This global effort should include continued consideration of more proliferation-resistant nuclear fuel cycles, including concepts that might offer a long-term option for nearly complete elimination of the world's plutonium stocks.

On September 27, 1993, the Clinton administration announced a non-proliferation initiative that included some first steps in the directions recommended above, among them a proposal for a global convention banning production of fissile materials for weapons; a voluntary offer to put U.S. excess fissile materials under International Atomic Energy Agency (IAEA) safeguards; and a recognition that plutonium disposition is an important nonproliferation problem requiring renewed interagency, and ultimately international, attention. This is a much needed and timely start; more, however, remains to be done.

CRITERIA AND CONTEXT

The steps we recommend are designed to meet three key security objectives:

1. to minimize the risk that either weapons or fissile materials could be obtained by unauthorized parties;
2. to minimize the risk that weapons or fissile materials could be reintroduced into the arsenals from which they came, thereby halting or reversing the arms reduction process; and
3. to strengthen the national and international arms control mechanisms and incentives designed to ensure continued arms reductions and prevent the spread of nuclear weapons.

Other key criteria include protecting worker and public health and the environment; being acceptable to the public and the institutions whose approval is needed; and, to the extent consistent with other criteria, minimizing costs and delays.

We note that the expenditures implied by all our recommendations combined would total at most several billion dollars, spread over a period of a decade or decades. Since the primary objective is the reduction of major security risks, these expenditures should be considered in the context of the far larger sums being spent every year to provide national and international security. Thus, although the costs of alternate approaches are important and are discussed in the report, cost is not the primary criterion in choosing among competing options. Moreover, exploiting the energy value of plutonium should not be a central criterion for decision making, both because the cost of fabricating

4 EXECUTIVE SUMMARY

and safeguarding plutonium fuels makes them currently uncompetitive with cheap and widely available low-enriched uranium fuels, and because whatever economic value this plutonium might represent now or in the future is small by comparison to the security stakes.

World Stocks of Fissile Materials

The problem of management and disposition of excess weapons plutonium must be considered in the context of the large world stocks of fissile materials. While all but a small fraction of the world's HEU is in military use, civilian stocks of plutonium are several times larger than military stocks and are growing much faster, by some 60 to 70 tons each year. Most of these civilian stocks, however, are in the form of radioactive spent fuel from the world's power reactors, from which the plutonium is difficult to extract. The difficulty of extracting this plutonium declines substantially as the radioactivity of the fuel decays over the decades after it leaves the reactor. Roughly 130 tons of plutonium have been separated from spent fuel for reuse as reactor fuel, of which some 80 to 90 tons remains in storage in separated form.

Plutonium customarily used in nuclear weapons (weapons-grade plutonium) and plutonium separated from spent reactor fuel (reactor-grade plutonium) have different isotopic compositions. Plutonium of virtually any isotopic composition, however, can be used to make nuclear weapons. Using reactor-grade rather than weapons-grade plutonium would present some complications. But even with relatively simple designs such as that used in the Nagasaki weapon—which are within the capabilities of many nations and possibly some subnational groups—nuclear explosives could be constructed that would be assured of having yields of at least 1 or 2 kilotons. Using more sophisticated designs, reactor-grade plutonium could be used for weapons having considerably higher minimum yields. Thus, the difference in proliferation risk posed by separated weapons-grade plutonium and separated reactor-grade plutonium is small in comparison to the difference between separated plutonium of any grade and unseparated material in spent fuel.

While plutonium and HEU can both be used to make nuclear weapons, there are two important differences between them. The first is that HEU can be diluted with other, more abundant, naturally occurring isotopes of uranium to make low-enriched uranium (LEU), which cannot sustain the fast-neutron chain reaction needed for a nuclear explosion. LEU is the fuel for most of the world's nuclear power reactors. In contrast, plutonium cannot be diluted with other isotopes of plutonium to make it unusable for weapons. "Re-enriching" LEU to the enrichment needed for weapons requires complex enrichment technology to which most potential proliferators do not have access, while separating plutonium from other elements with which it might be mixed in fresh reactor fuel requires only straightforward chemical processing. Thus, the management of plutonium in any form requires greater security than does the management of LEU.

Second, as noted earlier, in the current nuclear fuel market, the use of plutonium fuels is generally more expensive than the use of widely available LEU fuels—even if the plutonium itself is "free"—because of the high fabrication costs resulting from plutonium's radiological toxicity and from the security precautions required when handling it. As a result, while most of the world's roughly 400 nuclear reactors could in principle burn plutonium in fuel containing a mixture of uranium and plutonium (mixed-oxide or MOX fuel), few—and none in the United States—are currently licensed to do so.

The United States has agreed to buy 500 tons of surplus Russian HEU, blended to LEU, for $11.9 billion over the next 20 years, provided certain conditions are met. The United States will later resell the material to fulfill the demand for nuclear fuel on the domestic and world markets. While the purchase of Russian plutonium could, similarly, be justified on security grounds, both the security aspects and the economics of using plutonium as reactor fuel would be less attractive than in the case of LEU.

Because of the more difficult technical and policy issues involved, this report focuses primarily on the disposition of plutonium rather than HEU.

The International Environment

The management and disposition of plutonium from dismantled nuclear weapons will take place within a complex international context that includes the arms reduction and nonproliferation regimes of which this problem is an element, the continuing crisis in the former Soviet Union, worldwide plans for civilian nuclear energy (particularly the use of separated plutonium), and existing approaches to safeguards and security for nuclear materials.

Recent *nuclear arms reduction* agreements and pledges, along with national decisions concerning what stocks of plutonium are to be declared "excess," will largely set the parameters of how much plutonium will require disposition and when it will become available. The reductions agreements entail a complex and uneven schedule of reductions in deployed launchers between now and 2003. As yet, no agreement exists to govern the dismantlement of the surplus nuclear weapons, or the modes of storage and eventual disposition of the fissile materials, although discussions of some aspects of the problem are under way. Mutually agreed, monitored provisions for the disposition of fissile materials could help enhance political support for implementation of START II and for agreement on deeper reductions.

6 EXECUTIVE SUMMARY

The current *crisis in the former Soviet Union* creates a variety of risks with respect to the management and disposition of nuclear weapons and fissile materials. We categorize these as dangers of:

- "breakup," meaning the emergence of multiple nuclear-armed states where previously there was only one;
- "breakdown," meaning erosion of government control over nuclear weapons and materials within a particular state; and
- "breakout," meaning repudiation of arms reduction agreements and pledges, and reconstruction of a larger nuclear arsenal.

Breakup is the most immediate threat, mainly because of uncertainty over whether Ukraine will carry out its denuclearization pledges. Security concerns may well be the driving factors in Ukraine's ultimate decision, but that decision could be affected by measures that ensure that weapons and fissile materials transferred to Russia will not be reused for military purposes, and that provide compensation for these materials.

Breakdown of the elaborate system of control of nuclear weapons and fissile materials in the former Soviet Union remains a possibility, despite Russian efforts to maintain the former Soviet systems for this purpose. The thefts of conventional weapons and nuclear materials other than plutonium and HEU that have already occurred are disturbing. Enhanced assistance in improving security and accounting for fissile materials in the former Soviet Union is a potentially high-leverage area deserving urgent attention. The broad regime of accounting we recommend could provide an important basis for additional steps to improve security of these materials.

Breakout seems unlikely in the near term. The significant nuclear arsenals that each side will retain under START II will further reduce any motivation that a future Russian government might have for taking such a step. Ratification and implementation of START I and START II are not yet assured, however. The steps that we outline would reduce the potential for breakout, and provide a foundation for deeper reductions and for the inclusion of additional parties in the future.

The foundation of the *nuclear nonproliferation regime* is the Non-Proliferation Treaty (NPT), which is up for extension in 1995. Agreements for secure, safeguarded management and disposition of fissile materials from surplus nuclear weapons could help make clear that the nuclear powers are fulfilling their disarmament obligations under Article VI of the NPT. Moreover, acceptance by the major nuclear powers of safeguards and constraints on substantial portions of their nuclear programs would help to reduce the inherently discriminatory nature of the nonproliferation regime. These steps, while probably not dissuading all nations that might be attempting to acquire nuclear weapons, would help build global political support for indefinite extension of the NPT and strengthening the regime, which are major U.S. policy goals.

International efforts to reduce the proliferation risks posed by the existence of civilian plutonium and enriched uranium rest on *safeguards*, which are national and international measures designed to detect diversion of materials and enable a timely response, and *security*, which consists of (currently national) measures designed to prevent theft of materials through the use of barriers, guards, and the like. Standards for both vary widely. Those applied to civilian materials, even separated plutonium and HEU, are less stringent than those applied to nuclear weapons and fissile material in military stocks. Varying and lower standards may be justified in the case of spent fuel for the first decades outside the reactor, when its high radioactivity makes it difficult to steal or divert, but they are not justified in the case of separated civilian plutonium or HEU. New steps toward improved and consistent international standards should be pursued.

Choices regarding the fissile materials from dismantled weapons may also affect and be affected by *civilian nuclear power programs*, a topic that depends on economic, political, and technical factors outside the scope of this study. In some countries, nuclear power programs already include the use of plutonium in the fuel loaded into reactors. But the amount of weapons plutonium likely to be surplus is small on the scale of global nuclear power use—the equivalent of only a few months of fuel for existing reactors—and it is not essential to the future of civilian nuclear power. There is thus no reason that disposition of this weapons plutonium should drive decisions on the broader questions surrounding the future of nuclear power.

The production of tritium was not part of our charge, and we have not examined alternatives for this purpose in detail. We believe, however, that there is no essential reason why plutonium disposition and tritium production need be linked, and there appear to be good arguments why they should not be. Technically, the scale of the plutonium disposition task is very much larger than any tritium production requirement. From a policy perspective, producing weapons materials in the same facility that was destroying other weapons materials would raise political and safeguards issues.

THE PROPOSED WEAPONS AND FISSILE MATERIALS REGIME

We recommend a broad transparency regime for nuclear weapons and fissile materials, as outlined above. This regime could be approached step-by-step, with each step adding to security while posing little risk. The regime we envision would include a variety of measures applying to each phase of the life cycle of military fissile materials: production and separation of the materials;

8   EXECUTIVE SUMMARY

fabrication of fissile material weapons components; assembly, deployment, retirement, and disassembly of nuclear weapons; and storage and eventual disposition of fissile materials. These measures should be mutually reinforcing, to build confidence that the information exchanged is accurate and that the goals of the regime are being met.

There is likely to be some resistance to a regime of full accounting and monitoring of total weapons and fissile material stocks and facilities, but such a regime meets objectives shared by the United States and Russia (and, for that matter, by many other countries). Moreover, extensive data exchanges and verification measures have already been agreed for deployed strategic nuclear forces and other military systems.

Declarations of total stocks of weapons and fissile materials, with their locations, coupled with exchanges of operating records and inspections of material production sites, would reduce the large uncertainty in present estimates of these stocks. Fissile material production facilities and their operating records can be examined to confirm consistency with reported production figures, and stocks of fissile materials and weapons at declared sites can be confirmed through routine and occasional challenge inspections. The commitment of the Russian and U.S. governments to such declarations and the progressive opening of Russian society should make it less likely that a stockpile or production facility of any significant size could be hidden.

Dismantlement should also be monitored. The United States is dismantling its nuclear weapons at a rate of somewhat less than 2,000 per year, with a goal of increasing that rate to 2,000—the maximum rate permitted by available facilities; personnel; and environment, safety, and health (ES&H) considerations. The plutonium components ("pits") are being placed intact into containers and put in intermediate storage at the Pantex disassembly site near Amarillo, Texas. The HEU components are being shipped to the Y-12 plant at Oak Ridge, Tennessee, for storage and eventual use as naval or civilian reactor fuel. Russian spokesmen have declared that Russia is dismantling nuclear weapons at four sites, at a rate comparable to the U.S. rate, and is storing the materials at several existing sites.

Neither the United States nor Russia plans to monitor the other's dismantlement, although limited Ukrainian monitoring is reported to be in place in Russia. Means exist or could be developed to monitor dismantlement without undue interference or costs, while protecting sensitive information. As with other parts of the regime, some declassification would be necessary to permit effective monitoring. The basic approach would be a variant of the perimeter-portal monitoring system now in place to verify that missiles banned by the Intermediate-Range Nuclear Forces treaty are not being produced; warheads entering and leaving the facility would be counted, and amounts of fissile material measured. Such monitoring could be applied without undue interference with necessary maintenance and modification of the remaining military stockpile.

A *cutoff of production of weapons materials* would require monitoring of enrichment and reprocessing facilities. Still greater confidence could be achieved if all fuel cycle facilities were monitored. These tasks could be carried out by bilateral or international monitors (or both), using means that have met international acceptance in nonproliferation verification. Continued production of HEU for naval reactors and tritium for nuclear stockpile maintenance would introduce some complications, but these could readily be addressed through careful design of the agreement and the monitoring system.

The United States is no longer producing plutonium or HEU for weapons. Russia has also ceased production of HEU for weapons, but is still operating plutonium production reactors and separating the resulting weapons-grade plutonium. The Russian government asserts that these reactors provide necessary heat and power to surrounding areas, and that the fuel must be reprocessed for safety reasons. The United States has begun discussions with Russia about assistance in converting these reactors so that separated weapons plutonium is not generated, or in providing alternate power sources, but these discussions remain embryonic.

Internationalizing the Regime

The security goals outlined above would be best served if the standards set by this regime for managing U.S. and Russian excess weapons and fissile materials were extended worldwide. In particular, new agreements should be pursued to:

1. create consistent, stringent international standards of accounting and security for fissile materials;
2. end all production of fissile materials for nuclear weapons, worldwide;
3. create an international system of declarations and inspections covering declared nuclear weapons arsenals, including reserves, and fissile material stocks (complementing the declarations and inspections already required of non-nuclear-weapon-state parties to the Non-Proliferation Treaty); and
4. create an international safeguarded storage regime under which all civilian fissile materials not in immediate use would be placed in agreed safeguarded storage sites, with agreed levels of physical security.

The IAEA secretariat and organizations in several countries are now working on concepts for such universal reporting and safeguarding of civilian fissile materials. These steps, and others that we recommend, would require increased resources for the IAEA, as well as organizational improvements. In some cases resources could be provided specifically for a new task. But the agency also urgently needs more resources overall.

INTERMEDIATE STORAGE

Present and Planned Arrangements

It will be necessary to provide secure intermediate storage of surplus weapons plutonium for decades, since long-term disposition will take years to start and possibly decades to complete. In both the United States and Russia, fissile materials from dismantled weapons are currently stored in the form of weapons components, some at the dismantlement site and some elsewhere. Neither country has yet decided how much will be held in reserve. No monitoring or transparency measures relating to storage of these fissile materials are yet in place, although the Clinton administration has announced that U.S. excess fissile materials will be placed under international safeguards, and Russia has expressed willingness to do the same. Russia and the United States also have tens of tons of weapons-grade plutonium not incorporated in weapons that are stored in various forms at several sites in their weapons complexes.

In the United States, plutonium from weapons is being stored temporarily in simple "igloos" at Pantex, the dismantlement site. This arrangement provides high security and generally adequate standards of protection for environment, safety, and health. Given the stability of both the pits and the facilities at the site, there is no technical or economic reason why this arrangement could not be continued for a considerable time, but the public and the authorities in the area surrounding the site have been assured that interim storage there will not be extended beyond a decade. To meet that pledge, and to provide improved storage for plutonium in other forms now stored at several widely dispersed sites, the Department of Energy proposes to invest in a new, consolidated facility for long-term storage at a site to be selected. No full analysis of the advantages and disadvantages of this approach compared to upgrading existing storage facilities has been completed. We therefore do not offer a recommendation, though we recognize the safeguards and security advantages that a new consolidated facility might offer.

Less is known about Russian storage arrangements. Russia has requested, and the United States has agreed to provide, assistance in constructing a storage facility for excess fissile materials from weapons. We support construction of a facility designed to consolidate all these excess weapons materials, as this would facilitate security and international monitoring.

There is considerable debate concerning the optimum physical form in which to store plutonium. We recommend that, for the time being, plutonium continue to be stored in the form of intact weapons components. Decades of experience have demonstrated that pits are relatively safe and stable, and storage in this form would postpone the costs and ES&H issues of conversion to other forms. Although the design of pits is sensitive, international monitors could externally assay the amount of plutonium in a canister containing a pit without, in most cases, revealing sensitive design information. Intact pits can more easily be reused for weapons by the state that produced them than plutonium in other forms, but they probably do not pose substantially greater proliferation risks than storage as deformed pits or metal ingots. Deformation of pits and perhaps other steps to reduce the rearmament risk should be given serious consideration, and should be undertaken if they can be accomplished at relatively low cost and ES&H risk.

One cannot be confident, however, that plutonium in pits can be stored without degradation for more than a few decades. When a definite decision regarding long-term disposition has been made, the pits should be converted into the forms required for that disposition option, under agreed safeguards and security.

A New Storage Regime

The following measures constitute a regime for intermediate storage of surplus fissile materials that serves the objectives noted earlier with minimum disruption to the process of dismantlement and storage:

1. *Commitment to Non-Weapons Use.* The United States and Russia should commit a large fraction of the fissile materials from dismantled weapons to non-weapons use. They should agree on the specific amounts.

2. *Safeguarded Storage and Disposition.* The preceding commitment should be verified by monitoring of the present and future sites where fissile materials are stored, and continued monitoring of the material after it leaves these sites for long-term disposition.

3. *IAEA Involvement.* Although such monitoring might begin bilaterally, the IAEA should be brought into the process expeditiously, in an expansion and strengthening of its nonproliferation role. The IAEA would monitor the amount of material in the storage site and safeguard any material removed from the site to ensure its use for peaceful purposes. Such safeguards would be an extension of the existing safeguards system. Bilateral monitoring would probably continue as well.

Financial or other incentives could be provided to Russia for putting the material into storage. Management, control, or outright ownership of the stores and the material in them might be transferred to other parties, such as an international consortium formed for that purpose. The material might even be physically relocated to some other country, possibly in return for cash, as in the case of the HEU deal. Such incentives would not obviate the need for, and are secondary to, prompt agreement on a storage regime along the lines recommended here.

LONG-TERM DISPOSITION

Categories, Criteria, and Standards

The technical options for long-term disposition of excess weapons plutonium can be divided into three categories:

- *indefinite storage*, in which the storage arrangements outlined in the previous section would be extended indefinitely;
- *minimized accessibility*, in which physical, chemical, or radiological barriers would be created to reduce the plutonium's accessibility for use in weapons (either by potential proliferators or by the state from whose weapons it came), for example, by irradiating the plutonium in reactors or mixing it with high-level wastes; and
- *elimination*, in which the plutonium would be made essentially completely inaccessible, for example, by burning it in reactors so completely that only a few grams would remain in a truckload of spent fuel, or by launching it into deep space.

In both the "minimized accessibility" and the "elimination" categories, some of the options *use* the plutonium to generate electricity, while others *dispose* of the plutonium without using its energy content. Both classes of options would involve net economic costs. The electricity generation options would produce revenues, but the costs of using plutonium to produce this electricity would be higher than the costs of generating it using enriched uranium. The current Russian government nonetheless sees weapons plutonium as a valuable asset and therefore strongly prefers options that use the plutonium.

Risks of Storage. Although intermediate storage is an inevitable step preceding all disposition options, it should not be extended longer than necessary. Maintaining this material in a readily weapons-usable form over the long term would send negative political signals for nonproliferation and arms reduction, and the security offered by indefinite storage against the risks of breakout and theft is entirely dependent on the durability of the political arrangements. Indeed, one of the key criteria by which disposition options should be judged is the speed with which they can be accomplished, and thus how rapidly they curtail these risks of storage.

Risks of Handling—The "Stored Weapons Standard." Although options in the "minimized accessibility" and "elimination" classes decrease the long-term accessibility of the material for weapons use, they could increase the short-term risks of theft or diversion because of the required processing and transport steps. In order to ensure that the overall process reduces net security risks, an agreed and stringent standard of security and accounting must be maintained throughout the disposition process, approximating as closely as practicable the security and accounting applied to intact nuclear weapons. We call this the "stored weapons standard." These risks of handling are a second key criterion for judging disposition options.

Risks of Recovery—The "Spent Fuel Standard." A third key security criterion for judging disposition options is the risk of recovery of the plutonium after disposition. We believe that options for the long-term disposition of weapons plutonium should seek to meet a "spent fuel standard"—that is, to make this plutonium roughly as inaccessible for weapons use as the much larger and growing quantity of plutonium that exists in spent fuel from commercial reactors. Options that left the plutonium more accessible than these existing stocks would mean that this material would continue to pose a unique safeguards problem indefinitely. Conversely, the costs, complexities, risks, and delays of going beyond the spent fuel standard to eliminate the excess weapons plutonium completely, or nearly so, would not be justified unless the same approach were to be taken with the global stock of civilian plutonium. Over the long term, however, steps beyond the spent fuel standard will be necessary—for both the weapons plutonium and the larger civilian stock—as described below.

In addition, policymakers will have to take into account the political impact that the use of excess weapons plutonium in reactors, or the disposal of that plutonium, would have on nuclear fuel cycle debates abroad. Whatever choice it makes, the United States will have to explain how that choice fits into the broader context of its nonproliferation and fuel cycle policies.

The Preferred Approaches

The best means of plutonium disposition may well differ in the United States and Russia, given that the two countries have different economies, reactor and waste infrastructures, and plutonium fuel policies, and given that very different safeguards and security risks currently pertain.

As noted above, there are two options that hold especially strong promise of being able to meet the criteria just outlined: the use of plutonium as fuel in existing or modified reactors without reprocessing, and vitrification together with high-level wastes. A third option, burial in deep boreholes, might prove

14   EXECUTIVE SUMMARY

on further study to be on a par with the first two. We now describe each of these options in turn.

The Spent Fuel Option

Excess weapons plutonium could be used as fuel in reactors, transforming it into intensely radioactive spent fuel similar in most respects to the spent fuel produced in commercial reactors today. This use could probably begin within approximately 10 years (paced by obtaining the necessary fuel fabrication capability and the needed approvals and licenses) and be completed within 20 to 40 years thereafter (paced by the number of reactors used, the fraction of the reactor core using plutonium fuel, the percentage of plutonium that this fuel contains, and the amount of time that the fuel remains in the reactor). Examples include:

- *U.S. Light-Water Reactors.* The predominant commercial reactors in the world today are light-water reactors (LWRs). Without major modifications, typical LWRs could burn a fuel consisting of mixed oxides of plutonium and uranium (MOX) in one-third of their reactor cores. Four existing LWRs in the United States (three operational at Palo Verde in Arizona, and one 75 percent complete in Washington State) were designed to use MOX in 100 percent of their reactor cores; a single such reactor, using fuel containing somewhat more plutonium than would be used if energy production alone were the aim, could transform 50 tons of weapons plutonium into spent fuel in 30 years. Alternatively, other operating or partly completed reactors could also be modified to use full MOX cores, or a new full-MOX reactor might be built on a government site, with costs partly offset by later sales of electricity.

Although the United States has no operating MOX fuel fabrication capability, there is an unfinished facility at the Hanford site that could be completed and modified for this purpose; alternatively, a new MOX facility could be built in roughly a decade, at significantly higher cost.

This option is technically demonstrated, as LWRs in several countries are burning MOX fuels today. Environmental, health, and safety risks can be minimized with the application of money and good management, although some of the specifics of how best to do so require further study. Use of MOX fuels, however, would be controversial in the United States, where such fuels are not now used, and gaining licenses and public approval could raise difficulties. The subsidy required to transform 50 tons of plutonium into spent fuel in this way (compared to the cost of producing the same electricity by the means with which it would otherwise be produced) would probably fall in the range from a few hundred million to a few billion dollars, depending on assumptions and on the specific approach chosen.

EXECUTIVE SUMMARY 15

- *Russian Light-Water Reactors.* Similarly, Russian plutonium could be used as MOX in Russian VVER-1000 reactors (the only existing reactors in Russia likely to be safe enough and long-lived enough for this mission). VVER-1000s that are not yet operational, but that the Russian government plans to complete for electricity production, could be modified to handle full MOX cores, or such modifications could be incorporated in operating reactors during the shutdowns for safety improvements that are now planned. Because of the current political and social upheaval in Russia, safeguards and security risks would be substantial. The current Russian government's preference for storing plutonium until it can be used in the next generation of Russian liquid-metal fast reactors is not attractive because of the indefinite time before disposition could begin, the security liabilities of prolonged storage, and the high cost of these reactors.

- *CANDUs.* Existing Canadian deuterium-uranium (CANDU) reactors are a technically attractive possibility for this mission, because the reactor design allows them inherently to handle full-MOX cores, with less change from the usual physics of the reactor than in the case of LWRs. The cost of this option is difficult to estimate, as no one has yet attempted to fabricate MOX fuel for CANDU reactors on any significant scale. We do not know whether the opportunity for Canada to participate in an important disarmament process, combined with possible U.S. subsidies for the project, would be attractive enough to cause that country to reverse its long-standing policy against the use of fuels other than natural uranium in its power reactors.

- *Substitution for Civilian Plutonium.* Utilities in Europe and Japan currently plan to use more than 100 tons of reactor-grade plutonium in MOX fuels over the next decade. If excess weapons plutonium from Russia or the United States were substituted for this material—with an associated delay in separation of plutonium from civilian spent fuel, so that additional excess stocks of civilian plutonium did not build up as a result—disposition of 50 or even 100 tons of plutonium could be accomplished relatively rapidly (since the facilities required are already built and licensed, or scheduled to be) and with comparatively small *net additional* safeguards risks (since after the initial transport, all the facilities handling plutonium would have done so in any case). However, the agreements required to implement this option would be complex and probably difficult to reach. Substantial changes in a variety of existing contracts and programs would have to be made, and transport of weapons plutonium to these countries would be controversial.

- *New Reactors for the Plutonium Mission.* Given the high costs and long times required for the construction of new reactors, building such reactors for the mission of transforming weapons plutonium into spent fuel would be

16   EXECUTIVE SUMMARY

justifiable only if problems of licensing and public acceptance made currently operating or partly completed reactors unavailable (and only, of course, if the reactor-MOX option were deemed preferable to the vitrification and deep-borehole approaches). If that proves to be the case, the new reactors should be built on a government-owned site and should be of sufficiently well-proven design so as not to create additional technical and licensing uncertainties. Reactors we have examined of more advanced design do not offer sufficient advantages for this mission to offset the extra costs and delays that their use would entail. In particular, the use of advanced reactors and fuels to achieve high plutonium consumption without reprocessing is not worthwhile, because the consumption fractions that can be achieved—between 50 and 80 percent—are not sufficient to greatly alter the security risks posed by the material remaining in the spent fuel. Development of advanced reactors and fuel types is of interest for the future of nuclear electricity generation, including the minimization of safety and security risks, but the timing and scope of such development need not and should not be governed by the current weapons plutonium problem.

The Vitrification Option

An alternative means of creating similar radioactive and chemical barriers to weapons use of this material would be to mix it with radioactive high-level waste (HLW) left from the separation of plutonium from weapons and other defense activities. Under current plans, HLW will be mixed with molten glass (vitrified) to produce large glass logs. These logs, like spent reactor fuel, will be stored for an interim period and then placed in a geologic repository. The logs would pose radiological barriers to handling and processing similar to those of spent LWR fuel a few decades old. Incorporating plutonium into these logs appears feasible, although technical questions remain. These technical issues are more substantial than those facing the MOX options, but licensing and public approval appear easier to obtain in the vitrification case, at least in the United States. Vitrification raises fewer security risks in handling than the MOX option, because the process of mixing plutonium with HLW would be easier to safeguard than the more complex process of fabricating MOX. This might be of particular importance in the current Russian context. Russian vitrification efforts have so far focused on a phosphate glass that is less appropriate for this mission than the borosilicate glass used in the United States and elsewhere because it is less durable and offers less protection against the possibility of an unplanned nuclear chain reaction once plutonium is embedded in it. New technologies for comparatively small melters could be transferred to Russia for this purpose. So far, however, the Russian officials responsible for these issues have rejected disposal options such as vitrification.

The Deep-Borehole Option

Disposal in deep boreholes has been examined in several countries as an approach to spent fuel and HLW management, and is still being examined in Sweden. Because of the very great depth of the holes, there are good reasons to believe that the materials emplaced would remain isolated from the environment for periods comparable to or possibly longer than those expected for the geologic repository case, but significant uncertainties must be resolved. Plutonium in such boreholes would be extremely inaccessible to potential proliferators, but would be recoverable by the state in control of the borehole site. The method would be relatively inexpensive to implement, but developing sufficient confidence to permit licensing could be costly and time-consuming; the United States has expended decades and billions of dollars in preparation for such licensing in the case of geological repositories for spent fuel and HLW.

All three of these options have the potential to be satisfactory next steps beyond interim storage in the disposition of excess weapons plutonium. None of them, however, could be confidently selected until currently open questions, described in Chapter 6 of this report, are answered.

Other Approaches

A variety of other reactors have been proposed for this mission, such as high-temperature gas-cooled reactors, fast-neutron reactors, or various existing research or plutonium production reactors. Existing reactors other than the LWRs and CANDUs described above should be rejected on grounds of the uncertain availability and safety of those reactors with sufficient capacity. The advanced reactors, as noted above, are not competitive for this mission because of the cost and delay of their development, licensing, and construction.

A variety of exotic disposal options have also been proposed, including sub-seabed disposal, detonation in underground nuclear explosions, launching into deep space, and dilution in the ocean, among others. This report rejects all of these on grounds of retrievability, cost, delay, environmental concerns, or conflict with existing policies and international agreements.

Beyond the Spent Fuel Standard

Long-term steps will be needed to reduce the proliferation risks posed by the entire global stock of plutonium, particularly as the radioactivity of spent fuel decays. Options for reducing these risks could include placement of spent fuel in geologic repositories, or pursuit of fission options that would burn ex-

18   EXECUTIVE SUMMARY

isting plutonium stocks nearly completely. A variety of reprocessing-oriented reactor options have been proposed for this mission, ranging from the use of standard LWRs to challenging concepts such as accelerator-based conversion. The costs of these approaches would be in the tens or hundreds of billions of dollars, and the time scales would be many decades or centuries, depending on the choice of options. These technologies can only be realistically considered in the broader context of managing the future of nuclear power to provide energy while minimizing the risk of nuclear proliferation, an important task that is beyond the scope of this committee. To further refine these concepts, research on fission options for near-total elimination of plutonium should continue at the conceptual level.

Although all the plausible disposition options will take many years to implement, it is important to begin now to build consensus on a road map for decision. Such a road map would provide guidelines for the necessary national and international debate to come, focus further efforts on those options most likely to minimize future risks, and provide plausible end points for the process that the near-term steps will set in motion. Research and development should be undertaken immediately to resolve the outstanding uncertainties facing each of the options.

THE INSTITUTIONAL FRAMEWORK

The institutional and political issues involved in managing weapons dismantlement, intermediate storage of fissile materials, and long-term disposition may be more complex and difficult to resolve than the technical ones. Because disposition options will require decades to carry out, it is critical that decisions throughout be made in a way that can muster a sustainable consensus. The entire process must be carefully managed to provide adequate safeguards, security, and transparency; to obtain public and institutional approval, including licenses; and to allow adequate participation in the decision making by all affected parties, including the U.S. and Russian publics and the international community. Adequate information must be made available to give substance to the public's participation.

These issues cover a broad institutional and technical spectrum. Establishing fully developed arrangements for managing these tasks will require an unusually demanding integration of policy under conditions of dispersed authority and intense political sensitivity. In the United States, jurisdiction over fissile material and fabricated weapons is divided between the Department of Energy (DOE) and the Department of Defense (DOD) in different phases of the deployment cycle. Each department has many subordinate divisions involved. Related diplomacy is handled by the State Department and the Arms Control and Disarmament Agency, with input from DOE and DOD. Numerous other agencies perform supporting functions. The relevant installations are authorized and financed by Congress, regulated by independent agencies and commissions, constrained by state laws, and increasingly affected by public opinion in their surrounding communities. Policy debates too often focus on specific options, such as particular reactor types, rather than the comprehensive view required to make choices for this complex problem. The consequences of this fragmentation are illustrated in a related area by the fact that technical assessment of the U.S. high-level waste repository at Yucca Mountain is incomplete after two decades of work and billions of dollars of expenditure, and final licensing is not projected for another two decades. These challenges to comprehensive policymaking are at least as great in Russia, where they must be surmounted in the midst of continuing political and economic upheaval.

None of the governments involved have previously faced the problem of handling excess plutonium in the quantities now contemplated, and none appear to have developed policies and procedures likely to be adequate to the task. Yet decisions are urgent, since without new approaches even the near-term tasks of dismantlement and storage are not likely to meet all of the required security criteria.

In these areas, the United States bears a special burden of policy leadership. If demanding technical assessments are to be completed, if consensus is to be forged, and if implementation is to be accomplished in reasonable time, major advances in the formulation and integration of policy and in institutional coordination will be needed. The president should establish a more systematic process of interagency coordination to deal with the areas addressed in this report, with sustained top-level leadership. The new interagency examination of plutonium disposition options envisioned in President Clinton's September 27, 1993, nonproliferation initiative is a first step in that direction, but much more remains to be done.

Recommendations

• The president should establish a more systematic process of interagency coordination to deal with the areas addressed in this report, with sustained top-level leadership.

DECLARATIONS AND DISMANTLEMENT

• The United States and Russia should make formal commitments that specific quantities of fissile material from dismantled weapons (representing a very large fraction of those materials) will be declared excess and committed to non-weapons use or disposal. Storage and disposition of these materials should be subject to agreed standards of accountability, transparency, and security. The standards for accountability and security should approximate as closely as possible the stringent standards applied to stored nuclear weapons.

• The United States should negotiate with Russia to create, through a step-by-step process, a broad regime under which each side's stocks of nuclear weapons and fissile materials would be declared and monitored, and the size of both stocks would be verifiably reduced over time in line with current reductions in deployed delivery systems. This regime would include, in addition to the fissile material steps mentioned in the previous recommendation:

1. a system of mutual declarations of total inventories of nuclear weapons and of fissile materials in civilian and military inventories;

2. measures designed to increase confidence in the accuracy of the declarations, and the transparency of each side's nuclear weapons production complexes, including physical access to production facilities and production records for fissile materials;

22   EXECUTIVE SUMMARY

3. a monitored cutoff of production of HEU and plutonium for weapons—if necessary, the United States should be willing to provide limited funding to assist Russia in the measures necessary to cut off plutonium production; and

4. an agreement providing for perimeter portal monitoring of dismantlement facilities, counting warheads entering these facilities, and assaying the fissile material that leaves. If the *net* subtractions from each side's stockpile are to be confirmed, some monitoring of warhead assembly will be required as well.

- Information concerning the total stockpiles of weapons and fissile materials, and those weapons characteristics necessary for external monitoring, should be declassified as part of this transparency regime. Appropriate reviews to prepare for such declassification should be initiated promptly.

- Russia and the United States should dismantle their retired warheads as expeditiously as is practical, consistent with protection for the environment, safety, and health, and cost-effectiveness.

INTERMEDIATE STORAGE

- The United States and Russia should place plutonium excess to military needs in safeguarded storage as soon as practical.

- Stored excess fissile materials committed to non-weapons use or disposal by the United States and Russia should be placed under international safeguards (possibly combined with bilateral monitoring). In the interest of speed, monitoring of storage could initially be a bilateral U.S.-Russian effort, but the IAEA should be brought into the process rapidly.

- Plutonium from dismantled weapons should continue to be stored as intact pits for now. Deformation of these pits and perhaps other steps to reduce the rearmament risk should be given serious consideration, and should be undertaken if they can be accomplished at relatively low cost and risk to the environment, safety, and health.

- Pits should be stored in sealed containers, with monitors permitted to assay the containers externally without observing the pits' dimensions, to provide adequate safeguards without compromising sensitive weapons design information.

- Once definite disposition options have been chosen, the plutonium should be converted expeditiously to whatever form is required as part of the disposition process.

- Financial or other incentives might be provided to encourage Russia to place the maximum amount of material into monitored storage. With the condition that these not be an open-ended commitment or provide any incentive for continued production of separated plutonium, such incentives would be desirable and should continue to be explored.

- The United States should continue providing assistance for a Russian fissile material storage facility, which should be designed to consolidate all excess weapons materials under appropriate standards of security and international monitoring.

- The safeguards budget of the IAEA should be substantially increased, and other steps should be taken to strengthen that organization's ability to carry out its critical responsibilities. One promising approach would be the creation of a voluntary fund, to which nations interested in improved safeguards would make contributions above and beyond their fixed allocations.

- Appropriate arrangements for intermediate storage are to a large extent decoupled from long-term disposition decisions and should be considered more urgent.

DISPOSITION

- It is important to begin now to build consensus on a road map for decisions concerning long-term disposition of excess weapons plutonium. Because disposition options will take decades to carry out, it is critical to develop options that can muster a sustainable consensus.

- Storage should not be extended indefinitely, because of (1) the negative impact that maintaining this material in forms readily accessible for weapons use would have on nonproliferation and arms reduction, (2) the risk of breakout, and (3) the risks of theft from the storage site. One of the key criteria by which disposition options should be judged is the speed with which they can be accomplished, and thus the degree to which they curtail the risks of prolonged storage.

24   EXECUTIVE SUMMARY

- Disposition options beyond storage should be pursued only if they reduce overall security risks compared to leaving the material in storage, considering both the final form of the material and the risks of the various processes required to get to that state. In the current unsettled circumstances in Russia, this minimum criterion is a significant one.

- The United States and Russia should begin discussions with the aim of agreeing that whatever disposition options are chosen, an agreed, stringent standard of accounting, monitoring, and security will be maintained throughout the process—coming as close as practicable to meeting the standard of security and accounting applied to intact nuclear weapons.

- Disposition options should be designed to transform the weapons plutonium into a physical form that is at least as inaccessible for weapons use as the much larger and growing stock of plutonium that exists in spent fuel from commercial nuclear reactors. The costs, complexities, risks, and delays of going further than this "spent fuel standard" to eliminate the excess weapons plutonium completely or nearly so would not be justified unless the same approach were to be taken with the global stock of civilian plutonium.

- The two most promising alternatives for the purpose of meeting the spent fuel standard are:

1. *the spent fuel option*, which has several variants. The principal one is to use the plutonium as once-through fuel in existing commercial nuclear power reactors or their evolutionary variants. Candidates for this role are U.S. light-water reactors (LWRs), Russian LWRs, and Canadian deuterium-uranium (CANDU) reactors. The use of European and Japanese reactors already licensed for civilian plutonium should also be considered for Russian weapons plutonium.

2. *the vitrification option*, which would entail combining the plutonium with radioactive high-level wastes as these are melted into large glass logs. The plutonium would then be roughly as difficult to recover for weapons use as plutonium in spent fuel.

A third option, *burial in deep boreholes*, has until now been less thoroughly studied than alternatives 1 and 2, but could turn out to be comparably attractive.

- A coordinated program of research and development should be undertaken immediately to clarify and resolve the uncertainties we have identified regarding each of these three options. The aim should be to pave the way for a national discussion, with full public participation, in order to make a choice within a very few years.

• Applying the spent fuel standard narrows the options considerably:

1. Options that irradiate the weapons plutonium in reactors only briefly ("spiking"), leaving it far less radioactive than typical spent fuel, and with little change in its isotopic composition, should not be pursued except possibly as a preliminary step on the road toward the spent fuel option. (Even for that purpose, in those cases the committee has examined, the possible advantages of the spiking option over continued storage do not appear to be worth the substantial cost of such spiking approaches.)

2. Options that involve *only* a chemical barrier to reuse—such as vitrification of plutonium without HLW or other fission products—should not be pursued, except possibly as a first step toward adding radiological or physical barriers as well.

3. Advanced reactors should not be specifically developed or built for transforming weapons plutonium into spent fuel, because that aim can be achieved more rapidly, less expensively, and more surely by using existing or evolutionary reactor types.

4. Options that strive to destroy a large fraction of the plutonium without reprocessing and recycle, using existing or advanced reactors with nonfertile fuels, should not be pursued because such approaches cannot destroy enough of the plutonium to obviate the need for continuing safeguards, and the modest reduction in security risk that could be achieved is not worth the extra delay, cost, and uncertainty that the development of such approaches would entail.

• Production of tritium should not be a major criterion for choosing among disposition options.

• Institutional issues in managing plutonium disposition are complex and the process to resolve them must be carefully managed. The process must provide adequate safeguards, security, and transparency, as well as protection for the environment, safety, and health; obtain public and institutional approval, including licenses; and allow adequate participation in the decision making by all affected parties, including the U.S. and Russian publics and the international community. Adequate information must be made available to give substance to the public's participation.

26 EXECUTIVE SUMMARY

TOTAL PLUTONIUM INVENTORIES

• Although we did not conduct a comprehensive examination of the proliferation risks of civilian nuclear fuel cycles, which would have gone beyond our charge, the risks posed by all forms of plutonium must be addressed.

• While the spent fuel standard is an appropriate goal for next steps, further steps should be taken to reduce the proliferation risks posed by *all* of the world's plutonium stocks, military and civilian, separated and unseparated; the need for such steps exists already, and will increase with time. Options for near-total elimination of plutonium may have a role to play in this effort, and research on defining and exploring these options should be continued at a conceptual level. These options, however, can only realistically be considered in the broader context of the future of nuclear electricity generation, including the minimization of security and safety risks—the assessment of which is beyond the scope of this report. Studies of that broader context should have as one important focus minimizing the risk of nuclear proliferation, and should consider nuclear systems as a whole, from the mining of uranium through to the disposal of waste; should consider feasible safeguarding methods as elements of development and design; and should take an international approach, realizing that other nations' approaches reflect their differing economic, political, technical, security, and geographic situations and perceptions.

• Urgent steps are needed to improve safeguards and security for all fissile materials in the former Soviet Union, including materials beyond those considered excess. We recommend a comprehensive approach at a significantly higher level of funding, with an emphasis on cooperation in addressing the most immediate risks. Western countries, including the United States, should press Russia and the other states of the former Soviet Union to take a number of steps urgently—within weeks or months, rather than years—and should be willing to provide necessary equipment and funds for these purposes. In particular, Western countries should press for, and offer assistance for:

1. immediate installation of appropriate portal monitoring systems to detect any theft of fissile materials, and adequate armed guard forces at *all* sites where enough weapons-usable fissile material to make a nuclear weapon is stored;

2. an urgent program of security inspections and improvements at all of these sites;

3. improved economic conditions for personnel responsible for accounting and security of weapons and fissile materials, to reduce incentives for corruption and insider theft;

4. improved national oversight of security and safeguards, with a strengthened basis in law (in Russia, this would involve strengthening the role of GOSATOMNADZOR, while in other former Soviet states it would involve strengthening or creating comparable organizations);

5. consolidation of fissile material storage and handling where possible;

6. conversion of research reactors to run on low-enriched uranium fuels, reducing the number of sites where weapons-grade fissile materials are used;

7. greater Western participation and cooperation in safeguards and security, ideally at all fissile material sites, but—at a minimum—at all civilian sites; and

8. regularized, as well as emergency, working-level cooperation in monitoring reports of alleged diversions.

- The steps we have outlined to improve safeguards and physical security for fissile materials in the United States and Russia should set a standard for a regime of improved management of such materials in civil use throughout the world. Negotiations should be pursued to:

1. create a global cutoff of all unsafeguarded production of fissile materials;

2. use the U.S.-Russian safeguarded storage regime recommended above as a base for a broad international storage and management regime for fissile materials, including registration and safeguards for all civilian separated plutonium and HEU;

3. extend the U.S.-Russian declaratory regime mentioned above to a global regime of public declarations of stocks of fissile materials;

4. agree on higher standards of physical security for these materials, with an international organization given authority to inspect sites to monitor whether the standards are met; and

5. agree on cooperative international approaches to manage reprocessing and use of plutonium to avoid building up excess stocks.

○

ISBN 0-16-046780-2